V

DATE DUE

MOTIVATION AND LEADERSHIP AT WORK

McGraw-Hill Series in Management

CONSULTING EDITORS
Fred Luthans
and Keith Davis

MOTIVATION AND LEADERSHIP AT WORK

Sixth Edition

Richard M. Steers

Lundquist College of Business
University of Oregon

Lyman W. Porter

Graduate School of Management
University of California—Irvine

Gregory A. Bigley

Graduate School of Management
University of California—Irvine

The McGraw-Hill Companies, Inc.
New York   St. Louis   San Francisco   Auckland   Bogotá   Caracas
Lisbon   London   Madrid   Mexico City   Milan   Montreal   New Delhi
San Juan   Singapore   Sydney   Tokyo   Toronto

McGraw-Hill

*A Division of The **McGraw·Hill** Companies*

This book is printed on acid-free paper.

1 2 3 4 5 6 7 8 9 0   FGR   FGR   9 0 9 8 7 6 5

ISBN 0-07-061031-2

This book was set in Times Roman by Ruttle, Shaw & Wetherill, Inc.
The editor was Dan Alpert;
The production supervisor was Louise Karam.
The cover was designed by Top Desk Publishers' Group.
Project supervision was done by Hockett Editorial Service.
Quebecor Printing/Fairfield was printer and binder.

Library of Congress Catalog Card Number: 95-81666

ABOUT THE AUTHORS

Richard M. Steers is the Kazumitsu Shiomi Professor of Management and International Studies at the Lundquist College of Business at the University of Oregon. Professor Steers is the author of eighteen books and over seventy articles on topics ranging from employee motivation and performance to organizational effectiveness and comparative management. He is past president and fellow of the Academy of Management, as well as a fellow of both the American Psychology Association and the American Psychological Society. He has served on several editorial boards, including *Administrative Science Quarterly, Academy of Management Journal,* and *Academy of Management Review.* He holds a Ph.D. from the University of California, Irvine, and has served as a visiting professor at Irvine, Nijenrode School of Business (The Netherlands), and Oxford University (England).

Lyman W. Porter is Professor of Management in the Graduate School of Management at the University of California, Irvine, and was formerly dean of that school. Prior to joining UCI in 1967, he served on the faculty of the University of California, Berkeley, and as a visiting professor at Yale University. Professor Porter is past president of the Academy of Management. In 1983 he received that organization's Award for Scholarly Contributions to Management, and in 1994 its Distinguished Educator Award. He also has served as president of the Society of Industrial-Organizational Psychology and in 1989 received the Society's Distinguished Scientific Contributions Award. Professor Porter's major fields of interest are organizational psychology and management. He is the author (with Lawrence McKibbin) of *Management Education and Development* (McGraw-Hill, 1988), a major report on the state of business school education and postdegree management development.

Gregory A. Bigley is currently completing his doctorate at the University of California, Irvine. He received his MBA from UCI in 1991 and holds a bachelors' degree in economics from the University of California, Los Angeles. Prior to enrolling in UCI's MBA program, Mr. Bigley worked for Ford Motor Credit Corporation in a supervisory capacity. He has also worked for other major companies, including General Foods Corporations and Disney Corporation. Mr. Bigley's major areas of interest include leadership, trust in organizations, and organizational justice.

CONTENTS

PREFACE

The first edition of this book was published in 1975 and was devoted solely to articles relating to the topic of motivation in work organizations. Since that time, not only has interest in this subject grown, but so have the amount and sophistication of the scientific and scholarly literature relating to it. This indicates healthy progress in a major substantive area of study, but it is not the only positive development of note. In recent years in the broad field of organizational behavior (OB) there has been an increasing tendency for some topics that used to be considered as relatively separate to be regarded as more closely connected than they might seem at first glance. Two of these are motivation and leadership, as they relate to the workplace. Thus, in a major departure from the five previous editions of this book, we are revising the title and contents of the book to include a co-equal emphasis on *both* motivation *and* leadership.

The decision to include leadership along with motivation in this sixth edition was not an easy one. Although we had no doubts about the expanding interrelationships of the two topics, nor about the importance of leadership in the fields of management and OB, we were reluctant to alter our previous exclusive focus on motivation. To have both topics in the same book would require that the book be slightly longer, which it is in this new edition, and that there be a reduced number of readings relating to motivation in both a relative and an absolute sense. It was this latter reality that gave us the most pause. However, in the end we concluded that students and instructors would be better served by adding the topic of leadership even at the expense of reducing somewhat the coverage of motivation. Our hope, then, is that this book will bring together in one volume the major contemporary scholarly writing that addresses two of the most fundamental and critical behavioral topics facing today's work organizations: motivation and leadership.

As in previous editions, the approach taken in this book is to integrate text materials with selections authored by leading academic scholars. The major emphasis in the text and readings is on a blend of theoretical formulations, major research findings, and real-world organizational applications relating to our two principal topics. The objective is to help show students how insights gained from the science side of these two topics can inform those who are, or soon will be, engaging in managerial practice. The book is intended, therefore, for students of organizational behavior, general management, or industrial psychology who have had some previous exposure to the basic concepts in one or more of these fields and who want to gain a more in-depth knowledge and understanding about work motivation and leadership.

As instructors who have used previous editions of this book will note, a third author has been added to the former Steers & Porter team. Greg Bigley, at the time of the publication of this sixth edition, is completing his doctoral work in organizational behavior at the University of California, Irvine, and will shortly be embarking on his own academic career in this field. He has carried a significant share of the work in helping to select articles and draft text material for this sixth edition, and for that and for the exceptional quality of those efforts, the senior authors express their sincere appreciation.

The authors want to thank C. J. Farrar for her sterling administrative assistance on this sixth edition, and Rachel Youngman of Hockett Editorial Service for her friendly and expert help in the book's production. Also, as in the past, we thank our respective schools, the University of Oregon and UC Irvine, for providing good examples of academic leadership and stimulating motivational environments in which to work. Finally, as always, the two senior authors acknowledge with special thanks the continuing support and encouragement of their wives, Sheila and Meredith—both of whom are excellent motivators and leaders in their own right.

Richard M. Steers
Lyman W. Porter
Gregory A. Bigley

MOTIVATION AND LEADERSHIP AT WORK

PART ONE

MOTIVATION AND LEADERSHIP: AN INTRODUCTION

MOTIVATION AND LEADERSHIP IN ORGANIZATIONS

Motivation and leadership are, arguably, the two fundamental topic areas that organizational researchers and practicing managers look to in order to understand behavior inside organizations. The current intensity of interest in these subjects is evidenced by several factors. For example, the popular management literature abounds with books and periodical publications that focus on motivation, leadership, or both. Further, a multimillion-dollar global industry exists to show organizations how to motivate employees and how to train and develop leaders. In addition, since the scientific investigation of motivation and leadership began (independently of one another), in the early 1900s, literally thousands of scholarly articles and books on each of these topics have been published, and new work continues to be produced at a rapid rate and in high volume.

Motivation and leadership have received such considerable and sustained attention because most perspectives on these subjects have assumed that they involve principal behavioral factors that are especially critical to the functioning of contemporary organizations. Managers and researchers cannot avoid a concern with the behavioral requirements of an organization. In addition to deploying financial and physical resources, every organization must utilize its human resources effectively. Katz and Kahn (1978) have posited that organizations have three behavioral requirements in this regard: (1) people must be attracted not only to join the organization but also to remain in it; (2) people must perform the tasks for which they have been hired and must do so in a dependable manner; and (3) people must go beyond this dependable role performance and engage in some form of creative, spontaneous, and innovative behavior at work—a set of behaviors commonly called "extra-role behavior." In other words, for an organization to maximize the potential of its human resources, according to this reasoning, its managers must come to grips with the motivational and leadership problems of stimulating decisions to participate, choices to produce, and efforts to be innovative and solve problems.

Of these two basic topics, motivation may be the most all-encompassing. Motivation, as a concept, represents a highly complex phenomenon that affects, and is affected by, a multitude of factors in the work milieu. A comprehensive understanding of the ways in which organizations function requires that at least some attention be directed toward the question of why people behave as they do on the job—that is, the determinants of employee work behavior and the ramifications of such behavior for an organization. Thus, in order to comprehend more fully the effects of variations in those organizational factors of interest (e.g., job redesign, organizational reward systems) on important dependent variables (e.g., group effectiveness, organizational performance), an understanding of the topic of motivation seems essential. For example, one may be interested in predicting the effects of a change in the level of employee compensation (discussed in Chapter 7) on employee productivity. The relationship between these two variables will be difficult to specify, *a priori,* and hard to explain, *post hoc,* in the absence of some basic answer to the question of why people behave the way they do at work.

Such is also the case for the relationship between leadership behavior and a range of dependent variables. Although the concept of leadership may not be quite as pervasive as that of motivation, leadership is, nevertheless, assumed to be critical to the functioning of modern organizations. This assumption might appear questionable in light of the observation that most organizations consist of a set of structural features, such as stated objectives, rules, policies, procedures, and clear lines of authority, that seem to channel the behaviors of employees in narrow patterns. However, although substantial influence does flow from an organization's structural properties, these features, in and of themselves, are considered insufficient to support organized activity. Two important reasons for this are the following: organizational designs are incomplete, and individual membership in organizations is segmented in nature (Katz & Kahn, 1978).

First, the organization, as a formal and abstract blueprint (of sorts), is necessarily imperfect because actual human behavior is infinitely more complex and variable than any "plan" could accommodate. An organizational design cannot possibly account for every member's activity at all times. Consequently, in addition to various structural features, organizations must possess a mechanism that can ensure that human behavior is coordinated and directed toward task accomplishment. That mechanism is presumed to be leadership.

Second, individual organizational membership is segmented in nature in the sense that people belong to other groups (e.g., families) or organizations (e.g., churches), in addition to their work organizations. Furthermore, people have powerful experiences over the course of their lives (e.g., college education, raising children). The pattern and intensity of people's motives may change as they assimilate their continuing experiences. These changing needs and motives may result in behaviors, such as an expressed desire for greater independence and autonomy, that require some kind of response from the organization, a response that cannot always be handled by its existing structural features. Leadership, then, is proposed as a process to enable the organization to accommodate these kinds of individual predispositions and tendencies.

THE INTERACTION OF MOTIVATION AND LEADERSHIP

Scientific developments in the areas of motivation and leadership proceeded essentially independently of one another for several decades. Early approaches to motivation, such as instinct theories, emerged around the turn of the century. The scientific investigation of leadership commenced somewhat later, with trait theories being popular in the 1930s. From these two beginning points, progress in the study of motivation and leadership was made for many years with very little interaction between the two topic areas.

However, as more organizational researchers began to investigate behavioral phenomena with models of motivation or leadership, some interaction started to occur between the two topics. In fact, the importance of the research that has attempted to apply theories of motivation to organizational settings is largely due to its managerial leadership implications. For example, Herzberg's (Herzberg, Mausner, & Snyderman, 1959; Herzberg, 1966) motivator-hygiene theory of work motivation (discussed in Chapter 2) produced several important, at least at the time, recommendations for managers. It suggested, for instance, that managers could not raise the level of employee satisfaction by changing the work context (e.g., raising pay). Rather, to increase employee satisfaction, managers would have to change the intrinsic value of the work itself. Managers could do this in a number of ways, including providing recognition for a job well done or giving employees more opportunities for personal growth through their work.

Researchers in the area of leadership generally did not acknowledge a role for motivation in their theories until relatively recently. That is, early trait, behavior, and contingency theories of leadership (discussed in Chapter 3) did not use ideas from the area of motivation to identify relevant independent variables (i.e., traits, behaviors, or situation contingencies) or to explain the intervening processes between these independent variables and the dependent variables of interest (e.g., group effectiveness). Recently, however, leadership researchers, particularly those studying charismatic and transformational approaches (discussed in Chapters 3, 9, and 10) have started to draw more heavily on motivational concepts in an effort better to understand certain organizational phenomena.

A major impetus driving organizational researchers and practicing managers to emphasize both motivation and leadership comes from recent developments in contemporary organizations. Organizations function within, and depend upon, their environments. However, by every measure, the environments of most organizations are becoming more turbulent. The globalization of the world's markets, the dizzying pace of advances in information technologies, the impact of government regulations, and the growing sophistication of the world's capital markets have all been cited as reasons for the relentless escalation in the rate of environmental change and in the competitive intensity experienced by most organizations (e.g., Kanter, 1989; Kotter, 1988; Pfeffer, 1994). Under these circumstances, many of the structural features that are intended to guide behavior inside organizations quickly become ill-suited to shifting conditions.

As organizations attempt to adapt to increasing environmental volatility and competitive intensity, organizational effectiveness, or even survival, may depend on management's ability to energize and direct organizational employees to apply intense and sustained effort toward the goals of the organization, even when these goals may be subject to frequent modifications. Couched in this way, the importance of, and the connections between, the topics of motivation and leadership in an organizational context are apparent. Therefore, researchers and managers must draw on both topics to understand and then effectively influence behavior in today's organizations.

The link between motivation and leadership can be illustrated by their interaction with an overwhelming force which is affecting almost all organizations as the twenty-first century begins: advanced technology. Such technology, in one form or another, is crucial to the effective functioning of virtually every organization; yet it is *insufficient by itself* for guaranteeing the highest levels of performance. While technology provides a base for superior performance, it is inevitably up to the human resources to use that technology to its highest potential in order to help organizations reach their most far-reaching and challenging goals and objectives. Here is where motivation and leadership intersect: Without both high levels of motivated work behavior *and* exceptional leadership, an organization's technological capabilities are likely to remain underutilized and less-than-optimally applied.

Another example of a place where a joint consideration of motivation and leadership can help illuminate issues is the increasingly important topic of teams in organizations. Many contemporary organizations are attempting to develop a more team-oriented culture in order to maximize the efforts and initiatives of small groups of people. How leadership is distributed and displayed within such groups has a lot to do with whether a teamlike feeling is generated among the members, and this, in turn, is assumed to affect the resulting motivation of those group members. We can probably all think of organizational groups we have known where leadership appears to be missing and member motivation is essentially absent or at least quite low; likewise, it is not too difficult for most of us to point to groups we have observed—certain collegiate or professional sports teams are obvious examples—that exhibit exactly the opposite pattern: a combination of strong leadership and high motivation. When the subject is teams and teamwork, leadership and motivation seem inseparably linked.

Although these two concepts are interrelated, it is also important to point out that they are not totally intertwined and overlapping. There are certainly aspects of motivation that are strongly affected by variables other than leadership, and there are many consequences of leadership beyond its effects on motivation. Nevertheless, the degree of fundamental connection between the two areas has been growing in recent years, particularly as more comprehensive analyses of organizational behavior have been developed and as new organizational issues arise. For instance, in the past decade or so there has been considerable interest (see Chapters, 8, 9, 10) focused on such topics as high involvement management, self-management, transformational leadership, charismatic leadership, and learning organizations. Indeed, it is virtually impossible to pick up a popular business book or magazine article that does not make some mention of one or more of these topics. What is sometimes overlooked in such publications, but what is emphasized in many of the more scholarly articles in this book, however, is the fact that fundamental behavioral issues relating to both motivation and leadership are woven throughout these very "modern" managerial concerns, and any analysis is incomplete unless both factors are considered.

The objective of this book, therefore, is to provide the serious student of motivation and leadership with some tools to obtain a more comprehensive and empirically-based knowledge of these two concepts as they occur in work organizations. Thus, the book consists of a combination of text and readings on current theories, research, and applications in the field. Throughout an emphasis is placed on the comparative approach— that is, on the similarities and differences among and between various theories and models and their implications, rather than on the presentation or defense of one particular approach. Moreover, because of the centrality of these topics, we believe they can be best understood by considering how they affect, and are affected by, other important variables which, together, constitute today's ever-changing work environment. This results in particular emphasis being placed throughout this book on the study of relationships among major variables—for example, motivation and leadership as they relate to reward systems, group influences, and job design—rather than on a simple listing of facts and theoretical points.

PLAN OF THE BOOK

This book is divided into four parts. Part One consists of the introductory material presented in this chapter and two additional chapters that examine prominent theories of motivation and leadership, respectively. Each of these two latter chapters contains an extensive introduction which reviews the past development of the theories in each field.

On the basis of the groundwork laid in Part One, Part Two looks at several central issues in motivation and leadership at work. Included here are such topics as social influence (e.g., power, group influences, corporate culture), gender, job attitudes, absenteeism, and cross-cultural considerations, as each relates to motivation and/or leadership. This is followed, in Part Three, by a discussion of several of the more common applications of motivation and leadership concepts. Included here are the topics of job design, reward systems, self-managing teams, organizational change, and current leadership challenges. Finally, Part Four provides some concluding observations and implications for management.

In all, we present some forty articles on various aspects of employee motivation and leadership, written by some of the most respected scholars in the field. Some of these articles are more theoretical, while others are more applied. Some argue in support of one particular theory or technique, while others suggest more eclectic approaches. Taken together, however, these articles should provide a comprehensive portrait of the dynamics of motivation and leadership in the contemporary world of work.

REFERENCES

Herzberg, F. *Work and the nature of man.* Cleveland: World Publishing, 1966.
Herzberg, F., Mausner, B., & Snyderman, B. B. *The motivation to work.* New York: Wiley, 1959.
Kanter, R. M. *When giants learn to dance.* New York: Simon & Schuster, 1989.
Kotter, J. P. *The Leadership Factor.* New York: The Free Press, 1988.

Katz, D., & Kahn, R. L. *The Social Psychology of Organizations,* 2nd ed. New York: Wiley, 1978.

Pfeffer, J. *Competitive advantage through people.* Boston: Harvard Business School Press, 1994.

CHAPTER 1: Questions for Discussion

1 What are some specific examples of extra role behavior (the third behavioral requirement discussed by Katz & Kahn) in organizations? Can you think of some ways that leaders might motivate their subordinates to engage in such activity?

2 How would you compare the importance of the topics of motivation versus leadership in terms of understanding behavior in organizations?

3 Can you think of other examples where a joint knowledge of motivation and leadership would be helpful in understanding workplace situations?

MODELS OF
WORK MOTIVATION

The term "motivation" was originally derived from the Latin word *movere*, which means "to move." However, this one word is obviously an inadequate definition for our purposes here. What is needed is a description which sufficiently covers the various components and processes associated with how human behavior is activated. A brief selection of representative definitions indicates how the term has been used:

. . . the contemporary (immediate) influence on the direction, vigor, and persistence of action (Atkinson, 1964).

. . . how behavior gets started, is energized, is sustained, is directed, is stopped, and what kind of subjective reaction is present in the organism while all this is going on (Jones, 1955).

. . . a process governing choice made by persons or lower organisms among alternative forms of voluntary activity (Vroom, 1964).

. . . motivation has to do with a set of independent/dependent variable relationships that explain the direction, amplitude, and persistence of an individual's behavior, holding constant the effects of aptitude, skill, and understanding of the task, and the constraints operating in the environment (Campbell & Pritchard, 1976).

These definitions appear generally to have three common denominators which may be said to characterize the phenomenon of motivation. That is, when we discuss motivation, we are primarily concerned with (1) what energizes human behavior, (2) what directs or channels such behavior, and (3) how this behavior is maintained or sustained. Each of these three components represents an important factor in our understanding of human behavior at work. First, this conceptualization points to energetic forces within individuals that drive them to behave in certain ways and to environmental forces that often trigger these drives. Second, there is the notion of goal orientation on the part of individuals; their behavior is directed *toward* something. Third, this way of viewing motivation contains a *systems orientation*; that is, it considers those forces in individuals and in their surrounding environments that feed back to the individuals either to reinforce the intensity of their drive and the direction of their energy or to dissuade them from their course of action and redirect their efforts. These three components of motivation appear again and again in the theories and research that follow.

As indicated in Chapter 1, the concept of motivation has received considerable attention over the course of this century. Furthermore, the topic of motivation has become increasingly prominent in the efforts of organizational researchers and practicing managers to understand and influence organizational behavior. Despite the intense interest in the area, however, no overall, commonly accepted framework or approach to work motivation currently exists. Nevertheless, a survey of the organization studies literature indicates that the extant theories may be grouped into two general classes: content theories and process theories.

The *content theories* of work motivation assume that factors exist within the individual that energize, direct, and sustain behavior. These approaches to motivation are concerned with the identification of important internal elements and the explanation of how these elements may be prioritized within the individual. In contrast to content theories of motivation, *process theories* of motivation attempt to describe *how* behavior is energized, directed, and sustained. These theories focus on certain psychological processes underlying action. In particular, process theories place heavy emphasis on describing the functioning of the individual's decision system as it relates to behavior.

The remainder of this opening essay for the present chapter considers an array of motivational theories. We begin with a description of several early psychological approaches to motivation that involved the concepts of instinct, drive, and reinforcement, and which were the precursors of later theories. The next section describes four content models that have been applied to, or have been developed for, work settings: Maslow's hierarchy of needs, Alderfer's existence-relatedness-growth (ERG), Herzberg's motivator-hygiene, and McClelland's learned needs. Following this discussion of content theories, several basic cognitive-type frameworks that are relevant to process theories of work motivation will be briefly summarized. Then two major process conceptualizations are reviewed: Vroom's expectancy theory and the Porter-Lawler model. (Two other important process theories of work motivation—Adam's equity theory and Locke's goal setting theory—will be discussed later in two of this chapter's readings.) This introductory essay concludes with an overview of how practicing managers have approached motivational problems at work from the earliest days of this century up to recent times. A selection of readings on current issues in the area of work motivation completes the chapter.

EARLY PSYCHOLOGICAL APPROACHES

Most psychological theories of motivation, both early and contemporary, have their roots—at least to some extent—in the principle of hedonism. This principle, briefly defined, states that individuals tend to seek pleasure and avoid pain. Hedonism assumes a certain degree of conscious behavior on the part of individuals whereby they make intentional decisions or choices concerning future action. In theory, people rationally consider the behavioral alternatives available to them and act to maximize positive results and to minimize negative results. The concept of hedonism dates back to the early Greek philosophers; it later reemerged as a popular explanation of behavior in the eighteenth and nineteenth centuries, as seen in the works of philosophers such as Locke, Bentham, Mill, and Helvetius. Bentham even went so far as to coin the term "hedonic calculus" in 1789 to describe the process by which individuals calculate the pros and cons of various acts of behavior.

Toward the end of the nineteenth century, motivation theory began to move from the realm of philosophy toward the more empirically based science of psychology. As consideration of this important topic grew, it became apparent to those who attempted to use the philosophically based concept of hedonism that several serious problems existed. Vroom explained this dilemma as follows:

> There was in the doctrine no clear-cut specification of the type of events which were pleasurable or painful, or even how these events could be determined for a particular individual; nor did it make clear how persons acquired their conceptions of ways of attaining pleasure and pain, or how the source of pleasure and pain might be modified by experience. In short the hedonistic assumption has no empirical content and was untestable. Any form of behavior could be explained, after the fact, by postulating particular sources of pleasure or pain, but no form of behavior could be predicted in advance (1964, p. 10).

In an effort to fill this void, several theories of motivation began to evolve which attempted to formulate empirically verifiable relationships among sets of variables which could be used to predict behavior. The earliest such theory centered on the concept of instinct.

Instinct Theories

While not rejecting the notion of hedonism, psychologists like James, Freud, and McDougall argued that a more comprehensive explanation of behavior was necessary than simply assuming that a rational person pursues his or her own best interest. In short, they posited two additional variables that were crucial to our understanding of behavior: instinct and unconscious motivation.

Instead of seeing behavior as highly rational, these theorists saw much of it as resulting from instinct. McDougall, writing in 1908, defined an instinct as "an inherited or innate psychophysical disposition which determines its possessor to perceive, or pay attention to, objects of a certain class, to experience an emotional excitement of a particular quality upon perceiving such an object, and to act in regard to it in a particular manner, or at least, to experience an impulse to such an action." However, while McDougall saw instinct as purposive and goal-directed, other instinct theorists, like James, defined the concept more in terms of blind and mechanical action. James (1890) included in his list of instincts the following: locomotion, curiosity, sociability, love, fear, jealousy, and sympathy. James and McDougall believed that every person has such instincts in greater or lesser degree and that these instincts are the prime determinants of behavior. In other words, individuals were seen as possessing automatic predispositions to behave in certain ways, depending on internal and external cues.

The second major concept associated with instinct theories is that of unconscious motivation. While the notion is implicit in the writings of James, it was Freud (1915) who most ardently advocated the existence of such a phenomenon. On the basis of his clinical observations, Freud argued that the most potent behavioral tendencies are not necessarily those that individuals *consciously* determine would be in their best interests. Individuals are not always aware of all their desires and needs. Rather, such unconscious phenomena as dreams, slips of the tongue ("Freudian slips"), and neurotic symptoms were seen by Freud as manifestations of the hedonistic principle on an *unconscious* level. Thus, a major factor in human motivation was seen here as resulting from forces unknown even to the individual.

The instinct theory of motivation was fairly widely accepted during the first quarter of this century. Then, beginning in the early 1920s, it came under increasing attack on several grounds (Hilgard & Atkinson, 1967; Morgan & King, 1966). First, there was the disturbing fact that the list of instincts continued to grow, reaching nearly six thousand in number. The sheer length of such a list seriously jeopardized any attempt at parsimony in the explanation of motivation. Second, the contention that individuals varied greatly in the strengths or intensities of their motivational dispositions was becoming increasingly accepted among psychologists, adding a further complication to the ability of instinct theory to explain behavior fully. Third, some researchers found that at times there may be little relation between the strength of certain motives and subsequent behavior. Fourth, some psychologists came to question whether the unconscious motives as described by Freud were really instinctive or whether they were learned behavior. In fact, this fourth criticism formed the basis of the second "school" of motivation theorists, who later became known as "drive" theorists.

Drive and Reinforcement Theories

Researchers who have been associated with drive theory typically base their work on the influence that learning has on subsequent behavior. Thus, such theories have a historical component, which led Allport (1954) to refer to them as "hedonism of the past"; that is, drive theories generally assumed that decisions concerning present behavior are based in large part on the consequences, or rewards, of past behavior. Where past action led to positive consequences, individuals would tend to repeat such actions; where past actions led to negative consequences or punishment, individuals would tend to avoid repeating them. This position was first elaborated by Thorndike in his "law of effect." Basing his "law" on experimental observations of animal behavior, Thorndike posited:

Of several responses made to the same situation, those which are accompanied or closely followed by satisfaction to the animal will, other things being equal, be more firmly connected with the situation, so that when it recurs, they will be more likely to occur; those which are accompanied or closely followed by discomfort to the animal will, other things being equal, have their connection with that situation weakened, so that when it recurs, they will be less likely to occur. The greater the satisfaction or discomfort, the greater is the strengthening or weakening of the bond (1911, p. 244).

While this law of effect did not explain why some actions were pleasurable or satisfying and others were not, it did go a long way toward setting forth an empirically verifiable theory of motivation. Past learning and previous "stimulus-response" connections were viewed as the major causal variables of behavior.

The term "drive" was first introduced by Woodworth (1918) to describe the reservoir of energy that impels an organism to behave in certain ways. While Woodworth intended the term to mean a general supply of energy within an organism, others soon modified this definition to refer to a host of specific energizers (such as hunger, thirst, sex) toward or away from certain goals. With the introduction of the concept of drive, it now became possible for psychologists to predict in advance—at least in theory—not only what goals an individual would strive toward but also the strength of the motivation toward such goals. Thus, it became feasible for researchers to attempt to test the theory in a fairly rigorous fashion, a task that was virtually impossible for the earlier theories of hedonism and instinct.

A major theoretical advance in drive theory came from the work of Cannon in the early 1930s. Cannon (1939) introduced the concept of "homeostasis" to describe a state of disequilibrium within an organism which existed whenever internal conditions deviated from their normal state. When such disequilibrium occurred (as when an organism felt hungry), the organism was motivated by internal drives to reduce the disequilibrium and to return to its normal state. Inherent in Cannon's notion was the idea that organisms exist in a dynamic environment and that the determining motives for behavior constantly change, depending upon where the disequilibrium exists within the system. Thus, certain drives, or motives, may move to the forefront and then, once satisfied, retreat while other drives become paramount. This concept can be seen to a large extent in the later work of Maslow (discussed in a later section).

The first comprehensive—and experimentally specific—elaboration of drive theory was put forth by Hull. In his major work, *Principles of Behavior,* published in 1943, Hull set down a specific equation to explain an organism's "impetus to respond": Effort = Drive × Habit. "Drive" was defined by Hull as an energizing influence which determined the intensity of behavior, and which theoretically increased along with the level of deprivation. "Habit" was seen as the strength of relationship between past stimulus and response (S-R). Hull hypothesized that habit strength depended not only upon the closeness of the S-R event to reinforcement but also upon the magnitude and number of such reinforcements. Thus, Hull's concept of habit draws very heavily upon Thorndike's "law of effect." Hull argued that the resulting effort, or motivational force, was a multiplicative function of these two central variables.

If we apply Hull's theory to an organizational setting, we can use the following example to clarify how drive theory would be used to predict behavior. A person who has been out of work for some time (high deprivation level) would generally have a strong need or desire to seek some means to support himself or herself (goal). If, on the basis of *previous* experience, this person draws a close association between the securing of income and the act of taking a job, we would expect him or her to search ardently for employment. Thus, the motivation to seek employment would be seen, according to this theory, as a multiplicative function of the intensity of the need for money (drive) and the strength of the feeling that work has been associated with the receipt of money in the past (habit). Later, in response to empirical evidence which was inconsistent with the theory, Hull (1952) somewhat modified his position. Instead of positing that behavior was wholly a function of antecedent conditions (such as past experience), he added an incentive variable to his equation. His later formulation thus read: Effort = Drive × Habit × Incentive. This incentive factor, added largely in response to the attack by the cognitive theorists (discussed in a later section), was defined in terms of anticipatory reactions to future goals. It was thus hypothesized that one factor in the motivation equation was the size of, or attraction to, future potential rewards. As the size of the reward varied, so too would the motivation to seek such a reward. This major revision by Hull (as amplified by Spence, 1956) brought drive theory into fairly close agreement with the early cognitive theories. However, while cognitive theories have generally been applied to humans, including humans at work, drive theory research has continued, by and large, to study animal behavior in the laboratory.

Just as drive theory draws upon Thorndike's "law of effect," so do modern reinforcement approaches (e.g., Skinner, 1953). The difference is that the former theory emphasizes an internal state (i.e., drive) as a necessary variable to take into account, while reinforcement theory does not. Rather, the reinforcement model places total emphasis on the *consequences* of behavior. Behavior initiated by the individual (for whatever reason) that produces an effect or consequence is called *operant* behavior (i.e., the individual has "operated" on the environment), and the theory deals with the contingent relationships between this operant behavior and the pattern of consequences. It ignores the inner state of the individual and concentrates solely on what happens to a person when he or she takes some action. Thus, strictly speaking, reinforcement theory is not a theory of motivation because it does not concern itself with what energizes or initiates behavior. Nevertheless, since a reinforcement approach provides a powerful means of analysis of what controls behavior (its direction and maintenance), it is typically considered in discussions of motivation.

CONTENT THEORIES OF MOTIVATION

In this section, four of the most prominent content theories of work motivation will be discussed. The first two theories—Maslow's hierarchy of needs and Alderfer's existence-relatedness-growth (ERG)—view needs as sequentially activated. Although not developed explicitly for organizational settings, Maslow's needs hierarchy was the first major theory of motivation to be applied to individuals at work. Alderfer's ERG theory represents an important extension and refinement of the needs hierarchy; ERG theory attempted to deal with some of the deficiencies of Maslow's model. The third theory discussed in this section is Herzberg's motivator-hygiene model. His two-factor theory, as it is often called, was among the very first models of motivation to be developed specifically for work applications. McClelland's learned needs theory is the last framework discussed in the section. His theory represents somewhat of a departure from the other approaches, in that he views needs as socially acquired attributes of the individual, rather than as innate psychological characteristics.

Maslow's Hierarchy of Needs

Maslow's (1954, 1968) needs hierarchy is perhaps the most widely known theory relating individual needs to motivation. The theory attempts to show how the healthy personality grows and develops over time and how that personality comes to manifest itself in motivated behavior.

Maslow (1954) contends that people are wanting beings whose needs guide behavior. According to Maslow, a need influences a person's activities until it has been satisfied. Further, his theory holds that an individual's needs are arranged in a hierarchical fashion, from the very fundamental (e.g., food, shelter) to the most advanced (e.g., self-fulfillment). Individuals, it is hypothesized, attend to needs in a sequential fashion, moving from the bottom of the hierarchy toward the top, as lower-level needs are satisfied. According to Maslow, lower-level needs must be satisfied, in general, before higher-level needs are activated sufficiently to drive behavior. Further, only unsatisfied needs can influence behavior; those that are satisfied do not motivate.

Maslow (1968) distinguishes between two basic categories of needs: deficiency needs and growth needs. He posits that if the individual is to be healthy and secure, deficiency needs must be satisfied. "Needs for safety, the feeling of belonging, love and respect (from others) are all clearly deficits" (Maslow, 1954, p. 10). The individual will fail to develop a healthy personality to the extent that these needs are not met. In contrast, growth needs are those that relate to the development and achievement of one's potential. For Maslow the idea of growth needs is more vague than the concept of deficiency needs: "Growth, individuation, autonomy, self-actualization, self-development, productiveness, self-realization are all crudely synonymous, designating a vaguely perceived area rather than a sharply defined concept" (Maslow, 1968, p. 24).

According to Maslow, individuals are motivated by five general needs that may be classified into either the deficiency or the growth categories.

Deficiency Needs

1 Physiological: The most basic needs in Maslow's hierarchy center around needs related to survival and include the needs for oxygen, food, water, sleep, and so on. In the workplace, such needs are reflected in the individual's concern for basic working conditions (e.g., moderate temperature, clean air).

2 Safety and security: The second level of needs is associated with the safety and security of one's physical and emotional environment. These needs include a desire for stability, order, security, freedom from threats of emotional harm, and protection against accidents. At work, such needs may be represented by a concern for safe working conditions and job security.

3 Belongingness: The third level consists of those needs related to one's desire for acceptance by others, friendship, and love. In organizations, interacting frequently with fellow workers or experiencing employee-centered leadership may help to satisfy these needs.

Growth Needs

4 Esteem and ego: These are the needs for self-respect, self-esteem, and respect and esteem for others. In the workplace, these needs may be reflected in a concern for jobs with higher status and a desire for recognition for the successful accomplishment of a particular task.

5 Self-actualization. The highest need category consists of the need for self-ful-fillment. People with dominant self-actualization needs are concerned with developing to their full and unique potential as individuals. In organizations, these needs may be reflected in the desire for work assignments that challenge one's skills and abilities and that allow for creative or innovative approaches.

According to Maslow, individuals move up the needs hierarchy through a dynamic cycle of deprivation, domination, gratification, and activation (Steers and Black, 1994). That is, when the individual experiences deprivation (i.e., an unfulfilled need) at a particular level in the hierarchy, the unsatisfied need will direct the individual's thoughts and actions. For example, a person who is concerned about physical safety will ignore or disregard higher-order needs and devote all of his or her energies to se-curing a safer environment. However, once this need is met, or gratified, it will cease to dominate the person's consciousness. Instead, needs at the next level in the hierar-chy will be activated (in this case, belongingness needs). This cycle is repeated at each level in the hierarchy until the individual reaches the level of self actualization.

Evaluation of Maslow's Hierarchy of Needs Theory   Maslow's work has generated a great deal of research attempting to evaluate the utility of the theory in organizational settings. For example, Porter (1961) found that managers at higher levels of an organization were generally more able than lower-level managers to satisfy their growth needs. These findings follow from the idea that upper-level managers generally have more challenging and autonomous jobs than their lower-level counterparts. As a result, managers in the upper echelons of an organization are in a much better position to pursue their growth needs.

However, although studies have been able to differentiate between jobs that allow for growth need satisfaction and those that hinder it, research has not been able to es-tablish the validity of the need hierarchy itself. In fact, in an extensive review of the re-search findings associated with Maslow's hierarchy, Wahba and Bridwell (1976) con-cluded that Maslow's model presents the student of work motivation with a paradox: the theory is widely accepted, but there is little research evidence to support it.

The review evaluated three aspects of Maslow's model. First, no clear evidence was found indicating that human needs can be classified into five distinct categories, or that these categories are structured in a hierarchical way. However, there did seem to be some evidence to support a general classification scheme distinguishing deficiency from growth needs. Second, the review examined the proposition that an unsatisfied need leads an individual to focus exclusively on that need. Some studies supported this proposition while other studies did not. Finally, the review explored the idea that satis-faction of needs at one level activates needs at the next higher level. This proposition was not supported by the research evidence.

Although research findings have failed to support the needs hierarchy model and have questioned its conceptual validity, Maslow's theory continues to be useful in gen-erating ideas about the fundamental nature of human motives. For managers, in particular, the needs hierarchy idea has a commonsense appeal; it is relatively easy to comprehend and has clear implications for management. For example, assuming that many employees have met their deficiency needs, managers can focus on creating a work situation that is aimed at satisfying higher-level growth needs.

In an attempt to overcome some of the problems with Maslow's approach, Alderfer presented his existence-relatedness-growth (ERG) model of motivation. This model will be reviewed next.

Alderfer's Existence-Relatedness-Growth (ERG) Theory

The most popular extension and refinement of Maslow's theory of needs is the one proposed by Alderfer (1972) (Cherrington, 1989). While Maslow's model was not developed specifically for work organizations, Alderfer's theory attempted to establish a conceptualization of human needs that is relevant to organizational settings. In extending Maslow's theory, Alderfer argued that the need categories could be collapsed into three more general classes:

1 Existence. These are needs related to human existence and are comparable to Maslow's physiological needs and certain of his safety needs.

2 Relatedness. These are needs that involve interpersonal relationships in the workplace. Relatedness needs are similar to Maslow's belongingness needs and certain of his safety and esteem/ego needs.

3 Growth. These are needs associated with the development of the human potential. Included in this category are needs corresponding to Maslow's self-esteem and self-actualization needs.

Alderfer's model agrees with Maslow's in positing that individuals tend to move from existence, through relatedness, to growth needs, as needs in each category are satisfied. However, ERG theory differs from the needs hierarchy model in two important respects. First, Alderfer contends that, in addition to the satisfaction-progression process described by Maslow, a frustration-regression sequence also exists. For example, the ERG model predicts that if an individual is continually frustrated in his or her attempts to satisfy growth needs, then relatedness needs will be reactivated and become the primary drivers of behavior. Second, and especially important, in contrast to the needs hierarchy theory, the ERG model does not hold that one level of needs must be satisfied before needs in the next level can emerge to motivate behavior. Instead, the ERG model proposes that more than one need may be operative in a given individual at any point in time.

Evaluation of Alderfer's ERG Theory At present, only a few studies have attempted to test ERG theory. Therefore, empirical verification has not been established. However, the studies that have been reported appear to show stronger support for Alderfer's ERG model than for Maslow's hierarchy of needs (e.g., Schneider & Alderfer, 1973). The ERG model appears to be less rigid than the needs hierarchy theory, allowing for more flexibility in describing human behavior.

As with Maslow's theory, ERG theory appears to offer a useful way of thinking about employee motivation. Although there is disagreement between Maslow and Alderfer regarding the exact number of need categories, both theories acknowledge that opportunities for the satisfaction of needs constitute an important element in the motivation of individuals.

Herzberg's Motivator-Hygiene Theory

Herzberg's motivator-hygiene theory is, perhaps, the most controversial theory of work motivation. The original research used in developing the theory was conducted with several hundred accountants and engineers. Herzberg and his colleagues used the critical incident method of obtaining data for their research. That is, the subjects in the study where asked two questions: (1) "Can you describe, in detail, when you felt exceptionally good about your job?" and (2) "Can you describe, in detail, when you felt exceptionally bad about your job?" Herzberg's motivator-hygiene theory, as well as the supporting data, was first published in 1959 (Herzberg, Mausner, & Snyderman) and was subsequently amplified and developed in a later book (Herzberg, 1966).

On the basis of his study, Herzberg reported that employees tended to describe satisfying experiences in terms of factors that were intrinsic to the content of the job itself. These factors were called "motivators" and included such variables as achievement, recognition, the work itself, responsibility, advancement, and growth. Conversely, dissatisfying experiences, called "hygiene" factors, resulted largely from extrinsic, non-job-related factors, such as company policies, salary, coworker relations, and supervisory style. Herzberg argued, on the basis of these results, that eliminating the causes of dissatisfaction (through hygiene factors) would not result in a state of satisfaction. Instead, it would result in a neutral state. Satisfaction (and motivation) would occur only as a result of the use of motivators.

Evaluation of Herzberg's Motivator-Hygiene Theory   Since its inception, Herzberg's theory has been subject to several important criticisms. For example, it has been noted (King, 1970) that the model itself has five different theoretical interpretations and that the available research evidence is not entirely consistent with any of these interpretations. Second, a number of scholars believe the model does not give sufficient attention to individual differences (although Herzberg himself would dispute this) and assumes that job enrichment benefits all employees. Research evidence suggests that individual differences are, in fact, an important moderator of the effects of job enrichment. Finally, research has generally failed to support the existence of two independent factors (motivators and hygiene factors). Even so, the model has enhanced our understanding of motivation at work.

One of the most significant contributions of Herzberg's work was the strong impact it had on stimulating thought, research, and experimentation in the area of motivation at work. This contribution should not be overlooked. Before 1959, little research had been carried out on *work* motivation (with the notable exception of Viteles, 1953, and Maier, 1955), and the research that did exist was largely fragmentary. Maslow's work on needs hierarchy theory and Murray's, McClelland's, and Atkinson's work on achievement motivation theory were concerned largely with laboratory-based findings or clinical observations, and none had seriously addressed the problems of the workplace at that time. Herzberg filled this void by specifically calling attention to the need for increased understanding of the role of motivation in work organizations.

Moreover, he did so in a systematic manner and in language that was easily understood by managers. He advanced a theory that was simple to grasp, was based on some empirical data, and—equally important—offered managers specific recommendations for action to improve employee motivational levels. In doing so, he forced organizations to examine closely a number of possible misconceptions concerning motivation. For example, Herzberg argued that money should not necessarily be viewed as the most potent force on the job. Moreover, he stated that other "context" factors in addition to money which surround an employee's job (such as fringe benefits and supervisory style) should not be expected to affect motivation markedly either. He advanced a strong case that managers must instead give considerable attention to a series of "content" factors (such as opportunities for achievement, recognition, and advancement) that have an important bearing on behavior.

In addition, Herzberg probably deserves a good deal of credit for acting as a stimulus to other researchers who have advocated alternative theories of *work* motivation. A multitude of research articles have been generated as a result of the so-called "Herzberg controversy." Some of these articles (e.g., Bockman, 1971; Whitset & Winslow, 1967) strongly support Herzberg's position, while others (e.g., House & Wigdor, 1967; Vroom, 1964) seriously question the research methodology underlying the theory. Such debate is healthy for any science. The student of motivation should consider Herzberg's theory—or any other such theory—to be one attempt at modeling work behavior. In other words, it appears that a fruitful approach to this "controversial" theory would be to learn from it that which can help us develop better models, rather than to accept or reject the model totally.

It is interesting that, despite the voluminous criticism leveled against the model, Herzberg's motivation-hygiene theory is still popular among managers. Furthermore, Herzberg's theory appears to have an international appeal. Gibson, Ivancevich, and Donnelly (1994) report that in their discussions of motivation applications with numerous managers in Europe, the Pacific Rim, and Latin America, "the Herzberg explanation is referred to more often than any other theory" (p. 156).

McClelland's Learned Needs Theory

Another well-known content theory is the learned needs theory developed by McClelland (1961, 1962, 1965a,b, 1971). He contends that individuals acquire certain needs from the culture of a society by learning from the events that they experience, particularly in early life. Four of the needs that people may learn are the need for achievement (n Ach), the need for power (n Pow), the need for affiliation (n Aff), and the need for autonomy (n Aut). Once learned, these needs may be regarded as personal predispositions that affect the way people perceive work (and other) situations and that influence their pursuit of certain goals.

Need for Achievement (n Ach) McClelland defined n Ach as "behavior toward competition with a standard of excellence" (McClelland, Atkinson, Clark, and Lowell,

1953). He and his associates conducted their most thorough series of studies on this particular learned need, and identified four characteristics of individuals with a high need for achievement: (1) a strong desire to assume personal responsibility for finding solutions to problems or performing a task, (2) a tendency to set moderately difficult achievement goals and to take calculated risks, (3) a strong desire for concrete performance feedback on tasks, and (4) a single-minded preoccupation with task accomplishment.

The need for achievement is perhaps the most prominent learned need from the standpoint of studying organizational behavior. The challenging nature of a difficult task cues that motive which, in turn, activates achievement-oriented behavior. Many managerial and entrepreneurial positions are assumed to require such a need in individuals in order for them to be successful. However, when people with a high n Ach are given routine or unchallenging jobs, the achievement motive will probably not be activated. Therefore, there would be little reason to expect individuals with a high n Ach to perform in a superior fashion in such situations (McClelland, 1961).

Need for Power (n Pow)   The n Pow is defined as the need to control the environment, to influence the behavior of others, and to be responsible for them. McClelland contends that individuals with a high n Pow may be characterized by: (1) a desire to direct and control someone else, and (2) a concern for maintaining leader-follower relations. Research evidence suggests that individuals with high n Pow tend to be superior performers, to be in supervisor positions, to have above-average attendance records, and to be rated by others as having good leadership abilities (Steers & Braunstein, 1976).

Need for Affiliation (n Aff)   The need for affiliation is defined as an "attraction to another organism in order to feel reassured from the other that the self is acceptable" (Birch & Veroff, 1966). Individuals with a high n Aff desire to establish and maintain friendly and warm relationships with others. McClelland identified three characteristics of individuals with a high need for affiliation (1) a strong desire for approval and reassurance from others, (2) a tendency to conform to the wishes and norms of others when pressured by people whose friendship they value, and (3) a sincere interest in the feelings of others.

People who have a high n Aff prefer to work with others rather than to work alone. Therefore, high n Aff individuals tend to take jobs characterized by a high amount of interpersonal contact, such as sales, teaching, public relations, and counseling. There is some evidence to suggest that employees with high n Aff have better attendance records than those with low n Aff (Birch & Veroff, 1966). In addition, some research findings indicate that employees with a high n Aff perform somewhat better in situations where personal support and approval are tied to performance (Chung, 1977; French, 1958).

The organizational implications of the n Aff appear to be fairly clear. McClelland's theory would suggest that n Aff employees will be productive to the extent that supervisors can create a cooperative, supportive work environment where positive feedback is tied to task performance. The explanation for this is that by working hard in such an environment, an individual with a high n Aff can satisfy his or her affiliation needs.

Need for Autonomy (n Aut)   Need for autonomy is defined as a desire for independence. Individuals with a high n Aut want to work alone, prefer to control their own work place, and do not want to be hampered by excessive rules or procedures (Birch & Veroff, 1966). Research has found that individuals with a high n Aut tend not to be committed to the goals and objectives of their organizations, not to perform well unless they are allowed to participate in the determination of their tasks, and not to respond to external pressures for conformity to group norms.

Evaluation of McClelland's Learned Needs Theory   Most research evidence offered in support of McClelland's learned needs theory has been provided by McClelland or his associates, with the need for achievement receiving most of the attention from other organizational behavior theorists and researchers. Over the years, there have been a number of serious criticisms of McClelland's work. First, it is argued that the primary research instrument (a projective psychological test called the TAT) used in the studies by McClelland and his colleagues has questionable predictive validity. Second, McClelland's claim that needs, especially n Ach, can be learned by adults conflicts with a large body of literature stating that motives are normally acquired in childhood and that they are difficult to alter in adulthood. McClelland (1962) recognizes this problem but points to evidence from politics and religion that suggests otherwise. Third, McClelland's notion of acquired needs is questioned by some scholars on the grounds that needs may not be acquired *permanently*.

Despite these and other criticisms of McClelland's research and theory, the concept of learned or acquired needs is an important one and has clear applicability to organizational and work settings. It emphasizes, to use psychological terminology, that *nurture*—that is, what kinds of life circumstances people encounter and experience—is as important as *nature*—that is, what people are "born with"—in understanding what motivates human behavior.

PROCESS THEORIES OF MOTIVATION

Content theories of motivation conceptualize behavior as the product of innate psychological characteristics (e.g., needs). In contrast, process theories view behavior as the result, at least in part, of human decision processes. This section begins with a discussion of some of the early cognitive theories that are relevant to motivation, and which establish a foundation for the process theories of work motivation. Two of the most important of these process theories will then be examined. The first is Vroom's expectancy theory. The second is the Porter-Lawler model of work motivation, which represents an extension and elaboration of Vroom's theory.

Early Cognitive Theories Relevant to Motivation

The basic tenet of this theoretical framework is that a major determinant of human behavior is the beliefs, expectations, and anticipations individuals have concerning future events. Behavior is thus seen as purposeful, goal-directed, and based on conscious intentions. Two of the most prominent early researchers who developed such cognitive approaches were Tolman and Lewin. While Tolman studied animal behavior and

Lewin human behavior, both took the position that organisms make conscious decisions concerning future behavior on the basis of cues from their environment. Such a theory is largely *ahistorical* in nature (as opposed to the historical notion inherent in drive theory, discussed in an earlier section). Tolman (1932) argued, for example, that learning results more from changes in beliefs about the environment than from changes in the strengths of past habits. Cognitive theorists did not entirely reject the concept that past events may be important for present behavior, however. Lewin (1938), whose work is characterized by an ahistorical approach, noted that historical and ahistorical approaches were in some ways complementary. Past occurrences could have an impact on present behavior to the extent that they modified present conditions. For example, the past experience of a child who burned a finger on a hot stove may very likely carry over into the present to influence behavior. In general, however, the cognitive theorists posited that it is the "events of the day" that largely influence behavior; past events are important only to the extent that they affect present and future beliefs and expectations.

In general, cognitive theories of motivation—or expectancy/valence theories (also called "instrumentality" theories), as they later became known—view motivational force as a multiplicative function of two key variables: expectancies and valences. "Expectancies" were seen by Lewin (1938) and Tolman (1959) as beliefs individuals had that particular actions on their part would lead to certain outcomes. "Valence" denoted the amount of positive or negative value placed on *anticipated* outcomes by an individual.

Typically, the early cognitive theories were developed to have general applications. Later, however, cognitive-type models were produced specifically for use in work situations. Two of these process theories will be discussed next.

Vroom's Expectancy Theory

Vroom (1964) presented the first systematic formulation of expectancy theory developed specifically for work situations. His model is based on the assumption that individuals make conscious and rational choices about their work behavior. This perspective contrasts sharply with the idea that people are inherently motivated or unmotivated, as many noncognitive models presume. According to Vroom (1964), employees rationally evaluate various work behaviors (e.g., working overtime versus leaving work early) and then choose those that they believe will lead to the work-related rewards that they value most (e.g., promotions). Put another way, employees will decide to apply effort to those tasks that they find attractive and that they believe they can perform. The attractiveness of a particular task depends upon the extent to which the employee believes that its accomplishment will lead to valued outcomes (John, 1992). A useful way of viewing the model is presented below.

1 Outcomes: These are the anticipated consequences that are relevant to the individual and that are perceived to follow certain of his or her work behaviors, such as a pay raise, a sense of accomplishment, acceptance by peers, fatigue, and so on.

2 Valence: This is the extent to which the *anticipated* outcomes appear attractive or unattractive to the individual. The valance of an outcome can range from –1.0 (a highly undesirable outcome, such as being fired) to +1.0 (a very desirable outcome, such as a promotion). Work-related outcomes, such as good pay, a good job, group support, being fired, and so forth, vary in their attractiveness from person to person. Typically, pay raises have high valences for employees. For example, a pay raise may appear very attractive, (e.g., the valence is 1.0) to a particular salesperson.

3 E → P Expectancy: This is the *effort-performance* (E → P) *expectancy* (called simply "expectancy" in Vroom's original work) and is defined as an individual's subjective probability that effort will actually lead to performance on some job or task. This degree of belief can vary from 0 (the individual is certain that behavior will *not* lead to performance) to 1.0 (the individual is sure that behavior will lead to performance). For example, a salesperson may feel fairly confident (e.g., an expectancy of 0.8) that working an extra hour per day will result in a 10% increase in his or her product sales for the quarter.

4 P → O Expectancy: This is the *performance-outcome* (P → O) *expectancy* (also called "instrumentality" in Vroom's work) and is defined as an individual's belief that a particular level of performance in a given situation will result in a particular set of outcomes. As with the effort-performance expectancy, the performance outcome expectancy can range from 0 to 1.0, and a person may have any number of outcome expectancies regarding performance. For example, a salesperson may strongly believe (e.g., an expectancy of 0.9) that a 0% increase in his or her product sales for the quarter will result in a pay raise. He or she may believe that there is a slim chance (e.g., an expectancy of 0.1) that this 10% increase in performance will lead to a promotion.

According to the theory, E→ P expectancies, P → O expectancies, and the valences of various outcomes (considered by the employee) influence the person's level of motivation. Further, these variables are assumed to operate in a multiplicative fashion. Using the example above, if a pay raise appears very attractive to a salesperson (e.g., valence = 1.0), if the person is fairly confident that an increase in effort will lead to an increase in performance (E → P = 0.8), and if he or she strongly believes that an increase in performance will result in a desired outcome (e.g., a pay raise) (P → O = 0.9), then the individual appears to have a relatively high motivational force (1.0 × .8 × .9 = .72). However, if the salesperson did not believe that an increase in performance will lead to a pay raise (e.g., P → O = 0.1), then the motivational force would not be nearly so high (1.0 × .8 × .1 = .08). With this multiplicative model, all three factors must be high for the motivational level of an individual to be high.

Evaluation of Vroom's Expectancy Theory   This theory has generated a considerable body of research, much of which suggests that difficulties are encountered when testing the model (Harrell & Stahl, 1986; Miner, 1980). One problem involves the concept of effort, or motivation, itself. As noted above, the theory attempts to predict the amount of effort that the individual will expend on one or more tasks. However, there is limited agreement about the meaning of effort. Further, expectancy theory, as a process theory, does not specify which outcomes are relevant to a particular individual in a particular situation. Each researcher has tended to address this issue in a unique way. Consequently, no systematic approach has been used across investigations. In addition, and especially important, the expectancy approach contains the implicit assumption that motivation is a conscious rational choice process. That is, individuals are assumed consciously to calculate the pleasure or pain that they expect to attain or avoid when making a choice. However, it is generally accepted that individuals are not always conscious of their motives, expectancies, and perceptual processes. Yet expectancy theory tends to ignore habitual behavior and subconscious motivation.

The Porter-Lawler Model

Porter and Lawler (1968) refined and extended Vroom's (1964) expectancy model. They agree with Vroom that employee effort is jointly determined by the valence that employees place on certain outcomes and the degree to which people believe that their efforts will lead to the attainment of these rewards. However, Porter and Lawler emphasize that effort may not necessarily result in performance. Furthermore, they contend that the relationship between valences and expectancies, on the one hand, and effort or motivation, on the other, is more complicated than Vroom's model suggests. The Porter-Lawler model is presented in Exhibit 2-1.

The Porter-Lawler model holds that effort may not necessarily result in job performance for two reasons. First, the individual may not have the ability to accomplish the

EXHIBIT 2-1
The Porter-Lawler model of work motivation. (From Lyman W. Porter & Edward E. Lawler III, Managerial attitudes and performance. Homewood, Ill.: Irwin, 1968, p. 165. Reprinted by permission.)

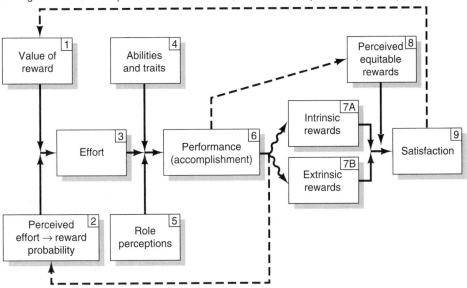

tasks that constitute his or her job. In this case, even if the employee is highly motivated (i.e., expends a lot of effort), performance may not be obtained. Second, the person may not have a good understanding of the task to be performed (i.e., there may be a lack of role clarity). High motivation will not result in job performance if the employee does not have a clear grasp of the ways in which effort may be appropriately directed.

In addition, this model highlights the point that performance and satisfaction may not necessarily be related to each other. Porter and Lawler define satisfaction as "the extent to which rewards actually received meet or exceed the perceived equitable level of rewards" (p. 31). The relationship between performance and satisfaction depends on several factors. For example, in organizations, performance may not always result in expected rewards. Employees are not likely to be satisfied in situations where they are not given the amount of rewards to which they think they are entitled.

Furthermore, the Porter-Lawler model indicates that the nature of the task has implications for the satisfaction-performance linkage. That is, performance on a task may provide the employee with intrinsic rewards, extrinsic rewards, or both. Moreover, the authors suggest that intrinsic rewards can be more closely linked with good performance than extrinsic rewards, because intrinsic rewards can result directly from task performance. In contrast, extrinsic rewards are administered by the organization. In other words, extrinsic rewards depend upon outside sources both for recognition that performance has been attained and for the administration of appropriate compensation.

In addition, the model holds that employees' self-ratings of performance have a major impact on their beliefs about what levels of rewards are equitable. The theory posits that rewards are not evaluated in absolute terms; rather they are assessed subjectively. For example, if employees believe that they have achieved a high level of performance, they will think that they are entitled to greater rewards than would be the case if they thought that their performance was at a low level.

Finally, Porter and Lawler suggest what may happen after an employee performs. Specifically, the rewards that result from a particular level of performance will interact with the employee's perception of them to determine satisfaction. Thus, this model suggests that performance leads to satisfaction, rather than the opposite. This was a significant departure from the traditional thinking.

Evaluation of the Porter-Lawler Model   Some research evidence supports aspects of the model (Roberts & Glick, 1981); however, the model has also been criticized on several grounds (Pinder, 1984). For example, the generalizability of the model may be limited by the fact that the research accompanying the development of the model focused exclusively on pay as it relates to employee motivation. Additional research is needed to test whether other consequences of performance, both positive and negative (e.g., promotion, demotion, fatigue), have the same impact on employees. Also, Porter and Lawler tested their propositions cross-sectionally rather than longitudinally, and this may result in overestimates of the validity of the model (Taylor and Griess, 1976).

On the other hand, this model can provide managers with a useful basis for analyzing and understanding motivational situations in organizational settings. In addition, this model focuses on, and provides guidelines for, how organizations can critically evaluate the effectiveness of their current reward policies and practices.

MANAGERIAL APPROACHES TO MOTIVATION

As we have seen, there has been a gradual evolution in psychological theories of motivation. Similarly, there have been major developments and trends in the way that managers in work organizations approach motivational challenges in the employment situation. Therefore, we now shift our attention directly to the workplace itself and review the changing pattern of managerial approaches to motivating employees. It will be apparent in the following discussion that, although psychological theories and managerial practices relating to motivation developed roughly during the same span of time across the decades of the twentieth century, there have been few signs of any sort of cross-fertilization of ideas until relatively recently.

Before the industrial revolution, the major type of "motivation" took the form of fear of punishment—physical, financial, or social. However, as manufacturing processes became more complex, large-scale factories emerged which destroyed many of the social exchange relationships which had existed under the "home industries," or "putting out," system of small manufacturing. These traditional patterns of behavior between workers and their "patrons" were replaced by the more sterile and tenuous relationship between employees and their company. Thus, the industrial revolution was a revolution not only in a production sense, but also in a social sense.

The genesis of this social revolution can be traced to several factors. First, the increased capital investment necessary for factory operation required a high degree of efficiency in order to maintain an adequate return on investment. This meant that an organization had to have an efficient work force. Second, and somewhat relatedly, the sheer size of these new operations increased the degree of impersonalization in superior-subordinate relationships, necessitating new forms of supervision. Third, and partly as a justification of the new depersonalized factory system, the concept of social Darwinism came into vogue. In brief, this philosophy argued that no person held responsibility for other people and naturally superior people were destined to rise in society, while naturally inferior ones would eventually be selected out of it. In other words, it was "every person for him- or herself" in the workplace.

These new social forces brought about the need for a fairly well defined philosophy of management. Many of the more intrinsic motivational factors of the home industry system were replaced by more extrinsic factors. Workers—or, more specifically, "good" workers—were seen as pursuing their own best economic self-interests. The end result of this "new" approach in management was what has been termed the "traditional" model of motivation.

Traditional Model

This model is best represented by the writings of Frederick W. Taylor (1911) and his associates in the scientific management school. Far from being exploitative in intent, scientific management was viewed by these writers as an economic boon to the worker as well as to management. Taylor saw the problem of inefficient production as a problem primarily with management, not workers. It was management's responsibility to find suitable people for a job and then to train them in the most efficient methods for their work. The workers having been thus well trained, management's next responsibility was to install a wage incentive system whereby workers could maximize their income by doing exactly what management told them to do and doing it as rapidly as possible. Thus, in theory, scientific management represented a joint venture of management and workers to the benefit of both. If production problems arose, they could be solved either by altering the technology of the job or by modifying the wage incentive program.

This approach to motivation rested on several very basic contemporary assumptions about the nature of human beings. Specifically, workers were viewed as being typically lazy, often dishonest, aimless, dull, and, most of all, mercenary. To get them into the factories and to keep them there, an organization had to pay a "decent" wage, thus outbidding alternative forms of livelihood (e.g., farming). To get workers to produce, tasks were to be simple and repetitive, output controls were to be externally set, and workers were to be paid bonuses for beating their quotas. The manager's major task was thus seen as closely supervising workers to ensure that they met their production quotas and adhered to company rules. In short, the underlying motivational assumption of the traditional model was that, for a price, workers would tolerate the routinized, highly fractionated jobs of the factory. These assumptions and expectations, along with their implied managerial strategies, are summarized in Exhibit 2-2.

As this model became increasingly applied in organizations, several problems began to arise. To begin with, managers, in their quest for profits, began modifying the basic system. While jobs were made more and more routine and specialized (and "efficient" from a mass-production standpoint), management began putting severe constraints on the incentive system, thereby limiting worker income. Workers soon discovered that, although their output was increasing, their wages were not (at least not proportionately). Simultaneously fear of job security arose. As factories became more "efficient," fewer workers were needed to do the job and layoffs and terminations became commonplace. Workers responded to the situation through elaborate and covert methods of restricting output in an attempt to optimize their incomes while protecting their jobs. Unionism began to rise, and the unparalleled growth and efficiency that had occurred under scientific management began to subside.

In an effort to overcome such problems, some organizations began to reexamine the simplicity of their motivational assumptions about employees and to look for new methods to increase production and maintain a steady work force. It should be pointed out, however, that the primary economic assumption of the traditional model was not eliminated in the newer approaches and that it remains a central concept of many motivational approaches today. Recent studies among both managers and workers indicate that money is a primary motivational force and that many workers will, in fact, select jobs more on the basis of salary prospects than job content. However, newer approaches have tended to view the role of money in more complex terms as it affects motivational force. Moreover, these newer theories argue that additional factors are also important inputs into the decision to produce. One such revisionist approach to motivation at work is the "human relations" model.

EXHIBIT 2-2
GENERAL PATTERNS OF MANAGERIAL APPROACHES TO MOTIVATION

Traditional model	Human relations model	Human resources model
Assumptions		
1 Work is inherently distasteful to most people.	1 People want to feel useful and important.	1 Work is not inherently distasteful. People want to contribute to meaningful goals which they have helped to establish.
2 What they do is less important than what they earn for doing it.	2 People desire to belong and to be recognized as individuals.	
3 Few want or can handle work which requires creativity, self-direction, or self-control.	3 These needs are more important than money in motivating people to work.	2 Most people can exercise far more creative, responsible self-direction and self-control than their present jobs demand.
1 The manager's basic task is closely to supervise and control subordinates.	1 The manager's basic task is to make each worker feel useful and important.	1 The manager's basic task is to make use of "untapped" human resources.
2 He or she must break tasks down into simple, repetitive, easily learned operations.	2 He or she should keep subordinates informed and listen to their objections to his or her plans.	2 He or she must create an environment in which all members may contribute to the limits of their ability.
3 He or she must establish detailed work routines and procedures, and enforce these firmly but fairly.	3 The manager should allow subordinates to exercise some self-direction and self-control on routine matters.	3 He or she must encourage full participation on important matters, continually broadening subordinate self-direction and control.
Policies		
1 People can tolerate work if the pay is decent and the boss is fair.	1 Sharing information with subordinates and involving them in routine decisions will satisfy their basic needs to belong and to feel important.	1 Expanding subordinate influence, self-direction, and self-control will lead to direct improvements in operating efficiency.
2 If tasks are simple enough and people are closely controlled, they will produce up to standard.	2 Satisfying these needs will improve morale and reduce resistance to formal authority—subordinates will "willingly cooperate."	2 Work satisfaction may improve as a "by-product" of subordinates making full use of their resources.
Expectations		

Human Relations Model

Beginning in the late 1920s, initial efforts were made to discover why the traditional model was inadequate for motivating people. The earliest such work carried out by Mayo (1933, 1945) and Roethlisberger and Dickson (1939) pointed the way to what was to become the human relations school of management by arguing that it was necessary to consider the "whole person" on the job. These researchers posited that the increased routinization of tasks brought about by the industrial revolution had served to drastically reduce the possibilities of finding satisfaction in the task itself. They believed that, because of this change, workers would begin seeking satisfaction elsewhere (such as from their coworkers). On the basis of this early research, many of the traditional assumptions were replaced with a new set of propositions concerning the nature of human beings (see Exhibit 2-2). Bendix (1956, p. 294) best summarized this evolution in managerial thinking by noting that the "failure to treat workers as human beings came to be regarded as the cause of low morale, poor craftsmanship, unresponsiveness, and confusion."

The new assumptions concerning the "best" method of motivating workers were characterized by a strong social emphasis. It was argued here that management had a responsibility to make employees *feel* useful and important on the job, to provide recognition, and generally to facilitate the satisfaction of workers' social needs. Attention was shifted away from the study of worker-machine relations and toward a more thorough understanding of interpersonal and group relations at work. Behavioral research into factors affecting motivation began in earnest, and morale surveys came into vogue in an attempt to measure and maintain job satisfaction. The basic ingredient that typically was *not* changed was the nature of the required tasks on the job.

The motivational strategies which emerged from such assumptions were several. First, as noted above, management felt it had a new responsibility to make workers feel important. Second, many organizations attempted to open up vertical communication channels so that employees would know more about the organization and would have greater opportunity to have their opinions heard by management. Company newsletters emerged as one source of downward communication. Employee "gripe sections" were begun as one source of upward communication. Third, workers were increasingly allowed to make routine decisions concerning their own jobs. Finally, as managers began to realize the existence of informal groups with their own norms and role prescriptions, greater attention was paid to using group incentive systems. Underlying all four of these developments was the presumed necessity of viewing motivation as largely a social process. Supervisory training programs began emphasizing the idea that a supervisor's role was no longer simply that of a taskmaker. Supervisors had also to be understanding and sympathetic to the needs and desires of their subordinates. However, as pointed out by Miles (1965), the basic goal of management under this strategy remained much the same as it had been under the traditional model; that is, both strategies aimed at securing employee compliance with managerial authority.

Human Resources Model

In recent years the assumptions of the human relations model have been widely challenged, not only as an oversimplified and incomplete statement of human behavior at work, but also for being as manipulative as the traditional model. In response to the criticism, a different approach was proposed under various titles, including McGregor's (1960) "Theory Y," Likert's (1967) "System 4," Schein's (1972) "Complex Man," and Miles' (1965) "Human Resources" model. The latter term will be used here as being more descriptive of the underlying philosophy inherent in these new perspectives.

Human resources models generally view humans as being motivated by a complex set of interrelated factors (such as money, need for affiliation, need for achievement, and desire for meaningful work). It is assumed that different employees often seek quite different goals in a job and have a diversity of talents to offer. Under this conceptualization, employees are regarded as reservoirs of potential talent, and management's responsibility is to learn how best to tap such resources.

Inherent in such a philosophy are several fairly basic assumptions about the nature of people. First, it is assumed that people want to contribute on the job. In this sense, employees are viewed as being, to a degree, "premotivated" to perform. In fact, the more people become involved in their work, the more meaningful the job can often become. Second, it is assumed that work does not necessarily have to be distasteful. Many of the current efforts at job enrichment and job redesign are aimed at increasing the potential meaningfulness of work by adding greater task variety, autonomy, responsibility, and so on. Third, it is argued that employees are quite capable of making significant and rational decisions affecting their work and that allowing greater latitude in employee decision making is actually in the best interests of the organization. Finally, it is assumed that increased self-control and direction allowed to employees on the job, plus the completion of more meaningful tasks, can in large measure determine the level of satisfaction on the job. In other words, it is generally assumed that good and meaningful performance leads to job satisfaction and not the reverse, as is assumed in the human relations model.

Certain implied managerial strategies follow naturally from this set of assumptions. In general, this approach would hold that it is management's responsibility first to appreciate the complex nature of motivational patterns. On the basis of such knowledge, management should attempt to determine how best to use the potential resources available to it through its work force. It should assist employees in meeting some of their own personal goals within the organizational context. Moreover, such a philosophy implies a greater degree of participation by employees in relevant decision-making activities, as well as increased autonomy over task accomplishment. Thus, in contrast to the traditional and human relations models, management's task is seen not so much as one of manipulating employees to accept managerial authority as it is of setting up conditions in which employees can meet their own goals at the same time as meeting the organization's goals.

In conclusion, it should be pointed out that the human resources approach to motivation has only lately begun to receive concentrated attention. Many organizations have attempted to implement one or more aspects of it, but full-scale adoptions of the approach, including the multitude of strategic implications for managers, are still not common. In fact, when one looks across organizations, it becomes readily apparent that aspects of all three models have their advocates. In recent years, in fact, the notion of a multiple strategy—using all three approaches at one time or another depending upon the nature of the organization, its technology, its people, and its goals and priorities—has come to be labeled a "contingency approach" to management. In effect, a contingency perspective allows one to dispense with the unlikely assumption that a single approach will be equally effective under any and all circumstances, and rather substitutes an emphasis on diagnosis of the situation to determine which approach will be more useful and appropriate under the *particular* circumstances.

OVERVIEW OF THE READINGS

The first article, by Komaki and her colleagues, discusses how reinforcement theory applies to the workplace. The primary emphasis in reinforcement theory is on how the environment can be "constructed" or modified to bring about particular types of effects on a person's behavior. For some time, there has been strong interest in applications of reinforcement theory in the everyday work environment. Komaki's article, based on research studies carried out over the past 20 years, highlights the issues and problems involved in the implementation of this approach. As the article demonstrates, the theory has been used to improve performance in a wide variety of work situations, on a wide set of behaviors, and with a range of consequences. Of particular interest, and representing a unique contribution of the article, is the later section that explores the issue of how reinforcement theory can help us better understand, from a motivational perspective, why people do what they do.

The second article, by Mowday, examines a theory—equity theory—that was originally developed in the 1960s. The article describes the basic formulation of this theory, which is grounded in social exchange processes, and summarizes a considerable body of related research. The emphasis of equity theory on social comparisons involved in interactions or "exchanges" among people makes it relevant to many aspects of behavior in work situations, especially those involving the effects of compensation on individuals' levels of motivation for task performance.

Although there have not been many advances in the development of equity theory in the last decade or so, the theory has nevertheless led to some interesting and relatively new (in terms of concerted research attention) issues. One such issue is that of procedural justice in the workplace, which is explored in the third article in this chapter, by Cropanzano and Folger. These authors highlight the distinction between two types of justice: distributive justice, which is at the heart of equity theory and which deals with the differing amounts of rewards (or punishments) "distributed" to different individuals; and procedural justice, which focuses on how decisions to distribute particular rewards or punishments are made. As Cropanzano and Folger emphasize, distributive justice is concerned with "ends," whereas procedural justice is concerned with "means." Thus, strictly speaking, procedural justice is not a component of equity theory but rather a logical extension of it in terms of understanding the motivated behavior of individuals. In light of society's increasing attention to procedural due process—especially in the employment situation—a focus on procedural justice seems particularly relevant in today's world of work.

The subject of the fourth article, by Wood and Bandura, is social learning theory. This theory has received noteworthy attention in recent years from the field of psychology, and it seems especially applicable to work situations, since almost all such situations are, to some degree, "social." The authors (Bandura is the primary developer of social learning theory) provide an elaboration of the fundamental theory. They emphasize the importance of beliefs in one's own competencies and explain how self-regulation of motivation operates by means of individuals' internal standard or goals and their comparisons of their behavior with those goals.

Goal-setting is the topic of the fifth reading, by Locke and Latham. Locke is generally credited with producing the seminal work on goal-setting in 1968. The basic premise of this approach to work motivation is that employees' conscious goals influence their work. The article traces the history of the concept of goal and sets forth the theoretical foundation of the goal-setting approach to motivation. Notably, Locke and Latham discuss the relationship between goal-setting theory and other models or frameworks of work motivation.

Klein presents a control theory model of motivation in the sixth article. From a control theory perspective, motivation is regulated by means of a negative feedback loop in which an individual compares his or her perceived performance against a goal standard. According to the theory, behavior is directed toward the reduction of discrepancies between goal standards and the perceived state of affairs. Although control theory has come in for heavy criticism (e.g., Locke, 1991), it has been receiving recent attention in the organizational studies literature as a theory of work motivation.

In the final article in this chapter, Shamir observes that most recent models of motivation developed by organizational researchers have assumed that individuals are simply rational calculators attempting to maximize their own utility. However, he argues that the literature dealing with motivation suggests that much observed organizational behavior cannot be explained on the basis of this assumption. In order to overcome the limitations imposed by this restrictive premise, Shamir presents a self-concept-based theory of work motivation. From this perspective, he argues that individuals are not just motivated to maximize utility on the basis of some rational calculus. In addition, individuals are intrinsically motivated to maintain and increase their self-worth and self-esteem, and people are motivated to maintain consistency among the various parts of their self-concepts and between their self-concepts and behavior.

REFERENCES

Alderfer, C. P. *Existence, relatedness, and growth.* New York: Free Press, 1972.

Allport, G. W. The historical background of modern psychology. In G. Lindzey (Ed.), *Handbook of social psychology.* Cambridge, Mass.: Addison-Wesley, 1954.

Atkinson, J. W. *An introduction to motivation.* Princeton, N.J.: Van Nostrand, 1964.

Bendix, R. *Work and authority in industry.* New York: Wiley, 1956.

Birch, D., & Veroff, J. *Motivation: A study of action.* Monterey, Calif.: Brooks/Cole, 1966.

Bockman, V. M. The Herzberg controversy. *Personnel Psychology,* 1971, 24, 155–189.

Campbell, J. P., & Pritchard, R. D. Motivation theory in industrial and organizational psychology. In M. D. Dunnette (Ed.), *Handbook of industrial and organizational psychology.* Chicago: Rand McNally, 1976.

Cannon, W. B. *The wisdom of the body.* New York: Norton, 1939.

Cherrington, D. J. *Organizational behavior.* Needham Heights, Mass.: Allyn & Bacon, 1989.

Chung, K. H. *Motivation theories and practices.* Columbus, Oh.: Grid, 1977, pp. 47–48.

French, E. Effects of the interaction of motivation and feedback on task performance. In J.

Atkinson (Ed.), *Motives in fantasy, action and society,* Princeton, N.J.: Van Nostrand, 1958, pp. 400–408.

Freud, S. The unconscious. In *Collected papers of Sigmund Freud,* Vol. IV (J. Rivière, Trans.). London: Hogarth, 1949. (First published in 1915.)

Gibson, J. L., Ivancevich, J. M., & Donnelly, J. H., Jr. *Organizations: Behavior, structure, processes.* Boston: Irwin, 1994.

Harrell, A., & Stahl, M. J. Additive information processing and the relationship between expectancy of success and motivational force. *Academy of Management Journal,* 1986, 29, 424–433.

Herzberg, F. *Work and the nature of man.* Cleveland: World Publishing, 1966.

Herzberg, F., Mausner, B., & Snyderman, B. B. *The motivation to work.* New York: Wiley, 1959.

Hilgard, E. R., & Atkinson, R. C. *Introduction to psychology.* New York: Harcourt, Brace & World, 1967.

House, R. J., & Wigdor, L. A. Herzberg's dual-factor theory of job satisfaction and motivation. *Personnel Psychology,* 1967, 20, 369–390.

Hull, C. L. *Principles of behavior.* New York: Appleton-Century-Crofts, 1943.

Hull, C. L. *A behavior system: An introduction to behavior theory concerning the individual organism.* New Haven, Conn.: Yale University Press, 1952.

James, W. *The principles of psychology,* Vols. I and II. New York: Henry Holt, 1890.

John, G. *Organizational behavior: Understanding life at work,* 3rd ed. New York: Harper-Collins, 1992.

Jones, M. R. (Ed.). *Nebraska symposium on motivation.* Lincoln: University of Nebraska Press, 1955.

King, N. Clarification and evaluation of the two-factor theory of job satisfaction. *Psychological Bulletin,* 1970, 74, 18–31.

Lewin, K. *The conceptual representation and the measurement of psychological forces.* Durham, N.C.: Duke University Press, 1938.

Likert, R. *The human organization.* New York: McGraw-Hill, 1967.

Locke, E. A. Toward a theory of task motivation and incentives. *Organizational Behavior and Human Performance,* 1968, 3, 157–189.

Locke, E. A. Goal theory vs. control theory: Contrasting approaches to understanding work motivation. *Motivation and Emotion,* 1991, 15(1), 9–28.

Maier, N. R. F. *Psychology in industry,* 2d ed. Boston: Houghton Mifflin, 1955.

Maslow, A. H. *Motivation and personality.* New York: Harper & Row, 1954.

Maslow, A. H. *Toward a theory of being.* New York: Van Nostrand Reinhold, 1968.

Mayo, E. *The human problems of an industrial civilization.* New York: Macmillan, 1933.

Mayo, E. *The social problems of an industrial civilization.* Cambridge, Mass.: Harvard University Press, 1945.

McClelland, D. C. *The achieving society.* Princeton, N.J.: Van Nostrand, 1961.

McClelland, D. C. Business drive and national achievement. *Harvard Business Review,* 1962, 40, 99–112.

McClelland, D. C. Achievement motivation can be developed. *Harvard Business Review,* 1965a, 43, 6–24, 178.

McClelland, D. C. Toward a theory of motive acquisition. *American Psychologist,* 1965b, 20, 321–333.

McClelland, D. C. *Assessing human motivation.* New York: General Learning Press, 1971.

McClelland, D. C., Atkinson, J. W., Clark, R. A., & Lowell, E. L. *The achievement motive.* New York: Appleton-Century-Crofts, 1953.

McClelland, D. C., & Burnham, D. H. Power is the great motivator. *Harvard Business Review,* 1976, 54, 100–110.

McDougall, W. *An introduction to social psychology.* London: Methuen, 1908.

McGregor, D. *The human side of enterprise.* New York: McGraw-Hill, 1960.

Miles, R. E. Human relations or human resources? *Harvard Business Review,* 1965, 43(4), 148–163.

Miner, J. *Theories of organizational behavior.* Hinsdale, Ill.: Dryden Press, 1980.

Morgan, C. T., & King, R. A. *Introduction to psychology.* New York: McGraw-Hill, 1966.

Pinder, C. C. *Work motivation: Theories, issues, and applications.* HarperCollins, 1984.

Porter, L. W. A study of perceived need satisfaction in bottom and middle management jobs. *Journal of Applied Psychology,* 1961, 45, 1–10.

Porter, L. W., & Lawler, E. E. III. *Managerial attitudes and performance.* Homewood, Ill.: Richard D. Irwin, 1968.

Roberts, K., & Glick, W. The job characteristics approach to task design: A critical review. *Journal of Applied Psychology,* 1981, 66, 193–217.

Roethlisberger, F., & Dickson, W. J. *Management and the worker.* Cambridge, Mass.: Harvard University Press, 1939.

Schein, E. *Organizational psychology.* Englewood Cliffs, N.J.: Prentice-Hall, 1972.

Schneider, B., & Alderfer, C. P. Three studies of measures of need satisfaction in organizations. *Administrative Science Quarterly,* 1973, 18, 489–505.

Skinner, B. F. *Science and human behavior.* New York: Macmillan, 1953.

Spence, K. W. *Behavior theory and conditioning.* New Haven, Conn.: Yale University Press, 1956.

Steers, R. M., & Black, J. S. *Organizational behavior,* 5th ed. New York: HarperCollins, 1994.

Steers, R. M., & Braunstein, D. N. Behaviorally based measure of manifest needs in work settings. *Journal of Vocational Behavior,* 1976, 9, 251–266.

Taylor, E. K., & Griess, T. The missing middle in validation research. *Personnel Psychology,* 1976, 29, 5–11.

Taylor, F. W. *Scientific management.* New York: Harper, 1911.

Thorndike, E. L. *Animal intelligence: Experimental studies.* New York: Macmillan, 1911.

Tolman, E. C. *Purposive behavior in animals and men.* New York: Appleton-Century-Crofts, 1932.

Tolman, E. C. Principles of purposive behavior. In S. Koch (Ed.), *Psychology: A study of science,* Vol. 2. New York: McGraw-Hill, 1959.

Viteles, M. S. *Motivation and morale in industry.* New York: Norton, 1953.

Vroom, V. H. *Work and motivation.* New York: Wiley, 1964.

Wahba, M. A., & Bridwell, L. G. Maslow reconsidered: A review of research on the need hierarchy theory. *Organizational Behavior and Human Performance,* 1976, 15, 212–240.

Whitset, D. A., & Winslow, E. K. An analysis of studies critical of the motivation-hygiene theory. *Personnel Psychology,* 1967, 20, 391–416.

Woodworth, R. S. *Dynamic psychology.* New York: Columbia University Press, 1918.

Motivational Implications of Reinforcement Theory

Judith L. Komaki
Timothy Coombs
Stephen Schepman

Two decades ago in the heady, idealistic times of the late 1960s, reports began streaming in that illustrated the application of reinforcement theory, a motivational theory emphasizing the consequences of performance. When consequences—such as feedback and recognition—were judiciously rearranged, dramatic improvements occurred in clinical, educational, and work settings. Children who were thought to be autistic and destined to spend the remainder of their lives in institutions began to communicate and to help themselves when they were reinforced for successive approximations to desired behaviors.[1] First-graders in a disadvantaged neighborhood learned skills critical to further achievement.[2] When dockworkers at Emery Air Freight were recognized for their efforts and received feedback, they worked more efficiently.[3] Even Army recruits in boot camp met the rigorous standards of their superiors when a token economy program was used.[4] Given these indications of the positive impact of reinforcement theory, industrial/organizational psychologists began discussing the promise of an innovative approach to motivation.[5–8]

Twenty years later, legitimate questions have been raised, particularly where adults in complex organizations are concerned, as to whether or not the reinforcement approach has lived up to its promise. In the first section of this article we review how it has been used in the past two decades to *promote* performance. We survey over 50 studies, all of them meticulously controlled. We outline the major findings as well as the people, the places, and the duration of the studies. We describe the types of reinforcers that have been used and the range of target behaviors.

The next section of the article discusses how reinforcement theory can lead to a better *understanding* of why people in organizations do seemingly perplexing things. We discuss how employees who do an outstanding job are inadvertently punished and why professors who genuinely believe in the importance of education sometimes neglect their teaching. The chapter ends with a forecast of what is likely to occur in the next two decades.

First, let us talk about reinforcement theory: what it hopes to do, what it is, and how it is typically used in work settings.

REINFORCEMENT THEORY IN APPLIED SETTINGS

Aims

The importance of motivating workers to maintain their performance over extended periods is eloquently portrayed by Isak Dinesen.[9] Responsible for a coffee plantation

This paper was written especially for the previous edition of this volume. A special note of thanks to Terry Coombs.

near Nairobi, she describes how workers must do many things over and over—setting plants in regular rows of holes, 600 trees to the acre; and how they must coordinate among themselves, first hulling, then grading and sorting the coffee, and then packing the coffee in sacks, 12 to a ton. These tasks are not unimportant. They must be done day in and day out, season after season, in just the right way. Motivating workers to sustain their performance is a formidable challenge that continues to elude practitioners and scholars alike.[10,11] Reinforcement theory, referred to as operant conditioning theory, behavior modification, or applied behavior analysis, identifies ways of helping persons like Dinesen secure the continued cooperation of workers.[12-14] Of the three aspects of motivation—initiating, directing, and maintaining performance[15,16]—reinforcement theory is particularly suited to maintaining performance on an ongoing basis.

Reflecting the visionary values of the late 1960s, reinforcement theorists hope to make a difference. When they work in applied settings, they aim to enhance behaviors of importance in a meaningful way. The studies, for example, aim at ensuring that mental health staff consistently implement residents' programs[17] and that policy board members learn how to work together to solve problems.[18] In fact, three spokespersons have gone on record, voicing their hope that "better application...will lead to a better state of society."[19]

Features

Reinforcement theory has two features which distinguish it from other motivation theories: its emphasis on the consequences of performance, and its techniques for assessing performance and evaluating effectiveness.

Focus on Performance Consequences   The consequences of our performance—the feedback we receive, the comments we hear—are thought to make a powerful impact on what we do from day to day. When frequent, contingent, positive consequences have been arranged to follow performance, substantial and meaningful improvements have occurred in literally thousands of experiments conducted on animals at all levels of the phylogenetic scale, including humans.[20-23] In fact, one of the major tenets of reinforcement theory is that behavior is a function of its consequences.

A distinction is made between consequences which occur *after* the behavior of interest and antecedents which occur *before* the behavior. When bosses do something which occurs after subordinate's behavior, for example, these actions are called consequences. Because the providing of feedback, recognition, and incentives typically follow subordinate performance, they would generally be categorized as consequences. When a packaging supervisor grins, thrusts out his hand for a quick congratulatory shake, and says to workers: "Good running last night. 537 cases," his actions and his statement are considered consequences.[24] On the other hand, when bosses do something *before* the occurrence of a subordinate's particular behavior, these actions are called antecedents. Because the providing of training, the setting of goals, and the communication of company policy typically precede subordinate performance, they would generally be categorized as antecedents. When Hector in the *Iliad* "sprang from his chariot clad in his suit of armour, and went about among the host brandishing his two spears, exhorting the men to fight and raising the terrible cry of battle,"[25] his exhortations were antecedent to the event.

How do consequences differ from antecedents? Consequences function in a motivational role, increasing or decreasing the probability of behaviors recurring, whereas antecedents serve in an educational or cuing role, clarifying expectations for performance, specifying the relationship between behavior and its consequences, and/or signaling occasions in which consequences are likely to be provided. For example, even though antecedents were provided (e.g., workers were exhorted to perform safely, they were provided information about proper safety procedures, and rules were posted), workers did not change their safety practices.[26] Only when consequences (in the form of feedback) were delivered did they consistently perform safely on the job. This study is consistent with other studies, which show that antecedents alone do not result in substantial improvements over an extended period in ongoing work settings.[27-29] Thus, antecedents are not considered sufficient to act as the sole motivating force. Consequences are critical. In fact, close examination of studies successful in sustaining performance, whether they are positive reinforcement studies or even Japanese management cases,[30] shows that they include at least one consequence.

Emphasis on Rigorous Evaluation Another noteworthy feature of reinforcement theory is its emphasis on evidence of a particular sort, that is, on empirical data.[31] No number of expert opinions substitutes for evidence that A actually changed and that B was truly responsible for A.

The development of fair and accurate ways of obtaining information about workers' performance has been a priority for reinforcement theorists. Referred to as *applied operant measures,*[32-35] these differ from traditional methods in two ways. First, they directly sample workers' performance, rather than rely on self-reports or indirect measures. For example, when assessing the service provided to customers, reinforcement theorists look at what the salesperson actually said to the customer rather than at "helpfulness" scores on rating scales or at sales volume or customer traffic, which are typically affected by many extraneous factors of which sales performance is only one tiny aspect. Similarly, when measuring safety, the focus is on the practices of workers on the job rather than on their reports of safety awareness or on accident statistics.

Secondly, the test of interrater reliability plays a critical role during three stages of the measurement process:

1 *During the developmental stage.* Two observers independently record and then calculate a percentage agreement score (number of agreements divided by number of agreements and disagreements). Revisions continue until agreement is reached on the scoring of virtually all checklist items all the time. When this criterion is achieved, then and only then are the terms considered objectively defined.

2 *In the training of observers.* Trainees are not considered trained until they can pass the test of interrater reliability.

3 *During the formal data collection.* Checks are made regularly to see whether observers have become stricter or more lenient than they were when they were trained. In short, when reinforcement theorists measure performance in applied settings, they directly sample what workers do and/or produce and they rely on the test of interrater reliability.

These applied operant measures form the foundation for the providing of consequences that are related to performance.

This empirical emphasis also makes imperative the rigorous evaluation of the effectiveness of programs. Reinforcement theorists want to know if the relationship between A and B is a result of happenstance or cause and effect. To evaluate with confidence requires the use of a particular type of research design, referred to as an *internally valid design*. Two families of designs are considered internally valid: (1) the traditional control-group designs such as the pretest-posttest control group design[36] and (2) the within-group designs such as the reversal and the multiple-baseline designs.[37,38]

Within-group designs, commonly used by reinforcement theorists, have the advantage of allowing one to draw cause-and-effect conclusions with assurance. At the same time, they do not require the random assignment of subjects to either treatment and control group, as the control-group design does. Rarely is it possible in the wrapping and makeup departments of a bakery, for example, to randomly assign workers so that two new groups are formed, one of which is treated and one of which is not treated. With within-group designs, each group serves as its own control. In the reversal design, for example, there are at least three phases: (1) a baseline phase, during which performance is measured before introducing any program, (2) an intervention phase, during which the program is introduced, while continuing to measure performance, and (3) a reversal phase, during which the treatment is discontinued or altered. The group's performance is assessed during baseline, intervention, and reversal phases. When performance improves during the intervention stage and "reverses" back to baseline during the reversal stage, it is possible to rule out the possibility that other factors such as technological innovations or practice were responsible and say with assurance that the program was responsible for the changes.

Another type of within-group design, the multiple-baseline design, is also used when evaluating the effectiveness of programs. A multiple-baseline design was used to assess the impact of a reinforcement program in two departments of a wholesale bakery (described in the next section). A versatile design, the multiple-baseline design can be used with intact groups (e.g., Crenshaw, Baldwin Hills branches), with individual workers, and with different behaviors (e.g., smiling, talking to customers). Perhaps not surprisingly, the reversal and multiple-baseline designs are used in many reinforcement studies.

Four-Step Process

A positive reinforcement program typically includes four steps: specifying desired performance, measuring workers' progress, judiciously rearranging consequences, and evaluating the effectiveness of the program. To get an idea of how this process typically works, let us take an example of a program carried out by the first author and two students at Georgia Tech.[39] Injuries had jumped sharply at a wholesale bakery, and management was naturally alarmed. To encourage employees to maintain safe practices, management introduced a four-step positive-reinforcement program that was very different from the usual approach of posting signs and admonishing workers to be careful.

1 *Specify desired behavior.* First, desired work practices were defined. To establish what workers should do to avoid having similar accidents in the future, verbs such as "turn off" and "release," rather than adjectives such as "careful" and "conscientious," were encouraged. A list of definitions was generated (e.g., "Walk around conveyer belt," "Look toward knife being sharpened"). To ensure that the definitions were objective, each definition had to meet the test of interrater reliability. When the criterion of 90 percent or better was achieved, then and only then were the terms considered objectively defined.

2 *Measure desired performance.* Observers, trained until they passed the test of interrater reliability, went to the work site and recorded the percent of incidents performed in a safe or unsafe manner. The observations were made frequently, four times a week on average. Checks on interrater reliability were conducted regularly.

3 *Provide frequent, contingent, positive consequences.* The consequence for safe practices was feedback. The department's safety scores were presented on a graph so that workers could see at a glance how their group had done and how this compared to their previous record. The graph was posted publicly in the work area, thus fostering a healthy competition between departments. When workers asked, they were also told what they had done correctly and incorrectly.

4 *Evaluate effectiveness on the job.* To assess whether or not the program was effective, a within-group research design—the multiple-baseline design across groups—was used. The two groups were the wrapping and makeup departments. Data were collected in both groups. The program was introduced in a staggered manner: after $5\frac{1}{2}$ weeks in the wrapping department and after $13\frac{1}{2}$ weeks in the makeup department.

The results: From performing safely 70 percent and 78 percent of the time, employees in the two departments substantially improved their safety performance to 96 percent and 99 percent, respectively. Within a year, the number of lost-time injuries dropped from 53 to 10. Although this is only one of a series of examples, it shows the four steps involved in sustaining the motivation of workers.

The next section surveys the reinforcement studies that have been conducted in work settings over the past 20 years.

USING REINFORCEMENT THEORY TO PROMOTE PERFORMANCE

Reinforcement theory has been found to work with a variety of target behaviors, for extended durations, with a range of subjects and settings, and using a variety of different consequences. A recent review shows that at least 51 well-controlled studies have been reported, addressing whether or not positive reinforcement results in improvements of performance on the job.[40] Of the 51 studies, 47 resulted in substantial improvements in performance, for a success rate of 92.2 percent of the studies. The positive results are consistent with previous reviews of the literature.[41–46]

With a Variety Of Target Behaviors

The studies, as a group, show broad generality. The target areas ranged from soliciting suggestions from mental health employees for solving common problems[47] to encouraging field salespersons to keep in touch with the home office.[48]

Productivity improvements have been reported in both the quantity and the quality of the work. Increases were obtained in the amount of time resource room teachers actually spent instructing pupils[49] and the percentage of pages that staff correctly types.[50]

Among the most popular target areas has been that of increasing *attendance and punctuality.* Approximately 20 studies have examined one or both of these topics.[51] Attending work on time is critical in organizations which rely on having a certain number of qualified workers present before running equipment or assembly lines. In some industries, the absenteeism rate can run as high as 10 to 20 percent of the work force on any given day, with costs estimated in the billions of dollars each year.[52] Thus, the decline in absenteeism from 3.01 percent to 2.4 percent at a unionized manufacturing and distribution center was significant both statistically and financially.[53]

In addition to these traditional areas, *safety and health*—an area of concern to both management and workers—has been the topic of over a dozen studies. Workers showed improvements in safety practices,[26,39] as well as other performance areas (housekeeping,[54] hazards,[55] and earplug usage[56]), thus lessening the chance of incurring a disabling injury. Working together, employees in a fiber-glass-reinforced plastics plant were also able to reduce their exposure to likely carcinogenic substances such as styrene and to enhance their chances of remaining healthy.[57]

A critical area for consumers, the *quality of service*, has been a regular subject of interest. Tellers in banks[58] and salespersons in department stores[59,60] upgraded their interactions with customers. Besides approaching customers more quickly, salespersons learned to assess customers' needs and then to provide relevant information.

With a Wide Range of Subjects and Settings

The settings of the studies ranged from real-estate offices to the U.S. Marine Corps.[61,62] Approximately half of the studies were conducted in the private sector, in manufacturing or service industries. The other half took place in the public sector, in social service agencies or in institutional or educational settings. The locations included the United States, as well as Scandinavia[54] and the Middle East.[56,58]

Among the subjects were bus drivers[63] and baseball players.[64] White- (e.g., supervisors), pink- (e.g., real estate agents), and blue-collar (e.g., factory workers) workers were represented. Sample sizes included the staff of 12 residential units in a psychiatric hospital[65] and over 1000 miners.[66]

With a Range of Different Types of Consequences

At least five different classes of consequences were used. Because all of the classes are not in everyday parlance, they are described in more detail.

1 *Organizational.* Indigenous to work settings, organizational consequences include promotions, pay raises, and special training opportunities. In a regional transportation authority, benefits such as free gasoline and free monthly passes on the bus system were offered to workers as an incentive for reducing accidents.[63]

2 *Generalized.* Generalized reinforcers derive their potency from the fact that they can be exchanged for backup reinforcers. Examples of generalized reinforcers include cash, frequent flyer coupons, and trading stamps. Trading stamps were given to miners who had not suffered a lost-time injury during the month.[66] Backup reinforcers include choices such as what, where, and with whom you work. The opportunity to select a clerical assignment was used as a backup reinforcer in a job training center for trainees who had earned coupons.[67]

3 *Activity.* Another class of consequences, derived from the Premack principle, is referred to as an activity consequence.[68] Basically, the Premack principle states that any activity which workers engage in more regularly than another activity can be used as a positive reinforcer. A novel application of the Premack principle took place in a sales organization.[69] When it was found that the callers liked to make renewal calls, rather than new service calls, the opportunity to sell five renewal contracts was made contingent upon one new service contract sale. When callers could only make renewal calls after making a service sale, they substantially increased new service sales.

4 *Social.* Typically expressed by individuals, social consequences include commendations, compliments, criticism, reviews, and recognition for a job well done. For example, winning teams were "personally congratulated by the director of operations."[63] In another example, hospital supervisors made comments to staff members, such as, "I'm pleased to see you interacting with clients, but I'm sure Mary [the client] is even more pleased."[70]

5 *Informational.* Informational consequences, as the label suggests, are ones in which information is provided about a person's performance. The information can be conveyed a variety of different ways. For example, feedback notes were passed on to supervisors to encourage the completion of accident reports; the number of total items that had been included, as well as any increases in completeness over prior submissions were mentioned.[71] In other studies, graphs of baseline and intervention levels of workers' performance were used.[26,39,54,55,59,62] The information itself can also vary. In the area of safety, the information provided included the percentage of incidents performed safely by the group,[26,39] the frequency of hazards,[55] the percentage of correct housekeeping practices,[54] and audiograms at the beginning and at the end of workers' shifts, showing the temporary hearing losses that occurred when earplugs were not worn.[72]

Consequences are often used in combination. Lessening the perennial procrastination associated with long-range, relatively unstructured projects—such as completing master's theses—was the aim of one study.[73] Realizing how easy it is to let more immediately pressing activities disrupt progress, the authors set up a system of weekly deadlines, monitoring, and a host of consequences. To help maintain a steady rate of work, they used social, informational, and organizational consequences. For the organizational consequences, the authors incorporate their evaluations of a student's progress on his or her master's thesis in the letters of recommendation they sent out for the student.

For Extended Durations

Each of the 51 studies was conducted in the field over a considerable amount of time. In fact, the median length of time that an intervention lasted was not 1, not 2, but 8 weeks. Illustrating the potential longevity of any positive reinforcement program, a token economy program was successful in reducing accidents for 11 years in one mine in Arizona and for 12 years in another mine in Wyoming.[66]

The next section takes a different perspective and describes how reinforcement theory can be used to explain workers' actions.

USING REINFORCEMENT THEORY TO UNDERSTAND WHY PEOPLE DO WHAT THEY DO

Have you ever wondered why normally long-sighted individuals end up taking short-term solutions? By analyzing the consequences for performance, you can gain insight into why workers do the sometimes perplexing things they do. The following principles, all involving performance consequences, aid in our understanding: (1) positive reinforcement, (2) negative reinforcement, (3) punishment by application, (4) punishment by withdrawal, and (5) extinction.[74] The first two principles, positive reinforcement and negative reinforcement, help explain why some behaviors are inadvertently strengthened. The last three principles explain why some behaviors are mistakenly weakened.

How Undesired Behaviors Are Mistakenly Reinforced

Rewarding A While Hoping for B   The principle of positive reinforcement can be used to promote either desired *or* undesired behavior. Its placement is critical. In an article aptly titled "On the Folly of Rewarding A, While Hoping for B," Kerr gives examples of how organizations "hope for" employee efforts in such areas as cooperation, creativity, and long-term strategic planning, while formally rewarding none of these.[75] Organizations "hope" that managers will be willing to incur huge start-up costs for programs that will potentially yield fruit in 60 months, while these same organizations promote persons who show bottom-line results in 60 days. Charting this example in Table 1, we can see a case of positive reinforcement inappropriately applied. The consequences, the rewards of promotion and additional staff, are positive. Unfortunately, the behavior they follow is the one favoring the short-term strategy. Thus, these positive reinforcers inadvertently encourage an undesired perspective. By looking at the consequences accruing to the individual, it helps us to understand how "rational" it is to sacrifice long-term growth despite the exhortations of the CEO who continually stresses strategic planning for the future.

Another example is presented in Table 1. The company's tenth anniversary is 6 months away. The public relations staff knows they need to produce a report describing the company's history and its current activities. The staff believes that the project will take very little time. Two months before the anniversary celebration, the public relations staff begins to gather information and finds that the report is far more com-

TABLE 1
POSITIVE REINFORCEMENT AT WORK

Behavior	Consequence	Principle
Efforts to change profit picture in 60 days	Followed by positive reinforcers: promotion to vice president, additional staff	Positive reinforcement
Staff procrastinates until 2 months before deadline	Followed by positive reinforcers: extra personnel hired, workload lightened, bonus paid for effort extended	Positive reinforcement

plicated than originally expected. Because the deadline must be met, the staff is permitted to hire temporary staff at company expense and set all other work aside. When the report is finally completed in a frenzy of activity, the staff are given a bonus for working so hard to meet the deadline. Seeing how the staff was inappropriately reinforced for their procrastination, it becomes easier to understand why they might procrastinate on future projects.

Take a moment now to analyze a situation you are faced with every day, the instruction you receive. What are the consequences for your professors for the desired behavior of teaching? What are the consequences for publishing? Do you think that your professors will devote the necessary time it takes to prepare lectures and examinations when they are promoted for the length of their publication records?

Negative Reinforcement at Work The principle of negative reinforcement, like positive reinforcement, also helps to explain why behavior is strengthened. Negative reinforcement, unlike positive reinforcement, involves escaping from or avoiding negative consequences such as nagging or litigation.

The case of a unionized production shop having a promotion-by-seniority policy is portrayed in Table 2. Though the boss firmly believes that there is an exemplary candidate who merits a promotion, she recommends for that promotion a person with a merely adequate record. The reason: the latter happens to be higher in seniority and the boss thus avoids complaints of favoritism or bias. In the past, such grievances have taken hours in litigation. By recommending the senior candidate, the boss has avoided exposing herself to unnecessary problems. Analyzing this situation from the point of view of negative reinforcement helps explain why the boss ends up recommending for promotion the person with a less than exemplary record.

TABLE 2
NEGATIVE REINFORCEMENT AT WORK

Behavior	Consequence	Principle
Boss recommends for promotion individual with adequate record, who is highest in seniority	Avoids complaints of favoritism and a grievance being filed with union	Negative reinforcement

How Desired Behaviors Are Inadvertently Discouraged

We have seen how two principles—positive and negative reinforcement—aid us in understanding why some behaviors are strengthened. Now, let us look at how three principles—punishment by application, punishment by removal, and extinction—help explain why workers get discouraged from doing the very things they are being encouraged to do.

Punishment by Application   The most typical reason why workers fail to do what they are expected to do is that they are punished for doing as desired.[76] The inherent punishment involved in pioneering new areas helps to explain why some engineers shun such endeavors (Table 3). As a necessary part of forging these new frontiers, engineers are presented with negative consequence after negative consequence. They are frustrated by time-consuming, seemingly fruitless literature searches. They work with concepts which are, as yet, incomprehensible to their peers, whose companionship they therefore lack. And because they are pioneering new fields, they must spend inordinate amounts of time in research and setup before having anything to show for their efforts. As a result of all of these negative consequences being applied (hence, the term "punishment by application"), it is no wonder that some eventually forgo their pioneering efforts and return to more tried-and-true research topics.

Here is another example of punishment by application: In a delightful, well-written book on analyzing performance problems, Mager and Pipe describe how one of them was called in to solve an "attitude problem" on the part of physicians who were resisting the using of computers to place prescriptions.[76] An analysis of the situation revealed that there were many negative consequences attached to using the computer. The environs of the terminals were crowded, noisy, and busy, with no room to work. Moreover, the terminals were placed so as to make their use fairly uncomfortable for those who wear bifocals. Not surprisingly, physicians were less than enthusiastic about using the computers when the result was inconvenient, slightly embarrassing and, for some, even mildly painful. When these negative consequences were changed, their "attitude problem" disappeared and the physicians began using the computers regularly.

What would you predict? Employees at Emery Air Freight were supposed to fill out damage forms about packages damaged during shipment. The paperwork was time-

TABLE 3
PUNISHMENT BY APPLICATION

Behavior	Consequence	Principle
Engineers pioneering new areas	Endure frustrating, time-consuming literature searches	Punishment by application
	Have trouble communicating with peers	
	Have problems demonstrating accomplishments	

consuming, airline representatives were likely to give them flak, and it took time away from other priorities that the company was striving toward. For a description of how the employees actually reacted, refer to the article, "At Emery Air Freight."[77]

Punishment by Removal   The principle of punishment by removal, which involves the withdrawal of a positive reinforcer following a person's behavior, also helps explain why some behaviors are weakened. For example, an administrator of a government-sponsored program is extremely careful of funds and displays outstanding efficiency to end the fiscal year under budget (Table 4). The government "rewards" this efficiency by cutting the following year's budget. It is small wonder that next year the administrator's efficiency tends to weaken.

Another example of punishment by removal: Tom Wolfe, in the book *The Right Stuff*,[78] refers to the reluctance of the young fighter pilots to admit when they had maneuvered themselves into a bad corner they couldn't get out of. Such an admission triggered a complex and very public chain of events at the field: all other incoming flights were held up, fire trucks trundled out to the runway, and the bureaucracy geared up to investigate. Perhaps most importantly, the pilot's peers started to question whether the pilot had "the right stuff." As Table 5 shows, the desired behavior (that of responsibly admitting to a problem) is weakened by (1) the certainty that such an admission will cause a great deal of trouble for the pilot (punishment by application) and (2) the loss of that most important conviction on the part of the pilot's peers (punishment by removal).

It should be noted that reinforcement theorists do *not* recommend punishment procedures as a way of changing behavior. Instead, as we trust is illustrated here, these weakening procedures can best be used to analyze why people don't do what they are

TABLE 4
PUNISHMENT BY REMOVAL

Behavior	Consequence	Principle
Administrator comes in under budget	Gets positive reinforcer withdrawn, i.e., budget slashed for next fiscal year	Punishment by removal

TABLE 5
PUNISHMENT BY APPLICATION AND REMOVAL

Behavior	Consequence	Principle
Fighter pilot declaring emergency	Complex and public set of events is triggered: flights held up, fire trucks sent out, paperwork flow starts	Punishment by application
	Gets positive reinforcer withdrawn, e.g., peers don't think pilot has "right stuff"	Punishment by removal

supposed to do. Based on this better understanding, we can then devise ways to positively reinforce the performance that is desired.

Extinction   The principle of extinction—that is, stopping or not delivering positive reinforcers—also explains why workers don't always do what it seems they should. In the area of occupational safety, for example, it is frequently perplexing that workers continue to perform unsafely despite compelling arguments to perform otherwise. To understand why, it is helpful to raise questions about the consequences of performing safely. An analysis of the performance consequences, as shown in Table 6, helps explain why workers persist in acting unsafely, despite cogent reasons for conduction themselves in a safe manner. When one closely examines what happens when workers perform as desired, one finds relatively few positive consequences occur when workers perform safely. Coworkers rarely comment. Management recognition is rare. The fact that there are few, if any, positive reinforcers delivered for performing as desired illustrates the principle of extinction.

Further analysis of situations involving safety reveals that even when workers are performing safely, an accident may occur; for example, a truck lid flies up, and through no fault of the workers, he ends up with a broken nose. Thus, there is some chance for a punishing consequence such as an accident to occur. On the other hand, when one examines what happens when workers perform in an undesired manner, one finds a lack of punishment. The "natural" consequence of performing unsafely, having an accident, is typically, albeit fortunately, missing; studies have shown that workers can perform unsafely literally hundreds of times without incurring an accident. As you can see by examining the consequences of performance, one can better understand why workers perform the way they do, despite cogent reasons to the contrary.

Using All the Principles to Analyze a Situation

To see how the principles, as a group, can be used to better understand a given situation, let us turn to a final example. The management of a manufacturing engineering group was particularly interested in upgrading the quality of the work so as to reduce the lag time, that is, the time it took from gear design to tooling. One of the authors and a class of graduate students looked in depth at the consequences for producing high-quality work. Table 7 describes what we found. In the first place, pay raises and promotions were not awarded on the basis of merit. Instead, the same percentage raise was given to each worker. Few opportunities existed for promotions of any kind. Em-

TABLE 6
EXTINCTION AT WORK

Behavior	Consequence	Principle
Workers perform safely	Few positive reinforcers, e.g., little management recognition, few coworker comments	Extinction

TABLE 7
HOW THE PRINCIPLES OF BEHAVIOR CAN BE USED IN TANDEM

Consequence	Principle
Workers doing quality work	
Pay and raises not contingent on performance; promotions rare; little management recognition; few peer comments; little, if any, task feedback	Extinction
Being asked to check peers' work	Punishment by application
Avoid having the shop return the design work	Negative reinforcement
Workers doing poor-quality work	
Infrequent reprimands; few peer comments	Lack of punishment by application
Pay and raises still forthcoming; no loss of friends on job	Lack of punishment by removal
Avoid being asked to check	Negative reinforcement

ployees received little or no overt feedback from either peers or management. What the exceptional employees received was extra work. Those who were most capable were assigned the unpleasant task of checking on the design work of their peers. These checkers, however, discovered that they need not critique the work of their peers. They could simply OK the work and pass it on to the shop where prototypes were built from the designs. If the design work was shoddy, the shop returned it to the designer, thereby avoiding the problem of peer criticism. Having failed to "catch" the design problems, the checkers were not again asked to critique the work of the others, thus lightening their workload and keeping their friends.

As you can see, this example illustrates how workers are sometimes inadvertently reinforced for undesired behavior. At the same time, this example shows how employees are sometimes punished for desired behavior and how desired performance is extinguished. By using the strengthening principles—positive and negative reinforcement—and the weakening principles—punishment by application and removal and extinction—to analyze situations, we can better understand why people do what they do.

LOOKING AHEAD

What does the future hold? As we move into the twenty-first century with its changing demographic and organizational forces, three developments are forecast.[79,80]

Shoring Up and Shifting Content

Our first prediction is that reinforcement theory will be employed to fully utilize the fewer number of young people entering the job market and to upgrade the level of literacy and basic skills of entry-level workers. We also predict that it will be employed in manufacturing as well as the rapidly expanding service sector, and in jobs involving routine assembly work as well as those requiring the troubleshooting of computerized equipment. The same four-step process of specifying desired performance, measuring performance, rearranging consequences, and evaluating effectiveness will be used. What will be different is that a shift will occur in the content of workers' performance so that more studies will focus on troubleshooting and service-related behaviors.[58–60]

Expanding Upward

With the nature of organizations themselves changing as they rebound from mergers and downsizing, we predict that reinforcement theory can be used beneficially at the upper echelons of organizations. The idea that reinforcement principles can be used to satisfy the demand for savvy and successful leaders has been suggested.[81–83] Recently, a model of effective supervision has been developed, based on reinforcement theory.[84] Two categories in particular are identified as being key in motivating others: monitoring and providing consequences.[85,86] Effective managers are much more likely than so-so managers to monitor, that is, to examine the work and observe workers in action. They do not leave this fact finding a chance. The data also show that effective managers provide consequences. They let workers know how they are doing. They compliment workers in a casual, off-the-cuff fashion. Reinforcement theory can be used to bolster how leaders interact with their subordinates, and thus improve the functioning of organizations as a whole.

Helping Workers to Help Themselves

Lastly, we predict that workers will learn to use reinforcement theory to design their own motivational programs. The idea of self-management is well established in clinical settings.[87–88] The idea has been broached by industrial/organizational psychologists,[89–92] but, with few exceptions,[93–95] it has not been extensively applied in work settings. Recently, however, a study in a unionized state government agency illustrates how workers can successfully learn to help themselves improve their own attendance.[96] First, the employees specified what they wished to attain; they set attendance goals and, just as important, they identified ways of overcoming obstacles preventing them from coming to work. Then, they kept track of their attendance and how they coped. Lastly, they identified and delivered consequences for attaining or failing to attain the goals they had set. The results showed that employees substantially improved their attendance at work. Furthermore, they raised their confidence in their ability to control their own behavior.

Thus, from the heady, idealistic era of the late 1960s to the changing demographics of the twenty-first century, we can see how reinforcement theory has been and can be beneficially employed. In the past two decades, reinforcement theory has been used to promote a wide variety of behaviors with diverse populations in different work settings. It has also yielded valuable insights into why workers behave as they do. Reinforcement theory holds considerable promise for addressing the challenges of the twenty-first century.

NOTES

1 Lovaas, O. I. (1966). A program for the establishment of speech in psychotic children. In J. K. Wing (Ed.), *Early childhood autism.* London: Pergamon.

2 Becker, W. C., Madsen, C. H. Jr., Arnold, C. R., & Thomas, D. R. (1967). The contingent use of teacher attention and praise in reducing classroom behavior problems. *The Journal of Special Education,* 1(3), 287–307.

3 Where Skinner's theories work. (1972, December), *Business Week,* pp. 64–65.

4 Datel, W. E., & Legters, L. J. (1970, June). *The psychology of the army recruit.* Paper presented at the meeting of the American Medical Association, Chicago.

5 Hamner, W. C. (1974). Reinforcement theory and contingency management in organizational settings. In H. L. Tosi & W. C. Hamner (Eds.), *Organizational behavior and management: A contingency approach.* Chicago: St. Clair Press.

6 Nord, W. R. (1969). Beyond the teaching machine: The neglected area of operant conditioning in the theory and practice of management. *Organizational Behavior and Human Performance,* 4, 375–401.

7 Porter, L. W. (1973). Turning work into nonwork: The rewarding environment. In M. D. Dunnette (Ed.), *Work and nonwork in the year 2001* (pp. 113–133). Belmont, Calif.: Wadsworth.

8 Whyte, W. F. (1972). Skinnerian theory in organizations. *Psychology Today,* April, pp. 67–68, 96, 98, 100.

9 Dinesen, I. (1937). *Out of Africa.* New York: Vintage.

10 Campbell, J. P., & Pritchard, R. D. (1976). Motivational theory in industrial organizational psychology. In M. D. Dunnette (Ed.), *Handbook of industrial and organizational psychology* (pp. 63–130). New York: Wiley.

11 Mitchell, T. R. (1982). Motivation: New directions for theory, research, and practice. *Academy of Management Review,* 7, 80–88.

12 Kazdin, A. E. (1989). *Behavior modification in applied settings* (4th ed.). Pacific Grove, Calif.: Brooks/Cole.

13 Skinner, B. F. (1974). *About behaviorism.* New York: Vintage.

14 Stolz, S. B., Wienckowski, L. A., & Brown, B. S. (1975, November). Behavior modification: A perspective on critical issues. *American Psychologist,* 1027–1048.

15 Cofer, C. N., & Appley, M. H. (1964). *Motivation: Theory and research.* New York: Wiley.

16 Steers, R. M., & Porter, L. W. (1987). *Motivation and work behavior* (4th ed.). New York: McGraw-Hill.

17 Pommer, D. A., & Streedbeck, D. (1974). Motivating staff performance in an operant learning program for children. *Journal of Applied Behavior Analysis,* 7, 217–221.

18 Briscoe, R. V., Hoffman, D. B., & Bailey, J. S. (1975). Behavioral community psychology: Training a community board to problem solve. *Journal of Applied Behavior Analysis,* 8, 157–168.

19 Baer, D. M., Wolf, M. M., & Risley, T. R. (1968). Some current dimensions of applied behavior analysis. *Journal of Applied Behavior Analysis,* 1, 91–97.

20 Honig, W. K. (1966). *Operant behavior: Areas of research and application.* New York: Appleton-Century-Crofts.

21 Ulrich, R., Stachnik, T., & Mabry, J. (Eds.) (1966). *Control of human behavior* (Vol. 1). Glenview, Ill.: Scott, Foresman.

22 Ulrich, R., Stachnik, T., & Mabry, J. (Eds.) (1970). *Control of human behavior* (Vol. 2). Glenview, Ill.: Scott, Foresman.

23 Ulrich, R., Stachnik, T., & Mabry, J. (Eds.) (1974). *Control of human behavior: Behavior*

modification in the workplace (Vol. 3). Glenview, Ill.: Scott, Foresman.

24 Gellerman, S. W. (1976, March–April). Supervision: Substance and style. *Harvard Business Review,* 89–99.

25 Homer (1952). The Iliad of Homer (Book 5, Verse 493). In R. M. Hutchins (Ed.), *Great books of the Western world.* Chicago: Encyclopedia Britannica.

26 Komaki, J., Heinzmann, A. T., & Lawson, L. (1980). Effect of training and feedback: component analysis of a behavioral safety program. *Journal of Applied Psychology,* 65, 261–270.

27 Geller, E. S., Eason, S. L., Phillips, J. A., & Pierson, M. D. (1980). Interventions to improve sanitation during food preparation. *Journal of Organizational Behavior Management,* 2(3), Summer.

28 Kreitner, R., & Golab, M. (1978). Increasing the rate of salesperson telephone calls with a monetary refund. *Journal of Organizational Behavior Management*, 1, 192–195.

29 Quilitch, H. R. (1975). A comparison of three staff-management procedures. *Journal of Applied Behavior Analysis,* 8, 59–66.

30 Schonberger, R. J. (1982). *Japanese manufacturing techniques: Nine hidden lessons in simplicity.* New York: The Free Press.

31 Whaley, D. L., & Surratt, S. L. (1967). *Attitudes of science: A program for a student-centered seminar* (3rd ed.). Kalamazoo, Mich.: Behaviordela.

32 Bellack, A. S., & Hersen, M. (1988). *Behavioral assessment: A practical handbook.* New York: Pergamon.

33 Ciminero, A. R., Calhoun, K. S., & Adams, H. E. (1977). *Handbook of behavioral assessment.* New York: Wiley.

34 Komaki, J., Collins, R. L., & Thoene, T. J. F. (1980). Behavioral measurement in business, industry, and government. *Behavioral Assessment,* 2, 103–123.

35 Nelson, R. O., & Hayes, S. C. (1986). *Conceptual foundations of behavioral assessment.* New York: Guilford.

36 Campbell, D. T., & Stanley, J. C. (1963). Experimental and quasiexperimental designs for research. In N. L. Gage (Ed.), *Handbook of research on teaching.* Chicago: Rand McNally.

37 Kazdin, A. E. (1982). *Single case research designs: Methods for clinical and applied settings.* New York: Oxford University Press.

38 Komaki, J., & Jensen, M. (1986). Within-group designs: An alternative to traditional control group designs. In M. F. Cataldo & T. J. Coates (Eds.), *Health & industry* (pp. 86–138). New York: Wiley.

39 Komaki, J. L., Barwick, K. D., & Scott, L. R. (1978). A behavioral approach to occupational safety: Pinpointing and reinforcing safety performance in a food manufacturing plant. *Journal of Applied Psychology,* 63, 434–445.

40 Komaki, J. L., Coombs, T., & Schepman, S. (1990). *A review of two decades of the operant conditioning literature in business and industry.* Purdue University, Department of Psychological Science, West Lafayette, Ind.

41 Andrasik, F. (1979). Organizational behavior modification in business settings: A methodological and content review. *Journal of Organizational Behavior Management,* 2(2), 85–102.

42 Babb, H. W., & Kopp, D. G. (1978). Applications of behavior modifications in organizations: A review and a critique. *Academy of Management Review,* 3, 281–292.

43 Hopkins, B. L., & Sears, J. (1982). Managing behavior for productivity. In L. W. Frederiksen (Ed.), *Handbook of organizational behavior management.* New York: Wiley.

44 Merwin, G. A., Jr., Thomason, J. A., & Sanford, E. E. (1989). A methodology and content review of organizational behavior management in the private sector: 1978–1986. *Journal of Organizational Behavior Management,* 10(1), 39–57.

45 O'Hara, K., Johnson, C. M., & Beehr, T. A. (1985). Organizational behavior management in the private sector: A review of empirical research and recommendations for further investigation. *Academy of Management Review,* 10, 848–864.

46 Schneier, C. E. (1974). Behavior modification in management: A review and a critique. *Academy of Management Journal,* 17, 528–548.

47 Quilitch, H. R. (1978). Using a simple feedback procedure to reinforce the submission of written suggestions by mental health employees. *Journal of Organizational Behavior Management,* 1(2), 155–163.

48 Kreitner, R., & Golab, M. (1978). Increasing the rate of salesperson telephone calls with a monetary refund. *Journal of Organizational Behavior Management,* 1(3), 192–195.

49 Maher, C. A. (1982). Improving teacher instructional behavior: Evaluation of a time management training program. *Journal of Organizational Behavior Management,* 4(3/4), 27–36.

50 Nordstrom, R., Hall, R. V., Lorenzi, P., & Delquadri, J. (1988). Organizational behavior modification in the public sector: Three field experiments. *Journal of Organizational Behavior Management,* 9(2), 91–112.

51 Hermann, J. A., DeMontes, A. I., Dominguez, B., Montes, F., & Hopkins, B. L. (1973). Effects of bonuses for punctuality on the tardiness of industrial workers. *Journal of Applied Behavior Analysis,* 6, 563–570.

52 Steers, R. M., & Rhodes, S. R. (1978). Major influences on employee attendance: A process model. *Journal of Applied Psychology,* 63, 391–407.

53 Pedalino, E., & Gamboa, V. U. (1974). Behavior modifications and absenteeism: Intervention in one industrial setting. *Journal of Applied Psychology,* 59, 694–698.

54 Nasanen, M., & Saari, J. (1987). The effects of positive feedback on housekeeping and accidents at a shipyard. *Journal of Occupational Accidents,* 8, 237–250.

55 Sulzer-Azaroff, B., & De Santamaria, M. C. (1980). Industrial safety hazard reduction through performance feedback. *Journal of Applied Behavior Analysis,* 13, 287–295.

56 Zohar, D., & Fussfeld, N. (1981). Modifying earplug wearing behavior by behavior modification techniques. An empirical evaluation. *Journal of Organizational Behavior Management,* 3(2), 41–52.

57 Hopkins, B. L., Conard, R. J., & Smith, M. J. (1986). Effective and reliable behavioral control technology. *American Industrial Hygiene Association Journal,* December.

58 Elizur, D. (1987). Effect of feedback on verbal and non-verbal courtesy in a bank setting. *Applied Psychology: An International Review,* 36, 147–156.

59 Komaki, J. L., Collins, R. L., & Temlock, W. (1987). An alternative performance measurement approach: Applied operant measurement in the service sector [Special Issue]. *Applied Psychology: An International Review,* 36(1), 71–89.

60 Luthans, F., Paul, R., & Taylor, L. (1985). The impact of contingent reinforcement on retail salespersons' performance behaviors: A replicated field experiment. *Journal of Organizational Behavior Management,* 7(1/2), 25–35.

61 Anderson, D. C., Crowell, C. R., Sponsel, S. S., Clarke, M., & Brence, J. (1982). Behavior management in the public accommodations industry: A three-project demonstration. *Journal of Organizational Behavior Management,* 4(1/2), 33–66.

62 Komaki, J., & Collins, R. L. (1982). Motivation of preventive maintenance performance. In R. M. O'Brien, A. M. Dickinson, & M. Rosow (Eds.), *Industrial behavior modification: A learning-based approach to business management* (pp. 243–265). New York: Pergamon.

63 Haynes, R. S., Pine, R. C., & Fitch, H. G. (1982). Reducing accident rates with organizational behavior modification. *Academy of Management Journal*, 25, 407–416.

64 Heward, W. L. (1978). Operant conditioning of a .300 hitter? The effects of reinforcement on the offensive efficiency of a barnstorming baseball team. *Behavior Modification*, 2, 25–40.

65 Prue, D. M., Krapfl, J. E., Noah, J. C., Cannon, S., & Maley, R. F. (1980). Managing the treatment activities of state hospital staff. *Journal of Organizational Behavior Management*, 2(3), 165–181.

66 Fox, D. K., Hopkins, B. L., & Anger, W. K. (1987). The long-term effects of a token economy on safety performance in open-pit mining. *Journal of Applied Behavior Analysis*, 20, 215–224.

67 Deluga, R. J., & Andrews, H. M. (1985–1986). A case study investigating the effects of a low-cost intervention to reduce three attendance behavior problems in a clerical training program. *Journal of Organizational Behavior Management*, 7(3/4), 115–124.

68 Premack, D. (1965). Reinforcement theory. In D. Levine (Ed.), *Nebraska symposium on motivation*. Lincoln: University of Nebraska Press.

69 Gupton, T., & LeBow, M. D. (1971). Behavior management in a large industrial firm. *Behavior Therapy*, 2, 78–82.

70 Brown, K. M., Willis, B. S., & Reid, D. H. (1981). Differential effects of supervisor verbal feedback and feedback plus approval on institutional staff performance. *Journal of Organizational Behavior Management*, 3(1), 57–68.

71 Fox, C. J., & Sulzer-Azaroff, B. (1987). Increasing completion of accident reports. *Journal of Safety Research*, 18, 65–71.

72 Zohar, D., Cohen, A., & Azar, N. (1980). Promoting increased use of ear protectors in noise through information feedback. *Human Factors*, 22(1), 69–79.

73 Dillon, M. J., Kent, H. M., & Malott, R. W. (1980). A supervisory system for accomplishing long-range projects: An application to master's thesis research. *Journal of Organizational Behavior Management*, 2(3), 213–228.

74 Miller, L. K. (1980). *Principles of everyday behavior analysis* (2nd ed.). Belmont, Calif.: Wadsworth.

75 Kerr, S. (1975). On the folly of rewarding A, while hoping for B. *Academy of Management Journal*, 18, 769–782.

76 Mager, R. F., & Pipe, P. (1984). *Analyzing performance problems: You really oughta wanna* (2nd ed). Belmont, Calif.: Lake.

77 "At Emery Air Freight: Positive reinforcement boosts performance." (1973) *Organizational Dynamics*, 1(3), 41–50.

78 Wolfe, T. (1979). *The right stuff.* New York: Bantam.

79 Offermann, L. R., & Gowing, M. K. (1990). Organizations of the future: Changes and challenges. *American Psychologist*, 45(2), 95–108.

80 Katzell, R. A., & Thompson, D. E. (1990). Work motivation: Theory and practice. *American Psychologist*, 45(2), 144–153.

81 Luthans, F., Hodgetts, R. M., & Rosenkrantz, S. A. (1988). *Real managers.* Cambridge, Mass.: Ballinger.

82 Scott, W. E., Jr., & Podsakoff, P. M. (1985). *Behavioral principles in the practice of management.* New York: Wiley.

83 Sims, H. P. (1977). The leader as a manager of reinforcement contingencies: An empirical example and a model. In J. G. Hunt & L. L. Larson (Eds.), *Leadership: The cutting edge* (pp. 121–137). Carbondale, Ill.: Southern Illinois University Press.

84 Komaki, J. L., & Desselles, M. (in press). *Leadership from an operant perspective: Making it work.* Boston: Hyman & Unwin.

85 Komaki, J. L. (1986). Toward effective supervision: An operant analysis and comparison of managers at work. *Journal of Applied Psychology,* 71, 270–279.

86 Komaki, J. L., Desselles, M. L., & Bowman, E. D. (1989). Definitely not a breeze: Extending an operant model of effective supervision to teams. *Journal of Applied Psychology,* 74, 522–529.

87 Meichenbaum, D. H. (1973). Cognitive factors in behavior modification: Modifying what clients say to themselves. *Annual Review of Behavior Therapy Theory & Practice,* 1, 416–431.

88 Thoresen, C. E., & Mahoney, M. J. (1974). *Behavioral self-control.* New York: Holt, Rinehart & Winston.

89 Blood, M. R. (1978). Organizational control of performance through self rewarding. In B. T. King, S. Streufert, & F. E. Fiedler (Eds.), *Managerial control and organizational democracy.* Washington, D. C.: Winston & Sons.

90 Manz, C. C., & Sims, H. P., Jr. (1980). Self-management as a substitute for leadership: A social learning theory perspective. *Academy of Management Review,* 5, 361–367.

91 Wexley, K. N. (1984). Personnel training. *Annual Review of Psychology,* 35, 519–551.

92 Brief, A. P., & Hollenbeck, J. R. (1985). An exploratory study of self-regulating activities and their effects on job performance. *Journal of Occupational Behaviour,* 6, 197–208.

93 Gaetani, J. J., Johnson, C. M., & Austin, J. T. (1983). Self-management by an owner of a small business: Reduction of tardiness. *Journal of Organizational Behavior Management,* 5(1), 31–39.

94 Lamal, P. A., & Benfield, A. (1978). The effect of self-monitoring on job tardiness and percentage of time spent working. *Journal of Organizational Behavior Management,* 1(2), 142–149.

95 Luthans, F., & Davis, T. R. V. (1979, Summer). Behavioral self-management: The missing link in managerial effectiveness. *Organizational Dynamics,* pp. 42–60.

96 Frayne, C. A., & Latham, G. P. (1987). Application of social learning theory to employee self-management of attendance. *Journal of Applied Psychology,* 72, 387–392.

Equity Theory Predictions of Behavior in Organizations

Richard T. Mowday

Employees are seldom passive observers of the events that occur in the workplace. They form impressions of others and the events that affect them and cognitively or behaviorally respond based on their positive or negative evaluations. A great deal of theory and research in the social sciences has been devoted to understanding these evaluative processes. More specifically, research has attempted to uncover the major influences on individual reactions in social situations and the processes through which these reactions are formed. One useful framework for understanding how social interactions in the workplace influence employee reactions to their jobs and participation in the organization is provided by theories of social exchange processes (Adams, 1965; Homans, 1961; Jacques, 1961; Patchen, 1961; Simpson, 1972).

Exchange theories are based on two simple assumptions about human behavior. First, there is an assumed similarity between the process through which individuals evaluate their social relationships and economic transactions in the market. Social relationships can be viewed as exchange processes in which individuals make contributions (investments) for which they expect certain outcomes. Individuals are assumed to have expectations about the outcomes that should result when they contribute their time or resources in interaction with others.

The second assumption concerns the process through which individuals decide whether or not a particular exchange is satisfactory. Most exchange theories assign a central role to social comparison processes in terms of how individuals evaluate exchange relationships. Information gained through interaction with others is used to determine whether an exchange has been advantageous. For example, individuals may compare their outcomes and contributions in an exchange with the outcomes and contributions of the person with whom they are interacting. Where there is relative equality between the outcomes and contributions of both parties to an exchange, satisfaction is likely to result from the interaction.

The popularity of social exchange theories may be attributable to their agreement with commonsense observations about human behavior in social situations. Exchange theories suggest that individuals in social interaction behave in a manner similar to the "economic man" of classical economics. Most theories of motivation assume that individuals are motivated to maximize their rewards and minimize their costs (Vroom, 1964; Walster, Bercheid, & Walster, 1976). The major difference between assumptions made about economic man and social exchange theories is that the latter recognize that individuals exist in environments characterized by limited and imperfect information. The ambiguity present in most social situations results in individuals relying

This paper was written especially for the previous edition of this volume. Support for the preparation of the manuscript was partially provided by a grant from the Office of Naval Research, Contract No. N00014-76-C-0164, NR 170-812. The assistance of Thom McDade in the early stages of preparing the paper is gratefully acknowledged.

heavily on information provided by others to evaluate their actions and those of others (Darley & Darley, 1973). Social interactions therefore play a central role in providing information to individuals on the quality of their relationships with others. Our reliance upon others for valued information, however, may place constraints on how we behave in our interactions with others. In order to maintain our social relationships it may be necessary to conform to certain social norms that prevent us from maximizing our outcomes without regard to the outcome of others.

The purpose of this paper is to examine one prominent theory of social exchange processes: Adams' (1963a, 1965) theory of equity. Although Adams' theory is only one of several exchange theories that have been developed, it deserves special attention for several reasons. First, Adams' theory is perhaps the most rigorously developed statement of how individuals evaluate social exchange relationships. The careful formulation of the theory has led to considerable research interest in testing its specific predictions. The large number of studies available on equity theory provides evidence upon which to evaluate the adequacy of social exchange models. Second, the majority of research on equity theory has investigated employee reactions to compensation in employer-employee exchange relationships. The theory and supporting research are therefore highly relevant to increasing our understanding of behavior in organizational settings.

In the sections that follow, Adams' equity theory will be briefly summarized and the research evidence reviewed. The major empirical and conceptual questions surrounding the theory will then be discussed. Finally, the generalizability of the theory will be considered and suggestions made for applying equity theory to several previously neglected areas of organizational behavior.

EQUITY THEORY

Antecedents of Inequity

The major components of exchange relationships in Adams' theory are inputs and outcomes. Inputs or investments are those things a person contributes to the exchange. In a situation where a person exchanges his or her services for pay, inputs may include previous work experience, education, effort on the job, and training. Outcomes are those things that result from the exchange. In the employment situations, the most important outcome is likely to be pay. In addition, other outcomes such as supervisory treatment, job assignments, fringe benefits, and status symbols may also be considered in evaluating the exchange. To be considered in evaluating exchange relationships, inputs and outcomes must meet two conditions. First, the existence of an input or outcome must be recognized by one or both parties to the exchange. Second, an input or outcome must be considered relevant to the exchange (i.e., have some marginal utility). Unless inputs or outcomes are both recognized and considered relevant, they will not be considered in evaluating an exchange relationship.

Adams suggests that individuals weight their inputs and outcomes by their importance to the individual. Summary evaluation of inputs and outcomes are developed by separately summing the weighted inputs and weighted outcomes. In the summation process, inputs and outcomes are treated as independent even though they may be highly related (e.g., age and previous work experience would be considered as separate inputs). The ratio of an individual's (called "person's") outcomes to inputs is compared to the ratio of outcomes to inputs of another individual or group (called "other"). Other may be a person with whom you are engaged in a direct exchange, another individual engaged in an exchange with a common third party, or person in a previous or anticipated work situation. The selection of comparison others is discussed in more detail below. The important consideration at this point is that person evaluates his or her outcomes and inputs by comparing them with those of others.

Equity is said to exist whenever the ratio of person's outcomes to inputs is equal to the ratio of other's outcomes and inputs.

$$\frac{O_p}{I_p} = \frac{O_o}{I_o}$$

Inequity exists whenever the two ratios are unequal.

$$\frac{O_p}{I_p} < \frac{O_o}{I_o} \quad \text{or} \quad \frac{O_p}{I_p} > \frac{O_o}{I_o}$$

Several important aspects of this definition should be recognized. First, the conditions necessary to produce equity or inequity are based on the individual's perceptions of inputs and outcomes. In behavioral terms, the objective characteristics of the situation are of less importance than the person's perceptions. Second, inequity is a relative phenomenon. Inequity does not necessarily exist if person has high inputs and low outcomes as long as the comparison other has a similar ratio. Employees may therefore exhibit satisfaction on a job that demands a great deal and for which they receive very little if their comparison other is in a similar position. Third, inequity exists when a person is relatively underpaid and relatively overpaid. It is this implication of Adams' theory that has generated the most attention since it suggests that people will react in a counterintuitive fashion when they are overpaid. Research evidence indicates, however, that the threshold for underpayment is lower than that associated with overpayment (Leventhal, Weiss, & Long, 1969). As might be expected, individuals are somewhat more willing to accept overpayment in an exchange relationship than they are to accept underpayment. The relationship between the ratios of outcomes to inputs of person and other might best be considered along a continuum reflecting different degrees of inequity ranging from overpayment on one extreme to underpayment on the other. The midpoint of the continuum represents the point at which the two ratios are equal. Equity is defined as a zone which is asymmetric about the midpoint. The asymmetry reflects the fact that the thresholds for overpayment and underpayment may differ.

One final aspect of Adams' formulation should be mentioned. Walster et al. (1976) have shown that the formula relating to two ratios of person and other is inadequate in situations where inputs might be negative. Following their example, consider the situation where person's inputs have a value of 5 and outcomes are −10 while other's inputs and outcomes are –5 and 10, respectively. Using Adams' formula, these two ratios are equal and thus a condition of equity would be said to exist.

$$\frac{O_p}{I_p} = \frac{-10}{5} = -2 \quad \text{and} \quad \frac{O_o}{I_o} = \frac{10}{-5} = -2$$

Obviously, a situation in which person makes positive inputs but receives negative outcomes is inequitable when compared to another who makes negative inputs but receives positive outcomes. Walster et al. (1976) have proposed an alternative formulation that overcomes this problem. Equity and inequity are defined by the following relationship.

$$\frac{\text{Outcomes}_p - \text{Inputs}_p}{(|\text{Inputs}_p|)^{k_p}} \quad \text{compared with} \quad \frac{\text{Outcomes}_o - \text{Inputs}_o}{(|\text{Inputs}_o|)^{k_o}}$$

The reader interested in pursuing this subject further can find a more detailed discussion of this formula and its terms in Walster et al. (1976).

Consequence of Inequity

The motivational aspects of Adams' theory are derived from the hypothesized consequences of perceived inequity. The major postulates of the theory can be summarized simply: (1) perceived inequity creates tension in the individual; (2) the amount of tension is proportional to the magnitude of the inequity; (3) the tension created in the individual will motivate him or her to reduce it; and (4) the strength of the motivation to reduce inequity is proportional to the perceived inequity (Adams, 1965). In other words, the presence of inequity motivates the individual to change the situation through behavioral or cognitive means to return to a condition of equity.

The methods through which individuals reduce inequity are referred to as methods of inequity resolution. Adams describes six alternative methods of restoring equity: (1) altering inputs; (2) altering outcomes; (3) cognitively distorting inputs or outcomes; (4) leaving the field; (5) taking actions designed to change the inputs or outcomes of the comparison other; or (6) changing the comparison other. The choice of a particular method of restoring equity will depend upon the characteristics of the inequitable situation. Adams suggests, however, that the person will attempt to maximize positively valent outcomes and minimize increasingly effortful inputs in restoring equity. In addition, person will resist changing the object of comparison and distorting inputs that are considered central to the self-concept. In general, it is considered easier to distort other's inputs and outcomes than the person's own inputs or outcomes. Finally, leaving the field (e.g., turnover from an organization) as a method of reducing inequity will only be considered in extreme cases of inequity.

RESEARCH ON EQUITY THEORY PREDICTIONS OF EMPLOYEE REACTIONS TO PAY

Considerable research interest has been generated in testing predictions from Adams' theory. The most recent review of equity theory research summarized the results from over 160 investigations (Adams & Freedman, 1976). Although equity considerations are relevant to a number of different types of social relationships (cf. Walster et al., 1976), most early research focused attention on the employer-employee exchange relationship. These studies were generally laboratory investigations in which subjects were hired to perform relatively simple tasks such as proofreading or interviewing. The simple nature of the tasks suggests that differences found between subjects in the quantity or quality of performance would be attributable to motivation levels rather than differences in skills or abilities. Perceived inequity was induced by either manipulating the subject's perceived qualifications to be hired for the task (qualifications manipulation) or by actual differences in pay rates (manipulation by circumstances).

Predictions from equity theory about employee reactions to pay distinguish between two conditions of inequity (underpayment versus overpayment) and two methods of compensation (hourly versus piece rate). Specific predictions are summarized for each condition in Table 1. The methodology and results of selected studies designed to test these predictions are presented in Table 2. More extensive reviews of this literature can be found in Adams and Freedman (1976), Campbell and Pritchard (1976), Goodman and Friedman (1971), Lawler (1968a), Opsahl and Dunnette (1966), and Pritchard (1969).

A review of the studies summarized in Table 2 suggests general support for equity theory predictions. In the overpayment-hourly condition, a number of studies have provided some support for the prediction that overpaid subjects will produce higher quantity than equitably paid subjects (Adams & Rosenbaum, 1962; Arrowood, 1961; Goodman & Friedman, 1968; Lawler, 1968b; Pritchard, Dunnette, & Jorgenson, 1972; Wiener, 1970). Several studies have either failed to support or provided mixed support for equity theory predictions in this condition, although they often differed from the supporting studies in the manner in which perceived inequity was experimentally manipulated (Anderson & Shelly, 1970; Evans & Simmons, 1969; Friedman & Goodman, 1967; Valenzi & Andrews, 1971). In the overpayment-piece-rate condition, support for the theory has been found by Adams (1963b), Adams and Jacobsen (1964), Adams and Rosenbaum (1962), Andrews (1967), and Goodman and Friedman (1969). Mixed or marginal support for the theory was provided by Lawler, Koplin, Young, and Fadem (1968), and Wood and Lawler (1970). Although fewer studies have examined the underpayment conditions, support for both the hourly and piece-rate predictions

TABLE 1

EQUITY THEORY PREDICTIONS OF EMPLOYEE REACTIONS TO INEQUITABLE PAYMENT

	Underpayment	Overpayment
Hourly payment	Subjects underpaid by the hour produce less or poorer-quality output than equitably paid subjects	Subjects overpaid by the hour produce more or higher-quality output than equitably paid subjects
Piece-rate payment	Subjects underpaid by piece rate will produce a large number of low-quality units in comparison with equitably paid subjects	Subjects overpaid by piece rate will provide fewer units of higher quality than equitably paid subjects

TABLE 2
SUMMARY OF EQUITY THEORY RESEARCH ON EMPLOYEE REACTIONS TO PAY

Study	Equity condition	Method of induction	Task	Dependent variables	Results
Adams (1963b)	Overpayment: hourly and piece rate	Qualifications	Interviewing	Productivity, work quality	Hourly-overpaid subject produced greater quantity and piece-rate overpaid subjects produced higher quality and lower quantity than equitably paid subjects.
Adams and Jacobsen (1964)	Overpayment: piece rate	Qualifications	Proofreading	Productivity, work quality	Overpaid subjects produced less quantity of higher quality.
Adams and Rosenbaum (1962)	Overpayment: hourly and piece rate	Qualifications	Interviewing	Productivity	Hourly-overpaid subjects produced more quantity while piece-rate-overpaid subjects produced less quantity.
Anderson and Shelly (1970)	Overpayment: hourly	Qualifications, importance of task	Proofreading	Productivity, work quality	No differences were found between groups.
Andrews (1967)	Overpayment and underpayment: piece rate	Circumstances, previous wage experiences	Interviewing Data checking	Productivity, work quality	Overpaid subjects produced higher quality and underpaid subjects produced greater quantity and lower quality.
Arrowood (1961)	Overpayment: hourly	Qualifications, work returned	Interviewing	Productivity	Overpaid subjects had higher productivity.
Evans and Simmons (1969)	Overpayment and underpayment: hourly	Competence, authority	Proofreading	Productivity, work quality	Underpaid subjects produced more of poorer quality in competence condition. No differences found in other conditions.
Friedman and Goodman (1967)	Overpayment: hourly	Qualifications	Interviewing	Productivity	Qualifications induction did not affect productivity. When subjects were classified by perceived qualifications, unqualified subjects produced less than qualified subjects.
Goodman and Friedman (1968)	Overpayment and underpayment: hourly	Qualifications, quantity versus quality emphasis	Questionnaire coding	Productivity, work quality	Overpaid subjects produced more than equitably paid subjects. Emphasis on quantity versus quality affected performance.
Goodman and Friedman (1969)	Overpayment: piece rate	Qualifications, quantity versus quality emphasis	Questionnaire scoring	Productivity, work quality	Overpaid subjects increased productivity or work quality, depending upon induction.

Study	Payment condition	Variables	Task	Dependent measures	Results
Lawler (1968b)	Overpayment: hourly	Qualifications, circumstances	Interviewing	Productivity, work quality	Overpaid (unqualified) subjects produced more of lower quality. Subjects overpaid by circumstances did not differ from equitably paid group.
Lawler, Koplin, Young, and Fadem (1968)	Overpayment: piece rate	Qualifications	Interviewing	Productivity, work quality	Overpaid subjects produced less of higher quality in initial work session. In later sessions, subject's perceived qualifications and productivity increased. The need for money was related to productivity for both groups.
Lawler and O'Gara (1967)	Underpayment: piece rate	Circumstances	Interviewing	Productivity, work quality	Underpaid subjects produced more of lower quality and also perceived their job as more interesting but less important and complex.
Pritchard, Dunnette, and Jorgenson (1972)	Overpayment and underpayment: hourly and piece rate	Circumstances, actual change in payment	Clerical task	Performance satisfaction	Circumstances induction did not result in performance differences for piece rate, but some support was found for hourly overpay and underpay. Changes in pay rate supported hourly predictions. Some support found for piece-rate-overpayment prediction but not for underpayment.
Valenzi and Andrews (1971)	Overpayment and underpayment: hourly	Circumstances	Clerical task	Productivity, work quality	No significant differences found between conditions. 27 percent of underpaid subjects quit. No other subjects in other conditions quit.
Wiener (1970)	Overpayment: hourly	Qualifications, inputs versus outcomes, ego-oriented versus task oriented	Word manipulation	Productivity, work quality	Outcome-overpayment subjects produced more. Input-overpaid subjects produced more only on ego-oriented task.
Wood and Lawler (1970)	Overpayment: piece rate	Qualifications	Reading	Amount of time reading, quality	Overpaid subjects produced less, but this could not be attributed to striving for higher quality.

have been reported (Andrews, 1967; Evans & Simmons, 1969; Lawler & O'Gara, 1967; Pritchard et al., 1972).

Although the support for Adams' theory appears impressive, several questions concerning the interpretation of the study results need to be considered. Following Vroom (1964), Goodman and Friedman (1971) suggest that the following concepts must be operationalized to provide a complete and unambiguous test of equity theory: (1) person's evaluation of his or her inputs; (2) person's perception of the relevance of the inputs for task performance; (3) person's perception of the experimenter's perception of the inputs; (4) person's perception of other's outcome-input ratio; (5) person's perception of future outcomes; (6) person's perception of the outcomes relative to alternative outcomes (e.g., past outcomes); and (7) relative importance person attaches to using 4, 5, and 6 as comparison objects. Control over these factors is central to ensuring a high degree of internal validity for the results of experimental studies. To the extent these factors may remain uncontrolled, conclusive tests of the theory become very difficult and alternative explanations for the study results can be raised. It should be apparent that many of these factors remain uncontrolled in even the most rigorous laboratory experiment. For example, Goodman and Friedman (1971) point out that the comparison other used by subjects is ambiguous in most studies. To the extent subjects use different comparison others than intended by the experimenter, interpretation of the study results becomes problematic.

A number of writers have been critical of research on equity theory precisely because several alternative explanations may exist for observed differences in the performance of subjects, particularly in the overpayment condition (Campbell & Pritchard, 1976; Goodman & Friedman, 1971; Lawler, 1968a; Pritchard, 1969). Two problems are commonly raised in interpreting the results of research on overpayment inequity, and both have to do with experimental manipulations of perceived inequity. Inequity is commonly induced in subjects by challenging their qualifications for the job. Subjects are led to believe they do not possess the necessary experience or training to qualify for the rate of pay they are to receive. Although seldom verified, it is assumed that this will result in experienced overpayment inequity (i.e., subjects believe they are being paid more than they should receive given their qualifications).

Challenging the qualifications of subjects, however, may also be experienced as threatening their self-esteem or perceived job security. Subjects may therefore work harder to prove to themselves (and to the experimenter) that they are capable of performing the task or to protect their job security. In other words, subjects may perform as predicted by the theory for reasons related to the experimental treatment but not to perceived inequity. Support for these alternative explanations for results of research on overpayment inequity comes from several sources. Andrews and Valenzi (1970) had subjects role-play an overpayment inequity situation in which subject qualifications to perform the task were challenged. When asked to indicate how they would respond in this situation, none of the subjects responded in terms of wage inequity. A majority of subjects, however, responded in terms of their self-image as a worker. In another study, Wiener (1970) found that overpaid subjects produced more than equitably paid subjects only when the task was ego-involving (i.e., task performance was central to the self-concept). Based on this finding, he argued that the performance of subjects in the overpayment condition was more highly attributable to devalued self-esteem brought about by challenges to their qualifications than to feelings of inequity. In studies where perceived inequity has been manipulated by means other than challenging the subject's qualifications (e.g., by actual changes in pay rates), less support is commonly found for equity theory predictions (Evans & Simmons, 1969; Pritchard et al., 1972; Valenzi & Andrews, 1971).

Several writers have seriously questioned the extent to which overpayment in work organizations may lead to perceived inequity. Locke (1976), for example, argues that employees are seldom told they are overpaid or made to feel incompetent to perform their job duties as is the case in laboratory experiments. He argues that employees are more likely to simply adjust their idea of equitable payment to justify what they are getting. This raises the possibility that employees in organizations use their pay rates as a primary source of information about their contributions (e.g., "if the organization is willing to pay this much, I must be making a valuable contribution"). Campbell and Pritchard (1976) also point out that employer-employee exchange relationships are highly impersonal when compared to exchanges between two close friends. Perceived overpayment inequity may be more likely in the latter exchange relationship than in the former. Individuals may react to overpayment inequity only when they believe their actions have led to someone else's being treated unfairly (Campbell & Pritchard, 1976; Walster et al., 1976). From the employee's standpoint in work organizations, there may be little objective evidence that the organization feels it is being treated unfairly.

In summary, predictions from Adams' theory about employee reactions to wage inequities have received some support in the research literature. Research support for the theory appears to be strongest for predictions about underpayment inequity. Although there are fewer studies of underpayment than of overpayment, results of research on underpayment are relatively consistent and subject to fewer alternative explanations. There are both theoretical and empirical grounds for being cautious in generalizing the results of research on overpayment inequity to employee behavior in work organizations. Where such studies have manipulated perceived inequity by challenging subjects' qualifications for the job, observed differences in performance can be explained in ways that have little to do with inequity. Where other methods of inducing overpayment inequity are used, considerably less support is often found for the theory. Predicted differences in productivity and satisfaction due to overpayment inequity are often in the predicted direction but fail to reach acceptable levels of statistical significance.

Conceptual Issues in Equity Theory

In addition to the methodological considerations discussed with respect to research on equity theory, several writers have also raised questions about the conceptual adequacy of the theory (e.g., Weick, 1967). Since theories or models of social processes are ways of making sense out of our environment by simplifying relationships between variables, it should not be surprising that any given theory fails to capture the complexity we know to exist in the real world. Consequently, there are usually a number of limitations that can be pointed out in any given theory, and equity theory is no different from other motivation approaches in this regard. The conceptual issues to be discussed below point to several limitations of the present formulation of equity theory, and they should be viewed as areas in which the theory may be clarified or extended through further research.

Concept of Equity

The concept of equity is most often interpreted in work organizations as a positive association between an employee's effort or performance on the job and the pay he or she receives (Goodman, 1977). In other words, it is believed that employees who contribute more to the organization should receive higher amounts of the rewards the organization has to offer. This belief is often referred to as the "equity norm." Adams (1965) suggests that individual expectations about equity or "fair" correlations between inputs and outcomes are learned during the process of socialization (e.g., in the home or at work) and through comparison with the inputs and outcomes of others. Although few would question the existence of an equity norm governing social relationships, the derivation of this norm and its pervasiveness remain somewhat unclear. In addition, it is important to determine the extent to which the equity norm is defined by an individual's effort and performance or by other types of contributions they may make to organizations.

Walster et al. (1976) suggest the norm of equity originates in societal attempts to develop methods of allocating rewards that maximize the amount of collective reward. Through evolving ways to "equitably" distribute rewards and costs among its members, groups or organizations can maximize the total rewards available. Groups therefore induce their members to behave equitably and establish reinforcement systems to ensure this norm is followed in social relationships. It should be apparent, however, that groups or society in general frequently deviate from the equity norm in distributing rewards. Social welfare programs and old-age medical assistance, for example, are instances in which resources are distributed on the basis of need rather than an assessment of the individual's contribution to the larger group.

The equity norm appears to be only one of several norms that govern the distribution of rewards in social relationships. An important question concerns what factors influence the extent to which rewards are distributed equitably or allocated on some other basis. In an analysis of reward allocation in small groups, Leventhal (1976) suggests that the particular distribution rule adopted in allocating rewards is related to both the goals of the reward system and characteristics of the allocator. Table 3 contrasts three decision rules that can be used in allocating rewards (equity, equality, and responsiveness to needs) and the situations where each rule is most likely to be used. The equity norm appears to be most closely associated with the goal of maximizing productivity in a group, while rewards are most likely to be distributed equally when the goal is to minimize group conflict.

Distribution rules represent an important concept in understanding reward systems (Cook, 1975; Goodman, 1977). Distribution rules identify the association between any dimension of evaluation and the levels of outcomes to be distributed. A consideration of distribution rules suggests both that different norms may govern the distribution of rewards in organizations and that different factors may weight more heavily in allocating rewards using any given norm. For example, in organizations where an equity

TABLE 3
DISTRIBUTION RULES FOR ALLOCATING REWARDS

Distribution rule	Situations where distribution rule is likely to be used	Factors affecting use of distribution rule
Equity/contributions (outcomes should match contributions)	1 Goal is to maximize group productivity. 2 A low degree of cooperation is required for task performance.	1 What receiver is expected to do 2 What others receive 3 Outcomes and contributions of person allocating rewards 4 Task difficulty and perceived ability 5 Personal characteristics of person allocating rewards and person performing
Social responsibility/needs (outcomes distributed on the basis of needs)	1 Allocator of rewards is a close friend of the receiver, feels responsible for the well-being of the receiver, or is successful or feels competent.	1 Perceived legitimacy of needs 2 Origin of need (e.g., beyond control of the individual)
Equality (equal outcomes given to all participants)	1 Goal is to maximize harmony, minimize conflict in group. 2 Task of judging performer's needs or contribution is difficult. 3 Person allocating rewards has a low cognitive capacity. 4 A high degree of cooperation is required for task performance. 5 Allocator anticipates future interactions with low-input member.	1 Sex of person allocating rewards (e.g., females more likely to allocate rewards equally than males) 2 Nature of task

Source: Adapted from Leventhal (1976).

norm is followed, it is common to find that an individual's contribution in terms of seniority is a more important basis for rewards than is actual job performance. Our ability to predict how individuals react to reward systems therefore depends upon identifying the particular norm they believe should be followed and the specific dimension (i.e., input) they feel is most important in allocating rewards. Equity theory often assumes that rewards should be given in relation to a person's contribution and, further, that performance is the most important contribution in the work setting. The accuracy of our predictions of employee reactions to reward systems can be increased, however, by recognizing the existence of several norms governing the distribution of rewards and the differential importance that may be attached to employee inputs.

Choice of a Method of Inequity Resolution

Although the several factors Adams (1965) suggested individuals will take into consideration in choosing among alternative methods of reducing inequity make the theory more testable, they do not allow a totally unequivocal set of predictions to be made from the theory (Wicklund & Brehm, 1976). In any situation, a given method of restoring inequity may satisfy one of these rules while at the same time violating another. Cognitively distorting inputs as a method of reducing inequity, for example, may allow the individual to maximize positively valent outcomes, but at the expense of threatening aspects central to his or her self-concept. When such a conflict occurs, it is difficult to specify how an individual will react to inequity. Opsahl and Dunnette (1966) have pointed out that the inability to predict how individuals will react to inequity makes conclusive tests of the theory problematic. If an overcompensated group fails to respond to inequity by increasing inputs, can this be interpreted as a disconfirmation of the theory or as an instance in which other methods of reducing inequity (e.g., cognitively distorting your own or other's inputs or outcomes) are being used? This ambiguity associated with equity theory appears to result in a situation where almost any result of empirical research can be explained in terms of the theory.

Many of the studies of equity theory have failed to capture the complexity of inequity resolution processes (Adams & Freedman, 1976). It is common in such studies to set up an inequitable situation and determine the extent to which subjects reduce inequity by changing work quantity or quality. In more personal exchange relationships, however, the method of reducing inequity chosen may be sensitive to cues from the other party to the exchange (Adams & Freedman, 1976). For example, in overpayment situations, an organization may suggest employees increase their skills and abilities through further education rather than increasing their effort on the job. Research also suggests that strategies for reducing inequity are dynamic and may change over time. Lawler et al. (1968) found that subjects reduced overpayment-piece-rate inequity by increasing work quality in an initial work session but increased their perceived qualifications to perform the task in subsequent sessions. Cognitively changing perceived inputs (qualifications) may have allowed subjects to reduce the overpayment inequity in a manner that permitted increased quantity of production and thus increased rewards to be received.

The way in which individuals reduce perceived inequity appears to be a complex process. A greater understanding of this process is essential to increasing the accuracy of predictions from equity theory.

Choice of a Comparison Other

One area of recent concern in equity theory is to develop a greater understanding of how individuals choose comparison standards against which to evaluate inputs and outcomes. Adams (1965) suggested that comparison others may be the other party to the exchange or another individual involved in an exchange with the same third party.

Until recently, little has been known about the actual comparison standards people use or the process through which alternative comparisons are chosen.

Goodman (1974) differentiated between three classes of referents: (1) others, (2) self-standards, and (3) system referents. Others are people who may be involved in a similar exchange either with the same organization or with some other organization. Self-standards are unique to the individual but different from his or her current ratio of outcomes and inputs; for example, individuals may compare their current ratio against inputs and outcomes associated with an earlier job. System referents are implicit or explicit contractual expectations between an employer and employee. At the time of being hired, an employee may be promised future rewards and this can become a basis for evaluating the exchange. In a study of 217 managers, Goodman (1974) found each of these referents was used in determining the degree of satisfaction with pay. Perhaps his most important finding was that a majority of managers reported using multiple referents in assessing their satisfaction. For example, 28 percent of the managers indicated they compared their present situation against both those of others and self-standards. He also found that higher levels of education were associated with choosing a comparison referent outside the organization.

Based on his research, Goodman (1977) has developed a model of the factors that may influence the selection of comparison person or standard. This model is presented in Figure 1. He postulates that the choice of a referent is a function of both the availability of information about the referent and the relevance or attractiveness of the referent for the comparison. Availability of information about referents is primarily determined by the individual's propensity to search and his or her position in an organization (i.e., access to information). The relevance or attractiveness of a referent is determined jointly by the instrumentality of the referent for satisfying the individual's comparison needs and the number and strength of needs related to a referent. A more detailed discussion of this model can be found in Goodman (1977).

Goodman's (1974, 1977) work represents an important step in increasing our understanding of how social comparison processes are made. If his model is supported by subsequent research, it will provide an important tool for both researchers and managers in determining who or what employees use in making comparisons about their present level of rewards.

Individual and Situational Differences in Reactions to Inequity

One area of research on equity theory that has received little attention is the impact of individual and situational differences on employee perceptions and reactions to inequity. The importance of considering individual differences was first demonstrated by Tornow (1971). Recognizing that the classification of something as an input or an outcome is often ambiguous in equity comparisons, he suggested that individuals may have a stable tendency to classify ambiguous job elements as either inputs or outcomes. Using the data collected by Pritchard et al. (1972), he subsequently classified subjects as either input- or outcome-oriented and found this factor had an impact on their reactions to inequity. For example, outcome-oriented individuals were found to be more sensitive to overpayment than were subjects with an input orientation. Individual differences were therefore having an effect on how individuals reacted to per-

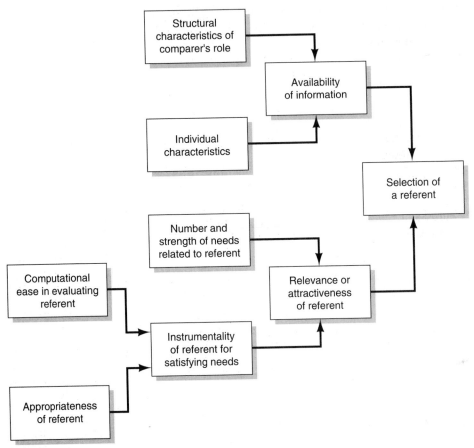

FIGURE I
Factors influencing the selection of a referent in social comparison processes. (*Adapted from Goodman, 1977.*)

ceived inequity. This is an area in which more research is needed to isolate the stable traits of individuals that can affect inequity perceptions. One variable that may be promising is the individual's level of internal/external control (Rotter, 1966). It is possible that individuals who believe events that happen to them are under their control (internals) would have a greater propensity to attempt to reduce perceived inequity than individuals who believe events are largely beyond their control (externals).

The importance of considering situational factors in employee reactions to inequity has already been noted in discussing Campbell and Pritchard's (1976) personal-impersonal exchange continuum. In the overpayment situation, employees may not react strongly to perceived inequity since the exchange with the larger organization is quite impersonal. However, where exchanges are between two close friends, both parties to the exchange may be highly sensitive to any inequities. Walster et al. (1976) have noted that an individual who feels responsible for an inequitable situation may express greater tension than someone who inadvertently finds himself or herself in an inequitable relationship. The locus of cause for a perceived inequity may therefore represent an important consideration in how individuals react to perceived inequity, particularly when the inequity is favorable to themselves.

RELATIONSHIP OF EQUITY THEORY TO EXPECTANCY THEORY

Much of the original interest in equity theory came from the fact that it made predictions about individual behavior that were difficult to incorporate into existing theories of motivation (Weick, 1967). For example, in the overpayment-piece-rate situation equity theory predicted that employees will increase quality and reduce quantity of performance. In contrast, expectancy theory appears to suggest that individuals attempt to maximize the attainment of valued outcomes and that motivation levels should be high whenever attractive outcomes (e.g., pay) are made directly contingent upon performance. Considerable research interest has been generated in trying to test these seemingly competing predictions.

Lawler (1968a) was one of the first to suggest that equity theory and expectancy theory may not be irreconcilable in terms of their predictions. A review of the equity theory literature led Lawler to conclude that the results of studies of the hourly payment condition could be explained equally well by expectancy theory. In the piece-rate conditions, expectancy theory could make the same predictions as equity theory if it was assumed that perceived inequity influenced the valence or attractiveness of rewards. It is possible that increasingly large piece-rate rewards have a decreasing valence for employees and that the amount of reward that has been received influences the valence of additional amounts of the reward. Lawler felt that if perceived equity were explicitly recognized as one of the factors affecting the valence of outcomes, expectancy theory could explain the results of equity theory research. Lawler (1973) and others (Campbell & Pritchard, 1976) have therefore concluded that equity considerations could be subsumed under the more general expectancy theory of motivation.

Although the two theories do not really appear to be in conflict, it is unclear whether this reflects genuine similarity or the ambiguity with which the theories are stated. As noted by Campbell and Pritchard (1976), both theories are somewhat ambiguous and thus it always is possible to come up with some previously unrecognized outcome that will reconcile competing predictions. In addition, the effects of perceived inequity on the valence of outcomes remains to be demonstrated. Although Lawler et al. (1968) found that the need for money correlated more highly with productivity for overpaid subjects than for equitably paid subjects, need for money was not experimentally manipulated and thus the direction of causality is difficult to establish. In addition, a composite measure of need for money was constructed based on measures taken both before and after the manipulation of perceived overpayment. Consequently, the effects of the inequity manipulation on the subject's need for money (an indicator of valence of money) cannot be determined.

In view of the ambiguity surrounding the two theories and the lack of evidence concerning the effects of perceived inequity on the valence of outcomes, it is perhaps premature to conclude that equity theory can be incorporated into expectancy theory. As Adams (1968) has argued, it may be less useful to debate which theory can be incorporated into the other than to identify the conditions in which individual behavior is guided by either equity or expectancy considerations.

CONCLUSIONS AND DIRECTIONS FOR FUTURE RESEARCH

Evaluating the current status of equity theory presents something of a dilemma; depending upon the particular body of literature one examines, very different conclusions can be drawn. On the one hand, researchers interested in organizations have largely moved away from equity theory to other motivation approaches in explaining behavior in the workplace. After a high level of initial research interest, organization researchers appear to have followed the arguments of Lawler (1973) and others that equity theory can be incorporated into expectancy theory. Consequently, research involving applications of equity theory to organizational settings has decreased in recent years. If the current literature in social psychology is examined, on the other hand, a very different picture emerges. Walster et al. (1976) recently introduced a reformation of Adams' original theory, and it has been heralded as a general theory of social behavior capable of integrating a number of the minitheories (e.g., reinforcement theory, cognitive consistency theory) that currently exist. Berkowitz and Walster (1976, p. xi) go so far as to talk about "a new mood of optimism" emerging in social psychology, at least in part attributable to the promise of equity theory for developing a more comprehensive understanding of social behavior.

Has equity theory largely outlived its usefulness as a theory of motivation in organizations, or is it a theory capable of providing general explanations of behavior in a number of different social settings? This is a difficult question to answer at the present time. However, it appears that equity theory has more to contribute to our understanding of organizational behavior than previous research would suggest. The early emphasis of organizational research on equity theory predictions of employee reactions to pay was perhaps both its greatest strength and weakness. On the positive side, focusing on monetary rewards provided a research setting in which the variables were easily quantifiable and the predictions were relatively unambiguous (or so it seemed at the time). On the negative side, exclusive interest in employee reactions to pay prevented the extension of equity theory to other areas of social relationships in organizations. Adams (1965) was careful to note that equity theory was relevant to any social situations in which exchanges may take place (e.g., between coworkers, between superiors and subordinates, etc.). With the exception of Goodman's (1977) recent work on social comparison process in organizations, the extension of the theory to a broad range of social relationships has been left to social psychologists (see Berkowitz & Walster, 1976). Several areas of behavior in organizations that might profitably be examined in equity theory terms are discussed below.

Previous research on equity theory has largely been concerned with individual reactions to perceived inequity. What appears to have been neglected are the instrumental uses of inequity in interpersonal relationships (Adams & Freedman, 1976). Individuals in organizations, for example, may purposely create perceived inequity in social relationships as a way of improving their situation or achieving certain goals. Supervisors may routinely attempt to convince employees that they are not contributing as much as another employee or at a level expected for the pay they receive. Creating perceptions of overpayment inequity may therefore be viewed as a strategy designed to increase the level of employee performance. Just as routinely, employees may attempt the same strategy, but in reverse. Ingratiation attempts (Wortman & Linsenmeier, 1977) may be viewed as strategies on the part of lower-status employees to increase the outcomes of those in higher-level positions. To the extent that those in higher positions perceive an inequity in their social relationships with lower-level employees, they will feel obligated to reciprocate. Research evidence that individuals may create perceived inequity in social relationships as a means of accomplishing certain objectives was presented by Leventhal and Bergman (1969). They found that subjects who were moderately underrewarded attempted to reduce the inequity by taking some of their partner's money when given the opportunity. Subjects who were extremely underrewarded, however, increased the discrepancy between their own rewards and those of their partner by increasing his or her advantage. By intensifying the inequity, subjects may have been following a deliberate strategy designed to convince their partner that a more equitable distribution of rewards was necessary.

Campbell, Dunnette, Lawler, and Weick (1970) have suggested the importance of viewing leadership processes in terms of exchanges between superiors and subordinates. In describing what they call the "unilateral fiction" in leadership research, they point out that managers are most often viewed as initiating the action of others and that superior-subordinate interactions are assumed to end when the manager issues a directive. Relationships between superiors and subordinates in organizations, however, are more accurately characterized by reciprocal-influence processes. A great deal of interaction between managers and employees in organizations may involve bargaining processes in which the terms of an exchange are established to the satisfaction of each party. When the manager issues a directive that is carried out by the employee, it is reasonable to assume that expectations of repayment are formed in the employee. Furthermore, when employees do a favor for the manager it may result in a perceived obligation to reciprocate on the part of the manager. Reciprocal relationships between managers and employees can be described in terms of equity theory; taking such a perspective may increase our understanding of the leadership process.

Equity theory appears to offer a useful approach to understanding a wide variety of social relationships in the workplace. Additional research is needed to extend predictions from the theory beyond simple questions about how employees react to their pay. As Goodman and Friedman (1971) have noted, equity theory predictions about employee performance levels may be one of the less interesting and useful applications of the theory. The effects of perceived inequity on employee performance levels are often slight and of limited time duration. The utility of equity theory may be greatest for increasing our understanding of interpersonal interactions at work (e.g., supervisory-subordinate relationships). In this regard, researchers interested in organizations may want to follow the lead of social psychologists in extending applications of the theory.

REFERENCES

Adams, J. S. Toward an understanding of inequity. *Journal of Abnormal and Social Psychology,* 1963, 67, 422–436. (a)

Adams, J. S. Wage inequities, productivity and work quality. *Industrial Relations,* 1963, 3, 9–16. (b)

Adams, J. S., Inequity in social exchange. In L. Berkowitz (Ed.), *Advances in experimental social psychology,* Vol. 2. New York: Academic Press, 1965. Pp. 267–299.

Adams, J. S. Effects of overpayment: Two comments on Lawler's paper. *Journal of Personality and Social Psychology,* 1968, 10, 315–316.

Adams, J. S., & Freedman, S. Equity theory revisited: Comments and annotated bibliography. In L. Berkowitz & E. Walster (Eds.), *Advances in experimental social psychology,* Vol. 9. New York: Academic Press, 1976. Pp. 43–90.

Adams, J. S., & Jacobsen, P. R. Effects of wage inequities on work quality. *Journal of Applied Psychology,* 1964, 69, 19–25.

Adams, J. S., & Rosenbaum, W. B. The relationship of worker productivity to cognitive dissonance about wage inequities. *Journal of Applied Psychology,* 1962, 46, 161–164.

Anderson, B., & Shelly, R. K. Reactions to inequity, II: A replication of the Adams experiment and a theoretical reformulation. *Acta Sociologica,* 1970, 13, 1–10.

Andrews, I. R. Wage inequity and job performance: An experimental study. *Journal of Applied Psychology,* 1967, 51, 39–45.

Andrews, I. R., & Valenzi, E. Overpay inequity or self-image as a worker: a critical examination of an experimental induction procedure. *Organizational Behavior and Human Performance,* 1970, 53, 22–27.

Arrowood, A. J. Some effects on productivity of justified and unjustified levels of reward under public and private conditions. Unpublished doctoral dissertation, University of Minnesota, 1961.

Berkowitz, L., & Walster, E. (Eds.), *Advances in experimental social psychology,* Vol. 9. New York: Academic Press, 1976.

Campbell, J. P., Dunnette, M. D., Lawler, E. E., & Weick, K. E. *Managerial behavior, performance, and effectiveness.* New York: McGraw-Hill, 1970.

Campbell, J., & Pritchard, R. D. Motivation theory in industrial and organizational psychology. In M. Dunnette (Ed.), *Handbook of industrial and organizational psychology.* Chicago: Rand McNally, 1976. Pp. 63–130.

Cook, K. S. Expectations, evaluations and equity. *American Sociological Review,* 1975, 40, 372–388.

Darley, J. M., & Darley, S. A. *Conformity and deviation.* Morristown, N.J.: General Learning Press, 1973.

Evans, W. M., & Simmons, R. G. Organizational effects of inequitable rewards: Two experiments in status inconsistency. *Administrative Science Quarterly,* 1969, 14, 224–237.

Friedman, A., & Goodman, P. Wage inequity, self-qualifications, and productivity. *Organizational Behavior and Human Performance,* 1967, 2, 406–417.

Goodman, P. S. An examination of referents used in the evaluation of pay. *Organizational Behavior and Human Performance,* 1974, 12, 170–195.

Goodman, P. S. Social comparison processes in organizations, In B. Staw & G. Salancik (Eds.), *New directions in organizational behavior.* Chicago: St. Clair, 1977. Pp. 97–132.

Goodman, P. S., & Friedman, A. An examination of the effect of wage inequity in the hourly condition. *Organizational Behavior and Human Performance,* 1968, 3, 340–352.

Goodman, P. S., & Friedman, A. An examination of quantity and quality of performance under conditions of overpayment in piece-rate. *Organizational Behavior and Human Performance,* 1969, 4, 365–374.

Goodman, P. S., & Friedman, A. An examination of Adams' theory of inequity. *Administrative Science Quarterly,* 1971, 16, 271–288.

Homans, G. C. *Social behavior: Its elementary forms.* New York: Harcourt, Brace & World, 1961.

Jaques, E. *Equitable payment.* New York: Wiley, 1961.

Lawler, E. E. Equity theory as a predictor of productivity and work quality. *Psychological Bulletin,* 1968, 70, 596–610. (a)

Lawler, E. E. Effects of hourly overpayment on productivity and work quality. *Journal of Personality and Social Psychology*, 1968, 10, 306–313. (b)

Lawler, E. E. *Motivation in work organizations.* Belmont, Calif.: Brooks/Cole, 1973.

Lawler, E. E., Koplin, C. A., Young, T. F., & Fadem, J. A. Inequity reduction over time and an induced overpayment situation. *Organizational Behavior and Human Performance*, 1968, 3, 253–268.

Lawler, E. E., & O'Gara, P. W. Effects of inequity produced by underpayment on work output, work quality, and attitudes toward the work. *Journal of Applied Psychology,* 1967, 51, 403–410.

Leventhal, G. S. Fairness in social relationships. In J. Thibaut, J. Spence, & R. Carson (Eds.), *Contemporary topics in social psychology.* Morristown, N.J.: General Learning Press, 1976.

Leventhal, G. S., & Bergman, J. T. Self-depriving behavior as a response to unprofitable inequity. *Journal of Experimental Social Psychology,* 1969, 5, 153–171.

Leventhal, G. S., Weiss, T., & Long, G. Equity, reciprocity, and reallocating rewards in the dyad. *Journal of Personality and Social Psychology,* 1969, 13, 300–305.

Locke, E. A. The nature and causes of job satisfaction. In M. Dunnette (Ed.), *Handbook of industrial and organizational psychology.* Chicago: Rand McNally, 1976. Pp. 1297–1349.

Opsahl, R. L., & Dunnette, M. The role of financial compensation in industrial motivation. *Psychological Bulletin,* 1966, 66, 94–118.

Patchen, M. *The choice of wage comparisons.* Englewood Cliffs, N.J.: Prentice-Hall, 1961.

Pritchard, R. D. Equity theory: A review and critique. *Organizational Behavior and Human Performance*, 1969, 4, 176–211.

Pritchard, R. D., Dunnette, M. D., & Jorgenson, D. O. Effects of perceptions of equity and inequity on worker performance and satisfaction. *Journal of Applied Psychology,* 1972, 56, 75–94.

Rotter, J. B. Generalized expectancies for internal versus external control of reinforcement. *Psychological Monographs,* 1966, 80, (1, Whole No. 609).

Simpson, R. L. *Theories of social exchange.* Morristown, N.J.: General Learning Press, 1972.

Tornow, W. W. The development and application of an input-outcome moderator test on the perception and reduction of inequity. *Organizational Behavior and Human Performance,* 1971, 6, 614–638.

Valenzi, E. R., & Andrews, I. R. Effect on hourly overpay and underpay inequity when tested with a new induction procedure. *Journal of Applied Psychology,* 1971, 55, 22–27.

Vroom, V. H. *Work and motivation.* New York: Wiley, 1964.

Walster, E., Bercheid, E., & Walster, G. W. New directions in equity research. In L. Berkowitz & E. Walster (Eds.), *Advances in experimental social psychology,* Vol. 9. New York: Academic Press, 1976. Pp. 1–42.

Weick, K. E. The concept of equity in the perception of pay. *Administrative Science Quarterly,* 1967, 2, 414–439.

Wicklund, R. A., & Brehm, J. W. *Perspectives on cognitive dissonance.* Hillsdale, N.J.: Lawrence Erlbaum, 1976.

Wiener, Y. The effects of "task-" and "ego-oriented" performance on 2 kinds of overcompensation inequity. *Organizational Behavior and Human Performance,* 1970, 5, 191–208.

Wood, I., & Lawler, E. E. Effects of piece-rate overpayment on productivity. *Journal of Applied Psychology,* 1970, 54, 234–238.

Wortman, C. B., & Linsenmeier, J. A. W. Interpersonal attraction and methods of ingratiation in organizational settings. In B. M. Staw & G. R. Salancik (Eds.), *New directions in organizational behavior.* Chicago: St. Clair, 1977. Pp. 133–178.

Procedural Justice and Worker Motivation

Russell Cropanzano
Robert Folger

When people do not receive the rewards to which they feel entitled, they are often motivated to do something about it. The problem comes in specifying which types of actions most employees will take. Some are likely to become angry and work less hard, increase their absenteeism, or even leave their jobs. Others will work even harder in the hope of eventually obtaining what they want. Because not all employees receive what they think they deserve, managers need to know the conditions under which each reaction is likely to occur.

We argue that when employees react to the way they are treated at work, their motivation to respond in one fashion or another cannot be understood adequately without taking into account two separate notions of fairness. Traditionally the organizational science literature has considered only one way of describing what it means to be fairly treated, namely, the notion of distributive justice. That way of conceptualizing fairness is illustrated by equity theory (Adams, 1965). According to equity theory, people determine whether they have been treated fairly at work by examining their own payoff ratio of outcomes (e.g., size of a raise) to inputs (e.g., level of performance) and comparing that ratio with the corresponding outcome-input ratio obtained by others such as their coworkers.

A second way of thinking about what it means to be treated fairly—namely, the notion of procedural justice—focuses not on the results of compensation decisions or other administrative decisions that involve allocations of scarce resources among employees (i.e., the payoff ratio of outcomes to inputs), but instead focuses on the fairness of the manner in which the decision-making process is conducted. In other words, the focus shifts from *what* was decided to *how* the decision was made. Someone who says that "the ends do not justify the means," for example, calls attention to the importance of following some general guidelines of fairness with respect to the *process* of making an allocation decision. The implication is that certain procedures are not justified, even though they might produce equitable results.

The way courtroom trials are conducted helps to illustrate the distinction between distributive and procedural justice. Judges, as the persons with administrative authority in a courtroom, are responsible for ensuring that the procedures used to conduct a trial (e.g., procedures regulating how evidence can be presented) have been administered impartially and in accordance with the law. Juries, on the other hand, may be given the responsibility for ensuring that verdicts are in some sense equitable—that is, making the verdict as an outcome fit with the "inputs" or actions of the person on trial. Clearly it is possible for a jury's decision to seem inequitable even though the judge was completely fair and impartial with respect to all rulings regarding the presentation of evidence, as well as with respect to every other matter concerning how the trial was conducted.

This paper was written especially for the previous edition of this volume.

In light of the distinction between procedural and distributive justice, it is plausible for a person to have reasons for believing that a (procedurally) fair hearing might result in an (inequitably) unfair verdict; similarly, a fair (equitable) outcome might result from an unfair (procedurally inappropriate or unlawfully conducted) hearing. The point is that the fairness of the end results and the fairness of the determining processes can be evaluated independently of one another. The two types of fairness may, at times, even conflict with one another, for example, when the strict observance of a defendant's procedural rights seems to interfere with obtaining the evidence necessary for determining that person's guilt or innocence.

PROCEDURAL JUSTICE AS A SUPPLEMENT TO EQUITY THEORY

Equity theory (Adams, 1965) says that people assess fairness by first dividing their own outcomes (such as pay or status) by their inputs (such as effort or time), then calculating the corresponding ratio that involves the outcomes and inputs of some referent other. These two quotients are compared. If a person's own ratio is bigger, the person may feel remorse and guilt. If the referent's ratio is larger, the person with the smaller ratio may feel angry and resentful. In both cases the emotions are unpleasant, and the person is motivated to reduce these negative feelings. For example, people can lower their inputs (i.e., work less) or cognitively distort the outcomes of the other person. Indeed, any of the four terms in the equation can be altered, and this can be done by either cognitions or behaviors.

Although equity theory has received broad support, it has also been criticized as not being particularly "useful" (e.g., Locke & Henne, 1986). A major limitation to equity theory's usefulness is the difficulty of specifying what type of action an aggrieved employee will take. Serious consequences for organizations can arise when perceived unfair treatment leads to some form of retaliation by employees. In defining unfair treatment by outcome-input ratios, equity theory provides grounds for predicting that retaliation (e.g., work slowdowns as a way of lowering employee inputs) might accompany underpayment. Unfortunately, the same formula also provides a basis for exactly the opposite prediction: If the inequity is resolved via cognitive adjustment (e.g., perceptually raising own outcomes), then the underpaid employee might well become one of the organization's hardest workers.

Equity theory's failure to resolve these opposing predictions may stem from placing too much emphasis on the results of reward allocations and ignoring the process that led up to them. Similarly, the research done to test equity has focused only on distributive justice issues and has neglected procedural justice issues. Experience suggests that two people may react very differently to the same inequity if they believe different things about how that inequity was created (e.g., if two different decision-making processes were used). As Bies (1987) has argued, for example, employees disadvantaged by a two-tier pay system are likely to respond very differently depending on whether the system is seen as being the only way for a company to stay in business or as a union-busting ploy by management.

Leventhal (1980) lists some possible determinants of procedural justice. For example, procedures should remain consistent across different people and different times. A fair procedure would be one that is based on society's shared ethical standards and takes into account the concerns of everyone involved. Justice also requires that the procedure be free from bias and based on accurate information. Finally, a fair procedure should include some system that allows erroneous decisions to be corrected.

Tyler (1989) has recently found evidence for three aspects of concern about procedural fairness as administered by an authority or decision maker: (1) the extent to which the decision maker exhibits neutrality, (2) the extent to which the intentions of the decision maker can be trusted, and (3) the extent to which the decision maker shows respect for the rights of the parties to a decision (those whom the decision affects). These three types of considerations represent the central features of what it means for decisions to be made in a procedurally fair manner. Note that this perspective emphasizes the importance of the behavior and inferred qualities of the decision maker, as well as the characteristics of the decision-making process.*

The following sections review in greater detail the advantages of considering procedural justice. In particular we will note the implications of procedural justice for specific predictions about employee attitudes and behavior. Each of these will be considered in turn.

PROCEDURAL JUSTICE AND EMPLOYEE ATTITUDES

Ample evidence attests to the importance of procedural justice, but much of it has been collected outside of the organizational context. For example, Tyler (1984) examined defendants' perceptions of courtroom fairness. In this study, questionnaire items assessed distributive fairness (i.e., whether the verdict was fair) and procedural justice (i.e., whether the procedures were administered impartially). The pattern of results would have been impossible to predict with equity theory. Tyler found that distributive justice was indeed related to outcome satisfaction. The defendants' evaluation of the judicial system, however, was only predicted by the fairness of the procedures. More to the point, if a person was treated in a procedurally fair manner and still received an unfavorable verdict, that person would derogate the verdict (a distributive inequity) but not the court system.

Those results have been replicated by Tyler (1987), who found that perceived legitimacy and support for legal authorities (such as police officers) were predicted by procedural fairness rather than distributive justice. This finding has also been extended into the realm of political behavior. Tyler, Rasinski, and McGraw (1985) found that "trust in national government" was predicted only by the perceived extent of procedural fairness. Finally, Barrett-Howard and Tyler (1986) have shown that procedures are the fundamental determinants of perceived fairness in a wide variety of situations, including the workplace. Findings such as this have caused Lind and Tyler to state that "procedural justice has especially strong effects on attitudes about institutions and au-

---

*Throughout our presentation we use the term "procedures" very broadly to include various aspects of the decision maker's conduct. In particular, we mean the term to be inclusive of procedurally related behavior that may occur even after the decision itself (such as providing explanations), thereby encompassing what some authors (e.g., Bies & Shapiro, 1987) have termed *interactional* fairness judgments pertaining to conduct associated with the implementation of a procedure.

thorities, as opposed to attitudes about the specific outcome in question" (1988, p. 179).

In the field of organizational behavior, procedural justice gained prominence by a less direct route. In particular, problems with the equity or distribution factors caused researchers to consider administration and procedural variables. A good example occurs in the work of Dyer and Theriault (1976), who examined Lawler's (1971) model of pay satisfaction. Generally speaking, in the Lawler model pay is a function of two cognitions: the amount to which an employee feels entitled, and the amount he or she actually receives. When the two cognitions are compared, the employee is unhappy if a discrepancy exists. Lawler had noted that this model borrows heavily from equity theory.

Dyer and Theriault pointed out that Lawler had excluded pay administration variables (such as the superior's accuracy in work assessments and the superior's influence over pay decisions). That is, the discrepancy framework has not examined the effects of a fair (or unfair) system of administering organizational rewards. To alleviate this problem, Dyer and Theriault added 12 administration items to their questionnaire. They assessed fairness over three different samples. Although the absolute level of pay was the best predictor of satisfaction, the procedural administration variables significantly improved the fit of the model for each sample. Weiner (1980) conducted a similar assessment of the Lawler model. Weiner found that by considering pay administration she could predict pay satisfaction, absenteeism, and turnover better than with the distributive justice variables alone.

Similar findings have come from research on performance appraisal satisfaction. Landy, Barnes, and Murphy (1978) mailed a short fairness questionnaire to 711 employees at a large manufacturing firm. They found that five items predicted whether "performance [had] been fairly and accurately evaluated." In descending order these were: the opportunity for the subordinate to express his or her feelings, the existence of a formal appraisal program, the supervisor's knowledge of the subordinate's performance, the existence of action plans to improve performance weaknesses, and the frequency of evaluations. These are all procedural items. Although Landy et al. did not directly assess distributive justice, they did do a follow-up of the managers about a year later (Landy, Barnes-Farrell, & Cleveland, 1980). The results showed that their original findings were not affected by the actual level of the evaluation (i.e., whether the evaluation had been favorable or unfavorable).

A second study on appraisal satisfaction and fairness was conducted by Dipboye and de Pontbriand (1981). The methodology was essentially the same as Landy, Barnes, and Murphy (1978). This time a short survey was mailed to 971 exempt employees at a research and development firm. Dipboye and de Pontbriand found that four of their independent variables were related to the evaluation of both the rater and the rating system. Only one of these (favorability of the appraisal) was a distributive item. The other three (discussion of plans, relevance, opportunity to participate, and goal-setting) were administration variables. Interestingly, the favorability of the appraisal was highly related to the rating of the appraiser but had a smaller relationship to the rating of the system as a whole. That finding, of course, is consistent with the work of Tyler and his colleagues discussed earlier.

Greenberg (1986) had a sample of 217 managers generate statements concerning their most fair and unfair performance evaluations. Using a Q-sort technique, a second subsample of these managers placed the items into seven categories. When these categories were factor-analyzed, Greenberg found that only two factors emerged. Five of the categories loaded on a procedural factor, and two loaded on a distributive factor. Greenberg reported no significant differences between the two factors. Together they accounted for 94.7 percent of the variance. He cautioned future researchers not to neglect either dimension at the expense of the other.

Greenberg's warning is especially important in light of the legal and political findings reviewed above. It could be that distributive and procedural justice exert their influence on different attitudes. In particular, distribution predicts satisfaction with the outcome received, whereas procedural justice influences the evaluation of the organization. Such a pattern would certainly be consistent with the work of Tyler and his colleagues. Unfortunately, except for Dipboye and de Pontbriand's study (which found supportive results) none of the organizational studies were set up to examine this issue in detail. Specifically, there was either a limited number of criterion variables (outcome satisfaction and commitment were not both included), independent variables (adequate measures of both types of justice were absent), or both.

Recently, a more extensive series of studies has examined the effects of procedural justice in the workplace. These studies yielded highly consistent results. The first of these examined employee attitudes in a company's head office (Konovsky, Folger, & Cropanzano, 1987). Stepwise regression analysis showed that procedural factors influenced organizational commitment, whereas distributive factors predicted satisfaction with pay. These findings were extended in a second study by Folger and Konovsky (1989). The authors examined employee responses to pay raise decisions. Causal analyses showed that once again procedural justice accounted for more variance in attitudes about the organization and its authorities (i.e., trust-in-supervision and organizational commitment), whereas distributive justice was a better predictor of pay satisfaction. Finally, in the most extensive project to date, Martin (1987) assessed the pay satisfaction of 1685 workers at a financial services company. Martin stated that "both distributive and procedural justice determined satisfaction, while organizational commitment was determined by perceptions of procedural fairness" (p. ix).

There are significant implications regarding these findings about the relationship between procedural justice and employees' attitudes toward the organization and its authorities, especially because such attitudes may be related to important employee behaviors. Bateman and Organ (1983) found that satisfaction with supervision had a strong relationship with good "citizenship" behavior, for example, which included such things as dependability, keeping the work space clean, avoiding waste, and taking time to train new workers. Similarly, committed employees are less likely to leave the organization (Mowday, Porter, & Steers, 1982) and more likely to engage in voluntary prosocial behavior (O'Reilly & Chatman, 1986). Given these findings, the role of procedural justice in increasing the individual's evaluation of the organization takes on added significance. If employees can be guaranteed fair procedural treatment, they are less likely to leave and more likely to become loyal organizational members. Further, besides the ethical and moral reasons for justice, fair procedures can often be implemented in a relatively inexpensive manner. Recall from our review that when individuals perceived a fair allocation of rewards, they were satisfied with the institution even in the face of negative outcomes (e.g., Folger & Konovsky, 1989).

One limitation of the above studies is that they operationalize distributive and procedural justice as competing constructs. That is, both are measured and the amount of variance each accounts for is assessed. On this basis one is considered "more" or "less" important for predicting a given phenomenon. We have already mentioned Greenberg's (1986) warning against this approach, and it bears repeating here. Recent research has shown that outcomes and allocations work together to create a sense of injustice. A full understanding of fairness cannot be achieved by examining the two constructs separately. Rather, one needs to consider the interaction between outcomes and procedures.

A TWO-COMPONENT MODEL OF JUSTICE

Perceptions of injustice or unfair treatment can be broken down into two components (e.g., Cropanzano & Folger, 1989; Folger, 1987). One component involves a person's perception of having received an inequitable or negative outcome—for example, a low raise based on a poor performance rating. This component is the domain traditionally addressed by equity theory. The second component involves perceptions of the events leading up to and accompanying the unfavorable outcome. Such perceptions influence how an individual assesses procedural fairness. If the events associated with the allocation are just, it is more difficult to question the outcomes that have resulted. For example, it is more difficult to press a claim of unfair treatment if the poor performance rating stemmed from the supervisor's having conducted a rating process generally regarded as fair and impartial. There should still be a desire to do something about the low rating, but there should be less motivation to retaliate in some fashion against the supervisor or the organization.

The two-component approach assumes that the perception of an unfair or negative outcome (the distributive component) energizes behavior. Simply put, when people receive outcomes they do not want, they are motivated to do something. Some of the things a person might be motivated to do under such circumstances can be called "destructive" because of the harmful effects on other people, their property, or their sources of livelihood. Employees seeking to rectify perceived injustice by working less, by quitting, or by going on strike, for example, are threatening their employers' profits. Obviously employers are likely to regard other actions as examples of "constructive" motivation, such as when an employee redoubles his or her efforts in order to prove that a low performance rating unfairly characterized his or her ability.

According to this two-component approach, the motivational route an employee will travel—in other words, whether in a constructive or destructive direction—is predicted to be determined by the perceived fairness of the procedures. Specifically, if the procedures are fair then the system under which the employee works is also assumed to be fair. Hence, the negative outcome will be addressed constructively. Conversely, if the system is determined to be unfair, then the worker is expected to retaliate by using destructive tactics. Thus a two-component approach suggests that although the distribution of outcomes provides an energizing or motivational force, procedures determine the direction in which behavior will travel (i.e., whether action will be taken *against* an employer or the agents of employers such as supervisors and managers).

This line of reasoning implies that both components are crucial for influencing perceptions of injustice. Folger and Martin (1986) have described such an approach by saying that before someone will take action against another person in the name of rectifying unfair treatment, two types of questions must be answered affirmatively. One question considers whether more favorable outcomes were possible: Would outcomes have been better under some other set of conditions? This is the distributive component. Can the individual imagine a reasonable and positive alternative outcome? If so, then behavior is energized.

A second type of question addresses interpersonal behavior (other people's actions, such as the steps taken by a supervisor in appraising performance) and asks whether those in authority followed appropriate norms of conduct: Should a different decision-making process have been used? This is the procedural component. If the answer to this second question is yes, then the potential for hostile (destructive) attitudes and behaviors will be increased. If the answer is no, then the experience of injustice will be reduced and perhaps eliminated; certainly there will be less of a tendency for someone to "blame the system," and hence actions taken against the organization are diminished.

It is important to note that if the individual perceives the procedures to be fair, then even if the distribution is inequitable, he or she will be less inclined to take destructive actions against those in authority. This fair-process effect (Folger, Rosenfield, Grove, & Corkran, 1979) has been widely documented (see reviews by Folger & Greenberg, 1985; and Lind & Tyler, 1988). It should also be noted that dual-component formulations are fairly recent, however, and many parameters and implications have not yet been subjected to rigorous examination. Having issued that caveat, we turn to examining the existing empirical evidence.

Three sections compromise the discussion that follows. In the first, we examine the case where the allocation is favorable but the procedures are unfair. In the second, attention shifts to the situation where outcomes are inequitable but the procedures are perceived as fair. Finally, we review the negative reactions that occur when both the distribution and administration rules are unjust. Within each of these sections the reader should be attentive to three sets of dependent variables: attitudinal effects, individual behavioral effects, and collective action.

Fair Distribution with Unfair Procedures

To date the research seems to indicate that people are not concerned with procedural fairness following a fair distribution. If their outcome is positive (Greenberg, 1987) or if a favorable alternative is unimaginable (Cropanzano & Folger, 1989), then subjects are not upset about inequity. The clearest example of this can be found in Greenberg (1987). In this study people achieved either high, moderate, or low outcomes because of fair or unfair procedure. In the fair procedure condition, Greenberg paid subjects for high performance; the unfair procedure was to use the room in which subjects had worked as the basis for their pay (a completely arbitrary decision).

Greenberg found that even when it worked to their advantage, people were able to clearly recognize an unfair administration rule. However, individuals did not become upset about this procedure until a negative outcome took place. Specifically, Greenberg had subjects rate the unfairness of procedures and the extent to which this unfairness concerned them. He found that paying subjects based on the room in which they worked was always rated as unfair. However, subjects did not report concern about this outcome until it caused them to earn less money. Further, although the unfair treatment caused subjects to like the experimenter less, they tended to voice complaints only when a low outcome was paired with an unfair procedure.

As a dual-component model would predict, it seems that the motivating "kick" of a low outcome is an important stimulus to action. Whereas by itself an inequitable allocation does not predict the direction a response will take, this study indicates that alone a procedural injustice is sometimes unlikely to provoke any action at all. This finding is consistent with the work of Cropanzano and Folger (1989), who found that low levels of resentment were reported in a situation similar to the one described above. Although further evidence is required to clarify the extent of this effect, for now it appears that when the outcome is positive and the procedures are negative, people will note the injustice without becoming particularly upset. They know the rules are unjust, and they do not like the person responsible for them (i.e., the experimenter). They seem relatively unmotivated, however, to take any action to alleviate the problem.

Presumably these findings could be qualified. For example, if a person expects to interact with the system again, that person should be concerned with procedures. Such increased concern would be reasonable; although procedural unfairness might not cause much of a negative effect in the short run (and may even result in a short-term increase in one's own outcomes), a fundamentally unfair set of procedural practices does represent an ever-present threat of unfair outcomes over the long run. On the other hand, if the procedural unfairness is both stable and advantageous (e.g., tending to favor one sex or race), then perhaps the favored person will continue to ignore it. That this prediction has yet to be tested is unfortunate, because the case of repeated interactions would be most applicable to the workplace.

Altruism, social consciousness, and humanitarian interests could also lead people to express concern about others who are victims of unjust procedures. This may be particularly true if the wronged individual is a friend or similar other. In such a case, unfair procedural rules could be motivating even for the person not directly affected. Once again, more research is needed to clarify this point. However, even given these potential moderators, at present is seems safe to state that a procedural injustice that hurts no one will not be very motivating.

Unfair Distribution with Fair Procedures

The findings reviewed above stand in marked contrast to what occurs when an inequitable distribution is assigned by a fair administrative procedure. In that case people may express some dissatisfaction with their outcomes (e.g., Greenberg, 1987), but they tend not to report much unfairness and not to express much resentment (Cropanzano & Folger, 1989). In fact, Cropanzano and Folger found some evidence that when a negative outcome was assigned by fair procedures, subjects became angry at themselves rather than angry at an experimenter. These findings are consistent with the field studies reviewed earlier. For example, recall that Folger and Konovsky (1989) found that low wages were related to pay satisfaction but not to organizational commitment or the evaluation of the company's authorities.

The evidence also indicates that just administration rules curb behavioral retaliation. In the Greenberg (1987) and Folger and Martin (1986) studies, subjects did not attempt to report the experimenter's behavior unless there was a procedural injustice. Even after the loss of a desired reward, individuals did not tend to retaliate so long as the allocation rules were fair. Other researchers have found similar results (Taylor, Moghaddam, Gamble, & Zellerer, 1987): After being denied membership in a high-status group, participants tended to avoid collective action if the reasons for the refusal were perceived as just. The Taylor et al. study offers additional evidence for a two-component approach. Subjects were allowed to work on the task a second time and reapply for group membership. When a negative outcome occurred under a fair procedure condition, individual performance increased significantly. Participants simply worked harder. When a negative outcome was followed by an unfair procedure, Taylor et al. found that performance dropped.

Taylor et al. is the first experiment to take performance measures. As a result, their findings need to be replicated and extended. It is likely that various situational factors may limit the generalizability of this study. For example, the unfair procedure used in this experiment may have offered little likelihood of future success. Therefore, procedures may influence performance by changing reward contingencies. Even given this limitation, the situation was hardly an unusual one. Consider, for example, possible charges of sex discrimination with respect to procedures. When promotion decisions will be made by an all-male group, then suspected procedural unfairness might lower the performance of females.

Unfair Distribution with Unfair Procedures

Once an inequitable outcome is paired with an unfair decision rule, the typically negative things associated with injustice began to occur. Even though people may tolerate poor procedures following a positive outcome, they respond vigorously after a negative one. For example, Cropanzano and Folger (1989) had subjects fail to achieve a desired reward as a result of working on a difficult task. Even though the objective outcome was always negative, they found that if subjects were allowed to select the task for themselves, they reported low levels of resentment (this is the poor-outcome, fair-procedure case mentioned above). When a free choice was not granted, however, subjects reported high levels of resentment, low levels of a willingness to be understanding, and a sense of having been treated unfairly within the experiment.

Greenberg (1987) and Folger and Martin (1986) gave individuals the opportunity to report an unfair experimenter to the human subjects committee. Both studies found that subjects only expressed an intent to report the injustice if both an unfair outcome and an unfair procedure were simultaneously present. Lacking either of these components, the individuals were unlikely to take action against the experimenter.

In a more extensive study, Taylor et al. (1987) gave individuals the opportunity to organize against a group that had denied them membership for either fair or unfair reasons. Alternatively, subjects could apply for membership a second time. Performance measures were taken following the unfair treatment. These authors found that when both the outcomes and the procedures were negative, workers did indeed become motivated, but not to work harder. Performance dropped significantly following the dual injustice. Instead, subjects expressed an intent to organize into a group and take action against the individuals who had wronged them. This activity did not take place when the procedures were fair—even when subjects failed to attain membership in the desired organization.

Collective action, it would seem, can be a prominent response used to correct a procedural injustice that has caused poor outcomes. There are probably at least two reasons for this. First, a distributive inequity tends to involve more individualized and idiosyncratic perceptions, such as those regarding which inputs are relevant and what the respective contributions of various group members are. Because the relative values of both outcomes and inputs are "in the eye of the beholder," judgments about distributive justice present difficulties with respect to mustering collective support. A procedural injustice, on the other hand, is more likely to involve the treatment of a substantial number of organization members (e.g., a companywide policy). Hence, since many people may be affected simultaneously, collective action should be facilitated.

A second reason why procedural injustices trigger collective action can be found in the work of Tyler (1987), Folger and Konovsky (1989), and others. Procedural injustice lowers the evaluation of the entire organization. It undermines loyalty to both the institution and to its appointed representatives. To move against an organization requires the strength found in numbers. On the other hand, by itself a distributive inequity has a more localized effect on outcome satisfaction. Addressing a distributive inequity, as a matter of individualized dissatisfaction, is less apt to require a large group.

CONCLUSION

The incorporation of procedural justice into organizational research has been a recent innovation. Thus far, it seems to have been a productive one. Field studies have shown that outcomes and procedures exert their influence on different employee attitudes. The amount that people receive affects outcome satisfaction, whereas procedures (and the related actions of authorities) affect organizational commitment. More recently, a two-component model of injustice has been proposed. One component is a distributive inequity that energizes behavior. Although people can recognize an unfair decision-making process, they may not be motivated to change it until a negative outcome occurs. The second component is a procedural injustice that directs the individual's response in a specific direction. If administrative conduct and procedures are just, people are predicted to work within the system (e.g., increase performance). If procedures are implemented in an unfair manner, however, employees lower their commitment and take retaliatory action (e.g., lower performance). Most evidence so far has been supportive, but a great deal more research is needed.

In a work of finite resources people cannot have all of the things they want. Although organizations should strive for the best allocations possible, some perceptions of unfavorable outcomes are inevitable. The existence of fair procedures may be a more realistic goal. If procedures are just, then the negative consequences of unfavorable outcomes are less likely. Procedural fairness should motivate employees away from activities viewed by management as being destructive and should motivate employees toward activities seen as being more constructive.

REFERENCES

Adams, J. S. (1965). Inequity in social exchange. In L. Berkowitz (Ed.), *Advances in experimental social psychology* (Vol. 2). New York: Academic Press.

Barrett-Howard, E., & Tyler, T. R. (1986). Procedural justice as a criterion in allocation decisions. *Journal of Personality and Social Psychology,* 50, 296–305.

Bateman, T. S., & Organ, D. W. (1983). Job satisfaction and the Good Soldier: The relationship between affect and employee "citizenship." *Academy of Management Journal,* 26, 163–169.

Bies, R. J. (1987). The predicament of injustice: The management of moral outrage. In L. L. Cummings & B. M. Staw (Eds.), *Research in organizational behavior* (Vol. 9). Greenwich, Conn.: JAI Press.

Bies, R. J., & Shapiro, D. (1987). Interactional fairness judgments: The influence of causal accounts. *Social Justice Research,* 1, 199–218.

Cropanzano, R., & Folger, R. (1989). Referent cognitions and task decision autonomy: Beyond equity theory. *Journal of Applied Psychology,* 74, 293–299.

Dipboye, R. L., & de Pontbriand, R. (1981). Correlates of employee reactions to performance appraisals and appraisal systems. *Journal of Applied Psychology,* 66, 248–251.

Dyer, L., & Theriault, R. (1976). The determinants of pay satisfaction. *Journal of Applied Psychology,* 61, 596–604.

Folger, R. (1987). Reformulating the preconditions of resentment: A referent cognitions model. In J. C. Masters & W. P. Smith (Eds.), *Social comparison, social justice, and relative deprivation* (pp. 183–215). Hillsdale, N.J.: Lawrence Erlbaum Associates.

Folger, R., & Greenberg, J. (1985). Procedural justice: An interpretive analysis of personnel systems. In K. Rowland & G. Ferris (Eds.), *Research in personnel and human resources management* (Vol. 3). Greenwich, Conn.: JAI Press.

Folger, R., & Konovsky, M. A. (1989). Effect of procedural and distributive justice on reactions to pay raise decisions. *Academy of Management Journal,* 32, 115–130.

Folger, R., & Martin C. (1986). Relative deprivation and referent cognitions: Distributive and procedural justice effects. *Journal of Experimental Social Psychology,* 22, 531–546.

Folger, R., Rosenfield, D., Grove, J., & Corkran, L. (1979). Effects of "voice" and peer opinions on responses to inequity. *Journal of Personality and Social Psychology,* 37, 2253–2261.

Greenberg, J. (1986). Determinants of perceived fairness of performance evaluations. *Journal of Applied Psychology,* 71, 340–342.

Greenberg, J. (1987). Reactions to procedural injustice in payment distributions: Do the means justify the ends? *Journal of Applied Psychology,* 72, 55–61.

Konovsky, M. A., Folger, R., & Cropanzano, R. (1987). Relative effects of procedural and distributive justice on employee attitudes. *Representative Research in Social Psychology,* 17, 15–24.

Landy, F. J., Barnes, J. L., & Murphy, K. R. (1978). Correlates of perceived fairness and accuracy of performance evaluation. *Journal of Applied Psychology,* 63, 751–754.

Landy, F. J., Barnes-Farrell, J. L., & Cleveland, J. N. (1980). Perceived fairness and accuracy of performance evaluation: A follow-up. *Journal of Applied Psychology,* 65, 355–356.

Lawler, E. E. (1971). *Pay and organizational effectiveness: A psychological view.* New York:

McGraw-Hill.

Leventhal, G. S. (1980). What should be done with equity theory? In R. J. Gergen, M. S. Greenberg, & R. H. Willis (Eds.), *Social exchange: Advances in theory and research* (pp. 27–55). New York: Plenum Press.

Lind, E. A., & Tyler, T. R. (1988). *The social psychology of procedural justice.* New York: Plenum Press.

Locke, E. A., & Henne, D. (1986).Work motivation theories. In C. L. Cooper & I. Robertson (Eds.), *International review of industrial and organizational psychology: 1986* (pp. 1–35). New York: Wiley.

Martin, C. L. (1987). *Distributive and procedural justice effects on satisfaction and commitment.* Unpublished doctoral dissertation, Georgia Institute of Technology, Athens, Georgia.

Mowday, R., Porter, L., & Steers, R. (1982). *Organizational linkages: The psychology of commitment, absenteeism, and turnover.* New York: Academic Press.

O'Reilly, C., & Chatman, J. (1986). Organizational commitment, and psychological attachment: The effects of compliance, identification, and internalization on prosocial behavior. *Journal of Applied Psychology, 71,* 492–499.

Taylor, D. M., Moghaddam, F. M., Gamble, I., & Zellerer, E. (1987). Disadvantaged group responses to perceived inequity: From passive acceptance to collective action. *Journal of Social Psychology,* 127(3), 259–272.

Tyler, T. R. (1984). The role of perceived injustice in defendants' evaluations of their courtroom experience. *Law and Society Review,* 18, 51–74.

Tyler, T. R. (1987). Conditions leading to value-expressive effects in judgments of procedural justice: A test of four models. *Journal of Personality and Social Psychology,* 42, 333–344.

Tyler, T. R. (1989). The psychology of procedural justice: A test of the group-value model. *Journal of Personality and Social Psychology,* 57, 830–838.

Tyler, T. R. (1990). *Why people obey the law: Procedural justice, legitimacy, and compliance.* New Haven, Conn.: Yale University Press.

Tyler, T. R., Rasinski, K., & McGraw, K. M. (1985). The influence of perceived injustice on the endorsement of political leaders. *Journal of Applied Social Psychology,* 15, 700–725.

Weiner, N. (1980). Determinants and behavioral consequences of pay satisfaction: A comparison of two models. *Personnel Psychology,* 33, 741–757.

Social Cognitive Theory of Organizational Management

Robert Wood
Albert Bandura

Many theories have been proposed over the years to explain human psychosocial functioning. They differ in the conceptions of human nature they adopt and in what they regard as the basic determinants and mechanisms of human motivation and action. Human behavior often has been explained in terms of one-sided determinism. In such models of unindirectional causation, behavior is depicted as being shaped and controlled either by environmental influences or by internal dispositions. Social cognitive theory explains psychosocial functioning in terms of triadic reciprocal causation (Bandura, 1986). In this model of reciprocal determinism, behavior, cognitive, and other personal factors and environmental events operate as interacting determinants that influence each other bidirectionally (see Figure 1). Reciprocality does not mean that the different sources of influences are of equal strength. Nor do the reciprocal influences occur simultaneously. It takes time for a causal factor to exert its influence and to activate reciprocal influences. Because of the bidirectionality of influence, people are both products and producers of their environment.

This article focuses on how personal factors contribute to this dynamic transaction in the management of organizations. In the analysis of the personal determinants in this interactional causal structure, social cognitive theory accords a central role to cognitive, vicarious, self-regulatory, and self-reflective processes. Three aspects of social cognitive theory are especially relevant to the organizational field (Bandura, 1988d): the development of people's cognitive, social, and behavioral competencies through mastery modeling, the cultivation of people's beliefs in their capabilities so that they will use their talents effectively, and the enhancement of people's motivation through goal systems.

DEVELOPMENT OF COMPETENCIES THROUGH MASTERY MODELING

Psychological theories traditionally have emphasized learning through the effects of one's actions. If knowledge and skills could be acquired only through direct experience, the process of human development would be greatly retarded, not to mention exceedingly tedious, costly, and hazardous. Fortunately, people can expand their knowledge and skills on the basis of information conveyed by modeling influences. Indeed, virtually all learning phenomena resulting from direct experience can occur vicariously by observing people's behavior and the consequences of it (Bandura, 1986; Rosenthal & Zimmerman, 1978).

From *Academy of Management Review,* 1989, 14(3), 361–383. Adapted by permission.

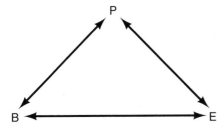

FIGURE 1
Schematization of the relations among behavior (B), cognitive and other personal factors (P), and the external environment (E).

Mechanisms Governing Modeling

Observational learning is governed by four component processes. *Attentional processes* determine what people selectively observe in the profusion of modeling influences and what information they extract from ongoing modeled activities. People cannot be much influenced by observed accomplishments if they do not remember them. A second major subfunction governing observational learning concerns cognitive *representational processes*. Retention involves an active process of transforming and restructuring information about events in the form of rules and conceptions. Retention is greatly aided when people symbolically transform the modeled information into memory codes and mentally rehearse the coded information.

In the third subfunction in modeling—*behavioral production processes*—symbolic conceptions are translated into appropriate courses of action. This is achieved through a conception-matching process, in which people's centrally guided patterns of behavior are enacted and the adequacy of their actions is compared against their conceptual model (Carroll & Bandura, 1987). Individuals then modify their behavior on the basis of the comparative information in order to achieve close correspondence between their conceptions and their action. The richer the repertoire and subskills that people possess, the easier it is to integrate these skills in the production of new behavior patterns.

The fourth subfunction in modeling concerns *motivational processes.* Social cognitive theory distinguishes between acquisition and performance because people do not do everything they learn. Performance of observationally learned behavior is influenced by three major types of incentive motivators—*direct, vicarious,* and *self-produced.* People are most likely to adopt modeled strategies if the strategies produce valued outcomes, rather than unrewarding or punishing effects. The observed cost and benefits that are accrued to others influence observers' adoption of modeled patterns in much the same way as do directly experienced consequences. People are motivated by the successes of others who are similar to themselves, but they are discouraged from pursuing behaviors that they have seen often result in adverse consequences. Personal standards of conduct provide a further source of motivation. The self-evaluations people generate about their own behavior regulate which observationally learned activities they are most likely to pursue. They express what they find self-satisfying and reject what they disapprove of.

Modeling is not merely a process of behavioral mimicry. People may adopt functional patterns of behavior, which constitute proven skills and established customs, in essentially the same form as they are exemplified. However, for many activities, subskills must be improvised to suit changing circumstances. Modeling influences also convey rules for generative and innovative behavior. In this form of abstract modeling, observers extract the rules governing the specific judgments or actions exhibited by others. Once they learn the rules, they can use them to judge events and to generate courses of action that go beyond what they have seen or heard. Much human learning is aimed at developing cognitive skills on how to acquire and use knowledge for different purposes. Observational learning of thinking skills is greatly facilitated if models verbalize their thought processes in conjunction with their action strategies (Bandura, 1986; Meichenbaum, 1984).

Guided Mastery Modeling

Mastery modeling has been widely used with good results to develop intellectual, social, and behavioral competencies (Bandura, 1986, 1988d). The method that produces the best results includes three major elements. First, the appropriate skills are modeled to convey the basic competencies. Effective modeling teaches people general rules and strategies for dealing with different situations, rather than specific responses. People need to learn how the rules can be widely applied and adjusted to fit changing conditions. Modeling influences must be designed to build self-assurance in one's capabilities as well as to convey skills. The impact that modeling has on beliefs about one's capabilities is greatly increased by one's perceived similarity to the models.

The second aspect involves guided skill mastery. After individuals understand the new skills, they need guidance and opportunities to perfect them. Initially, they test their newly acquired skills in simulated situations in which they need not fear making mistakes or appearing inadequate. This is best achieved by role-playing, in which they practice handling the types of situations they must manage in their work environment and they receive instructive feedback. The feedback that is most informative and helps to achieve the greatest improvements is based on corrective modeling.

Modeling and guided performance under simulated conditions are well suited for creating competencies, but it is unlikely that the new skills will be used for long, unless they prove useful when they are put into practice in work situations. The third aspect of mastery modeling is a transfer program aimed at providing self-direct success. People must experience sufficient success when using what they have learned in order to believe both in themselves and the value of the new ways. This is best achieved by a transfer program, in which newly acquired skills are first tried on the job in situations that are likely to produce good results. As individuals gain skill and confidence in handling easier situations, they gradually take on more difficult problems. If they do not gain sufficient success to convince themselves of their new effectiveness, they will apply the new skills weakly and inconsistently, and they will rapidly abandon their newly acquired skills when they either fail to get quick results or experience difficulties.

Mastery modeling programs have been successfully applied to help supervisors develop competencies. Mastery modeling produces lasting improvements in supervisors' skills (Latham & Saari, 1979). Simply explaining to supervisors the rules and giving them strategies on how to handle problems on the job without using modeling and guided practice does not improve their supervisory competencies. To enhance competencies, people need instructive modeling, guided practice with corrective feedback, and help in transferring new skills to everyday situations. Porras and his colleagues have shown that mastery modeling affects the morale and productivity of organizations as well as supervisors' skills (Porras et al., 1982). Supervisors who had the benefit of the modeling program improved and maintained their supervisory problem-solving skills, as rated by their employees. The plant in which the modeling program was applied had a lower absentee rate, lower turnover of employees, and a higher level of productivity in follow-up assessments.

SELF-EFFICACY REGULATORY MECHANISM

In social cognitive theory (Bandura, 1986, 1988a), self-regulation of motivation and performance attainments is governed by several self-regulatory mechanisms that operate together. One of the mechanisms that occupies a central role in this regulatory process works through people's beliefs in their personal efficacy. Perceived self-efficacy concerns people's beliefs in their capabilities to mobilize the motivation, cognitive resources, and courses of action needed to exercise control over events in their lives. There is a difference between possessing skills and being able to use them well and consistently under difficult circumstances. To be successful, one not only must possess the required skills, but also a resilient self-belief in one's capabilities to exercise control over events to accomplish desired goals. People with the same skills may, therefore, perform poorly, adequately, or extraordinarily, depending on whether their self-beliefs of efficacy enhance or impair their motivation and problem-solving efforts.

Sources of Self-Efficacy Beliefs

People's beliefs about their efficacy can be instilled and strengthened in four principal ways. The most effective way individuals develop a strong sense of efficacy is through *mastery experiences*. Performance successes strengthen self-beliefs of capability. Failures create self-doubts. However, if people experience only easy successes, they come to expect quick results and are easily discouraged by failure. To gain a resilient sense of efficacy, people must have experience in overcoming obstacles through perseverant effort. Some setbacks and difficulties in human pursuits serve a useful purpose in teaching that success usually requires sustained effort. After people become assured of their capabilities through repeated successes, they can manage setbacks and failures without being adversely affected by them.

The second way to strengthen self-beliefs is through *modeling*. Proficient models build self-beliefs of capability by conveying to observers effective strategies for managing different situations. Modeling also affects self-efficacy beliefs through a social comparison process. People partly judge their capabilities in comparison with others. Seeing similar others succeed by sustained effort raises observers' beliefs about their own capabilities, whereas observing similar others fail despite high effort lowers observers' judgments of their own capabilities and undermines their efforts.

Social persuasion is a third way of increasing people's beliefs that they possess the capabilities to achieve what they seek. If people receive realistic encouragements, they will be more likely to exert greater effort and to become successful than if they are troubled by self-doubts. However, if their beliefs of personal efficacy are raised to unrealistic levels, they run the risk of failures that undermine their perceptions of personal efficacy. Successful motivators and efficacy builders do more than convey positive appraisals. In addition to raising people's beliefs in their capabilities, they assign tasks to them in ways that bring success and avoid placing them prematurely in situations in which they are likely to fail. To ensure progress in personal development, success should be measured in terms of self-improvement, rather than through triumphs over others.

People also rely partly on judgments of their *physiological states* when they assess their capabilities. They read their emotional arousal and tension as signs of vulnerability to poor performance. In activities involving strength and stamina, people judge their fatigue, aches, and pains as signs of physical incapability. The fourth way of modifying self-beliefs of efficacy is for people to enhance their physical status, to reduce their stress levels, or to alter their dysfunctional construals of somatic information.

Diverse Effects on Self-Efficacy Beliefs

People's beliefs in their efficacy can affect their psychological well-being and performance through several intervening processes (Bandura, 1990). People can exert some influence over their lives through the environments they select and the environments they create. One's judgments of personal efficacy affect one's choice of activities and environments. People tend to avoid activities and situations they believe will exceed their coping capabilities, but they readily undertake challenging activities and pick social environments they judge themselves capable of managing. The social influences in the selected environments can set the direction of personal development through the competencies, values, and interests these influences promote. This process is well illustrated in research on the impact that perceived self-efficacy has on choice of career paths. The stronger the people's self-beliefs of efficacy, the more career options they consider to be possible and the better they prepare themselves educationally for different occupational pursuits (Betz & Hackett, 1986; Lent & Hackett, 1987; Miura, 1987). People often restrict their career options because they believe they lack the necessary capabilities, although they have the actual ability. This self-limitation arises more from self-doubts, rather than from inability. Women are especially prone to limit their interests and range of career options through the self-beliefs that they lack the necessary capabilities for occupations that are traditionally dominated by men, even when they do not differ from men in actual ability.

People's self-beliefs of efficacy also determine their level of motivation, which is reflected in how much effort they will exert and how long they will persevere. The stronger the belief in their capabilities, the greater and more persistent are their efforts (Bandura, 1988a). When faced with difficulties, people who have self-doubts about their capabilities slacken their efforts or abort their attempts prematurely and quickly settle for mediocre solutions. Those who have a strong belief in their capabilities exert greater effort to master the challenge (Bandura & Cervone, 1983, 1986; Cervone & Peake, 1986; Jacobs, Prentice-Dunn, & Rogers, 1984; Weinberg, Gould, & Jackson, 1979). Strong perseverance usually pays off in performance accomplishments. Studies of manufacturing industries indicate that the impact that training programs have on the acceptance of production goals and level of productivity is party mediated by changes in employee's self-beliefs of efficacy (Earley, 1986).

People's self-beliefs of efficacy affect how much stress and depression they experience in threatening or taxing situations, as well as their level of motivation. People who believe they can exercise control over potential threats do not conjure up apprehensive cognitions and, therefore, are not perturbed by them. But those who believe they cannot manage potential difficulties experience high levels of stress. They tend to dwell on their deficiencies and view many aspects of their environment as threatening (Ozer & Bandura, 1990). Disbelief in one's capabilities to attain valued goals that affect one's sense of self-worth or to secure things that bring satisfaction to one's life also creates depression (Bandura, 1988a; Holahan & Holahan, 1987a, b; Kanfer & Zeiss, 1983). Through inefficacious thought, such people distress and depress themselves and constrain and impair their level of functioning (Bandura, 1988b, 1988c; Lazarus & Folkman, 1984; Meichenbaum, 1977; Sarason, 1975).

Self-beliefs of efficacy also affect thought patterns that may be self-aiding or self-hindering. These cognitive effects take various forms. Much human behavior is regulated by forethought in the form of cognized goals. Personal goal setting is influenced by one's self-appraisal of capabilities. The stronger the perceived self-efficacy, the higher the goals people set for themselves and the firmer are their commitments to these goals (Bandura & Cervone, 1986; Locke, Frederick, Lee, & Bobko, 1984; Taylor, Locke, Lee, & Gist, 1984). Many activities involve analytic judgments that enable people to predict and control events in probabilistic environments. Strong belief in one's problem-solving capabilities fosters efficient analytic thinking. And finally, people's perceptions of their efficacy influence the types of anticipatory scenarios they construct and reiterate. Highly self-efficacious individuals visualize success scenarios that provide positive guides for performance, whereas those who judge themselves as inefficacious are more inclined to visualize failure scenarios, which undermine performance. One's perceived self-efficacy and cognitive simulation affect each other bidirectionally. People's high sense of efficacy fosters cognitive constructions of effective actions, and people's cognitive reiteration of efficacious courses of action strengthens their self-beliefs of efficacy (Bandura & Adams, 1977; Kazdin, 1979).

The sociocognitive benefits of a sense of personal efficacy do not arise simply from the incantation of capability. Saying something is so should not be confused with believing it. Self-efficacy beliefs are the product of a process of self-persuasion that relies on diverse sources of efficacy information that must be selected, weighted, and integrated (Bandura, 1986). If people's self-efficacy beliefs are firmly established, they remain resilient to adversity. In contrast, individuals with weakly held self-beliefs are highly vulnerable to change, and negative experiences readily reinstate their disbelief in their capabilities.

SELF-REGULATION OF MOTIVATION AND ACTION THROUGH GOAL SYSTEMS

Social cognitive theory also emphasizes human capacities for self-direction and self-motivation (Bandura, 1988a). The self-regulation of motivation and action operates partly through people's internal standards and their evaluations of their own behavior. People seek self-satisfactions from fulfilling valued goals, and they are motivated by discontent with substandard performances. Thus, discrepancies between behavior and personal standards generate self-reactive influences, which serve as motivators and guides for action designed to achieve desired results. Through self-evaluative reactions, people keep their conduct in line with their personal standards.

Hierarchical Dual Control Mechanism

Many theories of motivation and self-regulation are founded on a negative feedback control model (Carver & Scheier, 1981; Kanfer, 1977; Lord & Hanges, 1987). This type of system functions as a motivator and regulator of action through a discrepancy reduction mechanism. Perceived discrepancy between performance and an internal standard triggers action to reduce the incongruity. In negative feedback control, if the performance matches the standard, the person does nothing. A regulatory process in which matching a standard occasions inactivity does not characterize human self-motivation. Such a feedback control system would produce circular action that leads nowhere. In fact, people transcend feedback loops by setting new challenges for themselves.

Human self-motivation relies on *discrepancy production* as well as on *discrepancy reduction*. It requires both *active control* and *reactive control* (Bandura, 1988a; 1989). People initially motivate themselves through active control by first setting valued standards that create a state of disequilibrium and then by mobilizing their effort on the basis of what it would take to accomplish what they seek. Feedback control comes into play in one's subsequent adjustments of effort to achieve desired results. After people attain the standards they have been pursuing, they generally set higher standards for themselves. Their adoption of further challenges creates new motivating discrepancies to be mastered. Thus, self-motivation involves a dual control mechanism that operates through discrepancy production, which is followed by discrepancy reduction.

Diverse Effects of Goals

Many of the activities that people perform are aimed at obtaining future outcomes. Therefore, they must create guides and motivators in the present for activities that lead to outcomes in the future. This is achieved by adopting goals and evaluating one's progress in relation to those goals. Goals can improve individuals' psychological well-being and accomplishments in several ways. First, goals have strong motivational effects. Goals provide a sense of purpose and direction, and they raise and sustain the level of effort needed to reach them. When people are unclear about what they are trying to accomplish, their motivation is low and their efforts are poorly directed. Investigations of varied domains of functioning under both laboratory and naturalistic conditions provide substantial converging evidence that explicit, challenging goals enhance and sustain people's motivation (Latham & Lee, 1986; Locke, Shaw, Saari, & Latham, 1981; Mento, Steel, & Karren, 1987).

Goals not only guide and motivate performance, they also help to build people's beliefs in their capabilities. Without standards against which to measure their performances, people have little basis either for judging how they are doing or for evaluating their capabilities. Subgoals serve this purpose well (Bandura & Schunk, 1981). Success in attaining challenging subgoals increases people's self-beliefs in their capabilities. Accomplishing challenging goals also creates self-satisfaction and increases one's interest in what one is doing. The closer the attainments match valued goals, the greater are the positive self-reactions (Bandura & Cervone, 1986; Locke, Cartledge, & Knerr, 1970). Goals have these beneficial effects when they serve as challenges, rather than as onerous dictates.

The beneficial effects of goals are partly determined by how far into the future they are set. Short-term, or proximal, goals raise one's effort and direct what one does during the short run. Distant goals are too far removed in time to be effective self-motivators. Usually, there are too many competing influences in everyday life for distant aims to exert much control over one's current behavior. Motivation is best regulated by long-range goals that set the course for one's endeavors combined with a series of attainable subgoals that guides and sustains the efforts along the way (Bandura & Schunk, 1981; Bandura & Simon, 1977; Morgan, 1985). Making complex tasks manageable by breaking them down into a series of subgoals also helps to reduce one's self-demoralization through high aspiration. A person's accomplishment may indicate significant progress when evaluated against a proximal subgoal, but it may appear disappointing if compared against long-range lofty aspirations. People can be making good progress but deriving little sense of accomplishment because of the wide disparity between current standing and distal aspiration.

Recent research into the effects that goals have on complex decision making has shown that challenging goals lead people to use more effort in the development of strategies (Earley, Wojnaroski, & Prest, 1987). However, challenging goals also may lead to suboptimal cognitive processing (Huber, 1985) and the selection of less effective strategies (Earley, Connolly, & Ekegren, 1989). Managerial goals that are difficult to attain increase the likelihood of failure and one's vulnerability to self-debilitating modes of thought.

Self-Influence Governing Cognitive Motivation

Motivation based on personal standards or goals involves a cognitive comparison process. By making self-satisfaction conditional on matching adopted goals, people give direction to their actions and create self-incentives to help them persist in their effort until their performances match their goals. The motivational effects do not stem from the goals themselves, but rather from people responding evaluatively to their own behavior. Their goals specify the conditional requirements for positive self-evaluation.

Activation of self-evaluation processes through internal comparison requires both comparative factors—a personal standard and knowledge of the level of one's own performance. Neither performance knowledge without goals, nor goals without performance knowledge has any lasting motivational impact (Bandura & Cervone, 1983; Becker, 1978; Strang, Lawrence, & Fowler, 1978). However, the combined influence of goals and performance feedback heightens motivation.

Cognitive motivation based on goal intentions is mediated by three types of self-influences: affective self-evaluation, perceived self-efficacy for goal attainment, and adjustment of personal standards. As already noted, goals motivate by enlisting self-evaluative involvement in the activity, and perceived self-efficacy determines whether discrepancies between standards and attainments are motivating or discouraging. The goals people set for themselves at the outset of an endeavor are likely to change, depending on the pattern and level of progress they are making (Campion & Lord, 1982). Individuals may maintain their original goal, they may lower their sights, or they may adopt an even more challenging goal. Thus, the third constituent, self-influence in the ongoing regulation of motivation, concerns the readjustment of one's goals in light of one's attainments. Taken together, these self-reactive influences account for a major share of the variation in motivation under different goals structures (Bandura & Cervone, 1983, 1986).

Concluding Remarks

The value of psychological theory is judged not only by its explanatory and predictive power, but also by its operational power to improve human functioning. Social cognitive theory provides a conceptual framework for clarifying the psychological mechanisms through which social-structural factors are linked to organizational performance. Within the model of triadic reciprocal causation, both personal and organization factors operate through a bidirectionality of influence. Many conceptual systems are dressed up in appealing terminology, but they remain prescriptively ambiguous on how to effect psychosocial changes. Social cognitive theory provides explicit guidelines about how to equip people with the competencies, the self-regulatory capabilities, and the resilient sense of efficacy that will enable them to enhance both their well-being and their accomplishments.

REFERENCES

Bandura, A. (1986) *Social foundations of thought and action: A social cognitive theory.* Englewood Cliffs, NJ: Prentice-Hall.

Bandura, A. (1988a) Self-regulation of motivation and action through goal systems. In V. Hamilton, G. H. Bower, & N. H. Frijda (Eds.), *Cognitive perspectives on emotion and motivation* (pp. 37–61). Dordrecht, Netherlands: Kluwer Academic Publishers.

Bandura, A. (1988b) Perceived self-efficacy: Exercise of control through self-belief. In J. P. Dauwalder, M. Perrez, & V. Hobi (Eds.), *Annual series of European research in behavior therapy* (Vol. 2, pp. 27–59). Lisse, Netherlands: Swets & Zeitlinger.

Bandura, A. (1988c) Self-efficacy conception of anxiety. *Anxiety Research,* 1, 77–98.

Bandura, A. (1988d) Organizational applications of social cognitive theory. *Australian Journal of Management,* 13, 137–164.

Bandura, A. (1989) Human agency in social cognitive theory. *American Psychologist* 44, 1175–1184.

Bandura, A. (1990) Reflections on nonability determinants of competence. In J. Kolligan, Jr., & R. J. Sternberg (Eds.), *Competence considered: Perceptions of competence and incompetence across the lifespan.* New Haven, CT: Yale University Press.

Bandura, A., & Adams, N. E. (1977) Analysis of self-efficacy theory of behavioral change. *Cognitive Therapy and Research,* 1, 287–308.

Bandura, A. & Cervone, D. (1983) Self-evaluative and self-efficacy mechanisms governing the motivational effects of goal systems. *Journal of Personality and Social Psychology,* 45, 1017–1028.

Bandura, A., & Cervone, D. (1986) Differential engagement of self-reactive influences in cognitive motivation. *Organizational Behavior and Human Decision Processes,* 38, 92–113.

Bandura, A., & Schunk, D. H. (1981) Cultivating competence, self-efficacy and intrinsic interest through proximal self-motivation. *Journal of Personality and Social Psychology*, 41, 586–598.

Bandura A., & Simon, K. M. (1977) The role of proximal intentions in self-regulation of refractory behavior. *Cognitive Therapy and Research*, 1, 177–193.

Becker, L. J. (1978) Joint effect of feedback and goal setting on performance: A field study of residential energy conservation. *Journal of Applied Psychology*, 63, 428–433.

Betz, N. E., & Hackett, G. (1986) Applications of self-efficacy theory to understanding career choice behavior. *Journal of Social and Clinical Psychology*, 4, 279–289.

Campion, M. A., & Lord, R. G. (1982) A control systems conceptualization of the goal-setting and changing process. *Organizational Behavior and Human Performance*, 30, 265–287.

Carroll, W. R., & Bandura, A. (1987) Translating cognition into action: The role of visual guidance in observational learning. *Journal of Motor Behavior*, 19, 385–398.

Carver, C. S., & Scheier, M. F. (1981) *Attention and self-regulation: A control-theory approach to human behavior.* New York: Springer-Verlag.

Cervone, D., & Peake, P. K. (1986) Anchoring, efficacy, and action: The influence of judgmental heuristics on self-efficacy judgments and behavior. *Journal of Personality and Social Psychology*, 50, 492–501.

Earley, P. C. (1986) Supervisors and shop stewards as sources of contextual information in goal setting: A comparison of the United States with England. *Journal of Applied Psychology*, 71, 111–117.

Earley, P. C., Connolly, T., & Ekegren, G. (1989) Goals, strategy development and task performance: Some limits on the efficacy of goal-setting. *Journal of Applied Psychology*.

Earley, P. C., Wojnaroski, P., & Prest, W. (1987) Task planning and energy expended: Exploration of how goals affect performance. *Journal of Applied Psychology*, 72, 107–114.

Holahan, C. K., & Holahan, C. J. (1987a) Self-efficacy, social support, and depression in aging: A longitudinal analysis. *Journal of Gerontology*, 42, 65–68.

Holahan, C. K., & Holahan, C. J. (1987b) Life stress, hassles, and self-efficacy in aging: A replication and extension. *Journal of Applied Social Psychology*, 17, 574–592.

Huber, V. L. (1985) Effects of task difficulty, goal-setting and strategy on performance of a heuristic task. *Journal of Applied Psychology*, 70, 492–504.

Jacobs, B., Prentice-Dunn, S., & Rogers, R. W. (1984) Understanding persistence: An interface of control theory and self-efficacy theory. *Basic and Applied Social Psychology*, 5, 333–347.

Kanfer, F. H. (1977) The many faces of self-control, or behavior modification changes its focus. In R. B. Stuart (Ed.), *Behavioral self-management* (pp. 1–48). New York: Brunner/Mazel.

Kanfer, R., & Zeiss, A. M. (1983) Depression, interpersonal standard-setting, and judgments of self-efficacy. *Journal of Abnormal Psychology*, 92, 319–329.

Kazdin, A. E. (1979) Imagery elaboration and self-efficacy in the covert modeling treatment of unassertive behavior. *Journal of Consulting and Clinical Psychology*, 47, 725–733.

Latham, G. P., & Lee, T. W. (1986) Goal setting. In E. A. Locke (Ed.), *Generalizing from laboratory to field settings* (pp. 101–117). Lexington, MA: Heath.

Latham, G. P., & Saari, L. M. (1979) Application of social learning theory to training supervisors through behavioral modeling. *Journal of Applied Psychology*, 64, 239–246.

Lazarus, R. S., & Folkman, S. (1984) *Stress, appraisal, and coping.* New York: Springer.

Lent, R. W., & Hackett, G. (1987) Career self-efficacy: Empirical status and future direction. *Journal of Vocational Behavior*, 30, 347–382.

Locke, E. A., Cartledge, N., & Knerr, C. S. (1970) Studies of the relationships between satisfaction, goal setting, and performance. *Organizational Behavior and Human Performance*, 5, 135–158.

Locke, E. A., Frederick, E., Lee, C., & Bobko, P. (1984) Effect of self-efficacy, goals, and task strategies on task performance. *Journal of Applied Psychology,* 69, 241–251.

Locke, E. A., Shaw, K. N., Saari, L. M., & Latham, G. P. (1981) Goal setting and task performance: 1969–1980. *Psychological Bulletin,* 90, 125–152.

Lord, R. G., & Hanges, P. J. (1987) A control system model or organizational motivation: Theoretical development and applied implications. *Behavioral Science,* 32, 161–178.

Meichenbaum, D. H. (1977) *Cognitive-behavior modification: An integrative approach.* New York: Plenum Press.

Meichenbaum, D. (1984) Teaching thinking: A cognitive-behavioral perspective. In R. Glaser, S. Chipman, & J. Segal (Eds.), *Thinking and learning skills* (Vol. 2): *Research and open questions* (pp. 407–426). Hillsdale, NJ: Erlbaum.

Mento, A. J., Steel, R. P., & Karren, R. J. (1987) A meta-analytic study of the effects of goal setting on task performance: 1966–1984. *Organizational Behavior and Human Decision Processes,* 39, 52–83.

Miura, I. T. (1987) The relationship of computer self-efficacy expectations to computer interest and course enrollment in college. *Sex Roles,* 16, 303–311.

Morgan, M. (1985) Self-monitoring of attained subgoals in private study. *Journal of Educational Psychology,* 77, 623–630.

Ozer, E., & Bandura, A. (1990) *Mechanisms governing empowerment effects: A self-efficacy analysis. Journal of Personality and Social Psychology,* 58, 472–486.

Porras, J. I., Hargis, K., Patterson, K. J., Maxfield, D. G., Roberts, N., & Bies, R. J. (1982) Modeling-based organizational development: A longitudinal assessment. *Journal of Applied Behavioral Science,* 18, 433–446.

Rosenthal, T. L., & Zimmerman, B. J. (1978) *Social learning and cognition.* New York: Academic Press.

Sarason, I. G. (1975) Anxiety and self-preoccupation. In I. G. Sarason & D. C. Spielberger (Eds.), *Stress and anxiety* (Vol. 2, pp. 27–44). Washington, DC: Hemisphere.

Strang, H. R., Lawrence, E. C., & Fowler, P. C. (1978) Effects of assigned goal level and knowledge of results on arithmetic computation: Laboratory study. *Journal of Applied Psychology,* 63, 446–450.

Taylor, M. S., Locke, E. A., Lee C., & Gist, M. E. (1984) Type A behavior and faculty research productivity: What are the mechanisms? *Organizational Behavior and Human Performance,* 34, 402–418.

Weinberg, R. S., Gould, D., & Jackson, A. (1979) Expectations and performance: An empirical test of Bandura's self-efficacy theory. *Journal of Sport Psychology,* 1, 320–331.

Goal Setting Theory: An Introduction

Edwin A. Locke
Gary P. Latham

In this chapter we present the conceptual base of goal setting theory, the history of the concept of goal and related concepts in psychology and management, and the relationship between goal setting theory and other work motivation theories.

GOALS AS REGULATORS OF ACTION

As budding industrial/organizational psychologists in the 1960s, we were interested in the topic of motivation because this concept provided, in principle, a partial answer to the question, Why do some people perform better on work tasks than others? We agreed with the conventional assumption that human action is determined by both cognitive (e.g., knowledge) and motivational factors.

In approaching the study of motivation, however, we were faced with the problem of how to study it. Since motivation is something within the individual, it can only be observed directly within ourselves. While introspective observation is of scientific importance, motivation in other people cannot be observed directly but must be inferred. While inference is epistemologically abhorrent to some psychologists and leads them to reject internal states as explanatory concepts, it is not to us or to cognitive psychologists in general. As Arnold (1960) pointed out, to do away with inference in science, if one hopes to understand the world, is never possible—even in the hard sciences.

Given our belief that it was legitimate to look for explanations of action within the individual, the next question became, What should we look at? There were many competing concepts in the field: drives, needs, values, attitudes, motives, instincts, and so on. We were greatly influenced here by T. A. Ryan (1970), who was working on his treatise *Intentional Behavior* while the first author was a doctoral student at Cornell between 1960 and 1964. Ryan, who had in turn been influenced by the Würzburg school, by Lewin (a Gestalt psychologist), and by C. A. Mace (1935), argued that the most immediate and simplest way to explain, from a motivational standpoint, an individual's action in a specific situation was to look at what the person was trying to do in that situation.

Ryan (1970) observed that "to the layman it seems a simple fact that human behavior is affected by conscious purposes, plans, intentions, tasks and the like" (p. 18). At about the same time, Locke observed that "the man in the street, taking for granted the causal efficacy of purposes, uses this term every day to explain goal-directed action. He explains his changing jobs by his consciously held *purpose* to further his career and . . . his son's going to college by his conscious *purpose* to get an education" (1969b, p. 991). In short, goal setting theory had its ultimate roots in the simplest type

Edwin A. Locke & Gary P. Latham, *A theory of goal setting & test performance,* ©1990, pp. 1–26. Reprinted by permission of Prentice Hall, Upper Saddle River, New Jersey.

of introspection, the kind that can be performed by anyone. Furthermore, also based on introspective evidence, it unapologetically assumes that goals (ideas of future, desired end states) play a causal role in action. Such assumptions were virtually banned from psychology when behaviorism was the dominant American school, but with the cognitive revolution of the 1970s, such views have become respectable and properly so.

Consider now the question posed earlier as to why some people perform better on work tasks than others. Of course, there are many answers to this question. People differ greatly in their ability, their knowledge, and the strategies they use to perform tasks. However, another important but frequently overlooked reason why people perform differently is that they have different goals. They try for different outcomes when they work on a task. We use the term *goal* as the generic concept that encompasses the essential meaning of terms such as intention, task, deadline, purpose, aim, end, and objective. All of these have in common the element that there is something that the person wants to achieve. (The differences between these concepts are explained later in this chapter.)

The concept of goal-directed action, however, has wider significance. Goal directedness is "a cardinal attribute of the behavior of living organisms. . . . It may be observed at all levels of life: in the assimilation of food by an amoeba, in the root growth of a tree or plant, in the stalking of prey by wild animals, and in the activities of a scientist in a laboratory" (Locke, 1969b, p. 991).

Among living organisms there are two categories of goal-directed action (Binswanger, 1986; Locke, 1969b): (a) nonconsciously goal-directed or vegetative actions such as photosynthesis, digestion, and blood circulation; and (b) consciously goal-directed or purposeful actions such as hunting for food and productive work. The former can be found at all levels of life from plants on up, whereas the latter only occur in animals and human beings.

Binswanger (1986) argued that both types of goal-directed action share three common features that justify calling the action goal-directed:

1 *Self-generation.* The actions of living organisms are fueled by energy sources integral to the organism as a whole, i.e., the energy source is not "put into it" as the motor into a torpedo but is integral to every cell. Furthermore, this energy is available for many different actions—depending on environmental circumstances and the organism's needs.

2 *Value-significance.* A living organism can go out of existence; its survival is conditional. To maintain its existence, every living organism must take specific actions to fulfill its needs. If it does not take such actions, it dies. Life maintenance is the ultimate explicit or implicit end of such action and the standard of successful action. Thus all goal-directed action has value significance for the organism. In contrast, the continued existence of inanimate objects does not require them to take any action; they will remain "as is" unless changed or destroyed by external forces. Their movements have no value significance.

3 *Goal-causation.* There has been much confusion since the time of Aristotle about the cause of goal-directed or teleological action. For example, it has been claimed that final causation, that is, causation by the goal of the action, is a contradiction in terms in that it suggests that the future is the cause of the present. Actually, there are two types of goal causation and neither one involves a contradiction.

In purposeful action, it is the individual's *idea* of and desire for the goal or end that causes action. The idea serves as the efficient cause, but the action is aimed toward a future state.

In nonconsciously goal-directed action (e.g., the actions of the heart and lungs), the principle is the same, but the explanation is more complex. Binswanger (1986) observed that natural selection explains the adaptation of actions to survival in the same way that it explains the adaptation of structural features of the organism to survival:

> For example, my heart will be able to beat tomorrow only if I am alive tomorrow. But I will survive only if my blood is circulated today. The present blood circulation is thus an indirect cause of the future heartbeat. And since blood circulation is the *goal* of the heartbeat, this means that subsequent heartbeats are caused by the survival value of that action's goal, as attained in earlier instances of that very action. . . . The vegetative actions of living organisms are teleological—i.e., goal directed—because these actions have been naturally selected for their efficacy in attaining ends having survival value for the agent. . . . in vegetative action a *past instance* of the "final cause" functions as the efficient cause. (pp. 4–5)

To summarize, *the ultimate biological basis of goal-directed action is the organism's need to sustain its life by taking the actions its nature requires.* In the lower organisms such as plants, these actions are automatic and nonconscious. In people and animals, some of the required actions must be consciously goal-directed. Purposefully goal-directed actions, which are the concern of this theory, are a subcategory of goal-directed action in which goal attainment is caused by consciousness (e.g., by the individual's desire, vision, expectation, anticipation, imagination, aspiration).

The denial of the causal efficacy of consciousness is a fundamental reason why behaviorism failed as a model for explaining human action (Bandura, 1986; Locke, 1977, 1980b). Behaviorists argued that behavior was controlled by past reinforcements, by events that followed previous responses or actions. They never explained, however, the nature of the link between the past and the future. The so-called law of effect or law of reinforcement was at best descriptive, namely: a reinforcer is something that follows a response and somehow makes subsequent responses more likely. When pressed, behaviorists will claim that the connecting events are strictly physiological, but this reductionist argument has never been proven.

The actual explanation of what is called the reinforcement effect is that every consequent that has a subsequent effect becomes an antecedent in that it generates expectations about the future, which in turn regulate action (Bandura, 1977; 1986). To offer as an explanation, as the behaviorists do, that "the behavior changed because it was reinforced" simply cuts off search for the actual causes of the action. For example: Why does a reinforcer reinforce and by what means? What is a reinforcer? What makes it work? Behaviorists have at best a superficial technology of behavior rather than a science of behavior.

The concept of purposeful action applies to both people and animals, although not to the same extent. People share the perceptual level of awareness with the lower animals but unlike them have the power to regulate their own consciousness. Animals are guided by sensory-perceptual mental contents and processes (i.e., desires for specific objects); their time frame is limited to the immediate past, immediate future, and the present. The capacity to grasp the language of even the most "intelligent" species is not even remotely close to the capacity of human children in this respect (see Terrace, 1979).

Human beings have the capacity to go beyond sensory material. They possess the capacity for reason. They can form concepts based on sensory information and go on to form higher-order concepts based on integrations of lower-order concepts (Rand, 1969). They can project thoughts backward in time and forward through millennia; they can detect objects that no human eye can see; they can imagine things being different from what they are; they can project what might be and what ought to be; they can infer and deduce theories and conclusions; they can count and measure from milliseconds to light years; they can make machines and write documents that change the course of history; and they can study themselves. None of this is possible to animals.

Depending on the amount of quality of people's thinking, they may program their minds with few goals or with many, with clear goals or vague ones. They may set goals that either further their happiness and well-being or undermine and negate them. They can also fail to focus their minds and try to exist in an unfocused or drugged stupor. Thus people have a choice as to whether they set goals, and as to what type of goals they set. But since rational, goal-directed action is essential for happiness and survival, we can say that purposeful action is action that is quintessentially human.

Goal setting theory assumes that human action is directed by conscious goals and intentions. However, it does not assume that all human action is under fully conscious control. Furthermore, there are degrees of conscious self-regulation. For example, some actions are not consciously intended, such as sneezing, tics, and mannerisms. There are also actions that reflect a conflict between conscious intent and subconscious desire, as in a person who feels subconscious hostility toward another person but consciously tries to be polite. An insulting or critical comment may slip out in a conversation. Such actions may be more common among people with severe psychological problems but are certainly not confined to such people.

We agree with Ach (Ryan, 1970) and more recently with Klinger (1987) that a goal or purpose does not have to be in conscious awareness every second during goal-oriented action in order for it to regulate action. Klinger noted, for example, that a student pursuing a Ph.D. degree does not think of that goal every minute. Once the student begins the doctoral program, he or she will normally focus on subgoals such as mastering the material in a given course, finding a thesis topic, or developing plans for reaching those subgoals (e.g., how to study; how to carry out the dissertation research). Getting the degree is the integrating goal behind those subgoals and plans. While not always in conscious awareness, the end goal is easily called into awareness—e.g., the student's asking himself or herself, Why am I here? Furthermore, it may go in and out of awareness at different times. For example, a student who is tired and wants to avoid homework one evening may remind himself or herself that studying is necessary to get the degree. Focusing on the end goal all the time would actually be disruptive to performance in many situations, because it would distract the individual from taking the actions needed to reach it, especially actions requiring new learning. Usually, a goal, once accepted and understood, will remain in the background or periphery of consciousness, as a reference point for guiding and giving meaning to subsequent mental and physical actions leading to the goal.

In habitual action, there is some degree of conscious initiation of the action, but once initiated, the action flows with minimal (but not zero) conscious regulation. A case in point would be driving to work using the same route day after day and year after year. After a while, only minimal attention needs to be paid to the action. In fact, more conscious control would be needed to break the pattern (e.g., take a different route) than to maintain it.

In the case of learned skills, aspects of an action sequence (such as dribbling and shooting a basketball) that were originally conscious may become automatized through repeated practice. The individual only needs to focus on the component motions if something goes wrong. Otherwise he or she is free to focus on the performance outcome desired and the means to attain it, such as game strategy.

Goal theory does not assume that every aspect of a consciously intended action is consciously intended. For example, if one has an intent to lift one's arm, the arm normally goes up even though there is no conscious intent to move each muscle involved, nor to send specific electric signals to the brain and back down to the arm. The end result is intended, but the means, which in this case are physiological, involve automatized processes that do not require direct conscious control in order to operate. Control over such actions is indirect.

There are also actions, that, although consciously initiated, do not correspond to the intended action or do not achieve the desired goal (Locke, 1968b). This can be due to many reasons, including lack of sufficient knowledge or ability, external blocks to performance, illness, subconscious conflicts (as noted above), or changed circumstances. Such actions could be called goal-directed, but unsuccessful. It is an empirical question as to just what circumstances facilitate or prevent goal-performance correspondence.

Nor does goal setting theory assume that every performance outcome is consciously foreseen. For example, a businessperson with a goal to double sales will not necessarily intend or foresee all the consequences of achieving such a goal (e.g., greater strains on company resources and on family life). People can, in crucial respects, foresee and plan for the future, but they are not omniscient.

Caveats aside, goal setting theory does assume that the goals people have on a task influence what they will do and how well they will perform. Goal setting theory specifies the factors that affect goals, and their relationship to action and performance.

THE CONCEPT OF GOAL AND RELATED CONCEPTS

Since we have chosen to use the term *goal* in preference to other related concepts such as intention, task, or purpose, it will be useful to give our reasons and to show the relationship between the term *goal* and these other concepts.

Figure 1 shows our classification of these concepts. First, we distinguish between concepts that stress the conscious or psychological element and those that stress the nonconscious or external element, even though in each case the other is implied. Next

Type of Concept	Conscious aspect stressed; external aspect implied	Borderline	Nonconscious (external or physiological) aspect stressed; conscious aspect implied
Emphasis on behavior or action	intent, intention	norm	task
Emphasis on the end or aim of action	level of aspiration	goal (personal goal) aim	budget deadline bogey
	purpose ↕	end objective standard	assigned goal quota
Emphasis on the motivational element underlying goals	purpose value motive desire wish attitude		drive need instinct

FIGURE 1
Classification of goal related concepts.

we classify on the basis of whether the term stresses behavior or action itself, the end or aim of the action, or the motivational force underlying the aim or goal.

Starting in the upper left cell, the term *intention* refers specifically to a psychological state. It may refer to a goal (e.g., I intend to score twenty points in this basketball game), but it more often refers to a determination to take a certain action (e.g., I intend to mail this letter, get dressed, go to work, call my lawyer). The term *norm* is placed between the two top cells because it refers to an appropriate or desirable way of acting shared by a group of people; thus it refers to what the actor feels is appropriate, but it also stresses what other people believe to be acceptable behavior. In the upper right cell, the term *task* refers to a piece of work to be accomplished. The emphasis is on the work (the external), but it is implied that the work is intended to be accomplished by somebody.

Moving to the left cell in the second row, *level of aspiration* refers clearly to the level of performance one is trying to attain on a task (but see Chapter 5 for different meanings of this concept). *Purpose* refers unambiguously to a consciously held goal, but it may also refer to a motive underlying a goal (what is your purpose in trying to buy out company X?); thus the arrow to the bottom cell.

The term *goal* (the aim or end of an action) is placed between the left and right columns because we usually think of goals as something we consciously want to attain, yet the thing we want to attain is usually something outside us (my goal is to increase sales by 10%). The term *personal goal* distinguishes between assigned and actual (operative) goals. Similarly, the term *aim* also suggests a conscious desire (I am aiming for a scholarship) but also indicates there is something out there we are aiming for. The terms *end* and *objective* place emphasis on the end result of our planned efforts or the place where we are going, but there is a strong implication that somebody is deliberately trying for them. In the same way the term *standard* (something set up as a rule to measure or evaluate things) implies an internalized concept of appropriate action but also may refer to an external criterion (company standard—often a minimal level of acceptable performance).

Turning to the next cell to the right, the emphasis is more external. A *budget* specifies a limit on the amount of money to be spent by an individual, department, or organization. The stress is on the "out there," although it is implied that somebody is trying to meet it. Similarly, a *deadline* refers to a time goal, the time by which some task is supposed to be completed. The focus is on the external (time) aspect, but again the deadline is implicitly somebody's deadline. A *bogey* is a somewhat outdated term referring to an amount of production expected of the employees by management. The bogey is out there, but it is expected that the workers will accept it as their personal goal. The terms *assigned goal* and *quota* are similar in meaning.

Turning to the last row, the concepts of *value, motive, desire, wish* and *attitude* can be viewed as concepts that underlie an individual's choice of goal or decision to accept a goal (e.g., I am trying to increase sales by 10% because I want to please the boss, get promoted, prove that I can do the job, see myself as a good person, etc.). Fishbein and Azjen's (1975) model explicitly used attitudes as predictors of intentions. All these terms refer to consciousness (although values and motives can be subconscious as well as conscious). In contrast, terms in the bottom-right cell such as *drive, need,* and *instinct* (disregarding the issue of whether they are all valid concepts) most typically refer to physiologically based energizers that could affect goal choice, although some theories that rely on such concepts would claim that they control action directly (e.g., Hull).

Combined terms such as "task goal" have occasionally been used in the literature, but such terms seem unnecessarily complicated and redundant. Goal or personal goal would do just as well. Some researchers use the term *intentions* to refer to personal goals in order to distinguish them from assigned goals, but the term *personal goal* seems more consistent.

Why, then, did we choose the term *goal* as the key concept in our theory? First, we were interested in how people perform on tasks so we wanted a term that stresses the end result rather than the behavior alone. Thus our preference for goal over intention. The term *task*, used by Ryan (1958), had too much of an external focus for our needs. *Purpose* was a less than desirable choice because of its frequent reference to underlying motives. The term *level of aspiration* was too narrow because it ruled out goals that did not involve a specific level of performance, and yet which we frequently studied (e.g., try to do your best). *Aim* and *end* also seemed a bit narrow, as did *standard*, which focuses mainly on a minimum amount of work. *Objective* was already widely used in the Management by Objectives literature and, for our purposes, put too much focus on end results (e.g., profits) and too little on shorter-range ends that could guide actions. *Budget, deadline,* and *bogey* had narrower meanings and focused mainly on the external. Thus we found that the term *goal* was the most appropriate concept while recognizing that there were many other terms whose meanings were highly similar. Thus it is not surprising that in the literature one often sees many of these concepts used interchangeably.

LEVELS OF EXPLANATION

Explaining human actions by specifying a person's goal does not constitute a full explanation of that action. Explanations, including explanations of human action, exist on different levels (Ryan, 1970). Goal setting theory provides an immediate or first-level explanation of action. Goals and intentions are viewed as immediate precursors and regulators of much, if not most, human action.

A second-level explanation of action would deal with the question, Where do the goals come from? At this level we would try to account for the goals themselves by reference to other motivational concepts as well as to events and conditions outside the person. We would look, for example, at the individual's motives or values (what he or she seeks to gain and/or keep, considers desirable, beneficial, etc.; Locke, 1976). Values are more general than goals; goals are more situationally and task specific. For example, one might value ambition, whereas one's goal would be to become a company president or a full professor within fifteen years. We could also look at value or personality syndromes that would predispose individuals to set certain types of goals in certain classes of situations. McClelland (1961) argued that people high in the achievement motive are prone to set moderately challenging goals in situations where they have immediate feedback, and can control the outcome, and where external incentives are not stressed. The Type A personality is characterized as a compulsive goal setter who will try to do more and more in less and less time, especially when threatened by competition from others.

Situational factors would include such influences as the demands or requests of authority figures, peer pressure, role models, cultural standards, incentives, rewards, and punishments. An individual's task-specific goals might also be connected to other, longer-range goals such as "I want to double sales this year because I want this to be the biggest company in the U.S. in ten years."

A third-level explanation would attempt to identify the sources and roots of the individual's values, motives, and personality. The only motivational concept broader and more fundamental than that of values is that of needs: the objective requirements of the individual's survival and well-being. For example, the goal to go shopping for specific dinner items could be tied to the value of nutritious food, which would in turn derive (motivationally) from the individual's need for food. As Nuttin (1984) observed, "a subject's motivational direction toward a specific object [goal] should be conceived as the concretization or canalization of a more general need" (p. 67).

The concept of needs does not account for individual differences, however, because people have the same basic needs (everyone needs food, water, sleep, self-esteem, etc.) But the concept of needs is necessary to explain why people act at all, and to explain why certain broad categories of action (e.g., eating) are universal.

One assumption of this division into levels is that the higher-level factors (second and third levels) affect action through the lower levels—i.e., that needs affect action through their effect on values and values through their effect on goals (Locke & Henne, 1986). This assumption has seldom been tested, and it may not even be true as stated. Subconscious values may affect action without the individual's having conscious awareness of any goals based on such values. Our assumption appears somewhat plausible, however, if only because immediate level theories, focusing on task-specific motives and perceptions (e.g., goal setting theory, turnover intention theory, and social-cognitive theory) seem to have been far more successful in accounting for human action than the more general value theories such as McClelland's "need" achievement theory (Locke & Henne, 1986).

THE DOMAIN OF GOAL SETTING THEORY

Goal setting theory, as developed in this book, is confined mainly to the first level of explanation and goes somewhat into the second. At the first level we ask the fundamental question, What is the relationship between goals and action, or more specifically, goals and task performance? And what factors affect this relationship? Cognitive factors, especially feedback and expectancy/self-efficacy and, to an increasing degree, task strategies, play a major role in the theory. At the second level we look at some of the factors that may affect goal choice and goal commitment, and also briefly at the relation of goal choice to personality.

As noted earlier, the reason for developing the theory was our interest in understanding work motivation. We wanted to explain why some people worked harder than others or performed better than others on a task independently of their ability and knowledge. The most direct way to explain it seemed to be to look at the goals people were trying to attain. From there we looked at how such factors as feedback, participation, commitment, and incentives combined or interacted with goals.

We could, of course, have made our theory "look better" by making predictions regarding only direction rather than level of performance. For example, we could have predicted that people with an intention to go to work are more likely to go there rather than to the ball game. This procedure would certainly have produced very good results (e.g., see Locke, Bryan, & Kendall, 1968, experiments 3, 4 and 5), but it would not have explained differences in performance on the job. (Intention-behavior theories are now well developed in social psychology, as we shall see below.)

COGNITION AND MOTIVATION

At all levels of explanation, cognitive factors play a role in explaining both the choice of action and its degree of success. For example, goals, if chosen by people themselves, are based on such factors as their beliefs about what they can achieve, their recollections of past performance, their beliefs about consequences, and their judgments of what is appropriate to the situation. And their degree of success will depend on knowing if they are, in fact, performing in line with the goals (feedback) and their knowledge of appropriate task strategies. At the second level, value choice would depend on the individual's conscious or subconscious philosophy (e.g., What is the good? What values should a person have?). At the third level, cognition is relevant to needs in that how people go about satisfying their needs depends on whether they correctly identify their needs, on their beliefs about what actions will satisfy them, and again on their philosophical premises.

Although cognition and motivation can be separated by abstraction for the purpose of scientific study, in reality they are virtually never separate. All knowledge or beliefs are appraised automatically by the subconscious and can be appraised consciously (by choice) as well (e.g., Is this fact good for me or bad for me or irrelevant?). This is how knowledge is translated into action. On the other side of the same coin, all motivation is based on conscious or subconscious cognitive input (e.g., "I want high-fiber cereal because it is good for my health"). Most action is guided cognitively ("What is the best way to attain this goal?") as well as motivationally.

Another aspect of cognition, alluded to earlier, must be mentioned here, and that is *volition.* We view volition as involving the choice to raise one's level of cognitive focus from the perceptual level to the conceptual level. To quote Rand (1964, pp. 20–21):

> Man's sense organs function automatically; man's brain integrates his sense data into percepts automatically; but the process of integrating percepts into concepts—the process of abstraction and of concept-information—is *not* automatic.
>
> The process of concept-formation does not consist merely of grasping a few simple abstractions. . . . It is not a passive state of registering random impressions. It is an actively sustained process of identifying one's impressions in conceptual terms, of integrating every event and every observation into a conceptual context, of grasping relationships, differences, similarities in one's perceptual material and of abstracting them into new concepts, of drawing inferences, of making deductions, of reaching conclusions, of asking new questions and discovering new answers and expanding one's knowledge into an ever-growing sum. The faculty that directs this process...is: reason. The process is *thinking.*
>
> Reason is the faculty that identifies, and integrates the material provided by man's senses. It is a faculty that man has to exercise *by choice.* Thinking is not an automatic function. In any hour and issue of his life, man is free to think or to evade that effort. . . . The act of focusing one's consciousness is volitional. Man can focus his mind to a full, active, purposefully directed awareness of reality—or he can unfocus it and let himself drift in a semi-conscious daze, merely reacting to any chance stimulus of the immediate moment, at the mercy of his undirected sensory-perceptual mechanism and of any random, associational connections it might happen to make.

In terms of its connection to action, the nature of an individual's thinking, as noted earlier, will affect whether he or she sets specific or vague goals, long-range or short-range goals, consistent or contradictory goals, personally meaningful or meaningless goals, and realistic or unrealistic goals. It will also affect the degree of commitment to goals and the degree to which rational plans are developed for achieving them. Thinking is also pertinent after goals have been formulated. The individual also has to *choose* to take action in accordance with each chosen goal by keeping in focal awareness what is to be achieved, the means needed to achieve it, and the reasons for or benefits of such action.

GOAL SETTING THEORY: A BRIEF HISTORY

As we have noted, the most direct precursor of and direct influence on goal setting theory was the work of T. A. Ryan (1970). But goal setting theory has precursors that go back at least to the turn of the century. Broadly, there are two strands of influence, one connecting the theory to the academic world and the other to the world of business. More specifically, the strands tie into experimental psychology and management theory. These strands of influence are shown in Figure 2. This dual heritage, while only coincidental, seems especially appropriate for a theory of work motivation. It is also fortunate, especially in retrospect, that one of the present authors is especially comfortable with laboratory experiments and theorizing while the other author is especially comfortable with field experiments and applying psychological theories to work organizations.

Academic Precursors

The academic strand began with the Würzburg school in Germany in the early 1900s, directed by O. Kulpe (see Ryan, 1970, for an overview). He and his colleagues were interested in the study of mental processes. They used the term *task* to refer to that which the subject was asked to do. One member of the school, Ach, used the term *determining tendency* to describe the fact, identified by Watt, that a task assigned earlier could affect later action without the individual's being consciously aware of the task at the time of action. For example, if the task was "to add" when presented with the numbers "4 and 6", the subjects will say "10" without conscious deliberation. Ryan incorporated the concept of determining tendency into his 1970 model (Figure 2–1, p. 25) to describe the fact that intentions may affect action even when separated in time from the relevant action.

It is doubtful whether Ach was correct in asserting that there was no awareness at all of the intent at the time of action. The individual must have retained the task in memory or else could not have responded appropriately to the numbers 4 and 6. The concept of determining tendency is most logically interpreted as a memory of a previously assigned task held, perhaps, in peripheral awareness.

FIGURE 2
Historical precursors of goal setting theory.

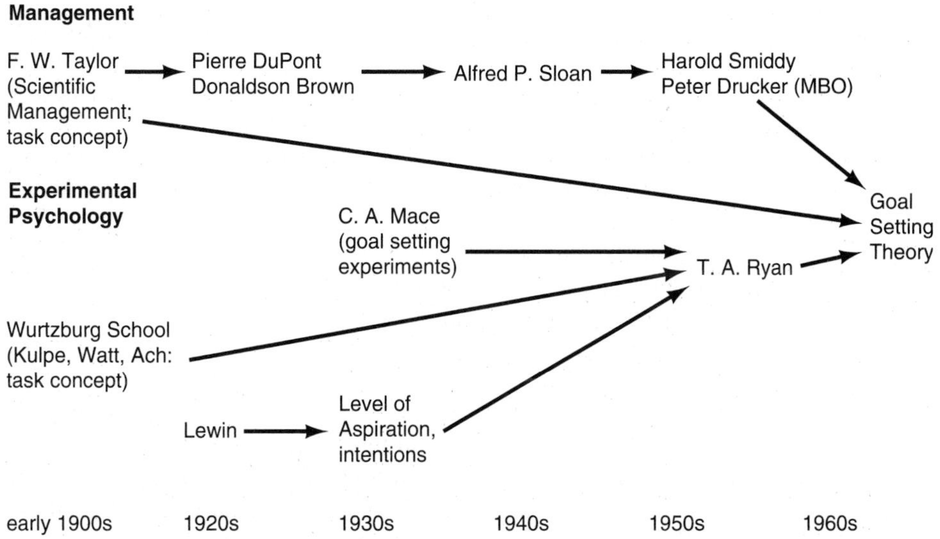

Management

F. W. Taylor (Scientific Management; task concept)   Pierre DuPont   Donaldson Brown   Alfred P. Sloan   Harold Smiddy   Peter Drucker (MBO)

Experimental Psychology

C. A. Mace (goal setting experiments)   T. A. Ryan   Goal Setting Theory

Wurtzburg School (Kulpe, Watt, Ach: task concept)

Lewin   Level of Aspiration, intentions

early 1900s   1920s   1930s   1940s   1950s   1960s

Another contribution of Ach (and his student Hillgruber) was the formulation of the "difficulty law of motivation," which stated that volitional effort increased as the difficulty of a task or action increased (Ach, 1935). This law is clearly the precursor of the "goal difficulty function."

Lewin, a Gestalt psychologist, criticized some of Ach's work on the grounds that the effect of the task on performance was even stronger than Ach had acknowledged. Ach had pitted the laws of association (e.g., repetition) in word association experiments against the effect of the task.

Lewin also seems to have introduced the specific term *intention* to the field. His work gave it respectability as a psychological concept. Lewin (1961) argued that an intention was a quasi-need and was associated with a state of tension that was maintained until reduced by the performance or completion of the intended activity or a substitute activity. Lewin's work led to experiments on the resumption of interrupted tasks (the Ovsiankina effect), on the recall of interrupted tasks (the Zeigarnik effect), to voluminous studies of the effect of intention on learning (intentional vs. incidental learning), to studies of "mental set," and—most importantly for goal setting theory— to studies of level of aspiration (i.e., goal setting; Ryan, 1970). Unlike goal setting theory, however, level-of-aspiration research focused almost exclusively on the determinants rather than the effects of level of aspiration. (This work is reviewed along with the more recent work on determinants of goals in Chapters 5 and 9.) Lewin's work, including his later studies of group decision making, influenced the studies of goal setting and participation in factory settings by French and his colleagues at both the Harwood Manufacturing Company and the General Electric Company (e.g., Coch & French, 1948; French, Kay, & Meyer, 1966).

Another academic influence on our work was the series of experiments conducted in England by Mace (1935). It is not clear what had influenced Mace to do this research, but so far as we know, his were the earliest experimental studies ever done of goal setting as an independent variable. He was the first to compare the effects of specific, challenging goals with goals such as "do your best," and to compare the effects of goals differing in level of difficulty. The results of one of his most successful experiments were reported in Ryan and Smith's (1954) early industrial psychology textbook, which the present first author was assigned to read as a graduate student. Mace also suggested that task liking and enjoyment were affected by degree of success in relation to performance goals or standards. Finally, he suggested that incentives such as praise, criticism, feedback, supervision, and assigned standards affected performance through their effects on the individual's personal goals. While Mace did not perform any statistical tests on his experimental data, his work was certainly an important impetus to goal setting theory. The first known study to statistically show a relationship between goals and subsequent performance was that by Bayton (1943).

Applied Precursors

The strand of thought stemming from the field of management started with Frederick W. Taylor, the father of Scientific Management. He published his major work, the *Principles of Scientific Management*, in 1911, which was about the same time that the

Würzburg school was flourishing. This book focused on how to select, train, and motivate shop workers. For Taylor, the two key motivational devices were the task and the bonus. Taylor wrote:

> Perhaps the most important law belonging to this class, in its relation to scientific management, is the effect which the task idea has upon the efficiency of the workman. This, in fact, has become such an important element of the mechanism of scientific management, that by a great number of people scientific management has come to be known as "task management."
>
> There is absolutely nothing new in the task idea. Each one of us will remember that in his own case this idea was applied with good results in his schoolboy days. No efficient teacher would think of giving a class of students an indefinite lesson to learn. Each day a definite, clear-cut task is set by the teacher before each scholar, stating that he must learn just so much of the subject; and it is only by this means that proper, systematic progress can be made by the students. The average boy would go very slowly if, instead of being given a task, he were told to do as much as he could . . . the average workman will work with the greatest satisfaction, both to himself and to his employer, when he is given each day a definite task which he is to perform in a given time, and which constitutes a proper day's work for a good workman. This furnishes the workman with a clear-cut standard, by which he can throughout the day measure his own progress, and the accomplishment of which affords him the greatest satisfaction. (Taylor, 1967 edition, pp. 120–122)

Under Taylor's system, a large bonus was paid if the worker succeeded in attaining his assigned task. While Taylor's classic book was published not long after many of the Würzburg school publications, there is no evidence that Taylor had ever heard of them. Thus his use of the same key concept (task), while remarkable, seems coincidental.

Taylor's ideas, through a circuitous route, played a role in the emergence of Management by Objectives, or MBO (Greenwood, 1981; Locke, 1982a; Wren, 1987). MBO is a system of motivating and integrating the efforts of business managers by setting goals for the organization as a whole and then cascading these objectives down through each management level, so that goal attainment at each level helps attain goals at the next-highest level and ultimately the goals of the whole firm (Carroll & Tosi, 1973). Greenwood (1981) and Wren (1987) outlined the history of MBO as follows: Pierre DuPont adapted some of Taylor's ideas on accounting and cost control (another aspect of his theory of Scientific Management) at the DuPont Power Company. For example, ROI (return on investment) was developed as a measure of organizational performance. One of DuPont's subordinates, Donaldson Brown, further adapted this concept so that it could be used to evaluate the performance of various department or divisions within the DuPont Company. When Pierre DuPont later became head of General Motors, he took Brown with him and hired Alfred P. Sloan, who eventually succeeded him as president of GM. Sloan institutionalized the ROI concept as a means of maintaining some centralized control when he decentralized GM. It appears that Sloan was the first executive to actually use MBO to motivate and evaluate managers, although he did not call it by that name. Sloan claimed that "the guiding principle" was to make our standard [goals] difficult to achieve, but possible to attain, which I believe is the most effective way of capitalizing on the initiative, resourcefulness, and capabilities of operating personnel" (cited in Odiorne, 1978, p. 15). This claim turned out to foreshadow, in part, the empirical findings of goal setting research that emerged in our own work.

The name and formal concept of MBO came some years later (Greenwood, 1981). Harold Smiddy had been a partner in the consulting firm of Booz, Allen and Hamilton and while there had learned of the concept of the "manager's letter." Each manager was required to submit to his superior each month a list of the goals he planned to achieve and the means he would use to achieve them. In 1948 Smiddy joined the General Electric Company and introduced the idea of the manager's letter there. *His* outside consultant, Peter Drucker (later to become the famous writer on management), convinced him to develop it into a management philosophy that Drucker named Management by Objectives (Drucker, 1954). Drucker apparently knew about Sloan's prior use of MBO at GM (Greenwood, 1981; Odiorne, 1978), even though Sloan did not use the term or develop MBO into a philosophy of management. MBO can be viewed as goal setting applied to the macro or organizational level.

GOAL SETTING IN CONTEMPORARY WORK MOTIVATION THEORY

Aside from being a motivation theory in its own right, the concept of goal setting has been incorporated sooner or later, explicitly or implicitly, into a number of work motivation theories. Consider, for example, Human Relations theory, which stresses an approach to motivating employees based on cohesive work groups, considerate supervision, two-way communication, and employee participation in decision making. Especially in its early years, Human Relations theories denigrated top-down styles of leadership, as well as incentives as a means of motivating employees to accept goals (e.g., Whyte, 1955).

Eventually, Human Relations theory, possibly as a result, in part, of Lewin's influence, incorporated both goal setting and money into its body of techniques, even if not into its theory, by combining them with participation. In the famous Harwood studies (Marrow, Bowers, & Seashore, 1967), goal setting in the form of work standards, plus incentives and participation, were all used.

Today Human Relations advocates more openly concede the importance of goals and monetary incentives. A well-known book on the Scanlon Plan, a participative, Human Relations-oriented plan than entails the use of economic rewards to motivate employees, asserts that ". . . standards are not inconsistent with a Scanlon Plan if they are used as a tool for meeting the cost and not for restrictive control. Everyone needs a benchmark and a set of criteria to evaluate himself" (Frost, Wakeley, & Ruh, 1974, p. 121).

Similarly, Likert, while emphasizing the importance of managers acting supportively toward subordinates, acknowledges that "superiors in System 4 organizations . . . should have high performance aspirations, but this is not enough. Every *member* should have high performance aspirations as well" (Likert, 1967, p. 51). This emphasis is taken seriously in practice, as demonstrated in a report of the application of System 4 at GM's Lakewood assembly plant (Dowling, 1975). Management set explicit goals for such areas as production, scrap, grievances, and labor costs and then had employees set their own goals on the basis of higher-management input and as well as their own knowledge of the operation. With respect to feedback concerning goal accomplishment, "employees at Lakewood were given more information about how they were doing and were given it more frequently than ever before" (p. 36).

Organizational development (OD), an outgrowth of the Human Relations movement, considers MBO to be an OD technique (French & Bell, 1984) because, in theory, goals are to be set particularly when MBO is used. Another OD technique, survey feedback, typically involves goal setting in practice in that its aim is to identify specific problem areas in the organization by means of attitude surveys and then take specific steps to eliminate those problems.

Goal setting has also been incorporated into another major work motivation theory: VIE, or valence-instrumentality-expectancy theory. The major premise of VIE theory is that in making choices, an individual mentally sums the expected pleasures to be derived from each possible alternative, subtracts the sum of the expected pains, and chooses the alternative with the highest positive net value. VIE theory did not recognize the importance of goal setting in its original, organizational psychology version (Vroom, 1964), probably due to VIE theory's hedonistic emphasis. Its major focus was on the way in which people's beliefs and feelings allegedly lead them to choose a particular course of action.

The hedonistic and other assumptions of VIE theory have been criticized in detail elsewhere (Locke, 1975). Suffice it to say that some revised models have put less stress on hedonism and, more pertinent to the present discussion, have expanded VIE theory to include an explicit goal setting stage (Campbell, Dunnette, Lawler, & Weick, 1970). One possible way to integrate some of the VIE constructs with goal setting is to view values and expectancies as factors that influence the goals an individual chooses or accepts while viewing goals themselves as the more direct determinants of action (Hollenbeck & Klein, 1987). However, expectancies also influence performance directly.

Two other work motivation theories have never shown any explicit theoretical recognition of the importance of goal setting to employee motivation. Both schools, however, have recognized its importance implicitly, since when these theories are put into practice, goal setting is virtually always involved.

The Cognitive Growth school, associated mainly with Herzberg and to an extent Maslow (1954), promulgated in the early 1960s, emphasized people's psychological or growth needs (e.g., knowing more, integrating one's knowledge, being creative, being effective in ambiguity, developing a genuine sense of self-worth, etc.). It was asserted that these needs could best be satisfied through one's work. According to Herzberg, jobs that did not allow for such growth needed to be enriched by providing the employee with increased responsibility and autonomy.

Herzberg never mentioned goal setting as an element of job enrichment. In fact, the idea was explicitly rejected by him (Herzberg, 1975, pp. 98–99) and his followers (Ford, 1969, p. 28). This may have been due to its association with Scientific Management, whose emphasis on extreme division of labor Herzberg (1966) disparaged. In practice, goal setting was unwittingly incorporated into the procedure of job enrichment under the name of feedback. The explicit purpose of feedback in job enrichment programs is to increase the employee's feeling of achievement and to provide him or her with a sense of personal responsibility for the work. Two obvious questions that arise in this context are, How does an employee know when he or she has achieved something? and How does that employee know when he or she has adequately or successfully fulfilled his or her responsibility? The answer must be, When the feedback is compared, by management or by the employee, with some standard of appropriate performance, i.e., when the feedback is appraised in terms of some goal. Thus whenever management gives its employees feedback, one can be confident that some performance standard is involved, implicitly if not explicitly.

Numerous studies have shown that feedback in itself does not have the power to motivate performance directly (Annett, 1969; Latham, Mitchell, & Dossett, 1978; Locke, Cartledge, & Koeppel, 1968). It has been argued that feedback motivates action only indirectly, through its relationship to goal setting. For example, if the feedback shows that one's prior performance was below the desired standard, one can increase one's subsequent effort, or change one's tactics, in order to meet the standard in the future.

In practice, job enrichment has involved so many different types of job changes, often within the same study, that isolating specific effects of the different elements is virtually impossible (Locke, 1975). Noticeable progress in this direction was made in a simulated field study by Umstot, Bell, and Mitchell (1976). They found that job enrichment procedures from which goal setting elements had been specifically deleted led to increased job satisfaction but failed to improve productivity. In contrast, assigning the employees explicit, challenging goals accompanied by feedback led to higher productivity even in the absence of job enrichment. When goal setting and job enrichment were combined, both productivity and satisfaction improved. In some studies alleged to involve job enrichment, employee goal setting has been advocated explicitly (Walters, 1975).

It is probable, therefore, that increases in the quantity or quality of productivity found in job enrichment studies (Ford, 1969; Lawler, 1970) are at least partially attributable to an implicit goal setting element. Locke, Sirota, and Wolfson (1976), in their field study of job enrichment, attributed some of the performance improvement found to goals and feedback. They also suggested that productivity might increase under such programs as a result of the elimination of unnecessary tasks or of a more efficient use of labor. This could occur when employees are allowed to work where they are needed rather than where they are arbitrarily assigned by a supervisor (see also Locke, Feren, McCaleb, Shaw, & Denny, 1980).

If the incorporation of goal setting has been subtle among advocates of the Cognitive Growth school, it is much more obvious among advocates of a more recent school, Organizational Behavior Modification (OBM), which became popular in the 1970s as a method of motivating employees. The OBM technique of goal smuggling consists of openly advocating the use of "performance standards," a term used as a synonym for goal, accompanied by feedback and possibly praise and/or money, but describing these procedures at the theoretical level in behavioristic language (Locke, 1977). Thus performance standards or goals become "controlling stimuli" or "discriminative stimuli," and feedback, praise, and money become "reinforcers" or "conditioned reinforcers" (Fellener & Sulzer-Azaroff, 1984; Luthans & Krietner, 1975).

These labels add nothing to our understanding of how or why goal setting works. Worse, they are misleading and, in many cases, incorrect. Consider first the claim that the goal is a stimulus or discriminative stimulus. Even if the stimulus referred to here is an assigned goal, such a stimulus only affects action if the individual commits himself or herself to that goal. *Thus the efficient cause of goal-directed action is internal, not external.* A goal is an idea. Furthermore, some goals are set by the individual without any external prod (Brief & Hollenbeck, 1985).

Bandura (1986) has shown that even the behaviorist emphasis on consequents is misleading at best and mistaken at worst. Reinforcement does not affect behavior unless individuals believe that they can make the requisite response. Furthermore, making such a response presupposes that the individual knows what response to make (Levine, 1971) and wants the rewards that it brings (Dulany, 1968). Finally, goals can affect behavior in a single trial *before* any behavior has been reinforced (Locke, 1982b).

Similarly, consider the claim that feedback is a reinforcer for goal-directed activity. First, feedback is simply information. How one responds to information depends on if and how it is understood and appraised (Arnold, 1960). Feedback may lead to a negative appraisal, an appraisal of indifference, or a positive appraisal depending on the individual's values and the circumstances. In turn such appraisals can lead to many different responses, including no change in effort, greater effort, reduced effort, modified strategies, change of tasks, leaving the situation, aggression, or various defensive maneuvers. Calling feedback a reinforcer simply obscures the decision process that follows it and discourages the search for the actual mechanisms by which it does affect subsequent action (Locke, 1977, 1980a, 1980c).

Behavior modification advocates argue that feedback effects vary with the circumstances due to differences in individuals' "reinforcement history." Such a claim, like the concept of instinct, can "explain" everything and therefore nothing. Other OBM advocates have claimed that since goal setting theory refers to internal mental states, it is untestable and therefore unscientific unless rephrased in terms of "objective," that is, external concepts. Since numerous studies show that goals and goal commitment can be measured and can be related to actual performance, their claim is invalid.

As noted earlier, all the sciences, including physics, chemistry, and biology, depend on inferences that go beyond what can be observed directly. Trying to pretend otherwise simply leads to the distortion of scientific concepts (Locke, 1969b, 1972); this is especially true in psychology, where all the key concepts refer to mental states. Mental states and processes, as noted earlier, can be directly observed in oneself. They need only be inferred in other people. The emergence of cognitive psychology as the dominant paradigm in the field over the past ten to fifteen years, and the simultaneous decline of the influence of behaviorism in all subfields of psychology, testify to an overwhelming consensus, supported by introspection, logic, and empirical findings (e.g., see Bandura, 1986) in favor of the use of such inference.

As the influence of behaviorism has declined, a neo-behaviorist theory is emerging to take its place. It is called control theory and can be viewed as a combination or integration of behaviorism, machine-computer theory (cybernetics), goal setting theory, and, by implication, drive-reduction theory. It is derived most directly from Miller, Galanter, and Pribram's TOTE model (1960). The major concepts of control theory have been presented by Campion and Lord (1982), Carver and Scheier (1982), Hyland (1988), Lord and Hanges (1987), Powers (1973), and others. In brief, the theory asserts that there is *input* (a stimulus), which is detected by a *sensor*. This is fed into a *comparator*, which compares the input with a *reference standard*. If there is a deviation (also called a "disturbance"), a *signal* is sent to an *effector*, which generates modified *output* (a response). This output becomes the input for the next cycle. In goal theory language, the input is feedback from previous performance, the reference signal is the goal, the comparator is the individual's conscious judgment, and the effector or response is his or her subsequent action which works to reduce the discrepancy between goal and performance.

While control theory acknowledges the importance of goal setting, there are serious, if not irredeemable, flaws in the model. First, observe that the major "motive" for action under control theory is to remove disturbances or discrepancies between the goal and the input (feedback). The natural state of the organism is seen to be one of motionlessness or rest. This is true of machines, but not of living organisms which are naturally active. It is, in effect, a mechanistic version of long discredited drive-reduction theory (Cofer & Appley, 1967). Nuttin (1984) has observed that in this aspect, control theory fundamentally misstates the actual source of motivation: "The behavioral process . . . does not begin with a 'test' of the discrepancy between the standard and the actual states of affairs. Instead, it begins with a preliminary and fundamental operation, namely the construction of the standard itself, which, as a goal, is at the origin of the action and directs its further course" (p. 145). Similarly, Bandura (1990) noted that *goal setting is first and foremost a discrepancy creating process*. Control theory begins in the middle rather than at the beginning of the motivational sequence. To quote Bandura (in press):

> Human self-motivation relies on both *discrepancy production* and *discrepancy reduction*. It requires *feedforward* control as well as *feedback* control. People initially motivate themselves through feedforward control by setting themselves valued challenging standards that create a state of disequilibrium and then mobilizing their effort on the basis of anticipatory estimation of what it would take to reach them. After people attain the standard they have been pursuing, they generally set a higher standard for themselves. The adoption of further challenges creates new motivating discrepancies to be mastered. Similarly, surpassing a standard is more likely to raise aspiration than to lower subsequent performance to conform to the surpassed standard. Self-motivation thus involves a dual cyclic process of disequilibrating discrepancy production followed by equilibrating discrepancy reduction. (p. 23 of preprint)

Figure 3 illustrates how little of the motivational process control theory, in its "core" version, incorporates.

The above is important because if discrepancy reduction is the major motive, as implied by control theory, then the most logical thing for an individual to do would simply be to adapt his or her goal to the input. This would guarantee that there would be no disturbance or discrepancy. Machines, of course, cannot do this because the standard has been fixed by people at a certain level (as in setting a thermostat). But people can and do change standards that diverge from present performance. If the individual's major motive were to remove disturbances, people would never do this. Control theorists argue that lower-level goals are actually caused by goals at a higher level in the individual's goal hierarchy (Carver & Scheier, 1982). But this only pushes the problem back a step. Why should people set higher-level goals if they only want to reduce

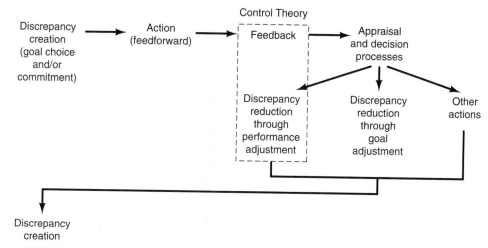

FIGURE 3
Aspects of the motivation process incorporated into the "core version" of control theory.

tension? But in reality, people do set goals and then act to attain them; they do not focus primarily on eliminating disturbances. Removal of discrepancies and any associated tension is a *correlate* of goal-directed action, not its cause. The causal sequence begins with setting the goal, not with removing deviations from it.

At a fundamental level, discrepancy reduction theories such as control theory are inadequate because if people consistently acted in accordance with them by trying to eliminate all disturbances, they would all commit suicide—because it would be the only way to totally eliminate tension. If people chose instead to stay alive but set no goals, they would soon die anyway. By the time they were forced into action by desperate, unremitting hunger pangs, it would be too late to grow and process the food they would need to survive.

In their major work, Carver and Scheier (1981) denied that discrepancy reduction is motivated by a desire to reduce a drive or state of tension. But their own explanation as to why people act to reduce discrepancies is quite puzzling. "The shift [of action in the direction of the goal or standard] is a natural consequence of the engagement of a discrepancy-reducing feedback loop" (p. 145). This statement, of course, explains nothing. Why is discrepancy reduction a "natural consequence"? According to goal theory, *both* discrepancy creation *and* discrepancy reduction occur for the same reason: because people need and desire to attain goals. Such actions are required for their survival, happiness, and well-being.

A second problem with control theory is its very use of a machine as a metaphor. The problem with such a metaphor is that it cannot be taken too literally or it becomes highly misleading (e.g., see Sandelands, Glynn, & Larson, 1988). For example, people do not operate within the deterministic, closed-loop system that control theory suggests. In response to negative feedback, for example, people can try harder or less hard. They can focus on the cause and perhaps change their strategy. They can also lower the goal to match their performance; in some cases they may raise their goal. Furthermore, they can reinterpret the discrepancy as unimportant and ignore it or can even totally deny it. They can also question the accuracy of the feedback. They can go outside the system (by leaving the situation). They can attack the person they hold responsible for the discrepancy. They can become paralyzed by self-doubt and fear and do nothing. They can drink liquor to blot out the pain. In short, they can do any number of things other than respond in machinelike fashion. Furthermore, people can feel varying degrees of satisfaction and dissatisfaction, develop varying degrees of commitment to goals, and assess their confidence in being able to reach them (Bandura, 1986). These emotions, decisions, and estimates affect what new goals they will set and how they will respond to feedback indicative of deviations from the goal (Bandura, 1988). Control theory, insofar as it stresses a mechanistic model, simply has no place for these alternatives, which basically means that it has no place for consciousness. Insofar as this is the case, the theory must fail for the same reason behaviorism failed. Without studying and measuring psychological processes, one cannot explain human action.

One might ask why control theory could not be expanded so as to accommodate the ideas and processes noted above. Attempts have been made to do this, but when it is done, the machine language may be still retained. Hyland (1988), for example, described the effects of goal importance or commitment in terms of "error sensitivity," which is represented diagrammatically by a box called an "amplifier." Expectations and memory are represented as "symbolic control loops." Decision making is done not by a person but by a "selector." What is the benefit of translating relatively clear and well-accepted concepts that apply to human beings into computer language that is virtually incomprehensible when used to describe human cognition? The greater the number of concepts referring to states or actions of consciousness that are relabeled in terms of machine language, the more implausible and incomprehensible the whole enterprise becomes. Nuttin (1984, p. 148) wrote on this: "When behavioral phenomena are translated into cybernetic and computer language, their motivational aspect is lost in the process. This occurs because motivation is foreign to all machines."

On the other hand, if additional concepts are brought into control theory and not all relabeled in machine language (e.g., Lord & Hanges, 1987), then control theory loses its distinctive character as a machine metaphor and becomes superfluous—that is, a conglomeration of ideas borrowed from *other* theories. And if control theory does not make the needed changes and expansions, it is inadequate to account for human action. Control theory, therefore, seems to be caught in a triple bind from which there is no escape. If it stays strictly mechanistic, it does not work. If it uses mechanistic language to relabel concepts referring to consciousness, it is incomprehensible. And if it uses nonmechanistic concepts, it is unoriginal. It has been argued that control theory is useful because it provides a general model into which numerous other theories can be integrated (Hyland, 1988). However, a general model that is inadequate in itself cannot successfully provide an account of the phenomena of other theories.

In their book, Carver and Scheier (1981) examined the effect of individual differences in degree of internal focus versus external focus in action. While this presentation is more plausible than the mechanistic versions of control theory, most of it actually has little to do with control theory as it relates to goal setting. For example, they discuss how expectancies and self-focus affect performance but do not examine the goal-expectancy literature. And some of their conclusions (such as that self-efficacy does not affect performance directly) contradict actual research findings. Only one actual goal setting study (not in Carver and Scheier's book) has used the self-focus measure. Hollenbeck and Williams (1987) found that self-focus only affected performance as part of a triple interaction in which ability was not controlled. Thus it remains to be seen how useful the measure is, either as a moderator or as a mediator of goal setting effectiveness.

There is also a conceptual problem with the prediction that the relation between goals and performance will be higher among those high in self-focus than those in self-focus. Goal attainment requires, over and above any internal focus, an *external* focus; most goals refer to something one wants to achieve in the external world. Thus the individual must monitor external feedback that shows progress in relation to the goal in order to make progress toward it. Individuals might focus internally as well (a) to remind themselves of what the goal is—though this can also be done externally, as on a feedback chart; (b) to retain commitment by reminding themselves of why the goal is important; and (c) to assess self-efficacy. Furthermore, depending on what is focused on, (e.g., self-encouraging thoughts or self-doubt), an internal focus could either raise or lower goal-relevant effort. In sum, the relation between where one is focused and goal-relevant performance seems intuitively far more complex than is recognized by the cognitive version of control theory.

Finally, some have argued that control theory is original because it deals with the issue of goal change (e.g., Campion & Lord, 1982). However, goal change was actually studied first by level-of-aspiration researchers in the 1930s and 1940s, so control theory can make no claim of originality here. Nor can a mechanistic model hope to deal adequately with issues involving human choice as noted above.

In sum, the present authors do not see what control theory has added to our understanding of the process of goal setting; all it has done is to restate a very limited aspect of goal theory in another language, just as was done by behavior mod advocates. Worse, control theory, in its purest form, actually obscures understanding by ignoring or inappropriately relabeling crucial psychological processes that are involved in goal-directed action.

In contrast to behavior modification and control theory, Bandura's (1986) social-cognitive theory is highly compatible with goal setting theory. It not only includes goal setting as part of its content but adds two important dimensions to goal theory. The first is role modeling, which Bandura has shown to be an important social influence on action. Studies have shown that modeling has significant effects on goal choice and goal commitment. The second added dimension is self-efficacy. Though related in meaning to expectancy (from valence-instrumentality-expectancy theory), self-efficacy has a wider meaning and is measured somewhat differently from the way expectancy is usually measured. Self-efficacy has been found to play multiple roles in goal setting theory. It affects goal choice, goal commitment, and response to feedback, and it also has a direct effect on performance. Social-cognitive theory is also highly compatible with the metatheoretical approach of goal setting theory; both stress the importance of cognitive self-regulation.

Some mention should be made of two related theories having some similarity to goal setting literature in the area of social psychology. These are the theories of "reasoned action" and of "planned behavior" put forth by Ajzen (1987), Ajzen and Fishbein (1980), and Fishbein and Ajzen (1975). These models are mainly concerned with predicting behaviors such as purchasing coffee or using birth-control pills from measured intentions to take those actions. Intentions in turn are predicted by attitudes toward the action and subjective norms. Ajzen (1987) added perceived behavioral control to his model.

There are clearly strong parallels between such theories and goal setting theory. As we noted earlier, intentions are similar in meaning to goals. Attitudes, in the form of valences, and norms are integrated into goal setting theory in several places. And perceived control is similar in meaning to self-efficacy and plays a similar role in both theories. Reviews of the literature on these models show them to have substantial validity (Ajzen, 1987; Sheppard, Hartwick, & Warshaw, 1988).

The term *goal* is distinguished from that of intention by Sheppard, Hartwick, and Warshaw (1988) by using *goal* to refer to the desire to attain outcomes that require overcoming obstacles (such as getting enough money to implement the desire to buy a car). The term *intention* is used if there are no substantial obstacles, such as in the case of the intention to buy coffee. Our use of the term *goal,* however, is different. We use it to refer to desired outcomes in terms of level of performance to be attained on a task rather than to the desire to take a specific action. The two types of theories are therefore complementary in that they pertain to different domains but use similar approaches. Goal setting theory, as we shall see, is also more elaborated and is based on a more extensive research base than the intention theories.

Another modern movement focused on the understanding of volitional and goal-directed action is centered in West Germany; this interest is perhaps not a coincidence, since, as already noted, the academic roots of goal setting trace back to Würzburg (Figure 2). Researchers such as U. Kleinbeck, H. Heckausen, J. Kuhl, and P. Gollwitzer have all written about and done research on goal-directed activity (e.g., see Halisch & Kuhl, 1987). W. Meyer (1987) has studied perceived ability, which is similar in meaning to self-efficacy. C. Antoni and J. Beckman (1987) have specifically looked at the individual difference variables of attentional focus and persistence as a moderator of goal setting effects. Kleinbeck (1986) has studied the effects of the goals when individuals are performing two tasks at once. Gollwitzer, Heckausen, and Ratajczak (1987) looked at the effects of what we in Chapter 6 call goal intensity on commitment. Frese and Sabini (1985) call this West German movement, along with its American counterparts, *action theory,* which, they argue, "begins with a conception of human behavior: that it is directed toward the accomplishment of goals, that it is directed by plans, that those plans are hierarchically arranged, and that feedback from the environment articulates with plans in the guidance of action" (p. xxiii). Action theory, in terms of its basic assumptions, is clearly compatible with goal setting theory.

Finally, in Belgium, Nuttin (1984) published a book entitled *Motivation, Planning and Action.* In addition to his incisive critiques (cited earlier) of tension-reduction and cybernetic (control) theories, he made many astute observations about the relationship between goals and needs, goals and feedback, and goals and planning, which are quite compatible with goal theory (see also Nuttin, 1985).

DIMENSIONS OF GOALS

Goals, like other mental processes (Rand, 1969), have two main attributes: content and intensity. *Goal content* refers to the object or result being sought—e.g., buying a house, getting a raise, winning a tennis match, getting a score of 26 or better on a task. Usually the content will refer to some aspect of the external world, although it is also possible for people to have psychological goals such as happiness, higher self-esteem or less anxiety and self-doubt. The content of different goals may differ qualitatively. An individual may have a career goal, a job goal, a financial goal, or a goal in sports or hobbies or in his or her social life. Goal content may vary quantitatively. The individual may have few or many goals, short-term or long-term goals (close or distant deadlines), or easy or difficult goals. Goals may also vary in degree of specificity or clarity, the clearest or most specific goals usually being quantitative (e.g., try for a 5% productivity improvement) and the least clear being more verbal (e.g., do the best you can, do a good job). An individual's goals may also be consistent or conflicting.

Most research on goal content to date has focused on the effects, alone and in various combinations, of degree of goal specificity and degree of goal difficulty. Multiple goals and goals differing in time span have been studied to some degree. Goal setting has been studied with scores of different tasks and in many different settings.

It is worth making the distinction here between goal difficulty and task difficulty, since there has been some confusion in the literature over the meanings of these two terms (see Locke, Shaw, Saari, & Latham, 1981). A *task* is a piece of work to be accomplished. A *difficult task* is one that is hard to do. A task can be hard because it is complex, that is, requires a high level of skill and knowledge. For example, writing a book on physics is a harder task than writing a thank-you note. A task can also be hard because it requires a great deal of effort: digging the foundation for a swimming pool takes more effort than digging a hole in which to plant a flower seed. The only goal setting study to have explicitly separated goal and task difficulty is that by Campbell and Ilgen (1976). Using chess problems, they found that both goal and task difficulty affected performance. Harder goals led to better performance than easier goals, and initial assignment of more-difficult problems led to better subsequent performance than initial assignment of less-difficult problems. The authors attributed the latter effect to increased task knowledge fostered by working on the more-difficult problems.

Since a goal is the object or aim of an action, it is possible for the completion of a task to be a goal. In most goal setting studies, however, the term *goal* refers to attaining a specific standard of proficiency on a given task, usually within a specified time limit. For example, two individuals are given the same task (e.g., simple addition), but one is asked to complete a large number of problems within thirty minutes and the other, a small number. The harder goal would be achieved by expending greater effort and attention than would be expended to achieve the easy goal. Harder goals, like harder tasks, can also require more knowledge and skill than easier goals (e.g., winning a chess tournament vs. coming in next to last). Harder tasks usually lead to more effort but lower performance scores than easier tasks. For example, the average person's score would be lower on a calculus test than on a test of simple addition (though as Campbell and Ilgen found, working on a harder task may lead to better subsequent performance than working on an easier task when all subjects are subsequently given tasks of equal difficulty to work on). To summarize the distinction between the terms, *goal difficulty* specifies a certain level of task proficiency measured against a standard, whereas *task difficulty* refers simply to the nature of the work to be accomplished.

The second dimension of goals, *intensity*, refers to such factors as the scope and integration of the goal setting process, the effort required to form the goals, the place of the goal in the individual's goal hierarchy, the degree to which the individual is committed to the goal, and the importance of the goal. Most research on goal intensity has focused on the determinants and effects of goal commitment, although there have been a few studies on the intensity of the goal setting process.

It should be noted that goal content and intensity are not always easy to separate. For example, a more-intense psychological process could be involved in setting clear, specific goals than vague goals in a situation where a great deal of information had to be analyzed and integrated before the goals could be clearly formulated. In such a case, clearer goals would be more intense than vague goals. In other situations, however, there might be no difference, as in a laboratory experiment in which different people were assigned specific and general goals. The different goals might lead to different degrees of effort, even though they would not necessarily differ in intensity.

REFERENCES

Ach, N. (1935). *Analyse des willens.* Berlin: Urban & Schwarzenberg.

Ajzen, I. (1987). Attitudes, traits, and actions: Dispositional prediction of behavior in personality and social psychology. *Advances in Experimental Social Psychology, 20,* 1–63.

Ajzen, I., & Fishbein, M. (1980). *Understanding attitudes and predicting social behavior.* Englewood Cliffs, NJ: Prentice Hall.

Annett, J. (1969). *Feedback and human behavior.* Baltimore: Penguin.

Antoni, C. H., & Beckmann, J. (1987). An action control conceptualization of goal setting and feedback effects. University of Mannheim, W. Germany, unpublished manuscript.

Arnold, M. B. (1960). *Emotion and personality: Psychological aspects, Vol 1.* New York: Columbia University Press.

Bandura, A. (1977). *Social learning theory.* Englewood Cliffs, NJ: Prentice Hall.

Bandura, A. (1986). *Social foundations of thought and action: A social-cognitive view.* Englewood Cliffs, NJ: Prentice Hall.

Bandura, A. (1988). Self-regulation of motivation and action through goal systems. In V. Hamilton, G. Bower, & N. Frijda (Eds.), *Cognitive perspectives on emotion and motivation.* Dordrecht: Kluwer Academic Publishers.

Bandura, A. (1990). Reflections on nonability determinants of competence. In J. Kolligan & R. Sternberg (Eds.), *Competence considered: Perceptions of competence and incompetence across the lifespan.* New Haven: Yale University Press.

Bayton, J. A. (1943). Interrelations between levels of aspiration, performance, and estimates of past performance. *Journal of Experimental Psychology, 33,* 1–21.

Binswanger, H. (1986). The goal-directedness of living action. *The Objectivist Forum,* 7(4), 1–10.

Brief, A. P., & Hollenbeck, J. R. (1985). An exploratory study of self-regulating activities and their effects on job performance. *Journal of Occupational Behavior,* 6, 197–208.

Campbell, D. J., & Ilgen, D. R. (1976). Additive effects of task difficulty and goal setting on subsequent task performance. *Journal of Applied Psychology,* 61, 319–24.

Campbell, J. P., Dunnette, M. D. Lawler, E. E., & Weick, K. E., (1970). *Managerial behavior, performance, and effectiveness.* New York: McGraw-Hill.

Campion, M. A., & Lord, R. G. (1982). A control systems conceptualization of the goal-setting and changing process. *Organizational Behavior and Human Performance, 30,* 265–87.

Carroll, S. J., & Tosi, H. L. (1973). *Management by objectives.* New York: Macmillan.

Carver, C. S., & Scheier, M. F. (1981). *Attention and self-regulation: A control-theory approach to human behavior.* New York: Springer-Verlag.

Carver, C. S., & Scheier, M. F. (1982). Control theory: A useful conceptual framework for personality-social, clinical, and health psychology, *Psychological Bulletin, 92,* 111–35.

Coch, L., & French, J. R. P. (1948). Overcoming resistance to change. *Human Relations,* 1, 512–32.

Cofer, C. N., & Appley, M. H. (1967). *Motivation: Theory and research.* New York: Wiley.

Dowling, W. F. (1975). At General Motors: System-4 builds performance and profits. *Organizational Dynamics,* 3, 23–38.

Drucker, P. F. (1954). *The practice of management.* New York: Harper.

Dulany, D. E., Jr. (1968). Awareness, rules and propositional control: A confrontation with S-R behavior theory. In D. Horton & T. Dixon (Eds.), *Verbal behavior and general behavior theory.* New York: Prentice Hall.

Fellner, D. J., & Sulzer-Azaroff, B. (1984). A behavioral analysis of goal setting. *Journal of Organizational Behavior Management,* 6, 33–51.

Fishbein, M., & Ajzen, I. (1975). *Belief, attitude, intention and behavior: An introduction to theory and research.* Reading, MA: Addison-Wesley.

Ford, R. N. (1969). *Motivation through the work itself.* New York: American Management Association.

French, J. R. P., Kay, E., & Meyer, H. H. (1966). Participation and the appraisal system. *Human Relations,* 19, 3–20.

French, W. L., & Bell, C. H. (1984). *Organization development: Behavioral science interventions for organization improvement.* Englewood Cliffs, NJ: Prentice Hall.

Frese, M., & Sabini, J. (1985). *Goal directed behavior: The concept of action in psychology.* Hillsdale, NJ: L. Erlbaum.

Frost, C. F., Wakeley, J. H., & Ruh, R. A. (1974). *The Scanlon plan for organizational development: Identity, participation, and equity.* East Lansing, MI: Michigan State University.

Gollwitzer, P. M., Heckhausen, H., & Ratajczak, H. (1987). From weighing to willing: Approaching a change decision through pre- or postdecisional mentation. Max-Planck-Institute for Psychologische Forschung, Munich, West Germany, unpublished manuscript.

Greenwood, R. G. (1981). Management by objectives: As developed by Peter Drucker, assisted by Harold Smiddy. *Academy of Management Review,* 6, 225–30.

Halisch, F., & Kuhl, J. (Eds.) (1987). *Motivation, intention, and volition.* New York: Springer-Verlag.

Herzberg, F. (1966). *Work and the nature of man.* Cleveland: World Publishing Co.

Herzberg, F. (1975). One more time: How do you motivate employees? In R. M. Steers & L. W. Porter (Eds.), *Motivation and work behavior.* New York: McGraw-Hill.

Hollenbeck, J. R., & Klein, H. J. (1987). Goal commitment and the goal setting process: Problems, prospects and proposals for future research. *Journal of Applied Psychology,* 72, 212–220.

Hollenbeck, J. R., & Williams, C. R. (1987).Goal importance, self-focus, and the goal-setting process. *Journal of Applied Psychology,* 72, 204–211.

Hyland, M. E. (1988). Motivational control theory: An integrative framework. *Journal of Personality and Social Psychology,* 55, 642–51.

Kleinbeck, U. (1986). Effects of goal-setting on motivation and performance in dual-task situations. Presented at the 21st International Congress of Applied Psychology.

Klinger, E. (1987). Current concerns and disengagement from incentives. In F. Halisch and J. Kuhl (Eds.), *Motivation, intention and volition.* New York: Springer-Verlag.

Latham, G. P., Mitchell, T. R., & Dossett, D. L. (1978). Importance of participative goal setting and anticipated rewards on goal difficulty and job performance. *Journal of Applied Psychology,* 63, 163–71.

Lawler, E. E. (1970). Job design and employee motivation. In V. H. Vroom & E. L. Deci (Eds.), *Management and motivation.* Baltimore: Penguin.

Levine, M. (1971). Hypothesis theory and nonlearning despite ideal s-r reinforcement contingencies. *Psychological Review,* 78, 130–40.

Lewin, K. (1961). Intention, will and need. Reprinted in T. Shipley (Ed.), *Classics in psychology.* New York: Philosophical Library. (This article originally appeared, in German, in *Psychol. Forsch.,* 1926.)

Likert, R. (1967). *The human organization.* New York: McGraw-Hill.

Locke, E. A. (1968b). Toward a theory of task motivation and incentives. *Organizational Behavior and Human Performance,* 3, 157–89.

Locke, E. A. (1969b). Purpose without consciousness: A contradiction. *Psychological Reports,* 25, 991–1009.

Locke, E. A. (1972). Critical analysis of the concept of causality in behavioristic psychology. *Psychological Reports,* 31, 175–97.

Locke, E. A. (1975). Personnel attitudes and motivation. *Annual Review of Psychology,* 26, 457–80.

Locke, E. A. (1976). The nature and causes of job satisfaction. In M. D. Dunnette (Ed.), *Handbook of industrial and organizational psychology.* Chicago: Rand McNally.

Locke, E. A. (1977). The myths of behavior mod in organizations. *Academy of Management Review,* 2, 543–53.

Locke, E. A. (1980a). Attitudes and cognitive processes are necessary elements in motivational models (Debate). In B. Karmel (Ed.), *Point and counterpoint in organizational behavior.* Hinsdale, IL: Dryden.

Locke, E. A. (1980b). Behaviorism and psychoanalysis: Two sides of the same coin. *Objectivist Forum* 1(1), 10–15.

Locke, E. A. (1980c). Latham versus Komaki: A tale of two paradigms. *Journal of Applied Psychology,* 65, 16–23.

Locke, E. A. (1982a). The ideas of Frederick W. Taylor: An evaluation. *Academy of Management Review,* 7, 14–24.

Locke, E. A. (1982b). Relation of goal level to performance with a short work period and multiple goal levels. *Journal of Applied Psychology,* 67, 512–14.

Locke, E. A., Bryan, J. F., & Kendall, L. M. (1968). Goals and intentions as mediators of the effects of monetary incentives on behavior. *Journal of Applied Psychology,* 52, 104–21.

Locke, E. A., Cartledge, N., & Koeppel, J. (1968). Motivational effects of knowledge of results: A goal-setting phenomenon? *Psychological Bulletin,* 70, 474–85.

Locke, E. A., Feren, D. B., McCaleb, V. M., Shaw, K. N., & Denny, A. T. (1980). The relative effectiveness of four methods of motivating employee performance. In K. D. Duncan, M. M. Gruneberg, & D. Wallis (Eds.), *Changes in working life.* London: Wiley Ltd.

Locke, E. A., & Henne, D. (1986). Work motivation theories. In C. Cooper & I. Robertson (Eds.), *International review of industrial and organizational psychology.* Chichester England: Wiley Ltd.

Locke, E. A., Shaw, K. M., Saari, L. M., & Latham, G. P. (1981). Goal setting and task performance: 1969–1980. *Psychological Bulletin,* 90, 125–52.

Locke, E. A., Sirota, D., & Wolfson, A. D. (1976). An experimental case study of the successes and failures of job enrichment in a government agency. *Journal of Applied Psychology,* 61, 701–11.

Lord, R. G., & Hanges, P. J. (1987). A control system model of organizational motivation: Theoretical development and applied implications. *Behavioral Science,* 32, 161–78.

Luthans, F., & Kreitner, R. (1975). *Organizational behavior modification.* Glenview, IL: Scott Foresman.

Mace, C. A. (1935). *Incentives: Some experimental studies.* Industrial Health Research Board (Great Britain), Report No. 72.

Marrow, A. J., Bowers, D. G., & Seashore, S. E. (1967). *Management by participation.* New York: Harper & Row.

Maslow, A. H. (1954). *Motivation and personality.* New York: Harper.

McClelland, D. C. (1961). *The achieving society.* Princeton, NJ: Van Nostrand.

Meyer, W. U. (1987). Perceived ability and achievement-related behavior. In F. Halisch and J. Kuhl (Eds.), *Motivation, intention and volition.* New York: Springer-Verlag.

Miller, G. A., Galanter, E., & Pribram, K. H. (1960). *Plans and the structure of behavior.* New York: Henry Holt.

Nuttin, J. (1984). *Motivation, planning and action.* Hillsdale, NJ: L. Erlbaum.

Nuttin, J. (1985). *Future time perspective and motivation.* Hillsdale, NJ: L. Erlbaum.

Odiorne, G. S. (1978). MBO: A backward glance. *Business Horizons,* October, 14–24.

Powers, W. T. (1973). Feedback: Beyond behaviorism. *Science,* 179, 351–56.

Rand, A. (1964). The Objectivist ethics. In A. Rand (Ed.), *The virtue of selfishness.* New York: New American Library.

Rand, A. (1969). *Introduction to Objectivist epistemology.* New York: The Objectivist.

Ryan, T. A. (1958). Drives, tasks, and the initiation of behavior. *American Journal of Psychology,* 71, 74–93.

Ryan, T. A. (1970). *Intentional behavior.* New York: Ronald Press.

Ryan, T. A., & Smith, P. C. (1954). *Principles of industrial psychology.* New York: Ronald Press.

Sandelands, L. E., Glynn, M. A., & Larson, J. R. (1988). Task performance and the "control" of feedback. Columbia University, unpublished manuscript.

Sheppard, B. H., Hartwick, J., & Warshaw, P. R. (1988). The theory of reasoned action: A meta-analysis of past research with recommendations for modifications and future research. *Journal of Consumer Research,* 15, 325–43.

Taylor, F. W. (1967). *Principles of scientific management.* New York: Norton (originally published in 1911).

Terrace, H. (1979). *Nim: A chimpanzee who learned sign language.* New York: Knopf.

Umstot, D. D., Bell, C. H., & Mitchell, T. R. (1976). Effects of job enrichment and task goals on satisfaction and productivity: Implications for job design. *Journal of Applied Psychology,* 61, 379–94.

Vroom, V. (1964). *Work and motivation.* New York: Wiley.

Walters, R. W. (1975). *Job enrichment for results: Strategies for successful implementation.* Reading, MA: Addison-Wesley.

Whyte, W. F. (1955). *Money and motivation: An analysis of incentives in industry.* New York: Harper.

Wren, D. A. (1987). *The evolution of management thought.* New York: Wiley.

An Integrated Control Theory Model of Work Motivation

Howard J. Klein

Work motivation typically has been described within the organizational behavior literature as the set of psychological processes that cause the initiation, direction, intensity, and persistence of behavior (Campbell & Pritchard, 1976; Pinder, 1984). Despite some definitional agreement, current approaches to motivation appear as a splintered and perplexing array of theories, few with overwhelming empirical support and most with unresolved theoretical ambiguities or inadequacies. This situation is both undesirable and unnecessary. It is undesirable because of the confusion created, the absence of intelligible guidelines for application, and clear transgression of the principle of scientific parsimony (Hollenbeck, 1989). It is unnecessary because the constructs overlap considerably and because the different perspectives rarely contradict and often augment each other (Campbell & Pritchard, 1976; Landy & Becker, 1987).

One form of synthesis is the development of a metatheory, a framework that reasonably links existing theories (Landy & Becker, 1987). In a metatheory, the current component theories would be consigned to the role of middle range theories (Pinder, 1984) and would remain useful for application to specific motivational problems, whereas the integrated metatheory would provide a more general framework for understanding work motivation and would guide the refinement of the component theories. The purpose of this paper is to propose one possible metatheory, using control theory as the integrating framework. To achieve this goal, the basic elements of control theory are briefly reviewed, an integrated control theory model of work motivation is presented, and this model is contrasted with existing ones.

Using control theory as the integrating framework is advantageous for several reasons. First, as noted by Lord and Hanges (1987), although control theory is not a fully developed theory of motivation, its dynamic structure easily allows the integration of other theories. In this paper, it will be shown that a control theory model of motivation explicitly incorporates feedback, goal-setting, expectancy, and attribution theories, and it can be extended to include several other theories (e.g., social learning theory). In addition to providing the impetus for integration, control theory is parsimonious because even as the others are incorporated, it can remain a simple heuristic. Another benefit is that focus is directed to the cognitive processes underlying motivation, the absence of which has been a criticism of current approaches (Ilgen & Klein, 1989; Landy & Becker, 1987).

CONTROL THEORY

Control theory, present for some time (e.g., Wiener, 1948), has been a useful framework for theoretical development in many fields (Carver & Scheier, 1981). According

From *Academy of Management Review,* 1989, 14(2), 150–172. Reprinted by permission.

to the cybernetic hypothesis (Wiener, 1948), the feedback loop is the fundamental building block of action. In its simplest form, the feedback loop consists of four elements: a referent standard or goal, a sensor or input function, a comparator, and an effector or output function. In the often-used example of a thermostat controlling the temperature of a room, the referent standard is the temperature the thermostat is set at, the sensor is the element monitoring the current room temperature, the comparator is the mechanism that compares the current and desired temperatures, and the effector is the furnace or air conditioner. In this simple feedback sequence, illustrated in Figure 1, an input is perceived by the sensor, which sends a signal to the comparator, where it is tested against the standard (Powers, 1973). If this comparison reveals a discrepancy, an error signal is generated, and the system takes some action via the effector to reduce the discrepancy. This process of sensing, comparing, and effecting is repeated until the discrepancy subsides.

In human control systems, feedback involves much more than the mechanical sensing of the environment, goals are not predetermined inflexible standards, and there are several alternatives for reducing discrepancies (Lord & Hanges, 1987). As a result, control theory can represent a very flexible, nonmechanical view of behavior (Lord & Hanges, 1987). Although human control systems are more complex, they do operate in the same basic way—utilizing feedback to ensure the attainment of goals. Consider, for example, a salesperson who has accepted a quarterly sales quota as a personal goal (the standard). The input function would be information the salesperson perceives about his or her current sales performance. When this information is compared to the standard, the salesperson forms a perception of how well he or she is meeting the quota. If this comparison reveals a discrepancy, the salesperson will take some corrective action, possibly increasing the number of new contacts.

When framed as a theory of behavior, control theory has two primary elements: one cognitive, the other affective (Carver & Scheier, 1981). The cognitive component con-

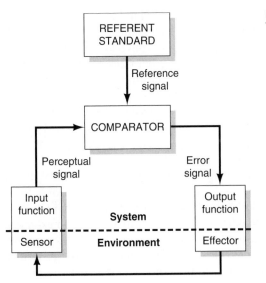

FIGURE 1
The simple feedback loop.

sists of internal goals, the processing of information about one's current state, and the comparison of that state with those goals. The affective component arises from perceived discrepancies between one's desired and current states, and behavior is initiated from one's desire to resolve those discrepancies (Carver & Scheier, 1981). Complex behaviors can be explained by hierarchies of feedback loops. In such hierarchies, the *means* to reduce discrepancies in higher order feedback loops become the *standards* of lower order loops (Lichtenstein & Brewer, 1980; Powers, 1973). That is, the output function of one feedback loop might consist of a string of other loops, and each of those, in turn, might contain other strings of loops, and so on (Miller, Galanter, & Pribram, 1960).

For example, the output function in the previous example—increasing new contacts—is made up of several actions, including finding potential customers and making the initial contact. Thus, on closer inspection, this output consists of at least two feedback loops—finding and contacting. Each of these could, in turn, be broken down further with the hierarchy extended down to a loop involving neural signals and changes in muscle tension associated with turning the pages in a phone book. The result is a hierarchical plan for increasing sales through increasing new contacts. Powers (1973) proposed that the human nervous system embodies a detailed hierarchy of such feedback loops.

This hierarchy of control also could be extended upward. That is, the action of meeting the sales quota could be part of the output function of a higher order standard, perhaps getting a monetary bonus. Getting that bonus may, in itself, be part of the effector of yet a higher standard (e.g., buying a new house). Therefore, in order to achieve any given standard, chains of subgoals, necessary partial accomplishments, may need to be established, with each subgoal being pursued sequentially as attention shifts from one control loop to another (Lord & Hanges, 1987; Powers, 1973; Shank & Albeson, 1977). This shifting of attention within goal hierarchies is an important component of control theory, given the limited human capacity for conscious processing.

The feedback loops discussed above are referred to in cybernetics as negative feedback loops because the response to an error is the reduction of that error (Powers, 1973). In cybernetics, positive feedback results in an enlargement of the discrepancy, and a positive feedback loop is a system that tries to maximize distance from, rather than match, a standard. The assumption underlying these definitions is that discrepancies in either direction are equally undesirable. Although this is true for many mechanical systems, it usually is not the case with human systems. To avoid confusion, the more common organizational behavior usage of the terms positive and negative will be employed rather than the cybernetic definitions. That is, *positive feedback* will refer to information denoting one has exceeded a goal, *negative feedback* to information indicating the standard was not attained.

Several authors have recognized the potential explanatory power of control theory and have used it to examine behavior in organizations (e.g., Campion & Lord, 1982; Hollenbeck & Brief, 1988; Taylor, Fisher, & Ilgen, 1984). Even though these authors have laid the groundwork for a control theory model of work motivation, an examination of these models reveals some inconsistencies. The problem is not that these models are incongruent with the tenets of control theory or with empirical findings. Rather, the problem is that their different perspectives prohibit any one of them from providing a comprehensive model. In addition, inconsistencies in their assumptions and treatments do not allow a coherent model to be arrived at through a simple aggregation of the available literature. Given that these perspectives can be integrated, doing so should aid future research and conceptual development by focusing efforts and preventing further divergence. Thus, this paper not only integrates several motivational perspectives into a control theory model, but it also unifies the different existing control theory models.

AN INTEGRATED CONTROL THEORY MODEL

The model presented in Figure 2 is a control theory model of work motivation that integrates the works of Carver and Scheier, Lord, Taylor, Hollenbeck, and their colleagues (Campion & Lord, 1982; Carver, 1979; Carver, Blaney, & Scheier, 1979; Carver & Scheier, 1981, 1982; Hollenbeck, in press; Hollenbeck & Brief, 1988; Hollenbeck & Williams, 1987; Lord & Hanges, 1987; Taylor et al., 1984). In comparing

FIGURE 2
An integrated control theory model of work motivation.

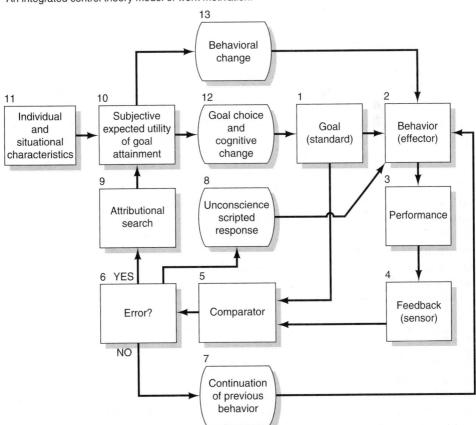

this model to Figure 1, goals are equivalent to the referent standard, the comparator remains the same, behavior represents the effector, and feedback represents the sensor. The primary difference is the inclusion of several cognitive processes between the comparator and the effector. These additional processes reflect that in human systems neither the sensor, standards, nor effector are necessarily fixed quantities. The nature and function of the elements in this integrated model are delineated below. The specific hypotheses generated in explicating the model are summarized in tabular form at the end of the section.

Goals

In line with the extensive goal-setting literature, an individual's personal goals (Box 1) are the immediate precursors of behavior (Box 2) (Locke, Shaw, Saari, & Latham, 1981; Mento, Steel, & Karren, 1987). Given a control theory framework, however, action actually initiates from perceived discrepancies (Miller et al., 1960). In addition, it is acknowledged that intentions do not always get translated into behaviors (Ajzen & Fishbein, 1977) and that behaviors, reflecting the magnitude and direction of effort, are but partial determinants of performance (Box 3). Goals may differ on several dimensions, including difficulty and specificity (Locke et al., 1981). In control theory, the goal difficulty–performance relationship is explained by noting that difficult goals require greater efforts to avoid discrepancies (Campion & Lord, 1982; Lord & Hanges, 1987). Returning to the example used earlier, assume a salesperson achieves $20,000 in sales during the first month of a quarter. If that salesperson's quarterly quota is $100,000, he or she is much more likely to perceive a discrepancy and the need to take corrective action than if that quota was an easier goal of $70,000.

The goal specificity–performance relationship also can be explained by control theory. Vague goals make poor referent standards because there are many situations in which no discrepancy would be indicated and, therefore, there would be no need for corrective action (Campion & Lord, 1982). A first-month performance level of $20,000 is likely to be perceived as inadequate with a specific quarterly goal of $100,000. This same initial performance level is less likely to be perceived as a problem with a more general goal of between $75,000 and $125,000 or a vague nonquantitative goal such as do your best. Klein, Whitener, and Ilgen (1988) provided support for this position when they found that specific goals were found associated with smaller goal-performance discrepancies. Because vague goals allow more levels of performance to be considered goal attainment, specificity also would affect the variability of performance across individuals, with specific goals resulting in less variability in performance (Klein et al., 1988; Locke, Chah, Harrison, & Lustgarten, 1989).

Feedback

At some point during or after task performance, feedback (Box 4) is provided or sought out by the individual. *Task feedback*, as defined by Ilgen, Fisher, and Taylor (1979), is a message an individual receives from a source that contains information about the individual's task performance. Feedback may be available continuously, intermittently, or only after task completion, depending on its source. Feedback may originate from others who are in a position to evaluate the individual's behavior, from the task environment, or from within the individual (Greller & Herold, 1975; Ilgen et al., 1979). Additional feedback can be actively sought out through inquiry or monitoring to supplement the feedback that is provided (Ashford, 1986; Ashford & Cummings, 1983). Therefore, for almost all tasks, some knowledge of performance is available (Ammons, 1956).

The way that feedback is acquired and processed varies, however, according to the person's awareness (Taylor et al., 1984). Conscious processing of feedback is most likely to occur (a) when an individual is unfamiliar with a situation, (b) when the feedback obtained is dramatically incongruent with expectations, and (c) when others cue the individual to attend to feedback (Taylor et al., 1984). All of these factors would serve to increase the salience of the feedback. How feedback is processed is important because it influences the nature of subsequent information processing and because unconsciously processed feedback may be biased towards the recipient's expectations (Taylor et al., 1984).

In addition, feedback may be ignored, intentionally or unintentionally, for a multitude of reasons, including the perceived inaccuracy, irrelevance, or triviality of the information (Ilgen et al., 1979). Two conditions thought to decrease the likelihood that feedback will be ignored are valued goals (Power's, 1973, concept of controlled quantity) and self-focus or self-attention. Individuals high in self-focus are more aware of inconsistencies between their ideal and actual selves (Wicklund, 1975), and this awareness increases the desire for consistency (Taylor & Fiske, 1978).

From a control theory perspective, self-attention and salient standards increase both the probability that a discrepancy will be discerned and the desire to reduce that discrepancy. There is considerable evidence that the relationship between goal difficulty and performance is enhanced when goals are important and when subjects are high in self-focus (e.g., Hollenbeck & Williams, 1987). Finally, the feedback individuals compare to their goals at any given time will likely be a composite of information selectively obtained from a variety of sources and weighted by their evaluation of its value (Taylor et al., 1984). Therefore, it is the perceived situation, not the objective environment, that enters the comparator (Powers, 1973).

Goals and Feedback as Dual Elements Results from studies in which goals and feedback were systematically varied (e.g., Bandura & Cervone, 1983; Becker, 1978) suggest that both are necessary to improve performance. Control theory provides an elegant explanation for this interaction (Taylor, 1983): It is knowledge of one's previous performance relative to some goal that influences the amount of effort subsequently exerted (Becker, 1978). In addition to goals and feedback being of little value alone, it appears that when only one exists, individuals often will try to provide the other. When feedback is received in the absence of a goal, it often will be perceived as meaningless and will be ignored (Ashford, 1986; Taylor et al., 1984). Such feedback may, however, cue the individual to spontaneously set a goal (Ammons, 1956; Taylor et al., 1984). Likewise, in the absence of externally provided feedback, it is likely that individuals with goals will engage in feedback-seeking behavior in order to monitor the progress of goals (Ammons, 1956; Ashford & Cummings, 1983; Lord

& Hanges, 1987). Control theory also emphasizes the need for congruence between goals and feedback in order for the system to operate effectively (Taylor et al., 1984).

Previous authors have pointed to the goal-feedback interaction and called for the integration of the two literatures (e.g., Taylor, 1983). Control theory suggests not only that goals and feedback can and should be integrated, but that they are inseparable— dual elements of a single motivational process. Similarities in the definition and function of goals and feedback support this position. Regarding definition, one is rarely described without mention of the other. For example, Ashford and Cummings (1983) define feedback as "information that denotes how well individuals are meeting various goals" (p. 372). In addition, feedback may be evaluative, referring to performance level, or descriptive, referencing actions or behaviors (Herold & Greller, 1977). Similarly, goals can be set for either the desired outcomes or the required behaviors. Concerning the functions of these constructs, both goals and feedback have been discussed as directing attention and action (Ashford & Cummings, 1983; Ilgen et al., 1979; Locke et al., 1981). Goals and feedback also both serve to clarify role expectations and, as such, are both often cited as useful for the reduction of role ambiguity (e.g., Naylor, Pritchard, & Ilgen, 1980). Finally, research in both literatures supports the notion that both factors serve to increase task interest and persistence (Elwell & Grindley, 1938; Locke & Bryan, 1967).

If goals and feedback are viewed as dual elements, as control theory suggests, the similarities between them lead to a number of hypotheses regarding the nature of these constructs and their relationship with performance. In general, the specificity of both feedback and goals has been related to performance (Ammons, 1956; Ilgen et al., 1979; Locke et al., 1981; Mento et al., 1987), although specificity often has been confounded with difficulty in the goal-setting literature. The evidence that goal specificity affects the variability of performance across individuals (Locke et al., 1989) suggests that feedback specificity, similarly, may relate to performance variance. Likewise, the evidence that overly specific feedback early in the learning process may be dysfunctional (Ammons, 1956) suggests that in such contexts, overly specific goals may be similarly unproductive.

The feedback literature also asserts that, in general, the more frequent and immediate the feedback, the greater its impact (Ammons, 1956; Ilgen et al., 1979). Additionally, goals contain a time dimension, and the feedback findings suggest that goals with a shorter time frame may be more effective, a position supported by Bandura and Schunk (1981). Given, however, that excessively frequent feedback can be detrimental (Ilgen et al., 1979), goals with too short a time frame may be dysfunctional. Another important dimension of feedback is its sign. Although the sign of a goal (i.e., to increase versus decrease something) is distinct from the sign of feedback, goal difficulty is clearly related to sign of feedback. The more difficult the goal, the greater the possibility that feedback regarding goal progress or attainment will be negative, and negative feedback is less likely to be accepted than is positive feedback (Ilgen et al., 1979). Similarly, the more difficult the goal, the less likely it is to be accepted (Matsui, Okada, & Mizuguchi, 1981).

A final similarity is the parallel between feedback receipt versus feedback seeking and individual goal setting versus the receipt of external goals. Ashford and Cummings (1983) suggested several conditions in which individuals are likely to engage in feedback-seeking behaviors. These same factors (e.g., the drive to self-evaluate) could, conceivably, instigate the setting of personal goals. In addition, acceptance of external feedback and the acceptance of assigned goals are a concern in both literatures. Furthermore, similar factors, for example, the power of the source and providing a rationale, have been identified as influencing the acceptance of both (Ilgen et al., 1979; Leskovec, 1967; Locke, Latham, & Erez, 1988).

Comparator

Regardless of its source or how it is processed, when feedback is perceived, it is tested (Box 5) against the goal through a psychological process represented by the comparator (Carver, 1979; Miller et al., 1960). There are three results of this comparison process (Carver & Scheier, 1981): (a) the individual is on target toward meeting the goal, (b) the individual is behind schedule, or (c) the individual is ahead of schedule. If a person is on target, no error (Box 6) is detected, and the person, in most instances, will return to his or her previous behavior (Box 7). The failure to detect an error implies that the actions being employed are appropriate and, thus, they will tend to be repeated. There are, however, exceptions. For example, individuals may become bored and want to try something new, or they may anticipate that conditions have changed and, thus, alter their behavior in preparation for those changes (Wood & Locke, 1986).

If the comparison process reveals an error, a response will be initiated in order to correct that error. As with the processing of feedback, the processing of an error need not be conscious. Taylor et al. (1984) pointed out that the acquisition and processing of information can vary from a highly controlled to a virtually automatic series of activities. Similarly, Lord and Hanges (1987) held that the decision mechanism in their model operated differently in different situations. This distinction between conscious and unconscious processing in response to discrepancies is analogous to the distinction made by Carver and Scheier (1981) and Hollenbeck and Brief (1988) between an interrupted versus uninterrupted feedback loop. These positions are also in line with March and Simon's (1958) routinized and problem-solving responses, as well as the view of cognitive psychologists who have suggested there are two models of processing information, one automatic and one controlled (e.g., Shiffrin & Schneider, 1977).

Reflecting these dual processes, the model in Figure 2 indicates two alternatives following the perception of an error. These two options represent parallel levels of processing, not simply alternative paths for discrepancy reduction. According to Carver and Scheier's model, the matching-to-standard process usually occurs automatically and unconsciously. Whether or not a discrepancy is perceived consciously is most likely dependant on the salience of the error (Taylor & Fiske, 1978) and whether or not the feedback leading to the error perception was consciously processed (Taylor et al., 1984). Likewise, the response to any perceived errors may be either conscious or unconscious.

It is likely that whether or not the response is conscious will depend on whether the discrepancy was consciously perceived (Taylor et al., 1984) and the individual's familiarity with the situation (Lord & Hanges, 1987). Given that feedback, especially from internal or task sources, often is acquired and processed unconsciously (Taylor et al., 1984), frequently the response to discrepancies will be corrected using unconscious scripted responses (Box 8) (Lord & Kernan, 1987; March & Simon, 1958; Schank & Ableson, 1977). In addition, because of the hierarchical structure of goals, processing may be controlled at a particular level, and it may be automatic at lower levels. Controlled processing, because it requires conscious attention, prevents simultaneous controlled processing at other levels. Conversely, automatic processing, by minimizing the need for conscious attention, permits conscious attention to be directed elsewhere.

Unconscious Scripted Response

Scripts are overlearned performance programs, cognitive structures that provide sequences of events for familiar situations (Lord & Kernan, 1987; Schank & Abelson, 1977). Schank and Abelson suggested that individuals have scripts for situations that are frequently encountered and that a script becomes stronger as the sequence is repeated. Scripts also can be tied to the goals of individuals (Lichtenstein & Brewer, 1980; Lord & Kernan, 1987); therefore, many routine work behaviors are executed via scripts. People can adapt to novel situations by utilizing more general plans, the mechanisms that underlie scripts (Schank & Abelson, 1977). A *plan* is an accumulation of more general information connecting events that have not been encountered frequently enough to be linked in the form of a script. Behavior can initiate from either a plan or a script, and each has equal status in the overall strategy for realizing goals (Schank & Abelson, 1977). Using plans is more difficult because it requires an individual to use considerably more thought and attention. It is likely, therefore, that an experienced salesperson will have a well-developed script for closing a deal, whereas a new salesperson may have only a general plan.

Schank and Abelson also discussed how distractions and interferences can cause the interruption of a script. Script interference results from obstacles in the environment or mistakes on the part of the individual. In either case, the person is in the position of seeking corrective actions. That is, script interruption often will result in the perception of an error and a shift to conscious processing. In well-practiced scripts, certain obstacles or errors will have been encountered often enough for the corrective responses to become scripts themselves. In the example used here, an experienced salesperson may have a subscript for dealing with customers who try to back out of a deal. The other potential interrupters of scripts, *distractions*, are conditions or actions that result in a temporary or permanent change in the relative importance of the goal. An emergency phone call made to a salesperson who is in the process of closing a deal would be an example of a script distraction.

To summarize the distinctions made between conscious and unconscious information processing, both feedback and goal-performance discrepancies may or may not be recognized, and if processed, they may or may not be consciously perceived. Likewise, the response to a discrepancy and the decision of how to respond may or may not be conscious. If a script exists for resolving a discrepancy, that script will be enacted. If no script is available, planning is required, and the decision process will shift to one of conscious problem solving. The distinction between scripted and conscious responses is important because there is evidence to suggest that goals are more effective when scripted responses are available.

It has been suggested that without well-learned responses, the attentional demands of goals may undermine performance (Wood, Mento, & Locke, 1987). Given that the capacity for conscious processing is limited, when a script is unavailable for a set of behaviors, a goal that is focusing a person's attention on a task requiring those behaviors may interfere with the conscious processing required to learn or plan those behaviors. Studies employing heuristic tasks (e.g., Earley, Ekegren, & Connolly, 1987) and a meta-analysis of the effects of task complexity (Wood et al, 1987) demonstrate that specific, difficult goals are dysfunctional for novel and complex tasks. Individuals clearly would not have scripts for a heuristic task and would be less likely to have strong scripts for all aspects of a complex task.

Conscious Response

If a programmed response is unavailable, problem-solving activities directed toward finding an appropriate response will be initiated (March & Simon, 1958). Even though these processes essentially involve rational choice, it is recognized that rationality is bounded and that choice is always exercised with respect to a narrow, simplified perception of reality (March & Simon, 1958). The importance of the decision and the time constraints will influence the degree of rationality that is approached (Lord & Hanges, 1987).

According to Carver and Scheier's (1981) model, when the automatic feedback loop is interrupted, an individual will reassess the likelihood of meeting the goal. This assessment entails processing the available information, and it results in an *outcome expectancy*, a subjective estimate of the likelihood that the goal can be attained, given the nature of the situation and the available options (Carver, 1979). Outcome expectancies are similar to, but differ subtly from, both performance to outcome expectancies in expectancy theory (Lawler, 1973) and efficacy expectations in social learning theory (Bandura, 1977, 1986). Those differences are discussed in depth both by Carver and Scheier (1981) and by Bandura (1977).

Attributional Search

Carver and Scheier (1981) outlined a number of factors that might influence outcome expectancies, including past performance, locus of control, social influence, and attributions. As part of the conscious problem-solving response, individuals will embark on attributional searches (Box 9) to develop causal explanations for being unable to meet their goals (Carver & Scheier, 1981). This search may entail seeking additional feedback. Based on this causal analysis, individuals form new outcome expectancies that may or may not differ from previous expectations. It has been demonstrated that individuals do engage in spontaneous attributional searches and that such searches are most likely to happen when an unexpected event occurs (i.e., when expectancies are disconfirmed) (e.g., Pyszczynski & Greenberg, 1981; Wong & Weiner, 1981).

In the area of organizational behavior, researchers have relied primarily on the model presented by Weiner et al. (1971). That model posits that there are four main causal elements (ability, effort, luck, and task difficulty) representing the influence of two orthogonal dimensions (stability and locus). More recently, a third dimension, controllability, has been added (Weiner, 1985). In addition, unstable, internal, controllable factors (i.e., effort) can be broken down further by making the distinction between the amount of effort and the direction of that effort (Taylor et al., 1984).

The primary dimension of interest relating to the reevaluation of outcome expectancies is stability (McMahan, 1973). Weiner, Heckhausen, Meyer, and Cook (1972), for example, found that ascriptions of an outcome to stable factors produce greater shifts in expectancy, increments following success, and decrements following failure, than do ascriptions to unstable causes. If a salesperson is behind in meeting a quota and attributes that failure to deficiencies in the product line (i.e., a stable factor), it is likely that the outcome expectancy for meeting that quota will fail. If, instead, the salesperson attributes such failure to unstable factors (e.g., to bad luck or to not trying hard enough), changes in expectancy will be smaller. Similarly, if a salesperson is ahead of schedule, his or her outcome expectancy would be expected to increase more if that success is attributed to ability than if it is attributed to a couple of lucky deals.

Subjective Expected Utility

Although previous control theory models have explicitly included the role of outcome expectancies, both Taylor et al. (1984) and Carver and Scheier (1981) also suggested that the importance, or value, of goals plays a role. Taylor et al. (1984), for example, suggested that task persistence is determined by factors that would affect the attractiveness of goal attainment. Similarly, Campion and Lord (1982) suggested that valences (as well as expectancies and attributions) may have an impact on motivation through their impact on goal commitment or goal change. Other authors have suggested using both expectancies and attractiveness to predict goal commitment (e.g., Hollenbeck & Klein, 1987; Mento, Cartledge, & Locke, 1980). Therefore, using an expectancy theory, or, in more general terms, a subjective expected utility (SEU) framework (Edwards, 1961), to predict the decision to retain a goal when confronted with a performance-standard discrepancy is consistent with these authors.

This utility (Box 10) is construed to be a multiplicative function of the attractiveness of goal attainment and the expectancy of attaining that goal. Other things being equal, individuals are more likely to remain committed to a goal when they have a high expectancy of reaching it and when their perceived value of goal attainment is high (Matsui, Okada, & Mizuguchi, 1981; Mento et al., 1980). Although the probability of goal attainment may be less for difficult goals, this is often offset by their correspondingly higher valence (Campbell, 1982; Matsui et al., 1981). Carver and Scheier (1981) concluded that the judgment regarding outcome expectancies was a critical decision point, with responses falling into one of two categories: renewed effort or withdrawal. In the current model, this decision is a function of the SEU of goal attainment. Given that numerous authors have suggested that the choice of personal goals is influenced by expectancy and attractiveness (e.g., Mento et al., 1980), initial goal choice is also believed to be a function of the SEU of goal attainment.

Individual and Situational Factors

The judgments that determine SEU are, in turn, influenced by a host of individual and situational characteristics (Box 11) in addition to causal attributions (Campion & Lord, 1982; Taylor et al., 1984). Outcome expectancies, for example, may be influenced by individual factors, such as ability and past experiences, as well as by situational causes, including social comparisons and performance constraints. Likewise, the attractiveness of goal attainment will be influenced by many individual (e.g., needs, values, higher order goals) and situational (e.g., reward structure) considerations. More complete lists of such factors have been outlined elsewhere (e.g., Campbell, 1982; Hollenbeck & Klein, 1987; Taylor et al., 1984). Although not explicit in Figure 2, these individual and situational factors have direct effects on behavior and performance and may influence other elements in the model (e.g., attributions).

Response Decision

If the resulting SEU of goal attainment is high, continued effort toward that goal should result. If, however, the SEU is low, the predicted response is withdrawal. A similar position was taken by Lewin, Dembo, Festinger, and Sears (1944), who stated that although the decision for a person to continue or stop may be influenced by a large number of factors, stopping or not stopping will ultimately depend on the force toward that goal. If the SEU is low, the withdrawal impetus can be expressed either behaviorally or cognitively (Carver & Scheier, 1981). The primary withdrawal response is to leave the situation, if such a response is possible and not associated with aversive consequences. Laboratory research indicates that physical withdrawal from a situation is likely when goal-performance discrepancies are combined with negative expectancies, especially for persons high in self-focus (Carver et al., 1979; Steenbarger & Aderman, 1979).

An individual may withdraw either from the particular task causing the discrepancy or from the job. If a salesperson is having difficulty with only the bookkeeping aspects of the job, finding someone else to complete those duties is a more probable response than leaving the job. If withdrawal from the problematic task is not possible, or if that task is central to the job, withdrawal from the job would be expected, contingent on the perceived consequences of leaving. When physical withdrawal from the situation is precluded, the withdrawal impetus may be expressed mentally. Essentially, this cognitive withdrawal involves giving up, resignation to failure, and disengagement from the situation. An individual who has withdrawn mentally would be expected to reduce his or her efforts, to simply go through the motions, and to avoid feedback that would increase the salience of the discrepancy (Carver & Scheier, 1981).

Cognitive Reactions   Predicting the specific response of an individual who chooses to persist is complicated because persistence may result in cognitive (Box 12) and/or behavioral (Box 13) changes. Cognitive reactions may take the form of changes in goal commitment, changes in the level of the goal, or changes in the goal itself (Campion & Lord, 1982; Taylor et al., 1984). In general, commitment toward a goal could increase, remain the same, or decrease. In instances in which the SEU of goal attainment changes, but the force toward the goal remains sufficiently high for the individual to persist and is still greater than the force toward alternative goals, there should be no change in the goal, but an incremental change in goal commitment. For example, assume that the motivational force toward a quarterly quota drops because the expectancy of meeting that goal is lowered following a poor first month. That goal may still be retained if the SEU of the goal is still higher than that toward an easier goal. Yet the force toward that goal is not as strong as it was, and this change should be evident in the commitment the individual demonstrates toward that goal.

In instances in which the SEU changes to the extent that the force toward a goal becomes less than that toward an alternative goal, the individual should abandon the original goal and replace it with the goal with the greatest SEU. In the above example, if the expectancy of attaining the sales quota drops to the extent that its attractiveness cannot compensate (i.e., the SEU of the easier goal becomes greater than that of the original goal), it is likely that the individual will lower his or her goal. In addition to changing the level of the original goal, the individual could replace that goal with a different goal. Another possible cognitive reaction would be to deny or distort the feedback so that the previously perceived error is rationalized (Lord & Hanges, 1987).

In general, cognitive changes are less likely to occur than behavioral changes. Campion and Lord (1982) suggested that cognitive changes are longer term, secondary responses and that different behavioral responses would be tried before changing goals. Similarly, March and Simon (1958) proposed that individuals will first try to find or develop a satisfactory performance program, but if unsuccessful, will try to relax the criteria. The explanation for this lies in the hypothesized causes of the above cognitive changes—changes in the SEU of goal attainment. The value of attaining a particular goal is likely to be a fairly stable factor in the short term. In the example used here, the attractiveness of meeting an established sales quota, because of its instrumentality in obtaining other outcomes (e.g., a bonus, promotion, praise), is unlikely to change during the performance period.

Also, outcome expectancies will tend to remain constant, depending on attributions, as long as the individual believes that an untried behavioral response will remedy the situation. If, for example, a salesperson feels it is possible to catch up by trying harder or by changing strategies, or if he or she is confident that luck will change, it is likely that outcome expectancies will remain high. As alternative behavioral responses are exhausted, the likelihood of making a stable attribution increases, enhancing the likelihood that expectancies will drop (Taylor et al., 1984). Support for this position was provided by Campion and Lord (1982), who found that the number of failures participants experienced was an important determinant of their response. This relative stability of SEUs in the short run also suggests that changes in commitment are more likely than changes in goals.

Behavioral Reactions Behavioral reactions may occur either as a result of cognitive changes or in the absence of cognitive changes. That is, a change in goal commitment, or goal change, will likely require corresponding changes in behavior. The absence of cognitive change, however, also indicates persistence with behavioral changes needed to reduce the perceived discrepancy. There are two primary ways for an individual to change behaviors: the intensity of effort can be altered (i.e. trying harder) or the direction of behavior can be changed (i.e., trying a different strategy)

(Carver & Scheier, 1981; Lord & Hanges, 1987; Taylor et al., 1984). For example, a salesperson either can work more hours and make more calls per week or he or she can change the type of calls (e.g., focusing on new customers at the expense of follow-up calls). Furthermore, an individual may change both the intensity and direction of his or her efforts. Another possible behavioral reaction would be to react against the system (Taylor et al., 1984).

The choice between altering the intensity or the direction of behavior is hypothesized to depend upon the causal attributions made for past performance. Kelley (1973) suggested that attributions have a more direct influence on behavior than was discussed earlier, positing that causal attributions influence decisions among alternative courses of action. Along these lines, Taylor et al. (1984) hypothesized that "changes in the direction of behavior will only occur when the individual attributes past performance to incorrect behavioral strategies" and that "if past failure is attributed to a noncontrollable factor, then changing behavior would not be seen as potentially effective" (p. 107). Whereas the evaluative dimension of feedback is important for the comparison process, it is the descriptive aspect that is important for forming attributions.

Reactions to Positive Discrepancies   In mechanical systems, overshooting a standard is as serious as a negative deviation and results in the same corrective response. In human systems, however, exceeding a standard usually is a desired outcome (Taylor et al., 1984). Carver and Scheier (1981) and Hollenbeck (1989) have suggested that reactions to positive errors will not be as extreme or direct as with a negative error because the dissatisfaction resulting from failing to meet a goal may not be present. Although the reaction to a positive discrepancy may not be as strong, the cognitive processes determining that response should be the same. Given a positive discrepancy, if one feels that the higher level of performance can be maintained and if that level of performance is perceived as more attractive, an upward goal change would be expected. If, however, the SEU of this higher level of performance is not greater than that of the current goal, no such change would be expected. Under these conditions, direct action to reduce the discrepancy is unlikely, but its reduction may occur as the indirect result of directing attention and effort elsewhere (Carver & Scheier, 1981; Hollenbeck, 1989). In some situations, however, the SEU of the higher performance level may be lower, for instance, with a just-in-time inventory system or where there are strong group norms regarding rate busting. In these situations, it is likely that active steps will be taken to reduce the discrepancy.

Assume that a salesperson is well ahead of schedule after the first month in meeting a quarterly sales quota. If the SEU of exceeding the goal is higher than that of meeting the goal, it is likely that the salesperson will raise his or her personal goal and continue the actions that have proven successful. If, however, the SEU of exceeding the quota is about the same as meeting the quota, the salesperson can be expected to retain the current goal. More time may be devoted to nonwork interests or to other dimensions of the job (e.g., increasing product knowledge), the indirect result being lower performance in subsequent months. The third possibility is that the SEU of the higher performance level is lower than the SEU of meeting the goal. The salesperson may, for example, perceive that exceeding the quota will result in higher quotas being set for subsequent quarters, quotas the salesperson may feel unable or unwilling to meet. In such a case, the salesperson will actively try to reduce his or her performance in subsequent quarters, and he or she may even try to distort the first month's performance, perhaps by delaying reports of some of the first month's sales.

Hierarchical Nature of Control Loops

As noted earlier, any complex activity requires many subsidiary functions, and a number of theorists have suggested that behavior is hierarchically organized into goal-subgoal relationships (e.g., Powers, 1973). Locke, Cartledge, and Knerr (1970) suggested that when individuals have goals on tasks, they will set subgoals according to their perceived instrumentality in achieving the end goal. The force toward an end goal should therefore be related to the force toward subgoals through its influence on the attractiveness of attaining that subgoal. This suggests that a salesperson who does not perceive meeting quarterly sales goals as important for the attainment of higher order goals may quickly abandon those subgoals in the face of adversity.

It has been suggested that the lower the subgoal, the more flexible the individual will be in altering it in response to perceived discrepancies (Powers, 1973). Campion and Lord (1982), for example, found that following failure, increasing exam goals (a subgoal) and increasing effort (a subsubgoal) were common student responses, whereas lowering course grades (the end goal) occurred only after repeated failure. One explanation is that lower level goals typically will have lower SEUs because their attractiveness is based largely on their instrumentality in achieving higher level goals. This hierarchical structure also suggests that when goal progress is impeded or when a goal is changed, other goals in the hierarchy will require adjustment. If initial subgoals are not met, subsequent subgoals may be raised in the hopes of catching up and eventually meeting the higher order goal (Campion & Lord, 1982). The other alternative is to lower the higher order goal and, correspondingly, to lower the remaining subgoals.

Individuals have multiple goal hierarchies for the multiple work and nonwork roles they face. The operation of work-related goal hierarchies cannot be completely understood independent of nonwork hierarchies. When an individual has competing goals, either within or across goal hierarchies, there is competition for the individual's time and effort (Miller et al., 1960). It is therefore important to understand where, both within and across goal hierarchies, a person will focus his or her attention. It has been suggested that within Power's (1973) hierarchy attention typically is directed at the program level because behavioral sequences (i.e., scripts) are initiated at this level (Carver & Scheier, 1981; Hollenbeck, 1989; Schank & Abelson, 1977). That is, a person's attention should be directed toward the level just above his or her operating script. If that script were interrupted, attention would shift down a level. If, for example, a salesperson is employing a closing-a-deal script with a customer, his or her attention will be directed elsewhere, perhaps to planning the rest of the day's schedule. If, however, that script is interfered with, the salesperson's attention will shift to dealing with the customer. Being able to perform tasks automatically allows the diversion of attention from those tasks to other concerns, either higher in the same goal hierarchy or in some other hierarchy.

With competing goals, attention will be directed to the most salient hierarchy at the time (Taylor & Fiske, 1978). Factors influencing salience include situational cues (Taylor et al., 1984), the relative importance of the goals, and the magnitude of the perceived discrepancies. If a salesperson perceives equal discrepancies in goals for completing paperwork and making follow-up calls, and if follow-up calls are viewed as more important, the salesperson will focus his or her attention on calls rather than paperwork. Likewise, if the larger discrepancy is perceived in spending time with family than in meeting a sales quota (assuming at least equal importance), it is likely that the salesperson would attend to the nonwork hierarchy. Schank and Abelson's (1977) notion of script distractions also is relevant here. A script distraction changes the relative salience of goals, and attention will shift to the hierarchy causing the distraction. For example, if a salesperson employing a work-related script receives a phone call indicating that his or her child is ill, the script will be abandoned and his or her attention will shift from the salesperson hierarchy to a parent hierarchy.

Summary of the Integrated Model

Numerous hypotheses have been implicitly and explicitly suggested in delineating the proposed model. These propositions are reiterated in Table 1. Also, the primary theoretical perspectives that the hypotheses were derived from are indicated in this table. In viewing these hypotheses, note that the primary value of a metatheory is its ability to account for the hypotheses of the perspectives it incorporates. Although this is clearly the case, the majority of the hypotheses presented are derived from control theory. In addition, many of these have not been stated in previous models.

COMPARISONS WITH OTHER MODELS

The model in Figure 2 is an integration of several theories of motivation as well as several previous control theory models. The specific ways that the current model integrates those models and theories are examined below.

Previous Control Theory Models

In presenting the integrated control theory model, the models of Carver and Scheier, Lord, Taylor, and Hollenbeck have been referred to frequently. To indicate precisely how those models differ from each other and how the current model combines their positions, these models are contrasted in Table 2. These models differ primarily in (a) their orientation, (b) where the decision mechanism is placed, (c) the nature of the decision processes, (d) the determinants of conscious versus unconscious processing, (e) the primary consequences of the decision mechanism, (f) the general and specific responses to discrepancies, and (g) their treatment of positive discrepancies. As is evident in Table 2, the current model consolidates the different positions of the previous models on these issues.

Motivation Theories Explicitly Integrated

TABLE 1

SUMMARY OF PROPOSITIONS DERIVED FROM THE MODEL AND THEIR ORIGINS

Proposition 1: Difficult goals will lead to higher levels of performance (G).

Proposition 2: Specific goals will lead to higher levels of performance and less performance variance across individuals (G).

Proposition 3: Goals and feedback interact in influencing performance (C).

Proposition 4: Goal setting in the absence of feedback will result in feedback-seeking behavior, and feedback in the absence of goals will result in spontaneous goal setting (C).

Proposition 5: Specific feedback will lead to higher levels of performance (F) and less performance variance across individuals (C).

Proposition 6: Moderately frequent feedback (F) and moderately short-term goals (C) will result in the greatest performance improvements.

Proposition 7: Overly specific feedback (F) and overly specific goals (C) will be dysfunctional in novel settings.

Proposition 8: The same factors initiate feedback-seeking behavior and spontaneous goal setting (C).

Proposition 9: The same factors relate to the acceptance of feedback and the acceptance of goals (C).

Proposition 10: Whether or not feedback regarding a goal is noticed depends upon both the importance of the goal and self-focus (C).

Proposition 11: The salience of feedback will influence whether or not it is processed consciously (I).

Proposition 12: The salience of an error and the way feedback was processed will influence whether or not the discrepancy is consciously perceived (I).

Proposition 13: If no error is detected, neither goals nor behavior will change. If an error is perceived, a response will be initiated to try and correct it (C).

Proposition 14: If a script exists for a discrepancy, that script will be enacted. If a script is unavailable or interrupted, the decision process will shift to one of conscious problem solving (I).

Proposition 15: Goal setting is more effective when scripted responses are available (C).

Proposition 16: When consciously responding to errors, individuals will embark on attributional searches (A).

Proposition 17: Attributions to stable causes will lead to greater changes in outcome expectancies than attributions to unstable causes, positive shifts following positive errors, negative following negative errors (A).

Proposition 18: The decision to persist versus the decision to withdraw is a function of the SEU of goal attainment, as is the initial choice of a goal (E).

Proposition 19: The SEU of goal attainment is a multiplicative function of outcome expectancies and the attractiveness of goal attainment (E).

Proposition 20: The judgments that determine SEU are influenced by a host of individual and situational factors (E).

Proposition 21: The SEU of goal attainment is related to goal commitment, and changes in SEU relate to changes in commitment (E).

Proposition 22: When the SEU of a goal becomes less than the SEU of an alternative goal, the individual will change goals (E).

Proposition 23: Cognitive changes are less likely to occur initially than are behavioral changes, and changes in goals are less likely to occur initially than are changes in commitment (C).

Proposition 24: Causal attributions to the amount of effort expended or the distribution of that effort will be related to subsequent changes in effort expenditure or distribution (A).

Proposition 25: Individuals employ the same processes in reacting to positive discrepancies as to negative discrepancies (C).

Proposition 26: The SEU of an end goal will influence the SEU of the subgoal through its influence on the attractiveness of the subgoal's attainment (E).

Proposition 27: Within a goal hierarchy, higher order goals have higher SEUs than do lower order goals and, therefore, are more resistant to change (E).

Proposition 28: Any change in a goal will result

TABLE 1
SUMMARY OF PROPOSITIONS DERIVED FROM THE MODEL AND THEIR ORIGINS *(CONTINUED)*

in accompanying changes in lower and/or same-level goals to maintain equilibrium in the hierarchy (C).

Proposition 29: People have multiple goal hierarchies reflecting multiple role demands (C).

Proposition 30: Attention is given to the most salient hierarchy at a particular time (C).

Proposition 31: The relative importance of the

end-goal and the magnitude of the perceived discrepancy influence the saliency of a goal hierarchy (C).

Proposition 32: Within a hierarchy, attention is at the level above an operating script (C).

Proposition 33: If there is a distraction from a script, attention will be shifted to the hierarchy causing the distraction (C).

Note: Letters in parentheses indicate the primary theoretical perspective from which the hypothesis is derived: A = attribution theory, C = control theory, E = expectancy theory, F = feedback, G = goal setting, and I = information processing.

Goal Setting Adopting a control theory framework provides explanations for important aspects of goal setting, including the origins of personal goals, the importance of goal commitment, and the ways that goal characteristics (e.g., specificity, difficulty) affect behavior (Campion & Lord, 1982). Control theory also addresses goal-setting issues that, although identified as important, have been virtually unexplored (Locke et al., 1981). These include the existence and interplay of subgoals, multiple competing goals, goal hierarchies, task strategies, and the modification of goals over time. These processes also highlight control theory's conceptualization of goals as dynamic antecedents of behavior (Campion & Lord, 1982).

Feedback Control theory, similarly, can account for findings in the feedback literature, for example, the positive relationships between specificity and frequency of feedback and performance (Ilgen et al., 1979). The model presented here also takes into consideration many other aspects from feedback research, including multiple dimensions of feedback, multiple sources for feedback, feedback-seeking behavior, selective perception of feedback, and conscious and unconscious processing of feedback. In addition, control theory predicts the goal by feedback interaction consistently found in the literature and suggests that goals and feedback are dual elements of a single motivational process.

Expectancy Theory A criticism of expectancy theory has been its inability to account for meaningful amounts of variation in behavior (Campbell & Pritchard, 1976). Expectancy theory is not, however, designed to predict actual behavior but the force to act (Parker & Dyer, 1976). It is better suited, therefore, to account for intentions (i.e., goals) than either effort or performance. Expectancy theory also has been criticized as being overly rational for most situations, and the current model suggests such processes are brought into play only in certain circumstances. In discussing the role of expectancy theory, a fairly simple version has been employed (i.e., outcome expectancy × attractiveness). More complex SEU models (e.g., Lawler,

TABLE 2
A COMPARISON OF PREVIOUS CONTROL THEORY MODELS AND THE PROPOSED MODEL

Issue	Cybernetics	Carver & Scheier's	Lord's	Taylor's	Hollenbeck's	Current Model
Orientation	Mechanical Systems	Self-Regulation	Goal-Setting Processes	Feedback Processes	Organizational Behavior	Motivation
Placement of the Decision Mechanism	No decision mechanism	Outside the feedback loop, initiated when the loop is interrupted	Within the feedback loop	Same as Lord's	Same as Carver & Scheier's	Within the feedback loop (Box 10)
Decision Processes	Not applicable	Unconscious: Routinized response Conscious: Outcome expectancies Attributions	Unconscious: Routinized choice Conscious: Action-first choice Choice avoidance Rational choice	Unconscious: Automatic processing Conscious: Attributions Expectancy beliefs	Same as Carver & Scheier's	Unconscious: Scripted response Conscious: Attributions Subjective expected utility
Determinants of Conscious Processing	Not applicable	Interruption of the feedback loop (difficulty in meeting the goal)	Familiarity of mean-end relations Frequency of environmental feedback	Familiarity with the situation Size of discrepancy Salience of feedback	Not specifically addressed	Familiarity with the situation Discrepancy salience Salience of feedback
Primary Consequence of Decision Processes	Not applicable	Persistence versus withdrawal	Cognitive versus behavioral response	Same as Lord's	Same as Carver & Scheier's	Persistence versus withdrawal; If persistence, cognitive versus behavioral response

Responses to Perceived Discrepancies	Mechanical	Behavioral: Persistence versus withdrawal Affective: Satisfaction	Behavioral: Amount of effort Change strategy Cognitive: Change standard Distort feedback	Behavioral: Direction of effort Amount of effort Persist versus quit React against the feedback system Cognitive: Discredit feedback Alter expectancies Change standards Affective: Satisfaction	Behavioral: Absenteeism Voluntary turnover Affective: Satisfaction Organizational Commitment	Behavioral: Direction of effort Amount of effort React against system Cognitive: Distort feedback Change goal commitment Change goals
Positive Versus Negative Discrepancies	Reactions to positive discrepancies are treated in the same manner as negative discrepancies	Reactions to positive discrepancies may not be as extreme or direct as for negative discrepancies, but the processes are the same	Reactions to positive discrepancies may not be as important, depending on the nature of the goal	Reactions to positive discrepancies are the same as perceiving no discrepancy	Same as Carver & Scheier's	Same as Carver & Scheier's

1973; Naylor et al., 1980) could easily be employed instead.

Attribution Theory Two major propositions from attribution theory are incorporated in the proposed model, one regarding the reevaluation of outcome expectancies, the other the choice of behavioral responses. There is strong empirical support for the first of these roles from the social psychology literature, but attributions have not proven successful in predicting specific behaviors (Weiner, 1985). One explanation is that attributions have not been measured specifically enough to predict specific actions (Weiner, 1983). The conditional use of attributions in the current model also is consistent with the research about when attributional searches are most likely to occur.

Other Theories and Constructs Integrated

Social Learning Theory Some authors, interested in self-regulation, have built upon social learning (or social-cognitive) theory rather than control theory. There are a number of parallels between these two perspectives, including the similarities between efficacy expectations and outcome expectancies alluded to earlier. According to social learning theory, motivation involves a cognitive process in which goals are compared with knowledge about one's performance (Bandura, 1977, 1986; Bandura & Cervone, 1983, 1986). In addition, perceived negative discrepancies are viewed as creating dissatisfaction and motivating corrective changes. Also, according to social learning theory, people process, weigh, and integrate diverse sources of information concerning their capabilities, and they regulate their behavioral choices and effort expenditure accordingly. All of the above positions are consistent with the proposed model. In addition, social comparison is explicitly recognized in the proposed model as a situational factor affecting outcome expectancies and, in turn, goal choice.

Other Theories of Motivation To the extent that other theories of motivation have been integrated into the four perspectives incorporated into the proposed model, those theories can be assimilated. For example, Lawler (1973) and others have argued that expectancy theory can explain equity theory concerns if perceived equity is explicitly recognized as a factor affecting the attractiveness of outcomes. Similar arguments have been made regarding need theories. Need theories generally hold that behavior is motivated to satisfy some basic need, be it need for achievement or the need to self-actualize. According to expectancy theory, outcomes become attractive when they can be used to satisfy such needs (Vroom, 1964). In addition, goal-setting theory has explicitly recognized needs and values as influencing goal choice (Locke et al., 1981). A final example would be the arguments of those who have claimed that findings from reinforcement theory can be explained by goal setting and feedback (e.g., Locke, 1977).

Satisfaction As is evident in Table 2, control theory also predicts affective reactions. These reactions depend primarily on the direction and magnitude of the goal-performance discrepancy and the importance of the goal (Taylor et al., 1984).

Typically, feedback indicating that one is at or beyond the standard will yield positive emotions, whereas perceiving one is below standard will result in negative affect (Locke et al., 1970; Taylor et al., 1984). The more valued the goal, the stronger the reaction. Outcome expectancies and attributions also have been hypothesized to moderate the magnitude of the resulting emotions. If having perceived a negative discrepancy, one maintains a high outcome expectancy, dissatisfaction will be considerably less than if the expectancy is low (Carver & Scheier, 1981). Regarding attributions, emotional reactions are thought to be amplified when success or failure is attributed to internal causes and diminished when attributions are external (Weiner, Russell, & Lerman, 1979).

Escalation to Commitment   According to Staw (1982), escalation of commitment to a failing course of action may occur when there are a series of goal-directed behaviors, negative feedback, and the opportunity to commit further effort to goal attainment. These components certainly are present in the current model. Carver and Scheier (1982) similarly discussed the dysfunctional consequences of individuals who remain committed to standards that cannot be obtained. Such a reaction occurs when expectancies remain unrealistically high following failure. This could result from selective perception of feedback, distortion of feedback, and/or inaccurate attributions for failure. Cognitive dissonance theory (Festinger, 1957) would suggest that individuals use responses such as these to reduce the dissonance following disconfirmed expectancies, rather than admit that an inappropriate goal was chosen.

Other Constructs   The hypotheses regarding physical and mental withdrawal have implications for organizational withdrawal behaviors such as organizational commitment, absenteeism, and turnover, and Hollenbeck's (1989) model focuses on such behaviors. In addition, many models of these withdrawal behaviors (e.g., Mowday, Porter, & Steers, 1982; Steers & Rhodes, 1978) include the affective and cognitive elements discussed in the proposed model. The elaborated operation of the proposed feedback loop also is compatible with theories of social cognition, information processing, and decision making. Examples include the encoding of behavioral specifications, the coexistence of controlled and automatic processes, and goal-directed, script-based responses.

Other Levels of Analysis   Even though the proposed model is concerned solely with personal goals, this is not a serious limitation. It has been argued that all concepts of motivation are essentially concepts of self-regulation (Bandura, 1986; Carver & Scheier, 1981; Manz, 1986). Furthermore, often the effects of externally originating goals are recognized as mediated by personal goals (e.g., Garland, 1983). Thus, another advantage of the control theory perspective is that it shifts the focus of attention not only to the individual but also to the individual's self-regulation of his or her behavior. In addition, the proposed model, and control theory in general, could be modified and employed at other levels of analysis (e.g., work groups, organizations) because goals and feedback are also relevant at those levels.

CONCLUSIONS

Control theory is well suited as a framework for the development of a metatheory for understanding work motivation. An integrated model of motivation should aid future conceptual development, research, and application by providing a more general framework for understanding motivation while guiding the refinement of the component theories. The model presented here is a useful heuristic that provides an integration on two levels. First, a control theory perspective explicitly integrates goal setting, feedback, expectancy, and attribution theories as well as implicitly integrating several other theories and constructs such as social learning theory, need theories, and information processing. Second, the proposed model unifies the work of previous authors who have applied control theory to motivated behavior. Even in its expanded form, control theory remains a simple framework while encompassing all of these theories, constructs, and perspectives.

In addition, a control theory model of motivation is advantageous for several other reasons. First, it focuses attention on the cognitive processes underlying motivation. In articulating these cognitive processes, control theory provides a structure for the simultaneous application of different cognitive processes at different levels of attention. Hierarchically organized feedback loops provide an explanation of how automatic and conscious processes operate simultaneously to initiate and direct behavior. Second, control theory focuses attention on the self-regulation of behavior. Although most motivational theories are aimed at understanding the behavior of individuals, they generally emphasize the effects of external influences (e.g., providing goals, incentives) on motivation, not the individual's self-regulation in response to those influences. Both of the above further differentiate the integrated model from the component theories it incorporates.

Finally, numerous propositions can be derived from the integrated model regarding (a) the nature of goals and feedback; (b) cognitive, behavioral, and affective reactions over time to goals, performance, and feedback; and (c) the role of attributions, expectancies, and goal hierarchies in determining those reactions. These propositions, as a whole, could not be derived without the control theory perspective (Lord & Hanges, 1987). As is evident in Table 1, although some of the hypotheses could be derived from expectancy theory and others from attribution, feedback, or goal setting, none of these theories alone can account for all of the propositions. Furthermore, none of those four theories, either alone or in concert, are well suited to predict the functioning of goal hierarchies, multiple and competing goals, or the modifications of goals over time.

Therefore, even though the current model integrates several other motivational perspectives, it is much more than a simple aggregation of the perspectives it incorporates. This is evident in the number of hypotheses presented in Table 1 that are unique to control theory. As a result, control theory generates research programs that would not emerge from either goal-setting or the other component theories. Examples of these programs would include examining the links between motivation and learning (Lord & Kernan, 1987) and between work attitudes and goal-based withdrawal behaviors (Hollenbeck, 1989). Control theory also generates research examining the functioning of goal hierarchies, multiple and competing goals, and the modifications of goals over time. Though the hypotheses derived from these programs may not contradict the component theories, it is likely that they would not emanate from those perspectives.

Similarly, the propositions in Table 1, taken as a whole, could not have been derived from any one of the previous control theory models. This is partly because of the differing orientations of those authors, and it is also because of the unique contributions of the current model. Specifically, the current model goes beyond past control theory models in specifying (a) the implications of viewing goals and feedback as dual processes; (b) the nature, determinants, and consequences of conscious and unconscious information processing; (c) the role of expectancy and attribution theories; (d) the antecedents of and relationship between behavioral and cognitive reactions; and (e) the operations of goal hierarchies and the direction of attention within hierarchies and across competing hierarchies. The result is an integrated, dynamic, and parsimonious model that focuses on self-regulation and the underlying cognitive mechanisms of motivation.

REFERENCES

Ajzen, I., & Fishbein, M. (1977) Attitude-behavior relations: Theoretical analysis and review of empirical research. *Psychological Bulletin,* 84, 888–918.

Ammons, R. B. (1956) Effects of knowledge of performance: A survey and tentative theoretical formulation. *Journal of General Psychology,* 54, 279–299.

Ashford, S. J. (1986) Feedback seeking in individual adaptation: A resource perspective. *Academy of Management Journal*, 29, 465–487.

Ashford, S. J., & Cummings, L. L. (1983) Feedback as an individual resource: Personal strategies of creating information. *Organizational Behavior and Human Performance,* 32, 370–398.

Bandura, A. (1977) Self-efficacy: Toward a unifying theory of behavioral change. *Psychological Review,* 84, 191–215.

Bandura, A. (1986) *Social foundations of thought and action: A social-cognitive view.* Englewood Cliffs, NJ: Prentice-Hall.

Bandura, A., & Cervone, D. (1983) Self-evaluation and self-efficacy mechanisms governing the motivational effects of goal systems. *Journal of Personality and Social Psychology,* 45, 1017–1028.

Bandura, A., & Cervone, D. (1986) Differential engagement of self-reactive mechanisms governing the motivational effects of goal systems. *Organizational Behavior and Human Decision Processes,* 38, 92–113.

Bandura, A., & Schunk, D. H. (1981) Cultivating competence, self-efficacy, and intrinsic motivation through proximal self-motivation. *Journal of Personality and Social Psychology,* 41, 586–598.

Becker, L. J. (1978) Joint effects of feedback and goal setting on performance: A field study of residential energy conservation. *Journal of Applied Psychology,* 63, 428–433.

Campbell, D. J. (1982) Determinants of choice of goal difficulty level: A review of situational and personality influences. *Journal of Occupational Psychology,* 55, 79–95.

Campbell, J. P., & Pritchard, R. D. (1976) Motivation theory in industrial and organizational psychology. In M. D. Dunnette (Ed.), *Handbook of industrial and organizational psychology* (pp. 63–130). Chicago: Rand McNally.

Campion, M. A., & Lord, R. G. (1982) A control systems conceptualization of the goal setting and changing process. *Organizational Behavior and Human Performance*, 30, 265–287.

Carver, C. S. (1979) A cybernetic model of self-attention. *Journal of Personality and Social Psychology*, 37, 1251–1281.

Carver, C. S., Blaney, P. H., & Scheier, M. F. (1979) Reassertion and giving up: The interactive role of self-directed attention and outcome expectancy. *Journal of Personality and Social Psychology*, 37, 1859–1870.

Carver, C. S., & Scheier, M. F. (1981) *Attention and self-regulation: A control theory approach to human behavior.* New York: Springer-Verlag.

Carver, C. S., & Scheier, M. F. (1982) Control theory: A useful conceptual framework for personality—social, clinical, and health psychology. *Psychological Bulletin*, 92, 111–135.

Earley, P. C., Ekegren, G., & Connolly, T. (1987) *Goals, strategy development, and task performance: Toward boundary conditions for the goal setting model.* Unpublished manuscript, University of Arizona, Tucson.

Edwards, W. (1961) Behavioral decision theory. *Annual Review of Psychology*, 12, 473–498.

Elwell, L. J., & Grindley, G. C. (1938) The effect of knowledge of results on learning and performance: A coordinated movement of the two hands. *British Journal of Psychology*, 39, 39–54.

Festinger, L. A. (1957) *A theory of cognitive dissonance.* Evanston, IL: Row, Peterson.

Garland, H. (1983) Influence of ability, assigned goals, and normative information on personal goals and performance: A challenge to the goal attainability assumption. *Journal of Applied Psychology*, 68, 20–30.

Greller, M. M., & Herold, D. M. (1975) Sources of feedback: A preliminary investigation. *Organizational Behavior and Human Performance*, 13, 244–256.

Herold, D. M., & Greller, M. M. (1977) Feedback: The definition of a construct. *Academy of Management Journal*, 20, 142–147.

Hollenbeck, J. R. (1989) Control theory and the perception of work environments: The effects of focus of attention on affective and behavioral reactions to work. *Organizational Behavior and Human Decision Processes*.

Hollenbeck, J. R., & Brief, A. P. (1988) Self-regulation in the workplace: Towards a unified approach to understanding worker attitudes and behaviors. In R. Schuler (Ed.), *Readings in personnel and human resource management* (pp. 496–508). St. Paul, MN: West.

Hollenbeck, J. R., & Klein, H. J. (1987) Goal commitment and the goal setting process: Problems, prospects and proposals for future research. *Journal of Applied Psychology*, 72, 212–220.

Hollenbeck, J. R., & Williams, C. R. (1987) Goal importance, self-focus, and the goal setting process. *Journal of Applied Psychology*, 72, 204–211.

Ilgen, D. R., Fisher, C. D., & Taylor, M. S. (1979) Consequences of individual feedback on behavior in organizations. *Journal of Applied Psychology*, 64, 349–371.

Ilgen, D. R., & Klein, H. J. (1989) Organizational behavior. In M. R. Rosenzweig & L. W. Porter (Eds.), *Annual review of psychology* (Vol. 40). Palo Alto, CA: Annual Reviews.

Kelley, H. H. (1973) The process of causal attribution. *American Psychologist*, 28, 107–128.

Klein, H. J., Whitener, E. M., & Ilgen, D. R. (1988) *The role of goal specificity in the goal setting process.* Unpublished manuscript, Ohio State University, Columbus.

Landy, F. J., & Becker, L.J. (1987) Motivation theory reconsidered. *Research in Organizational Behavior*, 9, 1–38.

Lawler, E. E. (1973) *Motivation in work organizations.* Belmont, CA: Brooks/Cole.

Leskovec, E. W. (1967) A guide for discussing the performance appraisal. *Personnel Journal*, 46, 150–152.

Lewin K., Dembo, T., Festinger, L., & Sears, P. S. (1944) Level of aspiration. In J. J. Hunt (Ed.), *Personality and the behavior disorders* (pp. 333–378). New York: Roland Press.

Lichtenstein, E. H., & Brewer, W. F. (1980) Memory for goal-directed events. *Cognitive Psychology*, 12, 412–445.

Locke, E. A. (1977) The myths of behavior modification in industry. *Academy of Management Review*, 2, 543–553.

Locke, E. A., & Bryan, J. F. (1967) Performance goals as determinants of level of performance and boredom. *Journal of Applied Psychology*, 51, 120–130.

Locke, E. A., Cartledge, N. D., & Knerr, C. S. (1970) Studies of the relationships between satisfaction, goal setting and performance. *Organizational Behavior and Human Performance*, 5, 135–158.

Locke, E. A., Chah, D., Harrison, S., & Lustgarten, N. (1989) Separating the effects of goal specificity from goal difficulty. *Organizational Behavior and Human Performance.*

Locke, E. A., Latham, G. P., & Erez, M. (1988) The determinants of goal commitment. *Academy of Management Review*, 13, 23–39.

Locke, E. A., Shaw, K. N., Saari, L. M., & Latham, G. P. (1981) Goal setting and task performance: 1969–1980. *Psychological Bulletin*, 90, 125–152.

Lord, R. G., & Hanges, P. J. (1987) A control systems model of organizational motivation: Theoretical development and applied implications. *Behavioral Science*, 32, 161–178.

Lord, R. G., & Kernan, M. C. (1987) Scripts as determinants of purposeful behavior in organizations. *Academy of Management Review*, 12, 265–277.

Manz, C. C. (1986) Self-leadership: Toward an expanded theory of self-influence processes in organizations. *Academy of Management Review*, 11, 585–600.

March, J. G., & Simon, H. A. (1958) *Organizations.* New York: Wiley.

Matsui, T., Okada, A., & Mizuguchi, R. (1981) Expectancy theory prediction of the goal theory postulate: The harder the goals, the higher the performance. *Journal of Applied Psychology*, 66, 54–58.

McMahan, I. D. (1973) Relationships between causal attributions and expectancy of success. *Journal of Personality and Social Psychology*, 28, 108–114.

Mento, A. J., Cartledge, N. D., & Locke, E. A. (1980) Maryland vs. Michigan vs. Minnesota: Another look at the relationship of expectancy and goal difficulty to task performance. *Organizational Behavior and Human Performance*, 25, 419–440.

Mento, A. J., Steel, R. P., & Karren, R. J. (1987) A meta-analytic study of the effects of goal setting on task performance: 1966–1984. *Organizational Behavior and Human Decision Processes*, 39, 52–83.

Miller, G. A., Galanter, E., & Pribram, K. H. (1960) *Plans and the structure of behavior.* New York: Holt, Rinehart & Winston.

Mowday, R. T., Porter, L. W., & Steers, R. M. (1982) *Employee-organization linkages.* New York: Academic Press.

Naylor, J. D., Pritchard, R. D., & Ilgen, D. R. (1980) *A theory of behavior in organizations.* New York: Academic Press.

Parker, D. F., & Dyer, L. (1976) Expectancy theory as a within-person behavioral choice model: An empirical test of some conceptual and methodological refinements. *Organizational Behavior and Human Performance*, 17, 97–117.

Pinder, C. (1984) *Work motivation.* Glenview, IL: Scott, Foresman.

Powers, W. T. (1973) *Behavior: The control of perception.* Chicago: Aldine.

Pyszczynski, T. A., & Greenberg, J. (1981) Role of disconfirmed expectations in the instigation of attributional processing. *Journal of Personality and Social Psychology*, 40, 31–38.

Schank, R., & Abelson, R. (1977) *Scripts, plans, goals, and understanding.* New York: Halsted.

Shiffrin, R. M., & Schneider, W. (1977) Controlled and automatic human information processing: II. Perceptual learning, automatic attending, and a general theory. *Psychological Review,* 84, 127–190.

Staw, B. M. (1982) Counterforces to change. In P. S. Goodman & Associates (Eds.), *Change in organizations* (pp. 87–121). San Francisco: Jossey-Bass.

Steenbarger, B. N., & Aderman, D. (1979) Objective self-awareness as a nonaversive state: Effect of anticipating discrepancy reduction. *Journal of Personality,* 47, 330–339.

Steers, R. M., & Rhodes, S. R. (1978) Major influences on employee attendance: A process model. *Journal of Applied Psychology,* 63, 391–407.

Taylor, M. S. (1983) *A control theory integration of performance goal and performance feedback research: Current findings, practical implications and future research issues.* Symposium presented at the meeting of the Academy of Management, Dallas.

Taylor, M. S., Fisher, C. D., & Ilgen, D. R. (1984) Individuals' reactions to performance feedback in organizations: A control theory perspective. *Research in Personnel and Human Resources Management,* 2, 81–124.

Taylor, S. E., & Fiske, S. T. (1978) Salience, attention, and attribution: Top of the head phenomena. In L. Berkowitz (Ed.), *Advances in experimental social psychology* (Vol. 11, pp. 249–288). New York: Academic Press.

Vroom, V. H. (1964) *Work and motivation.* New York: Wiley.

Weiner, B. (1983) Some methodological pitfalls in attributional research. *Journal of Educational Research,* 75, 530–543.

Weiner, B. (1985) An attributional theory of achievement motivation and emotion. *Psychological Review,* 92, 548–573.

Weiner, B., Frieze, I., Kukla, A., Reed, L., Rest, S., & Rosenbaum, R. M. (1971) Perceiving the causes of success and failure. In E. Jones, D. Kanouse, H. Kelley, R. Nisbett, S. Valins, & B. Weiner (Eds.), *Attribution: Perceiving the causes of behavior* (pp. 95–120). Morristown, NJ: General Learning Press.

Weiner, B., Heckhausen, H., Meyer, W., & Cook, R. E. (1972) Causal ascriptions and achievement behavior: A conceptual analysis of effort and reanalysis of locus of control. *Journal of Personality and Social Psychology,* 21, 239–248.

Weiner, B., Russell, D., & Lerman, D. (1979) Affective consequences of causal ascriptions. In J. H. Harvey, W. J. Ickes, & R. F. Kidd (Eds.), *New directions in attribution research* (Vol. 2, pp. 59–90). Hillsdale, NJ: Erlbaum.

Weiner, N. (1948) *Cybernetics: Control and communication in the animal and the machine.* Cambridge: MIT Press.

Wicklund, R. A. (1975) Objective self-awareness. In L. Berkowitz (Ed.), *Advances in experimental social psychology* (Vol. 8, pp. 233–275). New York: Academic Press.

Wong, P. T. P., & Weiner, B. (1981) When people ask "why" questions, and the heuristic of attributional search. *Journal of Personality and Social Psychology,* 40, 650–663.

Wood, R. E., & Locke, E. A. (1986) *Goal setting and strategy effects on complex tasks: A theoretical analysis.* Unpublished manuscript, University of New South Wales.

Wood, R. E., Mento, A. J., & Locke, E. A. (1987) Task complexity as a moderator of goal effects: A meta-analysis. *Journal of Applied Psychology,* 72, 416–425.

Meaning, Self and Motivation in Organizations
Boas Shamir

INTRODUCTION

Current reviews of work motivation theories (Pinder 1984; Locke and Henne 1986; Landy and Becker 1987) are unanimous in their dissatisfaction with the 'state of the art'. Locke and Henne write: 'of all the subject areas in organizational behaviour and industrial organizational psychology, motivation has consistently been one of the most confusing. Theories abound, yet somehow they do not seem to fit in with either research findings or with each other' (1986: 1). Pinder has observed: 'We seem to be adding increasingly smaller increments to our base of knowledge about work motivation and behaviour, as more and more research is conducted into the topic' (1984: 307). Following an earlier review by Campbell and Pritchard (1976) he also notes that existing work motivation theories are under-utilized by managers.

Yet all the above-mentioned reviews suggest that the problem is not with the theories themselves, but with their implicit claim to be universally applicable. According to these reviews, advances in the field are likely to come from the reconceptualization of current principles and the reordering of current theories, rather than from the addition of more theories or the empirically based refinement of existing theories. This view is stated most strongly by Landy and Becker, who claim that we have more than enough theories of motivation and more than enough data on motivational phenomena. 'We need to be more clever with what we already have.' (Landy and Becker 1987: 3).

'What we already have' is defined by the above-mentioned reviews, to consist mainly of need theories (Maslow 1954; McClelland 1985), equity or social comparison theory (Adams 1965), expectancy theory (Vroom 1964), reinforcement theory (Hamner 1975), goal-setting theory (Locke and Latham 1984) and a task-centered version of intrinsic motivation theory (Hackman and Oldham 1980). The reader's general familiarity with these models is assumed.

It is the thesis of this paper that 'what we already have' is not enough, and current models should be supplemented by a self-concept based theory of work motivation. The paper discusses some of the shortcomings of current models stemming from their overreliance on hedonistic assumptions and an instrumental model of man: namely, their bias toward individualistic behaviours in individualistic cultures, their inapplicability to 'weak' situations (Mischel 1973), their emphasis on predicting discrete acts and their oversight of the role of values and moral obligations in work motivation. Following this discussion it is argued that, in order to correct these biases, current thinking should be expanded by adding a self-concept based model of work motivation grounded in assumptions derived from the literature on the relationships between the self-concept and behaviour. The assumptions underlying such a model are then presented followed by a series of propositions about work motivation and some research suggestions.

From *Organization Studies*, 1991, 12(3), 405–424. Reprinted by permission.

SOME SHORTCOMINGS OF CURRENT WORK MOTIVATION THEORIES

An Individualistic Bias

Most psychological theories of motivation, both early and contemporary, have their roots, at least to some extent, in the principle of hedonism (Steers and Porter 1987: 8). Their main focus is on the individual who is assumed to be a rational maximizer of personal utility. As such, they reflect the philosophical and ideological assumptions of the neoclassical paradigm which has dominated both economics and psychology (Etzioni 1988). Need theories differ from other current theories in that they emphasize 'expressive individualism' rather than 'utilitarian individualism' (to use the terms coined by Bellah et al. 1985) but they both focus on individual satisfaction. In contrast, the highly publicized Japanese model of motivation, for instance, stresses attachment to the organization and achievement of organizational goals. A persistent theme dividing the two models is the relative emphasis upon collective versus individual motivation (Staw 1984). Other cultures also emphasize collective concerns more than individual concerns in connection with work motivation (Hofstede 1980). Hence American or Western motivational models may be less valid in other cultures.

Cultural bias, though, is only part of the problem. The over-emphasis on utilitarian individualism in current motivation theories renders many work-related phenomena unexplainable, even in Western cultures. Transformational leadership is a case in point. It has recently been pointed out (Burns 1978; Bass 1985) that, while some leadership effects can be explained by 'transactional' models of leadership, which are based on exchange notions and conform with current motivation models, other leadership effects cannot be accounted for within such models. The main effect attributed to 'transformational' leaders is their ability to persuade followers to transcend their own self-interest for the sake of the team, the organization or some other collective. Such an effect has no place in individualistic utilitarian motivation theories (Shamir et al. 1990). The recent literature on organizational citizenship behaviour (Organ 1988) also points out the need for a more collective oriented theory of work motivation.

A Bias Towards 'Strong' Situations

There is a fundamental situational bias in current cognitive motivation theories. These models stress the importance of clear and specific goals and of reward–performance expectancies for individual motivation. They are useful in situations where goals can be clarified, where there is an abundance of rewards, and where rewards can be closely linked to performance. This is simply not the case in many situations, for instance in the public sector (Perry and Porter 1982) or in cultures where rewards are less abundant, or there is less tolerance of power distance (Hofstede 1980) between individuals, and less tendency or cultural sanction to differentiate among individuals on the basis of their work performance.

Another aspect of the situational bias is even more fundamental. Situations characterized by clear goals, availability of rewards and strong rewards–performance relationship are high in 'situational strength' (Mischel 1973). According to Mischel, 'strong' situations are characterized by well-recognized rules of conduct that constrain behaviour, induce uniform expectancies regarding appropriate response patterns and provide adequate incentives for the performance of these response patterns.

The fundamental problem is that such situations are liable to produce uniformity in behaviour, and therefore dispositional variables such as individual motivation are less likely to be relevant for the explanation of behaviour in those situations (Weiss 1986). In other words, current motivation theories may be particularly useful in situations that strongly determine behaviour and relatively useless in 'weak' situations where the variation in behaviour is both larger and more reflective of variation in individual motivation.

An Emphasis on the Explanation and Prediction of Discrete Behaviours

As Landy and Becker (1987) have argued, current motivation theories do not specify the level of behaviour addressed by them and therefore contain an implicit claim to be equally valid for all categories of behaviour—the broad and the specific, the immediate and the long term, the discrete and the continuous.

This state of affairs is problematic in view of the tendency of current theories to emphasize easily observable and measurable and relatively discrete behaviours. The problem with such a reductionist approach is two-fold: First, in many cases the interest of social scientists and practitioners is not in specific acts, but rather in large units of analysis and complex patterns of behaviour. Second, it leads to judging the validity and usefulness of theories in terms of their ability to explain and predict specific acts. Since the prediction of such acts is enhanced by focusing on immediate antecedents such as 'intentions to behave' in a specific way (Ajzen and Fishbein 1977), or specific goals (Locke and Latham 1984), certain theories and explanations are likely to be judged as being generally more valid in spite of their unproven ability to explain or predict larger patterns of behaviour.

For example, Locke and Henne state: 'The more task specific and closer the concepts (processes) are to the point of action the more valid the theory' (1986: 25). 'Valid' in Locke and Henne's terms means being able to predict what a particular person will do in a specific task situation. But is this what we are always interested in, and are these point-of-action theories equally valid for the prediction of work behaviour patterns that extend over time and situations and may not even have an identifiable 'point-of-action'?

Most conceptions of commitment, in contrast, 'point to a shifting number and range of rather ill-delineated performances rather than to ironclad and numerically constant behaviours having clearly defined parameters that everyone knows' (Marks 1977: 929). Such a 'diffuse' and open-ended concept of commitment may be useless for explaining or predicting specific acts. It may be useful, however, for explaining or predicting longitudinal or horizontal consistency of behaviour around a theme—be it an idea, a value, a person, a relationship, a group or an organization. It is therefore important to distinguish theories of motivation that are concerned with specific acts, from those that are concerned with the repetition or continuation of such acts or those that focus on broader patterns of behaviour containing many different acts performed over time and space, which are nevertheless consistent in the sense of being reflective of a certain theme.

A Limited Concept of Intrinsic Motivation

While there is no single conception of intrinsic motivation in the field of organization behaviour, the majority of current concepts include one or both of the following propositions: (1) that intrinsic motivation stems from the expected pleasure of the activity itself rather than from its results; (2) that intrinsic motivation is based on self-administered rewards rather than on rewards distributed by an external agent. Both assumptions reflect an individualistic hedonistic bias and a thinking in terms of 'outcomes', 'rewards' and 'reinforcements'. Further, both of them incorporate a 'task' focused view of intrinsic motivation. Thus, it has been claimed that intrinsic motivation operates according to the principles of expectancy theory (Staw 1976) and intrinsic 'outcomes' have valences and expectancies associated with them; and that intrinsic outcomes occur, when they occur, immediately upon the performance of the acts that produce them (Pinder 1984).

Even those views that make a stronger distinction between intrinsic and extrinsic motivation based on assumptions about the psychologically gratifying properties of optimal arousal, achievement, competence, increased competence or self-determination, (e.g. Deci and Ryan 1985) tend to be task-oriented and neglect the symbolic and expressive aspects of human beings. They do not acknowledge the possibility that the above-mentioned properties may be absent from the immediate task, and that the performance of this task may not lead to any rewards, not even pleasure, and yet the task would be motivating due to its meaning for the individual, for instance in terms of the affirmation of his or her identity and collective affiliations.

The human capacity to attach meaning to objects, symbols and events is commonly treated as irrelevant or reduced to calculative considerations and global emotions. Excluding the term 'meaning' from the vocabulary of motives, and limiting this vocabulary to 'needs' 'drives' 'rewards' 'outcomes' and 'satisfactions' reflects the view of the person as an entity disconnected from society, without larger concerns than the satisfaction of individual needs (Frankl 1963). Yet there is evidence that even in Western societies one of the major functions of work is to connect the individual to concerns that transcend his own limited personal existence, which therefore cannot be reduced to individual need satisfaction (Jahoda 1979).

The Exclusion of Values and Moral Obligations

Another manifestation of the limited concept of intrinsic motivation is the exclusion of values and moral obligations from current theories of work motivation. The concept of denotic motivation or the motivation to discharge one's moral obligations was introduced to the organizational literature by Schwartz (1983) but has not been adopted by mainstream motivation theories. Values do not constitute a major part of any current work motivation theory. They have probably been rejected by current theories on the basis of their poorly observed relationships with specific behaviours, but it is precisely this characteristic of values, that 'they may be experienced in many different ways in many different situations' (Locke and Henne 1986: 3) that makes them potentially suitable for theories dealing with the molar level of behaviour.

To the extent that values appear in current motivation theories they are conceptualized in terms of order of preferences or of 'what the individual' acts to gain and/or keep', (which is essentially identical to the concept of valence in expectancy theory). What is missing, however, is the sociological concept of values as 'conceptions of the desirable' as distinct from the desired (Kluckhohn 1962). Such a concept of values has little to do with need satisfaction. It is not reflective of what the person wants to get. On the contrary: it demands something of the person. Without such a concept of values it is difficult to account for the motivation to fulfil one's moral obligations (Etzioni 1988), or for individual contributions to collective concerns which cannot be translated into individual rewards (Shamir 1990).

To recapitulate: currently accepted work motivation theories are useful for explaining discrete behaviours in 'strong' situations and individualistic cultures. We need to supplement existing models with theories that can explain behaviour at a more molar level in 'weak' situations and in different cultures. We also need theories that can explain individual sacrifices for collective concerns and can account for the role of values and moral obligations in energizing and directing work behaviour. What follows is an attempt to lay the foundations of such a theory on the basis of the literature on the relationships between the self-concept and behaviour.

PRIOR CONCEPTIONS OF THE RELATIONSHIP BETWEEN THE SELF-CONCEPT AND WORK MOTIVATION

The idea that self-concept is a relevant work motivation construct is not new, but its full implications have not been developed. Katz and Kahn (1966) posited value-expression and self-idealization, which they defined as the motivation to establish and maintain a satisfactory self-concept, as an important motivational pattern in organizations. They referred to 'expressing in words and in acts one's important values and thus identifying oneself and maintaining a satisfactory self-image'. 'As a result, satisfaction accrues to the person from the expression of attitude and behaviour reflecting his or her cherished belief and self-image. The reward is not so much a matter of social recognition as one of establishing one's self-identity, confirming one's notion of the sort of person one sees oneself to be and expressing the values appropriate to the self-concept' (Katz and Kahn 1966: 346). However, they also claimed that the pattern of motivation associated with value expression and self-identification is generally confined to the upper echelons of the organization and that it is only in voluntary organizations that it extends to the rank and file.

Korman (1970) presented two hypotheses derived from cognitive balance or consistency approaches: (1) individuals will be motivated to perform on a task or a job in a manner which is consistent with the self-image with which they approach the task or job situation; and (2) individuals will tend to choose and find most satisfying those job and task roles which are consistent with their self-cognitions. Unfortunately the subsequent development of this theory and related research has focused only on self-esteem and self-perceived competence and their relationships with task performance and satisfaction to the exclusion of other possible implications of the initial propositions (Korman 1977).

Subsequent literature on the relationships between self-concept and work motivation has an instrumental focus on task performance, hence the emphasis in this literature on self-efficacy perceptions (Brief and Aldag 1981), a sense of competence, and self-assessments of abilities, skills and level of performance (Ashford 1989). Undoubtedly, such perceptions, beliefs and assessments are important sources of work motivation and important moderators of other motivational influences. However, recent literature on the self-concept suggests that it includes much more than perceptions of competence or self-efficacy, and that the motivations associated with the self-concept are much wider than a concern with successful task performance.

UNDERLYING MOTIVATIONAL ASSUMPTIONS

In order to develop a self-concept based theory of work motivation it is necessary to supplement the model of humans implied in current work motivation formulations with a model of humans which rests on different assumptions. By doing this, we do not reject the hedonistic–utilitarian model as useless but merely emphasize its insufficiency. A self-concept based theory may rest on the following assumptions, some of which are derived from Bandura's (1986) social cognitive theory, but most of which are derived from the sociological literature on the self-concept, particularly the approach known as 'structural' symbolic interactionism (Stryker 1980):

1 *Humans are not only goal-oriented but also self-expressive.* This means that, in contrast to the current cognitive emphasis in motivation theories, behaviour is not always goal-oriented, instrumental and calculative but is also expressive of feelings, attitudes and self-concepts. Allport (1955) has claimed that the core tendency of human behaviour is not opportunistic functioning but rather functioning in a manner expressive of the self. Making this assumption enables us to account for behaviours that are not instrumental for the individual and do not even contribute to the individual's satisfaction. The most extreme expression of such behaviour is self-sacrifice (Strauss 1969). Such extreme personally destructive acts cannot be explained within the logic of instrumental or hedonistic motivation theories, but only in terms of a different logic in which the individual, by sacrificing himself, makes a statement about his identity and his relationship with a common cause. While the sacrifice of one's life is not a common work behaviour, many smaller sacrifices are regularly made by individuals in work roles.

There is convincing evidence that possessions (Csikszentmihalyi and Rochberg-Halton 1981) and attitudes (Prentice 1987) serve both instrumental and expressive functions for the individual. A large body of research suggests that people choose to spend time in situations that allow them to express their dispositions, attitudes and self-conceptions (Snyder and Ickes 1985). Many studies on consumer behaviour have found a relationship between the consumer's self-concept and product choice (for a review, see Malhotra 1988). We can therefore assume that behaviour may serve instrumental functions or expressive functions and that a full account of motivation requires reference to both.

2 *People are motivated to maintain and enhance their self-esteem and self-worth.* We distinguish between self-esteem and self-worth because they rely on different evaluative standards and thus constitute different (although related) sources of motivation. Self-esteem is based on a sense of competence, power or achievement. Self-worth is

based on a sense of virtue and moral worth and is grounded in norms and values concerning conduct (Gecas 1982). Bandura (1986) makes a similar distinction between self-esteem stemming from evaluations based on competence, and self-esteem based on the possession of attributes that have been culturally invested with positive or negative value. Both competence standards and cultural values are internalized into the self-concept in the form of evaluative standards.

In a similar vein, Higgins et al. (1987) make a distinction between two types of self-guides: the 'ideal self' and the 'ought self'. The ought self is a person's representation of the attributes that he or she believe they should or ought to possess, i.e. their sense of personal duties, obligations and responsibilities.

We can assume that these two types of internalized standards or guides have behavioural consequences: 'Much of (peoples') behaviour is motivated and regulated by internal standards and self-evaluative reactions to their own actions' (Bandura 1986: 20). Thus self-evaluation is an important form of intrinsic motivation. To the extent that these self-evaluations reflect the 'ought self' and hence an anticipated sense of self-worth, they are closely linked to social values as cultural 'conceptions of the desirable' (Kluckhohn 1962).

3 *People are also motivated to retain and increase their sense of self-consistency* (Gecas 1982). The self-concept is thought of as pertaining a multiplicity of meanings or elements (Gordon 1968). Consistency refers to three dimensions: (a) correspondence among components of the self-concept at a given time (Higgins et al. 1987); (b) continuity of the self-concept along the time dimension (Turner 1968); and (c) congruence between the self-concept and behaviour (Burke and Reitzes 1981). People derive a sense of 'meaning' from a sense of unity of their self-concept, from continuity between the past, the present and the projected future (McHugh 1968) and from the correspondence between their behaviour and self-concept.

Some motivation theories (e.g. Rokeach 1979) locate the motivating mechanism in the discrepancy between behavioural or cognitive elements and the person's self-conception, but we can assume that self-consistency is not only a 'corrective' mechanism activated in cases of discrepancy but also a positive motivation. In a sense, the self-concept is an ideology that people attempt to express and validate in their behaviour (Schlenker 1985). The confirmation of the self-concept has long been assumed by 'sociological' social psychologists from G. H. Mead onwards to be one of the fundamental human motives (Turner 1987).

Convincing evidence for the strength of the self-consistency motive is provided by the recent literature on the escalation of commitment to an ineffective course of action. (Brockner et al. 1986). Such an escalation is not only non-instrumental, it is anti-instrumental. ('Throwing good money after bad'). It can be explained by the self-consistency motive. According to this explanation, if the initial behaviour was reflective of the actor's self-concept, and deviations from that line of behaviour are perceived to be inconsistent with the self-concept, the actor will be motivated to continue that line of behaviour regardless of its instrumental consequences. The experiments conducted by Brockner et al. (1986) support this interpretation.

4 *Self-concepts are composed, in part, of identities.* Identities are the second link of the self-concept to society (the first is values). They locate the self in socially recognizable categories. People derive meaning from being linked to social collectives through their identities. Further, identities are expressed in activities that are congruent with the identity. An illustration of this is the identification of alumni with their alma mater which leads to them donating to that institution, to recruiting offspring and others, and to their attendance at functions (Ashforth and Mael 1989).

According to identity theory (Stryker 1980), identities are organized in the self-concept according to a hierarchy of salience. Identity salience is defined as the importance of an identity for defining one's self, relative to other identities held by the individual. This view argues that the higher the salience of an identity within the self-concept the greater its motivational significance. More specifically, the higher an identity on the salience hierarchy, the greater the probability that a person will perceive a given situation as an opportunity to perform in terms of the identity, and the greater the probability that a person will actively seek out opportunities to perform in terms of that identity. There is some empirical support for these propositions (Santee and Jackson 1979; Callero 1985).

A theoretical rationale for these propositions has been provided by Gecas (1986), who suggests the existence of an 'authenticity' motive. According to this suggestion, people are motivated to reflect in their actions their 'true identity', or 'real self'. The more the behaviour reflects salient identities, the more it is perceived by the actor to be an authentic reflection of his/her 'real self'.

5 *Self-concept based behaviour is not always related to clear expectations or to immediate and specific goals.* Rather, it is often guided by imagined possibilities and faith. Levinson (1978) has been concerned with the imagined possibilities of the self as motivating forces. He described 'the Dream' as a personal construction that contains the imagined self associated with a variety of aspirations, goals and values. More recently, Markus and Nurius (1986) have advanced the concept of 'possible selves' as a central motivational construct. According to Markus and Nurius, possible selves represent individuals' ideas of what they might become, what they would like to become and what they are afraid of becoming. An individual's repertoire of possible selves can be viewed as the cognitive and personalized carriers of enduring goals, aspirations, motives, fears and threats and of the associated affective states. Thus they provide a specific self-relevant form, meaning, organization and direction to these dynamics and an essential link between the self-concept and motivation.

It is important to note that as representations of the self in future states, possible selves are views of the self that often have not been verified or confirmed by social experience. Furthermore, according to the theory, this type of self-knowledge does not always exert its influence on the individual in direct proportion to the ease with which it can be formulated or to the likelihood of being realized. For instance, being rich, famous or thin are fairly remote possibilities for many people. The probabilities attached to these events are low, yet they are greater than zero and, as such, can have powerful influence on the individual. Purchasing decisions, for instance, may often be affected by such remote possibilities.

The above stated assumptions lay a foundation for a theory that views work behaviour as self-expressive, self-maintaining and self-guided. Before using these assumptions to derive some propositions about work motivation it is necessary to specify what is to be explained by the theory, the conditions under which it is most likely to be useful, and the people to whom it is most likely to apply.

WHAT IS TO BE EXPLAINED?

It was claimed earlier that one of the weaknesses of current work motivation theories is their failure to specify the level of behaviour they seek to explain. It should therefore be stressed that a self-concept based theory of work motivation is not proposed for the explanation of the motivation to perform a specific task in a specific task situation. Such an explanation would be better achieved by existing motivation theories such as expectancy and goal-setting theory. Rather, it is proposed for the explanation of general work motivation and general job motivation. General work motivation is the motivation to invest efforts in the work role—whatever the specific job one holds at a certain time. General job motivation is the tendency to invest efforts in one's current job. The two are, of course, related—general job motivation is partially a function of general work motivation (for a similar distinction between work involvement and job involvement see Kanungo 1982).

We are interested here in work motivation and job motivation at the molar level—which extends beyond specific tasks and task situations. Thus we assume that certain individuals are consistently more work motivated than other individuals, and that individuals are consistently more motivated in certain jobs than in other jobs and consistently more motivated in certain jobs than in other jobs and consistently more motivated in certain periods of their life than in other periods. In saying 'consistently' we refer to two dimensions—longitudinal (over a time period) and horizontal (across specific situations, specific tasks and specific behaviours). The latter type of consistency has been called coherence (Magnusson and Endler 1977). It refers to the existence of meaningful patterns of behaviour across situations (Snyder and Ickes 1985). In other words, it is assumed that the individual's customary level of attendance, tardiness, work effort, donating personal time to work, etc., reflect, at least in part, a common element of motivation. It is this common element, neglected by most current models of work motivation, that the self-concept based theory endeavours to address.

CONDITIONS UNDER WHICH THE THEORY APPLIES

Another weakness of most existing theories is their failure to specify the conditions under which they apply, and their implicit bias towards 'strong' situations. It should therefore be stressed that the proposed self-concept theory is likely to be particularly useful for the explanation of behaviour in weak situations, i.e. under the following conditions:

1 Goals are not clearly specified. Recall that in many cases they cannot be clearly specified due to the nature of the task or the organization.

2 Means for achieving goals are not clear or not established. This may reflect the unanalyzability of the task or the weakness of technology.

3 External rewards are not clearly related to performance or goal attainment, due to difficulties in performance evaluation, the dearth of external rewards, or cultural and organizational restrictions imposed on the reward distribution system.

The theory is expected to be less useful for the explanation of behaviour in strong situations, except for the explanation of 'deviant', non-conforming behaviour such as 'whistle-blowing'.

INDIVIDUALS TO WHOM THE THEORY APPLIES

A self-concept based theory of work motivation is not likely to apply to all individuals to the same extent. Several individual differences are likely to moderate its applicability. First, individuals may differ on the dimension of 'instrumental' vs. 'expressive' orientation to work (Goldthorpe et al. 1969) and on the related dimension of being 'pragmatic' vs. 'moral' in their social relations (Snyder 1979). To the extent that these are stable characteristics, the theory should apply to 'expressive' and 'moral' individuals more than to 'instrumental' or 'pragmatic' individuals.

Second, individuals differ in the extent to which they have a crystallized self-concept. For instance, a body of literature by Brockner and his colleagues (Brockner 1988) shows that persons who have characteristically high self-esteem have a more crystallized self-concept than low self-esteem workers, and this is an important moderator of individual reactions to job conditions and job-related events. Consequently, we may expect persons with a characteristically high self-esteem to be more likely to express their self-concept on the job, and to behave on the job in a manner which is consistent with their self-concept. A self-concept based theory should be less applicable to low self-esteem individuals with a non-crystallized self-concept. Such individuals are less likely to be guided by their self-concepts and more likely to adapt their self-concepts to the realities of their jobs.

THEORETICAL PROPOSITIONS AND RESEARCH SUGGESTIONS

On the basis of the above stated assumptions, and bearing in mind the above specified situational and individual limitations, we can propose that general job motivation will be enhanced to the extent that:

1 Job-related identities are salient in the person's self-concept.
2 The job offers opportunities for self-esteem enhancement.
3 The job offers opportunities for increased self-worth.
4 Actions required on the job are congruent with the person's self-concept or can be performed in a way which is consistent with the person's self-concept.
5 Career opportunities on the job are congruent with the person's possible selves.

General job motivation will be lower to the extent that:

1 The job or its context contain elements that are detrimental to the person's self-esteem.
2 The job or its context contain elements that are detrimental to the person's self-worth.

These propositions are interactional in the sense of conceiving job motivation to be a function of the interaction between the person's self-concept, the attributes of the job and the context in which it is performed. Accordingly, job motivation is determined by the level of congruence between the job (and its context) and the person's self-concept. Further development and refinement of the theory requires research efforts that try to examine parts of the theory. In order to advance such research we need to be able to measure the self-concept components implied by the theory, to assess the relevant job aspects in a way that would allow us to determine their congruence with the self-concept, and to assess general job performance in a way that would reflect horizontal and longitudinal consistency. The measurement and operationalization difficulties involved in such research are considerable. However, we can draw from the literature some ideas and measures that have not yet been widely applied in the field of organizational behaviour.

General job performance, the dependent variable, can be assessed by a composite of measures of output quantity and quality, absenteeism, tardiness, voluntary unpaid overtime, extra-role cooperative behaviour and other relevant behaviours. This assessment can rely on direct observations as well as on superior, peer and client evaluations. Much attention has been given to the differences between direct measures and performance evaluations and to the differences between various sources of evaluation. More attention should be given to the similarities among them and to their combination into a general job performance measure (Fisher 1980). Statistical methods such as factor analysis can be used to identify the general common factor and to determine the weights that should be assigned to each indicator in the composite score.

Assuming such a composite score is available, our first proposition concerning the relationship between identity salience and job performance can be relatively easily tested. Identity salience has been operationalized as the perceived importance of an identity for self-definition relative to other identities held by an individual. The measurement procedure requires obtaining the individual's rating of each of several relevant identities on common dimensions such as 'central to who I am/not central to who I am' or 'defines me/does not define me'. Some studies use three dimensions for each identity (Hoelter 1985); others use more (Callero 1985). The ratings for each identity are summed and the results are used to obtain a score of how salient the focal identity (in our case: organizational, departmental, occupational, etc.) is relative to that individual's other identities (spouse, parent, religion, leisure, etc.).

In most cases, a set of seven or eight identities (national, ethnic, or family, for example) can be identified as being the most relevant for the population studied, and the relative salience of job-related identities can be determined through comparisons with the average salience of the other identities for the individual. These scores can be correlated with a composite job performance score to examine our hypothesis regarding the relationships between identity salience and job behaviour.

Testing the other propositions is more difficult since it requires not only the measurement of relevant self-concept components but also the measurement of job aspects on commensurate dimensions. We give some illustrations now of how the congruence between job aspects and self-concept components can be assessed.

Chatman (1989) has recently demonstrated how the congruence between personal values and organizational values can be assessed. She has presented an interactional model in which commitment, performance and tenure are consequences of person–organization fit, defined as the congruence between the norms and value of the organization and the values of persons. In her studies, person–organization fit is assessed by asking the person to Q-sort 54 value statements into nine categories according to their importance, and asking a representative sample of organization members to Q-sort the same items into nine categories according to how characteristic is each attribute of their organization. Organization member profiles are combined to form a mean organization profile, and person–organization fit is measured by calculating the correlation between each person's profile and that of his/her organization. This method can be extended to assess the congruence between other components of the self-concept and other aspects of the job. For instance, individual's self-perceived attributes can be compared with those of characteristic or exemplary job holders using a similar Q-sort method.

Higgins' approach to the measurement of discrepancies among components of the self-concept can also be extended to the measurement of discrepancies between components of the self-concept and some job aspects. Higgins et al. (1987) asked subjects to list up to ten attributes associated with their actual or present self-concept and each of the self-guides–the ideal self and the ought self. After the subjects listed the attributes they were asked to rate the extent to which they believed they actually possessed, ideally would like to possess, or ought to possess each attribute listed.

To calculate the magnitude of discrepancy between the actual self and each self-guide, the attributes and ratings in the actual self were compared to the attributes and ratings in the self-guide, and the total number of attributes pairs and ratings that matched (i.e. synonyms) was subtracted from the total number of attribute pairs that mismatched (i.e. antonyms). Zero order and partial correlations were then performed to examine the relationships between emotional problems and the discrepancy scores. This approach can be extended by asking the person or a sample of current job holders to list their attributes or the attributes of successful job holders and compare these lists with the lists that describe the focal person's actual self and his or her ideal self and ought self. Congruence or discrepancy scores can be calculated following the Higgins method and correlated with a composite job performance index.

Both the Chatman method and the extended Higgins method are based on the assumption that environments are best conceptualized and measured in terms of the attributes and perceptions of the people in the environment, since 'it is the people that make the place' (Schneider 1987). A different approach has been suggested by Burke and Reitzes (1981). They view performance as the externalization of the content of the self, in the sense that the meanings of the behaviours in the performance are the meanings of the self content, and the link between identity and performances lies in the process of assessing each on the same dimensions of meaning.

Assuming that the self—and by extension the identities that comprise the self—is an object whose meaning can be identified in semantic space, Burke and Reitzes (1981) suggested that people will select from behaviours it is possible to perform those whose meaning is located in semantic space most closely to the meaning attached to the relevant identity. They employed the semantic differential technique to identify the meaning of a certain identity for individuals, and then used the same dimensions to assess the meaning of alternative behaviours for the same individuals, and for predicting which behaviour will be chosen on the basis of the similarity of meaning profiles between the identity and the behaviours. This method can possibly be extended to assess the meaning of jobs, job behaviours and job products for the person and compare their meanings to those of the person's identities to determine their level of similarity or congruence.

This brief discussion of research possibilities illustrates the variety of multiplicity of potential research methods that pertain to empirical investigation of a self-concept based theory of work motivation. The above-mentioned methods do not cover all aspects of the theory and do not exhaust all research possibilities. The purpose of the review was merely to suggest that our theoretical propositions can be empirically validated in principle, demonstrate that the variables implied by the theory are accessible through common research methods, and encourage researchers to begin the effort of testing some parts of the theory.

IMPLICATIONS

Our theoretical framework has several theoretical and managerial implications beyond those already specified. First, it enables a clearer conceptualization of organizational commitment. While many writers originally defined organizational commitment in terms of identification with the organization (Sheldon 1971; Hall and Schneider 1972) or the attachment of personality systems to organizational systems (Kanter 1968), subsequent applications of the concept have confounded this aspect with other motivational constructs and with behavioural consequences of commitment (Mowday et al. 1982; O'Reilly and Chatman 1986). In addition, confusion exists regarding the distinctiveness of organizational commitment from other work-related commitments (Morrow 1983). Our framework suggests defining and measuring organizational commitment, occupational commitment and other work-related commitments in terms of the salience of the relevant identity in the individual's self-concept. Such conceptualization not only enables a distinction among the various commitments but it clearly distinguishes commitment from other motivational constructs and from its presumed consequences.

Second, a self-concept based theory provides a basis for accounting for individual work efforts that are collectively oriented and cannot be accounted for by an individual calculative logic (Shamir 1990). This is done by positing values and identities as major components of the self-concept that the individual seeks to validate in his or her work behaviour. Since both values and identities have their origins in collectivities, they can serve to link individual behaviour with collective concerns. 'It is only through identification as the sharing of identity that individual motives become social values, and social values, individual motives' (Foote 1951: 20).

The transformational leadership effect of getting followers to transcend their own self interests for the sake of the collectivity (Burns 1978; Bass 1985), for instance, can be explained in terms of leadership actions that raise the salience of certain identities and values in the person's self-concept, and link collective goals and required behaviours to those identities and values (Shamir et al. 1990).

Third, the theory provides a version of intrinsic motivation that is less closely linked to the way particular tasks are engineered and more related to the broader meaning of these tasks in terms of the person's values, identities, self-perceived attributes and possible selves. Thus it supplements the current emphasis on job characteristics and job scope with an emphasis on the symbolic meaning of jobs and job facets for workers. In support of this emphasis, it has recently been suggested, for instance, that the main negative impact of assembly-line work on employee motivation should not have been attributed to monotony, lack of challenge or other direct effects of task design, but to the symbolic meaning of this work system for employees' self-concept, i.e. to its dehumanizing implications (Nord et al. 1988).

Perhaps the main managerial implication of our framework is that of modesty. Our theoretical propositions imply that, in contrast with the illusion reinforced by current motivation theories, a great deal of employee motivation may not be under managers' immediate control. This is because the meanings of organizations, jobs, products, clients and behaviours for workers reflect social judgments and social values that originate, at least in part, outside the organizational system. Managers can influence these meanings through their role as leaders whose primary function is the creation of shared meanings through their own actions as role models and their use of language, symbols and rituals. Thus the self-concept based theory provides a potential link between management as symbolic action (Pfeffer 1981), organizational culture (Schein 1985) and employee motivation.

REFERENCES

Adams, J. Stacy 1965 'Inequity in social exchange' in *Advances in experimental social psychology,* Vol. 2. L. Berkowitz (ed.), 267–300. New York: Academic Press.

Ajzen, Icek, and M. Fishbein 1977 'Attitude-behavior relations: A theoretical analysis and review of empirical studies'. *Psychological Bulletin* 84: 888–902.

Allport, Gordon W. 1955 *Becoming: Basic considerations for a psychology of personality.* New Haven: Yale University Press.

Ashford, Susan J. 1989 'Self assessments in organizations: A literature review and integrative model'. *Research in Organizational Behaviour* 11: 133–174.

Ashforth, Blake E., and F. Mael 1989 'Social identity theory and the organization'. *Academy of Management Review* 14: 20–29.

Bandura, Albert 1986 *Social foundations of thought and action: A social cognitive theory.* Englewood Cliffs, N.J.: Prentice Hall.

Bass, Bernard M. 1985 *Leadership and performance beyond expectations.* New York: The Free Press.

Bellah, Robert N., R. Madsen, W. M. Sullivan, A. Swidler, and S. M. Tipton 1985 *Habits of the heart: Individualism and commitment in American life.* New York: Harper and Row.

Brief, Arthur P., and R. J. Aldag 1981 'The self in work organizations: A conceptual review'. *Academy of Management Review* 6: 75–88.

Brockner, Joel 1988 *Self-esteem at work.* Lexington, MA: Lexington.

Brockner, Joel, R. Mouser, G. Birnbaum, K. Lloyd, J. Deitcher, S. Nathanson, and J. S. Rubin 1986 'Escalation of commitment to an ineffective course of action'. *Administrative Science Quarterly* 31: 109–126.

Burke, Peter J., and D. C. Reitzes 1981 'The link between identity and role performance'. *Social Psychology Quarterly* 44: 83–92.

Burns, James McGregor 1978 *Leadership.* New York: Harper and Row.

Callero, Peter J. 1985 'Role identity salience'. *Social Psychology Quarterly* 48: 203–215.

Campbell, John P., and R. D. Pritchard 1976 'Motivation theory' in *Handbook of industrial and organizational psychology.* M. D. Dunnette (ed.), 63–130. Chicago: Rand McNally.

Chatman, Jennifer A. 1989 'Improving interactional organizational research: A model of person-organization fit'. *Academy of Management Review* 14: 333–349.

Csikszentmihalyi, Mihalyi, and E. Rochberg-Halton 1981 *The meaning of things: Domestic symbols and the self.* New York: Cambridge University Press.

Deci, Edward L., and R. M. Ryan 1985 *Intrinsic motivation and self determination in human behavior.* New York: Plenum Press.

Etzioni, Amitai 1988 *The moral dimension: Toward a new economics.* New York: The Free Press.

Fisher, Cynthia D. 1980 'On the dubious wisdom of expecting job satisfaction to correlate with performance'. *Academy of Management Review* 5: 607–612.

Foote, Nelson 1951 'Identification as the basis for a theory of motivation'. *American Sociological Review* 26: 14–21.

Frankl, Victor 1963 *Man's search for meaning.* New York: Washington Square Press.

Gecas, Viktor 1982 'The self concept'. *Annual Review of Sociology* 8: 1–33.

Gecas, Viktor 1986 'The motivational significance of self-concept for socialization theory' in *Advances in Group Processes,* Vol. 3. E. J. Lawler (ed.), 131–156.

Goldthorpe, John H. D. Lockwood, F. Bechoffer, and S. Platt 1969 *The affluent worker in the class structure.* Cambridge: Cambridge University Press.

Gordon, Chad 1968 'Self-conceptions: Configurations of content' in *The self in social interaction.* C. Gordon and K. J. Gergen (eds.), 115–135. New York: Wiley.

Hackman, J. Richard, and G. R. Oldham 1980 *Work redesign.* Reading, MA: Addison Wesley.

Hall, Douglas T., and B. Schneider 1972 'Correlates of organizational identification as a function of career patterns and organizational types'. *Administrative Science Quarterly* 17: 240–350.

Hamner, W. Clay 1975 'Reinforcement theory and contingency management in organizational settings' in *Motivation and work behavior.* R. M. Steers and L. W. Porter (eds.), 477–504. New York: McGraw-Hill.

Higgins, E. Tory, R. L. Klein, and T. J. Strauman 1987 'Self discrepancies: Distinguishing among self-states, self-state conflicts, and emotional vulnerabilities' in *Self and identity: psychosocial contributions.* K. Yardley and T. Honess (eds.), 173–186. New York: Wiley.

Hoelter, Jon W. 1985 'The structure of self-conception: conceptualization and measurement'. *Journal of Personality and Social Psychology* 49: 1392–1407.

Hofstede, Geert 1980 *Culture's consequences: international differences in work-related values.* Beverly Hills, CA: Sage.

Jahoda, Marie 1979 'The psychological consequences of unemployment in the 1930s and the 1970s'. *Bulletin of the British Psychological Society* (September): 429–434.

Kanter, Rosabeth Moss 1968 'Commitment and social organization: A study of commitment mechanisms in utopian communities'. *American Sociological Review,* 33: 499–517.

Kanungo, Rabindra N. 1982 'Measurement of job and work involvement'. *Journal of Applied Psychology* 67: 341–343.

Katz, Daniel, and R. L. Kahn 1966 *The social psychology of organizations.* New York: Wiley.

Kluckhohn, Clyde 1962 'Values and value orientations in a theory of action' in *Toward a general theory of action.* T. Parsons and E. Shils (eds.), 338–34. New York: Harper.

Korman, Abraham K. 1970 'Toward a hypothesis of work behavior'. *Journal of Applied Psychology* 56: 31–41.

Korman, Abraham K. 1977 *Organizational behavior.* Englewood Cliffs, N.J.: Prentice Hall.

Landy, Frank J., and W. S. Becker 1987 'Motivation theory reconsidered'. *Research in Organizational Behavior* 9: 1–31.

Levinson, Daniel J. 1978 *The seasons of man's life.* New York: Ballantine Books.

Lock, Edwin A., and G. P. Latham 1984 *Goal setting: a motivational technique that works.* Englewood Cliffs, NJ: Prentice Hall.

Locke, Edwin A., and D. Henne 1986 'Work motivation theories' in *International Review of Industrial and Organizational Psychology* C. L. Cooper and I. Robertson (eds.), 1–35. Chichester, England: Wiley.

Magnusson, D., and N. S. Gerber, *editors* 1977 *Personality at the crossroads: Current issues in interactional psychology.* Hillsdale, NJ: Erlbaum.

Malhotra, Naresh K. 1988 'Self concept and product choice: An integrated perspective'. *Journal of Economic Psychology* 9: 1–28.

Marks, Stephen 1977 'Multiple roles and role strain: Some notes on human energy, time and commitment'. *American Sociological Review* 42: 921–936.

Markus, Hazel, and P. Nurius 1986 'Possible selves'. *American Psychologist* (September): 954–969.

Maslow, Abraham H. 1954 *Motivation and personality.* New York: Harper and Row.

McClelland, David 1985 *Human motivation.* Chicago: Scott Foresman.

McHugh, Peter 1968 *Defining the situation: The organization of meaning in social interaction.* Indianapolis: Bobbs-Merrill.

Mischel, Walter 1973 'Toward a cognitive social learning reconceptualization of personality'. *Psychological Review* 80: 200–213.

Morrow, Paula 1983 'Concept redundancy in organizational research: The case of work commitment'. *Academy of Management Review* 8: 486–500.

Mowday, Richard T., L. W. Porter, and R. W. Steers 1982 *Employee organization linkages.* New York: Academic Press.

Nord, W. R., A. P. Brief, J. M. Atieh, and E. M. Doherty 1988 'Work values and the conduct of organizational behavior'. *Research in Organizational Behavior* 10: 1–42.

O'Reilly, Charles, and J. Chatman 1986 'Organizational commitment and psychological attachment'. *Journal of Applied Psychology* 71: 492–499.

Organ, Dennis W. 1988 *Organizational citizenship behavior.* Lexington, MA: Lexington.

Perry, James L., and L. W. Porter 1982 'Factors affecting the context of motivation in public organizations'. *Academy of Management Review* 7: 83–98.

Pfeffer, Jeffrey 1981 'Management as symbolic action'. *Research in Organizational Behavior* 3: 1–52.

Pinder, Craig C. 1984 *Work motivation.* Glenview, Ill.: Scott Foresman.

Prentice, Deborah A. 1987 'Psychological correspondence of possessions, attitudes and values'. *Journal of Personality and Social Psychology* 53: 993–1003.

Rokeach, Milton 1979 'Some unresolved issues in theories of beliefs, attitudes and values'. *Nebraska Symposium on Motivation:* 261–304. Lincoln: University of Nebraska Press.

Santee, R., and S. Jackson 1979 'Commitment to self-identification: A sociopsychological approach to personality'. *Human Relations* 32:141–158.

Schein, Edgar H. 1985 *Organizational culture and leadership.* San Francisco: Jossey Bass.

Schlenker, Barry R. 1985 'Identity and self-identification' in *The self and social life.* B. R. Schlenker (ed.), 15–99. New York: McGraw-Hill.

Schneider, Benjamin 1987 'The people make the place'. *Personnel Psychology* 45: 437–453.

Schwartz, Howard S. 1983 'A theory of denotic work motivation'. *Journal of Applied Behavioral Science* 14: 204–214.

Shamir, Boas 1990 'Calculations, values and identities: The sources of collectivistic work motivation'. *Human Relations* 43: 313–332.

Shamir, Boas 1990 'The transformational effects of charismatic leadership'. Submitted for publication.

Sheldon, M., R. J. House, and M. B. Arthur 1971 'Investments and involvements as mechanisms producing commitment to the organization'. *Administrative Science Quarterly* 16: 143–150.

Snyder, Mark 1979 'Self-monitoring processes' in *Advances in experimental social psychology* 12. L. Berkowitz (ed.), 85–128. New York: Academic Press.

Snyder, Mark, and W. Ickes 1985 'Personality and social behavior' in *Handbook of social psychology,* 3rd ed. G. Lindzey and E. Aronson (eds.), 874–916. New York: Random House.

Staw, Barry M. 1976 *Intrinsic and extrinsic motivation.* Morristown, NJ: General Learning Press.

Staw, Barry M. 1984 'Organizational behavior: A review and reformulation of the field's outcome variables'. *Annual Review of Psychology* 35: 627–666.

Steers, Richard M., and L. W. Porter, *editors* 1987 *Motivation and work behavior.* New York: McGraw-Hill.

Strauss, Anselm L. 1969 *Mirrors and masks.* London: M. Robertson.

Stryker, Sheldon 1980 *Symbolic interactionism: A social structural version.* Menlo Park, Cal.: Benjamin/Cummings.

Turner, Jonathan H. 1987 'Toward a sociological theory of motivation'. *American Sociological Review* 52: 15–27.

Turner, Ralph H. 1968 'The self conception in social interaction' in *The self in social interaction.* C. Gordon and K. R. Gergen (eds.), 93–106. New York: Wiley.

Vroom, Victor H. 1964 *Work and motivation.* New York: Wiley.

Weiss, Howard M. 1986 'Personality, situational strength and work behavior'. Paper delivered at the International Congress of Applied Psychology, Jerusalem, Israel, July.

CHAPTER 2: Questions for Discussion

1 Exactly what is meant by the term "motivation"?

2 In general, why have the various need theories of work motivation been so popular among practicing managers?

3 If high n Ach people tend to be superior performers, would you suggest that an organization simply hire only those people who appear to have a high n Ach? Why or why not?

4 Would the general principles of operant conditioning be as applicable to solving the problems of turnover or absenteeism as they would to solving those of performance? Why or why not? Cite examples to illustrate your answer.

5 How would you compare expectancy theory with the need theories of motivation?

6 Why do you think equity theory has been largely ignored by many managers and writers working in the field of organizational behavior?

7 Consider a case in which two employees are passed over for a promotion. Using the concepts of procedural and distributive justice, explain why the two employees might have entirely different reactions—one works even harder, while the other decreases effort.

8 Social learning theory suggests that behavior may be maintained through direct reinforcement and punishment or through a person's observation (or modeling) of the reinforcing or punishing outcomes of other people's behavior. How might the effects of these two methods (i.e., direct and indirect) differ?

9 How would you compare control theory with goal-setting theory? Which do you think is more useful in work settings?

10 According to the self-concept approach to motivation, people are motivated to maintain consistency among the various parts of their self-concepts and between their self-concepts and behavior. What are the managerial implications of this assertion?

MODELS OF LEADERSHIP

Researchers and practitioners have conceptualized leadership in work settings as a social influence process through which one individual exerts influence, intentionally, over others to structure the behaviors and relationships within a group or organization (Yukl, 1994). However, within this broad notion of leadership, the specific definitions of the construct vary considerably. Even a cursory examination of leadership definitions in the organization studies literature reveals a diverse array of usages. For example, over the past 50 years, leadership has been defined in terms of personal traits, individual behaviors, interpersonal influence, situational factors, and combinations of these.

One reason for this lack of consensus is that researchers have formulated definitions of leadership calibrated to their own individual interests and concerns. Further, the variations in what has interested leadership scholars have been broad. In fact, interests among scholars have varied so much that there appear to be almost as many different definitions of leadership as there are people who have attempted to define the concept (Stogdill, 1974).

From the standpoint of understanding the behavior of people at work, Katz and Kahn (1978) present a particularly useful definition of leadership. These authors contend that the essence of organizational leadership is "the influence increment over and above mechanical compliance with the routine directives of the organization" (Katz & Kahn, 1978, p. 528). From Katz and Kahn's perspective, leadership occurs when one individual influences others to perform voluntarily above the minimum requirements of their work roles. These authors argue that the voluntary aspect of followers' responses to leadership distinguishes leadership from other influence processes, such as position power or formal authority. This voluntary feature will be apparent in the various approaches to leadership that will be discussed later in this chapter.

EARLY LEADERSHIP FRAMEWORKS

The first major theoretical framework in the scientific study of leadership was the leader trait approach. From this perspective, researchers concentrated on identifying a common set of attributes that distinguished leaders from followers or effective leaders from ineffective ones. The second significant development in leadership theory was the behavioral approach. Scholars interested in leader behaviors focused on trying to discover leadership styles that would be effective across all situations. Both of these approaches to leadership are discussed in this section, which reviews early leadership frameworks.

Leader Traits

The scientific analysis of leadership began by focusing on leaders themselves. More specifically, the early approaches concentrated on those personal attributes—physical, mental, and social—that seemed to differentiate leaders from followers. The trait theory of leadership, as it is often called, was originally grounded in the assumption that some people are simply "natural" leaders by virtue of the fact that they have been endowed with certain characteristics not possessed by others. From this perspective, researchers hypothesized that leaders could be distinguished from followers on the basis of remarkable personal attributes such as superior intelligence, boundless energy, faultless memory, uncanny intuition, and overwhelming persuasive power.

Hundreds of trait studies were conducted during the 1930s and 1940s. In general, these studies were rather unsophisticated, both theoretically and methodologically. For example, explanatory processes linking traits to various outcomes were typically not posited. Further, the predominant research procedure was correlation analysis; that is, researchers simply looked for significant associations between leader traits and various indicators of leader success.

The results of much of this research were brought together in a classic review by Stogdill in 1948. He examined over one hundred empirical studies of leader attributes covering 27 recurring characteristics. His review suggested that the trait research effort was somewhat of a disappointment. Of the numerous attributes examined by researchers, only intelligence and height seemed to distinguish leaders from followers, at least with any degree of consistency. To this point, the only conclusion that this extensive body of research could apparently offer was that leaders are slightly taller and slightly smarter than other individuals.

Since traits appeared to have little analytical or predictive value, leadership researchers shifted their emphasis in the late 1940s and early 1950s from leader traits to leader behaviors as the basic units of analysis. Consequently, trait theories of leadership fell into a state of disrepute for a number of years. However, before proceeding to the discussion of behavioral approaches to leadership, it should be noted that traits and trait theories are not dead, as will be seen in the first reading in this chapter by Kirkpatrick and Locke (1991). As evidence from better designed studies has been amassed, traits seem to have reemerged as promising explanatory variables. The investigation of leader traits has been more productive because researchers have constructed more appropriate theories (e.g., including intervening variables), used better measures of traits, included more relevant traits, and used longitudinal data (Yukl, 1994). Consequently a variety of personal attributes, such as energy level and emotional maturity, have now been linked to effective leadership (e.g., Bass, 1990). Further, traits associated with socialized or learned motivational patterns, such as the need for power and the need for achievement, have been empirically connected with effective managers (McClelland, 1975; McClelland & Boyatzis, 1982; McClelland & Burnham, 1976). In addition, different types of skills—that is, interpersonal skills, technical skills, and cognitive skills—appear to be relevant to managerial success (Bass, 1990). Finally, traits figure prominently in charismatic and transformational frameworks of leadership. These latter approaches will be discussed in a later section.

Leader Behaviors

As discussed above, the apparent failure of trait approaches to the study of leadership, by the end of the 1940s, led researchers to adopt a new focus for their work during the 1950s. Instead of personal attributes, investigators began to concentrate on leader behaviors as explanatory variables. This approach compares the behaviors of effective leaders with those of ineffective ones.

Two major research projects investigating leader behaviors were initiated at about the same time. One was a research effort conducted at Ohio State University under the direction of Stogdill, Fleishman, Hemphill, and associates. The other was a program undertaken at the University of Michigan by Likert and his colleagues. Both projects resulted in similar conclusions—that leadership behaviors could be classified into two content categories. One category contained those behaviors that pertained to interpersonal relationships; the other category consisted of those behaviors that related to task completion. The findings from the Ohio State University and University of Michigan studies are discussed in more detail below.

The Ohio State Leadership Studies.   The Ohio State University program was launched in the late 1940s. To start with, researchers developed a questionnaire that subordinates could use to describe the behaviors of their immediate supervisors or managers. To construct this instrument, researchers compiled a list of approximately 1800 examples of leadership behaviors. Then this list was reduced to 150 items that seemed to be good examples of the most important ones. These items were used in a questionnaire that was administered to a diverse sample of military and civilian personnel. The questionnaire responses were subjected to a factor analysis, which revealed that subordinates viewed supervisors' behavior in terms of two basic categories labeled "consideration" and "initiating structure."

Consideration was defined as the degree to which a leader shows concern for subordinates and acts in a friendly and supportive manner. Leaders with this style are likely to have relationships with subordinates characterized by mutual trust, and they demonstrate respect for employees' ideas and feelings. Examples of behaviors which fall into this category include finding time to listen to subordinates' concerns, acting on subordinates' suggestions, and "going to bat" for subordinates.

Initiating structure was defined as the extent to which a leader organizes and structures his or her own work and the work of subordinates. Leaders with this style tend to direct group work through planning activities, assigning tasks, scheduling, and setting deadlines. Examples of other behaviors which fall into this category include maintaining definite standards of performance, criticizing poor work, asking subordinates to follow standard procedures, and offering new approaches to problems.

The results of the initial study led to the development of several shorter questionnaires. Two of the most prominent are the Leader Behavior Description Questionnaire (LBDQ) and the Supervisory Behavior Description Questionnaire (SBDQ). Over the last four decades, these instruments, and modified versions of them, have been used in hundreds of leadership studies by many different researchers.

The University of Michigan Studies. The Michigan studies investigated the relationships between leader behavior and group performance. In the original study, twelve high-low productivity pairs of work units were selected for examination at the Prudential Insurance Company (Katz, Macoby, & Morse, 1950). Each pair represented a high-producing section and a low-producing section, with other variables (e.g., type of work, conditions, methods) being held constant. Interviews were used to collect information about supervisors' behavior. Managers were classified as being relatively effective or ineffective on the basis of various objective measures of group performance.

In comparing effective with ineffective managers, the Michigan studies found that these managers could be distinguished from each other along two dimensions of leader behavior (e.g., Likert, 1961, 1967). These dimensions were similar to the ones discovered in the Ohio State studies and were labeled relationship-oriented and task-oriented behaviors.

Relationship-oriented behavior referred to behaviors such as acting friendly toward subordinates, showing appreciation for subordinates' contributions, recognizing their accomplishments, and showing concern for their welfare and needs. These relationship-oriented behaviors were similar to the dimension of consideration in the Ohio State University studies. Task-oriented behavior referred to behavior such as planning and scheduling work, coordinating subordinates' activities, and providing necessary supplies, equipment, and technical assistance. This category was similar to the dimension called initiating structure by Ohio State researchers.

Furthermore, it was discovered that, for effective managers, these two categories of behavior were not inversely related. In other words, findings suggested that relationship-oriented behavior need not occur at the expense of task centered activities, and vice versa.

Evaluation of the Leader Behavior Approaches. Much of the subsequent work attempting to validate the task-oriented (or initiating structure) and relationship-oriented (or consideration) categories of leadership behavior has been produced by researchers using the Ohio State approach. Therefore, this approach will be briefly assessed below.

The empirical support for the impact of the consideration and initiating structure dimensions of leadership behavior has been somewhat weak, although scores of studies have been conducted (e.g., Kerr & Schriesheim, 1974). In fact, the only relationship that has demonstrated any degree of consistency has been the effect of consideration on various measures of satisfaction. Subordinates tend to be more satisfied when leaders are considerate (e.g., Fleishman & Harris, 1962).

Furthermore, the methodologies used in these studies have been criticized. For example, there is some debate concerning whether the questionnaires are measuring leadership behaviors. Critics contend that they may in fact be measuring the respondents' behavior or their attitudes toward their leaders (e.g., Mitchell, Larson, & Green, 1977). Furthermore, most of the studies examining the effects of leader behavior variables on the criterion variables (e.g., various measures of satisfaction) collected data on both independent and dependent variables at the same point in time. Employing this methodology, when significant correlations are found, provides no way to determine the direction of causality.

Two major theoretical weaknesses have been observed. First, the behavior content categories—that is, consideration and initiating structure—seem to have been defined too broadly to allow for meaningful empirical results. Currently, researchers are attempting to develop more useful content categories. For example, Yukl (1989) argues for fourteen categories: planning, problem solving, clarifying, monitoring, motivating, conflict management, recognizing, rewarding, supporting, mentoring, networking, consulting, delegating, and informing.

Second, these research programs gave too little attention to the effects of the situation on leadership behavior and/or leader effectiveness. In other words, although leader-follower interactions were carefully considered, the situational differences that might influence leader effectiveness were not sufficiently examined. These situational differences, or contingencies, were, however, emphasized in the subsequent leadership research that commenced in the 1960s, and several of these contingency theories of leadership will be considered in the next section.

In spite of the methodological and theoretical drawbacks, some scholars have argued that findings based on the early leader behavior approaches to leadership were definitely informative and useful. For example, House and Baetz (1979) contend that research on leader behaviors indicates that both consideration and initiating structure are necessary (perhaps at different times) for group effectiveness. Further, they argue that the research suggests that if a manager cannot provide leadership for his or her work group along both of these dimensions then the group may find someone else who can provide it.

CONTINGENCY THEORIES OF LEADERSHIP

After trait and behavior approaches fell short as overall theories for understanding the complexities of leadership, attention turned to situational aspects of leadership. Researchers looked for situation-type variables that permitted certain leader traits and behaviors to be effective within a given work group or organizational context. Several contingency approaches to leadership can be identified. Three of them will be reviewed briefly below: (1) Fiedler's contingency model, (2) House's path-goal theory, and (3) Vroom, Yetton, and Jago's normative decision model of leadership.

Fiedler's Contingency Model

Fiedler (1964, 1967) and his associates developed the first coherent contingency model of leadership. His theory contained three types of variables: (1) a leader orientation variable, called "least preferred coworker" (LPC); (2) a complex situation variable, termed "situation favorability"; and (3) various outcome criteria of group performance or effectiveness. Essentially, Fiedler argued that group performance or effectiveness depends on the interaction of leader orientation and situation favorability.

Leader Orientation. In an adaptation of the earlier research discussed in the previous section, Fiedler (1964, 1967) distinguished two basic leader orientations—a relationship orientation (where concern for people is central) and a task orientation (where concern for work accomplishment is most important). The operational technique that Fiedler developed to measure leadership orientation is noteworthy. Leadership orientation is measured by his least preferred coworker (LPC) scale. To arrive at an LPC score, the leader is asked to think of the person with whom he or she has worked that was least preferred as a coworker. Then, the leader is asked to rate that person on several bipolar scales (e.g., friendly-unfriendly, trustworthy-untrustworthy, cooperative-uncooperative). The LPC score is the sum of the ratings on all of these scales. A favorable description of the least preferred coworker (i.e., high LPC) is indicative of a relationship-oriented leader, whereas an unfavorable description (i.e., low LPC) is suggestive of a task-oriented leader.

Situation Favorability. As noted above, group effectiveness or performance depends on the interaction between the leader's LPC score and situation favorability. Fiedler defines favorability as the extent to which the situation gives the leader control over his or her subordinates. Favorability is measured in terms of three aspects of the work situation.

1 Leader-member relations. This refers to the degree of loyalty, trust, and respect that followers have for the leader. If others are willing to follow on the basis of loyalty or mutual respect, then the leader has little need to rely on task structure or position power (see below).

2 Task structure. This refers to the extent to which task-related goals can be specified, problems can be solved with procedures, decision correctness can be verified, and so forth. The more structured the task, the easier it is for the leader to tell group members how to perform it.

3 Position power. This refers to the degree to which the leader has authority to evaluate subordinates' performance and to administer rewards and punishments. The more rewards and punishments that the leader can use, the more influence the leader will have.

These three factors, in combination, determine the extent to which the leader controls the work situation. The differentiation of these factors yield eight leadership situations (or octants), which are depicted in Exhibit 3-1. As the exhibit shows, leader-member relations are described as good (octants 1–4) or bad (octants 5–8); task structure is classified as high (octants 1, 2, 5, 6) or low (octants 3, 4, 7, 8); and leader position power is rated as strong (octants 1, 3, 5, 7) or weak (octants 2, 4, 6, 8).

Once the situation is defined in terms of some combination of the three situation variables, the situation may be rated in terms of its favorableness to the leader. Fiedler contends that situation favorableness, from the leaders' perspective, is highest in octant 1 and lowest in octant 8. In other words, when leader-member relations are good, when task structure is high, and when position power is strong (as is the case in octant 1), the leader is in a superior position to influence the group, compared with a situation in which the reverse is true (as is the case in octant 8).

Combining situation favorableness with LPC scores, Fiedler examined the statistical correlations between LPC scores and group performance for each situation octant. The results of his analyses indicated that low-LPC (i.e., task-oriented) leaders were more effective in facilitating group performance when the situation was either highly favorable or highly unfavorable (i.e., at either end of the continuum presented in Exhibit 3-1). According to Fiedler, if the situation is highly favorable (i.e., everyone gets along, the task is clear, and the leader has power), then the group only needs someone to show direction (that is, the low-LPC leader). If the situation is highly unfavorable, then the group requires a low-LPC leader to counterbalance the power of the group and to show direction in an ambiguous task environment.

In contrast to low-LPC leaders, high-LPC leaders were more effective in facilitating group performance when the situation was moderately favorable or moderately unfavorable (i.e., toward the middle of the continuum). In a range in the middle of the continuum, the leader is moderately liked, has some power, and supervises jobs that are somewhat vague. In such situations, a high-LPC leader exerts the necessary influence to clarify task ambiguity through discussion and participation that utilizes the contributions of the subordinates.

EXHIBIT 3-1
Fiedler's classification of situation favorableness.

Leader/ member relations	Good				Poor			
Task structure	High		Low		High		Low	
Position power	Strong	Weak	Strong	Weak	Strong	Weak	Strong	Weak
Situation	I	II	III	IV	V	VI	VII	VIII
	Very favorable ⟵						⟶ Very unfavorable	

Source: Fred E. Fiedler, *A Theory of Leadership Effectiveness* (New York, McGraw-Hill, 1967). Reprinted by permission.

Evaluation of Fiedler's Model. Fiedler's theory and research have elicited pointed criticisms over the last three decades. Several of the more important criticisms follow: First, Graen et al. (1971) suggest that research support for the model is weak, especially if studies conducted by researchers not associated with Fiedler are examined. In most cases, even though the correlations may be in the right directions, they fail to achieve statistical significance (Graen et al., 1970; Graen et al., 1971).

Second, the LPC scale has been criticized as an invalid instrument for measuring leadership orientation or style (Schriesheim & Kerr, 1977; Schriesheim, Bannister, & Money, 1979). As evidence of this, some scholars point to the fact that Fiedler has changed his interpretation of the LPC score in a somewhat arbitrary fashion. Further, researchers are still debating its meaning. According to Fiedler's (1978) interpretation, the LPC score indicates a leader's motive hierarchy. However, Rice's (1978) review of the research on LPC scores suggests that the data support a value-attitude interpretation better than a motive hierarchy interpretation of leadership orientation (Yukl, 1994).

Third, the situational measures have been criticized as not being independent of the leader's LPC score (e.g. Kerr & Harlan, 1973). In most cases, the leader provided both the LPC score and the measure of leader-member relations. Therefore, the two may be confounded with each other.

Finally, in many work situations, the task can be changed by the leader. Consequently, the task is not totally an independent variable in the model.

As a result of these criticisms and others, the initial interest in Fiedler's contingency theory of leadership has diminished in recent years. However, although Fiedler's theory is not as prominent today as it once was, its central idea—that the leader's impact on group performance depends, to some extent, on a set of situational contingency factors—has endured. Even though most of the more popular approaches to leadership today may be more sophisticated than Fiedler's model (e.g., they consist of more relevant variables, or they include better measures of the model's components), nearly all acknowledge a role for systematic analysis of situational elements in determining the causes of leader effectiveness.

House's Path-Goal Theory of Leadership

House's (1971; House and Dessler, 1974) path-goal theory of leaderships builds heavily on the expectancy/valence model of work motivation (see Chapter 2) and emphasizes the ways in which leaders can facilitate task performance by showing subordinates how performance can be instrumental in achieving desired rewards. More specifically, House's theory holds that subordinates' satisfaction and performance depends on their expectancies and valances, which, in turn, depend on the leader's behavior or style. Furthermore, the expectancies and valences of subordinates are also affected by two basic contingency variables: characteristics of the subordinates and characteristics of the environment faced by the subordinates. These contingency variables moderate the relationship between leader behaviors and subordinates' satisfaction and performance. The relationship among these variables is shown in Exhibit 3-2. The components of this model will be discussed below.

Leadership Styles.   The original version of House's (1971) path-goal theory contained only two leader functions. The first was termed "path clarification." It dealt with the extent to which the leader helps subordinates understand the types of behaviors necessary to achieve goals and obtain rewards. A second type of leader behavior was to increase the number of rewards available to subordinates by being supportive and attending to their welfare.

In a later version of the theory (House and Dessler, 1974), the path-goal model identified four distinct types of leader behaviors:

1 Supportive leadership. Leaders with this style show concern for the well-being and personal needs of subordinates. These leaders attempt to develop satisfactory interpersonal relations among group members and to create a friendly climate in the work group. This category of behavior is similar to the consideration dimension in the Ohio State research program.

2 Directive leadership. Leaders with this style provide specific guidance for subordinates by setting standards of performance, scheduling and coordinating work efforts, and asking subordinates to follow rules and regulations. Leaders who exhibit directive leadership let subordinates know what is expected of them. This category of behavior is similar to the Ohio State initiating structure dimension.

3 Achievement-oriented leadership. This style of leadership involves setting challenging goals, seeking improvements in performance, emphasizing excellence in performance, and showing confidence that subordinates will achieve high levels of performance.

EXHIBIT 3-2
Components of the path-goal model.

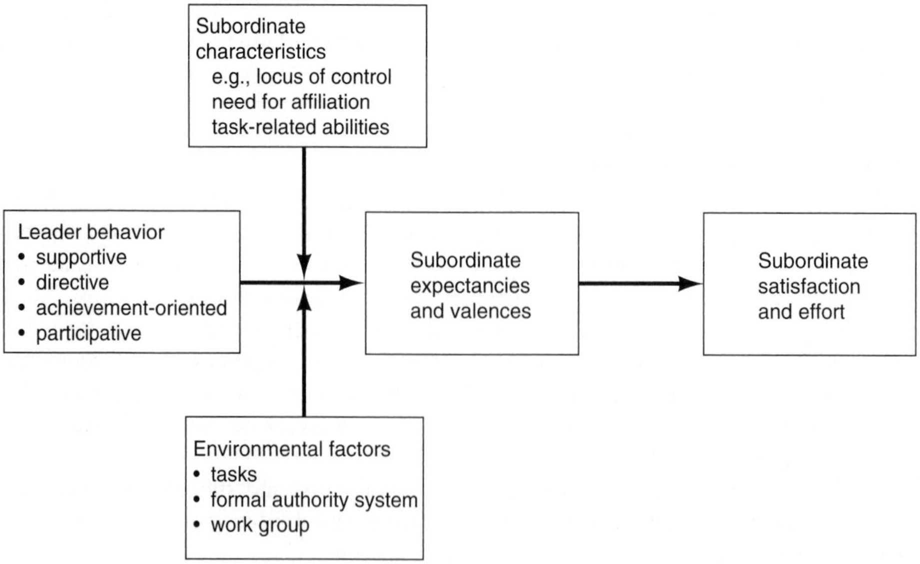

4 Participative leadership. Leaders with this style solicit suggestions and advice from subordinates and take this information into account when making decisions.

Subordinates' Expectancies and Valences.   As indicated above, a central component of House's path-goal theory is an expectancy theory of work motivation. According to expectancy models (see Chapter 2), employees make conscious and rational decisions about their work behavior. They will choose to apply effort to those tasks that they find attractive and that they believe they can perform. The attractiveness of a task depends on the extent to which the employee thinks that its accomplishment will lead to a valued outcome. The effect of a leader's behavior is to modify subordinates' perceptions regarding the valued outcomes that are attainable and to influence the perceived probabilities of attaining them.

Subordinate Characteristics.   Subordinate characteristics are one set of situation variables that moderate the relationship between leader behavior and the outcome variables of subordinate satisfaction and effort. In other words, the personal characteristics of employees partially determine how they will react to a leader's behavior. For example, employees who have an internal locus of control (i.e., who believe rewards are contingent upon their own efforts) may be more satisfied with a participative leadership style, whereas employees who have an external locus of control (who believe rewards are beyond their own control) may be more satisfied with a directive style. For another example, employees with strong needs for acceptance and affiliation may find their needs satisfied with a supportive leader, while employees with strong needs for autonomy may be motivated more by participative leaders than by supportive ones. Finally, individuals who feel that they have high levels of task-related abilities may not respond well to directive leader behavior. Instead, they may prefer an achievement-oriented style of leadership.

Environmental Factors.   Environmental factors are another set of situation variables that moderate the relationship between leader style and outcomes. House's path-goal theory posits three categories of such factors: the tasks, the formal authority system of the organization, and the work group. Variables in these categories may function either to motivate or to constrain the subordinate. For example, an intrinsically satisfying job may serve to motivate employees. On the other hand, the technological features of a task, such as an assembly line, may constrain behavior variability. Or, the work group may motivate the subordinate by praising individuals who did the most to help the group achieve its performance objectives.

According to the path-goal theory, the variables described above interact to determine employee satisfaction and effort. For example, if the task is unstructured, if the subordinates are inexperienced, and if few formal rules and procedures exist to guide work, then the directive leadership style may be the most effective for motivating employees, resulting in higher subordinate satisfaction and effort. In contrast, if the task is routine and boring, if the subordinates are experienced, and if many formal rules and procedures exist to direct work, then a supportive leadership style may be the most effective.

Evaluation of Path-Goal Theory. Empirical research designed to test House's path-goal theory has tended to focus on the dimensions of directive and supportive leadership (Szilagyi & Wallace, 1990). Research has generally supported the position that directive leadership behavior is most effective on ambiguous and unstructured tasks (House & Dessler, 1974; House & Mitchell, 1974; Filley, House, & Kerr, 1976). Further, there seems to be some evidence supporting the hypothesis that supportive behavior is most beneficial for unstructured tasks (House & Dessler, 1974; House & Mitchell, 1974; Filley, House, & Kerr, 1976; 1986a). Far fewer studies have been conducted to test hypotheses about achievement-oriented and participative leadership; however, some results are encouraging (Indvik, 1986b).

Although results of the empirical research testing path-goal theory have shown some promise, many of the findings are questionable because the theory itself contains some deficiencies. For example, the theory does not suggest how different situation variables are likely to interact (Osborn, 1974). In addition, the theory considers the effects of the four leader behaviors separately, even though it is likely that interactions among the various behaviors exist (Yukl, 1994). Further, House's path-goal model is limited by the theoretical deficiencies of the expectancy model of work motivation on which it is based (Schriesheim & Kerr, 1977). As we saw in Chapter 2, expectancy theory has been criticized, along with other rational choice models, for presenting an unrealistic account of the human decision-making process. Finally, some of the studies attempting to test the theory have contained various methodological problems.

Despite criticisms, however, House's path-goal theory has made a significant contribution to the topic of leadership because it specified important leadership behaviors and situation variables that should be considered in almost any organizational setting. Furthermore, like Fielder's theory (discussed in the previous section), House's model emphasizes that the relationship between leaders and their subordinates does not exist in a vacuum. Researchers and managers obviously need to take into account situational factors before they can predict the effects of specific leader behaviors on subordinates' satisfaction and performance.

Vroom, Yetton, and Jago's Normative Decision Model of Leadership

Vroom and his colleagues, Yetton, initially, and Jago, later, developed a model of leadership that emphasized the role played by leaders in making decisions (Vroom & Yetton, 1973; Vroom & Jago, 1988). Basically, the model focuses on the degree to which employees should be allowed to participate in decisions. According to this model, the decision procedures used by the leader influence the overall effectiveness of a decision through a number of intervening variables. Three of these—decision quality, decision acceptance, and decision timeliness—are discussed below.

1 Decision quality. The quality of a decision is highest when the "best" alternative is selected, independent of effects that may be associated with the necessity that the decision be accepted by subordinates. This dimension, quality, is a central consideration when the decision is important for facilitating group performance and when significant variation exists among the alternatives. For example, a decision concerning where to place a water cooler in a plant does not require high decision quality, whereas a decision on performance goals does require high decision quality.

2 Decision acceptance. Decision acceptance is important whenever a decision has implications for subordinates' work motivation and whenever a decision must be implemented by subordinates. Some decisions do not require group acceptance to be successfully implemented (e.g., what color of carpet to use for office floors), whereas others must be accepted by group members in order to be executed successfully (e.g., selecting strategies to increase sales).

3 Decision timeliness. Decision timeliness is an important consideration whenever time imposes constraints on decisions. For example, some decisions can be made at a work group's discretion (e.g., whether to change secretarial reporting relationships), whereas others can demand immediate action (e.g., whether to introduce a new product in the next quarter).

Leader Decision-Making Styles. The Vroom-Yetton-Jago model suggests that leaders with multiple subordinates have five basic decision-making styles or procedures available to them. Further, this approach suggests that these five styles can be placed on a continuum that is anchored at one end by a highly autocratic procedure (called "AI") and at the other end by a highly participative procedure (called "GII"). According the Vroom and Yetton (1973), the five decision-making styles may be described as follows:

AI The manager makes the decision or solves the problem alone, using only the information available to him or her at the time.

AII The manager asks for information from subordinates but makes the decision alone. Subordinates function only as information sources.

CI The manager shares the problem with the relevant subordinates individually, getting their ideas and suggestions, without bringing them together as a group. Then the manager makes the decision alone. The decision may or may not reflect the influence of the subordinates.

CII The manager and subordinates meet as a group to discuss the problem, but the manager makes the decision. The decision may or may not reflect subordinates' influence.

GII The manager and subordinates meet as a group to discuss the problem, and the group makes the decision. The manager and the subordinates generate and evaluate alternatives together. Then they attempt to reach an agreement (consensus) on a solution. The manager accepts and implements any solution which has the support of the entire group.

Using the Normative Model. The Vroom-Yetton-Jago normative decision model of leadership provides the leader with, in effect, a decision tree to help him or her choose an effective decision style. A recent version of the decision tree is shown in Exhibit 3-3 (Vroom and Jago, 1988). The decision process entails answering a series of questions about the nature of the problem. After working his or her way through the decision tree, the leader selects the style that is most appropriate for the situation.

QR Quality Requirement: *How important is the technical quality of this decision?*

CR Commitment Requirement: *How important is subordinate commitment to the decision?*

LI Leader's Information: *Do you have sufficient information to make a high-quality decision?*

ST Problem Structure: *Is the problem well structured?*

CP Commitment Probability: *If you were to make the decision by yourself, is it reasonably certain that your subordinate(s) would be committed to the decision?*

GC Goal Congruence: *Do subordinates share the organizational goals to be attained in solving this problem?*

CO Subordinate Conflict: *Is conflict among subordinates over preferred solutions likely?*

SI Subordinate Information: *Do subordinates have sufficient information to make a high-quality decision?*

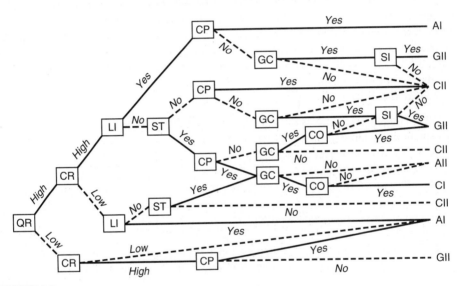

EXHIBIT 3-3
The normative model of decision making.
Source: From *The new leadership: Managing participation in organizations,* by Victor H. Vroom and Arthor G. Jago (Englewood Cliffs, N.J.: Prentice-Hall, 1988). Copyright 1987 by V.H. Vroom and A.G. Jago. Used with permission of the authors.

Evaluating the Vroom-Yetton-Jago Model. Since the normative decision model of leadership was first proposed by Vroom and Yetton in 1973, a number of studies have been conducted to test it. In general, the results of the empirical research have been supportive (e.g., Field, Reed, & Louviere, 1990; Field, Wedley, & Hayward, 1989). However, the revised version of the model (i.e., Vroom & Jago, 1988) is still too new to have been tested extensively.

The model has several important limitations that should be noted. For example, the model treats the decision-making process as the outcome of a single, discrete episode. However, many important decisions typically require multiple meetings with a variety of different groups at different times and with changing environmental circumstances (Yukl, 1994). In addition, the model erroneously assumes that all leaders are sufficiently skilled to use each of the decision procedures (Crouch & Yetton, 1987; Field, 1979).

EMERGING LEADERSHIP THEORIES

As has been discussed, the trait, behavior, and contingency frameworks, or theories, of leadership have all come in for serious criticism. These, as well as most other leadership theories, are subject to conceptual and methodological shortcomings, and they all currently lack strongly consistent empirical support. In fact, after over half a century of scientific research, scholars still have not been able to reach a high degree of consensus regarding a comprehensive conceptualization of the entire leadership process. However, given the presumed importance of this topic to organizations trying to cope with increasingly turbulent environments, researchers have persisted in attempts to generate viable approaches. Several such relatively recent developments in the area of leadership theory that appear to be attracting increasing attention will be described in the next two subsections. These are leader-member exchange, and charismatic and transformational frameworks.

Leader-Member Exchange (LMX) Theory

Leader-member exchange (LMX) theory was formerly called the "vertical dyad linkage theory" (Dansereau, Graen, and Hage, 1975). This model focuses on reciprocal influence processes within leader/subordinate dyads. According to the theory, supervisors or leaders do not treat all subordinates equally. Over time, leaders establish close interpersonal relationships with some subordinates (called the "in-group"), but keep their distance from other subordinates (called the "out-group"). In-group members have relationships with their supervisor that are marked by trust, loyalty, and a sense of a common fate. These individuals come to function as the leader's assistant or advisors. Members of the out-group do not have such relationships with the leader. Consequently, they tend to be excluded from important decisions or activities. Although it is not always clear why these different relationships occur, they appear to be established early in the leader-subordinate relationship as the two parties mutually define the role of the subordinate.

Evaluation of the LMX Theory. The LMX theory requires further development and testing. Regarding leadership effectiveness, Yukl (1994) claims that the theory is still more descriptive than prescriptive. That is, LMX theory specifies a typical role-making process that occurs between leaders and their subordinates; however, the theory does not suggest what patterns of exchange between the leader and his or her subordinates are optimal for leadership effectiveness. Furthermore, the theory does not recognize that leaders potentially may establish special exchange relationships with all members of the subordinate group and that these relationships may all be different in nature. For example, the leader may delegate authority to a few subordinates while maintaining a relationship of mutual respect and trust with others (Yukl, 1994).

Charismatic and Transformational Leadership Theories

Charismatic and transformational models are among the newest developments in the area of leadership. It is important to note here that a central concept in most of these models is the notion of charisma. Charisma is a Greek word meaning "divinely inspired gift," such as the ability to perform miracles. Weber (1947) used the term to describe a basis of power or influence grounded in followers' perceptions that a leader is endowed with exceptional personal qualities. This general idea has been carried forward into current organizational leadership theories. Three such theories are briefly discussed below: House's charismatic leadership theory, Conger and Kanungo's charismatic leadership theory, and Bass' transformational leadership theory.

House's Charismatic Leadership Theory. House's (1977) theory of charismatic leadership developed a set of testable propositions concerned with identifying the traits of charismatic leaders, the behaviors used by these leaders, and the conditions under which such leaders may emerge. Insofar as leader traits are concerned, House argued that charismatic leaders are likely to have a strong need for power, a high level of self-confidence, and a strong conviction in their own beliefs. Concerning behaviors, House posited that charismatic leaders are likely to engage in impression management (to increase followers' trust in leaders' decisions), to articulate an appealing vision (to give the work meaning), to model desirable behavior that followers admire and identify with, to communicate high expectations that induce followers to set higher performance goals and become committed to them, and to act in ways that arouse motives relevant to the group's mission. Finally, regarding necessary conditions, charismatic leaders must be able to define task roles in ideological terms for followers.

House (1977) contended that the identification of leader traits, leader behaviors, and situation characteristics that may result in the emergence of charismatic leaders is important because these types of leaders have such extraordinary effects on followers. Followers of charismatic leaders generally accept the leader and his or her views without question. They feel affection toward, and willingly obey, the leader; and they are likely to become emotionally involved with the mission of the group or organization. They believe they have the ability to contribute to the organization's goals, and they set high performance goals for themselves.

Conger and Kanungo's Charismatic Leadership Theory. According to Conger and Kanungo (1987), charismatic leadership is, essentially, an attribution of the followers. Therefore, these theorists are concerned with identifying those variables that may result in such an attribution. According to their theory, leaders who advance a radical vision (but one still within the realm of possible acceptance by followers) are more likely to be perceived as charismatic. In addition, leaders who act in unconventional or unorthodox ways to achieve their visions are more likely to be viewed as charismatic by subordinates. Followers are more likely to attribute charisma to leaders who make self-sacrifices and take personal risks than those who do not. Charisma is more likely to be attributed to leaders who use personal persuasion to gain followers' commitment to a new course than to leaders who use participative decision-making processes or formal authority. Leaders who set forth their proposals with confidence are more likely to be viewed as charismatic than leaders who seem to be unsure. A later version of this theory holds that leader behaviors affect follower attributions through the influence processes of personal identification (based on followers' desire to please an admired leader) and internalization (the incorporation of values into the psyches of followers), especially if followers are dissatisfied with the status quo (Conger, 1989).

Bass's Transformational Leadership. Bass (1985) built on the work of Burns (1978), a political scientist who studied presidential leadership, to describe a leadership process that resulted in exceedingly high levels of performance on the part of followers within organizations. According to Bass (1985; Bass and Avolio, 1990), transformational leadership consists of four behavioral components: charisma, inspiration, intellectual stimulation, and individualized consideration. Charisma is viewed as the process through which leaders arouse strong emotions in followers, an important outcome being the identification of the followers with the leader. Inspiration refers to leader behaviors, such as articulating an appealing vision, using symbols to focus followers' efforts, and modeling appropriate behavior. Intellectual stimulation includes those behaviors which encourage followers to be creative problem solvers. Finally, individualized consideration includes leader behaviors that provide special support to followers, such as expressing appreciation for a job well done and assigning special projects that will promote subordinate self-confidence.

According to this theory, the behavioral components of leadership interact to affect changes in followers' level of awareness and in their motive patterns. First, transformational leaders make followers cognizant of the importance of work objectives and task outcomes. Second, by exhibiting various combinations of these behaviors, leaders elevate followers to their "better selves." Consequently, the followers of transformational leaders tend to be motivated by such high order needs as achievement and self-actualization, rather than by baser needs (e.g., security). Additionally, the theory would predict that these followers are more likely to transcend their own short-term self-interests for the sake of their work group or organization.

Evaluation of Charismatic and Transformational Leadership Theories. Since these conceptual approaches to leadership are still quite new, insufficient empirical evidence exists to evaluate them adequately. Furthermore, they are likely to be very difficult theories to test with conventional research methods. However, these theories and others like them appear to make a contribution to our understanding of leadership in work settings. For example, they all attempt to describe levels of influence/performance that the earlier theories of leadership would find awkward to explain. Furthermore, they consider the emotional attributes as well as the rational aspects, of the individual. Earlier theories of leadership tended to emphasize only the rational dimensions of individual thought and action. In addition, these approaches, especially the charismatic theories, recognize collective processes in motivation (e.g., social identification), whereas earlier leadership theories typically acknowledged only dyadic influences between a leader and an individual follower (Yukl, 1994).

OVERVIEW OF READINGS

The first selection in this chapter, by Kirkpatrick and Locke, reviews a number of traits that distinguish leaders from nonleaders. As was discussed earlier, although leader traits fell out of favor with organizational researchers for a number of years following Stogdill's (1948) classic review, they have since reemerged as promising explanatory variables. Kirkpatrick and Locke identify six key traits—drive, leadership motivation, honesty and integrity, self-confidence, cognitive ability, knowledge of the business—that, they contend, help individuals to perform effectively in leadership situations.

In the second article, Schriesheim and Neider argue that organizational researchers have not yet developed an approach to the topic of leadership which, when used as the basis of leadership training and development programs, can clearly improve organizational performance. These authors hold that the extant perspectives on leadership are too narrow and simplistic to be useful. However, according the Schriesheim and Neider, many of the problems associated with current leadership approaches will be remedied in the coming "new phase" in leadership work. This perspective treats leadership as only one part of the manager's job, employs a much more sophisticated conceptualization of leadership style, and views leadership as a multidimensional process of interpersonal influence.

The third article in this chapter, by Shamir, House, and Arthur, attempts to establish a motivational basis of charismatic leadership. Charismatic leaders are purported to have profound effects on their followers' values, goals, needs, and aspirations. In fact, research has suggested that charismatic leaders are able to elevate followers' needs from lower to higher levels in the Maslow hierarchy, raise followers to higher levels of morality, and motivate followers to transcend their own self-interests. Yet, according to these authors, an adequate motivational explanation to account for this profound effect of charismatic leaders does not exist. In an effort to bridge this gap in the literature, Shamir and his colleagues present a self-concept-based theory of motivation. They attempt to show how charismatic leaders activate self-concept-related motivators, and how these motivators can explain the effects that charismatic leaders have on their followers.

The last two articles in this section take rather radical perspectives on the topic of leadership. In the fourth article, Meindl, Ehrlich, and Dukerich suggest that modern organizations consist of causal processes that are so complex that they are beyond human comprehension. In such systems, leadership may not be a central organizational process; rather, it may be the consequence of a bias on the part of organizational members to understand important but causally indeterminate organizational events in particular terms. In other words, instead of being a determinant of organizational events, leadership may be best understood as an explanatory category that can be used by members to account for particular organizational outcomes (e.g., increased organizational performance).

Similarly, Gemmill and Oakely suggest that leadership is a social myth that serves to strengthens members' convictions that leaders and hierarchy are necessary in organizations. The problem with the concept of leadership, according to these authors, is that it is indicative of, and contributes to, a social pathology. Leadership induces massive learned helplessness among members of social systems. Further, since the major function of the leader myth is to preserve existing social arrangements, the myth encourages dysfunctions and difficulties within the system to be attributed to the lack of "leadership." Therefore, dysfunctions of the social system and the corresponding personal behaviors of members go unexamined.

REFERENCES

Bass, B. M. *Leadership and performance beyond expectations.* New York: Free Press, 1985.

Bass, B. M. *Handbook of leadership: A survey of theory and research.* New York: Free Press, 1990.

Bass, B. M., & Avolio, B. J. The implications of transactional and transformational leadership for individual, team, and organizational development. In W. Pasmore & R. W. Woodman (Eds.), *Research in organizational change and development,* Vol. 4. Greenwich, Conn.: JAI Press, 1990, pp. 231–272.

Burns, J. M. *Leadership.* New York: Harper & Row, 1978.

Conger, J. A. *The charismatic leader: Behind the mystique of exceptional leadership.* San Francisco, Calif.: Jossey-Bass, 1989.

Conger, J. A., & Kanungo, R. Toward a behavioral theory of charismatic leadership in organizational settings. *Academy of Management Review,* 1987, **12**, 637–647.

Crouch, A. G., & Yetton, P. Manager behavior, leadership style, and subordinate performance: An empirical extension of the Vroom-Yetton conflict rule. *Organizational Behavior and Human Decision Processes,* 1987, **19**, 384–396.

Dansereau, F., Graen, G., & Hage, W. J. A vertical dyad linkage approach to leadership in formal organizations. *Organizational Behavior and Human Performance,* 1975, **13**, 46–78.

Fiedler, F. E. A contingency model of leadership effectiveness. In L. Berkowitz (Ed.), *Advances in experimental social psychology,* Vol. 1. New York: Academic Press, 1964.

Fiedler, F. E. *A theory of leadership effectiveness.* New York: McGraw-Hill, 1967.

Fiedler, F. E. The contingency model and the dynamics of the leadership process. In L. Berkowitz (Ed.), *Advances in experimental social psychology,* Vol. 11. New York: Academic Press, 1978.

Field, R. H. G. A critique of the Vroom-Yetton contingency model of leadership behavior. *Academy of Management Review,* 1979, **4**, 249–257.

Field, R. H. G., Read, P. C., & Louviere, J. J. The effect of situation attributes on decision making choice in the Vroom-Jago model of participation in decision making. *Leadership Quarterly,* 1990, **1**, 165–176.

Field, R. H. G., Wedley, W. C., & Hayward, M. W. J. Criteria used in selecting Vroom-Yetton decision styles. *Canadian Journal of Administrative Science,* 1989, **6**(2), 18–24.

Filley, A. C., House, R. J., & Kerr, S. *Managerial process and organizational behavior,* 2d ed. Glenview, Ill.: Scott, Foresman, 1976.

Fleishman, E. A., & Harris, E. F. Patterns of leadership behavior related to employee grievances and turnover. *Personnel Psychology,* 1962, **15**, 43–56.

Graen, G., Alvares, D., Orris, J. B., & Martella, J. A. Contingency model of leadership effectiveness: Antecedent and evidential results. *Psychological Bulletin,* 1970, **74**, 285–296.

Graen, G., Orris, J. B., & Alvares, K. M. Contingency model of effectiveness: Some experimental results. *Journal of Applied Psychology,* 1971, **55**, 196–201.

House, R. J. A path-goal theory of leader effectiveness. *Administrative Science Quarterly,* 1971, **16,** 321–339.

House, R. J., A 1976 theory of charismatic leadership. In J. G. Hunt & L. L. Larson (Eds.), *Leadership: The cutting edge.* Carbondale, Ill.: Southern Illinois University Press, 1977, pp. 189–207.

House, R. J., & Baetz, M. L. Leadership: Some empirical generalizations and new research directions. *Research in Organizational Behavior,* 1979, **1**, 341–423.

House, R. J., & Dessler, G. The path-goal theory of leadership: Some post hoc and a priori tests. In J. Hunt & L. Larson (Eds.), *Contingency approaches to leadership.* Carbondale, Ill.: Southern Illinois Press, 1974.

House, R. J., & Mitchell, T. R. Path-goal theory of leadership. *Journal of Contemporary Business,* 1974, **3**, 81–97.

Indvik, J. Path-goal theory of leadership: A meta-analysis. Procedings, Academy of Management, Chicago, 1986a, 189–192.

Indvik, J. A path-goal theory investigation of achievement-oriented and participative leader message behavior. Paper, Academy of Management, Chicago, 1986b.

Katz, D., & Kahn, R. L. *The social psychology of organizations,* 2d ed. New York: John Wiley, 1978.

Katz, D., Maccoby, N., & Morse, N. *Productivity, supervision, and morale in an office situation.* Ann Arbor, Mich.: Institute for Social Research, 1950.

Kerr, S., & Harlan, A. Predicting the effects of leadership training and experience from the contingency model: Some remaining problems. *Journal of Applied Psychology.* 1973, **57**, 114–117.

Kerr, S., & Schriesheim, C. A. Consideration, initiating structure, and organizational criteria— An update of Korman's 1966 review. *Personnel Psychology,* 1974, **27**, 555–568.

Likert, R. *New patterns of management.* New York: McGraw-Hill, 1961.

Likert, R. *The human organization: Its management and value.* New York: McGraw-Hill, 1967.

McClelland, D. C. *Power: The inner experience.* New York: Irvington, 1975.

McClelland, D. C., & Boyatzis, R. E. Leadership motive pattern and long-term success in management. *Journal of Applied Psychology,* 1982, **67**, 737–743.

McClelland, D. C., & Burnham, D. H. *Power is the great motivator.* Harvard Business Review, 1976, **54**, 100–110.

Mitchell, T. R., Larson, J. R., Jr., & Green, S. G. Leader behavior, situational moderators, and group performance: An attributional analysis. *Organizational Behavior and Human Performance,* 1977, **18**, 254–268.

Osborn, R. N. Discussant comments. In J. G. Hunt & L. L. Larson (Eds.), *Contingency approaches to leadership.* Carbondale, Ill.: Southern Illinois University Press, 1974.

Rice, R. W. Construct validity of the least preferred coworker score. *Psychological Bulletin,* 1978, **85**, 1199–1237.

Schriesheim, C. A., Bannister, B. D., & Money, W. H. Psychometric properties of the LPC scale: An extension of Rice's review. *Academy of Management Review,* 1979, **4**, 287–290.

Schriesheim, C. A., & Kerr, S. Theories and measures of leadership: A critical appraisal. In J. G. Hunt & L. L. Larson (Eds.), *Leadership: The cutting edge.* Carbondale, Ill.: Southern Illinois University Press, 1977, pp. 9–45.

Stogdill, R. M. Personal factors associated with leadership: A survey of the literature. *Journal of Psychology,* 1948, **25**, 35–71.

Stogdill, R. M. Handbook of leadership: A survey of the literature. *Journal of Psychology,* 1974, **25**, 35–71.

Szilagyi, A. D., & Wallace, M. J., Jr. *Organizational behavior and performance.* New York:

HarperCollins, 1990.

Vroom, V. H., & Jago, A. G. *The new leadership: Managing participation in organizations.* Englewood Cliffs, N.J.: Prentice-Hall, 1988.

Vroom, V. H., & Yetton, P. W. *Leadership and decision making.* Pittsburgh: University of Pittsburgh Press, 1973.

Weber, M. *The theory of social and economic organization* (T. Parsons, Trans.). New York: Free Press, 1947.

Yukl, G. Managerial leadership: A review of theory and research. *Journal of Management,* 1989, **15**, 251–289.

Yukl, G. *Leadership in organizations,* 3d ed. Englewood Cliffs, N.J.: Prentice-Hall, 1994.

Leadership: Do Traits Matter?

Shelley A. Kirkpatrick
Edwin A. Locke

Few issues have a more controversial history than leadership traits and characteristics. In the 19th and early 20th centuries, "great man" leadership theories were highly popular. These theories asserted that leadership qualities were inherited, especially by people from the upper class. Great men were born, not made (in those days, virtually all business leaders were men). Today, great man theories are a popular foil for so-called superior models. To make the new models plausible, the "great men" are endowed with negative as well as positive traits. In a recent issue of the *Harvard Business Review,* for example, Slater and Bennis write,

> "The passing years have . . . given the coup de grace to another force that has retarded democratization—the 'great man' who with brilliance and farsightedness could preside with dictatorial powers as the head of a growing organization."[1]

Such great men, argue Slater and Bennis, become "outmoded" and dead hands on "the flexibility and growth of the organization." Under the new democratic model, they argue, "the individual *is* of relatively little significance."

Early in the 20th century, the great man theories evolved into trait theories. ("Trait" is used broadly here to refer to people's general characteristics, including capacities, motives, or patterns of behavior.) Trait theories did not make assumptions about whether leadership traits were inherited or acquired. They simply asserted that leaders' characteristics are different from non-leaders. Traits such as height, weight, and physique are heavily dependent on heredity, whereas others such as knowledge of the industry are dependent on experience and learning.

The trait view was brought into question during the mid-century when a prominent theorist, Ralph Stogdill, after a thorough review of the literature concluded that "A person does not become a leader by virtue of the possession of some combination of traits."[2] Stogdill believed this because the research showed that no traits were universally associated with effective leadership and that situational factors were also influential. For example, military leaders do not have traits identical to those of business leaders.

Since Stogdill's early review, trait theory has made a comeback, though in altered form. Recent research, using a variety of methods, has made it clear that successful leaders are not like other people. The evidence indicates that there are certain core traits which significantly contribute to business leaders' success.

Traits *alone*, however, are not sufficient for successful business leadership—they are only a precondition. Leaders who possess the requisite traits must take certain *actions* to be successful (e.g., formulating a vision, role modeling, setting goals). Possessing the appropriate traits only makes it more likely that such actions will be taken

From *Academy of Management Executive,* 1991, **5**(2), 48–60. Reprinted by permission.

and be successful. After summarizing the core leadership traits, we will discuss these important actions and the managerial implications.

THE EVIDENCE: TRAITS DO MATTER

The evidence shows that traits do matter. Six traits on which leaders differ from non-leaders include: drive, the desire to lead, honesty/integrity, self-confidence, cognitive ability, and knowledge of the business.[3] These traits are shown in Exhibit 1.

Drive

The first trait is labeled "drive" which is not be confused with physical need deprivation. We use the term to refer to a constellation of traits and motives reflecting a high effort level. Five aspects of drive include achievement motivation, ambition, energy, tenacity, and initiative.

Achievement.   Leaders have a relatively high desire for achievement. The need for achievement is an important motive among effective leaders and even more important among successful entrepreneurs. High achievers obtain satisfaction from successfully completing challenging tasks, attaining standards of excellence, and developing better ways of doing things. To work their way up to the top of the organization, leaders must have a desire to complete challenging assignments and projects. This also allows the leader to gain technical expertise, both through education and work experience, and to initiate and follow through with organizational changes.

The constant striving for improvement is illustrated by the following manager who took charge of a $260 million industrial and office-products division.[4]

> After twenty-seven months on the job, Tom saw his efforts pay off: the division had its best first quarter ever. By his thirty-first month, Tom felt he had finally mastered the situation. . . . [Tom] finally felt he had the structure and management group in place to grow the division's revenues to $400 million and he now turned his attention to divesting a product group which no longer fit in with the growth objectives of the division.

Drive: achievement, ambition, energy, tenacity, initiative

Leadership Motivation (personalized vs. socialized)

Honesty and Integrity

Self-Confidence (including emotional stability)

Cognitive Ability

Knowledge of the Business

Other Traits (weaker support): charisma, creativity/originality, flexibility

EXHIBIT 1.
Leadership traits.

Managers perform a large amount of work at an unrelenting pace. To perform well, a leader needs to constantly work toward success and improvement. Superior managers and executives are concerned with doing something better than they or others have ever done it. For example, at PepsiCo only "aggressive achievers" survive. Similarly, Thomas Watson of IBM has been described as "driven throughout by a personal determination to create a company larger than NCR."[5] This brings us to a second related motive: ambition.

Ambition. Leaders are very ambitious about their work and careers and have a desire to get ahead. To advance, leaders actively take steps to demonstrate their drive and determination. Ambition impels leaders to set hard, challenging goals for themselves and their organizations. Walt Disney, founder of Walt Disney Productions, had a "dogged determination to succeed" and C. E. Woolman of Delta Air Lines had "inexhaustible ambition."

Effective leaders are more ambitious than nonleaders. In their 20-year study, psychologists Ann Howard and Douglas Bray found that among a sample of managers at AT&T, ambition, specifically the desire for advancement, was the strongest predictor of success twenty years later. The following character sketches of two managers who successfully progressed illustrate the desire for advancement.[6]

> "I want to be able to demonstrate the things I learned in college and get to the top," said Al, "maybe even be president. I expect to work hard and be at the third level within 5 years, and to rise to much higher levels in the years beyond that. I am specifically working on my MBA to aid in my advancement. If I'm thwarted on advancement, or find the challenge is lacking, I'll leave the company.

> [He] had been promoted to the district level [after 8 years] and certainly expected to go further. Although he still wouldn't pinpoint wanting to be president (his wife's dream for him), he certainly had a vice presidency (sixth level) in mind as early as year 2 in the study, after his first promotion.

The following sketches characterize two less ambitious individuals:

> Even though Chet had the benefits of a college degree, his below-average scholastic performance did not fill him with confidence in his capabilities. He hedged a bit with his interviewer when asked about his specific aspirations, saying he wasn't sure what the management levels were. When pressed further, he replied, "I'd like to feel no job is out of my reach, but I'm not really possessed of a lot of ambition. There are times when I just want to say, 'To hell with everything.' "

> After [his] promotion to the second level, he looked more favorably upon middle management, but he still indicated he would not be dissatisfied to stay at the second level. [He] just seemed to take each position as it came; if he ever looked ahead, he didn't appear to look up.

Energy. To sustain a high achievement drive and get ahead, leaders must have a lot of energy. Working long, intense work weeks (and many weekends) for many years, requires an individual to have physical, mental, and emotional vitality.

Leaders are more likely than nonleaders to have a high level of energy and stamina and to be generally active, lively, and often restless. Leaders have been characterized as "electric, vigorous, active, full of life" as well as possessing the "physical vitality to maintain a steadily productive work pace."[7] Even at age 70, Sam Walton, founder of Wal-Mart discount stores, still attended Wal-Mart's Saturday morning meeting, a whoop-it-up 7:30 a.m. sales pep rally for 300 managers.

The need for energy is even greater today than in the past, because more companies are expecting all employees, including executives, to spend more time on the road visiting the organization's other locations, customers, and suppliers.

Tenacity. Leaders are better at overcoming obstacles than nonleaders. They have the "capacity to work with distant objects in view" and have a "degree of strength of will or perseverance."[8] Leaders must be tirelessly persistent in their activities and follow through with their programs. Most organizational change programs take several months to establish and can take many years before the benefits are seen. Leaders must have the drive to stick with these programs, and persistence is needed to ensure that changes are institutionalized.

An example of heroic perseverance in the face of obstacles, from American history, is the tale of John Paul Jones, a captain in the newly formed American Navy. On September 25, 1779, John Paul Jones, aboard the Bonhomme Richard, engaged in battle with the English ship, Serapis, off the coast of England. After being bombarded with cannon fire by the Serapis, having two old cannons explode causing a fire, and being fired at by their supposed ally, the Alliance, Jones appeared to have lost the battle. When asked to surrender in the face of almost certain defeat, Jones made his immortal reply: "I have not yet begun to fight."

Determined to sink the Serapis, Jones spotted an open hatch on the Serapis' deck and ordered a young sailor to climb into the rigging and toss grenades into the hatch, knowing the English had stored their ammunitions there. After missing with the first two grenades, the third grenade disappeared into the hatchway and was followed by a thunderous explosion aboard the Serapis. Engulfed in flames, the English captain surrendered to Jones. Even though the entire battle had gone against him, John Paul Jones was determined not to give up, and it was this persistence that caused him to finally emerge victorious.

It is not just the direction of action that counts, but sticking to the direction chosen. Effective leaders must keep pushing themselves and others toward the goal. David Glass, CEO of Wal-Mart, says that Sam Walton "has an overriding something in him that causes him to improve every day. . . . As long as I have known him, he has never gotten to the point where he's comfortable with who he is or how we're doing." Walt Disney was described as expecting the best and not relenting until he got it. Ray Kroc, of McDonald's Corporation, was described as a "dynamo who drove the company relentlessly."[9] Kroc posted this inspirational message on his wall:

Nothing in the world can take the place of persistence.
Talent will not; nothing is more common than unsuccessful men with great talent.
Genius will not; unrewarded genius is almost a proverb.
Education will not; the world is full of educated derelicts.
Persistence, determination alone are omnipotent.

Persistence, of course, must be used intelligently. Dogged pursuit of an inappropriate strategy can ruin an organization. It is important to persist in the right things. But what are the right things? In today's business climate, they may include the following: satisfying the customer, growth, cost control, innovation, fast response time, and quality. Or, in Tom Peters' terms, a constant striving to improve just about everything.

Initiative.   Effective leaders are proactive. They make choices and take action that leads a change instead of just reacting to events or waiting for things to happen; that is, they show a high level of initiative. The following two examples from consultant Richard Boyatzis of McBer and Company illustrate proactivity.[10]

> I called the chief, and he said he couldn't commit the resources, so I called the budget and finance people, who gave me a negative response. But then I called a guy in another work group who said he was willing to make a trade for the parts I needed. I got the parts and my group was able to complete the repairs.

> One of our competitors was making a short, half-inch component and probably making $30,000–$40,000 a year on it. I looked at our line: we have the same product and can probably make it better and cheaper. I told our marketing manager: "Let's go after that business." I made the decision that we would look at it as a marketplace rather than looking at it as individual customers wanting individual quantities. I said, here's a market that has 30,000 pieces of these things, and we don't give a damn where we get the orders. Let's just go out and get them. We decided we were going to charge a specific price and get the business. Right now we make $30,000–$40,000 on these things and our competitor makes zero.

Instead of sitting "idly by or [waiting] for fate to smile upon them," leaders need to "challenge the process."

Leaders are achievement-oriented, ambitious, energetic, tenacious, and proactive. These same qualities, however, may result in a manager who tries to accomplish everything alone, thereby failing to develop subordinate commitment and responsibility. Effective leaders must not only be full of drive and ambition, they must *want to lead others.*

Leadership Motivation

Studies show that leaders have a strong desire to lead. Leadership motivation involves the desire to influence and lead others and is often equated with the need for power. People with high leadership motivation think a lot about influencing other people, winning an argument, or being the greater authority. They prefer to be in a leadership rather than subordinate role. The willingness to assume responsibility, which seems to coincide with leadership motivation, is frequently found in leaders.

Sears psychologist Jon Bentz describes successful Sears executives as those who have a "powerful competitive drive for a position of . . . authority . . . [and] the need to be recognized as men of influence."[11] Astronauts John Glenn and Frank Borman built political and business careers out of their early feats as space explorers, while other astronauts did not. Clearly, all astronauts possessed the same opportunities, but it was their personal makeup that caused Glenn and Borman to pursue their ambitions and take on leadership roles.

Psychologist Warren Bennis and colleague Burt Nanus state that power is a leader's currency, or the primary means through which the leader gets things done in the organization. A leader must want to gain the power to exercise influence over others. Also, power is an "expandable pie," not a fixed sum; effective leaders give power to others as a means of increasing their own power. Effective leaders do not see power as something that is competed for but rather as something that can be created and distributed to followers without detracting from their own power.

Successful managers at AT&T completed sentence fragments in the following manner:[12]

"When I am in charge of others I find my greatest satisfactions."
"The job I am best fit for is one which requires leadership ability."
"I depend on others to carry out my plans and directions."

A manager who was not as successful completed the sentence fragment "Taking orders . . ." with the ending "is easy for it removes the danger of a bad decision."

Successful leaders must be willing to exercise power over subordinates, tell them what to do, and make appropriate use of positive and negative sanctions. Previous studies have shown inconsistent results regarding dominance as a leadership trait. According to Harvard psychologist David McClelland, this may be because there are two different types of dominance: a personalized power motive, or power lust, and a socialized power motive, or the desire to lead.[13]

Personalized Power Motive. Although a need for power is desirable, the leader's effectiveness depends on what is behind it. A leader with a personalized power motive seeks power as an end in itself. These individuals have little self-control, are often impulsive, and focus on collecting symbols of personal prestige. Acquiring power solely for the sake of dominating others may be based on profound self-doubt. The personalized power motive is concerned with domination of others and leads to dependent, submissive followers.

Socialized Power Motive. In contrast, a leader with a socialized power motive uses power as a means to achieve desired goals, or a vision. Its use is expressed as the ability to develop networks and coalitions, gain cooperation from others, resolve conflicts in a constructive manner, and use role modeling to influence others.

Individuals with a socialized power motive are more emotionally mature than those with a personalized power motive. They exercise power more for the benefit of the whole organization and are less likely to use it for manipulation. These leaders are also less defensive, more willing to take advice from experts, and have a longer-range view. They use their power to build up their organization and make it successful. The socialized power motive takes account of followers' needs and results in empowered, independent followers.

Honesty and Integrity

Honesty and integrity are virtues in all individuals, but have special significance for leaders. Without these qualities, leadership is undermined. Integrity is the correspondence between word and deed and honesty refers to being truthful or non-deceitful. The two form the foundation of a trusting relationship between leader and followers.

In his comprehensive review of leadership, psychologist Bernard Bass found that student leaders were rated as more trustworthy and reliable in carrying out responsibilities than followers. Similarly, British organizational psychologists Charles Cox and Cary Cooper's "high flying" (successful) managers preferred to have an open style of management, where they truthfully informed workers about happenings in the company. Morgan McCall and Michael Lombardo of the Center for Creative Leadership found that managers who reached the top were more likely to follow the following formula: "I will do exactly what I say I will do when I say I will do it. If I change my mind, I will tell you well in advance so you will not be harmed by my actions."[14]

Successful leaders are open with their followers, but also discreet and do not violate confidences or carelessly divulge potentially harmful information. One subordinate in a study by Harvard's John Gabarro made the following remark about his new president: "He was so consistent in what he said and did, it was easy to trust him." Another subordinate remarked about an unsuccessful leader, "How can I rely on him if I can't count on him consistently?"[15]

Professors James Kouzes, Barry Posner, and W. H. Schmidt asked 1500 managers "What values do you look for and admire in your supervisors?" Integrity (being truthful and trustworthy, and having character and conviction) was the most frequently mentioned characteristic. Kouzes and Posner conclude:

> Honesty is absolutely essential to leadership. After all, if we are willing to follow someone, whether it be into battle or into the boardroom, we first want to assure ourselves that the person is worthy of our trust. We want to know that he or she is being truthful, ethical, and principled. We want to be fully confident in the integrity of our leaders.

Effective leaders are credible, with excellent reputations, and high levels of integrity. The following description (from Gabarro's study) by one subordinate of his boss exemplifies the concept of integrity: "By integrity, I don't mean whether he'll rob a bank, or steal from the till. You don't work with people like that. It's whether you sense a person has some basic principles and is willing to stand by them."

Bennis and Nanus warn that today credibility is at a premium, especially since people are better informed, more cautious, and wary of authority and power. Leaders can gain trust by being predictable, consistent, and persistent and by making competent decisions. An honest leader may even by able to overcome lack of expertise, as a subordinate in Gabarro's study illustrates in the following description of his superior: "I don't like a lot of the things he does, but he's basically honest. He's a genuine article and you'll forgive a lot of things because of that. That goes a long way in how much I trust him."

Self-Confidence

There are many reasons why a leader needs self-confidence. Being a leader is a very difficult job. A great deal of information must be gathered and processed. A constant series of problems must be solved and decisions made. Followers have to be convinced to pursue specific courses of action. Setbacks have to be overcome. Competing interests have to be satisfied. Risks have to be taken in the face of uncertainty. A person riddled with self-doubt would never be able to take the necessary actions nor command the respect of others.

Self-confidence plays an important role in decision-making and in gaining others' trust. Obviously, if the leader is not sure of what decision to make, or expresses a high degree of doubt, then the followers are less likely to trust the leader and be committed to the vision.

Not only is the leader's self-confidence important, but so is others' perception of it. Often, leaders engage in impression management to bolster their image of competence; by projecting self-confidence they arouse followers' self-confidence. Self-confident leaders are also more likely to be assertive and decisive, which gains others' confidence in the decision. This is crucial for effective implementation of the decision. Even when the decision turns out to be a poor one, the self-confident leader admits the mistake and uses it as a learning opportunity, often building trust in the process. Manor Care, Inc., for example, lost over $21 million in 1988 when it was caught holding a large portion of Beverly Enterprise's stock. Chairman and CEO Stewart Bainum, Jr. stated, "I take full and complete responsibility for making the acquisition."[16] Considered to be the "best managed company in the [nursing home] industry," Manor Care's stock has rebounded, and it seems to be making a comeback. Less successful managers are more defensive about failure and try to cover up mistakes.

Emotional Stability. Self-confidence helps effective leaders remain even-tempered. They do get excited, such as when delivering an emotionally charged pep talk, but generally do not become angry or enraged. For the most part, as long as the employee did his/her homework leaders remain composed upon hearing that an employee made a costly mistake. For example, at PepsiCo, an employee who makes a mistake is "safe . . . as long as it's a calculated risk."

Emotional stability is especially important when resolving interpersonal conflicts and when representing the organization. A top executive who impulsively flies off the handle will not foster as much trust and teamwork as an executive who retains emotional control. Describing a superior, one employee in Gabarro's study stated, "he's impulsive and I'm never sure when he'll change signals on me."

Researchers at the Center for Creative Leadership found that leaders are more likely to "derail" if they lack emotional stability and composure. Leaders who derail are less able to handle pressure and more prone to moodiness, angry outbursts, and inconsistent behavior, which undermines their interpersonal relationships with subordinates, peers, and superiors. In contrast, they found the successful leaders to be calm, confident, and predictable during crisis.

Psychologically hardy, self-confident individuals consider stressful events interesting, as opportunities for development, and believe that they can influence the outcome. K. Labich in *Fortune* magazine argued that "By demonstrating grace under pressure, the best leaders inspire those around them to stay calm and act intelligently."[17]

Cognitive Ability

Leaders must gather, integrate, and interpret enormous amounts of information. These demands are greater than ever today because of rapid technological change. Thus, it is not surprising that leaders need to be intelligent enough to formulate suitable strategies, solve problems, and make correct decisions.

Leaders have often been characterized as being intelligent, but not necessarily brilliant and as being conceptually skilled. Kotter states that a "keen mind" (i.e., strong analytical ability, good judgement, and the capacity to think strategically and multidimensionally) is necessary for effective leadership, and that leadership effectiveness requires "above average intelligence," rather than genius.

An individual's intelligence and the perception of his or her intelligence are two highly related factors. Professors Lord, DeVader, and Alliger concluded that "intelligence is a key characteristic in predicting leadership perceptions."[18] Howard and Bray found that cognitive ability predicted managerial success twenty years later in their AT&T study. Effective managers have been shown to display greater ability to reason both inductively and deductively than ineffective managers.

Intelligence may be a trait that followers look for in a leader. If someone is going to lead, followers want that person to be more capable in *some* respects than they are. Therefore, the follower's perception of cognitive ability in a leader is a source of authority in the leadership relationship.

Knowledge of the Business

Effective leaders have a high degree of knowledge about the company, industry, and technical matters. For example, Jack Welch, president of GE had a PhD in engineering; George Hatsopolous of Thermo Electron Corporation, in the years preceding the OPEC boycott, had both the business knowledge of the impending need for energy- efficient appliances and the technical knowledge of thermodynamics to create more efficient gas furnaces. Technical expertise enables the leader to understand the concerns of subordinates regarding technical issues. Harvard Professor John Kotter argues that expertise is more important than formal education.

Effective leaders gather extensive information about the company and the industry. Most of the successful general managers studied by Harvard's Kotter spent their careers in the same industry, while less successful managers lacked industry-specific experiences. Although cognitive ability is needed to gain a thorough understanding of the business, formal education is not a requirement. Only forty percent of the business leaders studied by Bennis and Nanus had business degrees. In-depth knowledge of the organization and industry allows effective leaders to make well-informed decisions and to understand the implications of those decisions.

Other Traits

Charisma, creativity/originality, and flexibility are three traits with less clear-cut evidence of their importance to leadership.[19] Effective leaders may have charisma; however, this trait may only be important for political leaders. Effective leaders also may be more creative than nonleaders, but there is no consistent research demonstrating this. Flexibility or adaptiveness may be important traits for a leader in today's turbulent environment. Leaders must be able to make decisions and solve problems quickly and initiate and foster change.

There may be other important traits needed for effective leadership; however, we believe that the first six that we discussed are the core traits.

THE REST OF THE STORY

A complete theory of leadership involves more than specifying leader traits. Traits only endow people with the potential for leadership. To actualize this potential, additional factors are necessary which are discussed in our forthcoming book *The Essence of Leadership* (written with additional authors).

Three categories of factors are discussed here: skills, vision, and implementing the vision. *Skills* are narrower than traits and involve specific capacities for action such as decision making, problem solving, and performance appraisal.

The core job of a leader, however, is to create a *vision*—a concept of what the organization should be. To quote Bennis and Nanus, "a vision articulates a view of a realistic, credible, attractive future for the organization, a condition that is better in some important ways than what now exists. A vision is a target that beckons."[20] Next the leader must *communicate* this vision to followers through inspirational speeches, written messages, appeals to shared values and above all through acting as a role model and personally acting in a way that is consistent with the vision. Third, the leader must develop or at least help to develop a general *strategy* for achieving the vision (i.e. a strategic vision).

Implementing the vision requires at least six activities:

1 *Structuring*. Today's effective organizations have minimal bureaucracy: small corporate staffs, few layers of management and large spans of control. The leader must insure that the organization's structure facilitates the flow of information (downward, upward, and diagonally). Information from customers regarding product quality and services is especially crucial.

2 *Selecting and Training*. Leaders must make sure that people are hired who have the traits needed to accept and implement the vision. Maintaining and upgrading skills is assured by constant training, as is commitment to the organization's vision.

3 *Motivating*. Leaders cannot achieve the vision alone; they must stimulate others to work for it too. They must generate enthusiasm, commitment, and compliance. Besides communicating the vision, effective leaders use at least six procedures to motivate followers.

Formal authority. The leader is the "boss" and must use his or her legitimate power constructively. The leader must start by asking directly for what he or she wants. *Thriving on Chaos* author Tom Peters said that if one wants something, then "Just ask for it."

Role models. Leaders must behave the way they wish their followers would behave. For example, if they want subordinates to be customer-oriented, they should spend time themselves talking to customers. This has far more influence on employees than just telling them that customers are important.

Build subordinate self-confidence. If employees have been carefully selected and trained, such confidence will be justified. Jay Conger calls the process of strengthening subordinates' belief in their capabilities "empowerment."[21]

Delegation of authority. Giving autonomy and responsibility to employees also creates empowerment. In their book *Superleadership,* Charles Manz and Henry Sims[22] argue that delegating authority actually enhances the power of leaders by helping their subordinates become capable of attaining organizational goals. Effective delegation, of course, presupposes that subordinates are capable of holding the responsibilities they are given (as a result of extensive training and experience).

Specific and challenging goals.[23] Ensuring that subordinates have specific and challenging goals lead to higher performance than ambiguous goals. Challenging goals are empowering, because they demonstrate the leader has confidence in the follower. Goals must be accompanied by regular feedback indicating progress in relation to the goals. Feedback, in turn, requires adequate performance measurement.

For goals to be effective employees must be committed to them. Inspiration, modeling, training, and delegation all facilitate commitment.

Rewards and punishments. Effective leaders are *not* tolerant of those who reject the vision or repeatedly fail to attain reasonable goals. Rewards (and punishments) send messages not only to the employee in question but also to others; followers often direct their own actions by looking at what happens to their peers. People may learn as much or more by observing models than from the consequences of their own actions.[24] Rewards may include pay raises, promotions and awards, as well as recognition and praise. Effective leaders do not just reward achievement, they celebrate it.

4 *Managing Information.* Leaders have a profound influence on how information is managed within the organization. Effective leaders are effective information gatherers because they are good listeners and encourage subordinates to express their opinions. They stay in contact with the rest of the organization by, in Tom Peters' terms, "wandering around." Leaders actively seek information from outside the organization. Good leaders also disseminate information widely so that followers will understand the reasons for decisions that are made and how their work fits into the organization's goals. At the same time, effective leaders try not to overwhelm subordinates with too much information.

5 *Team Building.* Achieving goals requires collaboration among many (in some cases, hundreds of thousands) individuals. Leaders need to help build effective teams, starting with the top management team.[25] While an effective leader cannot do everything, he or she can insure that everything gets done by hiring, training, and motivating skilled people who work together effectively. And they, in turn, can build effective teams of their own.

6 *Promoting change and innovation.* Finally, effective leaders must promote change and innovation. The vision, since it pertains to a desired future state, is the starting point of change. This must be reinforced by constant restructuring, continual retraining to develop new skills, setting specific goals for innovation and improvement, rewarding innovation, encouraging a constant information flow in all directions and emphasizing responsiveness to customer demands.

• • •

It is clear that leadership is a very demanding activity and that leaders who have the requisite traits—drive, desire to lead, self-confidence, honesty (and integrity), cognitive ability, and industry knowledge—have a considerable advantage over those who lack these traits. Without drive, for example, it is unlikely that an individual would be able to gain the expertise required to lead an organization effectively, let alone implement and work toward long-term goals. Without the desire to lead, individuals are not motivated to persuade others to work toward a common goal; such an individual would avoid or be indifferent to leadership tasks. Self-confidence is needed to withstand setbacks, persevere through hard times, and lead others in new directions. Confidence gives effective leaders the ability to make hard decisions and to stand by them. A leader's honesty and integrity form the foundation on which the leader gains followers' trust and confidence; without honesty and integrity, the leader would not be able to attract and retain followers. At least a moderate degree of cognitive ability is needed to gain and understand technical issues as well as the nature of the industry. Cognitive ability permits leaders to accurately analyze situations and make effective decisions. Finally, knowledge of the business is needed to develop suitable strategic visions and business plans.

MANAGEMENT IMPLICATIONS

Individuals can be *selected* either from outside the organization or from within non- or lower-managerial ranks based on their possession of traits that are less changeable or trainable. Cognitive ability (not be confused with knowledge) is probably the least trainable of the six traits. Drive is fairly constant over time although it can change; it is observable in employees assuming they are given enough autonomy and responsibility to show what they can do. The desire to lead is more difficult to judge in new hires who may have had little opportunity for leadership early in life. It can be observed at lower levels of management and by observing people in assessment center exercises.

Two other traits can be developed through experience and *training.* Knowledge of the industry and technical knowledge come from formal training, job experience, and a mentally active approach toward new opportunities for learning. Planned job rotation can facilitate such growth. Self-confidence is both general and task specific. People differ in their general confidence in mastering life's challenges but task-specific self-confidence comes from mastering the various skills that leadership requires as well as the technical and strategic challenges of the industry. Such confidence parallels the individual's growth in knowledge.

Honesty does not require skill building; it is a virtue one achieves or rejects by choice. Organizations should look with extreme skepticism at any employee who behaves dishonestly or lacks integrity, and should certainly not reward dishonesty in any form, especially not with a promotion. The key role models for honest behavior are those at the top. On this issue, organizations get what they model, not what they preach.

CONCLUSIONS

Regardless of whether leaders are born or made or some combination of both, it is unequivocally clear that *leaders are not like other people.* Leaders do not have to be great men or women by being intellectual geniuses or omniscient prophets to succeed, but they do need to have the "right stuff" and this stuff is not equally present in all people. Leadership is a demanding, unrelenting job with enormous pressures and grave responsibilities. It would be a profound disservice to leaders to suggest that they are ordinary people who happened to be in the right place at the right time. Maybe the place matters, but it takes a special kind of person to master the challenges of opportunity. Let us not only give credit, but also use the knowledge we have to select and train our future leaders effectively. We believe that in the realm of leadership (and in every other realm), the individual *does* matter.

ENDNOTES

This article is based on a chapter of a forthcoming book by Edwin A. Locke, Shelley A. Kirkpatrick, Jill K. Wheeler, Jodi Schneider, Kathryn Niles, Harold Goldstein, Kurt Welsh, & Dong-OK Chah, entitled *The Essence of Leadership*. We would like to thank Dr. Kathryn Bartol for her helpful comments on this manuscript.

1 P. Slater and W. G. Bennis, "Democracy is Inevitable," *Harvard Business Review*, Sept-Oct, 1990, 170 and 171. For a summary of trait theories, see R. M. Stogdill's *Handbook of Leadership* (New York: Free Press, 1974). For reviews and studies of leadership traits, see R. E. Boyatzis, *The Competent Manager* (New York: Wiley & Sons, 1982); C. J. Cox and C. L. Cooper, *High Flyers: An Anatomy of Managerial Success* (Oxford: Basil Blackwell); G. A. Yukl, *Leadership in Organizations* (Englewood Cliffs, NJ: Prentice Hall, 1989), Chapter 9.

2 R. M. Stogdill, "Personal Factors Associated with Leadership: A Survey of the Literature," *Journal of Psychology*, 1948, 25, 64.

3 See the following sources for evidence and further information concerning each trait: 1) drive: B. M. Bass's *Handbook of Leadership* (New York: The Free Press, 1990); K. G. Smith and J. K. Harrison, "In Search of Excellent Leaders" (in W. D. Guth's *The Handbook of Strategy*, New York: Warren, Gorham & Lamont, 1986). 2) desire to lead: V. J. Bentz, "The Sears Experience in the Investigation, Description, and Prediction of Executive Behavior" (In F. R. Wickert and D. E. McFarland's *Measuring Executive Effectiveness*, (New York: Appleton-Century-Croft, 1967); J. B. Miner, "Twenty Years of Research on Role-Motivation Theory of Managerial Effectiveness," *Personnel Psychology*, 1978, 31, 739–760. 3) honesty/integrity: Bass, op. cit.; W. G. Bennis and B. Nanus, *Leaders: The Strategies for Taking Charge* (New York: Harper & Row, 1985); J. M. Kouzes and B. Z. Posner, *The Leadership Challenge: How to Get Things Done in Organizations* (San Francisco: Jossey-Bass); T. Peters, *Thriving on Chaos* (New York: Harper & Row, 1987); A. Rand, *For the New Intellectual* (New York: Signet, 1961). 4) self-confidence: Bass, op. cit. and A. Bandura, *Social Foundations of Thought and Action: A Social Cognitive Theory* (Englewood Cliffs, NJ: Prentice-Hall). Psychological hardiness is discussed by S. R. Maddi and S. C. Kobasa, *The Hardy Executive: Health Under Stress* (Chicago: Dorsey Professional Books, 1984); M. W. McCall Jr. and M. M. Lombardo, *Off the Track: Why and How Successful Executives get Derailed* (Technical Report No. 21, Greensboro, NC: Center for Creative Leadership, 1983). 5) cognitive ability: R. G. Lord, C. L. DeVader, and G. M. Alliger, "A Meta-analysis of the Relation Between Personality Traits and Leadership Perceptions: An Application of Validity Generalization Procedures," *Journal of Applied Psychology*, 1986; 61, 402–410; A. Howard and D. W. Bray, *Managerial Lives in Transition: Advancing Age and Changing Times* (New York: Guilford Press, 1988).   6)

knowledge of the business: Bennis and Nanus, op. cit.; J. P. Kotter, *The General Managers* (New York: Macmillan); Smith and Harrison, op. cit.

4 From J. J. Gabarro, *The Dynamics of Taking Charge* (Boston: Harvard Business School Press, 1987).

5 All PepsiCo references are from B. Dumaine, "Those highflying managers at PepsiCo," *Fortune,* April 10, 1989, 78–86. The Watson quote is from Smith and Harrison, op. cit., as are the Disney and Woolman quotes in the following paragraph.

6 The four quotes are from Howard and Bray, op. cit.

7 From Kouzes and Posner, op. cit., pp. 122 and V. J. Bentz, op. cit. The Sam Walton quote is from J. Huey, "Wal-Mart: Will it take over the world?," *Fortune,* January 30, 1989, 52–59.

8 From Bass, op. cit.

9 The Walton quote is from Huey, op. cit., and the Kroc quote is from Smith and Harrison, op. cit. The quote on Kroc's wall is taken from Bennis and Nanus, op. cit.

10 From Boyatzis, op. cit. Also, Kouzes and Posner, op. cit. stress the importance of leader initiative.

11 From Bentz, op. cit.

12 From Howard and Bray, op. cit.

13 The distinction between a personalized and a socialized power motive is made by D. C. McClelland, "N-achievement and entrepreneurship: A longitudinal study," *Journal of Personality and Social Psychology,* 1965, 1, 389–392. These two power motives are discussed further by Kouzes and Posner, op. cit.

14 From McCall and Lombardo, op. cit.

15 From Gabarro, op. cit.

16 K. F. Girard examines Manor Care in "To the Manor Born," *Warfield's,* March, 1989, 68–75.

17 From K. Labish, "The Seven Keys to Business Leadership," *Fortune,* October 24, 1988, 58–66.

18 From Lord, DeVader, and Alliger, op. cit.

19 For research on charisma, see Bass, op. cit. and R. J. House, W. D. Spangler, and J. Woycke, "Personality and charisma in the U.S. presidency: A psychological theory of leadership effectiveness (Wharton School, University of Pennsylvania, 1989, unpublished manuscript), on creativity/originality, see Howard and Bray, op. cit. and A. Zaleznik, *The Managerial Mystique* (New York: Harper and Row, 1989); on flexibility, see Smith and Harrison, op. cit.

20 From Bennis and Nanus, op. cit.

21 From J. A. Conger, *Charismatic Leadership: The Elusive Factor in Organizational Effectiveness* (San Francisco: Jossey-Bass, 1988).

22 C. Manz and H. P. Sims, *Superleadership: Leading Others to Lead Themselves* (New York: Prentice Hall, 1989).

23 See E. A. Locke and G. P. Latham, *A Theory of Goal Setting & Task Performance* (Englewood Cliffs, NJ: Prentice Hall, 1990).

24 See Bandura, op. cit.

25 See D. C. Hambrick, "The top management team: Keys to strategic success," *California Management Review,* 1987, 30, 1–20.

Leadership Theory and Development: The Coming "New Phase"

Chester A. Schriesheim
Linda L. Neider

Over the years numerous programmes have been employed to develop managers to be more successful leaders. Organisations generally seem to believe that their performance will increase as a result of leadership development and, because of this belief, some type of leadership development is usually included in an organisation's human resource programme. In fact, Bures and Banks (1985) recently found that 48 per cent of companies conduct management development programmes that could be called "leadership development".

Dozens of leadership "theories" or "models" exist (Bass, 1981; Yukel, 1981) and organisations may employ any of the hundreds or thousands of different leadership development interventions (Bolt, 1985; McCauley, 1986; Strong, 1986). Yet the question still remains, "Have we developed general approaches to leadership which, when applied to the training and development of leaders, clearly increase their organisational performance?" Unfortunately, the answer to this question seems to be "Probably not" (Tetrault *et al.,* 1988), although we do know that enhanced leadership effectiveness does increase organisational effectiveness (House, 1988). For these reasons, the purpose of this article is (1) to briefly note why much of the leadership development work, based on current and past approaches, does not seem to work, and (2) to summarise new research directions which promise to change this situation. This recent research has already yielded an enhanced understanding of basic leadership processes and, in the future, practical applications appear possible through management development programmes.

WHY CURRENT LEADERSHIP DEVELOPMENT DOES NOT ALWAYS SEEM TO WORK

Previous Approaches to Leadership Theory and Practice

Leadership development currently conducted in organisations may be viewed as existing on a continuum. At one end very specific training is involved, aimed at enhancing concrete skills (such as providing performance feedback to subordinates, conducting counselling interviews, and so on). At the other end of the continuum more abstract and conceptual development occurs (focusing on such things as selecting a leadership style).

Although it is difficult to evaluate leadership training and development overall, it should be noted that the specific-skills type of leadership training is typically implemented in unique or idiosyncratic ways in most organisations. This makes it impossi-

From *Leadership & Organization Development Journal,* 1989, **10**(6), 17–26. Reprinted by permission.

ble to draw any firm conclusions about the general effectiveness of these types of training programmes (Beer and Walton, 1987). Thus, little of general value is known about skill-based leadership training programmes and, consequently, these types of programme are not considered further in this review (Goldstein, 1980; Wexley, 1984). We do, however, know that many of the broader forms of leadership development have been almost uniformly unsuccessful (Tetrault *et al.,* 1988), and this will be our focus. Specifically, why have these forms of leadership development not "worked"?

Virtually all of the broader forms of leadership development have been based on one or more leadership "theories", "models", or "approaches". In this regard, it should be noted that most textbook treatments of leadership highlight that modern leadership theory and practice has gone through three distinct phases (Behling and Schriesheim, 1976; Berkman and Neider, 1987). The first, commonly referred to as the "trait phase", involved attempting to identify either a common or universal set of characteristics that distinguished leaders from non-leaders or effective leaders from those who were ineffective. This phase, which ran from the turn of the century to about 1950, was largely unsuccessful in pinpointing universal leadership characteristics (Stogdill, 1974; Bass, 1981). Although some traits, such as intelligence, were more often than not associated with leadership success, the general pattern of research evidence indicated that no common set of "success" characteristics seemed to exist. Thus, the second phase of leadership theory and practice, which has come to be called the "behavioural phase", was initiated.

The behavioural phase focused on first identifying various leadership styles and then trying to determine which style was generally most effective across all situations. Although it is appealing to believe that such a style could exist, the evidence which accumulated through the late 1960s indicated otherwise (Bass, 1981; Kerr *et al.,* 1974). As a consequence, research on the behavioural approach was largely abandoned and leadership theory and practice entered its third and current phase, the contingency approach, in the early 1970s.

The contingency approach treats leadership effectiveness as arising from the dynamic interplay of three factors: the leader, the followers, and the situation in which both find themselves (Bass, 1981; Yukl, 1981). Although this approach is intuitively more appealing than the two which preceded it, it too is not without problems. In particular, the evidence which has accumulated on these various leadership theories has generally been ambiguous, at best (Field, 1979; Graeff, 1983; Lueder, 1985; Schriesheim and Kerr, 1977; Vecchio, 1987). Likewise, the accumulated evidence on practical applications of contingency approaches to the development of managers, for example, is generally negative (Burke and Day, 1986; Clegg, 1987; Tetrault *et al.,* 1988).

There may be a positive aspect to the trend that, overall, the trait, behavioural and situational approaches to leadership theory and research have not been particularly successful. The fact that the trait approach has not generally been supported may, for example, indicate that leaders can be "made" (in contrast to being born or not born with "leadership characteristics"). On the other hand, the fact that no clear set of leader characteristics can be said strongly to predict leadership success indicates that trying to select potential leaders via traditional paper-and-pencil tests or inventories is unlikely to be very fruitful. This, of course, does not imply that an organisation's attempts to predict managerial success are doomed to failure. It may very well be that researchers have not yet identified the appropriate categories of traits to use as predictors of managerial success (House and Baetz, 1979).

The failure of behavioural phase researchers to identify an optimum leadership style for all situations belies a number of currently popular major programmes (Blake and Mouton, 1978, 1985), as well as consultants who preach that there is a universally best way to lead (Schriesheim, 1982). Such lack of success also indicated that simple-minded approaches to leadership will not work and that quality leadership development must be sophisticated and involve subtitles. Efforts would seem well-advised to focus, at a minimum, on teaching participants to diagnose situations so as to know what behaviours are most appropriate, and to develop the ability to display different leadership styles, depending on situational demands (Latham and Saari, 1979).

Although failure of the contingency approach to leadership theory and practice is, at least partly, disappointing, it may also be seen in a positive light. On the one hand, time and effort have been "wasted" in pursuing a "blind alley". On the other hand, had contingency research and practice not been undertaken, we would not be poised on the threshold of what may be considered the coming phase of leadership theory and development: a managerial phase which considers realistic complexities and views leadership from an interpersonal influence perspective.

The Coming Phase of Leadership Theory and Practice

It seems intuitively appealing, and much research supports the general proposition, that how a leader acts in a given situation critically determines whether he or she will be effective (Bass, 1981; Yukl, 1981). Why then has behavioural and contingency leadership research and practice yielded little fruit? Although a number of answers may be proposed, the one which seems most plausible at this time is that these approaches have been too narrow or myopic—they have approached leadership from too simple a perspective.

All existing major situational and behavioural approaches to leadership have ignored the broader managerial roles which leaders must perform, and they have treated the concept of leadership style in an unnecessarily simplified manner. Current leadership approaches have also ignored the fact that leadership is inherently a process of interpersonal influence and have, instead, treated it from a very naive point of view. Specifically,

> . . . leadership is the only way in which the manager contributes to organizational effectiveness. The manager also performs duties which are *externally oriented* so far as his unit is concerned . . . Similarly, not all of the manager's *internally oriented* activities can be labelled leadership acts. . . . Clearly, the manager must perform a mix of internal and external activities if his unit is to perform well. Leadership is only one of the internal activities performed by managers (Behling and Schriesheim, 1976, p. 294).

Based on research, such as that by Mintzberg (1973), managers may be seen as performing a multitude of roles, only one of which is the interpersonal role which we commonly label "leadership". Clearly, then, leadership theory and practice must acknowledge these broader role requirements and, in fact, there is evidence that this is beginning to occur (Hunt *et al.,* 1982, 1984, 1988). When leadership is viewed from a managerial perspective, instead of the isolated way in which it has been treated, we may expect theory and practice to begin to deal with the more significant issues facing leaders. As a result, leadership theory and practice may begin to make serious progress in helping us better develop managers for enhanced leadership effectiveness.

The coming of age of leadership theory and research will also, of necessity, employ a more sophisticated conceptualisation of leadership style. Historically, most approaches to leadership style have treated it either as a single-dimensional continuum (Tannenbaum and Schmidt, 1958; Vroom and Yetton, 1973), or as involving two types of behaviour—typically person-centred and task-centred (Blake and Mouton, 1978, 1985; Hersey and Blanchard, 1977; House, 1971; Kerr *et al.,* 1974). It seems obvious that leaders display a whole host of behaviours and that this complexity needs to be taken into account in future research and practice (Schriesheim and Kerr, 1977; Yukl, 1981).

As a final consideration, most major existing treatments have not focused on leadership as a multidimensional process of interpersonal influence. Specifically, the terms "influence" and "influence processes" have rarely appeared in the leadership literature (Bass, 1981; Yukl, 1981), and they have only recently begun to be investigated (Schriesheim and Hinkin, 1986). Thus, it is perhaps not surprising that both past research and practice could not meaningfully advance since the fundamental nature of leadership as a process was largely ignored. There is substantial evidence that the coming age of leadership theory and development will not repeat this or the two other major mistakes of the past (which were mentioned above). In fact, some "new wave" work which is currently being conducted very much typifies this coming phase of leadership theory and practice. Examples of this current work, as well as its potential applications, are presented below.

CURRENT "NEW PHASE" LEADERSHIP WORK

As one might expect, the newest research on leadership is generally managerial in focus: it treats leadership as one part of the manager's job. It also involves examining more than just one or two elements of "style", focusing instead on leadership as a multidimensional, interpersonal process. Specifically, there are three major "new phase" trends which appear to be emerging in a leadership theory and development—(1) a focus on leadership as one aspect of management, (2) an elaboration on interpersonal influence processes and (3) a concentration on much broader conceptualisations of style. Each of these trends is discussed below.

Focus on Leadership as an Aspect of Management

One outcome of focusing on leadership as an aspect of the larger job of managing is a new-found interest in fundamental management processes. In this respect, it should be noted that practising managers have long had an interest in issues surrounding delegation and employee participation in decision-making processes (McConkey, 1974;

Steinmetz, 1976). However, academics have ignored delegation altogether and, additionally, have often examined participation from a normative or value-laden perspective (Leana, 1986; Locke and Schwieger, 1979).

Although Bass *et al.*, (1975) should be credited with the first serious consideration of viewing participation and delegation as distinct management activities, Leana (1986, 1987) has most recently made significant contributions in this area. The results of her innovative studies indicate several differences in the relative use of delegation and participation on the part of managers. Specifically, she found that adept managers chose to relinquish, instead of share, decision-making authority based on characteristics of the decision situation (e.g. workload pressures) as well as characteristics of the employees involved (e.g. their ability levels).

Our recent research (Schriesheim and Neider, 1988) has expanded on Leana's work and the classic decision-making framework of Vroom and Yetton (1973). Briefly, Vroom and Yetton developed a decision tree model to assist managers in choosing an appropriate decision facing a manager and various situational constraints, one of several decision styles is suggested as appropriate. In their "individual" model, these styles range from having a manager make the decision him/herself (AI style) to delegating a problem to a subordinate (DI). Although highly creative, the Vroom and Yetton individual model is incomplete with respect to delegative decision styles. Thus, so as to increase the utility of their model, we decided to expand and clarify their treatment of delegative decision-making subtypes.

As a result of such research, we have identified three different forms or types of delegation and have started to examine how these forms are associated with the motivation, commitment, satisfaction and performance of employees. Table I presents these three delegative forms, along with four other forms of leadership decision making. Also summarised in Table I are the relationships which have been obtained in our research to date with job satisfaction and commitment to the employing organisation (commitment is defined in involving (1) willingness to invest effort in furthering the goals of the organisation, (2) reluctance to leave the organisation and (3) viewing one's values as congruent with those of the organisation (Mowday *et al.*, 1982).

Although the data are preliminary, it appears that a middle-ground delegational strategy is best. That is, leaders who are seen as delegating to subordinates but, at the same time, as neither abdicating nor requiring excessive permissions or approvals, are most likely to find that subordinates report job satisfaction and commitment to their organisations. Interestingly, as shown in Table I, a middle form of delegation was also superior to the various forms of autocratic, consultative and participative leadership in our research. Thus, while more studies are clearly needed on such things as practical guidelines for effective delegation, it appears important to distinguish among different forms of delegation. It also seems important to emphasise the use of what we call "advisory" and "informational" delegation over the more extreme or "abdicational" kind. Based on these findings, then, the implementation of management development programmes which focus on distinctions among the different types of delegation, as well as on some of the simple guidelines which have developed in the world of practice (McConkey, 1974; Steinmetz, 1976), would appear reasonable. This would seem to be a useful change in the way current leadership development programmes are conducted.

TABLE I
SEVEN FORMS OF LEADERSHIP DECISION MAKING AND THEIR RELATIONSHIPS WITH
SUBORDINATE JOB SATISFACTION AND COMMITMENT TO THE ORGANISATION

Decision-making form	Definition	Relationship with job satisfaction and organisational commitment
Extreme autocratic	Leader makes decision without any input from the subordinate	Weakly negative with satisfaction; strongly negative with commitment
Autocratic	Leader makes decision after first obtaining information from the subordinate	Zero with satisfaction; weakly positive with commitment
Consultative	Leader makes decision after obtaining the subordinate's advice or recommendation	Zero with satisfaction; weakly negative with commitment
Joint or participative	Leader makes decision jointly with subordinate; both decide as equals	Weakly positive with both
Advisory delegation	Subordinate makes decision after first obtaining recommendation from the leader	Zero with satisfaction; highly positive with commitment
Informational delegation	Subordinate makes decision after first getting needed information from the leader	Moderately positive with satisfaction; zero with commitment
Extreme delegation	Subordinate makes decision without any input from the leader	Moderately negative with satisfaction; zero with commitment

Focus on Interpersonal Influence Processes

Hollander (1985) aptly states that "Leadership has been defined in a great many ways. The most consistent element noted is that leadership involves a process of influence between a leader and followers . . ." and that "The term power is used as a substitute for influence in some definitions of leadership. But . . . the distinction between these terms is meaningful . . ." (p. 486). Despite the importance of understanding the dynamic aspect of how managers and subordinates influence one another, little research has been done in this area until very recently.

The work of Kipnis *et al.* (1980) represents one of the earliest breakthroughs in this area. These researchers began their investigation inductively, by asking 165 students who were employed to write a paragraph describing "How I get my way with my boss, co-workers, and subordinates". The 370 influence tactics identified were then classified into 14 categories by the authors and 58 survey questionnaire items developed to measure them. These survey questionnaire items were next administered to 754 employed students, to obtain from them descriptions of how frequently in the previous six months they had used the influence tactic described by each item to influence their boss, co-workers and subordinates. Finally, these descriptions were factor-analysed and the results used to construct multi-team questionnaire scales to measure eight dimensions of influence in work organisations.

Further refinement of the Kipnis *et al.* work (Hinkin and Schriesheim, 1986; Schriesheim and Hinkin, 1986), has further confirmed seven key influence strategies which appear to be operative in a variety of different organisational settings: rationality, assertiveness, bargaining, coalition, upward appeals, ingratiation and sanctions. Table II briefly defines these seven influence tactics and presents a summary of major findings obtained in recent investigations. Without excessive detail, research has generally found that the use of rationality ("reason", "rational arguments", or "expertise") is clearly the preferable way of trying to get one's way. On the other hand, more forceful strategies, such as the use of personal assertiveness or the use of organisationally derived sanctions, are more likely to be ineffective and to generate defensive or negative reactions on the part of others. Again, while further investigation into these basic influence patterns and processes is desirable, it appears that meaningful and useful new knowledge has been generated about the various influence tactics which might be considered for use by a manager who is trying to influence his/her employees. Also, while it may seem only "intuitive", comfort may be taken in the fact that this research has supported the use of rationality as a preferable way of influencing others in organisational settings. Perhaps it would make sense, based on this research, to consider designing leadership development interventions which focus on how rationality might be best used and on how effective rational arguments may be constructed and presented to others.

A whole literature on rational argumentation and persuasion exists, and it would

TABLE II

SEVEN INFLUENCE TACTICS USED IN ORGANISATIONS AND THEIR RELATIONSHIPS WITH SUBORDINATE JOB SATISFACTION AND COMMITMENT TO THE ORGANISATION

Influence tactic	Definition: Attempts to get one's way by the use of . . .	Relationship with job satisfaction and organisational commitment
Rationality	Logic, data, and rational arguments	Highly positive with both satisfaction and commitment
Assertiveness	Forcefulness in presenting what one wants done	Moderately negative with both satisfaction and commitment
Bargaining	Making trades or offering exchanges	Zero with either satisfaction or commitment
Coalitions	Obtaining support for one's way from peers and subordinates	Zero with either satisfaction or commitment
Upward appeals	Requests which are directed towards higher levels in the organisation	Moderately negative with satisfaction; none with commitment
Ingratiation	Flattery and sycophancy	Zero with either satisfaction or commitment
Sanctions	Organisationally based rewards or punishments (or threats/promises or reward and/or punishment)	Very negative with satisfaction; zero with commitment

thus seem reasonable to begin integrating such material into "new phase" leadership development programmes. Additionally, it would make sense at this point to continue investigating other influence styles to determine more effectively which styles are most appropriate under varying situational and subordinate characteristics. Ultimately, such research should lead to a set of prescriptions for new managers concerning how best to achieve organisational goals.

Focus on Broader Conceptualisations of "Style"

The research summarised above clearly takes a more holistic view of leadership "style". For example, delegation is treated as but one form of leadership decision making (others include autocratic, consultative and participative), and several subtypes of delegation are also considered (advisory, informational and extreme delegation). The same is true of the research on interpersonal influence processes. Here, seven influence tactics are the focal point, instead of only one or two.

In addition to current investigations of delegation and influence processes, research is now examining expanded treatments of leadership as a multidimensional, dynamic interpersonal process. For example, Fred Fiedler, generally credited with launching contingency theories of leadership, has recently expanded his original LPC model to elaborate on the process by which a manager may obtain effective group performance (Fiedler and Garcia, 1987). To achieve high performance, these authors now contend that organisations must enhance group support for managers, select experienced managers for high stress positions and train intelligent leaders to be more directive in their interactions with subordinates. Although still in its infancy, this new "cognitive resource" approach does represent one example of the emerging "new phase" in leadership conceptualisations.

Other examples which highlight placing attention on broader perspectives of leadership style include recent work in the areas of transformational leadership styles (Avolio and Bass, 1988; Bass, 1985; Hollander, 1978; Kuhnert and Lewis, 1987) help subordinates understand what sorts of behaviours they must engage in to receive desired outcomes. Research by Graen and his associates (1982; Dienesh and Liden, 1986) is a particularly good representation of innovations in this area. On the other hand, the stylistic characteristics associated with the transformational leader include motivating subordinates to work for transcendental organisational goals, delegating opportunities for new learning experiences, and intellectually stimulating subordinates to think creatively (Avolio and Bass, 1988). The transformational leader is one who possesses a high level of charisma and thus induces loyalty, commitment and, in some instances, devotion from followers (House *et al.*, 1986; Conger and Kanungo, 1987). With respect to both transactional and transformational leader styles, the natural questions that arise are: "What types of organisations foster such styles and how can managers learn to use effectively the behaviours inherent in these approaches?" Obviously, it is these questions that are being addressed in the new phase of leadership development.

Finally, in addition to current studies of transformational and transactional leadership styles, research is now examining an expanded treatment of leadership as a process in which leaders encourage or discourage the performance of their subordinates through either rewarding or punishing them *contingently* (appropriately—based on their performance) or *non-contingently* (inappropriately—with no relationship to performance) (Hinkin *et al.*, 1987; Hinkin and Schriesheim, 1988; Podsakoff and Schriesheim, 1984, 1985). This perspective views leadership style as consisting of four different reward and punishment strategies and it represents what appears to be a significant breakthrough with substantial potential for development to enhance leadership effectiveness, particularly at supervisory and mid-management levels.

The four major reinforcement strategies mentioned above and their effects are summarised in Table III and, as one might expect, the use of contingent rewards by a supervisor has been generally associated with the satisfaction and commitment of subordinates (and with performance as well). The surprising fact has also been uncovered that employees often respond positively (in terms of enhanced satisfaction and commitment) to supervisors who use contingent punishment (on the subordinates themselves and on others). This appears most likely to occur when that punishment is seen as appropriate and when it is accompanied by coaching on how to perform better in the future. Non-contingent rewards, on the other hand, do not generally result in improved subordinate commitment, although sometimes satisfaction is a result. Non-contingent punishment, however, almost always results in decrements in both subordinate satisfaction and commitment.

Besides having immediate applicability for supervisory interactions with subordinates, the use of this perspective also allows the application of many highly specific and practical guidelines (for the use of rewards and punishments) which have been developed in the general area of psychology which is known as "reinforcement theory" (Sims, 1979). Again, although future research in this domain will, undoubtedly, be forthcoming, it appears that this research is very much consonant with the coming new phase of leadership theory and practice and it opens the door to what would appear to

TABLE III

FOUR FORMS OF LEADER REWARD AND PUNISHMENT BEHAVIOUR AND THEIR RELATIONSHIPS WITH SUBORDINATE JOB SATISFACTION AND COMMITMENT TO THE ORGANISATION

Reinforcement behaviour	Definition: Leader behaviour which provides subordinates with . . .	Relationship with job satisfaction and organisational commitment
Contingent reward behaviour	Rewards when they perform as expected (but not when their performance is unacceptable)	Highly positive with both satisfaction and commitment
Contingent punishment behaviour	Punishments when they fail to perform as expected (but not when their performance is acceptable)	Moderately positive with satisfaction; zero with commitment
Non-contingent reward behaviour	Rewards whether or not they perform as expected	Zero or weakly positive with satisfaction; zero with commitment
Non-contingent punishment behaviour	Punishments whether or not their performance is unacceptable	Highly negative with both satisfaction and commitment

be potentially valuable applications of existing behavioural management concepts to the leadership of employees in work organisations.

CONCLUSION

Some writers in the leadership area have spent considerable time and energy complaining about the current state of theory and practice. Although it must be acknowledged that much previous work did not lead to concrete and tangible benefits, the three previous phases of leadership theory and practice did set the stage for emerging new approaches (see Table IV) which will form the basis for what may very well be a renaissance in leadership development.

Although only time will tell whether this prediction is true or not, interested readers are urged to "stay tuned". It seems quite reasonable to expect that we will know some very significant things about leadership in the coming years, and people interested in staying up-to-date and remaining at the cutting edge of leadership development should not lose heart. The search for meaningful and practical leadership theory and development is, it appears, about to bear significant fruit.

TABLE IV
THREE MAJOR "NEW PHASE" TRENDS IN LEADERSHIP THEORY AND RESEARCH DEVELOPMENT

Trend	Examples of relevant issues	Selected research in the area
Focus on leadership as just one aspect of management	• When is participation in decision making an appropriate strategy? • What types of delegation strategies work most effectively for different employees, in different situations?	• Bass *et al.* (1975) • Leana (1987) • Schriesheim and Neider (1988) • Vroom and Yetton (1973)
Focus on interpersonal influence processes	• What are the major ways in which leaders "get their way" with subordinates? • How can influence tactics be used to obtain desired organisational outcomes?	• Hinkin and Schriesheim (1986, 1988) • Kipnis *et al.* (1984) • Schriesheim and Hinkin (1986)
Focus on broader conceptualisations of style	• What behaviours and techniques are characteristic of charismatic leaders? • How should a manager organise social exchange with subordinates to obtain increases in performance and commitment? • What are the effects of differential rewards and punishments on subordinates' behaviours?	• Avolio and Bass (1988) • Bass (1985) • Hinkin and Schriesheim (1987) • Hollander (1978) • Podsakoff and Schriesheim (1984, 1985)

REFERENCES

Avolio, B.J. and Bass, B.M. (1988), "Transformational Leadership, Charisma and Beyond", in Hunt, J.G., Baliga, B.R., Dachler, H.P. and Schriesheim, C.A. (Eds.), *Emerging Leadership Vistas,* Lexington, Boston.

Bass, B.M. (1981), *Stogdill's Handbook of Leadership,* rev. ed., Free Press, New York.

Bass, B.M. (1985), "Leadership: Good, Better, Best", *Organizational Dynamics,* Vol. 13 No. 3, pp. 26–40.

Bass, B.M., Valenzi, E.R., Farrow, D.L. and Solomon, R.J. (1975), "Management Styles Associated with Organizations, Task, Personal and Interpersonal Contingencies", *Journal of Applied Psychology,* Vol. 60 pp. 720–29.

Beer, M. and Walton, A.E. (1987), "Organization, Change and Development", *Annual Review of Psychology,* Vol. 38, pp. 339–67.

Behling, O. and Schriesheim, C. (1976), *Organizational Behavior: Theory, Research and Application,* Allyn and Bacon, Boston.

Berkman, H.W. and Neider, L.L. (1987), *The Human Relations of Organizations,* Kent, Boston.

Blake, R.R. and Mouton, J.S. (1978), *The New Managerial Grid,* Gulf, Houston.

Blake, R.R. and Mouton, J.S. (1985), *The Managerial Grid III,* Gulf, Houston.

Bolt, J.F. (1985), "A Revolution in Management Training and Development", *Training and Development Journal,* Vol. 39 No. 1, pp. 60–62.

Bures, A.L. and Banks, M.C. (1985), "Managerial Perceptions of Management Development Programs and Needs", *Training and Development Journal,* Vol. 39, No. 1, pp. 62–4.

Burke, M.J. and Day, R.R. (1986), "A Cumulative Study of the Effectiveness of Managerial Training", *Journal of Applied Psychology,* Vol. 71, pp. 232–45.

Clegg, W.H. (1987), "Management Training Evaluation: An Update," *Training and Development Journal,* Vol. 41 No. 1, pp. 65–71.

Conger, J.A. and Kanungo, R.N. (1987), "Toward a Behavioral Theory of Charismatic Leadership in Organizational Settings", *Academy of Management Review,* Vol. 12, pp. 637–47.

Dienesch, R.K. and Liden, R.C. (1986), "Leader-Member Exchange Model of Leadership: A Critique and Further Development", *Academy of Management Review,* Vol. 11, pp. 618–34.

Fiedler, F.E. and Garcia, J.E. (1987), *New Approaches to Effective Leadership: Cognitive Resources and Organizational Performance,* Wiley, New York.

Field, R.H.G. (1979), "A Critique of the Vroom-Yetton Contingency Model of Leadership Behavior", *Academy of Management Review,* Vol. 4, pp. 249–57.

Goldstein, I.L. (1980), "Training in Work Organizations", *Annual Review of Psychology,* Vol. 31, pp. 229–72.

Graeff, C.L. (1983), "The Situational Leadership Theory: A Critical View", *Academy of Management Review,* Vol. 8, pp. 285–91.

Graen, G., Novak, M.A. and Sommerkamp, P. (1982), "The Effects of Leader-Member Exchange and Job Design on Productivity: Testing a Dual Attachment Model", *Organizational Behavior and Human Performance,* Vol. 30, pp. 109–31.

Hersey, P. and Blanchard, K.H. (1977), *Management of Organization Behavior: Utilising Human Resources,* 3rd ed., Prentice-Hall, Englewood Cliffs, NJ.

Hinkin, T.R., Podsakoff, P.M. and Schriesheim, C.A. (1987), "The Mediation of Performance-contingent 'Compensation' by Supervisors in Work Organizations", in Gomez-Mejia, L., and Balkin, D. (Eds.), *New Perspectives in Compensation,* Prentice-Hall, Englewood Cliffs, NJ.

Hinkin, T.R. and Schriesheim, C.A. (1986), "Relationships between Perceived Supervisory Power and Influence and Subordinate Satisfaction and Commitment", paper presented at the annual Southern Management Association meetings, Atlanta, Georgia.

Hinkin, T.R. and Schriesheim, C.A. (1987), "Relationships between Perceived Bases of Power and Perceived Leader Reward and Punishment Behaviour: An Exploratory Investigation", paper presented at the annual Southern Management Association meetings, New Orleans, LA.

Hinkin, T.R. and Schriesheim, C.A. (1988), "Power and Influence: The View from Below", *Personnel,* Vol. 65 No. 5, pp. 47–50.

Hollander, E.P. (1978), *Leadership Dynamics,* Free Press, New York.

Hollander, E.P. (1985), "Leadership and Power", in Lindzey, G., and Aronson, E. (Eds.), *Handbook of Social Psychology,* Vol. II, 3rd ed., Random House, New York.

House, R.J. (1971), "A Path-goal Theory of Leader Effectiveness", *Administrative Science Quarterly,* Vol. 16, pp. 321–38.

House, R.J. (1988), "Leadership Research: Some Forgotten, Ignored, or Overlooked Findings", in Hunt, J.G., Baliga, B.R., Dachler, H.P., and Schriesheim, C.A. (Eds.), *Emerging Leadership Vistas,* Lexington, Boston.

House, R.J. and Baetz, M.L. (1979), "Leadership: Some Empirical Generalizations and New Research Directions", in Staw, B.M. (Ed.), *Research in Organizational Behavior,* Vol. 1, JAI Press, Greenwich, pp. 341–424.

House, R.J., Woycke, J. and Fodor, E.M. (1986), "Charismatic Leadership in US Presidential Office", paper presented at the annual Academy of Management Meetings, San Diego, California.

Hunt, J.G., Baliga, B.R., Dachler, H.P. and Schriesheim, C.A. (Eds.) (1988), *Emerging Leadership Vistas,* Lexington, Boston.

Hunt, J.G., Hosking, D.M., Schriesheim, C.A. and Stewart, R. (Eds.) (1984), *Leaders and Managers: International Perspectives on Managerial Behavior and Leadership,* Pergamon, New York.

Hunt, J.G., Sekaran, U. and Schriesheim, C.A. (Eds.) (1982), *Leadership: Beyond Establishment Views,* Southern Illinois University Press, Carbondale.

Kerr, S., Schriesheim, C.A., Murphy, C.J. and Stogdill, R.M. (1974), "Toward a Contingency Theory of Leadership Based upon the Consideration and Initiating Structure Literature", *Organizational Behavior and Human Performance,* Vol. 12, pp. 62–82.

Kipnis, D., Schmidt, S.M., Swaffin-Smith, C. and Wilkinson, I. (1984), "Patterns of Managerial Influence: Shotgun Managers, Tacticians and Bystanders", *Organizational Dynamics,* Vol. 13, pp. 58–67.

Kipnis, D., Schmidt, S.R. and Wilkinson, I. (1980), "Intraorganisational Influence Tactics: Explorations in Getting One's Way", *Journal of Applied Psychology,* Vol. 65, pp. 440–52.

Kuhnert, K. and Lewis, P. (1987), "Transactional and Transformational Leadership: A Constructive Development Analysis", *Academy of Management Review,* Vol. 12, pp. 648–57.

Latham, G.P. and Saari, L.M. (1979), "The Application of Social Learning Theory to Training Supervisors through Behavior Modeling", *Journal of Applied Psychology,* Vol. 64, pp. 239–46.

Leana, C.R. (1986), "Predictors and Consequences of Delegation", *Academy of Management Journal,* Vol. 29, pp. 754–74.

Leana, C.R. (1987), "Power Relinquishment vs. Power Sharing: Theoretical Clarification and Empirical Comparison of Delegation and Participation", *Journal of Applied Psychology,* Vol. 72, pp. 228–33.

Locke, E.A. and Schwieger, D. (1979), "Participation in Decision-making: One More Look", in Staw, B.M. (Ed.), *Research in Organizational Behavior,* Vol. 1, JAI Press, Greenwich.

Lueder, D.C. (1985), "Don't be Misled by LEAD", *Journal of Applied Behavioral Science,* Vol. 21, pp. 243–51.

McConkey, D.D. (1974), *No-nonsense Delegation,* AMACON, New York.

McConkey, D.D. (1986), *Developmental Experiences in Managerial Work: A Literature Review,* Technical Report No. 26, Center for Creative Leadership, Greensboro, NC.

Mintzberg, H. (1973), *The Nature of Managerial Work,* Harper & Row, New York.

Mowday, R.T., Porter, L.W. and Steers, R.M. (1982), *Employee Organization Linkages: The Psychology of Commitment, Absenteeism, and Turnover,* Academic Press, New York.

Podsakoff, P.M. and Schriesheim, C.A. (1984), "Leader Reward and Punishment Behavior: A Theoretical and Methodological Review", paper presented at the annual Southern Management Association meeting, New Orleans.

Podsakoff, P.M. and Schriesheim, C.A. (1985), "Field Studies of French and Raven's Bases of Power: Critique, Reanalysis, and Suggestions for Future Research", *Psychological Bulletin,* Vol. 97, pp. 387–411.

Schriesheim, C.A. (1982), "The Great High Consideration-High Initiating Structure Leadership Myth: Evidence on its Generalizability", *Journal of Social Psychology,* Vol. 112, pp. 221–8.

Schriesheim, C.A. and Hinkin, T.R. (1986), "Influence Tactics Used by Subordinates: A Theoretical and Empirical Analysis and Refinement of the Kipnis, Schmidt, and Wilkinson Subscales", paper presented at the annual Academy of Management meetings, San Diego.

Schriesheim, C.A. and Kerr, S. (1977), "Theories and Measures of Leadership: A Critical Appraisal of Current and Future Directions", Hunt, J.G. and Larson, L.L. (Eds.), *Leadership: The Cutting Edge,* Southern Illinois University Press, Carbondale.

Schriesheim, C.A. and Neider, L.L. (1988), "Distinctions among Subtypes of Perceived Delegation and Leadership Decision-making: A Theoretical and Empirical Analysis", paper presented at the American Psychological Association Convention (Division 14, Industrial and Organizational Psychology), Atlanta.

Sims, H.P. (1979), "Managing Behavior through Learning and Reinforcement", Hellriegel, D. and Slocum, J.W. (Eds.) *Organisational Behavior,* 2nd ed., West, St. Paul, Minnesota.

Steinmetz, L.L. (1976), *The Art and Skill of Delegation,* Addison-Wesley, Reading, Massachusetts.

Stogdill, R.M. (1974), *Handbook of Leadership,* Free Press, New York.

Strong, G. (1986), "Taking the Helm of Leadership Development", *Training and Development Journal,* Vol. 40, pp. 43–5.

Tannenbaum, A. and Schmidt, W. (1958), "How to Choose a Leadership Style", *Harvard Business Review,* Vol. 36, pp. 95–101.

Tetrault, L.A., Shriesheim, C.A. and Neider, L.L. (1988), "Leadership Training Interventions: A Review", *Organization Development Journal,* Vol. 6 No. 3, pp. 77–83.

Vecchio, R.P. (1987), "Situational Leadership Theory: An Examination of a Prescriptive Theory", *Journal of Applied Psychology,* Vol. 72, pp. 444–51.

Vroom, V.H. and Yetton, P.W. (1973), *Leadership and Decision Making,* University of Pittsburg Press, Pittsburg.

Wexley, K.N. (1984), "Personnel Training", *Annual Review of Psychology,* Vol. 35, pp. 519–51.

Yukl, G. (1981), *Leadership in Organizations,* Prentice-Hall, Englewood Cliffs, NJ.

The Motivational Effects of Charismatic Leadership: A Self-Concept Based Theory

Boas Shamir
Robert J. House
Michael B. Arthur

INTRODUCTION

In the past 15 years a new genre of leadership theory, alternatively referred to as "charismatic," "transformational," "visionary," or "inspirational," has emerged in the organizational literature (House 1977, Burns 1978, Bass 1985, Bennis and Nanus 1985, Tichy and Devanna 1986, Boal and Bryson 1988, Conger and Kanungo 1987, Kuhnert and Lewis 1987, Sashkin 1988).

These theories focus on exceptional leaders who have extraordinary effects on their followers and eventually on social systems. According to this new genre of leadership theory, such leaders transform the needs, values, preferences and aspirations of followers from self-interests to collective interests. Further, they cause followers to become highly committed to the leader's mission, to make significant personal sacrifices in the interest of the mission, and to perform above and beyond the call of duty. We refer to this new genre of theories as charismatic because charisma is a central concept in all of them, either explicitly or implicitly.

Theories of charismatic leadership highlight such effects as emotional attachment to the leader on the part of the followers; emotional and motivational arousal of the followers; enhancement of follower valences with respect to the mission articulated by the leader; follower self-esteem, trust, and confidence in the leader; follower values; and follower intrinsic motivation.

The leader behavior specified by charismatic theories is different from the behavior emphasized in earlier theories of organizational leadership. The earlier theories describe leader behavior in terms of leader/follower exchange relationships (Hollander 1964, Graen and Cashman 1975), providing direction and support (Evans 1970, House 1971), and reinforcement behaviors (Ashour 1982; Podsakoff, Todor and Skov 1982). In contrast, the new leadership theories emphasize symbolic leader behavior, visionary and inspirational messages, nonverbal communication, appeal to ideological values, intellectual stimulation of followers by the leader, display of confidence in self and followers, and leader expectations for follower self-sacrifice and for performance beyond the call of duty. Such leadership is seen as giving meaningfulness to work by infusing work and organizations with moral purpose and commitment rather than by affecting the task environment of followers, or by offering material incentives and the threat of punishment.

Research based on these theories has yielded an impressive set of findings concerning the effects of charismatic leaders on follower attitudes, satisfaction and performance. However, there is no motivational explanation to account for the profound ef-

From *Organization Science*, 1993, **4**(4), 577–594. ©1993, The Institute of Management Science. Reprinted by permission.

fects of such leaders, some of which are difficult to explain within currently dominant models of motivation. The purpose of this paper is to offer a motivational theory to account for the effects of charismatic leaders on their followers.

Empirical Evidence

In the last decade, at least 35 empirical investigations of charismatic leadership in organizations have been conducted. These studies relied on a variety of research methods, including two case studies (Roberts 1985, Roberts and Bradley 1988), two longitudinal observational studies (Trice and Beyer 1986), numerous field surveys (for examples see Smith 1982; Yukl and Van Fleet 1982; Hater and Bass 1988; Podsakoff, MacKenzie, Moorman, and Fetter 1990), an analysis of behavior in a management game (Avolio, Waldman, and Einstein 1988), three rigorous laboratory experiments (Howell and Frost 1989, Kirkpatrick 1992, and Puffer 1990), an interpretative analysis of interviews (Bennis and Nanus 1985), a rigorous content analysis of interviews (Howell and Higgins 1990), a rigorous analysis of historical archival information (House, Spangler and Woycke 1991), and four longitudinal analyses of the effects of leader behavior on U.S. Air Force Academy cadets (Curphy 1990, Koene et al. 1991, Keller in press, Howell and Avolio 1993, and Waldman and Ramirez 1993).

These studies were conducted across a wide variety of samples, including students who served as laboratory subjects (Howell and Frost 1989, Kirkpatrick 1992, and Puffer 1990), military combat and noncombat leaders (Yukl and Van Fleet 1982, Curphy 1990), numerous samples of middle and lower level managers (for examples see Smith 1982, Avolio and Bass 1987, Waldman et al. 1987, Bass and Yammarino 1988, Hater and Bass 1988), world class leaders of nations (Bass, Avolio and Goodheim 1987), educational leaders (Roberts 1985, Roberts and Bradley 1988, Sashkin 1988), Asian Indian middle managers (Pereria 1987), top level corporate leaders (Bennis and Nanus 1985), U.S. presidents (House, Spangler, and Woycke 1991), Dutch supermarket managers (Koene et al. 1991), educational administrators in Singapore (Koh et al. 1991), presidents of alcoholic rehabilitation organizations (Trice and Beyer 1986), and emergent informal project champions (Howell and Higgins 1990).

Space limitations prevent a detailed review of the findings of these studies (for reviews see Bass 1990; House, Howell, Shamir, Smith and Spangler 1991). While the studies were not guided by a unified theoretical perspective, there is a considerable convergence of the findings from studies concerned with charismatic leadership and those concerned with transformational and visionary leadership. Collectively, these findings indicate that leaders who engage in the theoretical charismatic behaviors produce the theoretical charismatic effects. In addition, they receive higher performance ratings, have more satisfied and more highly motivated followers, and are viewed as more effective leaders by their superiors and followers than others in positions of leadership. Further, the effect size of charismatic leader behavior on follower satisfaction and performance is consistently higher than prior field study findings concerning other leader behavior, generally ranging well below 0.01 probability of error due to chance, with correlations frequently ranging in the neighborhood of 0.50 or better.

The Problem

Unfortunately, the literature on charismatic leadership does not provide an explanation of the process by which charismatic leadership has its profound effects. No motivational explanations are provided to explain how charismatic leaders bring about changes in followers' values, goals, needs and aspirations.

Three types of changes that have been emphasized by previous theories present a particular theoretical challenge. First, Burns (1978) and Bass (1985) suggested that transformational or charismatic leaders are able to elevate followers' needs from lower to higher levels in the Maslow hierarchy. Second, Burns (1978) claimed that such leaders raise followers to higher levels of morality, to "more principled levels of judgment" (p. 455). Third, House (1977), Burns (1978) and Bass (1985) proposed that such leaders are successful in motivating followers to transcend their own self-interests for the sake of the team, the organization or the larger polity. We shall refer to these effects as "the transformational effects of charismatic leadership."

However, none of these theorists offers a motivational explanation that can account for these important effects. It is very difficult, for instance, to envision how any of the existing individual-focused theories of motivation—whether an exchange theory, a reinforcement theory, or a cognitive theory—can account for a transformation such as that called for by Kennedy in his famous challenge, "Ask not what your country can do for you, ask what you can do for your country."

The problem is that current theories of charismatic leadership claim that a variety of leadership behaviors transform followers from an individual-oriented, hedonistic, rational-economic mode of operation to a collective, moral and value-oriented mode of operation. However, these claims cannot be accounted for by current psychological theories of motivation, which assume either a rational-economic or a highly idiosyncratic need-satisfying model of human beings. Therefore, we need to supplement current theories of charismatic leadership with a motivational theory that will be able to better explain the relationships between leader behaviors and effects on followers, and account for the transformational effects of charismatic leaders.

In the following sections of this paper, we first present some assumptions about the motivational significance of the self-concept. We then show how charismatic leaders activate self-concept related motivations, and how these motivations can explain the effects that are not well explained by current theories. Following, we specify leader behaviors that are likely to activate these processes. We derive from our motivational analysis testable propositions about the effects of these behaviors on followers' self-concepts, and their further effects on followers. We then discuss some follower attributes that moderate the hypothesized relationships. Finally, we specify organizational conditions under which charismatic leadership is likely to emerge and be effective.

ASSUMPTIONS

In this section, we explicate a set of assumptions which underlie the motivational theory which we then advance. In developing these assumptions, we have drawn mainly on Bandura's (1986) Social-Cognitive Theory, Stryker's (1980) Identity Theory, and

Tajfel and Turner's Social Identity Theory (Tajfel and Turner 1985, Ashforth and Mael 1989). For a more detailed account of these assumptions see Shamir (1991).

(a) Humans are not only pragmatic and goal-oriented but are also self-expressive. We assume that behavior is not only instrumental-calculative, but also expressive of feelings, aesthetic values and self-concepts. (For supporting empirical evidence, see Csikszentmihalyi and Rochberg-Halton 1981, Kinder and Sears 1985, Snyder and Ickes 1985, Prentice 1987). We "do" things because of what we "are," because by doing them we establish and affirm an identity for ourselves. Making the assumption that humans are self-expressive enables us to account for behaviors that do not contribute to the individual's self-interest, the most extreme expression of which is self-sacrifice (Strauss 1969). Earlier theories of leadership addressed the instrumental aspects of motivation. We will argue later that charismatic leadership addresses the expressive aspects.

(b) People are motivated to maintain and enhance their self-esteem and self-worth. Self-esteem is based on a sense of competence, power, achievement or ability to cope with and control one's environment. Self-worth is based on a sense of virtue and moral worth and is grounded in norms and values concerning conduct (Gecas 1982). Both competence standards and cultural norms are internalized into the self-concept in the form of evaluative standards (Bandura 1986).

Self-evaluation is an important source of intrinsic motivation: people's anticipatory self-reactions to their own performances serve as principal sources of reward and sanction. Furthermore, these self-reactions, at least in part, reflect social values, thus providing an important link between the individual and the collectivity.

(c) People are also motivated to retain and increase their sense of self-consistency. Self-consistency refers to correspondence among components of the self-concept at a given time, to continuity of the self-concept over time (Turner 1968) and to correspondence between the self-concept and behavior. People derive a sense of "meaning" from continuity between the past, the present and the projected future (McHugh 1968), and from the correspondence between their behavior and self-concept (Gecas 1982, Schlenker 1985).

(d) Self-concepts are composed, in part, of identities. In addition to values, identities—sometimes referred to as role-identities (McCall and Simmons 1978, Stryker 1980—also link the self-concept to society. According to social identity theory (Tajfel and Turner 1985), the self-concept comprises a personal identity encompassing idiosyncratic characteristics and a social identity encompassing salient group classifications. Social identities locate the self in socially recognizable categories such as nations, organizations, and occupations, thus enabling people to derive meaning from being linked to social collectives (Ashforth and Mael 1989).

According to one view of structural symbolic interactionism (Stryker 1980), identities are organized in the self-concept according to a hierarchy of salience. The higher an identity in the salience hierarchy, the greater the probability that a person will perceive a given situation as an opportunity to perform in terms of that identity, and the greater the probability that a person will actively seek out opportunities to perform in terms of that identity. Santee and Jackson (1979) and Callero (1985) provide empirical support for these assertions.

(e) Humans may be motivated by faith. We assume that when goals cannot be clearly specified or the subjective probabilities of accomplishment and rewards are not high, people may be motivated by faith, because being hopeful in the sense of having faith in a better future is an intrinsically satisfying condition. Note that faith is not synonymous with expectancies. By definition, faith cannot be reduced to subjective probabilities since the mere translation of faith into calculations implies loss of faith.

THE THEORY

Our assumptions about the self-concept and its motivational implications allow us to propose a theory to explain the transformational effects of charismatic leadership. The theory has four main parts: (a) leader behaviors; (b) effects on followers' self-concepts; (c) further effects on followers; and (d) the motivational processes by which the leader behaviors produce the charismatic effects. These processes link the leader behaviors to their effects on followers' self-concepts, and the effects on followers' self-concepts to further effects on followers. The theory is outlined in Figure 1.

At the heart of our theory are five processes by which charismatic leaders motivate followers through implicating their self-concepts. These processes are presented first. We then derive from our motivational analysis a set of empirically observable leader behaviors that are hypothesized to activate the self-implicating processes, a set of effects on followers' self-concepts that are triggered by the leader behaviors, and a set of further effects on followers that are mediated by the self-concept effects.

We do not view the variables specified within each set as constituting exhaustive sets. Nor can we rule out the possibility that the variables within each set are intercorrelated and constitute syndromes (Meindl 1990). At this stage, our propositions refer to the relationships between the sets of variables. Hopefully, empirical research guided by these propositions will enable a more parsimonious and more exact formulation of the relationships implied by the theory.

The Self-implicating Effects of Charismatic Leadership[1]

We suggest that charismatic leaders motivate their followers in the following manner:

(a) *Increasing the intrinsic valence of effort.* This is accomplished by emphasizing the symbolic and expressive aspects of the effort—the fact that the effort itself reflects

---

[1]In the analysis that follows, we do not distinguish between "good" or "moral" and "evil" or "immoral" charismatic leadership. Indeed, our analysis suggests that the psychological mechanisms relied upon by the "Hitlers" and the "Gandhis" may be similar in certain respects. This means that the risks involved in following charismatic leaders are at least as large as the promises. The motivational processes and the creation of personal commitment described in this paper can lead to blind fanaticism in the service of megalomaniacs and dangerous values, no less than to heroic self-sacrifice in the service of a beneficial cause. An awareness of these risks is missing from most of the current literature on organizational charismatic or transformational leadership. We believe that these risks should not be neglected, but rather that we need more studies of the nature and effects of charismatic leadership and the conditions under which it produces harmful versus beneficial effects for followers and collectives. "Beware Charisma!. . . . But to beware does not necessarily mean or entail 'Avoid!'. . . . Be aware! Then choose" (Hodgkinson 1983). We hope that the analysis presented here will help lead to the awareness called for by Hodgkinson (1983). However, we do not endorse charismatic leadership as necessarily good or bad. For a theory that differentiates personalized authoritarian and exploitive charismatics from collective, egalitarian and not exploitive, see House and Howell (1992).

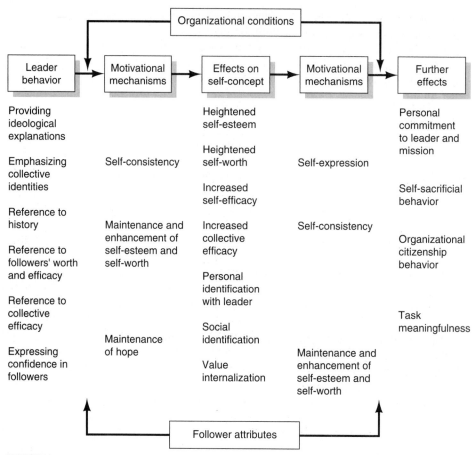

FIGURE 1.
An outline of the theory.

important values—that by making the effort, one makes a moral statement. Charismatic leadership is presumed to strengthen followers' belief in the necessity and propriety of "standing up and being counted."

The intrinsic valence of the effort may also be increased by making participation in the effort an expression of a collective identity, thus making the effort more meaningful for the follower. This implicates the self-concept of followers by increasing the salience of that identity in the follower's self-concept, thus increasing the likelihood of efforts and behaviors representing that identity. Charismatic leaders may use existing identities and emphasize their uniqueness or superiority ("Black is beautiful"), or they may create "new" desirable social categories for the followers ("the master race"). In both cases, the self-concepts of the followers are clearly engaged.

Meindl and Lerner (1983) have suggested that the salience of a shared identity can increase the "heroic motive" and the likelihood that self-interest oriented pursuits will voluntarily be abandoned for more altruistic or collectivistic endeavors. It follows that, when charismatic leaders increase the salience of collective identities in their followers' self-concepts, they also increase the likelihood of self-sacrificial, collective-oriented behavior on the part of followers.

It is important to note that, once followers choose to make the effort and through that effort identify themselves with certain values and with the leader and the collective, they are subject to considerable social and psychological forces that are likely to increase their commitment to that effort (Kanter 1967, Salancik 1977). We will return to this point in our discussion of personal commitment.

(b) *Increasing effort-accomplishment expectancies.* Charismatic leaders increase effort-accomplishment expectancies by enhancing the followers' self-esteem and self-worth. They enhance self-esteem by expressing high expectations of the followers and confidence in the followers' ability to meet such expectations (Yukl 1989, Eden 1990). By so doing, they enhance followers' perceived self-efficacy, defined as a judgment of one's capability to accomplish a certain level of performance. Self-efficacy is a strong source of motivation (Bandura 1986, p. 351).

Charismatic leaders also increase followers' self-worth through emphasizing the relationships between efforts and important values. A general sense of self-worth increases general self-efficacy; a sense of moral correctness is a source of strength and confidence. Having complete faith in the moral correctness of one's convictions gives one the strength and confidence to behave accordingly.

Another aspect of charismatic leadership that is likely to increase effort-accomplishment expectancies is its emphasis on collective efficacy. "Perceived collective efficacy will influence what people choose to do as a group, how much effort they put into it, and their staying power when group efforts fail to produce results" (Bandura 1986, p. 449). Thus, being a member of an efficacious collective enhances one's self-efficacy.

(c) *Increasing the intrinsic valence of goal accomplishment.* This is one of the most important motivational mechanisms of charismatic leadership. Articulation of a vision and a mission by charismatic leaders presents goals in terms of the values they represent. Doing so makes action oriented toward the accomplishment of these goals more meaningful to the follower in the sense of being consistent with his or her self-concept.

Charismatic leadership also increases the meaningfulness of goals and related actions by showing how these goals are consistent with the collective past and its future and thus creating the sense of "evolving" which is central for self-consistency and a sense of meaningfulness (McHugh 1968). In addition, such leadership stresses the importance of the goal as a basis for group identity and for distinguishing the group or collective from other groups. This brings meaning to the followers' lives and efforts by connecting them to larger entities and to concerns that transcend their own limited existence (Jahoda 1981). By these leadership actions, certain identities are evoked and made more salient and therefore more likely to be implicated in action.

(d) *Instilling faith in a better future.* The "rewards" involved in the charismatic leadership process involve self-expression, self-efficacy, self-worth and self-consistency, which emerge from the process and cannot be exchanged. In most cases, charismatic leadership de-emphasizes extrinsic rewards and their related expectancies in order to emphasize the intrinsic aspects of the effort. Refraining from providing pragmatic extrinsic justification for the required behavior increases the chances that followers will attribute their behavior to internal self-related causes and thus adds to followers' commitment to that course of action.

Note that while noncharismatic leadership emphasizes proximal, specific goals and increases the subjective likelihood that goal attainment would lead to specific outcomes (Locke and Lathan 1990, House 1971) charismatic leadership tneds to emphasize vague and distal goals and utopian outcomes. It is here that Bass refers to charismatic leaders' use of "symbolism, mysticism, imaging and fantasy" (1985, p. 6). In order to understand the motivational impact of such messages (that contradict current motivational models which stress goal specificity and proximity), we have to resort to our assumption that having faith in a better future is a satisfying condition in itself. People would therefore follow leaders who provide hope (a vision) for a better future and faith in its attainment, even if such faith cannot be translated into specific proximal goals whose attainment is highly probable.

(e) *Creating personal commitment.* Another important aspect of charismatic motivational influence is the creation of a high level of commitment on the part of the leader and the followers to a common vision, mission or transcendent goal (Bennis and Nanus 1985, House 1977). "Their art is to manufacture ethics to give life through commitment to the spirit of the organization" (Hodgkinson 1983, p. 218).

When we speak about commitment in the context of charismatic leadership, we refer to unconditional commitment—internalized "personal" or "moral" commitment (Johnson 1982). This is a motivational disposition to continue a relationship, a role or a course of action and to invest efforts regardless of the balance of external costs and benefits and their immediate gratifying properties.

We propose that such commitment is achieved when the relationship or role under consideration becomes a component of the individual's self-concept and when the course of action related to that relationship or role is consistent with and expressive of the individual's self-concept; in other words, when "action is not merely a means of doing but a way of being" (Strauss 1969, p. 3).

Such a concept of commitment fits very well into our analysis of charismatic leadership. By recruiting the self-concept of followers, increasing the salience of certain identities and values, and linking behaviors and goals to those identities and values and to a mission that reflects them, charismatic leadership motivates followers through the creation of personal commitments.

These processes are self-reinforcing because the behavioral manifestations of such a commitment are likely to further bind the self-concept of the individual to the leader and the mission. Faced with their own voluntary and public action on behalf of the leader, the collective or the mission, individuals are likely to integrate these relationships and values even further into their self-concepts as a result of self-attribution and self-justification processes and the need to reduce or avoid cognitive dissonance (Salancik 1977, Staw 1980). When the self is engaged in a situation, the need for self-justification and dissonance reduction is particularly strong.

Generated and reinforced in these ways, personal commitment is perhaps the most intrinsic of all intrinsic motivators since in the final analysis it is a commitment to one's own self-concept and evaluative standards, "to a conception of (oneself) as a certain kind or kinds of person who is expected and expects to act in a certain way in certain situations" (Strauss, 1969, p. 3).[2]

Summary. To recapitulate, we have suggested that charismatic leaders achieve transformational effects through implicating the self-concepts of followers. More specifically, we have argued that such leaders increase the intrinsic value of efforts and goals by linking them to valued aspects of the follower's self-concept, thus harnessing the motivational forces of self-expression, self-consistency, self-esteem and self-worth. We have further argued that charismatic leaders change the salience hierarchy of values and identities within the follower's self-concept, thus increasing the probability that these values and identities will be implicated in action. Since values and identities are socially based, their control of behavior is likely to represent a shift from the instrumental to the moral and from concern with individual gains to concern with contributions to a collective. Finally, we have argued that charismatic leaders increase self-efficacy and collective efficacy through expressing positive evaluations, communicating higher performance expectations of followers, showing confidence in followers' ability to meet such expectations, and emphasizing the individual's ties to the collective. The differences between these processes and the motivational processes implied by more traditional leadership theories are outlined in Table 1.

Leader Behavior

The motivational processes described above are activated by two classes of leader behavior: (a) role modeling, and (b) frame alignment.

(a) *Role Modeling.* Vicarious learning occurs when the relevant messages are inferred by followers from observation of leaders' behavior, life style, emotional reactions, values, aspirations, preferences, and the like. The leader becomes a "representative character" (Bellah et al. 1985)—a symbol which brings together in one concentrated image the way people in a given social environment organize and give meaning and direction to their lives. He or she becomes an image that helps define for the followers just what kinds of traits, values, beliefs and behaviors it is good and legitimate to develop. Thus, the leader provides an ideal, a point of reference and focus for followers' emulation and vicarious learning.

This is sometimes exemplified by leaders' display of self-sacrificial behavior in the interest of the mission. By taking risks, making personal sacrifices, and engaging in unconventional ideological behavior (Conger and Kanungo 1987, Sashkin 1988), charismatic leaders demonstrate their own courage and conviction in the mission and

---

[2]From an organizational perspective, however, commitment is a double-edged sword. To the extent that the leader's goals and values are congruent with the goals and values of the organization, charismatic leadership is likely to provide a strong link between organizational goals and member commitment to such goals. To the extent that the leader's goals and values are in conflict with those of the organization, such as when leaders represent a challenge to the status quo, charismatic leadership is likely to induce negative attitudes toward the organization and resistance to directives from management by organizational members. Thus, charismatic leadership represents a strong force for *or against* member commitment to organizational goals.

TABLE 1
SUMMARY OF THE MOTIVATIONAL EFFECTS OF TRADITIONAL AND CHARISMATIC LEADER-
SHIP PROCESSES

Motivational charismatic component processes	Traditional leadership processes	Charismatic leadership
Intrinsic value of behavior	Making the task more interesting, varied, enjoyable, challenging, as in job enrichment	Linking behavior to followers' self-concepts, internalized values and cherished identities
Behavior-Accomplishment expectancy	Coaching; training; providing material, instrumental and emotional support; clarifying goals	Increasing general self-efficacy (through increasing self-worth and communicating confidence and high expectations). Emphasizing collective efficacy
Instrinsic value of goal accomplishment	Setting goals, increasing task identity, providing feedback	Linking goals to the past and the present and to values in a framework of a "mission" which serves as a basis for identification
Accomplishment-Reward expectancies	Establishing clear performance evaluation and tying rewards to performance	Generating faith by connecting behaviors and goals to a "dream" or a utopian ideal vision of a better future.
Valence of Extrinsic Rewards	Taken into consideration in rewarding performance	Not addressed

thus both earn credibility and serve as a role model of the values of the vision and the mission.

(b) *Frame alignment* (Snow et al. 1986) refers to the linkage of individual and leader interpretive orientations, such that some set of followers' interests, values and beliefs and the leader's activities, goals and ideology become congruent and complementary. The term "frame" denotes "schemata of interpretation" (Goffman 1974) that enables individuals to locate, perceive and label occurrences within their life and the world at large. By rendering events or occurrences meaningful, frames function to organize experience and guide action, whether individual or collective (see also Boal and Bryson 1988).

Charismatic leaders engage in communicative processes that affect frame alignment and "mobilize" followers to action. They interpret the present and past. They link present behaviors to past events by citing historical examples (Willner 1984). They articulate an ideology clearly, often using labels and slogans. They provide a vivid image of the future. Further, they amplify certain values and identities and suggest linkages between expected behaviors, amplified values and identities, and their vision of the future.

By articulating an ideological vision and recruiting a number of followers who share the values of the vision, charismatic leaders provide for followers a sense of identity with the collectivity and a sense of efficacy resulting from membership in the collectivity. Articulation of high performance expectations, together with display of confidence in followers, results in enhancing both follower self-esteem and self-worth. By relating the vision to significant historical events and projecting it into the future, charismatic leaders provide for followers a sense of continuity.

These general behavioral principles can be translated into more specific and observable behaviors.

PROPOSITION 1.

In order to implicate the followers' self-concepts, compared to noncharismatic leaders, the deliberate and nondeliberate messages of charismatic leaders will contain:

(a) *more references to values and moral justifications,*
(b) *more references to the collective and to collective identity,*
(c) *more references to history,*
(d) *more positive references to followers' worth and efficacy as individuals and as a collective,*
(e) *more expressions of high expectations from followers,*
(f) *more references to distal goals and less reference to proximal goals.*

Effects on Followers' Self-concept

Several effects on the followers' self-concept evolve directly from our preceding discussion. These are specified in the following proposition:

PROPOSITION 2.

The more leaders exhibit the behaviors specified above, the more their followers will have:

(a) *a high salience of the collective identity in their self-concept,*
(b) *a sense of consistency between their self-concept and their actions on behalf of the leader and the collective,*
(c) *a high level of self-esteem and self-worth,*
(d) *a similarity between their self-concept and their perception of the leader,*
(e) *a high sense of collective efficacy.*

These effects on the self-concept represent three common processes of psychological attachment: personal identification, social identification, and value internalization. The distinction among these processes requires further clarification.

Personal identification, sometimes called classical identification, refers to a situation in which a person "attempts to be like or actually to be the other person" (Kelman 1958). This identification is predicated on the desire to emulate or vicariously gain the qualities of the other—in this case, the leader. Identification with the leader will increase with the extent to which he or she represents desirable identities, values and attributes in his or her behavior.

Social identification is the definition of self in terms of a social category. Increased social identification means increased salience of the relevant social identity in the individual's self-concept. Leader behaviors that define the boundaries of the collectivity emphasize its distinctiveness, prestige and competition with other groups. Such leader behavior increases the salience of the collective identity in members' self-concepts (Ashford and Mael 1989). Identification with the leader and social identification may overlap when the leader is perceived as a representative character, but each may exist independently of the other.

Value internalization refers to the incorporation of values within the self as guiding principles. Although certain values are associated with the leader and/or group, value internalization can occur in the absence of personal or social identification, and identification may exist in the absence of value internalization (Kelman 1958). Identification and internalization represent different types of commitment (O'Reilly and Chatman 1986) and different processes of social influence (Howell 1988). It should be noted that, while personal identification with the leader is consistent with our theory, our main emphasis is on social identification and value internalization processes.

Self-concept as an Intervening Variable and Further Effects on Followers

The theory suggests that the above specified effects on followers' self-concepts mediate other effects of charismatic leaders on the followers. The changes in followers' self-concepts will produce these effects through the motivational mechanisms of self-expression, self-consistency, and the maintenance and enhancement of self-esteem and self-worth. These further effects are observable manifestations of the transformational effects of charismatic leadership.

First, it is proposed that the linkage formed by charismatic leaders between followers' self-concepts and the leader's mission will be evidenced by increased personal commitment of the followers to the leader and the mission. Second, increased social identification and value internalization will lead to a high willingness among followers to make personal sacrifices for the collective mission as articulated by the leader, and a high level of "extra role," organizational citizenship behaviors (O'Reilly and Chatman 1986, Organ 1988, Podsakoff et al. 1990). Such behaviors are of particular interest because they are the voluntary behavioral manifestations of performance beyond expectations—exertion of effort and self-sacrifice in the interest of the work team or the larger organization.

In addition, followers of charismatic leaders are expected to have a high sense of "meaningfulness" associated with the task. Such meaningfulness stems from a high sense of consistency between their self-concepts and their actions on behalf of the leader and the collective, and from the implications of these actions for their self-esteem and self-worth. Thus,

PROPOSITION 3.
The more leaders exhibit the behaviors specified in the theory the more followers will demonstrate:

(a) *personal commitment to the leader and the mission,*
(b) *a willingness to make sacrifices for the collective mission,*
(c) *organizational citizenship behavior,*
(d) *meaningfulness in their work and lives.*

It is further proposed that the increased self-efficacy and collective efficacy, together with the high personal commitment to the mission and the sense of "meaningfulness" associated with the tasks, will produce heightened performance motivation among followers, which will in turn result in higher levels of performance. These final effects are not specified in our propositions because they are not unique to the proposed theory and may be produced by other leader behaviors triggering other motivational mechanisms. They are reinforced, however, by the self-processes outlined in our model.

FOLLOWER ATTRIBUTES

Our theory implies that charismatic leaders will not have similar effects on all followers. We now turn to a discussion of some follower characteristics that may moderate the hypothesized relationships between leader behaviors and effects on followers.

Follower Values and Identities

The theory presented here implies that the leader, in order to have the transformational effects specified in the theory, must appeal to existing elements of the followers' self-concepts—namely, their values and identities. In most cases, charismatic leaders do not instill totally new values and identities in the followers' self-concepts; rather they raise their salience and connect them with goals and required behaviors. In this sense, charismatic leaders must respond to their potential followers, no less than the followers respond to them. Furthermore, our theory gives followers a central place in implying that followers may actively choose a leader and decide to follow him or her, based on the extent to which the leader is perceived to represent their values and identities.

The relevant values and identities may or may not be well articulated in the minds of the followers. We believe that one of the effects of the articulation of a vision by charismatic leaders is that such a vision, being value and identity laden, articulates for followers values and identities that they hold but have not been able to articulate clearly to themselves. Note, however, that this can only occur when the values of the followers and the leader are not in opposition.

This line of reasoning leads to the following proposition:

PROPOSITION 4.

A necessary condition for a leader's messages to have charismatic effects is that the message is congruent with the existing values and identities held by potential followers.

Follower Orientations

Other follower characteristics may moderate the transformational effects of charismatic leadership. Organization members are known to differ on the dimension of having an "instrumental" or "expressive" orientation to work (Goldthorpe et al. 1968). Since charismatic leadership arouses expressive motivations, it can by hypothesized that it will have a higher appeal to people with an expressive orientation to work.

In addition, people differ in the extent to which they conceive of themselves as either pragmatic or principled in their relations with others (Snyder 1979). We propose

that people with a more principled orientation to social relations will be more susceptible to leadership messages that link their behaviors and actions to ideological values.

These considerations suggest the following propositions:

PROPOSITION 5.
*The more the potential followers have an expressive orientation toward work and
life, the more susceptible they will be to the influence of charismatic leaders.*

PROPOSITION 6.
*The more the potential followers have a principled orientation to social relations,
the more susceptible they will be to the influence of charismatic leaders.*

ORGANIZATIONAL CONDITIONS FOR CHARISMATIC LEADERSHIP

Current enthusiasm about charismatic and transformational leadership in the organizational literature tends to give the impression that this type of leadership is equally applicable to all organizational situations. Our analysis leads us to qualify this enthusiasm and to theoretically specify the conditions under which charismatic leadership is
more likely to emerge and to be effective.

First, the organizational task is a relevant consideration. Recall that charismatic
leadership gives meaning to efforts and goals by connecting them to followers' values.
These values are likely to reflect, at least in part, the dominant values of society or of
the subculture of potential followers. Thus, it follows that charismatic leadership is
more likely to emerge and be effective when the organizational task is closely related
to dominant social values to which potential followers are exposed than when it is unrelated to such values or contradicts them. In the former case, it is easier to translate
followers' dominant values into a mission.

To take an obvious example, at this time in the United States, charismatic leadership is more likely to emerge in high technology industries whose tasks can be easily
linked to values such as scientific and economic progress and national pride, than in
the production of tobacco, which may be perceived to contradict the dominant value of
health. In other words, the situation has to offer at least some opportunities for
"moral" involvement. Otherwise, charismatic leadership cannot emerge.

Second, charismatic leadership is more likely to be relevant under conditions that
do not favor leadership based on the use of extrinsic rewards and punishments. The
use of extrinsic incentives requires certain organizational conditions to be effective,
among them the ability of the leader to specify and clarify goals, considerable available knowledge about the means for achieving them, objective or highly consensual
ways of measuring performance, and a high degree of discretion in the allocation of
rewards on the basis of performance. Under such conditions, the utilitarian and calculative logic of a leader who uses extrinsic motivation can be clarified to the followers and adhered to by the leader (House 1971). We propose that charismatic leadership is more likely to emerge when performance goals cannot be easily specified and
measured, and when leaders cannot link extrinsic rewards to individual performance.

Mischel (1973) describes such conditions as "weak psychological situations,"
which are not uniformly construed in the same way by all observers, do not generate

uniform expectancies concerning desired behavior, do not provide sufficient performance incentives, or fail to provide the learning conditions required for successful construction of behavior. In such "weak" situations, followers' self-concepts, values and identities can be more readily appealed to and engaged. Furthermore, in the absence of clear extrinsic justifications for behavior, followers are more likely to look for self-related justifications for their efforts (Bem 1982) and thus become more prone to the influence of charismatic leadership.

Third, charismatic leadership may be more appropriate under exceptional conditions, such as those requiring nonroutine and unusually high performance, in order to prevail and be effective, such as crises of high levels of uncertainty. When conditions change or when the situation requires exceptional efforts, behaviors and sacrifices, extrinsically motivated leadership is not likely to be effective, since it is by definition "conditional" and these situations require "unconditional" commitment. Furthermore, in unstable conditions or when a new organization is being formed, there is more ambiguity and anxiety and a greater need for orientation on the part of organizational members. Under such conditions, members are more likely to look for charismatic leaders and to accept their definitions of the organization's identity and its mission.

Three related points are worth noting. First, exceptional circumstances are not a necessary condition for the emergence of charismatic leadership. Our analysis does not rule out the possibility of charismatic leadership in nonexceptional situations. For instance, members may be alienated from the existing organizational order under routine situations, and charismatic leadership may emerge to lead a movement to alleviate such alienating conditions (Boal and Bryson 1988). Second, exceptional conditions do not necessarily imply crisis situations. They may include situations of exceptional opportunities as well. Crises are not necessary for the emergence of charismatic leaders (Willner 1984, Conger and Kanungo 1987). Third, when crisis-handling leaders have charismatic effects, these effects will be short-term unless the leader can relate the handling of the crisis to a higher purpose that has intrinsic validity for the actors (Boal and Bryson 1988, p. 17).

Based on the above reasoning, we suggest the following proposition:

PROPOSITION 7.
The emergence and effectiveness of charismatic leaders will be facilitated to the extent to which:

(a) *There is an opportunity for substantial moral involvement on the part of the leader and the followers,*

(b) *Performance goals cannot be easily specified and measured,*

(c) *Extrinsic rewards cannot be made clearly contingent on individual performance,*

(d) *There are few situational cues, constraints and reinforcers to guide behavior and provide incentives for specific performance,*

(e) *Exceptional effort, behavior and sacrifices are required of both the leaders and followers.*

CONCLUSION

In this paper, we have focused on certain fundamental effects of charismatic leaders on followers. We have argued that these effects are produced by leadership actions that implicate the self-concept of the followers, and engage the related motivations for self-expression, self-esteem, self-worth and self-consistency. Our argument has resulted in a theory that links leader behavior and follower effects through follower self-concepts. According to this theory, leader behaviors activate self-concepts which in turn affect further motivational mechanisms. These intervening variables and processes in turn have a strong positive impact on the behaviors and psychological states of followers. Hopefully, our explanation helps to provide greater insights concerning the charismatic leadership phenomenon.

The outcome of our analysis is a theoretical extension of current theories of charismatic and transformational leadership. We recognize that the theory is speculative. However, we believe such speculation is warranted because it provides an explanation and accounts for the rather profound effects of charismatic leader behaviors demonstrated in prior research.

Some scholars have voiced skepticism concerning whether or not leaders can make a difference in organizational performance (Pfeffer 1977; Salancik and Pfeffer 1977; Meindl, Ehrlich and Dukerich 1985). This skepticism reflects the argument that people are biased toward over-attributing to leaders influence on events which are complex and difficult to understand. As a result, leadership in general, and charismatic leadership in particular, could be dismissed as an exaggerated perception on the part of the followers which does not have strong substantive effects on organizational outcomes, and is therefore not worthy of much attention by students of organizations.

Others, notably Meindl (1990), have criticized charismatic leadership theories for being much too "leader-centered." Meindl has offered a "follower-oriented" approach as an alternative to the conventional theories. In his view, the charismatic effects are a function of social psychological forces operating among followers, subordinates and observers, rather than arising directly out of the interactions between followers and leaders. According to Meindl, these social-psychological forces are functionally autonomous from the traits and behaviors of the leaders per se. Therefore, according to this radical perspective, leader behavior and leader traits should be deleted from explanations of charismatic leadership.

Obviously, we do not accept this extreme position. We believe that the evidence for the effects of charismatic leadership is too strong to be dismissed. We view Meindl's (1990) ideas as complementary, rather than contradictory, to the theory presented here. The self-processes we have described can be influenced by inter-follower processes as well as by leader behaviors. Followers' self-concepts and the related motivations can be engaged by informal role models and other social influence processes that occur among peers. This does not rule out, however, the potentiality for self-engagement as a result of charismatic leader behaviors, nor does it rule out the possibility that leaders will be instrumental in the initiation or orchestration of such inter-follower processes.

We have presented our arguments in the form of testable propositions. The theory presented here also suggests the ways in which follower attributes and organizational conditions can moderate the charismatic leadership process. Our assumptions and theoretical propositions do not contradict existing models of motivation; rather, they suggest the existence of additional motivational mechanisms without which the transformational effects of charismatic leadership cannot be explained. Hopefully, the theory advanced here will be pruned, modified and extended as a result of future empirical testing.

ACKNOWLEDGEMENTS

This paper was written while the first two authors were Visiting Professors at Suffolk University. The authors are indebted to Jane M. Howell, Susan Jackson, Raanan Lipshitz, Phillip Podsakoff and Jitendra Singh for their comments on an earlier draft of this paper.

REFERENCES

Ashforth, B. E. and F. Mael (1989), "Social Identity Theory and the Organization," *Academy of Management Review,* 14, 1, 20–39.

Ashour, A. S. (1982), "A Framework for A Cognitive Behavioral Theory of Leader Influence and Effectivness," *Organizational Behavior and Human Performance,* 30, 407–430.

Avolio, B. J. and B. M. Bass (1987). "Charisma and Beyond," in J. G. Hunt, B. R. Baliga, H. P. Dachler, and C. A. Schriesheim (Eds.), *Emerging Leadership Vistas,* Lexington: MA: D. C. Heath and Company.

———, D. A. Waldman and W. O. Einstein (1988), "Transformational Leadership in Management Game Simulation," *Group and Organization Studies,* 13, 1, 59–80.

Bandura, A. (1986), *Social Foundations of Thought and Action: A Social Cognitive Theory,* Englewood Cliffs, NJ: Prentice-Hall.

Bass, B. M. (1985), *Leadership and Performance Beyond Expectations,* New York: The Free Press.

——— (1990), *Bass & Stogdill's Handbook of Leadership,* 3rd ed., New York: The Free Press.

———, B. J. Avolio and L. Goodheim (1987), "Biographical Assessment of Transformational Leadership at the World-Class Level," *Journal of Management,* 13, 7–19.

——— and F. J. Yammarino (1988), "Long Term Forecasting of Transformational Leadership and Its Effects Among Naval Officers: Some Preliminary Findings," *Technical Report No. ONR-TR-2,* Arlington, VA: Office of Naval Research.

Bellah, R. N., R. Madsen, W. M. Sullivan, A. Swidler and S. M. Tipton (1985), *Habits of the Heart: Individualism and Commitment in American Life,* New York: Harper & Row.

Bem, D. J. (1982), "Self-Perception Theory," in L. Berkowitz (Ed.), *Advances in Experimental Social Psychology,* Vol. 6, New York: Academic Press.

Bennis, W. and B. Nanus (1985), *Leaders: The Strategies for Taking Charge,* New York: Harper & Row.

Boal, K. B. and J. M. Bryson (1988), "Charismatic Leadership: A Phenomenological and Structural Approach," in J. G. Hunt, B. R. Baliga, H. P. Dachler, and C. A. Schriesheim (Eds.), *Charismatic Leadership,* San Francisco: Jossey-Bass, 11–28.

Burns, J. M. (1978), *Leadership,* New York: Harper & Row.

Callero, P. J. (1985), "Role Identity Salience," *Social Psychology Quarterly,* 48, 3, 203–215.

Conger, J. A. and R. A. Kanungo (1987), "Towards a Behavioral Theory of Charismatic Leadership in Organizational Settings," *Academy of Management Review,* 12, 637–647.

Csikszentmihalyi, M. and E. Rochberg-Halton (1981), *The Meaning of Things: Domestic Symbols and the Self,* New York: Cambridge University Press.

Curphy, G. J. (1990), "An Empirical Study of Bass (1985) Theory of Transformational and Transactional Leadership," Unpublished Doctoral Dissertation, The University of Minnesota.

Eden, D. (1990), *Pygmalion in Management,* Lexington, MA: D. C. Heath and Co.

Evans, G. (1970), "The Effects of Supervisory Behavior on the Path-Goal Relationship," *Organizational and Human Performance,* 5, 277–298.

Gecas, V. (1982), "The Self Concept," *Annual Review of Sociology,* 8, 1–33.

Goffman, E. (1974), *Frame Analysis,* Cambridge: Harvard University Press.

Goldthorpe, J. G., D. Lockwood, R. Beechofer and J. Platt (1968), *The Affluent Worker: Industrial Attitudes and Behavior,* Cambridge: Cambridge University Press.

Graen, G. and J. F. Cashman (1975), "A Role-Making Model of Leadership in Formal Organizations: A Developmental Approach," in J. G. Hunt and L. L. Larson (Eds.), *Leadership Frontiers,* Kent, OH: Kent State University Press, 143–165.

Hater, J. J. and B. M. Bass (1988), "Supervisor's Evaluations and Subordinates' Perceptions of Transformational Leadership," *Journal of Applied Psychology,* 73, 695–702.

Hodgkinson, C. (1983), *The Philosophy of Leadership,* New York: St. Martin's Press.

Hollander, E. P. (1964), *Leaders, Groups, and Influence,* New York: Oxford University Press.

House, R. J. (1971), "A Path Goal Theory of Leader Effectiveness," *Administrative Science Quarterly,* 16, 3, 321–338.

——— (1977), "A 1976 Theory of Charismatic Leadership," in J. G. Hunt and L. L. Larson (Eds.), *Leadership: The Cutting Edge,* Carbondale: Southern Illinois University Press.

———, J. M. Howell, B. Shamir, B. J. Smith, and W. D. Spangler (1991), "A 1991 Theory of Charismatic Leadership," Graduate School of Business Administration, University of Western Ontario, London, Ontario, Canada.

———, W. D. Spangler, and J. Woycke (1991), "Personality and Charisma in the U.S. Presidency: A Psychological Theory of Leadership Effectiveness," *Administrative Science Quarterly* (in press).

Howell, J. M. (1988), "Two Faces of Charisma: Socialized and Personalized Leadership in Organizations," in J. A. Conger and R. N. Kanungo (Eds.), *Charismatic Leadership,* 213–236, San Francisco: Jossey-Bass.

——— and P. J. Frost (1989), "A Laboratory Study of Charismatic Leadership," *Organizational Behavior and Human Decision Processes,* 43, 2, 243–269.

——— and C. Higgins (1990), "Champions of Technological Innovation," *Administrative Science Quarterly,* 35, 317–341.

Jahoda, M. (1981), "Work Employment and Unemployment: Values, Theories and Approaches in Social Research," *American Psychologist,* 36, 184–191.

Johnson, M. P. (1982), "Social and Cognitive Features of the Dissolution of a Commitment to a Relationship," in S. Duch (Ed.), *Personal Relationships,* London: Academic Press.

Kanter, R. M. (1967), "Commitment and Social Organization: A Study of Commitment Mechanisms in Utopian Communities," *American Sociological Review,* 33, 4, 499–517.

Kelman, H. C. (1958), "Compliance, Identification and Internalization: Three Processes of Attitude Change," *Journal of Conflict Resolution,* 2, 51–60.

Kinder, D. R. and D. O. Sears (1985), "Public Opinion and Political Action, in Lindzey, G. and E. Aronson (Eds.), *Handbook of Social Psychology,* 3rd ed., New York: Random House.

Kuhnert, K. W. and P. Lewis (1987), "Transactional and Transformational Leadership: A Constructive/Developmental Analysis," *Academy of Management Review,* 12, 648–657.

McCall, G. H. and J. T. Simmons (1978), *Identities and Interaction,* revised ed., New York: Free Press.

McHugh, P. (1968), *Defining the Situation: The Organization of Meaning in Social Interaction,* Indianapolis: Bobbs-Merril.

Meindl, J. R. (1990), "On Leadership: An Alternative to the Conventional Wisdom," in B. M. Straw and L. L. Cummings (Eds.), *Research in Organizational Behavior,* 12, Greenwich, CT: JAI Press, 159–203.

———, S. B. Ehrlich, and J. M. Dukerich (1985), "The Romance of Leadership," *Administrative Science Quarterly,* 30, 78–102.

——— and M. J. Lerner (1983), "The Heroic Motive: Some Experimental Demonstrations," *Journal of Experimental Social Psychology,* 19, 1–20.

Mischel, W. (1973), "Toward a Cognitive Social Learning Reconceptualization of Personality," *Psychological Review,* 80, 200–213.

O'Reilly and J. Chatman (1986), "Organizational Commitment and Psychological Attachment: The Effects of Compliance, Identification and Internalization on Prosocial Behavior," *Journal of Applied Psychology,* 71, 3, 492–499.

Organ, D. W. (1988), *Organizational Citizenship Behavior,* Lexington, MA: Lexington Books.

Pereria, D. (1987), "Factors Associated with Transformational Leadership in an Indian Engineering Firm," Paper Presented at Administrative Science Association of Canada.

Pfeffer, J. (1977), "The Ambiguity of Leadership," *Academy of Management Review,* 2, 104–112.

Podsakoff, P. M., S. B. Mackenzie, R. H. Moorman and R. Fetter (1990), "Transformational Leader Behaviors and Their Effects on Followers' Trust in Leader, Satisfaction, and Organizational Citizenship Behaviors," *Leadership Quarterly,* 1, 2, 107–142.

Podsakoff, P. M., W. D. Todor and R. Skov (1982), "Effects of Leader Performance Contingent and Non-Contingent Reward and Punishment Behaviors on Subordinate Performance and Satisfaction," *Academy of Management Journal,* 25, 812–821.

Prentice, D. A. (1987), "Psychological Correspondence of Possessions, Attitudes and Values," *Journal of Personality and Social Psychology,* 53, 6, 993–1003.

Puffer, S. M. (1990), "Attributions of Charismatic Leadership: The Impact of Decision Style, Outcome, and Observer Characteristics," *Leadership Quarterly,* 1, 3, 177–192.

Roberts, N. (1985), "Transforming Leadership: A Process of Collective Action," *Human Relations,* 38, 1023–46.

Roberts, N. C. and R. T. Bradley (1988), "The Limits of Charisma," in J. A. Conger and R. N. Kanungo (Eds.), *Charismatic Leadership: The Elusive Factor in Organizational Effectiveness,* San Francisco: Jossey-Bass.

Salancik, G. R. (1977), "Commitment and the Control of Organizational Behavior and Belief," in Staw, B. M. and Salancik, G. R. (Eds.), *New Directions in Organizational Behavior,* Chicago: St. Clair, 1–54.

——— and J. Pfeffer (1977), "Constraints on Adminstrators Discretion: The Limited Influence of Mayors on City Budgets," *Urban Affairs Quarterly,* June.

Santee, R. and S. Jackson (1979), "Commitment to Self-Identification: A Sociopsychological Approach to Personality," *Human Relations,* 32, 141–158.

Sashkin, M. (1988), "The Visionary Leader," in J. A. Conger and R. A. Kanungo (Eds.), *Charismatic Leadership: The Elusive Factor in Organizational Effectiveness,* San Francisco: Jossey-Bass, 122–160.

Schlenker, B. R. (1985), "Identity and Self-Identification," in Schlenker, B. R. (Ed.), *The Self and Social Life,* New York: McGraw-Hill.

Shamir, B. (1991), "Meaning, Self and Motivation in Organizations," *Organization Studies,* 12, 405–424.

Smith, B. J. (1982), *An Initial Test of a Theory of Charismatic Leadership Based on the Re-*

sponses of Subordinates, Unpublished Doctoral Dissertation, University of Toronto, Canada.

Snow, D. A., E. B. Rochford, S. K. Worden and R. D. Benford (1986), "Frame Alignment Processes, Micromobilization and Movement Participation," *American Sociological Review,* 51, August, 464–481.

Snyder, M. (1979), "Self Monitoring Processes," in L. Berkowitz (Ed.), *Advances in Experimental Social Psychology,* 12, New York: Academic Press, 85–128.

———— and W. Ickes (1985), "Personality and Social Behavior," in Lindzey, G. and E. Aronson, *Handbook of Social Psychology,* 3rd ed., New York: Random House.

Staw, B. M. (1980), "Rationality and Justification in Organizational Life," in Staw, B. M. and L. L. Cummings (Eds.), *Research in Organizational Behavior,* 2, Greenwich, CT: JAI Press, 45–80.

Strauss, A. L. (1969), *Mirrors and Masks,* London: M. Robertson.

Stryker, S. (1980), *Symbolic Interactionism: A Social Structural Version,* Menlo Park, CA: The Benjamin/Cummings Publishing Company.

Tajfel, H. and J. C. Turner (1985), "Social Identity Theory and Intergroup Behavior," in S. Worchel and W. G. Austin (Eds.), *Psychology of Intergroup Relations,* 2nd ed., Chicago: Nelson-Hall, 7–24.

Tichy, N. M. and M. A. Devanna (1986), *The Transformational Leader,* New York: Wiley.

Trice, H. M. and J. M. Beyer (1986), "Charisma and Its Routinization in Two Social Movement Organizations," in B. M. Staw and L. L. Cummings (Eds.), *Research in Organizational Behavior,* Greenwich, CT: JAI Press, 113–164.

Turner, R. H. (1968), "The Self Conception in Social Interaction," in Gordon, G. and R. Gergen (Eds.), *The Self in Social Interaction,* New York: Wiley.

Waldman, D. A., B. M. Bass and W. O. Einstein (1987), "Leadership and Outcomes of Performance Appraisal Processes," *Journal of Occupational Psychology,* 60, 177–186.

Willner, A. R. (1984), *The Spellbinders: Charismatic Political Leadership,* New Haven, CT: Yale University Press.

Yukl, G. A. (1989), *Leadership in Organizations,* 2nd ed., Englewood Cliffs, NJ: Prentice-Hall.

———— and D. D. Van Fleet (1982), "Cross-Situational, Multimethod Research on Military Leader Effectiveness," *Organizational Behavior and Human Performance,* 30, 87–108.

REFERENCES ADDED IN PROOF

House, R. J. and J. M. Howell (1992), "Personality and Charismatic Leadership," *Leadership Quarterly,* 3, 2, 81–108.

Howell, J. M. and B. J. Avolio (1993), "Transformational Leadership, Transactional Leadership, Locus of Control and Support for Innovation: Key Predictors of Consolidated-business-unit Performance," *Journal of American Psychology,* 78, 6, in press.

Keller, R. T. (in press), "Transformational Leadership and the Performance of Research and Development Project Groups, *Journal of Management.*

Kirkpatrick, S. A. (1992), "Decomposing Charismatic Leadership: The Effects of Leader Content and Process on Follower Performance, Attitudes, and Perceptions," Unpublished Doctoral Dissertation, University of Maryland, College Park.

Koene, H., H. Pennings and M. Schreuder (1991), "Leadership, Culture, and Organizational Effectiveness," Paper Presented at the Center for Creative Leadership Conference, Boulder, Colorado.

Koh, W. L., J. R. Terborg, and R. M. Steers (1991), "The Impact of Transformational Leaders on Organizational Commitment, Organizational Citizenship Behavior, Teacher Satisfaction and Student Performance in Singapore," Academy of Management Meetings, August, 1991,

Miami, FL.

Locke, E. A. and G. P. Latham (1990), *A Theory of Goal Setting and Task Performance,* Englewood Cliffs, NJ: Prentice Hall.

Waldman, D. A. and Ramirez (1992), "CEO Leadership and Organizational Performance: The Moderating Effect of Environmental Uncertainty," Concordia University Working Paper 92-10-37, p. 59.

The Romance of Leadership

James R. Meindl
Sanford B. Ehrlich
Janet M. Dukerich

The sheer volume of theory and research devoted to the study of leadership over the decades is testimony to its prominence in our collective efforts to understand and improve organizations. However, it has become apparent that, after years of trying, we have been unable to generate an understanding of leadership that is both intellectually compelling and emotionally satisfying. The concept of leadership remains largely elusive and enigmatic. Critics have made us aware of a range of scientific deficiencies that have plagued relevant theories and research, citing poor methodology, conceptual problems, definitional ambiguities, inappropriate focus, lack of coherence, and so on (e.g., Bennis, 1959; Stogdill, 1974; Miner, 1975; Greene, 1976; Karmel, 1978; McCall and Lombardo, 1978). Others have told us that leadership is best construed as a mere substitute for and, thus, is functionally equivalent to other, more mundane organizational arrangements and processes (e.g., Kerr and Jermier, 1978). Still others confront us with disturbing evidence that our assumptions about the direct instrumental potency of leadership on organizational outcomes have vastly outstripped reality (e.g., Lieberson and O'Connor, 1972; Salancik and Pfeffer, 1977). Finally, there are persuasive arguments that cause one to suspect that the greater relevance of leadership as a concept for organizational science is that it is a phenomenologically important aspect of how observers and participants understand, interpret, and otherwise give meaning to organizational activities and outcomes (Calder, 1977; Pfeffer, 1977; Pfeffer and Salancik, 1978). Despite these assaults on traditional views, it appears that the concept of leadership is a permanently entrenched part of the socially constructed reality that we bring to bear in our analysis of organizations. And there is every sign that the obsessions with and celebrations of it will persist. The purpose of this analysis is to shed some light on this collective commitment to leadership.

In our view, the social construction of organizational realities has elevated the concept of leadership to a lofty status and level of significance. Such realities emphasize leadership, and the concept has thereby gained a brilliance that exceeds the limits of normal scientific inquiry. The imagery and mythology typically associated with the concept is evidence of the mystery and near mysticism with which it has been imbued. A sample listing of some articles on leadership that were found in recent volumes of the *Index of Business Publications* reflects this imagery: "Leadership and Magical Thinking"; "Black Art of Leadership"; "I Think Continually of Those Who Are Great"; "Protean Managerial Leadership"; and "Casting Out Organizational Demons: An Exorcise in Leadership."

It appears that as observers of and as participants in organizations, we may have de-

From "The Romance of Leadership" by James R. Meindl, Sanford B. Erhlich, and Janet M. Dukerich in *Administrative Science Quarterly,* 1985, 30, 78–102, adapted with permission of *Adminstrative Science Quarterly.* Copyright ©1985 Cornell University.

veloped highly romanticized, heroic views of leadership—what leaders do, what they are able to accomplish, and the general effects they have on our lives. One of the principal elements in this romanticized conception is the view that leadership is a central organizational process and the premier force in the scheme of organizational events and activities. It amounts to what might be considered a faith in the potential if not in the actual efficacy of those individuals who occupy the elite positions of formal organizational authority. The romanticization of leadership is hinted at in the observations made by a number of social and organizational analysts who have noted the esteem, prestige, charisma, and heroism attached to various conceptions and forms of leadership (e.g., Weber, 1946; Klapp, 1964; House, 1977; Burns, 1978; Good, 1978; McCall and Lombardo, 1978; Staw and Ross, 1980; March, 1981). We suspect that the romanticized conception of leaders and leadership is generalized and prevalent. The argument being advanced here is that the concept of leadership is a perception that plays a part in the way people attempt to make sense out of organizationally relevant phenomena. Moreover, in this sense-making process, leadership has assumed a romanticized, larger-than-life role.

An important part of the sense-making process involves an attempt to generate causal attributions for organizational events and occurrences (Thompson and Tuden, 1959; Weick, 1979). The possibility of taking an attributional perspective on leadership was first raised by Calder (1977) and by Pfeffer (1977). Since then, there has been a growing body of research and theory devoted to attributional analyses of leadership (see McElroy, 1982; Lord and Smith, 1983, for recent reviews). However, that literature, with but few exceptions (e.g., Phillips and Lord, 1981), has not dealt in a direct way with the basic issue raised by Calder and by Pfeffer, which we are addressing here: namely, leadership is perhaps best construed as an explanatory category that can be used to explain and account for organizational activities and outcomes. Staw (1975) reached a similar conclusion, but in a more general context, by arguing that the self-reported opinions and beliefs of organizational actors and observers regarding causality may in fact constitute attributional inferences rather than actual causal determinants of events and occurrences. Unfortunately, most researchers have responded by focusing narrowly on the methodological ramifications of this view (e.g., DeNisi and Pritchard, 1978; Downey, Chacko, and McElroy, 1979; Binning and Lord, 1980; McElroy and Downey, 1982), for the most part ignoring the wider, underlying implication that many organizational behavior concepts can be used by individuals to form coherent explanations of events and occurrences. This is precisely the premise from which the present analysis proceeds.

The significance placed on leadership is a response to the ill-structured problem of comprehending the causal structure of complex, organized systems. Imagine for a moment the problem faced by an observer who must comprehend a large and complex system: there are many causal forces to consider and they occur together in highly intricate and overlapping networks, complete with multiple inputs and outcomes, numerous feedback loops, and all existing in some dynamic state of flux. Total comprehension of the system will easily be beyond the power of the observer. In such a task, the particular understanding that is gained will depend at least as much on the characteristics of the observer as it does on the system itself. Our informal, implicitly held models and perhaps our more formal theories, as well, are limited responses to the task of comprehending the causal complexities that characterize all organizations. Of course, the potential ways in which an understanding can be achieved are many, and it would be difficult to choose among them on a purely rational, logical basis. However, what is attended to and what causal factors emerge as the "figure" against the background of all other possibilities, even if arbitrary with respect to the system, is not random but is a process guided by the psychology and sociology of the observer. In effect, the results represent a systematic bias about how a system is understood, how relevant events and outcomes are defined and explained, and to what factors they are attributed. The term "bias" is used here in the way Schlenker (1982: 205) defined it: "A bias in the interpretation and explanation of events is a subjective tendency to prefer one interpretation over another; such an interpretation may or may not be an error according to some 'objective' criterion for assessing the event." Such preferences occur, in part, because of the ambiguity of relevant information and the perceived importance of events. The romanticized conception of leadership results from a biased preference to understand important but causally indeterminant and ambiguous organizational events and occurrences in terms of leadership. Accordingly, in the absence of direct, unambiguous information that would allow one rationally to infer the locus of causality, the romanticized conception of leadership permits us to be more comfortable in associating leaders—by ascribing to them control and responsibility—with events and outcomes to which they can be plausibly linked.

The Present Research

The research reported here examined the hypothesis that the relative prominence of the use of leadership in understanding complex, organized systems varies to a significant degree with the performance levels of such systems. Generally speaking, the need to understand and make sense should correspond to the occurrence of salient events (Anderson, 1983). It is possible that observers are generally prone to overestimate the impact of leadership in their explanations of events; however, it seems likely that variations in events would be important for uncovering any bias toward understanding events in terms of leadership. One implication of a heroic, larger-than-life view of leadership is that its effects on an organization are not trivial. That is, associations between leadership and events will be consistent with the romanticized conception and will therefore be most appealing when those events are in some way defined as extraordinary (i.e., large cause, large effect). We reasoned that the romanticized conception will have greatest sway in extreme cases—either very good or very poor performance—causing observers to understand these events in terms of leadership. A stronger emphasis on leadership should occur under conditions in which high-magnitude outcomes obtain, and weaker preferences should be found when low-magnitude outcomes obtain. We know from past research that leaders are often held responsible and are "scapegoated" for poor organizational performance (e.g., Gamson and Scotch, 1964). Other evidence suggests that information about performance is sometimes used to infer the good and bad quality of leadership that must have existed (e.g., Staw, 1975). Thus, we expected that a bias toward leadership could be systematically related to performance levels in a positive or negative way. These ideas were tested in a series of archival and experimental studies.

ARCHIVAL STUDIES

In the archival studies, we attempted to find evidence of the bias represented in the romanticized conception of leadership by explaining how, if at all, an interest in leadership is associated with the performance of firms, industries, and the national economy. In order to do so, we examined published sources and dissertations for the appearance of leadership as a topic of interest and attention. The working assumption was that an analysis of the correspondence between attention to leadership and performances could provide an indirect and very broad indication of the extent to which outcomes are collectively understood in terms of and attributed to leadership. In Study 1, we examined the relative emphasis on corporate leaders and leadership in the popular press. In Studies 2 and 3, we focused on the correspondence between variations in national economic performance and the general emphasis placed on leadership by young scholars and by the business community in general. All three studies were designed to test the hypothesis that the amount of interest in and attention devoted to leadership in the publications studied would vary directly or inversely with general performance.

STUDY 1: THE POPULAR PRESS

Method

For this study, we examined titles of articles published in the *Wall Street Journal,* from 1972 through 1982, on a sample of 34 business firms drawn from the Fortune 500 list of large U.S. corporations. We measured the amount of attention and publicity this well-known publisher of business news devoted to the topic of corporate leadership and determined whether or not that attention bore any relationship to performance levels—defined here in general terms of the sales of profit growth of the firms and industries involved. The *Wall Street Journal* was chosen because it has an impeccable reputation as a highly credible source of business news, it has an extraordinary readership, and it is perhaps one of the most powerful, leading publications in the world (Neilson and Neilson, 1973). For performance data for the same period, we relied on the *Value Line Investment Survey.*

Our selection of firms was guided by several considerations. First, we attempted to sample a range of different industries, with several sample firms in each industry. We also tried to choose firms that showed a range of different performance curves over the time period. Finally, we wanted to select firms that we felt would have received ample press coverage during those years. We had originally sampled 35 firms; however, we realized later that we had unwittingly selected one firm that was a wholly owned subsidiary, and it was therefore dropped. The final sample of firms is listed in Table 1.

Emphasis on Leadership.   To get an estimate of the extent to which corporate leadership was emphasized for a given firm in a given year, we used the annual index of the *Wall Street Journal*, which contains a listing by title, under each large corporation, of every article on the corporation appearing in the *WSJ* in that year. Our procedure was to read the titles under the headings for each firm in the sample and for every year. An article was classified as leadership oriented (LA) if its title included a keyword or phrase that appeared in a "dictionary," developed specifically for this

TABLE 1
SAMPLE OF FIRMS

Abbott Labs	Ford Motor Company
Allied Chemical	General Electric
American Airlines	General Mills
American Cyanamid	General Motors
American Home Products	Hewlett-Packard
American Motors	IBM
Armco	Lilly
Bethlehem Steel	Lockheed
Boeing	McDonnell-Douglas
Bristol Myers	McGraw-Edison
Burroughs	NCR
Chrysler	Pan Am
Continental Airlines	RCA
Data General	Republic Steel
Delta Airlines	Texas Instruments
DuPont	U.S. Steel
Eastern Airlines	Westinghouse

research, containing a short, selected list of items. The items included references to names of corporate officers, references to senior executive positions, and phrases such as "top management," "senior executive," "top brass," and other descriptors commonly used to refer to corporate leadership. In some cases, whether or not an item was a keyword depended on its use in the context of the title. For example, the word "management" was included if it referred to the administrators of the firm, but it was excluded when the referent was a process, as in "the management of innovation." If the title did not include a listed item, then the article was assigned to an "other" (OA) category. Two coders had the task of scanning the titles and coding articles. Each coder was assigned responsibility for tabulating the frequencies in each category on a firm-by-firm, yearly basis, for half the sample. The two coders underwent several preliminary exercises in which they were asked to search and classify the articles from a number of pages of the *Index*, using the dictionary to guide their decisions. These exercises led to some modifications in the dictionary. In subsequent trial runs, each coder independently searched and classified the articles from two pages selected at random from the *Index*. The extent of their agreement was scored, revealing an error rate of less than 3 percent. The coders' tabulations summarizing the number of articles classified as LA relative to the number of articles classified as OA was taken as a rough indication of the degree to which leadership was being emphasized. This emphasis was captured in a "Leadership Quotient" (LQ), equivalent to the ratio, (LA/OA) $\times$ 100.

Of course, there are some obvious, inherent limitations in using titles to classify articles. If nothing else, measurement error would be increased through any misclassifications. However, there are several considerations that justified its use and provided us with at least some reassurance about its suitability for this research. First, this method allowed us to scan and code a very large number of references in a reasonable period of time, thus enabling us to expand the number of data points far beyond that possible through an analysis of the actual contents of articles. Second, titles are usually intended to highlight the main themes of an article, which suggest that there is a reasonable correspondence between title and content. Third, even if the correspondence between titles and content is a loose one, references to leaders in the title head of an article symbolically emphasize the concept of leadership, increasing its prominence relative to other concepts and thereby producing an implicit association between top management and whatever information then appears in the article or elsewhere about the firm. Fourth, our method is conceptually consistent with the systems used by a number of well-known and popular library data bases. For example, the *Social Sciences Citation Index (SSCI)* and the *Educational Resources Information Center (ERIC)* data bases both make use of title-keyword systems to classify publications into a variety of content areas. Although these considerations cannot give us perfect confidence, when taken together they allowed us to feel reasonably comfortable with our title scan and classification procedure.

Results and Discussion

A total of 33,248 articles about the firms in our sample appeared in the *WSJ* over the period examined. Of those, 2,832 had titles that were coded as emphasizing things other than leadership (OA). The average number of articles for any given firm, in any given year, was 88.90. Of those, an average of 7.57 were coded as LA, ranging from a minimum of zero to a maximum of 59. The average number of OA articles was 81.33, ranging from a minimum of 6 to a maximum of 995. The average yearly LQ was 14.48 percent, ranging from a minimum of 0 percent to a maximum of 70 percent. The comparable figure for mean annual sales growth was 13.33 percent, ranging from a low of –45.57 percent to a high of 131.03 percent.

Year-Wise Analysis. To find evidence that a general emphasis on leadership is associated with performance, we examined the yearly LQ's for the entire sample of firms in conjunction with their yearly performances. The results indicated that LQ scores were positively related to performance, measured here in terms of yearly annual sales growth, $r(9 \text{ df}) = .53$, $p<.05$. This suggests that years in which companies are on average doing well are also the years in which leadership on average tends to be more highly emphasized.

Analysis by Industry. To examine the relative emphasis on leadership with respect to different industry performances, we classified the 34 firms in our sample into ten major industrial groupings on the basis of the first two digits of their SIC designations. The mean annual increase in sales performance across these industries was 10.37 percent, with a standard deviation of 2.70 percent, ranging from a high of 15.80 percent, to a low of 6.92 percent. The number of firms in our sample in the same industrial group was quite small: usually three or four, but in one case two, and in another case six. Even so, a one-way ANOVA revealed that the mean LQ varied substantially across the industry groups, $F(9,34) = 2.28$, $p<.05$. Moreover, the variance in LQ appears to be systematically related to industry performance: a planned comparison revealed that firms associated with the five highest performance industries had, on average, significantly higher LQ's than those firms associated with the lowest performance industries, $F(1,33) = 8.99$, $p<.01$. That finding was corroborated by a significant correlation between average firm LQ and industry performance, $r(8 \text{ df}) = .64$, $p<.05$.

Company-by-Company Analysis.   To examine how the emphasis on leadership may vary in relationship to a firm's own performances over time and how that relationship may vary across firms, we conducted separate analyses for each firm, correlating LQ with annual performance. Since we have data available for only 11 years, the potential degrees of freedom available for these analyses are quite small (df = 9). However, we felt that the 34 replications could provide us with a reasonably good estimate of the pervasiveness of the expected effect. Given the inherent difficulties of specifying a priori what definition of performance will be used to make inferences about and associations to the leaders of any given firm, and since performance of a single firm is often judged in terms of how well it is doing relative to others in its own industry, we expanded the general performance outcomes for this analysis to include growth in profits and sales relative to the comparable industry-wide figures. The results of these analyses indicated that for 25 of the 34 firms (74 percent), LQ was significantly ($p<.09$ or greater) associated with at least some of our definintions of performance. If 50 percent is used as an extremely conservative expected value, then a simple one-degree-of-freedom chi-square test suggests this is a nonrandom pattern: $x^2(1 \text{ df}) = 6.89$, $p<.019$. Also, of the 25 firms showing an association between LQ and performance, 16 (64 percent) were positive, and the remaining 9 (36 percent) were negative.

Within-Year Analysis.   Our final analysis focused on the covariation of LQ and performance across companies in each of the 11 years. The data summarized in Table 2 show that, in every year examined, LQ was correlated ($p<.08$ or greater) with performance outcomes. In eight of those years, the significant correlations were negative, indicating that in each of those years, the poorer the performance, the more leadership was emphasized. In the remaining three years, the significant correlations were positive, such that the better the performances, the greater the emphasis on leadership.

The four sets of analyses gave us an opportunity to gain somewhat different perspectives on the data and provided us with different focal points for examining the tendency to associate leadership with performance. In each of the analyses, the weight of

TABLE 2
WITHIN-YEAR ANALYSIS: DIRECTION OF SIGNIFICANT CORRELATIONS BETWEEN LEADER-SHIP QUOTIENT AND COMPANY PERFORMANCE MEASURES

					Year					
1972	1973	1974	1975	1976	1977	1978	1979	1980	1981	1982
neg*	neg	neg	neg	neg	neg*	pos	pos	pos	neg	neg

*$p<.08$; all others are $p<.05$ or greater.

evidence supported our expectations that the emphasis on a firm's top management will vary significantly with performance levels. The industry and the year-wise analyses revealed that an emphasis on leadership increases with increasingly positive performance. The within-company and within-year analyses introduced additional evidence that, on some occasions and for some firms, leadership is more likely to be emphasized when performances are poor. These two major patterns of results, when taken together, provided us with initial support for the proposition that the perceived causal priority of and attributions to leadership in understanding organizational events and occurrences are likely to occur when performances are either very good or very bad.

STUDY 2: DISSERTATION TOPICS

With the evidence obtained from Study 1, we turned our attention to exploring the societal aspect of our theory, which suggests that the level of collective interest and significance invested in the concept of leadership is responsive to fluctuations in the general economic performance of the entire nation. In order to test the notion, we chose, in this study, to track the level of interest in leadership through the dissertation topics young scholars chose. We assumed that the commitment and devotion represented by a dissertation topic would provide us with a glimpse of the collective investment in the concept of leadership.

Method

We counted the number of doctoral dissertations devoted to the topic of leadership and related it to the general economic conditions over the years 1929–1983. Our primary source of information was *Dissertation Abstracts International (DAI),* an internationally recognized reference tool that summarizes and indexes virtually all the current dissertations accepted in the U.S. and Canada (*DAI User's Guide,* 1983). We used the subject index, which lists and groups dissertations into over 200 specialized subject headings, one of which is "leadership." The number of dissertations appearing every year under that heading ("LD") formed the basis of our analysis. However, because *DAI* did not give comparable data that would allow us to estimate easily the total number of dissertations in all the social sciences, we obtained an estimate from another source, *American Doctoral Dissertations.* We used their annual figures to find the total number of social science dissertations accepted each year ("TD"). In order to estimate general economic conditions, we relied on figures published by the Economic Statistics Bureau of Washington, DC, in their *Handbook of Basic Economic Statistics*, to compute year-to-year percentage changes in the GNP (delta GNP). This measure was chosen because it is a very broad and familiar indicator of swings in the nation's economy.

Results and Discussion

From 1929 to 1983 there was a dramatic increase in the number of dissertations awarded. In 1929, there were under 2,000; in 1979, there were over 35,000. This historical trend showed up in our preliminary analysis as a very strong correlation between years and TD, $r = .91$, $p<.001$, and LD, $r = .81$, $p<.001$. Thus, in light of this strong historical trend, we controlled for years, through partial correlations, to examine the relationship between economic conditions and interest in leadership. We also formed a ratio, LD/TD, which yielded a leadership quotient ($LD_{dissertations}$) conceptually similar to that used in Study 1. It also seemed reasonable to expect a lag of several years between economic conditions and completed dissertations, although we could not specify exactly what that lag would be. On the basis of these considerations, our analyses focused on the lagged (0 to +6 years) partial correlations between delta GNP and $LQ_{dissertations}$, controlling for linear, historical trends. Table 3 shows that the relationship between delta GNP and $LQ_{dissertations}$ was negative, indicating that downturns in the growth of the economy were subsequently followed by a greater interest in leadership, relative to all other topics and after controlling for historical trends. This relationship becomes reliable after a two-year lag, reaching its highest level in the plus-fourth year, and then drops off. These results, then, suggest that there is an association between good or bad economic times and the interest in leadership, at least among scholars choosing dissertation topics.

STUDY 3: GENERAL BUSINESS PERIODICALS

This study was conceptually similar to Study 2. This time, however, our strategy was to focus more specifically on the business community. Accordingly, we deliberately chose an available data base that was much wider in scope than that used in Study 2 and captured to a greater degree the interests of the general business community in the topic of leadership. Given the results of Study 2, we expected that the negative relationship between the state of the general economy and interest in leadership would be replicated here. This strategy allowed us to observe whether or not the general business community's collective interest in leadership is also responsive to fluctuations in the national economy. If so, then we could have added confidence in the generalizability of our guiding hypothesis. In addition, the study afforded us an opportunity to determine if interest is such that it tends to emphasize leadership to a greater degree during good or during bad economic times.

Method

We examined the annual volumes from 1958 to 1983 of the *Business Periodical Index (BPI)*, published by the H. W. Wilson Company, which consist of subject entries for a wide range of business-oriented publications. In 1981 alone, the contents of over 250 different periodicals were indexed and grouped into hundreds of subject headings, one of which is "leadership." Although scholarly journals such as *ASQ* and *AMJ* are indexed, the majority of the publications indexed are nonacademic and practitioner- oriented. For example, this index includes popular periodicals, such as *Barrons, Business Week, Forbes,* and *Fortune,* as well as more specialized, often industry-specific publications, such as *Chemical Week, Electronics World,* and *Pipeline and Gas Journal.* Because of these characteristics, this database was chosen over others, such as *ERIC,*

TABLE 3
LAGGED PARTIAL CORRELATIONS BETWEEN $LQ_{DISSERTATIONS}$ AND CHANGES IN THE GENERAL ECONOMY (DELTA GNP)

			Lag			
0	+ 1	+ 2	+ 3	+ 4	+ 5	+ 6
−15	−22	−28*	−27*	−39**	−17	−02

*$p<.05$; **$p<.01$.

or *SSCI*. In addition, the index was published from 1958 to the present—the longest running period we could find.

As in Study 2, obtaining a yearly estimate of the interest in leadership entailed a simple count of the number of titles listed under the subject heading, "leadership" (LA_{BPI}). However, no published data were available on the total number of articles indexed (TA_{BPI}), and this had to be estimated. Fortunately, because the format, page size, and type size have remained the same across volumes and years, we were able to obtain the average number of entries per page by drawing a sample of 50 pages (two pages for every year) and then counting the number of entries on each ($M = 65.24$; SD $= 7.15$). We then multiplied the number of pages in each volume by the average number of entries per page to arrive at a yearly estimate of TA_{BPI}.

Results and Discussion

There has been a strong growth in the number of business periodicals published over the years, and this historical trend was reflected in our data by the zero-order correlations between years and TA_{BPI}, $r = .88$, $p<.001$, and LA_{BPI}, $r = .83$, $p<.001$. In an analysis parallel to that in the previous study, we examined the relationship between LQ_{BPI} (LA/TA) and delta GNP, controlling for that linear historical trend. The partial correlations were lagged in the same manner as in Study 2 (0 to +6 years), although little delay was anticipated, given that the intent of the majority of the periodicals is to stay current. The results, summarized in Table 4, show that, as in Study 2, there appeared to be some association between economic performance and interest in leadership, after controlling for historical trends. However, unlike in the previous study, the relationship is predominantly positive, suggesting that the interest in leadership in the general business community, at least in terms of publications, seems to be at its greatest levels when there are

TABLE 4
LAGGED PARTIAL CORRELATIONS BETWEEN LQ_{BPI} AND CHANGES IN THE GENERAL ECONOMY (DELTA GNP)

			Lag			
0	+1	+2	+3	+4	+5	+6
.67***	.48**	.52**	.02	−.33	−.35	−.02

*$p<.05$; **$p<.01$; ***$p<.001$.

upswings in the nation's economic growth. Apparently, the relationship is more immediate in time than that found with the dissertation data, which is not surprising, given the differences in the nature and goals of those publications. However, why $LQ_{dissertations}$ in Study 2 varied inversely and why in this study LQ_{BPI} varied directly with delta GNP is intriguing. Perhaps those patterns represent some underlying differences between academic and practitioner-oriented views. Whatever the case, the relationships are not likely to represent random associations and are both generally consistent with our expectations, if not in direction, at least in terms of degree.

EXPERIMENTAL STUDIES

The preceding archival studies provided reasonably clear evidence of a general relationship between performance outcomes and degree of emphasis on leadership. The following series of experiments was designed to test more precisely the notion that the use of leadership as an explanatory concept—in the form of causal attributions—varies with performance. In particular, given the theoretical arguments and the pattern of studies, we sought to determine if, under controlled experimental conditions, leadership attributions would indeed be more likely to occur—and thereby create a stronger association—when performance is either very good or very bad. In the three experiments reported here, business school students were presented with minimal information and were asked to account for instances of performance that varied in terms of the magnitude of outcomes. In each case, they were asked to consider a leader as a possible reason for the outcome event. For comparison purposes, individuals' attributions to alternative determinants of performance other than to the leader were also obtained. Study 4 provided a partial test of the hypothesis by examining attributional patterns when observers were presented with information that varied the magnitude of *positive* performance outcomes. Study 5 provided a more complete test of the hypothesis by replicating and extending Study 4 and included conditions that varied the magnitude of *negative* as well as positive performance outcomes. Studies 4 and 5 laid the groundwork for Study 6, which attempted to replicate the pattern of results under more refined conditions and began to explore the role of expectations on leadership attributions. Although Studies 4 and 5 were preliminary, because they were instrumental to the development of Study 6, we will briefly describe them here.

STUDY 4

Method

Fifty-nine undergraduates enrolled in an introductory organizational behavior course at a large northeastern university participated in this study. Their mean age was 21.90 years, and on the average they reported having the equivalent of 2.56 years of work experience.

Subjects were randomly assigned to read one of three different versions of an extremely brief organizational performance-related vignette. Each version contained the same summary description of an organizational unit and its members, including the leader. The vignettes differed only in terms of the information they provided on performance outcomes, which were defined in terms of sales increase. Low, moderate, and high magnitude effects were conveyed to subjects by providing them with information that the unit had experienced either a slight (2 percent), moderate (10 percent), or large (25 percent) increase in sales performance. The vignettes read as follows:

> John Smith is the Director of Sales for a major northeastern appliance firm. John assumed this position five years ago following his attainment of an MBA degree. Prior to his MBA, John had completed a bachelor's degree in Marketing. In this position he has gained the respect of both his subordinates and superiors. On his last evaluation John was rated as a capable worker and his subordinates have indicated that they enjoy working for him. John currently is in charge of five subordinates. All of the subordinates working in John's department have a good working knowledge of marketing principles as demonstrated by their prior and current work experience. At the end of the fourth quarter, new customer accounts had shown a slight/moderate/large increase (2%/10%/25%) during the year, over last year's performance.

Immediately after reading the vignettes, subjects were asked to rate (on a 7-point scale) the extent to which they considered the leader to be an important causal determinant of the performance outcome. And, in order to insure that subjects were aware of and at least considered other, perhaps competing explanations for the outcome, parallel questions asked them to express the extent to which alternative, plausible factors may have contributed to the outcome, including other actors (subordinates), environmental factors (general economy), and anything else they felt should be considered (other). Responses to these last questions were considered together as "alternative" attributions and were therefore aggregated, for conceptual and analytic purposes.

Results and Discussion

Attributions ("leader" vs. "alternatives") were examined conjointly with outcome effects (low, moderate, and high magnitudes) in a 3×2 ANOVA. The data in Table 5 reveal that the general level of attribution making did not differ across the three magnitude conditions (overall low $M = 5.08$; overall moderate $M = 4.93$; overall large $M = 5.03$), $F(1,56) = .21$; ns. The analysis also revealed that in general, attributions to leader (overall $M = 5.27$) were preferred to attributions to alternatives (overall $M = 4.75$), $F(1,56) = 11.59$, $p<.001$. Most importantly, however, and as expected, the main

TABLE 5
MEAN ATTRIBUTION IN EACH MAGNITUDE CONDITION: STUDY 4

Attributions*	Magnitude of Increase		
	Low (N = 19)	Moderate (N = 20)	High (N = 20)
Leader	5.10	5.20	5.50
Alternatives	5.00	4.67	4.55

*7-point scales; higher scores indicate stronger attributions.

effects were qualified by an interaction between type of attribution and magnitude of outcome, $F(2,56)$, $p<.06$, indicating that larger magnitude outcomes caused *greater* use of the leader as an explanation and *less* use of alternative explanations. A planned comparison between the leader and alternative attributions in the large magnitude condition ($M = 5.50$ and $M = 4.55$, respectively) was significant, $F(1,56) = 13.43$, $p<.001$. These two types of attributions were not reliably different in the other low and moderate magnitude conditions.

Thus, the pattern of results provided initial support for the hypothesis that the preference to use leaders in understanding organizational outcomes increases with increasingly large magnitudes of positive effects. Although, by itself, the increase in attributions to the leader was not great, the trend upward is compelling when compared with the "baseline" provided by the use of alternative explanations. Such comparisons reveal that the increase in leadership attributions occurred despite the fact that attributions to alternatives decreased.

STUDY 5

The support found in Study 4, although suggestive, is limited by the fact that only positive performance conditions were examined. In its general form, the hypothesis is different to the direction of performance changes—the effect should occur in the negative as well as in the positive cases. Accordingly, the goal in Study 5 was to further verify the hypothesis by examining attributional responses for negative performance cases, as well, especially in light of the negative associations uncovered in our archival studies.

Method

One hundred and sixteen undergraduates enrolled in introductory behavior and human resource courses participated in this study. Their mean age was 22.32 years, and on average they reported having the equivalent of 2.24 years of work experience.

The vignettes used in Study 4 were modified to accommodate the inclusion of negative as well as positive outcomes of varying degrees. That resulted in six different versions: large negative (25 percent decrease), moderate negative (10 percent decrease), small negative (2 percent decrease), small positive (2 percent increase), moderate positive (10 percent increase), and large positive (25 percent increase) effects. Thus, the descriptions subjects received ranged from very poor sales performance at the high-magnitude, negative end, to very good sales performance at the high-magnitude, positive end. On the basis of feedback obtained from initial pre-testing, the brief description of the leader was made consistent with the general positive or negative direction of performance change, in order to insure that he remained an equally plausible explanation for all outcome effects. Thus, in three cases of increased performance, a somewhat positive impression was conveyed; in the decreased performance cases, a somewhat negative impression was conveyed. Of course, the description of the leader within each type (increase versus decrease in performance) was held constant.

Immediately after reading the vignettes, subjects were asked to rate the performance of the unit on a 7-point scale, from "extremely poor" to "extremely good." As in Study 4, subjects were then asked to attribute performance outcomes to the leader and to alternative causes.

Results and Discussion

The performance and attribution data are summarized in Table 6. Our prediction was that the greatest level of leader attributions would occur at both extremes of the performance continuum—i.e., where positive and negative magnitudes are greatest—implying a curvilinear relationship between performance level and leader attributions. The means across the six conditions suggest such a pattern did indeed occur. However, the most sensitive and useful test compares subjects' own perceptions of performance outcomes with the strength of their attributions to the leader. Accordingly, an orthogonal polynomial regression analysis was conducted, using subjects' own perceptions of performance to predict the extent to which leadership was used as an explantory concept. The hypothesis, in this case, is a quadratic ($2°$ polynomial) model. Linear, quadratic, and cubic models were examined, and, as predicted, the only coefficient to reach significance was associated with the quadratic component, $B = 3.09(1.02)$; $t = 3.02$, $p<.001$. In addition, goodness-of-fit tests for the polynomial model at each degree were conducted. These tests estimated the *lack* of fit of models at each degree, relative to the residual MS from fitting polynomials of higher degrees. Thus, a high F ratio is an indication of a poor fit. These tests revealed that the linear model produced a significantly poor fit, $F(2,112) = 4.87$, $p = .009$, while the quadratic model provided the best fit, $F(1,112) = .62$, $p = .43$. A scatter plot of the data confirmed the U-shaped distribution of scores. Figure 1 shows the mean attributions for subjects at each perceived performance level. Similar analyses conducted on the alternative attributions indicated that such curvilinear trends did not occur, lending added support to the hypotheses.

As an even better test of the hypothesis, the perceived performances were used to predict subjects' preferences for using the leader as a causal explanation *relative* to their tendency to make alternative attributions. Accordingly, a parallel regression

TABLE 6
MEAN PERCEIVED PERFORMANCE AND ATTRIBUTIONS IN EACH PERFORMANCE OUTCOME
CONDITION: STUDY 5

Dependent Variable	Performance condition					
	Large decrease ($N = 19$)	Moderate decrease ($N = 19$)	Slight decrease ($N = 20$)	Slight increase ($N = 18$)	Moderate increase ($N = 20$)	Large increase ($N = 20$)
Attributions*						
Leader	5.00	4.26	4.55	4.94	5.05	5.10
Alternatives	3.82	3.96	4.07	4.09	3.91	3.80
Perceived performance†	2.47	3.11	3.55	5.17	5.55	6.35

*7-point scales; higher scores indicate stronger attributions.
†7-point scales; higher scores indicate better perceived performance.

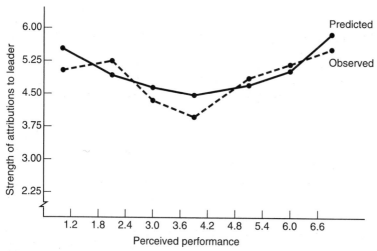

FIGURE 1.
Predicted values and mean attributions to leader at each level of perceived performance: Study 5.

analysis was conducted using the difference between the leader and alternative attributions as the dependent variable. Again, the quadratic component was significant, $B = 4.60(1.22)$; $t = 3.76$, $p<.001$. Also as expected, the subsequent fit test revealed a poor linear fit, $F(2,112) = 7.34$, $p<.001$, but a good fitting quadratic model, $F(1,112) = .57$, $p = .45$. These results, then, paralleled those of the previous regression analyses.

When taken together, the results provided good support for the hypothesis that larger outcomes—whether they are positive or negative—are most likely to lead observers to make the inference that a leader was an important cause. Nevertheless, several issues remained, and those became the focus of Study 6.

STUDY 6

This final study had two general objectives. One was to replicate the pattern of results found in the previous experiments under somewhat more refined conditions. The vignettes used in those experiments raised some issues that could be relevant to the observed effects. One issue concerned the salience and general prominence of the leader in the vignettes. Upon reflection, we had not paid much attention to the positioning and length of the leader's description in the vignettes. It was possible that we had unwittingly and artificially inflated the extent to which the leader was subsequently considered as an important causal determinant of performance. That is a concern, because other research indicates that attributions in general are highly sensitive to the contextual properties of causal information, such as saliency and primacy (e.g., Jones et al., 1968; Taylor and Fiske, 1978; McArthur, 1981). In fact, it is precisely for those reasons that the "main effects" for type of attribution (leader versus alternatives) observed in Studies 4 and 5 must be treated with caution. A less likely, but nevertheless present possibility is that extreme outcomes may somehow have been attributed to the leader in response to such artificial, externally induced prominence, rather than being the results of internal processes (e.g., Phillips and Lors, 1981). A related issue was the description of the leader: in Study 5, in order to insure that the leader remained an equally plausible, potential causal determinant across the entire span of positive and negative performance conditions, he was portrayed somewhat positively in the three positive, increased performance conditions and somewhat negatively in the three negative, decreased performance conditions. Although this is not necessarily a problem, Study 6 allowed us to make use of an alternative strategy in which all descriptive information on the leader was deleted from the various vignettes, and we were able to clear up any ambiguities that might have been associated with the previous strategy.

A second general purpose was to examine the role of performance expectations in making leader attributions. Other literature (e.g., Jones and Davis, 1965; Jones et al., 1971; Pyszczynski and Greenberg, 1981; Hastie, 1984; Weiner, 1985) suggests that spontaneous attribution making is exacerbated by, among other things, the degree to which events depart from observers' general and normative expectations. Surprising, extraordinary events increase the need to search for plausible causal determinants. In the present context, expectations may be strongly related to the magnitude of the performance outcome and to the subsequent tendency to make attributions to the leader and perhaps to alternative causes, as well. One reasonable hypothesis is that the more extreme performances deviated from observers' less extreme expectations of what performance changes are typical for an organization. If that is true, then perhaps it is the size of deviation from expectations—not simply the magnitude of performance—that is responsible for the observed pattern of leadership attributions. Although that reasoning is not inconsistent with the general perspective taken in this analysis, it does suggest that some attempt should be made to take into account observers' expectations, along with performance outcomes, in order to examine their effects on attributions.

Method

Seventy-two undergraduate business majors in sections of an evening introductory organizational behavior course participated in this experiment. Their mean age was 25.0 years, and on average reported having nearly five (4.87) years of full-time work experience.

The vignettes used in the previous studies were modified, in order to decrease the prominence of the leader relative to other potential causal determinants, by weaving into the text the mention of the leader, along with a number of other causal determinants. The final vignettes read as follows:

The Gemini Corporation is a large volume manufacturer of household appliances. They have been in business for a number of years and have several plants located throughout the country. The appliance industry is characterized by an environment whose market and economic factors have been changing over the past few years. Sales is one of the functional departments within this corporation and is headed by a Director, John Smith, who assumed this position at the beginning of the last fiscal year. At about the same time, a new group of sales representatives were hired and reported directly to Mr. Smith. At the end of the fiscal year, gross sales had shown a slight/moderate/large increase/decrease (2%/10%/25%) over last year's performance.

As a further precaution, subjects were asked on the rating form itself to consider all of the potential causes before they made their attributional ratings of the impact of any single causal determinant. Before making these ratings, however, subjects were first asked to rate the performance of the unit, as in the previous studies. And, in order to assess the extent to which the level of performance deviated from their own implicit and general expectations, after rating the unit's performance they were also asked to rate (on a 7-point scale) how surprising they found the increase or decrease in performance.

Results and Discussion

Initial Analyses. A series of analyses of variance was conducted on the six performance conditions, examining attributions, expectations, and perceived performance. These data are summarized in Figure 2. A one-way ANOVA of the perceived performance attested to the efficacy of the manipulation, $F(5,66) = 9.65$, $p<.001$. A similar analysis of the expectation measure revealed a significant effect of performance condition on expectations, $F(5,66) = 3.14$, $p = .013$. Attributions were examined in a two-way analysis of variance with one between factor (performance) and one within factor (leader versus alternative attributions). This analysis revealed a significant main effect for performance outcome, $F(5,66) = 2.55$, $p = .036$, and for type of attribution, $F(1,66) = 7.49$, $p = .008$. Moreover, both main effects were qualified by a significant interaction, $F(5,66) = 2.42$, $p = .045$.

FIGURE 2.
Graphic representation of attributions to leader and alternatives in each performance outcome condition: Study 6.

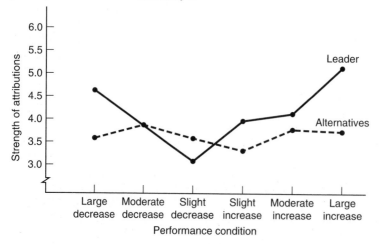

Expectations and Performance. First, in order to establish the relationship between performance and expectations, a polynomial regression analysis was conducted in which rated performance was used to predict the reported deviations from expectations. This analysis revealed that the coefficient on the quadratic component was significant, $B = 2.989(1.26)$; $t(69) = 2.38$, $p<.025$. Moreover, the goodness-of-fit tests indicated that the linear model provided a significant poor fit, $F(2.89)$, $p = .062$, while the U-shaped model ($2°$ polynomial) provided the best fit, $F(1.68) = .19$, $p = .67$. Thus, extremely good and extremely poor performance were judged to be more surprising and therefore represented larger deviations from subjects' general expectations.

Leader Attributions. The next task was to incorporate expectations into the model specified by the original hypothesis. However, the polynomial regression technique used in the previous experiment to test the predicted curvilinear relationship between perceived performance and leader attributions did not lend itself to the inclusion of more than a single predictor variable and, therefore, could not be used to control and test for the additional effect of expectations. Consequently, a more traditional multiple-regression procedure was employed as a reasonable approximation of the model. First, the relationship between leader attributions and perceived performance was estimated by including the performance variable and its squared term as predictors of leader attributions. If the hypothesized "quadratic" relationship were true, then a significant, but negative coefficient should be obtained on the performance variable, *in combination* with a significant but positive coefficient on the squared term. With only these two predictor terms, the overall equation was significant, $R^2 = .347$; $F(2.69) = 18.30$, $p<.001$. More importantly, however, and as expected, the coefficient associated with the performance term was significant and negative, $B = -2.41(.438)$, $p<.001$; and the coefficient associated with the squared term was significant and positive, $B = .322(.545)$, $p<.001$. In effect, then, these results replicated those of the previous study and, in light of the changes made in the vignettes, provided us with more confidence in the validity and generalizability of the effect.

The overall equation remained significant when the expectation ratings were added into the above model as a predictor, $R^2 = .344$; $F(3,68) = 13.41$, $p<.001$. However, the coefficient associated with the expectation rating was not significant, $B = .1829(.110)$, $p = .103$. The negative coefficient on the performance term remained significant, $B = -2.24(.444)$, $p<.001$, as did the positive coefficient on the squared term, $B = .297(.559)$, $p<.001$. Thus one must conclude that although extreme performances deviated from expectations and were generally viewed as more surprising than lower magnitude performances, in this case, such deviations probably did not, by themselves, have a large independent effect on the strength of leader attributions. Moreover, when controlling for expectations, the observed relationship between the magnitude of outcomes and the tendency to understand performance in terms of leadership persisted.

A plausible argument is that when faced with explaining a large magnitude outcome, individuals make more attributions to all relevant sources. According to that line of reasoning, the level of leadership attributions may simply be an artifact of a more general trend. Consequently, we performed one final set of analyses that attempted to control for individuals' general tendency to make attributions to all sources. In order to do that, the same set of variables was used to predict a ratio in which the strength of leadership attributions was divided by the strength of attributions to all other sources. This ratio roughly parallels the LQ measure used in the previous archival studies. According to the hypothesis, extreme performances should be associated with higher ratios. The prediction model was also significant for this dependent variable, $R^2 = .283$, $p<.001$. And, as with the previous dependent variable, the coefficient associated with the expectation term was not significant, $B = .238(.458)$, $p = .604$. However, as predicted, the coefficient on the performance term was significant and negative, $B = -.811(.184)$, $p<.001$; and the coefficient associated with the squared term was significant and positive, $B = .109(.232)$, $p<.001$. This last analysis, then, indicated that extreme performances did indeed lead to a proportional increase in the preference to use the leader as a causal explanation and provided a strong confirmation of our expectations.

GENERAL DISCUSSION

The romanticized conception of leadership suggests that leaders do or should have the ability to control and influence the fates of the organizations in their charge. This assumption of control and the responsibility it engenders is a double-edged sword: not only does it imply giving credit for positive outcomes, but it also entails laying blame for negative ones (Salancik and Meindl, 1984). Our experimental studies revealed that pattern. However, the results of our archival studies suggest that one or the other tendency, for whatever reasons, may predominate in any given case. The negative and positive associations in Studies 2 and 3, respectively, between an interest in leadership and the state of the national economy are particularly intriguing. The positive association uncovered in Study 3 suggests that the popular press that serves the general business community contributes to the credit-giving aspect of the romanticized view. Of course, the popular press is in part a reflection of the community it serves, and firms, by their own activities, can prompt an interest in and association to leadership factors. Thus, the finding that leadership is accentuated during times of economic prosperity is, in retrospect, not so difficult to understand. By the same token, the scholarly community may have less reason to favor giving credit over laying blame. In fact, the negative association between an interest in the topic of leadership and economic prosperity may reflect the problem-oriented response of young scholars to hard times.

Others (e.g., Pfeffer, 1977; Pfeffer and Salancik, 1978) have suggested that the tendency to ascribe high levels of control and influence to leaders arises from private needs to find causes among human actors. Accordingly, the exacerbation of those needs would tend to foster the development of a romantic conception in which leadership was indeed believed to be highly significant. In fact, a subsequent analysis of our experimental studies revealed that attributions to different personal causal agents (in this case, leader and subordinates) tended to be positively correlated ($r = .20, .22,$ and $.37$ in Studies 4, 5, and 6, respectively), as this general line of reasoning would suggest. A romanticized view of leadership is probably also an outgrowth of a general faith in human organizations as potentially effective and efficient value-producing systems that fulfill the various interests of their participants and perhaps, also, society at large. The potency and promise of human organizations and all the values they represent come to be symbolized in the formal hierarchy of authority and the officials who occupy the elite positions of power and status (Milgram, 1974). Given this, a faith in the significance of leadership may be one manifestation of internalized values about the validity of organizations and therefore, by implication, the roles occupied by people who are charged with the responsibility to maintain and control them.

Because observers are prone to overestimate the amount of control that leaders exert, particularly when the event or outcome in question is especially significant, a subscription to a romanticized view could be dysfunctional to the goals of an "objective" or rational assessment of important but causally indeterminant events. At the same time, however, it seems possible that an excessive belief in the potency of leadership could also be functional for those who will occupy positions of formal authority and status. If we assume that on some occasions leadership can, in reality, make a difference—but that we cannot be sure when—then it may be important for organizations to have leaders who operate, at some level, on the assumption that they do make a difference and that they are in control. Without the benefits of a working assumption that conveys a sense of efficacy and control, the initiation of and persistence in potentially relevant activity would be considerably more difficult. The end result may be somewhat depressed functioning and a sense of helplessness in situations in which control is in fact possible.

The present research may begin to provide us with some new insights about the reason for changing leadership or decisions to extend an incumbent's tenure in response to perceived variations in an organization's fortunes. For example, there is a small, but somewhat paradoxical literature that attempts to understand the causes and consequences of managerial succession. Several theoretical perspectives have been offered (e.g., Grusky, 1963; Gamson and Scotch, 1964; Gordon and Rosen, 1981), all of them based on more or less implicit assumptions about the attributions of relevant and powerful others to leadership factors in response to poor organizational performance. In fact, the theories and the empirical studies make a convincing case that poor performance increases the probability and rate of successions (Grusky, 1963; Helmich and Brown, 1972; Lieberson and O'Connor, 1972; Helmich, 1974, 1977; Osborn et al., 1981). There is less theoretical agreement about the effect of succession on subsequent organizational performance. Conventional wisdom implies that the effect on performance of changing leaders should be positive, since such events are ostensibly guided by the positive intentions and expectations of those in a position to induce them. Some (e.g., Grusky, 1963) argue that successions are disruptive to so many important processes that subsequent performances will decline. Still others (e.g., Gamson and Scotch, 1964) emphasize the symbolic aspects of successions and consider them exercises in "ritualistic scapegoating" that involve processes that are only incidentally or tangentially relevant for subsequent performance. The available empirical evidence tends to run contrary to the conventional wisdom, suggesting that although poor performances may often precipitate successions, such events have little or negative effects on subsequent performance (e.g., Allen, Panian, and Lotz, 1979; Brown, 1982). The paradox is that, despite the absence of clearly instrumental effects, successions are nevertheless a popular response to poor performance. At least a part of that paradox can be understood as reflecting an inclination to construe events and outcomes in terms of leadership. Pfeffer (1977) argued that the limited impact that many leadership successions have on performance outcomes is due in large part to the lack of variability in the pool of individuals from which both the incumbent and successor have been drawn. One interesting and testable hypothesis precipitated by the present analysis is that interested parties are very likely to overperceive the degree of relevant variation in that pool, seeing more heterogeneity than really exists between the old and the new leader and among the potential successors. Given the romanticization of leadership, it is less difficult to understand the optimistic faith in the effectiveness of successions—the shifting of commitment from the old to the new leader and the maintenance of positive expectations for outcomes, even in the face of contrary evidence.

Needless to say, organizations have always been influenced by their environments, yet it is only recently—within the last ten years—that organizational dependencies have been fully appreciated in our theoretical perspectives (e.g., Aldrich, 1979; Hall, 1982; Pfeffer and Salancik, 1978). In Study 1, the average company sales growth performance over the 11-year period and the corresponding figures for relevant industries were strongly correlated, $R(9 \text{ df}) = .80$, $p<.01$. That is not surprising, given the number of industries sampled and the size of the firms in our sample that were chosen to represent these industries. However, it does provide a rough indication that a given firm's fate, in terms of performance, is closely tied to external factors affecting whole industries, as opposed to being under the direct, unique control of its top management. As expected, however, we were able to find evidence that there is nevertheless a tendency to link leadership not only with variations in company performance, but also with the performance of entire industries, which are undoubtedly affected by factors well beyond the control of any single firm or management. Other researchers have also found systematic evidence indicating that traditional views have overestimated the amount of variance in performance outcomes that is logically and empirically attributable to leadership (e.g., Lieberson and O'Connor, 1972; Salancik and Pfeffer, 1977). Such evidence shifts attention and the locus of control away from top-level leaders and the positions they occupy to other causal entities and forces not directly tied to the qualities and activities of leadership. The implication is that perhaps leadership is not as important as we normally think—at least not in the traditional sense (Pfeffer, 1978, 1981). That implication is provocative, because it contradicts the romanticized conception of leadership, and some resistance to it is predictable. To the extent that observers are psychologically invested in a romanticized view of leadership, then, we might expect selective perceptions, confirmatory biases, and other processes (Ross, 1977) to be present that cause the observer to avoid or resist information and evidence that diminishes the significance of leadership to organizational functioning. Consider the reaction of Burke (1979: 121) to Pfeffer (1978):

> Pfeffer indeed went out on a limb by proclaiming that leaders do not matter that much. Many variables other than the leader per se account for organizational outcomes. Moreover, "leadership is the outcome of an attribution process in which observers—in order to achieve a feeling of control over their environment—tend to attribute outcomes to persons rather than

to context, and the identification of individuals with leadership positions facilitates this attribution process" (p. 31). An interesting belief, interpretation, hypothesis, or whatever, but methinks Pfeffer broke the limb and fell off. In other words, in an apparent attempt to be provocative, Pfeffer seems to have leaned too heavily toward iconoclasm.

It is possible to take the position that leadership may in fact contribute to a large portion of the variance that is controllable and thus warrants intense attention. However, the results of our analysis suggest that the faith in leadership is likely to exceed the reality of control and will be used to account for variance that is in fact uncontrollable. This is a convenient state of affairs for managements motivated to do just that. Salancik and Meindl (1984) presented evidence documenting the attempt by top managements to create an illusion of control through the manipulation of causal reasoning around performance issues. Such motivations appear to be strongest among managements whose firms have displayed the sorts of erratic performance histories that would imply little real control. Our analysis suggests that what otherwise might be considered patently obvious attempts to create the illusions of control where none exists is likely to be complemented by a high degree of receptivity among observers.

When considering the "symbolic role" of management (Pfeffer and Salancik, 1978; Pfeffer, 1981), the greater significance of leadership lies not in the direct impact on substantive matters but in the ability to exert control over the meanings and interpretations important constituencies give to whatever events and occurrences are considered relevant for the organization's functioning (Pondy, 1978; Daft and Weick, 1984). The manipulation of language and other organizationally relevant symbols allows leaders to manage the political and social processes that maintain organized activity in the face of potentially disruptive forces (Pondy et al., 1982). One plausible hypothesis is that the development of a romanticized conception of leadership causes participants more readily to imbue the symbolic gestures of leaders with meaning and significance. Accordingly, the psychological readiness to comprehend things in terms of leadership, whatever dysfunctions it represents, may play an important role in determining the ultimate effectiveness of symbolism as a political tool, benefiting most those leaders who are adept at its manipulation.

CONCLUSION

There has been in recent years some question concerning the viability of leadership, both as a concept and as an area of inquiry. Indeed, there is ample reason to modify our traditional assumptions about the instrumental potency of leadership factors in the larger scheme of things. Given the present analysis, however, it appears that the obsession with the concept will not easily be curtailed. While there are some obvious limitations to the studies reported here, together they provide reasonably coherent and compelling evidence for the premise that a romanticized conception of leadership is an important part of the social reality that is brought to bear in our informal analysis of organizations—and perhaps in our more formal theories as well. Ironically, though, a heroic vision of what leaders and leadership are all about virtually guarantees that a satisfying understanding will remain beyond the grasp of our best scientific efforts, particularly since the thrust of scientific inquiry is to do away with mysteries. The major effect is to objectify, quantify, and in some cases trivialize the unique import of leadership. In that sense, the product of such efforts is contrary and antithetical to the romanticized conception. And, if our analysis is correct, the continuing infatuation with leadership, for whatever truths it yields about the qualities and behavior of our leaders, can also be used to learn something about the motivations of followers. It may be that the romance and the mystery surrounding leadership concepts are critical for sustaining follower-ship and that they contribute significantly to the responsiveness of individuals to the needs and goals of the collective organization.

REFERENCES

Aldrich, Howard E. 1979 Organizations and Environments. Englewood Cliffs, NJ: Prentice-Hall.

Allen, Michael P., Sharon K. Panian, and Roy E. Lots 1979 "Managerial succession and organizational performance: A recalcitrant problem revisited." Administrative Science Quarterly, 24: 167–180.

Anderson, Craig A. 1983 "The causal structure of situations: The generation of plausible causal attributions as a function of type of event situation." Journal of Experimental Social Psychology, 19: 185–203.

Bennis, Warren 1959 "Leadership theory and administrative behavior: The problem of authority." Administrative Science Quarterly, 4: 259–301.

Binning, John F., and Robert G. Lord 1980 "Boundary conditions for performance cue effects on group process rating: Familiarity versus type of feedback." Organizational Behavior and Human Performance, 26: 115–130.

Brown, M. Craig 1982 "Administrative succession and organizational performance: The succession effect." Administrative Science Quarterly, 27: 1–16.

Burker, W. Warner 1979 Review of Morgan W. McCall and Michael M. Lombardo (eds.), Leadership: Where Else Can We Go? Journal of Applied Behavioral Science, 15: 121–122.

Burns, John M. 1978 Leadership. New York: Harper & Row.

Calder, Bobby J. 1977 "An attribution theory of leadership." In Barry M. Staw and Gerald R. Salancik (eds.), New Direction in Organizational Behavior: 179–204. Chicago: St. Clair.

Daft, Richard L., and Karl E. Weick 1984 "Toward a model of organizations as interpretation systems." Academy of Management Review, 9: 284–295.

DeNisi, Angelo S., and Robert D. Pritchard 1978 "Implicit theories of performance as artifacts in survey research: A replication and extension." Organizational Behavior and Human Performance, 21: 358–366.

Downey, H. Kirk, Thomas I. Chacko, and James C. McElroy 1979 "Attribution of the 'causes' of performance: A constructive, quasi-longitudinal replication of the Staw (1975) study." Organizational Behavior and Human Performance, 24: 287–299.

Elig, Timothy W., and Irene Hanson Frieze 1979 "Measuring causal attributions for success and failure." Journal of Personality and Social Psychology, 37: 621–634.

Gamson, William A., and Norman A. Scotch 1964 "Scapegoating in baseball." American Journal of Sociology, 70: 69–72.

Goode, William J. 1978 The Celebration of Heroes. Berkeley, CA: University of California Press.

Gordon, Gil E., and Ned Rosen 1981 "Critical factors in leadership succession." Organizational Behavior and Human Performance, 27: 227–254.

Greene, Charles N. 1976 "Disenchantment with leadership research: Some causes, recommendations, and alternative directions." In J. G. Hunt and L. L. Larson (eds.), Leadership: The Cutting Edge: 57–67. Carbondale, IL: Southern Illinois University Press.

Grusky, Oscar 1963 "Managerial succession and organizational effectiveness." American Journal of Sociology, 69: 21–31.

Hall, Richard H. 1982 Organizations: Structures and Process, 3rd ed. Englewood Cliffs, NJ: Prentice-Hall.

Hastie, Reid 1984 "Causes and effects of causal attributions." Journal of Personality and Social Psychology, 46: 44–56.

Helmich, Donald L. 1974 "Organizational growth and succession patterns." Academy of Management Journal, 17: 771–775.

Helmich, Donald L. 1977 "Executive succession in the corporate organization: A current integration." Academy of Management Review, 2: 252–266.

Helmich, Donald L., and W. B. Brown 1972 "Successor type and organizational change in the corporate enterprise." Administrative Science Quarterly, 17: 371–381.

House, Robert J. 1977 "A 1976 theory of charismatic leadership." In J. G. Hunt and L. L. Larson (eds.), Leadership: The Cutting Edge: 189–207. Carbondale, IL: Southern Illinois University Press.

Jones, Edward E., and Keith E. David 1965 "From acts to dispositions: The attribution process in person perception." In L. Berkowitz (ed.), Advances in Experimental Social Psychology, 2: 219–266. New York: Academic Press.

Jones, Edward E., Leslie Rock, Kelly O. Shaver, George Goethals, and L. M. Ward 1968 "Pattern of performance and ability attribution: An unexpected primacy effect." Journal of Personality and Social Psychology, 10: 317–340.

Jones, Edward E., Steven Worchel, George R. Goethals, and Judy Grumet 1971 "Prior expectancy and behavior extremity as determinants of attitude attribution." Journal of Experimental Social Psychology, 7: 59–80.

Karmel, Barbara 1978 "Leadership: A challenge to traditional research methods and assumptions." Academy of Management Review, 3: 475–482.

Kerr, Steven, and John M. Jermier 1978 "Substitutes for leadership: Their meaning and measurement." Organizational Behavior and Human Performance, 22: 375–403.

Klapp, Orrin E. 1964 Symbolic Leaders. Chicago: Aldine.

Lieberson, Stanley, and James F. O'Connor 1972 "Leadership and organizational performance: A study of large corporations." American Sociological Review, 37: 117–130.

Lord, Robert G., and Jonathan E. Smith 1983 "Theoretical information processing and situational factors affecting attribution theory models of organizational behavior." Academy of Management Review, 8: 50–60.

March, James G. 1981 "How we talk and how we act: Administrative theory and administrative life." Unpublished manuscript, Sanford University.

McArthur, Leslie Z. 1981 "What grabs you? The role of attention in impression formation and causal attribution." In E. T. Higgins, C. P. Herman, and M. P. Zanna (eds.), Social Cognition: The Ontario Symposium, 1: 201–246. Hillsdale, NJ: Erlbaum.

McCall, Morgan W., Jr., and Michael M. Lombardo (eds.) 1978 Leadership: Where Else Can We Go? Durham, NC: Duke University Press.

McElroy, James C. 1982 "A typology of attribution leadership research." Academy of Management Review, 7: 413–417.

McElroy, James C., and H. Kirk Downey 1982 "Observation in organizational research: Panacea to the performance-attribution effect?" Academy of Management Journal, 25: 822–835.

Milgram, Stanley 1974 Obedience to Authority. New York: Harper & Row.

Miner, John B. 1975 "The uncertain future of the leadership concept: An overview." In J. G. Hunt and L. L. Larson (eds.), Leadership Frontiers: 197–208. Kent, OH: Kent State University Press.

Neilson, Winthrop, and Frances Neilson 1973 What's News—Dow Jones. Radnor, PA: Chilton.

Osborn, Richard N., Lawrence R. Jauch, Thomas N. Martin, and William F. Glueck 1981 "The event of CEO succession, performance and environmental conditions." Academy of Management Journal, 24: 183–191.

Pfeffer, Jeffrey 1977 "The ambiguity of leadership." Academy of Management Review, 2: 104–112.

Pfeffer, Jeffrey 1978 "The ambiguity of leadership." In Morgan W. McCall and Michael M. Lombardo (eds.), Leadership: Where Else Can We Go?: 13–34. Durham, NC: Duke University Press.

Pfeffer, Jeffrey 1981 "Management as symbolic action: The creation and maintenance of organizational paradigm." In L. L. Cummings and B. M. Staw (eds.), Research in Organizational Behavior, 3: 1–52. Greenwich, CT: JAI Press.

Pfeffer, Jeffrey, and Gerald R. Salancik 1978 The External Control of Organizations: A Resource Dependence Perspective. New York: Harper & Row.

Phillips, James S., and Robert G. Lord 1981 "Causal attributions and perceptions of leadership." Organizational Behavior and Human Performance, 28: 143–163.

Pondy, Louis R. 1978 "Leadership is a language game." In M. W. McCall, Jr., and M. M. Lombardo (eds.), Leadership: Where Else Can We Go: 87–99. Durham, NC: Duke University Press.

Pondy, Louis R., Peter Frost, Gareth Morgan, and Thomas Dandridge (eds.) 1982 Organizational Symbolism. Greenwich, CT: JAI Press.

Pyszczynski, T. A., and Gerald Greenberg 1981 "Role of disconfirmed expectancies in the instigation of attributional processing." Journal of Personality and Social Psychology, 40: 31–38.

Ross, Lee 1977 "The intuitive psychologist and his shortcomings: Distortions in the attribution process." In Leonard Berkowitz (ed.), Advances in Experimental Social Psychology, 10: 174–220. New York: Academic Press.

Rush, Michael C., Jay C. Thomas, and Robert L. Lord 1977 "Implicit leadership theory: A potential threat to the internal validity of leader behavior questionnaires." Organizational Behavior and Human Performance, 20: 92–110.

Salancik, Gerald R., and James R. Meindl 1984 "Corporate attributions as strategic illusions of management control." Administrative Science Quarterly, 29: 238–254.

Salancik, Gerald R., and Jeffrey Pfeffer 1977 "Constraints on administrative discretion: The limited influence of mayors on city budgets." Urban Affairs Quarterly, 12: 475–498.

Schlenker, Barry R. 1982 "An identity-analytic approach to the explanation of social conduct." In Leonard Berkowitz (ed.), Advances in Experimental Social Psychology, 15: 194–248. New York: Academic Press.

Staw, Barry M. 1975 "Attribution of the 'causes' of performance: A general alternative interpretation of cross-sectional research on organizations." Organizational Behavior and Human Performance, 13: 414–432.

Staw, Barry M., and Jerry Ross 1980 "Commitment in an experimenting society: A study of the attribution of leadership from administrative scenarios." Journal of Applied Psychology, 65: 249–260.

Stogdill, Ralph M. 1974 Handbook of Leadership. New York: Free Press.

Taylor, Shelly E., and Susan G. Fiske 1978 "Salience, attention, and attribution: Top of the head phenomena." In L. Berkowitz (ed.), Advances in Experimental Social Psychology, 11:

250–288. New York: Academic Press.

Thompson, James D., and A. Tuden 1959 "Strategies, structures, and processes of organizational decision." In J. D. Thompson, P. B. Hammond, R. W. Hawkes, B. H. Lunker, and A. Tuden (eds.), Comparative Studies in Administration: 195–216. Pittsburgh: Pittsburgh University Press.

Weber, Max 1946 "The sociology of charismatic authority." In H. H. Gerth and C. W. Mills (eds.), From Max Weber: Essays in Sociology: 245–252. New York: Oxford University Press.

Weick, Karl E. 1979 The Social Psychology of Organizing, rev. ed. Reading, MA: Addison-Wesley.

Weiner, Bernard E. 1985 "Spontaneous causal thinking," Psychological Bulletin, 97: 74–84.

Leadership: An Alienating Social Myth?

Gary Gemmill
Judith Oakley

INTRODUCTION

As a result of deeply ingrained cultural assumptions, approaches to the study of leadership usually start with the idea that leaders are unquestionably necessary for the functioning of an organization. Belief in hierarchy and the necessity of leaders represents an unrecognized ideology which takes its power chiefly from the fact that it is an undiscussable aspect of reality based upon epistemological and ontological beliefs outside of conscious awareness (Anthony, 1977; Neumann, 1989; Gemmill, 1986). Campbell (1977) is quite accurate in pointing out that discussion of the purposes and problems for which leadership concepts and data are to be used is notably absent from studies in the field. Why is a leader really necessary? What problems or issues in an organization indicate a real need for a leader? Exactly what underlying existential needs or problems the concept of a leader is meant to address has not been clearly articulated.

Some of the confusion around the concept of leadership seems to stem from the process of reification. Reification is a social process which converts an abstraction or mental construct into a supposed real entity. Through reification the social construction of leadership is mystified and accorded an objective existence. It is a social fiction that represents a form of what Fromm labels "false consciousness" which refers to the content of the conscious mind that is fictitious and has been introjected or assimilated without awareness through cultural programming. With reification, social progress is viewed as "caused" by or "determined" by a leader, a cadre of leaders, or "leadership." It is assumed by researchers and practitioners that because there is a word ("leader" or "leadership") there must be an independent objective reality it describes or denotes. Reification functions to trap such labeled individuals within a mode of existence that serves to meet various unconscious emotional needs of members of an organization and of a society.

The leadership myth functions as a social defense whose central aim is to repress uncomfortable needs, emotions, and wishes that emerge when people attempt to work together (Gemmill, 1986; Jacques, 1955). Stated somewhat differently, when members of a group are faced with uncertainty and ambiguity regarding direction, they often report experiencing feelings of anxiety, helplessness, discomfort, disappointment, hostility, and fear of failure. Frightened by these emerging emotions and impulses, which are ordinarily held in check by absorption into the prevailing social system, they collude, largely unconsciously, to dispel them by projecting them onto "leadership" or the "leader" role. The projection allows organizational members to avoid directly confronting the emerging emotions and regress to a form of social order with which they are familiar. As Hirschhorn (1988) states, social defenses are rituals that induce mind-

From *Human Relations*, 1992, **45**(2), 113–129. Reprinted by permission of Plenum Publishing Corporation.

lessness and: ". . . by not thinking, people avoid feeling anxious" (p. 2). The undiscussability of the myth is rooted in the lack of questioning of the alienating consequences and resultant reification of the social forces that position "leadership" as a healthy concept.

The tendency of social groupings and individuals to create social defenses and mindlessly act out rituals results in a flawed process of reality construction. Morgan (1986) points out that while individuals create their reality, they often do so in confiding and alienating ways. People create worlds out of mental constructs, or psychic prisons, in which they become trapped by their own ideas. The thesis examined here is that the concepts of "leader" and "leadership" have become psychic prisons. While leadership is viewed as having a positive connotation, we suggest that contrariwise it is a serious sign of social pathology, that it is a special case of an iatrogenic social myth that induces massive learned helplessness among members of a social system. Learned helplessness is characterized by an experienced inability to imagine or perceive viable options, along with accompanying feelings of despair and a resistance to initiating any form of action (Seligman, 1977). It is our thesis that much of the current writing and theorizing on leadership stems from a deepening sense of social despair and massive learned helplessness. As social despair and helplessness deepen, the search and wish for a messiah (leader) or magical rescue (leadership) also begins to accelerate. We argue that the current popular writings and theories of leadership clearly reflect this social trend. When pain is coupled with an inordinate, widespread, and pervasive sense of helplessness, social myths about the need for great leaders and magical leadership emerge from the primarily unconscious collective feeling that it would take a miracle or messiah to alleviate or ameliorate this painful form of existence.

We further argue that the major significance of most recent studies on leadership is not to be found in their scientific validity but in their function in offering ideological support for the existing social order. The idea of a leadership elite explains in a Social Darwinistic manner why only certain members of a social system are at the apex of power and entitled to a proportionably greater share of the social wealth. So-called leader traits are woven into a powerful social myth, which while serving to maintain the status quo, also paradoxically sows the seeds of its own destruction by accentuating helplessness, mindlessness, emotionlessness, and meaninglessness. The social myth around leaders serves to program life out of people (non-leaders) who, with the social lobotomization, appear as cheerful robots (Mills, 1956). It is our contention that the myth making around the concept of leadership is, as Bennis asserts, an unconscious conspiracy, or social hoax, aimed at maintaining the status quo (Bennis, 1989).

LEADERSHIP AND ALIENATION

The radical humanist perspective on leadership incorporates a deconstructionist approach (Parker & Shotter, 1990). Deconstructionism is an approach to the philosophy of knowledge that aims to demonstrate how a discourse (leadership) is undermined by the very philosophy on which it is based (Culler, 1982). To deconstruct a discourse is to unravel hidden assumptions, internal contradictions, and repressed meanings. For example, by uncovering the underlying assumption that a leader or leadership is necessary in discourses on leadership, hidden presuppositions are identified, examined, and made visible in order to reveal the hidden political and social beliefs implied in the text.

Within the radical humanist paradigm alienation is viewed as a central concept, a concept Burrell and Morgan (1979) define as: "The state in which . . . a cognitive wedge is driven between man's consciousness and the objectified social world, so that man sees what are essentially the creations of his own consciousness in the form of a hard, dominating, external reality" (p. 298). Controversy exists concerning the nature of the relationship between reification and alienation (Marx, 1973). The radical structuralist viewpoint, represented by theorists such as Karl Marx, views forms of social structure as primary in the formation of alienation. From a Marxist viewpoint, changes in social structures result in changes in personal alienation and awareness. Radical humanists, on the other hand, view alienation as primary in forming social structure and social consciousness. Changing personal awareness, social structure, and social consciousness concurrently can result in lessening alienation.

Max Pages articulated the radical humanist viewpoint on alienation in his view of organizational change where change is seen as: " . . . a different kind of relationship with people. They [organization members] want to have the opportunity to express their needs and be able to pursue them. They want not to be bossed; they want to enter into relationships that will not be possessive. This is what I wish to mobilize when I work with people . . . I believe I can be more useful if I help people destroy the organizational forms in which they are imprisoned" (Tichy, 1974, pp. 9–10). Our viewpoint of this epistemiological issue is that alienation and reification are codeterminant and that changes in personal awareness of the process of reification is a necessary but not a sufficient condition for changes in experienced alienation, social structure, and social consciousness.

Erich Fromm (1955) and R. D. Laing (1967) have cogently argued that a statistical concept of "normal" can be pathological since it reflects only false consciousness. Alienation is seen as the dominant reality of modern man—an unauthentic existence resulting from the false consciousness of ideologies and norms imposed from outside the individual and resulting in social and organizational behaviors that are characteristically pathological and neurotic (Fromm, 1955). Laing has pointedly stated, "What we call 'normal' is a product of repression, denial, splitting, projection, introjection, and other forms of destructive action or experience . . . the condition of alienation, of being asleep, of being unconscious, of being out of one's mind, is the condition of the normal man" (pp. 27–28). Fromm (1955) expressed a similar diagnosis when he stated: "the danger of the future is that man may become robots. True enough, robots do not rebel. But given man's nature, robots cannot live and remain sane . . . they will destroy themselves because they cannot stand any longer the boredom of a meaningless life" (pp. 312–313).

Erich Fromm (1955) approaches alienation as a social as well as an individual issue. Alienation in organizations and society as a whole is viewed by Fromm (1955) as caused by the powerlessness and paralysis experienced by individuals as a result of their experiences in industrial societies which make it difficult to lead meaningful, self-directed lives. In Fromm's view, the socialization process in industrial societies has stripped us of our ability to take initiative due to the false belief that happiness comes as a result of material comfort and high levels of consumption. The false belief is reinforced by reified institutions, lifestyles, and ideologies that necessitate social organizations with a high degree of centralized control. In this alienated state, individuals disclaim responsibility for their lives by believing that their fate is not under their own personal control. In a similar vein, Steiner (1975) elaborates on the social factors operating in alienation. He views alienation as a form of social deception, in which the majority of people are mystified into believing that society is not depleting them of their humanity and vitality, and even if it were, there are good reasons for it. The net effect is that the average person, instead of sensing his oppression and being angry by it, decides that her feelings of emptiness and despair are her own fault and own responsibility. When this happens, the person feels alienated, since she is unaware of the social deception.

THE SOCIAL MYTH OF LEADERSHIP

According to Fromm (1960), each society becomes caught up in its own need to survive in the particular form in which it has developed. This is accomplished by fabricating a repertoire of fictions and illusions. The effect of society acting to preserve itself is not only to funnel fictions into consciousness, but also to prevent the awareness of reality that might threaten the existing "natural order." Because the social fiction of the leaders is inculcated outside of awareness, reality-testing is blocked and the development of genuine insight into social issues is threatened, as is any experimentation that might lead to more vital ways of relating in a work setting.

There exists a strong tendency to explain organization outcomes by attributing causality to "leadership" (Pfeffer, 1977; Calder, 1977). This attributional social bias creates the illusion that "leaders" are in control of events. The use of leadership as a cause or social myth seems to stem, in part, from the natural uncertainty and ambiguity embedded in reality which most persons experience as terrifying, overwhelming, complex, and chaotic (Pedigo & Singer, 1982). The terror of facing feelings of helplessness and powerlessness can lead a society, as Becker (1973) speculated, to focus emotions on one person who is imagined to be all powerful ("the leader"). The attribution of omnipotence and omniscience allows the terror to be focused in one place instead of it being experienced as diffused in a seemingly random universe.

The major function of the leader myth is to preserve the existing social system and structure by attributing dysfunctions and difficulties within the system to the lack, or absence of "leadership." The dysfunctional and destructive aspects of the social system itself and the corresponding personal behavior of the members go unexamined, as does the collusion among members in creating and maintaining the social myth of leadership. Because the myth is undiscussable by members, self-sealing nonlearning about the dynamics of the myth is constantly reinforced. As long as faults, imperfections, and hopes can be attributed to leadership, the social system itself remains unexamined and unchanged.

THE RESURGENCE OF THE GREAT LEADER MYTH

The recent fascination with leadership characteristics and traits in the management literature is reminiscent of a ghost dance, an attempt to resurrect and revive the spirit of a time gone by. Ghost dances were a predominant expression of religious movement that gained popularity among native American tribes in the latter half of the nineteenth century in reaction to the impending destruction of their way of life (Hultkrantz, 1987). The ghost dance was performed to receive the spirits of the ancestors in the hope that this would lead to a restoration of the past and prevent further disintegration of their dying civilization. Similarly, the revival of the "traitist" approach to leadership seems a "ghost dance" aimed at restoring and preventing disintegration of our own civilization. Increasing alarm and concern with the defection or total absence of leadership is a sign of increasing social despair and massive learned helplessness.

The current reemergence of the "traitist" approach to leaders and "charisma" is embodied in recent books by Bennis and Nanus (1985), Zaleznik (1989), and Tichy and Devanna (1987). The traits they attempt to identify are in a sense a different form of abstracted traits than the earlier studies done on leadership traits. For example, Zaleznik (1990) writes: "For a leader to secure commitment from subordinates he or she has to demonstrate extraordinary competence or other qualitites subordinates admire" (p. 12). In the same vein, Bennis and Nanus (1985) impute almost magical qualities to leaders: "leadership can move followers to higher degrees of consciousness, such as liberty, freedom, justice, and self-actualization" (p. 218).

"Charisma" is the leadership trait most often examined by members of the "leadership mafia." Charisma is a social phenomenon similar to the illusionary aspects of the reported U.F.O. phenomenon in the sense that it is viewed as of divine origin beyond our material world. Weber's (1968) most frequently cited definition is: "Charisma is a quality of an individual personality by virtue of which he is set apart from ordinary men and treated as endowed with supernatural, superhuman, or at least specifically exceptional qualities" (p. 48). The mistake in theory building and research on "charismatic" leaders is the belief that "charisma" is a measurable attribute of the person who it is attributed to that is entirely independent from the perceptual distortions of those attributing the "charisma." While leadership studies on charisma have largely been oriented toward identifying individual traits, Wasielewski (1985) has recently proposed it be considered an interactional relationship that is the product of an emotional interaction between charismatic leaders and followers. We argue along similar lines that the importance of "charisma" is to be found in its meaning as a social fiction or social delusion that allows "followers" to escape responsibility for their own actions and inactions. The label "charisma" is like the term leader itself; a "black hole" in social space that serves as a container for the alienating consequences of the social myth resulting from intellectual and emotional deskilling by organization members.

UNCONSCIOUS ASPECTS OF LEADERSHIP

The meaning of leadership in contemporary organizations can be discovered by examining the socially constructed meanings and behavior patterns that emerge from perceptions and reactions to the concept of leadership. In many organizations, a stable dichotomy exists between the leaders and the followers, with the leaders being viewed by their followers as performing both protective and nurturance functions, much as parents are viewed by their children. In this relationship, leaders are unconsciously perceived by their followers as providing protection against external threats and preventing internal infighting and destructive acts within the organization. By projecting their anxiety and aggression onto the leaders, followers perceive themselves as freed from the anxiety and responsibility of taking initiative, seeking autonomy, taking risks, or expressing their own fears and feelings of aggression and destructiveness. When organization members accept and act these feelings unreflectively, they adapt the authoritarian personality as described by Erich Fromm in *Escape from Freedom* (1941), and in much of the classical sociology literature such as Whyte's "organization man," C. Wright Mill's "cheerful robot," or David Riesman's "lonely crowd" (Mills, 1956; Riesman, 1961; Whyte, 1956). In contrast, those attracted to a leader role have an exaggerated narcissistic need to project their fears of inferiority and inadequacy onto persons of inferior social status and gain satisfaction from the enhanced power, superior status, and material rewards that accompany leadership positions (Schwartz, 1987).

A more complete understanding of the meaning of leadership in organizations can be gained by examining the collective unconscious assumptions about leadership and authority. Collective unconscious assumptions (basic assumptions) are formed concerning leadership and authority which affect both individual and group behavior (Bion, 1961). As Bion points out, under the influence of the pairing basic assumption in groups, members become preoccupied with the thought that sometime in the future a person (leader) or idea (leadership) will surface that will eventually solve all their problems without any effort on their part. There is a messianic hope that in the future everything will finally work and members will be delivered from their anxieties, fears, and struggles. The predominant emotions are manic-like forms of hope, faith, and utopianism. According to Bion (1961), these emotions can only persist as long as the leader or idea remains "unborn" and unmaterialized. Due to the unreality of the omnipotent and magical idealization, it is impossible for a person or idea ever to live up to the expectations. Eventually, the faith and hope of members is shattered, opening the door to despair, disappointment, and disillusionment, the emotions lurking behind the more manic ones such as hope. The manic emotions constitute a defense against depression (Winnicott, 1987). It is when the group is caught in a manic defense that members are least likely to feel they are defending against depression. At such times, they are most likely to feel elated, happy, busy, excited, humorous, omniscient, zestful, and are less inclined to look at the seriousness of life with its heaviness and sadness.

Bion (1961) describes another basic assumption that occurs in groups, the dependency basic assumption, as a social fiction that impairs work on the real issues in a group or organization. The dependency basic assumption group comes into operation when members act as if they were joining together in order to be sustained by a single leader on whom they depend for nourishment and protection. The essential aim of the dependency assumption group is to covertly attain security through establishing a fantasy that members of a group are coming together to be nurtured and protected by "a leader." Members act as if they know nothing, as if they are inadequate and helpless. Their behavior in this regard implies that the leader by comparison is omnipotent and omniscient. In over-idealizing the leader, members deskill themselves from their own critical thinking, visions, inspirations, and emotions.

In the emotional state of dependency, the members want extremely simple explanations and act as if no one can do anything that is difficult. A person in a leader role functions as an emotional container for other members that results in an alienating intellectual and emotional deskilling in them. The person designated as the leader can function as a central figure for containing both positive and negative projections of followers. As Muktananada (1980) states: "there is a great mirror in the Guru's eyes in which everything is reflected" (p. 34). There is similarly a great mirror in the eyes of the leader in which the intrapsychic conflicts of the group members at large are reflected. However, in projecting their own senses of completeness and incompleteness onto a leader, people become alienated and caught in an illusion of helplessness and failure without realizing that they limit the leader's power as well as their own by their denial, projection, and passivity.

Looking toward people in authority to define what is meaningful work activity occurs without much conscious thought and reflection. The childlike dependency basis of the leader myth is seen clearly in the writing of Smircich and Morgan (1982) who view leadership as a process whereby "followers" give up their mindfulness to a "leader" or "leadership." As they state: "Leadership is realized in the process whereby one or more individuals succeeds in attempting to frame and define the reality of others" (p. 257). Milgram's (1974) classic studies on obedience to authority as well as studies on cult groups such as Jim Jones' "People's Temple" (Ulman & Abse, 1983) attest to the primitive unreflected acceptance and unconscious compliance with an authority figure's definition of what aspects of reality are to be given conscious attention. The unreflected acceptance of the authority figure's or power elite's definition of how the world of work is to be enacted is the infrastructure of false consciousness.

In addition to providing a focus for dependency issues, the person assigned a leader role often represents and acts as a voice for the intrapsychic conflicts of followers and is unconsciously used to act our a shared collective issue. For example, repressed anger is often projected onto someone in a leader role who then acts it out for the group in such a way that group members become vicariously satisfied. Projecting violent, aggressive, and hostile feelings onto a leader allows people to reduce the discomfort of having to openly confront these feelings either in themselves or with each other. From the standpoint of projecting away positive attributes and emotions, people engage in a deskilling process that leaves them feeling empty, helpless, and powerless. Maslow (1971) seems to capture well the underlying dynamics of the deskilling process that accompanies alienation with what he termed the "Jonah Complex." He used the term in reference to an individual evading and running away from his or her undeveloped potential for creativity and greatness. He believed that people paradoxically fear not only their worst qualities but also their best qualities. With the projective numbing and relinquishing of their abilities to create and nourish themselves, they experience confusion, feel overwhelmed, and feel helpless. When this happens, alienated members of an organization willingly submit themselves to spoon feeding, preferring safe and easy security to the possible pains and uncertainty of learning by their own effort and mistakes. In this respect, Freud (1960) believed that members of a group desperately seek illusions to protect themselves from emotional truths and avoid reality.

THE CONTEMPORARY IDEOLOGY OF LEADERSHIP

Leadership theories espousing "traits" or "great person" explanations reinforce and reflect the widespread tendency of people to deskill themselves and idealize leaders by implying that only a select few are good enough to exercise initiative. This view of leadership must be questioned in light of the dysfunctional and alienating consequences perpetrated by this social myth. The deconstruction of leadership and the creation of alternative definitions necessitates placing a value on inverting and debunking cultural assumptions that hold in place the current leader myth. Proposing alternative realities in organizations is often viewed as taking a dangerous risk since it challenges prevailing perceptions of reality held by the current leadership. Throughout history, successful challenges have been made by persons acting in the role of the sage-fool (Kets de Vries, 1990). Traditionally, the sage-fool's role has been institutionalized in the roles of court jester, clown, and anti-hero. In these roles, sage-fools balance the hubris of the kings or other powerful persons by parodying the foolishness and stupidity of the leader's false consciousness and misuse of power by using humor to cushion the impact of uncovering unspeakable truths and other information considered to be socially destructive (Kets de Vries, 1990). In contemporary organizations, this role is often taken up by outsiders such as O.D. consultants. From the radical humanist perspective, however, an O.D. consultant cannot succeed just by presenting his or her version of the alternative reality to the organization's members and their leaders. Real change occurs only when members can learn to liberate themselves through expanded awareness and self-created programs of action (Tichy, 1974). As noted psychoanalyst Alan Wheelis (1975) so poignantly expresses it: "Freedom is the awareness of alternatives and the ability to choose" (p. 15).

Increasing awareness of alienation and reification in work settings means finding ways to examine consciously the beliefs about existing structures and attitudes concerning power authority. Neumann (1989) proposes that many people automatically adopt a traditional "work ideology" and subsequently feel uncomfortable with organizational interventions designed to increase participation in decision making. This commonly occurs because of the widespread acceptance of organizational norms that promote abdication of decision-making authority to those above. In recent years, empowerment has emerged as an idea designed to increase involvement and participation in decision making by those perceived as working in environments where taking orders and being told what to do is the norm and self-management is not practiced. The idea of empowerment has gained popularity in corporate and academic circles due to the widespread perception that by delegating more decision-making authority to organization members, productivity and performance will be enhanced (Bennis, 1989; Kanter, 1979; Lawler, 1986; Manz & Sims, 1980; Peters & Austin, 1985).

To some, the idea of empowerment has become another magic solution designed to promote widespread changes in organizational perceptions and practices. Without an examination of deeply held beliefs about leadership constructs and power and authority relationships, however, it is unlikely that fundamental change will occur. Encouraging subordinates to take increased responsibility for outcomes and managing themselves may have little impact if intellectual and emotional deskilling and other problems arising from constructs around leadership are not directly addressed. Under present conditions in organizations, many of the changes involving empowerment may be seen as an attempt to shift blame and responsibility for organizational problems from the top management to other organization members without a corresponding change in actual power relationships. Alternatively, implementing empowerment programs may also be viewed by other organization members as an attempt to co-opt them by creating the illusion that a decrease in top management control and an increase in self-monitoring is equivalent to equal participation in decision-making processes (illusionary power equalization). Focusing attention on the leader myth and its role in shaping individually- and collectively-held beliefs can create awareness of choices and the predisposition for risk and experimentation necessary for changing behaviors and creating new paradigms.

EXPERIMENTING WITH NEW PARADIGMS

Chris Argyris (1969) points out that one danger in conducting only "naturalistic" and "descriptive" research on behavior within organizations is a tendency to view what exists at the present time as inevitable or immutable. Truly, if only the prevailing human conditions in organizations were studied, the risk would be one of reinforcing a concept of a person whose "natural" behavior is concealing feelings, playing games, mistrusting, being bored with work, being passive, feeling powerless, and not taking risks (Argyris, 1990). The basic danger of descriptive research is failing to consider alternative systems in which meaninglessness and powerlessness are minimized or eliminated. With limited awareness and lack of experimentation with alternative realities, resignation in accepting as human nature the pathological status quo evidence in the descriptive data is likely.

Acceptance of the leader myth promotes alienation, deskilling, reification of organizational forms, and dysfunctional organizational structures. Contrariwise, the dynamics of leadership, when viewed as a social process, are quite different from the idea of a leadership elite, where acceptance of a leader requires abdicating authority to a power outside the self. Leadership as a social process can be defined as a process of dynamic collaboration, where individuals and organization members authorize themselves and others to interact in ways that experiment with new forms of intellectual and emotional meaning. Experimenting in this sense is similar to Weick's (1977) concept of enactment, where proactive behavior occurs and is not necessarily linked to specific goals. The presence of well-defined leaders often decreases the ability of a group to experiment, whereas a revolt against leaders and efforts to work without them may give rise to new, more amorphous forms of leadership where organization members work at their boundaries through a process of dynamic collaboration (Smith & Gemmill, 1991). Working in dynamic collaboration requires individuals to change their perceptions and develop new norms and structures which create a variety of new options and increases the possibility that new structures will be found which are better suited to the current environment (Ashby, 1970; Bronowski, 1970).

An alternative view of leadership has emerged in recent decades from the expanding body of feminist theory on the nature of power and authority. Radical feminists view power as exercised in contemporary society as "power over," representative of a masculine, or patriarchal worldview in which social relationships originate from primary relationships defined by male "power over" women and children (Rich, 1976). Alternatively, a feminist conception of leadership re-defines power as the ability to influence people to act in their own interests, rather than induce them to act accordingly to the goals and desires of the leader (Carroll, 1984). Feminists envision new paradigms that reconceptualize leadership and power relationships based on supportive and cooperative behaviors. Feminist theory, therefore, points to the need for new forms of leadership by re-defining the meanings attached to leadership behavior, as in Bunch and Fisher's (1976) definition of leadership as "people taking the initiative, carrying things through, having ideas and the imagination to get something started, and exhibiting particular skills in different areas" (p. 3). Unawareness of viable alternatives to present behavior associated with leadership, and limited experimentation have been, perhaps, the greatest impediments to creation of less alienating work relationships.

Michels' (1915) iron law of oligarchy could easily be recast into the iron law of nonlearning in organizations or social systems. According to Michels, organizations that start out with egalitarian or anarchistic political values tend to become as, or perhaps more authoritarian and alienating than the organizations they were designed to reform or replace. The issue seems to be that people cannot simply will themselves into a new way of operating. They inevitably end up enacting and reacting the prior structures because experientially and behaviorally they are unable to transcend them. Awareness of alienation, social defenses, and false consciousness is a necessary but not sufficient condition for changes in a social system or organization (Hirschhorn, 1988). For example, Argyris (1990) suggests that executives are often aware of ineffectual interpersonal behavior in other executives they perceive as ineffectual, yet they themselves exhibit the same ineffectual behavior. Even when they become aware of their own ineffectual behavior, however, it is not enough to effect change in their behavior. For change to occur, it is necessary to experiment with new paradigms and new behaviors to find more meaningful and constructive ways of relating and working together. While such social experimentation is a process marked by uncertainty, difficulties, awkwardness, disappointment, and tentativeness of actions, it is indispensable if people are to experience a non-alienated mode of existence in a work environment or in society as a whole.

CONCLUSION

Jung (1958), in writing on the phenomena of reported flying saucers, seems accurately to describe how illusionary social processes perpetuate such social myths and reflect the pervasive sense of helplessness. He hypothesizes that the reports of U.F.O.s, flying saucers, and alien beings represent an intrapsychic longing for wholeness and unity which seems impossible to accomplish in our existing world. In a Sartre-like drama (Sartre, 1955), people become alienated from their true creative and vital life force and project it outward so that they see it coming to them in an alien form. The longing or wish is projected via a quasi-hallucinatory process where it is perceived as alien to the self, or extraterrestrial. Jung (1958) contended that aside from whether the U.F.O.s objectively exist, it seems clear that they psychologically exist in the experience of many humans in a wide variety of cultures.

Similarly, we speculate that leadership as a social myth symbolically represents a regressive wish to return to the symbolic environment of the womb: to be absolved of consciousness, mindfulness, and responsibility for initiating responses to our environment to attain what we need and want. The womb represents a protected environment that we have all experienced where we did not have to take risk, experience angst and pain, feel frightened, and expose our inadequacy or incompetence. To become completely infantilized is the ultimate form of deskilling and learned helplessness. Jung (1957) may have had this in mind when he wrote:

> Where there are many, there is security; what the many believe must of course be true; what the many want must be worth striving for, and necessary, and therefore good. In the clamor of the many there lies the power to snatch wish-fulfillments by force; sweetest of all, however, is that gentle and painless slipping back into the kingdom of childhood, into the paradise of parental care, into happy-go-luckiness and irresponsibility. All the thinking and looking after are done from the top; to all questions there is an answer, and for all needs the necessary provision is made. The infantile dream state of the mass man is so unrealistic that he never thinks to ask who is paying for this paradise (pp. 70–71).

It is a fact of existence that everyone has had a unitive experience of being completely taken care of without any conscious effort on their part. Hence, the regressive wish is not just something spun out of thin air but is borne of an actual experience with a symbiotic environment, albeit prelinguistic and preverbal. The unitive experience of a symbolic environment is the basis for the regressive wish.

Members of a social system often behave as alienated robots in work relationships. They often seem paralyzed by their fears and cannot bear to experience their work relationships as a changing process in which nothing is ever really fixed. The work process is imbued with meaning by every individual; therefore it has no objective meaning of its own. At times, the creative possibilities of events and experiences carry us in directions and toward goals of which at the time we are only dimly aware. This process can be fraught with both fascination and fright since these is no fixed end point or closed system of behavior, actions, or unchanging set of principles by which work relationships develop creatively and constructively. In reality, there are multiple ways of being together in the work process. Members of an organization can be free to relate to each other in the work process any way they choose. They are limited only by their fears, imagination, cultural programming, and psychohistories. Admittedly, these are significant limitations, but not necessarily insurmountable.

Hopefully, we have provided a foundation, a beginning, in our analysis that can serve to both encourage and guide much needed future research on leadership and alienation. Interventions designed to demythologize leadership and lessen alienating consequences need to be more precisely developed and tested in the crucible of experience. At present, the Tavistock group relations-type conference can be used as a powerful intervention for demythologizing leadership as well as a research methodology for investigating unconscious behavior associated with leadership. Making discussable what is typically undiscussable about leadership and alienation is a step toward demythologizing and personal "reskilling." Amplifying personal awareness of the leadership myth and its social function allows one to examine their own projective identification and ways of deskilling themselves unnecessarily. It is our contention that only disenchantment and detachment from the central social myth and ritual of dependency on leadership can promote the change necessary for opening up new possibilities for creativity and change in the ways we structure life at work so it loses the toxicity associated with alienation.

REFERENCES

Anthony, P. D. *The ideology of work.* London: Tavistock Publications, 1977.

Argyris, C. The incompleteness of the social psychological theory. *American Psychologist,* 1969, 24, 893–908.

Argyris, C. *Overcoming organizational defenses.* Boston, Massachusetts: Allyn & Bacon, 1990.

Ashby, W. R. *Design for a brain* (3rd ed.). London: Methuen, 1970.

Becker, E. *The denial of death.* New York: Free Press, 1973.

Bennis W. *Why leaders can't lead: The unconscious conspiracy continues.* San Francisco: Jossey-Bass, 1989.

Bennis, W., & Nanus, B. *Leaders: The strategies for taking charge.* New York: Harper & Row, 1985.

Bion, W. R. *Experiences in groups.* New York: Basic Books, 1961.

Bronowski, J. New concepts in the evolution of complexity. *Synthese,* 1970, 21, 228–246.

Bunch, C., & Fisher, B. What future for leadership. *Quest,* Spring 1976, 2, 2–13.

Burrell, G., & Morgan, G. *Sociological paradigms and organisational analysis.* Portsmouth, New Hampshire: Heinemann, 1979.

Calder, B. An attribution theory of leadership. In B. Staw and B. Salanck (Eds.), *New directions in organizational behavior.* Chicago: St. Clair, 1977.

Campbell, J. P. The cutting edge of leadership: An overview. In J. C. Hunt and L. Larson (Eds.), *Leadership: The cutting edge.* Carbondale: Southern Illinois University Press, 1977.

Carroll, S. J. Feminist scholarship on political leadership. In B. Kellerman (Ed.), *Leadership: Multidisciplinary perspectives.* Englewood Cliffs, New Jersey: Prentice-Hall, 1984.

Culler, J. *On deconstruction: Theory and criticism after structuralism.* Ithaca: Cornell University Press, 1982.

Freud, S. *Group psychology—The awareness of the ego.* New York: Bantam. 1960.

Fromm, E. *Escape from freedom.* New York: Rinehart & Co, 1941.

Fromm, E. *The sane society.* New York: Fawcett Premier Books, 1955.

Fromm, E. Psychoanalysis and Zen Buddhism. In D. Suzuki, E. Fromm, and R. DeMartino, *Zen Buddhism and Psychoanalysis.* New York: Harper & Row, 1960.

Gemmill, G. The mythology of the leader role in small groups. *Small Group Behavior,* 1986, 17(1), 41–50.

Hirschhorn, L. *The workplace within: The psychodynamics of organizational life.* Cambridge, Massachusetts: MIT Press, 1988.

Hultkrantz, A. *Native religions of North America: The power of visions and fertility.* San Francisco: Harper & Row, 1987.

Jacques, E. Social systems as a defense against persecutory and depressive anxiety. In M. Klein, P. Heiman, and R. Mohey-Kyrle (Eds.), *New directions in psychoanalysis.* London: Tavistock, 1955, pp. 478–498.

Jung, C. G. *The undiscovered self.* New York: Mentor, 1957.

Jung, C. G. Flying saucers: A modern myth of things seen in the sky. In G. Adler, M. Fordham, W. McGuire, and H. Read (Eds.), *The collected works of C. G. Jung* (Vol. 10). Princeton, New Jersey: Princeton University Press, 1958.

Kanter, R. M. Power failure in management circuits. *Harvard Business Review,* 1979, 57(4).

Kets De Vries, M. F. R. The organizational fool: Balancing a leader's hubris. *Human Relations,* 1990, 43(8), 751–770.

Laing, R. D. *The politics of experience.* Baltimore, Maryland: Ballantine Books, 1967.

Lawler, E. *High-involvement management: Strategies for improved organizational performance.* San Francisco: Jossey-Bass, 1986.

Manz, C., & Sims, H. Self-management as a substitute for leadership: A social learning perspective. *Academy of Management Review,* 1980, 5, 361–367.

Marx, K. *Grundisse: Foundations of the critique of political economy* (translated by M. Nicolaus). New York: Vintage, 1973.

Maslow, A. *The further reaches of human nature.* New York: Viking Press, 1971.

Masterson, J. F. *The search for the real self: Unmasking the personality disorders of our age.* New York: The Free Press, 1988.

Michels, R. *Political parties: A sociological study of oligarchical tendencies of modern democracy.* London: Jarrold & Sons, 1915.

Milgram, S. *Obedience to authority.* New York: Harper & Row, 1974.

Mills, C. W. *The power elite.* Oxford, England: Oxford University Press, 1956.

Morgan, G. *Images of organizations.* Beverly Hills, California: Sage, 1986.

Muktananada, S. *The perfect relationship.* Geneshpuri, India: Gurudeu Siddha Peeth, 1980.

Neumann, J. E. Why people don't participate in organizational change. In R. W. Woodman and W. A. Pasmore (Eds.), *Research in organizational change and development* (Vol. 3). Greenwich, Connecticut: JAI Press, 1989.

Parker, I., & Shotter, J. (Eds.). *Deconstructing social psychology.* New York: Routledge, 1990, pp. 1–14.

Pedigo, J., & Singer, B. Group process development: A psychoanalytic view. *Small Group Behavior,* 1982, 13, 496–517.

Peters, T., & Austin, N. *A passion for excellence: The leadership difference.* New York: Random House, 1985.

Pfeffer, J. The ambiguity of leadership. *Academy of Management Review,* January 1977, 104–112.

Rich, A. *Of woman born.* New York: W. W. Norton & Co, 1976.

Riesman, D. *The lonely crowd: A study of the changing American character.* New Haven, Connecticut: Yale University Press, 1961.

Sartre, J. P. *No exit, and three other plays.* New York: Vintage, 1955.

Schwartz, H. The psychodynamics of organizational totalitarianism. *Journal of General Management,* 1987, 13(1), 41–54.

Seligman, M. E. P. *Helplessness: On depression, development, and death.* San Francisco: W. H. Freeman & Co., 1977.

Smircich, L., & Morgan, G. Leadership: The management of meaning. *Journal of Applied Behavioral Science,* 1982, 18(3), 257–273.

Smith, C., & Gemmill, G. Change in the small group: A dissipative structure perspective. *Human Relations,* 1991, 44, 697–716.

Steiner, C. et al. *Readings in radical psychiatry.* New York: Grove Press, 1975.

Tichy, N. An interview with Max Pages. *Journal of Applied Behavioral Science,* 1974, 10(1), 8–26.

Tichy, N., & Devanna, M. *The transformational leader.* New York: John Wiley & Sons, 1987.

Ulman, R., & Abse, D. The group psychology of mass madness: Jonestown. *Political Psychology,* 1983, 4(4), 637–661.

Wasielewski, P. The emotional basis of charisma. *Symbolic Interaction,* 1985, 8(2), 207–222.

Weber, M. *Economy and society: An outline of interpretive sociology.* Guenther, Roth, and C. Wiltick (Eds.). New York: The Bedminister Press, 1968.

Weick, K. E. Organizational design: Organizations as self-designing systems. *Organizational Dynamics,* 1977, 6, 31–46.

Wheelis, A. *How people change.* New York: Harper & Row, 1975.

Whyte, W. *The organization man.* New York: Simon & Schuster, 1956.

Winnicott, D. W. *Through paediatrics to psychoanalysis.* London: Hogarth, 1987.

Zaleznik, A. *The managerial mystique: Restoring leadership in business.* New York: Harper & Row, 1989.

Zaleznik, A. The leadership gap. *Academy of Management Executive,* 1990, 4(1), 7–22.

Chapter 3 Questions for Discussion

1 What does the term "leadership" mean, as it has been applied to work settings?

2 Select an individual trait that might be associated with effective leadership in an organization? Why did you choose this personal attribute? Can you think of a circumstance under which this trait may actually detract from a leader's effectiveness?

3 Can you think of a situation where it would be most effective for a work group to have two people perform the leadership functions of initiating structure and consideration? When would it not be advisable for a group to split up these functions?

4 Compare Fiedler's contingency theory with House's path-goal theory of leadership. Do you think that leadership style is flexible? Why or why not?

5 Can you think of an example where it would be best if the entire work group participated in the decision-making process? Conversely, can you identify a situation in which it would be best for the leader alone to decide? Describe the situations that you chose in terms of the Vroom-Yetton-Jago normative decision-making model.

6 Why would a manager be interested in attribution theory?

7 Under what conditions would a charismatic leader have a negative impact on the organization? Provide some examples.

8 What does the coming "new phase" mean for leadership training and development?

9 Compare and contrast House's path-goal theory with the charismatic approach of Shamir et al. regarding the fundamental assumptions that each perspective makes about what motivates individuals.

PART TWO

TWO

CENTRAL ISSUES IN MOTIVATION AND LEADERSHIP

SOCIAL INFLUENCE
AND POWER

Nothing much happens between or among people in work organizations unless social influence occurs. Indeed, any attempt to understand the roles of leadership and motivation in affecting employee behavior in the work environment must necessarily involve attention to the process of social influence and the associated exercise of power. Leadership, as we have discussed earlier, is itself a type of social influence. It is social in that it involves people—on both the sending (the influencer) and receiving (the influenced) sides. It is a form of influence in that it has the potential to modify or alter behavior, and a major area of behavior that is often affected—but certainly not the only area—is motivation.

As soon as one starts to think about the term "social influence," the idea of "power" is almost always close at hand. It is difficult to consider one concept without the other. In fact, most definitions of power involve "the capacity to influence." Thus, in organizational settings, power is, in effect, a resource that leaders can use to exert social influence. However, whether leaders are actually motivated to use that resource is a different issue, as is the question of what effects the use of power will have on the motivation of others to whom it is applied. Power represents potential, but that potential often remains latent and dormant in many organizational circumstances, rather than being manifested.

One reason that power is sometimes not utilized to the extent that it could be is that it is seen by some as carrying negative overtones. In the terms of Whetten and Cameron (1995, p. 296), "for many people, power is a 'four-letter word.'" The classic pronouncement of this view of power is the famous statement by Lord Acton when writing to Bishop Mandell Creighton (in the nineteenth century): "Power tends to corrupt [and] absolute power corrupts absolutely" (Catlin, 1962, p. 71). However, the idea that the use (or even mere possession) of power is inherently negative is an overly narrow view. Adverse, even disastrous, consequences can of course result from the exercise of power, but equally likely are potential positive consequences that might be widely acclaimed. Regardless of whether negative, neutral, or positive effects can occur when power is used, the fact remains that no organization could function for very long without power as a basis of influence. Within the organizational work environment power is virtually as omnipresent as the weather is in the external environment. Unlike the weather, however, it is possible for managers and leaders to do something with and about power.

When organizational scholars consider the topic of power, especially interpersonal or social power, they frequently talk about different types of power. While there is no one categorization scheme that is universally accepted, the typology put forth some years ago by French and Raven (1968) is still widely applicable. They identified five major bases, or types, of power:

• **Legitimate power:** This is power conferred on a person by the organization. It is ordinarily what we think of when we use the term "authority" or "formal authority." In the organizational context, legitimate power or authority gives one person or persons (e.g., supervisors) a designated "right" to require compliance by someone else. Such a right is "recognized" in the sense that the person responding to the exercise of legitimate power has accepted or agreed in advance to comply, within identified limits, when requested.

• **Reward power:** This power exists when one person controls the rewards that someone else desires or needs. In an organization, this is a power that higher-level managers typically have over lower-level managers or subordinates. However, it is possible to think of situations at work where someone on the same level or even a lower level can exercise this type of power (e.g., by promising to obtain for a peer or superior a desired piece of information that may not otherwise be available).

• **Coercive power:** This is, in effect, the capability of causing harm to others, whether physically, emotionally, financially, or otherwise. It is the power to apply or withhold punishment, and it is often used in conjunction with attempts to generate fear in order to gain others' compliance. In organizations a typical use of such power might be the threat by a manager of firing or laying off a subordinate if a certain performance level or other conditions are not met.

• **Expert power:** This is power based on knowledge, especially specialized knowledge not easily available to a wide range of people. A typical example of such power operating in everyday life is the influence that a physician has over a patient. No organizationally legitimate power exists in this instance, but nevertheless the patient usually complies with a doctor's order because of the assumed negative consequences of not acknowledging that person's expertise. Within contemporary organizations, as contrasted with many business firms and other organizations in past decades, expert power is not confined to the top of the hierarchy. Consequently, this has the effect of providing certain employees at lower levels with the means to counterbalance the greater legitimate power of those at higher levels. It could be said, from a power perspective, that the dispersal of expertise throughout an organization is a great leveler.

• **Referent power:** This is a power that a person gains if others show admiration for, or a desire to be like, that person. Thus, it is a power that is, in effect, "given" to someone by those who relate (or "refer") in some way, either directly or indirectly.

Typically, it is not a power that relates in any particular way to a formal position in an organization. Potentially, anyone in an organization can gain referent power by their actions, behavior or appearance, although certainly a person's reputation and status have a lot to do with the amount of referent power they have.

Several points can be made about this and similar lists of sources of interpersonal power within organizations. First, the various types involve different combinations of personal and positional attributes. Legitimate power derives primarily from a position that a person occupies, not from the characteristics of the person. Likewise, the bases of reward power and coercive power are largely, but not totally, determined by the type and level of a person's position within the organization. At the other extreme, referent power is primarily based on the attributes of the person and has relatively little to do with the position that the person holds. Expertise as a source of power is the property of an individual but is also partly determined by a person's position. Individuals can gain expertise irrespective of their particular positions in an organizational hierarchy, but often the positions they occupy provide widely varying access to specialized information and training and hence affect the ease with which expertise can be acquired.

A second important point to keep in mind about the different types of power discussed above involves the amount and type of impact that their use has on those on the "receiving" end. While a leader or manager may have the option of using one or several types of power, it makes a difference which types are selected. (See, especially, the article by Yukl et al. later in this chapter.) The explicit use of coercive or even legitimate power in a particular situation, for example, may result in negative reactions on the part of subordinates, when a more subtle use of referent power would have brought about equal compliance without adverse side effects. Or, an attempt to use only expert power may not be sufficient in a situation where that expertise is questioned by those to be influenced. In such a case, the use of reward or legitimate power may be necessary, even if those powers carry risks of creating negative reactions on the part of others. The adroit use of different types of powers in particular kinds of circumstances is, in itself, a type of expertise that can be learned and developed. In addition, it is important to emphasize that the total amount of power that a person possesses at any point in time is not a fixed quantity but is subject to expansion or contraction based on when and how each type of power is used.

OVERVIEW OF THE READINGS

The readings in this chapter open with a provocative essay by Pfeffer on the necessity of acknowledging and appreciating the role of power in organizations. He argues that potential leaders must come to grips with the need deliberately and overtly to exert influence and power over others rather than to rely only on one's own skills: "One can be quite content, quite happy, quite fulfilled as an organizational hermit, but one's influence is limited and the potential to accomplish great things, which requires interdependent action, is almost extinguished." Pfeffer particularly focuses on the need for greater attention to the uses of power and political influence in the implementation of decisions.

The second reading, by Bower and Weinberg, is also concerned with political dimensions of organizations. They contend that a particular kind of political skill, which they term "statecraft," is a key ingredient in achieving successful leadership in organizations. From their perspective, such statecraft must be displayed at the very top of organizations and cannot be delegated, because it is there that corporate strategy is formulated, and it is from there that the most powerful signals about the purposes and direction of the organization are sent. Their thesis about the importance of statecraft and how it can be exhibited are illustrated by analyses of two corporate executives who have recently held top leadership positions. The article concludes by identifying a set of political statecraft skills required of chief executives if they are to be effective.

The next reading, by Eagly and Johnson, provides a detailed analysis of studies of whether men and women differ in how they approach the tasks of influence and leadership. For those believing that there are distinct gender differences in this regard, the article's conclusions will be a disappointment. Likewise, however, for those who believe there are no differences, the conclusions will also be contrary to their view. In fact, based on an extremely careful and comprehensive review of the scientific research literature available at the time the article was published (1990), the authors find that in studies carried out in organizational contexts, where the leadership role is somewhat sharply defined, men and women did not differ appreciably in their leadership styles. On the other hand, in studies conducted in nonorganizational contexts, where leadership roles were more ambiguously defined, men and women tended to behave in different and so-called stereotypical styles—that is, women were more interpersonally oriented, and men were more task-oriented. The article is an especially good antidote to the many oversimplified conclusions about men's and women's leadership styles that frequently appear in the popular press.

The following article, by Porter, Lawler, and Hackman, discusses and analyzes the ways in which groups (as opposed to individual leaders) can and do influence employee behavior. In particular, they include a consideration of how managers may be able to modify the work environment in order to help align group and organizational goals for mutual benefit.

The fifth article in this chapter, by Yukl and colleagues, reports a research study that examined patterns of managers' influence tactics. The article contains a number of interesting hypotheses about the use of particular influence tactics by those in leadership positions, and the study confirmed many of these hypotheses. Some tactics were found to be particularly effective in certain sets of conditions, but they could also be used ineptly or in the wrong circumstances. As the authors explain, "determining what tactics are appropriate is not just a matter of 'common sense.'"

The chapter's final article focuses on a somewhat different source of social influence. In this article, a prominent organizational scholar, O'Reilly, describes how the "culture" of an organization can influence employee motivation and commitment. A central feature of O'Reilly's analysis is the role that organizational norms—widely shared and accepted standards of behavior—play in affecting these variables.

REFERENCES

Catlin, G. E. G. *Systematic politics*. Toronto: University of Toronto Press, 1962.
Whetten, D. A., & Cameron, K. S. *Developing management skills,* 3d ed. New York: Harper-Collins, 1995.

Understanding Power in Organizations

Jeffrey Pfeffer

Norton Long, a political scientist, wrote, "People will readily admit that governments are organizations. The converse—that organizations are governments—is equally true but rarely considered."[1] But organizations, particularly large ones, are like governments in that they are fundamentally political entities. To understand them, one needs to understand organizational politics, just as to understand governments, one needs to understand governmental politics.

Ours is an era in which people tend to shy away from this task. As I browse through bookstores, I am struck by the incursion of "New Age" thinking, even in the business sections. New Age can be defined, I suppose, in many ways, but what strikes me about it are two elements: (1) a self-absorption and self-focus, which looks toward the individual in isolation; and (2) a belief that conflict is largely the result of misunderstanding, and if people only had more communication, more tolerance, and more patience, many (or all) social problems would disappear. These themes appear in books on topics ranging from making marriages work to making organizations work. A focus on individual self-actualization is useful, but a focus on sheer self-reliance is not likely to encourage one to try to get things done with and through other people—to be a manager or a leader. "Excellence can be achieved in a solitary field without the need to exercise leadership."[2] In this sense, John Gardner's (former secretary of HEW and the founder of Common Cause) concerns about community are part and parcel of a set of concerns about organizations and getting things accomplished in them.[3] One can be quite content, quite happy, quite fulfilled as an organizational hermit, but one's influence is limited and the potential to accomplish great things, which requires interdependent action, is almost extinguished.

If we are suspicious of the politics of large organizations, we may conclude that smaller organizations are a better alternative. There is, in fact, evidence that the average size of establishments in the United States is decreasing. This is not just because we have become more of a service economy and less of a manufacturing economy; even within manufacturing, the average size of establishments and firms is shrinking. The largest corporations have shed thousands, indeed hundreds of thousands of employees—not only middle managers, but also production workers, staff of all kinds, and employees who performed tasks that are now contracted out. Managers and employees who were stymied by the struggles over power and influence that emerge from interdependence and differences in point of view have moved to a world of smaller, simpler organizations, with less internal interdependence and less internal diversity, which are, as a consequence, less political. Of course, such structural changes only increase interdependence among organizations, even as they decrease interdependence and conflict within these organizations.

I see in this movement a parallel to what I have seen in the management of our human resources. Many corporations today solve their personnel problems by getting rid of the personnel. The rationale seems to be that if we can't effectively manage and motivate employees, then let's turn the task over to another organization. We can use leased employees or contract workers, or workers from temporary help agencies, and let those organizations solve our problems of turnover, compensation, selection, and training.

It is an appealing solution, consistent with the emphasis on the individual, which has always been strong in U.S. culture, and which has grown in recent years. How can we trust large organizations when they have broken compacts of long-term employment? Better to seek security and certainty within oneself, in one's own competencies and abilities, and in the control of one's own activities.

There is, however, one problem with this approach to dealing with organizational power and influence. It is not clear that by ignoring the social realities of power and influence we can make them go away, or that by trying to build simpler, less interdependent social structures we succeed in building organizations that are more effective or that have greater survival value. Although it is certainly true that large organizations sometimes disappear,[4] it is also true that smaller organizations disappear at a much higher rate and have much worse survival properties. By trying to ignore issues of power and influence in organizations, we lose our chance to understand these critical social processes and to train managers to cope with them.

By pretending that power and influence don't exist, or at least shouldn't exist, we contribute to what I and some others (such as John Gardner) see as the major problem facing many corporations today, particularly in the United States—the almost trained or produced incapacity of anyone except the highest-level managers to take action and get things accomplished. As I teach in corporate executive programs, and as I compare experiences with colleagues who do likewise, I hear the same story over and over again. In these programs ideas are presented to fairly senior executives, who then work in groups on the implications of these ideas for their firms. There is real strength in the experience and knowledge of these executives, and they often come up with insightful recommendations and ideas for improving their organizations. Perhaps they discover the wide differences in effectiveness that exist in different units and share suggestions about how to improve performance. Perhaps they come to understand more comprehensively the markets and technologies of their organizations, and develop strategies for both internally oriented and externally oriented changes to enhance effectiveness. It really doesn't matter, because the most frequently heard comment at such sessions is, "My boss should be here." And when they go back to their offices, after the stimulation of the week, few managers have either the ability or the determination to engineer the changes they discussed with such insight.

I recall talking to a store manager for a large supermarket chain with a significant share of the northern California grocery market. He managed a store that did in excess of $20 million in sales annually, which by the standards of the average organization makes him a manager with quite a bit of responsibility—or so one would think. In this organization, however, as in many others, the responsibilities of middle-level managers are strictly limited. A question arose as to whether the store should participate in putting its name on a monument sign for the shopping center in which the store was located. The cost was about $8,000 (slightly less than four hour's sales in that store). An analysis was done, showing how many additional shoppers would need to be attracted to pay back this small investment, and what percentage this was of the traffic count passing by the center. The store manager wanted the sign. But, of course, he could not spend even this much money without the approval of his superiors. It was the president of the northern California division who decided, after a long meeting, that the expenditure was not necessary.

There are many lessons that one might learn from this example. It could be seen as the result of a plague of excessive centralization, or as an instance of a human resource management policy that certainly was more "top down" than "bottom up." But what was particularly interesting was the response of the manager—who, by the way, is held accountable for this store's profits even as he is given almost no discretion to do anything about them. When I asked him about the decision, he said, "Well, I guess that's why the folks at headquarters get the big money; they must know something we don't." Was he going to push for his idea, his very modest proposal? Of course no, he said. One gets along by just biding one's time, going along with whatever directives come down from the upper management.

I have seen this situation repeated in various forms over and over again. I talk to senior executives who claim their organizations take no initiative, and to high-level managers who say they can't or won't engage in efforts to change the corporations they work for, even when they know such changes are important, if not essential, to the success and survival of these organizations. There are politics involved in innovation and change. And unless and until we are willing to come to terms with organizational power and influence, and admit that the skills of getting things done are as important as the skills of figuring out what to do, our organizations will fall further and further behind. The problem is, in most cases, not an absence of insight or organizational intelligence. Instead the problem is one of passivity, a phenomenon that John Gardner analyzed in the following way:

> In this country—and in most other democracies—power has such a bad name that many good people persuade themselves they want nothing to do with it. The ethical and spiritual apprehensions are understandable. But one cannot abjure power. Power, as we are now speaking of it . . . is simply the capacity to bring about certain intended consequences in the behavior of others. . . . In our democratic society we make grants of power to people for specified purposes. If for ideological or temperamental reasons they refuse to exercise the power granted, we must turn to others. . . . To say a leader is preoccupied with power is like saying that a tennis player is preoccupied with making shots his opponent cannot return. Of course leaders are preoccupied with power! The significant questions are: What means do they use to gain it? How do they exercise it? To what ends do they exercise it?[5]

If leadership involves skill at developing and exercising power and influence as well as the will to do so, then perhaps one of the causes of the so-called leadership crisis in organizations in the United States is just this attempt to sidestep issues of power. This diagnosis is consistent with the arguments made by Warren Bennis and his colleagues, who have studied leaders and written on leadership. For instance, Bennis and Nanus noted that one of the major problems facing organizations today is not that too many people exercise too much power, but rather the opposite:

These days power is conspicuous by its absence. Powerlessness in the face of crisis. Powerlessness in the face of complexity. . . . power has been sabotaged. . . . institutions have been rigid, slothful, or mercurial.[6]

They go on to comment on the importance of power as a concept for understanding leadership and as a tool that allows organizations to function productively and effectively:

However, there is something missing . . . POWER, the basic energy to initiate and sustain action translating intention into reality, the quality without which leaders cannot lead. . . . power is at once the most necessary and the most distrusted element exigent to human progress. . . . power is the basic energy needed to initiate and sustain action or, to put it another way, the capacity to translate intention into reality and sustain it.[7]

Such observations about power are not merely the province of theorists. Political leaders, too, confirm that the willingness to build and wield power is a prerequisite for success in public life. In this consideration of power and leadership, Richard Nixon offered some observations that are consistent with the theme of this article:

Power is the opportunity to build, to create, to nudge history in a different direction. There are few satisfactions to match it for those who care about such things. But it is not happiness. Those who seek happiness will not acquire power and would not use it well if they did acquire it.

A whimsical observer once commented that those who love laws and sausages should not watch either being made.

By the same token, we honor leaders for what they achieve, but we often prefer to close our eyes to the way they achieve it. . . .

In the real world, politics is compromise and democracy is politics. Anyone who would be a statesman has to be a successful politician first. Also, a leader has to deal with people and nations as they are, not as they should be. As a result, the qualities required for leadership are not necessarily those that we would want our children to emulate—unless we wanted them to be leaders.

In evaluating a leader, the key question about his behavioral traits is not whether they are attractive or unattractive, but whether they are useful.[8]

OUR AMBIVALENCE ABOUT POWER

That we are ambivalent about power is undeniable. Rosabeth Kanter, noting that power was critical for effective managerial behavior, nevertheless wrote, "Power is America's last dirty word. It is easier to talk about money—and much easier to talk about sex—than it is to talk about power."[9] Gandz and Murray did a survey of 428 managers whose responses nicely illustrate the ambivalence about power in organizations.[10] Some items from their survey, along with the percentage of respondents reporting strong or moderate agreement, are reproduced in Table 1. The concepts of power and organizational politics are related; most authors, myself included, define organizational politics as the exercise or use of power, with power being defined as a potential force. Note that more than 90% of the respondents said that the experience of work-

TABLE 1
MANAGERS' FEELINGS ABOUT WORKPLACE POLITICS

Statement	Percentage expressing strong or moderate agreement
The existence of workplace politics is common to most organizations	93.2
Successful executives must be good politicians	89.0
The higher you go in organizations, the more political the climate becomes	76.2
Powerful executives don't act politically	15.7
You have to be political to get ahead in organizations	69.8
Top management should try to get rid of politics within the organization	48.6
Politics help organizations function effectively	42.1
Organizations free of politics are happier than those where there are a lot of politics	59.1
Politics in organizations are detrimental to efficiency	55.1

Source: Jeffrey Gandz and Victor V. Murray, "The Experience of Workplace Politics," *Academy of Management Journal,* 23 (1980).

place politics is common in most organizations, 89% said that successful executives must be good politicians, and 76% said that the higher one progresses in an organization, the more political things become. Yet 55% of these same respondents said that politics were detrimental to efficiency, and almost half said that top management should try to get rid of politics within organizations. It is as if we know that power and politics exist, and we even grudgingly admit that they are necessary to individual success, but we nevertheless don't like them.

This ambivalence toward, if not outright disdain for, the development and use of power in organizations stems from more than one source. First, there is the issue of ends and means—we often don't like to consider the methods that are necessary to get things accomplished, as one of the earlier quotes from Richard Nixon suggests. We are also ambivalent about ends and means because the same strategies and processes that may produce outcomes we desire can also be used to produce results that we consider undesirable. Second, some fundamental lessons we learn in school really hinder our appreciation of power and influence. Finally, in a related point, the perspective from which we judge organizational decisions often does not do justice to the realities of the social world.

Ends and Means   On Saturday, September 25, 1976, an elaborate testimonial dinner was held in San Francisco for a man whose only public office was as a commissioner on the San Francisco Housing Authority board. The guest list was impressive—the mayor, George Moscone; Lieutenant Governor Mervyn Dymally, at that time the highest-ranking Afro-American in elected politics; District Attorney Joe Freitas; Democratic Assemblyman Willie Brown, probably the most powerful and feared individual in California politics; Republican State Senator Milton Marks; San Francisco Supervisor Robert Mendelsohn; the city editor of the morning newspaper; prominent attorneys—in short, both Democrats and Republicans, a veritable who's who of the northern California political establishment. The man they were there to honor had recently met personally with the president's wife, Rosalynn Carter. Yet when the world heard more of this guest of honor, some two years later, it was to be with shock and horror at what happened in a jungle in Guyana. The person being honored that night in September 1976—who had worked his way into the circles of power in San Francisco using some of the very same strategies and tactics described in this article—was none other than Jim Jones.[11]

There is no doubt that power and influence can be acquired and exercised for evil purposes. Of course, most medicines can kill if taken in the wrong amount, thousands die each year in automobile accidents, and nuclear power can either provide energy or mass destruction. We do not abandon chemicals, cars, or even atomic power because of the dangers associated with them; instead we consider danger an incentive to get training and information that will help us to use these forces productively. Yet few people are willing to approach the potential risks and advantages of power with the same pragmatism. People prefer to avoid discussions of power, apparently on the assumption that "If we don't think about it, it won't exist." I take a different view. John Jacobs, now a political editor for the *San Francisco Examiner*, co-authored a book on Jim Jones and gave me a copy of it in 1985. His view, and mine, was that tragedies such as Jonestown could be prevented, not by ignoring the processes of power and influence, but rather by being so well schooled in them that one could recognize their use and take countermeasures, if necessary—and by developing a well-honed set of moral values.

The means to any end are merely mechanisms for accomplishing something. The something can be grand, grotesque, or, for most of us, I suspect, somewhere in between. The end may not always justify the means, but neither should it automatically be used to discredit the means. Power and political processes in organizations can be used to accomplish great things. They are not always used in this fashion, but that does not mean we should reject them out of hand. It is interesting that when we use power ourselves, we see it as a good force and wish we had more. When others use it against us, particularly when it is used to thwart our goals or ambitions, we see it as an evil. A more sophisticated and realistic view would see it for what it is—an important social process that is often required to get things accomplished in interdependent systems.

Most of us consider Abraham Lincoln to have been a great president. We tend to idealize his accomplishments: he preserved the Union, ended slavery, and delivered the memorable Gettysburg Address. It is easy to forget that he was also a politician and a pragmatist—for instance, the Emancipation Proclamation freed the slaves in the Confederacy, but not in border states that remained within the Union, whose support he needed. Lincoln also took a number of actions that far overstepped his Constitutional powers. Indeed, Andrew Johnson was impeached for continuing many of the actions that Lincoln had begun. Lincoln once explained how he justified breaking the laws he had sworn to uphold:

> My oath to preserve the Constitution imposed on me the duty of preserving by every indispensable means that government, that nation, of which the Constitution was the organic law. Was it possible to lose the nation and yet preserve the Constitution? . . . I felt that measures, otherwise unconstitutional, might become lawful by becoming indispensable to the preservation . . . of the nation.[12]

Lessons to Be Unlearned   Our ambivalence about power also comes from lessons we learn in school. The first lesson is that life is a matter of individual effort, ability, and achievement. After all, in school, if you have mastered the intricacies of cost accounting, or calculus, or electrical engineering, and the people sitting on either side of you haven't, their failure will not affect your performance—unless, that is, you had intended to copy from their papers. In the classroom setting, interdependence is minimized. It is you versus the material, and as long as you have mastered the material, you have achieved what is expected. Cooperation may even be considered cheating.

Such is not the case in organizations. If you know your organization's strategy but your colleagues do not, you will have difficulty accomplishing anything. The private knowledge and private skill that are so useful in the classroom are insufficient in organizations. Individual success in organizations is quite frequently a matter of working with and through other people, and organizational success is often a function of how successfully individuals can coordinate their activities. Most situations in organizations resemble football more than golf, which is why companies often scan resumes to find not only evidence of individual achievement but also signs that the person is skilled at working as part of a team. In achieving success in organizations, "power transforms individual interests into coordinated activities that accomplish valuable ends."[13]

The second lesson we learn in school, which may be even more difficult to unlearn, is that there are right and wrong answers. We are taught how to solve problems, and for each problem, that there is a right answer, or at least one approach that is more correct than another. The right answer is, of course, what the instructor says it is, or what is in the back of the book, or what is hidden away in the instructor's manual. Life appears as a series of "eureka" problems, so-called because once you are shown the correct approach or answer, it is immediately self-evident that the answer is, in fact, correct.

This emphasis on the potential of intellectual analysis to provide the right answer—the truth—is often, although not invariably, misplaced. Commenting on his education in politics, Henry Kissinger wrote, "Before I served as a consultant to Kennedy, I had believed, like most academics, that the process of decision-making was largely intellectual and all one had to do was to walk into the President's office and convince him of the correctness of one's view. This perspective I soon realized is as dangerously immature as it is widely held."[14] Kissinger noted that the easy decisions, the ones with right and wrong answers that can be readily discerned by analysis, never reached the president, but rather were resolved at lower levels.

In the world in which we all live, things are seldom clearcut or obvious. Not only do we lack a book or an instructor to provide quick feedback on the quality of our approach, but the problems we face often have multiple dimensions—which yield multiple methods of evaluation. The consequences of our decisions are often known only long after the fact, and even then with some ambiguity.

AN ALTERNATIVE PERSPECTIVE ON DECISION MAKING

Let me offer an alternative way of thinking about the decision-making process. There are three important things to remember about decisions. First, a decision by itself changes nothing. You can decide to launch a new product, hire a job candidate, build a new plant, change your performance evaluation system, and so forth, but the decision will not put itself into effect. As a prosaic personal example, recall how many times you or your friends "decided" to quit smoking, to get more exercise, to relax more, to eat healthier foods or to lose weight. Such resolutions often fizzle before producing any results. Thus, in addition to knowledge of decision science, we need to know something about "implementation science."

Second, at the moment a decision is made, we cannot possibly know whether it is good or bad. Decision quality, when measured by results, can only be known as the consequences of the decision become known. We must wait for the decision to be implemented and for its consequences to become clear.

The third, and perhaps most important, observation is that we almost invariably spend more time living with the consequences of our decisions than we do in making them. It may be an organizational decision, such as whether to acquire a company, change the compensation system, fight a union-organizing campaign; or a personal decision, such as where to go to school, which job to choose, what subject to major in, or whom to marry. In either case, it is likely that the effects of the decision will be with us longer than it took us to make the decision, regardless of how much time and effort we invested. Indeed, this simple point has led several social psychologists to describe people as rationalizing (as contrasted with rational) animals.[15] The match between our attitudes and our behavior, for instance, often derives from our adjusting our attitudes after the fact to conform to our past actions and their consequences.[16]

If decisions by themselves change nothing; if, at the time a decision is made, we cannot know its consequences; and if we spend, in any event, more time living with our decisions than we do in making them, then it seems evident that the emphasis in much management training and practice has been misplaced. Rather than spending inordinant amounts of time and effort in the decision-making process, it would seem at least as useful to spend time implementing decisions and dealing with their ramifications. In this sense, good managers are not only good analytic decision makers; more important, they are skilled in managing the consequences of their decisions. "Few successful leaders spend much time fretting about decisions once they are past. . . . The only way he can give adequate attention to the decisions he has to make tomorrow is to put those of yesterday firmly behind him."[17]

There are numerous examples that illustrate this point. Consider, for instance, the acquisition of Fairchild Semiconductor by Schlumberger, an oil service company.[18] The theory behind the merger was potentially sound—to apply Fairchild's skills in electronics to the oil service business. Schlumberger wanted, for example, to develop more sophisticated exploration devices and to add electronics to oil servicing and drilling equipment. Unfortunately, the merger produced none of the expected synergies:

> When Schlumberger tried to manage Fairchild the same way it had managed its other business units, it created many difficulties. . . . resources were not made available to R&D with the consequence of losing technical edge which Fairchild once had. Creative . . . technical people left the organization and the company was unable to put technical teams together to pursue new technological advancement.[19]

A study of 31 acquisitions found that "problems will eventually emerge after acquisitions that could not have been anticipated. . . . both synergy and problems must be actively managed."[20] Moreover, firms that see acquisitions as a quick way of capturing some financial benefits are often insensitive to the amount of time and effort that is required to implement the merger and to produce superior performance after it occurs. Emphasis on the choice of a merger partner and the terms of the deal can divert focus away from the importance of the activities that occur once the merger is completed.

Or, consider the decision to launch a new product. Whether that decision produces profits or losses is often not simply a matter of the choices made at the time of the launch. It also depends on the implementation of those choices, as well as on subsequent decisions such as redesigning the product, changing the channels of distribution, adjusting prices, and so forth. Yet what we often observe in organizations is that once a decision is made, more effort is expended in assigning credit or blame than in working to improve the results of the decision.

I can think of no example that illustrates my argument as clearly as the story of how Honda entered the American market, first with motorcycles, and later, of course, with automobiles and lawn mowers. Honda established an American subsidiary in 1959, and between 1960 and 1965, Honda's sales in the United States went from $500,000 to $77 million. By 1966, Honda's share of the U.S. motorcycle market was 63%,[21] starting from zero just seven years before. Honda's share was almost six times that of its closest competitors, Yamaha and Suzuki, and Harley-Davidson's share had fallen to 4%. Pascale showed that this extraordinary success was largely the result of "miscalculation, serendipity, and organizational learning," not of the rational process of planning and foresight often emphasized in our efforts to be successful.[22]

Sochiro Honda himself was more interested in racing and engine design than in building a business, but his partner, Takeo Fujisawa, managed to convince him to turn his talent to designing a safe, inexpensive motorcycle to be driven with one hand and used for package delivery in Japan. The motorcycle was an immediate success in Japan. How and why did Honda decide to enter the export market and sell to the United States? Kihachiro Kawashima, eventually president of American Honda, reported to Pascale:

> In truth, we had no strategy other than the idea of seeing if we could sell something in the United States. It was a new frontier . . . and it fit the "success against all odds" culture that Mr. Honda had cultivated. I reported my impressions . . . including the seat-of-the-pants target of trying, over several years, to attain a 10 percent share of U.S. imports. . . . We did not discuss profits or deadlines for breakeven.[23]

Money was authorized for the venture, but the Ministry of Finance approved a currency allocation of only $250,000, of which less than half was in cash and the rest in parts and motorcycle inventory. The initial attempt to sell motorcycles in Los Angeles was disastrous. Distances in the United States are much greater than in Japan, and the motorcycles were driven farther and faster than their design permitted. Engine failures were common, particularly on the larger bikes.

The company had initially focused its sales efforts on the larger, 250cc and 350cc bikes, and had not even tried to sell the 50cc Supercub, believing it was too small to have any market acceptance:

> We used the Honda 50s . . . to ride around Los Angeles on errands. They attracted a lot of attention. One day we had a call from a Sears buyer. . . . we took note of Sears' interest. But we still hesitated to push the 50cc bikes out of fear they might harm our image in a heavily macho market. But when the larger bikes started breaking, we had no choice. We let the 50cc bikes move. And surprisingly, the retailers who wanted to sell them weren't motorcycle dealers, they were sporting goods stores.[24]

Honda's "you meet the nicest people on a Honda" advertising campaign was designed as a class project by a student at UCLA, and was at first resisted by Honda. Honda's distribution strategy—sporting goods and bicycle shops rather than motorcycle dealers—was made *for* them, not *by* them. And its success with the smaller motorbike was almost totally unanticipated. It occurred through a combination of circumstances: the use of the motorbike by Honda employees, who couldn't afford anything fancier; the positive response from people who saw the bike; and the failure of Honda's larger bikes in the American market.

Honda did not use decision analysis and strategic planning. In fact, it is difficult to see that Honda made any decisions at all, at least in terms of developing alternatives and weighing options against all assessment of goals and the state of the market. Honda succeeded by being flexible, by learning and adapting, and by working to have decisions turn out right, once those decisions had been made. Having arrived with the wrong product for a market they did not understand, Honda spent little time trying to find a scapegoat for the company's predicament; rather, Honda personnel worked vigorously to change the situation to their benefit, being creative as well as opportunistic in the process.

The point is that decisions in the world of organizations are not like decisions made in school. There, once you have written down an answer and turned in the test, the game is over. This is not the case in organizational life. The important actions may not be the original choices, but rather what happens subsequently, and what actions are taken to make things work out. This is a significant point because it means that we need to be somewhat less concerned about the quality of the decision at the time we make it (which, after all, we can't really know anyway), and more concerned with adapting our new decisions and actions to the information we learn as events unfold. Just as Honda emerged as a leader in many American markets more by accident and trial-and-error learning than by design, it is critical that organizational members develop the fortitude to continue when confronted by adversity, and the insight about how to turn situations around. The most important skill may be managing the consequences of decisions. And, in organizations in which it is often difficult to take any action, the critical ability may be the capacity to have things implemented.

WAYS OF GETTING THINGS DONE

Why is implementation difficult in so many organizations, and why does it appear that the ability to get decisions implemented is becoming increasingly rare? One way of thinking about this issue, and of examining the role of power and influence in the implementation process, is to consider some possible ways of getting things done.

One way of getting things to happen is through hierarchical authority. Many people think power is merely the exercise of formal authority, but it is considerably more than that, as we will see. Everyone who works in an organization has seen the exercise of hierarchical authority. Those at higher levels have the power to hire and fire, to measure and reward behavior, and to provide direction to those who are under their aegis. Hierarchical direction is usually seen as legitimate, because the variation in formal authority comes to be taken for granted as a part of organizational life. Thus the phrase, "the boss wants . . . " or "the president wants . . . " is seldom questioned or challenged. Who can forget Marine Lieutenant Colonel Oliver North testifying, during the Iran-contra hearings, about his willingness to stand on his head in a corner if that was what his commander-in-chief wanted, or maintaining that he never once disobeyed the orders of his superiors?

There are three problems with hierarchy as a way of getting things done. First, and perhaps not so important, is that it is badly out of fashion. In an era of rising education and the democratization of all decision processes, in an era in which participative management is advocated in numerous places,[25] and particularly in a country in which incidents such as the Vietnam War and Watergate have led many people to mistrust the institutions of authority, implementation by order or command is problematic. Readers who are parents need only reflect on the difference in parental authority between the current period and the 1950s to see what I mean. How many times have you been able to get your children to do something simply on the basis of your authority as a parent?

A second, more serious problem with authority derives from the fact that virtually all of us work in positions in which, in order to accomplish our job and objectives, we need the cooperation of others who do not fall within our direct chain of command. We depend, in other words, on people outside our purview of authority, whom we could not command, reward, or punish even if we wanted to. Perhaps, as a line manager in a product division, we need the cooperation of people in human resources for hiring, people in finance for evaluating new product opportunities, people in distribution and sales for getting the product sold and delivered, and people in market research for determining product features and marketing and pricing strategy. Even the authority of a chief executive is not absolute, since there are groups outside the focal organization that control the ability to get things done. To sell overseas airline routes to other domestic airlines requires the cooperation of the Transportation and Justice Departments, as well as the acquiescence of foreign governments. To market a drug or medical device requires the approval of the Food and Drug Administration; to export products overseas, one may need both financing and export licenses. The hierarchical authority of all executives and administrators is limited, and for most of us, it is quite limited compared to the scope of what we need in order to do our jobs effectively.

There is a third problem with implementation accomplished solely or primarily through hierarchical authority: what happens if the person at the apex of the pyramid, the one whose orders are being followed, is incorrect? When authority is vested in a single individual, the organization can face grave difficulties if that person's insight or leadership begins to fail. This was precisely what happened at E.F. Hutton, where Robert Fomon, the chief executive officer, ruled the firm through a rigid hierarchy of centralized power:

> Fomon's strength as a leader was also his weakness. As he put his stamp on the firm, he did so more as monarch than as a chief executive. . . . Fomon surrounded himself with . . . cronies and yes men who would become the managers and directors of E.F. Hutton and who would insulate him from the real world.[26]

Because Fomon was such a successful builder of his own hierarchical authority, no one in the firm challenged him to see the new realities that Hutton, and every other securities firm, faced in the 1980s.[27] Consequently, when the brokerage industry changed, Hutton did not, and it eventually ceased to exist as an independent entity.

Another way of getting things done is by developing a strongly shared vision or organizational culture. If people share a common set of goals, a common perspective on what to do and how to accomplish it, and a common vocabulary that allows them to coordinate their behavior, then command and hierarchical authority are of much less importance. People will be able to work cooperatively without waiting for orders from the upper levels of the company. Managing through a shared vision and with a strong organizational culture has been a very popular prescription for organizations.[28] A number of articles and books tell how to build commitment and shared vision and how to socialize individuals, particularly at the time of entry, so that they share a language, values, and premises about what needs to be done and how to do it.[29]

Without denying the efficacy and importance of vision and culture, it is important to recognize that implementation accomplished through them can have problems. First, building a shared conception of the world takes time and effort. There are instances when the organization is in crisis or confronts situations in which there is simply not sufficient time to develop shared premises about how to respond. For this very reason, the military services rely not only on techniques that build loyalty and esprit de corps,[30] but also on a hierarchical chain of command and a tradition of obeying orders.

Second, there is the problem of how, in a strong culture, new ideas that are inconsistent with that culture can penetrate. A strong culture really constitutes an organizational paradigm, which prescribes how to look at things, what are appropriate methods and techniques for solving problems, and what are the important issues and problems.[31] In fields of science, a well-developed paradigm provides guidance as to what needs to be taught and in what order, how to do research, what are apprpriate methodologies, what are the most pressing research questions, and how to train new students.[32] A well-developed paradigm, or a strong culture, is overturned only with great difficulty, even if it fails to account for data or to lead to new discoveries.[33] In a similar fashion, an organizational paradigm provides a way of thinking about and investigating the world, which reduces uncertainty and provides for effective collective action, but which also overlooks or ignores some lines of inquiry. It is easy for a strong culture to produce groupthink, a pressure to conform to the dominant view.[34] A vision focuses attention, but in that focus, things are often left out.

An organization that had difficulties, as well as great success, because of its strong, almost evangelical culture is Apple Computer. Apple was founded and initially largely populated by counterculture computer hackers, whose vision was a computer-based form of power to the people—one computer for each person. IBM had maintained its market share through its close relations with centralized data processing departments. IBM was the safe choice—the saying was, no one ever got fired for buying IBM. The Apple II was successful by making an end run around the corporate data processing manager and selling directly to the end-user, but "by the end of '82 it was beginning to seem like a good idea to have a single corporate strategy for personal computers, and the obvious person to coordinate that strategy was the data processing manager."[35] Moreover, computers were increasingly being tied into networks; issues of data sharing and compatibility were critical in organizations that planned to buy personal computers by the thousands. Companies wanted a set of computers that could run common software, to save on software purchasing as well as training and programming expenses. Its initial vision of "one-person–one machine," made it difficult for Apple to see the need for compatibility, and as a consequence:

> The Apple II wouldn't run software for the IBM PC; the PC wouldn't run software for Lisa, Lisa wouldn't run software for the Apple II; and none of them would run software for the Macintosh. . . . Thanks largely to Steve [Jobs], Apple had an entire family of computers none of which talked to one another.[36]

Apple's strong culture and common vision also helped cause the failure of the Apple III as a new product. The vision was not only of "one person–one machine," but also of a machine that anyone could design, modify, and improve. Operating systems stood between the user and the machine, and so the Apple culture denigrated operating systems: The problem with an operating system, from the hobbyist point of view, was that it made it more difficult to reach down inside the computer and show off your skills; it formed a barrier between the user and the machine. Personal computers meant power to the people, and operating systems took some of that power away. . . . It wasn't a design issue; it was a threat to the inalienable rights of a free people.[37]

Apple III had an operating system known as SOS for Sophisticated Operating System, which was actually quite similar to the system Microsoft had developed for IBM's personal computer—MS DOS (Microsoft Disk Operating System), except it was even better in some respects. Yet Apple was too wary of operating systems to try to make its system *the* standard, or even *a* standard, in personal computing. As a result the company lost out on a number of important commercial opportunities. The very zeal and fervor that made working for Apple like a religious crusade and produced extraordinary levels of commitment from the work force made it difficult for the company to be either cognizant of or responsive to shifts in the marketplace for personal computers.

There is a third process of implementation in organizations—namely, the use of power and influence. With power and influence the emphasis is on method rather than structure. It is possible to wield power and influence without necessarily having or using formal authority. Nor is it necessary to rely on a strong organizational culture and the homogeneity that this often implies. Of course, the process of implementation through power and influence is not without problems of its own. What is important is to see power and influence as one of a set of ways of getting things done—not the only way, but an important way.

From the preceding discussion we can see that implementation is becoming more difficult because: (1) changing social norms and greater interdependence within organizations have made traditional, formal authority less effective than it once was, and (2) developing a common vision is increasingly difficult in organizations composed of heterogeneous members—heterogeneous in terms of race and ethnicity, gender, and even language and culture. At the same time, our ambivalence about power, and the fact that training in its use is far from widespread, mean that members or organizations are often unable to supplement their formal authority with the "unofficial" processes of power and influence. As a result their organizations suffer, and promising projects fail to get off the ground. This is why learning how to manage with power is so important.

THE MANAGEMENT PROCESS: A POWER PERSPECTIVE

From the perspective of power and influence, the process of implementation involves a set of steps, which are outlined below.

- Decide what your goals are, what you are trying to accomplish.
- Diagnose patterns of dependence and interdependence; what individuals are influential and important in your achieving your goal?
- What are their points of view likely to be? How will they feel about what you are trying to do?
- What are their power bases? Which of them is more influential in the decision?
- What are your bases of power and influence? What bases of influence can you develop, to gain more control over the situation?
- Which of the various strategies and tactics for exercising power seem most appropriate and are likely to be effective, given the situation you confront?
- Based on the above, choose a course of action to get something done.

The first step is to decide on your goals. It is, for instance, easier to drive from Albany, New York, to Austin, Texas, if you know your destination than if you just get in your car in Albany and drive randomly. Although this point is apparently obvious, it is something that is often overlooked in a business context. How many times have you attended meetings or conferences or talked to someone on the telephone without a clear idea of what you were trying to accomplish? Our calendars are filled with appointments, and other interactions occur unexpectedly in the course of our day. If we don't have some clear goals, and if we don't know what our primary objectives are, it is not very likely that we are going to achieve them. One of the themes Tom Peters developed early in his writing was the importance of consistency in purpose. Having the calendars, knowing the language, what gets measured, and what gets talked about—all focus on what the organization is trying to achieve.[38] It is the same with individuals; to the extent that each interaction, in each meeting, in each conference, is oriented toward the same objective, the achievement of that objective is more likely.

Once you have a goal in mind, it is necessary to diagnose who is important in getting your goal accomplished. You must determine the patterns of dependence and interdependence among these people and find out how they are likely to feel about what you are trying to do. As part of this diagnosis, you also need to know how events are likely to unfold, and to estimate the role of power and influence in the process. In getting things accomplished, it is critical to have a sense of the game being played, the players, and what their positions are. One can get badly injured playing football in a basketball uniform, or not knowing the offense from the defense. I have seen, all too often, otherwise intelligent and successful managers have problems because they did not recognize the political nature of the situation, or because they were blindsided by someone whose position and strength they had not anticipated.

Once you have a clear vision of the game, it is important to ascertain the power bases of the other players, as well as your own potential and actual sources of power. In this way you can determine your relative strength, along with the strength of other players. Understanding the sources of power is critical in diagnosing what is going to happen in an organization, as well as in preparing yourself to take action.

Finally, you will want to consider carefully the various strategies, or, to use a less grand term, the tactics that are available to you, as well as those that may be used by others involved in the process. These tactics help in using power and influence effectively, and can also help in countering the use of power by others.

Power is defined here as the potential ability to influence behavior, to change the course of events, to overcome resistance, and to get people to do things that they would not otherwise do.[39] Politics and influence are the processes, the actions, the behaviors through which this potential power is utilized and realized.

WHAT DOES IT MEAN, TO MANAGE WITH POWER?

First, it means recognizing that in almost every organization, there are varying interests. This suggests that one of the first things we need to do it to diagnose the political landscape and figure out what the relevant interests are, and what important political subdivisions characterize the organization. It is essential that we do not assume that everyone necessarily is going to be our friend, or agree with us, or even that preferences are uniformly distributed. There are clusters of interests within organizations, and we need to understand where these are and to whom they belong.

Next, it means figuring out what point of view these various individuals and subunits have on issues of concern to us. It also means understanding why they have the perspective that they do. It is all too easy to assume that those with a different perspective are somehow not as smart as we are, not as informed, not as perceptive. If that is our belief, we are likely to do several things, each of which is disastrous. First, we may act contemptuously toward those who disagree with us—after all, if they aren't as competent or as insightful as we are, why should we take them seriously? It is rarely difficult to get along with those who resemble us in character and opinions. The real secret of success in organizations is the ability to get those who differ from us, and whom we don't necessarily like, to do what needs to be done. Second, if we think people are misinformed, we are likely to try to "inform" them, or to try to convince them with facts and analysis. Sometimes this will work, but often it will not, for their disagreement may not be based on a lack of information; it may, instead, arise from a different perspective on what our information means. Diagnosing the point of view of interest groups as well as the basis for their positions will assist us in negotiating with them in predicting their response to various initiatives.

Third, managing with power means understanding that to get things done, you need power—more power than those whose opposition you must overcome—and thus it is imperative to understand where power comes from and how these sources of power can be developed. We are sometimes reluctant to think very purposefully or strategically about acquiring and using power. We are prone to believe that if we do our best, work hard, be nice, and so forth, things will work out for the best. I don't mean to imply that one should not, in general, work hard, try to make good decisions, and be nice, but that these and similar platitudes are often not very useful in helping us get things accomplished in our organizations. We need to understand power and try to get it. We must be willing to do things to build our sources of power, or else we will be less effective than we might wish to be.

Fourth, managing with power means understanding the strategies and tactics through which power is developed and used in organizations, including the importance of timing, the use of structure, the social psychology of commitment and other forms of interpersonal influence. If nothing else, such an understanding will help us become astute observers of the behavior of others. The more we understand power and its manifestations, the better will be our clinical skills. More fundamentally, we need to understand strategies and tactics of using power so that we can consider the range of approaches available to us, and use what is likely to be effective.

Again, as in the case of building sources of power, we often try not to think about these things, and we avoid being strategic or purposeful about employing our power. This is a mistake. Although we may have various qualms, there will be others who do not. Knowledge without power is of remarkably little use. And power without the skill to employ it effectively is likely to be wasted.

Managing with power means more than knowing the ideas discussed in this article. It means being, like Henry Ford, willing to do something with that knowledge. It requires political savvy to get things done, and the willingness to force the issue. For years in the United States, there had been demonstrations and protests, court decisions and legislative proposals attempting to end the widespread discrimination against minority Americans in employment, housing, and public accommodations. The passage of civil rights legislation was a top priority for President Kennedy, but although he had charisma, he lacked the knowledge of political tactics, and possibly the will to use some of the more forceful ones, to get his legislation passed. In the hands of someone who knew power and influence inside out, in spite of the opposition of Southern congressmen and senators, the legislation would be passed quickly.

In March 1965, the United States was wracked by violent reactions to civil rights marches in the South. People were killed and injured as segregationists attacked demonstrators, with little or not intervention by the local law enforcement agencies. There were demonstrators across from the White House holding a vigil as Lyndon

Johnson left to address a joint session of Congress. This was the same Lyndon Johnson who, in 1948, had opposed federal antilynching legislation, arguing that it was a matter properly left to the states. This was the same Lyndon Johnson who, as a young congressional secretary and then congressman, had talked conservative to conservatives, liberal to liberals, and was said by many to have stood for nothing. This was the same Lyndon Johnson who in eight years in the House of Representatives had introduced not one piece of significant legislation and had done almost nothing to speak out on issues of national importance. This was the same Lyndon Johnson who, instead, had used some of his efforts while in the House to enrich himself by influencing colleagues at the Federal Communications Commission to help him obtain a radio station in Austin, Texas, and then to change the operating license so the station would become immensely profitable and valuable. This was the same Lyndon Johnson who, in 1968, having misled the American people, would decide not to run for reelection because of his association with both the Vietnam War and a fundamental distrust of the presidency. On that night Johnson was to make vigorous use of his power and his political skill to help the civil rights movement:

> With almost the first words of his speech, the audience . . . knew that Lyndon Johnson intended to take the cause of civil rights further than it had ever gone before. . . . He would submit a new civil rights bill . . . and it would be far stronger than the bills of the past. . . . "their cause must be our cause, too," Lyndon Johnson said. "Because it is not just Negroes, but really it is all of us, who must overcome the crippling legacy of bigotry and injustice. . . . And we shall overcome."[40]

As he left the chamber after making the speech, Johnson sought out the 76-year-old chairman of the House Judiciary Committee, Emmanuel Celler:

> "Manny," he said, "I want you to start hearings tonight."
> "Mr. President," Cellar protested, "I can't push that committee or it might get out of hand. I am scheduling hearings for next week."
> . . . Johnson's eyes narrowed, and his face turned harder. His right hand was still shaking Celler's, but the left hand was up, and a finger was out, pointing, jabbing.
> "Start them *this* week, Manny," he said. "And hold night sessions, too."[41]

Getting things done requires power. The problem is that we would prefer to see the world as a kind of grand morality play, with the good guys, and the bad ones easily identified. Obtaining power is not always an attractive process, nor is its use. And it somehow disturbs our sense of symmetry that a man who was as sleazy, to use a term of my students, as Lyndon Johnson was in some respects, was also the individual who almost single-handedly passed more civil rights legislation in less time with greater effect than anyone else in U.S. history. We are troubled by the issue of means and ends. We are perplexed by the fact that "bad" people sometimes do great and wonderful things, and that "good" people sometimes do "bad" things, or often, nothing at all. Every day, managers in public and private organizations acquire and use power to get things done. Some of these things may be, in retrospect, mistakes, although often that depends heavily on your point of view. Any reader who always does the correct thing that pleases everyone should immediately contact me—we will get very wealthy together. Mistakes and opposition are inevitable. What is not inevitable is passivity, not trying, not seeking to accomplish things.

In many domains of activity we have become so obsessed with not upsetting anybody, and with not making mistakes, that we settle for doing nothing. Rather than rebuild San Francisco's highways, possibly in the wrong place, maybe even in the wrong way, we do nothing, and the city erodes economically without adequate transportation. Rather than possibly being wrong about a new product, such as the personal computer, we study it and analyze it, and lose market opportunities. Analysis and forethought are, obviously, fine. What is not so fine is paralysis or inaction, which arise because we have little skill in overcoming the opposition that inevitably accompanies change, and little interest in doing so.

Theodore Roosevelt, making a speech at the Sorbonne in 1910, perhaps said it best:

It is not the critic who counts; not the man who points out how the strong man stumbles, or where the doer of deeds could have done them better. The credit belongs to the man who is actually in the arena, whose face is marred by dust and sweat and blood; who strives valiantly; who errs, and comes short again and again; because there is not effort without error and shortcoming; but who does actually strive to do the deeds; who knows the great enthusiasms, the great devotions; who spends himself in a worthy cause, who at the best knows in the end the triumphs of high achievement and who at the worst, if he fails, at least fails while daring greatly, so that his place shall never be with those cold and timid souls who know neither victory or defeat.[42]

It is easy and often comfortable to feel powerless—to say, "I don't know what to do, I don't have the power to get it done, and besides, I can't really stomach the struggle that may be involved." It is easy, and now quite common, to say, when confronted with some mistake in your organization, "It's not really my responsibility, I can't do anything about it anyway, and if the company wants to do that, well that's why the senior executives get the big money—it's their responsibility." Such a response excuses us from trying to do things; in not trying to overcome opposition, we will make fewer enemies and are less likely to embarrass ourselves. It is, however, a prescription for both organizational and personal failure. This is why power and influence are not the organization's last dirty secret, but the secret of success for both individuals and their organizations. Innovation and change in almost any arena requires the skill to develop power, and the willingness to employ it to get things accomplished. Or, in the words of a local radio newscaster, "If you don't like the news, go out and make some of your own."

REFERENCES

1 Norton E. Long, "The Administrative Organization as a Political System," in S. Mailick and E. H. Van Ness, eds., *Concepts and Issues in Administrative Behavior* (Englewood Cliff, NJ: Prentice-Hall, 1962), p. 110.
2 Richard M. Nixon, *Leaders* (New York, NY: Warner Books, 1982), p. 5.
3 John W. Gardner, *On Leadership* (New York, NY: Free Press, 1990).
4 Michael T. Hannan and John Freeman, *Organizational Ecology* (Cambridge, MA: Harvard University Press, 1989).
5 Gardner, *op. cit.*, pp. 55–57.
6 Warren Bennis and Burt Nanus, *Leaders: The Strategies for Taking Charge* (New York, NY: Harper and Row, 1985), p. 6.

7   Ibid., pp. 15–17.

8   Nixon, *op. cit.*, p. 324.

9   Rosabeth Moss Kanter, "Power Failure in Management Circuits," *Harvard Business Review,* 57 (July/August 1979): 65.

10 Jeffrey Gandz and Victor V. Murray, "The Experience of Workplace Politics," *Academy of Management Journal,* 23 (1980): 237–251.

11 Tim Reiterman with John Jacobs, *Raven: The Untold Story of the Rev. Jim Jones and His People* (New York, NY: E. P. Dutton, 1982), pp. 305–307.

12 Nixon, *op. cit.,* p. 326.

13 Abraham Zaleznick and Manfred F. R. Kets de Vries, *Power and the Corporate Mind* (Boston, MA: Houghton Mifflin, 1975), p. 109.

14 Henry Kissinger, *The White House Years* (Boston, MA: Little, Brown, 1979), p. 39.

15 Elliot Aronson, *The Social Animal* (San Francisco, CA: W. H. Freeman, 1972), chapter 4; Barry M. Staw, "Rationality and Justification in Organizational Life," *Research in Organizational Behavior,* B. M. Staw and L. L. Cummings, eds. (Greenwich, CT: JAI Press, 1980), vol. 2, pp. 45–80; Gerald R. Salancik, "Commitment and the Control of Organizational Behavior and Belief," *New Directions in Organizational Behavior,* Barry M. Staw and Gerald R. Salancik, ed. (Chicago, IL: St. Clair Press, 1977), pp. 1–54.

16 Leon Festinger, *A Theory of Cognitive Dissonance* (Stanford, CA: Stanford University Press, 1957).

17 Nixon, *op. cit.*, p. 329.

18 Alok K. Chakrabarti, "Organizational Factors in Post-Acquisition Performance," *IEEE Transactions on Engineering Management,* 37 (1990): 259–268.

19 Ibid., p. 259.

20 Ibid., p. 266.

21 D. Purkayastha, "Note on the Motorcycle Industry—1975," #578-210, Harvard Business School, 1981.

22 Richard T. Pascale, "Perspectives on Strategy: The Real Story Behind Honda's Success," *California Management Review,* 26 (1984): 51.

23 Ibid., p. 54.

24 Ibid., p. 55.

25 William A. Pasmore, *Designing Effective Organizations: The Sociological Systems Perspective* (New York, NY: John Wiley, 1988); David L. Bradford and Allan R. Cohen, *Managing for Excellence* (New York, NY: John Wiley, 1984).

26 Mark Stevens, *Sudden Death: The Rise and Fall of E. F. Hutton* (New York, NY: Penguin, 1989), p. 98.

27 Ibid., p. 121.

28 Thomas J. Peters and Robert H. Waterman, Jr., *In Search of Excellence* (New York, NY: Harper and Row, 1982); Terrence Deal and Allan A. Kennedy, *Corporate Cultures* (Reading, MA: Addison-Wesley, 1982); Stanley Davis, *Managing Corporate Culture* (Cambridge, MA: Ballinger, 1984).

29 Richard T. Pascale, "The Paradox of 'Corporate Culture': Reconciling Ourselves to Socialization," *California Management Review,* 26 (1985): 26–41; Charles O'Reilly, "Corporations, Culture, and Commitment: Motivation and Social Control in Organizations," *California Management Review,* 31 (1989): 9–25.

30 Sanford M. Dornbusch, "The Military Academy as an Assimilating Institution," *Social Forces* 33 (1955): 316–321.

31 Richard Harvey Brown, "Bureaucracy as Praxis: Toward a Political Phenomenology of Formal Organizations," *Administrative Science Quarterly,* 23 (1978): 365–382.

32 Janice Lodahl and Gerald Gordon, "The Structure of Scientific Fields and the Functioning of University Graduate Departments," *American Sociological Review,* 37 (1972): 57–72.

33 Thomas S. Kuhn, *The Structure of Scientific Revolutions,* 2d ed. (Chicago, IL: University of Chicago Press, 1970).

34 Irving L. Janis, *Victims of Groupthink* (Boston, MA: Houghton Mifflin, 1972).

35 Frank Rose, *West of Eden: The End of Innocence at Apple Computer* (New York, NY: Viking Penguin, 1989), p. 81.

36 Ibid., p. 85.

37 Ibid., p. 97.

38 Thomas J. Peters, "Symbols, Patterns, and Settings: An Optimistic Case for Getting Things Done," *Organizational Dynamics,* 7 (1978): 3–23.

39 Jeffrey Pfeffer, *Power in Organizations* (Marshfield, MA: Pitman Publishing, 1981); Kanter, *op. cit.,*; Richard M. Emerson, "Power-Dependence Relations," *American Sociological Review* 27 (1962): 31–41.

40 Robert A. Caro, *Means of Ascent: The Years of Lyndon Johnson* (New York, NY: Alfred A. Knopf, 1990), pp. xix-xx.

41 Ibid., p. xxi.

42 Nixon, *op. cit.*, p. 345.

Statecraft, Strategy, and Corporate Leadership

Joseph Lyon Bower
Martha Wagner Weinberg

Like love, death, and war, the subject of leadership is one we cannot leave alone. For practitioners and poets, for chiefs, for visionaries and their critics, the art and craft of mobilizing human effort is a constant source of fascination and inspiration. Machiavelli's *Prince*, Shakespeare's *King Lear,* Barnard's *Functions of the Executive,* and Neustadt's *Presidential Power* are merely four examples of classic analyses of the complex and difficult work of leaders: in each, the description and analysis of both the subtlety and range of executive work rings true.

Unfortunately, much of the literature on the leadership of contemporary American business has lacked this breadth, particularly in its treatment of the political dimensions of managerial competence. In volume after volume, analysts have enumerated the skills and tools associated with the direction of the functional units or operating systems of the firm.[1] An implicit assumption in many of these studies is that when this "technocratic" work is going well, it is "apolitical" and insulated from the *ad hoc* struggles for power and influence that we often associate with troubled, "politicized" firms. Indeed, the management of power and influence within the corporation is often treated as a distasteful though necessary task which has little to do with fostering or furthering superior performance in the marketplace.

Frequently, analysts of the political work of executives have focused on the management of relationships with relevant constituencies in the world *outside* the boundaries of the company. Underlying many of these studies is the notion that, in formulating plans to handle the ongoing work of government affairs or in building coalitions to deal with problems imposed by a meddlesome government or a hostile trading nation, top managers behave quite differently and work toward much different objectives than they do when they are operating inside their companies. Often these activities are considered to be the domain of government affairs "specialists" who are valued for their ability to understand and explain to chief executives a world governed by *quid pro quos* and defensive reaction to irrational but significant sources of risk.

In this article, we draw on our research with CEOs to argue that a certain kind of political skill that we call "statecraft"—the essence of which involves the use of persuasion and informal authority to mobilize coalitions to accomplish goals—is a critical component of business leadership. Furthermore, we argue that the exercise of statecraft crosses the boundary between the firm and a wide variety of constituencies in the external world other than the market. Because the constituencies that support, operate, and manage all firms have goals that are more than merely economic, astute executives must include in their repertoire activities that often lend themselves poorly to measures of economic performance.

Three premises underlie our argument:

- that it is useful in examining top executive work to regard all firms as political economies, that is, organizations in which the distribution of rewards is at least as critical as is economic efficiency;
  - that political work in the firm is the particular domain of top management; and
- that skill at management of the political economy of the firm, or what we choose to call "statecraft," although seldom captured by systems designed to measure economic performance, is central to the achievement of corporate purpose and to strategic redirection of all organizations.

It is useful to comment briefly on each of these premises.

The Firm Is a Political Economy   The conventional wisdom on which much of the analysis of the contemporary American firm is predicated is that the firm is first and foremost an economic entity.[2] Many have been reluctant to acknowledge the political dimensions of private-sector organizations, even in the face of empirical research that has consistently pointed to their significance, because they do not like to think of politics pervading "good organizations." In the United States, "politics" has always carried with it the pejorative connotation of being manipulative and exploitative of human beings. It is also ideologically suspect since politics is not "governed" by the market's invisible hand. In no element of society are these pejorative connotations more firmly attached to "politics" than in American business. But it is clear that politics, "who gets what, when, how," to use Harold Lasswell's classic definition, is necessary in any organization in which there are many constituencies imposing excessive or conflicting demands, or in which resources for accomplishing objectives or incentives for mobilizing organization members are limited. Because firm, like other organizations, are more than market-driven entities, they require management of allegiances and political direction. We think of this sort of activity as a form of benevolent politics, infused with purpose. It is an essential component of leadership of the firm.

Benevolent Politics Is the Job of Top Management   A source of the prevalent, almost instinctive abhorrence of the notion of "politics" in the private-sector firm is the fear of the chaos that often occurs when there is mobilization of competing factions in an effort to "win" control over the firm's direction.

Within the firm, there are many possible sources of disagreement about purpose that may lead to politicization. Among them are competing professional norms, strong personal loyalties, or resource constraints that pit functional groups against one another. Individuals, organizational units, and professional groups invest heavily over time in programs and procedures aimed at economic efficiency as they perceive it. Disputes among such groups are often much more serious than their substance would suggest because the real stakes are self- and organizational esteem associated with the viability of these investments, as well as the power and influence that go with their recognition. The resolution of disputes among those individuals or groups cannot be carried out successfully without paying attention to the consequences of decisions for the resource-base and motivation of those involved.

In dealing with conflicts among constituencies which are endemic to organizations, it is critical that the process be perceived as corporately legitimate. If the process entails only a mechanical division of the spoils, the firm may be quickly politicized. Instead, the resolution must be perceived as legitimate because of its contribution to corporate purpose through an efficient allocation of resources and the maintenance of the total organization's commitment.

There are at least two reasons statecraft must be exercised at the top and cannot be delegated. First, successful dispute resolution usually requires interpretation of the corporate purpose. It is only the top executive whose *position* confers the authority and legitimacy necessary for articulating corporate strategy. Although many individual products and ideas may bubble up from within the organization, corporate strategy is by definition a function performed on behalf of the entire organization. It is therefore only the top executives of the firm who can combine formal authority, a widely acknowledged mandate, and the political skill and influence necessary to move the firm in consistent and purposeful directions.

Second, it is the chief executive who personifies the firm and who therefore serves as the single most important source of cues about the organization's purpose and direction.[3] Instinctively, when an organization succeeds or fails, we turn to the top to see who is responsible and to ask what sort of person led this organization to its present state. In fact, while much of the day-to-day output of the firm is the product of the technocratic organization, and, correspondingly, while much of the activity of the top manager may not appear to be either inspired or heroic, it is usually only the visible man or woman at the top who has the ability to disseminate the powerful signals so necessary to direct the difficult organizational work of cementing loyalty and allegiance to the firm.

Statecraft Is a Component of the Leadership of All Healthy Organizations   Because all firms are more than economies, it is not only firms under siege from the external environment or troubled firms that require executive attention to the delicate balancing of the demands of both internal and external constituencies. Indeed, we would argue that the executives of all healthy firms must have not only a well-articulated view of their economic missions and "product," but also a vision of how to manage the political dimensions of their work. At the heart of this vision must be implicit or explicit attention to the performance of the two primary functions of leadership. These are the composition and maintenance of the coalition necessary to ensure achievement of corporate purpose and the stabilization of balance among the technocratic, organizational, and interpersonal dimensions of the firm to allow the maximum benefits of each to flow to the organization.

In any well-led firm at any point in time, an astute executive may pay more attention to dealing with one of these dimensions than another. Indeed, one can define a continuum along which all firms fall that helps explain the style of work necessary to keep the firms on an even strategic keel. At one end of the continuum are those firms in which all of the underlying premises of organization are unstable: the environment is changing rapidly; markets are uncertain; or the rules of the game are being rewritten.

In such circumstances, a manager may well feel quite uncertain about what in fact is going on, and which individuals or groups will support his continued efforts to lead.

Organizations in this state require "process" work of the most visible kind. In this situation, the identification and mobilization of potentially salient constituencies into a coalition that provides a stable base from which to launch a successful effort in the marketplace must be a dominant strategic focus of the executive. Lee Iacocca is the contemporary prototype of this sort of leader.

At the other end of the continuum are those firms in which leadership feels comfortable with its understanding of the present and prospects of its company, as well as its control over the organization and constituencies whose support is necessary for success. The basic organizational premises are stable and the need for political management may be less easily detectable. "Statecraft in the shadows," the work of the management of the "steady state" firm, requires a more focused concentration on the other major function of the manager of the firm, the accumulation of influence to protect the technocratic system as it does its work and to maintain a healthy balance between the political and technocratic influences on corporate purpose. The virtually anonymous top management of IBM exemplifies this mode.

Although all leaders must ultimately pay attention to both functions, it is useful to describe briefly the situations faced by two top managers in order to demonstrate the two ends of the continuum and to illustrate these two dimensions of strategic work.

FRANK LORENZO: THE POLITICAL MANAGER IN THE WORLD TURNED UPSIDE DOWN

Perhaps one of the most telling examples in recent years of a firm in which almost all of the organizing principles were in a state of flux is the story of Continental Airlines (CAL) in the period between 1982, when the airline was taken over by Texas International Airlines, and 1984, when it began to operate in the black despite having sought protection under Chapter 11 of the federal bankruptcy laws.[4] Frank Lorenzo, the chairman and major stockholder of the firm, was faced with extreme uncertainty at several levels. Texas International had taken over larger Continental Airlines despite the bitter opposition of Continental's employees and in the face of mounting financial losses. In addition, the climate of the airline industry as a whole was volatile and, in many respects, troubled. The industry had traditionally experienced instability, both because the volume of air travel correlated with the state of the economy and because jet fuel, with its shifting supply and price, was one of the key components of cost. Finally, and perhaps most significantly, as a result of the Airline Deregulation Act of 1977, the industry was undergoing a massive restructuring. The established carriers like Continental were faced with the need to adapt aircraft use and routes to meet customers demand in a marketplace set free from government intervention. At the same time, they needed to become profitable when challenged by new nonunion entrants with significantly lower labor costs.

In this turbulent environment, one of the central strategic decisions that Lorenzo had to make was to decide what combination of constituencies (the groups and individuals who cared about the success or failure of Continental Airlines) he and the top management of CAL needed to assemble into a coalition that would allow them to succeed in the marketplace and ensure the company a sustainable position in the evolving industry. Gordon Donaldson and Jay Lorsch have argued that the three most significant constituencies to which top managers must pay attention are the capital markets, the product markets, and employees.[5] Although these market-defined categories of constituencies are often significant, it is useful to look at how Lorenzo, in the face of a situation in which all of the rules were being rewritten, turned away from some, segmented others, and introduced new, nonmarket-defined constituencies as central elements of his new ongoing coalition.

In filing for Chapter 11 protection in September 1983, CAL argued labor costs were so crippling that unless the company was allowed to abrogate its labor contracts, it would be forced to liquidate. By doing this, the CAL management also sent a clear message to one of its main market-defined constituencies, its unionized employees, that their claims would no longer dominate the company's agenda and, indeed, may have been written off. The bankruptcy was also a strong signal to a second main market-defined constituency, the traditional sources of capital, that something was sorely amiss. However, this marked no point of great discontinuity for Lorenzo. Since he had first become involved with Texas International Airlines, Lorenzo had had a tenuous relationship with Wall Street investment analysts, preferring to rely in arranging financings on an informal network of long-term personal associates in the investment community and on his own judgment of the financial markets.

If Lorenzo was willing to back away from cultivating some of the market-defined constituencies, what was the composition of his new coalition and how did it reflect his own assessment of which groups he needed to have with him as he repositioned CAL? Certainly one forum in which Lorenzo demonstrated both confidence and skill was in the arena of government. By putting the company into Chapter 11 bankruptcy, he and the CAL management were also ensuring that many of the significant business decisions that would be made in the short run would thus be made in the courtroom. Although the constraints involved in operating a company in bankruptcy were many and severe, the CAL managers had been successful in their legal actions in the past. And, as the bankruptcy proceedings unfolded, they had a high degree of success in their pleadings before the judge.

In addition, Lorenzo had always demonstrated an understanding of and a facility for dealing with the regulatory apparatus of the government, and he had a thorough understanding of the premises on which the policy of deregulation was based. Indeed, many of the top managers of CAL and its parent company, Texas Air Corporation, had had extensive government experience. The boards of directors of CAL and New York Air included John Robson and Alfred Kahn, two of the architects of deregulation. Lorenzo had reinforced his relationship with the regulatory apparatus by focusing his efforts in Washington on the substance of the public policy debate and by choosing to avoid the route of making large campaign contributions or hiring lobbyists. As Texas Air's vice president for government affairs put it:

> We don't have lots of money and we're too small to cover all the bases. A proactive stance of influencing the policy before it hurts us, or at least knowing in advance what it's going to be, and where it came from is the way we do business.[6]

Lorenzo also counted on his ability to read the broad political and social climate, both in assessing his ability to deflect challenges to his business by parts of the government and in understanding the preferences and tolerances of customers. Given Lorenzo's sensitivities to the political climate, it is plausible to conclude that it was no accident that he originated the concept of "peanuts fares" during the Carter Administration and took a tough stand on escalating wages in the airline industry following Ronald Reagan's dismissal of the striking air traffic controllers. In addition, he and several of his former associates such as Donald Burr, the founder of People Express, had throughout their careers banked on a view of airline customers as willing to trade off price and service in highly sophisticated ways. In the days immediately following CAL's filing for Chapter 11 protection, the top CAL management bet the airline both on their ability to call the fare and route structure that would allow them to fill their planes and on their ability to communicate to the public that CAL was sound but was troubled by the quite normal but unfair bane of the existence of American society, a labor problem.

Equally significant in the shaping of his coalition were Lorenzo's calls on the kinds of people he wanted to have with him in the organization as he faced an industry environment characterized by extreme uncertainty. Rather than being made up of career airline employees, the key decision-making group that guided CAL through the bankruptcy was small, relatively young, and consisted largely of lawyers, former government employees, and financial specialists with long-standing relationships with Lorenzo. These managers each came with considerable experience at dealing with one or more of the external constituencies of government, the courts and the entrepreneurial financial community that were all to form the base of Lorenzo's new coalition. Most of these men, when quizzed about their motivation, expressed little concern for job security, compensation, or formal position. Instead, they described themselves as being driven by a fascination with the complexity of the task and with the entrepreneurial vision guiding it. In this respect, Lorenzo's ability to sustain his coalition of loyalists both outside and inside the firm depended much less on his marshalling of formal authority than it did on his ability to build informal influence and loyalty to his style of operating and to his goals and view of the world.

This description of Lorenzo and his management style is not designed to hold him up as a paragon of managerial excellence: the jury is still out on the questions of whether Lorenzo will ultimately be judged a "successful" leader of Continental Airlines and what "success" means in the context of the CAL drama. Rather it is meant to illustrate the central position that the work of coalition identification and mobilization plays in the formulation of strategy for an executive in an environment in which all the rules are being rewritten. Lorenzo's "call" on the line-up of constituencies necessary to compete in a restructuring industry is a strategic one, as is his implicit or explicit decision to flaunt the convention of showing respect and deference to groups traditionally defined as overwhelmingly significant because of their role in the marketplace. This set of decisions is both strategic and political. The formulation, execution, and implementation of his strategy depends much more heavily on judgments about credibility and vision than on economic feasibility; on influence rather than on formal authority; and on a consistent and imaginative view of the nature of the uncertain world outside the firm than on a rational analysis of how the technocratic tasks of the firm should be divided and categorized.

BERNARD O'KEEFE: THE ACKNOWLEDGED CHIEF OF A SUCCESSFUL FIRM

The story of Bernard O'Keefe (chairman and, until 1984, CEO of EG&G, Inc.) provides an example of "statecraft in the shadows," the kind of work required of leaders in companies that have stable organizing principles and, by all objective measures, are successful. In firms such as these, the constituency-identification and coalition-building function so central to the job of Frank Lorenzo is still necessary, particularly when the company faces a crisis. But its importance in day-to-day work of top management pales in comparison to the significance of the other major organizational functions of the executive, the protection of the operations of the technocratic system, and the maintenance of a healthy balance between political and technocratic influences.

EG&G, Inc., a *Fortune 500* company with approximately 20,000 employees and almost $1 billion in sales in 1984, is a diversified firm that produces a variety of technical and scientific products and services for commercial, industrial, and government customers throughout the world.[7] Since its founding in 1947, EG&G has enjoyed remarkably stable economic success: in 1983, a typical year for EG&G, *Forbes* listed EG&G first among firms in the electronics industry in return on equity (29.4%), first in return on total capital (25.2%), and second in growth of earnings per share (26.8%).[8]

O'Keefe joined the firm shortly after its founding and, even before being named president in 1965, managed the business development of EG&G, a task that none of the three more technically focused founding partners relished. O'Keefe, himself a electronic engineer who had received significant on-the-job technical training as a navy ensign assigned to the Los Alamos project during World War II, did not at any time during his career restrict his interest to his initial area of technical expertise, the management of atomic tests. As early as the 1950s, he made a commitment to himself to devote at least one day a week to external affairs. As he explains it:

> I had never had time to get advanced degrees. I decided early on that I needed to get outside what was an ingrown technological company for two reasons: I needed to find out how other businesses ran and I needed to understand a broader spectrum of social activity. I relied on having an information base outside the company. And I liked it, enjoyed it. It allowed me to grow.[9]

Throughout his years at EG&G, he consistently maintained this commitment. Early in his career, he became involved with the activities of the Boston Chamber of Commerce and, as a result of his contacts there with local executives was asked to join several boards of directors. In addition to accepting these invitations, he worked in state government, serving as chairman of the Massachusetts Board of Higher Education and the Governor's Management Task Force. Despite the fact that EG&G is not primarily a manufacturing company, in the late 1970s O'Keefe became active in the National Association of Manufacturers, and in 1982 he became its chairman. Throughout his career, he has frequently testified before Congress and contributed guest columns and statements to the news media on a range of public policy issues. And, in 1983, he published *Nuclear Hostages,* an impassioned plea to cease the arms race.[10]

In addition to being an enjoyable and educational experience and a vehicle for garnering publicity for the company, O'Keefe's work in the areas outside his company represented an expansion of his operating arena and significantly bolstered his ability to exercise his leadership role inside his company. EG&G historically has been a company run by well-trained engineers interested in the development of technical products. By freeing himself up from a focus on the technical work of the company, O'Keefe reinforced his own ability to perform two crucial jobs of the astute political leader. First, he reserved to himself the role of scanning the external environment for potentially damaging or useful nonmarket-generated cues which would affect EG&G. And, second, he served as an interpreter of these cues back into his company. His ability to do this, and to translate among the technically focused groups within EG&G, gave him a base within the company of tremendous informal authority and leverage, the staples of the leader of the political system. As one of the top managers of EG&G described it:

> Barney owns a piece of this company that nobody else can touch. . . . I can't tell you why I've always believed that he knows more about the world than I do. I guess, objectively speaking, there's no basis for it. But I *believe,* and so does everybody in the company.[11]

Especially significant about O'Keefe's work with groups outside the company was the fact that in doing this work he also stepped back from running many of the technocratic functions in the company. In 1969, following a disastrous cost overrun on a government contract that resulted in EG&G's only year of financial losses, O'Keefe brought in Dean Freed, an outsider with experience in the management of high-technology, fast-growth companies and turned over to him control of the operations of the commercial businesses. Freed and his colleagues in turn developed a rigorous planning and control process that dominates the day-to-day operations of the company. Although this elaborate administrative process, which was to change entirely the company's way of doing business, was not at all in keeping with O'Keefe's own much more informal style, O'Keefe resisted the temptation to meddle and to assert his own authority directly in the process. As Freed described it:

> Barney was quite magnificent about moving me into his company. I'd say I wanted to do something and he'd say "fine, just keep me informed." He didn't meddle in my areas, and in fact, would open doors that allowed me to get control.[12]

Ironically, in giving away control over the management of day-to-day operations of the technocratic system, O'Keefe increased his stature and ability to function as a leader of the organizational system of the firm. His ceding of control over an area that could be run according to a system of rules and tasks known to and accepted by the employees put in place a basic "constitution," an agreed-upon method of operating those parts of the business that were suited to management by the technocratic system. As O'Keefe himself put it:

> This is a nonadversarial company. It's got to be to work well. It simply couldn't function with a sense of betrayal. Much of my legitimacy came from my setting the contract, then letting people work within known rules. If this hadn't been the norm, this company would have

dissolved into battling fiefdoms long ago.[13]

The credibility and informal influence that flowed from this willingness to protect and not tamper with the technocratic part of the company also enhanced O'Keefe's ability to change the direction of the company at crucial times when he needed to make stick his own assessment of the direction that a strategic change should take. Even in 1969, when EG&G took a loss because of the inadequacy of its control systems and plunged those associated with the company into a period of distress, O'Keefe's job was not in jeopardy, and his proposals for redirection of the company were not seriously questioned.[14] As a long-time director of EG&G described it:

> There was no move to get Barney. The founders trusted him; the directors trusted him; and the employees trusted him. We have no reason to believe that he wasn't agile enough to fix things for the benefit of everybody. And he'd already demonstrated that he was comfortable and extremely good at dealing with uncertainty.[15]

Although a less overt and visible form of organizational "process" work than Lorenzo's, O'Keefe's "stagecraft in the shadows" consisted of three activities that proved critical in allowing him to manage the company and lead its membership toward the achievement of the corporate purpose. First, by focusing on the development of his relationships with groups in the world outside EG&G that could potentially provide important information or ultimately affect the company's long-term position, O'Keefe served as a conduit for the nonmarket-generated cues that technocratic systems are often designed to filter out. Second, he took on as a primary job for himself the role of determining which part of the management work of the company should be allocated to the technocratic organization.

In so doing, he effectively protected the technocratic system from politicization by delegating feasible tasks and allowing them to be completed. At the same time, he reserved for himself the critical decisions (fraught with uncertainty) about when that system needed to change and what the company should do when the ongoing predictable systems and measures of marketplace performance did not provide sufficient information to answer questions about long-term directions. Third, because of his experience outside the company. O'Keefe was able to gain access to information and advice and to mobilize supporters at times when he needed to refashion the company's strategy. In turn, his ability to mobilize and deal with groups on the outside increased his influence and leverage inside at precisely those times when the formal authority and legitimacy that came with his position might not have been sufficient to carry the day.

THE ELEMENTS OF STATECRAFT

As the examples of Frank Lorenzo and Bernard O'Keefe illustrated, the two central components of statecraft will be more or less visible depending on the stability of the basic organizing principles of the enterprise; on whether the changes in corporate strategy that are required challenge the needs of key individuals or groups; on the temperamental proclivities of the individual who holds the jobs the job; and on the point in time at which one chooses to analyze the company. But in addition to recognizing the significance of the management of a core coalition committed to corporate purpose, and the central importance of purposive maintenance of a balance between technocratic and political systems, it is possible to generalize from descriptions of chief executives about the skills that leaders require to practice successful statecraft.

Managing the Face of the Issue Whereas technocratic work is often discussed in words and numbers, all astute leaders recognize that they conduct their political work in two different languages. The first language is based in symbols and consists of the signals top managers give off about their vision of the firm and their role in it. The second is the language of process, and involves the rhetoric and gestures that they use to conduct the daily activities of the firm. To be successful at statecraft, the messages in both languages must be consistent.

For example, in his role as the formal leader of the economic activity of EG&G, O'Keefe could easily have asserted his authority in the operations of the business— even after having ceded control to Freed. However, the perception of inconsistency between his symbolic gesture and his actions that would almost certainly have resulted would have cost him dearly in resources needed to deal with both internal and external constituencies.

Identifying Targets Setting goals and objectives is almost universally thought of as an intellectual activity. In fact, astute leaders recognize that "objectives" are the outcome of a process of translating a personal vision of what the company might be into a strategy that is explicit and can be implemented. For that to happen, subordinates who have expertise or who control the resources and operations that are required for action must be identified or recruited, and they must be persuaded to contribute to the process of articulating the new objectives of the firm. In this sense, making strategy is a process of hitting moving targets.

Leaders must work continually to preserve the coalition of those ongoing constituencies whose activities maintain and enhance their vision of the corporate purpose. They have as well the primary responsibility for developing new constituencies that will help achieve the corporate purpose and for ridding their organization of the groupings that become useless. For example, in the account of the development of the 360 computer series at IBM, it is striking how Tom Watson, Jr. introduced new kinds of people into the top levels of the company (which he inherited from his father); and it is equally impressive how Vincent Learson beat down and rearranged those pieces of the company that would not focus on the chosen goal of a compatible line of computers.[16]

Often the constituencies whose commitment is required in order to achieve corporate purpose are in disagreement. Then, maintaining the coalition of interest is demanding work. Schlumberger's Jean Riboud notes that "running a company is like politics. You are always balancing interests and personalities and trying to keep people motivated."[17] The trick is not merely to balance forces, but to align them with corporate purpose or even to shift the corporate purpose.

Managing the Core Coalition   All management involves resolving conflicts, and many of these are interpersonal. But the work of making strategy involves a distinct sort of conflict resolution. The process of change involves reordering the priorities and claims of constituencies within and outside the firm and also managing the change in status and authority that may result. It is this activity that permits the firm to move in new directions. In the process, "far out" ideas may become respectable, well-established ideas may face strong challenge, and resources may be moved to support new approaches.

There are two key problems that relate directly to two principal functions of the leader. First, the government coalition of any organization almost inevitably reflects deep commitments to existing strategy. Consideration of change is deeply threatening to some, not the least because they believe it ill considered. A second problem arises because strategic change has the potential for destroying the balance between the technocratic and political systems of the firm. In fact, the redirection of strategy constitutes a form of revolution in which the structure, systems, and leadership of the firm are rearranged to address a new view of how success can be achieved and sustained.

Lorenzo and O'Keefe provide polar examples of the variations in subtlety or boldness with which this process may occur. Another example of the process of changing strategy is provided by the work of Jack Busby, who during the 1960s and 1970s successfully guided Pennsylvania Power and Light through phases of growth, conservation, and entry into the nuclear age. When asked how he persuaded the members of his organization (at that point a group totally oriented toward growth) to change their focus to the need for energy conservation, he spoke in language that demonstrated his consciousness of the significance of the political process:

> We began with a few people, a kind of new coalition, made up of people with different viewpoints but with a common understanding of problems facing us . . .
>
> With this group of friends and allies we adopted what could be called a mechanized guerrilla warfare approach. You don't try to besiege the strong points, you go around them. You go into middle management, to the people you think are smart, capable and in positions from which they can contribute to the turnaround if they can be persuaded. At the same time you hope these people are smart enough to keep in touch with their bosses and not become sacrificial lambs. It is not that you do this secretly, but you don't go and ask the department heads whether you can go talk to some of their lieutenants because if you do you are not going to have the right kind of discussion. But at the same time you don't make a secret of the fact that you are doing this. You just can't sit in your office praying and writing memos. You have to go out there and talk to the guys who can produce some change and develop the data that can go into studies to help convince others.[18]

Busby also describes his posture toward the members of the organization who resisted the new ways of doing business: "You surround that individual with an environment in which he or she begins to feel a little bit out of step. You don't make it a direct personal confrontation. You set up a situation where people feel they can change without having to say they were wrong."[19]

Picking Issues for Management   Unlike the management of operations and other technocratic activity, statecraft is not easily carved up for delegation to others. By its nature, the work is personal work: its products—influence and a reservoir of loyalty and informal authority—cannot be assigned or given away. (Perhaps this is the most significant reason that we find example after example in which the transition from an owner-founder to a hired professional manager has been difficult.) Because these "products" are especially necessary to the manager at times when formal authority will not carry the day, they constitute an important reserve currency in the organization and, as such, must be constantly guarded and nurtured. The true organizational statesman must be comfortable working by himself, without the bolstering of organizational reassurance and without the satisfaction of periodic quantifiable marks of success.

Although they do not delegate the central responsibility for statecraft, astute leaders set and maintain the pattern of delegation of operating and administrative problems as part of their balancing between political and technocratic systems. They are careful to use the technocratic systems to manage all those issues that can be handled without politicization or threat to corporate purpose. As O'Keefe has done at EG&G, it is not uncommon to see corporate chief executives give over much of the running of the existing portfolio of businesses to their seconds in command, or for presidents to give over responsibility to a cadre of operating chiefs. One CEO noted that the only issues he attended to regularly were strategy, key people, and the overall finances of the company. All other issues he would consider only in order to determine to what part of his technocratic structure he would delegate them.[20]

As a corollary, astute leaders seek to "lift out" from the technocratic structure those issues that have become politicized, or isolate a disoriented fragment of a coalition or recast the definition of responsibility so as to contribute to overall coherence. At IBM, Learson quickly eliminated a key study committee that had turned into a forum for conflict between those committed and those uncommitted to the new strategy.[21] And in the example of PP&L, once the conservation phase got underway, Busby helped his somewhat confused marketers see their new mission by renaming their department "community relations." Interestingly, after they acquired the ability to teach the community about the emerging world of scarce energy, they also proved themselves able to use those same skills to persuade that same community of the usefulness of nuclear power. (This occurred despite their geographic proximity to Three Mile Island.) Thus the symbolic recasting of the marketing function resulted over time in the development of new and useful operating capability.[22]

Meeting the Constituents   All manuals for chief executives urge them to track important changes in the environment. But in the fine print, this often takes the form of an admonition to use staff for careful monitoring of commercially significant events. Astute leaders do more than this. They develop, cultivate, and maintain ties with a broader range of constituencies than those within the grasp of the technocratic system. It may be this function, together with the formal authority that they enjoy as chief executives, that gives them the advantage in setting the direction of the organization that others will accept. Sometimes this merely involves work with the board of directors or with the company bankers, but often this is done through a personal network.

Again and again we see executives cultivating and using such relationships. It is for this reason that busy chief executives sit on the boards of other companies and of community organizations. They then use these connections to help their companies. Examples abound, Paul Casey, president of McCord, sat on the board of Tecumseh Products with Edward Giblin, president of Excello. Through that relationship, each was able to determine that a merger might help their companies. It was through the same kind of process that Reginald Jones learned that GE might be able to buy Utah Mining.

EG&G's O'Keefe constantly relied on the network of friends developed while working at Los Alamos during the Second World War to help the company deal with the government as a customer. He continued to develop his outside contacts through work with the National Association of Manufacturers. Through this work, he learned how to broaden his board and the capabilities of his company. In the same spirit, Frank Lorenzo has assiduously cultivated his relationships with sources of finance and ideas in Wall Street and in the government. This helped him guide Continental Airlines through the hurricane of deregulation. One top manager noted that he "tried to learn enough about new things to be able to ask an intelligent question," and then when the organization answered "to have a probing follow-up."[23]

The process of getting out into other worlds, especially finance and government, is important. It acclimates executives to dealing in the world of influence and bargaining as opposed to the more formal control or orderly norms of the technocratic system. These skills are necessary for moving their company through sea changes or extreme uncertainty. This may be one reason why high-level government executives often have successful careers in business, while the reverse is seldom true. Managers of large corporations are frustrated by the fluidity, fragmentation, and lack of responsiveness in our federal government. On the other hand. Donald Rumsfeld, Fred Malek, James Lynn, William Ruckelshaus, and George Schultz are examples of government executives who successfully made the transition to managing large businesses.

Choosing Quiescence   If the examples of O'Keefe and others are instructive, a final element of the art of statecraft depends on knowing when not to act. Perhaps the most significant area of executive action is what astute organizational statesmen *don't* do. They often have the patience to do nothing. They resist the temptation to meddle with smoothly functioning technocratic systems, even if by doing this they remain aloof from making decisions in their own area of expertise or distance themselves from the excitement of "good news," sales closed, or breakthroughs accomplished.

On issues involving a high degree of uncertainty, astute managers resist the temptation to fortify themselves with a group of like-minded supporters. Organizational statecraft involves delicate balancing. It cannot be done with committees or by a band of zealots. It must be done in private, alone or with a very lean organization, with the recognition that "the buck stops here" on the most difficult issues. In recounting his experience at restructuring his company, Mario Schinberni, the widely respected chairman and CEO of Italy's powerful Montedison, begins his description by emphasizing that he "entered Montedison alone, without a team. . . . I then tried to build my organization. . . . My first decision was taken without consulting anyone. Only after nine months did I share my decision with two young assistants."[24]

While they must be willing to operate alone in making some of the most difficult choices about the direction of the firm, the most astute leaders must be willing to give credit for victories to their valued colleagues in their organizations, even at the expense of downplaying their own hard work. Frequently, sophisticated top managers eschew publicly any sense of personal profit or gain in power. There are no public victories. In order to avoid the negative connotations of power, they have to resist the need for personal reassurance and must seem to thrive on ambiguity, while at the same time making successes seem possible only because of the efforts of others. Reginald Jones' response to a proposal by an employee that a history be written of the "Jones Era" of the General Electric Company exemplifies this. Jones, when approached with the idea, vetoed it, saying:

> I wouldn't want, even when I retire, to make it appear that General Electric is the Jones story, because this is an institution, and I'm a steward here. I have it for a while, and then I move on, and the whole company is doing this.[25]

The effective leader, in other words must exercise a mix of skills to keep the efforts of selected constituencies aligned on some compromise of their objectives that translates into coherent and implemented corporate purpose. The process of managing both the technocratic and political systems is a dynamic one: the successful leader must therefore respect each system for its own contribution and make sophisticated judgments about the appropriate balance between the two at any point. The management of the organizational and technocratic processes is essential to the achievement of purpose; in this basic sense, purpose and process are inseparable. Indeed, we have argued that frequently successful leaders speak of purpose through the medium of nonmarket organizational activity, and they use the organizational system both to build the coalitions necessary to pursue agreed-upon goals and to ensure the supply of the reserve currency of influence necessary in times of change or redirection. In this fundamental sense, then, statecraft is the vehicle through which strategy is managed; and its practice, rather than being destructive and manipulative, is a benevolent and essential component of the job of leadership of the firm.

REFERENCES

1 Elsewhere, Bower has developed the distinction between "technocratic" systems designed to help managers use resources selectively so as to achieve high levels of efficiency and effectiveness, and "political" systems designed to insure legitimacy and accountability. See Joseph Bower, *The Two Faces of Management* (Boston, MA: Houghton Mifflin, 1983). For the purpose of this article, it is sufficient to recognize that modern organizations of any size require a high degree of sophistication in the way goals are developed, budgets set, capital invested, managers recruited, trained, and compensated, and organization designed and built. Desirable as well is a degree of continuity almost unimaginable in democratic political process. Generally speaking, we will refer to these as administrative and operating systems of organizations, but where it seems convenient, we may call them technocratic.

2 This is true despite the fact that leading students and practitioners of management such as Chester Barnard, Philip Selznick, Richard Cyert, James March, Alfred Sloan, and Jean Riboud have emphasized the political work of the executive. See Chester Barnard, *The Functions of the Executive* (Cambridge, MA: Harvard University Press, 1938); Philip Selznick, *Leadership in Administration* (Evanston, IL: Row Peterson and Company, 1957); Richard Cyert and James March, *A Behavioral Theory of the Firm* (Englewood

Cliffs, NJ: Prentice-Hall Inc., 1983); and Alfred Sloan, *My Years with General Motors* (New York, NY: Doubleday, 1969). For descriptions of Sloan's work, see Alfred Chandler, *Strategy and Structure* (Cambridge, MA: MIT Press, 1962). For a description of Riboud's work, see Ken Auletta, *The Art of Corporate Success* (New York, NY: Putnam, 1984).

3 For excellent discussions of the symbolic role of the chief executive, see Jeffrey Pfeffer and Gerald Salancik, *The External Control of Organizations* (New York, NY: Harper & Row, 1976), and Murray Edelman, *The Symbolic Uses of Politics* (Urbana, IL: University of Illinois Press, 1964).

4 For a more detailed description of this period, see *Continental Airlines* (A), Harvard Business School case 9-385-006.

5 Gordon Donaldson and Jay Lorsch, *Decision Making at the Top* (New York, NY: Basic Books, 1983).

6 Interview with Clark Onstad, April 10, 1984.

7 For a more detailed description of EG&G and an analysis of O'Keefe's career there, see Martha Weinberg, "The Private Sector Political Entrepreneur: Bernard O'Keefe at EG&G," in Jameson Doig and Erwin Hargrove, eds., *Leadership and Innovation* (Baltimore, MD: Hopkins University Press, 1987).

8 *Forbes,* January 3, 1983.

9 Weinberg, op. cit., p. 351.

10 Bernard O'Keefe, *Nuclear Hostages* (Boston, MA: Houghton Mifflin, 1983).

11 Weinberg, op. cit., p. 361.

12 Ibid., p. 357.

13 Ibid., p. 362.

14 In 1969, during a period of very rapid growth, EG&G experienced a cost overrun on one of its major contracts and the profitability of the company deteriorated badly.

15 Interview with William Pounds, June 18, 1984.

16 Thomas Wise, "IBM's $5 Billion Gamble: The Rocky Road to the Marketplace," *Fortune,* September 1966.

17 Ken Auletta, op. cit., p. 123.

18 *Pennsylvania Power and Light Company,* Harvard Business School case #9-384-082.

19 Ibid.

20 Interview with William Sneath, CEO, Union Carbide Corporation, 1972.

21 Wise, op. cit.

22 Pennsylvania Power and Light, op. cit.

23 Interview with Michael Sachar, joint managing director, Marks and Spencer, 1975.

24 Interview with Dr. Mario Schinberni, April 25, 1984.

25 Reginald Jones, as quoted in Harry Levinson and Stuart Rosenthal, *CEO: Corporate Leadership in Action* (New York, NY: Basic Books, 1984), p. 49.

Gender and Leadership Style: A Meta-Analysis

Alice H. Eagly
Blair T. Johnson

In recent years many social scientists, management consultants, and other writers have addressed the topic of gender and leadership style. Some authors with extensive experience in organizations who write nontechnical books for management audiences and the general public have argued for the presence of sex differences in leadership style. For example, Loden (1985) maintained that there is a masculine mode of management characterized by qualities such as competitiveness, hierarchical authority, high control for the leader, and unemotional and analytic problem solving. Loden argued that women prefer and tend to behave in terms of an alternative feminine leadership model characterized by cooperativeness, collaboration of managers and subordinates, lower control for the leader, and problem solving based on intuition and empathy as well as rationality. Loden's writing echoes the androgynous manager theme developed earlier by Sargent (1981), who accepted the idea that women and men, including those who are managers in organizations, behave stereotypically to some extent. Sargent advocated that managers of each sex adopt "the best" of the other sex's qualities to become more effective, androgynous managers. In a somewhat different rendition of this sex-difference theme, Hennig and Jardin (1977) also acknowledged sex-differentiated managerial behavior, which they ascribed to personality traits acquired in early socialization, particularly through differing male and female resolutions of the Oedipus complex.

In contrast to these generalizations about gender-stereotypic leadership styles promulgated in books written primarily for practicing managers and the general public, social scientists have generally maintained that there are in fact no reliable differences in the ways that women and men lead. Although a few social scientists have acknowledged that there is some evidence for sex differences in leadership style among research participants who have not been selected for occupancy of leadership roles in natural settings (e.g., Brown, 1979; Hollander, 1985), most have agreed that women and men who occupy leadership roles in organizations do not differ (but see Shakeshaft, 1987, for a contrasting opinion). Illustrating this consensus among social scientists are the following representative statements summarizing research comparing the styles of female and male leaders: "The preponderance of available evidence is that no consistently clear pattern of differences can be discerned in the supervisory style of female as compared to male leaders" (Bass, 1981, p. 499); "Contrary to notions about sex specialization in leadership styles, women leaders appear to behave in similar fashion to their male colleagues" (Nieva & Gutek, 1981, p. 91); "There is as yet no research evidence that makes a case for sex differences in either leadership aptitude or style" (Kanter, 1977a, p. 199); "In general, comparative research indicates that there

From *Psychological Bulletin,* 1990, 108 (2), 251–273. Copyright © 1985, The American Psychological Association. Adapted by permission.

are few differences in the leadership styles of female and male designated leaders" (Bartol & Martin, 1986, p. 278).

Underlying this divergence in the opinions voiced in popular and social scientific writings is the fact that authors in these two camps have based their conclusions on quite different kinds of data. Authors such as Loden (1985) who have written books for managers and the general public based their conclusions primarily on their own experience in organizations as well as on the impressions they gleaned from interviews with practicing managers. Social scientists typically based their conclusions on more formal studies of managerial behavior in which data were gathered via questionnaires or behavioral observations and then analyzed quantitatively. In view of these contrasting methods, it is tempting for social scientists to dismiss the generalizations that are based on personal experience and interviews, and to accept as valid only those conclusions that stem from more formal empirical research on leadership. However, the generalizations that social scientists appear to have accepted in this area, which stem from reviews of empirical research (e.g., Bartol & Martin, 1986), are quite vulnerable to error because of the relatively informal methods by which reviewers have drawn conclusions from the available research. With only one exception, these reviews were traditional, narrative reviews and, therefore, were not based on any clear rules about how one derives conclusions from research findings. Moreover, none of the existing reviews was based on more than a small proportion of the available studies. For example, both Bartol and Martin (1986) and Dobbins and Platz (1986) based their generalizations on eight studies that compared the leadership styles of men and women, yet we located 162 studies pertaining only to the four types of leadership style we included in our meta-analysis (see *Method*). Moreover, prior reviewers did not state the criteria by which they selected their small samples of studies. As we became aware of these selection problems and of the severe underuse of available research on gender and leadership style, we decided that a thorough survey of this domain was long overdue. Our meta-analysis thus provides a systematic, quantitative integration of the available research in which the leadership styles of men and women were compared and statistical analyses were performed on the resulting data.

Theoretical Analysis of Sex Differences in Leadership Style

Leaving aside the claims of both the social scientists and the management experts who have written about gender and leadership style, we face a topic of considerable complexity that we analyze from several perspectives. One of our perspectives takes into account existing knowledge about sex differences in social behaviors such as aggression, helping, and conformity as well as numerous nonverbal and communicative behaviors. Large numbers of laboratory and field studies have been performed on such behaviors, primarily by social psychologists, and in many of these studies female and male behavior has been compared. Quantitative reviews of this research have established the presence rather than the absence of overall sex differences (see overviews by Eagly, 1987; Eagly & Wood, in press; Hall, 1984). These differences, although typically not large, tend to be comparable in magnitude to most other findings reported in social psychological research. On the average, sex appears to be a variable that has neither especially impactful nor especially weak effects on social behavior and that produces findings consistent with laypeople's ideas about how the sexes differ (see Eagly, 1987).

Reasons to Expect the Absence of Sex Differences in Leadership Style   Despite the gender-stereotypic findings generally produced in studies of social behavior, similar results would not necessarily be obtained for leaders and managers because of important differences between leadership research and typical research in social psychology. In particular, the majority of leadership studies have been performed in organizations. In contrast, most social psychological research has been carried out in experimental laboratories and to a lesser extent in field settings not embedded within organizations (e.g., on street corners). In such environments, subjects interact with strangers on a short-term basis, and the constraints of organizational and familial roles are generally minimal or absent. Consequently, there is often considerable ambiguity about how one should behave, and people may react in terms of quite global and readily observable attributes of themselves and others (e.g., sex, age, race, and general physical appearance). In situations of this type, gender roles, which are rules about how one should behave as a male or female, may provide more guidance than they otherwise would and thus produce gender-stereotypic behavior.

Behavior may be less stereotypic when women and men who occupy the same managerial role are compared because these organizational leadership roles, which typically are paid jobs, usually provide fairly clear guidelines about the conduct of behavior. Managers become socialized into their roles in the early stages of their experience in an organization (see Feldman, 1976; Graen, 1976; Terborg, 1977; Wanous, 1977). In addition, male and female managers have presumably been selected by organizations (and have selected themselves into these roles) according to the same set of organizationally relevant criteria, further decreasing the likelihood that the men and women who occupy these roles differ substantially in their style. Thus, reasonable assumptions about socialization into leadership roles and selection for these roles suggest that male and female leaders *who occupy the same organizational role* should differ very little. Managers of both sexes are presumably more concerned about managing effectively than about representing sex-differentiated features of societal gender roles.

This argument that organizational roles should override gender roles is consistent with Kanter's (1977a) structural interpretation of organizational behavior. Kanter argued that apparent sex differences in the behavior of organizational leaders are in fact a product of the differing structural positions of the sexes within organizations. Because women are more often in positions of little power or opportunity for advancement, they behave in ways that reflect their lack of power. Kanters' reasoning thus suggests that women and men who are equivalent in terms of status and power would behave similarly, even though sex differences may appear to be substantial when women and men are compared without control of their organizational status.

Reasons to Expect the Presence of Sex Differences in Leadership Style   Despite these reasons for arguing that differences between female and male organizational leaders should be minimal, other perspectives suggest that sex differences may be common, especially in some types of leadership research. As our reasoning has already implied, the social structural rationale for the absence of differences between occupants of the same managerial role within organizations is fully consistent with the presence of differences in leadership studies that compare women and men in other circumstances. In the leadership literature, there are two major types of studies that did not examine organizational leaders—namely, laboratory experiments, usually conducted with college students, and assessment studies, which we defined as research assessing the styles of people who were not selected for occupancy of leadership positions. Because the social structural rationale for the absence of differences between women and men in the same organizational role is not relevant to studies of these two types, sex-differentiated leadership styles are likely to be prevalent in such research, just as gender-stereotypic behavior is commonly found in social psychological research more generally.

There are, in addition, several reasons to suggest that male and female organizational leaders, even those who occupy the same positions, may differ to some extent in their leadership style despite the structural forces for minimizing differences that we have already noted. One such reason acknowledges the possibility of ingrained sex differences in personality traits and behavioral tendencies, differences that are not nullified by organizational selection or socialization. For example, some psychologists have maintained that sex differences in adult social behavior are in part a product of biological influences such as the greater prenatal androgynization of males (e.g., Money & Ehrhardt, 1972). Other psychologists have emphasized the importance of childhood events that are different for the sexes such as experiences that occur in sex-segregated play groups in which girls and boys play in different styles and use different methods of influencing one another (Maccoby, 1988). Thus, it is possible that biological sex differences and sex-differentiated prior experiences cause men and women to be somewhat different kinds of people, even if they do occupy the same managerial role. It may not be possible to find men and women who are so nearly equivalent that trait-level differences disappear entirely, even though sex differences in the behavior of organizational leaders may be smaller than those in the general population. In particular, men and women may come to managerial roles with a somewhat different set of skills. Especially relevant is the evidence meta-analyses have provided for women's social skills: Women as a group, when compared with men as a group, can be described as friendly, pleasant, interested in other people expressive, and socially sensitive (see Eagly, 1987; Hall, 1984). To the extent that such findings reflect ingrained sex differences that are not leveled by organizational selection or socialization, male and female managers may behave differently, despite structural forces toward sameness.

Another perspective suggesting that leader behavior may be somewhat sex differentiated in organizations postulates *gender-role spillover,* which is "a carryover into the workplace of gender-based expectations for behavior" (Gutek & Morasch, 1982, p. 58; see also Nieva & Gutek, 1981). The spillover concept suggests that gender roles may contaminate organizational roles to some extent and cause people to have different expectations for female and male managers. In support of this idea, Russell, Ruth, and Herd (1988) found that university women described an effective female (vs. male) leader as exhibiting higher levels of both the interpersonally oriented and the task-oriented aspects of leadership (i.e., higher in consideration and initiation of structure; see discussion of these variables in next subsection).

Consistent with the idea that gender roles spill over to organizational roles, several social scientists have claimed that female leaders and managers experience conflict between their gender role and their leadership role (see Bass, 1981; Bayes & Newton, 1978; Kruse & Wintermantel, 1986; O'Leary, 1974). This conflict arises for female leaders because the stereotype of manager and the normative expectations associated with being a good manager include more masculine than feminine qualities (see Powell, 1988). The idea that women are subjected to incompatible expectations from the managerial and the female role thus presumes that gender roles are important within organizations.

Another manifestation of the spillover of gender roles onto organizational roles is that people who hold positions in organizations tend to have negative attitudes about women occupying managerial roles. Reflecting the subordinate status of women in the society, numerous studies have shown that people are often reluctant to have a female supervisor and think that women are somewhat less qualified for leadership and that female managers would have negative effects on morale (see reviews by O'Leary, 1974; Riger & Galligan, 1980; Terborg, 1977). Because these attitudes and beliefs raise questions about women's competence, ability to lead, and potential for advancement, female managers often face a less supportive environment than male managers. Sex differences in leadership style might result from this aspect of gender-role spillover as well as from the other aspects we have noted.

Finally, some of the fine-grained features of the structural interpretation of organizational behavior suggest other possible sources of sex differences in the behavior of organizational leaders. One such consideration is that, as Kanter (1977b) pointed out, women in managerial roles often have the status of *token* because of their rarity in such positions. Thus, female managers commonly are members of a numerically small minority, whereas their male counterparts are members of a majority group. As Kanter and others argued, token status increases one's visibility (Taylor, Fiske, Etcoff, & Ruderman, 1978) and can have a number of negative implications for how one is perceived and treated, especially when the token is a woman (Crocker & McGraw, 1984; Ott, 1989; Yoder & Sinnett, 1985). In addition, even those female and male leaders who occupy the same organizational role may differ systematically in seniority, salary, the availability of mentoring and informal collegial support, and other characteristics that convey some of the subtleties of organizational status. Women, especially as relative newcomers in many managerial roles, tend to have less status in these ways, and this difference may be reflected in their behavior.

In summary, ingrained sex differences in traits and behavioral tendencies, a spillover of gender roles onto organizational roles, and subtle differences in the structural position of women and men could cause leadership behavior to be somewhat sex-differentiated even when occupants of the same organizational role are compared. Therefore, some evidence of sex differences in leadership style in organizational studies would not be surprising. Nonetheless, our reasoning that organizational roles are more important than gender roles led us to predict that differences between men and women occupying the same leadership role in organizations would be smaller than differences between men and women observed in other types of leadership research, namely laboratory experiments and assessment studies.

Design of the Meta-Analysis

Types of Leadership Style   The fact that investigators have examined many facets of leadership style (see Bass, 1981) requires that reviewers decide which facets to include and how to organize them into types. In examining this issue, we found that the majority of the studies had assessed the extent to which leaders or managers were concerned with two aspects of their work. The first of these aspects we termed *task accomplishment* (or, for brevity, task style)—that is, organizing activities to perform assigned tasks. The second aspect we termed *maintenance of interpersonal relationships* (or, for brevity, interpersonal style)—that is, tending to the morale and welfare of the people in the setting.

This distinction between task and interpersonal styles was first represented in leadership research by Bales (1950), who proposed two categories of leaders, those with an orientation to task accomplishment and those with a socioemotional orientation indicative of concern for morale and relationships among group members. This distinction was developed further in the Ohio State studies on leadership (e.g., Halpin, 1957; Halpin & Winer, 1957; Hemphill & Coons, 1957; Stogdill, 1963). In this research, task orientation, labeled *initiation of structure,* included behavior such as having subordinates follow rules and procedures, maintaining high standards for performance, and making leader and subordinate roles explicit. Interpersonal orientation, labeled *consideration,* included behavior such as helping and doing favors for subordinates, looking out for their welfare, explaining procedures, and being friendly and available. Task and interpersonal orientations are typically regarded as separate, relatively orthogonal dimensions (e.g., in the Leader Behavior Description Questionnaire [LBDQ] constructed by the Ohio State researchers; Halpin & Winer, 1957). Less commonly, these orientations are treated as two ends of a single continuum (e.g., in the Least Preferred Co-Worker [LPC] instrument; Fiedler, 1967).

Task and interpersonal styles in leadership research are obviously relevant to gender because of the stereotypes people have about sex differences in these aspects of behavior (see Ashmore, Del Boca, & Wohlers, 1986; Eagly & Steffen, 1984). Men are believed to be more self-assertive and motivated to master their environment (e.g., more aggressive, independent, self-sufficient, forceful, dominant). In contrast, women are believed to be more selfless and concerned with others (e.g., more kind, helpful, understanding, warm, sympathetic, aware of others' feelings). In research on gender, these two orientations have been labeled *masculine* and *feminine, instrumental* and *expressive,* and *agentic* and *communal.* Although the task and interpersonal dimensions studied in leadership research are not as broad as these very general tendencies examined in gender stereotype research, the ideas are quite similar. Therefore, leadership research provides an excellent opportunity to determine whether the behavior of leaders is gender stereotypic.

The only other aspect of leadership style studied frequently enough to allow us to represent it in our meta-analysis is the extent to which leaders (a) behave democratically and allow subordinates to participate in decision making, or (b) behave autocratically and discourage subordinates from participating in decision making. The dimension of *democratic* versus *autocratic* leadership (or participative vs. *directive* leadership) follows from early experimental studies of leadership style (e.g., Lewin & Lippitt, 1938) and has been developed since that time by a number of researchers (e.g., Likert, 1961; Vroom & Yetton, 1973). Although democratic versus autocratic style is a different (and narrower) aspect of leader behavior than task-oriented and interpersonally oriented styles (see Bass, 1981), the democratic–autocratic dimension also relates to gender stereotypes, because one component of the agentic or instrumental aspect of these stereotypes is that men are relatively dominant and controlling (i.e., more autocratic and directive than women).

Methods of Assessing Leadership Style   The diversity of the methods that have been used to assess style complicates the task of integrating research in this area. Moreover, a substantial methodological literature criticizes and compares these measures (see Bass, 1981). Because the methodological issues that have been raised remain largely unresolved by leadership researchers, we did not attempt to settle these issues in order to base our meta-analytic generalizations on only those measures that we or other investigators might regard as most valid. Instead, we included all measures that researchers regarded as assessing task-oriented and interpersonally oriented styles or autocratic versus democratic style. We coded our studies on a number of these measures' features, many of which may be regarded as having implications for the quality of the measures. For example, measures differed in how directly or indirectly they assessed leadership style; the most direct measures were based on observers' coding of ongoing leadership behavior, and the most indirect measures were based on leaders' responses to questionnaire measures of attitudes or personality. Representing such features in our coding scheme (see *Method*) allowed us to determine whether they covaried with sex differences in leadership style.

Congeniality of Leadership Roles for Men and Women   When we thought about gender in relation to the available studies of leadership style, we were struck by the variation in the extent to which the leadership roles investigated in this research (e.g., elementary school principal, nursing supervisor, military officer) would be perceived as congenial mainly for women or men. For leadership roles that are typically regarded as especially suitable for women, negative attitudes toward female leaders presumably would not be prevalent, nor would conflict between the female and the leader role be an issue. Presumably women would be under less pressure to adopt male-stereotypic styles of leadership in such positions.

To enable us to take account of the gender congeniality of leadership roles, we conducted a questionnaire study to obtain judgments of each role, and analyzed these judgments to estimate the extent to which women or men were more interested in each role and believed themselves more competent to perform it. In addition, because people associate task-oriented qualities with men and interpersonally oriented qualities with women, we also determined the extent to which each role was judged to require each set of these gender-stereotypic qualities. These features of our meta-analysis allowed us to determine whether the ascription of gender-stereotypic qualities to leadership roles related to sex differences in the styles by which people carry out these roles.

Predictions for Meta-Analysis.   As we have already stated, our major prediction is that gender-stereotypic sex differences in leadership style are less pronounced in organizational studies comparing occupants of the same managerial role than in leadership studies of other types. Beyond this prediction, our purposes as reviewers are primarily descriptive and exploratory, even though other predictions might follow from the issues we have discussed. For example, if, as we suggested, female managers often face a less supportive environment than do male managers, these women might strive so hard to overcome antifemale prejudices that they behave counterstereotypically as a result. Additional complexities enter if we reason that ratings of leaders' behavior could produce findings that are more stereotypic than those produced by measures grounded more firmly in behavior. Rather than set forth a series of speculative hypotheses that take these and other considerations into account, we prefer to present our review and to discuss such issues as they become relevant to interpreting our meta-analytic findings.

METHOD

Sample of Studies

Computer-based information searches were conducted using the keywords *leadership style* as well as *leader* and *leadership* when paired with terms such as *gender, sex, sex differences,* and *women.* These keywords were searched in the following data bases: *Psychological Abstracts* (PsycINFO: 1967 to April, 1987), *Dissertation Abstracts International* (DISS: 1961 to May, 1987), Educational Resources Information Center (ERIC: 1966 to November, 1986), Social Science Citation Index (Social SciSearch: 1971 to October, 1986), *Sociological Abstracts* (1963 to October, 1986), and a worldwide business and management data base (ABI/INFORM: 1971 to February, 1987). We also searched through the reference lists of numerous review articles, chapters, and books as well as the reference lists of all located studies.

Criteria for including studies in the sample were that (a) the study included one or more measures that assessed task- and interpersonally oriented styles or autocratic versus democratic style; (b) subjects were adults or adolescents from the United States or Canada who were not sampled from abnormal populations; (c) the study assessed the leadership style of at least five people of each sex; and (d) the reported results were sufficient either to calculate a sex-of-subject effect size or to determine the statistical significance or direction of the sex difference. This last criterion eliminated studies that provided only a multiple regression equation in which sex appeared as one of the predictors (e.g., Gustafson, 1982) as well as studies that provided only a multivariate analysis of variance on leadership style combined with other measures (e.g., Martinez, 1982; Rice, Instone, & Adams, 1984).

Studies were omitted if the people whose leadership style was assessed had been selected to equalize their status on a personality or attitudinal variable (e.g., an index of masculinity or femininity) that probably correlates with both sex and leadership style (e.g., Sirianni-Brantley, 1985; Stake, 1981); accurate estimation of any sex difference in leadership style is not possible from such studies. In addition, studies were rejected if the leadership measure assessed only a narrow aspect of style such as methods of dealing with poorly performing subordinates or managing conflict (e.g., Dobbins, 1986; Dobbins, Pence, Orban, & Sgro, 1983; Koberg, 1985; Renwick, 1977). If leadership was assessed on several narrow indexes (e.g., Baugher, 1983; Lanning, 1982), these were combined, when appropriate, into a measure of one of the styles considered in this article (e.g., task orientation), based on our independent choices of the indexes that best matched the item content of the most popular measures of the broader style. The indexes were combined using Rosenthal and Rubin's (1986) suggested formula and assuming that the average interindex correlation was .25. This correlation was estimated by averaging the interitem correlations given (or derived from coefficient alphas) for multiple-item style measures used in the studies included in the meta-analysis. These combined measures aggregated five indexes whenever possible (and fewer otherwise). If the report was not sufficiently detailed to allow such combinations, the study was eliminated (e.g., Hughes, Copeland, Ford, & Heidt, 1983; Moore, Shaffer, Goodsell, & Baringoldz, 1983).

Studies were also eliminated if the only measures of leadership style assessed ideal rather than actual style (e.g., Arcy, 1980). Studies were omitted if they assessed, not people's naturally occurring styles, but the impact of treatments designed to instill a certain leadership style (e.g., Crudge, 1983; Hall, 1983; Heft & Deni, 1984). Finally, we excluded studies of T groups, encounter groups, and therapy groups (e.g., Hurst, Stein, Korchin, & Soskin, 1978), because their measures of leader behavior reflected a tradition quite different from that of the other leadership style research we located. Application of these criteria yielded 162 studies reported in 161 documents. . . .

RESULTS

Characteristics of Studies

Before considering the sex differences reported in studies of leadership style, we examined the characteristics of these studies. Table 1 shows 18 of these study characteristics aggregated over all of the 370 sex comparisons that we encountered as well as summarized separately within each of the types of leadership style.

As shown by the central tendencies of the characteristics listed in Table 1, studies typically (a) were published relatively recently; (b) were published as dissertations; (c) based the statistical analysis on a moderate number of observations; (d) aggregated a moderate number of observations into each data point; (e) compared the sexes in such a way that some confounding with other variables was likely; and (f) were carried out in organizations. In addition, these studies typically (a) assessed middle managers; (b) assessed adults in their thirties; (c) assessed people in male-dominated roles or from populations with male majorities; (d) assessed leaders with predominantly female subordinates; and (e) unsuccessfully attempted random sampling of the people whose style was assessed or randomly selected them. Finally, the measuring instruments typically (a) had people rate their own leadership styles or had subordinates rate their leaders; and (b) used ratings presumably based on observation of leaders' behavior but without control of the behaviors available for observation.

The means for the last five characteristics represent the variables constructed from questionnaire respondents' judgments of the leadership roles examined in the studies.

TABLE 1
SUMMARY OF STUDY CHARACTERISTICS

Variable and class	All comparisons ($n = 370$)	Interpersonal style comparisons ($n = 153$)	Task style comparisons ($n = 154$)	Interpersonal vs. task style comparisons ($n = 35$)	Democratic vs. autocratic style comparisons ($n = 28$)
Median date of publication	1981	1981	1981	1981	1980
Publication form					
Journal article	91	34	35	6	16
Other published document	10	4	5	0	1
Dissertation	256	110	109	27	10
Unpublished document	13	5	5	2	1
Median no. of observations for analysis	88	88	81	105	84
Median no. of observations aggregated into each data point	12	12	12	16	15
Confounding of male–female comparison					
Controlled via matching	42	20	20	2	0
Known	92	38	38	9	7
Unknown and likely	175	79	77	12	7
Unknown and unlikely	61	16	19	12	14
Type of study					
Organizational	289	131	128	17	13
Assessment	56	15	15	16	10
Laboratory	25	7	11	2	5
Level of leadership					
First or line	58	23	27	4	4
Second or middle	184	84	83	7	10
Third or higher	11	3	3	4	1
Ambiguous, mixed, or unkown	61	28	26	4	3
People not selected for leadership	56	15	15	16	10
Mean age of people whose style was assessed (years)	37.85	39.26	38.39	32.80	31.24
Median percentage of men among people whose style was assessed	73.00	73.00	73.00	61.60	61.84

Median percentage of men among subordinates	16.32	16.17	16.25	25.49	18.66
Basis of selection for people whose style was assessed					
Random sample	103	42	42	11	8
Unsuccessful random sample	131	59	57	10	5
Self-selected	58	21	23	6	8
Unknown	78	31	32	8	7
Identity of rates for style measure					
People rated selves	197	73	72	34	18
Supervisors rated leaders	15	8	7	0	0
Subordinates rated leaders	120	57	58	1	4
Peers rated leaders	4	1	1	0	2
Judges rated leaders	22	8	11	0	3
Mixed or unclear	12	6	5	0	1
Type of rating for style measure					
Responses to attitude or personality scale	67	17	17	31	2
Responses to hypothetical leadership situations	62	27	26	2	7
Presumed observation of leader's behavior	205	97	95	1	12
Actual observation of leader's behavior	36	12	16	1	7
Mean respondent judgments of rules					
Competence sex difference[a]	−0.11*	−0.12*	−0.11*	−0.06	−0.10
Interest sex difference	−0.09*	−0.09*	−0.09*	−0.02	−0.05
Stereotypic interest difference	−0.10*	−0.11*	−0.10*	−0.02	−0.06
Interpersonal ability rating[b]	11.04	11.05	11.06	10.94	10.91
Task ability rating	10.88	10.91	10.90	10.83	10.54

Note: For categorical variables, numbers in table represent frequency of sex comparisons in each class. Summaries of continuous variables are based on reports for which information was available on each variable.

[a]For the first three variables constructed from judgments of the leadership roles, values are positive for differences in the masculine direction (greater male estimates of competence and of interest; ascription of greater interest to average men).

[b]For the last two variables constructed from judgments of the leadership roles, values are larger to the extent that a role was judged to require more interpersonal or task ability (on 15-point scales with 15 indicating high ability).

*Differs significantly (p < .05 or smaller) from 0.00 (exactly no difference).

As shown by these means, women judged themselves as significantly more competent in these leadership roles and as more interested in occupying the roles than men did. In addition, respondents of both sexes judged the average woman more interested in occupying the roles than the average man. They also judged that the roles required "quite a lot" of both interpersonal and task ability.

When these study characteristics were examined separately within the types of leadership style (see Table 1), notable exceptions to these overall patterns were that (a) journal articles were especially common in studies of autocratic versus democratic style, (b) measures of interpersonal versus task style and democratic versus autocratic style were based more exclusively on self-ratings, and (c) measures of interpersonal versus task style were based primarily on responses to attitude scales.

Table 2 lists the measuring instruments that assessed leadership style and names all measures that were used for two or more of the sex comparisons. As Table 2 shows, the majority of the studies used standard instruments; the Leader Behavior Description Questionnaire, which places task and interpersonal orientations on separate dimensions, received the most use. The Least Preferred Co-Worker instrument predominated among studies placing interpersonal and task orientation on two ends of a single dimension. In contrast, unique measures predominated in studies of democratic versus autocratic style

Table 3 describes the settings of the organizational studies and the subject populations of the assessment and laboratory studies. Among the organizational studies, educational settings predominated; the greatest number of these studies examined elementary school principals or university administrators. College undergraduates predominated in both the assessment and the laboratory studies.

Overall Sex Differences in Leadership Style

The summary given in Table 4 allows one to determine if men and women differed in leadership style. An overall sex difference is shown by a mean effect size that differed significantly from the 0.00 value that indicates exactly no difference (i.e., by a confidence interval that did not include 0.00). The sign of these means is positive for stereotypic differences and negative for counterstereotypic differences. These means and confidence intervals are given both aggregated over all types of style and computed separately for each style.

In general, leadership styles were slightly gender stereotypic: The weighted mean computed across all types of style was slightly but significantly stereotypic (see Table 4). However, computed within each type, these means indicated *no sex difference* for (a) the task comparisons and (b) the interpersonal versus task comparisons. These means indicated *stereotypic differences* for (a) the interpersonal comparisons (women were more interpersonally oriented) and (b) the democratic versus autocratic comparisons (women were more democratic). Yet the mean effect size for interpersonal style was quite small. The largest overall sex difference was obtained for the democratic versus autocratic comparisons: Sex comparisons for this type of style were significantly more stereotypic than those for each of the other three types of style (as shown by appropriate contrasts; see description of contrast procedure in next subsection). This pattern was similar for the unweighted means, although the task style difference became significant in the counterstereotypic direction (i.e., women were more task oriented). The medians of the effect sizes were similar to the weighted and unweighted means.

As shown by the homogeneity statistics given in Table 4, the sex comparisons were not homogeneous (i.e., consistent) across the studies. As also indicated in Table 4, the removal of various numbers of outliers allowed homogeneity to be attained. Suggesting relatively stable findings, the procedure eliminated small proportions of effect sizes for all of the types of style except the democratic versus autocratic style, which required eliminating 22% to attain homogeneity. The confidence intervals associated with the weighted means after outlier removal showed that the overall tendencies for women to be more interpersonally oriented, more task oriented, and more democratic than men were all significant.

There is no completely satisfactory method to compute a mean effect size that takes into account the nonsignificant comparisons that could not be represented as effect sizes because of a lack of sufficient information. Nevertheless, one possible solution is to give these comparisons the value of 0.00 (indicating exactly no sex difference). When this step was taken, the mean unweighted effect sizes (see means reported in Table 4 under "All reports") became slightly smaller than the unweighted means (before outlier removal) that omitted these 0.00 values, but the pattern was the same (i.e., women were more interpersonally oriented, more task oriented, and more democratic).

Table 4 also reports the proportion of sex comparisons that were stereotypic in direction. These proportions differed significantly from .50, the proportion expected under the null hypothesis, for the interpersonal, task, and democratic versus autocratic comparisons ($ps < .01$ or smaller). Consistent with the pattern we have already described, these differences were counterstereotypic for the task style and interpersonal and the democratic versus autocratic styles.

Accounting for Variability in the Effect Sizes

Categorical and continuous models were fitted to the effect sizes following Hedges and Olkin's (1985) statistical procedures (see *Method*).

Test of Our Major Hypothesis   To test our hypothesis that sex differences in leadership style are less stereotypic in organizational settings than in other settings, we classified the effect sizes into the three types of studies: organizational, assessment, and laboratory. Consistent with the significant between-classes effects for type of study shown in Table 5, the expected pattern was obtained for interpersonal style and task style. For interpersonal style, a priori comparisons among the mean weighted effect sizes for the three classes of studies (see Hedges & Becker, 1986; Hedges & Olkin, 1985) showed that the sex difference for the organizational studies was significantly less stereotypic than that for the assessment studies ($p < .01$) or the laboratory studies ($p < .001$). For task style, these comparisons also showed that the sex difference for the organizational studies was significantly less stereotypic than that for the assessment studies ($p < .05$) or the laboratory studies ($p < .025$). For measures of interpersonal versus task styles as well as democratic versus autocratic style, type of

TABLE 2
SUMMARY OF LEADERSHIP STYLE MEASURES USED IN STUDIES

Measure	Reference[a]	All comparisons (n = 370)	Interpersonal style comparisons (n = 153)	Task style comparisons (n = 154)	Interpersonal vs. task style comparisons (n = 35)	Democratic vs. autocratic style comparisons (n = 28)
Leader Behavior Description Questionnaire (Form XII)[b]	Stogdill (1963), Stogdill, Goode, & Day (1962)	93	47	46	—	—
Leader Behavior Description Questionnaire (early form)	Halpin (1957), Halpin & Winer (1957), Hemphill & Coons (1957)	42	21	21	—	—
Leadership Effectiveness and Adaptability Description	Hersey & Blanchard (1977, 1982)	46	23	23	—	—
Leadership Opinion Questionnaire	Fleishman (1953, 1957, 1960)	28	14	14	—	—
Organizational Climate Description Questionnaire[c]	Halpin (1960)	12	6	6	—	—
Interaction Process Analysis and variants	Bales (1950)	9	4	5	—	—
Supervisory Behavior Description Questionnaire	Fleishman (1970)	6	3	3	—	—
Styles of Management Inventory	Blake & Mouton (1964, 1978)	6	3	3	—	—
Educational Administrative Style Diagnosis Test	Reddin & Reddin (1979)	4	2	2	—	—
Organization Climate Survey	Coleman (1979)	4	2	2	—	—
Measures of McGregor's Theory X, Theory Y	Barone (1982), Jacoby & Terborg (1975), Marnani (1982), Myers (1970), Tanner (1982)[d]	8	3	3	2	—

Least Preferred Co-Worker	Fiedler (1967)	29	—	—	29	—
Vroom and Yetton Problem Set	Vroom & Yetton (1973)	6	—	—	—	6
Principal Behavior Checklist	Alpren (1954), Grobman & Hines (1956), Van Aken (1954)	4	—	—	—	4
Sargent and Miller Leadership Questionnaire	Sargent & Miller (1971)	2	—	—	—	2
Unique measure or measure constructed by authors from components given in document		71	25	26	4	16

[a]References listed provide information regarding the development of each measure of style.
[b]Used consideration and initiation of structure scales.
[c]Used consideration and production emphasis scales.
[d]Scales developed by authors listed to assess McGregor's (1960) Theory X and Theory Y concepts.

TABLE 3
SUMMARY OF SETTING OR SUBJECT POPULATION FOR ORGANIZATIONAL, ASSESSMENT, AND LABORATORY STUDIES

Type of study/setting or subject population	All comparisons ($n = 370$)	Interpersonal style comparisons ($n = 153$)	Task style comparisons ($n = 154$)	Interpersonal vs. task style comparisons ($n = 35$)	Democratic vs. autocratic style comparisons ($n = 28$)
Organizational studies					
Educational	210	94	93	11	12
Elementary school	93	41	41	5	6
Middle or junior high school	4	2	2	0	0
High school	13	6	6	1	0
University or college	47	22	21	2	2
Student organizations	6	2	2	0	2
Athletic teams	3	1	1	1	0
Other, mixed, or unknown	44	20	20	2	2
Business	26	11	11	3	1
Governmental	19	9	8	2	0
Miscellaneous[a]	34	17	16	1	0
Assessment studies					
College undergraduates	29	6	6	10	7
Business graduate students	2	0	0	1	1
Other graduate students	4	2	2	0	0
Other or mixed subjects[b]	21	7	7	5	2
Laboratory studies					
College undergraduates	21	6	10	2	3
Other or mixed subjects[c]	4	1	1	0	2

[a]Includes military, religious, hospital, and other settings.
[b]Includes candidates for managerial positions, participants in management training programs, and nonmanagerial employees of business firms.
[c]Includes graduate students and mixed samples of undergraduate and graduate students.

TABLE 4
SUMMARY OF SEX DIFFERENCES IN LEADERSHIP STYLE

Criterion	All comparisons	Interpersonal style comparisons	Task style comparisons	Interpersonal vs. task style comparisons	Democratic vs. autocratic style comparisons
Known effect sizes					
Sample size (n)	329	136	139	31	23
Mean weighted d (d_+)[a]	0.03	0.04	0.00	−0.03	0.22
95% CI for d_+	0.01/0.05	0.01/0.07	−0.03/0.03	−0.10/0.03	0.15/0.29
Homogeneity (Q) of ds comprising d_+[b]	1234.44*	373.87*	501.46*	70.40*	252.63*
Mean unweighted d	0.02	0.08	−0.10	−0.03	0.42
95% CI for mean unweighted d	−0.03/0.07	0.01/0.14	−0.17/−0.02	−0.17/0.10	0.17/0.66
Median d	0.02	0.07	−0.07	0.00	0.25
Known effect sizes excluding outliers					
Sample size (n)	275	118	125	27	18
n removed outliers	54(16%)	18(13%)	14(10%)	4(13%)	5(22%)
Mean weighted d (d_+)	0.02	0.13	−0.06	0.02	0.27
95% CI for d_+	−0.00/0.05	0.10/0.17	−0.10/−0.03	−0.06/0.09	0.19/0.35
Homogeneity (Q) of ds comprising d_+	311.19	140.12	142.76	32.97	27.40
All reports					
Sample size (n)	370	153	154	35	28
Mean weighted d	0.02	0.07	−0.09	−0.03	0.34
95% CI for mean unweighted d	−0.03/0.06	0.01/0.13	−0.16/−0.02	−0.15/0.09	0.13/0.55
Stereotypic differences[c]	175/341 (.51)	87/141 (.62)	52/144 (.36)	14/32 (.44)	22/24 (.92)

Note: When all reports were included, a value of 0.00 (exactly no difference) was assigned to sex differences that could not be calculated and were reported as nonsignificant. Effect sizes were calculated for all significant differences. Effect sizes are positive for differences that are stereotypic and negative for differences that are counterstereotypic. CI = confidence interval; d = effect size; d_+ = mean weighted effect size; Q = homogeneity of effect sizes.

[a]Effect sizes were weighted by the reciprocal of the variance.

[b]Significance indicates rejection of the hypothesis of homogeneity.

[c]Frequencies are number of differences in the stereotypic direction divided by the number of differences of known direction. The proportion appears in parentheses.

*p < .001.

331

TABLE 5
CATEGORICAL MODELS FOR PREDICTING SEX DIFFERENCES IN LEADERSHIP STYLE FROM TYPE OF STUDY AND TYPE OF STYLE

Type of study	All effect sizes			Interpersonal style effect sizes			Task style effect sizes			Interpersonal vs. task style effect sizes			Democratic vs. autocratic style effect sizes			Between types of style effect
	n	d_{i+}	Q_{wi}^a	n	d_{i+}	Q_{wi}	n	d_{i+}	Q_{wi}	n	d_{i+}	Q_{wi}	n	d_{i+}	Q_{wi}	Q_B
Organizational	269	−0.00	1009.37***	120	−0.01	284.54***	120	−0.02	439.90***	16	−0.03	38.73***	13	0.21†	224.58***	21.62***
Assessment	43	0.12†	138.77***	12	0.25†	28.64**	12	0.08	31.48***	13	−0.04	28.08***	6	0.29†	18.51**	32.06****
Laboratory	17	0.22†	50.43***	4	0.37†	16.34**	7	0.19	20.96**	2	0.12	3.27	4	0.20†	8.52*	1.34
Q_a (Between types of study effect)		35.87***			44.35***			9.12**			0.32			1.03		

Note: Effect sizes are positive for differences that are stereotypic and negative for differences that are counterstereotypic; d_{i+} = weighted means of effect sizes for the *ith* class; Q_{wi} = homogeneity of effect sizes within the *ith* class; Q_B = between-classes goodness-of-fit statistic.
[a]Significance indicates rejection of the hypothesis of homogeneity.
*$p < .05$. **$p < .01$. ***$p < .001$.
†Differs significantly ($p < .05$ or smaller) from 0.00 (exactly no difference).

study had no significant effect. The significant effect that type of study produced when all the effect sizes were analyzed thus reflects primarily the trends observed for the interpersonal and task styles.

Table 5 also reports categorical models that were based on classifying the effect sizes into the four types of style and were computed within each type of study (i.e., organizational, assessment, laboratory). The significant between-styles effect for the organizational studies primarily reflects the relatively large mean for the democratic versus autocratic style, and the significant effect for the assessment studies primarily reflects the relatively large means for the interpersonal and the democratic versus autocratic styles. The nonsignificance of the between-styles effect for the laboratory studies suggest that leadership styles were stereotypic in laboratory studies regardless of the type of style assessed. Although the number of laboratory studies on leadership style is unfortunately quite small, the relative consistency of this stereotypic trend across the types of style lends confidence to our generalization that leaders' behavior is somewhat gender stereotypic in experimental settings.

Models Involving Characteristics of Research Report   The sex of the authors of the research reports also related to the effect sizes; female authors obtained more stereotypic findings on the whole ($p < .001$ for categorical model). Yet when the effect sizes were examined within the four types of styles, this overall trend was intact only for the interpersonal and the democratic versus autocratic styles ($ps < .001$) for categorical models). To the extent that women especially value interpersonally oriented and democratic styles, this finding suggests a tendency for authors to portray their own sex favorably. Eagly and Carli (1981) and Wood (1987) reported this tendency in earlier meta-analyses.

As shown by one of the models given in Table 6, date of publication related significantly to all of the sets of effect sizes. On an overall basis, sex differences were more stereotypic in the more recent studies, and this trend was also obtained for the interpersonal and the task styles, which predominated among our effect sizes. However, sex differences became less stereotypic over time in our two smaller samples of effect sizes, namely interpersonal versus task style and democratic versus autocratic style. This lack of consistency over the four types of style and the confounding of publication date with various study attributes clouds interpretation of these secular trends.

Among the characteristics of the research reports that did not relate to the magnitude of the sex differences is whether the report was published (i.e., journal article or other published document) or unpublished (i.e., dissertation or other unpublished document). Although it is common in meta-analyses that effects are larger in published than unpublished studies (see Glass, McGaw, & Smith, 1981), this relation is often absent in meta-analyses of sex differences in social behavior, presumably because these reports are often incidental to studies' main hypotheses and therefore have little impact on publishability (see Eagly, 1987).

Models Involving Characteristics of Studies' Methods   Most aspects of the studies' methods that we coded either did not relate to the effect sizes or related relatively weakly. Furthermore, interpretation of those few relations that did prove significant was often hampered by skewed distributions of many of these features (see Table 1) as well as by (a) confounding between these features and (b) relatively small numbers of effect sizes for two of the styles (i.e., interpersonal vs. task and democratic vs. autocratic). Nonetheless, we note some of the many analyses we performed.

We were particularly interested, for example, in whether studies in which sex was known to be confounded with personal attributes such as age and job seniority (or was likely to have been so confounded) would produce more stereotypic sex comparisons. We did not obtain such tendencies. Nor did sex comparisons appear to be more stereotypic in self-selected samples or in samples for which random selection was seriously compromised. Furthermore, sex comparisons did not become less stereotypic when the rating underlying the style measure was more directly linked to behavior and therefore presumably less vulnerable to biases based on gender stereotypes. The impact of the specific measuring instrument used to assess style (see Table 2) was difficult to evaluate because of small sample sizes for most measures and the confounding of measures with characteristics of the instruments such as the identity of the raters.

The identity of the raters who provided the data for the style measure did have some impact on sex differences in both interpersonal and task orientation. Most of the measures of these two styles were based on self ratings or subordinate ratings (see Table 1), and self ratings were significantly more stereotypic than subordinate ratings for interpersonal style ($p < .01$) and task style ($p < .001$). For the two other types of style, skewed distributions of the raters' identity precluded meaningful analyses. In addition, sex of the raters showed no relation to the effect sizes.

As shown in one of the models given in Table 6, the level of aggregation of the style measure related significantly to the total set of effect sizes as well as to the effect sizes for the task, interpersonal versus task, and autocratic versus democratic styles. Specifically, as the number of judgments underlying each data point increased, women became relatively more task oriented than men and relatively more democratic. Thus, in the case of the task and the democratic versus autocratic styles, the overall tendencies for women to be more task oriented and more democratic than men (see Table 4) were more pronounced in studies using measures that can be presumed to be more reliable by virtue of their higher level of aggregation.

Models Involving Characteristics of Social Settings and Leadership Roles Organizational size had little effect on the sex differences, but information necessary to code this variable was often missing from the reports. The organizational level of leaders had little impact on the effect sizes except for task style: A tendency for men to be more task oriented than women obtained for first-level (i.e., line) managers reserved slightly for the midlevel managers ($p < .001$ for contrast). The basis by which leaders were selected in laboratory studies also related to the effect sizes: Leaders who were appointed on a random basis or on the basis of their own qualifications behaved more stereotypically than leaders who emerged on their own ($p < .025$ for categorical model).

The percentage of men among the people whose style was assessed related significantly to sex differences in both the interpersonal and the democratic versus autocratic styles (see Table 6). To the extent that men predominated, the tendencies weakened for women (vs. men) to show more concern about interpersonal relations and to be more democratic.

Two additional variables—the percentage of men among leaders' subordinates and the age of the people whose style was assessed—related significantly to the effect sizes for some of the styles within the organizational sample, which maintained moderate numbers of effect sizes for these analyses. Specifically, larger proportions of male subordinates were associated with male leaders being more task-oriented than female leaders ($p < .001$), but more interpersonally oriented on interpersonal versus task measures ($p < .05$) and less democratic ($p < .01$). Also within the organizational studies, age was a significant predictor of sex differences in task and interpersonal styles: Older leaders were more stereotypic in their interpersonal style but less stereotypic in their task style ($ps < .001$). However, interpretation of these relations involving age and the sex distribution of subordinates was limited by relatively large amounts of missing data as well as by confounding of these variables with types of studies (i.e., organizational, assessment, laboratory).

Models Involving Gender Congeniality of Leadership Roles As shown by the analyses using our gender congeniality measures as predictors (see Table 6), questionnaire respondents' judgments of the leadership roles related significantly to sex differences in task style. In general, leaders of each sex were especially task oriented when their role was viewed as congenial to their gender. Specifically, these effect sizes were larger (i.e., positive, indicating men were more task oriented than women) to the extent that (a) male (compared with female) respondents rated themselves as more competent in the role, (b) male respondents rated themselves as more interested in occupying the role, (c) respondents of both sexes judged the average man more interested in occupying the role than the average woman, and (d) respondents of both sexes judged that the role required relatively little interpersonal ability. Similarly, these effect sizes were smaller (i.e., negative, indicating women were more task oriented than men) to the extent that the roles were more congenial to women on these indexes. Because respondents' judgments of the leadership roles were significantly related only to sex differences in task style, the significant relations obtained when all the effect sizes were analyzed reflected primarily the task style findings.

DISCUSSION

Interpersonal and Task Styles

Our major hypothesis was that stereotypic sex differences would be less pronounced in organizational studies than in assessment or laboratory studies. Indeed, this hypothesis was confirmed for both interpersonal and task styles. These findings support our arguments that the criteria organizations use for selecting managers and the forces they maintain for socializing managers into their roles minimize tendencies for the sexes to lead or manage in a stereotypic manner. Yet these data also suggest that people not selected or trained for leadership roles do manifest stereotypic leadership behavior when placed in these roles, as shown by the data from the assessment and the laboratory studies. Moreover, our claim that selection criteria lessen sex differences is strengthened by the finding that those few laboratory leaders who gained their posi-

TABLE 6
CONTINUOUS MODELS FOR SEX DIFFERENCES IN LEADERSHIP STYLE

Predictor	All effect sizes		Interpersonal style effect sizes		Task style effect sizes		Interpersonal vs. task style effect sizes		Democratic vs. autocratic style effect sizes	
	b	b^*	b	b^*	b	b^*	b	b^*	b	b^*
Date of publication	0.01***	.14	0.01***	.19	0.03***	.37	-0.02*	-.25	-0.02**	-.20
n of observations aggregated into each data point	-0.00***[a]	-.13	-0.00	-.06	0.00***[b]	-.26	-0.03***	-.53	-0.02***	.42
Percentage of men among people whose style was assessed	-0.00***[c]	-.13	-0.00***[d]	-.21	-0.00	-.03	-0.00	-.12	-0.01***	-.32
Respondent judgments of roles										
Competence sex difference[e]	0.18***	.16	-0.01	-.01	0.46***	.40	-0.04	-.06	-0.02	-.01
Interest sex difference	0.22***	.15	0.09	.07	0.48***	.32	-0.13	-.11	-0.14	-.05
Stereotypic interest difference	0.11***	.16	0.01	.01	0.28***	.40	-0.09	-.17	0.01	.01
Interpersonal ability rating[f]	-0.05***	-.12	-0.01	-.02	-0.10***	-.20	-0.07	-.26	-0.04	-.07
Task ability rating	-0.01	-.02	0.01	.02	0.04	.08	-0.05	-.26	-0.05	-.08
Minimum n[g]	288		124		127		20		17	

Note: Models are weighted least squares simple linear regressions calculated with weights equal to the reciprocal of the variance for each effect size. Effect sizes are positive for differences that are stereotypic and negative for differences that are counterstereotypic. b = unstandardized regression coefficient. b^* = standardized regression coefficient.

[a] $b = -0.0092$, $SE(b) = .000016$.
[b] $b = -0.0017$, $SE(b) = .000029$.
[c] $b = -0.0028$, $SE(b) = .000052$.
[d] $b = -0.0040$, $SE(b) = .000099$.
[e] For the first three variables constructed from judgments of the leadership roles, values are positive for differences in the masculine direction (greater male estimates of competence and of interest; ascription of greater interest to average men).
[f] For the last two variables constructed from judgments of the leadership roles, values are larger to the extent that a role was judged to require more interpersonal or task ability.
[g] n varied across the analyses because of missing data (e.g., the absence of judgments of the leadership roles for the assessment studies).
* $p < .05$.
** $p < .01$.
*** $p < .001$.

tions through emergence did not manifest the stereotypic styles of laboratory leaders who were appointed. Evidently sex differences were leveled even by the implicit leader selection criteria of initially leaderless groups.

When we ignored whether the sex comparisons were from organizational, assessment, or laboratory studies (see Table 4), sex differences in interpersonal and task styles were quite small, with overall trends toward women being more concerned about both maintenance of interpersonal relationships and task accomplishment. In view of these trends, it is not surprising that measures placing interpersonal and task orientation on the ends of a single dimension produced no sex difference in any of the overall summaries. On such bipolar measures, the stereotypic interpersonal sex difference and the counterstereotypic task difference would cancel one another, resulting in no difference.

Given the variety of settings, roles, and measures encountered in this research, the sex comparisons for the task and interpersonal styles were expected to be inconsistent across the studies. Yet the removal of relatively small numbers of the effect sizes (10% to 13%) produced homogeneous sets of effect sizes consistent with description in terms of single means. This aspect of the findings lends some confidence to our statements that if we take the entire research literature into account, women's leadership styles emphasize both interpersonal relations and task accomplishment to a slightly greater extent than men's styles.

Democratic versus Autocratic Style

The strongest evidence we obtained for a sex difference in leadership style occurred on the tendency for women to adopt a more democratic or participative style and for men to adopt a more autocratic or directive style. Moreover, this sex difference did *not* become smaller in the organizational studies, as did the differences in the interpersonal and task styles. Although the overall mean weighted effect size ($d_+ = 0.22$) was not large, the mean became larger once outliers were removed ($d_+ = 0.27$), and 92% of the available comparisons went in the direction of more democratic behavior from women than men. Despite this impressive consistency in the direction of the sex difference, the effect sizes themselves were quite heterogeneous, requiring the removal of 22% to obtain a set that did not reject the hypothesis of homogeneity. Yet substantial inconsistency across the studies is not unexpected for this type of style in view of the tendency for investigators to construct unique measures and not to rely on standard instruments, as did most investigators of the other types of leadership style that we reviewed (see Table 2).

Our interpretation of the sex difference in the extent to which leaders behave democratically versus autocratically is necessarily speculative, but follows from some of the considerations that we presented early in this article (see *Reasons to Expect the Presence of Sex Differences in Leadership Style*). We thus argued that women and men recruited into leadership roles in organizations may not be equivalent in personality and behavioral tendencies, even though they satisfy the same selection criteria. In particular, we noted that women's social skills might enable them to perform managerial roles differently than men. Interpersonal behavior that is skillful (e.g., in terms of understanding others' feelings and intentions) should facilitate a managerial style that is democratic and participative. Making decisions in a collaborative style requires not only the soliciting of suggestions from one's peers and subordinates, but also the preservation of good relationships with them when evaluating and perhaps rejecting their ideas. The give-and-take of collaborative decision making introduces interpersonal complexity not encountered by leaders who behave in an autocratic or directive manner. This interpretation is supported by research showing that teachers who lacked social skills, as indexed by their relative inability to decode nonverbal cues, had more autocratic attitudes and were generally more dogmatic (Rosenthal, Hall, DiMatteo, Rogers, & Archer, 1979).

Another perspective on the democratic-autocratic sex difference acknowledges the attitudinal bias against female leaders that we considered in the beginning of the article. The skepticism that many people have expressed concerning women's capabilities in managerial and leadership roles may be exacerbated by any tendency for women in these roles to take charge in an especially authoritative manner. Placating subordinates and peers so that they accept a woman's leadership may to some extent require that she give them input into her decisions and allow some degree of control over these decisions. Moreover, to the extent that women leaders have internalized to some degree the culture's reservations about their capability for leadership, they may gain confidence as leaders by making collaborative decisions that they can determine are in line with their associates' expectations. Thus, proceeding in a participative and collaborative mode may enable many female leaders to win acceptance from others, gain self-confidence, and thereby be effective. Because men are not so constrained by attitudinal bias, they are freer to lead in an autocratic and nonparticipative manner should they so desire.

The Impact of Gender Congeniality of Leadership Roles and Sex Distribution of Role Occupants

Our findings suggested that leaders of each sex emphasized task accomplishment when they were in a leadership role regarded as congruent with their gender. Thus, only the sex differences in task style were significantly correlated with the tendency for the leadership roles to be regarded as more congenial for men or women, as indexed by our questionnaire respondents' judgments (see Table 6). Male leaders tended to be more task oriented than female leaders to the extent that a leadership role was more congenial to men; female leaders tended to be more task oriented than male leaders to the extent that a leadership role was more congenial to women. Furthermore, women tended to be more task oriented than men in leadership roles that are feminine in the sense that our respondents judged they require considerable interpersonal ability.

These findings suggest that being out of role in gender-relevant terms has its costs for leaders in terms of some decline in their tendency to organize activities to accomplish relevant tasks. Because our meta-analytic data are not informative concerning the mediation of these effects, these provocative findings should be explored in primary research. Perhaps people who are out of role lack (or are perceived to lack) the skills necessary to organize the task-relevant aspects of their environment. Out-of-role leaders may be somewhat deficient in the knowledge and authority required to organize people and resources to accomplish task-relevant goals.

The extent to which leadership roles were male dominated numerically also related to sex differences in leadership style. Specifically, the tendencies for female leaders to be more interpersonally oriented and more democratic than male leaders weakened to the extent that a role was male dominated. Thus, when women were quite rare in leadership roles and therefore tended to have the status of token in organizations or groups, they abandoned stereotypically feminine styles characterized by concern for the morale and welfare of people in the work setting and consideration of these people's views when making decisions. These findings suggest that women may tend to lose authority if they adopt distinctively feminine styles of leadership in extremely male-dominated roles. Women who survive in such roles probably have to adopt the styles typical of male role occupants.

CONCLUSION

The view, widely accepted by social scientists expert on leadership, that women and men lead in the same way should be very substantially revised. Similarly, the view, proclaimed in some popular books on management, that female and male leaders have distinctive, gender-stereotypic styles also requires revision. Our quantitative review has established a more complex set of findings. Although these findings require further scrutiny before they should be taken as definitive, the agreement of these findings with our role theory framework substantiates our interpretation of them. Thus, consistent with research on sex differences in numerous social behaviors (Eagly, 1987; Hall, 1984), we have established that leadership style findings generated in experimental settings tend to be gender stereotypic. Indeed, these findings concur with the generalizations of those narrative reviewers who noted that male and female leaders often differ in laboratory experiments (Brown, 1979; Hollander, 1985). In such settings, people interact as strangers without the constraints of long-term role relationships. Gender roles are moderately important influences on behavior in such contexts and tend to produce gender-stereotypic behavior (see Eagly, 1987). In addition, somewhat smaller stereotypic sex differences were obtained in assessment studies, in which people not selected for leadership responded to instruments assessing their leadership styles. Because respondents not under the constraints of managerial roles completed questionnaires in these studies, some tendency for leadership styles to appear stereotypic was expected from the perspective of our social role framework.

When social behavior is regulated by other, less diffuse social roles, as it is in organizational settings, behavior should primarily reflect the influence of these other roles and therefore lose much of its gender-stereotypic character. Indeed, the findings of this meta-analysis for interpersonal and task styles support this logic. Nonetheless, women's leadership styles were more democratic than men's even in organizational settings. This sex difference may reflect underlying differences in female and male personality or skills (e.g., women's superior social skills) or subtle differences in the status of women and men who occupy the same organizational role. Deciding among the various causes that we have discussed would require primary research targeted to this issue.

The magnitude of the aggregate effect sizes we obtained in this meta-analysis deserves comment. When interpreting effect sizes, reviewers should take the methods of the studies into account, and, as Glass, McGaw, and Smith (1981) argued, they should avoid applying numerical guidelines to identify effect sizes as small or large. One feature of research on leadership style that is especially relevant to interpreting the magnitude of our aggregate effect sizes is that investigators face many barriers to achieving well-controlled studies. In organizational studies, the environments in which managers carry out their roles are quite diverse, even within a single organization. Because managers' leadership styles are evaluated either by themselves or by their associates, the various managers in a study are not necessarily evaluated by the same standard. Although more control of environmental influences can be achieved in laboratory studies of leadership (e.g., all leaders can be observed in a similar social setting), even these studies are relatively uncontrolled because each leader interacts with a unique group of followers. Counterbalancing the greater control of environmental factors in laboratory than organizational studies is the less rigorous selection of research participants for laboratory research and the resulting greater variability of leadership style within each sex. In general, uncontrolled variability in both organizational and laboratory studies of leadership would inflate the standard deviations that are the denominators of the effect sizes and thereby decrease the magnitude of these effect sizes. As a consequence, neither sex nor other variables would ordinarily produce large effect sizes in studies of leadership style. Therefore, we believe that effect sizes of the magnitude we obtained are considerably more consequential than effect sizes of the same magnitude obtained in more controlled forms of research.

Our review has not considered the extent to which the sex differences in leadership style that we have documented might produce differences in the effectiveness of leaders. Whether men or women are more effective leaders as a consequence of their differing styles is a complex question that could be addressed meta-analytically only by taking measures of group and organizational outcomes into account along with measures of leadership style. Because experts on leader effectiveness ordinarily maintain that the effectiveness of leadership styles is contingent on features of the group or organizational environment (e.g., Fiedler, 1967; Vroom & Yetton, 1973), we are unwilling to argue that women's relatively democratic and participative style is either an advantage or disadvantage. No doubt a relatively democratic style enhances a leader's effectiveness under some circumstances, and a relatively autocratic style enhances it under other circumstances. Nonetheless, we note that in recent years many management and organizational consultants have criticized traditional management practices for what they believe are overly hierarchical and rigidly bureaucratic forms (Fox, 1980; Heller & Van Til, 1986; Kanter, 1983; Naisbett, 1982; Ouchi, 1981; Peters & Waterman, 1982). Moreover, it is consistent with many feminist theorists' descriptions of hierarchy and domination (e.g., Elshtain, 1981; Miller, 1976) to argue that employment would be less alienating if forms of interaction in the workplace were less hierarchical and instead characterized by cooperation and collaboration between collegial groups of coworkers. Indeed, both consultants and feminists have advocated organizational change toward the more democratic and participative leadership styles that our meta-analysis suggests are more prevalent among women than men.

REFERENCES

Alpren, M. (1954). The development and validation of an instrument used to ascertain a school principal's pattern of behavioral (Doctoral dissertation, University of Florida). *Dissertation Abstracts International,* 33, 1579A.

Arcy, J. A. B. (1980). Self-perceptions of leader behavior of male and female elementary school principals in selected school districts in the midwest United States (Doctoral dissertation, Iowa State University, 1979). *Dissertation Abstracts International,* 40, 3638A.

Ashmore, R. D., Del Boca, F. K., & Wohlers, A. J. (1986). Gender stereotypes. In R. D. Ashmore & F. K. Del Boca (Eds.), *The social psychology of female-male relations: A critical analysis of central concepts* (pp. 69–119). Orlando, FL: Academic Press.

Bales, R. F. (1950). *Interaction process analysis: A method for the study of small groups.* Reading, MA: Addison-Wesley.

Barone, F. J. (1982). A comparative study of Theory X–Theory Y attitudes among managers and OD agents. *Dissertation Abstracts International,* 42, 4260A. (University Microfilms No. 82-07, 156).

Bartol, K. M., & Martin, D.C. (1986). Women and men in task groups. In R. D. Ashmore & F. K. Del Boca (Eds.), *The social psychology of female-male relations: A critical analyses of central concepts* (pp. 259–310). Orlando, FL: Academic Press.

Bass, B. M. (1981). *Stogdill's handbook of leadership: A survey of theory and research* (rev. ed.). New York: Free Press.

Baugher, S. L. (1983). Sex-typed characteristics and leadership dimensions of vocational education administrators in a midwest region of the United States (Doctoral dissertation, University of Missouri–Columbia, 1982). *Dissertation Abstracts International,* 44, 22A.

Bayes, M., & Newton, P. M. (1978). Women in authority: A sociopsychological analysis. *Journal of Applied Behavioral Science,* 14, 7–20.

Blake, R. R., & Mouton, J. S. (1964). *The managerial grid.* Houston, TX: Gulf.

Blake, R. R., & Mouton, J. S. (1978). *The new managerial grid.* Houston, TX: Gulf.

Brown, S. M. (1979). Male versus female leaders: A comparison of empirical studies. *Sex Roles,* 5, 595–611.

Butterfield, D. A., & Powell, G. N. (1981). Effect of group performance leader sex, and rater sex on ratings of leader behavior. *Organizational Behavior and Human Performance,* 28, 129–141.

Coleman, D. G. (1979). *Barnard's effectiveness and efficiency applied to a leader style model.* Unpublished manuscript, Northeast Missouri State University, Kirksville, MO.

Crocker, J., & McGraw, K. M. (1984). What's good for the goose is not good for the gander: Solo status as an obstacle to occupational achievement for males and females. *American Behavioral Scientist,* 27, 357–369.

Crudge, J. (1983). The effect of leadership styles on the rehabilitation training of student-workers (Doctoral dissertation, United States International University, 1982). *Dissertation Abstracts International* 43, 3300A.

Dobbins, G. H. (1986). Equity vs equality: Sex differences in leadership. *Sex Roles,* 15, 513–525.

Dobbins, G. H., Pence, E. C., Orban, J. A., & Sgro, J. A. (1983). The effects of sex of the leader and sex of the subordinate on the use of organizational control policy. *Organizational Behavior and Human Performance,* 32, 325–343.

Dobbins, G. H., & Platz, S. J. (1986). Sex differences in leadership: How real are they? *Academy of Management Review,* 11, 118–127.

Eagly, A. H. (1987). *Sex differences in social behavior: A social-role interpretation.* Hillsdale, NJ: Erlbaum.

Eagly, A. H., & Carli, L. L. (1981). Sex of researchers and sex-typed communications as determinants of sex differences in influence ability: A meta-analysis of social influence studies. *Psychological Bulletin,* 90, 1–20.

Eagly, A. H., & Steffen, V. J. (1984). Gender stereotypes stem from the distribution of women and men into social roles. *Journal of Personality and Social Psychology,* 46, 735–754.

Eagly, A. H., & Wood, W. (in press). Explaining sex differences in social behavior: A meta-analytic perspective. *Personality and Social Psychology Bulletin.*

Elshtain, J. (1981). *Public man, private woman: Women in social and political thought.* Princeton, NJ: Princeton University Press.

Feldman, D. C. (1976). A contingency theory of socialization. *Administrative Science Quarterly,* 21, 433–452.

Fiedler, F. E. (1967). *A theory of leadership effectiveness.* New York: McGraw-Hill.

Fleishman, E. A. (1953). The management of leadership attitudes in industry. *Journal of Applied Psychology,* 36, 153–158.

Fleishman, E. A. (1957). The Leadership Opinion Questionnaire. In R. M. Stogdill & A. E. Coons (Eds.), *Leader behavior: Its description and measurement* (pp. 120–133). Columbus, OH: Bureau of Business Research, Ohio State University.

Fleishman, E. A. (1960). *Manual for the Leadership Opinion Questionnaire.* Chicago: Science Research Associates.

Fleishman, E. A. (1970). *Manual for the Supervisory Behavior Description Questionnaire,* Washington, DC: American Institutes for Research.

Foy, N. (1980). *The yin and yang of organizations.* New York: Morrow.

Glass, G. V., McGraw, B., & Smith, M. L. (1981). *Meta-analysis in social research.* Beverly Hills, CA: Sage.

Graen, G. (1976). Role-making processes within complex organizations. In M. D. Dunnette (Ed.), *Handbook of industrial and organizational psychology* (pp. 1201–1245). Chicago: Rand McNally.

Grobman, H., & Hines, V. A. (1956). What makes a good principal? *National Association of Secondary School Principals Bulletin,* 40, 5–16.

Gustafson, L. C. (1982). The leadership role of the public elementary school meda librarian as perceived by the principal and its relationship to the factors of the sex, educational background and the work experience of the media librarian (Doctoral dissertation, University of Maryland). *Dissertation Abstracts International,* 43, 2206A.

Gutek, B. A., & Morasch, B. (1982). Sex-ratios, sex-role spillover, and sexual harassment of women at work. *Journal of Social Issues,* 38, 55–74.

Hall, A. H. (1983). The influence of a personal planning workshop on attitudes toward managerial style (Doctoral dissertation, University of Maryland, 1983). *Dissertation Abstracts International* 44, 2953A.

Hall, J. A. (1984). *Nonverbal sex differences: Communication accuracy and expressive style.* Baltimore, MD: Johns Hopkins University Press.

Halpin, A. W., (1957). *Manual for the Leader Behavior Description Questionnaire.* Columbus, OH: Bureau of Business Research, Ohio State University.

Halpin, A. W. (1966). *Theory and research in administration.* New York: Macmillan.

Halpin, A. W., & Winer, B. J. (1957). A factorial study of the leader behavior descriptions. In R. M. Stogdill & A. E. Coons (Eds.), *Leader behavior: Its description and measurement* (pp. 39–51). Columbus, OH: Bureau of Business Research, Ohio State University.

Hedges, L. V., & Becker, B. J. (1986). Statistical methods in the meta-analysis of research on gender differences. In J. S. Hyde & M. C. Linn (Eds.), *The psychology of gender: Advances through meta-analysis* (pp. 14–50). Baltimore, MD: Johns Hopkins University Press.

Hedges, L. V., & Olkin, I. (1985). *Statistical methods for meta-analysis.* Orlando, FL: Academic Press.

Heft, M., & Deni, R. (1984). Altering preferences for leadership style of men and women undergraduate residence advisors through leadership training. *Psychological Reports,* 54, 463–466.

Heller, T., & Van Til, J. (1986). Leadership and followership: Some summary propositions. In T. Heller, J. Van Til, & L. A. Zurcher (Eds.), *Contemporary studies in applied behavioral science: Vol. 4. Leaders and followers: Challenges for the future* (pp. 251–263). Greenwich, CT: JAI Press.

Hemphill, J. K., & Coons, A. E. (1957). Development of the Leader Behavior Description Questionnaire. In R. M. Stogdill & A. E. Coons (Eds.), *Leader behavior: Its description and measurement* (pp. 6–38). Columbus, OH: Bureau of Business Research, Ohio State University.

Hennig, M., & Jardin, A. (1977). *The managerial woman.* New York: Anchor Press.

Hersey, P., & Blanchard, K. H. (1982). *Management of organizational behavior: Utilizing human resources* (4th ed.). Englewood Cliffs, NJ: Prentice-Hall.

Hollander, E. P. (1985). Leadership and power. In G. Lindzey & E. Aronson (Eds.), *Handbook of social psychology* (3rd ed., Vol. 2, pp. 485–537). New York: Random House.

Hughes, H., Jr., Copeland, D. R., Ford, L. H., & Heidt, E. A. (1983). *Leadership and management education and training (LMET) course requirements for recruit company and "A" school instructors* (Tech. Rep. No. 154, Report No. AD-A137306). Orlando, FL: Department of the Navy.

Hurst, A. G., Stein, K. B., Korchin, S. J., & Soskin, W. F. (1978). Leadership style determinants of cohesiveness in adolescent groups. *International Journal of Group Psychotherapy,* 28, 263–277.

Jacoby, J., & Terborg, J. R. (1975). *Managerial Philosophies Scale.* Conroe, TX: Teleometrics International.

Kanter, R. M. (1977a). *Men and women of the corporation.* New York: Basic Books.

Kanter, R. M. (1977b). Some effects of proportions on group life: Skewed sex ratios and responses to token women. *American Journal of Sociology,* 82, 965–990.

Kanter, R. M. (1983). *The change masters: Innovations for productivity in the American corporation.* New York: Simon and Schuster.

Koberg, C. S. (1985). Sex and situational influences on the use of power: A follow-up study. *Sex Roles,* 13, 625–639.

Kruse, L., & Wintermantel, M. (1986). Leadership Ms.-qualified: I. The gender bias in everyday and scientific thinking. In C. F. Graumann & S. Moscovici (Eds.), *Changing conceptions of leadership* (pp. 171–197). New York: Springer-Verlag.

Lanning, G. E., Jr. (1982). A study of relationships and differences between management styles and staff morale as perceived by personnel in the colleges of the Ventura County community district. *Dissertation Abstracts International,* 43, 996A. (University Microfilms No. 82-20, 739).

Lee, D. M., & Alvares, K. M. (1977). Effects of sex on descriptions and evaluations of supervisory behavior in a simulated industrial setting. *Journal of Applied Psychology,* 62, 405–410.

Lewin, K., & Lippitt, R. (1938). An experimental approach to the study of autocracy and democracy: A preliminary note. *Sociometry,* 1, 292–300.

Likert, R. (1961). *New patterns of management.* New York: McGraw-Hill.

Loden, M. (1985). *Feminine leadership or how to succeed in business without being one of the boys.* New York: Times Books.

Maccoby, E. E. (1988). Gender as a social category. *Developmental Psychology,* 24, 755–765.

Marnani, E. B. (1982). Comparison of preferred leadership styles, potential leadership effectiveness, and managerial attitudes among black and white, female and male management students (Doctoral dissertation, United States International University, 1981). *Dissertation Abstracts International,* 43, 1271A.

Martinez, M. R. (1982). A comparative study on the relationship of self-perceptions of leadership styles between Chicano and Anglo teachers (Doctoral dissertation, Bowling Green State University). *Dissertation Abstracts International,* 43, 766A.

McGregor, D. (1960). *The human side of enterprise.* New York: McGraw-Hill.

Miller, J. B. (1976). *Toward a new psychology of women.* Boston: Beacon Press.

Money, J., & Ehrhardt, A. A. (1972). *Man & woman, boy & girl.* Baltimore, MD: Johns Hopkins University Press.

Moore, S. F., Shaffer, L., Goodsell, D. A., & Baringoldz, G. (1983). Gender or situationally determined spoken language differences? The case of the leadership situation. *International Journal of Women's Studies,* 6, 44–53.

Myers, M. S. (1970). *Every employee a manager.* New York: McGraw-Hill.

Naisbitt, J. (1982). *Megatrends: Ten new directions transforming our lives.* New York: Warner Books.

Nieva, V. F., & Gutek, B. A. (1981). *Women and work: A psychological perspective.* New York: Praeger.

O'Leary, V. E. (1974). Some attitudinal barriers to occupational aspirations in women. *Psychological Bulletin,* 81, 809–826.

Ott, E. M. (1989). Effects of the male-female ratio at work: Police women and male nurses. *Psychology of Woman Quarterly,* 13, 41–57.

Ouchi, W. G. (1981). *Theory Z: How American business can meet the Japanese challenge.* Reading, MA: Addison-Wesley.

Peters, T. J., & Waterman, R. H., Jr. (1982). *In search of excellence: Lessons from America's best-run companies.* New York: Harper & Row.

Powell, G. N. (1988). *Women & men in management.* Newbury Park, CA: Sage.

Reddin, W. J., & Reddin, M. K. (1979). *Educational Administrative Style Diagnosis Test (EASDT).* Fredericton, New Brunswick, Canada: Organizational Tests.

Renwick, P. A. (1977). The effects of sex differences on the perception and management of superior-subordinate conflict: An exploratory study. *Organizational Behavior and Human Performance,* 19, 403–415.

Rice, R. W., Instone, D., & Adams, J. (1984). Leader sex, leader success, and leadership process: Two field studies. *Journal of Applied Psychology,* 69, 12–31.

Riger, S., & Galligan, P. (1980). Women in management: An exploration of competing paradigms. *American Psychologist,* 35, 902–910.

Rosenthal, R., Hall, J. A., DiMatteo, M. R., Rogers, P. L., & Archer, D. (1979). *Sensitivity to nonverbal communication: The PONS test.* Baltimore, MD: Johns Hopkins University Press.

Rosenthal, R., & Rubin, D. B. (1986). Meta-analytic procedures for combining studies with multiple effect sizes. *Psychological Bulletin,* 99, 400–406.

Russell, J. E. A., Rush, M. C., & Herd, A. M. (1988). An exploration of women's expectations of effective male and female leadership. *Sex Roles,* 18, 279–287.

Sargent, A. G. (1981). *The androgynous manager.* New York: Amacom.

Sargent, J. F., & Miller, G. R. (1971). Some differences in certain communication behaviors of autocratic and democratic group leaders. *Journal of Communication,* 21, 233–252.

Shakeshaft, C. (1987). *Women in educational administration.* Newbury Park, CA: Sage.

Sirianni-Brantley, K. (1985). The effect of sex role orientation and training on leadership style (Doctoral dissertation, University of Florida, 1984). *Dissertation Abstracts International,* 45, 3106B.

Stake, J. E. (1981). Promoting leadership behaviors in low performance-self-esteem women in task-oriented mixed-sex dyads. *Journal of Personality,* 49, 401–414.

Stogdill, R. M. (1963). *Manual for the Leader Behavior Description Questionnaire-Form XII.* Columbus. OH: Bureau of Business Research, Ohio State University.

Stogdill, R. M., Goode, O. S., & Day, D. R. (1962). New leader behavior description subscales. *Journal of Psychology.* 54, 259–269.

Tanner, J. R. (1982). Effects of leadership, climate and demographic factors on school effectiveness: An action research project in leadership development (Doctoral dissertation, Case Western Reserve University, 1981). *Dissertation Abstracts International,* 43, 333A.

Taylor, S. E., Fiske, S. T., Etcoff, N., & Ruderman, A. (1978). The categorical and contextual bases of person memory and stereotyping. *Journal of Personality and Social Psychology,* 36, 778–793.

Terborg, J. R. (1977). Women in management: A research review. *Journal of Applied Psychology,* 62, 647–664.

Van Aken, E. W. (1954). An analysis of the methods of operations of principals to determine working patterns (Doctoral dissertation, University of Florida). *Dissertation Abstracts International,* 14, 1983.

Vroom, V. H., & Yetton, P. W. (1973). *Leadership and decision-making.* Pittsburgh, PA: University of Pittsburgh Press.

Wanous, J. P. (1977). Organizational entry: Newcomers moving from outside to inside. *Psychological Bulletin,* 84, 601–618.

Wood, W. (1987). Meta-analytic review of sex differences in group performance. *Psychological Bulletin,* 102, 53–71.

Yoder, J. D. & Sinnett, L.M. (1985). Is it all in the numbers? A case study of tokenism. *Psychology of Women Quarterly,* 9, 413–418.

Ways Groups Influence Individual Work Effectiveness

Lyman W. Porter
Edward E. Lawler III
J. Richard Hackman

To analyze the diversity of group and social influences on individual work effectiveness, it may be useful to examine group effects separately on each of four summary classes of variables that have been shown to influence employee work behavior. These four classes of variables are:

1 The job-relevant knowledge and skills of the individual
2 The level of psychological arousal the individual experiences while working
3 The performance strategies the individual uses during his or her work
4 The level of effort the individual exerts in doing his or her work

Below, we shall examine the ways in which work groups influence each of these four major influences on individual performance.

GROUP INFLUENCES BY AFFECTING MEMBER KNOWLEDGE AND SKILLS

Performance on many tasks and jobs in organizations is strongly affected by the job-relevant knowledge and skills of the individuals who do the work. Thus, even if an employee has both high commitment toward accomplishing a particular piece of work and well-formed strategy about how to go about it, the implementation of that plan can be constrained or terminated if he or she does not know how to carry it out, or if he or she knows how but is incapable of doing so. While ability is relevant to the performance of jobs at all levels in an organization, its impact probably is somewhat reduced for lower-level jobs. The reason is that such jobs often are not demanding of high skill levels. Further, to the extent that organizational selection, placement, and promotion practices are adequate, *all* jobs should tend to be occupied by individuals who possess the skills requisite for adequate performance.

Discussion in the previous chapter focused on how groups can improve the job-relevant knowledge and skills of an individual through direct instruction, feedback, and model provision. For jobs in which knowledge and skill are important determiners of performance effectiveness, then, groups can be of help. Nevertheless, the impact of groups on member performance effectiveness by improving member knowledge and skill probably is one of the lesser influences groups can have—both because employees on many jobs tend already to have many or all of the skills needed to perform them effectively and because there are other sources for improving skills which may be

Slightly revised from L. W. Porter, E. E. Lawler, & R. J. Hackman, *Behavior in organizations.* New York: McGraw-Hill, 1975, pp. 411–422. Used by permission.

more useful and more potent than the work group, such as formal job training programs and self-study programs.

GROUP INFLUENCES BY AFFECTING MEMBER AROUSAL LEVEL

A group can substantially influence the level of psychological arousal experienced by
a member—through the mere pressure of the other group members and by those others sending the individual messages which are directly arousal-enhancing or arousal-
depressing. The conditions under which such group-promoted changes in arousal level
will lead to increased performance effectiveness, however, very much depend upon the
type of task being worked on (Zajonc, 1965).

In this case, the critical characteristics of the job have to do with whether the initially *dominant task responses* of the individual are likely to be correct or incorrect.
Since the individual's output of such responses is facilitated when he is in an aroused
state, arousal should improve performance effectiveness on well-learned tasks (so-
called performance tasks) in which the dominant response is correct and needs merely
to be executed by the performer. By the same token, arousal should impair effectiveness for new or unfamiliar tasks (learning tasks) in which the dominant response is
likely to be incorrect.

It has sometimes been argued that the *mere* presence of others should heighten the
arousal of individuals sufficiently for the predicted performance effects to be obtained.
However, the evidence now seems to indicate that the *mere* presence of others may not
result in significant increases in arousal. Instead, only when the other group members
are—or are seen as being—in a potentially evaluative relationship vis-à-vis the performer are the predictions confirmed (cf. Zajonc & Sales, 1966; Cottrell et al., 1968;
Hency & Glass, 1968).

Groups can, of course, increase member arousal in ways other than taking an evaluative stance toward the individual. Strongly positive, encouraging statements also
should increase arousal in some performance situations—for example, by helping individuals become personally highly committed to the group goal, and making sure
they realize that they are a very important part of the team responsible for reaching
that goal. What must be kept in mind, however, is that such devices represent a double-
edged sword: while they may facilitate effective performance for well-learned tasks,
they may have the opposite effect for new and unfamiliar tasks.

What, then, can be said about the effects on performance of group members when
their presence (and interaction) serves to *decrease* the level of arousal of the group
member—as, for example, when individuals coalesce into groups under conditions of
high stress? When the other members of the group are a source of support, comfort, or
acceptance to the individual (and serve to decrease his arousal level), it would be predicted that performance effectiveness would follow a pattern exactly opposite to that
described above: the group would impair effectiveness for familiar or well-learned
performance tasks (because arousal helps on these tasks and arousal is being lowered)
and facilitate effectiveness for unfamiliar or complicated learning tasks (because in
this case arousal is harmful, and it is being lowered).

The relationships predicted above are summarized in Figure 1. As the group becomes increasingly threatening, evaluative, or strongly encouraging, effectiveness

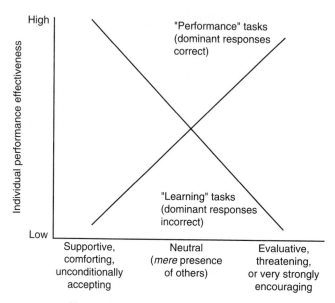

FIGURE 1
Individual performance effectiveness as a function of type of task and experienced relationship to the group.

should increase for performance tasks and decrease for learning tasks. When the group is experienced as increasingly supportive, comforting, or unconditionally accepting, effectiveness should decrease for performance tasks and increase for learning tasks. And when no meaningful relationship at all is experienced by the individual between him- or herself and the group, performance should not be affected. While some of the predictions have been tested and confirmed in small group experimental settings, others await research.

Even that research which has focused on these relationships has not been designed or conducted in actual organizational settings, and the findings must be generalized with caution. It is clear, however, that individuals in organizations do use their group memberships as a means of achieving more comfortable levels of arousal. Individuals in high-pressure managerial jobs, for example, often find that they need to gather around themselves a few trusted associates who can and do provide reassurance and continuing acceptance when the going gets especially tough. This, presumably, should help reduce the manager's level of arousal and thereby increase the likelihood that he or she will be able to come up with *new and original* ways of perceiving and dealing with the immediate problem. If the theory is correct, however, this practice should not facilitate performance of the more "routine" (i.e., well-learned) parts of his or her job.

It is well known that overly routine jobs can decrease a worker's level of arousal to such an extent that his or her performance effectiveness is impaired. It seems quite possible, therefore, that the social environment of workers on such jobs can be designed so as to compensate partially for the deadening effects of the job itself and thereby lead to an increment of performance on well-learned tasks.

Finally, the supervisor probably has a more powerful effect on level of arousal of a worker than any other single individual in the immediate social environment. By close supervision (which usually results in the worker's feeling more or less constantly evaluated) supervisors can and do increase the level of arousal experienced by workers. While this may, for routine jobs, have some potential for improving performance effectiveness, it also is quite likely that the worker's negative reactions to being closely supervised ultimately will result in his or her attention being diverted from the job itself and focused instead on ways of either getting out from "under the gun" of the supervisor or somehow getting back at the supervisor to punish him or her for unwanted close supervision.

GROUP INFLUENCES BY AFFECTING LEVEL OF MEMBER EFFORT AND MEMBER PERFORMANCE STRATEGIES

The level of effort a person exerts in doing his or her work and the performance strategies he or she follows are treated together here because both variables are largely under the performer's *voluntary* control.

Direct versus Indirect Influences on Effort and Strategy

We have used a general "expectancy theory" approach to analyze those aspects of a person's behavior in organizations which are under his or her voluntary control. From this perspective a person's choices about effort and work strategy can be viewed as hinging largely upon (1) *expectations* regarding the likely consequences of choices and (2) the degree to which he or she *values* those expected consequences. Following this approach, it becomes clear that the group can have both a direct and an indirect effect on the level of effort a group member exerts at the job and on his or her choices about performance strategy.

The *direct* impact of the group on effort and strategy, of course, is simply the enforcement by the group of its own norms regarding what is an "appropriate" level of effort to expend on the job and what is the "proper" performance strategy. We previously discussed in some detail how groups use their control of discretionary stimuli to enforce group norms, and thereby affect such voluntary behaviors. Thus, if the group has established a norm about the level of member effort or the strategies members should use in going about their work, the group can control individual behavior merely by making sure that individual members realize that their receipt of valued group-controlled rewards is contingent upon their behaving in accord with the norm.

The *indirect* impact of the group on the effort and performance strategies of the individual involves the group's control of information regarding the state of the organizational environment outside the boundaries of the group. Regardless of any norms the group itself may have about effort or strategy, it also can communicate to the group member "what leads to what" in the broader organization, and thereby affect the individual's *own* choices about behavior.

For example, it may be the case in a given organization, that hard work (i.e., high effort) tends to lead to quick promotions and higher pay; the group can influence the effort of the individual by helping him or her realize this objective state of affairs. Similarly, by providing individual members with information about what performance strategies are effective in the organization, the group can indirectly affect the strategy choices made by the person. Whether high quality of output or large quantities of output are more likely to lead to organizational rewards, for example, is information that the group can provide the individual with to assist him in making his or her own choices about work strategy.

Moreover, groups can affect the *personal preferences and values* of individual members—although such influences tend to occur relatively slowly and over a long period of time. When such changes do occur, the level of desire (or the valence) individuals have for various outcomes available in the organizational setting will change as well. And as the kinds of outcomes valued by the individual change, his or her behavior also will change to increase the degree to which the newly valued outcomes are obtained at work. The long-term result can be substantial revision of the choices made by the individual about the effort he or she will expend and the performance strategies he or she will use at work.

It should be noted, however, that such indirect influences on a member's effort and performance strategy will be most potent early in the individual's tenure in the organization when he or she has not yet had a chance to develop through experience his or her own personal "map" of the organization. When the individual becomes less dependent upon the group for data about "what leads to what" and "what's good" in the organization, the group may have to revert to direct norm enforcement to maintain control of the work behavior of individual members.

In summary, the group can and does have a strong impact on both the level of effort exerted by its members and the strategies members use in carrying out their work. This impact is realized both directly (i.e., by enforcement of group norms) and indirectly (i.e., by affecting the beliefs and values of the members). When the direct and indirect influences of a group are congruent—which is often the case—the potency of the group's efforts on its members can be quite strong. For example, if at the same time that a group is enforcing its *own* norm of, say, moderately low production, it also is providing a group member with data regarding the presumably *objective* negative consequences of hard work in the particular organization, the group member will experience two partially independent and mutually reinforcing influences aimed at keeping his rate of production down.

Effort, Strategy, and Performance Effectiveness

What, then, are the circumstances under which groups can improve the work *effectiveness* of their members through influences on individual choices about the level of effort and about strategy? Again, the answer depends upon the nature of the job. Unless a job is structured so that effort or performance strategy actually can make a real difference in work effectiveness, group influences on effort or strategy will be irrelevant to how well individual members perform.

Strategy: In general, groups should be able to facilitate member work effectiveness by influencing strategy choices more for complex jobs than for simple, straightforward, or routine ones. The reason is that on simple jobs, strategy choices usually cannot make much of a difference in effectiveness; instead, how well one does is determined almost entirely by how hard one works. On jobs characterized by high variety and autonomy, on the other hand, the work strategy used by the individual usually is of considerable importance in determining work effectiveness. By helping individuals develop and implement an appropriate work strategy—of where and how to put in their effort—the group should be able to substantially facilitate their effectiveness.

Effort: In the great majority of organizational settings, most jobs are structured such that the harder one works, the more effective one's performance is likely to be. Thus, group influences on the effort expended by members on their jobs are both very pervasive and very potent determiners of individual work effectiveness. There are, nevertheless, some exceptions to this generalization; the success of a complicated brain operation, for example, is less likely to depend upon effort expended that it is upon the strategies used and the job-relevant knowledge and skills of the surgeon.

When neither effort or strategy or both are in fact important in determining performance effectiveness, the individual has substantial personal control over how well he or she does in his work. In such cases, the degree to which the group facilitates (rather than hinders) individual effectiveness will depend jointly upon (1) the degree to which the group has accurate information regarding the task and organizational contingencies which are operative in that situation and makes such information available to the individual and (2) the degree to which the norms of the group are congruent with those contingencies and reinforce them.

Participation

One management practice which in theory should contribute positively to meeting both of the above conditions is the use of group participation in making decisions about work practices. Participation has been widely advocated as a management technique, both on ideological grounds and as a direct means of increasing work effectiveness. And, in fact, some studies have shown that participation can lead to higher work effectiveness (e.g., Coch & French, 1948; Lawler & Hackman, 1969). In the present framework, participation should contribute to increased work effectiveness in two different ways.

1 Participation can increase the amount and the accuracy of information workers have about work practices and the environmental contingencies associated with them. In one study (Lawler & Hackman, 1969), for example, some groups themselves designed new reward systems keyed on coming to work regularly (a task clearly affected by employee effort—i.e., trying to get to work every day). These groups responded both more quickly and more positively to the new pay plans than did groups which had technically identical plans imposed upon them by company management. One reason suggested by the authors to account for this finding was that the participative groups simply may have understood their plans better and had fewer uncertainties and worries about what the rewards were (and were not) for coming to work regularly.

2 Participation can increase the degree to which group members feel they "own" their work practices—and therefore the likelihood that the group will develop a norm of support of those practices. In the participative groups in the study cited above, for example, the nature of the work-related communication among members changed from initial "shared warnings" about management and "things management proposes" to helping members (especially new members) come to understand and believe in "our plan." In other words, as group members come to experience the work or work practices *as under their own control or ownership,* it becomes more likely that informal group norms supportive of effective behavior vis-à-vis those practices will develop. Such norms provide a striking contrast to the "group protective" norms which often emerge when control is perceived to be exclusively and unilaterally under management control.

We can see, then, that group participative techniques can be quite facilitative of individual work effectiveness—but only under certain conditions:

1 The topic of participation must be relevant to the work itself. There is no reason to believe that participation involving task-irrelevant issues (e.g., preparing for the Red Cross Bloodmobile visit to the plant) will have facilitative effects on work productivity. While such participation may indeed help increase the cohesiveness of the work group, it clearly will not help group members gain information or develop norms which are facilitative of high work effectiveness. Indeed, such task-irrelevant participation may serve to direct the attention and motivation of group members *away from* work issues and thereby even lower productivity (cf. French, Israel, & As, 1960).

2 The objective task and environmental contingencies in the work setting must actually be supportive of more effective performance. That is, if through participation group members learn more about what leads to what in the organization, then it is increasingly important that there be real and meaningful positive outcomes which result from effective performance. If, for example, group members gain a quite complete and accurate impression through participation that "hard work around here pays off only in backaches," then increased effort as a consequence of participation is most unlikely. If, on the other hand, participation results in a new and better understanding that hard work can lead to increased pay, enhanced opportunities for advancement, and the chance to feel a sense of personal and group accomplishment, then increased effort should be the result.

3 Finally, the work must be such that increased effort (or a different and better work strategy) objectively can lead to higher work effectiveness. If it is true—as argued here—that the main benefits of group participation are (1) increased understanding of work practices and the organizational environment and (2) increased experienced "ownership" by the group of the work and work practices, then participation should increase productivity only when the *objective determinants of productivity are under the voluntary control of the worker.* There is little reason to expect, therefore, that participation should have a substantial facilitative effect on productivity when work outcomes are mainly determined by the level of skill of the worker and/or by his or her arousal level (rather than effort expended or work strategy used) or when outcomes are controlled by objective factors in the environment over which the worker can have little or no control e.g., the rate or amount of work which is arriving at the employee's station).

IMPLICATIONS FOR DIAGNOSIS AND CHANGE

This section has focused on ways that the group can influence the performance effectiveness of individual group members. While it has been maintained throughout that the group has a substantial impact on such performance effectiveness, it has been emphasized that the nature and extent of this impact centrally depends upon the characteristics of the work being done.

To diagnose and change the direction or extent of social influences on individual performance in an organization, then, the following three steps might be taken.

1 An analysis of the task or job would be made to determine which of the four classes of variables (i.e., skills, arousal, strategies, effort) objectively affect measured performance effectiveness. This might be done by posing this analytical question: "If skills (or arousal, or effort, or strategies) were brought to bear on the work differently than is presently the case, would a corresponding difference in work effectiveness be likely to be observed as a consequence?" By scrutinizing each of the four classes of variables in this way, it usually is possible to identify which specific variables are objectively important to consider for the job. In many cases, of course, more than one class of variables will turn out to be of importance.

2 After one or more "target" classes of variables have been identified, the work group itself would be examined to unearth any ways in which the group was blocking effective individual performance. It might be determined, for example, that certain group norms were impeding the expression and use of various skills which individuals potentially could bring to bear on their work. Or it might turn out that the social environment of the worker created conditions which were excessively (or insufficiently) arousing for optimal performance on the task at hand. For effort and strategy, which are under the voluntary control of the worker, there are two major possibilities to examine: (a) that norms are enforced in the group which coerce individuals to behave in ineffective ways or (b) that the group provides information to the individual members about task and environmental contingencies in an insufficient or distorted fashion, resulting in their making choices about their work behavior which interfere with task effectiveness.

3 Finally, it would be useful to assess the group and the broader social environment to determine if there are ways that the "people resources" in the situation could be more fully utilized in the interest of increased work effectiveness. That is, rather than focusing solely on ways the group may be blocking or impeding performance effectiveness, attention should be given as well to any unrealized *potential* which resides in the group. It could turn out, for example, that some group members would be of great help to others in increasing the level of individual task-relevant skills, but these individuals have never been asked for help. Alternatively, it might be that the group could be assisted in finding new and better ways of ensuring that each group member has available accurate and current information about those tasks and environmental contingencies which determine the outcomes of various work behaviors.

The point is that the people who surround an individual at work can facilitate as well as hinder his or her performance effectiveness—and that any serious attempt to diagnose the social environment in the interest of improving work performance should explicitly address unrealized possibilities for enhancing performance as well as issues for which remedial action may be required.

When particular organizational changes will be called for on the basis of such a diagnosis—or what techniques should be used to realize these changes—will, of course, largely depend upon the particular characteristics of the organization and of the resources which are available there. The major emphasis of this section has been that there is *not* any single universally useful type of change or means of change—and that, instead, intervention should always be based on a thorough diagnosis of the existing social, organizational, and task environment. Perhaps especially intriguing in this regard is the prospect of developing techniques of social intervention which will help groups see the need for (and develop the capability of) making such interventions *on their own* in the interest of increasing the work effectiveness of the group as a whole.

REFERENCES

Coch, L., & French, J. R. P., Jr., Overcoming resistance to change. *Human Relations,* 1948, 1, 512–532.

Cottrell, N. B., Wack, D. L., Sekerak, F. J., & Rittle, R. H. Social facilitation of dominant responses by the presence of an audience and the mere presence of others. *Journal of Personality and Social Psychology,* 1968, 9, 245–250.

French, J. R. P., Jr., Israel, J., & As, D. An experiment on participation in a Norwegian factory. *Human Relations,* 1960, 19, 3–19.

Hency, T., & Glass, D. C. Evaluation apprehension and the social facilitation of dominant and subordinate responses. *Journal of Personality and Social Psychology,* 1968, 10, 446–454.

Lawler, E. E., & Hackman, J. R. The impact of employee participation in the development of pay incentive plans: A field experiment. *Journal of Applied Psychology,* 1969, 53, 467–471.

Zajonc, R. B. Social facilitation, *Science,* 1965, 149, 269–274.

Zajonc, R. B., & Sales, S. M. Social facilitation of dominant and subordinate responses. *Journal of Experimental Social Psychology,* 1966, 2, 160–168.

Patterns of Influence Behavior for Managers

Gary Yukl
Cecilia M. Falbe
Joo Young Youn

One of the most important determinants of managerial effectiveness is success in influencing people and developing commitment to task objectives (Yukl, 1989). Several studies have examined issues such as the types of influence tactics used by managers and the objectives of their influence attempts (Ansari & Kapoor, 1987; Erez, Rim, & Keider, 1986; Kipnis, Schmidt, & Wilkinson, 1980; Schilit & Locke, 1982; Schmidt & Kipnis, 1984; Schriesheim & Hinkin, 1990; Yukl & Falbe, 1990). However, we have only begun to investigate a number of important research questions about influence behavior that have implications for understanding and improving the effectiveness of managers. Only a few studies have examined the pattern of influence behavior used by managers with subordinates, peers, and superiors. Potentially relevant aspects of the influence pattern include differences in choice of tactics to use with subordinates, peers, and superiors *(directional differences),* which tactics are used together in the same influence attempt *(tactic combinations),* and differences in the choice of tactics for successive influence attempts made with the same target person *(sequencing differences).*

The extent to which managers vary their use of tactics with different targets has been examined in four questionnaire studies (Erez et al., 1986; Kipnis et al., 1980; Yukl & Falbe, 1990; Yukl & Tracey, 1992). Significant directional differences were found in these studies, but the magnitude of the effect was small. Regardless of the direction of influence, the various tactics had a similar ranking in terms of mean frequency of use. This finding may reflect common biases among the respondents. For example, it is possible that both agents and targets report more agent use of socially desirable tactics, such as rational persuasion, as compared to "undesirable" tactics, such as pressure. Directional differences in the use of various tactics have not been investigated with a research method less susceptible to these biases and attributions.

We know almost nothing about the way in which different tactics are combined in the same influence attempt. It is extremely difficult to investigate this subject in questionnaire studies. The profiles used by Kipnis and Schmidt (1988) indicate which tactics are emphasized by a manager, but they do not reveal which tactics are used alone and which are used together in the same influence attempt. Tactic combinations can be studied more directly with descriptions of specific influence incidents than with questionnaires, but this was not a research objective in prior incident studies, such as those by Keys and Case (1990) and Schilit and Locke (1982).

We have very limited knowledge about the way in which different influence tactics are sequenced in influence attempts involving repeated interactions between an agent

Condensed from *Group & Organization Management*, 1993, 18 (1) 5–28. Copyright © 1993, Sage Publications, Inc. Reprinted by permission of Sage Publications, Inc.

and a target. Kipnis and Schmidt (1983) proposed that most managers use simple requests or rational persuasion in an initial influence attempt, whereas in a follow-up influence attempt, ingratiation or a coalition is likely to be used with a powerful target, and pressure is likely to be used with a weak target. No empirical results were presented to support this proposition. In their article on how to become an influential manager, Keys and Case (1990) proposed that most contemporary managers try positive tactics initially but quickly resort to threats or manipulation if necessary, especially when the target is a subordinate. Once again, no empirical evidence was presented. It is time for a systematic investigation to determine if these propositions can be verified and to study the sequencing of tactics in more detail.

The present research was conducted to learn more about how managers use different tactics to influence subordinates, peers, and superiors. The research had three specific objectives:

1 to assess directional differences in the use of influence tactics
2 to identify tactics used together frequently and tactics used alone
3 to identify typical patterns in the sequencing of tactics

The first research question has been investigated by analysis of questionnaire data, and our objective in the current study was to determine if the results could be replicated with a different research method. The second and third objectives involve research questions not examined in previous empirical studies. A conceptual framework and specific hypotheses are presented in the next section, and relevant prior research is reviewed briefly.

MODEL AND HYPOTHESES

The research deals with the nine influence tactics defined in Table 1. These influence tactics are representative of the ones studied in prior research with questionnaires and influence incidents. The tactics are based on results from factor analysis studies of questionnaires and other types of validation research (Schriesheim & Hinkin, 1990; Yukl, Lepsinger, & Lucia, 1992).

Building on the preliminary model proposed by Yukl and Tracey (1992), the following interrelated factors determine how frequently an influence tactic is used in a particular direction (a) consistency with prevailing social norms and role expectations about use of the tactic in that context, (b) agent possession of an appropriate power base for use of the tactic in that context, (c) appropriateness for the objective of the influence attempt, (d) level of target resistance encountered or anticipated, and (e) costs of using the tactic in relation to likely benefits. The underlying assumption is that most managers will prefer to use tactics that are socially acceptable, that are feasible in terms of the agent's position and personal power in relation to the target, that are not costly (in terms of time, effort, loss of resources, or alienation of the target), and that are likely to be effective for a particular objective—given the anticipated level of resistance by the target. These factors may be used to derive specific hypotheses about directional differences in patterns of influence behavior and about patterns in the sequencing of tactics.

TABLE 1
DEFINITION OF INFLUENCE TACTICS

Rational persuasion: The agent uses logical arguments and factual evidence to persuade the target that a proposal or request is viable and likely to result in the attainment of task objectives.

Inspirational appeals: The agent makes a request or proposal that arouses target enthusiasm by appealing to target values, ideals, and aspirations, or by increasing targets self-confidence.

Consultation: The agent seeks target participation in planning a strategy, activity, or change for which target support and assistance are desired, or the agent is willing to modify a proposal to deal with target concerns and suggestions.

Ingratiation: The agent uses praise, flattery, friendly behavior, or helpful behavior to get the target in a good mood or to think favorably of him or her before asking for something.

Personal appeals: The agent appeals to target feelings of loyalty and friendship toward him or her when asking for something.

Exchange: The agent offers an exchange of favors, indicates willingness to reciprocate at a later time, or promises a share of the benefits if the target helps accomplish a task.

Coalition tactics: The agent seeks the aid of others to persuade the target to do something or uses the support of others as a reason for the target to agree also.

Pressure: The agent uses demands, threats, frequent checking, or persistent reminders to influence the target to do what he or she wants.

Legitimating tactics: The agent seeks to establish the legitimacy of a request by claiming the authority or right to make it or by verifying that it is consistent with organizational policies, rules, practices, or traditions.

Directional Differences in the Use of Tactics

Directional differences in the use of specific tactics may occur for a variety of reasons. Prior studies show that influence objectives vary by direction (Erez et al., 1986; Kpinis et al., 1980; Yukl & Falbe, 1990), and there is evidence that particular tactics tend to be used more with particular objectives (Erez et al., 1986; Kipnis et al., 1980; Schmidt & Kipnis, 1984). Some tactics are easier to use in a particular direction, because the agent's authority and position power are greater in that direction or because their use is consistent with role expectations, Finally, research with questionnaires indicates that some tactics are more likely to be effective in a particular direction (Falbe & Yukl, 1992; Yukl & Tracey, 1992). Based on these components of the model and on prior research findings, Yukl and Tracey (1992) proposed specific hypotheses for the nine tactics. Because all but one hypothesis was supported in their study, we will test the same hypotheses in the current study (the explanation for each hypothesis can be found in the Yukl and Tracey article).

Hypothesis 1: Rational persuasion is used more often in an upward direction than in a lateral or downward direction.

Directional differences in frequency of use for rational persuasion were not consistent in four prior studies that used questionnaires. More upward use of rational persuasion was found for two agent samples (Erez et al., 1986; Kipnis et al., 1980) and one target sample (Yukl & Tracey, 1992), but not for another agent sample (Yukl & Falbe, 1990) or for two other target samples (Erez et al., 1986; Yukl & Falbe, 1990).

Hypothesis 2: Inspirational appeals are used more often in a downward direction than in a lateral or upward direction.

Two prior studies (Yukl & Falbe, 1990; Yukl Tracey , 1992) found that inspirational appeals were used more in downward influence attempts than in lateral or upward influence attempts.

Hypothesis 3: Consultation is used more often in a downward direction than in a lateral or upward direction.

In the study by Yukl and Falbe (1990), agents reported greater use of consultation in a downward direction, but directional differences were not significant for target reports in the same study or in the study by Yukl and Tracey (1992).

Hypothesis 4: Ingratiation is used more often in a downward and lateral direction than upward.

Yukl and Tracey (1992) found that ingratiation was used most in downward influence attempts and least in upward influence attempts. In studies by Kipnis et al. (1980) and Yukl and Falbe (1990), agents reported that ingratiation was used more in downward and lateral influence attempts than in upward influence attempts. No significant differences were found for target reports in the study by Yukl and Falbe (1990), and no clear pattern emerged for agent and target reports in the study by Erez et al. (1986).

Hypothesis 5: Personal appeals are used more often in a lateral direction than in a downward or upward direction.

In the only study that examined directional differences for this tactic, Yukl and Tracey (1992) found that personal appeals were used most often for lateral influence attempts and least often for upward influence attempts.

Hypothesis 6: Exchange tactics are used more in a downward and lateral direction than upward.

Three prior studies (Erez et al., 1986; Kipnis et al., 1980; Yukl & Falbe, 1990) found that exchange was used more in downward and lateral influence attempts than in upward influence attempts. Yukl and Tracey (1992) found that exchange was used most often in lateral influence attempts and least often in upward influence attempts.

Hypothesis 7: Coalition tactics are used more in a lateral and upward direction than downward.

Yukl and Tracey (1992) found that coalition tactics were used most often in lateral influence attempts and least often in downward influence attempts. In a study by Erez et al. (1986), coalitions were used most often in a lateral direction according to agents, but no significant directional differences were found for targets. Likewise, directional differences were not significant for coalition tactics in two other studies (Kipnis et al., 1980; Yukl & Falbe, 1990).

Hypothesis 8: Legitimating tactics are used more in a lateral direction than in a downward or upward direction.

In the only prior study to examine directional differences for legitimating tactics, Yukl and Tracey (1992) found more use in lateral influence attempts than in downward or upward influence attempts.

Hypothesis 9: Pressure tactics are used more in a downward direction than in a lateral or upward direction.

Four questionnaire studies found more use of pressure in a downward direction than in a lateral or upward direction (Erez et al., 1986; Kipnis et al., 1980; Yukl & Falbe, 1990; Yukl & Tracey, 1992).

Initial and Follow-up Influence Attempts

The sequencing of tactics depends in part on the relative advantages and costs of each tactic. In general, it is reasonable to assume that a manager will initially select tactics that are likely to accomplish an objective with the least effort and cost. Simple requests and weak forms of rational persuasion (e.g., a brief explanation of the agent's request or proposal, an assertion made without supporting evidence) are easy to use and entail little in the way of agent costs. Thus initial influence attempts often involve either a simple request or a relatively weak form of rational persuasion, especially when the agent desires only compliance rather than commitment. If the agent doubts that a simple request or rational persuasion alone is likely to be effective, then an initial influence attempt is likely to include other "soft" tactics, such as personal appeals, ingratiation, consultation, or inspirational appeals. These tactics may be used alone, in various combinations with each other, or in combination with rational persuasion. In the face of continued resistance by a target, the agent will either escalate to "harder" tactics or abandon the effort if the request does not justify the risks of escalation. Pressure, exchange, and coalitions are likely to be saved for follow-up influence attempts, because they involve the greatest costs and risks. Based on this analysis, some specific hypotheses can be made for timing differences in the use of individual tactics.

Hypothesis 10: Rational persuasion is used more in initial influence attempts than in follow-up attempts.

Rational persuasion is a flexible tactic that is suitable for most types of influence attempts, and weak forms of rational persuasion are especially easy to use. Thus it is reasonable to expect that rational persuasion will be used frequently in initial influence attempts. In follow-up influence attempts, managers use a greater variety of tactics, and the proportionate use of rational persuasion is necessarily lower.

Hypothesis 11: Ingratiation is used more in initial influence attempts than in follow-up influence attempts.

Ingratiation is likely to be used early rather than late, because this tactic is intended to make the target more receptive to the agent's request. Ingratiation is unlikely to be successful unless it appears sincere, and it is more likely to appear manipulative if used after the agent has already encountered some resistance to a request or proposal.

Hypothesis 12: Personal appeals are used more in initial influence attempts than in follow-up influence attempts.

Personal appeals are used most for unusual requests for which there is not a clear rationale or legitimate basis. The agent needs a special favor and is asking the target to do something as a friend that would not be asked of a casual acquaintance or impersonal colleague. Because this tactic is the primary basis for some types of requests, it is likely to be used more often in initial influence attempts than as a follow-up tactic.

Hypothesis 13: Exchange is used more in follow-up influence attempts than in initial influence attempts.

Exchange requires some payoff to the target in return for compliance, and the payoff often has a direct cost to the agent. Thus exchange will not be used in an initial influence attempt, unless the request is important enough to justify an immediate offer of benefits.

Hypothesis 14: Coalition tactics are used more in follow-up influence attempts than in initial influence attempts.

Coalitions require effort to arrange, and some coalition tactics are risky because they may be perceived as manipulative. It is unlikely that an agent will go to the extra effort to enlist the aid of others unless the target resists a request important enough to justify this effort. In most cases, coalitions are used as a follow-up tactic to enhance an initial request that has not been as successful as the agent would like. A coalition is not likely to be used for an initial influence attempt except for a very important request for which some target resistance is anticipated.

Hypothesis 15: Pressure is used more in follow-up influence attempts.

Pressure tends to be resented by the target, especially when it appears coercive, and it hardly ever results in commitment. Pressure is a tactic that is used primarily to get compliance, and it is most appropriate when the target has already resisted an initial influence attempt. Because the potential costs (including the risk that a cooperative relationship will be undermined) are substantial in relation to the potential benefits, pressure tactics are less likely to be used in an initial influence attempt than in a follow-up influence attempt.

Use of Individual Tactics versus Tactic Combinations

Little is known about the extent to which each of the nine tactics is used alone or in combination with other tactics. Except for the idea that multiple tactics are more likely when resistance is anticipated, there is little basis for predicting this aspect of influence behavior. It is likely that complex interactions occur among aspects of the situation such as the influence objective, the expectation of likely target resistance, and the timing of the influence attempt. No specific hypotheses were developed for relative use of tactics alone or in combinations.

METHOD

Sample and Data Collection

Descriptions of influence incidents in organizations were obtained from night MBA students at a large state university. The students worked in regular jobs during the day in a variety of large and small private companies and public agencies. Nearly one half of the students were managers or supervisors, and most of the rest were nonmanagerial professionals. A total of 145 students provided incidents as part of a course project in three MBA courses. The students reported on their own experiences as an agent or target, and each student was asked to provide at least three incidents. Students were asked to provide an equal number of incidents in the same direction resulting in commitment, compliance, and resistance, and these outcomes were defined for the students beforehand. Direction of influence for the incidents was randomly assigned, but students who were not managers were not asked to provide downward agent incidents or upward target incidents because they did not have any subordinates. The students were encouraged to obtain examples of influence attempts that involved important issues or substantive requests for assistance or support, rather than routine task assignments for which only a simple request is necessary to ensure target compliance or commitment.

Students were provided forms for writing the critical incidents. The incident forms had fixed-response items to indicate the direction of the influence attempt (i.e., down, lateral, or up) and the initial and final outcome of the influence attempt (i.e., resistance, compliance, or commitment). On the blank part of the form, students were asked to describe in a paragraph or two what was said or done by the agent to influence the target and how the target reacted to the request. If a sequence of influence attempts occurred, respondents were asked to describe each episode in the sequence. Students were instructed to provide details, including quotes and examples of what the agent said. They were assured that the information in their incidents would remain confidential and would not be seen by anybody except the researchers.

Additional incidents were obtained by 16 MBA students for an optional research project that was not part of a regular course. These students interviewed managers in their own company and in other organizations. Each student was asked to collect 18 incidents, balanced by outcome and direction (randomly assigned). Ten students collected target incidents, and the remaining 6 students collected agent incidents. The students were given instructions on how to conduct the interview and how to report the results on the incident forms. To ensure that the instructions were understood, the first three incidents collected by a student were reviewed by the researchers, and students were given feedback about any deficiencies. . . .

RESULTS

The results are reported in three separate sections: (a) use of tactics alone and in combinations, (b) directional differences in use of tactics, and (c) use of tactics in initial

TABLE 2
USE OF EACH TACTIC ALONE AND IN COMBINATIONS

Influence tactic		Single tactic	Combinations	Z test
Rational persuasion	Target	270 (54%)	165 (30%)	7.89**
	Agent	148 (70%)	89 (42%)	5.83**
Inspiration	Target	10 (2%)	48 (9%)	−4.96**
	Agent	1 (0%)	13 (6%)	−3.25**
Consultation	Target	11 (2%)	33 (6%)	−3.23**
	Agent	1 (0%)	8 (4%)	−2.35*
Ingratiation	Target	32 (6%)	56 (10%)	−2.34*
	Agent	5 (2%)	19 (9%)	−2.93**
Personal appeal	Target	36 (7%)	43 (8%)	−0.61
	Agent	4 (2%)	6 (3%)	−0.63
Exchange	Target	34 (7%)	44 (8%)	−0.62
	Agent	16 (8%)	16 (8%)	−0.01
Coalition	Target	31 (6%)	50 (9%)	−1.82
	Agent	13 (6%)	16 (8%)	−0.56
Legitimating	Target	16 (3%)	45 (8%)	−3.46**
	Agent	3 (1%)	10 (5%)	−1.96*
Pressure	Target	64 (13%)	62 (11%)	1.00
	Agent	24 (11%)	35 (17%)	−1.52
Incidents	Target	504	273	
	Agent	211	106	
Tactics	Target	504	546	
	Agent	211	212	

Note: Percentages are based on column total for number of tactics.
*$p < .05$; **$p < .01$.

and follow-up influence attempts. Given the unequal distribution of incidents and small cell sizes for many tactics, most analyses were done separately rather than testing for interactions between direction, timing, source, and use of single tactics or combinations. Because of the large number of pairwise comparisons, a conservative two-tailed test was used even when a specific hypothesis would justify use of a one-tailed test.

Use of Tactics Alone and in Combinations

Table 2 shows how frequently each tactic was used alone or in combination with another tactic in the same influence episode. Proportions were based on total number of tactics used by agents or targets. A Z test of proportions (Loether & McTavish, 1980) indicated that the differences for several influence tactics were significantly greater than would be expected by chance. Results were very similar for data from agents and targets. Rational persuasion was more likely to be used alone than in combinations. Inspirational appeals, consultation, ingratiation, and legitimating tactics were more likely to be used in combinations than alone. The differences were not significant for the other five tactics.

Some tactics were more likely to be combined than others. . . . Rational persuasion is a very flexible tactic that can be used with any of the other eight tactics, and it was the tactic selected most often for combinations used in both initial (68%) and follow-up (66%) influence attempts. Rational persuasion was clearly the first choice for most combinations, but the second choice varied considerably across the remaining tactics. For example, consultation was paired more often with inspirational appeals or ingratiation than with other tactics (excluding rational persuasion) in initial influence attempts.

DIRECTIONAL DIFFERENCES

Consistent with Hypothesis 1, rational persuasion was used more in an upward direction than in a lateral or downward direction. Consistent with Hypothesis 2, inspirational appeals were used more in a downward direction than in a lateral or upward direction. Consultation was used more in a downward and lateral direction than upward, providing partial support for Hypothesis 3 (which stated that it would be used more in a downward direction than laterally or upward). Consistent with Hypothesis 4, ingratiation was used more in a downward and lateral direction than in an upward direction. Consistent with Hypothesis 5, personal appeals were used more in a lateral direction than in a downward or upward direction. Consistent with Hypothesis 6, exchange was used more in a downward and lateral direction than in an upward direction. Consistent with Hypothesis 7, coalition tactics were used more in a lateral and upward direction than in a downward direction. Hypothesis 8 was not supported; legitimating tactics were used most in a downward direction, not in a lateral direction. Consistent with Hypothesis 9, pressure was used more in a downward direction than in a lateral or upward direction.

Directional differences were sometimes reflected in the frequencies for particular components of the tactic categories. These findings are based on a qualitative examination of patterns of results rather than on statistical tests because of the small number of cases. Pressure in the form of threats to get the target dismissed occurred most often in a downward direction, whereas pressure in the form of persistent nagging or threats to quit occurred most often in an upward direction. An upward appeal to the boss of the target is a type of coalition tactic that occurred most often in lateral influence attempts, whereas asking peers to influence the target was a type of coalition tactic that occurred most often in upward influence attempts. Exchange in downward influence attempts often involved specific incentives (e.g., promise of a pay increase, promotion, or better assignment), whereas in lateral influence attempts exchange usually involved offers to trade favors or a reminder that a favor was owed.

Initial and Follow-up Attempts

The initial influence attempt in sequential incidents often involved either a simple request (43%) or the use of rational persuasion alone as a single tactic (22%). The relatively small number of sequential incidents and the high incidence of simple requests and weak cases of rational persuasion in initial influence attempts limited analysis of complex tactic sequences in the present data set. Nevertheless, the combined data from agents and targets was sufficient to test our hypotheses about the use of tactics in initial and follow-up influence attempts. . . .

. . . Consistent with Hypotheses 10, 11, and 12, rational persuasion, ingratiation, and personal appeals were used most often in initial influence attempts. Consistent with Hypothesis 13, exchange was used most often in immediate follow-up attempts. Although no hypothesis was made for legitimating tactics, this type of tactic was used more often in immediate follow-up attempts than in delayed follow-up attempts. Consistent with Hypotheses 14 and 15, coalition tactics and pressure were used most often in delayed follow-up influence attempts; in other words, they were usually saved until last.

As in the case of directional differences, a qualitative analysis of major components of the tactic categories revealed some differences related to sequencing. For example, an initial influence attempt often involved a weak form of rational persuasion (e.g., a brief explanation, an assertion without supporting evidence), whereas follow-up influence attempts usually involved a stronger form of rational persuasion (e.g., a detailed proposal, elaborate documentation, a convincing reply to concerns raised by the target person). A proactive form of consultation (e.g., requests for target suggestions or participation in planning) was more likely to be used in an initial influence attempt, whereas a reactive form of consultation (e.g., the agent offered to modify a proposal or assignment to deal with target concerns) was more likely to be used in an immediate or delayed follow-up attempt. A relatively weak form of pressure (e.g., insistent demand, sarcasm, vague threat) was more likely to be used in an initial influence attempt or an immediate follow-up attempt, whereas in a delayed follow-up attempt a strong form of pressure was more likely to be used (e.g., explicit threat or warning, disciplinary action, overt sanction). Persistent reminders, checking, or nagging were other (weak) forms of pressure unique to delayed follow-up attempts. The form of coalition tactic used in an initial influence attempt or an immediate follow-up attempt was likely to involve statements to identify others who endorsed the agent's proposal, whereas in a delayed follow-up attempt a coalition was more likely to involve getting other people to lobby directly with the target, or an upward appeal to the target's boss.

DISCUSSION

This was the first study to use critical incidents to examine directional differences in use of influence tactics. Directional differences were significant for all nine tactics, and the results mostly supported the hypotheses based on our model (see Table 3 for a summary of results). The results also confirmed most of the findings in the earlier research by Yukl and Tracey (1992) using questionnaires.

The current study is the first to report empirical results on the sequencing of tactics by managers. The results verified some propositions about sequencing made by other social scientists, and most of the hypotheses based on our model were supported. As

TABLE 3
SUMMARY OF RESULTS FOR EACH INFLUENCE TACTIC

Influence tactic	Directional hypothesis	Directional results	Sequencing hypothesis	Sequencing results
Rational persuasion	More up than down or lateral	Supported	More initial	Supported
Inspirational appeal	More down	Supported	No hypothesis	No difference
Consultation	More down than lateral or up	More down and lateral than up	No hypothesis	No difference
Ingratiation	More down and lateral than up	Supported	More initial	Supported
Personal appeal	More lateral than down or up	Supported	More initial	Supported
Exchange	More down and lateral than up	Supported	More follow-up	Supported for immediate follow-up
Coalition	More lateral and up than down	Supported	More follow-up	Supported for delayed follow-up
Legitimating	More lateral than down or up	More down and lateral than up	No hypothesis	Most in immediate follow-up, least in delayed follow-up
Pressure	More down than lateral or up	Supported	More follow-up	Supported

365

expected, many initial influence attempts consisted of simple requests or weak forms of rational persuasion. Ingratiation and personal appeals were used more in initial influence attempts, exchange and legitimating tactics were used more in immediate follow-up influence attempts, and coalitions and pressure tactics were used more in delayed follow-up influence attempts. A supplementary qualitative analysis of the influence incidents identified some apparent directional and sequencing differences involving various forms of the same influence tactic. However, these qualitative findings need to be verified and extended by additional research with quantitative methods of analysis.

The combined results for direction and sequencing supported the Kipnis and Schmidt (1983) proposition that pressure is used more as a follow-up tactic with weak targets and that coalition is used more as a follow-up tactic with strong targets. However, the results did not support their proposition that ingratiation is used more as a follow-up tactic with strong targets. Nor did the results support the Keys and Case (1990) proposition that managers quickly resort to use of threats and manipulation when meeting resistance by subordinates. Most of the managers in our study appeared reluctant to use coercive power and did so only as a last resort after trying less extreme tactics, such as mild forms of pressure and efforts to get a subordinate to take responsibility for helping to solve a performance problem.

This study was the first to examine how often various tactics are used alone and in combinations. Some tactics (inspirational appeals, consultation, ingratiation, and legitimating tactics) were more likely to be used in combination with another tactic than alone. The finding that consultation and inspirational appeals are seldom used as single tactics may explain why they did not emerge as separate categories in the early incident study by Kipnis et al. (1980), in which each influence attempt was coded into only one tactic category. More research is needed to discover why some combinations occur frequently and others seldom occur. A promising possibility to investigate is the idea suggested by Yukl (1990) that some tactics are more compatible with each other because they are easier to use together and enhance each other's effectiveness.

The results from our analysis of directional differences, sequencing differences, and tactic combinations provide the following summary of the way the nine influence tactics are typically used by managers. Rational persuasion was the tactic used most often both alone and in combinations. Although used proportionally more often in upward influence attempts, rational persuasion was used frequently in downward and lateral influence attempts as well. Inspirational appeals were used most often in influence attempts with subordinates, usually in combination with another tactic, such as rational persuasion, consultation, or ingratiation. Consultation was used most often in influence attempts with subordinates or peers, and it was usually combined with another tactic, such as rational persuasion, inspirational appeals, or ingratiation. Personal appeals were used most often in initial influence attempts or immediate follow-up attempts with a peer. Ingratiation was used most often in initial influence attempts with subordinates or peers, and it was typically used in combination with another tactic. Note, however, that our study investigated the use of ingratiation as an immediate influence tactic, and in an upward direction ingratiation is more likely to be used as a long-term impression management technique. Exchange was used most often in immediate follow-up attempts with subordinates and peers. A legitimating tactic was used most often in immediate follow-up attempts with subordinates and peers, and it was typically used in combination with rational persuasion or a pressure tactic. Pressure was used mostly as a follow-up tactic, and the target was usually a subordinate. Coalitions were used mostly as a follow-up tactic, and the target was usually a peer or superior.

The research method used in this study has some limitations that should be acknowledged. Any conclusions about the frequency of use for various tactics and tactic combinations rests on the assumption that the sampling of incidents was representative of influence attempts made in organizations. Some tactics or combinations may have occurred more frequently or less frequently merely because our set of incidents included a higher percentage of resistance outcomes than normally occurs in organizations. The absolute frequency of use for each tactic is probably somewhat inflated, because respondents were instructed not to include incidents involving only a simple request, which our unpublished research with diaries indicates is a very common form of influence attempt. As noted earlier, because of the unequal distribution of incidents and small cell sizes for many tactics, most analyses were done without regard to possible interactions between direction, timing, source, and use of single tactics or combinations. Future research should examine the possibility that our results for "main effects" may have been distorted by such interactions.

In the present study, we did not directly investigate an agent's reasons for selecting a particular tactic at a particular time for a particular target person. More research is needed to determine why managers select particular combinations and sequences of tactics and how these choices affect target compliance and commitment. Finally, the research on influence tactics has largely ignored the fact that an influence attempt made by a manager is seldom an isolated episode but is instead part of a sequence of reciprocal influence processes that occur in an evolving relationship between the parties. Research on proactive influence tactics needs to be integrated with the extensive research literature on other ways in which managers influence people at work (e.g., use of contingent rewards and punishments, goal setting, coaching and instruction, role modeling).

The findings in this study have some important practical implications. Recent studies have found that the influence behavior of managers is related to their effectiveness (Keys & Case, 1990; Kipnis & Schmidt, 1988; Yukl & Tracey, 1992). Effective managers select influence tactics that are appropriate for the situation (Yukl, 1989). Determining what tactics are appropriate is not just a matter of "common sense." Our set of incidents contained many examples of inept influence attempts (e.g., use of pressure when unnecessary; use of ingratiation in a clumsy way, use of incompatible tactics in the same influence attempt). Empirically based guidelines would help managers identify appropriate tactics and could be used in management training to improve a manager's skills in influencing people at work.

The present study increases our knowledge about aspects of the situation likely to be relevant for selecting appropriate tactics, and the results move us closer to development of an influence model with practical guidelines for managers. The following tentative guidelines are based on findings in the present study and findings about outcomes of using different tactics from the parallel research by Falbe and Yukl (1992) and Yukl and Tracey (1992).

• Ingratiation is sometimes useful for influencing subordinates and peers, but it is seldom useful for an immediate influence attempt with the boss.

• Exchange tactics are sometimes useful for influencing subordinates and peers, but they are seldom useful for influencing the boss.

• Ingratiation should be used in an initial influence attempt rather than in a follow-up influence attempt.

• Pressure tactics should be used in a follow-up influence attempt rather than in an initial influence attempt, and only when justified by the importance of the request.

• Legitimating tactics should be used only when there is a clear, verifiable basis for a request that is unknown to the target.

• A strong form of rational persuasion (e.g., a clear explanation of the reason for the request or proposal, a review of evidence supporting it) should be used rather than a weak form whenever possible.

• Rational persuasion may be used in combination with any of the other tactics, and it usually increases their effectiveness.

• Ingratiation should be used with another compatible tactic, such as rational persuasion or inspirational appeals, rather than alone.

• Pressure should be used with another compatible tactic, such as rational persuasion or legitimating, rather than alone.

• Strong forms of pressure (e.g., demands or threats) should not be used in combination with a soft tactic that is based on mutual trust and friendship, such as ingratiation, consultation, or personal appeals.

• Each tactic category includes a broad variety of behaviors; when planning an influence attempt, it is important to consider not only what tactics to use but also what forms of each tactic are most appropriate for the situation.

In conclusion, our research examined some questions that have received little attention, and some other questions for which prior research found mostly inconsistent results. The results supported our theoretical propositions in most cases, and they provide a better understanding about the use of different influence tactics by managers. Follow-up research is currently in progress to refine and extend the model.

REFERENCES

Ansari, M. A., & Kapoor, A. (1987). Organizational context and upward influence tactics. *Organizational Behavior and Human Decision Processes, 40*, 39–49.

Erez, M., Rim, Y., & Keider, I. (1986). The two sides of the tactics of influence: Agent vs. target. *Journal of Occupational Psychology, 59*, 25–39.

Falbe, C. M., & Yukl, G. (1992). Consequences for managers of using single influence tactics and combinations of tactics. *Academy of Management Journal, 35*, 638–652.

Keys, B., & Case, T. L. (1990). How to become an influential manager. *The Executive, 4*(4), 38–51.

Kipnis, D., & Schmidt, S. M. (1983). An influence perspective on bargaining within organizations. In M. Bazerman & R. Lewicki (Eds.), *Negotiating in organizations* (pp. 303–319). Beverly Hills, CA: Sage.

Kipnis, D., & Schmidt, S. M. (1988). Upward influence styles: Relationship with performance evaluations, salary, and stress. *Administrative Science Quarterly, 33*, 528–542.

Kipnis, D., Schmidt, S. M., & Wilkinson, I. (1980). Intra-organizational influence tactics: Explorations in getting one's way. *Journal of Applied Psychology, 65,* 440–452.

Loether, H. J., & McTavish, D. G. (1980). *Descriptive and inferential statistics: An introduction.* Boston: Allyn & Bacon.

Schilit, W. K., & Locke, E. (1982). A study of upward influence in organizations. *Administrative Science Quarterly, 27,* 304–316.

Schmidt, S. M., & Kipnis, D. (1984). Manager's pursuit of individual and organizational goals. *Human Relations, 37,* 781–794.

Schriesheim, C. A., & Hinkin, T. R. (1990). Influence tactics used by subordinates: A theoretical and empirical analysis and refinement of the Kipnis, Schmidt, and Wilkinson subscales. *Journal of Applied Psychology, 75,* 246–257.

Yukl, G. (1989). *Leadership in organizations.* Englewood Cliffs, NJ: Prentice-Hall.

Yukl, G. (1990). *Skills for managers and leaders.* Englewood Cliffs, NJ: Prentice-Hall.

Yukl, G., & Falbe, C. M. (1990). Influence tactics in upward, downward, and lateral influence attempts. *Journal of Applied Psychology, 75,* 132–140.

Yukl, G., Lepsinger, R., & Lucia, T. (1992). Preliminary report on the development and validation of the Influence Behavior Questionnaire. In K. Clark & M. Clark (Eds.), *The impact of leadership.* Greensboro, NC: Center for Creative Leadership.

Yukl, G., & Tracey, B. (1992). Consequences of influence tactics used with subordinates, peers, and superiors. *Journal of Applied Psychology, 77,* 525–535.

Corporations, Culture and Commitment: Motivation and Social Control in Organizations

Charles O' Reilly

Corporate culture is receiving much attention in the business press. A recent article in *Fortune* describes how the CEO at Black & Decker "transformed an entire corporate *culture,* replacing a complacent manufacturing mentality with an almost manic, market-driven way of doing things."[1] Similarly, the success of Food Lion (a $3 billion food-market chain that has grown at an annual rate of 37% over the past 20 years with annual returns on equity of 24%) is attributed to a culture which emphasizes "hard work, simplicity, and frugality."[2] Other well-known firms such as 3M, Johnson & Johnson, Apple, and Kimberly-Clark have been routinely praised for their innovative cultures.[3] Even the success of Japanese firms in the U.S. has been partly attributed to their ability to change the traditional culture developed under American managers. Peters and Waterman report how a U.S. television manufacturing plant, under Japanese management, reduced its defect rate from 140 to 6, its complaint rate from 70% to 7%, and the turnover rate among employees from 30% to 1%, all due to a changed management philosophy and culture.[4]

Even more dramatic is the turnaround at the New United Motors Manufacturing Incorporated (NUMMI) plant in Fremont, California. When General Motors closed this facility in 1982, it was one of the worst plants in the GM assembly division with an 18 percent daily absenteeism rate and a long history of conflict in its labor relations. The plant reopened as a joint venture between Toyota and GM in 1983. Over 85 percent of the original labor force was rehired, and workers are still represented by the UAW. Although the technology used is vintage 1970s and the plant is not as automated as many others within GM and Toyota, productivity is almost double what GM gets in other facilities. In 1987, it took an estimated 20.8 hours to produce a car at NUMMI versus 40.7 in other GM plants and 18.0 at Toyota. Quality of the NUMMI automobiles is the highest in the GM system, based on both internal audits and owner surveys, and absenteeism is at 2 percent compared to 8 percent at other GM facilities. What accounts for this remarkable success? According to one account, "At the system's core is a *culture* in which the assembly line workers maintain their machines, ensure the quality of their work, and improve the production process."[5]

But a culture is not always a positive force. It has also been implicated when firms run into difficulties. The CEO of financially troubled Computerland, William Tauscher, has attempted to restructure the form, noting that "a low-cost culture is a must."[6] Henry Wendt, CEO of SmithKline Beckman, has attributed his firm's current difficulties to complacency. "We've been victims of our own success. . . . I want to create a new culture."[7] Corporate culture has also been implicated in problems faced by Sears, Caterpillar, Bank of America, Polaroid, General Motors, and others. Even difficulties in mergers and acquisitions are sometimes attributed to cultural conflicts which make integration of separate units difficult. Failure to merge two cultures can lead to debilitating conflict, a loss of talent, and an inability to reap the benefits of synergy.

But what is really meant when one refers to a firm's "culture"? Do all organizations have them? Are they always important? Even if we can identify cultures, do we know enough about how they work to manage them? Four major questions need to be answered.

- What is culture?
- From a manager's perspective, when is culture important?
- What is the process through which cultures are developed and maintained?
- How can cultures be managed?

WHAT IS CULTURE?

If culture is to be analyzed and managed, it is important that we be clear about what is meant by the term. Failure to clearly specify what "culture" is can result in confusion, misunderstanding, and conflict about its basic function and importance.

Culture as Control

Clearly, little would get done by or in organizations if some control systems were not in place to direct and coordinate activities. In fact, organizations are often seen to be efficient and effective solely because control systems operate.[8]

But what is a "control system"? A generic definition might be that a control system is "the knowledge that someone who knows and cares is paying close attention to what we do and can tell us when deviations are occurring?" Although broad, this definition encompasses traditional formal control systems ranging from planning and budgeting systems to performance appraisals. According to this definition, control systems work when those who are monitored are aware that someone who matters, such as a boss or staff department, is paying attention and is likely to care when things aren't going according to plan.

Several years ago a large toy manufacturer installed, at considerable expense, a management-by-objectives (MBO) performance and appraisal system. After a year or so, top management became aware that the system was working well in one part of the organization but not another. They conducted an investigation and discovered the reason for the failure. In the part of the organization where MBO was working well, senior management was enthusiastic and committed. They saw real benefits and conveyed their belief up and down the chain of command. In the part of the organization where the system had failed, senior management saw MBO as another bureaucratic exercise to be endured. Subordinate managers quickly learned to complete the paperwork but ignore the purpose. The lesson here was that a control system, no matter how carefully designed, works only when those being monitored believe that people who matter care about the results and are paying close attention. When Jan Carlzon became head of SAS Airline, he was concerned about the poor on-time record. To correct this, he personally requested a daily accounting of the on-time status of all flights. In the space of two years, SAS on-time record went from 83% to 97%.[9]

In designing formal control systems, we typically attempt to measure either outcomes or behaviors. For example, in hospitals it makes no sense to evaluate the nursing staff on whether patients get well. Instead, control systems rely on assessing behaviors. Are specified medical procedures followed? Are checks made at appropriate times? In other settings, behavior may not be observable. Whenever possible, we then attempt to measure outcomes. Sales people, for instance, are usually measured on their productivity, since the nature of their job often precludes any effective monitoring of their behavior. In other situations, control systems can be designed that monitor both behaviors and outcomes. For example, for some retail sales jobs both behaviors (how the customer is addressed, how quickly the order is taken, whether the sales floor is kept stocked) and outcomes (sales volume) can be measured.

However, it is often the case that neither behavior nor outcomes can be adequately monitored.[10] These are the activities that are nonroutine and unpredictable, situations that require initiative, flexibility, and innovation. These can be dealt with only by developing social control systems in which common agreements exist among people about what constitutes appropriate attitudes and behavior.

Culture may be thought of as a potential social control system. Unlike formal control systems that typically assess outcomes or behaviors only intermittently, social control systems can be much more finely tuned. When we care about those with whom we work and have a common set of expectations, we are "under control" whenever we are in their presence. If we want to be accepted, we try to live up to their expectations. In this sense, social control systems can operate more extensively than most formal systems. Interestingly, our response to being monitored by formal and social control systems may also differ. With formal systems people often have a sense of external constraint which is binding and unsatisfying. With social controls, we often feel as though we have great autonomy, even though paradoxically we are conforming much more.

Thus, from a management perspective, culture in the form of shared expectations may be thought of as a social control system. Howard Schwartz and Stan Davis offer a practical definition of culture as "a pattern of beliefs and expectations shared by the organization's members. These beliefs and expectations produce norms that powerfully shape the behavior of individuals and groups."[11]

Culture as Normative Order

What Schwartz and Davis are referring to as culture are the central norms that may characterize an organization. Norms are expectations about what are appropriate or inappropriate attitudes and behaviors. They are socially created standards that help us interpret and evaluate events. Although their content may vary, they exist in all societies and, while often unnoticed, they are pervasive. For instance, in our society we have rather explicit norms about eye-contact. We may get uncomfortable when these are violated. Consider what happens when someone doesn't look at you while speaking or who continues to look without pause. In organizations we often find peripheral or unimportant norms around issues such as dress or forms of address. In the old railroads, for example, hats were a must for all managers, while everyone addressed each other with a formal "mister."

More important norms often exist around issues such as quality, performance, flexibility, or how to deal with conflict. In many organizations, it is impolite to disagree publicly with others. Instead, much behind-the-scenes interaction takes place to anticipate or resolve disputes. In other organizations, there may be norms that legitimate and encourage the public airing of disputes. Intel Corporation has an explicit policy of "constructive confrontation" that encourages employees to deal with disagreements in an immediate and direct manner.

In this view, the central values and styles that characterize a firm, perhaps not even written down, can form the basis for the development of norms that attach approval or disapproval to holding certain attitudes or beliefs and to acting in certain ways. For instance, the fundamental value of aggressiveness or competition may, if widely held and supported, be expressed as a norm that encourages organizational participants to stress winning competition. Pepsico encourages competition and punishes failure to compete.[12] Service is a pivotal norm at IBM; innovation is recognized as central at 3M. It is through norms—the expectations shared by group members and the approval or disapproval attached to these expectations—that culture is developed and maintained.

However, there is an important difference between the guiding beliefs or vision held by top management and the daily beliefs or norms held by those at lower levels in the unit or organization. The former reflect top managements' beliefs about how things ought to be. The latter define how things actually are. Simply because top management is in agreement about how they would like the organization to function is no guarantee that these beliefs will be held by others. One CEO spoke at some length about the glowing corporate philosophy that he believed in and felt characterized his firm's culture. After spending some time talking to mid-level managers in the organization, a very different picture emerged. A central norm shared by many of these managers was "Good people don't stay here." It is a common occurrence to find a noble sounding statement of corporate values framed on the wall and a very different and cynical interpretation of this creed held by people who have been around long enough to realize what is really important.

Moreover, norms can vary on two dimensions: the intensity or amount of approval/disapproval attached to an expectation; and the crystallization or degree of consensus or consistency with which a norm is shared. For instance, when analyzing an organization's culture it may be that for certain values there can be wide consensus but no intensity. Everyone understands what top management values, but there is no strong approval or disapproval attached to these beliefs or behaviors. Or, a given norm, such as innovation, can be positively valued in one group (e.g., marketing or R&D) and negatively valued in another (manufacturing or personnel). There is intensity but no crystallization.

It is only when there exist both intensity and consensus that strong cultures exist. This is why it is difficult to develop or change culture. Organizational members must come to know and share a common set of expectations. These must, in turn, be consistently valued and reinforced across divisions and management levels.[13] Only when this is done will there be both intensity and consensus. Similarly, a failure to share the central norms or to consistently reinforce them may lead to vacuous norms, conflicting interpretations, or to micro-cultures that exist only within subunits.

To have a strong culture, an organization does not have to have very many strongly held values. Only a few core values characterize strong culture firms such as Mars, Marriott, Hewlett-Packard, and Walmart. What is critical is that these beliefs be widely shared and strongly held; that is, people throughout the organization must be willing to tell one another when a core belief is not being lived up to. . . .

Culture and Commitment

Culture is critical in developing and maintaining levels of intensity and dedication among employees that often characterize successful firms. This strong attachment is particularly valuable when the employees have knowledge that is instrumental to the success of the organization or when very high levels of motivation are required. When IBM bought ROLM, the critical resource was not the existing product line but the design and engineering expertise of ROLM's staff. A failure to gain the commitment of employees during mergers and acquisitions can diminish or destroy the value of the venture. In contrast, a highly dedicated workforce represents a significant competitive advantage. Under turbulent or changing conditions, relying on employees who wait to be told exactly what to do can be a liability.

How, then, do strong culture organizations develop intensity and commitment? A 20-year veteran of IBM was quoted in a *Wall Street Journal* article as saying, "I don't know what a cult is and what it is those bleary-eyed kids selling poppies really do, but I'm probably that deeply committed to the IBM company."[14] To understand this process, we need to consider what commitment is and how it is developed. By understanding the underlying psychology of commitment, we can then think about how to design systems to develop such an attachment among employees.

Organizational Commitment   What is meant by the term "organizational commitment"? It is typically conceived of as an individual's psychological bond to the organization, including a sense of job involvement, loyalty, and a belief in the values of the organization. There are three processes or stages of commitment: *compliance, identification,* and *internalization.*[15] In the first stage, *compliance,* a person accepts the influence of others mainly to obtain something from others, such as pay. The second stage is *identification,* in which the individual accepts influence in order to maintain a satisfying, self-defining relationship. People feel pride in belonging to the firm. The final stage of commitment is *internalization,* in which the individual finds the values of the organization to be intrinsically rewarding and congruent with personal values.

Conceiving of commitment as developing in this manner allows us to understand how a variety of organizations—ranging from cults to strong culture corporations—generate commitment among their members. In fact, these organizations can be categorized based on the type of commitment displayed by their members. Cults and religious organizations, for example, typically have members who have internalized the values of the organization and who become "deployable agents," or individuals who can be relied upon to go forth and proselytize.[16] Japanese organizations, Theory Z, and strong culture firms are characterized by members who have a strong identification with the organization. These employees identify with the firm because it stands for something they value. In typical corporations, members comply with directions but may have little involvement with the firm beyond self-interest; that is, there is no commitment with the firm beyond that of a fair exchange of effort for money and, perhaps, status.

HOW CULTURE IS DEVELOPED

How do people become committed to organizations? Why, for example, would someone choose to join a cult? How do firms such as NUMMI get the incredible levels of productivity from their employees (as one team member said, "I like the new system so much it scares me. I'm scared because it took me 18 years to realize that I blew it at GM. Now we have a chance to do things a different way.")? The answer to this puzzle is simultaneously simple and nonobvious. As Jerry Salancik has noted, "commitment is too easy," yet it relies on an understanding of human motivation that is counter-intuitive.[17]

Constructing Social Realities

Most discussions of motivation assume a stable set of individual needs and values.[18] These are seen as shaping expectations, goals, and attitudes. In turn, these are presumed to guide behavior and people's responses to situations. In Maslow's theory, for instance, people are assumed to have a hierarchy of needs.[19] The managerial consequence of this view can be seen in our theories of job design in which jobs are supposed to be designed to take advantage of the desire of people to grow and self-actualize.[20] But are such theories correct? The empirical evidence is weak at best.[21] In spite of numerous efforts to demonstrate the effect of needs and personality, there is little support for the power of individual differences to predict behavior.

Consider the results of two experiments. In the first, Christian seminary students were approached and given one of two requests. Both asked them to extemporaneously address a visiting class in a discussion of the parable of the Good Samaritan. They were told to walk over to a classroom building to do this. In one condition they were informed that the class was already there and that they should hurry. In the other condition they were told that the class would arrive in several minutes. As they walked to the classroom, all subjects passed an old man (the "victim") dressed in shabby clothes and in obvious need of help. The experimenters were interested in what proportion of Christian seminarians thinking of the Good Samaritan would stop and help this person. Surprisingly, in the condition in which the subjects were told to hurry, only 30 percent paid any attention. Think about this. Seventy percent of a group of individuals with religious values who were training to be ministers failed to stop. Ninety-five percent of those who were not in a hurry, stopped to help.

In another experiment, researchers observed when students using a campus restroom washed their hands. They discovered that when another person was visible in the restroom, 90 percent washed their hands. When no other person was visible, less than 20 percent did so.

What explains these and other findings? What often seems to account for behavior are the expectations of others. As individuals, we are very susceptible to the informational and normative influence of others. We pay attention to the actions of others and learn from them. "In actuality, virtually all learning phenomena resulting from direct experience occur on a vicarious basis by observing other people's behavior and its consequences for them." We watch others and form expectations about how and when we should act.[22]

Yet, we are not sensitive to how much of our world is really a social construction—one that rests on shared agreements. We often tend to underestimate the degree to which situations and the expectations of others can constrain and shape behavior. Strong situations—ones in which there are very clear incentives and expectations about what constitutes appropriate attitudes and behavior—can be very powerful. When we care what others think, the power of these norms or social expectations can be heightened.

Mechanisms for Developing Culture

How can cultures be developed and managed in organizations? All organizations—from cults to strong culture corporations—draw on the same underlying psychology and create situations characterized by strong norms that focus people's attention, provide a clear guidance about what is important, and provide for group reinforcement of appropriate attitudes and behavior. Four common mechanisms are used to accomplish this. What varies across these organizations is not what is done but only the degree to which these mechanisms are used.

Participation   The first mechanism that is critical in developing or changing a culture are systems that provide for participation. These systems encourage people to be involved and send signals to the individual that he or she is valued. These may range from formal efforts such as quality circles and advisory boards to less formal efforts such as suggestion systems and opportunities to meet with top managers and informal social gatherings. What is important about these processes is that people are encouraged to make incremental choices and develop a sense of responsibility for their actions. In some cases, such as work design, the specific choices made may be less important for future success than the fact that people had the chance to make them.

From a psychological perspective, choice is often associated with commitment. When we choose of our own volition to do something, we often feel responsible.[23] When the choice is volitional, explicit, public, and irrevocable, the commitment is even more binding.[24] For instance, direct sales companies have learned that by getting the customer to fill out the order sheet, they can cut cancellations dramatically. A large number of psychological experiments have convincingly shown that participation can lead to both commitment and enjoyment, even when people are induced to engage in physically and emotionally stressful activities such as eating earthworms and becoming bone marrow donors.[25]

How do organizations use participation? Marc Galanter has documented how members of the Unification Church use processes of incremental commitment to recruit cult members.[26] Individuals are invited to dinner, convinced to spend the weekend for a seminar, and in some cases, induced to remain permanently with their new found "friends." Interestingly, there is no evidence that people who join cults under these circumstances are suffering from any psychopathology. Religious organizations often use elaborate systems of incremental choice and participation leading to greater and greater involvement. Japanese-managed automobile companies in the U.S. also have elaborate systems of selection and orientation that rely heavily on these approaches, as do American "strong culture" firms.

Management as Symbolic Action   The second mechanism commonly seen in strong culture organizations is that of clear, visible actions on the part of management in support of the cultural values.[27] In organizations, participants typically want to know what is important. One way we gain this information is to carefully watch and listen to those above us. We look for consistent patterns. When top management not only says that something is important but also consistently behaves in ways that support the message, we begin to believe what is said. When the CEO of Xerox, David Kearns, began his quest for improved quality, there was some initial uncertainty about whether he meant it. Over time, as the message was repeated again and again, and as resources continued to be devoted to the quality effort, norms developed setting expectations about the role and importance of quality throughout the corporation.[28]

An important function of management is to provide interpretations of events for the organization's members. Without a shared meaning, confusion and conflict can result. Managers need to be sensitive to how their actions are viewed. Interpreting (or reinterpreting) history, telling stories, the use of vivid language, spending time, and being seen as visible in support of certain positions are all potential ways of shaping the organization's culture. This does not mean that managers need to be charismatic. However, managers need to engage in acts of "mundane symbolism." By this they can insure that important issues get suitable amounts of time, that questions are continually asked about important topics, and that the subject gets on the agenda and it is followed up.

The appropriate use of symbols and ceremonies is also important. When Jerry Sanders, CEO of Advanced Micro Devices, decided to shift the firm's strategy toward innovation, he not only made substantive changes in budget, positions, and organizational structure, he also used a symbol. As a part of the many talks he had with employees describing the need to change, Sanders would also describe how important it was to invest in areas that others could not easily duplicate—such as investing in proprietary products. He would describe how a poor farmer would always need a cash crop at the end of the year if he was to survive. But if he began to prosper, a smart farmer would begin to plant crops that others might not be able to afford—crops, for example, that took more than a year to come to fruition, crops like asparagus. The notion of asparagus became a visible and important symbol for change within AMD, even to the point where managers begin referring to revenues from new proprietary products as "being measured on asparagus."

Symbols are not a substitute for substance, and ceremonies cannot replace content. Rather, many of the substantive changes that occur in organizations, such as promotions or reorganizations, have multiple meanings and interpretations. Over time, people may lose a clear sense for what the superordinate goals are and why their jobs are important. In strong culture organizations, managers frequently and consistently send signals helping to renew these understandings. They do this by continually calling attention to what is important, in word and in action.

Information from Others   While clear messages from management are an important determinant of a culture, so too are consistent messages from coworkers. If control comes from the knowledge that someone who matters is paying attention, then the degree to which we care about our coworkers also gives them a certain control over us. Years ago, several researchers conducted an experiment in which subjects were placed in a room to complete a questionnaire. While they were doing this, smoke began to flow from an air vent. While 75% of the subjects who were alone responded by notifying the experimenter of a possible fire, only 38% did so when in the company of two other subjects. When these other two were confederates of the experimenter and deliberately said nothing, only 10% of the subjects responded. One conclusion from this and other similar experiments is that we often take our cue from others when we are uncertain what to do.

In organizations, during periods of crisis or when people are new to the situation, they often look to others for explanations of what to do and how to interpret events. Strong cultures are typically characterized by consensus about these questions. In these settings there are often attempts made to insure a consistency of understanding and to minimize any us-them attitudes between parts of the organization. For instance, strong culture firms often pride themselves on the equality of treatment of all employees. At Mars, all employees punch a time clock and no one has a private secretary. At Gore-Tex, Walmart, Disney, and others there are no employees or managers, only associates, team members, and hosts. At NUMMI, Honda, and Nissan there are no private dining rooms for managers and workers often wear uniforms. In the Rajneesh Commune, everyone wore clothes with the color magenta.

The goal here is to create a strong social construction of reality by minimizing contradictory interpretations. In cults, this is often done by isolating the members from family and friends. Some religious organizations do this by encouraging extensive involvement in a variety of church activities and meetings. Japanese firms expect after-work socializing. At NUMMI, for instance, each work team is given a semiannual budget to be spent only on team-sponsored activities where the entire team participates. In corporations, 60-hour work weeks can also isolate people from competing interpretations. Some electronics firms in Silicon Valley have provided employee T-shirts with slogans such as "Working 80 hours a week and loving it." With this commitment of time, workers may be as isolated as if they had joined a cult.

Comprehensive Reward Systems   A final mechanism for promoting and shaping culture is the reward system, but not simply monetary rewards. Rather, these systems focus on rewards such as recognition and approval which can be given more frequently than money. These rewards also focus on the intrinsic aspects of the job and a sense of belonging to the organization. Recognition by your boss or coworkers for doing the right thing can be more potent in shaping behavior than an annual bonus. In the words of a popular management book, the trick is to catch someone doing

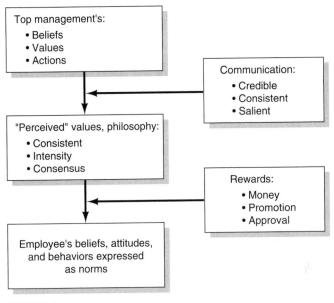

FIGURE 1

something right and to reward it on the spot. While tokens such as scrolls or badges can be meaningless, under the right circumstances they can also be highly valued.

It is easy to desire one type of behavior while rewarding another. Often management professes a concern for quality while systematically rewarding only those who meet their goals, regardless of the quality. Innovation may be espoused but even the slightest failure is punished. At its simplest, people usually do what they are rewarded for and don't do what they're punished for. If this is true and to be taken seriously, then a simple analysis of what gets management's attention should give us a sense for what the culture supports. Who gets promoted? At 3M, one important aspect of success is to be associated with a new product introduction. If innovation is espoused, but doing things by-the-book is what is rewarded, it doesn't take a psychologist to figure out what the firm actually values. In fact, if there are inconsistencies between what top management says and what is actually rewarded, the likely outcome will be confusion and cynicism.

MANAGING CULTURE

Each of these can affect the development of a shared set of expectations. As shown in Figure 1, the process begins with words and actions on the part of the group's leaders. Even if no explicit statements are made, subordinates will attempt to infer a pattern. If management is credible and communicates consistently, members of the group may begin to develop consistent expectations about what is important. When this consensus is also rewarded, clear norms can then emerge.

Whether or not these norms constitute a desirable culture depends on the critical tasks to be accomplished and whether the formal control system provides sufficient leverage to attain these. If culture *is* important, four steps can help a manager understand how to manage it.

• Identify the strategic objectives of the unit. Once identified, specify the short-term objectives and critical actions that need to be accomplished if the strategic objectives are to be accomplished.

• Analyze the existing values and norms that characterize the organization. This can be done by focusing on what people in the unit feel is expected of them by their peers and bosses and what is actually rewarded. What does it take to get ahead? What stories are routinely told? Who are the people who exemplify the group? Look for norms that are widely shared and strongly felt.

• Once these are identified, look for norms that may hinder the accomplishment of critical tasks; norms that would help but are not currently present; and conflicts between what is needed and what is currently rewarded.

• Once these are identified, programs can be designed to begin to shape or develop the desired norms. These can draw upon the psychological mechanisms discussed previously.

The logic here is straightforward and links culture to those activities critical for the implementation of strategy and for generating widespread understanding and commitment among the organization's members. Obviously, these actions take time and management resources to accomplish. However, to ignore them is to ignore a social control system that may already be operating in the organization. The issue is whether this system is helping or hindering. Managers need to be sensitive to what the central organizational norms are and how they can affect them. To not be sensitive to these issues is to ignore the advice of a CEO who said, "We will either be a victim or a successful result of our culture."

REFERENCES

1 *Fortune,* January 2, 1989.
2 *Fortune,* August 15, 1988.
3 *Fortune,* June 6, 1988.
4 T. Peters and R. H. Waterman, *In Search of Excellence: Lessons From America's Best-Run Companies* (New York, NY: Harper & Row, 1982), p. 32.
5 *Fortune,* January 30, 1989.
6 *Business Week,* October 10, 1988.
7 *Business Week,* October 10, 1988.
8 A. Wilkins and W. Ouchi, "Efficient Cultures: Exploring the Relationship between Culture and Organizational Performance," *Administrative Science Quarterly,* 28 (1983): 468–481; O. Williamson, *Markets and Hierarchies* (New York, NY: The Free Press, 1975).
9 J. Carlzon, *Moments of Truth* (Cambridge, MA: Ballinger, 1987).
10 S. Dornbusch and W. R. Scott, *Evaluation and the Exercise of Authority* (San Francisco, CA: Jossey-Bass, 1975).

11 H. Schwartz and S. Davis, "Matching Corporate Culture and Business Strategy," *Organizational Dynamics* (1981), pp. 30–48.

12 *Fortune,* April 10, 1989.

13 D. Feldman, "The Development and Enforcement of Group Norms," *Academy of Management Review,* 9 (1984): 45–53.

14 *Wall Street Journal,* April 7, 1986.

15 C. O'Reilly and J. Chatman, "Organizational Commitment and Psychological Attachment: The Effects of Compliance, Identification and Internalization on Prosocial Behavior," *Journal of Applied Psychology,* 71 (1986): 492–499.

16 W. Appel, *Cults in America* (New York, NY: Holt, Rinehart and Winston, 1983); D. Gerstel, *Paradise Incorporated: Synanon* (San Francisco, CA: Presidio Press, 1982).

17 G. Salancik, "Commitment Is Too Easy!" *Organizational Dynamics* (Summer 1977), pp. 62–80.

18 For example, see F. Herzberg, B. Mausner, and B. Snyderman, *The Motivation to Work* (New York, NY: John Wiley, 1959); A. Maslow, *Motivation and Personality* (New York, NY: Harper & Row, 1970).

19 Maslow, op. cit.

20 For example, see J. R. Hackman and G. Oldham, *Work Redesign* (Reading, MA: Addison-Wesley, 1980).

21 For example, see G. Salancik and J. Pfeffer, "A Social Information Processing Approach to Job Attitudes and Task Design," *Administrative Science Quarterly,* 23 (1978): 224–253.

22 For example, see S. Milgram, *Obedience to Authority* (New York, NY: Harper & Row, 1969); A. Bandura, *Social Learning Theory* (Englewood Cliffs, NJ: Prentice-Hall, 1977).

23 For example, see R. Caldini, *Influence: The New Psychology of Modern Persuasion* (New York, NY: Quill, 1984).

24 Salancik, op. cit.

25 For example, see I. Janis and L. Mann, *Decision Making: A Psychological Analysis of Conflict, Choice, and Commitment* (New York, NY: Free Press, 1977).

26 M. Galanter, "Psychological Induction into the Large Group: Findings from a Modern Religious Sect," *American Journal of Psychiatry,* 137 (1980): 1574–1579.

27 J. Pfeffer, "Management as Symbolic Action: The Creation and Maintenance of Organizational Paradigms," in L. Cummings and B. Staw, eds., *Research in Organizational Behavior,* Volume 3 (Greenwich, CT: JAI Press, 1981).

28 G. Jacobsen and J. Hillkirk, *Xerox: American Samuri* (New York, NY: Collier Books, 1986).

Chapter 4: Questions for Discussion

1 Can you think of organizations in which you have worked or been a member where "power tended to corrupt and absolute power corrupted absolutely"?

2 Can you provide an example of an organizational situation you have personally experienced where power was used to bring about results that you considered positive and for the good of the organization?

3 To what extent does the *explicit* use of legitimate power reduce or enhance the effectiveness of a leader? (Again, think of examples from your own experience.)

4 Can the use of power by a leader directly increase the motivation of subordinates in work settings? Or, will such attempts, especially if obvious, result in no effect or lower motivation?

5 Is the term "political influence" synonymous with the term "power"?

6 Would your own observations and experiences confirm Eagly and Johnson's findings about the kinds of differences in leadership approach that do, and do not, appear to exist between the two genders?

7 Under what circumstances will groups be more effective than an individual leader or manager in influencing the behavior of employees?

8 Do you agree with Yukl and his colleagues that "determining what [influence] tactics are appropriate is not just a matter of 'common sense' "? How convincing is their evidence on this point?

JOB ATTITUDES AND EMPLOYEE BEHAVIOR

One of the most controversial issues in the fields of both motivation and leadership concerns the relationship between job attitudes and employee performance. The origins of the controversy stem from disagreements not only about the potential causal relationships between these two sets of variables but also about the meanings and measurements of the two. For example, what do we mean by an attitude and how should we most accurately measure attitudes? What constitutes good job performance? Should we measure job performance at the individual level or at the group level? Should we focus on short-term or long-term results? And finally, do positive attitudes lead to good performance or does good performance lead to positive attitudes? Alternatively, is there a third intervening variable that moderates or in some way affects the relationship between the two? How we resolve this controversy has a major impact both on theory development and on managerial practice.

WHAT IS AN ATTITUDE?

To begin with, let us consider what we mean by job attitudes. Briefly defined, an "attitude" represents a predisposition to respond in a favorable or unfavorable way to persons or objects in one's environment. When we say we "like" something or "dislike" something, we are in effect expressing an attitude toward the person or object. When we look at the specific attitude of job satisfaction, for example, we are considering the extent to which one's job or job experiences are pleasurable or unpleasurable.

Three important assumptions underlie the concept of attitudes. First, an attitude is a hypothetical construct. We cannot actually see attitudes. Instead, we have to infer the existence of attitudes from people's statements and behaviors. Second, an attitude is a unidimensional construct; it usually ranges from very positive to very negative. As such, an attitude can be measured along a continuum. Third, attitudes are believed to be somewhat related to subsequent behavior, although this relationship is unclear, as we shall see.

ATTITUDES AND BEHAVIOR

Traditionally, job attitudes have been described as consisting of three related parts: (1) beliefs about the job, (2) the attitude itself, and (3) the behavioral intentions that result from the attitude. As shown in Exhibit 5-1, negative beliefs about the job (e.g., this is a dull, dirty job) lead to negative job attitudes (e.g., job dissatisfaction), which in turn lead to behavior intentions (e.g., intent to leave). These behavioral intentions are then often translated into actual behavior, such as leaving the organization, assuming the person is able to carry out the intention. Or, an individual who is dissatisfied may decide to put forth less effort on the job as a way of expressing his or her frustrations with the job. In both cases, the traditional model suggests that behaviors (including performance) are largely influenced by attitudes.

The problem with the traditional model is that real life experiences tell us that this relationship must be more complicated than the one we just described. For example, negative job attitudes do not always lead to poor performance, turnover, or absenteeism. Clearly, there must be other factors that influence the relationship between attitude and behavior. For instance, an unhappy employee may wish to leave his or her job but have no alternative employment and thus remain on the job. Moreover, some unhappy employees may be driven by a strong work ethic to continue to produce on the job.

OVERVIEW OF THE READINGS

As we shall see in the following three articles, considerable thought has gone into trying to identify the myriad of factors that can influence the attitude-behavior relationship. In the first article, Organ takes a closer look at the so-called "satisfaction-performance hypothesis." In the past, it has been generally believed that the satisfied worker is a productive worker. Organ asks us to reexamine this supposition. Suppose we viewed "performance" as the behavior of a good citizen within an organization's cul-

EXHIBIT 5-1
Job attitudes and behavior *(After Fishbein, 1967).*

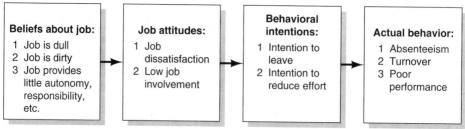

Beliefs about job:	Job attitudes:	Behavioral intentions:	Actual behavior:
1 Job is dull 2 Job is dirty 3 Job provides little autonomy, responsibility, etc.	1 Job dissatisfaction 2 Low job involvement	1 Intention to leave 2 Intention to reduce effort	1 Absenteeism 2 Turnover 3 Poor performance

ture? Suppose we viewed "satisfaction" as the extent to which employees feel that they are being fairly treated by management? What happens to our hypothesized relationships between these two variables? Moreover, what implications follow for the practice of management?

In the second selection, Staw furthers our analysis of the "happy worker is a productive worker" hypothesis. First, he argues that attitudes such as job satisfaction may be "dispositional"; that is, employees may have relatively stable attitudes over time that are largely unrelated to their experiences in the workplace. As a result, some people are naturally happy, regardless of what tasks they perform. Second, Staw asks us to consider the possibility that job performance is mainly unrelated to job attitudes Rather, performance is driven by many other factors, including technological and manufacturing processes. He concludes by considering the implications of this for changing organizations.

In the last reading in this chapter we turn to the subject of major influences on employee absenteeism. Most research on employee motivation and leadership behavior focuses on performance as the outcome variable. Here, the focus is shifted to another form of behavior that costs industry billions of dollars each year. In this article, Rhodes and Steers review various approaches to understanding absenteeism, considering both economic and psychological perspectives. Based upon this review, a diagnostic model of attendance motivation is presented that attempts to account for both voluntary and involuntary absenteeism.

A Restatement of the
Satisfaction-Performance Hypothesis

Dennis W. Organ

It appears that management scholars will not, perhaps cannot, let the job satisfaction-performance hypothesis fade away. Over 30 years have elapsed since Brayfield and Crockett (1955) reviewed a large body of evidence generally unsupportive of the proposition that there is any "appreciable" relationship between these variables, let alone the idea that "job satisfaction causes performance." Nearly a decade later, Vroom (1964) saw no reason to alter this conclusion. Yet recently we have seen two in-dependent meta-analytic reviews updating the assessment of the empirical record (Iaf-faldano and Muchinsky, 1985; Petty, McGee, & Cavender, 1984). Interestingly, the former review came to much the same conclusions as the earlier assessments, suggest-ing that high productivity and worker satisfaction form only "an illusory correla-tion . . . between two variables that we logically think should interrelate, but in fact do not" (Iaffaldano & Muchinsky, 1985, p. 270). On the other hand, Petty et al. (1984) concluded that the support for this relationship is perhaps greater than indicated by previous reviews. But even more interesting is the continued fascination of the man-agement research community with an issue presumably settled by previous investiga-tion.

Perhaps the fascination derives from the discomforting discrepancy between the empirical record and the apparently strong intuitive belief among practitioners (Gan-non & Noon, 1971; Katzell & Yankelovich, 1975) that job satisfaction is indeed an im-portant determinant of productivity. On the one hand, management scholars certainly do not feel obligated to have their research confirm conventional wisdom and may even take pride in the ability to disconfirm apparent common sense with scientific data. On the other hand, perhaps management theorists also feel an abiding need to ex-plain such contradictions in such a way as to offer points of reconciliation between re-search findings and the opinions of presumably intelligent, experienced observers of work behavior.

Over a decade ago, Organ (1977) suggested that one means of reconciling the dis-crepancy lay in the various meanings we might attach to the concept "performance." Conceivably, the practitioner attaches multiple meanings to this term, including such non-productivity or extra-role dimensions as cooperation, informal modes of helping coworkers and superiors, and generalized tendencies toward compliance. Research measures of performance may not adequately capture the variance in some of these more qualitative aspects of the practitioner's conception of performance. Organ drew upon social psychological exchange theory (e.g., Blau, 1964) to offer a defensible ra-tionale why job satisfaction might account for more variance in informal helping and compliance than in more narrow measures of productivity or in-role performance.

However, Organ (1977) had scant data to support his argument. Furthermore, though concerned with the interpretation of the concept "performance," he took no

From *Journal of Management*, 1988, 14(4), 547–557. Reprinted by permission.

note of the strong possibility that the "satisfaction" part of the proposition also demands scrutiny. Just what is it in what we call "satisfaction" that particularly influences "performance" of the sort that practitioners have in mind?

The purpose of this paper is to contribute toward a more precise and defensible version of the satisfaction-performance hypothesis by (a) reviewing recent empirical work that addresses extra-role contributions as "performance" correlates of satisfaction; (b) specifying the "satisfaction" referent that is tied to extra-role contributions and doing so in a way that links the issue to a potentially rich body of theory; and (c) considering the problems and prospects for both research and practice of the resulting reformulation of the satisfaction-performance proposition.

"PERFORMANCE" AS ORGANIZATIONAL CITIZENSHIP BEHAVIOR

Baseman and Organ (1983) used the term "citizenship behavior" to denote helpful, constructive gestures exhibited by organization members and valued or appreciated by officials, but not related directly to individual productivity nor inhering in the enforceable requirements of the individual's role. Bateman and Organ cited two rationales, either or both of which could support conceptually a link between job satisfaction and individual citizenship behavior. The first, drawn from social exchange concepts (e.g., Blau, 1964) suggests that individuals will feel bound by the norm of reciprocity when given the resources, treatment, and opportunities that induce satisfaction. Furthermore, given the constraints exerted by technology, work flow, and individual skills on productivity, they frequently will choose to reciprocate in the form of such citizenship behaviors as cooperation, supportiveness of the supervisor, helping behaviors, and gestures that enhance the reputation of the work unit internal and external to the organization. The second rationale, drawn from extensive naturalistic experiments on prosocial and altruistic behavior (e.g., as summarized in Brown, 1985, pp. 56–60) notes the accumulating evidence for a "mood state" or "positive affect" explanation of many forms of helping behavior. Thus, if job satisfaction represents the chronic or modal mood state of an organizational member, then presumably those most satisfied should have a characteristic predisposition toward prosocial gestures within the organization environment, and among those prosocial acts would number various forms of citizenship behavior.

Bateman and Organ (1983) tested the satisfaction-citizenship behavior hypothesis in a two-wave, two-variable cross-correlation panel research design, using a homemade measure of citizenship behavior that included 30 items on which immediate supervisors rated nonacademic university employees. The Job Descriptive Index (JDI: Smith, Kendall, & Hulin, 1969) provided measures of overall and facet satisfaction. The researchers found at each time of testing a static correlation of .41 between overall satisfaction and citizenship behavior. They could not, however, reject the null hypothesis of some common cause of both variables, because the cross-lagged correlations were approximately equal to each other and to both static correlations.

Smith, Organ, and Near (1983), working with a shorter but more refined measure of Organizational Citizenship Behavior (OCB), tested its relationship to satisfaction—in this instance, defined by the "Me at Work" semantic differential scale from Scott's (1967) measure—among 220 employees of two large banks. The researchers identified a two-factor structure in the OCB measure. Altruism, representing OCB gestures aimed at specific individuals, correlated .31 with job satisfaction. Compliance (or perhaps more aptly termed "conscientiousness"), which seemed to capture more impersonal forms of citizenship striving, correlated .21 with satisfaction. Separate causal models constructed from the interrelationships among these and other variables confirmed the link between satisfaction and Altruism, but not the link with Compliance.

Puffer (1987), guided by the concept "prosocial behavior," devised a measure of extra-role contributions by appliance salespeople whose earnings depended solely on sales commissions. Prosocial behavior (as rated by superiors) correlated .27 with a measure of "satisfaction with material rewards." Puffer also contributed a note of discriminant validity in this context, because the prosocial measure correlated only .16 with actual sales performance, which in turn correlated only .18 with satisfaction.

Motowidlo (1984) extended these findings to leader performance. Among 134 managers, he noted a correlation of .27 between managerial satisfaction and independent ratings by superiors of the manager's display of consideration toward subordinates. To the extent that certain forms of consideration and supportiveness of group members qualify as OCB, Motowidlo's finding adds a note of generality and robustness to the satisfaction-OCB hypothesis.

More recently, Motowidlo, Packard, and Manning (1986) have tested the flip side of the satisfaction-OCB hypothesis—i.e., that job-related distress inhibits the flow of OCB gestures. Motowidlo et al. surveyed the extent of prosocial behaviors by nurses toward patients, colleagues, and physicians. They found consistently negative correlations between self-reports of job stress and five different measures of prosocial behaviors; the absolute value of the correlations averaged about .20. In a path-analytic reconstruction of the linkages among the measured variables, they found that feelings of depression mediated the relation between job stressors and prosocial behaviors.

Thus, five published studies, using varied subject groups and procedurally independent assessments of the important variables, have reported significant relationships between measures of OCB and job satisfaction. The correlations range from the teens to over .40, with a weighted mean in the high twenties to low thirties—somewhat greater than Vroom's (1964) estimate of .14 from studies of satisfaction and traditional performance measures, or the .15 of Iaffaldano and Muchinsky's (1985) meta-analysis.

Interestingly, Iaffaldano and Muchinsky found that the correlations were significantly higher when the performance measures used in past studies were either subjective or global in nature. It seems likely that those types of performance measures would be the ones most likely to capture variance in some forms of OCB. Katzell and Yankelovich (1975), reporting the results of a survey of 563 managers and 69 union leaders, noted that respondents in both groups attached to the definition of "productivity" such attributes as "loyalty" and "less tangible features such as the absence of disruption . . ." (pp. 19–20) and other factors "even when their impact on output cannot be measured easily" (p. 103). It therefore seems likely that subjective, global ratings of subordinates' performance or productivity will reflect varying but substantial estimates of their tendencies to render OCB.

It would seem, then, that when we take into account what practitioners include in their concept of performance, that the empirical record provides some support for the "common sense" notion that satisfaction is related to performance.

But is this the same thing as saying "a happy worker is a productive worker," even when "productive" is couched in the terms described above? This inference follows only if we equate satisfaction with happiness and/or assume that job satisfaction scores bear a monotonic relationship to the psychological state of "happiness." The interpretation of the OCB-satisfaction correlation requires first some analysis of the underlying referent of satisfaction measures.

"SATISFACTION" AS FAIRNESS

There are well-developed theories of job satisfaction (e.g., Locke, 1976) and some measures of job satisfaction (such as the JDI) that are well-grounded and systematically developed from such theories. However, in recent years it seems that job satisfaction researchers have had little inclination to qualify or interpret their findings in light of some of the characteristic "behaviors" of job satisfaction scores or to consider possible distinguishable referents of such scores. Yet there do exist some data and relevant theoretical frameworks that permit some elaboration upon such referents.

Almost by convention, we use the terms "job satisfaction" and "job attitudes" interchangeably. Measures of job satisfaction are based on the techniques of attitude scale construction. And psychologists (e.g., Berkowitz, 1980) have long defined attitude in terms of constituent cognitions (beliefs) and affect (feeling). Not unreasonably, therefore, job satisfaction measures are assumed to reflect cognitions and affect in roughly equal proportion. Thus, Locke (1976, p. 1300) defines job satisfaction as "a pleasurable or positive emotional state [affect] resulting from the appraisal [cognition] of one's job or job experiences." Similarly, Smith, Kendall, and Hulin (1969) regard "job satisfactions" as "feelings or affective responses to facets of the situation," but in the next sentence "hypothesize that these feelings are associated with a perceived difference between what is expected as a fair return . . . and what is experienced . . ." (Smith et al., 1976, p. 6). Both Locke and Smith et al. seem to imply that responses of job satisfaction directly reflect affect but, because cognitions are such a direct and immediate determinant of these feelings, both components of attitude are strongly represented in responses.

However, Campbell (1976) has reviewed a series of studies of "quality of life" that show satisfaction measures behaving quite differently from happiness measures. Andrews and Withey (1976) factor analyzed 12 global subjective measures of well-being, finding that satisfaction-type measures load on a factor suggestive of "cognition" (i.e., a controlled assessment of external circumstances). Happiness-type measures load on what appears to be an "affect" factor, or the individual's internal emotional state. The two sets of measures correlate around .50, but correlate differently with other things; for example, the cognition measures correlate positively with age, whereas the affect indicators correlate negatively. Organ and Near (1985), reviewing these findings, suggested that job satisfaction measures capture more cognition than affect.

In support of this argument, Brief and Robertson (1987) found that a separate job cognitions measure was far superior to measures of positive and negative affect in accounting for unique variance in job satisfaction scores of 144 subjects.

Thus, consistent with recent work by Zajonc (1980), it appears that cognition and affect are not as tightly conjoined as once thought. They can operate in semi-independent fashion. And to the extent that they are separable, it appears that job satisfaction measures reflect more cognition than affect, not necessarily affect as a direct result of cognitions.

But what kind of cognition about the behavior of job satisfaction? To confront this question requires drawing upon some observations about the behavior of job satisfaction responses—how they are distributed and broken down—and the developing theory of social cognition (Folger, 1986).

The distribution of job satisfaction scores is almost invariably negatively skewed. Smith et al. (1969) reported this finding in the large samples with which they developed the JDI, even after weighting the neutral (i.e., "?") response closer to the dissatisfied response; presumably the skewness was even more pronounced with the neutral response given a value midway between the positive and negative responses. This is precisely the type of distribution found by Helson (1964) when subjects were asked to render psychophysical judgments of various stimuli when accompanied by an anchor or reference stimulus. The distribution of responses is negatively skewed, and subjects' judgments are less variable as well as more accurate in the vicinity of the value of the anchor stimulus. Helson (1964) has suggested that the same phenomenon that underlies subjective perception of audible tones, color, and other physical stimuli might also characterize judgments of social stimuli and attitudinal objects.

Indeed, Smith et al. (1969) drew upon Helson's adaptation level theory in developing the theoretical basis of the JDI as a measure of job satisfaction. They regard responses to the JDI items as resulting from comparisons of job circumstance to some anchor point. They also comment frequently on the respondent's "frame of reference." It seems that they implicitly regard this frame of reference as functioning like a standard of fairness, as they conclude that "satisfaction can be regarded as an evaluation of equitableness of treatments or conditions" (Smith et al., 1969, p. 166).

Herzberg, Mausner, and Snyderman's (1959) analysis of secondary or internal states, correlated with critical incidents of satisfaction and dissatisfaction, revealed that "feelings of fairness or unfairness" were the psychological state related to dissatisfaction. Fairness was seldom referred to in connection with satisfaction episodes.

We have some basis, then, for thinking that job satisfaction measures reflect more cognition than affect and that the cognition in question is an appraisal or comparison of the situation with a standard of fairness. The empirical distribution of scores, when coupled with Herzberg et al. (1959), suggested that most of the available scale or range of responses is used by subjects to appraise outcomes up to the approximate point regarded as fair or equitable. Thus, Smith et al. (1969) find the distribution ". . . sloping off steeply toward the satisfied end and gently toward the dissatisfied end" (pp. 79–80). This echoes Blau (1964), who marshals considerable support for the premise that outcomes that bring a person's situation up to the normatively expected level are more important than those that surpass it.

To interpret job satisfaction responses as largely representing judgments of fairness is not to imply any specific rule of fairness, such as the proportionate contributions rule in Adams' Equity Theory (1965). Blau (1964) has argued convincingly that any expectation—whether based on social comparison, past experience, the going rate, or prior implied promise—can and often does function much like a standard of justice with a quasi-moral character. More recently Leventhal (1980) has broadened our awareness of alternatives to the contributions rule, noting that needs, equality, conventional agreement, or status—but more typically some mix of the foregoing—can operate as rules of justice.

Thinking about job satisfaction in this fashion finds a useful point of contact with Folger's (1986) theory and experimental research concerning "referent cognitions." Folger argues that dissatisfaction is "inherently referential," in the sense that outcomes are compared with a referent cognition (p. 147). The psychological closeness or availability of a referent cognition is a function of the ease with which it can be imagined. The referent cognition, or "what the outcomes might have been," may derive from social comparison, but could also take the form of a previously held expectation or a promise made to the subject alone (in fact, in the experiments reviewed by Folger, 1986, the manipulation of referent cognition always takes the form of a stated or implied promise of what the probable outcomes would be). Folger has found that dissatisfaction is an interactive function of (a) the discrepancy between actual outcomes and the referent cognition; (b) the perceived likelihood of amelioration of outcomes; and (c) the perceived justification for the events or actions that caused the outcomes to fall short of referent cognition. He concludes that the combination of these factors determines whether outcomes determine "mere discontent" (affect?) or a sense of injustice (Folger, 1986, p. 151).

Folger raises as a problem for future research how responses to unfairness go beyond verbal expressions of satisfaction/dissatisfaction. Perhaps in organizations an important overt response is the extent of OCB.

WHY IS OCB A FUNCTION OF FAIRNESS?

One rationale for restraining OCB in response to cognitions of unfairness would make use of the terms drawn from Adams' (1965) Equity theory (i.e., a form of reducing inputs in order to effect equity). However, one need not endorse the proportionate contributions rule as the definitive criterion of justice in order to suggest that people perceiving unfairness will withhold something. But are they likely to diminish performance in terms of explicit job requirements? To do so invites potential sanctions and/or sacrifice of the incremental rewards provided by the system, and such a tactic probably would be painful for professionals and skilled artisans whose egos and self-esteem are so closely bound to pride in performance. A less painful, more flexible means of responding to perceived unfairness lies in calculated, discriminating withholding of discretionary gestures of the sort suggested by OCB.

Yet to characterize this response as merely an attempt to reestablish equity somehow seems to miss the point. It does not seem likely that an individual, perceiving himself or herself as a victim of injustice, really believes that the situation is made right by any degree of reduction of OCB, even though the response is elicited by conceptions of justice. What is suggested is that perceived unfairness evokes a fundamental redefinition of the relationship between the individual and the organization. The change is interpretable as one from social exchange, described by Blau (1964) as consisting of diffuse obligations and precise terms of exchange. Contributions are now limited to those of a contractually binding character.

In contrast, someone who senses general fairness in a social exchange relationship with the organization need not quibble over whether this or that mundane contribution tips the balance of equity. In any given instance, there is ambiguity about the value of the gesture and what should represent its appropriate recompense. Similarly, there is ambiguity concerning what degree of reciprocation is binding for any specific valued outcome. What is important is that the person be able to think of the organization as a microcosm of a just world (Lerner, 1980). If the long-run dynamic is toward fairness, the ambiguity attendant to the here-and-now discretionary contribution is tolerable. Indeed, there comes to mind a possible advantage to organizational reward systems that strive for long-term, global appraisals of fairness rather than one-to-one correspondence of micro-reward for micro-contribution. The inherent ambiguity of such a system frees the individual to contribute in discretionary fashion without thinking that this will be acquiescence to exploitation; on the other hand, there is enough cognitive slippage in attribution of the cause of the behavior to permit the person to infer some degree of intrinsic causation (Deci, 1975).

Interpreting the correlation between OCB and satisfaction as essentially a functional relationship between OCB and fairness cognitions finds support in a study by Scholl, Cooper, and McKenna (1987). They constructed a 10-item, self-report measure of "extra-role behavior," based on examples of such discretionary behavior as offered by Katz and Kahn (1978). Items included suggestions for improvement, helping others with problems, taking on extra responsibility, and continuing education. Scores on this measure correlated .41 with a measure of the person's report of perceived pay equity vis-à-vis others with a similar job. A smaller, but still statistically significant ($p < .01$) correlation was found between the extra-role behavior and report of pay equity in the context of the larger organization as a system. These correlations are quite in line with the trend of relationships elsewhere reported between OCB (or Prosocial Behavior) and the more general measures of job satisfaction.

THE FAIRNESS-OCB HYPOTHESIS: PROBLEMS AND IMPLICATIONS

Although recasting the satisfaction-performance hypothesis in terms of a fairness-OCB proposition has a reasonable logical basis and some degree of empirical support, and possibly resolves some issues, we still must reckon with some loose ends and with the plausibility of what it implies for theory, research, and practice.

Theory and Research

The discussion has assumed a direction of causality not inferrable from the research on OCB. The one longitudinal study attempting to ascertain cause-effect (Bateman & Organ, 1983) could not unequivocally do so. Causal models have been tested only against correlational data. Arguably, the correlation could reflect OCB as cause of satisfaction, either because OCB often elicits at the very least informal reinforcements from coworkers or superiors or because it brings satisfaction in its own right. One must also consider the justification phenomenon: having rendered OCB, a person might well experience a cognitive strain toward positive evaluation of the various dimensions of job circumstance. More convincing evidence that fairness cognitions temporally precede OCB is required before we can confidently develop theoretical frameworks within this area.

Another problem that arises is how to fit the person within the issue. Schneider and Dachler (1978) and Staw, Bell, and Clausen (1986) have marshalled impressive data arguing that satisfaction could be largely a dispositional variable. Does it seem plausible to think that this represents stable tendencies to perceive fairness or unfairness? Or is it more reasonable to anchor dispositional causes of satisfaction in something like Watson and Clark's (1984) concept of negative affectivity as a trait? A recent study (Atich, Brief, Burke, Robinson, & Webster, 1987) found a correlation of only −.24 between negative affectivity and job satisfaction, but the correlation was −.46 with life satisfaction, suggesting that this trait may be less influential in satisfaction measures as the domain of satisfaction becomes more circumscribed.

Whether the disposition accounting for stability in measured job satisfaction is primarily affective or cognitive, it presents a serious challenge to researchers trying to sort out causal paths among the person, environment, and OCB. Almost certainly there are feedback loops among those variables: for example, OCB has consequences that might well augment any disposition to exercise OCB, and, conversely, to withhold OCB.

If cognitions are taken as the major influence on OCB, what then do we make of the extensive social psychological research implicating affect as the cause of helping behavior (Brown, 1985)—research that apparently inspired much of the work examining the correlation between job satisfaction and OCB? Perhaps a distinction should be drawn between one-shot episodes of helping in nonorganizational contexts versus sustained patterns over time of OCB in the work environment. Conceivably more refined measures of OCB in the future would show that affect is more influential in certain types of OCB (e.g., helping a coworker in a direct, personal way), whereas fairness cognitions (net of affect) have more to do with less personal forms of OCB.

Addressing these questions would seem to require, at a minimum, the use of separate measures of affect as experienced at work and indices of fairness cognitions in respect to outcomes.

Management Practices

If OCB contributes appreciably to organizational effectiveness, if it is at least somewhat independent of in-role performance level, and if it is in considerable degree determined by fairness cognitions, what then follow as implications for management?

First, considering the apparent variety of fairness criteria and their weightings by different individuals (Leventhal, 1980), it would seem prudent for organizational officials to eschew any pure formula for fair outcomes based on any one criterion (e.g., a pay formula mechanically determined by measured in-role performance). A studied compromise among various criteria (e.g., technical excellence, market valuations, tenure, status), runs less risk of triggering cognitions of unacceptable unfairness (the tradeoff being, of course, that no group is likely to see perfect fairness). Perhaps organization theorists have overemphasized the virtues of a reward system dictating a one-to-one correspondence between increments of reward and specific individual actions; a system that permits some degree of ambiguity in this regard, yet on an overall basis continues to approximate most participants' notions of fairness, has much to recommend it.

Second, to the extent that stable dispositions enter into characteristic appraisals of fairness, some consideration of this tendency is important at selection time. Evidence that a given individual has some sort of persecution complex, reporting consistent victimization by unfair systems, employers, teachers, should be weighed against promise of ability to contribute in-role.

Finally, just as job satisfaction surveys have aided not only researchers but practitioners as well, perhaps organization officials would benefit by systematic inclusion of specific measures of fairness cognitions in periodic surveys.

REFERENCES

Adams, J. S. (1965). Inequity in social exchange. In L. Berkowitz (Ed.). *Advances in experimental psychology* (Vol. 2, pp. 267–299). New York: Academic Press.

Andrews, F. M., & S. B. Withey. (1976). *Social indicators of well-being.* New York: Plenum Press.

Atich, J. M., Brief, A. P., Burke, M. J., Robinson, B. S., & Webster, J. (1987, August). *Should negative affectivity remain an unmeasured variable in the study of job stress?* Paper presented at the meeting of the Academy of Management, New Orleans.

Bateman, T. S., & Organ, D. W. (1983). Job satisfaction and the good soldier: The relationship between affect and employee "citizenship." *Academy of Management Journal, 26,* 587–595.

Berkowitz, L. (1980). *A survey of social psychology.* New York: Holt, Rinehart, & Winston.

Blau, P. (1964). *Exchange and power in social life.* New York: Wiley.

Brayfield, A. H., & Crockett, W. H. (1955). Employee attitudes and employee performance. *Psychological Bulletin, 52,* 396–424.

Brief, A. P., & Robertson, L. (1987, August). *Job attitude organization: An exploratory study.* Paper presented at the meeting of the Academy of Management, New Orleans.

Brown, R. (1985). *Social psychology.* New York: Free Press.

Campbell, A. (1976). Subjective measures of well-being. *American Psychologist, 31,* 117–124.

Deci, E. L. (1975). *Intrinsic motivation.* New York: Plenum.

Folger, R. (1986). Rethinking equity theory. In Bierhof, H. W., Cohen, R. L., & Greenberg, J. (Eds.), *Justice in social relations* (pp. 145–162). New York: Plenum.

Gannon, M. J., & Noon, J. P. (1971). Management's critical deficiency. *Business Horizons, 14,* 49–56.

Helson, H. (1964). Current trends and issues in adaptation-level theory. *American Psychologist, 19,* 26–38.

Herzberg, F. H., Mausner, B., & Snyderman, B. S. (1959). *The motivation to work.* New York: Wiley.

Iaffaldano, M. T., & Muchinsky, P. M. (1985). Job satisfaction and job performance: A Meta-Analysis. *Psychological Bulletin, 97,* 251–273.

Katz, D., & Kahn, R. L. (1978). *The social psychology of organizations.* New York: Wiley.

Katzell, R. A., & Yankelovich, D. (1975). *Work, productivity, and job satisfaction.* New York: The Psychological Corporation.

Lerner, M. J. (1980). *The belief in a just world: A fundamental delusion.* New York: Plenum.

Leventhal, G. S. (1980). What should be done with Equity Theory? New approaches to the study of fairness in social relationships. In K. G. Gergen, M. S. Greenberg, & R. H. Willis (Eds.), *Social exchange: Advances in theory and research* (pp. 27–55). New York: Plenum.

Locke, E. A. (1976). The nature and causes of job satisfaction. In M. D. Dunnette (Ed.), *Handbook of industrial and organizational psychology* (pp. 1297–1349). Chicago: Rand McNally.

Motowidlo, S. J. (1984). Does job satisfaction lead to consideration and personal sensitivity? *Academy of Management Journal, 27,* 910–915.

Motowidlo, S. J., Packard, J. S., & Manning, M. R. (1986). Occupational stress: Its causes and consequences for job performance. *Journal of Applied Psychology, 71,* 618–629.

Organ, D. W. (1977). A reappraisal and reinterpretation of the satisfaction-cause-performance hypothesis. *Academy of Management Review, 2,* 46–53.

Organ, D. W., & Near, J. P. (1985). Cognition vs. affect in measures of job satisfaction. *International Journal of Psychology, 20,* 241–253.

Petty, M. M., McGee, G. W., & Cavender, J. W. (1984). A meta-analysis of the relationships between job satisfaction and individual performance. *Academy of Management Review, 9,* 712–721.

Puffer, S. M. (1987). Prosocial-behavior, noncompliant behavior, and work performance among commission salespeople. *Journal of Applied Psychology, 72,* 615–621.

Schneider, B., & Dachler, P. (1978). A note on the stability of the job descriptive index. *Journal of Applied Psychology, 63,* 650–653.

Scholl, R. W., Cooper, E. A., & McKenna, J. F. (1987). Referent selection in determining equity perceptions: Differential effects on behavioral and attitudinal outcomes. *Personnel Psychology, 40,* 113–124.

Scott, W. E., Jr. (1967). The development of semantic differential scales as measures of "morale." *Personnel Psychology, 20,* 179–198.

Smith, C. A., Organ, D. W., & Near, J. P. (1983). Organizational citizenship behavior: Its nature and antecedents. *Journal of Applied Psychology, 68,* 653–663.

Smith, P. C., Kendall, L. M., & Hulin, C. L. (1969). *The measurement of satisfaction in work and retirement.* Chicago: Rand McNally.

Staw, B. M., Bell, N. E., & Clausen, J. A. (1986). The dispositional approach to job attitudes: A lifetime longitudinal test. *Administrative Science Quarterly, 31,* 56–77.

Vroom, V. H. (1964). *Work and motivation.* New York: Wiley.

Watson, D., & Clark, L. A. (1984). Negative affectivity: The disposition to experience aversive emotional states. *Psychological Bulletin, 96,* 465–490.

Zajonc, R. B. (1980). Feeling and thinking: Preferences need no inferences. *American Psychologist, 35,* 151–175.

Organizational Psychology and the Pursuit of the Happy/Productive Worker

Barry M. Staw

What I am going to talk about in this article is an old and overworked topic, but one that remains very much a source of confusion and controversy. It is also a topic that continues to attract the attention of managers and academic researchers alike, frequently being the focus of both popular books and scholarly articles. This issue is how to manage an organization so that employees can be both happy and productive—a situation where workers and managers are both satisfied with the outcomes.

The pursuit of the happy/productive worker could be viewed as an impossible dream from the Marxist perspective of inevitable worker-management conflict. Such a goal could also be seen as too simple or naive from the traditional industrial relations view of outcomes being a product of necessary bargaining and compromise. Yet, from the psychological perspective, the pursuit of the happy/productive worker has seemed a worthwhile though difficult endeavor, one that might be achieved if we greatly increase our knowledge of work attitudes and behavior. In this article, I will examine this psychological perspective and try to provide a realistic appraisal of where we now stand in the search for satisfaction and productivity in work settings.

APPROACHES TO THE HAPPY/PRODUCTIVE WORKER

One of the earliest pursuits of the happy/productive worker involved the search for a relationship between satisfaction and productivity. The idea was that the world might be neatly divided into situations where workers are either happy and productive or unhappy and unproductive. If this were true, then it would be a simple matter to specify the differences between management styles present in the two sets of organizations and to come up with a list of prescriptions for improvement. Unfortunately, research has never supported such a clear relationship between individual satisfaction and productivity. For over thirty years, starting with Brayfield and Crockett's classic review of the job satisfaction-job performance literature,[1] and again with Vroom's discussion of satisfaction-performance research,[2] organizational psychologists have had to contend with the fact that happiness and productivity may not necessarily go together. As a result, most organizational psychologists have come to accept the argument that satisfaction and performance may relate to two entirely different individual decisions—decisions to participate and to produce.[3]

Though psychologists have acknowledged the fact that satisfaction and performance are not tightly linked, this has not stopped them from pursuing the happy/productive worker. In fact, over the last thirty years, an enormous variety of theories have attempted to show how managers can reach the promised land of high satisfaction and

TABLE 1
PATHS TO THE HAPPY/PRODUCTIVE WORKER

Worker Participation	The Pursuit of Excellence
Supportive Leadership	Socio-Technical Systems
9–9 Systems	Organizational Commitment
Job Enrichment	High Performing Systems
Behavior Modification	Theory Z
Goal Setting	Strong Culture

productivity. The theories shown in Table 1 constitute only an abbreviated list of recent attempts to reach this positive state.

None of the theories in Table 1 has inherited the happy/productive worker hypothesis in the simple sense of believing that job satisfaction and performance generally co-vary in the world *as it now exists*. But, these models all make either indirect or direct assumptions that *it is possible* to achieve a world where both satisfaction and performance will be present. Some of the theories focus on ways to increase job satisfaction, with the implicit assumption that performance will necessarily follow; some strive to directly increase performance, with the assumption that satisfaction will result; and some note that satisfaction and performance will be a joint product of implementing certain changes in the organization.

Without going into the specifics of each of these routes to the happy/productive worker, I think it is fair to say that most of the theories in Table 1 have been oversold. Historically, they each burst on the scene with glowing and almost messianic predictions, with proponents tending to simplify the process of change, making it seem like a few easy tricks will guarantee benefits to workers and management alike. The problem, of course, is that as results have come in from both academic research and from wider practical application, the benefits no longer have appeared so strong nor widespread. Typically, the broader the application and the more well-documented the study (with experimental controls and measures of expected costs and benefits), the weaker have been the empirical results. Thus, in the end, both managers and researchers have often been left disillusioned, skeptical that any part of these theories are worth a damn and that behavioral science will ever make a contribution to management.

My goal with this article is to *lower our expectations*—to show why it is so difficult to make changes in both satisfaction and performance. My intention is not to paint such a pessimistic picture as to justify not making any changes at all, but to inoculate us against the frustrations of slow progress. My hope is to move us toward a reasoned but sustainable pursuit of the happy/productive worker—away from the alternating practice of fanfare and despair.

CHANGING JOB ATTITUDES

Although organizational psychologists have accepted the notion that job satisfaction and performance do not necessarily co-vary, they have still considered job attitudes as something quite permeable or subject to change. This "blank state" approach to job attitudes comes from prevailing psychological views of the individual, where the person is seen as a creature who constantly appraises the work situation, evaluates the merits of the context, and formulates an attitude based on these conditions. As the work situation changes, individuals are thought to be sensitive to the shifts, adjusting their attitudes in a positive or negative direction. With such an approach to attitudes, it is easy to see why job satisfaction has been a common target of organizational change, and why attempts to redesign work have evolved as a principal mechanism for improving job satisfaction.

Currently, the major debate in the job design area concerns whether individuals are more sensitive to objective job conditions or social cues. In one camp are proponents of job redesign who propose that individuals are highly receptive to concrete efforts to improve working conditions. Hackman and Oldham, for example, argue that satisfaction can be increased by improving a job in terms of its variety (doing a wider number of things), identity (seeing how one's various tasks make a meaningful whole), responsibility (being in charge of one's own work and its quality), feedback (knowing when one has done a good job), and significance (the meaning or relative importance of one's contribution to the organization or society in general).[4] In the opposing camp are advocates of social information processing. These researchers argue that jobs are often ambiguous entities subject to multiple interpretations and perceptions.[5] Advocates of social information processing have noted that the positive or negative labeling of a task can greatly determine one's attitude toward the job, and that important determinants of this labeling are the opinions of co-workers who voice positive or negative views of the work. These researchers have shown that it may be as easy to persuade workers that their jobs are interesting by influencing the *perception* of a job as it is to make objective changes in the work role.

The debate between job design and social information processing has produced two recent shifts in the way we think about job attitudes. First, organizational psychology now places greater emphasis on the role of cognition and subjective evaluation in the way people respond to jobs. This is probably helpful, because even though we have generally measured job conditions with perceptual scales, we have tended to confuse these perceptions with objective job conditions. We need to be reminded that perceptions of job characteristics do not necessarily reflect reality, yet they can determine how we respond to that reality.

The second shift in thinking about job attitudes is a movement toward situationalism, stressing how even slight alterations in job context can influence one's perception of a job. It is now believed that people's job attitudes may be influenced not only by the objective properties of the work, but also by subtle cues given off by co-workers or supervisors that the job is dull or interesting. I think this new view is a mistake since it overstates the role of external influence in the determination of job attitudes. The reality may be that individuals are quite resistant to change efforts, with their attitudes coming more as a function of personal disposition than situational influence.

THE CONSISTENCY OF JOB ATTITUDES

Robert Kahn recently observed that, although our standard of living and working conditions have improved dramatically since World War II, reports of satisfaction on national surveys have not changed dramatically.[6] This implies that job satisfaction might be something of a "sticky variable," one that is not so easily changed by outside influence. Some research on the consistency of job attitudes leads to the same conclusion. Schneider and Dachler, for example, found very strong consistency in satisfaction scores over a 16-month longitudinal study (averaging .56 for managers and .58 for non-managers).[7] Pulakos and Schmitt also found that high school students' pre-employment expectations of satisfaction correlated significantly with ratings of their jobs several years later.[8] These findings, along with the fact that job satisfaction is generally intertwined with both life satisfaction and mental health, imply that there is some on-going consistency in job attitudes, and that job satisfaction may be determined as much by dispositional properties of the individual as any changes in the situation.

A Berkeley colleague, Joseph Garbarino, has long captured this notion of a dispositional source of job attitudes with a humorous remark, "I always told my children at a young age that their most important decision in life would be whether they wanted to be happy or not; everything else is malleable enough to fit the answer to this question." What Garbarino implies is that job attitudes are fairly constant, and when reality changes for either the better or worse, we can easily distort that reality to fit our underlying disposition. Thus, individuals may think a great deal about the nature of their jobs, but satisfaction can result as much from the unique way a person views the world around him as from any social influence or objective job characteristics. That is, individuals predisposed to be happy may interpret their jobs in a much different way than those with more negative predispositions.

The Attitudinal Consistency Study

Recently, I have been involved with two studies attempting to test for dispositional sources of job attitudes. In the first study, Jerry Ross and I reanalyzed data from the National Longitudinal Survey, a study conducted by labor economists at Ohio State.[9] We used this survey to look at the stability of job attitudes over time and job situations. The survey's measure of attitudes were not very extensive but did provide one of the few available sources of data on objective job changes.

The National Longitudinal Survey data revealed an interesting pattern of results. We found that job satisfaction was fairly consistent over time, with significant relationships among job attitudes over three- and five-year time intervals. We also found that job satisfaction showed consistency *even when people changed jobs.* This later finding is especially important, since it directly contradicts the prevailing assumptions of job attitude research.

Most job design experiments and organizational interventions that strive to improve job attitudes change a small aspect of work, but look for major changes in job satisfaction. However, the National Longitudinal Survey data showed that when people changed their place of work (which would naturally include one's supervisor, working conditions, and procedures), there was still significant consistency in attitudes. One could, of course, argue that people leave one terrible job for another, and this is why such consistency in job attitudes arises. Therefore, we checked for consistency across occupational changes. The National Longitudinal Survey showed consistency not only across occupational changes, but also when people changed *both* their employers and their occupations. This evidence of consistency tells us that people may not be as malleable as we would like to think they are, and that there may be some underlying tendency toward equilibrium in job attitudes. If you are dissatisfied in one job context, you are also likely to be dissatisfied in another (perhaps better) environment.

The Dispositional Study

The consistency data from the National Longitudinal Survey, while interesting, do not tell us what it is that may underlie a tendency to be satisfied or dissatisfied on the job. Therefore, Nancy Bell (a doctoral student at the Berkeley Business School), John Clausen (a developmental sociologist at Berkeley), and I undertook a study to find some of the dispositional sources of job satisfaction.[10] We sought to relate early personality characteristics to job attitudes later in life, using a very unusual longitudinal data source.

There are three longitudinal personality projects that have been running for over fifty years at Berkeley (the Berkeley Growth Study, the Oakland Growth Study, and the Guidance Study), and they have since been combined into what is now called the Intergenerational Study. Usually when psychologists speak of longitudinal studies, they mean data collected from one- or two-year intervals. These data span over 50 years. Usually, when psychologists refer to personality ratings, they mean self-reports derived from the administration of various questionnaires. Much of the Intergenerational Study data are clinical ratings derived from questionnaires, observation, and interview materials evaluated by a different set of raters for each period of the individual's life. Thus, these data are of unusual quality for psychological research.

Basically what we did with data from the Intergenerational Study was to construct an affective disposition scale that measured a very general positive-negative orientation of people. We then related this scale to measures of job attitudes at different periods in people's lives. The ratings used for our affective disposition scale included items such as "cheerful," "satisfied with self," and "irritable" (reverse coded), and we correlated this scale with measures of job and career satisfaction. The results were very provocative. We found that affective dispositions, from as early as the junior-high-school years, significantly predicted job attitudes during middle and late adulthood (ages 40–60). The magnitude of correlations was not enormous (in the .3 to .4 range). But, these results are about as strong as we usually see between two attitudes measured on the same questionnaire by the same person at the same time—yet, these data cut across different raters and over fifty years in time.

What are we to conclude from this personality research as well as our reanalyses of the National Longitudinal Survey? I think we can safely conclude that there is a fair amount of consistency in job attitudes and that there may be dispositional as well as situational sources of job satisfaction. Thus, it is possible that social information processing theorists have been on the right track in viewing jobs as ambiguous entities that necessitate interpretation by individuals. But, it is also likely that the interpretation of jobs (whether they are perceived as positive or negative) can come as much from internal, dispositional causes (e.g., happiness or depression) as external sources. Consequently, efforts to improve job satisfaction via changes in job conditions will need to contend with stable personal dispositions toward work—forces that may favor consistency of equilibrium in the way people view the world around them.

THE INTRANSIGENCE OF JOB PERFORMANCE

Although we have not conducted research on the consistency of performance or its resistance to change, I think there are some parallels between the problems of changing attitudes and performance. Just as job attitudes may be constrained by individual dispositions, there are many elements of both the individual and work situation that can make improvements in job performance difficult.[11]

Most of the prevailing theories of work performance are concerned with individual motivation. They prescribe various techniques intended to stimulate, reinforce, or lure people into working harder. Most of these theories have little to say about the individual's limits of task ability, predisposition for working hard, or the general energy or activity level of the person. Somewhat naively, our theories have maintained that performance is under the complete control of the individual. Even though there are major individual differences affecting the quantity or quality of work produced, we have assumed that *if the employee really wants to perform better, his or her performance will naturally go up.*

There already exist some rather strong data that refute these implicit assumptions about performance. A number of studies[12] have shown that mental and physical abilities can be reliable predictors of job performance, and it is likely that other dispositions (e.g., personality characteristics) will eventually be found to be associated with effective performance of certain work roles. Thus, influencing work effort may not be enough to cause wide swings in performance, unless job performance is somewhat independent of ability (e.g., in a low skill job). Many work roles may be so dependent on ability (such as those of a professional athlete, musician, inventor) that increases in effort may simply not cause large changes in the end product.

In addition to ability, there may also be other individual factors that contribute to the consistency of performance. People who work hard in one situation are likely to be the ones who exert high effort in a second situation. If, for example, the person's energy level (including need for sleep) is relatively constant over time, we should not expect wide changes in available effort. And, if personality dimensions such as dependability and self-confidence can predict one's achievement level over the lifecourse,[13] then a similar set of personal attributes may well constitute limitations to possible improvements in performance. Already, assessment centers have capitalized on this notion by using personality measures to predict performance in many corporate settings.

Performance may not be restricted just because of the individual's level of ability and effort, however. Jobs may *themselves* be designed so that performance is not under the control of the individual, regardless of ability or effort. Certainly we are aware of the fact that an assembly line worker's output is more a product of the speed of the line than any personal preference. In administrative jobs too, what one does may be constrained by the work cycle or technical procedures. There may be many people with interlocking tasks so that an increase in the performance of one employee doesn't mean much if several tasks must be completed sequentially or simultaneously in order to improve productivity. Problems also arise in situations where doing one's job better may not be predicated upon a burst of energy or desire, but upon increases in materials, financial support, power, and resources. As noted by Kanter, the administrator must often negotiate, hoard, and form coalitions to get anything done on the job, since there are lots of actors vying for the attention and resources of the organization.[14] Thus, the nature of the organization, combined with the abilities and efforts of individuals to maneuver in the organization, may serve to constrain changes in individual performance.

ASSESSING THE DAMAGE

So far I have taken a somewhat dark or pessimistic view of the search for the happy/productive worker. I have noted that in terms of satisfaction and performance, it may not be easy to create perfect systems because both happiness and performance are constrained variables, affected by forces not easily altered by our most popular interventions and prescriptions for change. Should organizational psychologists therefore close up shop and go home? Should we move to a more descriptive study of behavior as opposed to searching for improvements in work attitudes and performance?

I think such conclusions are overly pessimistic. We need to interpret the stickiness of job attitudes and performance not as an invitation to complacency or defeat, but as a realistic assessment that it will take very strong treatments to move these entrenched variables. Guzzo, Jackson, and Katzell have recently made a similar point after a statistical examination (called meta-analysis) of organizational interventions designed to improve productivity.[15] They noted that the most effective changes are often *multiple treatments,* where several things are changed at once in a given organization. Thus, instead of idealistic and optimistic promises, we may literally need to throw the kitchen sink at the problem.

The problem of course is that we have more than one kitchen sink! As noted earlier, nearly every theory of organizational behavior has been devoted to predicting and potentially improving job attitudes and performance. And, simply aggregating these treatments is not likely to have the desired result, since many of these recommendations consist of conflicting prescriptions for change. Therefore, it would be wiser to look for compatible *systems* of variables that can possibly be manipulated in concert. Let us briefly consider three systems commonly used in organizational change efforts and then draw some conclusions about their alternative uses.

THREE SYSTEMS OF ORGANIZATIONAL CHANGE

The Individually-Oriented System

The first alternative is to build a strong individually-oriented system, based on the kind of traditional good management that organizational psychologists have been advocating for years. This system would emphasize a number of venerable features of Western business organizations such as:

- Tying extrinsic rewards (such as pay) to performance.
- Setting realistic and challenging goals.
- Evaluating employee performance accurately and providing feedback on performance.

- Promoting on the basis of skill and performance rather than personal characteristics, power, or connections.
- Building the skill level of the workforce through training and development.
- Enlarging and enriching jobs through increases in responsibility, variety, and significance.

All of the above techniques associated with the individually-oriented system are designed to promote both satisfaction and productivity. The major principle underlying each of these features is to structure the work and/or reward system so that high performance is either intrinsically or extrinsically rewarding to the individual, thus creating a situation where high performance contributes to job satisfaction.

In practice, there can be numerous bugs in using an individually-oriented system to achieve satisfaction and performance. For example, just saying that rewards should be based on performance is easier than knowing what the proper relationship should be or whether there should be discontinuities at the high or low end of that relationship. Should we, for instance, lavish rewards on the few highest performers, deprive the lowest performers, or establish a constant linkage between pay and performance? In terms of goal-setting, should goals be set by management, workers, or joint decision making, and what should the proper baseline be for measuring improvements? In terms of job design, what is the proper combination of positive social cues and actual job enrichment that will improve motivation and satisfaction?

These questions are important and need to be answered in order to "fine-tune" or fully understand an individually-oriented system. Yet, even without answers to these questions, we already know that a well-run organization using an individually-oriented system *can* be effective. The problem is we usually don't implement such a system, either completely or very well, in most organizations. Instead, we often compare poorly managed corporations using individually-oriented systems (e.g., those with rigid bureaucratic structures) with more effectively run firms using another motivational system (e.g., Japanese organizations), concluding that the individual model is wrong. The truth may be that the individual model may be just as correct as other approaches, but we simply don't implement it as well.

The Group-Oriented System

Individually-oriented systems are obviously not the only way to go. We can also have a group-oriented system, where satisfaction and performance are derived from group participation. In fact, much of organizational life could be designed around groups, if we wanted to capitalize fully on the power of groups to influence work attitudes and behavior.[16] The basic idea would be to make group participation so important that groups would be capable of controlling both satisfaction and performance. Some of the most common techniques would be:

- Organizing work around intact groups.
- Having groups charged with selection, training, and rewarding of members.
- Using groups to enforce strong norms for behavior, with group involvement in off-the-job as well as on-the-job behavior.
- Distributing resources on a group rather than individual basis.

• Allowing and perhaps even promoting intergroup rivalry so as to build within-group solidarity.

Group-oriented systems may be difficult for people at the top to control, but they can be very powerful and involving. We know from military research that soldiers can fight long and hard, not out of special patriotism, but from devotion and loyalty to their units. We know that participation in various high-tech project groups can be immensely involving, both in terms of one's attitudes and performance. We also know that people will serve long and hard hours to help build or preserve organizational divisions or departments, perhaps more out of loyalty and altruism than self-interest. Thus, because individuals will work to achieve group praise and adoration, a group-oriented system, effectively managed, can potentially contribute to high job performance and satisfaction.

The Organizationally-Oriented System

A third way of organizing work might be an organizationally-oriented system, using the principles of Ouchi's Theory Z and Lawler's recommendations for developing high-performing systems.[17] The basic goal would be to arrange working conditions so that individuals gain satisfaction from contributing to the entire organization's welfare. If individuals were to identify closely with the organization as a whole, then organizational performance would be intrinsically rewarding to the individual. On a less altruistic basis, individuals might also gain extrinsic rewards from association with a high-performing organization, since successful organizations may provide greater personal opportunities in terms of salary and promotion. Common features of an organizationally-oriented system would be:

• Socialization into the organization as a whole to foster identification with the entire business and not just a particular subunit.
• Job rotation around the company so that loyalty is not limited to one subunit.
• Long training period with the development of skills that are specific to the company and not transferable to other firms in the industry or profession, thus committing people to the employing organization.
• Long-term or protected employment to gain organizational loyalty, with concern for survival and welfare of the firm.
• Decentralized operations, with few departments or subunits to compete for the allegiance of members.
• Few status distinctions between employees so that dissension and separatism are not fostered.
• Economic education and sharing of organizational information about products, financial condition, and strategies of the firm.
• Tying individual rewards (at all levels in the firm) to organizational performance through various forms of profit sharing, stock options, and bonuses.

The Japanese have obviously been the major proponents of organizationally-oriented systems, although some of the features listed here (such as profit sharing) are very American in origin. The odd thing is that Americans have consistently followed an organizationally-oriented system for middle and upper management and for members of professional organizations such as law and accounting firms. For these high-level employees, loyalty may be as valued as immediate performance, with the firm expecting the individual to defend the organization, even if there does not seem to be any obvious self-interest involved. Such loyalty is rarely demanded or expected from the lower levels of traditional Western organizations.

EVALUATING THE THREE SYSTEMS

I started this article by noting that it may be very difficult to change job performance and satisfaction. Then I noted that recognition of this difficulty should not resign us to the present situation, but spur us to stronger and more systemic actions—in a sense, throwing more variables at the problem. As a result, I have tried to characterize three syndromes of actions that might be effective routes toward the happy/productive worker.

One could build a logical case for the use of any of the three motivational systems. Each has the potential for arousing individuals, steering their behavior in desired ways, and building satisfaction as a consequence of high performance. Individually-oriented systems work by tapping the desires and goals of individuals and by taking advantage of our cultural affinity for independence. Group-oriented systems work by taking advantage of our more social selves, using group pressures and loyalty as the means of enforcing desired behavior and dispensing praise for accomplishments. Finally, organizationally-oriented systems function by building intense attraction to the goals of an institution, where individual pleasure is derived from serving the collective welfare.

If we have three logical and defensible routes toward achieving the happy/productive worker, which is the best path? The answer to this question will obviously depend on how the question is phrased. If "best" means appropriate from a cultural point of view, we will get one answer. As Americans, although we respect organizational loyalty, we often become suspicious of near total institutions where behavior is closely monitored and strongly policed—places like the company town and religious cult. If we define "best" as meaning the highest level of current performance, we might get a different answer, since many of the Japanese-run plants are now outperforming the American variety. Still, if we phrase the question in terms of *potential* effectiveness, we may get a third answer. Cross-cultural comparisons, as I mentioned, often pit poorly managed individually-oriented systems (especially those with non-contingent rewards and a bureaucratic promotion system) against more smoothly running group or organizationally-oriented systems. Thus, we really do not know which system, managed to its potential, will lead to the greatest performance.

Mixing the Systems

If we accept the fact that individual, group, and organizationally-oriented systems may each do *something* right, would it be possible to take advantage of all three? That is, can we either combine all three systems into some suprasystem or attempt to build a hybrid system by using the best features of each?

I have trepidations about combining the three approaches. Instead of a stronger treatment, we may end up with either a conflicted or confused environment. Because the individually-oriented system tends to foster competition among individual employees, it would not, for example, be easily merged with group-oriented systems that promote intragroup solidarity. Likewise, organizationally-oriented systems that emphasize how people can serve a common goal may not blend well with group-oriented systems that foster intergroup rivalry. Finally, the use of either a group- or organizationally-oriented reward system may diminish individual motivation, since it becomes more difficult for the person to associate his behavior with collective accomplishments and outcomes. Thus, by mixing the motivational approaches, we may end up with a watered-down treatment that does not fulfill the potential of *any* of the three systems.

In deciding which system to use, we need to face squarely the costs as well as benefits of the three approaches. For example, firms considering an individually-oriented system should assess not only the gains associated with increases in individual motivation, but also potential losses in collaboration that might result from interpersonal competition. Similarly, companies thinking of using a group-oriented system need to study the tradeoffs of intergroup competition that can be a byproduct of increased intragroup solidarity. And, before thinking that an organizationally-oriented system will solve all the firm's problems, one needs to know whether motivation to achieve collective goals can be heightened to the point where it outweighs potential losses in motivation toward personal and group interests. These trade-offs are not trivial. They trigger considerations of human resource policy as well as more general philosophical issues of what the organization wants to be. They also involve technical problems for which current organizational research has few solutions, since scholars have tended to study treatments in isolation rather than the effect of larger systems of variables.

So far, all we can be sure of is that task structure plays a key role in formulating the proper motivational strategy. As an example, consider the following cases: a sales organization can be divided into discrete territories (where total performance is largely the sum of individual efforts), a research organization where several product groups are charged with making new developments (where aggregate performance is close to the sum of group efforts), and a high-technology company where success and failure are due to total collaboration and collective effort. In each of these three cases, the choice of the proper motivational system will be determined by whether one views individual, group, or collective efforts as the most important element. Such a choice is also determined by the degree to which one is willing to sacrifice (or trade-off) a degree of performance from other elements of the system, be they the behavior of individuals, groups, or the collective whole. Thus, the major point is that each motivational system has its relative strengths and weaknesses—that despite the claims of many of our theories of management, there is no simple or conflict-free road to the happy/productive worker.

CONCLUSION

Although this article started by noting that the search for the happy/productive worker has been a rather quixotic venture, I have tried to end the discussion with some guarded optimism. By using individual, group, and organizational systems, I have shown how it is *at least possible* to create changes that can overwhelm the forces for stability in both job attitudes and performance. None of these three approaches is a panacea that will solve all of an organization's problems, and no doubt some very hard choices must be made between them. Yet, caution need not preclude action. Therefore, rather than the usual academic's plea for further research or the consultant's claim for bountiful results, we need actions that are flexible enough to allow for mistakes and adjustments along the way.

REFERENCES

1 A. H. Brayfield and W. H. Crockett, "Employee Attitudes and Employee Performance," *Psychological Bulletin,* 51 (1955):396–424.
2 Victor H. Vroom, *Work and Motivation* (New York, NY: Wiley, 1969).
3 James G. March and Herbert A. Simon, *Organizations* (New York, NY: Wiley, 1958).
4 Richard J. Hackman and Greg R. Oldham, *Work Redesign* (Reading, MA: Addison-Wesley, 1980).
5 E.g., Gerald R. Salancik and Jeffrey Pfeffer, "A Social Information Processing Approach to Job Attitudes and Task Design," *Administrative Science Quarterly,* 23 (1978):224–253.
6 Robert Kahn (1985).
7 Benjamin Schneider and Peter Dachler, "A Note on the Stability of the Job Description Index," *Journal of Applied Psychology,* 63 (1978):650–653.
8 Elaine D. Pulakos and Neal Schmitt, "A Longitudinal Study of a Valence Model Approach for the Prediction of Job Satisfaction of New Employees," *Journal of Applied Psychology,* 68 (1983):307–312.
9 Barry M. Staw and Jerry Ross, "Stability in the Midst of Change: A Dispositional Approach to Job Attitudes," *Journal of Applied Psychology,* 70 (1985):469–480.
10 Barry M. Staw, Nancy E. Bell, and John A. Clausen, "The Dispositional Approach to Job Attitudes: A Lifetime Longitudinal Test," *Administrative Science Quarterly* (March 1986).
11 See, Lawrence H. Peters, Edward J. O'Connor, and Joe R. Eulberg, "Situational Constraints: Sources, Consequences, and Future Considerations," in Kendreth M. Rowland and Gerald R. Ferris, eds., *Research in Personnel and Human Resources Management,* Vol. 3 (Greenwich, CT: JAI Press, 1985).
12 For a review, see Marvin D. Dunnette, "Aptitudes, Abilities, and Skills," in Marvin D. Dunnette, ed., *Handbook of Industrial and Organizational Psychology* (Chicago, IL: Rand McNally, 1976).
13 As found by John Clausen, personal communications, 1986.
14 Rosabeth M. Kanter, *The Change Masters* (New York, NY: Simon & Schuster, 1983).
15 Richard A. Guzzo, Susan E. Jackson, and Raymond A. Katzell, "Meta-analysis Analysis," in Barry M. Staw and Larry L. Cummings, eds., *Research in Organizational Behavior,* Volume 9 (Greenwich, CT: JAI Press, 1987).
16 See, Harold J. Leavitt, "Suppose We Took Groups Seriously," in E. L. Cass and F. G. Zimmer, eds., *Man and Work in Society* (New York, NY: Van Nostrand, 1975).
17 William Ouchi, *Theory Z: How American Business Can Meet the Japanese Challenge* (Reading, MA: Addison-Wesley, 1981); Edward E. Lawler, III, "Increasing Worker Involvement to Enhance Organizational Effectiveness," in Paul Goodman, ed., *Change in Organizations* (San Francisco, CA: Jossey-Bass, 1982).

Major Causes of Absenteeism

Susan R. Rhodes
Richard M. Steers

BACKGROUND FOR MODEL DEVELOPMENT

As one reviews the available research on employee absenteeism, one is struck by the general absence, until recently, of any systematic or comprehensive theory development. As Nicholson (1977, p. 232) pointed out, much of the early research focused on "tentative speculations and propositions *ex post facto* to case studies, and a number of more general theories of organizational behavior in which absence is only a minor element." Following Nicholson, these findings and theories can be categorized into three types of explanatory models: (1) *pain-avoidance models,* in which absence behavior is viewed as a flight from negative work experiences; (2) *adjustment-to-work models,* in which absence is seen as resulting largely from employee responses to changes in job conditions leading to a renegotiation of the psychological contract; (3) *decision models,* in which absence behavior is viewed primarily as a rational (or at least quasi-rational) decision to attain valued outcomes. In addition, a final category called "integrated models" can be identified that attempt to go beyond narrow sets of parameters and offer a more complex view of the causes of attendance.

Pain-Avoidance Models

Pain-avoidance models have guided much of absence research over the years (see Hackett and Guion, 1985) and have their origins in the early job satisfaction research. The underlying assumption is that job dissatisfaction (or negative job attitudes in general) represents the primary cause of absenteeism. Although concluding that there was little empirical evidence for a job satisfaction–performance relationship, Brayfield and Crockett (1955) ventured the opinion that dissatisfied workers would be absent more if their work dissatisfaction was symptomatic of being in a punishing situation. Moreover, Argyle (1972) noted that when work is satisfying people will show up to enjoy it.

Several meta-analyses of the absence–job satisfaction relationship, although presenting somewhat conflicting results, tend to support the conclusions that the pain-avoidance model is overly simplistic (Farrell and Stamm, 1988; Hackett and Guion, 1985; McShane, 1984). McShane's review of twenty-four published studies supported the notion that employees who are dissatisfied with various aspects of their jobs are more likely to be absent. The relationship was strongest for overall and work satisfaction, but coworker, pay, and supervision dissatisfaction also led to higher absenteeism. His results indicated that satisfaction with promotions was the only dimension unre-

Condensed from Susan R. Rhodes & Richard M. Steers, *Managing Employee Absenteeism.* Reading, Mass.: Addison-Wesley, 1990, pp. 33–42, 55–63.

lated to absenteeism. Finally, he found job satisfaction to be more highly related to frequency of absences than to number of days lost.

Farrell and Stamm's (1988) study found significant negative weighted correlations between overall job satisfaction and both total time absent and absence frequency. Finally, Hackett and Guion's meta-analysis results showed that less than 4 percent of the variance in absence measures was explained by overall job satisfaction and its dimensions. Although they did find all corrected mean correlations to be negative, they concluded that the strength of the relationship was very weak. They further argued against third-factor variables moderating the job satisfaction–absence relationship in that too much of the variance in correlations reported across studies could be accounted for by statistical artifacts. Although these studies offer slightly different viewpoints on the absence–job satisfaction relationship, none of them reported particularly strong mean correlations.

In addition to the meta-analysis technique, which is based on bi-variate correlations, an examination of multivariate studies of absence in which satisfaction is included as one of the variables is revealing. When considered along with other variables (for example, demographic, prior absenteeism, organizational), work attitudes (including overall job satisfaction, organizational commitment, job involvement) generally were not found to be significant predictors of absenteeism. Nonsignificant absence-attitude findings were reported for overall job satisfaction, satisfaction with supervision, and satisfaction with pay, working conditions, coworkers, and equipment. In Popp and Belohlav's study, overall satisfaction was a significant predictor of absence frequency but accounted for the smallest amount of variance among the significant variables.

When taken together, the meta-analysis and the multivariate studies provide little support for the "absence as pain-avoidance" theory. Therefore, like Hackett and Guion (1985), we conclude that it is not fruitful to test further any models that are based on the assumption that dissatisfaction is the primary cause of absence. However, sufficient findings are present to warrant the inclusion of attitudinal variables in more comprehensive models of employee absenteeism. Attitudes can at times serve to "pull" the individual toward the organization assuming the attitudes are positive, and the reverse can be expected when attitudes are more negative.

Adjustment-to-Work Models

In adjustment-to-work models, absence from work is viewed as a consequence of organizational socialization and other adaptive processes in response to job demands. Included among adjustment models are the earlier theorizing of Hill and Trist (1953) and Gibson (1966), as well as the more recent models of Rosse and Miller (1984) and Chadwick-Jones et al. (1982).

Hill and Trist's Model   Following Hill and Trist (1953), absence is viewed as one of the means of withdrawal from stressful work situations. Other means of withdrawal include turnover and accidents. In the early phase of "induction crisis," turnover is often the preferred mode of withdrawal. During this phase, newcomers typically lack knowledge about absence norms. Unsanctioned absence is the characteristic mode during the middle period of "differential transit." After this, in the "settled connection" phase, the individual substitutes sanctioned absences for unsanctioned absences, and levels of absence are reduced. This model is described as basically one of organizational socialization. That is, in becoming aware of the absence culture of the firm, individuals internalize these norms such that a change in withdrawal behavior consistent with the norms occurs. Accidents become a means of withdrawal if the sanctioned outlets for withdrawal are insufficient.

In providing evidence based on collective trends of accidents and absence to explain individual reactions, Hill and Trist's theory can only be considered to be highly speculative. Not only is there no direct evidence supporting their model, but also it is not clear that testable hypotheses could be developed from it (Chadwick-Jones et al., 1982). Their theory, however, makes a contribution by introducing the concept of social norms of absence.

Gibson's Model Gibson (1966) set forth a comprehensive conceptual model of organizational behavior to explain absence behavior based on the contractual relationship between the individual and the organization. According to Gibson's model, individuals and organizations enter into an exchange relationship in which the individual agrees to contribute his or her competencies in exchange for certain rewards, and the organization agrees to provide rewards for a certain level of effort on the part of the individual. Fundamental to the satisfactory implementation of the contract is the attitude of commitment to both the contract's intent and its terms, or what is termed "authenticity." The more the tasks and rewards of the organization are viewed as satisfying the individual's needs, the stronger will be the individual's identification with and commitment to the organization.

Gibson then applied the model to explain conflicting research in the absence literature. Work identification was viewed as a strong influence on absence behavior, and any factor that served to increase identification operated to reduce absence. Other important influences on absence behavior were the ease of legitimating absences, and the perceived authenticity of management. Using his framework, he explained research findings on the relationship between absence and gender, length of service, age, job status, size of organization, and cosmopolitans and locals. Although the research findings he presented appeared to be consistent with his theory, they in no way represent a test of his theory. Moreover, as Chadwick-Jones et al. (1982) point out, there is a considerable gap in the level of abstraction of the conceptual model and the methods and data used to support it. Finally, although Gibson provided propositions that were suitable for testing, there have been no following comprehensive tests of his model by absenteeism researchers.

Rosse and Miller's Model More recently Rosse and Miller (1984) focused on the adaptive responses or coping mechanisms available to a worker in coping with his or her work environment. Absence behavior is one of the adaptive responses available to the worker. Because their model was developed in response to the question "What do workers do when they are dissatisfied?" it is concerned with behavioral shifts and is not meant to be a general theory of behavior. According to this view, then, absence behavior would represent a break from normal routine. Although their approach is primarily an adjustment model, it also contains elements of a decision model.

According to Rosse and Miller, a stimulus event (for example, the first warm, sunny day of spring) leads to a state of relative dissatisfaction. This relative state equates with an awareness of a new standard, a negative response (or affect) resulting from not being at the new standard, and an action tendency to achieve the new standard. Next, the individual is viewed as considering behavioral alternatives to achieve the better state. Factors influencing the person's consideration include personal experience, exposure to role models, the presence of clear social norms, and the perception of constraints (that is, ability-induced or environmentally-induced limitations to behavior). The result of this consideration is a set of alternatives, ordered according to the perceived likelihood that they will lead to the person's being better off. The alternative chosen will be the one resulting in the highest positive utility, defined as "the anticipation that the behavior will improve the person's situation" (p. 211).

The environmental responses to the behavior will be experienced by the person as either positive, neutral, or negative. If the consequences are positive, the source of relative dissatisfaction has been eliminated and successful adaptation has occurred. On the other hand, if the consequences are negative or neutral, the source of relative dissatisfaction is still present, and the individual continues to repeat the adaptation cycle until successful adaptation occurs.

Rosse and Miller's model was examined empirically by a correlational field study designed and carried out prior to the development of the full model (Rosse and Hulin, 1985). As such, the study was not intended to be a formal test, but Rosse and Hulin concluded that the results provided an empirical basis for the model. Their findings indicated that job satisfaction indices were good predictors of intentions to quit, turnover, change attempts, and health symptoms. On the other hand, only satisfaction with work content and coworkers were related to absence behavior. According to Rosse and Miller, however, an adequate test of the model requires a longitudinal within-subject design permitting analysis of work perceptions, decision processes, enacted behavior, and the consequences of that behavior on subsequent cycles. This requires rigorous, labor-intensive studies.

In summary, Rosse and Miller's model makes three useful contributions. First, it focuses on absence as one of several behavioral responses available to individuals in dealing with relative dissatisfaction. This means that it is necessary to consider the relationship between absence and other behaviors. Second, it draws attention to the dynamic nature of absence behavior. Third, in acknowledging that the stimuli leading to relative dissatisfaction can come from within the work environment or outside it, absence behavior as an adaptive response can be viewed within the context of the individual's total life space.

Chadwick-Jones, Nicholson, and Johns's Model   The final adjustment model can be distinguished from the other models discussed thus far in that it focuses on the notion of social exchange rather than individual motivations. Moreover, the amount of absences taken is influenced by the prevailing absence culture. This framework was first developed by Chadwick-Jones et al. (1982) and later expanded by Nicholson and Johns (1985).

In viewing absence as part of a social exchange, Chadwick-Jones et al. stress that this is not simply an exchange that occurs between the individual and the organization, as in Gibson's model, but also one that occurs among individuals in the organization. First, the exchange between the individuals and the organization is a "negative exchange" in that the employees are withholding their presence from work, perhaps to make up for workload pressures, stress, or the constraints imposed by fixed work schedules. In some cases, management might tacitly collude with employees in the exchange, for example, in encouraging employees to use up sick days rather than lose them. Second, among employees, absences might be allocated to ensure that workload pressures can be met. Employees might take turns in being absent: "If you were absent last week, then it's all right for me to be absent tomorrow."

Because the absence of one person affects others in the organization, the absence culture sets limits on the appropriate levels of absence. Although interindividual variations in absence do occur, these differences operate within the limits prescribed by the particular culture. Chadwick-Jones et al. (1982, p. 7) define absence culture as "the beliefs and practices influencing the totality of absences—their frequency and duration—as they currently occur within an employee group or organization." Employees are aware, albeit imperfectly, of the nature of this culture. The absence culture then influences the absence norm, which is what employees "collectively recognize (usually with management collusion) as suitable and appropriate for people in the job, their unit, their organization, given the particular conditions, both physical and social, of tasks, pay, status, and discipline" (p. 7).

Following Nicholson and Johns (1985), variations in absence cultures across organizations or groups are predicted to arise from the degree of salience of the culture and the level of trust inherent in the psychological contract (see Fig. 1). First, the *salience* of the culture refers to the degree of distinctiveness of beliefs about absence, assumptions underlying employment, and views toward self-control. The more salient the culture, the more homogeneous it is and the more it impacts the individual directly, frequently resulting in clear norms regarding attendance behavior. On the other hand, cultures that are less salient exert more subtle influences on behavior and lead to greater individual variations in absences. Cultural salience is influenced by the organization's absence control system, its technology, and social ecology. Second, the level of *trust* refers to whether the tasks surrounding one's job are high or low in discretion. The four types of absence cultures are: (1) the *dependent* culture (low salience, high trust), characterized by deviant absence; (2) the *moral* culture (high salience, high trust), typified by constructive absence; (3) the *fragmented* culture (low salience, low trust), characterized by calculative absence; and (4) the *conflictual* culture (high salience, low trust) with its resultant defiant absence.

This absence culture framework makes a significant contribution to our understanding of absence behavior in recognizing how constraints can be placed on individual behavior by the collective reality of the organization. Group norms defining what constitutes acceptable behavior must be recognized as an important factor here. However, such an approach can be somewhat limited because it does not give sufficient attention to individual variations in behavior within an absence culture. That is, there is an equally important need to recognize individual differences as a factor in absenteeism.

**Cultural salience
(Horizontal integration)**

Low salience   High salience

		Low salience	High salience
Psychological contract (Vertical integration)	High trust	Type I Dependent Deviant absence	Type II Moral Constructive absence
	Low trust	Type III Fragmented Calculative absence	Type IV Conflictual Defiant absence

FIGURE 1
A typology of organizational absence cultures. *(From N. Nicholson & G. Johns, 1985, The absence of culture and the psychological contract: Who's in control of absence?* Academy of Management Review, 10, 402. *Reprinted with permission.)*

Decision Models

Two primary streams of influence have contributed to the development of decision models of absence. These are the rational decision models provided by economists and sociologists and the expectancy-valence framework posited by organizational psychologists. What these groups have in common is that they view absence behavior as largely rational in nature and determined by the individual's subjective evaluation of the costs and benefits associated with absence and its alternative.

Economic Models Economists have drawn on microeconomic theory and labor-economics analysis. First, Gowler (1969) presented a model of the labor supply of the firm. According to this model, absence is used by employees as a way to restore the balance of effort-rewarded ratios disturbed by fluctuations in levels of overtime. Second, following Gowler's lead, Allen, drawing on the concepts of work-leisure tradeoff and income substitution effects, developed a model of work attendance. According to his model, absence permits the worker to control wage levels and other rewards for work when considering desired levels of work, leisure, and risk. Absence results when the benefits of not working on any particular day are greater than the costs. Third, economists have examined the effect of the wage and fringe benefit structure on absence. For example, we know that when fringe benefits are not tied to hours worked, an incentive for absence is created. This is due to the fact that as work hours decrease, the paid benefits per hour increase, thus creating an income effect that fosters absence. Supporting the models based on economic theory are studies showing an increase in absence associated with an increase in the difference between a worker's marginal rate of substitution of income for leisure and his or her marginal wage rate (Dunn and Youngblood, 1986), increased fringe benefits (Allen, 1981; Chelius, 1981), and higher levels of paid sick and absence days (Dalton and Perry, 1981; Winkler, 1980).

Psychological Models Perhaps the most prominent psychological model of decision-making that has been applied to absence behavior is the expectancy-valence theory of employee motivation as developed by Vroom (1964) and extended by

Lawler and Porter (1967). This approach integrates decision theory with an analysis of motivational processes. Individuals are regarded as making choices about their behavior based on the probability that they will receive valued outcomes. Although the theory was not originally developed to explain absence, Lawler and Porter argue that it could apply to absence behavior. And although there has not been an empirical test of expectancy-valence theory in relation to absence behavior, the theory has had a pervasive influence on the study of absenteeism (for example, Ilgen and Hollenback, 1977; Morgan and Herman, 1976). Moreover, it had an influence on the development of the original Steers and Rhodes (1978, 1984) model, particularly in explaining the linkage between satisfaction with the job situation and attendance motivation.

Absence behavior is also treated in equity theory (Adams, 1965) as one of the means of restoring equity with regard to the ratio of outcomes received from work and one's inputs in comparison with a relevant other. Absence is a form of leaving the field in order to restore equity. Although notions of equity have been explored in absence research, the ambiguous role of absence in equity theory and the minor role it plays does not make the theory suitable for examining absence behavior.

Finally, integrating psychological and economic approaches to time valuation, Youngblood (1984) viewed absence as a function of motivation processes associated with both work and nonwork domains. First, similar to pain-avoidance models, absence was considered to be a reactive response to an unfavorable work environment. Second, drawing from economic theory, absence was viewed as reflecting proactive behavior for the purpose of restructuring the workweek. Correlational research results provided support for his framework. Youngblood's theory with supporting research suggests the importance of considering the centrality of the nonwork domain in understanding absence rather than simply viewing absence as "organizational" behavior.

TOWARD A DIAGNOSTIC MODEL OF ATTENDANCE

Based on the above discussion and the progress that has been made in recent years on the topic, we are now in a position to use this current knowledge to build a diagnostic model of employee attendance. The proposed model is designed to be integrative in that it incorporates new empirical and theoretical developments and because it includes both avoidable and unavoidable absence. Although this model is similar to the original formulation by Steers and Rhodes in focusing on the individual employee's decision to attend, it differs in its increased attention to absence culture, organizational practices, societal context, and perceived ability to attend. These developments follow from recent literature and are included here in an effort to delineate more clearly the major factors influencing such behavior. The model is also meant to be diagnostic in that it is designed to be used not just by researchers but also by managers interested in better understanding the particular forces for absenteeism in their own organizations. . . . It is hoped that this model will also continue the research tradition in the field of absenteeism by making use of what we currently know and by challenging others to continue the developmental process.

The *diagnostic model* of employee attendance will be described in three parts: (1) major influences on attendance motivation; (2) major influences on perceived ability to attend and actual attendance; and (3) the role of societal context and reciprocal rela-

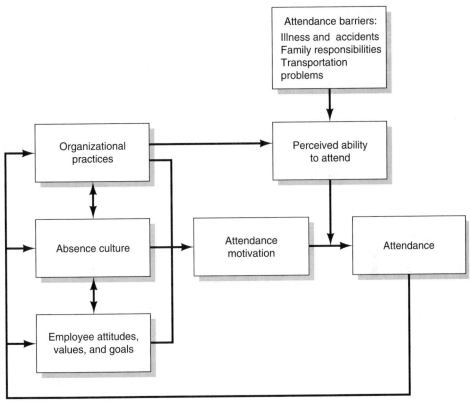

FIGURE 2
A diagnostic model of employee attendance.

tionships (see Fig. 2). Throughout, it is important to recognize that this is not an organizational or group model of absence; rather, the primary unit of analysis is individual behavior. Thus, the more macro variables are relevant to the extent that they influence individual attendance. In suggesting this paradigm, we recognize that any effort to model complex social behavior can lead to a situation in which some important variables might receive less attention than they deserve. Moreover, causal patterns are often complex or reciprocal, and this point too is sometimes lost or simplified in modeling attempts. Even so, while recognizing the limitations of parsimony, we have attempted in this model to highlight what appear to be the more salient factors that have a fairly significant and consistent influence on absence behavior.

Influences on Attendance Motivation

At least three sets of highly interactive factors can be identified that have an influence on an employee's attendance motivation. These are (1) the prevailing absence culture; (2) organizational policies and practices with respect to the workplace; and (3) employee attitudes, values, and goals. Hence, such influences can be found at the individual, group, and organizational levels throughout the organization. Let us see how each of these work.

Absence Culture   As discussed earlier in the paper, the concept of absence culture as originally introduced by Chadwick-Jones et al. (1982) and Johns and Nicholson (1982; see also Nicholson and Johns, 1985) represents one of the signal contributions to the study of employee absence. Absence culture can be defined as "the set of shared understandings about absence legitimacy . . . and the established 'custom and practice' of employee absence behavior and its control" (Johns and Nicholson, 1982, p. 136). Absence cultures can influence attendance motivation and subsequent attendance in at least three ways (Nicholson and Johns, 1985). First, where specific norms exist regarding the appropriate level of absence, an individual's attendance motivation level will often reflect these norms. Second, in the case where no specific norms exist, an individual's behavior can be influenced by his or her observations of the absence behavior of others and the consequences of such behavior. Finally, absence cultures can moderate the relationship between individual values and attitudes and subsequent attendance motivation.

Absence cultures can be distinguished both in their *cultural salience* (that is, the degree to which all members of a group share similar or divergent beliefs about absenteeism) and in their *trust* (that is, the amount of discretion provided employees by their management). High cultural salience means that group members have similar views about what constitutes an acceptable level of absence; low salience means that far less homogeneity exists. It is important to note here that high salience does not imply a norm of low absenteeism; rather, it denotes a shared sense of what level or magnitude of absence (high or low) is acceptable.

High trust, on the other hand, occurs when people experience high job discretion (as we see, for example, in professional jobs), leading to a high-trust psychological contract that reinforces the work ethic and internalized commitment to the organization. Low trust results when people experience lower job discretion (for example, assembly line workers) and typically leads to a more detached view of organizational participation and commitment. As noted earlier in the paper (see Fig. 1), these two aspects of absence culture combine to determine which of four "cultures" emerge in an organization (Nicholson and Johns, 1985).

In the final analysis, the nature and quality of these two variables determine the extent to which absence culture influences attendance motivation. For example, when an absence culture is highly salient, it can represent the primary influence on an individual's motivation to attend. On the other hand, when an absence culture is low in salience, other factors (for example, organizational practices or employee attitudes) typically emerge to have a stronger influence on attendance motivation).

Organizational Practices   In addition to variations in absence cultures, we must also recognize differences in organizational practices as a major influence on attendance motivation. Such practices can provide either the "push" or the "pull" necessary to encourage attendance. Four such practices can be identified: (1) the nature of an organization's absence control policies; (2) the work design or task interdependencies that characterize a particular job; (3) organizational recruitment and selection practices; and (4) expressed job expectations by management. Although other factors could be added to this list, let us look at these four examples.

First, a company's *absence control policies* represent a particularly salient force for attendance. These policies embody what management thinks constitute acceptable—and unacceptable—levels of absence and reasons for absence. Some companies are noted for their "rigorous" policies and policy enforcement; others are often seen as "lax." Moreover, it is not uncommon to find companies that apply significantly different control policies to managers and nonmanagers; indeed, minimal absence controls are often seen as a fringe benefit for managers. Sometimes these control policies are determined solely by corporate representatives; at other times they follow from contractual negotiations with unions. In any case, they are meant to reflect the basic ground rules governing "acceptable behavior" for whatever group they apply to.

Second, the nature of the job itself can influence motivation. Such *work design factors* as work cycle time, role discretion, and task identity, as well as resulting job stressors can often influence how employees see their role in the organization. As noted by Nicholson and Johns (1985, p. 401), "technological and bureaucratic experience may encourage them to see themselves as isolated, dispensable functionaries whose temporary absence is of no fundamental purpose, or they may see themselves as people whose coordinated commitment and reliable attendance is vital to organizational success." Because nonmanagerial positions are more likely to be characterized by low degrees of job discretion, task interdependencies, and perceived importance to the organization, it is not surprising that attendance values at this level tend to be weaker.

A third influence on attendance behavior is the *recruitment and selection practices* of the organization. Recruitment and selection practices determine what kinds of people are hired and what kinds are not. To the extent that companies examine job applicants' previous attendance and tardiness records from earlier employment or other pertinent information, it is less likely that absence-prone individuals will actually be hired.

And, finally, to the extent that management communicates *clear job expectations* regarding acceptable levels of absence to both current and prospective employees, we would expect a higher attendance norm. One way to convey such expectations for prospective employees is through the use of realistic job previews (Wanous, 1980), where prospective employees are fully informed concerning job duties and expectations. For current employees, such expectations can be transmitted by management through the communication of attendance policies, measuring employee attendance, and performance appraisal and reward practices.

Employee Attitudes, Values, and Goals Interacting with absence culture and organizational practices in determining attendance motivation is a third critical variable, namely the differences found across employees with respect to their attitudes, values, and goals. These differences can vary considerably from person to person, depending upon what is salient for the individual at a particular point in time. As noted earlier, *work-related attitudes* (for example, job involvement) can play a significant role in determining how employees view the psychological contract between employees and management, as well as how committed they are to coming to work (Farrell and Stamm, 1988; Hackett, 1988). Moreover, attendance motivation can be affected by variations in *personal work ethics,* as well as the *centrality of work* to the employees (that is, how important work is in his or her life goals). In employees who have other interests outside that take precedence (for example, family responsibilities, hobbies) or to the extent that the work ethic itself is low, we would expect to see a resulting attitude that is conducive to high absenteeism. And, finally, changes in *employee job expectations* (for example, when an employee becomes more "marketable" and begins to reexamine what he or she expects from the job) can influence an employee's view of the importance of coming to work.

Other examples of employee characteristics that can influence attendance can be identified. Whatever the specific set of characteristics, it is important to remember the *interactive* nature between these characteristics and absence culture and organizational practices. For example, variations in work design (for example, a speed-up on the assembly line) or changes in an absence control policy can influence job attitudes. Moreover, a consistently poor work ethic among a group of employees can cause a company to "tighten up" on its absence control policies because the employees might be seen as less trustworthy or committed. And the specificity, consistency of enforcement, and severity of absence control policies can clearly influence cultural salience and the trust dimension of an absence culture. Hence, as shown in Fig. 2, these three sets of factors—absence culture; organizational practices; and employee attitudes, values, and goals—interact with each other in a variety of ways ultimately to determine an employee's motivation or desire to come to work.

Influences on Perceived Ability to Attend and Attendance

The second part of the proposed model deals with the link between attendance motivation and actual attendance. As indicated (see Fig. 2), attendance motivation leads to actual attendance as constrained by an employee's perceived ability to attend. This perceived ability on the part of the employee, in turn, is influenced by both attendance barriers and organizational practices. At least three attendance barriers can be noted. First, there is the issue of actual *illness or accidents* that physically prevent someone from attending. No responsible company wants sick employees to come to work. Second, *family responsibilities* (for example, a sick child at home) can prevent an otherwise healthy individual from attending. This problem is especially serious for single parents or parents with several children, and the severity of the problem is likely to increase as more young mothers enter the labor force. And, finally, a variety of *transportation problems* (for example, a car breakdown, missing one's bus) can inhibit attendance in spite of one's motivational level.

These problems can sometimes be alleviated with the help of the company through such means as company-sponsored day care, car or van pooling, and physical fitness programs. Such organizational practices have become popular solutions in recent years to the problem of how we make it easier for motivated employees to get to work.

As noted in the model, these absence barriers combine with organizational relief efforts and are then assessed by the employee to determine his or her perceived ease of attending. Clearly, the way employees interpret a situation—as opposed to how it "really" is —will influence their actual behavior, and such employees will often see the same situation quite differently. For example, a snowstorm or a car breakdown might cause one employee to yield; whereas another employee might see these events as a challenge to be met. However they see it, the resulting perceptions concerning what is possible or not possible can represent a major influence on subsequent attendance.

Societal Context and Reciprocal Relationships

Finally, it is important to recognize that this sequence of interactive events, although not represented explicitly in Fig. 2, is enacted within a particular societal context. Two aspects of this context are particularly relevant to our analysis here. First, general *societal norms* concerning work or the value of work can influence both employee characteristics and organizational practices. Consider the example of work ethics. In Japan, for instance, societal norms stress hard work and the value of being a dedicated employee. It is not surprising, therefore, to find a low average absence rate of one-half percent, compared to almost 5 percent in the United States. Employees in Japan are more committed to coming to work, and companies respond with commensurate and supportive organizational practices. Few control policies are needed because for all practical purposes there is no problem.

Norms can also vary across segments of a larger society, based on such factors as geographic region, occupational grouping, and so forth. For example, occupational groups that are characterized by unionization often feel less commitment to the organization and more to the union, a fact that is capable of influencing absence behavior. Moreover, many companies prefer to open new divisions or plants in rural areas, where it is believed that employee work values and attendance norms are stronger. Finally, norms concerning child-care responsibilities are often different for women and men.

In fact, one could argue that societal norms influence almost all aspects of employee and corporate behavior. Some countries (most notably those in Western Europe) place a high societal value on efficient public transportation systems, thereby alleviating transportation problems for most employees. Moreover, in some societies like Japan, China, and Korea, it is customary for grandparents to assume child-care responsibility for working parents, thus making ability to attend somewhat easier. Thus, the pervasive nature of societal norms and practices should not be overlooked in our efforts better to understand behavior in the workplace.

In addition to societal norms, *economic and labor market conditions* can influence employee characteristics and organizational practices. For example, in periods of tight employment, companies can be reticent to enforce control policies rigorously for valued employees for fear of losing them. Moreover, recruitment and selection practices might not lead to the hiring of "ideal" employees when few job candidates are available. On an individual level, when economic conditions are poor, employees might be more likely to do their best to attend so as not to risk being discharged.

Thus attendance behavior must be viewed within an appropriate societal context. In addition, however, we must recognize several reciprocal relationships that exist within any social dynamic. For example, actual absence behavior is not only influenced by the many variables we have discussed here but also it, in turn, feeds back to influence some of its precursors. High absenteeism within a company, for example, might influence management to tighten its control policies; conversely, high attendance might lead to the opposite effect. High attendance or absenteeism can also influence absence culture, by either reinforcing or challenging the existing culture. Finally, high or low attendance can affect employee attitudes in either positive or negative ways. Hence, the diagnostic model presented here is a dynamic one, where major forces on behavior must be viewed as being in a constant state of flux and where a significant change in one variable can set off a chain reaction that ultimately affects many of the other variables, including attendance behavior itself.

REFERENCES

Adams, J. C. (1965). "Injustice in Social Exchange." In L. Berkowitz (ed.), *Advances in Experimental Social Psychology* (Vol. 2). New York: Academic Press.

Allen, S. G. (1981). "An Empirical Model of Work Attendance." *The Review of Economics and Statistics, 63*, pp. 77–87.

Argyle, M. (1972). *The Social Psychology of Work.* Harmondsworth: Penguin.

Brayfield, A., and Crockett, W. (1955). "Employee Attitudes and Employee Performance." *Psychological Bulletin, 52*, pp. 396–424.

Chadwick-Jones, J. K., Nicholson, N., and Brown, C. (1982). *Social Psychology of Absenteeism.* New York: Praeger.

Chelius, J. R. (1981). "Understanding Absenteeism: The Potential Contribution of Economic Theory." *Journal of Business Research, 9*, pp. 409–418.

Dalton, D. R., and Perry, J. L. (1981). "Absenteeism and the Collective Bargaining Agreement: An Empirical Test." *Academy of Management Journal, 24*, pp. 425–431.

Dunn, L. F., and Youngblood, S. A. (1986). "Absenteeism as a Mechanism for Approaching an Optimal Labor Market Equilibrium: An Empirical Study." *The Review of Economics and Statistics, 68*, pp. 668–674.

Farrell, D., and Stamm, C. L. (1988). "Meta-Analysis of the Correlates of Employee Absence." *Human Relations, 41*, 211–227.

Gibson, R. O. (1966). "Toward a Conceptualization of Absence Behavior." *Administrative Sciences Quarterly, 11*, pp. 107–133.

Gowler, D. (1969). "Determinants of the Supply of Labour to the Firm." *Journal of Management Studies, 6*, pp. 73–95.

Hackett, R. D. (1988). "Yet Another Look at the Relationship of Employee Absenteeism to Job Satisfaction." Hamilton, Canada: Series #290.

Hackett, R. D., and Guion, R. M. (1985). "A Reevaluation of the Absenteeism-Job Satisfaction Relationship." *Organizational Behavior and Human Decision Processes, 35*, pp. 340–381.

Hill, J. M. M., and Trist, E. L. (1953). "A Consideration of Industrial Accidents as a Means of Withdrawal from the Work Situation." *Human Relations, 6*, pp. 357–380.

Ilgen, D., and Hollenback, J. H. (1977). "The Role of Job Satisfaction in Absence Behavior." *Organizational Behavior and Human Performance, 19*, pp. 148–161.

John, G., and Nicholson, N. (1982). "The Meaning of Absence: New Strategies for Theory and Research." In B. M. Staw and L. L. Cummings (eds.), *Research in Organizational Behavior* (Vol. 4). Greenwich, CT: JAI.

McShane, S. L. (1984). "Job Satisfaction and Absenteeism: A Meta-Analytic Re-Examination." *Canadian Journal of Administrative Sciences, 1*, pp. 61–77.

Morgan, L. G., and Herman, J. B. (1976). "Perceived Consequences of Absenteeism." *Journal of Applied Psychology, 61*, pp. 738–742.

Nicholson, N. (1977). "Absence Behavior and Attendance Motivation: A Conceptual Synthesis." *Journal of Management Studies,* 14, pp. 231–252.

Nicholson, N., and Johns, G. (1985). "The Absence Culture and the Psychological Contract—Who's in Control of Absence?" *Academy of Management Review,* 10, pp. 397–407.

Porter, L. W., and Lawler, E. E. (1968). *Managerial Attitudes and Performance,* Homewood, Ill.: Dorsey Press.

Rosse, J. G., and Hulin, C. L. (1985). "Adaptation to Work: An Analysis of Employee Health, Withdrawal, and Change." *Organizational Behavior and Human Decision Processes,* 36, pp. 324–347.

Rosse, J. G., and Miller, H. E. (1984). "Relationship between Absenteeism and Other Employee Behaviors." In P. S. Goodman and R. S. Atkin (eds.), *Absenteeism: New Approaches to Understanding, Measuring, and Managing Absence,* pp. 194–228. San Francisco: Jossey-Bass.

Steers, R. M., and Rhodes, D. R. (1978). "Major Influences on Employee Attendance: A Process Model." *Journal of Applied Psychology,* 63, pp. 391–407.

———. (1984). "Knowledge and Speculation about Absenteeism." In P. S. Goodman and R. S. Atkin (eds.), *Absenteeism: New Approaches to Understanding, Measuring, and Managing Absence,* pp. 229–275. San Francisco: Jossey-Bass.

Vroom, V. (1964). *Work and Motivation.* New York: Wiley.

Wanous, J. P. (1975). "Tell It Like It Is at Realistic Job Previews." *Personnel,* 52 (4), pp. 50–60.

———. (1980). *Organizational Entry: Recruitment, Selection, and Socialization of Newcomers.* Reading, Mass.: Addison-Wesley.

Winkler, D. R. (1980). "The Effects of Sick-Leave Policy on Teacher Absenteeism." *Industrial and Labor Relations Review,* 33, pp. 232–239.

Youngblood, S. A. (1984). "Work, Nonwork, and Withdrawal." *Journal of Applied Psychology,* 69, pp. 106–117.

CHAPTER 5: Questions for Discussion

1 How valuable is the concept of job attitudes for understanding employee behavior? What is the relationship between job attitudes and leader behavior?

2 Is the concept of organizational citizenship behavior (OCB) meaningful for managers facing serious on-the-job performance problems?

3 How important is perceived fairness in determining employee commitment to a workplace? How important is fairness in determining employee performance?

4 Do you believe employee job attitudes are relatively stable across time and work experiences, as Staw suggests, or do they vary considerably over time as a result of short-term job experiences?

5 If job attitudes are relatively volatile across time, what are the implications for managing a work group? If attitudes are stable over time, what are the implications for managing a work group?

6 What managerial implications follow from the Rhodes and Steers diagnostic model of employee absenteeism?

7 How would you design a work environment aimed at minimizing voluntary absenteeism?

8 Absenteeism in several Asian countries (like Japan and Korea) is substantially lower than that in most Western countries (including those in North America and Europe). What factors account for these differences?

CROSS-CULTURAL INFLUENCES ON MOTIVATION AND LEADERSHIP

One of the cofounders of Honda Motor Company observed many years ago that "Japanese management and American management are 95 percent the same *and differ in all important respects.*" What Mr. Fujisawa was saying was that while a manager's job may look the same the world over, subtle cultural differences exist that tend to define the success or failure of the individual manager. Without an appreciation of these cultural differences, it is difficult, if not impossible, to succeed in the global workplace. What makes this challenge even more difficult, however, is the fact that many of these differences are often invisible to the untrained eye. As the ancient Chinese philosopher Lao Tsu once observed, "Water is the last thing a fish notices." In other words, our own cultures are so embedded in us that we frequently fail to notice many of their defining characteristics. It is to this topic of culture and its influence on work and management that we now turn.

For this chapter we have chosen the title "Cross-cultural Influences . . ." However, we could as effectively have used the term "Cross-national Influences . . ." It is important to remember, however, that although cultures and nations frequently overlap, they do not always coincide directly. Belgium and Canada, for example, each tends to have two distinct cultures contained within one country. Likewise, one culture can overlap more than one country, as in the case of Norway, Sweden, and Denmark. The basic point is that when the term "cross-cultural" is used it generally also implies "cross-national," although there can be definite exceptions, as noted.

In considering different influences on motivation and leadership across nations and their associated cultures, it is helpful to define briefly what is meant by the term "culture." Unfortunately, as Ajiferuke and Boddewyn (1970) have pointed out, "Culture is one of those terms that defy a single all-purpose definition, and there are almost as many meanings of culture as people using the term." Nevertheless, a typical social science definition is that put forth by Kroeber and Parsons (1958, p. 583): "the transmitted and created content and patterns of values, ideas, and other symbolic-meaningful systems as factors in the shaping of human behavior and the artifacts produced through that behavior." A more succinct definition provided by a management scholar who has carried out extensive cross-cultural studies is: "the collective programming of the mind which distinguishes the members of one human group from another," or, as he has also put it: "culture is to a human collectivity what personality is to an individual" (Hofstede, 1980, p. 25).

The critical, or central, issue in cross-national analyses of managerial influences is whether individuals' responses to organizations' practices are more or less universal and therefore whether those practices can be transferred from one culture to another with essentially similar results (Nath, 1988). Perhaps a better way to put the question is: To what extent can what is learned about motivation and leadership in the work situation in one culture (e.g., the United States) be applied in another culture (e.g., Egypt) with predictable outcomes? As implied earlier, the research evidence to date does not provide clear-cut answers to this type of question. Part of the reason is that research methodologies and conceptual foundations have not been sufficiently developed to permit unambiguous interpretation of findings. For example, when significant differences are found between leadership patterns across countries, it is extremely difficult to pin down the causes for these differences (or similarities, for that matter). While improved research designs can help in this regard, it is still a major problem to disentangle the effects of culture from those of other key variables such as amount of industrialization, type of technology, size of organization, nature of specific legal statutes, and the like. Even if these factors can be controlled in an effective research design, the question remains as to what it is about the culture or country that is in fact causing the differences (or lack of them).

Despite all of the nettlesome complexities involved in interpreting data and information obtained in cross-cultural or cross-national comparisons, it remains important to attempt to do so. For one thing, it helps provide a good antidote to ethnocentrism (a belief in the inherent superiority of one's own culture or group). No nation or culture has a monopoly on the best ways of doing something. This is especially so when it comes to understanding motivation and leadership at work and attempting to implement practices based on this knowledge. Second, it is always easier to understand something by comparison rather than in an absolute sense. Thus, our comprehension of a particular situation (e.g., motivation in U.S. organizations) is enhanced. Third, the world is increasingly moving toward greater intercultural and international exchanges of knowledge and individuals, and, therefore, many more people than in the past will find that their work careers will involve experiences in more than a single culture.

OVERVIEW OF THE READINGS

The readings in this chapter focus on how cross-cultural or cross-national differences can affect employee motivation and leadership effectiveness. First, Hofstede examines several contemporary Western theories of motivation on a general level to see how they apply internationally. That is, can a theory of motivation developed in the United States, for example, incorporate factors from other countries that are important for understanding motivation and behavior? Consider the issue of "pay for performance," for instance. In the United States, considerable emphasis is given to tying pay raises to individual performance. What happens to this approach in several European countries, where personal income tax escalates rapidly in the higher income brackets to the point where most, if not all, the pay raise goes for taxes? What happens to the motivational value of the reward? Or, consider what happens to individual pay-for-performance systems in several Asian countries where group achievement is prized and individual (that is, independent) effort is not? Again, what happens to the original theory? Issues such as these are considered in this first reading.

Following this general discussion, we turn our attention to the managerial problems in specific countries. It is clearly not possible in the space provided to cover this subject in a global fashion. Instead, keeping in mind Hofstede's discussion of the situation in North American and Western European countries, we shall focus on three other very different countries: Japan, Russia, and China. This comparison should allow us to gain an appreciation of the complexities of motivating and leading employees around the world. First, Lincoln and Ichikawa look at motivation and leadership in Japanese companies. Considerable effort is made in these two articles to compare the Japanese situation with that in the United States. Next, Puffer examines motivation and leadership in a rapidly changing Russian commercial environment. Finally, Schermerhorn and Nyaw take a look inside Chinese bureaucracies and consider how Chinese managers attempt to lead employees within a complex political and economic environment. Throughout, implications for management are considered.

REFERENCES

Ajiferuke, M., and Boddewyn, J. Culture and other explanatory variables in management studies. *Academy of Management Journal,* 1970, 13, 153–163.

Hofstede, G. *Culture's consequence: International differences in work-related values.* Beverly Hills, Calif.: Sage, 1980.

Kroeber, A., and Parsons, T. The concepts of culture and of the social system. *American Sociological Review,* 1958, 23, 582–583.

Nath, R. *Comparative management: A regional view.* Cambridge, Mass.: Ballinger, 1988.

Cultural Constraints in Management Theories

Geert Hofstede

Management as the word is presently used is an American invention. In other parts of the world not only the practices but the entire concept of management may differ, and the theories needed to understand it may deviate considerably from what is considered normal and desirable in the USA. The reader is invited on a trip around the world, and both local management practices and theories are explained from the different contexts and histories of the places visited: Germany, Japan, France, Holland, the countries of the overseas Chinese, South-East Asia, Africa, Russia, and finally mainland China.

A model in which worldwide differences in national cultures are categorized according to five independent dimensions helps in explaining the differences in management found; although the situation in each country or region has unique characteristics that no model can account for. One practical application of the model is in demonstrating the relative position of the U.S. versus other parts of the world. In a global perspective, U.S. management theories contain a number of idiosyncrasies not necessarily shared by management elsewhere. Three such idiosyncrasies are mentioned: a stress on market processes, a stress on the individual, and a focus on managers rather than on workers. A plea is made for an internationalization not only of business, but also of management theories, as a way of enriching theories at the national level.

IN MY VIEW

Lewis Carroll's *Alice in Wonderland* contains the famous story of Alice's croquet game with the Queen of Hearts.

> Alice thought she had never seen such a curious croquet-ground in all her life; it was all ridges and furrows; the balls were live hedgehogs, and mallets live flamingoes, and the soldiers had to double themselves up and to stand on their hands and feet, to make the arches.

You probably know how the story goes: Alice's flamingo mallet turns its head whenever she wants to strike with it; her hedgehog ball runs away; and the doubled-up soldier arches walk around all the time. The only rule seems to be that the Queen of Hearts always wins.

Alice's croquet playing problems are good analogies to attempts to build culture-free theories of management. Concepts available for this purpose are themselves alive with culture, having been developed within a particular cultural context. They have a tendency to guide our thinking toward our desired conclusion.

As the same reasoning may also be applied to the arguments in this article, I better tell you my conclusion before I continue—so that the rules of my game are under-

From *Academy of Management Executive,* 1993, 7(1), 81–94. Reprinted by permission.

stood. In this article we take a trip around the world to demonstrate that there are no such things as universal management theories.

Diversity in management *practices* as we go around the world has been recognized in U.S. management literature for more than thirty years. The term "comparative management" has been used since the 1960s. However, it has taken much longer for the U.S. academic community to accept that not only practices but also the validity of *theories* may stop at national borders, and I wonder whether even today everybody would agree with this statement.

An article I published in *Organizational Dynamics* in 1980 entitled "Do American Theories Apply Abroad?" created more controversy than I expected. The article argued, with empirical support, that generally accepted U.S. theories like those of Maslow, Herzberg, McClelland, Vroom, McGregor, Likert, Blake, and Mouton may not or only very partly apply outside the borders of their country of origin—assuming they do apply within those borders. Among the requests for reprints, a larger number were from Canada than from the United States.

MANAGEMENT THEORISTS ARE HUMAN

Employees and managers are human. Employees as humans was "discovered" in the 1930s, with the Human Relations school. Managers as humans was introduced in the late 40s by Herbert Simon's "bounded rationality" and elaborated in Richard Cyert and James March's *Behavioral Theory of the Firm* (1963, and recently re-published in a second edition). My argument is that management scientists, theorists, and writers are human too: they grew up in a particular society in a particular period, and their ideas cannot help but reflect the constraints of their environment.

The idea that the validity of a theory is constrained by national borders is more obvious in Europe, with all its borders, than in a huge borderless country like the U.S. Already in the sixteenth century Michel de Montaigne, a Frenchman, wrote a statement which was made famous by Blaise Pascal about a century later: *"Vérite en-deça des Pyrenées, erreur au-delà"*—There are truths on this side of the Pyrenees which are falsehoods on the other.

FROM DON ARMADO'S LOVE TO TAYLOR'S SCIENCE

According to the comprehensive ten-volume Oxford English Dictionary (1971), the words "manage," "management," and "manager" appeared in the English language in the 16th century. The oldest recorded use of the word "manager" is in Shakespeare's "Love's Labour's Lost," dating from 1588, in which Don Adriano de Armado, "a fantastical Spaniard," exclaims (Act I, scene ii, 188):

> *"Adieu, valour! rust, rapier! be still, drum! for your manager is in love; yea, he loveth".*

The linguistic origin of the word is from Latin *manus,* hand, via the Italian *maneggiare,* which is the training of horses in the *manege;* subsequently its meaning was extended to skillful handling in general, like of arms and musical instruments, as Don Armado illustrates. However, the word also became associated with the French *menage,* household, as an equivalent of "husbandry" in its sense of the art of running a household. The theatre of present-day management contains elements of both *manege* and *menage* and different managers and cultures may use different accents.

The founder of the science of economics, the Scot Adam Smith, in his 1776 book *The Wealth of Nations,* used "manage," "management" (even "bad management") and "manager" when dealing with the process and the persons involved in operating joint stock companies (Smith, V.i.e.). British economist John Stuart Mill (1806–1873) followed Smith in this use and clearly expressed his distrust of such hired people who were not driven by ownership. Since the 1880s the word "management" appeared occasionally in writings by American engineers, until it was canonized as a modern science by Frederick W. Taylor in *Shop Management* in 1903 and in *The Principles of Scientific Management* in 1911.

While Smith and Mill used "management" to describe a process and "managers" for the persons involved, "management" in the American sense—which has since been taken back by the British—refers not only to the process but also to the managers as a class of people. This class (1) does not own a business but sells its skills to act on behalf of the owners and (2) does not produce personally but is indispensable for making others produce, through motivation. Members of this class carry a high status and many American boys and girls aspire to the role. In the U.S., the manager is a cultural hero.

Let us now turn to other parts of the world. We will look at management in its context in other successful modern economies: Germany, Japan, France, Holland, and among the overseas Chinese. Then we will examine management in the much larger part of the world that is still poor, especially South-East Asia and Africa, and in the new political configurations of Eastern Europe, and Russia in particular. We will then return to the U.S. via mainland China.

Germany

The manager is not a cultural hero in Germany. If anybody, it is the engineer who fills the hero role. Frederick Taylor's *Scientific Management* was conceived in a society of immigrants—where large numbers of workers with diverse backgrounds and skills had to work together. In Germany this heterogeneity never existed.

Elements of the mediaeval guild system have survived in historical continuity in Germany until the present day. In particular, a very effective apprenticeship system exists both on the shop floor and in the office, which alternates practical work and classroom courses. At the end of the apprenticeship the worker receives a certificate, the *Facharbeiterbrief,* which is recognized throughout the country. About two thirds of the German worker population holds such a certificate and a corresponding occupational pride. In fact, quite a few German company presidents have worked their way up from the ranks through an apprenticeship. In comparison, two thirds of the worker population in Britain have no occupational qualification at all.

The highly skilled and responsible German workers do not necessarily need a manager, American-style, to "motivate" them. They expect their boss or *Meister* to assign their tasks and to be the expert in resolving technical problems. Comparisons of similar German, British, and French organizations show the Germans as having the highest rate of personnel in productive roles and the lowest both in leadership and staff roles.

Business schools are virtually unknown in Germany. Native German management theories concentrate on formal systems. The inapplicability of American concepts of management was quite apparent in 1973 when the U.S. consulting firm of Booz, Allen and Hamilton, commissioned by the German Ministry of Economic Affairs, wrote a study of German management from an American view point. The report is highly critical and writes among other things that "Germans simply do not have a very strong concept of management." Since 1973, from my personal experience, the situation has not changed much. However, during this period the German economy has performed in a superior fashion to the U.S. in virtually all respects, so a strong concept of management might have been a liability rather than an asset.

Japan

The American type of manager is also missing in Japan. In the United States, the core of the enterprise is the managerial class. The core of the Japanese enterprise is the permanent worker group; workers who for all practical purposes are tenured and who aspire at life-long employment. They are distinct from the non-permanent employees—most women and subcontracted teams led by gang bosses, to be laid off in slack periods. University graduates in Japan first join the permanent worker group and subsequently fill various positions, moving from line to staff as the need occurs while paid according to seniority rather than position. They take part in Japanese-style group consultation sessions for important decisions, which extend the decision-making period but guarantee fast implementation afterwards. Japanese are to a large extent controlled by their peer group rather than by their manager.

Three researchers from the East-West Center of the University of Hawaii, Joseph Tobin, David Wu, and Dana Danielson, did an observation study of typical preschools in three countries: China, Japan, and the United States. Their results have been published both as a book and as a video. In the Japanese preschool, one teacher handled twenty-eight four-year-olds. The video shows one particularly obnoxious boy, Hiroki, who fights with other children and throws teaching materials down from the balcony. When a little girl tries to alarm the teacher, the latter answers "what are you calling me for? Do something about it!" In the U.S. preschool, there is one adult for every nine children. This class has its problem child too, Glen, who refuses to clear away his toys. One of the teachers has a long talk with him and isolates him in a corner, until he changes his mind. It doesn't take much imagination to realize that managing Hiroki thirty years later will be a different process from managing Glen.

American theories of leadership are ill-suited for the Japanese group-controlled situation. During the past two decades, the Japanese have developed their own "PM" theory of leadership, in which P stands for performance and M for maintenance. The latter is less a concern for individual employees than for maintaining social stability. In view of the amazing success of the Japanese economy in the past thirty years, many Americans have sought for the secrets of Japanese management hoping to copy them.

There are no secrets of Japanese management, however; it is even doubtful whether there is such a thing as management, in the American sense, in Japan at all. The secret is in Japanese society; and if any group in society should be singled out as carriers of the secret, it is the workers, not the managers.

France

The manager, U.S. style, does not exist in France either. In a very enlightening book, unfortunately not yet translated into English, the French researcher Philippe d'Iribarne (1989) describes the results of in-depth observation and interview studies of management methods in three subsidiary plants of the same French multinational: in France, the United States, and Holland. He relates what he finds to information about the three societies in general. Where necessary, he goes back in history to trace the roots of the strikingly different behaviors in the completion of the same tasks. He identifies three kinds of basic principles (*logiques*) of management. In the U.S.A., the principle is the *fair contract* between employer and employee, which gives the manager considerable prerogatives, but within its limits. This is really a labor *market*, in which the worker sells his or her labor for a price. In France, the principle is the *honor* of each class in a society which has always been and remains extremely stratified, in which superiors behave as superior beings and subordinates accept and expect this, conscious of their own lower level in the national hierarchy but also of the honor of their own class. The French do not think in terms of managers versus nonmanagers but in terms of *cadres* versus *non-cadres;* one becomes cadre by attending the proper schools and one remains it forever; regardless of their actual task, cadres have the privileges of a higher social class, and it is very rare for a non-cadre to cross the ranks.

The conflict between French and American theories of management became apparent in the beginning of the twentieth century, in a criticism by the great French management pioneer Henri Fayol (1841–1925) on his U.S. colleague and contemporary Frederick W. Taylor (1856–1915). The difference in career paths of the two men is striking. Fayol was a French engineer whose career as a *cadre supérieur* culminated in the position of Président-Directeur-Général of a mining company. After his retirement he formulated his experiences in a pathbreaking text on organization: *Administration industrielle et générale,* in which he focused on the sources of authority. Taylor was an American engineer who started his career in industry as a worker and attained his academic qualifications through evening studies. From chief engineer in a steel company he became one of the first management consultants. Taylor was not really concerned with the issue of authority at all; his focus was on efficiency. He proposed to split the task of the first-line boss into eight specialisms, each exercised by a different person, an idea which eventually led to the idea of a matrix organization.

Taylor's work appeared in a French translation in 1913, and Fayol read it and showed himself generally impressed but shocked by Taylor's "denial of the principle of the Unity of Command" in the case of the eight-boss-system.

Seventy years later André Laurent, another of Fayol's compatriots, found that French managers in a survey reacted very strongly against a suggestion that one employee could report to two different bosses, while U.S. managers in the same survey showed fewer misgivings. Matrix organization has never become popular in France as it has in the United States.

Holland

In my own country, Holland, or as it is officially called, the Netherlands, the study by Philippe d'Iribarne found the management principle to be a need for *consensus* among all parties, neither predetermined by a contractual relationship nor by class distinctions, but based on an open-ended exchange of views and a balancing of interests. In terms of the different origins of the word "manager," the organization in Holland is more *menage* (household) while in the United States it is more *manege* (horse drill).

At my university, the University of Limburg at Maastricht, every semester we receive a class of American business students who take a program in European Studies. We asked both the Americans and a matched group of Dutch students to describe their ideal job after graduation, using a list of twenty-two job characteristics. The Americans attached significantly more importance than the Dutch to earnings, advancement, benefits, a good working relationship with their boss, and security of employment. The Dutch attached more importance to freedom to adopt their own approach to the job, being consulted by their boss in his or her decisions, training opportunities, contributing to the success of their organization, fully using their skills and abilities, and helping others. This list confirms d'Iribarne's findings of a contractual employment relationship in the United States, based on earnings and career opportunities, against a consensual relationship in Holland. The latter has centuries-old roots; the Netherlands were the first republic in Western Europe (1609–1810), and a model for the American republic. The country has been and still is governed by a careful balancing of interests in a multi-party system.

In terms of management theories, both motivation and leadership in Holland are different from what they are in the United States. Leadership in Holland presupposes modesty, as opposed to assertiveness in the United States. No U.S. leadership theory has room for that. Working in Holland is not a constant feast, however. There is a built-in premium on mediocrity and jealousy, as well as time-consuming ritual consultations to maintain the appearance of consensus and the pretense of modesty. There is unfortunately another side to every coin.

The Overseas Chinese

Among the champions of economic development in the past thirty years we find three countries mainly populated by Chinese living outside the Chinese mainland: Taiwan, Hong Kong, and Singapore. Moreover, overseas Chinese play a very important role in the economies of Indonesia, Malaysia, the Philippines, and Thailand, where they form an ethnic minority. If anything, the little dragons—Taiwan, Hong Kong, and Singapore—have been more economically successful than Japan, moving from rags to riches and now counted among the world's wealthy industrial countries. Yet very little attention has been paid to the way in which their enterprises have been managed. *The Spirit of Chinese Capitalism* by Gordon Redding (1990), the British dean of the Hong Kong Business School, is an excellent book about Chinese business. He bases his insights on personal acquaintance and in-depth discussions with a large number of overseas Chinese businesspeople.

Overseas Chinese American enterprises lack almost all characteristics of modern management. They tend to be small, cooperating for essential functions with other small organizations through networks based on personal relations. They are family-owned, without the separation between ownership and management typical in the West, or even in Japan and Korea. They normally focus on one product or market, with growth by opportunistic diversification; in this, they are extremely flexible. Decision making is centralized in the hands of one dominant family member, but other family members may be given new ventures to try their skills on. They are low-profile and extremely cost-conscious, applying Confucian virtues of thrift and persistence. Their size is kept small by the assumed lack of loyalty of non-family employees, who, if they are any good, will just wait and save until they can start their own family business.

Overseas Chinese prefer economic activities in which great gains can be made with little manpower, like commodity trading and real estate. They employ few professional managers, except their sons and sometimes daughters who have been sent to prestigious business schools abroad, but who upon return continue to run the family business the Chinese way.

The origin of this system, or—in the Western view—this lack of system, is found in the history of Chinese society, in which there were no formal laws, only formal networks of powerful people guided by general principles of Confucian virtue. The favors of the authorities could change daily, so nobody could be trusted except one's kin-folk—of whom, fortunately, there used to be many, in an extended family structure. The overseas Chinese way of doing business is also very well adapted to their position in the countries in which they form ethnic minorities, often envied and threatened by ethnic violence.

Overseas Chinese businesses following this unprofessional approach command a collective gross national product of some 200 to 300 billion U.S. dollars, exceeding the GNP of Australia. There is no denying that it works.

MANAGEMENT TRANSFER TO POOR COUNTRIES

Four-fifths of the world population live in countries that are not rich but poor. After World War II and decolonization, the stated purpose of the United Nations and the World Bank has been to promote the development of all the world's countries in a war on poverty. After forty years it looks very much like we are losing this war. If one thing has become clear, it is that the export of Western—mostly American—management practices *and* theories to poor countries has contributed little to nothing to their development. There has been no lack of effort and money spent for this purpose: students from poor countries have been trained in this country, and teachers and Peace Corps workers have been sent to the poor countries. If nothing else, the general lack of success in economic development of other countries should be sufficient argument to doubt the validity of Western management theories in non-Western environments.

If we examine different parts of the world, the development picture is not equally bleak, and history is often a better predictor than economic factors for what happens today. There is a broad regional pecking order with East Asia leading. The little dragons have passed into the camp of the wealthy; then follow South-East Asia (with its overseas Chinese minorities), Latin America (in spite of the debt crisis), South Asia, and Africa always trails behind. Several African countries have only become poorer since decolonization.

Regions of the world with a history of large-scale political integration and civilization generally have done better than regions in which no large-scale political and cultural infrastructure existed, even if the old civilizations had decayed or been suppressed by colonizers. It has become painfully clear that development cannot be pressure-cooked; it presumes a cultural infrastructure that takes time to grow. Local management is part of this infrastructure; it cannot be imported in package form. Assuming that with so-called modern management techniques and theories outsiders can develop a country has proven a deplorable arrogance. At best, one can hope for a dialogue between equals with the locals, in which the Western partner acts as the expert in Western technology and the local partner as the expert in local culture, habits, and feelings.

Russia and China

The crumbling of the former Eastern bloc has left us with a scattering of states and would-be states of which the political and economic future is extremely uncertain. The best predictions are those based on a knowledge of history, because historical trends have taken revenge on the arrogance of the Soviet rulers who believed they could turn them around by brute power. One obvious fact is that the former bloc is extremely heterogeneous, including countries traditionally closely linked with the West by trade and travel, like Czechia, Hungary, Slovenia, and the Baltic states, as well as others with a Byzantine or Turkish past, some having been prosperous, others always extremely poor.

The industrialized Western world and the World Bank seem committed to helping the ex-Eastern bloc countries develop, but with the same technocratic neglect for local cultural factors that proved so unsuccessful in the development assistance to other poor countries. Free market capitalism, introduced by Western-style management, is supposed to be the answer from Albania to Russia.

Let me limit myself to the Russian republic, a huge territory with some 140 million inhabitants, mainly Russians. We know quite a bit about the Russians as their country was a world power for several hundreds of years before communism, and in the nineteenth century it has produced some of the greatest writers in world literature. If I want to understand the Russians—including how they could so long support the Soviet regime—I tend to re-read Lev Nikolayevich Tolstoy. In his most famous novel, *Anna Karenina* (1876), one of the main characters is a landowner, Levin, whom Tolstoy uses to express his own views and convictions about his people. Russian peasants used to be serfs; serfdom had been abolished in 1861, but the peasants, now tenants, remained as passive as before. Levin wanted to break this passivity by dividing the land among his peasants in exchange for a share of the crops; but the peasants only let the land deteriorate further. Here follows a quote:

> (Levin) read political economy and socialistic works . . . but, as he had expected, found nothing in them related to his undertaking. In the political economy books—in (John Stuart) Mill, for instance, whom he studied first and with great ardour, hoping every minute to find

an answer to the questions that were engrossing him—he found only certain laws deduced from the state of agriculture in Europe; but he could not for the life of him see why these laws, which did not apply to Russia, should be considered universal. . . . Political economy told him that the laws by which Europe had developed and was developing her wealth were universal and absolute. Socialist teaching told him that development along those lines leads to ruin. And neither of them offered the smallest enlightenment as to what he, Levin, and all the Russian peasants and landowners were to do with their millions of hands and millions of acres, to make them as productive as possible for the common good.

In the summer of 1991, the Russian lands yielded a record harvest, but a large share of it rotted in the fields because no people were to be found for harvesting. The passivity is still there, and not only among the peasants. And the heirs of John Stuart Mill (whom we met before as one of the early analysts of "management") again present their universal recipes which simply do not apply.

Citing Tolstoy, I implicitly suggest that management theorists cannot neglect the great literature of the countries they want their ideas to apply to. The greatest novel in the Chinese literature is considered Cao Xueqin's *The Story of the Stone,* also known as *The Dream of the Red Chamber,* which appeared around 1760. It describes the rise and fall of two branches of an aristocratic family in Beijing, who live in adjacent plots in the capital. Their plots are joined by a magnificent garden with several pavillions in it, and the young, mostly female members of both families are allowed to live in them. One day the management of the garden is taken over by a young woman, Tan-Chun, who states:

> I think we ought to pick out a few experienced trust-worthy old women from among the ones who work in the Garden—women who know something about gardening already—and put the upkeep of the Garden into their hands. We needn't ask them to pay us rent; all we need ask them for is an annual share of the produce. There would be four advantages in this arrangement. In the first place, if we have people whose sole occupation is to look after trees and flowers and so on, the condition of the Garden will improve gradually year after year and there will be no more of those long periods of neglect followed by bursts of feverish activity when things have been allowed to get out of hand. Secondly, there won't be the spoiling and wastage we get at present. Thirdly, the women themselves will gain a little extra to add to their incomes which will compensate them for the hard work they put in throughout the year. And fourthly, there's no reason why we shouldn't use the money we should otherwise have spent on nurserymen, rockery specialists, horticultural cleaners, and so on for other purposes.

As the story goes, the capitalist privatization—because that is what it is—of the Garden is carried through, and it works. When in the 1980s Deng Xiaoping allowed privatization in the Chinese villages, it also worked. It worked so well that its effects started to be felt in politics and threatened the existing political order; hence the knockdown at Tienanmen Square of June 1989. But it seems that the forces of privatization are getting the upper hand again in China. If we remember what Chinese entrepreneurs are able to do once they have become overseas Chinese, we shouldn't be too surprised. But what works in China—and worked two centuries ago—does not have to work in Russia, not in Tolstoy's days and not today. I am not offering a solution; I only protest against a naive universalism that knows only one recipe for development, the one supposed to have worked in the United States.

A THEORY OF CULTURE IN MANAGEMENT

Our trip around the world is over and we are back in the United States. What have we learned? There is something in all countries called "management," but its meaning differs to a larger or smaller extent from one country to the other, and it takes considerable historical and cultural insight into local conditions to understand its processes, philosophies, and problems. If already the word may mean so many different things, how can we expect one country's theories of management to apply abroad? One should be extremely careful in making this assumption, and test it before considering it proven. Management is not a phenomenon that can be isolated from other processes taking place in a society. During our trip around the world we saw that it interacts with what happens in the family, at school, in politics, and government. It is obviously also related to religion and to beliefs about science. Theories of management always had to be interdisciplinary, but if we cross national borders they should become more interdisciplinary than ever.

Cultural differences between nations can be, to some extent, described using first four, and now five, bipolar *dimensions.* The position of a country on these dimensions allows us to make some predictions on the way their society operates, including their management processes and the kind of theories applicable to their management.

As the word culture plays such an important role in my theory, let me give you my definition, which differs from some other very respectable definitions. Culture to me is *the collective programming of the mind which distinguishes one group or category of people from another.* In the part of my work I am referring to now, the category of people is the nation.

Culture is a *construct,* that means it is "not directly accessible to observation but inferable from verbal statements and other behaviors and useful in predicting still other observable and measurable verbal and nonverbal behavior." It should not be reified; it is an auxiliary concept that should be used as long as it proves useful but bypassed where we can predict behaviors without it.

The same applies to the *dimensions* I introduced. They are constructs too that should not be reified. They do not "exist"; they are tools for analysis which may or may not clarify a situation. In my statistical analysis of empirical data the first four dimensions together explain forty-nine percent of the variance in the data. The other fifty-one percent remain specific to individual countries.

The first four dimensions were initially detected through a comparison of the values of similar people (employees and managers) in sixty-four national subsidiaries of the IBM Corporation. People working for the same multinational, but in different countries, represent very well-matched samples from the populations of their countries, similar in all respects except nationality.

The first dimension is labelled *Power Distance,* and it can be defined as the degree of inequality among people which the population of a country considers as normal: from relatively equal (that is, small power distance) to extremely unequal (larger power distance). All societies are unequal, but some are more unequal than others.

The second dimension is labelled *Individualism,* and it is the degree to which people in a country prefer to act as individuals rather than as members of groups. The opposite of individualism can be called *Collectivism,* so collectivism is low individualism. The way I use the word it has no political connotations. In collectivist societies a child learns to respect the group to which it belongs, usually the family, and to differentiate between in-group members and out-group members (that is, all other people). When children grow up they remain members of their group, and they expect the group to protect them when they are in trouble. In return, they have to remain loyal to their group throughout life. In individualist societies, a child learns very early to think of itself as "I" instead of as part of "we." It expects one day to have to stand on its own feet and not to get protection from its group any more; and therefore it also does not feel a need for strong loyalty.

The third dimension is called *Masculinity* and its opposite pole *Femininity.* It is the degree to which tough values like assertiveness, performance, success and competition, which in nearly all societies are associated with the role of men, prevail over tender values like the quality of life, maintaining warm personal relationships, service, care for the weak, and solidarity, which in nearly all societies are more associated with women's roles. Women's roles differ from men's roles in all countries; but in tough societies, the differences are larger than in tender ones.

The fourth dimension is labelled *Uncertainty Avoidance,* and it can be defined as the degree to which people in a country prefer structured over unstructured situations. Structured situations are those in which there are clear rules as to how one should behave. These rules can be written down, but they can also be unwritten and imposed by tradition. In countries which score high on uncertainty avoidance, people tend to show more nervous energy, while in countries which score low, people are more easy-going. A (national) society with strong uncertainty avoidance can be called rigid; one with weak uncertainty avoidance, flexible. In countries where uncertainty avoidance is strong a feeling prevails of "what is different, is dangerous." In weak uncertainty avoidance societies, the feeling would rather be "what is different, is curious."

The fifth dimension was added on the basis of a study of the values of students in twenty-three countries carried out by Michael Harris Bond, a Canadian working in Hong Kong. He and I had cooperated in another study of students' values which had yielded the same four dimensions as the IBM data. However, we wondered to what extent our common findings in two studies could be the effect of a Western bias introduced by the common Western background of the researchers: remember Alice's croquet game. Michael Bond resolved this dilemma by deliberately introducing an Eastern bias. He used a questionnaire prepared at his request by his Chinese colleagues, the *Chinese Value Survey* (CVS), which was translated from Chinese into different languages and answered by fifty male and fifty female students in each of twenty-three countries in all five continents. Analysis of the CVS data produced three dimensions significantly correlated with the three IBM dimensions of power distance, individualism, and masculinity. There was also a fourth dimension, but it did not resemble uncertainty avoidance. It was composed, both on the positive and on the negative side, from items that had not been included in the IBM studies but were present in the Chinese Value Survey because they were rooted in the teachings of Confucius. I labelled this dimension: *Long-term* versus *Short-term Orientation.* On the long-term side one finds values oriented towards the future, like thrift (saving) and persistence. On the short-term side one finds values rather oriented towards the past and present, like respect for tradition and fulfilling social obligations.

TABLE 1
CULTURE DIMENSION SCORES FOR TEN COUNTRIES

	PD	ID	MA	UA	LT
USA	40 L	91 H	62 H	46 L	29 L
Germany	35 L	67 H	66 H	65 M	31 M
Japan	54 M	46 M	95 H	92 H	80 H
France	68 H	71 H	43 M	86 H	30*L
Netherlands	38 L	80 H	14 L	53 M	44 M
Hong Kong	68 H	25 L	57 H	29 L	96 H
Indonesia	78 H	14 L	46 M	48 L	25*L
West Africa	77 H	20 L	46 M	54 M	16 L
Russia	95*H	50*M	40*L	90*H	10*L
China	80*H	20*L	50*M	60*M	118 H

Key: PD = Power Distance; ID = Individualism; MA = Masculinity; UA = Uncertainty Avoidance; LT = Long Term Orientation. H = top third; M = medium third; L = bottom third (among 53 countries and regions for the first four dimensions; among 23 countries for the fifth).
*estimated

Table 1 lists the scores on all five dimensions for the United States and for the other countries we just discussed. The table shows that each country has its own configuration on the four dimensions. Some of the values in the table have been estimated based on imperfect replications or personal impressions. The different dimension scores do not "explain" all the differences in management I described earlier. To understand management in a country, one should have both knowledge of and empathy with the entire local scene. However, the scores should make us aware that people in other countries may think, feel, and act very differently from us when confronted with basic problems of society.

IDIOSYNCRACIES OF AMERICAN MANAGEMENT THEORIES

In comparison to other countries, the U.S. culture profile presents itself as below average on power distance and uncertainty avoidance, highly individualistic, fairly masculine, and short-term oriented. The Germans show a stronger uncertainty avoidance and less extreme individualism; the Japanese are different on all dimensions, least on power distance; the French show larger power distance and uncertainty avoidance, but are less individualistic and somewhat feminine; the Dutch resemble the Americans on the first three dimensions, but score extremely feminine and relatively long-term oriented; Hong Kong Chinese combine large power distance with weak uncertainty avoidance, collectivism, and are very long-term oriented; and so on.

The American culture profile is reflected in American management theories. I will just mention three elements not necessarily present in other countries: the stress on market processes, the stress on the individual, and the focus on managers rather than on workers.

The Stress on Market Processes

During the 1970s and 80s it has become fashionable in the United States to look at organizations from a "transaction costs" viewpoint. Economist Oliver Williamson has opposed "hierarchies" to "markets." The reasoning is that human social life consists of economic transactions between individuals. We found the same in d'Iribarne's description of the U.S. principle of the contract between employer and employee, the labor market in which the worker sells his or her labor for a price. These individuals will form hierarchical organizations when the cost of the economic transactions (such as getting information, finding out whom to trust, etc.) is lower in a hierarchy than when all transactions would take place on a free market.

From a cultural perspective the important point is that *the "market" is the point of departure or base model,* and the organization is explained from market failure. A culture that produces such a theory is likely to prefer organizations that internally resemble markets to organizations that internally resemble more structured models, like those in Germany or France. The ideal principle of control in organizations in the market philosophy is *competition* between individuals. This philosophy fits a society that combines a not-too-large power distance with a not-too-strong uncertainty avoidance and individualism; besides the U.S.A., it will fit all other Anglo countries.

The Stress on the Individual

I find this constantly in the design of research projects and hypotheses; also in the fact that in the U.S. psychology is clearly a more respectable discipline in management circles than sociology. Culture however is a collective phenomenon. Although we may get our information about culture from individuals, we have to interpret it at the level of collectivities. There are snags here known as the "ecological fallacy" and the "reverse ecological fallacy." None of the U.S. college textbooks on methodology I know deals sufficiently with the problem of multilevel analysis.

Culture can be compared to a forest, while individuals are trees. A forest is not just a bunch of trees: it is a symbiosis of different trees, bushes, plants, insects, animals, and micro-organisms, and we miss the essence of the forest if we only describe its most typical trees. In the same way, a culture cannot be satisfactorily described in terms of the characteristics of a typical individual. There is a tendency in the U.S. management literature to overlook the forest for the trees and to ascribe cultural differences to interactions among individuals.

A striking example is found in the otherwise excellent book *Organizational Culture and Leadership* by Edgar H. Schein (1985). On the basis of his consulting experience he compares two large companies, nicknamed "Action" and "Multi." He explains the differences in culture between these companies by the group dynamics in their respective boardrooms. Nowhere in the book are any conclusions drawn from the fact that the first company is an American-based computer firm, and the second a Swiss-based pharmaceutics firm. This information is not even mentioned. A stress on interactions among individuals obviously fits a culture identified as the most individualistic in the world, but it will not be so well understood by the four-fifths of the world population for whom the group prevails over the individual.

One of the conclusions of my own multilevel research has been that culture at the national level and culture at the organizational level—corporate culture—are two very different phenomena and that the use of a common term for both is confusing. If we do use the common term, we should also pay attention to the occupational and the gender level of culture. National cultures differ primarily in the fundamental, invisible values held by a majority of their members, acquired in early childhood, whereas organizational cultures are a much more superficial phenomenon residing mainly in the visible practices of the organization, acquired by socialization of the new members who join as young adults. National cultures change only very slowly if at all; organizational cultures may be consciously changed, although this isn't necessarily easy. This difference between the two types of culture is the secret of the existence of multinational corporations that employ, as I showed in the IBM case, employees with extremely different national cultural values. What keeps them together is a corporate culture based on common practices.

The Stress on Managers Rather than Workers

The core element of a work organization around the world is the people who do the work. All the rest is superstructure, and I hope to have demonstrated to you that it may take many different shapes. In the U.S. literature on work organization, however, the core element, if not explicitly then implicitly, is considered the manager. This may well be the result of the combination of extreme individualism with fairly strong masculinity, which has turned the manager into a culture hero of almost mythical proportions. For example, he—not really she—is supposed to make decisions all the time. Those of you who are or have been managers must know that this is a fable. Very few management decisions are just "made" as the myth suggests it. Managers are much more involved in maintaining networks; if anything, it is the rank-and-file worker who can really make decisions on his or her own, albeit on a relatively simple level.

An amusing effect of the U.S. focus on managers is that in at least ten American books and articles on management I have been misquoted as having studied IBM *managers* in my research, whereas the book clearly describes that the answers were from IBM *employees.* My observation may be biased, but I get the impression that compared to twenty or thirty years ago less research in this country is done among employees and more on managers. But managers derive their *raison d'être* from the people managed: culturally, they are the followers of the people they lead, and their effectiveness depends on the latter. In other parts of the world, this exclusive focus on the manager is less strong, with Japan as the supreme example.

CONCLUSION

This article started with *Alice in Wonderland.* In fact, the management theorist who ventures outside his or her own country into other parts of the world is like Alice in Wonderland. He or she will meet strange beings, customs, ways of organizing or disorganizing and theories that are clearly stupid, old fashioned or even immoral—yet they may work, or at least they may not fail more frequently than corresponding theories do at home. Then, after the first culture shock, the traveller to Wonderland will feel enlightened, and may be able to take his or her experiences home and use them advantageously. All great ideas in science, politics, and management have travelled from one country to another and been enriched by foreign influences. The roots of American management theories are mainly in Europe: with Adam Smith, John Stuart Mill, Lev Tolstoy, Max Weber, Henri Fayol, Sigmund Freud, Kurt Lewin, and many others. These theories were re-planted here and they developed and bore fruit. The same may happen again. The last thing we need is a Monroe doctrine for management ideas.

Employee Work Attitudes and Management Practice in the U.S. and Japan: Evidence from a Large Comparative Survey

James R. Lincoln

What do we really know about the work motivation of the Japanese and the role of Japanese management practice in shaping it? How deeply rooted in the culture of Japan and the psyches of the Japanese people is the legendary commitment and the discipline of the Japanese labor force? How important are Japanese work patterns and the internal management of the Japanese firm for explaining the Japanese economic miracle, as compared with the macro forces of state guidance, *keiretsu* enterprise groupings, corporate strategy, and low-cost capital? If Japanese management practice does provide part of the explanation for the cooperation and productivity of the Japanese, does it only work with Japanese employees? That is to say, how transportable is Japanese management style: do overseas Japanese firms produce similar results with foreign workers? Do American and European firms that organize in "Japanese" fashion achieve the labor discipline, cooperation, and commitment that seem to characterize Japan?

Attempts to answer these and similar questions have filled the pages of the business press as well as scholarly journals in the nearly 8 years since the publication of *Theory Z* and *The Art of Japanese Management* marked the onset of Japanese management boom.[1] The quality of these accounts has ranged widely. Too many are ill-informed and opportunistic efforts to capitalize on the explosive demand for information on Japan and Japanese business. Others are thoughtful, incisive discussions by expert journalists, scholars, and consultants able to bring to bear on the issue rich experience from studying, living, and working in Japan. Notably absent until quite recently is much prominent commentary by the Japanese themselves, who, to a surprising extent, have followed the lead and absorbed the claims of Western observers of the Japanese management scene.[2]

Even the recent expert testimony of writers like Abegglen, Dore, and Vogel on Japanese organization and its lessons for the West is based much more on long personal experience, intuitive understanding, and generally "soft" journalistic research.[3] What does quantitative social science have to say about the contrasts in work motivation and worker productivity between Japan and the U.S.? Though the United States arguably has the world's largest, best-funded, and technically most sophisticated behavioral science community, surprisingly little of this research expertise has been aimed at a problem of critical contemporary importance to Americans: the nature, scope, and origins of the Japanese labor productivity advantage in manufacturing.

This article reviews a large survey research investigation of 106 factories in the U.S. (central Indiana) and Japan (Kanagawa Prefecture) and 8,302 of their employees. Between 1981 and 1983, my colleagues and I interviewed factory executives about the management style and organization of the plant and distributed questionnaires to representative samples of employees. To the best of our knowledge, the resulting data is the largest and most detailed body of survey information on American and Japanese factory workers and their employing organizations.

ARE WORK ATTITUDES DIFFERENT IN JAPAN AND THE U.S.?

The Japanese Are Less Satisfied . . .

A twofold question motivated our research: how do the work attitudes of Japanese manufacturing employees differ between Japan and the U.S.; and do those differences depend on the management and organization of the factory? Let's take the question of work attitudes first. We sought to measure through questionnaire items two attitude dimensions: job satisfaction and commitment to the company. Many would expect Japanese workers to score higher than Americans on both. The long hours, low absenteeism and turnover, the productivity and esprit de corps, the careers spent within a single company, the reluctance even to take time off for vacation—these are all well-documented patterns of Japanese worker behavior. Surely they suggest that job satisfaction and commitment to a particular company are extraordinarily higher in Japan.

As Table 1 shows, however, what we initially found was quite different. If our survey data are to be believed, it appears that commitment to the company is essentially the same in our American and Japanese employee samples. The specific questionnaire items in the six-item factor-weighted scale likewise either show no difference or the Americans appear to give the "more committed" response. Is the much-touted loyalty of the Japanese employee, then, a myth? Does the stability and discipline of Japanese labor have no basis in the attitudes and values of Japanese workers? These results seemed so at odds with expectations and the impressions of previous scholars that we were quite taken aback.

On the other hand, Table 1 *does* show large country differences in the job satisfaction items, but the direction is *contrary* to expectations. American employees seem much more satisfied with their jobs than do the Japanese. We were not, in fact, surprised by this finding. Every prior survey contrasting Japanese and Western work attitudes has likewise found work satisfaction to be lowest among the Japanese.[4]

How are we to interpret these results? Any first-year MBA student knows that high job satisfaction does not spell high work motivation.[5] As Ronald Dore suggests, low job satisfaction in Japan may imply a restless striving for perfection, an ongoing quest for fulfillment of lofty work values and company goals.[6] By the same token, American observers have cautioned that the high percentages of the U.S. workforce routinely reporting satisfaction with their jobs may be more cause for concern than complacency.[7] It may signal low expectations and aspirations, a willingness to settle for meager job rewards, and a preoccupation with leisure-time pursuits.[8]

Another possibility, of course, is that the Japan-U.S. differences in work attitudes we found are due, not to real cultural contrasts in work motives and values, but to measurement biases.[9] Many would argue that a distinctly American impulse is to put the best face on things, to be upbeat and cheerful, to appear in control and successful even when uncertainty is high and the future looks bleak. The Japanese, it appears, bias

TABLE 1

DESCRIPTIVE STATISTICS FOR MEASURES OF ORGANIZATIONAL COMMITMENT AND JOB SATISFACTION

	U.S. mean (SD)	Japan mean (SD)
Organizational Commitment Scale[a] (alpha = .75, U.S., .79, Japan).	2.13 (.469)	2.04 (.503)[b]
"I am willing to work harder than I have to in order to help this company succeed." (1 = strongly disagree, 5 = strongly agree)	3.91 (.895)	3.44 (.983)[b]
"I would take any job in order to continue working for this company." (same codes)	3.12 (1.14)	3.07 (1.13)
"My values and the values of this company are quite similar." (same codes)	3.15 (1.06)	2.68 (.949)[b]
"I am proud to work for this company." (same codes)	3.70 (.943)	3.51 (1.02)[b]
"I would turn down another job for more pay in order to stay with this company." (same codes)	2.71 (1.17)	2.68 (1.08)
"I feel very little loyalty to this company." (1 = strongly agree, 5 = strongly disagree)	3.45 (1.13)	3.40 (1.03)
Job Satisfaction Scale (alpha = .78, U.S.; .65, Japan)	1.54 (.449)	.962 (.350)[b]
"All in all, how satisfied would you say you are with your job?" (0 = not at all, 4 = very)	2.95 (1.12)	2.12 (1.06)[b]
"If a good friend of yours told you that he or she was interested in working at a job like yours at this company, what would you say?" (0 = would advise against it, 1 = would have second thoughts, 2 = would recommend it)	1.52 (.690)	.909 (.673)[b]
"Knowing what you know now, if you had to decide all over again whether to take the job you now have, what would you decide?" (0 = would not take job again, 1 = would have some second thoughts, 2 = would take job again)	1.61 (6.30)	.837 (.776)[b]
"How much does your job measure up to the kind of job you wanted when you first took it?" (0 = not what I wanted, 1 = somewhat, 2 = what I wanted)	1.20 (.662)	.427 (.591)[b]

[a]Factor weighted composite of commitment (satisfaction) items. "Alpha" is Cronbach's measure of internal consistency reliability.
[b]Difference in means between countries significant at $p < .001$.

their assessments in the opposite direction. From the Japanese mother who turns aside praise of her child's piano playing with: "*ie, mada heta desu!*" (no, it is still bad) to the Japanese politicians who, despite Japan's booming economy, persist in protesting the country's weak and dependent posture in world affairs—the Japanese seem to color their evaluations of nearly everything with a large dose of pessimism, humility, and understatement.

. . . But More Committed.

In order to better understand the country differences in our sample's work attitudes, we estimated a statistical simultaneous equations model which assumed that satisfaction and commitment are each caused by the other (and by other variables as well). The results showed that commitment to the company is strongly determined by job satisfaction but the reverse relation is weak to nonexistent.[10] Moreover, with the causal reciprocity thus statistically controlled, we found satisfaction still lower in Japan but commitment to the company proved substantially higher. Our initial impression of no commitment difference, it appeared, was due to our earlier failure to adjust for the very large gap in reported job satisfaction. The resulting picture of Japanese work attitudes as combining low job satisfaction and high organizational commitment is not inconsistent with what some theories hold to be a state of strong work motivation. We thus took this evidence as support for our hypothesis that the discipline of the Japanese work force does have some basis in the work attitudes of Japanese employees.

WORK ATTITUDES AND JAPANESE-STYLE ORGANIZATION

What then about the other questions we raised—particularly the extent to which management and organization have something to do with Japan-U.S. differences in work attitudes? Much has been written on the distinctiveness of Japanese management and its power to motivate work effort and loyalty among employees. While our survey could not address all the ways the Japanese firm is thought to be successful at mobilizing its human assets, we were nonetheless able to examine several such hypotheses.

Seniority Systems Breed Workforce Commitment

First, consider the age and seniority of the worker. The pervasive age and seniority-grading (*nenko*) of Japanese organizations is a much discussed and documented phenomenon.[11] Once maligned as arational and feudalistic, more and more economic and organizational theory has come to recognize the inner logic to seniority systems, particularly in work settings where skills are hard to measure and are peculiar to the firm.[12] Moreover, part of the motivational logic to an employment system that couples permanent employment with seniority compensation is that it builds loyalty and identification with the company's goals. With time spent in the organization individuals accumulate investments and incur opportunity costs. To realize a fair return on these investments they must stick with the company and work to maximize its success. Moreover, the psychological phenomenon of cognitive dissonance—the need to seek congruence or equilibrium between one's acts and one's cognitions—leads people to justify to themselves their past organizational investments by embracing the company's values and goals as their own.

Our survey found, as previous studies had, that age and seniority are strong predictors of company commitment and job satisfaction. Moreover, we found pervasive evidence that these and other work attitudes were more age-dependent in Japan. Part of the reason, it appears, is that rewards and opportunities are more likely to be explicitly tied to age and seniority than in the American workplace. Another reason has less to do with age or seniority per se than with differences among generations. Given Japan's rapid postwar social change, older Japanese are apt to have the scarcity- and production-mentality typical of populations in the early stages of economic development. Younger Japanese are much more likely to share American-style values of leisure, consumption, and affluence. The latter fact evokes endless fretting by Japanese elders over the erosion of traditional values and its dire implications for Japan's future productivity and economic growth.

Strong Social Bonds Foster Positive Work Attitudes

One of the very distinctive features of Japanese work organization is the cohesiveness of work groups and the strong social bonds that develop between superiors and subordinates.[13] Our survey findings underscore these patterns. The Japanese employees in our sample reported an average of more than two close friends on the job, while the Americans averaged fewer than one. Moreover, the much-noted Japanese practice of *tsukiai* (work group socializing over food and drink) appears in our finding that Japanese employees were far more likely than Americans to get together after hours with workmates and supervisors. Our study found that employees enmeshed in such networks of coworker relationships, whether Japanese or American, had more positive attitudes toward the company and the job. The clear implication is that a rise in the cohesion of the U.S. workplace to the level typical of Japanese firms would help to narrow the U.S. "commitment gap" with Japan.

There is still the question of whether work group cohesion in the Japanese company is an outcome of rational management efforts at job and organizational design. The alternative interpretation is that Japanese people are simply culturally inclined to cluster into tight-knit cliques.[14] The cultural explanation has many advocates, and certainly a strong case can be made that Japanese values motivate people to bind themselves to groups. On the other side is all the evidence that the Japanese workplace is organized in ways that seem consciously aimed at fostering enterprise community.

AUTHORITY AND STATUS HIERARCHIES

Are Japanese Hierarchies "Flat"?

A number of observers have pointed to the shape of the management pyramid in Japanese companies as an example of organizational architecture whose logic is that of fostering commitment to the firm. While American executives and consultants commonly allude (often as a rationale for middle-management reductions at home) to the lean and flat hierarchies of Japanese firms,[15] most scholars generally agree that finely graded hierarchies and narrow spans of control are typical of Japanese organization.[16]

Japanese companies are on the average smaller, more specialized to particular industries, and less likely to use the decentralized, multidivisional structures typical of large, diversified U.S. firms.[17] These traits imply smaller corporate staffs and economies in the deployment of middle-level functional managers. But within a particular plant or business unit, one tends to find levels proliferating, as well as status rankings (based largely on seniority) which bear little direct relation to decision making and responsibility.

Does the shape of Japanese managerial hierarchies play a role in promoting workforce discipline, integration, and commitment? A number of thoughtful observers believe that they do. A finely layered management pyramid implies opportunities for steady progression up long career paths, a critical factor in motivation when employees expect to spend their working lives within a single firm. Status differentiation also works to avert the polarization and alienation, common in U.S. and British manufacturing, when a rigid class division is drawn between homogeneous "management" and "labor" groups. Japanese hierarchies incorporate many small steps which break up this homogeneity and serve as career ladders. Yet the inequality in status and reward between peak management and production rank-and-file is typically much smaller than in comparably-sized U.S. firms.[18] To many observers, this kind of structure figures importantly in the company-wide community and commitment for which the Japanese company is renowned.

Our survey of 51 Japanese factories and 55 American plants showed the Japanese organizations, despite their smaller mean size (461 vs. 571 employees), averaging 5.5 management levels compared with 4.9 for the American plants. The samples did not differ in average first-line supervisor's span of control, but we did find some evidence in the Japanese plants of more organizational subunits for the same number of employees; a pattern indicative of smaller spans of control.

Do Flat Hierarchies Produce Positive Work Attitudes?

Japanese plants may have taller hierarchies, but *in both countries* plants with more levels proved to have less committed and satisfied employees.[19] This was the only instance where an organizational design feature typical of U.S. manufacturing appeared to have the motivational advantage. And even here there were some indications that the Japanese approach had merit. We found clear and consistent evidence across a large number of indicators that work attitudes, behaviors, and relations were far less determined by the employee's status position than in the U.S. As we argued above, this is part of the motivational logic of a finely graded hierarchy—to blur the boundaries and reduce the distance between echelons and hence the potential for conflict.

Do Narrow Spans of Control Mean Domineering Supervisors?

Another highly distinctive feature of Japanese authority hierarchies is the nature of supervision and the quality of the superior-subordinate relationship. Rather than bosses exercising direct authority and issuing commands to subordinate employees, Japanese supervisors seem to function as counselor and confidante to their work groups, building communication and cohesion with a minimum of direct, authoritarian control.[20] In sharp contrast to American workers who generally favor an arm's-length, strictly business, low-intensity relationship with their supervisors, workforce surveys in Japan regularly turn up evidence that Japanese employees prefer a paternalistic, diffuse, and personal supervisory style.[21]

Our study revealed a number of differences in Japanese and U.S. patterns of supervision.[22] The Japanese were much more likely to get together socially with supervisors outside of work. This, of course, is part of *tsukiai,* the Japanese practice of after hours socializing with workgroups. The Japanese were also much less likely than the American respondents to report that their supervisors: *"let them alone unless they asked for help."*[23] Moreover, such contact with supervisors raised the morale of the Japanese employees but lowered that of the Americans. Finally, we found clear evidence in the American sample that narrow supervisory spans of control reduced commitment and satisfaction. This was not the case in Japan. It appears that narrow spans in the American workplace have a connotation, absent in Japan, of "close and domineering supervision."

These findings paint a consistent picture: frequent supervisor-subordinate interactions have a positive quality in Japanese work settings which is missing in the U.S. While American manufacturing employees keep their distance from supervisors, Japanese employees seek such contact and through it develop stronger bonds to the work group and the organization as a whole.

DECISION-MAKING STRUCTURES

Japanese Organizations Are Centralized but Participatory . . .

Japanese decision-making styles are commonly characterized as participatory, consensus-seeking, and "bottom-up."[24] At the management level, they involve less formal delegation of authority to individual managers and more informal networking (*nemawashi*) to draw people into the decision process. The ironic result is that the formal structure of Japanese decision making appears quite centralized. High-level executives bear at least symbolic responsibility for many decisions which, in U.S. firms, are typically delegated.[25]

The *ringi* system exemplifies this pattern. A middle-level manager drafts a document proposing a course of action (*ringi-sho*). It then circulates up through the hierarchy, acquiring the "chops" (personal stamps) of other managers symbolizing their participation in the decision and willingness to commit to it.

At the shop- or office-floor level, participation operates through small group activities such as quality circles, production teams, and high-responsibility systems that hold workers accountable for quality, minor maintenance, and clean-up in the conduct of their tasks.[26]

We measured decision making in our Japanese and U.S. plants in three ways. First, we used a modification of the standard Aston scale of centralization.[27] For each of 37 standard decision-items, the chief executive of the plant was asked to report the hierarchical level where: the formal authority for the decision was located; and where, in practice, the decision was usually made. Averaged over the 37 decisions, we found strong evidence that, compared with U.S. plants, authority was more centralized in the Japanese plants but there was also more *de facto* participation by lower ranks.

Secondly, in the Japanese plants, we measured the prevalence of *ringi* by asking whether, for each of the 37 decisions, the *ringi* system was used. Averaged across the

51 Japanese plants, our informants reported that the *ringi* method was applied to approximately one-third of this set of decisions.

Finally, we measured quality circle participation from our questionnaire survey of employees. We found that 81% of the Japanese plants had quality circle programs in which 94% of the employees of those plants participated; 62% of the U.S. plants had circles and 44% of their employees were members.

Our survey results are thus consistent with the impressions of more casual observers: Japanese organizations centralize authority but decentralize participation in decisions. The *ringi* system is used to a substantial degree in decision making in Japanese factories. And quality circle participating is close to universal in Japanese plants, though it is reasonably widespread in American plants as well.[28]

. . . A Pattern which Produces Positive Work Attitudes in Both Countries.

The question then becomes: do Japanese decision-making practices help shape the work attitudes of Japanese employees? As with work group cohesion, the motivational payoff to participation has been a central theme in management theory, at least since the Hawthorne studies. We found *in both countries* that organizations which in Japanese fashion coupled formal centralization with *de facto* participation had more committed and satisfied employees.

Why? This outcome fits the general proposition that Japanese-style management works in the U.S. as well as in Japan. But it is not obvious why this particular configuration should have greater motivational value than one in which formal and *de facto* authority are aligned and both decentralized. Our reasoning is that formal decentralization (as the Aston scale measures it) taps delegation of specialized decision-making roles to lower management positions. First- and second-line supervisors in American manufacturing commonly enjoy a good deal of power over narrow jurisdictional areas. Yet that kind of delegation opens up few opportunities for participation either by the rank-and-file *or* by supervisors in other areas.

When formal authority stays high in the organization but widespread participation occurs, the power of lower management is reduced and decision making becomes the diffuse, participatory kind typical of Japanese organization, not the individualistic, compartmentalized delegation found in American firms. Clark has argued that Japanese middle managers are delegated so little formal authority that they have no choice but to negotiate with their employees in order to get things done.[29] In his view, the networking and consensus-seeking found in Japanese organizations are a direct response to their centralized authority structures.

Ringi and Quality Circles Also Produce Positive Work Attitudes

What about the specific participatory practices of *ringi* and quality circles? Do they also foster job satisfaction and commitment to a company? Our data suggest that they do. In the sample of Japanese plants, we found a statistically significant positive association between a plant's use of the *ringi* system and the employee's commitment to the firm. This was a noteworthy finding, for the majority of our employee sample were rank-and-file people who would not ordinarily be involved in the *ringi* process. The use of *ringi* is probably symptomatic of a generally participatory decision-making climate which has motivational value for workers and managers alike.

There are good reasons to suppose that quality circle programs are quite different in the U.S. and Japan. Owing in large part to the centralized oversight of the Japan Union of Scientists and Engineers, quality circle programs in Japanese industry generally comprise a much more uniform set of practices than in the United States. They require a high level of technical training on the part of production workers and a substantial commitment of resources on the part of the firm. American quality circle programs, with much less centralized guidance from professional and managerial bodies, are generally a hodgepodge. Few such programs exhibit the rigor and structure of Japanese practice.

Yet quality circle participation proved to be positively associated with job satisfaction and organizational commitment in both the U.S. and Japan. Moreover, the effect was stronger in the U.S. sample. The reason may in part lie in the later inception of American quality circles which give them a novelty value that has worn off the more established Japanese programs. Recent observers of Japanese quality circle programs have commented on growing problems of maintaining worker interest and motivation.[30]

In summary, our evidence, with rather remarkable consistency, suggests that Japanese-style decision-making arrangements (quality circles, *ringi,* centralized authority combined with dispersed participation), have positive effects on the work attitudes of Japanese and American employees alike. The fact that such arrangements are much more prevalent in Japanese industry suggests a partial explanation for the Japanese edge in labor discipline and commitment.

COMPANY-SPONSORED EMPLOYEE SERVICES

Yet another distinctive feature of the Japanese employment system is the large bundle of services, programs, and social activities that Japanese firms sponsor and provide for their employees. Such services figure significantly in the traditional portrait of Japanese "paternalism" in industry.[31] The array of programs, activities, classes, ceremonies, peptalks, calisthenics, songs, and other practices that Japanese firms employ in the quest of building community and commitment among the workforce is downright dizzying.[32]

How effective are such programs as motivational devices? Would more ceremonies, company picnics, sports teams, newsletters, and the like create a stronger bond between the U.S. manufacturing worker and the firm? Or, as many Western observers seem to think, are individualistic British and American workers likely to be contemptuous of overt management gestures at creating a happy corporate family?[33] Once again, a case can be made that employee services in Japan are a reflection, not a cause, of Japanese work values and attitudes. Cultural and historical forces have bred within companies an inclusive enterprise community one sign of which is a profusion of company-planned activities and services.

Still, there are some indications in the historical record that Japanese employers set upon welfarism (along with permanent employment and other labor practices) as a rational instrument for curbing labor militancy and creating, in a time of labor shortage, a more docile and dependent workforce.[34] Its timing coincided with the era of "welfare capitalism" in the United States (the 1920s), which large firms ushered in for similar purposes of managing an unruly labor force and appeasing the growing ranks of muckrakers and progressivist reformers. Why welfarism seemed to "stick" in Japan but faded in the U.S., at least until the postwar period, may be due to several forces: the milder impact on Japan of the Great Depression (which in the U.S. led many firms to jettison expensive welfare programs); the heightened stress on industrial discipline produced by militarist and imperialistic policies; and, for cultural reasons, the greater receptivity of Japanese workers to corporate paternalism and the principle of an enterprise family.[35]

Employee Services Are More Abundant in Japan . . .

Our strategy for measuring the level of welfare, social, and ceremonial activity was a relatively simple one. We inquired of our informants in each plant whether a list of nine company-sponsored activities/services were present. The list included: outside training, inhouse training, an employee newsletter, company ceremonies, company-sponsored sports and recreation programs, new employee orientation programs, an employee handbook, regular plant-wide information-sharing/"pep-talk" sessions, and a morning calisthenics program.

Our hypothesis was that such programs are more prevalent in Japanese firms. That proved to be the case for most of them, specifically: in-house training (by a small margin), formal ceremonies (present in all Japanese plants), sports and recreational activities, formal orientation programs, peptalks, and morning exercise sessions (nonexistent in the U.S. plants we studied). On the other hand, the American plants were more likely to encourage and support enrollment in high school and college coursework (by a large margin) and (by a small one) to provide employees with a company handbook. We found no difference between Japanese and U.S. plants in the likelihood of publishing a company newspaper. The indices proposed by summing these items had acceptable internal consistency reliability levels of .60 in the Japanese sample and .62 in the U.S. sample, indicating that these services tended to cluster in the same firms.

. . . But Raise Commitment and Satisfaction in Both Countries.

When we estimated the effect of the services index on employee commitment to the company and satisfaction with the job, we found almost identical positive associations in the two countries. Individualistic or not, the Americans in our sample appeared to react every bit as favorably as the Japanese to company-sponsored employee-oriented services. Once again the lesson seems clear: were such services in American industry to rise to the level typical of Japanese manufacturers, we should witness a corresponding shrinkage in the Japan-U.S. commitment gap.

ENTERPRISE UNIONS

Finally we consider the structure of unions and their implications for employee work attitudes. A legacy of the postwar Occupation reforms, Japanese unions are organized on a per-enterprise basis, concentrated in the largest firms, and combined into weak federations at higher levels.[36] They organize all regular (blue- and white-collar) employees, up to second-line supervision. Much debate has centered on whether Japanese enterprise unions are truly independent labor organizations in the Western sense. Some writers see them as highly dependent upon and easily coopted by the company, avoiding confrontations to advance their members' interests and working to build commitment to the firm. Hanami expresses this view well:

> There exists a climate of collusion . . . between the employers and the union representing the majority of employees . . . Basically the relationship is one of patronage and dependence, though the unions frequently put on an outward show of radical militancy in their utterances and behavior. [Moreover] the president of an enterprise union is in effect the company's senior executive in charge of labor relations.[37]

Yet other observers argue that, despite the constraints posed by dependence on a single firm, Japanese unions bargain hard on wage and benefit issues and have effectively coordinated their militancy in the annual Spring offensives (*shunto*) which present groups of employers with a set of unified wage demands.[38] A study by Koshiro concludes that union militancy has been an important factor behind rising aggregate wage levels in the postwar Japanese economy.[39]

U.S. Unions Foster Negative Work Attitudes, Japanese Unions Do Not

What, however, about the impact of unionism on employee work attitudes? Much survey research shows that U.S. union members report *lower* job satisfaction than do nonunion employees.[40] This pattern seems consistent with the goals of American union strategy: to aggregate grievances, foster an adversarial industrial relations climate, and drive a wedge between the worker and the firm.

Yet unionized workers are less likely to quit their jobs than nonunion employees.[41] One interpretation is that "true" dissatisfaction is probably no higher among union members but that the union politicizes the employment relation and encourages workers to inflate and publicize their grievances. In the nonunion workplace, by contrast, workers have no such vehicle for airing dissatisfactions and therefore act on them by simply terminating their relationship with the firm. This view, grounded in Albert Hirschman's "exit-voice-loyalty" model,[42] is also supported by evidence that grievance rates are higher in union shops even when objective working conditions are no worse.[43]

We would not anticipate finding similar union effects on the work attitudes of Japanese unionists. Indeed, a reasonable argument can be made for the opposite prediction: that enterprise unions build support for and loyalty to the company—that they are, in effect, one more Japanese management device for building motivation and commitment.

Our data do not show that. We find no statistically significant effect of union membership on job satisfaction, although we do find a slight tendency for company commitment to be lower in union plants. Thus, it does not appear that Japanese unions are in some sense instruments of a proactive policy of building discipline and dedication in the workforce. On the other hand, what we find in the U.S. still poses a decisive contrast with the Japan case. Consistent with other research, our survey produced strong and clear evidence that unions in U.S. factories give rise to sharply more negative employee work attitudes. Holding constant a large number of variables pertaining to the pay, status, job, skills, and gender of the worker, plus the size, age, and technology of the plant, company commitment and job satisfaction in our Indiana sample were markedly lower among the unionized plants.

The implications appear to be as follows. Japanese unions are not the agents of management that some critics hold them to be. But neither do they present the challenge to harmonious labor-management relations or high workforce morale that U.S. unions historically have posed. Since enterprise-specific unions are generally absent from the U.S. economy, we have no evidence on how they might perform in an American setting.

Some circumstantial evidence from the New United Motors Manufacturing, Inc. (NUMMI) plant in Fremont, California (the Toyota-GM joint venture), suggests, however, that U.S. workers may react very well to Japanese-style collective bargaining.[44] The union at NUMMI is a local of the United Auto Workers, but it made a number of concessions to the company in the area of work rules and job classifications. In turn, the company provides the union with space in the plant, shares information extensively, and enlists the cooperation of the union in enforcing policy with respect to absenteeism, quality, safety, and other issues. Though a small dissident movement has been formed, the level of labor-management cooperation and the productivity and discipline of the workforce at NUMMI has few parallels in the American auto industry. The special relationship between the company and the UAW local, reminiscent of the interdependence between enterprise unions and firms in Japan, is clearly part of the reason.

DISCUSSION

What conclusions can be drawn from our survey evidence on Japanese and U.S. work attitudes and the role of plant organization and management practice in shaping them? First, though a preliminary reading of the data sends mixed signals, the Japanese employee's combination of high commitment coupled with low satisfaction is in line with the hypothesis of a highly motivated Japanese workforce. Second, we found quite consistent evidence that "Japanese-style" management and employment methods, whether practiced by Japanese or U.S. plants, produce very similar gains in employee work attitudes (see the summary of findings in Table 2). These include cohesive work groups, quality circles, participatory (but not delegated) decision making, and company-sponsored services. The fact that such practices are more widely deployed in Japanese than in U.S. industry does suggest they may provide part (though we would hardly argue all) of the reason for the Japan-U.S. "commitment gap" in manufacturing.

Other management and employment practices we examined are not directly comparable across countries and our results cannot therefore be interpreted in this way. They nonetheless testify that tangible differences in Japanese and U.S. management translate into competitive advantages for Japanese firms in the area of employee motivation and cooperative industrial relations. In both countries, rising age and seniority engender increasingly positive work attitudes. As career employment and seniority promo-

TABLE 2
DO "JAPANESE"-STYLE MANAGEMENT PRACTICES PRODUCE COMPANY COMMITMENT AND JOB SATISFACTION IN JAPAN AND IN THE U.S.?

"Japanese" management/employment practice	Impact on work attitudes
Long-term employment and age/seniority grading	Positive in both countries[a]
Cohesive work groups	Positive in both countries
Dense supervision; close supervisor-subordinate contact	Positive in Japan; negative in U.S.
"Tall," finely-layered hierarchies	Negative in both countries; but contributes to management-labor consensus in Japan
Formal centralization/de facto decentralization of decision-making	Positive in both countries
Ringi system	Positive in Japan[b]
Quality circle participation	Positive in both countries
Welfare services	Positive in both countries
Unions (enterprise-specific in Japan; industry/occupation-specific in the U.S.)	Weak negative to null in Japan; strongly negative in U.S.

[a]In the sense that psychological attachment to the firm is found in both countries to rise with age and seniority.
[b]No comparable measure from the U.S. survey.

tion and compensation are more central to Japanese than U.S. employment practice, Japanese companies are better able to capitalize on these motivational returns. The Japanese system of enterprise unions offers collective bargaining in an atmosphere of mutual dependence and cooperation, and, in sharp contrast to U.S. unions, does little to foster tension between the worker and the firm.

Our findings seem to contradict the argument that Japanese management styles are only effective with employees who hold Japanese-type work values. The credibility of this view, which has much face validity, is also undercut by the apparent success of Japanese manufacturing firms in managing their U.S. operations and their American employees. Japanese management is no panacea, and mindless attempts to copy from the Japanese are doubtless doomed to failure. Still, our study strongly suggests that Japanese management practices are in part responsible for the work motivation of Japanese employees and that similar practices in the American workplace yield similar returns. Careful attempts on the part of U.S. managers to move in the direction of Japanese organizational design and human resource management may well yield some long-run competitive payoffs for American manufacturing.

REFERENCES

1 William G. Ouchi, *Theory Z: How American Business Can Meet the Japanese Challenge* (Reading, MA: Addison-Wesley, 1981); Richard Tanner Pascale and Anthony G. Athos, *The Art of Japanese Management: Applications for American Managers* (New York, NY: Simon and Schuster, 1981).

2 But see, Masahiko Aoki, "Risk Sharing in the Corporate Group," in Masahiko Aoki, ed.,

The Economic Analysis of the Japanese Firm (Amsterdam: North-Holland, 1984) pp. 259–264; Taishiro Shirai, ed., *Contemporary Industrial Relations in Japan* (Madison, WI: University of Wisconsin Press, 1983).

3 James C. Abegglen and George Stalk, Jr., *Kaisha: The Japanese Corporation* (New York, NY: Basic Books, 1985); Ronald Dore, *Flexible Rigidities* (Stanford, CA: Stanford University Press, 1986); Ronald Dore, *Taking Japan Seriously* (Stanford, CA: Stanford University Press, 1987); Ezra F. Vogel, *Comeback* (New York, NY: Simon and Schuster, 1985).

4 See the review in James R. Lincoln and Kerry McBride, "Japanese Industrial Organization in Comparative Perspective," *Annual Review of Sociology,* 13 (1987): 289–312.

5 See, for example, Charles Perrow, *Complex Organizations: A Critical Essay,* 3rd edition (Glenview, IL: Scott, Foresman, 1986).

6 Ronald Dore, *British Factory, Japanese Factory: The Origins of Diversity in Industrial Relations* (Berkeley, CA: University of California Press, 1973).

7 Robert Blauner, "Work Satisfaction and Industrial Trends in Modern Society," in Walter Galenson and Seymour Martin Lipset, eds., *Labor and Trade Unionism* (New York, NY: John Wiley, 1960), pp. 339–360; HEW Report, *Work in America* (Cambridge, MA: MIT Press, 1973).

8 John H. Goldthorpe, David Lockwood, F. Bechhofer, and J. Platt, *The Affluent Worker: Industrial Attitudes and Behavior* (London: Cambridge University Press, 1968).

9 Dore, 1973, op. cit.

10 James R. Lincoln and Arne L. Kalleberg, "Work Organization and Workforce Commitment: A Study of Plants and Employees in the U.S. and Japan," *American Sociological Review,* 50 (1985): 738–760; James R. Lincoln and Arne L. Kalleberg, *Culture, Control, and Commitment: A Study of Work Organization and Work Attitudes in the U.S. and Japan* (Cambridge: Cambridge University Press, 1989).

11 Kazuo Koike, "Internal Labor Markets: Workers in Large Firms," in Taishiro Shirai, ed., op. cit., pp. 29–62.

12 Edward Lazear, "Why Is There Mandatory Retirement?" *Journal of Political Economy,* 87 (1979): 1261–1284.

13 Robert E. Cole, "Permanent Employment in Japan: Facts and Fantasies," *Industrial and Labor Relations Review,* 26 (1972): 612–630; Thomas P. Rohlen, *For Harmony and Strength* (Berkeley, CA: University of California Press, 1974).

14 See, for example, Chie Nakane, *Japanese Society* (Berkeley, CA: University of California Press, 1970).

15 Thomas J. Peters and Robert H. Waterman, Jr., *In Search of Excellence: Lessons from America's Best-Run Companies* (New York, NY: Harper and Row, 1982).

16 Michael Y. Yoshino, *Japan's Managerial System: Tradition and Innovation* (Cambridge, MA: MIT Press, 1968); Dore, 1973, op. cit.; Richard Tanner Pascale, "Zen and the Art of Management," *Harvard Business Review,* 56 (1978): 153–162.

17 Rodney C. Clark, *The Japanese Company* (New Haven, CT: Yale, 1979).

18 Abegglen and Stalk, op. cit.

19 Lincoln and Kalleberg, 1985, op. cit.

20 Dore, 1973, op. cit.; Cole, 1972, op. cit.

21 Robert M. Marsh and Hiroshi Mannari, *Modernization and the Japanese Factory* (Princeton, NJ: Princeton University Press, 1977); Arthur M. Whitehill and Shinichi Takezawa, *The Other Worker: A Comparative Study of Industrial Relations in the U.S. and Japan* (Honolulu, HI: East-West Center Press, 1968).

22 Lincoln and Kalleberg, 1989, op. cit., Chapter 4.

23 Pascale and Athos, op. cit., p. 183.

24 Ouchi, op. cit.

25 Ezra F. Vogel, *Modern Japanese Organization and Decision-Making* (Berkeley, CA: University of California Press, 1975); Yoshino, op. cit.

26 Robert E. Cole, *Work, Mobility, and Participation* (Berkeley, CA: University of California Press, 1979).

27 D. S. Pugh, D. J. Hickson, C. R. Hinings, and C. Turner, "Dimensions of Organization Structure," *Administrative Science Quarterly,* 13 (1968): 65–91; James R. Lincoln, Mitsuyo Hanada, and Kerry McBride, "Organizational Structures in Japanese and U.S. Manufacturing," *Administrative Science Quarterly,* 31 (1986): 338–364.

28 Robert E. Cole, *Strategies for Learning: Small Group Activities in American, Japanese, and Swedish Industry* (Berkeley, CA: University of California Press, 1989).

29 Clark, op. cit.

30 Kunio Odaka, "The Japanese Style of Workers' Self-Management: From the Voluntary to the Autonomous Group," in Velnko Rus, Akihiro Ishikawa, and Thomas Woodhouse, eds., *Employment and Participation* (Tokyo: Chuo University Press, 1982), p. 323.

31 John W. Bennett and Iwao Ishino, *Paternalism in the Japanese Economy* (Minneapolis, MN: University of Minnesota Press, 1963).

32 See, for example, Dore, 1973, op. cit.; Rohlen, op. cit.; Marsh and Mannari, op. cit.

33 See, for example, Goldthorpe et al., op. cit.

34 Cole, 1979, op. cit.

35 Yoshino, op. cit.

36 H. Kawada, "Workers and Their Organizations," In Bernard Karsh and Solomon B. Levine, eds., *Workers and Employers in Japan* (Tokyo: University of Tokyo Press), pp. 217–268; Shirai, op. cit.

37 Tadashi Hanami, *Labor Relations in Japan Today* (Tokyo: Kodansha International, Ltd., 1979), p. 56.

38 Jean Bounine-Cabale, Ronald Dore, and Kari Tapiola, "Flexibility in Japanese Labor Markets," Report of the OECD Team, 1988.

39 Kazutoshi Koshiro, "The Quality of Life in Japanese Factories," in Taishiro Shirai, ed., *Contemporary Industrial Relations in Japan* (1983), pp. 63–88.

40 Richard B. Freeman and James L. Medoff, *What Do Unions Do?* (New York, NY: Basic Books, 1984), Chapter 9.

41 Ibid., p. 139.

42 Albert O. Hirschman, *Exit, Voice, and Loyalty* (Cambridge, MA: Harvard University Press, 1970).

43 Freeman and Medoff, op. cit., p. 139.

44 Clair Brown and Michael Reich, "When Does Union-Management Cooperation Work: A Look at NUMMI and GM-Van Nuys," in Daniel J. B. Mitchell and Jane Wildhorn, eds., *Can California Be Competitive and Caring?* (Los Angeles, CA: Institute of Industrial Relations, University of California, 1989), pp. 115–147.

Leadership as a Form of Culture: Its Present and Future States in Japan*

Akira Ichikawa

THE NATURE AND FUNCTION OF LEADERSHIP

Leadership Driving People

Leadership can be understood either as the power to drive people, or as influence over people. Not only is leadership necessary for those who have subordinates and are in formal positions to guide them, but it also has a critical meaning for individuals to enable them to cope within their groups.

For example, a president of a firm, a head of a department, or a coach of an athletic club demonstrates his or her leadership to the people in his or her organization. It is a matter of course for the leader to drive people. Needless to say, leaders in these kinds of organizations are given formal authority with which they are expected to demonstrate leadership within their organizations.

However, in some cases it is possible or desirable to have situations in which a person who does not possess a formal authority drives people through influence. A President or a Prime Minister of a country has formal power in his or her own country, but is supposed to have mutually equal power with Presidents or Prime Ministers of other countries. The same can be said of a CEO of a business firm. However, a degree of difference in the power to drive through influencing people clearly exists among those who do not possess formal power. As a simple example, varying degrees in the power to influence people exist among colleagues or friends.

These differences are brought about by factors other than formal authority. Thus it is possible for subordinates to lead superiors if the subordinates learn and demonstrate the means to lead other people. It can also be possible for a business person to lead customers, or other people with whom he or she has business associations (Figure 1).

Although the word 'leader' may not be appropriate in the above cases, the author believes that it is genuine leadership. It is critical for formal superiors to master and demonstrate this genuine leadership if they want to fulfill their own roles and improve the performance of their organizations.

Importance of Respect to People's Willingness

We should now like to give some consideration to the power of driving and compelling people. In general, the most definite and strongest power is a formally approved authority. Here, the relationship between a position where the power is held and a scope

---

*Translated from Japanese by Professor Gen-Ichi Nakamura and Dr. Dae-Ryong Choi. See Editor's Note at end of chapter.

From *International Review of Strategic Management,* 1993, 11(4), 473–480. Copyright © 1993, John Wiley & Sons Ltd. Reprinted by permission.

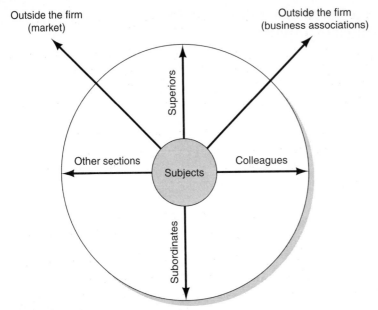

FIGURE 1
Omnidirectional leadership (middle managers of firms).

where the power extends is made explicitly. Furthermore, some punishment (e.g., de-motion in the case of business firms) may be imposed on a person who does not obey the order of his or her formal superior.

Even though authority bestows the power to drive subordinates, it is doubtful whether such authority comprises genuine leadership. Leadership should be consid-ered as a process for driving people through influencing them in a specific but broad sense, not as a driving power which aims at a small part of a group. Also, when lead-ership is applied for the improvement of the organization's performance and on the leader's own assessment, relying on formal power or position to drive subordinates through compulsion does not necessarily produce desirable consequences in the long run.

In other words, it is necessary to consider leadership as an instrument, means, or process for persuading people to comply willingly (Figure 2). How should we per-suade people to comply willingly without threatening or materially rewarding them? One of the objectives in studying leadership is to answer this question.

There are various factors in genuine leadership that drive people, besides formal power, threats, or material rewards. First, consider examples of acknowledged great leaders' behavior or that of people who do not possess any authority to drive others through compulsion. We can find a rational proof of the reasons why they drive peo-ple, and at the same time, a certain relationship between the condition of groups and the style of leaders.

This leads us to believe that leadership is a product of an epoch and a form of cul-

FIGURE 2
Means to drive people.

ture. When leadership is matched with its environment, it will prove significantly effective. In other words, it can be said that leadership is a form of a culture.

Rational and Cultural Aspects of Leadership

It can generally be said that a culture is a common value shared by a group of people, or a type of thought and behavior based on common values even though the existence of a culture can also be applied to an individual. There is a culture of a tribe or country. Furthermore, there may be one culture in a political world, and another culture in an economic world. Also, a particular culture can be seen in every industry or corporation.

Of course, because there are common characteristics in people or organizations over generations, or tribes, there are common conditions or factors with which certain aspects of leadership hold good in any country or field. However, in reality, different types of leadership or leaders can be seen in different countries, fields, or generations. This is the reason why we should understand that leadership is significantly related to a culture.

Therefore, in order to take people in a desired direction, and influence them so that they willingly go in that direction, it will be necessary to consider carefully the following two aspects.

The first is a rational aspect of leadership which corresponds to the elements that people or organizations hold in common, and appeals to the nature of people or the fundamental characteristics of organizations. Of course, there is no universal standard rational aspect because the people, organizations, or situations involved are extremely complicated.

The second is a cultural aspect which corresponds to particular characteristics of individuals, tribes, or groups. At first glance, a cultural aspect seems irrational. However, if it is matched with the values, styles, or rules of a group, persuading the people in the group will be easy. Also, it can be said that the cultural aspect is often appropriate to the objective of the group.

Before discussing the main issue of this article, which is the examination of this cultural aspect of leadership, we shall in the next section briefly discuss a rational aspect of leadership.

EFFECTIVE LEADERSHIP

Essential Attributes in Demonstrating Rational Leadership

What are the essential attributes needed to drive individuals or groups? The nature of the attributes is the same for individuals or groups even though we shall here focus on the attributes needed to drive groups. The essential attributes are the following:

1 Objectives or specific goals of a group.
2 External environments of a group.
3 Characteristics of a group.

An organization (or individuals or groups in an organization) can be naturally driven by an understanding of the above three attributes, and through proposals and guidance of the organization (that is, transmitting information) which match them. This will be discussed more specifically below.

If information which matches the objective of an organization, such as a business firm, is transmitted throughout the organization, it will be easier to persuade individuals or groups to follow it. There are various objectives for business firms. Some aims are based on corporate philosophy; there are also fundamentally common objectives such as improvement of profit, survival and expansion, response to customers' requests, or contribution to society. In any case, individuals or groups in an organization will be persuaded and driven if a leader proposes, guides, or requests a certain response from them after he or she has made it clear that this response is needed to achieve their objectives, or is related to the achievement of specific goals.

It is also important to understand and assess the external environments of an organization. Some say that external environments generate the behavior of organizations. In order to drive the people within an organization, it is necessary to explain their external environments to them, to make them realize what behavior is necessary, and sometimes even to build internal environments for guiding the organization. If necessary, leaders should suggest, or sometimes guide, the way to apply a certain behavior.

For example, when a firm faces a certain difficulty, a leader should make subordinates understand the meaning and characteristics of the problem and make them come up with appropriate behavior to deal with it. In some cases it will be enough to provide suggestions, in others it will be desirable to impose strong guidance or command. This depends on the degrees of importance and urgency of the difficulty or problem and the situations of the individuals or groups that the leader intends to drive.

It is also important to understand the characteristics of a group in a broad sense. That is both to understand and to match the level of experience, knowledge or characters of individuals or groups, and to understand and relate to the external environment.

If people are inexperienced, it may be necessary to provide some guidance, but if they are experienced it may be inadvisable to give fully detailed guidance. This also depends on the personal character or nature of each individual. Some people perform best when they have autonomy, but on the other hand, others do better when they are carefully guided. This involves the issue of a culture.

We also have to take into consideration the fact that many characteristics of a group depend on personal relationships. Is it a relationship between a person and his or her subordinate in an organization? Is it a relationship between a person and his or her colleague in an organization? Is it a relationship between a person and his or her customer? Is it a relationship between a person and his or her business partner? Every characteristic of a group will change depending on a specific human relationship or power relationship. Therefore, it will be necessary to drive people in ways which an understanding of those relationships shows to be appropriate.

Leadership Created by Personality

A rational leader is someone who can transmit essential information throughout a group by relating it clearly to the group's objectives, environments and characteristics.

In this context, it is important to know how subordinates perceive their leader. If the above mentioned essential information is perceived as unimportant by the subordinates, it will be impossible to drive them and make them behave willingly.

In order to make subordinates understand and to convince them to follow their leader's intention, it is necessary that the leader should be trusted by subordinates and receive their goodwill either as an individual or as an authority. Even though the information itself and the method of transmitting it are the same in every case, the information will be perceived differently by individual subordinates, depending on the person who transmits it. It is a fact of life that human beings cannot avoid having such differences of perception to some degree.

After all, this perception is created by an individual's personality or background. Here, it is important to note that we have to realize and distinguish between the power we possess naturally and the power of authority we are given.

Some leaders may confuse their formal power to drive subordinates with the natural power they personally possess. If one can motivate people and make them compliant without exerting any authority, it should be considered as genuine leadership. (Of course, this does not mean that a person in a position of authority should not take advantage of it. However, a senior person should not rely too heavily on the authority he or she possesses.)

This kind of leadership, generated by personality, contains more facets than a purely rational aspect of leadership, such as, for example, suitability, trust, and attractiveness. It may come primarily from inherent personal characteristics. However, it is possible in some degree to acquire it by learning techniques of rational persuasion, behaving with honesty and sincerity, and building up a track record of one's own achievements. Here the importance lies in a natural human desire to trust and respect others.

For instance, although it may not be an entirely appropriate example, if a man does not trust and love his dog, the dog does not love the man at all. The same is true of relationships between people.

LEADERSHIP AND CULTURE IN JAPAN

Characteristics of Japanese Culture and Requisites of Japanese Leaders

Some of the characteristics of leaders discussed in the previous section cannot be rationalized, because they might be related to individual characters and styles. However, as a whole, most of them are the common principles of leadership which hold good to some extent in all societies and groups.

On the other hand, there are particular leaders or styles of effective leadership which are suitable only to a specific community, society, or organization. In other words, different situations for leaders can be found by country or by activity, such as politics, economics, education, and sports. Different leaders can be found in different groups, with very varying requirements.

This, in a sense, can be considered as an aspect of the external environment discussed previously. However, it will be much easier to understand if the difference of leadership is related to culture. After all, the leader of any organization is bred, selected, and functions only when he or she possesses both the common characteristics of a leader and the conditions desired by that organization's culture.

We will now discuss the relationship between cultures and leaders mainly by taking cases in Japan and making comparisons between Japan and the Western world.

Essential Characteristics of Japanese Leaders Based on Japanese Culture

Who are the leaders of Japan? There are various views on this. First, we will take the political world. Formally, a political leader is a Prime Minister. In addition, those who have held the position before and those who are aspiring to the position are considered to be the leaders, or the top people, in the political world.

Consider the following case. In Japan, it is customary for journalists to interview acknowledged politicians by surrounding them and walking along with them before and after conferences at the Diet or a Cabinet council. We can see from this that most of the politicians are hidden by the group of journalists. That is because the height of politicians tends to be shorter than that of journalists. This is not only because of the generation gap (although young people have become taller recently); there is another reason for this gap in the height between leaders and journalists, which is that the height of political leaders tends to be short as a whole. For example, look at the Prime Ministers who have been supreme leaders in the political world: the present Prime Minister Miyazawa and ex-Prime Ministers Kaifu, Uno, or Takeshita are all of them short. Furthermore, the leaders of the Takeshita faction (the leading political faction in Japan), including Mr Kanamaru, are all shorter than the average height for their generation. The only recent exception might be Mr Nakasone. We can see the gap in height between the political leaders of Japan and the leaders of the Western countries, such as ex-President Bush of the USA and Chancellor Khol of Germany, at every summit conference.

Looking at this gap, many Japanese may wish they had a taller Prime Minister, but things are not as easy as that, because this has roots deep into their culture. It is not by chance but an inevitability because of Japanese culture, especially culture in the political world, that many Japanese Prime Ministers or other leaders are short.

The same applies even in the Japanese business world. It is not too much to say that there is a key to understanding the relationship between Japanese culture and the conditions of Japanese leaders or styles of Japanese leadership.

Physical Appearance of Japanese Leaders

The height of many leaders in the Japanese political and business world is short. This means that the physical appearance of not being tall is a major weighting factor in the nomination of leaders, or in Japanese selection criteria. Of course, this condition is not explicitly stated but, laying aside whether or not the Japanese are conscious of it, it is an undeniable fact.

More strictly speaking, a successor as a leader in Japan should not exceed a predecessor in terms of physical appearance. In other words, a Japanese leader does not select as his or her successor a subordinate who physically looks down at the leader. Although 'stout and short' is one of the images of leaders which the Japanese have, most leaders only become fat after achieving leadership. People who want to be leaders must not be fat before they become leaders. It is very rare for Japanese leaders (even though they themselves are physically stout) to select as their successors people who look bigger than them. This is not just a joke. It is a symbolic appearance of the Japanese culture.

Comparisons between Predecessors and Successors of Japanese Leaders

Based on the actual situations mentioned above, the conditions for becoming leaders and the styles of leadership in Japan can be considered as the following.

First, the essential condition is that people becoming leaders should not outdo their predecessors in either appearance or achievement. Successors should follow their predecessors' direction even after becoming leaders, and they should 'save the predecessors' faces,' and not despise them.

Current leaders should never have reason to suspect that their successors will ignore them and just do as they want after taking their place. Otherwise, the prospective successors will lose the opportunity of becoming the next leaders. A candidate who wishes to become a future leader should, for example, share the same interests as, and pledge loyalty to, the present leader as well as the leader's family. In addition, even if the candidate considers himself or herself to have greater ability than the current leader, such ability must be concealed.

The most comfortable choice of a successor, for a leader, is to select a member of his or her own family. That is heredity. Here, physical appearance is the second criterion. If you see a tall leader, it will be safe to assume that he or she comes from his or her predecessor's family.

We can find the main criterion for the selection of leaders in Japan by asking the following questions. What finally happened to the person who was listed as a candidate to be the new president in a company (other than a person from the same family as the current president)? Who was eventually elected as the president from among many candidates? What was the reason for the discord between a very important CEO and a president?

Selection Processes of Leaders in Japan

The reason why a successor should not surpass a predecessor in many ways may be a result of the processes of leader selection in Japan. As an example, a Prime Minister in Japan is not selected through direct election. A future president of a firm is selected from inside the firm. A proper person as a president is not sought from outside, neither does he or she fight to become a president (even a general meeting of stockholders does not substantially have much power to select a president).

Above all, a top manager is not selected openly. The selection is made in a closed society or group. Therefore it is natural that the present incumbent's intention should be emphasized.

There is another interesting fact. The physical appearance of many top managers of business ventures, where they seem to have established their positions through their own efforts, is short. They did not have any predecessors, so why are they short? Many of them have achieved their successes by having support, favors, and patrons from people outside their firms. Their supporters may be the top managers of clients, or corporate executives who help entrepreneurs. Here, the previously mentioned principle about physical appearance again applies. Very few people favor or patronize a taller man or woman who looks down at them even though he or she is younger than their supporters.

Critical Decision Factors for the Selection of Leaders among Various Choices in Japan

The above-mentioned conditions for the selection of leaders are certainly irrational. Many people may ask the question, 'Will the leaders who are selected by such criteria and processes ever function well?' However, in reality these physically small politicians and managers have established Japan as one of the leading countries, at least in the economic world. That is, they have brought leadership into play. In other words, we can say that this style of leadership has matched the culture of Japan's society and the cultures of its political or business world.

That is not to say that those leaders do not have any abilities or have succeeded only through apple-polishing. As one CEO says: 'There are many people who have the abilities to be a president of my company. But the critical factor to become a president is personality. Getting beloved by many people and getting along with them are requirements for the next president.'

In this sense, the political or business world in Japan may be a highly competitive society. Excellent top managers have controlled their subordinates well by making the subordinates compete at the last moment and keep a close eye on each other. It can be one of the leadership styles in Japan.

What are these leadership styles? Why do they work well? Before answering these questions, it is necessary to understand the characteristics of Japanese culture.

CHARACTERISTICS OF JAPANESE CULTURE AND TRADITIONAL JAPANESE-STYLE LEADERSHIP

Japanese Collectivism

The main characteristic of Japanese culture can be summed up in a word: collectivism. Although this collectivism has actually been changing gradually, the differences between collectivism in Japan and individualism in the Western countries are clearly seen.

We shall now discuss the three aspects of its typical characteristic as follows.

Relationships Between a Group and Its Members   In other words, this is the unification and identification of individuals to their group. This is quite different from the individuals' autonomous contribution to the group. Autonomy itself is left with the group.

Specifically, the interests of the group become those of each member. For the sake of the group, the members do not mind sacrificing themselves. Furthermore, they are proud of devoting all of what they have to the group and have no sense of being sacrificed.

Relationships among Members in the Group   An important key word to explain this is homogeneity. A member is expected to think and behave in the same way as others do. If there is a person who thinks and behaves differently from the others, that person will be pressured to conform. Failure to comply with the pressure means that he or she will be eliminated from the group. A heretic is ostracized by the villagers.

Strictly speaking, that is not to say that everyone has the same way of thinking or the same style of behavior. One person behaving differently or showing his or her excellent ability may destroy the order of the group, that is, cause the group to be in trouble. Above all, various negative reactions and emotions of jealousy will be aroused in the group. Rather than destroying the order of the group, the members may consider that it is easier to restrain themselves and keep pace with others. In this sense, they are homogeneous.

Relationships between the Group and Outsiders   A group protects its benefits and avoids any damage from outsiders. This is the natural tendency for a group. However, in the case of the group under collectivism, this appears in an extreme form. That is, a group justifies any means used to protect its interests, and does not care about outsiders at all. The group possesses egoistic thoughts and behavior and may even try to increase internal centralization by creating imaginary enemies outside.

A group in Japanese society is collective, comprised of the same sort of members who have strong loyalty to the group. When a group faces outside enemies or critical situations, the members of the group strongly unite to protect the group's interest. This is truly like a village or Japanese mafia (*Yakuza*) protecting its own territory. Of course a business firm also has the same characteristic.

Then what are the leader's characteristics in these kinds of societies? To understand them, it is necessary to go back to the society which became the basis of collectivism formation, a so-called agricultural society.

An Agricultural Society as the Origin of Japanese Culture

Characteristics of an agricultural society, compared with those of a hunting society, can be the following:

1 People settle down in one place. Naturally, the regional and blood relationships become closer, and the opportunities for human interaction and information exchange with outsiders will decrease.

2 As their work is based on the seasons, their life styles come to have periodicity. As people can anticipate the next opportunity coming round, they will possess a passive attitude rather than seeking active changes.

3 Everyone does the same work, such as rice-planting, weeding a rice field, and harvesting in rice-cropping. The difference between individual abilities is buried there and becomes an unimportant matter.

These characteristics of an agricultural society become much clearer by comparison with those of a hunting society. In a hunting society, people move around to chase animals, and their work does not have the same periodicity. So they make much of each moment. And that is the society in which an individual role is clear, and a leader who heads up the followers is needed.

Leaders in an Agricultural Society

The previously mentioned collectivism seems to be developed from a society with an agricultural-style culture. Further, this culture may characterize the culture of present Japanese society. Therefore, what types of leaders are suitable in this agricultural society? The answers are as follows:

1 Leaders should have the style of settlers. It is more important for leaders to listen to others, find a point of agreement, and settle down rather than to put themselves in the forefront and lead people. It is important to maintain the harmony of a group. This, for example, leads to the sentence, 'Harmony is precious' which was written in the Seventeen Article Constitution by Shotoku-Taishi. Apart from this, the constitution also says that plenty of discussion is important. This is to maintain and manage a group by bottom-up decision-making and consensus.

2 Leaders should possess the ability of extrapolating actual conditions from the past as specific knowledge. Even if leaders face some problems or obstacles, they are able to deal with them by drawing from a pile of past experiences as in most of the cases in an agricultural society. And it is also important to persuade people that good times will always come through bearing up under the present conditions.

3 Leaders should strengthen the feeling of unity and increase collectivity inside a group. At the same time, leaders should keep the group's feeling of tension and consciousness of competition against outside groups, such as neighboring villages. Specifically, many events such as village festivals were used to arouse a hostile feeling against the other groups.

Leader-Follower Relations Commonly Used Through the Modern Age in Japan

The above-mentioned portraits and functions of leaders, that is leadership, exactly overlap the portraits of current leaders in Japan. It is the traditional Japanese style of leadership. Although this may be to repeat what has been mentioned previously, a leader is selected from the group, based on his or her length of service and personality. A leader is the one who listens to others well and is trusted as a settling influence. A leader is the one who guides followers and increases collectivity by emphasizing the harmony of the group, arousing a competitive spirit against outsiders, and increasing a crisis atmosphere within the group.

In other words, a leader is not the person who establishes a position with their own high ability or activity, or with clear objectives based on a philosophy or vision, nor the one who is accepted as having strong characteristics to motivate people by using creativity and innovation.

This Japanese-style or agricultural-style leadership can function well with particular types of followers. These are people possessing high loyalty to their groups, being collective, respecting harmony, and willing to work for a long time without distinguishing between private and official time.

These followers do not possess any autonomy. They understand the relationship between individuals and groups as loyalty and sympathy not as an agreement of rights and obligations.

Essential Environmental Conditions for the Success of Traditional Japanese-Style Leadership

There is another important condition necessary for the achievement of successful results by these leaders and followers. That condition is related to the objectives, the characteristics, and the external environments of the society or group.

Stating the conclusion in advance, postwar Japan achieved surprising success in economic development because those factors matched well with each other. These matches are specified as the following:

1 The Japanese government set its priority of policies on economic rehabilitation to recover from the ruin of the war, and put the emphasis on industrial policy.

2 Many of the Japanese saw the difference between the spiritual and materiality as the reason for their defeat in the war, and aspired to the materialism of the Western countries, especially the materialistic culture of the USA.

3 After their defeat, many of the former political and business leaders in Japan lost power either by being ostracized or for some other reason. Therefore strong leadership allied to a philosophy did not come into existence. Also the leadership controlling operating activities became dominated.

4 By following the advanced countries, the Japanese objectives became very spe-

cific and persuasive. Having people who made efforts as a group to achieve their objectives of adapting to and catching up with the advanced countries was extremely effective.

5 The role of top managers was in stirring up and drawing on their followers' willingness, and creating conditions to realize that willingness.

6 The Japanese applied decision-making processes of bottom-up and consensus
such as the Ringi system, lifetime employment, a seniority system, and negativistic
personnel evaluation which phases out a person with problems. These Japanese-style
management systems were also very effective in the activities of achieving economic
growth and efficiency with suitable models for the moderately changing environment
in terms of both impact and speed.

In other words, leadership emphasizing the maintenance of passive, consensus-cen-
tered, and harmonious groups was the ideal style for the Japanese society that pursued
economic development in the postwar era.

This has been the case up to now. What is going to happen in the future? Will this
Japanese-style leadership continue to be effective? If not, what type of leadership will
be required? This issue will be discussed next.

FUTURE OF TRADITIONAL JAPANESE-STYLE LEADERSHIP

Future Environment and Culture of Japan

To discuss the future of leadership in Japan, it will be necessary to consider the two aspects stated previously. One is the issue of the future of the culture in Japanese society.
If the culture changes, that is changes occur in people's values and the behavioral
styles of the Japanese, traditional Japanese-style leadership will lose its effectiveness.

Another aspect is the issue of the external environment and the objectives of societies or groups, specifically Japan as a nation, or Japanese business entities. If those
too change, then traditional leadership will not function.

In fact, both of these aspects have already begun changing greatly. Even individuals' loyalty to their groups and their consciousness of respecting harmony have begun
to collapse in the Japanese younger generation. Also the Japanese management system, for example the seniority system, has faced difficulties caused by the end of high
economic growth. Furthermore, behavior which gives priority to a company or to
profit is a focus of censure, not only from outside but also inside Japan.

In addition, the world has been changing rapidly, and the West has been losing its
significance as a model to Japan. And Japan itself is now expected to act as a nation
which has a philosophy and autonomy with a global perspective.

This is not a subject only at the national level. The situation is exactly the same in
an industrial sector or a company. In other words, Japan has been greatly changing, or
is expected to change, its direction and culture. Therefore, Japanese leadership inevitably needs to change qualitatively.

Future Direction of Japanese Society

Therefore, what should leaders do? This is a very delicate issue. First, we shall consider Japanese culture. The characteristics of collectivism and egoism still remain

deeply embedded in Japanese cultures even though they are on the way to collapse. Consciousness of autonomy or co-existence still barely exists. Values or styles which give priority to the economy or to seeking materialistic sufficiency have grown stronger. What should leaders do in these situations?

Leaders have to aim at the following societies as well as business firms:

1 The society which puts importance on fairness and co-existence with the world by having a clear philosophy.

2 The society, as a nation, business firm, or individual, which establishes its own autonomy and respects others' autonomies.

3 The society which creates conditions for individuals to demonstrate their individual abilities and to live fruitful lives.

Needless to say, each culture or social structure has been established by various factors and processes over a long period. Therefore, it cannot be changed in a day, although undoubtedly, drastic remedy may be needed at some time. The collapse of Eastern Europe and the Soviet Union and the worsening of the world environment should be considered as good reasons for a change. In addition, the collapse of the economic bubble in Japan gives us many opportunities to reconsider our society.

However, we must not only break down the present situation, but also build up a new society. In order to do this, appropriate leadership for a new society is necessary.

From Traditional Japanese-Style Leadership to New Leadership for the Twenty-First Century in Japan

The new leadership for the twenty-first century should:

1 Have a clear philosophy, and be able to visualize it, to make it appeal adequately to people, and to get empathy for it. This philosophy must be based on a consciousness of co-existence and fairness.

2 Make clear what should be done to realize that philosophy and vision. In other words, leaders should provide specific schemes to make them materialize.

3 Respect and trust individuals, to find, improve, and utilize individuals' abilities and characters. In short, leaders should develop the conditions for positive participation by individuals.

4 Apply properly the means to induce individuals' autonomous behavior, such as taking the initiative, scolding and encouraging, or transmitting information according to the external environment or target individuals.

5 Have an unselfish and strong problem-finding consciousness or mission.

In every generation, the fact that leadership is exceedingly cultural will not change. Therefore the culture of a society or group itself needs to match with the leadership in order for the leadership outlined here to be accepted and become effective.

The priority of the whole world has been gradually changing from military strength or economic wealth to an emphasis on human beings. Within its change, Japanese culture has been shifting importance from collectivism to co-existence and individuality. However, we are still far from the desired situation.

The essential goal for the future of Japan will be to respect an individual and his or her characteristics and establish a society which has consciousness of being part of the world. This in itself needs proper leadership. After all, leadership changes a society, and the changed society breeds the leadership suitable to it.

EDITOR'S NOTE

The word translated as 'drive' is used in two senses:

1 To force people by compulsion to take a certain course of action.
2 To influence people through leadership.

After discussion with Professor Ichikawa through the translators, we believe that we have changed the word, or added qualifications, so that the appropriate difference in meaning is clear. However, it may be helpful to the reader to be aware of the two senses, in case I have done the translators and the author a disservice by making alterations at the wrong time.

A Riddle Wrapped in an Enigma: Demystifying Russian Managerial Motivation

Sheila Puffer

'Some people . . . may be Rooshans, and others may be Prooshans; they are born so, and will please themselves. Them which is of other naturs thinks different.' (Charles Dickens, *Mrs. Gamp*)

Russia and its people hold a fascination for many who have tried to understand that part of the world. Isolated for centuries, Russia gained the reputation, immortalized by Winston Churchill, of being 'a riddle wrapped in an enigma'. With Russia now opening its doors, Western business people are eager to solve the riddle in order to understand their Russian counterparts and do business successfully together.

One of the most perplexing aspects of the 'Russian mind' (Hingley, 1977) is motivation. Russian managers' motivation has been shaped by historical forces that are different from Western experience, causing Western managers to wonder whether their Russian counterparts can survive in the global market economy. My objective is to demystify Russian managerial motivation by analyzing it according to a framework that characterizes successful American managers. In this way I hope that the similarities and differences will become clear, and that Western business people will have a better sense of how to interpret the behavior of their Russian colleagues.

A FRAMEWORK OF MANAGERIAL MOTIVATION

The framework of managerial motivation or drive, developed by Kirkpatrick and Locke (1991), consists of five characteristics associated with the ability to expend a high level of effort in the managerial role. They are: (1) achievement motivation, (2) ambition, (3) energy, (4) tenacity, and (5) initiative. The framework will be applied to individuals in three eras in Russian history: the autocrat of tsarist times, comrade communist from the Russian revolution of 1917 to the collapse of the Soviet Union in 1991, and the emergent entrepreneur in the fledgling market-oriented economy of the 1990s.

Generally, managerial motivation took different forms in the three time periods. During tsarist times prior to the 1917 Russian revolution, autocratic leadership by strong individuals was the norm in a predominantly communal agrarian society. During the communist period, enterprise managers channeled their drive to meet plans handed down from government ministries. No effort was spared to meet plans, or at least to appear to meet plans. Regardless of its economic rationality, plan fulfillment was the key to rewards. Essentially, managers followed orders and played the game. In contrast, under current conditions managers and entrepreneurs must direct their efforts to leadership activities that include developing strategies for their enterprises, restructuring and streamlining them, and engaging in entrepreneurial thinking and behavior.

From *European Management Journal,* 1993, 11(4), 473–480. Reprinted by permission of Elsevier Science Ltd., Pergamon Imprint, Oxford, England.

To elaborate on the nature of Russian managerial motivation I now discuss the five components of motivation in three periods of Russian history. Many of the examples of managerial motivation are drawn from interviews, surveys, and field research that I have conducted over the past several years with a number of Russian and American colleagues.

Achievement

In the United States, high achievers have been found to gain satisfaction from performing challenging tasks, meeting high standards, and finding better ways of doing things.

The Autocrat of Tsarist Times   Achievement orientation was not fostered in traditional Russian society. In a rural communal society, the norm was for people to blend into the group, and not to challenge the standard way of doing things. In fact, primitive farming techniques in Russia remained unchanged for so long that, for years, grain yields were the lowest in all the long-settled countries, including India (Maynard, 1948, p. 30). Group harmony was maintained by having everyone work at the same level. Consequently, there was little motivation to strive to meet higher standards.

Comrade Communist   Conditions in most enterprises during the communist period were frustrating for managers with high achievement needs. Being a manager often involved such challenging tasks as striving to meet unrealistic deadlines and to manufacture products specified in the plan using raw materials of the wrong specification, on equipment of the wrong type, with unmotivated workers. While standards for production volume were often high, even unrealistic, quality standards were often abysmally low or easily subverted (Forker, 1991). However, some enterprises developed a reputation for higher quality, and goods bearing their label were in high demand.

Managers seldom had the opportunity to find better ways of doing things. Instead, as a matter of survival, they had to improvise methods to meet the plan based on insufficient resources (Puffer and McCarthy, 1993). For example, many plants had the problem of keeping antiquated equipment running or installing new equipment. At an electric motor manufacturing plant in 1988 our research team found that management had devised a complex makeshift system to perform a certain operation on the motors (Puffer and Ozira, 1992). The multimillion-dollar computerized machine tool purchased from Europe to perform the operation turned out to be incompatible with the existing machine tools on the assembly line. Several dozen workers were assigned to perform the operation by hand using outmoded tools in order to keep production moving—a costly and labor-intensive process. Ways of improvising to meet volume targets at other plants included using fewer raw materials, a practice that often resulted in products such as plastic or glass being flimsy and even dangerous. Another method consisted of eliminating time-consuming steps in the production process, such as omitting buttonholes on clothing.

One disillusioned achiever our research team encountered in 1988 was the chief design engineer of a large truck plant. In the 1970s he had registered an international patent for a revolutionary type of shock absorber he and his team had invented. Despite the undisputed technological advance of the product and the promise of bonuses for innovation, enterprise top management never adopted the innovation because of the retooling time and expense, as well as the initial drop in production output it would entail (Puffer, 1988; see Berliner, 1976).

An exception during the communist regime was the military sector. Higher standards of product quality were imposed primarily on enterprises that produced for that sector. Furthermore, conditions in such enterprises were more favorable in terms of the quality of raw materials and equipment, as well as wages. Consequently, talented, achievement-oriented managers gravitated to the military sector.

The Emergent Entrepreneur   Achievement motivation is a particularly important characteristic for successful entrepreneurs, and Russian entrepreneurs are no exception. In a 1991 survey of 109 actual and aspiring entrepreneurs in Russia, William Tullar (1992) found no difference between their achievement motivation and that of their American counterparts.

My colleagues and I also found evidence of achievement motivation among the forty Moscow entrepreneurs we studied in 1992 (McCarthy, *et al.,* 1993). Reflecting a desire for challenging tasks, a number of entrepreneurs had left the security of the state sector to start new businesses that would allow their scientific and technical expertise to flourish. Moreover, regarding high standards, the entrepreneurs rated the high quality of their products and services as the number one factor contributing to their firms' success.

Ambition

Ambition reflects the strong desire to advance in one's career, and to get to the top of the organization. It is a desire which gives individuals the need to demonstrate their abilities and determination, as well as the desire to succeed.

The Autocrat of Tsarist Times   In Russia, ambition is a dirty word. For centuries ambitious people have typically been viewed with resentment, suspicion, and envy. Such negative attitudes stemmed from communal living and farming, as well as the deeply rooted sentiment that social justice consisted of everyone being entitled to roughly the same things. According to egalitarian principles, no one was supposed to sink too low, nor rise too high. People who strived to be better than others were violating social norms, and were seen as taking away the rightful share of others (Connor, 1991). Russians relate many anecdotes about how deeply envy permeates their thoughts and behaviors. For instance, Anatoli Sobchak, mayor of St. Petersburg, recounted not long ago the story about a peasant to whom God would grant any wish, but would also give his neighbor twice as much. After much reflection, the peasant asked God to strike out one of his eyes—and both of his neighbor's eyes (Sobchak, 1990).

There is a traditional leveling instinct among Russians who, upon seeing someone who is better off, become preoccupied with bringing that person down to their level, instead of devising ways to become equally successful. Indeed, Nikolai Shmelev, the prominent market-oriented economist, criticized his fellow citizens for developing 'the syndrome of equal poverty for all' (Shmelev, 1990).

Comrade Communist   Under communism, ambitious people who aspired to a managerial career were attracted by the opportunity to exercise influence in their organizations, as well as by privileges and benefits such as chauffeured cars, country homes, and access to superior goods and services. Salaries were not much higher than those of skilled workers as a result of the government's practice of promoting wage convergence across occupations. The high social status of managers was evident from the responses of nearly 3,000 Soviet emigrés surveyed in the early 1980s about influence and privilege. They ranked managers of large industrial enterprises third among nine occupations, after first secretaries of the provincial (*oblast'*) party committee and colonels in the KGB (Swafford, 1987).

To be successful, upwardly striving managers had to cloak their ambition in service to the party and advancement of the common good of the organization. Their success depended both on talent and political factors, according to the emigrés cited earlier. Forty per cent reported that the most important criteria for job advancement were merit factors such as education, knowledge and experience, and organizational ability. Another 45 per cent cited party membership, protection, and connections, and 11 per cent mentioned ability to get along with superiors and loyalty (Gregory, 1987). In addition, a common career path for enterprise managers advancing to top management ranks was to spend several years working on loan in the communist party organization and subsequently returning to a line management position in their enterprise.

The Emergent Entrepreneur   Although there is no longer any legal restriction on fulfilling one's personal ambition by starting a private enterprise, there is still tremendous social pressure against ambitious entrepreneurs. In the words of former New York Times Moscow correspondent, Felicity Barringer: 'In America, it's a sin to be a loser, but if there's one sin in Soviet society, it's being a winner' (Barringer, 1989).

The new economic conditions have sparked a heated debate about social justice in the press, including the legitimacy and morality of private enterprise. In one article, for example, a woman complained about an acquaintance who earned extra money and enjoyed a few luxuries by growing and selling spring vegetables: 'I don't want to live like her—I want her to live like me' (Rogovin, 1986). The recent appearance of Russian millionaires flaunting their wealth has also fueled public suspicion and outcry.

Unfortunately, the battle over private enterprise and social justice has not been confined to verbal blows. Over the past several years a number of legitimate private businesses were shut down by government authorities because they were 'too' successful. Other firms closed their doors in anticipation of adverse action by the government, the public, or the criminal element (Jones and Moskoff, 1991). Articles in the press have referred derisively to entrepreneurs as latter-day NEPmen (entrepreneurs encouraged during Lenin's New Economic Plan) and kulaks (prosperous peasants who sometimes exploited other peasants). Some contemporary entrepreneurs recall how the NEPmen, kulaks, and other ambitious people were persecuted and even annihilated in earlier times, and fear they will suffer the same fate. According to Oleg Smirnov, a Russian representative of Pepsi-Cola: 'There is no tradition of law in this country, so some powerful official can strangle a cooperative [private business] in five minutes—there are sixty-four thousand ways to do it' (Smirnov, 1990).

The pervasiveness of envy in Russian society has led economist Nikolai Shmelev to charge that 'blind, burning envy of a neighbor's success . . . has become (virtually at all levels) a most powerful brake on the ideas and practice of restructuring. Until we at least muffle this envy, the success of restructuring will remain in doubt' (Shmelev, 1991). Envy exists in such proportions that many ambitious and successful people take great pains to downplay their accomplishments, as well as to conceal their material possessions behind high fences and closed doors in order to escape public censure and even violence.

In spite of the obstacles, a number of ambitious entrepreneurs have persevered and become highly successful. One of the 'new-age' entrepreneurs is Mikhail Efimovich Malkov, the forty-four-year-old general director of the Russian-German joint venture, Molkom (*Moscow Magazine,* 1991/1992). His ambition was evident at a very early age, judging from his claim that he 'did his first business deal from the moment he could talk.' Malkov's firm has a customs terminal on the outskirts of Moscow that provides shipping and storage for major international clients. His accomplishments include converting the Moscow Detachment of Underwater Technical Works from an unprofitable state enterprise into a highly profitable one, as well as leading one of the first efforts to transform a state enterprise into collective ownership. His need for challenge and risk taking are evident also in his hobbies of deep-sea diving and reading detective novels.

Energy

Effective managers typically have more energy than other people, along with greater physical, mental, and emotional vitality and stamina, enabling them to work long and intense hours.

The Autocrat of Tsarist Times   Russians traditionally have had their own brand of hard work. They are notorious for their bursts of energy, followed by long periods of lethargy. Historians have traced this behavior to peasants working the land under harsh climatic conditions. They would work feverishly during the spring and summer to bring in the harvest, and would lie idle throughout the long, cold winter months. The nineteenth-century Russian historian, Kliuchevskii, boldly concluded: 'No other nation in Europe can put forward such concentrated spasms of labor as the Russian. Nor, however, shall we find anywhere else in Europe such inexperience of steady, disciplined, evenly deployed work as in this same Russia' (Kliuchevskii 1987, p. 315).

Comrade Communist   During the communist period, conscientious managers had to have the stamina to work long hours and be all things to all people. Managers whom our team interviewed in 1988 would joke that they worked in 8-hour day—from 8 a.m. to 8 p.m., that is (Lawrence and Vlachoutsicos, 1990). In accordance with the Soviet administrative principle of one-person management, *edinonachalie,* the buck stopped with the head of the enterprise, and virtually all decision-making authority rested there. Heads of enterprises were deeply involved in issues ranging from important negotiations with ministry and party officials, to managing housing complexes and child care centers for the work force. Heads of enterprises, *direktora,* were required to hold weekly office hours and listen to problems of virtually anyone connected with the enterprise, including employees at all levels and their family members. They were 'hands on' managers who would tour their plants once or twice a day and concern themselves with operational problems. Although they did not usually take paperwork home with them in the evening, after work they would often attend social and sporting events sponsored by the enterprise.

The amount of energy required to be a successful enterprise manager took its toll on the health and well-being of many Russian managers. A team of researchers recently compared the stress and health of 1,000 heads of Soviet enterprises with managers in the United States, Japan, and India (Ivancevich, *et al.,* 1992). The Soviet managers reported the greatest stress of all the groups. In addition, they reported the greatest number of health problems, including illness, tension, and feelings of dissatisfaction.

An illustration of the demands placed on managers is provided by the wife of a plant manager who lamented that her husband's job was so stressful that she advised their son to choose a different career despite the perks and privileges it offered. She complained that July was the worse month because that was when he was at the ministry trying to reduce the plan to a level his enterprise could meet. He feared that the chief engineer, who was viewed as 'the ministry's man' would undercut him in the negotiations. Even at home in the evening the plant manager could not escape phone calls from employees reporting bottlenecks and supply shortages (Roberts and LaFollette, 1990, p. 31).

The Emergent Entrepreneur   The new entrepreneurs must also possess energy and stamina to start their own businesses and foster their growth. Some people are pursuing so many opportunities that they are working virtually around the clock. An outstanding example is Sviatoslav Fedorov, who was named Businessman of the Year in 1991 by *Moscow Magazine.* World-renowned as a scientist, Fedorov developed a surgical operation for correcting myopia using lasers, in addition to registering 50 patents, writing four books and nearly 400 articles, and lecturing in more than 60 countries. He established clinics in 12 cities, staffed by nearly 200 doctors, treating more than one-quarter million people a year. Fedorov's other ventures include two factories that manufacture lenses and surgical instruments, and two farms that provide food for his staff and patients. He has expanded beyond medicine and become engaged in controversial ventures including a cellular phone network, a hotel, and a gambling casino (Hofheinz, 1991/1992; Kirkland, 1990).

Perhaps the most energetic entrepreneurs are young people who have little experience with the communist regime. In Moscow, for example, teenagers could be found recently washing cars and fetching hamburgers for customers unwilling to wait in line. The most enterprising were earning as much as 300,000 rubles a month when the average monthly wage was less than 10,000. Such individuals 'were not tainted by all those years of "Glory to the Communists"' and they represent 'the first generation that will have no doubts about the need for a market economy,' according to Alexei Lasov, president of a large Moscow stock exchange (Auerbach, 1993). Already, some young people have distinguished themselves in important business ventures. For example, at age 16 Leonid Titov started working in a private enterprise that became the commodities exchange called The Russian Exchange. By 1992, at age 20, he had become one of its top managers (Klebnikov, 1992).

Tenacity

Effective managers possess tenacity, a characteristic that enables them to persevere under adversity and to pursue goals that may take many years to accomplish.

The Autocrat of Tsarist Times   The Russian people's ability to endure hardship and survive under adverse conditions is a hallmark of their character. Over the centuries, they have persevered through brutally harsh winters, the ravages of war, and severe shortages of basic material goods and comforts that the Western world takes for granted. Many believe that their destiny, reinforced by the teachings of the Russian Orthodox Church, is to endure suffering as a means to a brighter future. Two often-heard refrains are that life is a struggle, and that one must be patient. The communists redirected the Russians' tenacity toward the pursuit of communism. The people were told that they had to make personal sacrifices during the building of communism, a goal that would take many years to accomplish.

Comrade Communist   Effective managers during the communist period were those who persevered under adversity and fulfilled their enterprise's plans in spite of shortages of materials, equipment, and facilities. During our research project in 1988, we met a number of managers who refused to be defeated by bureaucracy and found ways to get the job done. For example, at a truck engine plant a new sandblasting machine could not be installed because headquarters would not authorize the hiring of laborers to dig the foundation. Consequently, the plant manager assigned production workers to do the work, paid them overtime, and disguised the wages in the budget (Puffer and Ozira, 1990). Similarly, at an electric motor plant we found that the plant manager had succeeded in constructing a new building using the volunteer labor of his employees on their days off (Puffer, 1988).

Tenacity was also a crucial trait needed by materials managers to keep supplies of critical resources flowing to enterprises. One highly effective materials (supply) manager we interviewed at an electric motor plant in 1988 described the problems he had getting a supplier to provide copper wire for a new model of motor. First, the manager went to see the supplier several hundred miles away. When this attempt failed, the plant used economic sanctions against the supplier, who paid them several thousand rubles in fines, yet still sent no wire. The materials manager tried to use rules and regulations to get the supplier to deliver the wire, but to no avail. Finally, he had higher authorities force his counterpart to meet with him at the ministry in charge of wire production. After all these actions, the motor plant finally began receiving the wire, but the shipments were consistently at least five per cent short (Puffer, 1989).

The Emergent Entrepreneur   Tenacity is also required of contemporary managers who face immense obstacles in the pursuit of their goals. There is virtually no legal or economic infrastructure to support private enterprise. Venture capital is extremely limited. The Moscow entrepreneurs my colleagues and I questioned in 1992 cited government regulation as the biggest obstacle to doing business (McCarthy, et al., 1993). For example, some laws are so ambiguous or rewritten so frequently that it is difficult for firms to develop long-term business strategies. The greatest challenge to private business people, however, may be the slowing of market reforms resulting from the appointment of the conservative Viktor Chernomydrin as prime minister in late 1992, and the waning popularity of President Boris Yeltsin.

Some entrepreneurs are tenaciously trying to hold onto their businesses and keep them from being overtaken by the criminal element. For instance, some private business owners have formed associations to find ways to deal with threats by organized crime. Similarly, a few years ago, one thousand taxi drivers staged a meeting at Moscow's Vnukovo Airport to discuss how to avoid paying protection money (Roberts and LaFollette, 1990). Still other entrepreneurs have resiliently rebuilt their businesses that were sabotaged or closed down by government officials (Jones and Moskoff, 1991).

One entrepreneur who is tenaciously pursuing her goals in spite of great hardship is Irina Razumnova, founder of *Gildiia* (Guild), a business advisory service in Moscow which caters primarily for women entrepreneurs. To get the organization off the ground she refused to be deterred by a lack of funding and facilities. She worked relentlessly, practically around the clock, sometimes by candlelight, in a delapidated building. Her perseverance resulted in an organization that offers training programs and consulting services in how to start a business (Levine, 1991/1992). A number of women have founded their own businesses and have joined business clubs to promote entrepreneurship among women (Puffer, 1993a).

Initiative

Effective managers take initiative and are proactive in making choices and taking actions that lead to change rather than being satisfied with the status quo, reacting to events, or waiting for things to happen.

The Autocrat of Tsarist Times   One prominent characteristic often associated with Russians is caution. The peasant admonition dating from the fifteenth century, 'to look both ways,' is thought to have originated with the rough terrain and harsh environment (Kliuchevskii, 1987). With such a high value placed on cautious behavior, it is little wonder that initiative was not a common feature of traditional Russian society.

Comrade Communist   During the communist regime initiative was not only discouraged, but was even punished. Officially, managers were rewarded for meticulously following rules and unquestioningly demonstrating loyalty to communist party principles.

However, unofficially, many managers showed exceptional initiative and creativity in order to overcome obstacles and meet the plan. For instance, managers at the truck plant our research team studied in 1988 convinced officials at the automotive ministry to eliminate from the plan requirements to produce trucks for export. Legally, once the plan was approved, it could not be changed. However, plant staff conducted a market study and determined that no market existed abroad for the trucks. Officials in the marketing department at the Ministry checked the analysis and agreed to eliminate the trucks from the plan (Walton and Naumov, 1990).

The Emergent Entrepreneur   Many new Russian entrepreneurs are demonstrating a great deal of initiative. For instance, a group of 109 entrepreneurs and aspiring entrepreneurs who completed a personality questionnaire were found to be more risk averse and less innovative than Americans (Tullar, 1992). Nevertheless, regardless of how they compare with Americans, hordes of entrepreneurs, brimming with initiative, have been unleashed in Russia. Claimed Herman Sterligov, president of the computerized commodity exchange, The Alysa System, in Moscow: 'Every day we have a thousand people who come to our Moscow office saying, "Please privatize us" or "I have this idea and I need funding"' (Sterligov, 1992).

In our study of 40 Moscow entrepreneurs, 60 percent had changed careers at least once, a concrete indicator of proactive behavior and dissatisfaction with the status quo (McCarthy, *et al.*, 1993). Many people have become engaged in multiple, unrelated activities as opportunities for making money arise. For instance, Makhmud Mazaev, a prominent urologist who heads a clinic in St Petersburg, wanted to purchase expensive medical equipment from the West. To finance the purchases, he came up with the idea of acting as a paid broker for people who want to study in business schools in the United States (Mazaev, 1993).

Another individual who believes in challenging the status quo is Yuri Lebedev. At the age of 37 he was appointed Minister of Innovation in the Russian government in 1990, a portfolio he created himself. Trained as a geologist, he began creating inventions while still a student. His own mining research company developed as a result of the compressed air machine he invented for quarrying rock. The company grew to include tourism and environmental development, and within a few years its annual sales had reached 25 million rubles. An iconoclast, Lebedev had never been a party member. True to form, on his first day as a government minister, he surprised his staff by wanting only one telephone. 'They looked at me as if I were crazy. They told me ministers need at least four telephones, otherwise no one will take them seriously. That's one reason why this country has so many problems' (Lebedev, 1990).

American executives who have joint ventures in Russia have also been impressed with the initiative and ingenuity of their Russian managers. Peter Hemingway, the first manager of Polaroid Corporation's Russian joint venture, Svetozor, praised the work of a Russian employee who, on his own, cut through exorbitant customs fees and saved the company a considerable amount of money (Puffer and Hemingway, 1992). Jack Medzorian of Baird Corporation, whose joint venture, Lomo, sells spectrometers in Russia, was equally impressed with the creativity and initiative that his Russian employees showed in selling a spectrometer. They contacted a firm that sold scrap metal to Western customers and showed them that, by using a spectrometer to sort the metal, they would receive ten times more revenues than for unsorted scrap (Puffer and Medzorian, 1992). The order for the spectrometer quickly followed. Nevertheless, Mr

Medzorian cautioned that one must watch out for misguided initiative of the part of employees. He recalled how the Russian managing director put into Baird's 1992 business plan a number of potentially profitable proposals that were unrelated to the spectrometer industry and did not fit the firm's strategy.

A PRACTICAL APPROACH TO RUSSIAN MANAGERIAL MOTIVATION

When working with Russians, Western managers can put an understanding of Russian managerial motivation to practical use in establishing a good relationship and conducting business effectively. A key attitude is to respect the differences in the ways that Russian managers approach their work. Russians' managerial motivation has been shaped by a set of economic, political, and social circumstances that give it a unique character. Western managers should take these factors into account in establishing their expectations about the attitudes and behaviors of their Russian partners.

Russian managerial motivation is the product of communal traditions and attitudes passed on from peasant society, as well as the egalitarian principles of communist ideology and the stultifying bureaucracy of the centrally planned economic system. Achievement, ambition, and initiative have been denigrated in Russia. People with a high need for achievement have been condemned for being individualistic, antisocial, and enemies of the people. Personal ambition has aroused feelings of envy, vindictiveness, and derision. And initiative has typically been received with indifference, at best, and punishment, at worst. Negative attitudes towards these characteristics are so deeply ingrained in the Russian psyche that many Russians who want to realize their ambitions feel pressure from two sources—public scorn and their own guilt from violating the values they were raised with. Western managers should carefully assess the extent to which their Russian associates feel these pressures. If Russians seem reluctant to take initiative or be ambitious, they might respond positively to proposals that emphasize benefits to the collective or that reward individuals in ways that do not arouse feelings of envy. One should respect requests for not publicizing personal achievements, material possessions or privileges.

Russians' energy and tenacity are valuable assets. Many successful managers and entrepreneurs have a demonstrated capacity for hard work. They can call upon large reserves of energy, and are capable of persevering in spite of immense obstacles. Western business people can help channel this energy by developing concrete action plans in collaboration with their Russian partners. Fixed deadlines, clear goals and procedures, regular feedback, and an emphasis on the importance and urgency of accomplishing the task are essential. These measures should be coupled with valued material and intrinsic rewards (Puffer, 1993b).

Another important consideration is the personal profile of the Russian business person. In general, older Russians with extensive managerial experience during the communist regime may be more conservative than younger entrepreneurs in taking risks and adapting to conditions of a market-oriented economy. However, there is wide personal variation in receptivity and adaptability to new conditions, and it is a matter of attitude, not necessarily age and background, that differentiates one manager from another.

It will take time for Russians to develop a new type of managerial motivation appropriate for their emergent market-oriented economy. Their motivational make-up may end up being based on both traditional Russian values and Western influences. Western business people and Russian business school educators will likely play important roles (Puffer, 1993c). Undoubtedly Russian managerial motivation will be unique and will never be completely demystified. Yet, Western managers, many of whom are cautiously optimistic about doing business in Russia (McCarthy, *et al.,* forthcoming; Welch, 1993), will increase the possibility of a successful business relationship by developing an understanding of Russian managerial motivation.

REFERENCES

Auerbach, J. Coming of Age in Capitalist Russia. *The Boston Globe,* pp. 20, 21, January 4, 1993.

Barringer, F. Comment at the conference, Chautauqua at Pitt: The Fifth General Chautauqua Conference on U.S. and Soviet Relations, October 30, 1989. Cited in H. Smith, *The New Russians,* New York: Random House, 1990, p. 203.

Berliner, J. S. Prospects for Technological Progress. In J. S. Berliner, *Soviet Industry from Stalin to Gorbachev.* Aldershot, England: Edward Elgar, pp. 222–245, 1988. [first published: 1976].

Connor, W. D. Equality of Opportunity. In A. Jones, W. D. Connor, and D. E. Powell (eds.), *Soviet Social Problems.* Boulder, CO: Westview, 1991, pp. 296–318.

Forker, L. B. Quality: American, Japanese, and Soviet perspectives. *The Academy of Management Executive,* Vol. 5, No. 4, pp. 63–74, 1991.

Gregory, P. R. Productivity, Slack, and Time Theft in the Soviet Economy. In J. R. Millar (ed.), *Politics, Work, and Daily Life in the USSR: A Survey of Former Soviet Citizens.* Cambridge: Cambridge University Pres, pp. 241–275, 1987.

Hingley, R. *The Russian Mind.* New York: Charles Scribner's Sons, 1977.

Hofheinz, P. The Pied-Piper of Capitalism. *Moscow Magazine,* pp. 50, 51, December 1991/January 1992.

Ivancevich, J. M., DeFrank, R. S., and Gregory, P. R. The Soviet Enterprise Director: An Important Resource Before and After the Coup. *The Academy of Management Executive,* Vol. 6, No. 1, pp. 42–55, 1992.

Jones, A., and Moskoff, W. *Ko-ops: The Rebirth of Entrepreneurship in the Soviet Union.* Bloomington: Indiana University Press, 1991.

Kirkland, R. I. Curing Communism. *Moscow Magazine,* pp. 64–68, October 1990.

Kirkpatrick, S. A., and Locke, E. A. Leadership: Do Traits Matter? *The Academy of Management Executive,* Vol. 5, No. 2, pp. 48–60, 1991.

Klebnikov, P. A Market Grows in Russia. *Forbes,* pp. 78–82, June 8, 1992.

Kliuchevskii, V. O. *Collected Works.* Vol. 1, Moscow: Mysl', 1967.

Lawrence, P. R., and Vlachoutsicos, C. A. *Managerial Patterns: Differences and Commonalities.* In P. R. Lawrence and C. A. Vlachoutsicos (eds.), *Behind the Factory Walls: Decision Making in Soviet and US Enterprises.* Boston: Harvard Business School Press, pp. 271–286, 1990.

Lebedev, Y. Cited in S. Handelman, Yuri Lebedev: Siberian Innovator. *Moscow Magazine,* p. 33, December 1990.

Levine, J. Enterprising Woman. *Moscow Magazine,* p. 7, December 1991/January 1992.

Maynard, J. *Russia in Flux.* New York: Macmillan, p. 30, 1948.

Mazaev, M. Personal communication with S. Puffer, Boston, 1993.

McCarthy, D. J., Puffer, S. M., and Shekshnia, S. V. The Resurgence of an Entrepreneurial Class in Russia. *Journal of Management Inquiry,* Vol. 2, No. 2, pp. 125–137, 1993.

McCarthy, D. J., Puffer, S. M., and Simmonds, P. J. Riding the Russian Roller Coaster: US Firms' Recent Experience and Future Plans in the Former USSR. *California Management Review,* forthcoming.

Moscow Magazine, Moscow, Magazine's Top 50, pp. 52–57, December 1991/January 1992.

Puffer, S. M. Unpublished field notes for *Behind the Factory Walls: Decision Making in Soviet and US Enterprises,* 1988.

Puffer, S. M. Women Managers in the Former USSR: A Case of 'Too Much Equality'? In N. J. Adler and D. N. Izraeli (eds.), *Competitive Frontiers: Women Managing Worldwide.* Cambridge, MA: Blackwell, 1993a.

Puffer, S. M. Three Factors Affecting Reward Allocations in the Former USSR: An Empirical Study. In J. B. Shaw and P. Kirkbride (eds.), *Research in Personnel and Human Resources Management: International Supplement.* Volume 3. Greenwich, CT: JAI Press, 1993b.

Puffer, S. M. Education for Management in a New Economy. In A. Jones (ed.), *Education and Society in the New Russia.* Armonk, NY: M. E. Sharpe, 1993c.

Puffer, S. M., and McCarthy, D. J. Decision-Making Authority of American and Former Soviet Managers: Not So Different After All? *The International Executive,* November/December, 1993.

Puffer, S. M., and Medzorian, J. Manufacturing Spectrometers in St Petersburg. In S. M. Puffer (ed.), *op. cit.,* pp. 248–257, 1992.

Puffer, S. M., and Ozira, V. I. *Capital Investment Decisions.* In P. R. Lawrence and C. A. Vlachoutsicos (eds.), *op cit.,* pp. 183–226, 1992.

Roberts, P. C., and LaFollette, K. *Meltdown Inside the Soviet Economy.* Washington, D.C.: The Cato Institute, 1990.

Rogovin, V.Z. Sotsial'naia Spravedlivost' i Sotsialisticheskoe Raspredelenie Zhiznennykh Blag (Social Equality and Social Distribution of Wealth). *Voprosy Filosofii* (Philosophical Issues), No. 9, p. 17, 1986.

Shmelev, N. Speech to the Third Congress of People's Deputies, March 12, reported in *Foreign Broadcast Information Service* (FBIS), March 14, 1990.

Shmelev, N. New Anxieties. In A. Jones and W. Moskoff (eds.), *The Great Market Debate in Soviet Economics.* Armonk, NY: M. E. Sharpe, pp. 3–35, 1991.

Smirnov, O. Cited in H. Smith, *op. cit.,* p. 285, 1990.

Sobchak, A. Cited in H. Smith, *op. cit.,* p. 204, 1990.

Sterligov, H. Cited in P. Klebnikov, *op. cit.,* pp. 79–82, 1992.

Swafford, M. Perceptions of Social Status in the USSR. In J. R. Millar (ed.), *Politics, Work, and Daily Life in the USSR: A Survey of Former Soviet Citizens.* Cambridge: Cambridge University Press, pp. 279–300, 1987.

Tullar, W. L. Cultural Transformation: Democratization and Russian Entrepreneurial Motives. Paper presented at the Academy of Management meetings, Las Vegas, 1992.

Walton E., and Naumov, A. *Planning.* In P. R. Lawrence and C. A. Vlachoutsicos (eds.), *op cit.,* pp. 111–150, 1990.

Welch, J. B. Investing in Eastern Europe: Perspectives of Chief Financial Officers. *The International Executive,* Vol. 35, No. 1, pp. 45–72, 1993.

Managerial Leadership in Chinese Industrial Enterprises: Legacies of Complex Structures and Communist Party Involvement

John R. Schermerhorn, Jr.
Mee-Kau Nyaw

The management literature is now replete with observations, commentary, and empirical research on continuing reforms of state-owned industrial enterprises in the People's Republic of China. The foundation work of Tung (1982) is complemented by an increasing number and variety of responsible contributions whose predominant concerns include management development (Warner, 1985), value comparisons (Lai and Lam, 1985; Shenkar and Ronen, 1987), structural arrangements (Warner and Nyaw, 1986), negotiating patterns and business style (Frankenstein, 1986), and broader political-economic perspectives (Bachman, 1988; Petras, 1988).

Among these books and articles, however, there is some inclination to focus attention on changes occurring in Chinese institutions as a result of recent reforms. This is the case even though Chinese society retains an underlying conservatism resulting in a pattern of "ups *and* downs" or "speed-ups *and* slow-downs" as it adjusts and readjusts on the political, economic, and business scenes (Henley and Nyaw, 1986b; Petras, 1988). The massacre in Beijing at Tiananmen Square on June 4, 1989, and subsequent reactionary treatment of student leaders and sympathizers of the "democracy" movement, are dramatic and most unfortunate cases-in-point.

Facing sanctions and criticisms from other nations of the world for its handling of this internal turmoil, China's communist leadership has had to reassess the country's economic reforms in the context of emerging sociopolitical developments. But even as another period of adjustment unfolds, the continuing strength and enduring influence of China's politically-based institutions and infrastructure remains apparent. There is a need, accordingly, for organization theorists to give increased attention to the historical aspects of institutional change and political control as they affect the management of industrial enterprises in China. Schermerhorn (1987) identifies three paradoxes that deserve special consideration in this regard.

1 *The paradox of the enterprise operating environment.* Chinese industrial enterprises operate in a reform environment that seeks greater economic growth and offers new market freedoms, yet the enterprises are still influenced by central planning tendencies that constrain them.

2 *The paradox of the enterprise organization structure.* Chinese industrial enterprises face pressures to increase productivity and business performance, yet they must simultaneously support multiple systems that serve political and social objectives.

3 *The paradox of the enterprise power structure.* Factory directors and the management cadre in Chinese industrial enterprises are assuming greater responsibilities

From *International Studies of Management & Organization,* 1990, 20, 9–21. Reprinted by permission.

for performance results, but internal checks and balances in parallel authority structures remain strongly influenced by the Chinese Communist Party.

Paradoxes such as these have important implications for the emergence of managerial leadership in Chinese firms. Many (if not most) enterprises have struggled over the past several years to respond to "new" administrative initiatives encouraged under the reforms (Burton, 1987). But the pace of truly transformational change is hampered by an entrenched state bureaucracy with strong roots to the past (Henley and Nyaw, 1986a), the failure of many managers to assume authority commensurate with their performance responsibilities (Boisot and Child, 1988), and political risk tracing to the continued influence and self-interests of the Chinese Communist Party (Bachman, 1988; Petras, 1988). As highlighted once again by the 1989 Tiananmen events, forty-plus years of socialism and a strong party presence in all aspects of Chinese society are proving to be conservative forces even in a reform environment.

At a minimum, therefore, what can be expected of this historical context for present-day action in Chinese enterprise is organizational change that will remain inherently incremental. The core nature of the contemporary Chinese sociopolitical milieu may constrain future developments to those which, as Cyert and March (1963) would suggest, fall "in the neighborhood" of past operations. Thus, the remainder of this paper examines the traditions established by complex enterprise structures and Communist Party involvement, with special interest in their implications for managerial leadership.

THE COMPLEX ORGANIZATION OF CHINESE INDUSTRIAL ENTERPRISE

State-owned Chinese industrial enterprises, as described by Henley and Nyaw (1986a), are structured quite differently from their typical Western counterparts. Many of their characteristic features are byproducts of China's socialist environment, and they are quite enduring. Even as the reforms continue to evolve, the presence of simultaneous systems and parallel authority structures lend a unique "Chinese" character to any firm (Schermerhorn, 1987).

Simultaneous Systems

Figure 1 portrays three systems that operate "simultaneously" to create the typical Chinese industrial enterprise: the life support, sociopolitical support, and business and operations systems. Of these, only the last is shared in common with most Western commercial enterprises. The other two systems are "ancillary" and have no direct relationship to the production of goods or services. They achieve meaning only in the broader setting of China's socialist society, which views all organizations as instruments of the state.

Components of the *enterprise life-support system* assist workers to fulfill such necessities of everyday life as housing, health care, child-care and education, and even recreation and entertainment. They involve the employing firm in assisting a worker's entire family in meeting their daily needs, and they represent a large proportion of any

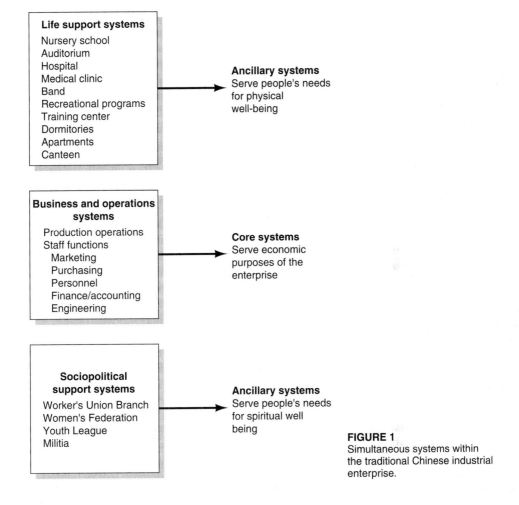

Life support systems
Nursery school
Auditorium
Hospital
Medical clinic
Band
Recreational programs
Training center
Dormitories
Apartments
Canteen

Ancillary systems
Serve people's needs
for physical
well-being

Business and operations systems
Production operations
Staff functions
 Marketing
 Purchasing
 Personnel
 Finance/accounting
 Engineering

Core systems
Serve economic
purposes of the
enterprise

Sociopolitical support systems
Worker's Union Branch
Women's Federation
Youth League
Militia

Ancillary systems
Serve people's needs
for spiritual well
being

FIGURE 1
Simultaneous systems within
the traditional Chinese industrial
enterprise.

enterprise's day-to-day operating concerns (Ignatius, 1989b). The extent of this commitment is illustrated at the First Automobile Works in Changchun, where some 80 percent of 60,000 total workers are employed in ways totally unrelated to car production—everything from barbering to police work. The factory director is quoted as saying: "Each year, I have to worry about housing for 2,000 couples getting married, nurseries for 2,000 newborn babies, and jobs for 2,500 school-leavers. I am mayor as well as factory head. Of course I have a bigger burden than my counterparts in the U.S." (Leung, 1989: A14).

Components of the *enterprise sociopolitical support system,* by contrast, are designed to advance socialist ideology. To this extent, Redding and Wong (1986) consider Chinese organizations as "politically dominated" and designed in part with ideological purposes in mind. The enterprise branch of the Chinese Communist Party is the center point for this ideology. Sociopolitical support systems such as the following exist within the firm and allow the party to exert a "political" presence:

Worker's Union: An enterprise branch of a national trade union with the objective of advancing worker welfare within the firm.

Women's Federation: An enterprise unit with the primary objective of safeguarding female rights.

Communist Youth League: An enterprise branch of a national youth league with the primary objective of helping the party express itself to young workers and young members of workers' families.

Militia: An enterprise unit with the primary objective of creating a paramilitary self-defense capability among workers.

Both the life-support and sociopolitical-support systems complicate the operating structures of Chinese organizations. They also extend managerial responsibilities into a far broader arena than is typical to most western organizations. The "Chinese" firm is, therefore, quite distinctive in the internal complications that result from its simultaneous systems.

Parallel Authority Structures

As shown in Figure 2, "administrative" and "party" authority co-exist within the Chinese industrial enterprise. Although reforms have sought broader roles for factory di-

FIGURE 2
Parallel internal authority structures in the traditional Chinese industrial enterprise.

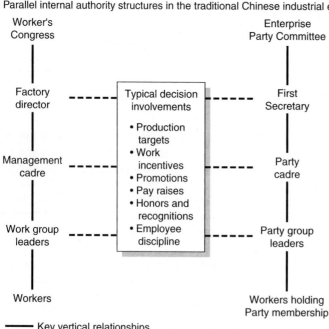

rectors and administrative cadre, enterprise party secretaries and the party cadre remain formally vested in the organization structure (Jiang, 1980; Tung, 1982; Zhu, 1985; Henley and Nyaw, 1986a; Petras, 1988). Through its presence in a "parallel" authority structure, the party reserves a potentially active and influential role in most enterprise decisions.

The party's authority within the enterprise has traditionally led to involvement in matters of managerial *control*—making sure that the factory director and other administrators work according to state and party plans and policies, and managerial *motivation*—stepping in to encourage people to work hard on behalf of the socialist state. At the Xian Department Store, for example, a policy to identify publicly the "Forty Worst Shop Assistants" was initiated to correct poor customer service. The store's Communist Party secretary was quoted as saying (Ignatius, 1989a: 1): "It's the only system we've found to pressure workers to do better. Those designated the 'worst' feel embarrassed. Otherwise, our efforts would have no effect." A contrite salesclerk whose name appeared on the list was quoted as lamenting: "I accept my punishment. . . . I view my little three-foot shop counter as a window of socialist civilization."

In this and many other ways, Chinese institutions thus operate in the boundaries of the parallel authority structure depicted in Figure 2. Within any individual enterprise, it is not uncommon for the party cadre to be involved in appointing the factory director and other high-level officials at one decision-making extreme, and in making employee compensation and discipline decisions at the other. Furthermore, this party involvement stands in addition to its active role in such ancillary units as the enterprise workers union and workers congress (Henley and Nyaw, 1986a)—many high-ranking trade unionists and representatives of workers congresses are themselves party members. This means that the party's influence in each firm is very highly integrated. In many cases, it is the party structure that serves as final arbiter of disputes arising within or among the many disparate internal units of the enterprise (Henley and Nyaw, 1987). In all cases, the existence of party influence through the parallel authority structures complicates management and administrative processes in Chinese industrial enterprises.

PERSPECTIVES ON THE EMERGENCE OF
MANAGERIAL LEADERSHIP

China's management reform program since 1979 has pressured enterprise administrators to think strategically, to be business oriented rather than production oriented, to take greater risks, and to be more entrepreneurial (Ma, 1980; Kasper, 1982; Byrd and Tydrick, 1984). Yet, when viewed from the structural perspective just presented, it is clear that the emergence of new "managerial leadership" in Chinese firms is constrained by forces of contemporary history.

At a most fundamental level, the traditional management functions have each been to some extent accomplished in the past by persons or groups other than a firm's administrative officials. *Planning* was largely done according to the mandates of state plans and by local government and ministerial interpretations of these plans into enterprise objectives. *Organizing* was minimized, since the complex internal organization of simultaneous systems and parallel authority structures permeated and restricted the very essence of Chinese industrial enterprise. *Leading* was constrained by a lack of managerial authority singularly to direct worker performance as the party cadre often assumed dominant roles in "encouraging" and "disciplining" workers in job performance. *Controlling* was largely an issue of ensuring conformity with the targets and budgets established by state-mandated plans, and was accomplished with the direct involvement of the party cadre on all matters of operating consequence.

Such historical legacies can make it difficult for true managerial leadership to emerge within a firm. Subtle suggestions of this conclusion are found in Burton's (1987) observation that the current reforms are designed to protect the status quo of the Chinese Communist Party. The forces of stability, even in times of change, therefore, run deep in this setting. They are found in an entrenched state bureaucracy whose officials have tendencies toward retaining central control (Henley and Nyaw, 1986b; Boisot and Child, 1988). They also exist in the failures of some, perhaps most, factory directors to assume the authority commensurate with the responsibility made available to them under the reforms (Petras, 1988; Boisot and Child, 1988).

This inherently conservative side of Chinese enterprises must be better understood—both to broaden the understandings of "outsiders" who seek to better understand these enterprises and even conduct business with them, and to help "insiders" establish an agenda for the development of enterprise managerial leadership that is more realistic, given the prevailing conditions in China. Two organizational phenomena of specific relevance here are the "substitutes for leadership" and "learned helplessness" effects.

Substitutes for Leadership

Kerr and Jermier (1978) originally identified *substitutes for leadership* as the situation where organizational, individual, and/or task variables substitute for direct managerial leadership in work situations. They point out, for example, the formalization (of rules, roles, plans, and goals), inflexibility (rigidity in operating protocols and in applying rules and procedures), and well-developed staff functions (serving in advisory and directive roles) can all provide task direction for individual workers as a substitute for direct leader initiatives. In leadership theory, this concept is important because it offers a way for managers to avoid "redundant" leadership behaviors—that is, attempting to do something already provided for in the situation. Instead, it encourages them to provide "complementary" leadership behaviors that fill needs otherwise unmet by situational and individual variables. For the short run at least, past legacies may make this difficult to accomplish in Chinese enterprises.

Observation: The contemporary history of Chinese organizations includes many substitutes for leadership whose legacies continue to make it difficult to satisfy reform expectations for the development of more personal managerial leadership among members of the administrative cadre.

Because substitutes for leadership have operated in the past—based on the external state bureaucracy, the enterprise party structure, and the historical lack of managerial authority—many of China's present administrative cadre may have a "trained incapacity" for personal managerial leadership. Because such leadership substitutes continue to exist, it can and should be expected that Chinese institutions are by their very natures still "training" many of the cadre to be "incapable" of personal managerial leadership in the future. Chinese socialist traditions, for example, include an important place for "emulation campaigns" designed to increase workforce motivation. Whereas the administrative cadre are involved in these campaigns, "leadership" of them has largely rested with enterprise party officials serving the important party role of raising political consciousness and commitment among workers (Henley and Nyaw, 1987).

If and where the party proves willing to extricate itself from providing "substitutes" for managerial leadership, one has to inquire whether or not members of the administrative cadre have the expertise and/or willingness to fill the void. *If* and where the party is *un*willing to extricate itself from such leadership, one has to wonder what implications this holds for the ultimate assumption of complementary leadership roles by the administrative cadre. Past leadership substitutes in Chinese firms have the potential to constrain managerial development in the present and future, even under the most progressive of conditions.

Learned Helplessness

"Alienation," "aimlessness," and "powerlessness" can develop among people who feel a lack of control over events shaping their lives. Social psychologists recognize that such feelings can arise in the workplace from a condition called *learned helplessness.* This is the tendency of persons who have been subject to tight controls, punishment for any misbehaviors, and repeated failures, to lose confidence that they have the skills required to succeed in their jobs (Martinko and Gardner, 1982, 1987). Learned helplessness occurs when a person learns from an experience of past inadequacies to feel incapable of future success.

Too many "signals" in the current Chinese economic and political environment foster learned helplessness and discourage personal leadership development among members of China's administrative cadre. In particular, the external state and party supervising external control over internal enterprise affairs has historically discouraged leadership initiatives by the administrative structure. Factory director Wu Changhai, for example, helped "turn around" the ailing Xian Food Machinery Factory (Clark, 1988). But he got into trouble with his superiors in the state bureaucracy after refusing their demands for what he considered an excessive share of his factory's new profits. They, in turn, harassed him by sending in state inspection teams and encouraging workers to denounce him. Wu was taken off his job for more than a year. Instead of a "success" experience based on his managerial leadership initiatives, Wu experienced a "failure." For Wu and others like him, who now have the added experience of the 1989 Tiananmen events to consider, future reticence to display personal leadership initiatives is even more likely.

The organizational structures and policies, evaluation and reward systems, and goals typical to Chinese enterprises further establish learned helplessness conditions. In China, bureaucratic *structures and policies* in the past have led to tight external state controls and ever-present internal supervision by the party cadre. Organizational *evaluation and reward systems* in the past have not discriminated among workers on a true performance basis, and were often tied to issues of good "citizenship" behavior as interpreted by the party cadre. Enterprise *goals* in the past have been set by state plans and supervised through the external state bureaucracy and internal party cadre. Learned helplessness in these and other aspects of management can create frustration and passivity within the administrative cadre, even to the point where managers are unable to respond to new expectations and opportunities made available to them.

Observation: The contemporary history of Chinese organizations displays a tendency toward learned helplessness among members of the administrative cadre. This, in turn, makes it difficult for them to satisfy reform expectations for the expression of more personal managerial leadership.

Unfortunately, learned helplessness effects will most likely prove insidious and longlasting as they continue to "trickle down" throughout the management levels of any Chinese enterprise. Someone who is expected *not* to exercise initiative at one level of managerial responsibility is *not* likely to encourage it on the part of lower-level personnel, or to view it with much favor if so exercised by them. As a result of this self-reinforcing cycle of learned helplessness in the administrative ranks, Chinese firms can be expected to struggle for some time to come with performance limitations founded more on a lack of managerial leadership than on actual industrial potential.

IMPLICATIONS FOR RESEARCH AND LEADERSHIP DEVELOPMENT

In order to better understand what is taking place within the Chinese industrial enterprises of today, one has to be aware of the historical and complex structural foundations from which Chinese firms are incrementally evolving. Substitutes for leadership and learned helplessness, both influenced by the role of the Chinese Communist Party in internal enterprise affairs, exemplify lingering constraints on the development of more truly personal managerial leadership by members of the administrative cadre.

Research Implications

Management theorists should be cautious when framing their research questions and conceptualizations on Chinese organization and management practices. They should view the present aspects of Chinese industrial enterprises in the context of the past, and they should avoid premature conclusions based more on the allure of future possibilities than on current realities. A research agenda sensitive to such issues might address questions such as these.

1 *What is the current role of the Chinese Communist Party as part of the parallel authority structure of enterprise decision making?* In various industries and in organizations of various types, how is authority distributed between party and administrative cadre for managerial decisions? In what ways and under what conditions is the party role changing in respect to these decisions? In what ways is it remaining stable? What are the implications of the party's enterprise presence for organizational design and managerial leadership in the future?

2 *Is there a difference between the managerial "leadership" required to achieve organizational effectiveness in each of the multiple and simultaneous systems of the Chinese industrial enterprise?* If the typical Chinese factory director assumes a broader role than his or her Western counterparts, one that is more of the "mayoral" role described by Schermerhorn (1987), can the director provide effective leadership to both ancillary and business systems of the enterprise? Or, does the Chinese firm operate with a group form of "executive office" responsible for ancillary as well as core business and commercial systems? If so, what are the consequences of this office and its political aspects to enterprise management and performance?

3 *Which structures within Chinese industrial enterprises provide appropriate and inappropriate "substitutes for leadership"?* What is known about past and present substitutes for leadership in Chinese organizations? What, if anything, can be done to maximize their advantages and minimize their disadvantages in the future? How is leadership responsibility in Chinese firms vested in people as opposed to structures, and to what extent is this investiture capable of changing in the present sociopolitical context of the economic reform environment?

4 *What practices and conditions within Chinese industrial enterprises are still fostering the development of "learned helplessness" among the administrative cadre?* How have the complex structures of the past and the traditional role of the party contributed to the emergence of learned helplessness? How pervasive is learned helplessness, and is there any "pattern" to its occurrence? What, if anything, can be done to overcome learned helplessness and establish true managerial leadership and confidence among China's administrative cadre?

Leadership Development Implications

To the extent that historical constraints on the development of managerial leadership are recognized in China, appropriate leadership development initiatives can and should be pursued. At the policy level, of course, the implications for change are complex and fundamental, especially in respect to the country's present political environment. Extreme limits on managerial leadership development seem indigenous to the prevailing system, especially now that the 1989 Tiananmen events have reconfirmed the strength of political influences over day-to-day affairs in all aspects of Chinese life. Yet at the level of enterprise operations, particularly in individual firms where special attention is given to improved management, modest initiatives of a leadership development nature may be possible.

Four training strategies identified by Martinko and Gardner (1982) for dealing more generally with learned helplessness may offer some potential short-run and local benefits. These strategies are:

1 *Immunization training:* Recognize that new entrants to the administrative cadre are likely to find that past legacies within the firm constrain leadership initiatives. Prepare them through training to expect these difficulties and to understand their personal reactions. Provide them with first-job managerial assignments that assure reasonable amounts of early success. This will help build their confidence for later dealings with more formidable leadership constraints at higher levels of managerial responsibility.

2 *Discrimination training:* Recognize that existing members of the administrative cadre will have special difficulty adapting to any changing expectations associated with management reforms. Increase their self-confidence by training them to better understand differences between past and present situations in the firm. Train and coun-sel them to understand how the future is expected to be even more different from the past and present, and to recognize the personal skills required to achieve managerial success in the future.

3 *Attributional training:* Recognize that the administrative cadre, already experi-encing a sense of learned helplessness, is likely to view past leadership failures and difficulties as being caused by external forces beyond its control. Train them to better understand their individual strengths and weaknesses as managers, and to recognize personal avenues for change and development. Train them to better understand new opportunities, even very small ones, that exist within the firm, and which allow them to further develop their leadership abilities.

4 *Modeling training:* Recognize that members of the administrative cadre can benefit from "role models" who demonstrate the desired managerial leadership and of-fer day-to-day reinforcement for the leadership development efforts of others. Train "high-potential" managers to become more confident and capable leaders by assigning them to work with and for others in the firm who already display the desired leader-ship qualities. Make sure such role models are available at all levels of managerial re-sponsibility in the firm.

CONCLUSION

Given the continuing novelty to the Western eye of reforms in the Chinese economic and political scenes, it has been tempting to interpret developments in enterprise man-agement from a narrow perspective dominated by prospects for change. Yet there can be little doubt that the managerial leadership in state-owned Chinese industrial enter-prises is limited by complex historical legacies of a structural and political nature. And while there certainly is some manifestation of personal managerial leadership among the administrative cadre in today's enterprises, it is unlikely that dramatic improve-ments in this important dimension of organizational life will occur either quickly or smoothly. China's past, simply put, holds too great a grasp on its present and future af-fairs—something demonstrated all too well in the 1989 Tiananmen massacre and party crack-down on the student-led "democracy movement." Management researchers and observers, accordingly, should give all due attention to the constraining legacies of tra-ditional organizational practices and the role of the Communist Party on the emer-gence of managerial leadership in Chinese industrial enterprises.

POSTSCRIPT

It is now July 1990. For all practical purposes, China's management and organiza-tional reforms are still severely constrained in the aftermath of the June 4, 1989, Tiananmen disaster. The party is asserting control over the country's institutions, and most enterprises seem to be taking "two steps back" on their difficult path to true in-dustrial progress. Once again, it seems, enterprise managers must live with the "down-side" of yet another of China's "speed-up and slow-down" cycles.

The difficulties of developing managerial leadership under such conditions are even more evident today than when our article was first drafted. After the turmoil and trauma of the past year, one has to wonder how members of the administrative cadre can sustain commitments to management and leadership development when their roles in enterprise affairs are subject to such externally-induced change and uncertainty.

By the time this postscript is read, some major transformation may have occurred to unlock the full productive potential of China's industries. It is more likely that social, political, and economic conditions will continue to limit both industrial development and the emergence of true managerial leadership in Chinese enterprises. As long as this continues to be the case, a great national resource—the managers of China's organizations—will remain largely underutilized.

REFERENCES

Bachman, D. (1988) "Politics and Political Reform in China." *Current History,* 87, pp. 249–256.

Boisot, M., and Child, J. (1988) "The Iron Law of Fiefs: Bureaucratic Failure and the Problem of Governance in the Chinese Economic Reforms." *Administrative Science Quarterly,* 33, pp. 507–527.

Burton, C. (1987) "China's Post-Mao Transition: The Role of the Party and Ideology in the 'New Period.' " *Pacific Affairs,* 60, pp. 431–446.

Byrd, W., and Tidrick, G. (1984) *Recent Chinese Economic Reforms: Studies of Two Industrial Enterprises.* Washington: The World Bank.

Clark, L. H., Jr. (1988) "China Must Avoid the 'Marble-boat' Syndrome." *The Wall Street Journal,* June 9, p. 28.

Cyert, R. M., and March, J. G. (1963) *A Behavioral Theory of the Firm.* Englewood Cliffs, NJ: Prentice Hall.

Frankenstein, J. (1986) "Trends in Chinese Business Practice: Changes in the Beijing Wind." *California Management Review,* 39, pp. 148–160.

Henley, J. S., and Nyaw, M. K. (1986a) "Introducing Market Forces into Managerial Decision-making in Chinese Industrial Enterprises." *Journal of Management Studies,* 23, pp. 635–656.

_____. (1986b) "Reforming Chinese Industrial Management." *Euro-Asia Business Review,* 5, pp. 10–15.

_____. (1987) "The Development of Work Incentives in Chinese Industrial Enterprises— Material versus Non-Material Incentives." Chapter 9 in M. Warner (ed.), *Management Reforms in China.* London: Frances Pinter Publishers.

Ignatius, A. (1989a) "Now if Ms. Wong Insults a Customer, She Gets an Award." *The Wall Street Journal,* January 24, p. 1.

_____. (1989b) "In this Factory Town, China's Welfare State Is Still Alive and Well." *The Wall Street Journal,* October 17, 1989, 1, p. 23.

Jiang, Y. (1980) "On the Leadership System of Socialist Enterprises." *Hongqi* [Red Flag], 21, pp. 9–13. (in Chinese)

Kasper, W. (1982) "Note on Sichuan Experiment." *The Australia Journal of Chinese Affairs,* 7, pp. 163–172.

Kerr, S., and Jermier, J. (1978) "Substitutes for Leadership: Their Meaning and Measurement." *Organizational Behavior and Human Performance,* 22, pp. 375–403.

Lai, G. T., and Lam, C. Y. (1985) "A Study on Work-Related Values of Managers in the People's Republic of China (Part II)." *Hong Kong Manager,* 22, 23–59.

Leung, J. (1989) "Socialism Burdens a Chinese Car Venture." *The Wall Street Journal,* April 13, A14.

Ma, H. (1980) "On the Reform of Industrial Enterprise Leadership System." *Jinqji Quanli* [Economic Management], 12, pp. 14–22. (in Chinese)

Martinko, M. J., and Gardner, W. L. (1982) "Learned Helplessness: An Alternative Explanation for Performance Deficits." *Academy of Management Review,* 7, pp. 195–204.

_____. (1987) "The Leader/Member Attribution Process." *Academy of Management Review,* 12, pp. 235–249.

Petras, J. (1988) "Contradictions of Market Socialism in China (Part I)." *Journal of Contemporary Asia,* 18, pp. 3–23.

Redding, S. G., and Wong, G. Y. Y. (1986) "The Psychology of Chinese Organizational Behavior." Chapter 7 in M. Bond (ed.), *The Psychology of the Chinese People.* Hong Kong: Oxford University Press.

Schermerhorn, J. R., Jr. (1987) "Organizational Features of Chinese Industrial Enterprise: Paradoxes of Stability in Times of Change." *Academy of Management Executive,* 1, pp. 345–349.

Shenkar, O., and Ronen, S. (1987) "Structure and Importance of Work Goals Among Managers in the People's Republic of China." *Academy of Management Journal,* 30, pp. 564–575.

Tung, R. (1982) *Chinese Industrial Society Post Mao.* New York: Lexington Books.

Warner, M. (1985) "Training China's Managers." *Journal of General Management,* 11, pp. 12–26.

_____. (1987) *Management Reforms in China.* London: Frances Pinter Publishers.

Zhu, Y. (ed.) (1985) *Contemporary China Economic Management.* Beijing: China Shehui Kexue Chubanshe. (in Chinese)

CHAPTER 6: Questions for Discussion

1 If you were transferred into a multinational corporation in Japan and you wanted to apply the need theories and equity theories in managing your Japanese employees, what considerations would you have to take into account in this new environment?

2 Do you think that the differences in organizational commitment and job satisfaction between Japanese and American employees are due more to cultural factors or national factors—or some other set of factors?

3 Discuss the implications of a socialist economy and political system (such as China) for equity theory and for goal-setting theory.

4 International operations require an understanding of the culture, economy, and political system of the host country. List several specific cultural and national factors which you think play an important role in the motivation and leadership of employees in different countries.

5 The tax system in many Western European countries (e.g., Holland and Germany) significantly limits many of the financial incentives that American companies often rely on to motivate their employees. In view of this constraint, how would you attempt to motivate Dutch or German workers if you couldn't use money?

6 How would you manage a group of culturally diverse employees (e.g., 50 percent Americans and 50 percent Russians)? What problems might you encounter? What positive outcomes might occur in such a culturally diverse group?

7 What do you think the differences would be between managing Chinese employees in the United States and managing them in their native country?

8 While there are obviously significant differences among people either within or between cultures, think for a moment about what you consider to be "typical" company presidents in Japan, Germany, and the United States In general, would you expect these presidents to exhibit basically the same personal characteristics? If so, what would these characteristics be? If not, what differences might you expect to find on a very general level?

PART THREE

THREE

APPLICATIONS OF MOTIVATION AND LEADERSHIP CONCEPTS

REWARD SYSTEMS IN ORGANIZATIONS

One of the central issues—if not *the* central issue—in considering motivation in work situations concerns the reward systems used in and by organizations. Applying the concept of reward in its broadest sense as something given in return for good received, we can see that reward systems in organizations involve exchange relationships. Organizations or those individuals functioning in their behalf (e.g., managers and supervisors) provide rewards to employees in exchange for "good received," that is, membership, attendance, and performance. The ways in which rewards are distributed within organizations and their relative amounts have considerable impact on the levels of employee motivation. Despite the obvious importance of reward systems to both employers and employees, experience has shown that they are neither simple nor easy to design and implement in ways that both parties will view as mutually beneficial and satisfactory.

TYPES OF REWARDS

There is a wide array of types of rewards that can be obtained in organizational settings, ranging from obvious ones such as pay, fringe benefits, and promotion, to praise, autonomy in decision making, and feelings of accomplishment and competency. These different types of rewards, however, can be classified along two major dimensions: intrinsic/extrinsic and systemwide/individual.

Intrinsic rewards are those that the individual provides himself or herself (e.g., feelings of accomplishment) as a result of performing some task. Extrinsic rewards, on the other hand, are those that are provided *to* the individual by someone else. Much of the conceptual work on intrinsic motivation is incorporated in the work of Deci (1975) and his *cognitive evaluation theory*. Briefly, this theory argues that an individual's level of effort on a task is determined largely by the nature of the rewards available for task accomplishment. Two processes by which rewards influence intrinsic motivation can be identified.

First, there is the notion of *locus of causality*. When behavior is intrinsically motivated, an individual's perceived locus of causality is thought to be internal; that is, individuals feel that task accomplishment is under their own control. Under such circumstances, they will engage in activities for *intrinsic* rewards. On the other hand, when individuals receive *extrinsic* rewards for task behavior, they will perceive their locus of causality to be external and will engage in those activities only when they believe that extrinsic rewards will be forthcoming (Deci, 1972, 1975; Deci & Ryan, 1985). The important point here is that, according to Deci, providing extrinsic rewards for an intrinsically satisfying task leads to a shift from internal to external locus of causality. As Deci (1972) states:

> Interpreting these results in relation to theories of work motivation, it seems clear that the effects of intrinsic motivation and extrinsic motivation are not additive. When extrinsic rewards such as money can certainly motivate behavior, they appear to be doing so at the expense of intrinsic motivation; as a result, contingent pay systems do not appear to be compatible with participative management systems. (pp. 224–225)

The empirical evidence that has been obtained with regard to the hypothesis that providing extrinsic rewards reduces the impact of intrinsic rewards is, however, decidedly mixed (Guzzo, 1979). This appears to be especially so the closer that situations approximate typical work settings.

Second, rewards can also influence intrinsic motivation through changes in feelings of *competence* and *self-determination*. Rewards or outcomes that reassure people they are competent or self-determining tend to increase their intrinsic motivation to perform. However, rewards or outcomes that convince people they are not competent or self-determining tend to decrease intrinsic motivation.

Several of the articles in this chapter will focus primarily on extrinsic rewards, those provided by the organization or some designated official (e.g., supervisor) *to* the individual. In considering extrinsic versus intrinsic rewards, however, the reader should be aware that in the literature on motivation at work these terms sometimes take on other meanings. Guzzo (1979) has made the excellent point that any particular reward has multiple attributes (self-generated or not, immediate or delayed, of long or short duration, etc.). Thus, it is important to keep in mind that there are many variations of types of rewards within the two broad categories of extrinsic and intrinsic. As just one example among many that could be provided, consider that while a simple pat on the back from a supervisor and a promotion to a higher-status job with a significant increase in pay are both extrinsic rewards, their effects on the individual's performance may be quite different.

The other major dimension that can be used to classify types of rewards in organizational settings is the distinction emphasized by Katz (1964): systemwide rewards versus individual rewards. The distinction is this: systemwide rewards are those that are provided by the organization to everyone in a broad category of employees. Examples would be certain fringe benefits (e.g., medical insurance) that everyone in the

	Systemwide	Individual
Extrinsic	Example: Insurance benefits	Example: Large merit increase
Intrinsic	Example: Pride in being part of a "winning" organization	Example: Feeling of self-fulfillment

EXHIBIT 7-1
Types of rewards.

organization receives simply by being an employee, or the dining room facilities provided to all managers above a certain level. Individual rewards, on the other hand, are provided to particular individuals but not to all individuals in a category. Examples would be bonuses and merit increases.

If we combine the two dimensions, intrinsic/extrinsic and systemwide/individual, we have a convenient way of categorizing any particular type of reward, as shown in Exhibit 7-1. It is useful to keep this classification system in mind when considering the intended functions of reward systems that are discussed in the next section. A particular type of reward will often be very effective for one function, but very ineffective for another function.

FUNCTIONS OF REWARD SYSTEMS

Organizations provide rewards for many reasons. These are summarized in Exhibit 7-2 (utilizing categorization schemes suggested by March & Simon, 1958, and Katz, 1964). As can be seen, rewards in and from organizations can potentially motivate two broad categories of behavior: participation in the organization and performance in the organization. The first of these categories, participation, can in turn be divided into

EXHIBIT 7-2
Functions of rewards systems.

A Participation
  1 Membership
    a Joining
    b Remaining
  2 Attendance (i.e., avoidance of absenteeism)
B Performance
  1 "Normal" role (job) performance
  2 "Extra-role behavior" (e.g., innovation, high commitment)

membership and attendance. "Membership" refers to the act of joining the organization as well as the decision to remain with it, and organizations clearly need to be concerned with both aspects. Thus, they devote considerable effort to designing reward systems which will induce individuals to become members of the organization in the first place and which also will instill a strong desire to stay with it once having become a part of it. It should be clear, though, that although the *design* of a reward system affects decisions to join and subsequently remain (or leave), *implementation* of a reward system also affects how long a person will stay with a particular organization. From the organization's perspective, excessive turnover can be a major problem, and thus well-designed reward systems may not be effective because of faulty implementation in practice. The other participation category involves attendance or, in other words, the avoidance of absenteeism. Although absenteeism may not be as severe a problem for many organizations as the difficulties of attracting people to join the organization or the problem of excessive turnover, it is nevertheless a type of behavior that most organizations want to reduce. Therefore, one of the objectives in the design of reward systems is to motivate high levels of attendance.

The other major category of behavior that reward systems are designed to facilitate is that of job performance (or the "decision to produce" in March & Simon's terminology). Here, again, there are two distinct subcategories: "normal" or expected role (job) performance, and what is called "extra-role behavior." The former refers to performance that meets the expected standards that the organization has designated for someone in a particular job. When this standard is met, the organization would consider that the employee's part of the psychological contract has been fulfilled. The employee has, in effect, exchanged adequate job performance for an agreed-upon level of compensation. Typically, to obtain an expected level of job performance the organization devotes considerable attention to the design and implementation of monetary compensation systems. The assumption is that if a pay system is set up in a way that appears fair and equitable in the amount and distribution of compensation, then most individuals in the organization can be depended upon to perform at least adequately if not outstandingly.

Extra-role behavior, on the other hand, goes "above and beyond" what is normally expected (by the organization) in the psychological contract. It is behavior that is spontaneous and innovative (Katz, 1964). Many examples could be offered, of course, such as the clerk who goes out of the way to placate a dissatisfied customer, or the manager who voluntarily stays overtime to solve some particular production problem. The essential point is that most organizations probably would not function very well if the only type of role behavior they received from all employees was routine minimally acceptable job performance. Hence, organizations need to find ways to motivate extra-role behavior from at least some of their employees (and particularly in certain types of circumstances—such as crises—that face organizations at particular times). The problem, from the organization's point of view, is that rewards which may be effective in generating normal job performance (such as certain systemwide rewards) may not be very useful in motivating extra-role behavior. Thus, to the extent that such extraordinary behavior is needed, the organization is presented with a considerable challenge in the design and application of reward systems, particularly as they involve individual extrinsic or intrinsic rewards.

IMPLEMENTATION AND ALLOCATION ISSUES

As noted several times already, the best-designed reward systems can often go awry in producing their intended results because of the manner in which they are implemented. Several of the articles in this chapter deal directly with reward allocation and implementation problems. As one reviews the detailed discussions in these articles, it is useful to keep in mind several of the broad issues involved.

One important issue in implementing reward systems, and perhaps the most basic issue of all, concerns the evaluation or appraisal of performance. If rewards are to be distributed in such a way that they have a positive impact on an individual's motivation to participate and to perform, it is crucial that the organization have effective means for assessing the quality and quantity of performance. If the appraisal systems that organizations use are unreliable or lack reasonable validity, it can hardly be expected that rewards distributed on the basis of such systems can have much effect in the desired direction.

A second issue involves the questions of how and whether rewards are in fact related to performance. While it might seem obvious, at first glance, that rewards should be distributed directly in relation to differences in performance, there are many reasons organizations do not do so. One reason was discussed above, the problem of accurately appraising performance. Another reason is the possibility that rewarding the particular type of performance will focus attention away from other desirable aspects of performance. In addition, rewarding certain individuals or groups for high performance may have a negative effect on other individuals or groups. Also, many organizations believe they are relating rewards directly to performance when, in fact, the relationship is not seen or believed by those receiving the rewards. This, of course, reduces the motivational impact of the reward system. The message here is threefold: first, it is not an easy matter to set up reward systems that relate rewards closely to performance; second, it may not always be desirable to do so, from the organization's perspective; and, third, even when organizations are both willing and able to tie rewards closely to particular types of employee job behavior, the link may not be perceived as close by the recipients of the rewards.

Another issue in reward systems implementation is the question of how well the systems in a particular organization relate to the management style that characterizes that organization (Porter, Lawler, & Hackman, 1975). Organization theorists often distinguish between two broad categories of management style, an open/participative style versus a more traditional/authoritarian style. (Of course, many organizations, if not most, represent a blend of these two styles.) To the extent that a particular firm or agency is managed in accordance with one or the other of these styles, the more likely it is that a reward system will be ineffective if it is implemented in a way that is inconsistent with the particular management style. For example, a participative appraisal system coupled with a highly participative approach in the decisions regarding reward distribution is not likely to work well in an organization that is otherwise run in a very hierarchical, authoritarian manner. Likewise, attempting to have a rigid reward system based only on highly quantified and objective measures of performance is unlikely to have positive effects in an organization that prides itself on its open and participative way of operating.

A final implementation issue revolves around the question of whether there should be relative openness or secrecy regarding various aspects of monetary compensation. This issue is particularly acute in the management parts of organizations, where typically there are fairly wide variations in pay for individuals at roughly the same level of the organization. Organizations vary considerably in how "open" the information provided is. Some provide extensive information about how rates of pay are determined but not very much information, if any, about the amount. Other organizations provide relatively little information about either. A minority of organizations (mostly in the public sector) provide open information both about methods of determining pay and about amounts. The issue, then, for most organizations (particularly in the private sector) is not so much whether to be open or secret, but rather the degree of openness.

OVERVIEW OF THE READINGS

The fact that rewards that are intended to affect one type of behavior can end up actually encouraging another (undesired) type is highlighted in the opening reading by Kerr. In this widely cited article, the author illustrates his points with examples from both work organizations and society and concludes with suggestions about how organizations and managers may increase the likelihood that rewards will produce their hoped-for effects.

The next two articles provide major cautionary signs about the casual or insufficiently considered use of rewards in organizational settings. The first of these is a provocative, but highly controversial, article published in the *Harvard Business Review* by Kohn. He argues forcefully for the view that "the failure of any given incentive [i.e., reward] program is due less to a glitch in that program than to the inadequacy of the psychological assumptions that ground all such plans." His central points are that: (1) "rewards succeed at securing one thing only: temporary compliance"; (2) rewards do not act as a motivator; and (3) rewards can potentially cause serious problems such as damaging cooperative relationships among employees and discouraging risk-taking. His basic thesis is that rewards are like bribes and "bribes in the workplace simply don't work."

The Kohn article generated considerable response from readers, both from the world of academia and from the world of practice. Although these responses (published in a subsequent issue of the *Review*) raised a variety of points, the most consistent issues were: (1) rewards can serve as a form of recognition, and not simply as a financial incentive; (2) "effectively designed" incentive systems *can* work if, for example, they are structured explicitly to encourage teamwork or to encourage innovation and creativity; (3) organizations cannot function solely on intrinsic rewards; and (4) if all (extrinsic) reward systems are to be abolished, what is the realistic alternative? Kohn's response to these counterarguments is that "organizations should pay people well and fairly, then do everything possible to help them forget about money"; organizations should also focus more on what choices employees have in what they do every day, on how greater collaboration can be encouraged, and on building more interesting and challenging content into jobs (as emphasized by Herzberg back in the 1960s) (*Harvard Business Review,* **71**(6), pp. 48–49).

The other article somewhat in the same vein is by Pearce. She looks specifically at the issue of merit pay and considers why such rewards often fail to achieve their intended objectives. In particular, the role of organizational uncertainty and complexity are mentioned as reasons for some of the failures of incentive compensation systems.

The final two articles in this chapter provide perspectives about how effective reward systems in organizations can, in fact, be designed and implemented. Lawler argues for the necessity of taking a strategic approach to compensation and rewards, tying rewards to the achievement of corporate strategic objectives. He makes the important point that organization design and management policies must be compatible with, and supportive of, a reward system if it is to be effective. Mejia and his colleagues, in the last article in this chapter, focus on the kinds of rewards and reward systems that are most appropriate for technical employees in such areas of companies as research and development (R&D). The authors contend that many conventional compensation systems will simply not motivate these types of employees and that a much more flexible and non-hierarchically based approach is needed. Accordingly, they provide a number of suggestions for the types of reward programs that may be effective for employees with technical and scientific backgrounds.

REFERENCES

Deci, E. L. The effects of contingent and non-contingent rewards and controls on intrinsic motivation. *Organizational Behavior and Human Performance,* 1972, 8, 217–229.

Deci, E. L. *Intrinsic motivation.* New York: Plenum, 1975.

Guzzo, R. A. Types of rewards, cognitions, and work motivation. *Academy of Management Review,* 1979, 4, 75–86.

Katz, D. The motivational basis of organizational behavior. *Behavioral Science,* 1964, 9, 131–146.

March, J. G., & Simon, H. A. *Organizations.* New York: Wiley, 1958.

Porter, L. W., Lawler, E. E., III, & Hackman, J. R. *Behavior in organizations.* New York: McGraw-Hill, 1975.

On the Folly of Rewarding A, While Hoping for B[1]

Steven Kerr

Whether dealing with monkeys, rats, or human beings, it is hardly controversial to state that most organisms seek information concerning what activities are rewarded, and then seek to do (or at least pretend to do) those things, often to the virtual exclusion of activities not rewarded. The extent to which this occurs of course will depend on the perceived attractiveness of the rewards offered, but neither operant nor expectancy theorists would quarrel with the essence of this notion.

Nevertheless, numerous examples exist of reward systems that are fouled up in that the types of behavior rewarded are those which the rewarder is trying to discourage, while the behavior desired is not being rewarded at all.

FOULED UP SYSTEMS

In Politics

Official goals are "purposely vague and general and do not indicate . . . the host of decisions that must be made among alternative ways of achieving official goals and the priority of multiple goals . . ."[2] They usually may be relied on to offend absolutely no one, and in this sense can be considered high acceptance, low quality goals. An example might be "All Americans are entitled to health care." Operative goals are higher in quality but lower in acceptance, since they specify where the money will come from, and what alternative goals will be ignored.

The American citizenry supposedly wants its candidates for public office to set forth operative goals, making their proposed programs clear, and specifying sources and uses of funds. However, since operative goals are lower in acceptance, and since aspirants to public office need acceptance (from at least 50.1 percent of the people), most politicians prefer to speak only of official goals, at least until after the election. They of course would agree to speak at the operative level if "punished" for not doing so. The electorate could do this by refusing to support candidates who do not speak at the operative level. Instead, however, the American voter typically punishes (withholds support from) candidates who frankly discuss where the money will come from, rewards politicians who speak only of official goals, but hopes that candidates (despite the reward system) will discuss the issues operatively.

In War

If some oversimplification may be permitted, let it be assumed that the primary goal of the organization (Pentagon, Luftwaffe, or whatever) is to win. Let it be assumed further that the primary goal of most individuals on the front lines is to get home alive.

From *Academy of Management Executive*, 1995, 9(1), 7–14. Reprinted by permission.

Then there appears to be an important conflict in goals—personally rational behavior by those at the bottom will endanger goal attainment by those at the top.

But not necessarily! It depends on how the reward system is set up. The Vietnam war was indeed a study of disobedience and rebellion, with terms such as "fragging" (killing one's own commanding officer) and "search and evade" becoming part of the military vocabulary. The difference in subordinates' acceptance of authority between World War II and Vietnam is reported to be considerable, and veterans of the Second World War were often quoted as being outraged at the mutinous actions of many American soldiers in Vietnam.

Consider, however, some critical differences in the reward system in use during the two conflicts. What did the GI in World War II want? To go home. And when did he get to go home? When the war was won! If he disobeyed the orders to clean out the trenches and take the hills, the war would not be won and he would not go home. Furthermore, what were his chances of attaining his goal (getting home alive) if he obeyed the orders compared to his chances if he did not? What is being suggested is that the rational soldier in World War II, whether patriotic or not, probably found it expedient to obey.

Consider the reward system in use in Vietnam. What did the soldier at the bottom want? To go home. And when did he get to go home? When his tour of duty was over! This was the case whether or not the war was won. Furthermore, concerning the relative chance of getting home alive by obeying orders compared to the chance if they were disobeyed, it is worth noting that a mutineer in Vietnam was far more likely to be assigned rest and rehabilitation (on the assumption that fatigue was the cause) than he was to suffer any negative consequence.

In his description of the "zone of indifference," Barnard stated that "a person can and will accept a communication as authoritative only when . . . at the time of his decision, he believes it to be compatible with his personal interests as a whole."[3] In light of the reward system used in Vietnam, wouldn't it have been personally irrational for some orders to have been obeyed? Was not the military implementing a system which rewarded disobedience, while hoping that soldiers (despite the reward system) would obey orders?

In Medicine

Theoretically, physicians can make either of two types of error, and intuitively one seems as bad as the other. Doctors can pronounce patients sick when they are actually well (a type 1 error), thus causing them needless anxiety and expense, curtailment of enjoyable foods and activities, and even physical danger by subjecting them to needless medication and surgery. Alternately, a doctor can label a sick person well (a type 2 error), and thus avoid treating what may be a serious, even fatal ailment. It might be natural to conclude that physicians seek to minimize both types of error.

Such a conclusion would be wrong. It has been estimated that numerous Americans have been afflicted with iatrogenic (physician *caused*) illnesses.[4] This occurs when the doctor is approached by someone complaining of a few stray symptoms. The doctor classifies and organizes these symptoms, gives them a name, and obligingly tells the patient what further symptoms may be expected. This information often acts as a self-fulfilling prophecy, with the result that from that day on the patient for all practical purposes is sick.

Why does this happen? Why are physicians so reluctant to sustain a type 2 error (pronouncing a sick person well) that they will tolerate many type 1 errors? Again, a look at the reward system is needed. The punishments for a type 2 error are real: guilt, embarrassment, and the threat of a malpractice suit. On the other hand, a type 1 error (labeling a well person sick) is a much safer and conservative approach to medicine in today's litigious society. Type 1 errors also are likely to generate increased income and a stream of steady customers who, being well in a limited physiological sense, will not embarrass the doctor by dying abruptly. Fellow physicians and the general public therefore are really *rewarding* type 1 errors while *hoping* fervently that doctors will try not to make them.

A current example of rewarding type 1 errors is provided by Broward County, Florida, where an elderly or disabled person facing a competency hearing is evaluated by three court-appointed experts who get paid much more *for the same examination* if the person is ruled to be incompetent. For example, psychiatrists are paid $325 if they judge someone to be incapacitated, but earn only $125 if the person is judged competent. Court-appointed attorneys in Broward also earn more—$325 as opposed to $175—if their clients lose than if they win. Are you surprised to learn that, of 598 incapacity proceedings initiated and completed in the county in 1993, 570 ended with a verdict of incapacitation?[5]

In Universities

Society hopes that professors will not neglect their teaching responsibilities but *rewards* them almost entirely for research and publications. This is most true at the large and prestigious universities. Clichés such as "good research and good teaching go together" notwithstanding, professors often find that they must choose between teaching and research-oriented activities when allocating their time. Rewards for good teaching are usually limited to outstanding teacher awards, which are given to only a small percentage of good teachers and usually bestow little money and fleeting prestige. Punishments for poor teaching are also rare.

Rewards for research and publications, on the other hand, and punishments for failure to accomplish these, are common. Furthermore, publication-oriented résumés usually will be well-received at other universities, whereas teaching credentials, harder to document and quantify, are much less transferable. Consequently it is rational for university professors to concentrate on research, even to the detriment of teaching and at the expense of their students.

By the same token, it is rational for students to act based upon the goal displacement[6] which has occurred within universities concerning what they are rewarded for. If it is assumed that a primary goal of a university is to transfer knowledge from teacher to student, then grades become identifiable as a means toward that goal, serving as motivational, control, and feedback devices to expedite the knowledge transfer. Instead, however, the grades themselves have become much more important for entrance to graduate school, successful employment, tuition refunds, and parental respect, than the knowledge or lack of knowledge they are supposed to signify.

It therefore should come as no surprise that we find fraternity files for examinations, term paper writing services, and plagiarism. Such activities constitute a personally rational response to a reward system which pays off for grades rather than knowledge. These days, reward systems—specifically, the growing threat of lawsuits—encourage teachers to award students high grades, even if they aren't earned. For example:

> When Andy Hansen brought home a report card with a disappointing C in math, his parents . . . sued his teacher. . . . After a year and six different appeals within the school district, another year's worth of court proceedings, $4000 in legal fees paid by the Hansens, and another $8500 by the district . . . the C stands. Now the student's father, auto dealer Mike Hansen, says he plans to take the case to the State Court of Appeals. . . . "We went in and tried to make a deal: They wanted a C, we wanted an A, so why not compromise on a B?" Mike Hansen said. "But they dug in their heels, and here we are."[7]

In Consulting

It is axiomatic that those who care about a firm's well-being should insist that the organization get fair value for its expenditures. Yet it is commonly known that firms seldom bother to evaluate a new TQM, employee empowerment program, or whatever, to see if the company is getting its money's worth. Why? Certainly it is not because people have not pointed out that this situation exists; numerous practitioner-oriented articles are written each year on just this point.

One major reason is that the individuals (in human resources, or organization development) who would normally be responsible for conducting such evaluations are the same ones often charged with introducing the change effort in the first place. Having convinced top management to spend money, say, on outside consultants, they usually are quite animated afterwards in collecting rigorous vignettes and anecdotes about how successful the program was. The last thing many desire is a formal, revealing evaluation. Although members of top management may actually *hope* for such systematic evaluation, their reward systems continue to *reward* ignorance in this area. And if the HR department abdicates its responsibility, who is to step into the breach? The consultants themselves? Hardly! They are likely to be too busy collecting anecdotal "evidence" of their own, for use on their next client.

In Sports

Most coaches disdain to discuss individual accomplishments, preferring to speak of teamwork, proper attitude, and one-for-all spirit. Usually, however, rewards are distributed according to individual performance. The college basketball player who passes the ball to teammates instead of shooting will not compile impressive scoring statistics and is less likely to be drafted by the pros. The ballplayer who hits to right field to advance the runners will win neither the batting nor home run titles, and will be offered smaller raises. It therefore is rational for players to think of themselves first, and the team second.

In Government

Consider the cost-plus contract or its next of kin, the allocation of next year's budget as a direct function of this year's expenditures—a clear-cut example of a fouled up reward system. It probably is conceivable that those who award such budgets and contracts really hope for economy and prudence in spending. It is obvious, however, that adopting the proverb "to those who spend shall more be given," rewards not economy, but spending itself.

In Business

The past reward practices of a group health claims division of a large eastern insurance company provides another rich illustration. Attempting to measure and reward accuracy in paying surgical claims, the firm systematically kept track of the number of returned checks and letters of complaint received from policyholders. However, underpayments were likely to provoke cries of outrage from the insured, while overpayments often were accepted in courteous silence. Since it was often impossible to tell from the physician's statement which of two surgical procedures, with different allowable benefits, was performed, and since writing for clarifications would have interfered with other standards used by the firm concerning percentage of claims paid within two days of receipt, the new hire in more than one claims section was soon acquainted with the informal norm: "When in doubt, pay it out!"

This situation was made even worse by the firm's reward system. The reward system called for annual merit increases to be given to all employees, in one of the following three amounts:

1 If the worker was "outstanding" (a select category, into which no more than two employees per section could be placed): 5 percent

2 If the worker was "above average" (normally all workers not "outstanding" were so rated): 4 percent

3 If the worker committed gross acts of negligence and irresponsibility for which he or she might be discharged in many other companies: 3 percent.

Now, since the difference between the five percent theoretically attainable through hard work and the four percent attainable merely by living until the review date is small, many employees were rather indifferent to the possibility of obtaining the extra one percent reward. In addition, since the penalty for error was a loss of only one percent, employees tended to ignore the norm concerning indiscriminant payments.

However, most employees were not indifferent to a rule which stated that, should absences or latenesses total three or more in any six-month period, the entire four or five percent due at the next merit review must be forfeited. In this sense, the firm was *hoping* for performance, while *rewarding* attendance. What it got, of course, was attendance. (If the absence/lateness rule appears to the reader to be stringent, it really wasn't. The company counted "times" rather than "days" absent, and a ten-day absence therefore counted the same as one lasting two days. A worker in danger of accumulating a third absence within six months merely had to remain ill—away from work—during a second absence until the first absence was more than six months old. The limiting factor was that at some point salary ceases, and sickness benefits take over. This was usually sufficient to get the younger workers to return, but for those with 20 or more years' service, the company provided sickness benefits of 90 percent of normal salary, tax-free! Therefore. . . .).

Thanks to the U.S. government, even the reporting of wrongdoing has been corrupted by an incredibly incompetent reward system that calls for whistleblowing employees to collect up to thirty percent *of the amount of a fraud* without a stated limit. Thus prospective whistleblowers are encouraged to delay reporting a fraud, even to actively participate in its continuance, in order to run up the total and, thus, their percentage of the take.

I'm quite sure that by now the reader has thought of numerous examples in his or her own experience which qualify as "folly." However, just in case, Table 1 presents some additional examples well worth pondering.

CAUSES

Extremely diverse instances of systems which reward behavior A although the rewarder apparently hopes for behavior B have been given. These are useful to illustrate the breadth and magnitude of the phenomenon, but the diversity increases the difficulty of determining commonalities and establishing causes. However, the following four general factors may be pertinent to an explanation of why fouled-up reward systems seem to be so prevalent.

1. Fascination with an "Objective" Criterion Many managers seek to establish simple, quantifiable standards against which to measure and reward performance. Such efforts may be successful in highly predictable areas within an organization, but are likely to cause goal displacement when applied anywhere else.

TABLE 1
COMMON MANAGEMENT REWARD FOLLIES

We hope for . . .	But we often reward . . .
• long-term growth; environmental responsibility	• quarterly earnings
• teamwork	• individual effort
• setting challenging "stretch" objectives	• achieving goals; "making the numbers"
• downsizing; rightsizing; delayering; restructuring	• adding staff; adding budget; adding Hay points
• commitment to total quality	• shipping on schedule, even with defects
• candor; surfacing bad news early	• reporting good news, whether its true or not; agreeing with the boss, whether or not (s)he's right

2. Overemphasis on Highly Visible Behaviors

Difficulties often stem from the fact that some parts of the task are highly visible while other parts are not. For example, publications are easier to demonstrate than teaching, and scoring baskets and hitting home runs are more readily observable than feeding teammates and advancing base runners. Similarly, the adverse consequences of pronouncing a sick person well are more visible than those sustained by labeling a well person sick. Team-building and creativity are other examples of behaviors which may not be rewarded simply because they are hard to observe.

3. Hypocrisy

In some of the instances described the rewarder may have been getting the desired behavior, notwithstanding claims that the behavior was not desired. For example, in many jurisdictions within the U.S., judges' campaigns are funded largely by defense attorneys, while prosecutors are legally barred from making contributions. This doesn't do a whole lot to help judges to be "tough on crime" though, ironically, that's what their campaigns inevitably promise.

4. Emphasis on Morality or Equity Rather than Efficiency

Sometimes consideration of other factors prevents the establishment of a system which rewards behavior desired by the rewarder. The felt obligation of many Americans to vote for one candidate or another, for example, may impair their ability to discuss the issues. Similarly, the concern for spreading the risks and costs of wartime military service may outweigh the advantage to be obtained by committing personnel to combat until the war is over. The 1994 Clinton health plan, the Americans with Disabilities Act, and many other instances of proposed or recent governmental intervention provide outstanding examples of systems that reward efficiency, presumably in support of some higher objective.

ALTERING THE REWARD SYSTEM

Managers who complain about lack of motivation in their workers might do well to consider the possibility that the reward systems they have installed are paying off for behavior other than what they are seeking. This, in part, is what happened in Vietnam, and this is what regularly frustrates societal efforts to bring about honest politicians and civic-minded managers.

A first step for such managers might be to explore what types of behavior are currently being rewarded. Chances are excellent that these managers will be surprised by what they find—that their firms are not rewarding what they assume they are. In fact, such undesirable behavior by organizational members as they have observed may be explained largely by the reward systems in use.

This is not to say that all organizational behavior is determined by formal rewards and punishments. Certainly it is true that in the absence of formal reinforcement some soldiers will be patriotic, some players will be team oriented, and some employees will care about doing their job well. The point, however, is that in such cases the rewarder is not *causing* the behavior desired but is only a fortunate bystander. For an organization to *act* upon its members, the formal reward system should positively reinforce desired behavior, not constitute an obstacle to be overcome.

POSTSCRIPT

An irony about this article's being designated a management classic is that numerous people claim to have read and enjoyed it, but I wonder whether there was much in it that they didn't know. I believe that most readers already knew, and act on in their nonwork lives, the principles that underlie this article. For example, when we tell our daughter (who is about to cut her birthday cake) that her brother will select the first piece, or inform our friends **before** a meal that separate checks will be brought at the end, or tell the neighbor's boy that he will be paid five dollars for cutting the lawn **after** we inspect the lawn, we are making use of prospective rewards and punishments to cause other people to care about our own objectives. Organizational life may seem to be more complex, but the principles are the same.

Another irony attached to this "classic" is that it almost didn't see the light of day. It was rejected for presentation at the Eastern Academy of Management and was only published in *The Academy of Management Journal* because Jack Miner, its editor at the time, broke a tie between two reviewers. Nobody denied the relevance of the content, but reviewers were quite disturbed by the tone of the manuscript, and therefore its appropriateness for an academic audience. A compromise was reached whereby I added a bit of the great academic cure-all, data (Table 1 in the original article, condensed and summarized in this update), and a copy editor strangled some of the life from my writing style. In this respect, I would like to acknowledge the extremely competent editorial work performed on this update by John Veiga and his editorial staff. I am grateful to have had the opportunity to revisit the article, and hope the reader has enjoyed it also.

ENDNOTES

[1] Originally published in 1975, *Academy of Management Journal,* 18, 769–783.

[2] Charles Perrow, "The Analysis of Goals in Complex Organizations," in A. Etzioni (ed.), *Readings on Modern Organizations* (Englewood Cliffs, NJ: Prentice-Hall, 1969), 66.

[3] Chester I. Barnard, *The Functions of the Executive* (Cambridge, MA: Harvard University Press, 1964), 165.

[4] L. H. Garland, "Studies of the Accuracy of Diagnostic Procedures," *American Journal Roentgenological, Radium Therapy Nuclear Medicine,* Vol. 82, 1959, 25–38; and Thomas J. Scheff, "Decision Rules, Types of Error, and Their Consequences in Medical Diagnosis," in

F. Massarik and P. Ratoosh (eds.), *Mathematical Explorations in Behavioral Science* (Homewood, IL: Irwin, 1965).

[5]*Miami Herald,* May 8, 1994, 1a, 10a.

[6]Goal displacement results when means become ends in themselves and displace the original goals. See Peter M. Blau and W. Richard Scott, *Formal Organizations* (San Francisco, CA: Chandler, 1962).

[7]*San Francisco Examiner,* reported in *Fortune,* February 7, 1994, 161.

Why Incentive Plans Cannot Work

Alfie Kohn

It is difficult to overstate the extent to which most managers and the people who advise them believe in the redemptive power of rewards. Certainly, the vast majority of U.S. corporations use some sort of program intended to motivate employees by tying compensation to one index of performance or another. But more striking is the rarely examined belief that people will do a better job if they have been promised some sort of incentive. This assumption and the practices associated with it are pervasive, but a growing collection of evidence supports an opposing view. According to numerous studies in laboratories, workplaces, classrooms, and other settings, rewards typically undermine the very processes they are intended to enhance. The findings suggest that the failure of any given incentive program is due less to a glitch in that program than to the inadequacy of the psychological assumptions that ground all such plans.

TEMPORARY COMPLIANCE

Behaviorist theory, derived from work with laboratory animals, is indirectly responsible for such programs as piece-work pay for factory workers, stock options for top executives, special privileges accorded to Employees of the Month, and commissions for salespeople. Indeed, the livelihood of innumerable consultants has long been based on devising fresh formulas for computing bonuses to wave in front of employees. Money, vacations, banquets, plaques—the list of variations on a single, simple behaviorist model of motivation is limitless. And today even many people who are regarded as forward thinking—those who promote teamwork, participative management, continuous improvement, and the like—urge the use of rewards to institute and maintain these very reforms. What we use bribes to accomplish may have changed, but the reliance on bribes, on behaviorist doctrine, has not.

Moreover, the few articles that appear to criticize incentive plans are invariably limited to details of implementation. Only fine-tune the calculations and delivery of the incentive—or perhaps hire the author as a consultant—and the problem will be solved, we are told. As Herbert H. Meyer, professor emeritus in the psychology department at the College of Social and Behavioral Sciences at the University of South Florida, has written, "Anyone reading the literature on this subject published 20 years ago would find that the articles look almost identical to those published today." That assessment, which could have been written this morning, was actually offered in 1975. In nearly forty years, the thinking hasn't changed.

Do rewards work? The answer depends on what we mean by "work." Research suggests that, by and large, rewards succeed at securing one thing only: temporary compliance. When it comes to producing lasting change in attitudes and behavior, however, rewards, like punishment, are strikingly ineffective. Once the rewards run out, people revert to their old behaviors. Studies show that offering incentives for losing weight, quitting smoking, using seat belts, or (in the case of children) acting generously is not only less effective than other strategies but often proves worse than doing nothing at all. Incentives, a version of what psychologists call extrinsic motivators, do not alter the attitudes that underlie our behaviors. They do not create an enduring *commitment* to any value or action. Rather, incentives merely—and temporarily—change what we do.

As for productivity, at least two dozen studies over the last three decades have conclusively shown that people who expect to receive a reward for completing a task or for doing that task successfully simply do not perform as well as those who expect no reward at all. These studies examined rewards for children and adults, males and females, and included tasks ranging from memorizing facts to creative problem-solving to designing collages. In general, the more cognitive sophistication and open-ended thinking that was required, the worse people performed when working for a reward. Interestingly enough, the researchers themselves were often taken by surprise. They assumed that rewards would produce better work but discovered otherwise.

The question for managers is whether incentive plans can work when extrinsic motivators more generally do not. Unfortunately, as author G. Douglas Jenkins, Jr., has noted, most organizational studies to date—like the articles published—have tended "to focus on the effects of *variations* in incentive conditions, and not on whether performance-based pay per se raises performance levels."

A number of studies, however, have examined whether or not pay, especially at the executive level, is related to corporate profitability and other measures of organizational performance. Often they have found slight or even *negative* correlations between pay and performance. Typically, the absence of such a relationship is interpreted as evidence of links between compensation and something other than how well people do their jobs. But most of these data could support a different conclusion, one that reverses the causal arrow. Perhaps what these studies reveal is that higher pay does not produce better performance. In other words, the very idea of trying to reward quality may be a fool's errand.

Consider the findings of Jude T. Rich and John A. Larson, formerly of McKinsey & Company. In 1982, using interviews and proxy statements, they examined compensation programs at 90 major U.S. companies to determine whether return to shareholders was better for corporations that had incentive plans for top executives than it was for those companies that had no such plans. They were unable to find any difference.

Four years later, Jenkins tracked down 28 previously published studies that measured the impact of financial incentives on performance. (Some were conducted in the laboratory and some in the field.) His analysis, "Financial Incentives," published in 1986, revealed that 16, or 57%, of the studies found a positive effect on performance. However, all of the performance measures were quantitative in nature: a good job consisted of producing more of something or doing it faster. Only five of the studies looked at the quality of performance. And none of those five showed any benefits from incentives.

Another analysis took advantage of an unusual situation that affected a group of welders at a Midwestern manufacturing company. At the request of the union, an incentive system that had been in effect for some years was abruptly eliminated. Now, if a financial incentive supplies motivation, its absence should drive down production. And that is exactly what happened, at first. Fortunately, Harold F. Rothe, former personnel manager and corporate staff assistant at the Beloit Corporation, tracked production over a period of months, providing the sort of long-term data rarely collected in this field. After the initial slump, Rothe found that in the absence of incentives the welders' production quickly began to rise and eventually reached a level as high or higher than it had been before.

One of the largest reviews of how intervention programs affect worker productivity, a meta-analysis of some 330 comparisons from 98 studies, was conducted in the mid-1980s by Richard A. Guzzo, associate professor of psychology at the University of Maryland, College Park, and his colleagues at New York University. The raw numbers seemed to suggest a positive relationship between financial incentives and productivity, but because of the huge variations from one study to another, statistical tests indicated that there was no significant effect overall. What's more, financial incentives were virtually unrelated to the number of workers who were absent or who quit their jobs over a period of time. By contrast, training and goal-setting programs had a far greater impact on productivity than did pay-for-performance plans.

WHY REWARDS FAIL

Why do most executives continue to rely on incentive programs? Perhaps it's because few people take the time to examine the connection between incentive programs and problems with workplace productivity and morale. Rewards buy temporary compliance, so it looks like the problems are solved. It's harder to spot the harm they cause over the long term. Moreover, it does not occur to most of us to suspect rewards, given that our own teachers, parents, and managers probably used them. "Do this and you'll get that" is part of the fabric of American life. Finally, by clinging to the belief that motivational problems are due to the particular incentive system in effect at the moment, rather than to the psychological theory behind all incentives, we can remain optimistic that a relatively minor adjustment will repair the damage.

Over the long haul, however, the potential cost to any organization of trying to fine-tune reward-driven compensation systems may be considerable. The fundamental flaws of behaviorism itself doom the prospects of affecting long-term behavior change or performance improvement through the use of rewards. Consider the following six-point framework that examines the true costs of an incentive program.

1. "Pay is not a motivator." W. Edward Deming's declaration may seem surprising, even absurd. Of course, money buys the things people want and need. Moreover, the less people are paid, the more concerned they are likely to be about financial matters. Indeed, several studies over the last few decades have found that when people are asked to guess what matters to their coworkers—or, in the case of managers, to their subordinates—they assume money heads the list. But put the question directly— "What do you care about?"—and pay typically ranks only fifth or sixth.

Even if people were principally concerned with their salaries, this does not prove that money is motivating. There is no firm basis for the assumption that paying people more will courage them to do better work or even, in the long run, more work. As

Frederick Herzberg, Distinguished Professor of Management at the University of Utah's Graduate School of Management, has argued, just because too little money can irritate and demotivate does not mean that more and more money will bring about increased satisfaction, much less increased motivation. It is plausible to assume that if someone's take-home pay was cut in half, his or her morale would suffer enough to undermine performance. But it doesn't necessarily follow that doubling that person's pay would result in better work.

2. Rewards punish. Many managers understand that coercion and fear destroy motivation and create defiance, defensiveness, and rage. They realize that punitive management is a contradiction in terms. As Herzberg wrote in HBR some 25 years ago ("One More Time: How Do You Motivate Employees?" January-February 1968), a "KITA"—which, he coyly explains, stands for "kick in the pants"—may produce movement but never motivation.

What most executives fail to recognize is that Herzberg's observation is equally true of rewards. Punishment and rewards are two sides of the same coin. Rewards have a punitive effect because they, like outright punishment, are manipulative. "Do this and you'll get that" is not really very different from "Do this or here's what will happen to you." In the case of incentives, the reward itself may be highly desired; but by making that bonus contingent on certain behaviors, managers manipulate their subordinates, and that experience of being controlled is likely to assume a punitive quality over time.

Further, not receiving a reward one had expected to receive is also indistinguishable from being punished. Whether the incentive is withheld or withdrawn deliberately, or simply not received by someone who had hoped to get it, the effect is identical. And the more desirable the reward, the more demoralizing it is to miss out.

The new school, which exhorts us to catch people doing something right and reward them for it, is not very different from the old school, which advised us to catch people doing something wrong and threaten to punish them if they ever do it again. What is essentially taking place in both approaches is that a lot of people are getting caught. Managers are creating a workplace in which people feel controlled, not an environment conducive to exploration, learning, and progress.

3. Rewards rupture relationships. Relationships among employees are often casualties of the scramble for rewards. As leaders of the Total Quality Management movement have emphasized, incentive programs, and the performance appraisal systems that accompany them, reduce the possibilities for cooperation. Peter R. Scholtes, senior management consultant at Joiner Associates Inc., put it starkly, "Everyone is pressuring the system for individual gain. No one is improving the system for collective gain. The system will inevitably crash." Without teamwork, in other words, there can be no quality.

The surest way to destroy cooperation and, therefore, organizational excellence, is to force people to compete for rewards or recognition or to rank them against each other. For each person who wins, there are many others who carry with them the feeling of having lost. And the more these awards are publicized through the use of memos, newsletters, and awards banquets, the more detrimental their impact can be. Furthermore, when employees compete for a limited number of incentives, they will most likely begin to see each other as obstacles to their own success. But the same result can occur with any use of rewards; introducing competition just makes a bad thing worse.

Relationships between supervisors and subordinates can also collapse under the weight of incentives. Of course, the supervisor who punishes is about as welcome to employees as a glimpse of a police car in their rearview mirrors. But even the supervisor who rewards can produce some damaging reactions. For instance, employees may be tempted to conceal any problems they might be having and present themselves as infinitely competent to the manager in control of the money. Rather than ask for help—a prerequisite for optimal performance—they might opt instead for flattery, attempting to convince the manager that they have everything under control. Very few things threaten an organization as much as a hoard of incentive-driven individuals trying to curry favor with the incentive dispenser.

4. Rewards ignore reasons. In order to solve problems in the workplace, managers must understand what caused them. Are employees inadequately prepared for the demands of their jobs? Is long-term growth being sacrificed to maximize short-term return? Are workers unable to collaborate effectively? Is the organization so rigidly hierarchical that employees are intimidated about making recommendations and feel powerless and burned out? Each of these situations calls for a different response. But relying on incentives to boost productivity does nothing to address possible underlying problems and bring about meaningful change.

Moreover, managers often use incentive systems as a substitute for giving workers what they need to do a good job. Treating workers well—providing useful feedback, social support, and the room for self-determination—is the essence of good management. On the other hand, dangling a bonus in front of employees and waiting for the results requires much less effort. Indeed, some evidence suggests that productive managerial strategies are less likely to be used in organizations that lean on pay-for-performance plans. In his study of welders' performance, Rothe noted that supervisors tended to "demonstrate relatively less leadership" when incentives were in place. Likewise, author Carla O'Dell reports in *People, Performance, and Pay* that a survey of 1,600 organizations by the American Productivity Center discovered little in the way of active employee involvement in organizations that used small-group incentive plans. As Jone L. Pearce, associate professor at the Graduate School of Management, University of California at Irvine, wrote in "Why Merit Pay Doesn't Work: Implications from Organization Theory," pay for performance actually "impedes the ability of managers to manage."

5. Rewards discourage risk-taking. "People will do precisely what they are asked to do if the reward is significant," enthused Monroe J. Haegele, a proponent of pay-for-performance programs, in "The New Performance Measures." And here is the root of the problem. Whenever people are encouraged to think about what they will get for engaging in a task, they become less inclined to take risks or explore possibilities, to play hunches or to consider incidental stimuli. In a word, the number one casualty of rewards is creativity.

Excellence pulls in one direction; rewards pull in another. Tell people that their income will depend on their productivity or performance rating, and they will focus on the numbers. Sometimes they will manipulate the schedule for completing tasks or even engage in patently unethical and illegal behavior. As Thane S. Pittman, professor and chair of the psychology department at Gettysburg College, and his colleagues point out, when we are motivated by incentives, "features such as predictability and simplicity are desirable, since the primary focus associated with this orientation is to get through the task expediently in order to reach the desired goal." The late Cornell University professor, John Condry, was more succinct: rewards, he said, are the "enemies of exploration."

Consider the findings of organizational psychologist Edwin A. Locke. When Locke paid subjects on a piece-rate basis for their work, he noticed that they tended to choose easier tasks as the payment for success increased. A number of other studies have also found that people working for a reward generally try to minimize challenge. It isn't that human beings are naturally lazy or that it is unwise to give employees a voice in determining the standards to be used. Rather, people tend to lower their sights when they are encouraged to think about what they are going to get for their efforts. "Do this and you'll get that," in other words, focuses attention on the "that" instead of the "this." Emphasizing large bonuses is the last strategy we should use if we care about innovation. Do rewards motivate people? Absolutely. They motivate people to get rewards.

6. Rewards undermine interest. If our goal is excellence, no artificial incentive can ever match the power of intrinsic motivation. People who do exceptional work may be glad to be paid and even more glad to be well paid, but they do not work to collect a paycheck. They work because they love what they do.

Few will be shocked by the news that extrinsic motivators are a poor substitute for genuine interest in one's job. What is far more surprising is that rewards, like punishment, may actually undermine the intrinsic motivation that results in optimal performance. The more a manager stresses what an employee can earn for good work, the less interested that employee will be in the work itself.

The first studies to establish the effect of rewards on intrinsic motivation were conducted in the early 1970s by Edward Deci, professor and chairman of the psychology department at the University of Rochester. By now, scores of experiments across the country have replicated the finding. As Deci and his colleague Richard Ryan, senior vice president of investment and training manager at Robert W. Baird and Co., Inc., wrote in their 1985 book, *Intrinsic Motivation and Self-Determination in Human Behavior,* "the research has consistently shown that any contingent payment system tends to undermine intrinsic motivation." The basic effect is the same for a variety of rewards and tasks, although extrinsic motivators are particularly destructive when tied to interesting or complicated tasks.

Deci and Ryan argue that receiving a reward for a particular behavior sends a certain message about what we have done and controls, or attempts to control, our future behavior. The more we experience being controlled, the more we will tend to lose interest in what we are doing. If we go to work thinking about the possibility of getting a bonus, we come to feel that our work is not self-directed. Rather, it is the reward that drives our behavior.

Other theorists favor a more simple explanation for the negative effect rewards have on intrinsic motivation: anything presented as a prerequisite for something else—that is, as a means toward another end—comes to be seen as less desirable. The recipient of the reward assumes, "If they have to bribe me to do it, it must be something I wouldn't want to do." In fact, a series of studies, published in 1992 by psychology professor Jonathan L. Freedman and his colleagues at the University of Toronto, confirmed that the larger the incentive we are offered, the more negatively we will view the activity for which the bonus was received. (The activities themselves don't seem to matter; in this study, they ranged from participating in a medical experiment to eating unfamiliar food.) Whatever the reason for the effect, however, any incentive or pay-for-performance system tends to make people less enthusiastic about their work and therefore less likely to approach it with a commitment to excellence.

DANGEROUS ASSUMPTIONS

Outside of psychology departments, few people distinguish between intrinsic and extrinsic motivation. Those who do assume that the two concepts can simply be added together for best effect. Motivation comes in two flavors, the logic goes, and both together must be better than either alone. But studies show that the real world works differently.

Some managers insist that the only problem with incentive programs is that they don't reward the right things. But these managers fail to understand the psychological factors involved and, consequently, the risks of sticking with the status quo.

Contrary to conventional wisdom, the use of rewards is not a response to the extrinsic orientation exhibited by many workers. Rather, incentives help create this focus on financial considerations. When an organization uses a Skinnerian management or compensation system, people are likely to become less interested in their work, requiring extrinsic incentives before expending effort. Then supervisors shake their heads and say, "You see? If you don't offer them a reward, they won't do anything." It is a classic self-fulfilling prophecy. Swarthmore College psychology professor Barry Schwartz has conceded that behavior theory may seem to provide us with a useful way of describing what goes on in U.S. workplaces. However, "It does this not because work is a natural exemplification of behavior theory principles but because behavior theory principles . . . had a significant hand in transforming work into an exemplification of behavior theory principles."

Managers who insist that the job won't get done right without rewards have failed to offer a convincing argument for behavioral manipulation. Promising a reward to someone who appears unmotivated is a bit like offering salt water to someone who is thirsty. Bribes in the workplace simply can't work.

Why Merit Pay Doesn't Work: Implications from Organizational Theory

Jone L. Pearce

Compensation plans that base pay on an individual's recent performance, such as merit pay, enjoy prominence in both the professional compensation literature and in the popular imagination. Such plans have the attraction of clear communication of performance expectations and give employees the opportunity to increase their incomes through their own efforts. That these plans have become synonymous with "fairness" is reflected in the widespread support for President Reagan's call for merit pay for schoolteachers. Compensation textbooks and journals reflect the general belief in these plans through their devotion of substantial space to discussions of the design and implementation of such programs, despite the fact that individual performance-contingent pay makes up a very small portion of most employees' total compensation.

In practice, however, we know that such pay programs are fraught with problems (see Winstanley 1982; Pearce and Perry 1983; Pearce, Stevenson, and Perry 1985). Edward Morse from Hay put it bluntly as 1986 drew to an end: "Our traditional reward systems have failed. The decline in U.S. productivity growth during the past 20 years signals loudly that our current [pay-for-performance] system is no longer meeting our needs" (p. 85). Although the limitations of these plans have been known for decades (see Sayles 1952; Whyte 1955; Meyer 1975), it is a rare author who does not end the list of "merit pay problems" with upbeat suggestions for the successful implementation of such programs (e.g., Hamner 1975).

Here it will be suggested that advice concerning the improvement of the implementation of such plans has not substantially improved their success. Real organizations are messy, indeterminate places, and a compensation idea that is not feasible except in pristine laboratory environments needs to be reexamined. Further, it will be proposed that the failure of individual merit pay plans should not reflexively be blamed on the practitioners struggling to put these programs in place. Rather, it will be suggested that these failures are the result of a flawed theoretical assumption behind individually contingent pay. Practicing managers are aware of the deficiencies of their own organizations' performance-contingent pay systems, but they have an incomplete rationale to explain these inadequacies. The result is frustration. Individually contingent pay, as an idea, needs to be analyzed in its organizational context. Therefore in this paper, the implications of "organizational theory" for individually based pay are developed.

It is important to emphasize at the outset that the present argument is concerned only with the problems of merit pay based on *individual* performance, not on group or organizational performance-based merit pay or bonuses. Advocates of individual performance-based programs suggest that to be effective, performance expectations need to be clearly stated in advance. These true pay-for-performance systems (rather than

From D. B. Balkin & L. R. Gomez-Mejia (Eds.), *New Perspectives on Compensation* (pp. 169–178). Englewood Cliffs, N.J.: Prentice-Hall, 1987. Reprinted by permission.

the ones based mostly on retrospective subjective judgments) are the focus of the present discussion.

These pay programs are based on the assumption that overall organizational performance is the simple additive combination of individual employees' separate contributions. Alternatively, it will be proposed that the greater the uncertainty, interdependence, and complexity of organizational work, the greater the cooperation among employees required for successful organizational performance, and that individual performance-based pay can provide powerful disincentives for cooperation. This is not the traditional suggestion that money is not a powerful motivator (Deci 1975). Quite to the contrary, individually contingent pay programs can be pernicious because they so effectively direct and sustain individuals' motivation; but such plans can direct motivation away from the actions that are most functional for organizations.

The idea itself seems to hold such power that these programs are usually explained as failures of implementation or intention that, at best, suggest additions to the list of moderating or limiting conditions. Most often managers are blamed for not implementing such programs properly. For example, Hamner (1975) states that "it is not the merit pay theory that is defective. Rather, the history of the actual implementation of the theory is at fault" (p. 220).

This is not to suggest that individually based incentive pay programs are always correctly implemented but that too often evidence of "failure" receives reflexive condemnation rather than thoughtful analysis. This unexamined belief in the idea of pay for individual performance has led to a straining for explanations. The dazzle of high individual motivation has deflected theoretical attention away from a focus on what actions are being motivated. The following arguments and testable propositions derived from them are more fully developed in Pearce (1985).

ORGANIZATION THEORY AND MERIT PAY

Individual performance-contingent pay derives from an assumption that the organization's effectiveness is the simple additive combination of individual's separate performances. Such pay programs are based on the development of "compensation contracts" in which pay is linked to the employee's performance in an explicit agreement. The clarity, "fairness," and motivating potential of these compensation contracts distract us from the fact that the employee-employer relationship has not been based on such "fixed contracts" for the simple reason that this is a less productive relationship for the kinds of uncertain, interdependent, and complex work organizations undertake.

Uncertainty in Organizations

The authority relationship between supervisors and subordinates has been a long-standing interest of organization and management theorists. Simon's (1957) definition of authority bears repeating: Subordinates accept authority whenever they permit their behavior to be guided by the decision of a supervisor, *without independently examining the merits of that decision.* When exercising authority, the supervisor does not seek to convince subordinates, only to obtain acquiescence. Organization theorists have argued that the authority of supervisors is accepted by employees in exchange for wages. It is important to recognize that this "employment contract" is an open-ended one. In exchange for pay, employees offer not specific services but their undifferentiated time and effort, which can be directed by the supervisors as they see fit. This is because, as Simon notes, from the viewpoint of the organization, there is no point in offering inducements to employees unless their actions could be brought into the coordinated system of organizational actions through their acceptance of its authority. Simon argues that open-ended employment contracts allow organizations the flexibility to respond to future uncertainty.

If performance requirements are indeed uncertain, the writing of a fixed-compensation contract restricts the ability of managers to respond to these changes. Pay for individual performance attempts to modify these traditional employment contracts so that they are less open-ended and more like the closed-ended (behaviors specified in advance) contracts of the marketplace. Simon (1957) implies that under circumstances of uncertainty, closed-ended performance contracts would be difficult to write. If conditions are genuinely uncertain, how can these contracts be detailed in advance?

In practice, these pay programs are frequently adapted to uncertainty by combining "subjective judgment" with objective measures (Lawler, 1981). Such adaptations certainly help to retain open-ended authority relationships, but they have side effects of their own. For example, Carroll and Schneier (1982) note that the more subjective the rating criterion, the more rater judgment is required, not only regarding the degree to which the rate meets the criterion but also regarding what the measure actually means. Therefore, as Lawler (1981) notes, subjectively based judgments require high levels of trust. Thus attempts to retain the authority relationship by using subjective supervisory judgments remove the clarity and fairness advantages of fixed contracts.

Recognition of the importance of uncertainty in organizational life helps us to understand otherwise inexplicable research findings. For example, researchers have found only a slight positive correlation between merit raises and performance ratings. Others usually interpret these data as missed opportunities to use a valued reward to increase motivation (e.g., Lawler 1971). Alternatively, supervisors may no tie such a salient reward to individually measured performance because they recognize not only that good performance is not completely represented in performance appraisals but also that these closed-ended contracts reduce their own ability to respond to unanticipated events. Supervisors face myriad uncertainties, requiring levels of flexibility that cannot be captured in individual performance contracts. Such supervisors use the discretion that merit raises afford to reward critical accomplishments, to cope with such concerns as inflation and salary compression, and to compensate for a particularly unattractive assignment or absence of an expected promotion. Pay does, in fact, serve a multitude of purposes in organizations, and mandating that it be dominated by an individual's measured performance in the most recent performance period impedes the ability of managers to manage.

Interdependence in Organizations

In describing the ways in which individually contingent pay interferes with the dependence of individuals on their organizations, it is useful to draw on Thompson's (1967) three-part categorization of dependence relations in organizations. First, individuals are most interdependent when they must work together, interacting during task performance, in order to complete their work. Individually contingent pay would rarely be advocated in the case of this "reciprocal interdependence," since credit and blame are virtually impossible to assign to individuals. However, Thompson's two other kinds of interdependence—sequential and pooled—are not readily seen as prohibiting individually contingent pay.

Sequentially dependent employees rely on others for either their inputs, for the disposal of their outputs, or for both. It is for this kind of interdependence that we have the most vivid descriptions of contingent pay dysfunctions (e.g., Whyte 1955; Babchuk and Goode 1951). Since the problems resulting from the use of individually contingent pay for sequentially dependent employees have been well documented, this discussion focuses on pooled interdependence.

Pooled interdependence is the collective dependence of employees on the continued success of the organization; Thompson argues that employees may not be directly independent with others for their task performance but are still jointly dependent with all other participants on their organization's ability to provide employment and other resources.

Individually contingent compensation contracts distract employees' attention from this more abstract dependence relationship and interfere with members' commitment to their colleagues and employer. By treating them as labor contractors, employees are encouraged to work only on activities represented in their contracts. Drawing on Kerr (1975), we might hope that they will cooperate with their colleagues and supervisors, but we are rewarding them for fulfilling the terms of a fixed contract.

Thus employees are seen by the organization and come to view themselves as "contractors," with a written "track record" provided by the compensation system that can be marketed to another employer. It can be speculated that it is this growing use of performance-based compensation contracts for professionals and managers, rather than massive changes in personal values, that has led to the popularly perceived shift among American managers and professionals from "organization men" (Whyte 1956) to "job-hopping professional managers" ("The Money Chase" 1981). Therefore, it should be no surprise to find that recent advocates of Japanese-style concern with fostering employee loyalty advocate abandoning individually contingent pay in favor of organizationwide bonuses (Ouchi 1981).

It is further suggested that pay for individual performance, since it provides incentives that run counter to the pooled interdependence among organization members, can actually undermine the quality of employer-employee relationships. Numerous scholars have attempted to articulate the positive attitude that frequently emerges among employees in their relationship with their employing organization (e.g., Pearce and Peters 1985). For example, Barnard (1938) describes the importance of "cooperation," and recently there has been a renewed interest in "organizational commitment" (Mowday, Porter, and Steers, 1982; Wiener 1982).

These pay plans can damage organizational commitment, since they treat the employee as a labor contractor. Such contracts communicate that the employer is only concerned with the employee's performance as it is reflected in the "contract measures" and is, in effect, indifferent to past contributions and experience (since the employer pays only for the recent performance period), to the employee's potential for other kinds of work, and to any extenuating circumstances that may have influenced the recent performance measures. There is recent evidence that merit pay programs do have significant and long-lasting (fifteen months) negative effects on organizational commitment (Pearce and Porter 1985).

Complexity in Organizations

The work of Williamson (1975) illustrates the complexity of organizational work and helps to clarify why the fixed contracts of individually contingent pay can be dysfunctional for overall organizational effectiveness. This economist has sought to understand the conditions under which economic activity takes place either in markets—in which transactions involve exchange between autonomous economic entities—or in organizations. He suggests that organizations are more efficient than marketplace contracting under conditions of future uncertainty, complex transactions, and dependence on individuals willing to exploit their advantage.

Under these circumstances, employment contracts in organizational settings have certain advantages over labor market contracting that makes employment more efficient. Particularly relevant to the present discussion, Williamson argues that organizations are better able to encourage cooperation among opportunistic specialists (employees). Thus organizations are the more efficient forms under certain circumstances because they can more easily compensate individuals for cooperation.

Williamson's work has important implications for the design of pay systems. It suggests that despite its advantages of clarity and apparent fairness, market contracting is not suited to all types of economic exchange. Employment relationships dominate the labor market today because work has become more complex, more dependent on particular individuals, and must be conducted under conditions of future uncertainty. If such conditions are not present, Williamson suggests that it is more efficient to use marketplace contracting for services rather than employment.

Therefore, individually contingent pay, by tying an employee's pay to his or her performance during a specific time period, is an attempt to reformulate the employer-employee relationships into a pseudocontract between buyer and seller. Under conditions of uncertainty, interdependence, and complexity, such pseudocontracts cannot be completely specified. They can, at best, cover only a portion of the desired actions and become a forced and artificial representation of the kind of performance that would be most effective for the organization (a familiar problem for those who have had experience with merit pay programs). Further, since pay can be such a powerful motivator, all the problems in the use of pseudocontracting in organizations are made worse when pay is attached to fulfilling the terms of the contract.

Pay-for-individual-performance systems, despite their motivating power, would not, then, be expected to result in enhanced organizational effectiveness. Such systems build in disincentives for the management of uncertainty, interdependence, and complexity and so discourage the kinds of cooperative actions that lead the organizational form to be more efficient than labor contracting. If the organization does, in fact, have individual tasks that are predictable, simple, and independent, this analysis suggests that it would be more efficient to hire contractors than employees. Pay for individual performance is neither a labor contract (since the authority relationship remains) nor a conventional employment relationship (with rewards allocated based on *post hoc* judgments of overall employee historical and potential contributions). Thus organizations that use such forms of compensation would be expected to have less effective performance than those not using such systems, since their compensation system is working against the advantages of the organizational form. We certainly could not expect the greater overall organizational effectiveness implied by pay-for-performance advocates.

This suggests a reinterpretation of the research reporting that executives' pay is uncorrelated (Redling 1981; Perham 1971) or, at best, weakly associated (Patton 1961; Gomez-Mejia, Tosi, and Hinkin 1984) with their organizations' financial performance. Instead of deploring this evidence as representing a lack of "the will to pay for performance" (Redling 1981), it may more accurately reflect attempts to pay for performance that simply have no influence on corporate performance. Booz-Allen and Hamilton (1983) reported that while the "shareholder value" of Standard and Poor's 400 corporations declined 10.5 percent from 1970 to 1982, the use of performance-based bonuses for these firms' chief executive officers nearly doubled (from 23 percent of total compensation in 1971 to 41 percent in 1981). This appears to reflect an increasing effort to tie a larger proportion of executive pay to measures of performance. These compensation committees were apparently trying to pay for individual performance, despite the fact that organizational performance was declining during this period. This certainly doesn't prove that individually contingent pay caused the decline in firm performance, but it does suggest that the absence of a strong positive relationship between executive pay and firm performance does not necessarily reflect a lack of "the will to pay for performance." Rather, perhaps, corporate compensation committees have been using the wrong model of the ways in which individual's performances contribute to overall organizational performance.

IMPLICATIONS

The argument developed here has implications for both research and practice. Research hypotheses derived from these arguments need to be tested empirically; a discussion of possible tests appears in Pearce (1985).

Regarding compensation practice, this article was intended to help explain the gap between the popular belief in the power of merit pay and the actual track record of these programs by examining one of the relatively neglected assumptions behind individually contingent pay. At this point one could reasonably ask, Since virtually no compensation system is actually dominated by individual performance-contingent compensation, what practical difference does it make if an important assumption is flawed?

Such a large discrepancy between compensation practice and popular theory is demoralizing to practitioners and can lead to poor practice. Professional compensation specialists are led to feel uncomfortable that their own organization's actual system deviates so far from "accepted advice," and they have no way to explain coherently *why* true pay for performance plays such a limited role in their employees' overall compensation. This discussion is intended to confirm that there is no need to feel guilty about the small role of merit pay.

Virtually all compensation textbooks note that pay is intended to attract and retain employees as well as motivate greater individual performance (Nash and Carroll 1975; Ellig 1982; Wallace and Fay 1983). Wallace and Fay argue that compensation systems must meet employees' expectations for equity or fairness and that individual job performance is only one of many factors—including prevailing labor market wages, the responsibility of the position, and skill and knowledge requirements—that contribute to perceived compensation fairness. Pay systems are already burdened by spiraling labor market demand, pay compression, demands for comparable worth, inflation, and the like, and advocating that they also be harnessed as the primary short-term performance-contingent incentive is not realistic.

In conclusion, individually contingent pay plans are based on a false assumption. These plans attempt to mimic marketplace contracts under conditions of uncertainty, complexity, and dependence for which they are not appropriate. Pay can be a powerful incentive, but compensation specialists need to ensure that the dazzle of high performance motivation doesn't distract from a concern with *what* performance is being motivated. Paying people on the basis of their recent measured individual performance simply does not build on the relative advantages of the organizational form. Most kinds of organizations succeed because of cooperation among their members, not because of members' discrete, independent performance. Such cooperation is particularly critical among employees with either valuable expertise (which may be the basis for the organization's competitive advantage) or the discretion to commit the organization's resources (i.e., managers). It is simply not in the organization's interest to encourage short-term single-transaction expectations among such important employees. Pay is important, and the ways in which organizations dispense it tell us a lot about the actions they expect from their employees. Compensation theory could reflect organizational realities better if it had as great a concern for the organizational context in which employees must work as it does for their levels of individual effort.

REFERENCES

Babchuk, N., and W. J. Goode (1951), "Work Incentives in a Self-determined Group," *American Sociological Review* 16, 679–687.

Barnard, C. I. (1938), *The Functions of the Executive.* Cambridge, Mass.: Harvard University Press.

Booz-Allen, and Hamilton Inc. (1983), *Creating Shareholder Value: A New Mission for Executive Compensation.* New York: New York.

Carroll, S. J., and C. E. Schneier (1982), *Performance Appraisal and Review Systems: The Identification, Measurement, and Development of Performance in Organizations.* Glenview, Ill.: Scott, Foresman.

Deci, E. L. (1975), *Intrinsic Motivation.* New York: Plenum.

Ellig, B. R. (1982), *Executive Compensation: A Total Pay Perspective.* New York: McGraw-Hill.

Gomez-Mejia, L. R., H. Tosi, and T. Hinkin (1984, August), *Organizational Determinants of Chief Executive Compensation.* Paper presented at the meeting of the Academy of Management, Boston.

Hamner, W. C. (1975), "How to Ruin Motivation with Pay," *Compensation Review* 7, no. 3, 17–27.

Kerr, S. (1975), "On the Folly of Rewarding A while Hoping for B," *Academy of Management Journal* 18, 769–783.

Lawler, E. E. (1971), *Pay and Organizational Effectiveness: A Psychological View.* New York: McGraw-Hill.

——— (1981), *Pay and Organization Development,* Reading, Mass.: Addison-Wesley.

Morse, E. (Fall 1986), "Productivity Rewards for Non-Management Employees," in *Topics in Total Compensation,* ed. R. C. Ochsner. Greenvale, New York: A Panel Publication.

Meyer, H. H. (1975), "The Pay-for-Performance Dilemma," *Organizational Dynamics* 3, no. 3, 39–50.

"The Money Chase: Business School Solutions May Be Part of the U.S. Problem," *Time,* May 4, 1981, p. 20.

Mowday, R. T., L. W. Porter, and R. M. Steers (1982), *Employee-Organization Linkages: The Psychology of Commitment, Absenteeism, and Turnover.* New York: Academic Press.

Nash, A. N., and S. J. Carroll (1975), *The Management of Compensation.* Belmont, Calif.: Wadsworth.

Ouchi, W. G. (1981), *Theory Z.* Reading, Mass.: Addison-Wesley.

Patton, A. (1961), *Men, Money, and Motivation.* New York: McGraw-Hill.

Pearce, J. L. (1985), *An Organization Is Not the Sum of Its Employees: An Unexamined Assumption of Performance-contingent Compensation.* Working paper, Graduate School of Management, University of California, Irvine.

———, and J. L. Perry (1983), "Federal Merit Pay: A Longitudinal Analysis," *Public Administration Review* 43, 315–325.

———, and R. H. Peters (1985), "A Contradictory Norms View of Employer-Employee Exchange," *Journal of Management* 11, 19–30.

———, and L. W. Porter (1985), *Employee Responses to Formal Performance Appraisal Feedback.* Working paper, Graduate School of Management, University of California, Irvine.

———, W. B. Stevenson, and J. L. Perry (1985), "Managerial Compensation Based on Organizational Performance: A Time-Series Analysis of the Impact of Merit Pay," *Academy of Management Journal* 28, 261–279.

Perham, J. (1971), "What's Wrong with Bonuses?" *Dun's Review and Modern Industry* 98, 40–44.

Redling, E. T. (1981), "Myth vs. Reality: The Relationship Between Top Executive Pay and Corporate Performance," *Compensation Review* 13, no. 4, 16–24.

Sayles, L. R. (1952), "The Impact of Incentives on Inter-group Work Relations: A Management and Union Problem," *Personnel* 28, 483–490.

Simon, H. A. (1957), *Administrative Behavior,* 2nd ed. New York: Free Press.

Thompson, J. D. (1967), *Organizations in Action.* New York: McGraw-Hill.

Wallace, M. J., and C. H. Fay (1983), *Compensation Theory and Practice.* Boston: Kent.

Whyte, W. F. (1955), *Money and Motivation.* New York: Harper & Row.

——— (1956), *The Organization Man.* New York: Simon & Schuster.

Wiener, Y. (1982), "Commitment and Organizations: A Normative View," *Academy of Management Review* 7, 418–428.

Williamson, O. E. (1975), *Markets and Hierarchies: Analysis and Antitrust Implications.* New York: Free Press.

Winstanley, N. B. (1982), "Are Merit Increases Really Effective?" *Personnel Administrator* 4, 37–41.

The Design of Effective Reward Systems
Edward E. Lawler III

Reward systems are one of the most prominent and frequently discussed features of organizations. Indeed, the organizational behavior and personnel-management literature is replete with examples of their functional and dysfunctional roles (see, for example, Whyte 1955). Too seldom, however, do writers examine thoroughly the potential impact of reward systems on organizational effectiveness and how they relate to the strategic objectives of the organization.

This chapter will focus on the strategic design choices that are involved in managing a reward system, and their relationship to organizational effectiveness, rather than on specific pay-system technologies. The details of pay-system design and management have been described in numerous books (e.g., Henderson 1979; Patten 1977; and Ellig 1982). The underlying assumption in this chapter is that a properly designed reward system can be a key contributor to organizational effectiveness. But careful analysis is required of the role reward systems should play in the strategic plan of the organization.

OBJECTIVES OF REWARD SYSTEMS

Reward systems in organizations have six kinds of impact that can influence organizational effectiveness: attraction and retention of employees, motivation of performance, motivation of skill development, cultural effects, reinforcement of structure, and cost.

Attraction and Retention

Research on job choice, career choice, and turnover clearly shows that the rewards an organization offers influences who is attracted to work for it and who will continue to work for it (see, for example, Lawler 1973; Mobley 1982). Overall, organizations that give the greatest rewards tend to attract and retain the most people. High reward levels apparently lead to high satisfaction, which in turn leads to lower turnover. Individuals who are currently satisfied with their jobs expect to remain so, and thus want to stay with the same organization.

The relationship between turnover and organizational effectiveness is not simple. It is often assumed that the lower the turnover rate, the more effective the organization is likely to be. Turnover is expensive. Replacing an employee can cost at least five times his or her monthly salary (Macy and Mirvis 1976). However, not all turnover is harmful to organizational effectiveness. Organizations may actually profit from losing poor performers. In addition, if replacement costs are low, as they may be in unskilled jobs, it can be more cost effective to keep wages low and accept high turnover. Thus, the ef-

From J. W. Lorsch (Ed.), *Handbook of Organizational Behavior* (pp. 255–271). Copyright © 1987, Englewood Cliffs, N.J.: Prentice Hall. Reprinted by permission.

fect of turnover depends on its rate, the employees affected, and their replacement cost.

The objective should be to design a reward system that is very effective at retaining the most valuable employees. To do this, the system must distribute rewards in a way that will lead the more valuable employees to feel satisfied when they compare their rewards with those received by individuals performing similar jobs in other organizations. The emphasis here is on *external* comparisons, for it is the prospect of a better situation elsewhere that induces an employee to leave. One way to accomplish this is to reward everyone at a level above that prevailing in other organizations. This strategy can be very costly, however. Moreover, it can cause feelings of intraorganizational inequity. The better performers are likely to feel unfairly treated if they are rewarded at the same level as poor performers in the same organization, even though they fare better than their counterparts elsewhere. They may not quit, but they are likely to be dissatisfied, complain, look for internal transfers, and mistrust the organization.

The best solution is to have competitive reward levels and to base rewards on performance. This should satisfy the better performers and encourage them to stay with the organization. It should also attract achievement-oriented individuals, because they like environments in which their performance is rewarded. However, it is important that the better performers receive *significantly more* rewards than poor performers. Rewarding them only slightly more may simply make the better and poorer performers *equally* dissatisfied.

In summary, managing turnover means managing anticipated satisfaction. Ideally, rewards will be effectively related to performances. When this difficult task cannot be accomplished, an organization can try to reward individuals at an above-average level. If turnover is costly, this should be cost-effective strategy, even if it involves giving out expensive rewards.

Research has shown that absenteeism and satisfaction are related, although not as strongly as satisfaction and turnover. When the workplace is pleasant and satisfying, individuals come to work regularly; when it isn't, they don't.

One way to reduce absenteeism is to administer pay in ways that maximize satisfaction. Several studies have also shown that absenteeism can be reduced by tying pay bonuses and other rewards to attendance (Lawler 1981). This approach is costly, but sometimes less costly than absenteeism. In many ways such a system is easier to administer than a performance-based one, because attendance is more readily measured. It is a particularly useful strategy in situations where both the work content and the working conditions are poor and do not lend themselves to meaningful improvements. If such improvements are possible, they are often the most effective and cost-efficient way to deal with absenteeism.

Motivation of Performance

Under certain conditions, reward systems have been shown to motivate performance (Lawler 1971; Vroom 1964). Employees must perceive that important rewards are tied in a timely fashion to effective performance. Individuals are inherently neither motivated nor unmotivated to perform effectively. Rather, they each use their own mental maps of what the world is like to choose behaviors that lead to outcomes that satisfy their needs. Thus, organizations get the kind of behavior that leads to the rewards their employees value. Performance motivation depends on the situation, how it is perceived, and the needs of people.

The most useful approach to understanding how people develop and act on their mental maps is called "expectancy theory" (Lawler 1973). Three concepts serve as the key building blocks of the theory.

Performance-Outcome Expectancy Each individual mentally associates every behavior with certain outcomes (rewards or punishments). In other words, people believe that if they behave in a certain way, they will get certain things. Individuals may expect, for example, that if they produce ten units, they will receive their normal hourly pay rate, while if they produce fifteen units, they will also receive a bonus. Similarly, they may believe that certain levels of performance will lead to approval or disapproval from members of their work group or their supervisor. Each performance level can be seen as leading to a number of different kinds of outcomes.

Attractiveness Each outcome has a certain attractiveness for each individual. Valuations reflect individual needs and perceptions, which differ from one person to another. For example, some workers may value an opportunity for promotion because of their needs for achievement or power, while others may not want to leave their current work group because of needs for affiliation with others. Similarly, a pension plan may have much greater value for older workers than for young employees on their first job.

Effort-Performance Expectancy Individuals also attach a certain probability of success to behavior. This expectancy represents the individual's perception of how hard it will be for him or her to achieve such behavior. For example, employees may have a strong expectancy (e.g., 90 percent) that if they put forth the effort, they can produce ten units an hour, but may feel that they have only a 50-50 chance of producing fifteen units an hour if they try.

Together, these concepts provide a basis for generalizing about motivation. An individual's motivation to behave in a certain way is greatest when he or she believes that the behavior will lead to certain outcomes (performance—outcome expectancy), feels that these outcomes are attractive, and believes that performance at a desired level is possible (effort-performance expectancy).

Given a number of alternative levels of behavior (ten, fifteen, or twenty units of production per hour, for example), a person will choose the level of performance with which the greatest motivational force is associated, as indicated by a combination of the relevant expectancies, outcomes, and values. In other words, he or she considers questions such as Can I perform at that level if I try? If I perform at that level, what will happen? and How do I feel about those things that will happen? The individual then decides to behave in a way that seems to have the best chance of producing positive, desired outcomes.

On the basis of these concepts, it is possible to construct a general model of behavior in organizational settings (see Figure 1). Motivation is seen as a force impelling an individual to expend effort. Performance depends on both the level of the effort put

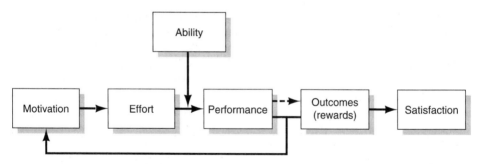

A person's motivation is a function of:
1 Effort-to-performance expectancies
2 Performance-to-outcome expectancies
3 Perceived attractiveness of outcomes

FIGURE 1
The expectancy-theory model.

forth *and* the individual's ability—which in turn reflects his or her skills, training, information, and talents. Effort thus combines with ability to produce a given level of performance. As a result of performance, the individual attains certain outcomes (rewards). The model indicates this relationship in a dotted line, reflecting the fact that people sometimes are not rewarded although they have performed. As this process of performance reward occurs repeatedly, the actual events provide information that influences an individual's perception (particularly expectancies) and thus influences motivation in the future. This is shown in the model by the line connecting the performance-outcome link with motivation.

Rewards can be both external and internal. When individuals perform at a given level, they can receive positive or negative outcomes from supervisors, coworkers, the organization's reward system, or other environmental sources. A second type of reward comes from the performance of the task itself (e.g., feelings of accomplishment, personal worth, achievement). In a sense individuals give these rewards to themselves when they feel they are deserved. The environment cannot give them or take them away directly; it can only make them possible.

The model also suggests that satisfaction is best thought of as a result of performance rather than as a cause of it. Strictly speaking, satisfaction does influence motivation in some ways. For instance, when it is perceived to come about as a result of performance, it can increase motivation because it strengthens people's beliefs about the consequences of performance. Also, satisfaction can lead to a decrease in the importance of certain outcomes (a satisfied need is no longer a motivation), and as a result, it can decrease motivation.

The expectancy model is a deceptively simple statement of the conditions that must exist if rewards are to motivate performance. It suggests that all an organization has to do is relate pay and other frequently valued rewards to obtainable levels of performance. But if the reward system is to be an effective motivator, the connection between performance and rewards must be visible, and a climate of trust and credibility must exist in the organization. The belief that performance will lead to rewards is essentially a prediction about the future. Individuals cannot make this kind of prediction unless they trust the system that is promising them the rewards. Unfortunately, it is not always clear how a climate of trust in the reward system can be established. However, as will be discussed later, research suggests that a high level of openness and the use of participation can contribute to trust in the pay system.

Skill Development

Just as reward systems can motivate performance they can motivate skill development. They can do this by tying rewards to skill development. To a limited degree most pay-for-performance systems do this indirectly by rewarding the performance that results from the skill. Pay systems that pay the holders of higher-level, more complex jobs also reward skill development when and if it leads to obtaining a higher-level job.

Technical ladders, which are often used in research and development settings, are intended to reward skill development more directly. As will be discussed later, some skill-based pay plans have recently been installed in some settings. They give individuals more pay as they develop specific skills. Like merit pay systems these systems are often difficult to manage because skill acquisition can be hard to measure. When they are well designed and administered, however, there is little question that they can motivate skill development (Lawler 1981).

The relationship between skill development and organizational effectiveness is not always a direct one. The nature of the technology an organization deals with or the availability of skilled labor may make this a low priority for an organization. Thus, although the reward system may be used to motivate skill development, in some instances this may not have a positive impact on organizational effectiveness.

Culture

Reward systems contribute to the overall culture or climate of an organization. Depending upon how they are developed, administered, and managed, reward systems can help create and maintain a human-resources-oriented, entrepreneurial, innovative, competence-based, bureaucratic, or participative culture.

Reward systems can shape culture precisely because of their important influence on motivation, satisfaction, and membership. The behaviors they evoke become the dominant patterns of behavior in the organization and lead to perceptions about what it stands for, believes in, and values.

Perhaps the most obvious connection between reward systems and culture concerns the practice of performance-based pay. A policy of linking—or not linking—pay and performance can have a dramatic impact on the culture because it so clearly communicates what the norms of performance are in the organization. Many other features of the reward system also influence culture. For example, relatively high pay levels can produce a culture in which people feel they are an elite group working for a top-flight company, while innovative pay practices such as flexible benefits can produce a culture of innovativeness. Finally, having employees participate in pay decisions can produce a participative culture in which employees are generally involved in business decisions and as a result are committed to the organization and its success.

Reinforcement and Definition of Structure

The reward system can reinforce and define the organization's structure (Lawler 1981). Because this effect is often not fully considered in the design of reward systems, their structural impact may be unintended. This does not mean it is insignificant. Indeed, the reward system can help define the status hierarchy, the degree to which people in technical positions can influence people in line-management positions, and the kind of decision structure used. As will be discussed later, the key issues here seem to be the degree to which the reward system is hierarchical and the degree to which it allocates rewards on the basis of movements up the hierarchy.

Cost

Reward systems are often a significant cost factor. Indeed, the pay system alone may represent over 50 percent of the organization's operating cost. Thus, it is important in strategically designing the reward system to focus on how high these costs should be and how they will vary as a function of the organization's ability to pay. For example, a well-designed pay system might lead to higher costs when the organization has the money to spend and lower costs when it does not. An additional objective might be to lower overall reward-system costs than business competitors.

In summary, reward systems in organizations should be assessed from a cost-benefit perspective. The cost can be managed and controlled and the benefits planned for. The key is to identify the outcomes needed for the organization to be successful and then to design the reward system in such a way that these outcomes will be realized.

RELATIONSHIP TO STRATEGIC PLANNING

Figure 2 presents a way of viewing the relationship between strategic planning and reward systems. It suggests that once the strategic plan is developed, the organization needs to focus on the kinds of human resources, climate, and behavior that are needed to make it effective. The next step is to design reward systems that will motivate the right kind of performance, attract the right kind of people, and create a supportive climate and structure.

Figure 3 suggests another way in which the reward system needs to be taken into consideration in strategic planning. Before the strategic plan is developed, it is important to assess a variety of factors, including the current reward system, and to determine what kind of behavior, climate, and structure they foster. This step is needed to ensure that the strategic plan is based on a realistic assessment of the organization's current condition and the changes likely to be needed to implement the new strategic plan. This point is particularly pertinent to organizations that are considering going into new lines of business, developing new strategic plans, and acquiring new divisions.

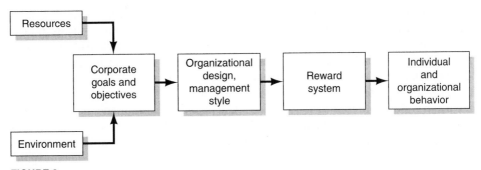

FIGURE 2
Goals and reward-system design.

Often, new lines of business require a different behavior and therefore a different reward system. Simply putting the old reward system in place can actually lead to failure in the new business. On the other hand, developing a new reward system for the new business can cause problems in the old business because of the comparisons that will be made between different parts of the same organization. The need for reward system changes must be carefully assessed before an organization enters into new business sectors.

DESIGN OPTIONS

Organizational reward systems can be designed and managed in virtually an infinite number of ways. A host of rewards can be distributed in a large number of ways. The rest of this chapter focuses on the visible extrinsic rewards that an organization can allocate to its members on a targeted basis: promotion, status symbols, and perquisites. Little attention will be given to such intrinsic rewards as feelings of responsibility, competence, and personal growth and development.

FIGURE 3
Determinants of strategic plan.

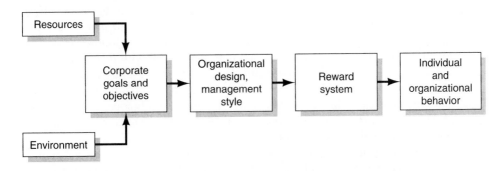

All organizational systems have a content or structural dimension as well as a process dimension. In a reward system, the content is the formal mechanisms, procedures, and practices (e.g., the salary structures, the performance-appraisal forms)—in short, the nuts and bolts of the system. Its communication and decision processes are also important. Key issues here are how much is revealed about how the reward system operates and how people are rewarded, and how much participation is allowed in the design and administration of the system. Many organizations administer rewards in a top-down, secretive way. Often this practice does not reflect a conscious choice. As discussed subsequently, organizations may wish to consider other ways that rewards can be administered.

Reward systems play important roles in organizational change efforts. They can aid or inhibit efforts to increase effectiveness. Ordinarily, major changes in other important organizational systems require a modification of the reward systems to ensure that all systems work well together. A key design decision then concerns the coordination of reward-system changes with other changes (for example, should they lead or lag?).

To begin the discussion of design choices, we will look at some key structural choices and then some key process choices. Finally the issue of pay and organizational change will be considered.

STRUCTURAL DECISIONS

Bases for Rewards

Job Based   Traditionally in organizations such rewards as pay and perquisites have been based on the type of job a person does. Indeed, with the exception of bonuses and merit salary increases, the standard policy in most organizations is to evaluate the job, not the person, and then to set the reward level. This approach is based on the assumption that job worth can be determined and that the person doing the job is worth only as much to the organization as the job itself is worth. This assumption is in many respects valid, because such techniques as job-evaluation programs make it possible to determine what other organizations are paying people to do the same or similar jobs. A job-based reward system assures an organization that its compensation costs are not dramatically out of line with those of its competitors, and it gives a somewhat objective basis to compensation practices.

Skill Based   An alternative to job-based pay that has recently been tried by a number of organizations is to pay individuals for their skills. In many cases this approach will not lead to pay rates very different from those of a job-based system. After all, people's skills are usually matched reasonably well with their jobs. A skill approach can, however, produce some different results in several respects. Often people have more skills than the job uses, in which case they would be paid more than under a job-based system. In other cases, newly appointed job-holders do not initially have all the skills associated with the position; they would have to earn the right to be paid whatever it is the job-related skills are worth.

Perhaps the most important changes introduced with skill-based or competence-based pay are in organizational climate and motivation. Instead of being rewarded for moving up the hierarchy, people are rewarded for increasing their skills and developing themselves. This policy can create a climate of concern for personal growth and development and produce a highly talented work force. It also can decrease the attractiveness of upward mobility and the traditional type of career progression. In factories where this system has been used, many people learn to perform multiple tasks, so that the work force becomes highly knowledgeable and flexible.

Skill-based pay tends to produce an interesting mix of positive and negative features as far as the organization is concerned (Lawler 1981). It typically produces somewhat higher pay levels for individuals, but this higher cost is usually offset by greater work-force flexibility. Lower staffing levels are also possible, there are fewer problems when absenteeism or turnover occur, and indeed absenteeism and turnover may be reduced, because people like the opportunity to utilize and be paid for a wide range of skills. On the other hand, skill-based pay can be rather challenging to administer. There is no easy way of determining how much a skill is worth, and skill assessment can often be difficult. Several systems have been developed for evaluating jobs and comparing them to the marketplace, but there are no analogous systems for workers' skills.

There are no well-established rules to determine which organizational situations best fit job-based pay and which best fit skill- or competence-based pay. In general, skill-based pay seems best suited to organizations that want to have a flexible, relatively permanent work force that is oriented toward learning, growth, and development. It also seems to fit particularly well with new plant start-ups and other situations in which the greatest need is for skill development. Despite its newness and the potential operational problems, skill-based pay seems to be a system that more and more organizations will be using.

Performance Based Perhaps the key strategic decision made in the design of any reward system is whether or not it will be based on performance. Once this decision is made, other features of the system tend to fall into place. The major alternative to basing pay on performance is to tie it to seniority. Many government organizations, for example, base their rates on the job the person does and then on how long he or she has been in that job. In Japan, individual pay is often based on seniority, although individuals may receive bonuses based on corporate performance.

Most business organizations in the United States say that they reward individual performance and describe their pay system and their promotion system as merit-based. A true merit pay or promotion system is often more easily aspired to than done, however. It has been observed that many organizations would be better off if they did not try to relate pay and promotion to performance, but relied on other bases for motivating performance (Kerr 1975; Goldberg 1977; Hills 1979). It is difficult to specify what kind of performance is desired and often equally difficult to determine whether that performance has been demonstrated. There is ample evidence that a poorly designed and administered reward system can do more harm than good (see, for example, Whyte 1955; Lawler 1971). On the other hand, when pay is effectively related to the desired performance, it clearly helps to motivate, attract, and retain outstanding performers. Thus, when it is feasible, it is usually desirable to relate pay to performance.

How to relate pay to performance is often the most important strategic decision an organization makes. The options are numerous. The kind of pay reward that is given can vary widely, and many include such things as stock and cash. In addition, the interval between rewards can range from a few minutes to many years. Performance can be measured at various levels. Each individual may get a reward based on his or her own performance. In addition, rewards based on the performance of a particular group can be given to each of its members. Or everyone in the organization can be given an award based on the performance of the total organization. Finally, many different kinds of performance can be rewarded. For example, managers can be rewarded for sales increases, productivity volumes, their ability to develop their subordinates, their cost-reduction ideas, and so on.

Rewarding some behaviors and not others has clear implications for performance. Thus decisions about what is to be rewarded need to be made carefully and with attention to the overall strategic plan of the business (see, for example, Galbraith and Nathanson 1978; Salscheider 1981). Consideration needs to be given to such issues as short- versus long-term performance, risk taking versus risk aversion, division performance versus total corporate performance, ROI (return on investment) maximization versus sales growth, and so on. Once key performance objectives have been defined for the strategic plan, the reward system needs to be designed to motivate the appropriate performance. Decisions about such issues as the use of stock options (a long-term incentive), for example, should be made only after careful consideration of whether they will encourage the kind of behavior that is desired (see, for example, Crystal 1978; Ellig 1982). In large organizations, it is quite likely that the managers of different divisions should be rewarded for different kinds of performance. Growth businesses call for different reward systems from those of "cash cows," because the managers are expected to produce different results (see Stata and Maidique 1980, for an example).

A detailed discussion of the many approaches to relating pay and performance is beyond the scope of this chapter. Table 1 gives an idea of some of the design features that are possible in a reward system, and some of the advantages and disadvantages of each.

The first column in the table rates each plan in terms of its effectiveness in creating the perception that pay is tied to performance. In general, this indicates the degree to which the approach leads employees to believe that higher pay will follow good performance. Second, each plan is evaluated in terms of whether it produced the negative side effects often associated with performance-based pay plans (such as social ostracism of good performers, defensive behavior, and giving false data about performance). Third, each plan is rated as to its ability to encourage cooperation among employees. Finally, employee acceptance of the plan is indicated. The ratings were developed on the basis of a review of the literature and my experience with the different types of plans (see, for example, Lawler 1971).

Several patterns appear in the ratings. Pay to performance are seen as most closely linked in the individual plans; group plans are rated next; and organizational plans are rated lowest. In organizational plans, and to a lesser extent in group plans, an individual's pay is not directly a function of his or her behavior, but depends on the behavior of many others. In addition, when some types of performance measures (e.g., profits) are used, pay is influenced by external conditions that employees cannot control.

TABLE 1
RATINGS OF VARIOUS PAY-INCENTIVE PLANS

		Tie pay to performance	Negative side effect	Encourage cooperation	Employee acceptance
Salary reward					
Individual plan	Productivity	4	1	1	4
	Cost effectiveness	3	1	1	4
	Superiors' rating	3	1	1	3
Group plan	Productivity	3	1	2	4
	Cost effectiveness	3	1	2	4
	Superiors' rating	2	1	2	3
Organizational plan	Productivity	2	1	3	4
	Cost effectiveness	2	1	2	4
Bonus					
Individual plan	Productivity	5	3	1	2
	Cost effectiveness	4	2	1	2
	Superiors' rating	4	2	1	2
Group plan	Productivity	4	1	3	3
	Cost effectiveness	3	1	3	3
	Superiors' rating	3	1	3	3
Organizational plan	Productivity	3	1	1	4
	Cost effectiveness	3	1	3	4
	Profit	2	1	2	4

Note: On a scale of 1 to 5, 1 = low and 5 = high.

Bonus plans are generally seen as more closely tied to performance than pay-raise and salary-increase plans. The use of bonuses permits substantial variation in an individual's pay from one time period to another. With salary-increase plans, in contrast, such flexibility is very difficult because past raises tend not to be rescinded.

Approaches that use objective measures of performance are rated higher than those that rely on subjective measures. In general, objective measures enjoy higher credibility; that is, employees will often accept the validity of an objective measure, such as sales volume or units produced, when they will not accept a superior's evaluation of their performance. When pay is tied to objective measures, therefore, it is usually clear to employees that it is determined by performance. Objective measures are also often publicly measurable. Thus the relationship between performance and pay is much more visible than when it is tied to a subjective, nonverifiable measure, such as a supervisor's rating. Overall, the data suggest that individually based bonus plans that rely on objective measures produce the strongest perceived connection between pay and performance.

The ratings indicate that most plans have little tendency to produce negative side effects. The notable exceptions here are individual bonus and incentive plans below the management level. These plans often lead to situations in which good performance leads to social rejection and ostracism, so that employees present false performance data and restrict their production. These side effects are particularly likely to appear where trust is low and subjective productivity standards are used.

In terms of the third criterion—encouraging cooperation—the ratings are generally higher for group and organizational plans than for individual plans. Under group and organizational plans, it is generally to everyone's advantage that an individual work effectively, because all share in the financial fruits of higher performance. This is not true under an individual plan. As a result, good performance is much more likely to be supported and encouraged by others when group and organizational plans are used.

Most performance-based pay plans achieve only moderate employee acceptance. The ratings show individual bonus plans to be least acceptable, particularly among nonmanagement employees, presumably because of their tendency to encourage competitive relationships between employees and the difficulty of administering such plans fairly.

No one performance-based pay plan represents a panacea, and it is unlikely that any organization will ever be completely satisfied with the approach it chooses. Furthermore, some of the plans that make the greatest contributions to organizational effectiveness do not make the greatest contributions to quality of work life, and vice versa. Still, the situation is not completely hopeless. When all factors are taken into account, group and organizational bonus plans that are based on objective data receive high ratings, as do individual-level salary-increase plans.

Many organizations employ multiple or combination reward systems. For example, they may use a salary-increase system that rewards workers for their individual performance while at the same time giving everybody in the division or plant a bonus based on divisional performance. Some plans measure group or company performance, calculate the bonus based on divisional performance. Some plans measure group or company performance, calculate the bonus pool generated by the performance of a group, and then divide it among group members on the basis of individual performance. By rewarding workers for both individual and group performance, the organization tries to motivate individuals to perform all needed behaviors (see, for example, Lincoln 1951; Fox 1979).

A common error in the design of many pay-for-performance systems is the tendency to focus no measurable short-term operating results because they are quantifiable and regularly obtained in any case. In particular, many organizations reward their top managers on the basis of quarterly or annual profitability (Fox 1979). Such a scheme can make managers very short-sighted in their behavior and encourage them to ignore strategic objectives important to the long-term profitability of the organization. A similar error is the tendency to depend on completely subjective performance appraisals for the allocation of pay rewards. There is considerable evidence that these performance appraisals are often biased and invalid, and instead of contributing to positive motivation and a good work climate that improves superior-subordinate relationships, they do just the opposite (see, for example, DeVries et al. 1981; Latham and Wexley 1981). Other common errors include the giving of too small rewards, failure to explain systems clearly, and poor administrative practices.

In summary, decision of whether to relate pay to performance is a crucial one in any organization. It can be a serious error to assume automatically that they should be related. A sound linkage can contribute greatly to organizational effectiveness. But a poor job can be harmful. Specifically, if performance is difficult to measure and/or rewards are difficult to distribute on the basis of performance, a pay-for-performance system can motivate counterproductive behaviors, invite lawsuits charging discrimination, and create a climate of mistrust, low credibility, and managerial incompetence. On the other hand, to declare that pay is unrelated to performance would be to give up a potentially important motivational tool and perhaps condemn the organization to a lower level of performance. The ideal, of course, is to foster conditions in which pay can be effectively related to performance and as a result contribute to the effectiveness of the organization.

Promotion, training opportunities, fringe benefits, and status symbols are important extrinsic rewards that, like pay, can be linked to performance. When they are linked to pay and are important, they, like pay, can motivate performance. The issues involved in relating them to performance are very similar to those involved in relating pay to performance, thus they will not be discussed in detail. As a general rule they are not usually tied to performance in organizations to the degree that pay is. They also are less flexible than is pay. This is, they are harder to give in varying amounts and to take away once they have been given.

Market Position

The reward structure of an organization influences behavior partially as a function of how the size of its rewards compares to what other organizations give. Organizations frequently have well-developed policies about how their pay levels should compare with the pay levels in other companies. For example, some companies (e.g., IBM) feel it is important to be a leader and consciously pay more than any of the companies with which they compete. Other companies are content to set their pay levels at or below the market for the people they hire. This structural issue in the design of reward systems is a critical one because it can strongly influence the kind of people that are attracted and retained by an organization as well as the turnover rate and the number of job applicants. Simply stated, organizations that pay above market end up attracting and retaining more people. From a business point of view this policy may pay off for them, particularly if turnover is a costly factor in the organization and if the business strategy requires a stable, highly talented staff.

On the other hand, if many of the jobs in the organization are low skilled and people are readily available in the labor market to do them, then a corporate strategy of high pay may not be effective. It can increase labor costs without offsetting benefits. Of course, organizations need not pay above market for all their jobs. Indeed, some organizations identify certain key skills that they need and pay generously for them, while offering average or below-average pay for other skills. This approach has some obvious business advantages, because it allows the organization to attract critically needed skills and at the same time to control costs.

Although it not often recognized, the market position that a company adopts with respect to its reward systems can also affect organization climate. For example, a policy of paying above market can make people feel that they are members of an elite organization that employs only competent people and that they are indeed fortunate to be there. A policy that awards extra pay to certain skilled employees but leaves the rest of the organization at a lower pay level can cause divisive social pressures within the organization.

Finally, some organizations try to offer more noncash compensation than the average as a way of competing for the talent they need. They talk in terms of producing an above-average quality of work life, and stress not only hygiene factors but interesting and challenging work. This stance potentially can be a very effective one and could give the organization a competitive edge, at least in attracting people who value these things. Still other organizations stress such noncash rewards as status symbols and perquisites. This approach also can be effective in attracting certain kinds of people.

In summary, the market position and mix of an organization's total reward package has a critical effect on both the behavior of members and the climate of the organization. This decision needs to be carefully related to the general business strategy of the organization, in particular, to the kind of human resources needed and the organization climate desired.

Internal/External-Pay-Comparison Oriented

Organizations differ in the degree to which they strive toward internal equity in their pay and reward systems. An internal-equity-oriented company tries to see that individuals doing similar work will be paid the same even though they are in very different parts of the country and/or in different businesses. Some corporations (e.g., IBM) base their national pay structure on the highest pay that a job receives anywhere in the country. Organizations that do not stress internal equity typically focus on the external labor market as the key determinant of what somebody should be paid. Although this approach does not necessarily produce different pay for people doing the same job, it may. For example, two industries—say, electronics and automobiles—may differ significantly in what they pay for the same job.

The internal-equity approach has both advantages and disadvantages. It can facilitate the transfer of people from one location to another, because there will be no pay difference to contend with. Similarly, it avoids the problems of rivalry and dissatisfaction that can develop within the organization if one location or division pays more than another. In addition, it can produce an organizational climate of homogeneity and the feeling that all work for the same company and all are treated fairly.

On the other hand, a focus on internal equity can be very expensive, particularly if pay rates across a diversified corporation are set at the highest level that the market demands anywhere in the corporation (Salscheider 1981). If it pays much more than is necessary to attract and retain good people, the organization may become noncompetitive in certain businesses and find that it has to limit itself to businesses in which its pay structures permit competitive labor costs. Overly high labor costs have, for example, often made it difficult for auto and oil and gas companies to compete in new business areas.

In summary, the difference between focusing on external equity and internal equity is a crucial one in the design of pay systems. It can influence the organization's cost structure as well as its climate and behavior. The general rule is that highly diversified companies are pulled more strongly toward an external market orientation, while organizations that are based on a single industry or single technology typically find themselves more comfortable with an internal-equity emphasis.

Centralized/Decentralized Reward Strategy

Closely related to the issue of internal versus external equity is the question of centralization. Organizations that adopt a centralized-reward-system strategy typically make the corporate staff responsible for seeing that such things as pay practices are similar throughout the organization. They ordinarily develop standard pay grades and pay ranges, standardized job-evaluation systems, and perhaps standardized promotion systems. In decentralized organizations, decisions about pay, promotion, and other rewards are left to local option. Sometimes the corporations suggest broad guidelines or principles to follow, but the day-to-day administration and design of the system is left up to the local entity.

The advantages of a centralized structure rest primarily in the expertise that can be accumulated at the central level and the homogeneity that is produced in the organization. This homogeneity can lead to a clear image of the corporate climate, feelings of internal equity, and the belief that the organization stands for something. It also eases the job of communicating and understanding what is going on in different parts of the organization. The decentralized strategy allows for local innovation and for closely fitting reward practices to the particular business.

There is no one right choice between the centralized and decentralized approaches to reward system design and administration. Overall, the decentralized system tends to make the most sense when the organization is involved in businesses that face different markets and perhaps are at different points in their life cycles (Greiner 1972; Galbraith and Nathanson 1978). It allows variation in practices that can give a competitive advantage to one part of the business but may prove to be a real hindrance in another. For example, such perquisites as cars are often standard operating procedure in one business but not in another. Similarly, extensive bonuses may be needed to attract one group of people, for example, oil-exploration engineers, but not others, for example, research scientists. Overall, then, an organization needs to look carefully at its mix of businesses and the degree to which it wants a single set of principles or policies to prevail across all its operating divisions, and then decide whether a centralized or decentralized reward strategy is likely to be more effective.

Degree of Hierarchy

Closely related to the issue of job-based versus competence-based pay is the strategic decision concerning the hierarchical nature of the organization's reward systems. Often no formal decision is ever made to have a relatively hierarchical or relatively egalitarian approach to rewards. A hierarchical approach simply happens because it is so consistent with the general way organizations are run. Hierarchical systems usually pay people more money and give them greater perquisites and symbols of office as they move higher up the organization ladder. This approach strongly reinforces the traditional hierarchical power relationships in the organization and fosters a climate of different status and power levels. In some cases, a hierarchical reward system may include more levels than the formal organization chart, creating additional status differences in the organization.

The alternative to a hierarchical system is one that downplays differences in rewards and perquisites based only on hierarchical level. For example, in large corporations that adopt an egalitarian stance to rewards (e.g., Digital Equipment Corporation), such privileges as private parking spaces, executive restrooms, and special entrances are eliminated. People from all levels in the organization eat together, work together, and travel together. Further, high levels of pay are not restricted to managers but can be earned by those who have worked their way up a technical ladder. This approach to rewards produces a distinctive climate in an organization, encouraging decision making by expertise rather than by hierarchy position, and minimizing status differentials in the organization.

In general, a steeply hierarchical system makes the most sense when an organization needs relatively rigid bureaucratic behavior, strong top-down authority, and a strong motivation for people to move up the organizational hierarchy. A more egalitarian approach fits with a more participative management style and the desire to retain technical specialists and experts in nonmanagement or lower-level-management roles. It is not surprising, therefore, that many of the organizations that emphasize egalitarian perquisites are in high-technology and knowledge-based industries.

Reward Mix

The kind of rewards that organizations give to individuals can vary widely. Monetary rewards, for example, can take many forms, from stock to medical insurance. When cash rewards are translated into fringe benefits, perquisites, or other trappings of office, they may lose their value for some people and as a result may be a poor investment for the employer (see, for example, Nealy 1963; Lawler 1971). On the other hand, certain benefits can best be obtained through mass purchase, and therefore many individuals want the organization to provide them. In addition, certain status symbols or perquisites may be valued by some individuals beyond their actual dollar cost to the organization and thus represent good buys. Finally, as was mentioned earlier there often are some climate and organizational structure reasons for paying people in the form of perquisites and status symbols.

One interesting development in the area of compensation is the flexible or cafeteria-style benefit program (Fragner 1975; Lawler 1981). The theory is that if individuals are allowed to tailor their own reward packages to fit their particular needs, the organization will get the best value for its money, because it will give people only those things that they desire. Such an approach also has the advantage of treating individuals as mature adults rather than as dependent people who need their welfare looked after in a structured way. While flexible benefit programs have not yet been widely implemented, the results of experiments to date have been favorable, and there is reason to believe that other organizations may adopt this approach in the near future, because it can offer a strategic cost-benefit advantage in attracting and retaining certain types of employees.

Overall, the forms in which the organization rewards its members should be consistent with the climate it hopes to foster. For example, a flexible compensation package is highly congruent with a participative open organization climate that treats individuals as mature adults and wants to attract talented mature people. A highly status-symbol-oriented approach, on the other hand, may appeal to people who value position power and need a high level of visible reinforcement for their position. This would seem to fit best in a relatively bureaucratic organization that relies on position power and authority to carry out its actions.

PROCESS ISSUES AND REWARD ADMINISTRATION

Reward system design and administration raise numerous process issues. Indeed, process issues are confronted more frequently than structure and content issues, because organizations must constantly make reward-system management, implementation, and communication decisions while structures tend to be relatively firmly fixed in place. Rather than discussing specific process issues here, the focus will be on broad process themes that can be used to characterize the way reward systems are designed and administered.

Communication Policy

Organizations differ widely in how much information they communicate about their reward systems. At one extreme, some organizations are extremely secretive, particularly in the area of pay. They forbid people to talk about their individual rewards, give minimal information to individuals about how rewards are decided upon and allocated, and have no publicly disseminated policies about such things as market position, the approach to gathering market data, and potential increases and rewards for individuals. At the other extreme, some organizations are so open that everyone's pay is a matter of public record, as is the overall organization pay philosophy (many new high-involvement plants operate this way; see, for example, Lawler 1978; Walton 1980). In addition, all promotions are subject to open job postings, and in some instances peer groups discuss the individual's eligibility for promotion.

The difference between an open and a closed communication policy in the area of rewards is enormous. There is no clear right or wrong approach. The issue is rather to choose a position on the continuum from open to secretive that is supportive of the overall climate and types of behavior needed for organizational effectiveness. An open system tends to encourage people to ask questions, share data, and ultimately be involved in decisions. A secretive system tends to put people in a more dependent position, to keep power concentrated at the top, and to allow an organization to keep its options open with respect to commitments to individuals. Secrecy can lead to considerable distortion in people's beliefs about the rewards given to other organization members, and can create a low-trust environment in which the relationship between pay and performance is not clear (see, for example, Lawler 1971; Steele 1975). Thus, a structurally sound pay system may end up being rather ineffective because its strong secrecy policies open it to misperceptions.

Open systems put considerable pressure on organizations to do an effective job of administering rewards. Thus, if such difficult-to-defend policies as merit pay are to be implemented, considerable time and effort needs to be invested in pay administration.

If such policies are poorly administered, strong pressures usually develop to eliminate discrimination and pay everyone the same (see, for example, Burroughs 1982). Ironically, therefore, if an organization wants to spend little time administering rewards but still wants to base pay on merit, secrecy may be the best policy, although secrecy in turn may limit the effectiveness of the merit pay plan.

Decision-Making Practices

Closely related to the issue of communication is the matter of how decisions about compensation are to be made. If individuals are to be actively involved in decisions concerning reward systems, they need to have information about policy and actual practice. Open communication makes it possible to involve a wide range of people in the decision-making process. Secrecy by its very nature limits the number of people who can be involved in pay decisions.

It is important to distinguish between decisions concerning the design and ongoing administration of reward systems. Traditionally, of course, organizations have made both design and administration decisions in a top-down manner. But it is possible to adopt a different decision-making style for each type of decision.

Systems typically have been designed by top management with the aid of staff support and administered by strict reliance on the chain of command. The assumption has been that this approach provides the proper checks and balances in the system and locates decision making where the expertise rests. In many cases this is a valid assumption and certainly fits well with an organizational management style that emphasizes hierarchy, bureaucracy, and control through the use of extrinsic rewards. It does not fit, however, with an organization that believes in more open communication, higher levels of employee involvement, and control through individual commitment to policies. Nor does it fit when expertise is broadly spread throughout the organization, as is often true in companies that rely heavily on knowledge workers or spend a great deal of effort training their people to become expert in technical functions.

Some organizations have experimented with involving employees in the design of pay systems (Lawler 1981). Favorable results have generally been achieved when employees help design their own bonus system. They tend to raise important issues and provide expertise not normally available to the designers of the system. And perhaps more importantly, once the system is designed, it is well accepted and understood. Employee involvement often makes possible a rapid start-up of the system and creates a commitment to see it survive long-term. In other cases systems have been designed by line managers, because they are the ones that need to maintain it. Unless they have had an opportunity for design input, it often is unrealistic to expect line people to have the same level of commitment to the pay system as the staff people have.

Some organizations have also experimented with having peer groups and low-level supervisory people handling the day-to-day decision making about who should receive pay increases and how jobs should be evaluated and placed in pay structures. The best examples are the new participative plants that use skill-based pay (see, for example, Walton 1980). In these plants, the work group typically reviews an individual's performance and decides whether he or she has acquired the new skills. This approach appears to work well. Peers often have the best information about performance and thus are in a good position to make a performance assessment. In traditional organizations their expertise is of no use, because they lack the motivation to give valid feedback and to respond responsibly. In more participative open systems, this motivational problem seems to be less severe, and as a result involvement in decision making is more effective.

In a few cases, executives have been asked to assess each other in a peer-group reward system (e.g., in Graphic Controls Corporation). Again, this approach can apparently work well in an organization that has a history of open and effective communication. Deciding on rewards is clearly not an easy task, and thus should not be assigned to a group unless members have good confrontation skills and can talk openly and directly about each other's performance.

Overall, there is evidence that some participative approaches to reward systems can be effective because of their congruence with the overall style and because the skills and norms needed to make them work are already in place. In more traditional organizations, the typical top-down approach to reward-system design and administration probably remains the best. From a strategic point of view, then, the decision about how much participation is desirable in reward-system design and administration depends on whether a participative, high-involvement type of organization is best suited to accomplish the strategic objectives of the business. If so, then participation in pay decisions and reward-system decisions should be considered.

REWARD SYSTEMS AND ORGANIZATIONAL CHANGE

In many major organizational changes, it is difficult to alter all the relevant systems in the organization simultaneously. Typically one change leads to another. Modification of the reward systems may either lead or lag in the overall change process.

Reward as a Lead

Perhaps the most widely discussed example of pay as a lead change is the use of a gain-sharing plan to improve plant productivity (Moore and Ross 1978; Lawler 1981). In these situations the initial change effort is the installation of a system of bonuses based on improvements in productivity. In the case of the Scanlon Plan, attempts are also made to build participative problem-solving groups into the organization, but the clear emphasis is on the gain-sharing formula and the financial benefits of improved productivity. The participative management structure is intended to facilitate productivity improvement, which in turn will result in gains to be shared. Not surprisingly, once gain-sharing starts and factors inhibiting productivity are identified, other changes follow. Typical of these are improvements in the organization structures, the design of jobs and work, and additional training programs. The gain-sharing plan itself provides a strong motivation to swiftly and effectively deal with those issues.

Other reward system changes can also lead to broader organizational change efforts. For example, the introduction of skill-based pay can potentially prompt a broad movement to participation because it gives people the skills and knowledge they need to participate. The movement to a more flexible fringe-benefit program can change organizational climate by creating one of innovation in the area of human-resource management.

In a somewhat different vein, a dramatic change in the pay-for-performance system can be very effective in shaping an organization's strategic directions. For example, installing bonus systems that reward previously neglected performance indicators can dramatically shift the directions of an organization. Similarly, a long-term bonus plan for executives can lead them to change their time horizons and their decision-making practices in important ways.

Rewards as a Lag

In most major organization change efforts, pay is a lag factor. As an organization moves toward participative management, for example, the initial thrust often comes in such areas as team building, job redesign, and quality circles. It is only after these practices have been in place for some time that the organization makes the associated changes in the reward system. Often, the organization does not originally anticipate a need to revise the reward system. But because all organizational systems are interconnected, it is almost inevitable that major changes in strategic direction or management style and practices will require that changes be made in the reward system as well.

New participative plants represent an interesting example of the simultaneous installation of participative reward systems and other participative practices (Lawler 1981). The success of these plants is probably due in part to the fact that all their systems have operated in a participative manner from the outset.

Rewards as a Motivator of Change

Major strategic changes are often difficult to accomplish even though they don't involve a change in management style. The forces of equilibrium have the effect of canceling out many changes. To the extent that changing one component of an organizational system reduces its congruence with other components, energy will develop to limit, encapsulate, or reverse the change. In addition, attention may be diverted from other important tasks by the need to direct a change, deal with resistance, and cope with the problems created by change.

Management is therefore faced with two key tasks if change is to be brought about. The first is *motivating change*—overcoming natural resistance and encouraging individuals to behave in ways that are consistent with both the immediate change goals and long-range corporate strategy. The second major task is *managing change*.

It is useful to think of organizational changes in terms of transitions (Beckhard and Harris 1977). The organization exists in a current state (C). An image has been developed of a future state of the organization (F). The period between C and F can be thought of as the transition period (T). The question is how to manage the transition. Too often, however, managers overlook the transition state, assuming that all that is needed is to design that best possible future. They think of change as simply a mechanical or procedural detail.

In most situations, the management systems and structures developed to manage either C or F are simply not appropriate for the management of T. They are steady-state management systems, designed to run organizations already in place rather than transitional management systems. During the transition period, different systems, and specifically different reward systems, may be needed temporarily. Many change efforts are resisted because organization members see them as a threat to their pay level. Particularly when the present system is highly standardized and tied to objective measures, such as the number of subordinates, people may resist a reorganization or other type of change whose impact on their pay is unclear but potentially negative. There is no magic formula for overcoming this resistance, but two approaches can help.

First, a floor should be put under individual pay rates throughout the transition period. That is, no one should have to fear losing pay during the change process. This point is critical in the case of a major reorganization, which may require some people to give up some subordinates and responsibilities, and to accept a lower salary if their jobs were reevaluated. If this problem is likely to be severe, the organization may want to assure individuals that their pay will not be cut, even after the change is in place.

A second important step is to appoint a group of high-level managers to develop an approach to compensation that will fit the new organization. This group should articulate a corporate rewards philosophy that includes the following:

1 The goals of the pay system
2 How the pay system will fit the new organizational structure
3 The fit between the management style of the organization and the process used to administer the pay system
4 How the pay system will be managed once it is developed

There are several reasons for developing a compensation system in this way. First, a philosophical base is needed for an effective pay system. More and more evidence is accumulating that, unless supported by some sort of widely accepted philosophy, corporate pay administration ends up being haphazard and a source of internal conflict. A philosophy cannot answer all the problems associated with rewards, but it can at least provide a touchstone against which new practices, policies, and decisions can be tested.

A second advantage of the group approach is that it will give key individuals a chance to influence how they will be paid in the future. A big unknown in the new organization thus becomes something under their control, rather than a potentially threatening factor about the reorganized structure. Moreover, by seriously considering how the pay system will have to change to fit other changes, the group can prevent "surprise" pay-system problems from occurring once the other changes have been implemented. Finally, as discussed further below, by assuring that an acceptable supporting pay system will exist, the group can promote institutionalization of the new organization structure.

Putting a floor under existing salaries helps reduce resistance, but it does nothing to encourage good implementation of change. It is possible, however, to use the reward system to support implementation of the reorganization. First of all, the organization needs to make it clear that the jobs and associated rewards given to managers after the transition will depend on their contribution to an effective transition process. One-time bonuses and payments may also ease the transition. In most cases, it makes sense to award these one-time financial payments on a group basis rather than on an individual basis.

It is important that transition goals specify, as precisely as possible, both the rate at which change is introduced and the process used to introduce it. One-time bonuses should be tied to meeting these goals, which can be a critical ingredient in the effective motivation of change. The organization should specify target dates for particular implementation events, such as having a new unit operating or completing the relocation of personnel. In addition, measures should be defined for the process used to implement change; examples might include people's understanding of the new system, the degree to which it was explained to them, the level of turnover among people that the organization wished to retain, signs of stress among people involved in the transition, and the willingness of managers to give up people to other parts of the organization where they can make a greater contribution.

Rewards, goals, and performance measures are critical tools in managing the transition process. They can help to assure that the change strategy is implemented rapidly and in a way that minimizes the dysfunctional consequences for both the organization and the people who work in it.

REWARD SYSTEM CONGRUENCE

For simplicity, we have so far treated each reward-system design feature as an independent factor. Overall system congruence is an important consideration, however. There is considerable evidence that reward-system design features affect each other and thus should be supportive of the same types of behavior, the same business strategy, and reflect the same overall managerial philosophy.

Table 2 illustrates one effort to define congruent sets of reward-system practices (Lawler 1977). The two management philosophies portrayed here are the traditional bureaucratic management style and a participative employee-involvement strategy. Their reward-system practices are different in every respect. The practices associated with traditional bureaucratic models tend to be more secretive, top-down, and oriented toward producing regularity in behavior. The participative practices, in contrast, encourage self-development, openness, employee involvement in reward-system allocation decisions, and ultimately more innovation and commitment to the organization.

Greiner (1972) and Galbraith and Nathanson (1978) have pointed out that reward-system practices need to be congruent with the maturity of the organization and the market in which the business operates. For example, rapidly developing businesses need to stress skill development, attraction, high-potential individuals, and incentives tied to business growth, while declining businesses need to reward expense reduction and to have a formalized job-evaluation system that closely tracks the market.

The reward system also needs to fit other features of the organization to ensure congruence in the total human-resource-management system. The reward system should be consistent with the way jobs are designed, the leadership style of the supervisors, and the types of career tracks available in the organization, to mention just a few examples. Unless this kind of fit exists, the organization will be riddled with conflicts, and the reward system practices may be canceled out by practices in other areas. For example, even the best performance-appraisal system will be ineffective unless ac-

TABLE 2
APPROPRIATE REWARD-SYSTEM PRACTICES

Reward system	Traditional or theory X	Participative or theory Y
Fringe benefits	Vary according to organizational level	Cafeteria—same for all levels
Promotion	All decisions made by top management	Open posting for all jobs; peer-group involvement in decision process
Status symbols	A great many carefully allocated on the basis of job position	Few present, low emphasis on organization level
Pay		
Type of system	Hourly and salary	All salary
Base rate	Based on job performed; high enough to attract job applicants	Based on skills; high enough to provide security and attract applicants
Incentive plan	Piece rate	Group and organization-wide bonus; lump sum increase
Communication policy	Very restricted distribution of information	Individual rates, salary-survey data, and all other information made public
Decision-making locus	Top management	Close to location of person whose pay is being set

companied by interpersonally competent supervisory behavior and jobs designed to allow for good performance measure (see DeVries et al. 1981).

CONCLUSION

An effective reward system should be designed to fit well with the other design features of the organization as well as with its business strategy. Thus there is no one best set of reward practices; indeed, it is impossible to design an effective reward system without knowing how other features of the organization are arrayed. Decisions about the reward system should be made in an interactive fashion: shaped by the business strategy, tentative reward-system design choices would then be tested against how other features of the organization are being designed. The ultimate goal is to develop an integrated human-resource-management strategy that is consistent in the ways it encourages people to behave, attracts the kind of people that can support the business strategy, and encourages them to behave appropriately.

REFERENCES

Beckhard, R., and R. Harris. 1977. *Organizational Transitions: Managing Complex Change.* Reading, Mass.: Addison-Wesley.

Burroughs, J. D. 1982. "Pay Secrecy and Performance: The Psychological Research." *Compensation Review* 14, no. 3:44–54.

Crystal, G. S. 1978. *Executive Compensation.* 2d ed. New York: AMACOM.

DeVries, D. L., A. M. Morrison, S. L. Shullman, and M. L. Gerlach, 1981. *Performance Appraisal on the Line.* New York: Wiley, Interscience.

Ellig, B. R. 1982. *Executive Compensation—A Total Pay Perspective.* New York: McGraw-Hill.

Fox, H. 1979. *Top Executive Bonus Plans.* New York: Conference Board.

Fragner, B. N. 1975. "Employees' 'Cafeteria' Offers Insurance Options." *Harvard Business Review* 53: 2–4.

Galbraith, J. R., and D. A. Nathanson. 1978. *Strategy Implementation: The Role of Structure and Process.* St. Paul, Minn.: West.

Greiner, L. 1972. "Evolution and Revolution as Organizations Grow." *Harvard Business Review* 50, no. 4:37–46.

Goldberg, M. H. 1977. "Another Look at Merit Pay Programs." *Compensation Review* 3:20–28.

Henderson, R. I. 1979. *Compensation Management: Rewarding Performance.* 2d ed. Reston, Va.: Reston.

Hills, F. S. 1979."The Pay-for-Performance Dilemma." *Personnel,* no. 5:23–31.

Kerr, S. 1975. "On the Folly of Rewarding A, While Hoping for B." *Academy of Management Journal* 18:769–783.

Latham, G. P., and K. N. Wexley. 1981. *Increasing Productivity Through Performance Appraisal.* Reading, Mass.: Addison-Wesley.

Lawler, E. E. 1971. *Pay and Organizational Effectiveness: A Psychological View.* New York: McGraw-Hill.

———. 1973. *Motivation in Work Organizations.* Monterey, Calif.: Brooks/Cole.

———. "Reward Systems." In *Improving Life at Work,* ed. J. R. Hackman and J. L. Suttle, pp. 163–226. Santa Monica, Calif.: Goodyear.

———. 1978. "The New Plant Revolution." *Organizational Dynamics* 6, no. 3:2–12.

———. 1981. *Pay and Organization Development.* Reading, Mass.: Addison-Wesley.

Lincoln, J. F. 1951. *Incentive Management.* Lincoln Electric Co., Cleveland, Ohio.

Macy, B. A., and P. H. Mirvis. 1976. "A Methodology for Assessment of Quality of Work Life and Organizational Effectiveness in Behavior-Economic Terms." *Administrative Service Quarterly* 21:217–26.

Mobley, W. H. 1982. *Employee Turnover: Causes, Consequences, and Control.* Reading, Mass.: Addison-Wesley.

Moore, B. E., and T. L. Ross. 1978. *The Scanlon Way to Improved Productivity.* New York: Wiley, Interscience.

Nealy, S. 1963. "Pay and Benefit Preferences." *Industrial Relations* 3:17–28.

Patten, T. H. 1977. "Pay: Employee Compensation and Incentive Plans." New York: Free Press.

Salscheider, J. 1981. "Devising Pay Strategies for Diversified Companies." *Compensation Review* 58, no. 6:15–24.

Stata, R., and M. A. Maidique. 1980. "Bonus System for Balanced Strategy." *Harvard Business Review* 58, no. 6:156–63.

Steele, F. 1975. *The Open Organization.* Reading, Mass.: Addison-Wesley.

Vroom, V. H. 1964. *Work and Motivation.* New York: Wiley.

Walton, R. E. 1980. "Establishing and Maintaining High Commitment Work Systems." In *The Organization Life Cycle,* ed. J. R. Kimberly, R. N. Miles, and associates. San Francisco: Jossey-Bass.

Whyte, W. F., ed. 1955. *Money and Motivation: An Analysis of Incentives in Industry.* New York: Harper.

Rethinking Rewards for Technical Employees

Luis R. Gomez-Mejia
David B. Balkin
George T. Milkovich

The scarcity of engineering and scientific talent is one of the most critical problems facing U.S. corporations today. Because of the difficulties that many companies face in retaining technical people, many also experience low rates of innovation and major delays in the marketing of new products. Rapid turnover at all levels for research and development (R&D) units is becoming the norm in such important industries as semiconductors and electronics. Technical employees behave as individual contractors, willing to change jobs with little remorse if their needs are not met by their current company.

Most disturbing to many of these firms is that an increasing number of top-level scientists and engineers are leaving corporate research labs to start their own companies. They are armed with venture capital and lured by the success stories of people such as Edson de Castro, who left Digital to start Data General, and Robert Noyce, a former Fairchild engineer who founded Intel. If successful, they could become major competitors eating away at the market share of their previous employers. But even if they fail, firms still suffer from the loss of some of their most valuable human resources.

One of the chief reasons that technical employees are so fickle about their employers is that they feel the contributions they provide their company are not adequately rewarded or recognized. Here are some actual examples of this syndrome:

- A research scientist for a large pharmaceutical corporation develops and patents a successful new drug that produces $100 million in revenue its first year on the market. The executives of the division receive large cash bonuses, and the top salespeople enjoy windfall commissions from the strong demand for the new product—but the scientist receives only a $500 honorarium for developing the drug.
- All of the engineers at a $7 billion electronics defense firm are either recent college graduates in their twenties with little work experience or plateaued engineers in their fifties who lack marketable skills and are merely waiting to retire. The shortage of experienced engineers with cutting-edge skills makes it more difficult for the firm to win important defense contracts and introduce new products to the market on time.
- Producing a major new memory chip takes enormous capital resources that only the largest firms such as Intel and Texas Instruments can afford. Yet top U.S. semiconductor companies have been steadily losing world market share to Japanese competitors that produce better-quality and superior-performing chips. The most talented electrical engineers in the U.S. are leaving large U.S. semiconductor firms for "boutique"

Reprinted by permission of the publisher, from *Organizational Dynamics,* Spring 1990. © 1990, American Management Association, New York. All rights reserved.

start-up companies that produce specialty chips for specific, limited markets. This trend hurts the large company's ability to compete in major semiconductor markets.

INEQUITABLE REWARDS

In each of the above cases scientists and engineers were compensated with a fixed salary and benefits package. This pay structure treats these innovators of new products as if they were generic employees. It does not reward them for the unique and indispensable contribution that they make to the organization. The traditional compensation systems that most organizations in the United States use were developed more than 50 years ago; they treat achieving "internal equity" and consistency across different employee groups as the ultimate goal. Under such a system, scientists and engineers, along with other employees, frequently are pigeonholed into predetermined grade levels with a standardized pay package.

These traditional pay methods are wreaking havoc with the morale and motivation of scientists and engineers in the 1990s. Research and development employees in technology-driven businesses are asked to produce innovations that are as critical to a firm's success as are the outputs of top salespeople or executives. Yet they operate under pay systems that often do not reward them accordingly. Top management in technology-intensive corporations needs to rethink reward policies for scientific talent, and to design pay policies that recognize their importance. Innovative ways to reward scientists and engineers should be based on strategic approaches to pay systems. Key contributor rewards, group rewards linked to company success, and increased budgetary discretion are examples of programs that can give technical innovators incentives to stay with their employer.

FLEXIBLE PAY SYSTEMS

How many times has a manager been frustrated when he or she loses a heavily-recruited engineer to a competitor because the human resources department refused to authorize a salary to match the competition? The HR manager typically justifies this refusal on the grounds that internal equity must be maintained: Other engineers would be dissatisfied and morale would suffer if pay guidelines were not followed. But as a result of his or her refusal, the company may lose rare and valuable technical talent.

Most firms face a dilemma between pressure to preserve equitable pay relationships among employees and the need to keep up with "going rates" in the labor market. When market forces are stable, it makes sense to develop a pay policy that gives high priority to salary equity among employees with jobs that require similar levels of effort, skill, and responsibility. The traditional, lockstep compensation system based on job evaluation does just that. Unfortunately, these systems often have difficulty adjusting to a changing economic environment. The market forces for technical employees are dynamic because of a severe scarcity of supply; therefore, it is more appropriate to develop a pay policy that permits flexibility and recognizes strategic and critical talent.

A flexible and adaptive pay system allows managers to respond to the jolts in the technical labor market. Under flexible pay systems, firms select a position in the market relative to their competitors for critical skill groups. The pay rate for a particular scientist or engineer is based more closely on his or her individual strategic importance than on "equitable" comparisons with the overall workforce. Managers must be supported with the necessary resources to put together an attractive pay package that becomes a competitive tool to bring scarce technical employees into the company where they are needed. Moreover, in addition to flexible pay systems, creative and innovative benefits and bonus packages can help firms to attract and retain technical talent.

A recent Peat Marwick survey found that 69% of Silicon Valley high-technology firms used "sign-on" bonuses to attract scientists and engineers. The sign-on bonus can take the form of cash, stock options, or a combination of both. The cash sign-on bonus was in the $3,000-$4,000 range. The sign-on bonus gives a manager greater flexibility to attract a recruit without provoking anger among current employees.

At some firms, special relocation benefits are available to bring technical employees on board. The company may buy and sell the employee's house, provide a settling-in allowance for a temporary residence, and offer equity in a new house to a recruit. These benefits may not be available to employees in other job categories.

Many firms that employ scientists and engineers provide market adjustments to their pay. Thus the employees do not perceive themselves as underpaid with respect to the market and may be less likely to be pirated away by a competitor. The market adjustment is an across-the-board salary increase given to affected employees, and it is separate from annual merit pay increases. According to findings of a recent survey of companies in the Boston high-technology corridor, more than 70% of the firms made market adjustments to the pay of their technical employees, and each of these employees received on average a 10% market adjustment on top of merit pay.

REWARDING KEY PEOPLE

A major problem faced by most technical managers is how to reward their top performers in proportion to the value their contributions add to the company. According to recent surveys by the Hay Group, today's typical merit-pay plan provides only a 2% difference between an outstanding and a satisfactory performer. A top-performing scientist may develop a new drug or create a software program worth millions of dollars in revenues. Clearly, this individual would not be recognized adequately with conventional merit pay.

In the United States a company is under no legal obligation to share with employed inventors the profits it collects from their inventions. Under U.S. patent law, employers own any invention or discovery an employee makes while working for them. Some U.S. firms provide a cash bonus for inventors who receive a patent on a commercial product, but many offer no special recognition for these important contributions. By contrast, West Germany and the United Kingdom have laws that obligate the employer to share returns with an employed inventor in proportion to the commercial returns of the patented invention. In the United States, organizations that recognize key scientists and engineers gain an edge over their competitors in recruiting and retaining top talent.

KEY CONTRIBUTORS

A key contributor is an employee who has demonstrated special skills or proprietary knowledge, who has made a significant impact on the firm's performance, and whose loss would pose a threat to the company. These individuals are unique and virtually impossible to replace. For example, a scientist doing leading-edge work on superconductivity may possess unique skills that are critical for the success of a company that is trying to bring to market a ceramic material with superconductor properties. Loss of this individual would seriously disrupt the firm's research and development activity and threaten the survival of the business.

Companies that are in the vulnerable position of relying on the contributions of a few key technical people need to devise schemes to retain them, especially when they are most critically needed. Key-contributor pay policies are designed to recognize the achievements of these people and to provide the incentive for them to remain with their employer.

Cash Rewards

According to a Hay Group national survey, 76% of high-technology industries have some kind of special pay policy for key technical people. They usually provide top technical contributors with cash or equity rewards. Cash is the most common reward and usually is given "after the fact" in recognition of an outstanding contribution.

To recognize the accomplishments of its top contributors, IBM offers cash bonuses at both the corporate and division levels. The IBM Corporate Award provides cash to the top technical people in the corporation each year during a special ceremony. IBM recently awarded $150,000 to each of two of its scientists who won the 1987 Nobel Prize in science for research in superconductivity.

At the division level, IBM gives Outstanding Innovation Awards to recognize individual achievements, such as important inventions or scientific discoveries. About 40 of these innovation awards, ranging from $2,500 to $25,000, are given each year.

Equity

Many companies also give equity to key technical people in the form of either a stock option or a stock grant. Restrictions placed on the exercise of the stock options allow the employer to retain the key person for several years before the restrictions lapse. The best opportunities to generate wealth from equity occur in small, private companies before the initial public offering of the stock. The IRS places tighter restrictions on the use of stock options on larger, public corporations. A technical employee, for example, may have to spend a considerable amount of personal cash to purchase stock when it is publicly traded, and he or she may be required to pay taxes on the gain before being permitted to sell the stock. As a result of the difficulties associated with stock options, some large, public corporations use unit performance shares or phantom stock to reward technical people in order to provide returns as great as those of venture-capital-financed start-ups.

Tektronix, a large, public, high-technology corporation, developed a unit performance shares program to reward key technical employees for the long-term commercial success of the venture unit in the corporation. Tektronix designed the payoff matrix of the unit performance shares to correspond to what would be available with equity participation in a small, private, start-up company. The shares are tied to the commercial success of the product in the market.

Budgetary Discretion

Another, less widely used reward is increased budgetary discretion, which comes in two forms. First, key contributors are often given special budgets over which they have discretion outside of normal accounting controls. Some use their budgets to buy additional project equipment, attend special conferences, travel to visit colleagues in other firms or foreign countries, or purchase computer software.

The second form of budgetary discretion allows key contributors to grant salary increases to support staff and colleagues who may have contributed to their success. For example, one scientist was able to grant a 10% bonus to his technicians and secretary. The logic underlying the budgetary discretion award is that key contributors know who contributed to their past successes—and will choose to reward them—and that these top contributors will allocate extra resources in ways that will allow them to become even more productive.

PENALTIES OF HIERARCHY

Many U.S. firms, particularly large, high-technology organizations, establish an elaborate hierarchy of grade levels for employees—including scientists and engineers. For example, one company producing electronic components in Massachusetts employs 500 technical employees in a research and development unit. It has 48 grade levels, each with a separate pay bracket. Employees enter the firm at lower grade levels and move up through the ranks over time. The pay and degree of responsibility of scientists and engineers are predicated largely on successive advancement in grade. And although promotions are supposedly based on performance, more often they come with seniority. Within each grade, assessments of each individual's performance generally determine pay allocation. This system has been borrowed from a manufacturing environment where division of labor and design of work flows are associated with the use of mechanistic and bureaucratic human resources procedures. The theory is that by partitioning jobs into multiple components, and making rewards contingent on fine distinctions in the nature of the tasks being accomplished, management can create a predictable and controllable work environment.

Unfortunately, applying a strict manufacturing mentality in a technical environment can be highly counterproductive. This mechanistic approach may create artificial barriers among people, fragmentation, and an individualistic climate in the workforce. These behaviors and the resulting culture often run counter to successful research and development environments. A successful research environment requires intense team effort, integration of activities by many individuals, fluid tasks, exchange of knowledge, and minimal status barriers. Scientists and engineers working on common problems need to feel that they are not in competition against each other.

The disruptive effects of an inflexible hierarchical grade system on research and development work are evident in a medium-size firm located in the Denver-Boulder area. As the company grew from 100 to 800 employees during a three-year period, it hired a consulting firm to establish a formal compensation plan. This plan called for 20 grade levels for the research and development workforce. A year after the plan was implemented, management began to realize that something had gone awry. Senior scientists were looking down on their junior counterparts, and the design engineers made it clear in a number of public remarks that they felt superior to the production engineers whose job was to "carry out orders." Only limited communication was taking place between these groups, backbiting became common, and crucial information (e.g., design flaws) was being withheld from top management.

The myopic view and parochialism this pay approach engendered in the scientists and engineers developed in part because jobs and the status hierarchy were narrowly defined. Many scientists and engineers tend to be more loyal to their discipline than they are to their employer, and many are chauvinistic about their technical specialty. The hierarchical grade system reinforced these tendencies with predictably negative results. The eventual success of a research and development program requires a businesswide orientation that goes well beyond the lab. People within the organization need to be willing to channel scarce resources to research and development projects. And those outside the organization who are relied upon for support will give that support only if they perceive the firm as having a strong research and development program.

THE PRODUCTIVITY PARADOX

Obviously, research and development projects in private firms have little value unless they lead to commercial applications. Some observers see the United States as the envy of the industrialized world in research and development. But others see the U.S. falling behind its major competitors when it comes to reaping the commercial benefits of research and development. This paradox can be explained partially by American management techniques and by the use of conventional approaches to rewarding research and development that fail to exploit American research and development superiority. A managerial obsession with specialization and hierarchy runs counter to the need for interaction, coordination, reciprocity, and inter-unit teamwork involved in mass producing new innovations. It is not unusual to find companies where research and developing is kept apart, both geographically and organizationally, from the rest of the firm. Findings of some surveys show that many employees in the production and manufacturing functions perceive research and development staff as being "weird" and disconnected from reality. On the other hand, those in research and development often view the former as drones who need close supervision in order to get things right.

Many human resources problems are difficult to solve because they seem to grow out of "human nature" and thus seem to be beyond management's control. People who do different kinds of work in separate departments may view each other with suspicion and contempt, and rivalries may develop between them. But, in fact, management has the ability to counteract this tendency. The pay system provides management with substantial clout to align the self-interests of scientists and engineers with those of other employees. Combining a conventional fixed compensation system with aggregate incentives can do much to create a unified workforce.

Promoting Team Elan

Many successful firms use team-based incentives as powerful tools to enhance the performance of research and development groups. They provide these incentives to an entire team of scientists and engineers working on a common problem when they achieve important milestones: reaching a scientific breakthrough, receiving a large government grant, obtaining a new patent, or finding a way to lower the costs of manufacturing a given product. These group-based incentives are remarkably instrumental in generating a tight and cohesive research and development team—a prerequisite for success. These rewards can also improve research and development performance by focusing employees' attention on high-priority tasks, bringing "free riders" into line, and encouraging people from diverse backgrounds to iron out their differences and work together for a shared goal and the common good.

One high-technology company in the Boston area offers a competitive bonus of 25% of an engineer's salary based on the performance of his or her entire team. Each team may submit a proposal to management explaining why it deserves a bonus based on costs saved or value added to the firm. Money for the bonus is generated by channeling into a special fund 1% of return on sales exceeding 5%. A companywide committee reviews the proposals twice a year. After consulting with supervisors, managers in other departments, and others who are involved with the teams in question, the committee makes a final determination. This special bonus fund may accumulate over time if only a few bonuses are awarded in a given year.

A company in Silicon Valley provides division managers with a pool of discretionary money that can be distributed to various research and development teams based on the difficulty of the work being done and its relative contribution to the firm. Confidential peer ratings are used to determine how the bonus is allocated among team members; in some cases the money is distributed equally among the members.

Fostering a Companywide Perspective

Successful start-up companies and mature high-technology firms have learned from experience that closely linking the fortunes of scientists and engineers to company performance is a powerful inducement to make them think like businesspeople rather than lab workers. Profit sharing leads to more variable compensation and requires the technical employee to share some of the firm's financial risks. As a result, scientists and engineers are forced to consider "bottom-line" commercial success as well as technical success. By focusing employees' attention on financial results, these plans pave the way for cooperation and integration of various units that might normally compete.

For example, every year that profitability goals are met, Hewlett-Packard awards a large cash bonus to each employee. Unlike many other high-technology firms, Hewlett-Packard has been in the black—and paying profit-sharing bonuses—for 25 years. In order to ensure that technical employees see a connection between their efforts and the firm's performance, and to make them feel that they share a common fate with others in the organization, Hewlett-Packard bases its profit-sharing plan at the divisional level. The company has a policy of splitting divisions soon after they exceed 1,000 employees.

Another example is provided by a Midwestern computer firm. The company gives employees involved in the development and manufacturing of a product 15% of any annual net profits attributed to the product whenever they exceed 1.6% of total sales.

Rewarding Long-Term Results

Perhaps no other activity in a corporation is more long-term oriented than research and development, both as an investment and as a process. It usually takes at least five years, and in many cases ten or more years, before the benefits of R&D efforts can be assessed. Because team-based bonuses and profit sharing are normally directed at short-term accomplishments (usually one year or less), successful high-tech firms often provide an additional layer of rewards designed to focus employees' attention on long-term results. These companies offer an extensive array of long-term incentives that treat research and development workers as executives by tying a portion of the income of scientists and engineers to the firm's stock values. Sharing equity with the employees enables management to use compensation as a form of communication: In this way management tells employees which outcomes the firm values. When they become part owners, technical employees may be more likely to understand the firm's perspective on their jobs. Long-term plans also encourage employees to share a vision of the firm's future financial success; research and development employees who share the vision may be particularly willing to initiate and sustain a common effort. Innovation relies on knowledge—a resource that resides in the employees themselves. Thus firms that base their success on continuing innovation are extremely vulnerable to the effects of attrition among R&D staff. Only by offering these employees incentives to remain with the firm can they hope to succeed.

THE SAIC EXAMPLE

Science Applications International Corporation (SAIC), a 20-year-old high-technology organization that employs some 9,000 workers in more than 200 offices throughout the United States, is one of the most profitable firms in the instrumentation and electronics industry. What is more, its turnover rate for scientists and engineers has a reputation for being well below the industry average. SAIC is a national leader in the use of equity compensation; it has offered an extensive menu of employee stock ownership plans (ESOPs) to its research and development employees for 20 years. The firm handles these stock dealings through its wholly-owned broker dealership. Some of the plans employees can choose from include:

- Contribution of up to 10% of their salary, to be matched by SAIC dollar-for-dollar, to purchase company stock.

- A performance award program that provides company stock to selected research and development teams based on their contribution.
- Yearly allocation of a pool of stock options to division managers. The managers can distribute these stocks to individual research and development employees or teams who are deemed exceptional performers.

PROFESSIONAL REWARDS

Attitude surveys conducted since the 1930s have established that job satisfaction is closely correlated with occupational level and education. However, scientists and engineers working in industry represent an extreme deviation from this norm, showing satisfaction levels that are sometimes even lower than those of menial laborers. The most common complaint expressed by technical employees is that a few years after one enters the workforce, perhaps within five years of graduating from school, one reaches a dead end in terms of both professional challenges and financial progress. Boredom can easily set in after a scientist or an engineer has been on the job performing a narrow set of tasks for several years. Because of the fast rate of technical obsolescence that makes new graduates highly attractive to employers and helps create a tight labor market, pay compression is so severe in many organizations that a freshly-minted engineer often commands a higher salary than a seasoned veteran does. Faced with an apparently bleak future in the organization, many senior scientists and engineers try to move into more lucrative and challenging management positions. Executive M.B.A. programs around the country enroll large numbers of scientists and engineers who hope that obtaining a business degree will help them make this transition. But the abilities and temperament of scientists and engineers are frequently quite removed from those of managers; thus an excellent engineer may turn out to be only a mediocre manager.

THE DUAL-CAREER LADDER OPTION

One solution to this problem, developed in the 1950s, is the use of dual-career ladders, which allow technical employees to move up in a grade hierarchy that is separate from but parallel to that of managerial employees. Consistent with the pay structures discussed earlier, this approach is often overly bureaucratic, and such attempts to solve the career stagnation problem for scientists and engineers have met with mixed results. One drawback of the dual-career ladder is that often it is based on the fragmentation of jobs, thus reinforcing pecking orders and impeding cooperation. A second, and perhaps greater, problem is that technical employees may not believe in the company line of "separate but equal." There is a widespread perception among scientists and engineers that parallel, dual-career ladders are a myth and that, in fact, upward mobility and influence in the organization, with their associated rewards, only come by moving into management ranks.

Alternatives to the dual-career ladder concept have blossomed in recent years at firms with successful research and development operations. These companies are experimenting with a wide variety of professional rewards that are valued highly by technical employees and that are not predicated on one's position in the organizational structure. Some of the most promising ideas are discussed below.

Expand the Nature of the Job

In order to prevent hierarchical barriers from arising, successful firms encourage the creation of large research and development teams composed of scientists and engineers from diverse areas in the organization. This allows technical employees to cross-fertilize ideas and experiment with a range of techniques, thereby reducing boredom and professional stagnation.

For example, one firm divides its technical people into teams of from five to thirteen employees guided by a leader. Each team is assigned a project. Team members have broad responsibility on a project and divide up the specific tasks themselves; each employee, theoretically, is able to do any job. By contrast with the dozens of job classifications for research and development personnel that exist in some other firms, under this system there is just one classification for all scientists and engineers. Moreover, more than half of these employees' pay is in the form of group and key contributor incentives.

Allow Technical Employees to Set Up New Ventures

One of the greatest fears in many high-technology companies is the potential loss of scientists and engineers who possess invaluable knowledge and who may become direct competitors by starting their own firms. Part of the motivation behind such a risky move by a scientist or an engineer is the wish to experience the thrills and challenges of entrepreneurship that they cannot feel in most large organizations. Firms with leading-edge research and development functions offer these employees the opportunity to start a new venture without incurring all the risks they would face if they went out on their own. After all, the mortality rate of such businesses is about 80% within a five-year period.

Firms such as 3M and Eastman Kodak have been enormously successful at setting up special "innovation banks" to fund internal enterprises. This not only allows a large venture to be supported inside the company as a separate business, but it also permits scientists and engineers to obtain resources that otherwise would find no place in a line manager's budget. At 3M, employees may request such funds from their division, from corporate research and development, or from the new venture division. These programs allow employees to satisfy their intellectual and entrepreneurial cravings without leaving the company. These programs also appeal to the employees' acquisitive side, since they receive large financial rewards if the new ventures succeed.

Support New Projects

Only a few technical employees may want to tackle the enormous task of starting a new business unit. But many may wish to develop their own projects of personal interest. Many firms with successful research and development staffs capitalize on these employees' interests by providing financial backing to scientists and engineers who choose to generate their own projects. Texas Instruments, for example, has an elaborate system that offers several options for funding projects, including a program called "wild hare grants" for ideas that are good but risky.

Allow Employees to Pursue Their Own Interests on Company Time

Another way to prevent career stagnation and alienation in the technical workforce is to allow a certain amount of discretionary time on the job, during which these employees may pursue their individual interests. This practice sometimes pays off handsomely when an employee comes up with a novel idea that eventually leads to a useful innovation. In one noteworthy example, 3M formalized its "15% rule"—up to 15% of an employee's time may be spent on projects of his or her own choosing.

REDUCING TECHNICAL OBSOLESCENCE

All organizations that employ scientists and engineers are concerned with maintaining state-of-the-art technical skills. Unfortunately, about five years after an engineer receives a university degree, half of his or her knowledge may be obsolete; in some fields, such as artificial intelligence, it may take only three years. As a result, it is not unusual for engineers to find that their careers have become plateaued by the time they reach their mid-thirties. The plateaued engineer may be a drain on company resources, since each additional year brings a decline in technical productivity—while payroll costs steadily increase.

By fine-tuning the benefits component of the pay package for technical employees, management may reduce the damage that technical obsolescence does to the firm. Providing educational benefits and sabbatical leaves for employees can help the company stay on the cutting edge.

Educational Benefits

Most technical companies provide full-tuition reimbursement for employees who take university courses in technical disciplines. Many companies also encourage their scientists and engineers to pursue advanced degrees, and they fully cover the costs. Funds are provided for travel and expenses to scientific meetings, seminars, and workshops in emerging fields of study. Costs are covered for professional association memberships, journal subscriptions, books, and publishing fees for writing articles in scientific journals.

Bell Labs, a leading research firm, places a heavy emphasis on continuing education. It has a huge in-house education center that provides technical training in many advanced scientific and engineering disciplines.

Wang recently provided funds for a school called the Wang Institute, which offers a master's degree in a skill that is in critical demand—software engineering. Graduates are free to work for any company they choose, but no doubt many will select Wang as their employer.

Merck also uses a variation on this theme. Believing that interaction with faculty and students will sharpen technical skills and stimulate creative thinking, the company encourages its scientists and engineers to teach at local universities.

Sabbatical Leaves

The sabbatical leave is another employee benefit that may be used to reduce technical obsolescence. Industry is starting to adopt this practice, which has been used for years in universities to provide time for faculty to renew their creative energies. A period of extended leave with pay, the sabbatical provides the opportunity for education or other meaningful activities that ultimately benefit both the employee and the firm. The educational sabbatical may be a good alternative for companies that do not have extensive in-house educational facilities and need to retrain their technical people. It also may be used to prevent job burnout, which develops frequently when scientists and engineers are working under high pressure to bring a new product to market on time.

At Intel, a technical employee who has worked at the company for seven years is entitled to take an eight-week sabbatical leave with pay in addition to his or her annual vacation. Employees also may apply for an additional six months off with pay to accomplish specified goals, such as doing service for the community, teaching, or continuing their education.

Xerox's technical employees may apply for management approval for sabbatical leaves that they use to perform social service for nonprofit organizations. If an employee's application is approved, he or she may take between three and twelve months' leave with full salary and benefits. This policy benefits both the employee and the firm. The community service performed by employees on sabbatical enhances the reputation of the company as a socially responsible employer. And the employee may return with a fresh perspective that may provide the inspiration for new innovations.

ENCOURAGING INNOVATIONS

All the reward programs examined in this article are designed to encourage technical employees to provide innovations that will lead to commercial success. Pay policies that treat innovators as "hired hands" and reward them according to inflexible methods clash with the interests of a firm and its scientists and engineers.

Executives who are interested in redesigning their reward systems for technical employees need to consider carefully the impact that any change will have on other organizational systems. The reward system is intimately related to job designs and organization structures, and changes in the rewards may result in some unpleasant surprises. Careful planning should precede the implementation of any new pay policy. Here are some suggestions for executives who may be considering making some adjustments to their technical reward systems:

• *Price the person, not the job, when rewarding a technical employee.* It is desirable to visualize each scientist and engineer as a unique individual with a unique market value. Executives and sales professionals are viewed this way in most organizations. A significant portion of the total earnings of the technical employee should come from variable compensation policies.

- *Provide a menu of pay incentives so that the total reward system for technical employees complements the goals and objectives of the organization.* Pay systems and policies should be compatible with other organization systems. The result is a multidimensional reward system that is in keeping with the goals of the organization and the interests of the technical employees.

- *Remove the professional reward system from the hierarchical structure.* Management needs to develop new ways of structuring jobs and building organizational units that meet more of the scientists' and engineers' needs.

- *Integrate the pay system for technical employees with the pay systems for other employee groups.* The more the pay system for technical employees is differentiated from that for other employees, the more buffering between the two clusters of employees is necessary. For example, because there is some interface between manufacturing and research and development, some of the production workers may feel that they are entitled to the same pay policies that apply to the design engineers. And, indeed, their demands should be considered. Where are the systems' lines drawn with respect to eligibility for a reward? One solution may be to allow production workers to share in the profit-sharing bonus (a share of company success) but restrict their inclusion in the team bonus (based on research and development success).

A PART OF THE TOTAL PICTURE

The pay system is a crucial element in research and development management. But it is only one part of the total picture in making the R&D operation effective. In some cases, variable pay systems succeed; in others, they fail. Success depends on fitting reward systems into a comprehensive and carefully integrated strategy. This strategy needs to include tough selection and hiring procedures, rigorous performance evaluation and feedback, increased discretion and flexibility and key contributors, and job designs that facilitate innovation.

SELECTED BIBLIOGRAPHY

For a general discussion on the use of innovative reward strategies for scientists and engineers, refer to Rosabeth Moss Kanter's article "The Attack on Pay" in *Harvard Business Review* (Volume 65, Number 2, 1987); "A Strategic Perspective to Compensation Management" by George Milkovich in *Research in Personnel and Human Resource Management* (JAI Press, Volume 6, 1988); "Managing a High-Tech Venture" by Luis Gomez-Mejia and David Balkin in *Personnel* (Volume 62, December, 1985); and *Managing High Technology Companies* by Henry Riggs (Lifetime Learning Publications, 1983).

Further detail about the empirical research upon which the ideas in this article are based can be found in these articles by the authors: "Determinants of R and D Compensation Strategies in the High Tech Industry," in *Personnel Psychology* (Volume 37,

Number 4, 1984); "Compensation Practices in High Tech Industries," in *Personnel Administrator* (Volume 30, November 6, 1985); "Toward a Contingency Theory of Compensation Strategy," in *Strategic Management Journal* (Volume 8, Number 2, 1987); and "Effectiveness of Individual and Aggregate Compensation Strategies," in *Industrial Relations* (Volume 28, Number 3, 1989).

Helpful references on the use of pay incentives and other specific rewards for scientists and engineers can be found in Michael Spratt and Bernadette Steele's article "Rewarding Key Contributors" in *Compensation and Benefits Review* (Volume 17, July–August 1985) and in Bernadette Steele and Richard Baker's article "Creating Entrepreneurial Pay Systems for Internal Venture Units" in *Topics in Total Compensation* (Volume 1, Number 1, 1986). David Balkin's article "Compensation Strategies for R&D Staff" in *Topics in Total Compensation* (Volume 2, Number 2, 1987) and Willard Marcy's article "New Approaches for Compensation of Inventors" in *Research Management* (Volume 21, Number 2, 1978) also provide helpful insights.

CHAPTER 7: Questions for Discussion

1 Given the causes of reward displacement by Kerr, what problems might you anticipate in trying to remedy the situation by altering the reward system?

2 How do Kerr's suggestions specifically deal with the causes of rewarding A while hoping for B? What other approaches might be suggested?

3 On balance, how do you assess the case that Kohn makes against the use of incentive plans in work organizations? Are the arguments convincing? Are they overstated? Are there major counterarguments that could be presented?

4 Critics of Kohn's article have raised the issue: If not reward or incentive systems in organizations, then what? What are the *realistic* alternatives?

5 If you were the CEO of a company, what policies regarding merit pay would you implement that would be consistent with both reinforcement theory and Pearce's recommendations?

6 How would you evaluate the compensation design options presented by Lawler? What would Kohn's response be to Lawler's major points?

7 Would the points made by Kerr in his "On the Folly of Rewarding A . . ." article have any implications for the approaches to compensation suggested by Lawler? Why or why not?

8 Are the issues of compensation and reward systems, and their relative effectiveness, any different for technical and research/development types of employees than for employees who have more general (i.e., nontechnical) backgrounds? Would some systems/approaches work for the former but not for the latter employees, and vice versa? Defend your reasoning based on some of the motivational models discussed in Chapter 2.

HIGH-INVOLVEMENT MANAGEMENT

Early managerial approaches to job design (discussed in Chapter 2) focused primarily on attempts to simplify an employee's required tasks insofar as possible in order to increase production efficiency. It was felt that, since workers were largely economically motivated, the best way to maximize output was to reduce tasks to their simplest forms and then reward workers with money on the basis of units of output—a piece-rate incentive plan. In theory, such a system would simultaneously satisfy the primary goals of both the employees and the company. Evidence of such a philosophy can be seen in the writings of Taylor and other scientific management advocates.

This approach to simplified job design reached its zenith from a technological standpoint in assembly-line production techniques such as those used by automobile manufacturers. (Piece-rate incentive systems have been largely eliminated here, however.) On auto assembly lines, in many cases, the average length of "work cycle" (i.e., the time allowed for an entire "piece" of work) ranges from 30 seconds to 1 1/2 minutes. This means that workers repeat the same task an average of at least 500 times per day. Such a technique, efficient as it may be, is not without its problems. As workers have become better educated and more organized, they have begun demanding more from their jobs. Not only is this demand shown in recurrent requests for shorter hours and higher wages, but it is also shown in several undesirable behavior patterns, such as increased turnover, absenteeism, dissatisfaction, and sabotage.

While organizational psychologists and practicing managers have long sought ways of reducing such behavior, only recently have they begun to study it rigorously in connection with the task performed. Now there exists a considerable body of knowledge concerning ways to attack the problem of job redesign as it affects motivation, performance, and satisfaction. Somewhat surprisingly, many of the new "solutions" bear a striking resemblance to the old craft-type of technology of pre-assembly-line days.

Considerable evidence has come to light recently in support of positive behavioral and attitudinal consequences of such job enrichment efforts. In general, such efforts have tended to result in (1) significantly reduced turnover and absenteeism; (2) improved job satisfaction; (3) improved quality of products; and (4) some, though not universal, improvements in productivity and output rates. On the negative side, the costs often associated with such programs are generally identified as (1) increased training time and expense and (2) occasionally, additional retooling costs where dramatic shifts toward group assembly teams have been instituted.

A major thrust of many of the contemporary efforts at job redesign research represents a blend of two central factors. On the one hand, researchers study the motivational processes associated with redesigning jobs. On the other hand, they are equally concerned with the practical applications of such knowledge as it affects attempts to improve the work environment. In this sense, investigations in this area have generally represented applied research in the truest sense.

HERZBERG'S TWO-FACTOR THEORY

As pointed out in Chapter 2, one of the earliest researchers in the area of job redesign as it affects motivation was Herzberg (Herzberg, Mausner, & Snyderman, 1959; Herzberg, 1966). The implications of his model of employee motivation are clear: motivation can be increased through basic changes in the nature of an employee's job (that is, job enrichment). Thus, jobs should be redesigned to allow for increased challenge and responsibility, opportunities for advancement and personal growth, and recognition.

Herzberg differentiated between what he described as the older and less effective job redesign efforts, known as job *enlargement,* and the newer concept of job *enrichment.* The term "job enlargement," as used by Herzberg, means a *horizontal* expansion of an employee's job, giving him or her more of the same kinds of activities but not altering the necessary skills. "Job enrichment," on the other hand, means a *vertical* expansion of an employee's job, requiring an increase in the skills repertoire, which ostensibly leads to increased opportunities. As Paul et al. (1969, p. 61) described it, job enrichment "seeks to improve both efficiency and human satisfaction by means of building into people's jobs, quite specifically, a greater scope for personal achievement and recognition, more challenging and responsible work, and more opportunity for individual advancement and growth."

ADDITIONAL EARLY MODELS OF JOB DESIGN

In addition to Herzberg's model, several other early models of job design can be identified (see Exhibit 8-1). These are (1) the requisite task attributes model, (2) the sociotechnical systems model, (3) activation theory, and (4) achievement motivation theory. While a detailed examination of these models is beyond the scope of this chapter, we can briefly review how the various models differ in their approach to the motivational properties of tasks.

The *requisite task attributes model,* proposed by Turner and Lawrence (1965), argued that an enriched job (that is, a job characterized by variety, autonomy, responsi-

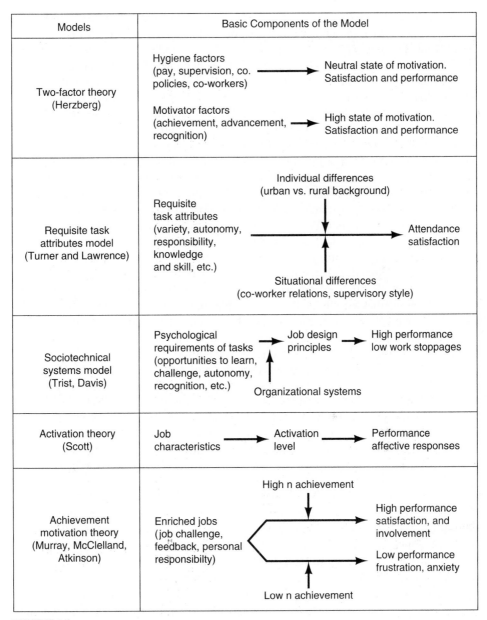

Models	Basic Components of the Model
Two-factor theory (Herzberg)	Hygiene factors (pay, supervision, co. policies, co-workers) ⟶ Neutral state of motivation. Satisfaction and performance Motivator factors (achievement, advancement, recognition) ⟶ High state of motivation. Satisfaction and performance
Requisite task attributes model (Turner and Lawrence)	Requisite task attributes (variety, autonomy, responsibility, knowledge and skill, etc.) with Individual differences (urban vs. rural background) and Situational differences (co-worker relations, supervisory style) ⟶ Attendance satisfaction
Sociotechnical systems model (Trist, Davis)	Psychological requirements of tasks (opportunities to learn, challenge, autonomy, recognition, etc.) ⟶ Job design principles ⟶ High performance low work stoppages; Organizational systems
Activation theory (Scott)	Job characteristics ⟶ Activation level ⟶ Performance affective responses
Achievement motivation theory (Murray, McClelland, Atkinson)	Enriched jobs (job challenge, feedback, personal responsibilty) with High n achievement ⟶ High performance satisfaction, and involvement; Low n achievement ⟶ Low performance frustration, anxiety

EXHIBIT 8-1
Conceptual models of the motivational properties of tasks. (*From R. M. Steers & R. T. Mowday, The motivational properties of tasks. Academy of Management Review, 1977, 2, 645–658. Reprinted by permission.*)

bility, etc.) would lead to increased attendance and job satisfaction. The model was similar to Herzberg's in that it viewed job enrichment as a motivating variable. It differed from Herzberg's in that Turner and Lawrence included absenteeism as a dependent variable. Moreover, Turnover and Lawrence acknowledged the existence of two sets of important moderators in the job scope—outcome relationship. First, they found that workers from urban settings were more satisfied with low-scope jobs than workers from rural settings. Second, it was found that situational factors (such as supervisory style and coworker relations) also moderated the impact of job scope on satisfaction and absenteeism. This acknowledgement of the role of individual and situational variables represents a significant contribution to our understanding of the ways in which job redesign affects employee attitudes and behavior. In fact, much of the subsequent work on the topic has taken the lead from the work of Turner and Lawrence.

A second and popular model, advanced by Trist and Davis, is known as the *sociotechnical systems model.* This model suggests that an appropriate starting point for understanding job design is to consider the psychological requirements of tasks in order for them to be motivating. These principles include the need for a job to provide (1) reasonably demanding content, (2) an opportunity to learn, (3) some degree of autonomy or discretion in decisions affecting the job, (4) social support and recognition, and (5) a feeling that the job leads to a desirable future.

On the basis of these principles, job design principles are derived which suggest, in brief, that enriched jobs meet these psychological requirements. As a consequence, enriched jobs would be expected to lead to such outcomes as high job performance and low labor stoppages. An important aspect of the sociotechnical model is that it clearly acknowledges the role of the social context (or organizational system) in which job redesign attempts are made. That is, the model argues that such changes cannot be successfully implemented without acknowledging and taking into account various social and organizational factors that also influence people's desire to perform on the job (reward system, work group norms, supervisory relations, etc.). Hence, the sociotechnical systems approach attempts to be a truly systematic (that is, comprehensive) approach to work design.

Activation theory focuses on the physiological processes involved in job redesign (Scott, 1966). Activation, defined as the degree of excitation of the brain stem reticular formation, has been found in laboratory experiments to have a curvilinear relationship to performance. Research has demonstrated that performance suffers at very low or very high levels of activation. Hence, jobs that are dull or repetitive may lead to low levels of performance because they fail to activate. On the other hand, more enriched jobs should lead to a state of activation with a resulting increase in performance. While many questions remain concerning the empirical support for activation theory, it does suggest how job design can affect employees physiologically, a relationship ignored in previous research.

Finally, *achievement motivation theory* (discussed in Chapter 2), proposed by Murray (1938) and refined by McClelland and Atkinson, also examines the process by which changes in the job situation influence behavior. The focus of this approach, however, is on employee personality, specifically, an employee's need for achievement. In essence, achievement motivation theory posits that employees with a high need for achievement will be more likely to respond favorably to enriched jobs than employees with a low need for achievement. Enriched jobs cue, or stimulate, the achievement motive, typically leading to higher levels of performance, involvement, and satisfaction. For employees with a low need for achievement, however, an enriched job may be threatening; that is, they may feel overchallenged. As a result, they may experience increased frustration and anxiety and exhibit lower performance.

HACKMAN AND OLDHAM'S JOB CHARACTERISTICS MODEL

More recently, Hackman and Oldham (1976, 1980) have suggested a model of job redesign that takes us one step closer to understanding the relationship between the nature of the job and employee performance. In their model, shown in Exhibit 8-2, five core job dimensions (skill variety, task identity, task significance, autonomy, and feedback) influence three critical psychological states. These three states are experienced meaningfulness of the work, experienced responsibility for work outcomes, and knowledge of actual results. These states, in turn, influence personal and work-related outcomes, including high internal work motivation, work quality, satisfaction, and attendance. Throughout this process, Hackman and Oldham caution us to remember the influence of various growth need strengths as potential moderators (see Chapter 2).

In conclusion, we have seen that several models of job design exist. Each model tends to focus on one aspect of the job situation (e.g., personality, social context, or

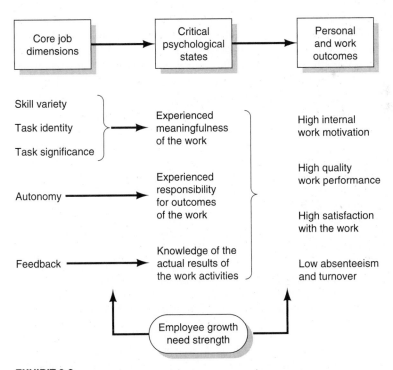

EXHIBIT 8-2
The job characteristics model of work motivation. (*From J. R. Hackman, Work design. In J. R. Hackman & J. L. Suttle (Eds.),* Improving life at work. *Glenview, Ill.: Scott, Foresman, 1977.*)

physiological response) and therefore makes a useful contribution by expanding our understanding of the relevant variables that must be included in a comprehensive model of work design. As the readings in this chapter will demonstrate, when one or more features of these models are implemented and job designs are actually changed, opinions about their efficacy for improving "quality of work life" are mixed. Results overall tend to be positive, but not uniformly so, and it is clear that the kinds of approaches discussed later in the chapter are not simple and do not constitute any type of panacea. In other words, there are a number of complexities involved in job design changes that are intended to improve the quality of work life. Nevertheless, these kinds of efforts have the *potential* for beneficial effects on the way the employee relates to the work situation, to supervision, and to the organization.

OVERVIEW OF THE READINGS

Based upon earlier work, several researchers have recently begun to focus on what has generally become known as "high-involvement management." High-involvement management represents an approach to management in which managers delegate substantial autonomy and decision making down through the ranks on the assumption that increased responsibility for task accomplishment leads to increased effort and performance. One variation on this approach is referred to as "self-management" or "self-leadership." The three readings that follow examine several aspects of this new approach to traditional job design. First, Lawler considers how new patterns of organization design can influence employee motivation and performance. Next, Manz reviews recent research on self-managing teams and presents the argument that, when done correctly, such an approach to group leadership can have surprising effects in the workplace. Finally, Pfeffer attempts to make the connection between having a high-involvement work force and achieving competitive advantage in the global marketplace. He argues, in essence, that an organization's human resources must be viewed as a strategic resource that can enhance an organization's competitive edge.

REFERENCES

Hackman, J. R., & Oldham, G. R. Motivation through the design of work: Test of a theory. *Organizational Behavior and Human Performance,* 1976, 16, 250–279.
Hackman, J. R., & Oldham, G. R. *Work redesign.* Reading, MA: Addison-Wesley, 1980.
Herzberg, F. *Work and the nature of man.* Cleveland: World Publishing, 1966.
Herzberg, F., Mausner, B., Peterson, R. O., & Capwell, D. F. *Job attitudes: Review of research and opinion.* Pittsburgh: Psychological Services of Pittsburgh, 1957.
Herzberg, F., Mausner, B., & Snyderman, B. *The motivation to work.* New York: Wiley, 1959.
Maier, N. R. F. *Psychology in industry,* 2d ed. Boston: Houghton Mifflin, 1955.
Murray, H. A. *Explorations in personality.* New York: Oxford University Press, 1938.
Paul, W. J., Robertson, K. B., & Herzberg, F. Job enrichment pays off. *Harvard Business Review,* 1969, 47(2), 61–78.
Scott, W. E. Activation theory and task design. *Organizational Behavior and Human Performance,* 1966, 1, 3–30.
Turner, A. N., & Lawrence, P. R. *Industrial jobs and the worker.* Boston: Harvard University, Graduate School of Business Administration, 1965.
Viteles, M. S. *Motivation and morale in industry.* New York: Norton, 1953.

The New Plant Approach: A Second Generation Approach

Edward E. Lawler III

The creation of a new manufacturing location represents an excellent opportunity to apply a new management approach. In a new setting, all the systems in an organization can be designed from the beginning to be consistent with a particular management strategy. Whole new methods of organizing and managing work can be put into place virtually overnight. In 1978 I wrote an article, "The New Plant Revolution" (*Organizational Dynamics,* Vol. 6, No. 3, 1978, pp. 2–12), which described a new approach to management that was being used by a number of companies when they created new plants. This New Plant Approach is much more participative in its management practices than is traditional management; its structure allows it to incorporate a number of innovations.

More recently, in 1990, I wrote an article that reviewed the New Plant Approach. "The New Plant Revolution Revisited" (*Organizational Dynamics,* Winter 1990) noted that companies such as Procter & Gamble and Mead used this management style for all their new plants, and that some companies have successfully converted their old plants to it as well. In addition, many of the specific practices that are part of the New Plant Approach have spread to existing plants and have become standard operating procedure in a large number of manufacturing settings.

Even though the New Plant Approach has proven to be quite successful, there are opportunities to improve upon it. After all, a great deal has changed in American business since its initial introduction more than 20 years ago. Significant new management technologies have developed, particularly in areas concerned with the management of quality and the use of information technology. In addition, the business environment has changed in many respects. Many markets have become global, and as a result performance standards with respect to quality, speed, and costs have grown.

The focus of this article is on the need to develop a new or next-generation management model for settings that are managed with a participative management approach. Although I am building on work that was originally done in manufacturing settings, much of what I have to say applies to any organizational setting in which a product or service is being produced or delivered.

The major feature that differentiates the Second Generation Approach from the New Plant Approach is the degree to which the former places information, power, knowledge, and rewards in the hands of individuals who are actually creating the products and services. The intention is to develop a high level of business involvement among all employees. The expectation is that doing so will lead to performance improvements in speed, quality, and costs because lower level employees will be able to act more quickly and in a more informed, more motivated manner.

The original New Plant Approach, for a variety of reasons, focused heavily on being sure that individuals had control over, and information about, their piece of the production process. It might best be called a productivity involvement or plant operations involvement approach to management. Getting individuals involved in the business of the organization represents a significant step beyond this type of involvement.

It requires the adoption of the same practices—for example, work teams, an all-salary workforce, and skill-based pay—that are part of the New Plant Approach, but it requires going beyond these in a number of areas as well. It requires that individuals receive new information, have additional skills, be rewarded differently, and ultimately have the power to influence many parts of the business process.

With this in mind, let us turn to a consideration of the features that need to be built into an organization if it is to involve individuals in the business.

ORGANIZATION DESIGN

The New Plant Approach includes a flat organization design and the extensive use of self-managing teams. This basic design approach is appropriate for a business involvement plant design as well. It is particularly important for business involvement that teams have the responsibility for producing a whole product or completely serving an identifiable customer base. Without this, it is impossible for individuals to feel that they have a business that they control in a bottom-line sense. In a manufacturing setting, a team needs to be given responsibility for producing an entire product and for dealing as directly as possible with both customers and suppliers. The teams, in essence, need to be responsible for all the value-added activities that occur with respect to a particular product.

In the case of service teams, the same principle holds. Employee teams need to be given responsibility for performing all activities with respect to a particular customer. This principle means, for example, that work teams charged with processing and managing mortgages, or handling credit card business, need to be given responsibility for the entire service process with respect to a particular customer.

In creating teams, a clear bias needs to exist toward establishing a customer-supplier relationship for each work team. These can be internal customer-supplier relationships; where possible, however, there is a definite advantage to creating external customer-supplier relationships. This provides the most "real" business experience for individuals and keeps them in contact with the competitive business environment that they are in and the kinds of demands that the organization faces from its external markets and suppliers.

To facilitate team management of a business, it often is important to include staff support members in the production teams. For example, engineers and accountants may need to be placed on the teams so that the teams can handle a full scope of business issues and, in effect, operate as mini-business enterprises.

The physical layout of the facility should be designed to facilitate teams owning an entire product or customer. Equipment needs to be positioned so that employees who are on the same teams are located together. Staff support individuals need to be located in the production areas they support. Blocks to communication, including walls, need to be minimized or eliminated, as do all symbols that indicate differences in power and status. Hierarchical symbols work against all individuals feeling responsible for organizational success, and they encourage decision making on the basis of hierarchy rather than expertise.

The sociotech approach to work design and the total quality management approach both argue for building teams around key workflow interdependencies. Total quality programs also stress the importance of establishing a clear customer relationship. Thus, both the total quality and sociotech approaches are compatible with creating business involvement plants. The sociotech approach has in fact frequently been used in the design of new plants. Neither the sociotech approach nor the quality approach, however, will necessarily create teams that are responsible for whole products or services—nor do they always create teams that have external customers. Both of these are critical elements in establishing the kinds of teams that encourage business involvement.

There are some interesting examples of organizations giving teams responsibility for taking a product from suppliers to completion. For example, the Digital Equipment plant at Enfield, Connecticut, allows work team members to deal directly with suppliers and gives them direct contact with the customers for the electronic boards that the teams make. This contact is facilitated by giving the team members business cards and including an 800 phone number with the product so that customers can call them directly with questions or problems. The teams are also encouraged to visit customers and to invite their suppliers into the plant to work with them in assuring high quality supplies.

Volvo's new Swedish car manufacturing facility carries the team model further than any other manufacturing facility of which I am aware. The customers, through information technology, place an order directly with the manufacturing team. The team informs the customer of the "build schedule" for the car and invites the customer to be on hand when the car is built. Once the car is completed, the team delivers the car to the customer—but the process does not end there. The team makes arrangements with the customer to maintain an ongoing performance record for the car. Team members can also communicate with the customer through information technology that ties them to the dealership and therefore to the customer. This approach has the potential to tie the entire manufacturing team to an individual customer over a sustained period of time. It allows the team to receive continuous feedback about the quality of each car produced, and to respond directly to customer questions and issues.

TOTAL TEAM ENVIRONMENT

The New Plant Approach stresses the use of teams at the production level, but it does not stress the use of teams in other areas of the plant. The jobs of managers, office personnel, and staff support individuals end up being different from what they are in a traditional plant because they have to deal with teams—yet they are not in a team structure. This inconsistency in some respects has limited the effectiveness of the New Plant Approach because staff support groups do not have the same kind of flexibility and performance gains that are characteristic of the production area.

The obvious solution to the problem of differences existing between the production area and the rest of the plant is to make the plant a total team environment. Several organizations have done this by placing as many support people as possible in production teams and by creating management and staff support teams. These teams meet regularly to allocate their time and effort and, like production teams, do a considerable amount of self-managing. They usually are not as flexible as the production teams, since it is harder for individuals to learn other jobs in staff and managerial roles. Nevertheless, with cross-training they are still in a good position to take advantage of some of the flexibility inherent in the team concept—and, consequently, to engage in a fair amount of self-management.

The use of team structures throughout the organization should contribute to an even flatter structure than is typical of the New Plant Approach. In plants using a team approach, the organization is usually quite flat with wide spans of control but there is a limit to just how flat it can be because of the need to have a supervisor for at least every three or four work teams. This can be partially overcome by having a team supervision approach so that individuals in managerial jobs can help each other out and cover the work load imbalances that are inherent in supervising a number of teams.

BUSINESS INTEGRATION

The typical New Plant Approach has been used primarily in locations that do only manufacturing. Consequently, employees in the manufacturing area have had little input or contact with individuals who are doing product development and little contact with individuals doing sales, customer service, or customer relations. This is an obvious limitation with respect to business involvement. Individuals who could provide valuable feedback are not involved in the total value creation process of the organization and do not have external customer contacts. This can be corrected, however, by co-locating and better integrating other functions with the manufacturing process. The use of concurrent engineering by an increasing number of organizations represents just such a positive step.

Product development and design can be co-located at manufacturing sites, so that individuals in the manufacturing areas can be involved in these issues and vice-versa. Production employees may not have great amounts of customer knowledge, but they do have a great deal of knowledge about manufacturability; it is important to capture this expertise in the product development process. Similarly, if the marketing and sales organizations are co-located with manufacturing, it can provide individuals in the manufacturing area with an opportunity to deal with customers more directly and to have inputs to the marketing and sales process.

The co-location of product development, manufacturing, and marketing/sales is not necessary in order to get individuals involved in all phases of the business process. Task forces represent one way to create involvement up and down the value-added chain without co-location. Information technology can also be used to allow individuals in the manufacturing area to have input to product design as well as sales and marketing activities. With networked computers, a task force can be given the opportunity to comment on new product designs and, in some cases, to answer marketing and sales questions about the products and services that they produce.

REWARD SYSTEM

Two important and visible features of the New Plant Approach are the extensive use of skill-based pay and the commitment to job security. In the Second Generation Approach, there is no reason to change either of these; both are consistent with a business involvement approach that pushes information, power, knowledge, and rewards downward. Indeed, what is needed is an extension of the commitment to skill-based pay.

In the New Plant approach, skill-based or competency pay is applied only to individuals who are in self-managing work teams, which in effect means it applies only to production area employees. With the use of teams throughout the organization, it is appropriate to extend skill-based pay to all employees in the organization. This means that staff, managerial, and clerical teams would all have skill-based pay just as do production teams. Few organizations have done this so far, although Polaroid stands out as a notable exception. The advantages of applying skill-based pay to all employees are essentially the same as those that are derived when it is applied to manufacturing divisions. It has the potential to create a more flexible and knowledgeable workforce, and it is highly congruent with a team-based management approach that stresses learning and continuous improvement.

Completely missing in the New Plant Approach are reward systems based on organization and business performance. This is an enormous void, and one that must be filled in a Second Generation Approach based on business involvement.

Individuals need to be accountable for the results of the business, and the best way to do this is to make their pay at least partially dependent on the success of the business for which they are responsible. This can be done through gainsharing plans, profit sharing plans, and employee ownership. The approach that works best is determined by specific organizational conditions. Critical factors are just how much of the business process an individual plant or location can be held accountable for and how those responsibilities relate to the rest of the organization. In many cases, more than one pay-for-performance method are likely to be needed. The key is to make compensation variable based on controllable performance. In the case of the new start-up, it may not be appropriate to put a gainsharing or other plant level plan in the beginning. It is often difficult to implement a good gainsharing plan then because it is hard to know what to measure and even harder to know what the standard is above which a bonus should be paid. What can be done at start-up is to make a commitment to the development of a gainsharing or profit sharing plan, and to begin the development process within several years after the start-up of the new location.

An important feature of the reward system in the New Plant Approach is skill-based pay. It helps assure the development of the right competencies in the work force. There is no reason to change this. In fact, with the greater use of teams in the Second Generation Approach, it is important to extend skill-based pay to white-collar and managerial teams. In some respects it can be harder to do skill-based pay in nonproduction areas because the quantification of performance and skill acquisition is more difficult. Nevertheless, this important feature needs to be built into these work teams as well. Without it, teams cannot control a very important feature of their environment that influences performance.

INFORMATION TECHNOLOGY

When the New Plant Approach was developed, there was very little use of computers and no use of computer networking by organizations. This limited the kinds of decisions that work team members could be involved in because it made it difficult to deliver information to them in a timely fashion. With the advent of relatively inexpensive computing and sophisticated information system networks, the situation has changed dramatically. It is now possible for all employees to have access to PCs or terminals that are linked to company-wide information systems. Employees can get a great deal of information about the business, their local operations, and, indeed, operations in other plants. This in turn means that they can be involved in a wide range of decisions and get feedback in areas where it was not practical before.

The Second Generation Approach needs to take advantage of information technology so that individuals have the ability to access the latest data about what is occurring in other areas of the company, how their product or service is performing, how customers are reacting to it, and how much it is costing to produce. This tremendous increase in the amount of feedback employees can get also changes decision-making processes so that more than just quality and production numbers are being considered. It can allow everyone to understand the economic tradeoffs that are involved in his or her performance and thus enable business involvement.

If adapted correctly, information technology can also help with problem solving and education. For example, it can allow employees to communicate with each other when they have a technical problem and avoid the entire process of going up and down the hierarchy to find out who has a particular expertise and what the correct solution is for a problem. In some Procter & Gamble plants, for example, individuals or teams with production problems can access an electronic bulletin board and ask for help from anyone within the organization. It is also possible for employees to compare production rates and numbers from plant to plant so that they are aware of how much can be done with the equipment for which they are responsible.

Networked computers can also be used to expand the input opportunities of employees. With the New Plant Approach, attitude surveys and focus groups are often used to sense how the employees are feeling about their job situation, but this is inherently a slow and limited approach to gathering data. IBM and other organizations are now converting this to an information technology-based system in which survey questions are simply put on the network and individuals are allowed to respond to them online. In addition, key strategy or policy decisions can be put on the information system for comment and debate. This can mean that even employees in overseas locations have a chance to give input on new policies and practices that previously would have been decided by a corporate staff group and senior management.

Finally, television screens can be used to help link employees who are involved in different aspects of the production or service process. This can take the form of video tapes that show employees in the manufacturing environment what employees outside that area are doing, or have been doing in some plants. Individuals earlier in the production process can be linked to those later in the production process by closed-circuit video. This has the obvious advantage of improving communication and understanding throughout the production process. It can also help individuals conceptualize what is going on elsewhere in the production process so that they can identify with the total product and suggest improvements.

Television and electronic mail can also be used to support business involvement by reporting on financial results and key company events. In some companies this is already being done on a regular basis. In one company, in fact, a quarterly state-of-the-business video tape is sent to every employee's home. Other companies do television broadcasts on a weekly basis in order to keep employees up-to-date on what is happening.

QUALITY TECHNOLOGY

When the New Plant Approach was first implemented in the late 1960s, very little was known in the United States about the quality programs being used in Japan. The situation has changed dramatically since then; virtually ever major corporation has a total quality management system based on the work of Juran, Deming, and Crosby. These so-called quality gurus have strongly transformed the way quality management is perceived in the United States. They stress the importance of employee involvement in producing high-quality products and offer a number of specific management tools to improve quality.

In many respects, the total quality concept of involvement is much more limited than that of the New Plant Approach. However, this does not mean that the quality tools they offer are inappropriate. Indeed, many of the tools need to be adopted because they can help work teams and plants do a better job of managing themselves and understanding their production processes.

Statistical process control, cost of quality measurement, and some of the problem-solving approaches inherent in the quality technology fit well with the Second Generation Approach. When these are installed in a business involvement-oriented plant, they can substantially improve the ability of teams to understand their production process and become more self-managing. Also potentially useful are quality improvement teams and task forces that are targeted at improving particular features of the production or service process. In contrast with traditionally managed locations, however, fewer of these teams should be needed in those organizations that adopt the Second Generation Approach. The reason for this is simple. The work teams should handle much of the improvement process activities themselves without the need for special groups and the extra cost that is involved in creating them and supporting them. Some organization-wide issues or some in-depth sticky problems may crop up that affect several teams; such problems may require individuals dedicated to solving them over a substantial period of time. In these cases the use of problem-solving teams makes sense.

Overall, the correct stance with respect to quality technology is to adopt those elements that improve the problem-solving process, bring more information and knowledge into the work teams, and allow them to be more self-managing. Several plants that started in the 1970s with the New Plant Approach have done a good job of this. They have trained their employees in statistical process control, problem analysis, and process management. This has helped them improve their organizational performance and advance further in the areas of business involvement and self-management.

HUMAN RESOURCE MANAGEMENT

A heavy commitment to selection and training is a critical element of the New Plant Approach. This typically includes realistic job previews as well as team-based selection processes. But the Second General Approach, if anything, requires a greater commitment to selection and development. In the area of development, for example, it requires a commitment to individuals learning a great deal about quality technology. It also requires individuals to learn more about the business impact of their roles in the organization. This means they need to get extensive economic education, as well as being educated in the technical details of the manufacturing or service process.

In essence, individuals in the production area need to be treated more like managers as far as the training, information, and pay rates they receive. In terms of skill-based pay, they need to be able to progress higher in total compensation in return for learning vertical or upward skills. This has implications for the kind of individuals that are selected, since much more is expected of them than just the ability to work in a team and control a production process. They need to develop an understanding of the business.

The Second Generation Approach demands a great deal of managers. They must be coaches, leaders, and expert resources. Getting the right kind of manager cannot be left to chance. The selection process needs to be able to identify them—and of course, training and support should be available to them. In the area of selection, assessment centers and simulations can help to identify the right individuals. The training and development process needs to include peer and staff assessment data and behavioral learning experiences.

RENEWAL/IMPROVEMENT PROCESS

The New Plant Approach does not have any built-in renewal or improvement structures. Total quality programs appropriately stress the importance of taking a continuous improvement approach to management. Such an approach can, and should, be combined with a focus on competitive benchmarking. This can help reinforce the necessity for continuous improvement because the simple fact of the matter is that performance standards, with respect to most products and services, are constantly rising.

Continuous improvement can be done within work teams if they are given the appropriate information and support, but it also may require separate structures to get the appropriate amount of attention and an organization-wide perspective. This suggests that organizations regularly need to create task forces or design teams that can assess the organization and look at its competitive position. They need to use such tools as attitude surveys and competitive benchmarking to see how well the organization is operating—and then to involve people within the organization in the improvement process.

It is difficult to predict exactly how often an extensive organizational renewal or assessment process should be undertaken, but a rough guess is that it should be done at least every two years, with benchmarking being done at least annually. One suggested approach that can help facilitate an assessment is to invite customers and suppliers to be involved in the assessment process. Similarly, outside experts in critical areas can be brought in to help describe the newest management technologies, as well as the newest manufacturing technologies. The key is to help the organization update itself and assure that it stays on the cutting edge.

THE SECOND GENERATION NEW PLANT IN PRACTICE

When I wrote my first article about the New Plant Approach, I was able to report that a number of plants already followed this model. The same is not true with respect to the Second Generation Model. I know of no example that fits it perfectly, although a number of organizations are clearly moving toward creating plants that will adhere to the new model. Organizations such as Mead, TRW, and Digital already have plants that possess many of the necessary features. Thus, my prediction is that before too long there will be a number of good examples.

Because the Second Generation Approach clearly represents a significant step beyond the New Plant Approach, adopting it involves some risk. But with the growing emphasis and acceptance of employee involvement as a management strategy, it is likely that more plants will explore Second Generation strategies. If, as seems likely, the new approach can offer efficiencies in the areas of reduced overhead, greater commitment to the business, and overall, greater flexibility and responsiveness, its use may very well grow rapidly and in fact become widespread.

SELECTED BIBLIOGRAPHY

My original article on this subject was "The New Plant Revolution" (*Organizational Dynamics,* Vol. 6 No. 3, 1978, pp. 2–12) and in 1990 I wrote an article reviewing the New Plant Approach entitled "The New Plant Revolution Revisited" (*Organizational Dynamics,* Winter 1990).

Data on the adoption of participative management practices are provided in Carla O'Dell's *People, Performance and Pay* (American Productivity Center, 1987) and in Edward E. Lawler, Gerald E. Ledford, and Susan A. Mohrman's *Employee Involvement in America* (American Productivity and Quality Center, 1989).

See the following for a description of the different approaches to participative management: Edward E. Lawler's *High Involvement Management* (Jossey-Bass, 1986); a chapter on "Beyond Self Managing Work Teams," by Charles Manz, published in a work edited by Robert W. Woodman and William A. Posmore, *Research in Organizational Change and Development,* Volume 4, JAL, 1990, pp. 273–299.

For a discussion of quality circles, see Edward E. Lawler and Susan A. Mohrman's "Quality Circles After the Fad" (*Harvard Business Review,* Volume 85 No. 1, pp. 64–71) and by the same authors "Quality Circles: After the Honeymoon" (*Organizational Dynamics,* Volume 15 No. 4, 1987, pp. 42–54).

For a discussion of team effectiveness, see *Groups that Work* edited by J. Richard Hackman (Jossey-Bass, 1990) and an article by J. P. MacDuffie, "The Japanese Auto Transplants: Challenges to Conventional Wisdom" (*ILR Report,* Volume 26 No. 1, 1988, pp. 12–18), which discusses the practices of Japanese companies.

Two works by Edward E. Lawler discuss gainsharing and skill-based pay, *Pay and*

Organizational Development (Addison-Wesley, 1981) and *Strategic Pay* (Jossey-Bass, 1990). There is also an article by Richard E. Walton and Leonard A. Schlesinger, "Do Supervisors Thrive in Participative Work Systems?" (*Organizational Dynamics,* Volume 8 No. 3, 1979, pp. 25–38) that looks at the role of managers in a participative management system.

Self-Leading Work Teams: Moving Beyond Self-Management Myths

Charles C. Manz[1,2]

INTRODUCTION

Employee self-management, both for individuals and for work teams (e.g., Hackman, 1986; Luthans & Davis, 1979; Manz, 1986, 1990, 1992; Manz & Sims, 1980, 1990), has been receiving increasing attention in the literature as a promising new management tool. At the same time, individual and team self-management application and theory has been the target of many criticisms and challenges. Some of these will be summarized in the next section. This literature suggests that "employee self-management" in many ways is often more of an illusion or myth than a reality.

In this paper a self-influence perspective will be proposed that promises the potential to move beyond self-management, and the limitations that have been ascribed to it. Specifically, the concept of self-leading teams will be introduced and discussed. The perspective taken here is that there are several limitations in the way that employee self-management and teams are often implemented. Pressures such as international competition requiring fuller utilization of human resources, frustrated needs of a changing workforce, insufficient organizational adaptability to meet rapidly changing environments, require that we continue to explore ways of more fully utilizing human resources. Furthermore, there is evidence suggesting that a number of factors that dilute the significance of participation in organizations often cause employees to place a low value on participative opportunities (Neumann, 1989). These forces taken together make exploring concepts and approaches that extend beyond so called self-management and self-managing teams, a worthwhile pursuit. Due to the magnitude of this undertaking some important considerations can not be adequately addressed (e.g., the role of unions) despite their obvious importance. Nevertheless, a number of issues and challenges to current thinking on self-managing teams will be raised as well as some contingencies and limitations to the self-leading team perspective proposed.

SELF-MANAGEMENT AND SELF-MANAGING TEAMS

What Is Employee Self-Management?

Self-management, as it has been conceptualized and applied in organizations, can be described as a set of strategies for managing one's own behavior to reduce discrepan-

[1]Department of Management, Arizona State University, Tempe, Arizona 85287.
[2]Requests for reprints should be addressed to Charles C. Manz, Department of Management, Arizona State University, Tempe, Arizona 85287.

From *Human Relations*, 1992, 45(11), 1119–1140. Reprinted by permission of Plenum Publishing Corporation.

cies from existing work standards (Manz, 1986). The focus is on behavior that helps meet the demands of the surrounding system. While the individual's immediate behavior might be described as self-controlled, the purpose of the overall process tends to serve the requirements of higher level control loops (e.g., self-management is practiced for the purpose of accomplishing what a superior or the wider organizational system directs be done). Following the negative feedback loop logic of cybernetic control theory (Carver & Scheier, 1981, 1982), self-management strategies tend to address short-run deviations from governing standards but not the appropriateness or the desirability of the standards themselves. While self-management applications do tend to allow employees significant self-influence regarding *how* to complete a task to meet a standard (as defined by the wider system, or higher management), they generally do not encompass self-influence in terms of *what* should be done and *why*.

Furthermore, as indicated by Manz (1986), self-management is typically dependent on extrinsic incentives—e.g., external rewards are needed to reinforce self-management activity in order for it to be continued (Manz & Sims, 1980; Thoresen and Mahoney, 1974). Also, self-management tends to address what "should" be done as defined by external sources, rather than what an individual is intrinsically motivated to do ("wants" to do) (Manz, 1986).

Self-Managing Work Team Theory

There are a number of different ways to describe and apply self-managing teams. Usually they involve an increased amount of behavioral control and decision making autonomy at the work group level (Manz & Sims, 1986). Self-managing work teams are typically introduced with the objective of simultaneously improving productivity for the organization as well as the quality of working life for employees (Manz & Sims, 1986, 1987). Self-managing teams have been described as possessing "a relatively whole task; members who each possess a variety of skills relevant to the group task; workers' discretion over such decisions as methods of work, task scheduling, and assignment of members to different tasks; and compensation and feedback about performance for the group as a whole" (Hackman, 1976).

The primary theoretical basis for self-managing teams in the work place is sociotechnical systems theory (e.g., Emery & Trist, 1969; Cummings, 1978; Susman, 1976), which advocates jointly optimizing both the social and technical components of the work environment. Training and skill development especially emphasizes employee technical (e.g., performing production tasks) and social (e.g., communication, dealing with conflict) skills. There is usually a shift in focus from individual to group methods for performing work. The logic for this shift is based on the view that a group can more effectively apply its resources to address work condition variances (particularly ones that are not easily predictable) within the group than can individual employees working separately (Susman, 1976). Self-managing work team members tend to experience enriched jobs (see, for example, Hackman & Oldham, 1975) and an increased focus on the success of the group as a whole.

As is true of the self-management concept, self-managing work teams typically entail less than complete self-influence for employees. These teams usually fall somewhere in a middle range on an imaginary continuum from external control to self-control (c.f., Hackman, 1986). In general, the introduction of self-managing work teams tends to increase the level of self-management opportunity and discretion of employees (especially when working on tasks with sufficient complexity and variability). On the other hand, the opportunity to exert control may actually be reduced for employees in jobs that naturally provide significant personal discretion (e.g., Manz & Angle, 1986). This paradoxical consequence can result from control limits exerted by the group, such as pressure to conform to group viewpoints and norms (Manz & Sims, 1982), and from leaders or supervisors of the group (Hackman, 1986; Manz & Sims, 1984, 1986, 1987).

It has been estimated that more than two hundred plants in the United States have adopted a self-managing work design (Lawler, 1986; Walton, 1985) and more than a thousand were recently undergoing significant change in that direction (Walton, 1985). The applications span many industries including both blue collar manufacturing and office settings. Some examples include: a pet food plant (Walton, 1977), coal mines (Trist, Susman, & Brown, 1977), a paint manufacturing plant (Poza & Markus, 1980), small parts manufacturing (Manz & Sims, 1982, 1984, 1987; & Sims & Manz, 1982), an independent insurance firm (Manz & Angle, 1986), a warehouse (Manz, Keating, & Donnellon, 1990) and paper mills (Manz & Newstrom, 1990).

Challenges to Self-Management Theory

It has been suggested that employee self-management can be more of a myth than a reality in actual practice. Dunbar (1981), drawing on the work of Perlmutter & Monty (1977), argued that people want to believe that they can exercise some self-influence even when the physical environment does not actually allow any real personal control. This creates what Dunbar describes as an illusion of control. He suggests that this illusion can have positive benefits such as enhanced confidence facilitating greater activity, ease in approach, and exploration (White, 1959) and increased motivation leading to the investment of resources, effort, and time that facilitate success (McClelland & Winter, 1969). On the negative side, an illusion of self-control can contribute to the discounting of relevant information (Fischoff & Beyth, 1975). Also, this illusion may create an artificial sense of involvement that reduces motivation to pursue actual self-control of behavior.

Furthermore, it has been argued that employees in so-called self-managing situations are in reality subject to significant control and supervision (Mills, 1983). This control and supervision includes establishment of clear task boundaries and support for the activities performed. Mills (1983) further indicates that "self-managed" individuals are subject to a variety of other controls: the normative systems within work groups, professional values stemming from an individual's specialized training, organizational socialization processes, and so on. External control, while potentially providing positive outcomes in many situations for the organization and the worker (e.g., by reducing ambiguity, by helping to coordinate effort of multiple people), nevertheless, can significantly limit the benefits resulting from employee self-management. This is particularly true when external control is unnecessary or suppresses individual potential contributions. In addition, Mulder (1971, 1976) has warned that implementing participation processes for the less powerful can ironically increase the power distance from the more powerful. That is, participative systems can create occasions for the powerful (often with the advantage of greater expertise and experience relative to participating workers) to exercise power over the less powerful.

In addition, employees will tend to choose not to participate in organizations when the area of participation is seen as being of limited value and importance (e.g., when participative discretion is parallel to, but separate from, significant organizational strategic issues; Neumann, 1989). Quality circles, Japanese management techniques, and so forth have sometimes been criticized for not providing any real self-control over actions. The philosophy of developing and allowing employees to be self-managed may be espoused, but the "theory in use" (Argyris, 1982a,b), which is based on hidden organizational agendas, is actually oriented toward external control.

Further challenges to self-management can be identified by comparing American views with international perspectives. For example, European organization theory was the focus of a seminar held in Fontainebleau, France, in 1975 (Hofstede & Kassem, 1976). In the opening chapter of the book based on this seminar, Kassem (1976) summarized some distinctions between European and American organization theory. These included: (1) Americans focus more on goals and people, Europeans focus more on structure and technology, (2) Americans tend to focus more on power processes, Europeans are more interested in power structures, (3) Americans focus more on informal participative management, Europeans focus on industrial democracy, and (4) Americans focus more on individual job enrichment, Europeans focus more on group-oriented socio-technical systems.

Kassem warned of the danger of oversimplifying distinctions between European and American organization theorists. More recently, Alioth, Muller, & Vaassen (1988), for example, found a variety of views held by Swiss managers regarding their role and the management of employee autonomy ranging from approaches resembling autocracy to empowerment. Kassem also noted several European theorists that take more of an American perspective and *vice versa*. Nevertheless, the broad brushstroke distinctions he draws are quite useful and reinforce some of the themes that emerged from a recent empowerment workshop involving international scholars and practitioners (Elden & Chisholm, 1988). In this workshop participants expressed contrasting views regarding self-direction at work, ranging from limited participation (a common American view) to more extensive empowerment (a more common European view).

Overall, Americans may be somewhat lagging in their orientation toward empowerment in the workplace. Walton (1987) found evidence supporting this assertion in the international shipping industry. The U.S. ranked last in an analysis of work-innovation practices (including several participative practices such as shipboard management teams) in comparison to Japan and seven European countries.

This paper will focus on the self-managed team concept, generally considered an advanced self-managed work system tool. The extent to which "self-managed" teams allow "real" worker self-influence will be discussed. Some alternatives regarding ways that work teams might be implemented so as to allow greater employee self-direction will be suggested.

BEYOND SELF-MANAGEMENT: TOWARD SELF-LEADERSHIP

Self-leadership can be described as a broader view of self-influence that includes the kind of self-management strategies addressed in the literature (e.g., Manz & Sims, 1980) as well as additional strategies for managing the natural motivational value of the task (intrinsic motivation) and the patterns in one's thinking (Manz, 1986, 1992). Self-leadership involves behavior but has a particular focus on cognition. It includes reduction of discrepancies from existing standards, as well as evaluating the appropriateness of the standards. It addresses what should be done and why in addition to how to do it. Self-leadership prescribes an active role for members in a work system and is represented as an advanced form of self-influence. (See Fig. 1 for a conceptual repre-

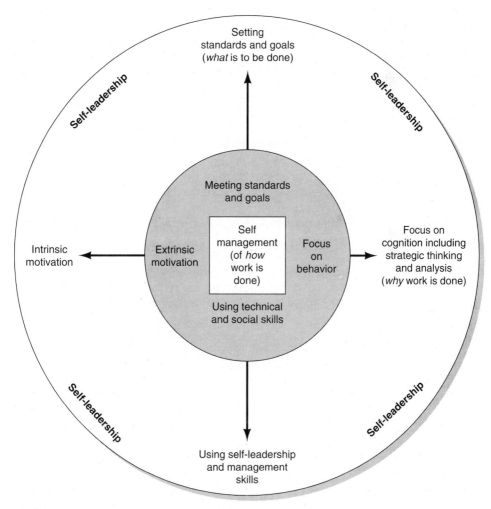

FIGURE 1
Some primary features involved in moving beyond self-management toward self-leadership.

sentation of some key features reflecting a movement beyond self-management toward self-leadership.)

On a continuum ranging from external control to complete employee self-control (cf. Manz & Angle, 1986) self-leadership falls significantly closer to the complete self-influence end than does self-management. In self-leadership–oriented organizations, workers play a greater role in influencing strategic processes and higher-level management decision making. Management and advanced self-influence skills need special emphasis as a part of employee training. In particular, self-leading employees need to develop significant abilities for strategic thinking and analysis. Initially, some employees will not possess the capacity or interest for this kind of activity. From a cybernetic control perspective, organization members become involved in setting governing standards as well as helping to achieve the standards. Both short-term processes of deviation reduction as well as longer-term processes of deviation amplification are involved. This includes establishing new standards or objectives that offer the potential to enhance the system rather than just maintain it (e.g., allowance for continuous improvement rather than maintenance of a static steady state).

In the following discussion, I will review some perspectives that especially shed light on the distribution of control resulting from different organizational forms. These organizational types also have significant implications for other functions such as enabling employees to perform. The primary focus here, however, will be on the issue of control. Various frameworks have been developed suggesting a progression of organizational forms specifying increasing self-control for organization members. They support the idea of a continuum ranging from an emphasis on external organizational and management control to organizational forms that move beyond "self-management" to more advanced forms of employee self-influence (e.g., self-leadership). A greater role for employees in establishing the standards that govern the system is implied in the more advanced forms.

Hackman (1986) identified four types of work units, based on the amount of organizational authority allocated. These include: the manager-led unit, the self-managing unit, the self-designing unit, and the self-governing unit. The amount of self-influence workers are allowed is reflected by the responsibility and authority of workers in four areas: (1) performing the work, (2) monitoring and managing the work process, (3) designing or modifying the work unit and its context, and (4) providing overall direction for the unit's efforts. The "manager-led" unit prescribes authority for performance of the task only and is similar to traditional organizational forms associated with the "scientific management" views of Taylor (1911). The "self-managing unit," has responsibility for monitoring and managing its own performance as well as performing the task. Some self-managing team applications in the U.S. (e.g., Walton, 1977; Manz & Sims, 1987) are examples of this form.

The "self-designing unit" and the "self-governing unit" suggest a movement beyond the self-managing team model. The "self-designing unit" has additional authority for changing the design of the unit and its context. Management sets direction for the unit but members possess the authority to do what needs to be done to perform the work. Top management task forces are exemplary of this type of unit. "Self-governing units" have the authority to decide what is to be done, as well as all of the responsibilities of the other three types of units. It can establish the direction (objective), change the structure and context of the unit, manage its own performance, and do the work. Corporate boards of directors, worker cooperatives, and sole proprietorships are representative of this type of unit.

The four different unit forms reflect differing amounts of authority and opportunity for employee self-influence. Note that the self-managed form specifies less employee involvement, authority and self-influence than do two of the other forms that Hackman identifies.

Lawler (1986, 1988) has distinguished between three organizational involvement strategies including: (1) parallel suggestion involvement, (2) job involvement, and (3) "high involvement." Lawler's criteria include the extent to which the lowest levels of the organization are provided with performance-related information, rewards, knowledge, and decision-making power.

"Parallel suggestion involvement" creates a separate parallel structure that provides employees with some increases in information, involvement, and rewards for profitable suggestions. Quality circles represent an example of one recent form of this employee involvement approach.

"Job involvement" tends to emphasize the enhancement of worker motivation through the enrichment of work. The job characteristics model (Hackman & Oldham, 1975), for example, suggests that work characteristics such as task variety, task wholeness, performance feedback, and so forth be increased to enrich work. Other approaches focus on the establishment of autonomous or self-managed work teams and thus, concentrate on the group as a unit as opposed to individual job relationships (e.g., Cummings, 1978; Hackman, 1986; Manz & Sims, 1987).

The management structure in the organization is significantly impacted by both the individual and group approaches to job enrichment. Worker skills, knowledge, decision breadth, and reward arrangements are affected, and Lawler suggests that the group approach tends to have the largest impact.

Lawler indicates that the "high involvement" approach provides the most extensive involvement and ability for self-influence. It entails passing power, information, knowledge, and rewards to the lowest levels of the organization. The logic is that if workers are going to care about the organization, they need to know about, be able to influence, be rewarded for, and have the knowledge and skills to contribute to, the performance of the organization. Workers are asked to be involved in decisions having to do with investment, strategy, and other key areas for the organization. Thus, Lawler's perspective suggests that high involvement clearly moves beyond the other two approaches and indicates that there are differences in the extent of self-influence allowed in different employee self-management–oriented strategies.

Walton (1985) addresses the movement from a control to a commitment form of organization management strategy. Organizations tend to emphasize rules and procedures, hierarchy, limited fixed jobs, minimum standards, status symbols, little information or authority distribution to lower organizational levels, adversarial labor relations, and so forth under the "control approach." The "commitment approach" is essentially the opposite. It emphasizes shared values and goals, flexible job definitions, dynamic "stretch" standards, minimum status differentials, flat organization forms with mutual influence systems, and so on.

Between these two opposing types is a middle ground that Walton calls the "transitional phase." Relatively few changes are allowed in terms of job designs; organizational structure or control mechanisms, and status symbols. However, workers are allowed greater responsibility and participation through mechanisms such as quality circles, QWL, and employee involvement programs, as well as increased access to information and input through *ad hoc* consultation mechanisms and some reduction of adversarial labor-management relations. Workers are provided with greater freedom and responsibility than under the control-oriented approach but significantly less than under the commitment condition.

Figure 2 suggests a continuum of types of teams representing increasing levels of employee self-influence. The figure suggests that self-managing work teams represent a less advanced level of worker self-control than do several other types. The primary issue implied by the figure is not a focus on self-management vs. external control. Rather, the figure suggests that self-management is not the end point of a control continuum. In order to appreciate a fuller set of organizational alternatives, particularly more advanced forms of employee empowerment, it is appropriate to begin to look beyond the concepts of self-management and self-managing teams.

The following discussion will address the concept of self-leading work teams as an alternative that can potentially provide an advancement beyond self-managed teams and many of the challenges to "self-management" raised earlier in this paper. Some potentially relevant contingencies involved in moving toward this advanced form of work design will also be discussed.

TOWARD A THEORY OF SELF-LEADING TEAMS

In several ways the concept of self-leading teams is similar to that of self-managing teams. Self-leading teams could consist of a relatively small group of individuals (e.g., 4–12 persons), although their membership would tend to be more fluid across different work teams. Team members would possess a greater level of discretion in their work than more traditional job structuring allows. They would normally make decisions regarding job assignments to different work tasks, methods for accomplishing production goals, ways of solving quality problems, strategies for addressing social problems within the group, and so forth. The group itself would be structured according to some natural divisions in the work process flow (where between-group interdependence exists) and would perform a relatively whole task process. Upon initial observation, a self-managing team would appear similar to a self-leading team.

Self-leading teams, however, would possess and exercise a greater level of influ-

FIGURE 2
A continuum of work team empowerment.

ence on decisions regarding what they do and why they do things, as well as how they do them, and thus would be located toward the right portion of Figure 2. Self-leading teams would be more involved with organizational strategic processes than self-managing teams. Thus, there would be a diminishing of distinctions between role definitions of higher-level managers and of the teams in a leadership sense. The team itself would be directly involved in establishing the direction for its work efforts, not just determining how to carry out the directions.

In a sense, examples of organizational forms similar to the way self-leading teams have been described here can be found in special cases involving professionals (e.g., professional partnerships, some academic departments, small theater companies, volunteer groups, etc.). In addition, Weick's (1979) notion of loosely coupled organizations, in which subunits (e.g., teams) have strong internal linkages but are somewhat insulated from external influences, is related as well. However, this paper is primarily concerned with work settings that traditionally have afforded employees with minimal self-influence and power (e.g., manufacturing environments, autocratically managed service environments).

Also, some overlap is apparent with European concepts of industrial democracy that allow worker influence and involvement in the governance as well as the performance process. Gulowsen (1979), for example, analyzed eight case studies of work systems involving various forms of self-managing teams in Scandinavia and Europe using criteria of autonomy, including the group's influence on: work performance methods, selection of group members, assignment of members to various tasks, the type of technology employed, when the group will work, selection of whether to have leaders within and outside the groups and who they are, and decisions regarding how much the group will do, whether it will add activities to the group's predetermined work purpose (goals), and what that purpose is to begin with (*what* does the group do). Each of these criteria strongly relate to the level of self-influence possessed by a team—the more of these elements controlled by the group the higher the level of the group's self-influence.

Two of the criteria appear to be particularly relevant to a movement beyond self-managing teams toward self-leading teams. First, the determination of whether the group will have designated leaders and who they will be (especially external to the group) is important. The leader is likely to significantly impact on what the group does and why it does what it does. Leadership often plays a pivotal role in determining the group's direction and purpose and the rationale involved in these choices. Thus, influence regarding selection of leaders represents an indirect impact on strategy related issues that are of central importance to the group.

The direct influence exerted on the decision of what the team's purpose will be is the second criterion of central importance. This implies group involvement in the underlying rationale (the *why*) and the ultimate decision of *what* the group will do. This is perhaps the most central means for moving a group toward the greater involvement in strategy determination implied by self-leading teams. Interestingly, not one of the eight cases analyzed by Gulowsen (1979) was found to involve a significant amount of influence on this latter criterion.

Another important distinguishing feature of self-leading teams is that workers perform work more for the natural (intrinsic) rewards that are built into the task rather than to receive externally administered rewards. Positive impact on the performer's feelings of competence and self-control (Deci, 1975a,b) and of purpose that extends beyond the immediate performance of the task (Manz, 1986, 1992), are central to this shift. Under conditions of self-leadership, workers tend to perform more because they "want" to rather than because they "should" perform.

This relates back to the process of determining what is performed. Employee involvement in deciding on what is to be accomplished enhances the potential for workers to accept (e.g., Vroom & Yetton, 1973) and be committed to work standards and objectives. Such involvement can contribute to employees' sense of competence, self-control, and purpose. While radical forms of co-determination such as those used in Europe (where influence is, at least in theory, more evenly shared by workers and management in terms of organizational governance) may not be necessary, a movement in this direction is often helpful and sometimes almost essential. A key is that workers are somehow represented in governance and strategic decision processes, and that information concerning why specific objectives and standards are adopted should be passed to lower levels of the organization. While it could be argued that many organizations claim that they attempt to build in these kinds of features under labels such as workplace democracy, employee involvement and participation, and even self-managing teams, this would be a significant shift for most organizations in practice. As a consequence, workers should better understand why specific objectives are being pursued, experience an increased sense of ownership, and be better equipped to contribute to setting the objectives and working to achieve them.

Specific organization characteristics employed to enable a team to move beyond self-management would vary from situation to situation. The common impact of these features would be that they enable and facilitate work team members to influence their own direction. Figure 3 suggests example features enabling a movement beyond self-managing teams in the direction of self-leading teams. For the most part, as additional features are introduced for self-leading teams, as implied in the right portion of the figure, the features listed for self-managing teams would be retained as well. Self-leadership adds to, expands, and encompasses the self-management process (Manz, 1986).

As suggested by Figure 3, the characteristics that enable a movement toward self-leading teams center on involvement of employees in strategic issues that enable them to have greater influence on what functions they serve and why. The figure indicates some contrasts between the focus of self-leading teams and self-managing teams. Self-managing designs sometimes claim more employee involvement in managerial issues than they actually deliver. Some work systems in fact fail because of a lack of follow-through, or a retreat from, the kinds of employee involvement characteristics originally designed into the system (Lawler, 1986).

The characteristics emphasized in Figure 3 are intended to add a further incremental advance toward workforce empowerment beyond traditional self-managing characteristics. Direct involvement in the decision of the team purpose and goals, empowerment to choose external group leaders, an emphasis on employee self-leadership skill development, passing "even more" information to lower levels of the organization, and in general charging workers with responsibility and authority to make strategic decisions, are clear examples of this movement. While some more advanced forms of self-

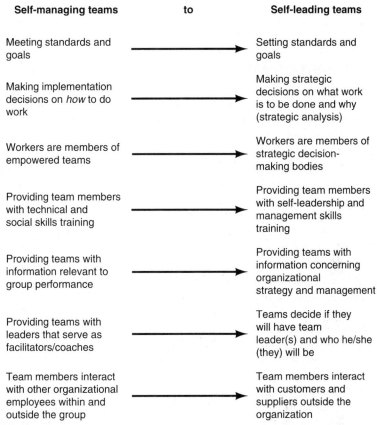

Self-managing teams	to	Self-leading teams
Meeting standards and goals	→	Setting standards and goals
Making implementation decisions on *how* to do work	→	Making strategic decisions on what work is to be done and why (strategic analysis)
Workers are members of empowered teams	→	Workers are members of strategic decision-making bodies
Providing team members with technical and social skills training	→	Providing team members with self-leadership and management skills training
Providing teams with information relevant to group performance	→	Providing teams with information concerning organizational strategy and management
Providing teams with leaders that serve as facilitators/coaches	→	Teams decide if they will have team leader(s) and who he/she (they) will be
Team members interact with other organizational employees within and outside the group	→	Team members interact with customers and suppliers outside the organization

FIGURE 3
Examples of organizational features consistent with a move beyond self-managing teams toward self-leading teams.

managing teams have included some of these features, many have not. The emphasis is on pressing the outer limits of employee self-influence. The work system itself moves well beyond a traditional autocratic management style and insulates the organization from the kind of self-management myths that have been suggested by the literature and that were summarized earlier in this paper.

In an in-progress study of a highly profitable American company, for example, it was discovered that employees have historically chosen their own job function and title. Clearly this unusual policy represents a step well beyond the *how* of performing work to the *what* and *why* of the work itself. Workers are also allowed to communicate directly with employees at different levels without having to go through a chain of command. No employee in the company needs approval to create a budget code and to begin spending financial resources to work on a new idea. The view within the company is that every employee is a leader and workers are allowed to essentially shape corporate strategy on the spot. For more information on this unusual organization see the article by Shipper and Manz (1992).

SOME CONTINGENCY FACTORS

Several organizational contingency factors are relevant to a movement toward a self-leading team type of work design. One key contingency is the *nature of the workers* involved. Neumann (1989) has discussed several factors that affect an employee's willingness to participate and noted that the literature has primarily focused on personality characteristics. One such contingency is the workers' need for autonomy (Harrell & Alpert, 1979). Both the employees and the organization may experience difficulties in implementation of a highly participative work system if enough individuals have a low need for autonomy (Manz, Mossholder, & Luthans, 1987).

In addition, the ability level of the workers involved is important. Manz et al. (1987) and Manz and Sims (1986) have indicated that there are at least two important sets of abilities. The first involves those that relate to work performance. For example, cognitive conceptual skills are of particular importance for higher-level managerial decision-making kinds of activities (Katz, 1974) that are called for in self-leading teams. Indeed, issues in human cognition such as information processing capacity, cognitive complexity, and so forth (c.f., Fiske and Taylor, 1984) become more relevant. They suggest a second important set of skills concerns self-managing abilities that enable an employee to be self-directing and self-motivating under autonomous conditions. If workers are significantly lacking in either of these ability categories a movement toward self-leadership will be difficult.

Some other characteristics of workers that are relevant to a movement toward self-leading teams in the workplace include: workers' level of perceived self-efficacy (Bandura, 1977a,b, 1982, 1986), locus of control (Mitchell, 1973; Strassberg, 1973), and self-esteem (Tharenou, 1979; Weiss, 1977). While each of these characteristics represents an important set of considerations, the view taken here is that with the aid of training, and guided work experience, workers can develop in ways that facilitate a movement toward self-leadership.

A movement toward self-leading teams will also be influenced by the *work context,* including the nature of the task, the technology employed, and the environment (Manz et al., 1987). For example, creative and nonroutine work tends to be more appropriate for increased levels of self-influence than does routine work (Manz et al., 1987; Slocum and Sims, 1980). Also, the potential for self-leadership tends to be higher in more ambiguous and changeable tasks that require more frequent adjustments and greater flexibility (Manz & Sims, 1980; Manz et al., 1987).

The type of technology will also tend to influence the dominant mode of control which will influence the degree of self-regulation that can be allowed in a work system (Van de Ven, 1979; Van de Ven & Delbecq, 1974; Van de Ven, Delbecq, & Koenig, 1976). Custom or continuous process technologies tend to fit better with self-regulation than do assembly line or mass production technologies (Slocum & Sims, 1980). A systemized control mode is often employed for mass production technologies. This implies top-down decision making and instructions. On the other hand, greater responsibility for the individual, providing the opportunity for workers to be significantly involved in their own regulation, is more often found with custom or continuous process technologies. Similarly, technology involving pooled interdependence (Thompson, 1967) may fit better with increased self-regulation than technology involving sequential interdependence (Manz et al., 1987; Slocum & Sims, 1980).

In addition, the recent emphasis on *new manufacturing techniques* such as "just in time" (JIT) and process controls may oppose significant worker self-influence (Klein, 1988, 1989). For example, when in-process inventory buffers are reduced toward zero to eliminate inefficiencies, with technologies based on sequential interdependence, the self-influence available to the workers can be largely eliminated. When inventory buffers are reduced within the manufacturing process, workers can become increasingly dependent on work flow time sequencing that is governed by the technology employed.

Finally, the nature of the *environment*—e.g., is it stable or dynamic? (Duncan, 1972)—can influence the potential and appropriateness of self-control. A dynamic environment usually calls for greater adaptability (Burns & Stalker, 1961; Lindsay & Rue, 1980) and consequently increased self-regulation.

Overall, the literature suggests that higher levels of self-regulation are more suitable for nonroutine more creative tasks, that rely on custom or continuous process technologies, and that are performed in dynamic environments. A number of other factors, however, can compensate for the influence of these forces, such as the social structure put into place (e.g., self-managing teams have been implemented in settings that lend themselves to systemized control with significant levels of self-regulation resulting). Here, the work context is viewed less as constraint and more as a strategic factor and tool. That is, conditions can be created that facilitate worker self-regulation.

A final consideration is the *organizational systems* that are addressed in the implementation of the team design. The focus of self-managing team applications tends to be on the work system in which the work is actually performed. A movement toward self-leading teams implies a special focus on the system of organizational governance. Saglio and Hackman (1982) have indicated that for worker cooperatives, the governance system centers on fostering organization members' influence and communication relevant to organization policy, and serves to protect their personal rights. Typical components of the governance system include the membership, its board of directors (the committee structure), and a grievance council. Clearly, if a movement toward self-leading teams requires employee involvement in organizational governance, we are addressing a potentially revolutionary change for most North American organizations.

Strauss (1982) has reviewed international experiences with elected worker representatives. In Yugoslavia, for example, elected worker councils actually hire and fire managers within certain guidelines. In Germany, where "co-determination" has been an important political issue, in the steel and coal industries there have been an equal number of worker and management representatives. Throughout Europe, efforts for involvement of workers in management issues (frequently related to governance) have been made (often accompanied by some amount of controversy and resistance). In the United States, on the other hand, with the exception of quality of work life efforts to make changes at the shop level (usually involving little participation in management except at very low levels), limited change has occurred. The changes that have taken place have been restricted to primarily a few experiments and some attempts at worker-owned cooperatives (Strauss, 1982).

Movement toward a self-leading team work system in many cases may not require major changes to the organizational governance system, although some change is usually required. Self-leading team-based work systems would likely require two central themes: (1) significant involvement of the work force in determining the direction of the organization as well as carrying out that direction, and (2) the opportunity for the work teams to influence that direction, especially as it relates to their specific work performance. For example, work teams might be involved in deciding on variations in product and/or service mixes that their group provides. This would require information flow to the work team level regarding market conditions and the costs and profitability of organization products and services. The work team's experience and knowledge of the work process, as it relates to its area of performance, could be applied to generate team proposals. These work team proposals could be evaluated by management and workforce representatives, discussed with the work team and/or representatives from the work team, and then integrated into organizational strategy.

Discretion to make significant decisions that might impact certain strategic issues relevant to the group's expertise could also be provided. In one manufacturing plant, for example, work teams had discretion to determine the product component parts they would produce at a given point in time depending on materials availability, defect problems, etc. (note that this required some level of between-team inventory buffers; Manz & Sims, 1987).

IMPLICATIONS AND RESEARCH QUESTIONS

This paper calls for organizational research and practice that explores organizational alternatives beyond self-managing teams. In many instances, what is currently referred to as employee self-management in reality may not provide employees with significant self-influence in their work. Rather, participative work systems, and in particular, self-managing work teams, can create an illusion of self-influence. In some cases they may establish the occasion for the powerful to exercise power over the powerless.

Self-leading work teams represent a more advanced employee self-influence alternative on a continuum away from external management and toward empowerment and self-leadership. Self-leading teams, as they have been discussed here, have similarities with what have been described as self-managing teams. However, the intention is that additional, significant, but sometimes subtle, features are emphasized that stretch the outer boundaries of employee self-influence. In particular, self-leading teams would influence the more strategic issues of what the team does and why, in addition to how it does its work. Overall, the self-leading team is proposed as an organizational form that challenges researchers and practitioners to look beyond the concept of self-management (which the literature suggests may be a middle point on a continuum ranging from external/control to advanced work team empowerment) in the pursuit of fuller utilization of human resources.

Some of the implications of moving toward self-leading teams include:

1 Employee self-influence may potentially move beyond illusions of worker empowerment and the tendency for management to sometimes have even greater power and influence over so-called self-managing workers.

2 Distinctions between managers and employees would become less clear as workers become more influential in areas that have been the domain of managers, especially concerning the establishment of direction for their own team and organization.

3 Changes in governance systems may need to be addressed that could represent a radical departure from typical participative systems used for organizations in the U.S.

Researchers and practitioners have already begun to explore movement toward greater employee involvement, perhaps most notably in Europe. To assist progress in this direction some research questions need to be explored. These include:

1 What new management perspectives and approaches can be developed for managing employees that recognize them as important sources of influence, especially for their teams and themselves? Self-managing team applications provide a starting base from which to explore this issue. For example, the team leader role, often described as a coordinator, facilitator, etc., has been studied (e.g., Hackman, 1986; Manz & Sims, 1986, 1987; Walton & Schlesinger, 1979) providing some guidance for addressing new leadership approaches.

2 What organizational governance systems are available throughout the world that might fit the demands of a self-leading team system? For example, could a system be developed that fits the North American culture based on the experiences of European companies?

3 What lessons can be learned from companies that have experimented with more radical forms of employee empowerment? Is there a generalizable sequence of steps that an organization can attempt to follow in moving to self-managing teams and then beyond toward self-leading teams?

4 Can organizational diagnostic tools and safeguards be created to help organizations avoid having employee empowerment efforts become simply illusions of employee self-influence or even disguised control mechanisms? Can we develop measurement and assessment tools for diagnosing the level of employee self-influence in so called participative or self-managing organizations?

The answers to these and many related questions could significantly contribute to the movement beyond self-managing work teams which offers the potential for enhanced organizational functioning under many conditions. Employee self-management may indeed represent only an intermediate stage of fuller development and utilization of human resources in increasingly complex and changing organizational environments. The usefulness of future organization thought and practice could be greatly assisted by research that explores the many paradoxes and challenges of pursuing management perspectives and organizational forms suitable for employees who in a very real sense become their own leaders.

REFERENCES

Alioth, A., Muller, W. R., & Vaassen, B. Managers' Conceptions of Their Own Roles and Employee Autonomy. Paper presented at the Academy of Management National Meeting, Anaheim, California, 1988.

Argyris, C. *Reasoning, learning and action: Individual and organizational.* San Francisco: Jossey Bass, 1982. (a)

Argyris, C. The executive mind and double-loop learning. *Organizational Dynamics,* 1982, 11, 5–22. (b)

Bandura, A. *Social learning theory.* Englewood Cliffs, New Jersey: Prentice-Hall, 1977. (a)

Bandura, A. Self-efficacy: Towards a unifying theory of behavioral change. *Psychological Review,* 1977, 84, 191–215. (b)

Bandura, A. Self-efficacy mechanism in human agency. *American Psychologist,* 1982, 37, 122–147.

Bandura, A. *Social foundations of thought and action. A social cognitive theory.* Englewood Cliffs, New Jersey: Prentice-Hall, 1986.

Burns, T. J., & Stalker, G. M. *The management of innovation.* London: Tavistock, 1961.

Carver, C. S., & Scheier, M.F. *Attention and self-regulation: A control theory approach to human behavior.* New York: Springer-Verlag, 1981.

Carver, C. S., & Scheier, M. F. Control theory: A useful conceptual framework for personality—social, clinical, and health psychology. *Psychological Bulletin,* 1982, 92, 111–135.

Cummings, T. Self-regulated work groups: A socio-technical synthesis. *Academy of Management Review,* 1978, 3, 625–634.

Deci, E. L. *Intrinsic motivation.* New York: Plenum, 1975. (a)

Deci, E. L. Notes on the theory and meta-theory of intrinsic motivation. *Organizational Behavior and Human Performance,* 1975, 15, 130–145. (b)

Dunbar, R. L. M. Designs for organizational control. In W. Starbuck and P. Nystrom (Eds.), *Handbook of organizations,* New York: Oxford University Press, 1981, pp. 85–115.

Duncan, R. Characteristics of organizational environments and perceived environmental uncertainty. *Administrative Science Quarterly,* 1972, 17, 313–327.

Elden, M., & Chisholm, R. (coordinators). Workshop on Empowering Work: An American, European and Scandinavian Exchange. National Academy of Management Meeting, Anaheim, California, 1988.

Emery, F. E., & Trist, E. L. Socio-technical systems. In F. E. Emery (Ed.), *Systems thinking.* London: Penguin Books, 1969, pp. 281–296.

Fischoff, B., & Beyth, R. I knew it would happen: Remembered probabilities of once future things. *Organizational Behavior and Human Performance,* 1975, 13, 1–16.

Fiske, S., & Taylor, S. *Social cognition.* Reading, Massachusetts: Addison-Wesley, 1984.

Gulowsen, J. A measure of work-group autonomy. In L. E. Davis and J. C. Taylor (Eds.), *Design of jobs* (second edition). Santa Monica, California: Goodyear Publishing, 1979.

Hackman, J. R. The Design of Self-Managing Work Groups. Technical Report No. 11, School of Organization and Management, Yale University, New Haven, Connecticut, December 1976.

Hackman, J. R. The psychology of self-management in organizations. In M. S. Pollack and R. O. Perloff (Eds.), *Psychology and work: Productivity change and employment,* Washington, D.C.: American Psychological Association, 1986, pp. 85–136.

Hackman, J. R., & Oldham, G. R. Development of the job diagnostic survey. *Journal of Applied Psychology,* 1975, 60, 159–170.

Harrell, T., & Alpert, B. The need for autonomy among managers. *Academy of Management Review,* 1979, 4, 259–267.

Hofstede, G., & Kassem, M. S. *European contributions to organization theory.* Amsterdam, The Netherlands: Van Gorcum, 1976.

Kassem, M. S. Introduction: European versus American organization theories. In G. Hofstede and M. S. Kassem (Eds.), *European contributions to organization theory.* Amsterdam, The Netherlands: Van Gorcum, 1976.

Katz, R. L. Skills of an effective administrator. *Harvard Business Review.* Sept.–Oct. 1974, 90–102.

Klein, J. JIT, SPC, and Teams. Working Paper, Division of Research, Harvard Business School, Boston, Massachusetts, 1988.

Klein, J. The human costs of manufacturing reform. *Harvard Business Review,* 1989, 67, 4–8.

Lawler, E. E. *High-involvement management.* San Francisco: Jossey-Bass, 1986.

Lawler, E. E., Choosing an involvement strategy. *Academy of Management Executive,* 1988, 2, 197–204.

Lindsay, W. M., & Rue, L. W. Impact of the organization environment on the long range planning process: A contingency view. *Academy of Management Journal,* 1980, 23, 385–404.

Luthans, F. & Davis, T. Behavioral self-management (BSM): The missing link in managerial effectiveness. *Organizational Dynamics,* 1979, 8, 42–60.

Manz, C. C. Self-leadership: Toward an expanded theory of self-influence processes in organizations. *Academy of Management Review,* 1986, 11, 585–600.

Manz, C. C. Beyond self-managing work teams: Toward self-leading teams in the workplace. In R. Woodman and W. Pasmore (Eds.), *Research in organizational change and development.* JAI Press, 1990.

Manz, C. C. *Mastering self-leadership: Empowering yourself for personal excellence.* Englewood Cliffs, New Jersey: Prentice-Hall, 1992.

Manz, C. C., & Angle, H. L. Can group self-management mean a loss of personal control: Triangulating on a paradox. *Group and Organization Studies,* 1986, 11, 309–334.

Manz, C. C., & Newstrom, J. Self-managing teams in a paper mill: Success factors, problems and lessons learned. *International Human Resource Management Review,* 1990, 1, 43–60.

Manz, C. C., & Sims, H. P., Jr. Self-management as a substitute for leadership: A social learning theory perspective. *Academy of Management Review,* 1980, 5, 361–367.

Manz, C. C., & Sims, H. P., Jr. The potential for groupthink in autonomous work groups. *Human Relations,* 1982, 35, 773–784.

Manz, C. C., & Sims, H. P., Jr. Searching for the unleader: Organizational member views on leading self-managed groups. *Human Relations,* 1984, 37, 409–424.

Manz, C. C., & Sims, H. P., Jr. Leading self-managed groups: A conceptual analysis of a paradox. *Economic and Industrial Democracy,* 1986, 7, 141–165.

Manz, C. C., & Sims, H. P., Jr. Leading workers to lead themselves: Th external leadership of self-managed work teams. *Administrative Science Quarterly,* 1987, 32, 106–128.

Manz, C. C., & Sims, H. P., Jr. *Super Leadership: Leading others to lead themselves.* New York: Berkeley, 1990.

Manz, C. C., Mossholder, K., & Luthans, F. An integrated perspective of self-control in organizations. *Administration and Society,* 1987, 19, 3–24.

Manz, C. C., Keating, D., & Donnellon, A. Preparing for an organizational change to employee self-management. The managerial transition. *Organizational Dynamics,* 1990, 19, 15–26.

McClelland, D. C., & Winter, D. G. *Motivating economic achievement.* New York: Free Press, 1969.

Mills, P. K. Self-management: Its control and relationship to other organizational properties. *Academy of Management Review,* 1983, 8, 445–453.

Mitchell, T. R. Motivation and participation: An integration. *Academy of Management Journal,* 1973, 16, 160–179.

Mulder, M. Power equalization through participation. *Administrative Science Quarterly,* 1971, 16, 31–38.

Mulder, M. Reduction of power differences in practice. In G. Hofstede and M. S. Kassem (Eds.), *European contributions to organization theory.* Amsterdam, The Netherlands: Van Gorcum, 1976.

Neumann, J. E. Why people don't participate in organizational change. In R. W. Woodman and W. A. Pasmore (Eds.), *Research in organizational change and development* (Vol. 3). Greenwich, Connecticut: JAI Press, 1989, pp. 181–212.

Perlmutter, L. C., & Monty, R. A. The importance of perceived control: Fact or fantasy. *American Scientist,* 1977, 65, 759–765.

Poza, E. J., & Markus, L. Success story: The team approach to work restructuring. *Organizational Dynamics,* Winter 1980, 3–25.

Saglio, J. H., & Hackman, J. R. The Design of Governance Systems for Small Worker Cooperatives. Working paper, Industrial Cooperative Association, Somerville, Massachusetts, 1982.

Shipper, F., & Manz, C. C. Employee self-management without formally designated teams: An alternative road to empowerment. *Organizational Dynamics,* 1992, 20, 48–61.

Sims, H. P., Jr., & Manz, C. C. Conversations within self-managed work groups. *National Productivity Review,* Summer 1982, 261–269.

Slocum, J. W., & Sims, H. P., Jr. A typology for integrating technology, organization and job design. *Human Relations,* 1980, 33, 193–212.

Strassberg, D. S. Relationships among locus of control, anxiety, and valued goal expectations. *Journal of Consulting and Clinical Psychology,* 1973, 41, 319.

Strauss, G. Workers' participation in management: An international perspective. In L. L. Cummings and B. M. Staw (Eds.), *Research in organizational behavior* (Vol. 4). Greenwich, Connecticut: JAI Press, 1982, pp. 173–265.

Susman, J. I. *Autonomy at work: A socio-technical analysis of participative management.* New York, Praeger, 1976.

Taylor, F. *The principles of scientific management.* New York: Harper, 1911.

Tharenou, P. Employee self-esteem: A review of the literature. *Journal of Vocational Behavior,* 1979, 15, 316–346.

Thompson, J. D. *Organizations in action.* New York: McGraw-Hill, 1967.

Thoresen, C. E., & Mahoney, M. J. *Behavioral self-control.* New York: Holt, Rhinehart and Winston, 1974.

Trist, E. L., Susman, G. I., & Brown, G. R. An experiment in autonomous working in an American underground coal mine. *Human Relations,* 1977, 30, 201–236.

Van de Ven, A. A revised framework for organizational assessment. In E. Lawler, D. Nadler, and C. Cammann (Eds.), *Organizational assessment: Perspectives on the measurement of organizational behavior and the quality of working life.* New York: Wiley-Interscience, 1979.

Van de Ven, A., & Delbecq, A. A task contingent model of work-unit structure, *Administrative Science Quarterly,* 1974, 19, 183–197.

Van de Ven, A., Delbecq, A., & Koenig, R. Determinants of co-ordination modes within organizations. *American Sociological Review,* 1976, 41, 322–328.

Vroom, V. H., & Yetton, P. W. *Leadership and decision making.* Pittsburgh: University of Pittsburgh Press, 1973.

Walton, R. E. Work innovations at Topeka: After six years. *Journal of Applied Behavioral Science,* 1977, 13, 422–433.

Walton, R. E. From control to commitment in the workplace. *Harvard Business Review,* 1985, 63, 77–84.

Walton, R. E. Innovating to compete: *Lessons for diffusing and managing change in the workplace.* San Francisco: Jossey-Bass, 1987.

Walton, R. E., & Schlesinger, L. A. Do supervisors thrive in participative work systems? *Organizational Dynamics,* 1979, 8, 24–39.

Weick, K. E. *The social psychology of organizing.* Reading, Massachusetts: Addison-Wesley, 1979.

Weiss, H. M. Subordinate imitation of supervisor behavior: The role of modeling in organizational socialization. *Organizational Behavior and Human Performance,* 1977, 19, 89–105.

White, R. W. Motivation reconsidered: The concept of competence. *Psychological Review,* 1959, 66, 297–333.

Producing Sustainable Competitive Advantage Through the Effective Management of People

Jeffrey Pfeffer

Suppose that in 1972, someone asked you to pick the five companies that would provide the greatest return to stockholders over the next 20 years. And suppose that you had access to books on competitive success that were not even written. How would you approach your assignment? In order to earn tremendous economic returns, the companies you picked should have some sustainable competitive advantage, something that (1) distinguishes them from their competitors, (2) provides positive economic benefits, and (3) is not readily duplicated.

Conventional wisdom then (and even now) would have you begin by selecting the right industries. After all, "not all industries offer equal opportunity for sustained profitability, and the inherent profitability of its industry is one essential ingredient in determining the profitability of a firm."[1] According to Michael Porter's now famous framework, the five fundamental competitive forces that determine the ability of firms in an industry to earn above-normal returns are "the entry of new competitors, the threat of substitutes, the bargaining power of buyers, the bargaining power of suppliers, and the rivalry among existing competitors."[2] You should find industries with barriers to entry, low supplier and buyer bargaining power, few ready substitutes, and a limited threat of new entrants to compete away economic returns. Within such industries, other conventional analyses would urge you to select firms with the largest market share, which can realize the cost benefits of economies of scale. In short you would probably look to industries in which patent protection of important product or service technology could be achieved and select the dominant firms in those industries.

You would have been very successful in selecting the five top performing firms from 1972 to 1992 if you took this conventional wisdom and turned it on its head. The top five stocks, and their percentage returns, were (in reverse order): Plenum Publishing (with a return of 15,689%), Circuit City (a video and appliance retailer; 16,410%), Tyson Foods (A poultry producer; 18,118%), Wal-Mart (a discount chain; 19,807%), and Southwest Airlines (21,775%).[3] Yet during this period, these industries (retailing, airlines, publishing, and food processing) were characterized by massive competition and horrendous losses, widespread bankruptcy, virtually no barriers to entry (for airlines after 1978), little unique or proprietary technology, and many substitute products or services. And in 1972, none of these firms was (and some still are not) the market-share leader, enjoying economies of scale or moving down the learning curve.

The point here is not to throw out conventional strategic analysis based on industrial economics but simply to note that the source of competitive advantage has always shifted over time. What these five successful firms tend to have in common is that for their sustained advantage, they rely not on technology, patents, or strategic position, but on how they manage their workforce.

THE IMPORTANCE OF THE WORKFORCE AND HOW IT IS MANAGED

As other sources of competitive success have become less important, what remains as a crucial, differentiating factor is the organization, its employees, and how they work. Consider, for instance, Southwest Airlines, whose stock had the best return from 1972 to 1992. It certainly did not achieve that success from economies of scale. In 1992, Southwest had revenues of $1.31 billion and a mere 2.6% of the U.S. passenger market.[4] People Express, by contrast, achieved $1 billion in revenues after only 3 years of operation, not the almost 20 it took Southwest. Southwest exists not because of regulated or protected markets but in spite of them. "During the first three years of its history, no Southwest planes were flown."[5] Southwest waged a battle for its very existence with competitors who sought to keep it from flying at all and, failing that, made sure it did not fly out of the newly constructed Dallas-Fort Worth international airport. Instead, it was restricted to operating out of the close-in Love Field, and thus was born its first advertising slogan, "Make Love, Not War." Southwest became the "love" airline out of necessity, not choice.

In 1978, competitors sought to bar flights from Love Field to anywhere outside Texas. The compromise Southwest wrangled permitted it to fly from Love to the four states contiguous to Texas.[6] Its competitive strategy of short-haul, point-to-point flights to close-in airports (it now flies into Chicago's Midway and Houston's Hobby airports) was more a product of its need to adapt to what it was being permitted to do than a conscious, planned move—although, in retrospect, the strategy has succeeded brilliantly. Nor has Southwest succeeded because it has had more access to lower-cost capital—indeed, it is one of the least leveraged airlines in the United States. Southwest's planes, Boeing 737s, are obviously available to all its competitors. It isn't a member of any of the big computerized reservation systems; it uses no unique process technology and sells essentially a commodity product—low-cost, low-frills airline service at prices its competitors have difficulty matching.

Much of its cost advantage comes from its very productive, very motivated, and by the way, unionized workforce. Compared to the U.S. airline industry, according to 1991 statistics, Southwest has fewer employees per aircraft (79 versus 131), flies more passengers per employee (2,318 versus 848), and has more available seat miles per employee (1,891,082 versus 1,339,995).[7] It turns around some 80% of its flights in 15 minutes or less, while other airlines on average need 45 minutes, giving it an enormous productivity advantage in terms of equipment utilization.[8] It also provides an exceptional level of passenger service. Southwest has won the airlines' so-called triple crown (best on-time performance, fewest lost bags, and fewest passenger complaints—in the same month) *nine* times. No competitor has achieved that even once.[9]

What is important to recognize is why success, such as that achieved at Southwest, can be sustained and cannot readily be imitated by competitors. There are two fundamental reasons. First, the success that comes from managing people effectively is often not as visible or transparent as to its source. We can see a computerized information system, a particular semiconductor, a numerically controlled machine tool. The culture and practices that enable Southwest to achieve its success are less obvious. Even when they are described, as they have been in numerous newspaper articles and even a segment on "60 Minutes," they are difficult to really understand. Culture, how people are managed, and the effects of this on their behavior and skills are sometimes seen as the "soft" side of business, occasionally dismissed. Even when they are not dismissed, it is often hard to comprehend the dynamics of a particular company and how it operates because the way people are managed often fits together in a system. It is easy to copy one thing but much more difficult to copy numerous things. This is because the change needs to be more comprehensive and also because the ability to understand the system of management practices is hindered by its very extensiveness.

Thus, for example, Nordstrom, the department store chain, has enjoyed substantial success both in customer service and in sales and profitability growth over the years. Nordstrom compensates its employees in part with commissions. Not surprisingly, many of its competitors, after finally acknowledging Nordstrom's success, and the fact that it was attributable to the behavior of its employees, instituted commission systems. By itself, changing the compensation system did not fully capture what Nordstrom had done, nor did it provide many benefits to the competition. Indeed, in some cases, changing the compensation system produced employee grievances and attempts to unionize when the new system was viewed as unfair or arbitrary.

THIRTEEN PRACTICES FOR MANAGING PEOPLE

Contrary to some academic writing and to popular belief, there is little evidence that effective management practices are (1) particularly faddish (although their implementation may well be), (2) difficult to understand or to comprehend why they work, or (3) necessarily contingent on an organization's particular competitive strategy. There are interrelated practices—I enumerate 13, but the exact number and how they are defined are somewhat arbitrary—that seem to characterize companies that are effective in achieving competitive success through how they manage people.

The following policies and practices emerge from extensive reading of both the popular and academic literature, talking to numerous people in firms in a variety of industries, and the application of some simple common sense. The particular way of subdividing the terrain is less important than considering the entire landscape, so the reader should realize that the division into categories is somewhat arbitrary. The themes, however, recur repeatedly in studies of organizations. It is important to recognize that the practices are interrelated—it is difficult to do one thing by itself with much positive result.

Employment Security

Security of employment signals a long-standing commitment by the organization to its workforce. Norms of reciprocity tend to guarantee that this commitment is repaid. However, conversely, an employer that signals through word and deed that its employees are dispensable is not likely to generate much loyalty, commitment, or willingness to expend extra effort for the organization's benefit. New United Motor Manufacturing (NUMMI), the Toyota-GM joint venture in California, guaranteed workers' jobs as part of the formal labor contract in return for a reduction in the number of job classifications and an agreement not to strike over work standards. This commitment was met even in the face of temporarily slow demand, and many observers believe that as a result, trust between employees and the organization increased substantially.

Taking on people not readily eliminated exerts pressure to be careful and selective in hiring. Moreover, "employment security enhances employee involvement because employees are more willing to contribute to the work process when they need not fear losing their own or their coworkers' jobs. Employment security contributes to training as both employer and employee have greater incentives to invest in training."[10] because there is some assurance that the employment relationship will be of sufficient duration to earn a return on the time and resources expended in skill development.

Selectivity in Recruiting

Security in employment and reliance on the workforce for competitive success mean that one must be careful to choose the right people, in the right way. Studies covering populations ranging from machine operators, typists, and welders to assembly workers—all in self-paced jobs so that individual differences mattered—indicate that the most productive employees were about twice as good as the least productive.[11] Southwest Airlines worries a lot about hiring the right people. In fact, it flies some of its best customers to Dallas and involves them in the flight attendant hiring process, believing that those who are in contact with the front-line employees probably know best what makes a good employee. At Lincoln Electric, hiring is done very carefully based on the desire to succeed and the capacity for growth.[12]

One of the practices of many of the Japanese automobile-manufacturing plants opened in the United States that proved especially newsworthy was their extensive screening of employees. Some of this was undoubtedly done to weed out those who were likely to be pro-union, but much of the screening was to find those people who could work best in the new environment, could learn and develop, and needed less supervision. There was little screening for particular skills, under the assumption that these could be readily learned. Nordstrom, the very effective specialty retailer whose sales per square foot are about double the industry average, tends to recruit sales clerks who are young and college-educated, seeking a career in retailing.[13]

Besides getting the right people in the door, recruiting has an important symbolic aspect. If someone goes through a rigorous selection process, the person feels that he or she is joining an elite organization. High expectations for performance are created, and the message sent is that people matter.

High Wages

If you want to recruit outstanding people, and want them to stay with the organization, paying more is helpful, although not absolutely necessary. High wages tend to attract more applicants, permitting the organization to be more selective in finding people who are going to be trainable and who will be committed to the organization. Perhaps most important, higher wages send a message that the organization values its people. Particularly if these wages are higher than required by the market, employees can perceive the extra income as a gift and work more diligently as a result.[14] Nordstrom typically pays its people an hourly wage higher than the prevailing rate for retail clerks at comparable stores. Coupled with incentive pay for outstanding work, Nordstrom salespeople often earn twice the average retail income.

Companies sometimes believe that lowering labor costs is essential for competitive success. This is not invariably the case, even in cost-competitive businesses, because in many organizations, labor costs are a small fraction of the total costs. Furthermore, even if labor costs (let alone labor rates) are higher, it may be that enhanced service, skill, and innovation more than compensate by increasing the level of overall profit. For instance, the CEO of Wendy's, facing declining company profitability, decided that the best way to become the customer's restaurant of choice was to become the employer of choice.[15] This entailed improving both benefits and base compensation, instituting a quarterly bonus, and creating an employee stock option plan. The results were dramatic: "Our turnover rate for general managers fell to 20% in 1991 from 39% in 1989, while turnover among co- and assistant managers dropped to 37% from 60%—among the lowest in the business. With a stable—and able—workforce, sales began to pick up as well."[16]

Incentive Pay

There has been a tendency to overuse money in an effort to solve myriad organizational problems. People are motivated by more than money—things like recognition, security, and fair treatment matter a great deal. Nevertheless, if people are responsible for enhanced levels of performance and profitability, they will want to share in the benefits. Consider the alternative—if all the gains from extra ingenuity and effort go just to top management or to shareholders (unless these are also employees), people will soon view the situation as unfair, become discouraged, and abandon their efforts. Thus, many organizations seek to reward performance with some form of contingent compensation.

Lincoln Electric is deservedly famous for its piecework and incentive bonus plan. Contrary to first impressions, the plan does much more than merely reward individual productivity. Although the factory workforce is paid on a piecework basis, it is paid only for good pieces—workers correct quality problems on their own time. Moreover, defects can be traced to the individual who produced them. Quality is emphasized as well as productivity. Additionally, piecework is only a part of the employee's compensation. Bonuses, which often constitute 100% of regular salary, are based on the company's profitability—encouraging employees to identify with the whole firm. They are also based on the individual's merit rating, and that rating is, in turn, based on four equally important aspects of performance: dependability, quality, output, and ideas and cooperation.[17] This broader evaluation mitigates the pernicious tendencies of simplistic incentive systems to go awry.

Employee Ownership

Employee ownership offers two advantages. Employees who have ownership interests in the organizations for which they work have less conflict between capital and labor—to some degree they are both capital and labor. Employee ownership, effectively implemented, can align the interests of employees with those of shareholders by making employees shareholders, too. Second, employee ownership puts stock in the hands of people, employees, who are more inclined to take a long-term view of the organization, its strategy, and its investment policies and less likely to support hostile takeovers, leveraged buyouts, and other financial maneuvers. Of course, to the extent that one believes this reduced risk of capital market discipline inhibits efficiency, significant employee shareholding is a disadvantage. However, the existing evidence largely contradicts this negative view.

It is probably no coincidence that all five of the companies mentioned as providing the best shareholder returns from 1972 to 1992 appear on The Employee Ownership 1000, a listing of "1000 companies in which employees own more than 4% of the stock of a corporation" traded on the New York or American stock exchanges or the over-the-counter market.[18] Although employee ownership is no panacea, and its effects depend largely on how it is implemented, the existing evidence is consistent with the view that employee ownership has positive effects on firm performance.[19]

Information Sharing

If people are to be a source of competitive advantage, clearly they must have the information necessary to do what is required to be successful. At the Advanced Micro Devices submicron development center, there are computer terminals throughout the plant that every employee has been trained to use in order to obtain information about product yields, development progress, production rates, or any other aspect of the operation. One reason sometimes given for not disclosing information to large numbers of employees is that it may leak to competitors. When Robert Beck was head of human resources for the Bank of America, he perceptively told the management committee, reluctant to disclose the bank's strategy and other information to its employees, that the competitors almost certainly knew the information already; typically, the only people in the dark are the firm's own employees.

Participation and Empowerment

Sharing information is a necessary precondition to another important feature found in many successful work systems: encouraging the decentralization of decision making and broader worker participation and empowerment in controlling their own work process. At Nordstrom, the written philosophy states:

> We also encourage you to present your own ideas. Your buyers have a great deal of autonomy, and are encouraged to seek out and promote new fashion directions at all times. . . . Nordstrom has a strong open-door policy and we encourage you to share your concerns, suggestions and ideas. . .
> Nordstrom Rules:
>   Rule #1: Use your good judgment in all situations. There will be no additional rules.[20]

The evidence is that participation increases both satisfaction and employee productivity.[21] Autonomy is one of the most important dimensions of jobs and was the focus of many job-redesign efforts undertaken as part of the quality of working life movement in the 1960s and 1970s.[22] The fundamental change involves moving from a system of hierarchical control and coordination of activity to one in which lower-level employees, who may have more or better information, are permitted to do things to enhance performance. At a Levi Strauss jeans factory, when it was time to purchase new forklift trucks, the drivers themselves got involved. They determined specifications, negotiated with suppliers, and made the final purchase decision, in the process saving the company money as well as obtaining equipment more appropriate for that plant. At Eaton, a unionized manufacturer, workers tired of fixing equipment that broke down and suggested that they build two new automated machines themselves. They did it for less than a third of what outside vendors would have charged and doubled the output of the department in the first year.[23]

Self-Managed Teams

Organizations that have tapped the power of teams have often experienced excellent results. Monsanto, a large chemical company, implemented work organization based on self-managed teams at its chemical and nylon complex near Pensacola, Florida. Teams of workers were responsible for hiring, purchasing, job assignments, and production.[24] Management was reduced from seven levels to four, and the plant experienced increases in both profitability and safety. At a 318-person submarine systems plant owned by AT&T, costs were reduced more than 30% through the use of teams.[25] Federal Express uses teams in its back-office operation with great success—service problems fell 13% in 1989 after the company's 1,000 clerical workers were organized in teams and given additional training and authority.[26] One of the more dramatic examples of the benefits of using teams occurred at Johnsonville Sausage. In 1986, a manufacturer asked Johnsonville to produce private-label sausage. The president was about to decline the new business, because he believed that the plant was already at capacity and could not handle the additional workload. However,

> before deciding, he assembled his 200 production workers, who are organized in teams of five to 20, and asked them to decide. . . . After . . . ten days, they came back with an answer: "We can do it." . . . The teams decided how much new machinery they would need and how many new people; they also made a schedule of how much to produce per day. Since Johnsonville took on the new project, productivity has risen over 50% in the factory.[27]

Teams work because of the peer monitoring and expectations of coworkers that are brought to bear to both coordinate and monitor work. Indeed, even critics of the team concept often argue that the problem with teams as a substitute for hierarchy is not that this approach doesn't work but that it works too well. Thus, a dissident union leader in the NUMMI plant noted: "[W]hen the team's under pressure, people try to meet the team's expectations and under peer pressure, they end up pushing themselves too hard. . . . The team concept is a nice idea, but when you put the teams under pressure, it becomes a damn effective way to divide workers."[28]

Training and Skill Development

An integral part of most new work systems is a greater commitment to training and skill development. Note, however, that this training will produce positive returns only if the trained workers are then permitted to employ their skills. One mistake many organizations make is to upgrade the skills of both managers and workers but not change the structure for work in ways that permit people to do anything different. Under such circumstances, it is little wonder that training has no apparent effect.

At Advanced Micro Devices' submicron development facility, some 70% of the technicians came from older facilities at AMD. In keeping with AMD's emphasis on employment stability, as old facilities were closed, people were evaluated with respect to their basic skills. If accepted, they were put through a seven-month program at Mission College—at full pay and at company expense—and then went to work in the new facility. This training not only demonstrated the firm's commitment to its employees, which was then reciprocated, but also ensured that the facility would be staffed with highly qualified people who had been specifically trained for their new jobs.

At a Collins and Aikman carpet plant in Georgia, more than a third of the employees were high school dropouts, and some could neither read nor write. When the firm introduced computers to increase productive efficiency, however, it chose not to replace its existing workforce but to upgrade its skills. After spending about $1,200 per employee on training, including lost job time, the company found that the amount of carpet stitched increased 10%. Moreover, quality problems declined by half. The employees, with more skills and better morale, submitted some 1,230 suggestions, and absenteeism fell by almost half.[29]

Cross-Utilization and Cross-Training

Having people do multiple jobs has a number of potential benefits. The most obvious is that doing more things can make work more interesting—variety is one of the core job dimensions that affect how people respond to their work. Variety in jobs permits a change in pace, a change in activity, and potentially even a change in the people with whom one comes in contact, and each of these forms of variety can make work life more challenging. Beyond its motivational effects, having people do multiple jobs has other important benefits. One is keeping the work process both transparent and as simple as possible. If people are expected to shift to new tasks readily, the design of those tasks has to be straightforward enough so they can be learned quickly. A second, somewhat related benefit is the potential for newcomers to a job to see things that can be improved that experienced people don't see, simply because they have come to take the work process so much for granted.

Multiskilling is also a useful adjunct to policies that promise employment security. After all, it is easier to keep people at work if they have multiple skills and can do different things. By the same token, maintaining employment levels sometimes compels organizations to find new tasks for people, often with surprising results. When Mazda, the Japanese automobile manufacturer, suffered a decline in business in the 1980s, rather than laying off factory workers, it put them to work selling cars, which, in Japan, are often sold door to door. At the end of the year, when awards were presented to the best salespeople, the company discovered that the top ten were all former factory workers. They could explain the product effectively, and of course, when business picked up, the fact that factory workers had experience talking to customers yielded useful ideas about product characteristics.

At Lechmere, a retail chain owned by Dayton-Hudson, the company experimented with cross-training and utilization of employees at a new store in Sarasota, Florida. The store offered the workers raises based on the number of jobs they learned to perform, a variant of a pay-for-skill plan. The workforce, composed of 60% full-time employees rather than the 30% typical for the chain, was substantially more productive than in other stores. "Cashiers are encouraged to sell records and tapes. Sporting goods salesmen get tutoring in forklifts. That way Lechmere can quickly adjust to changes in staffing needs simply by deploying existing workers. The pay incentives, along with the prospect of a more varied and interesting workday, proved valuable lures in recruiting."[30]

Symbolic Egalitarianism

One important barrier to decentralizing decision making, using self-managed teams, and eliciting employee commitment and cooperation is the symbols that separate people from each other. Consequently, it is not surprising that many of the firms that are known for achieving competitive advantage through people have various forms of symbolic egalitarianism—ways of signaling to both insiders and outsiders that there is comparative equality and it is not the case that some think and others do. At NUMMI, the executive dining room was eliminated, and everyone eats in the same cafeteria. Everyone wears a blue smock. There are no reserved places in the employee parking lot.

Communication across levels is greatly enhanced by the opportunity to interact and meet in less formal settings. This means that senior management is more likely to know what is actually going on and be able to communicate its ideas more directly to everyone in the facility. The reduction in the number of social categories tends to decrease the salience of various subdivisions in the organization, diminishes "us" versus "them" thinking, and provides more of a sense of everyone working toward a common goal. This egalitarianism makes cross-movement easier because there are fewer status distinctions to be overcome. At NUMMI, there is only one classification for Division 1 personnel compared to more than 80 previously. The number of skilled trades classifications shrank from 18 under the old General Motors systems to 2.[31]

Egalitarian symbols come in many forms. In some organizations, it is dress—few who have worked in a manufacturing facility have not heard the phrase "the suits are coming" when people from headquarters, typically more formally dressed, arrive. Physical space is another way in which common fate can be signaled, or not. The CEO of Solectron, a contract manufacturer that won the Malcolm Baldrige award, does not have a private office, and neither does the chairman. In contrast, John DeLorean's graphic description of the fourteenth-floor headquarters for General Motors is one of hushed, quiet offices reached by a private elevator that was secured—in other words, executives cut off from the rest of the organization.[32]

Although symbolic egalitarianism would seem easy to implement, the elimination of status symbols is often one of the most difficult things for a company to do. A friend bemoaned the fact that just as he had reached a managerial level that entitled him to use a private dining room, have preferential parking, and occupy a larger office, his employer embarked on a total quality movement and eliminated all of these perquisites.

Wage Compression

Although issues of wage compression are most often considered in terms of hierarchical compression, and particularly CEO pay relative to that of others, there is a horizontal aspect to wage compression as well. It can have a number of efficiency-enhancing properties for organizations.

It is important to remember that wage compression is distinct from incentive pay. Incentive pay simply means that people are rewarded, either individually or in groups, for their performance. These rewards can be large, producing wide variation in salaries, or small, producing substantially less variation. It is also important to recognize that incentive pay—particularly when applied to larger units such as work groups, departments, or the entire organization—can either reduce or increase the wage dispersion that would otherwise exist. Most gain-sharing and profit-sharing programs actually reduce pay dispersion, although they need not do so.

When tasks are somewhat interdependent and cooperation is helpful for accomplishing work, pay compression, by reducing interpersonal competition and enhancing cooperation, can lead to efficiency gains.[33] Furthermore, large differences in the allocation of organizational rewards can motivate people to achieve these rewards. Although increased motivation can produce greater efforts, large differences in rewards can as readily result in excessive time and energy spent on ingratiating oneself with one's supervisor or trying to affect the criteria for reward allocation.[34] By this reasoning, a more compressed distribution of salaries can actually produce higher overall performance, as there is less incentive for individuals to waste their time on gaming the system.

To the extent that wages are compressed, pay is likely to be deemphasized in the reward system and in the organization's culture. This has some obvious economic benefits—people are not constantly worrying about whether they are compensated appropriately and attempting to rebargain their salaries. A de-emphasis on pay can also focus attention on the other advantages of organizational membership such as good colleagues and work that is interesting and meaningful. There is a literature in psychology that suggests we attempt to figure out why we are doing what we are by looking at ourselves as an outsider observer would.[35] If we see we are very well paid, perhaps on a contingent basis, for what we do, we are likely to attribute our behavior to the economic rewards. If, however, we are not particularly well paid, or if pay is less salient, and if it is distributed on a less contingent basis (which will make it less salient), then we are likely to attribute our behavior to other, more intrinsic factors such as the inherent enjoyment of the work. In other words, being paid in a contingent fashion for what we do can actually undermine our intrinsic interest in and satisfaction with that activity.[36] Thus, pay compression, by helping to de-emphasize pay, can enhance other bases of satisfaction with work and build a culture that is less calculative in nature.

Promotion from Within

Promotion from within is a useful adjunct to many of the practices described. It encourages training and skill development because the availability of promotion opportunities within the firm binds workers to employers and vice versa. It facilitates decentralization, participation, and delegation because it helps promote trust across hierarchical levels; promotion from within means that supervisors are responsible for coordinating the efforts of people whom they probably know quite well. By the same token, those being coordinated personally know managers in higher positions. This contact provides social bases of influence so that formal position can loom less important. Promotion from within also offers an incentive for performing well, and although tied to monetary rewards, promotion is a reward that also has a status-based, nonmonetary component. Perhaps most important, it provides a sense of fairness and justice in the workplace. If people do an outstanding job but outsiders are being brought in over them, there will be a sense of alienation from the organization. One other advantage of promotion from within is that it tends to ensure that people in management positions actually know something about the business, the technology, and the operations they are managing. There are numerous tales of firms managed by those with little understanding of the basic operations, often with miserable results. David Halberstam's history of Ford Motor tells how finance took control of the company. Not only were these people not "car men," they knew little about automobiles, technology, production processes, or the market—anything that could not be conveyed via statistics—and had little interest in learning.[37] The problem with managing only through statistics is that without some understanding of the underlying processes that produce the measures, it is likely that managers will either focus on inappropriate measures or fail to fully comprehend what they mean.

By contrast, at Lincoln Electric, almost everyone who joins the company learns to weld—Lincoln's main product is, after all, arc welding equipment. Graduation from the welding program requires coming up with some innovation to the product. At Nordstrom, even those with advanced degrees start on the sales floor. Promotion is strictly from within, and when Nordstrom opens a new store, its key people are recruited from other stores around the country. This helps perpetuate the Nordstrom culture and values but also provides assurance that those running the store know what they are doing and have experience doing it the Nordstrom way.

TAKING THE LONG VIEW

The bad news about achieving some competitive advantage through the workforce is that it inevitably takes time to accomplish. By contrast, a new piece of equipment can be quickly installed; a new product technology can be acquired through a licensing agreement in the time it takes to negotiate the agreement; and acquiring capital only requires the successful conclusion of negotiations. The good news, however, is that once achieved, competitive advantage obtained through employment practices is likely to be substantially more enduring and more difficult to duplicate. Nevertheless, the time required to implement these practices and start seeing results means that a long-term perspective is needed. It also takes a long time horizon to execute many of these approaches. In the short term, laying off people is probably more profitable compared to trying to maintain employment security; cutting training is a quick way to maintain short-term profits; and cross-training and cross-utilization may provide insights and innovation in time, but initially, the organization foregoes the advantages of more narrow specialization and the immediate proficiency achieved thereby.

What determines an organization's time horizon is an important issue, but one outside the scope of this article. In general, however, there is some evidence that family ownership, employee ownership, or other forms of organization that lessen the immediate pressures for quick earnings to please the securities market are probably helpful. Lincoln Electric is closely held, and the Nordstrom family retains a substantial fraction of the ownership of that retailer. NUMMI has Toyota as one of the joint venture partners, and Toyota's own plans for the facility virtually dictate that it take a long-term view, which is consistent with its culture and tradition. Again, the Walton family's ownership position in Wal-Mart helps ensure that the organization takes a long view of its business processes.

It is almost inconceivable that a firm facing immediate short-term pressure would embark on activities that are apparently necessary to achieve some competitive advantage through people. This provides one explanation for the limited diffusion of these practices. If the organization is doing well, it may feel no need to worry about its competitive position. By the same token, if the organization is in financial distress, the immediate pressures may be too severe to embark on activities that provide productivity and profit advantages, but only after a longer, and unknown, period of time.

MEASUREMENT OF THE PRACTICES

Measurement is a critical component in any management process, and this is true for the process of managing the organization's workforce. Measurement serves several functions. First, it provides feedback as to how well the organization is implementing various policies. For example, many organizations espouse a promotion from within policy but don't fulfill this objective. Often, this is because there is no systematic collection and reporting of information such as what percentage of the positions at given levels have been filled internally. A commitment to a high-wage policy obviously requires information as to where in the relevant labor market the organization's wages fall. A commitment to training is more likely to be fulfilled if data are collected, not only on the total amount spent on training but also on what types of employees have received training and what sorts of training are being delivered.

Second, measurement ensures that what is measured will be noticed. "Out of sight, out of mind" is a principle that applied to organizational goals and practices as well as to people. One of the most consistent findings in the organizational literature is that measures affect behavior.[38] Most people will try to succeed on the measures even if there are no direct, immediate consequences. Things that are measured get talked about, and things that are not don't.

It is no accident that companies seriously committed to achieving competitive advantage through people make measurement of their efforts a critical component of the overall process. Thus, for example, at Advanced Micro Devices' submicron development facility, management made how people were managed a priority and measured employee attitudes regularly to see whether they were "achieving the vision." One survey asked questions such as: How many teams are you on in your own department and with members of other departments? How many hours per week do you spend receiving training and training others? The survey also asked the extent to which people agreed or disagreed with statements such as: there is problem solving at all levels in my work group; people in my work group are encouraged to take the initiative; a spirit of teamwork exists in our work group.

In a world in which financial results are measured, a failure to measure human resource policy and practice implementation dooms this to second-class status, oversight, neglect, and potential failure. The feedback from the measurements is essential to refine and further develop implementation ideas as well as to learn how well the practices are actually achieving their intended results.

OVERARCHING PHILOSOPHY

Having an overarching philosophy or view of management is essential. It provides a way of connecting the various individual practices into a coherent whole and also enables people in the organization to persist and experiment when things don't work out immediately. Moreover, such a philosophy makes it easier to explain what the organization is doing, justify it, and mobilize support from internal and external constituencies. Most simply put, it is hard to get somewhere if you don't know where you are going. In a similar fashion, practices adopted without a deeper understanding of what they represent and why they are important to the organization may not add up to much, may be unable to survive internal or external problems, and are likely to produce less than stellar results.

Many companies that seek competitive success through their people and practice a number of approaches really began with some underlying principles or else developed them early in the process. Levi Strauss's quality enhancement process began with the understanding that "manufacturing for quality and speed meant breaking the old paradigms," turning the culture upside down and completely reorienting the parameters of the business.[39] The company and its manufacturing senior vice president explicitly articulated the underlying assumptions of the old way of thinking and the new, as illustrated in Table 1.

SOME WORDS OF CAUTION

It would be difficult to find a single company that does all of these things or that does them all equally well. Some successful firms have tended to do a higher percentage, and it is useful to grade one's own company against the overall list. Nevertheless, there are few companies that do everything. Which practice is most critical does depend in part on the company's particular technology and market strategy.

A second important caution is to recognize that it is possible for a company to do all of these things and be unprofitable and unsuccessful, or to do few or none of them and be quite successful. How? These factors are almost certainly related to a company's ability to achieve competitive success through its workforce. But although that may be

TABLE 1
NEW VERSUS OLD PARADIGMS AT LEVI STRAUSS

Old paradigm	New paradigm
Economy of *scale* as basis for improvement logic	Economy of *time* as basis for improvement logic
Quality involves trade-offs	Quality is a "religion;" no compromise
Doers are separate from thinkers	Doers must also be thinkers
Assets are things	Assets are people
Profit is the primary business goal	Customer satisfaction is the primary business goal
Hierarchical organization; goal is to please the boss	Problem-solving network organization; goal is to please the internal or external customer
Measure to judge operational results	Measure to help people make operational improvements

Source: Presentation by Peter Thigpen at the Stanford School of Business, February 26, 1991.

an important basis of success, and one that is even increasing in importance, it is clearly not the *only* basis of success.

IBM, for instance, has done many of these things and has built a skilled and dedicated workforce. That in and of itself, however, could not overcome a product strategy that overemphasized large, mainframe computers. People Express, now defunct, also built a strong culture, selectively recruited, and used innovative compensation and work organization strategies to build flexibility and productivity in its operations. Indeed, it was one of the lowest-cost providers of airline services. But this cost advantage could not overcome other problems, such as the founder's edifice complex, which resulted in too-rapid expansion, acquisition of Frontier Airlines and becoming seriously financially overleveraged, and a growth rate that was not sustainable given the firm's fundamental human resource policies. In focusing on managing the workforce, I highlight only *one* dimension of the several that determine corporate performance.

By the same token, it is possible to be successful, particularly for a while, doing none of these things or even their opposite. Frank Lorenzo took over Continental Airlines and put it into bankruptcy in 1983 to break its union contracts. To say he played hardball with his employees was an understatement. Lorenzo's strategy was founded on financial and negotiating skills, not on his workforce. For a while, these strategies worked—although Continental lost $161 million in 1983, by 1985 it earned about $60 million, a very rapid turnaround. Similarly, Carl Icahn at Trans World Airlines made money, for a while, taking strikes and fighting with his workforce, seeking success through financial strategies. Neither airline succeeded in the long run, but in the short run, cutting wages and benefits, cutting employment levels, and managing through fear can produce temporary results.

A third word of caution is that these practices have potential downsides as well as benefits and are not necessarily easy to implement, particularly in a one-at-a-time fashion. One obvious problem is that they all necessarily entail more involvement and responsibility on the part of the workforce. There are many employees who would rather work only with their bodies and check their minds at the door—particularly if that is what they have become accustomed to—and instituting work practices that entail more effort and involvement may force turnover. These practices may be resisted by others in the company as well. The reader is cautioned that implementation issues loom large, regardless of how sensible the practices may be.

ENDNOTES

1 Michael E. Porter, *Competitive Advantage* (New York, NY: Free Press, 1985), 1.

2 *Ibid.,* 4.

3 "Investment Winners and Losers," *Money,* October 1992, 133.

4 Bridget O'Brian, "Southwest Airlines is a Rare Air Carrier: It Still Makes Money," *The Wall Street Journal,* October 26, 1992, A1.

5 James Campbell Quick, "Crafting an Organizational Culture: Herb's Hand at Southwest Airlines," *Organizational Dynamics* 21, Autumn 1992, 47.

6 O'Brian, *op cit.,* A7.

7 Quick, *op.cit.,* 50.

8 O'Brian, *op.cit.,* A1

9 *Ibid.,* A7.

10 Clair Brown, Michael Reich, and David Stern, "Becoming a High Performance Work Organization: The Role of Security, Employee Involvement, and Training," Working Paper 45, Institute of Industrial Relations (Berkeley, CA: University of California, 1992), 3.

11 Frank L. Schmidt and John E. Hunter, "Individual Differences in Productivity: An Empirical Test of Estimates Derived from Studies of Selection Procedure Utility," *Journal of Applied Psychology* 68, 1983, 407–414.

12 Harry C. Handlin, "The Company Built upon the Golden Rule: Lincoln Electric," in Bill L. Hopkins and Thomas C. Mawhinney (eds.), *Pay for Performance: History, Controversy, and Evidence* (New York, NY: Haworth Press, 1992), 157.

13 "Nordstrom: Dissension in the Ranks?" Case 9-191-002 (Boston, MA: Harvard Business School, 1990), 7.

14 George Akerlof, "Gift Exchange and Efficiency Wage Theory," *American Economic Review* 74, 1984, 79–83.

15 James W. Near, "Wendy's Successful 'Mop Bucket Attitude'," *The Wall Street Journal,* April 27, 1992, A16.

16 *Ibid.*

17 Handlin, *op. cit.,* 159.

18 Joseph R. Blasi and Douglas L. Kruse, *The New Owners* (New York, NY: Harper Business, 1991), 257.

19 Corey M. Rosen, Katherine J. Klein, and Karen M. Young, *Employee Ownership in America* (Lexington, MA: Lexington Books, 1986).

20 Richard T. Pascale, "Nordstrom, Inc.," unpublished case (San Francisco, CA: 1991), Exhibits 7 and 8.

21 David I. Levine and Laura D'Andrea Tyson, "Participation, Productivity, and the Firm's Environment," in Alan S. Blinder (ed.), *Paying for Productivity: A Look at the Evidence* (Washington, DC: The Brookings Institution, 1990), 183–243.

22 J. Richard Hackman and Greg R. Oldham, *Work Redesign* (Reading, MA: Addison-Wesley, 1980).

23 Thomas F. O'Boyle, "Working Together: A Manufacturer Grows Efficient by Soliciting Ideas from Employees," *The Wall Street Journal,* June 5, 1992, A4.

24 Barnaby Feder, "At Monsanto, Teamwork Works," *New York Times,* June 25, 1991, C1.

25 Barbara Presley Noble, "An Approach with Staying Power," *New York Times,* March 8, 1992, 23.

26 Brian Dumaine, "Who Needs a Boss?" *Fortune,* May 7, 1990, 54.

27 *Ibid.,* 55.

28 Paul S. Adler, "The 'Learning Bureaucracy': New United Motor Manufacturing, Inc.," In Barry M. Staw and Larry L. Cummings (eds.), *Research in Organizational Behavior* (Greenwich, CT: JAI Press, in press), 32.

29 Helene Cooper, "Carpet Firm Sets Up an In-House School to Stay Competitive," *The Wall Street Journal,* October 5, 1992, A1, A6.

30 Norm Alster, "What Flexible Workers Can Do," *Fortune,* February 13, 1989, 62.

31 Adler, *op. cit.,* 17.

32 J. Patrick Wright, *On a Clear Day You Can See General Motors* (Grosse Pointe, MI: Wright Enterprises, 1979).

33 Edward P. Lazear, "Play Equality and Industrial Politics," *Journal of Political Economy* 97, 1989, 561–580.

34 Paul Milgrom and John Roberts, "An Economic Approach to Influence Activities in Organizations," *American Journal of Sociology* 94, 1988, S154–S179.

35 Daryl J. Bem, "Self-Perception Theory," in Leonard Berkowitz (ed.), *Advances in Experimental Social Psychology,* vol. 6 (New York, NY: Academic Press, 1972), 1–62.

36 Mark R. Lepper and David Greene, "Turning Play into Work: Effects of Adult Surveillance and Extrinsic Rewards on Children's Intrinsic Motivation," *Journal of Personality and Social Psychology* 31, 1975, 479–486.

37 David Halberstam, *The Reckoning* (New York, NY: William Morrow, 1986).

38 See, for example, Peter M. Blau, *The Dynamics of Bureaucracy* (Chicago, IL: University of Chicago Press, 1955); and V. F. Ridgway, "Dysfunctional Consequences of Performance Measurement," *Administrative Science Quarterly* 1, 1956, 240–247.

39 Presentation by Peter Thigpen at Stanford Graduate School of Business, February 26, 1991.

CHAPTER 8: Questions for Discussion

1 How do the newer approaches discussed in this chapter relate to earlier theories of job design and work motivation?

2 Lawler's article reviews several "success stories" using the New Plant approach. Under what circumstances do you think this approach would have its greatest likelihood of success? Under what circumstances would it have its least likelihood of success? Explain.

3 What three or four key lessons for management follow from Lawler's article?

4 Manz's article on self-leading teams provides a controversial approach to group leadership. What primary obstacles exist in organizations that might inhibit the success of this approach? Can these obstacles be overcome? If so, how?

5 What special requirements does the self-leading teams approach have for group leaders? For group members?

6 Pfeffer argues that an organization's human resources can make the critical difference in global competition. On what basis does he make this assertion? Do you agree with this argument?

7 What advice does Pfeffer offer to managers? What limitations exist that may serve to moderate the effectiveness of these recommendations?

8 Looking back over the three readings on high-involvement management techniques, how might variations across cultures influence the effectiveness of these approaches? More specifically, would such approaches work in Japan? In China? In Mexico? What lessons can we draw from this material about managing across borders?

LEADERSHIP CHALLENGES

The managerial challenge of actually exercising leadership in organizational settings provides "real-world" tests of leadership theory and research. For the practicing manager or executive, the triad of traits, behavior, and situations all blend together to form a complex challenge. The seemingly ever-increasing emphasis on the importance of organizational leadership in popular books and articles has put a great deal of pressure on managers to "perform" at high levels in the leadership role. Much is expected, and potentially heavy penalties await those who don't "measure up." Thus, this chapter focuses on some of these leadership challenges and how they can be, and are being, met. As the reader will see, an examination of leadership challenges involves a consideration of the basic concept of leadership itself.

The collection of readings in this chapter forces the serious student of leadership to confront the issue of "what do we mean by effective leadership in organizations?" This fundamental question is especially apt in the context of contemporary organizations that operate in increasingly turbulent and complex environments. In essence, an important consideration is whether there are basic principles of successful leadership that can be distilled out of the welter of conflicting claims and prescriptions advanced by both behavioral scientists and practitioners. The reader is well advised to regard the arguments advanced in the articles in this chapter (as in all chapters in the book) with a healthy degree of skepticism and questioning. Many valid points are made, but "the evidence is certainly not all in," so to speak, in regard to many of the conclusions that are advanced. If this were not the case, then there would be no need for the many research studies and associated pieces of advice that seem constantly to appear on the topic of leadership. For this subject, more than for almost any other topic relating to the behavioral aspects of management in organizations, the advice of *caveat emptor* is exceedingly appropriate.

There is one other point that should be noted as one reads the articles in this chapter: More than one of the articles emphasizes the kinds of effects that particular leadership approaches or styles can have on the motivation of those who are, presumably, being led. As we have indicated throughout this book, one of the most important impacts of organizational leadership, whether it be effective or ineffective, is on the motivation of organizational members. In other words, the act of leadership creates effects, one of the most consequential of which is the intensification or, conversely, the dampening, of motivational force.

OVERVIEW OF THE READINGS

This chapter's readings begin with an article by Kotter that explores the issue of "what leaders really do." The author makes a clear-cut definitional distinction between "management" and "leadership." The former, according to Kotter, is about "coping with complexity," and the latter is about "coping with change." This line of reasoning results in a view that "management ensures plan accomplishment by controlling and problem solving," whereas "leadership [achieves] a vision [by] motivating and inspiring." In the words of Kotter, "good leaders motivate people in a variety of ways," including motivating other people to "provide leadership as well." The article concludes with some suggestions about how organizations can develop more effective leaders among their managers.

The following reading by Bass is probably one of the most cited articles for making the case for why organizations should promote and foster "*transformational* leadership," as opposed to "*transactional* leadership." Borrowing from the work of Burns (1978), a political scientist, the author elaborates on the distinction between the two types of leadership. He notes that the transactional leader tends to place much stronger emphasis on the "motivation" of employees through "the promise of rewards or the avoidance of penalties," that is, the control of rewards or penalties, than does the transformational leader. Especially emphasized in this article is the importance, for transformational leaders, of "attaining charisma," that is, of "inspiring and exciting . . . employees with the idea that they may be able to accomplish great things with extra effort." Bass also advances the argument that transformational leaders can "vary widely in their personal styles." The final sections of the article discuss a number of implications for organizations if they can succeed in increasing the amount of transformational leadership.

It is important to note that the advocacy of transformational leadership is not without its vigorous questioners. For example, Hollander (1992) contends that "transformational leadership can be seen as an *extension* of transactional leadership," rather than as a distinctly different type. He also raises the issue of whether there may be a downside to charismatic (that is, transformational) leaders and notes that "their potential for affecting large numbers of others adversely requires attention, if only because appeals based on emotional arousal provide ample opportunities for abuse" (p. 51).

The fundamental issue that Hollander raises is amplified in detail in the third reading in this chapter, by Krantz. Krantz notes that many contemporary commentators and organizational analysts talk about a "crisis of leadership," that is, a lack of effective leadership. In this author's view, "this diagnosis . . . is simplistic and is used defensively to avoid a confrontation with the more complex, and more intractable, problems underlying this leadership crisis." Put more succinctly, and focusing specifically on a central tenet of the advocates of charismatic leadership, Krantz suggests that "the leader's personality has been vastly overrated in attempts to understand leadership." He argues strongly against the easy acceptance of the idea of the "heroic" image of leadership. As he states, "a more pertinent and useful conceptualization of leadership will move away from focusing on the leader and toward a more complex appreciation of the variety of factors affecting leadership within a system."

A related view of leadership issues is provided in the fourth article, by Conger. He is concerned particularly with the possible downsides, or negative effects, of powerful leaders, while acknowledging their equal potential for creating positive results. "The very behaviors that distinguish leaders from managers," Conger argues, "also have the potential to produce problematic or even disastrous outcomes for their organizations." In this regard, he views with some alarm the excessive adulation of so-called "visionary" leaders and their resulting tendency to believe themselves invincible. This, Conger believes, lays the groundwork for possible, though obviously unintended, leadership calamities. The article provides some specific examples of how certain acknowledged "leaders" in business and industry who initially achieved a record of major achievement subsequently fell victim to those prior successes and proceeded to develop reliance solely on their own "superior" ideas and abilities. The major conclusion is that "many of the qualities of a strong leader have both a positive and a negative face."

The last article in this chapter, by Howell and his colleagues, deals with an interesting and crucial question: Is leadership always needed in all organizational situations, or can there be "substitutes" for leadership? The authors' basic thesis, and answer to the question, is that there are many circumstances in organizations where other "remedies" can be supplied that will reduce or eliminate the need for leadership, at least in the short run. Examples include teams of highly motivated individuals, prior professional education of certain employees, high levels of ability of some employees, extensive training, and the like. The authors also discuss factors that can "neutralize" or diminish the impact of leaders, such as physical distance and organizational reward systems that leave little discretion to the leader. They conclude by proposing that more explicit attention by organizations to a variety of options available for reducing their dependence on leaders "can itself [be] an act of leadership."

REFERENCES

Burns, J.M. *Leadership.* New York: Harper, 1978.
Hollander, E.P. Leadership, followership, self, and others. *Leadership Quarterly*, 1992, **3**(1), 43–54.

What Leaders Really Do

John P. Kotter

Leadership is different from management, but not for the reasons most people think. Leadership isn't mystical and mysterious. It has nothing to do with having "charisma" or other exotic personality traits. It is not the province of a chosen few. Nor is leadership necessarily better than management or a replacement for it.

Rather, leadership and management are two distinctive and complementary systems of action. Each has its own function and characteristic activities. Both are necessary for success in an increasingly complex and volatile business environment.

Most U.S. corporations today are overmanaged and underled. They need to develop their capacity to exercise leadership. Successful corporations don't wait for leaders to come along. They actively seek out people with leadership potential and expose them to career experiences designed to develop that potential. Indeed, with careful selection, nurturing, and encouragement, dozens of people can play important leadership roles in a business organization.

But while improving their ability to lead, companies should remember that strong leadership with weak management is no better, and is sometimes actually worse, than the reverse. The real challenge is to combine strong leadership and strong management and use each to balance the other.

Of course, not everyone can be good at both leading and managing. Some people have the capacity to become excellent managers but not strong leaders. Others have great leadership potential but, for a variety of reasons, have great difficulty becoming strong managers. Smart companies value both kinds of people and work hard to make them a part of the team.

But when it comes to preparing people for executive jobs, such companies rightly ignore the recent literature that says people cannot manage *and* lead. They try to develop leader-managers. Once companies understand the fundamental difference between leadership and management, they can begin to groom their top people to provide both.

THE DIFFERENCE BETWEEN MANAGEMENT AND LEADERSHIP

Management is about coping with complexity. Its practices and procedures are largely a response to one of the most significant developments of the twentieth century: the emergence of large organizations. Without good management, complex enterprises tend to become chaotic in ways that threaten their very existence. Good management brings a degree of order and consistency to key dimensions like the quality and profitability of products.

Leadership, by contrast, is about coping with change. Part of the reason it has become so important in recent years is that the business world has become more competitive and more volatile. Faster technological change, greater international competition, the deregulation of markets, overcapacity in capital-intensive industries, an unstable oil cartel, raiders with junk bonds, and the changing demographics of the work force are among the many factors that have contributed to this shift. The net result is that doing what was done yesterday, or doing it 5% better, is no longer a formula for success. Major changes are more and more necessary to survive and compete effectively in this new environment. More change always demands more leadership.

Consider a simple military analogy: a peacetime army can usually survive with good administration and management up and down the hierarchy, coupled with good leadership concentrated at the very top. A wartime army, however, needs competent leadership at all levels. No one yet has figured out how to manage people effectively into battle; they must be *led*.

These different functions—coping with complexity and coping with change—shape the characteristic activities of management and leadership. Each system of action involves deciding what needs to be done, creating networks of people and relationships that can accomplish an agenda, and then trying to ensure that those people actually do the job. But each accomplishes these three tasks in different ways.

Companies manage complexity first by *planning and budgeting*—setting targets or goals for the future (typically for the next month or year), establishing detailed steps for achieving those targets, and then allocating resources to accomplish those plans. By contrast, leading an organization to constructive change begins by *setting a direction*—developing a vision of the future (often the distant future) along with strategies for producing the changes needed to achieve that vision.

Management develops the capacity to achieve its plan by *organizing and staffing*—creating an organizational structure and set of jobs for accomplishing plan requirements, staffing the jobs with qualified individuals, communicating the plan to those people, delegating responsibility for carrying out the plan, and devising systems to monitor implementation. The equivalent leadership activity, however, is *aligning people*. This means communicating the new direction to those who can create coalitions that understand the vision and are committed to its achievement.

Finally, management ensures plan accomplishment by *controlling and problem solving*—monitoring results versus the plan in some detail, both formally and informally, by means of reports, meetings, and other tools; identifying deviations; and then planning and organizing to solve the problems. But for leadership, achieving a vision requires *motivating and inspiring*—keeping people moving in the right direction, despite major obstacles to change, by appealing to basic but often untapped human needs, values, and emotions.

A closer examination of each of these activities will help clarify the skills leaders need.

SETTING A DIRECTION VS. PLANNING AND BUDGETING

Since the function of leadership is to produce change, setting the direction of that change is fundamental to leadership.

Setting direction is never the same as planning or even long-term planning, although people often confuse the two. Planning is a management process, deductive in nature and designed to produce orderly results, not change. Setting a direction is more inductive. Leaders gather a broad range of data and look for patterns, relationships, and linkages that help explain things. What's more, the direction-setting aspect of leadership does not produce plans; it creates vision and strategies. These describe a business, technology, or corporate culture in terms of what it should become over the long term and articulate a feasible way of achieving this goal.

Most discussions of vision have a tendency to degenerate into the mystical. The implication is that a vision is something mysterious that mere mortals, even talented ones, could never hope to have. But developing good business direction isn't magic. It is a tough, sometimes exhausting process of gathering and analyzing information. People who articulate such visions aren't magicians but broad-based strategic thinkers who are willing to take risks.

Nor do visions and strategies have to be brilliantly innovative; in fact, some of the best are not. Effective business visions regularly have an almost mundane quality, usually consisting of ideas that are already well known. The particular combination or patterning of the ideas may be new, but sometimes even that is not the case.

For example, when CEO Jan Carlzon articulated his vision to make Scandinavian Airline Systems (SAS) the best airline in the world for the frequent business traveler, he was not saying anything that everyone in the airline industry didn't already know. Business travelers fly more consistently than other market segments and are generally willing to pay higher fares. Thus focusing on business customers offers an airline the possibility of high margins, steady business, and considerable growth. But in an industry known more for bureaucracy than vision, no company had ever put these simple ideas together and dedicated itself to implementing them. SAS did, and it worked.

What's crucial about a vision is not its originality but how well it serves the interests of important constituencies—customers, stockholders, employees—and how easily it can be translated into a realistic competitive strategy. Bad visions tend to ignore the legitimate needs and rights of important constituencies—favoring, say, employees over customers or stockholders. Or they are strategically unsound. When a company that has never been better than a weak competitor in an industry suddenly starts talking about becoming number one, that is a pipe dream, not a vision.

One of the most frequent mistakes that overmanaged and underled corporations make is to embrace "long-term planning" as a panacea for their lack of direction and inability to adapt to an increasingly competitive and dynamic business environment. But such an approach misinterprets the nature of direction setting and can never work.

Long-term planning is always time consuming. Whenever something unexpected happens, plans have to be redone. In a dynamic business environment, the unexpected often becomes the norm, and long-term planning can become an extraordinarily burdensome activity. This is why most successful corporations limit the time frame of their planning activities. Indeed, some even consider "long-term planning" a contradiction in terms.

In a company without direction, even short-term planning can become a black hole capable of absorbing an infinite amount of time and energy. With no vision and strategy to provide constraints around the planning process or to guide it, every eventuality deserves a plan. Under these circumstances, contingency planning can go on forever, draining time and attention from far more essential activities, yet without ever providing the clear sense of direction that a company desperately needs. After awhile, managers inevitably become cynical about all this, and the planning process can degenerate into a highly politicized game.

Planning works best not as a substitute for direction setting but as a complement to it. A competent planning process serves as a useful reality check on direction-setting activities. Likewise, a competent direction-setting process provides a focus in which planning can then be realistically carried out. It helps clarify what kind of planning is essential and what kind is irrelevant.

ALIGNING PEOPLE VS. ORGANIZING AND STAFFING

A central feature of modern organizations is interdependence, where no one has complete autonomy, where most employees are tied to many others by their work, technology, management systems, and hierarchy. These linkages present a special challenge when organizations attempt to change. Unless many individuals line up and move together in the same direction, people will tend to fall all over one another. To executives who are overeducated in management and undereducated in leadership, the idea of getting people moving in the same direction appears to be an organizational problem. What executives need to do, however, is not organize people but align them.

Managers "organize" to create human systems that can implement plans as precisely and efficiently as possible. Typically, this requires a number of potentially complex decisions. A company must choose a structure of jobs and reporting relationships, staff it with individuals suited to the jobs, provide training for those who need it, communicate plans to the work force, and decide how much authority to delegate and to whom. Economic incentives also need to be constructed to accomplish the plan, as well as systems to monitor its implementation. These organizational judgments are much like architectural decisions. It's a question of fit within a particular context.

Aligning is different. It is more of a communications challenge than a design problem. First, aligning invariably involves talking to many more individuals than organizing does. The target population can involve not only a manager's subordinates but also bosses, peers, staff in other parts of the organization, as well as suppliers, governmental officials, or even customers. Anyone who can help implement the vision and strategies or who can block implementation is relevant.

Trying to get people to comprehend a vision of an alternative future is also a communications challenge of a completely different magnitude from organizing them to fulfill a short-term plan. It's much like the difference between a football quarterback attempting to describe to his team the next two or three plays versus his trying to explain to them a totally new approach to the game to be used in the second half of the season.

Whether delivered with many words or a few carefully chosen symbols, such messages are not necessarily accepted just because they are understood. Another big challenge in leadership efforts is credibility—getting people to believe the message. Many things contribute to credibility: the track record of the person delivering the message, the content of the message itself, the communicator's reputation for integrity and trustworthiness, and the consistency between words and deeds.

Finally, aligning leads to empowerment in a way that organizing rarely does. One of the reasons some organizations have difficulty adjusting to rapid changes in markets or technology is that so many people in those companies feel relatively powerless. They have learned from experience that even if they correctly perceive important external changes and then initiate appropriate actions, they are vulnerable to someone higher up who does not like what they have done. Reprimands can take many different forms: "That's against policy" or "We can't afford it" or "Shut up and do as you're told."

Alignment helps overcome this problem by empowering people in at least two ways. First, when a clear sense of direction has been communicated throughout an organization, lower level employees can initiate actions without the same degree of vulnerability. As long as their behavior is consistent with the vision, superiors will have more difficulty reprimanding them. Second, because everyone is aiming at the same target, the probability is less that one person's initiative will be stalled when it comes into conflict with someone else's.

MOTIVATING PEOPLE VS. CONTROLLING AND PROBLEM SOLVING

Since change is the function of leadership, being able to generate highly energized behavior is important for coping with the inevitable barriers to change. Just as direction setting identifies an appropriate path for movement and just as effective alignment gets people moving down that path, successful motivation ensures that they will have the energy to overcome obstacles.

According to the logic of management, control mechanisms compare system behavior with the plan and take action when a deviation is detected. In a well-managed factory, for example, this means the planning process establishes sensible quality targets, the organizing process builds an organization that can achieve those targets, and a control process makes sure that quality lapses are spotted immediately, not in 30 or 60 days, and corrected.

For some of the same reasons that control is so central to management, highly motivated or inspired behavior is almost irrelevant. Managerial processes must be as close as possible to fail-safe and risk-free. That means they cannot be dependent on the unusual or hard to obtain. The whole purpose of systems and structures is to help normal people who behave in normal ways to complete routine jobs successfully, day after day. It's not exciting or glamorous. But that's management.

Leadership is different. Achieving grand visions always requires an occasional burst of energy. Motivation and inspiration energize people, not by pushing them in the right direction as control mechanisms do but by satisfying basic human needs for achievement, a sense of belonging, recognition, self-esteem, a feeling of control over one's life, and the ability to live up to one's ideals. Such feelings touch us deeply and elicit a powerful response.

Good leaders motivate people in a variety of ways. First, they always articulate the organization's vision in a manner that stresses the values of the audience they are addressing. This makes the work important to those individuals. Leaders also regularly involve people in deciding how to achieve the organization's vision (or the part most relevant to a particular individual). This gives people a sense of control. Another important motivational technique is to support employee efforts to realize the vision by providing coaching, feedback, and role modeling, thereby helping people grow professionally and enhancing their self-esteem. Finally, good leaders recognize and reward success, which not only gives people a sense of accomplishment but also makes them feel like they belong to an organization that cares about them. When all this is done, the work itself becomes intrinsically motivating.

The more that change characterizes the business environment, the more that leaders must motivate people to provide leadership as well. When this works, it tends to reproduce leadership across the entire organization, with people occupying multiple leadership roles throughout the hierarchy. This is highly valuable, because coping with change in any complex business demands initiatives from a multitude of people. Nothing less will work.

Of course, leadership from many sources does not necessarily converge. To the contrary, it can easily conflict. For multiple leadership roles to work together, people's actions must be carefully coordinated by mechanisms that differ from those coordinating traditional management roles.

Strong networks of informal relationships—the kind found in companies with healthy cultures—help coordinate leadership activities in much the same way that formal structure coordinates managerial activities. The key difference is that informal networks can deal with the greater demands for coordination associated with nonroutine activities and change. The multitude of communication channels and the trust among the individuals connected by those channels allow for an ongoing process of accommodation and adaptation. When conflicts arise among roles, those same relationships help resolve the conflicts. Perhaps most important, this process of dialogue and accommodation can produce visions that are linked and compatible instead of remote and competitive. All this requires a great deal more communication than is needed to coordinate managerial roles, but unlike formal structure, strong informal networks can handle it.

Of course, informal relations of some sort exist in all corporations. But too often these networks are either very weak—some people are well connected but most are not—or they are highly fragmented—a strong network exists inside the marketing group and inside R&D but not across the two departments. Such networks do not support multiple leadership initiatives well. In fact, extensive informal networks are so important that if they do not exist, creating them has to be the focus of activity early in a major leadership initiative.

CREATING A CULTURE OF LEADERSHIP

Despite the increasing importance of leadership to business success, the on-the-job experiences of most people actually seem to undermine the development of attributes needed for leadership. Nevertheless, some companies have consistently demonstrated an ability to develop people into outstanding leader-managers. Recruiting people with leadership potential is only the first step. Equally important is managing their career patterns. Individuals who are effective in large leadership roles often share a number of career experiences.

Perhaps the most typical and most important is significant challenge early in a career. Leaders almost always have had opportunities during their twenties and thirties to actually try to lead, to take a risk, and to learn from both triumphs and failures. Such learning seems essential in developing a wide range of leadership skills and perspectives. It also teaches people something about both the difficulty of leadership and its potential for producing change.

Later in their careers, something equally important happens that has to do with broadening. People who provide effective leadership in important jobs always have a chance, before they get into those jobs, to grow beyond the narrow base that characterizes most managerial careers. This is usually the result of lateral career moves or of early promotions to unusually broad job assignments. Sometimes other vehicles help, like special task-force assignments or a lengthy general management course. Whatever the case, the breadth of knowledge developed in this way seems to be helpful in all aspects of leadership. So does the network of relationships that is often acquired both inside and outside the company. When enough people get opportunities like this, the relationships that are built also help create the strong informal networks needed to support multiple leadership initiatives.

Corporations that do a better-than-average job of developing leaders put an emphasis on creating challenging opportunities for relatively young employees. In many businesses, decentralization is the key. By definition, it pushes responsibility lower in an organization and in the process creates more challenging jobs at lower levels. Johnson & Johnson, 3M, Hewlett-Packard, General Electric, and many other well-known companies have used that approach quite successfully. Some of those same companies also create as many small units as possible so there are a lot of challenging lower-level general management jobs available.

Sometimes these businesses develop additional challenging opportunities by stressing growth through new products or services. Over the years, 3M has had a policy that at least 25% of its revenue should come from products introduced within the last five years. That encourages small new ventures, which in turn offer hundreds of opportunities to test and stretch young people with leadership potential.

Such practices can, almost by themselves, prepare people for small- and medium-sized leadership jobs. But developing people for important leadership positions requires more work on the part of senior executives, often over a long period of time. That work begins with efforts to spot people with great leadership potential early in their careers and to identify what will be needed to stretch and develop them.

Again, there is nothing magic about this process. The methods successful companies use are surprisingly straightforward. They go out of their way to make young employees and people at lower levels in their organizations visible to senior management. Senior managers then judge for themselves who has potential and what the development needs of those people are. Executives also discuss their tentative conclusions among themselves to draw more accurate judgments.

Armed with a clear sense of who has considerable leadership potential and what skills they need to develop, executives in these companies then spend time planning for that development. Sometimes that is done as part of a formal succession planning or high-potential development process; often it is more informal. In either case, the key ingredient appears to be an intelligent assessment of what feasible development opportunities fit each candidate's needs.

To encourage managers to participate in these activities, well-led businesses tend to recognize and reward people who successfully develop leaders. This is rarely done as part of a formal compensation or bonus formula, simply because it is so difficult to measure such achievements with precision. But it does become a factor in decisions about promotion, especially to the most senior levels, and that seems to make a big difference. When told that future promotions will depend to some degree on their ability to nurture leaders, even people who say that leadership cannot be developed somehow find ways to do it.

Such strategies help create a corporate culture where people value strong leadership and strive to create it. Just as we need more people to provide leadership in the complex organizations that dominate our world today, we also need more people to develop the cultures that will create that leadership. Institutionalizing a leadership-centered culture is the ultimate act of leadership.

From Transactional to Transformational Leadership: Learning to Share the Vision

Bernard M. Bass

Sir Edmund Hillary of Mount Everest fame liked to tell a story about one of Captain Robert Falcon Scott's earlier attempts, from 1901 to 1904, to reach the South Pole. Scott led an expedition made up of men from the Royal Navy and the merchant marine, as well as a group of scientists. Scott had considerable trouble dealing with the merchant marine personnel, who were unaccustomed to the rigid discipline of Scott's Royal Navy. Scott wanted to send one seaman home because he would not take orders, but the seaman refused, arguing that he had signed a contract and knew his rights. Since the seaman was not subject to Royal Navy disciplinary action, Scott did not know what to do. Then Ernest Shackleton, a merchant navy officer in Scott's party, calmly informed the seaman that he, the seaman, was returning to Britain. Again the seaman refused—and Shackleton knocked him to the ship's deck. After another refusal, followed by a second flooring, the seaman decided he would return home. Scott later became one of the victims of his own inadequacies as a leader in his 1911 race to the South Pole. Shackleton went on to lead many memorable expeditions; once, seeking help for the rest of his party, who were stranded on the Antarctic Coast, he journeyed with a small crew in a small open boat from the edge of Antarctica to South Georgia Island.

LEADERSHIP TODAY

Most relationships between supervisors and their employees are quite different today. Few managers depend mainly on their legitimate power, as Scott did, or on their coercive power, as Shackleton did, to persuade people to do as they're told. Rather, managers engage in a transaction with their employees: They explain what is required of them and what compensation they will receive if they fulfill these requirements.

A shift in management style at Xerox's Reprographic Business Group (RBG) provides a good example. In the first step toward establishing management in which managers take the initiative and show consideration for others, 44 specific, effective management behaviors were identified. Two factors that characterize modern leadership were found in many of these behaviors. One factor—initiating and organizing work—concentrates on accomplishing the tasks at hand. The second factor—showing consideration for employees—focuses on satisfying the self-interest of those who do good work. The leader gets things done by making, and fulfilling, promises of recognition, pay increases, and advancement for employees who perform well. By contrast, employees who do not do good work are penalized. This transaction or exchange—this promise and reward for good performance, or threat and discipline for poor performance—characterizes effective leadership. These kinds of transactions took place in most of the effective 44 leadership behaviors identified at Xerox's RBG. This kind of leadership, which is based on transactions between manager and employees, is called "transactional leadership."

In many instances, however, such transactional leadership is a prescription for mediocrity. This is particularly true if the leader relies heavily on passive management-by-exception, intervening with his or her group only when procedures and standards for accomplishing tasks are not being met. My colleagues and I have arrived at this surprising but consistent finding in a number of research analyses. Such a manager espouses the popular adage, "If it ain't broken, don't fix it." He or she stands in back of the caboose of a moving freight train and says, "Now I know where we are going." This kind of manager may use disciplinary threats to bring a group's performance up to standards—a technique that is ineffective and, in the long run, likely to be counterproductive.

Moreover, whether the promise of rewards or the avoidance of penalties motivates the employees depends on whether the leader has control of the rewards or penalties, and on whether the employees want the rewards or fear the penalties. In many organizations, pay increases depend mainly on seniority, and promotions depend on qualifications and policies about which the leader has little to say. The breaking of regulations may be the main cause of penalties. Many an executive has found his or her hands tied by contract provisions, organizational politics, and inadequate resources.

TRANSFORMATIONAL LEADERSHIP

Superior leadership performance—transformational leadership—occurs when leaders broaden and elevate the interests of their employees, when they generate awareness and acceptance of the purposes and mission of the group, and when they stir their employees to look beyond their own self-interest for the good of the group. Transformational leaders achieve these results in one or more ways: They may be charismatic to their followers and thus inspire them; they may meet the emotional needs of each employee; and/or they may intellectually stimulate employees. Exhibit 1 lists the characteristics of transformational and transactional leadership; these listings are based on the findings of a series of surveys and on clinical and case evidence.

Attaining charisma in the eyes of one's employees is central to succeeding as a transformational leader. Charismatic leaders have great power and influence. Employees want to identify with them, and they have a high degree of trust and confidence in them. Charismatic leaders inspire and excite their employees with the idea that they may be able to accomplish great things with extra effort. Further, transformational leaders are individually considerate, that is, they pay close attention to differences among their employees; they act as mentors to those who need help to grow and develop. Intellectual stimulation of employees is a third factor in transformational leadership. Intellectually stimulating leaders are willing and able to show their employees new ways of looking at old problems, to teach them to see difficulties as problems to be solved, and to emphasize rational solutions. Such a leader was Lorenz Iversen, a former president of the Mesta Machine Company, who said to his employees, "We got

EXHIBIT 1
Characteristics of transformational and transactional leaders.

TRANSFORMATIONAL LEADER

Charisma: Provides vision and sense of mission, instills pride, gains respect and trust.

Inspiration: Communicates high expectations, uses symbols to focus efforts, expresses important purposes in simple ways.

Intellectual Stimulation: Promotes intelligence, rationality, and careful problem solving.

Individualized Consideration: Gives personal attention, treats each employee individually, coaches, advises.

TRANSACTIONAL LEADER

Contingent Reward: Contracts exchange of rewards for effort, promises rewards for good performance, recognizes accomplishments.

Management by Exception (active): Watches and searches for deviations from rules and standards, takes corrective action.

Management by Exception (passive): Intervenes only if standards are not met.

Laissez-Faire: Abdicates responsibilities, avoids making decisions.

---

this job because you're the best mechanics in the world!" He practiced management-by-walking-around and stimulated the development of many of Mesta's patented inventions. He is remembered for instilling pride and commitment in his employees.

THE BIG PAYOFF

Managers who behave like transformational leaders are more likely to be seen by their colleagues and employees as satisfying and effective leaders than are those who behave like transactional leaders, according to their colleagues', supervisors', and employees' responses on the Multifactor Leadership Questionnaire (MLQ). Similar results have been found in various organizational settings. Leaders studied have come from an extremely broad variety of organizations: chief executive officers and senior and middle level managers in business and industrial firms in the United States, Canada, Japan, and India; research and development project leaders; American, Canadian, and British Army field grade officers; United States Navy senior officers and junior surface fleet officers; Annapolis midshipmen; educational administrators; and religious leaders.

Moreover, various types of evaluations—including performance ratings by both supervisors and direct reports, as well as standard financial measures—have produced a similar correlation between transformational behavior and high ratings. Managers tagged as high performers by their supervisors were also rated, in a separate evaluation by their followers, as more transformational than transactional. Their organizations do better financially. The same pattern emerged between followers' descriptions of shipboard Naval officers and those officers' supervisors' performance appraisals and recommendations for early promotion. And among Methodist ministers, transformational—not transactional—leadership behavior was positively related to high church attendance among congregants and growth in church membership.

Results were the same for evaluation of team performance in complex business simulations. Considerable credit for Boeing's turn-around since its 1969 crisis can be given to its chief executive, T. A. Wilson, who has emphasized technological progress, aggressive marketing, and a willingness to take calculated business risks. The confidence that Boeing employees have in Wilson, and their respect for him as a brilliant engineer and an outstanding leader, have instilled in them great pride in the company and its products.

EXTRA EFFORT FROM BELOW

Transformational leaders have better relationships with their supervisors and make more of a contribution to the organization than do those who are only transactional. Moreover, employees say that they themselves exert a lot of extra effort on behalf of managers who are transformational leaders. Organizations whose leaders are transactional are less effective than those whose leaders are transformational—particularly if much of the transactional leadership is passive management-by-exception (intervening only when standards are not being met). Employees say they exert little effort for such leaders. Nevertheless, leader-follower transactions dependent on contingent reward may also work reasonably well if the leaders can provide rewards that are valued by the followers.

Exhibit 2 illustrates the effect that transformational, as compared with transactional, leadership has on employee effort. The data were collected from 228 employees of 58 managers in a large engineering firm. The managers were ranked according to their leadership factor scores, which were based on descriptions of leaders by their employees and colleagues on the Multifactor Leadership Questionnaire. "Four-star" leaders were those who ranked in the top 25% on a leadership factor score; "one-star" leaders were among the bottom 25% of managers on the leadership factor score. From 75% to 82% of the "four-star" transformational managers had employees who indicated they frequently exerted extra effort on their jobs. Of the "one-star" transformational managers, only 22% to 24% had employees who said they frequently exerted extra effort.

It is interesting to note that, as Exhibit 2 illustrates, being rated as "four-star" rather than "one-star" in *transactional* leadership did not have the same impact on employees' extra effort as a high rating had for the transformational leaders. Similar findings have emerged from studies of leaders and their immediate employees at a diverse range of organizations, including Digital Equipment Corporation and Federal Express.

DIFFERENT STYLES OF TRANSFORMATIONAL LEADERSHIP

As noted earlier, certain types of behavior characterize the transformational leader. Yet transformational leaders vary widely in their personal styles. H. Ross Perot is self-effacing: "I don't look impressive," he says. "To a lot of guys I don't look like I could afford a car." But Perot created the $2.5 billion EDS organization from his vision, initiative, emphasis on hard work, and a special organizational culture with strict codes of morality and dress and quasi-military management. His personal involvement in the rescue of two of his employees trapped as hostages in Iran in 1979 is an extreme example of individualized consideration, a transformational factor. Leslie Wexner of The

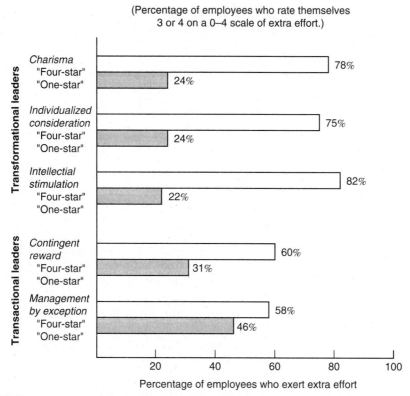

EXHIBIT 2
Employees' efforts under various leaders.

Limited, Inc. enjoys a more flamboyant lifestyle. But like Perot, Wexner converted his vision of a nationwide chain of women's sportswear stores into a reality through his own hard work. He stimulates employee participation in discussions and decisions and encourages them to share his vision of the company's future.

Many on *Fortune*'s list of the ten toughest bosses would not live up to modern behavioral science's prescriptions for the good leader: one who initiates the structure for interaction among his colleagues, and who does so with consideration for their welfare. Nevertheless, these tough bosses are highly successful as a consequence of the transformational qualities they display; Boeing's Wilson is a case in point. Although they do initiate structure and may be considerate of their employees, these leaders succeed through such transformational factors as charisma and the ability and willingness to treat different subordinates differently, as well as by providing intellectual stimulation for the employees. They frequently raise standards, take calculated risks, and get others to join them in their vision of the future. Rather than work within the organizational culture, they challenge and change that culture, as Roger Smith of General Motors Corporation did. Self-determination and self-confidence are characteristic of them. They succeed because of these transformational elements—even if they, like Wilson, have authoritarian tendencies.

TRANSFORMATIONAL LEADERS MAKE THE DIFFERENCE
BETWEEN SUCCESS AND FAILURE

Fighting with far fewer men and tanks than his enemy had, against superior equipment, Ernst Rommel, the Desert Fox, won a series of victories in 1941 and 1942 against the British in North Africa, until he was overwhelmed at El Alamein. Because he was up front at the scene of the action, he could make more rapid assessments and decisions than could his British counterparts, who stayed 20 miles back in headquarters. This, and his willingness to accept calculated risks, contributed to his legendary speed, surprise, and boldness, as well as to the continuing high morale of his troops.

Napoleon declared that an army of rabbits commanded by a lion could do better than an army of lions commanded by a rabbit. He was not far from the truth. With all due respect to social, economic, political, and market forces, and to human resources policies that affect an organization's health, having a lion—or, in Rommel's case, a fox—in command rather than a rabbit frequently means success for the organization. Lee Iacocca of Chrysler Corporation and John Welch of General Electric, who have become folk heroes (or folk devils, to some), are contemporary examples of the importance of transformational leaders to their organizations.

Leadership makes its presence felt throughout the organization and its activities. We have found that employees not only do a better job when they believe their supervisors are transformational leaders, but they also are much more satisfied with the company's performance appraisal system. Likewise, mass communications directed toward individual employees are much more likely to have an impact if the messages are reinforced face-to-face by their supervisors at all organizational levels.

Transformational leadership should be encouraged, for it can make a big difference in the firm's performance at all levels. Managers need to do more than focus on the exchange of material, social, and personal benefits for services satisfactorily rendered. The charismatic leader, like the flamboyant Ted Turner of Turner Broadcasting System, Inc., can instill a sense of mission; the individually considerate leader, like the shy and self-effacing Roberto Goizueta of the Coca Cola Corporation, can lead employees to take an interest in higher-level concerns; the intellectually stimulating leader, like the innovative Roger Smith at General Motors Corporation, can articulate a shared vision of jointly acceptable possibilities. This is not to say that transformational leaders are always prosocial in their efforts, for some fulfill grandiose dreams at the expense of their followers.

Despite the many successes with management development programs and the leadership development programs in our military academies, many executives still feel that leadership is like the weather—something to talk about, but about which not much can be done. Others say leadership ability is mystical—one needs to be born with it.

In fact, much can be done to improve leadership in an organization and to change the presiding style from transactional to transformational. The overall amount of transformational leadership in an organization can be increased substantially by suitable organizational and human resources policies. The new model of transformational leadership presents opportunities for enhancing a corporation's image and for improving its success in recruitment, selection, and promotion. This model also has implications for the organization's training and development activities and for the design of its jobs and organizational structure.

Implications for Corporate Image

It is no accident that many of the firms identified in Tom Peters and Robert Waterman's *In Search of Excellence* (Warner Books, 1982) as excellently managed have large numbers of transformational leaders. Conversely, the poorly managed "dinosaurs" among the firms they describe need to implement a lot more transformational leadership. A firm that is permeated with transformational leadership from top to bottom conveys to its own personnel as well as to customers, suppliers, financial backers, and the community at large that it has its eyes on the future; is confident; has personnel who are pulling together for the common good; and places a premium on its intellectual resources and flexibility and on the development of its people.

Implications for Recruiting

Increasing transformational leadership within the organization may help in recruitment. Candidates are likely to be attracted to an organization whose CEO is charismatic and enjoys a public image as a confident, successful, optimistic, dynamic leader. In addition, prospects are likely to be attracted by interview experiences with other members of management who exhibit individualized consideration. More intelligent prospects will be particularly impressed with intellectually stimulating contacts they make during the recruiting and hiring process.

Implications for Selection, Promotion, and Transfer

Since we can identify and measure the factors associated with transformational leadership, these factors should be incorporated into managerial assessment, selection, placement, and guidance programs—along with related assessments of relevant personal dimensions and individual differences. Somewhat more transformational leadership is generally expected and found as managers move to successively higher levels in the organization, but it is reasonable to expect that an individual's performance at one level will be similar to his or her performance at the next. Direct reports, peers, and/or supervisors can be asked to describe the manager's current leadership with the Multifactor Leadership Questionnaire; their responses should be considered when decisions are made regarding a manager's promotion or transfer into a position of greater supervisory responsibility. Feedback from these results can also be used for counseling, coaching, and mentoring.

Further, the organization can tap the personal characteristics and strengths that underlie the manager's transformational behavior. Charismatic leaders are characterized by energy, self-confidence, determination, intellect, verbal skills, and strong ego ideals. Each of these traits can be assessed in individual managers. Similarly, we can assess some of the traits underlying individualized consideration, such as coaching skills; preference for two-way, face-to-face communication; and willingness to delegate. Again, in the area of intellectual stimulation, candidates for promotion could be assessed with an eye toward the type of intellectual stimulation—general, creative, or mathematical—that would be most effective at the higher level of management. Appropriate intelligence tests may be used to select intellectually stimulating candidates.

Research findings indicate that when employees rate their managers on the MLQ, they describe new business leaders as significantly more transformational than established business leaders. Thus MLQ scores can be used profitably to identify executives to head new ventures.

Implications for Development

A management trainee's first supervisor can make a big difference in his or her subsequent career success. For example, six years after they joined Exxon, many managers who were highly rated by their supervisors reported that they had been given challenging assignments by their initial supervisor (i.e., they had received individualized consideration). Many had been assigned to supervisors with good reputations in the firm. It is important to note that managers tend to model their own leadership style after that of their immediate supervisors. Thus if more higher-ups are transformational, more lower-level employees will emulate transformational behavior—and will be likely to act as transformational leaders as they rise in the organization.

Organizational policy needs to support an understanding and appreciation of the maverick who is willing to take unpopular positions, who knows when to reject the conventional wisdom, and who takes reasonable risks. For example, when R. Gordon McGovern took over as president of Campbell Soup, he introduced the "right to fail" policy, which shook up the stodgy organization. On the other hand, the fine line between self-confidence and obstinacy needs to be drawn. The determined Winston Churchill who contributed so much to the survival of Britain in 1940 was the same Churchill whose obstinacy contributed to the mistakes in 1941 of failing to prepare Singapore adequately and of committing British troops to unnecessary disaster in Crete and Greece.

Intellectual stimulation also needs to be nurtured and cultivated as a way of life in the organization. The "best and the brightest" people should be hired, nourished, and encouraged. Innovation and creativity should be fostered at all levels in the firm.

Implications for Training

Despite conventional wisdom to the contrary, transformational leadership is a widespread phenomenon. True, more of it occurs at the top than at the bottom of an organization; but it has also been observed by many employees in their first-level supervisors. Transformational leadership can be learned, and it can—and should—be the subject of management training and development. Research has shown that leaders at all levels can be trained to be charismatic in both verbal and nonverbal performance. Successful programs have been conducted for first-level project leaders in hi-tech computer firms as well as for senior executives of insurance firms.

That transformational leadership can be increased through training was verified in an experiment when Multifactor Leadership Questionnaire scores were obtained on shop supervisors from their trainees, who were inmates in minimum, medium, and maximum security prisons. The supervisors worked directly with the inmates in industrial shops to produce various products for sale within and outside the prison system. The experiment compared four groups of supervisors on their pre- and post-training effectiveness in various industrial and vocational shops in the prison. One group was trained in transformational leadership, one group was trained in transactional leadership, one was untrained but measured "before and after," and one was untrained and measured only "after." The performances of both trained groups improved, but in comparison to the three other groups of supervisors, those who were trained in transformational leadership did as well or better at improving productivity, absenteeism, and "citizenship" behavior among the inmates; they also won more respect from the inmates.

TRAINING MANAGERS

Practical training that teaches people how to be transformational is similar to that used in the Xerox RPG strategy to modify management style. A counselor, mediator, or supervisor gives a manager a detailed, standardized description of his or her transformational and transactional leadership performance as rated by the manager's employees and/or colleagues. The Multifactor Leadership Questionnaire is used for this purpose. The manager also sees a chart showing the effects of his or her leadership on employee satisfaction, motivation, and perception of organizational effectiveness. Anonymity is maintained, although the manager sees the individual differences among the responses.

Participating managers complete a parallel questionnaire about their own leadership. The discrepancies between how they rate themselves and how their employees rate them may be examined scale-by-scale and item-by-item. The counselor may pose such questions as: "Why do you think you gave yourself a much higher score than your employees gave you in individualized consideration?" and "Why did your employees disagree with you on how rapidly you get to the heart of complex problems or the extent to which they trust you to overcome any obstacles?" It is important for managers to be aware of and accept their employees' view of their performance. A study of United States Naval officers found that those who agreed with their direct reports about their transformational leadership behavior were also likely to earn higher fitness ratings and recommendations for early promotion from their supervisors.

The manager and the counselor discuss in detail why certain results may have appeared and what can be done to improve ratings. For example, a manager may be asked: "What specific behavior on your part makes your employees say they are proud to work with you?" or "What have you done that results in your colleagues' saying you foster a sense of mission?" The collected responses to these questions can create a useful picture of what the manager can do to raise his or her performance on particular items.

In addition to working individually with a counselor, the manager also may participate in a workshop with other managers who are working toward becoming more transformational leaders. Workshop participants who received high ratings from their employees on a particular item are asked what they, the participants, specifically did to achieve these ratings. Questions might include: "Why did all of your employees say that you frequently enabled them to think about old problems in new ways?" or "Why did they all say that you increased their optimism for the future?"

Conversely, questions may focus on why a participant's employees varied widely in their ratings. If the data printout shows a wide divergence of opinion about whether a manager made the employees enthusiastic about assignments, he or she might be asked to suggest possible reasons for such differences of opinion among the employees.

Other Approaches to Training

Several other approaches to teaching transformational leadership make use of the specific data gathered in the workshop. For instance, participants are asked to think of an effective leader they have known and the behavior the leader displayed. Many examples of charisma, individualized consideration, and intellectual stimulation are usually noted. The effective leaders who are mentioned typically come from many levels inside and outside the organization; the workshop leader may point out that transformational leadership is neither particularly uncommon nor limited only to world class leaders. Moreover, these leaders' specific behaviors can be described, observed, and adopted. After viewing videotapes of charismatic, individually considerate, and intellectually stimulating managers in action, workshop participants may be asked to create their own scenarios and videotapes, in which they emulate the transformational leaders they have observed. The other participants may then offer critiques and suggest improvements.

The workshop also aims to increase other aspects of transformational leadership. The transformational leader develops and changes the organizational culture, and to show participants that they have such capabilities, the workshop leader asks them to imagine what the organization might be like in two to five years if it were fully aligned with their own ideas and interests. Then, in small teams based on their actual functions at work, they proceed to redesign the organization.

Similarly, training in mentoring can be used to promote the transformational factor of individualized consideration. For example, one participant can counsel another while a third acts as an observer and a source of feedback about the performance. And many creativity exercises show a manager how he or she can be more intellectually stimulating. Action plans emerge from workshop sessions. Examples include the following:

- I am going to sit down with all my employees and review these data with them.
- I am going to ask for another "reading" in a year; in the meantime I will try to reduce the discrepancies between where I am and where I should be.
- I'm going to talk with my mentor about these results and ask him what he thinks I should do about them.

Implications for Leadership Education

Military academies have traditionally emphasized leadership education, and today we are seeing a surge of interest in leadership courses in liberal arts colleges as well. At least 600 such courses were being offered, according to a recently completed survey of colleges. The Center for Creative Leadership holds conferences on leadership courses in undergraduate education, most recently in the summer of 1986. The subject of transformational leadership also has been added to leadership courses at the U.S. Air

Force Academy at Colorado Springs. In one such course, both faculty and students examined how Air Force officers who are transformational leaders serve as role models for cadets. Scales from the Multifactor Leadership Questionnaire were used to show that the transformational leaders among the instructors and staff provided role models for their students. The faculty and students discussed the questionnaire results and their implications.

Clearly, training cannot turn a purely transactional leader into a transformational leader. Moreover, some managers, while striving to be transformational leaders, misuse their training; their pseudotransformational efforts only further the manager's self-interest and values. Under the influence of such a manager, employees can be misdirected away from their own best interests and those of the organization as a whole. In one such case, Donald Burr of People's Express Airlines displayed many transformational qualities that rapidly built and then rapidly ruined the firm.

For too long, leadership development has been seen as mainly a matter of skill development. But leadership—particularly transformational leadership—should be regarded as an art and a science. It is encouraging to see that the Council for Liberal Learning of the Association of American Colleges now sponsors week-long conferences on leadership for scholars, prominent citizens, and national leaders.

Implications for Job Design and Job Assignment

As we have noted earlier, the results of a study of Exxon managers showed that highly rated managers had had challenging tasks delegated to them by their supervisors when they first joined the company. Jobs can—and should—be designed to provide greater challenges. Delegation with guidance and follow-up can become an individualizing and developmental way of life in a firm.

Transformational leaders show individualized consideration by paying attention to the particular development needs of each of their employees. Employees' jobs are designed with those needs in mind, as well as the needs of the organization. One employee needs experience leading a project team. Another needs an opportunity to reinforce what she has learned in an advanced computer programming class. Their transformational leader assigns them tasks accordingly.

Leaders can be intellectually stimulating to their employees if their own jobs allow them to explore new opportunities, to diagnose organizational problems, and to generate solutions. Leaders whose jobs force them to focus on solving small, immediate problems are likely to be less intellectually stimulating than those who have time to think ahead and in larger terms.

Implications for Organizational Structure

Transformational leadership is not a panacea. In many situations, it is inappropriate and transactional processes are indicated. In general, firms that are functioning in stable markets can afford to depend on their "one-minute" managers to provide the necessary, day-to-day leadership. If the technology, workforce, and environment are stable as well, then things are likely to move along quite well with managers who simply promise and deliver rewards to employees for carrying out assignments. And in stable organizations, even management-by-exception can be quite effective if the manager monitors employee performance and takes corrective action as needed. Rules and regulations for getting things done, when clearly understood and accepted by the employees, can eliminate the need for leadership under some circumstances.

But when the firm is faced with a turbulent marketplace; when its products are born, live, and die within the span of a few years; and/or when its current technology can become obsolete before it is fully depreciated; then transformational leadership needs to be fostered at all levels in the firm. In order to succeed, the firm needs to have the flexibility to forecast and meet new demands and changes as they occur—and only transformational leadership can enable the firm to do so.

Problems, rapid changes, and uncertainties call for a flexible organization with determined leaders who can inspire employees to participate enthusiastically in team efforts and share in organizational goals. In short, charisma, attention to individualized development, and the ability and willingness to provide intellectual stimulation are critical in leaders whose firms are faced with demands for renewal and change. At these organizations, fostering transformational leadership through policies of recruitment, selection, promotion, training, and development is likely to pay off in the health, well-being, and effective performance of the organization.

SELECTED BIBLIOGRAPHY

For nontechnical reading about transformational and transactional leadership, the following are suggested: James MacGregor Burns's *Leadership* (Harper, 1978); Bernard M. Bass's *Leadership and Performance Beyond Expectations* (Free Press, 1985) and "Leadership: Good, Better, Best" (*Organizational Dynamics,* 1985); Noel Tichy and Michelle Devanna's *Transformational Leadership* (Wiley, 1986); Warren G. Bennis and B. Nanus's *Leaders: The Strategies for Taking Charge* (Harper & Row, 1985); and Jan M. Kouzes and Barry Z. Posner's *The Leadership Challenge: How to Get Extraordinary Things Done in Organizations* (Jossey-Bass, 1987).

For more on transformational leadership that is selfish or antisocial, see Bernard M. Bass's "The Two Faces of Charismatic Leadership" *(Leaders Magazine,* forthcoming) and Jane Howell's "Two Faces of Charisma: Socialized and Personalized Leadership in Organizations" in *Charismatic Leadership: The Illusive Factor in Organizational Effectiveness* (Jossey-Bass, 1988), edited by Jay A. Conger and Rabindra N. Kanungo and Associates.

Several articles provide more specific evidence about and applications of transformational leadership. These include Bruce J. Avolio and Bernard M. Bass's "Charisma and Beyond," in *Emerging Leadership Vistas,* edited by Jerry G. Hunt (Lexington Books, 1988); Bernard M. Bass, Bruce J. Avolio, and Laurie Goodheim's "Biography and the Assessment of Transformational Leadership at the World Class Level" (*Journal of Management,* Volume 13, 1987); and John Hater and Bernard M. Bass's "Superiors' Evaluations and Subordinates' Perceptions of Transformational and Transactional Leadership" (*Journal of Applied Psychology,* November 1988).

Other very useful articles include Richard Crookall's "Management of Inmate Workers: A Field Test of Transformational and Situational Leadership" (Ph.D. dissertation, University of Western Ontario, 1989); and David A. Waldman, Bernard M.

Bass, and Francis J. Yammarino's "Adding to Leader-Follower Transactions: The Augmenting Effect of Charismatic Leadership" (Technical Report 3, Center for Leadership Studies, State University of New York, Binghamton, 1988). A detailed review of findings is presented in Bernard M. Bass and Bruce J. Avolio's "Implications of Transactional and Transformational Leadership for Individual, Team and Organizational Development" in *Research in Organizational Change and Development,* edited by Richard W. Woodman and William A. Pasmore (JAI Press, 1989).

Lessons from the Field: An Essay on the Crisis of Leadership in Contemporary Organizations

James Krantz

INTRODUCTION

This essay is about leadership and the crisis of leadership in our contemporary institutions. The point of departure for my thinking is the emerging literature in the field of applied behavioral and organizational research itself. In other words, this essay asks what one can learn about contemporary issues of leadership from reflecting on the themes and patterns that underlie the work of the field.[1]

This essay focuses on the relationship between the observer and what is observed. In it I address the crisis in leadership by analyzing the ways in which observers of organization and leadership make sense of their topics. Gleaning the lessons that reside in this intermediate zone requires turning to interpretative methods. In contrast to methods that aim for prediction or explanation, interpretation is concerned with understanding. It refers to making connections between previously disconnected data in order to illuminate the meanings that imbue some field of inquiry.

My intent here is to look across the field of organizational scholarship as it relates to issues of leadership and consider common themes and patterns. I take two "cuts" at the field. First, I take a broad look at the emerging ideas of leadership and authority that stem from changes in our economic order to a postindustrial society. Second, I examine in depth the recently published works by Warren Bennis, Peter Vaill, and Tom Gilmore about the crisis in leadership. Finally, I explore several underlying themes that link the concerns identified in the literature to larger social and cultural issues.

Because one's own theory or framework defines the questions asked and has an impact on the empirical "slice of life" one focuses upon, a final note of introduction may be useful to orient the reader to the author's interpretative stance. In this essay I view issues in leadership through the dual lenses of systems thinking and psychodynamic theory. How unconscious meanings, conflicts, fears, and beliefs are projected into organizations and how people collectively manage these forces is a central concern from this vantage point.

LEADERSHIP IN A NEW KEY

Leadership is in fashion now. Our society's preoccupation with leadership has spawned a large industry devoted to "leadership training" and "leadership development." The popular literature abounds with books extolling the heroic qualities of maverick business leaders who are taking on mythic proportions in our cultural landscape. No less telling is the massive volume of academic publication emerging in the area.[2] Although leadership has been widely and variously studied throughout the last century (Bass, 1981; Van Fleet & Yukl, 1989), the current explosion of interest in lead-

From *The Journal of Applied Behavioral Science*, 1990, 26(1), 49–64. Copyright © 1990 by NTL Institute. Reprinted by permission of Sage Publications, Inc.

ership, particularly the massive effort to find, create, foster, train, and develop more of it, speaks to important features of the historical moment.

At the same time, an understanding of leadership remains elusive enough for Warren Bennis to comment that leadership is both the most studied and least understood topic in all of social science. Although the studies agree on little, a consensus is emerging around the central requirements of effective leadership *at this time in history*—namely, the critical need to provide a vision around which members of an organization can coalesce and direct their productive energies (e.g., Bennis, 1989; Burns, 1978; Leavitt, 1986; Sashkin, 1988; Vaill, 1989).

The almost exclusive emphasis on this particular feature of leadership is relatively recent. Earlier, leadership and what is now distinguished as management were conflated, and classic managerial functions were considered essential to leadership (Barnard, 1938; Krantz & Gilmore, 1990; Selznick, 1957). Now they have been split apart. Managers and leaders are seen as different breeds (Bennis & Nanus, 1985; Burns, 1978; Zaleznik, 1978). Increasingly, the "managerial mentality" is viewed as a cause of our leadership crisis; the "manager," in contrast to the leader, is accused of doing damage by emphasizing order and efficiency rather than the sort of focus on mission and substance that can promote commitment and creativity (Vaill, 1989; Zaleznik, 1989).

A commonly expressed belief is that what is lacking is leadership in the new visionary sense (Sashkin, 1988; Zaleznik, 1989). The solution generally proposed for this lack of leadership is straightforward: find real leaders. The search for leaders with vision, leaders who can motivate people by articulating a purposeful direction, suffuses the academic literature and popular press. The massive leadership training and development industry is based on the same prescription: Provide leadership by developing leaders.

My central thesis is that this diagnosis of our crisis of leadership is simplistic and is used defensively to avoid a confrontation with the more complex, and more intractable, problems underlying this leadership crisis. I am not suggesting that the person of the leader is unimportant; there can be little doubt that the leader plays an enormously important part in the leadership of an enterprise. I am suggesting, however, that the leader's personality has been vastly overrated in attempts to understand leadership. Furthermore, in clinging to the hope that leaders themselves will solve our leadership crisis, we prevent ourselves from addressing the underlying problems that disable even enormously capable leaders.

The idea that leadership emanates from leaders was easier to maintain in an era that favored centralized bureaucratic hierarchies. Control was imposed from top to bottom; Taylorism enacted a view in which managers thought and workers labored; authority relations were based on obedience and contractual obligation; command and control systems were based on information held by few; and careers tended to imply a unitary trajectory through a single organization in which one was entirely dependent on one's higher authorities for progress. The era of more placid operating environments and economic expansion driven by mass production lent itself to organizational forms that reinforced the notion that leadership was provided by the top official(s) and that leadership is what "comes out" of leaders.

Even so, researchers have noticed features of organizational life that are inconsistent with the idea that control and leadership is such a top-down process (e.g. Mechanic, 1962). An intriguing example is a study by Nancy Roberts (1985), which explored the contextual determinants of charisma. Her study showed how an executive who helped an organization respond successfully to a crisis came to be considered "charismatic," even though she had not been thought of in those terms before or in her subsequent positions. In a similar vein, contingency theorists approach a systems paradigm by recognizing that leadership is effective under certain conditions and not others (House & Baetz, 1979; Vroom & Jago, 1988).

Similarly, psychoanalytically inclined researchers have explored the impact of unconscious processes on the capacity of leaders to function (Hirschhorn, 1988; Kernberg, 1980). To "group-as-a-whole" theorists, the leader is just as much a creature of the group's collective emotions as is any other member (Wells, 1985). Because they are active targets for other members' projections of love, hate, responsibility, and blame, leaders are profoundly affected by their followers (Turquet, 1974).

The major "fault lines" in the heroic image of leadership, however, are appearing in connection with the shift to the postindustrial order. The new postindustrial economic order is leading to dramatic changes in individuals' relationships with their organizations and in the character of authority relations, creating pressures to re-examine the attribution of leadership exclusively to formal leaders.

At the center of this evolving drama is the critical need for organizations to adapt to continually fluctuating environments to compete globally. This change renders large centralized bureaucratic hierarchies obsolete and favors systems in which response capability resides in the outer boundaries as well as in the center. To adapt, organizations have had to relax their hierarchical control systems (Cohen & Bradford, 1989; Kotter, 1985) and decentralize aggressively. They have had to introduce work designs enabling workers at all levels to exercise informed judgement. They have had to appreciate that participation and group collaboration and central determinants of quality and effectiveness. As a result of these changes, managers face the erosion of their traditional sources of power—the hierarchical organization (Kanter, 1989a) and a monopoly on information (Zuboff, 1988).

The new, highly decentralized organization makes it much more difficult to maintain the notion that top officials are "in control" than did its predecessor—the pyramidal, centralized structure that is receding. The illusory dimensions of this image of leadership have been exposed by changing conditions. With increasingly participative systems in which workers at all levels are expected to take up their roles more authoritatively, it becomes harder to sustain the myth of the lonely hero on top or the more recent myth of the brave maverick who saves the bureaucratically moribund organization (Reich, 1985).

New forms of organization, adapted to the turbulent conditions of contemporary operating environments, seek to replace obedience and obligation with commitment and personal involvement in work (Walton, 1985). The keys to success in these settings are collaboration and participation rather than deployment and command (Hirschhorn, 1984, 1988; Weisbord, 1987). Asking members at all levels to bring these parts of themselves into their work roles amounts to a renegotiation of authority relations, and requires a recognition of the fundamental interdependence between leaders and followers to create effective enterprise leadership.

Understanding the changing social, political, and economic terrain and searching for ways to go about coping with the new conditions that will enable organizations to thrive and allow people to find meaningful work within them calls for a reconceptualization of the concept of leadership that differs from traditional approaches. One implication of the basic premise explored in this article is that a more pertinent and useful conceptualization of leadership will move away from focusing on the leader and toward a more complex appreciation of the variety of factors affecting leadership within a system.

In systems terms, leadership is a property of the overall system and stems from the ongoing process of interaction among the important elements of the system. From this perspective, leaders and followers mutually co-produce overall system leadership. What leaders do cannot be considered independent from, but interdependent with, what followers do. To understand leadership within a system, one must appreciate the impact of systemic relationships among various subsystems (including the personalities of the leaders) that are dynamically and hierarchically related on the overall leadership capacity of an enterprise.

These subsystems include intergroup processes, task systems, and administrative structures of the organization. For example, without an effective relationship between the administrative structure and the task, leaders are doomed to fail. This "fit" is thus a property of a system's leadership capacity. It is also a view of leadership that highlights the dependency of the formal leader on her or his followers (Krantz, 1989) and puts into sharp focus the way intergroup relations within an organization shape leaders' capacity to exercise authority. In other words, it places followership and leader-follower relationships squarely in the center of systemic leadership capacity.

Each of the three authors discussed in depth below are grappling with the contemporary dilemmas of leadership. They each articulate a complex understanding of leadership than encompasses both what we need from our leaders as persons as well as the contextual requirements for effective systemic leadership. Warren Bennis (1989) has written an updated companion book to his earlier classic, *The Unconscious Conspiracy* (1976), that presents the parameters of the current crisis in leadership. In *Making a Leadership Transition* (1989) and *Managing as a Performing Art* (1989), Tom Gilmore and Peter Vaill, respectively, offer their own viewpoints for ways out of this current dilemma.

All three authors span the worlds of both academic practice and organizational consultation. Both Bennis, who is in his 60s, and Vaill, now in his 50s, have held senior administrative positions. Gilmore, a consultant and researcher in his 40s, is a senior member of a private consulting firm. In their efforts to link theory with experience, these authors begin with the commonly held understanding of the context within which this leadership crisis has arisen—the rapid and profound turbulence in the social, economic, and technological environments. Organizations must now contend with vastly different conditions in which former approaches no longer apply, and which require that they develop the capacity to change, learn, and adapt quickly and decisively.

Against the background of this "permanent white water," to use Vaill's (1989) term, former approaches to management and leadership well suited to earlier times in which operating environments were more placid and predictable (Emery & Trist, 1973) are rendered dysfunctional. Each of the three books is aimed at understanding conditions that foster the development and effective exercise of leadership.

Before turning to these books in some detail, I wish to underscore some of the human consequences of change of this magnitude. As Rosabeth Moss Kanter (1989b) points out, the shadow side of autonomy, freedom, discretion, and authorization is the sense of loss of control and greatly increased uncertainty. Facing the enormous uncertainties involved in operating in today's business environment is painful and disturbing, especially for managers who have been trained to "avoid surprises" or instilled with the belief that management is supposed to "control uncertainty." The uncertainty and ambiguity at the heart of any change can lead to psychological defensiveness and interpersonal rigidity.

Studies have illustrated how resistance to change has been, in part, rooted in the fear of the uncertain (Menzies, 1961; Jaques, 1955). Now that change is constant, robust psychological defenses against this painful reality appear quite frequently (e.g. Krantz & Gilmore, 1990). The kind of anxiety-laden, frightening changes that organizations are being called on to accomplish lead to a wide range of responses, from the most primitive and fragmented efforts to establish omnipotent relations with others to the mature achievement of collaboration and mutually respectful dialogue.

Shifting the focus for understanding leadership capacity from the person of the leader alone to the context of leadership is likely to stir up massive anxiety. In practice, this sort of reorientation calls established modes of thinking and relating into question. When responsibility for leadership is distributed around the system, people have to relinquish some of the shared notions they have developed with respect to more hierarchical authority systems. These notions serve, in part, as socially maintained defenses against painful anxieties (Jaques, 1955; Hirschhorn, 1988; Menzies, 1988), and dismantling them may threaten members with emotional disarray.

The belief that the people on top are "in control" and responsible for everything can be gratifying, partly because it is reassuring to know that at least *somebody* is in control is this world. This belief also enables people to relinquish the burden of responsibility for the groups and social systems in which they work and live (Milgrim, 1965; Rioch, 1971). Equating leadership with leaders reflects this kind of dependency, for it locates excessive responsibility at the top. The tendency in groups to believe in the unrealistic power and knowledge of their leaders is what Bion (1959) termed Basic Assumption Dependency, one of the main unconscious strategies employed to bind the troubling anxieties that arise in work situations. For centralized, bureaucratic hierarchies in which authority and command are concentrated in the hands of a few, this may seem an adaptive defense because it aligns people unconsciously with the task system.

The changes discussed in this essay render these defenses maladaptive and require people to relinquish them so that they may participate meaningfully in the new kinds of settings being created. An increase in anxiety can be expected whenever established defenses are threatened, as can efforts to shore them up. One hypothesis I propose is that the current search for heroic leaders represents just such an effort. The dramatic contrast between institutional changes occurring that are undercutting comfortable dependencies on one hand and what seem like nearly desperate efforts to locate organizational saviors and heroic leaders on the other requires interpretation. Trying to solve our institutional malaise and leadership vacuum by looking for leaders constitutes, following the argument in this article, a flight from confronting the deeper issues of institutional transformation and, equally, a flight from creating a context in which leaders can lead. Specifically, I hypothesize that efforts to find and create leaders as if that alone will solve our leadership crisis is a defense against recognizing the type of context for leadership is needed.

Efforts to shore up the heroic leader myth persist, despite the nearly overwhelming evidence that it is ill suited to emerging postindustrial conditions. The creation of cultural icons—such as Lee Iacocca—and the explosion in compensation given to chief executive officers serve to maintain the deified aura around our leaders and to deny their essential dependency on subordinates. Other defensive postures in response to these issues are boosterism and inspirational direction (e.g., Peters & Waterman, 1982). The three authors reviewed in this article are struggling with tendencies toward immature, defensive approaches to leadership and are striving toward a conceptualization of what mature, effective leadership will comprise under current conditions.

THREE STUDIES OF LEADERSHIP

In *Why Leaders Can't Lead* Warren Bennis has written a sequel to *The Unconscious Conspiracy* that filters the same basic argument through the last ten years of history. This newer book also presents Bennis's characteristic insightfulness and incisive observation, but the outcome is strikingly different—it is darker, more despairing, and angrier.

What a dramatic difference from his early work, which described how the behavioral scientist was developing tools to humanize work organizations (cf. Bennis, 1963)! If the course of his writing is any gauge, the OD that was rooted in the 1960s and grew in a climate of social hope and optimism has been tempered by experience. Bennis's dismay, anger, and sense of betrayal reflect a bitter recognition of how limited the social technology has been in the face of broader cultural forces.

In *Why Leaders Can't Lead* he addresses these cultural forces and the ways they affect the unconscious conspiracy he first described in his earlier book. The "unconscious conspiracy" refers to the context of leadership and the conditions presented to leaders that disable them. This set of tacit arrangements establishes the cultural and operational parameters of organizational life and, in Bennis's view, prevents leaders from "taking charge and making change." The situation he describes is critical. The crisis of leadership Bennis is trying to understand is rooted in a more general social disarray: "The business world is turbulent. . . . The political world is in upheaval . . . The very fabric of our society is being unravelled. . . . and unprecedented cynicism toward possible solutions [prevails]" (p.xii).

The book begins with the story of a 48-year-old university president who killed himself in 1969, the day after he left his office. This story exemplifies the impossibly complex conditions facing today's leaders and the ways these competing pressures become expressed in the personal travails of those trying to manage them. In attempting to account for this tragic death, Bennis weaves a complex explanation that includes multiple levels of analysis—of personality, leadership style, the historic moment, institutional history, and organizational factors—illustrating how the coalescence of these factors contributed to human destruction.

The relationship between the leader and the institution that Bennis sculpts is complex and sensitive: We need leaders who care deeply about their institutions, yet that implies they are also vulnerable to what happens within them. Identifying with the institution puts one at risk of psychic damage when others do not care for or identify with the institution as well. When the leader makes a personal investment in the institution but others simply use it to further personal or political ends, he or she is at risk. From an organizational standpoint, Bennis's diagnosis is that the university failed to provide sufficient mechanisms of protection and cushioning for the president.

High-quality leaders, he feels, withdraw from leadership positions because they are exposed and vulnerable to these destructive processes. The unconscious conspiracy produces "simply ridiculous" situations in which leaders are involved in and subjected to impossible situations, double-binding politics, and paralyzing conflicts. Bennis feels that leaders need to be passionately committed to quality and to people, and they must be allowed to express these aspects of themselves, without subjecting themselves to unmodulated destructiveness.

As to the question of whether leadership is in the person or in the context, Bennis's answer is "both": This polarity must be retained, or else understanding leadership will be impossible. To this Bennis adds a third component—the environment within which this dialectical accommodation between person and organization must be achieved.

He then paints a disturbing picture of a world in serious decline, in which we adapt to the compelling logic of mass markets by becoming shallow conformists and alienated consumers. Bennis depicts the current conditions within which institutions operate with a grim and acerbic brush. The central themes revolve around the pervasive narcissism in society that leads people to put their own ambitions above loyalty to institutions and above commitment to purposes beyond the self. In stark contrast to the 1960s, which Bennis recalls as a time of purpose and vision, now there is no social hope to rally around, nor any sense of shared values that serve as beacons. Bennis sees the organizational consequences of these societal developments—the idolatry of celebrity executives, the short-term bottom line obsessions that blind managers to the true importance of human resources, the willful distortion of reality to promote selfish interests, and the unbridled greed of the 1980s—as contributing profoundly to the unconscious conspiracy against leadership.

The primary hopeful note Bennis strikes is that the contemporary era is one of constant change. This holds out the possibility that changes will occur to reverse some of these trends that are draining the meaning out of life and sterilizing people's relatedness with their organizations. Maintaining the person-context tension to the very end, Bennis calls for special people of virtue to lead us out of this wilderness of materialism and isolated self-interest, people who can be trusted and can convince us to trust them. At the same time, he recognizes the deep-seated countervailing forces against innovation and creativity that reside in any established system of norms and interests, forces that work to neutralize their potential contributions.

In the end, he seems to feel that leadership can be exercised only by the self-actualized in today's world, whose sheer complexity and turbulence derail any but the most directed, purposeful leaders. In keeping with the dialectical tension throughout his book, he also recognizes that leaders alone cannot save us from the crisis he describes. We must also create institutions that let them lead.

In *Making a Leadership Change* (1989), Tom Gilmore takes a more hopeful stance in relation to the crisis in leadership. Gilmore stands for the idea of "working through." His appeal calls for responding to emergent postindustrial conditions adaptively through improved methods of leadership change, selection, and empowerment that take into account the increasingly complex set of factors impinging on successful leadership.

His argument serves as a counterpoint to calls for radical discontinuity or to appeals for epistemological transformation, which characterize Vaill's book (discussed below). From Gilmore's vantage point, the call for a radically altered mind-set or cultural paradigm can be understood as a form of magical thinking or a longing for a messianic vision or construct. His proposal is more sober: We must improve our ways of changing, finding, enabling, and replacing leaders if we are to develop the leadership that our organizations so desperately need.

Underlying his detailed and thoughtful presentation of a model for leadership transition is the enormously important idea that times of change provide perhaps the richest of all earning opportunities. In Gilmore's view, transitions are moments when crucial issues are grappled with, and when organizations enact their implicit theories in ways that make them more accessible than usual. In other words, if handled with self-awareness, leadership transitions are opportunities both for finding good leaders *and* for enhancing the organization's ability to enable its leaders by articulating, refining, and clarifying its purposes and priorities. Doing so depends on incorporating authentic self-review and careful thought into the process.

Gilmore begins with his own formulation of the crisis of leadership: "As our world becomes more complex, pluralistic, and interdependent, and as the pace of change quickens, we become increasingly dependent on authentic leaders" (p. 3). At the same time, unfortunately, these same factors both reduce the tenure of top executives and make them more vulnerable to competing and impairing demands. Leadership transitions become more frequent, and the "process costs" of leadership increase.

Yet transitions also afford the opportunity for important improvements in the organization and in its ability to bring in the sort of leadership it needs. Gilmore takes the reader through each step of a leadership transition: determining the organization's needs, developing a profile and expectations of the new leader, searching for and hiring a candidate, and coping with acting leaders and lame ducks in the interim. He discusses, also in illuminating detail, what new leaders must do to join with their organizations in meaningful and effective ways. This involves addressing the lingering impact of the predecessor, building alliances with the existing staff and building a new management team, incorporating an authentic new vision into the organization, managing the "inevitable reorganization" effectively, and preparing the organization for future transitions.

For the purposes of this article on leadership, what stands out is Gilmore's complex appreciation of the demands of leadership in postindustrial settings and an equally complex appreciation of the contemporary challenge of transition. This comes across primarily in two areas.

First, Gilmore recognizes the role of irrational forces in the exercise of leadership and authority. Of course, the irrational has always been a major factor in the exercise of authority. Now, however, the irrational is impinging upon and suffusing organizational dynamics to a far greater degree than before. Effective systemic leadership must find ways of working to harness its creative potential to the task.

By taking irrational forces into account, and by appreciating the impact of anxieties elicited in the course of leadership succession, Gilmore offers a sophisticated treatment of this daunting moment in an organization's life. At every step, he proposes the use of structures to bind the inevitable anxieties that arise and to preserve the all-important capacity for dialogue and reflection. As for the positive aspects of irrationality, Gilmore similarly argues for structures and social technology that enable new values, beliefs, and purposes to emerge and to be linked with organizational needs. Commitment is a more mature expression of irrationality than obedience, to be sure, but it depends on finding a way to link personal values to organizational purposes. Again, the conceptual movement is toward context and its enabling features.

Second, his image of leadership captures the evolving nature of authority. No longer can the leader command and direct as in earlier times of highly centralized hierarchical bureaucracies. Gilmore's emphasis on team building, forming alliances and networks, and working through collaboration all speak to the ways in which the nature of authority relations are changing. Paradoxically, this development de-emphasizes the person of the leader—with respect to the image of the commander or heroic warrior—and emphasizes the importance of leaders who work with and through people. His view of modern organizations is largely antithetic to charismatic leaders, for although Gilmore argues that organizations are increasingly dependent on effective leaders, he also says that leaders are increasingly dependent on their organizations to match them with their roles and enable them to work. Charisma breeds the sort of dependency that undermines an organization's ability to manage transitions effectively.

In *Managing as a Performing Art* (1989), Peter Vaill offers yet another perspective on the crisis in leadership, a viewpoint that calls into question the underlying world views that guide thinking on leadership and organizations. Instead of working through and refining our adaptive capacities, he suggests that we require nothing less than a transformation of our ways of thinking and understanding to meet the current challenges.

Vaill's understanding also centers on the state of dynamic fluctuation and turbulence that now characterizes the world. His concern with the implications of this situation lead him to explore the new emergent meanings of leadership, the sort of personal development required of people who lead, and the underlying philosophies of knowledge and action that support this development. As do Bennis and Gilmore, he focuses throughout on the dynamic interplay between person and context.

Vaill's metaphor for the new circumstances within which leaders and managers must operate is "permanent white water," a condition in which little can be taken for granted. He is speaking of a "revolution of the total situation" involving "not just new kinds of problems and opportunities that we are facing, but whole new contexts within which these problems and opportunities reside" (p. 2). Vaill does not say that we must now learn how to live within a newly configured context, as if in a Lewinian sense the situation will become "refrozen" after a systemic realignment. Rather, Vaill believes that contexts themselves have become destabilized. Because we orient ourselves to our contexts, the emergence of continuously shifting contexts presents major problems, one of which is that you can never completely know what your problems are.

Given this, the challenge for personal adaptation is no longer that of finding one's way within a context, but that of learning how to continuously learn emergent contexts. Thinking about this requires bumping our attention up a level to face the epistemological questions of how we know things rather than what we know. In other words, Vaill steers us toward what Bateson (1972) calls "deutero-learning," which refers to the capacity to learn how to learn (a new context). In Vaill's view, because managers work in a world of constant chaos, our existing paradigms of management and organization are inadequate. The new conditions call for abilities and attitudes that cannot be accommodated within the categories engendered by conventional paradigms. From this perspective, our paradigms are losing their relevance, and we must adopt new paradigms suited to the tumultuous, unpredictable world.

Vaill's critique of existing attitudes is multifaceted and spans our attitudes from the "micro" theories we hold about ourselves to the broader ideas we hold about the nature of organizations, authority, and the environments in which they operate. One common theme throughout concerns the ways our habits of thought tend to create our understanding of the world in which our selves and our consciousness are separated from our behavior, our goals, and our immediate contexts. For example, his critique of the theories of management based on competency notions is that these presume that managerial competency can be meaningfully understood apart from the whole person who exercises it. In the process of abstracting those bits of the person identified as a "competency," other elements that inform and give these "competencies" their meaning and potency are obliterated. The same type of argument can be applied to thinking about management as a set of functions, as if functions have any real meaning apart from the consciousness or context underlying the functioning.

Action taking involves the whole person; efforts to divide action taking into abstract, reified segments prevent us from recognizing some of the deepest and most profound sources of human creativity and effectiveness. According to Vaill, in the contemporary situation it is these elements of ourselves that we must locate and call on in order to navigate the white water.

Vaill also disputes the cherished belief in techniques or methods as ways of reaching goals. Dependence on techniques, which he terms "technoholism," presumes a stable context. The belief that following a specific sequence of steps or plan of action will produce a predictable outcome assumes that contingencies will not render the plan irrelevant. One way managers and leaders protect themselves from confronting the contingent nature of their work is by rigidly adhering to techniques and plans.

On the cultural level, Vaill sees parallel forces that lead to the denial of the deeper dimensions of human relatedness and meaning. Superficial "models of man" predominate in the social sciences and organizational practice. The commonly held, tacit understanding that binds people to a common organizational purpose and meaning are under attack from what he calls the "dialexic" impulse to comment on and expose everything. A perversion of self-reflection and introspection, "dialexic" mentality destroys cultural bonds and shared meaning. As cultural bonds weaken, people are thrown back onto themselves and their own personal interests, and this leads inevitably to alienation and the sense of purposelessness so characteristic of today's world.

Vaill's hope is that people can reintegrate themselves—reintegrate thought and action, intention and unconscious modes, the logical and nonlogical, behavior and consciousness—and thus enable themselves to engage holistically with the perplexing world they face. The kind of knowledge required to operate in the world Vaill pictures cannot be abstracted from past practices or based on proven methods. To operate under white water conditions of shifting contexts, one must depend on knowledge synthesized through complex, often nonrational means. This requires bringing all aspects of the self to the role. Unlike Bennis, Vaill does not consider the personal vulnerability that results from such a stance.

Established paradigms attempt to promote understanding of phenomena by breaking them into component parts. The synthetic or systems views that Vaill advocates do the opposite. One consequence of the atomistic approach is the creation of dualities and polarities that, when viewed from a broader perspective, appear as paradoxes. Vaill argues that paradox ought to be sought out and embraced, as a kind of bridging mechanism from the established framework into this more whole viewpoint. Along the way, numerous myths about authority, hierarchy, and organization are relinquished—not the least of which is that control is exercised through a pyramidal chain of command. For Vaill, organizational control arises from meaningful relatedness, from the development of common purposes, and from the bonding of shared commitment. Achieving this sense of collective purpose within the shifting contexts of white water depends on the articulation of and commitment to values. Because goals cannot be specified, values provide the only effective form of guidance. He goes so far as to say, "Leadership and management in the turbulent modern organization *are* values clarification" (p. 55, emphasis mine).

It is in the embracing of public, shared values that the person of the leader and the context of leadership come together for Vaill. To achieve this type of atunement to the unpredictable, novel context as it unfolds in the moment, Vaill believes that the leader's values, spiritual and otherwise, must serve as the primary organizing principle for action. Similarly, to achieve high performance and strategic clarity in the modern environment, organizations must organize themselves around economic, technological, communal, sociopolitical, and spiritual values. This brings the nonrational to the heart of management practice.

Vaill's image of the effective leader in today's organization is anything but the proficient technician or commanding presence. He likens the effective exercise of leadership to artistic performance, a kind of synthetic, harmonious immediacy. The leader is profoundly connected with his or her ensemble:

> . . . expressiveness . . . is more important than mere technical competence with the tools, actions, and traditions of the art and a mentality that is friendly to paradox will practice influence and control as an emanation of a growing, dawning comprehension of what is going on and of what is needed. (p. 124)

Because the writers discussed above have arisen in the same historical moment, their ideas are woven from commonly shared strands of experience. Several underlying themes, or subtexts, emerge. To complement the two already discussed—the need to consider the context of leadership (rather than leaders per se) in understanding the leadership crisis and the changing character of authority relations—three related subtexts emerging in the domain of organizational scholarship are addressed below.

THE INCREASING PROMINENCE OF IRRATIONALITY

Increasingly, leaders must contend with irrationality as the source of both destructiveness and creativity. Stable organizational arrangements are used by members to contain and manage the anxieties evoked by membership in groups and organizations (Menzies, 1961). The increasing pace of social, economic, and organizational change leads to a continual destabilization of boundaries and loss of established ways of containing anxiety (Hirschhorn, 1988). Heightened anxiety manifests itself as irrational group and individual behavior. In addition, the increased interdependence among subsystems eliminates buffers and prevents the containment of irrationality within subsystems, leading to more fluid parallel processes (Alderfer, 1984; Smith, 1989).

At the same time, the nonrational or irrational (I use the terms interchangeably here) is also a source of hope. If the emerging literature is any guide, then the issues of vision, purpose, and meaning are pivotal for developing leadership capacity in modern enterprises. These, too, are rooted in the irrational sphere, grounded in the realms of meaning, belief, value, and subjectivity. As the importance of things such as commitment, involvement, and creativity increase, then leaders will increasingly be called upon to embrace the irrational in constructive ways.

The emergent notion of organizational effectiveness and personal competence is one in which people link organizational purposes and missions with their personal value systems. One function of leadership is to help members make these connections. Because creativity, inspiration, and imaginativeness all reside in the irrational strata of the human mind, aligning the irrational dimension of peoples' functioning with their tasks and roles has become a prerequisite of high performing systems.

Similarly, functioning as an effective leader in today's chaotic environment requires that leaders be able to draw more readily on their own nonrational capabilities. The loss of "road maps" from past experience or proven techniques requires leaders to draw on their intuitive abilities to synthesize the complex information confronting them. A heightened receptivity to the unconscious and irrational spheres of organizational life depends on the ability to tolerate being vulnerable to often uncomfortable or frightening experiences. This amounts to a call for leaders with a high degree of personal integration and maturity, which stems from a recognition that the extraordinarily powerful social and psychological forces with which they must contend can easily derail the more fragile or rigid psyche. Without stable structures to rely on, leaders will have to draw on their inner resources to a far greater degree than before.

The Weberian legacy in organizational theory and managerial practice is increasingly becoming a liability in this respect. Certainly, organizations aim to relate means to ends rationally. But the normative orientation that devalues the irrational and "feeling-full" aspects of organizational membership[3] will attract people ill suited for modern settings (Kern, 1989), and will reinforce constricting norms that inhibit the kind of spirited, creative spontaneity required.

NARCISSISM IN THE MODERN AGE

Since the mid-century, psychoanalysts have been discovering a shift in common patterns of psychological functioning. Freud and his immediate followers discovered a type of incapacitating guilt, anxiety, phobia, and obsession that contemporary psychoanalysts see less and less. Today, they increasingly find people grappling with a lack of feeling, an inner emptiness, and a deep sense of frustration and unfulfillment.

The emergence of narcissism has a profound impact on the nature of organizational life and the exercise of leadership. Narcissism refers to a constellation of character traits centering around a particular relation of the self to the world. It refers to both a psychological and cultural condition. On the individual level, it refers to aspects of personality characterized by exaggerated investment in one's own image and interests. Narcissism is expressed by the untempered ambition and greed so common today, and by an attendant sense of isolation and detachment. It also refers to an unconscious exploitativenss and manipulativeness toward others, which involves a diminished concern for the social, for the other, and for community.

The impact of contemporary narcissism on our cultural and social life has been explored by various writers (e.g. Lasch, 1979; Lawrence, 1979). Some have written about excessive narcissism in leaders themselves (Horowitz & Arthur, 1988; Kets de Vries & Miller, 1985; Kernberg, 1980a, b), describing the corrosive impact on subordinate staff members of their striving for power and admiration.

There is equally good reason for concern about how this development erodes the domain in which leadership may be exercised. A central characteristic of narcissistic functioning is the difficulty in finding meaning and purpose outside of the self and beyond instrumental self-interest. In particular, it involves the use of work roles to seek power and prestige rather than meaningful activity through commitment to the task or to the ideals represented by the functions carried out by the institution. Although Bennis is most articulate and alarmed by an "everyone-for-him- or herself climate" in which people "rank their fealty to their own ambitions above any loyalty to the" organization (p. 63), Vaill and Gilmore also grapple with the attenuated connection to task and purpose that pervades modern organizations. Each recognizes that effective leadership depends on a context of followership in which people are related meaningfully to their work. Otherwise, a leader's "vision" cannot motivate anyone or coalesce activity.

The emergence of narcissism in society poses a severe problem for leaders and for the development of leadership capacity in institutions. Recognizing its profound impact on organizational membership leads to an additional hypothesis about the widespread call for leaders who can provide purpose and direction. Are we tacitly asking our leaders to provide this very sense of meaning and purpose, to enable people to experience commitment and involvement, and to help people overcome the sense of unconnected detachment from higher purposes? If so, then we are surely asking too much of them, and the tacit request is part of the unconscious conspiracy Bennis warns us about: By expecting the unexpectable of our leaders, we render them ineffective. Narcissism is a cultural problem; looking to our organizational leaders to compensate for it dooms them to failure.

MANAGING INTERGROUP RELATIONS IN CHAOTIC ENVIRONMENTS

The denser interdependencies and heightened adaptive challenges require increasingly sophisticated collaboration. More and more work is vested in teams and groups to accommodate greater complexity and draw upon collective problem-solving capacities (Weisbord, 1987). One function of organizational leadership is to foster this collaboration. But is "vision" enough to provide a facilitating medium?

Paradoxically, just as the need for robust and creative collaboration is increasing throughout organizations, the rising levels of diversity in the work force pose major barriers to achieving it.[4] Homogeneous work groups have the advantage of sharing tacit codes of communication and understanding. Although this can promote group blindness, it can also foster clear communication and understanding. With the introduction of women and nonwhite men into many levels of organizations, there is inevitably a fragmentation of the "world views" and cultural assumptions operating. Intergroup relationships as they are imported into work groups through their racial, ethnic, and gender-specific representatives pose an important challenge for leadership.

Similarly, the increased interdependence among functional, specialist, and regional work groups places a premium on another type of intergroup relationship. Leadership is faced with the need to oversee wide cultural, epistemological, and instrumental differences among groups. Failed collaboration among groups—for both identity groups and work groups—leads to heightened destructive irrationality. Genuine dialogue across these boundaries can produce creativity and enrichment.

It is unlikely that "vision" will be enough to forge these critical links across the perceptual and cultural gulfs these intergroup relationships represent. I expect that an increasingly essential component of leadership—whether this is exercised by formal leaders or others—will be the ability to manage intergroup processes and to promote negotiated understanding of shared tasks. My final hypothesis is that the emphasis on "vision" and "direction" is, at times, used in the hope that inspiration can be mobilized to avoid the complex and frightening issues raised by the increased work force diversity and subsystem interdependence in postindustrial settings.

CONCLUSION

The emerging consensus that effective leadership involves setting directions and providing vision is clearly grounded in the need for organizations to adapt continuously to changing, unstable environments. This essay has attempted to explore both the constructive aspects of this emerging consensus as well as the defensive uses of the search for visionary leaders.

Although the search for leaders who are passionately committed to a vision and who provide direction to their organizations is essential in this environment, it also lends itself to new forms of debilitating dependency and to a longing for saviors. Moving away from an excessive emphasis on formal leaders to a broader focus on the context of leadership renders visible the impact of a wider range of features—such as followership, structure, and intergroup relations—on systemic leadership capacity. Hoping for transformational leaders (Burns, 1978) or their "visions" to rescue us from the cultural malaise of narcissism, from the increasing need to exercise authority and judgement at all levels of organization, or from the unsettling confrontation with inter-group phenomena will undoubtedly perpetuate the crisis in leadership in our modern society.

One thing appears certain. The confusion, the accelerating rate of change, the breakdown in familiar boundaries, and the shifting contexts characteristic of organizational life will continue to put established patterns and ways of experiencing into disarray. Yet however discomforting and frightening they may be, in anxiety and disarray lie the seeds of change.

NOTES

1 Theoretically, the field of organizational research can be appreciated as a subsystem within the larger system of the field of organizations and management. As such, our field is in an isomorphic relationship with its larger enveloping system. The concept of isomorphy holds that the dynamics of any subsystem within a relevant system are defined by constructs that are similar in structure and function (von Bertalanfy, 1969). Thus, one could predict that the observer and what is observed will manifest parallel features.

2 The 1974 *Handbook of Leadership* referred to 3,000 studies performed from 1902 to 1967. The updated *Handbook* published seven years later (1981) reported that the number surpassed 5,000 (see Kets de Vries, 1985).

3 For example, Weber (1958) states that as bureaucracy "is developed the more perfectly [it] is 'dehumanized,' the more completely it succeeds in elimination from official business love, hatred, and all purely personal, irrational, and emotional elements" (pp. 215–216).

4 According to *Workforce 2000: Work and Workers for the 21st Century* (Johnston & Packer, 1987), by the year 2000 less than half of the work force will consist of white men.

REFERENCES

Alderfer, C. (1984). An intergroup perspective on group dynamics. In J. Lorsch (Ed.), *Handbook of organizational behavior.* Englewood Cliffs, NJ: Prentice-Hall.

Barnard, C. (1938). *The functions of the executive.* Cambridge, MA: Harvard University Press.

Bass, B. (1981). *Stogdill's handbook of leadership* (rev. ed.). New York: Free Press.

Bateson, G. (1972). *Steps to an ecology of mind.* New York: Random House.

Bennis, W. (1963). Effecting organizational change: A new role for the behavioral scientist: Effecting organizational change. *Administrative Science Quarterly, 8,* 125–168.

Bennis, W. (1976). *The unconscious conspiracy: Why leaders can't lead.* New York: AMACOM.

Bennis, W. (1989). *Why leaders can't lead: The unconscious conspiracy continues.* San Francisco: Jossey-Bass.

Bennis, W., & Nanus, B. (1985). *Leaders: The strategies for taking charge.* New York: Harper & Row.

Bion, W. (1959). *Experiences in groups and other papers.* New York: Basic Books.

Burns, J. M. (1978). *Leadership.* New York: Harper & Row.

Cohen, A., & Bradford, D. (1989). *Influence without authority.* New York: Wiley.

Emery, F., & Trist, E. (1973). *Toward a social ecology.* New York: Plenum.

Gilmore, T. (1989). *Making a leadership change.* San Francisco: Jossey-Bass.

Hirschhorn, L. (1984). *Beyond mechanization: Work and technology in a postindustrial age.* Cambridge, MA: MIT Press.

Hirschhorn, L. (1988). *The workplace within.* Cambridge, MA: MIT Press.

Horowitz, M., & Arthur, R. (1988). Narcissistic rage in leaders: The intersection of individual dynamics and group process. *The International Journal of Social Psychiatry, 34*(2), 135–141.

House, R., & Baetz, M. (1979). Leadership: Some empirical generalizations and new research directions. *Research in Organizational Behavior, 1,* 341–423.

Jacques, E. (1955). Social systems as a defense against persecutory and depressive anxiety. In M. Klein, P. Heimann, & R. Money-Kyrle (Eds.), *New directions in psychoanalysis.* London: Tavistock.

Johnston, W. B., & Packer, A. H. (1987). *Workforce 2000: Work and workers for the 21st century.* Indianapolis, IN: Hudson Institute.

Kanter, R. M. (1989a, November-December). The new managerial work. *Harvard Business Review,* pp. 85–92.

Kanter, R. M. (1989b). *When giants learn to dance—Mastering the challenges of strategy, management, and careers in the 1990s.* New York: Simon and Schuster.

Kern, J. (1989). *Gender, power, and authority in the bureaucracy: An examination of male supervisor-female subordinate professional relationships.* Unpublished manuscript.

Kernberg, O. (1980a). Organizational regression. In O. Kernberg, *Internal world and external reality.* New York: Jason Aronson.

Kernberg, O. (1980b). Regressive effects of pathology in leaders. In O. Kernberg, *Internal world and external reality.* New York: Jason Aronson.

Kets de Vries, M., & Miller, D. (1985). Narcissism and leadership: An object relations perspective. *Human Relations, 38*(6), 583–601.

Kotter, J. (1985). *Power and influence: Beyond formal authority.* New York: Free Press.

Krantz, J. (1989). The managerial couple: The superior-subordinate dyad as a unit of analysis. *Human Resource Management, 28*(2), 161–176.

Krantz, J., & Gilmore, T. (1990). The splitting of leadership and management as a social defense. *Human Relations, 43*(2), 183–204.

Lasch, C. (1979). *The culture of narcissism.* New York: W. W. Norton.

Lawrence, G. (1979). A concept for today: The management of oneself in role. In G. Lawrence (Ed.), *Exploring individual and organizational boundaries.* London: Wiley.

Leavitt, H. (1986). *Corporate pathfinders.* Homewood, IL: Dow Jones-Irwin.

Mechanic, D. (1962). Sources of power of lower participants in complex organizations. *Administrative Science Quarterly, 7*(2), 349–364.

Menzies, I. (1961). A case-study in the functioning of social systems as a defense against anxiety. *Human Relations, 13,* 95–121.

Menzies, I. (1988). A psychoanalytic perspective on social institutions. In E. Spillius (Ed.), *Melanie Klein today.* London: Routledge.

Milgrim, S. (1965). Some conditions of obedience and disobedience to authority. *Human Relations, 18*(1), 57–76.

Peters, T., & Waterman, P. (1982). *In search of excellence.* New York: Harper & Row.

Reich, R. (1985, May 13). The executive's new clothes. *The New Republic,* pp. 23–28.

Rioch, M. (1971). "All we like sheep" (Isaiah 53:6): Followers and leaders. *Psychiatry, 34,* 258–273.

Roberts, N. (1985). Transforming leadership: A process of collective action. *Human Relations, 38*(11), 1023–1046.

Sashkin, M. (1988). The visionary leader: A new theory of organizational leadership. In J. A. Conger & R. N. Kanungo (Eds.), *Charismatic leadership in management.* San Francisco: Jossey-Bass.

Selznik, P. (1957). *Leadership in administration.* New York: Harper & Row.

Smith, K. (1989). The movement of conflict in organizations: The joint dynamics of splitting and triangulation. *Administrative Science Quarterly, 34*(1), 1–20.

Trist, E. (1976). Critique of scientific management in terms of socio-technical theory. In M. Weir (Ed.), *Job satisfaction.* Glasgow: Fontana/Collins.

Turquet, P. (1974). Leadership: The individual and the group. In G. Gibbard, R. Hartmann, & J. Mann, (Eds.), *Analysis of groups.* San Francisco: Jossey-Bass.

Vaill, P. B. (1989). *Managing as a performing art.* San Francisco: Jossey-Bass.

Van Fleet, D. D., & Yukl, G. A. (1989). A century of leadership research. In W. Rosenbach & R. Taylor (Eds.), *Contemporary issues in leadership.* Boulder, CO: Westview Press.

von Bertalanffy, L. (1969). *General systems* (rev. ed.). New York: George Braziler.

Vroom, V., & Jago, A. G. (1988). *The new leadership: Managing participation in organizations.* Englewood Cliff, NJ: Prentice-Hall.

Walton, R. E. (1985). From control to commitment in the workplace. *Harvard Business Review, 63*(2), 77–84.

Weber, M. (1958). *From Max Weber: Essays in sociology* (H. Gerth & C. Wright Mills, Eds.). New York: Oxford University Press.

Weisbord, M. R. (1987). *Productive workplaces: Organizing and managing for dignity, meaning, and community.* San Francisco: Jossey-Bass.

Wells, L., Jr. (1985). The group-as-a-whole perspective and its theoretical roots. In A. Colman & M. Geller (Eds.), *Group Relations Reader* (Vol. 2). Washington, DC: A. K. Rice Institute.

Zaleznick, A. (1978, spring). Managers and leaders: Does it make a difference? *McKinsey Quarterly Review,* pp. 2–22.

Zaleznick, A. (1989). *The managerial mystique.* New York: Harper & Row.

Zuboff, S. (1988). *In the age of the smart machine.* New York: Basic Books.

The Dark Side of Leadership

Jay A. Conger

In recent years, business leaders have gained great popularity: Lee Iaccoca and Steven Jobs, for example, have stepped into the limelight as agents of change and entrepreneurship. But though we tend to think of the positive outcomes associated with leaders, certain risks or liabilities are also entailed. The very behaviors that distinguish leaders from managers also have the potential to produce problematic or even disastrous outcomes for their organizations. For example, when a leader's behaviors become exaggerated, lose touch with reality, or become vehicles for purely personal gain, they may harm the leader and the organization.

How do leaders produce such negative outcomes—and why? Three particular skill areas can contribute to such problems. These include leaders' strategic vision, their communications and impression-management skills, and their general management practices. We will examine each to discover its darker side.

PROBLEMS WITH THE VISIONARY LEADER

As we know, the 1970s and 1980s brought tremendous changes in the world's competitive business environment. Previously successful organizations that had grown huge and bureaucratic were suddenly faced with pressures to innovate and alter their ways. Out of these turbulent times came a new breed of business leader: the strategic visionary. These men and women, like Ross Perot of Electronic Data Systems and Mary Kay Ash of Mary Kay Cosmetics, possessed a twofold ability: to foresee market opportunities and to craft organizational strategies that captured these opportunities in ways that were personally meaningful to employees. When their success stories spread, "vision" became the byword of the 1980s. Yet though many of these leaders led their organizations on to great successes, others led their organizations on to great failures. The very qualities that distinguished the visionary leader contained the potential for disaster.

Generally speaking, unsuccessful strategic visions can often be traced to the inclusion of the leaders' personal aims that did not match their constituents' needs. For example, leaders might substitute personal goals for what should be shared organizational goals. They might construct an organizational vision that is essentially a monument to themselves and therefore something quite different from the actual wishes of their organizations or customers.

Moreover, the blind drive to create this very personal vision could result in an inability to see problems and opportunities in the environment. Thomas Edison, for example, so passionately believed in the future of direct electrical current (DC) for urban power grids that he failed to see the more rapid acceptance of alternating power (AC) systems by America's then-emerging utility companies. Thus the company started by

Edison to produce DC power stations was soon doomed to failure. He became so enamoured of his own ideas that he failed to see competing and, ultimately, more successful ideas.

In addition, such personal visions encourage the leader to expend enormous amounts of energy, passion, and resources on getting them off the ground. The higher their commitment, the less willing they are to see the viability of competing approaches. Because of the leader's commitment, the organization's investment is also likely to be far greater in such cases. Failure therefore will have more serious consequences.

Fundamental errors in the leader's perceptions can also lead to a failed vision. Common problems include (1) an inability to detect important changes in markets (e.g., competitive, technological, or consumer needs); (2) a failure to accurately assess and obtain the necessary resources for the vision's accomplishment; and (3) a misreading or exaggerated sense of the needs of markets or constituents. For example, with a few exceptions like the Chrysler minivan, Lee Iacocca inaccurately believed that automobile style rather than engineering was the primary concern of automotive buyers. At Chrysler, he relied on new body styles and his charisma to market cars built on an aging chasis (the K car) developed in the later 1970s. The end result was that, after several initial years of successful sales, Chrysler's sales plunged 22.8% in 1987. Today, the future of Chrysler looks equally cloudy.

Ultimately, then, the success of a leader's strategic vision depends on a realistic assessment of both the opportunities and the constraints in the organization's environment and a sensitivity to constituent's needs. If the leader loses sight of reality or loses touch with constituents, the vision becomes a liability. Visions may fail for a wide variety of reasons; Exhibit 1 outlines some of the more significant ones. We will examine several of these categories and illustrate them with the experience of some prominent business leaders.

Making the Leader's Personal Needs Paramount

As mentioned, one of the most serious liabilities of a visionary leader occurs when he or she projects purely personal needs and beliefs onto those of constituents. A common example is the inventor with a pet idea who acquires sufficient resources to initiate a venture that fails to meet the market's needs. When a leader's needs and wishes diverge from those of constituents, the consequences can be quite costly. Consider, for example, Edwin Land, inventor of the Polaroid camera. Dr. Land's experiences with a

EXHIBIT 1
The sources of failed vision.

The vision reflects the internal needs of leaders rather than those of the market or constituents.
The resources needed to achieve vision have been seriously miscalculated.
An unrealistic assessment or distorted perception of market and constituent needs holds sway.
A failure to recognize environmental changes prevents redirection of the vision.

camera he developed called the SX-70 illustrate how a leader can get sidetracked by his own personal goals.

As we know, Land's company, Polaroid, held a monopoly on the instant photography market for some three decades and became the household word for such cameras. Throughout the 1960s and 1970s, Polaroid's sales climbed with astonishing speed. By 1973, four million of the company's Colorpack cameras were being sold annually at $30 a piece. But Dr. Land was not content. His dream was to create what he called "absolute one-step photography"; the SX-70 camera was to embody his dream. "Photography will never be the same . . . With the gargantuan effort of bringing SX-70 into being, the company has come fully of age," Land remarked on the day of the camera's inauguration.

In setting the parameters for his new vision, Land outlined several demanding criteria: The camera was to be totally automatic and would have to fold to fit into a purse or pocket, possess a single-lens reflex-viewing system, and focus from less than a foot to infinity. It was to be a radically new design, making earlier versions of instant photography obsolete.

The SX-70 also represented a major strategic shift for the company. Before its advent, the manufacturing of Polaroid products, especially films, was subcontracted to outsiders. Plant and equipment were usually leased or rented. But Land's dream of the SX-70 required total integration of the company. A color-negative and camera-assembly plant were designed and built, and the company's existing chemical production and films-packaging facilities were expanded.

Although the total cost of the SX-70 strategy was never formally disclosed, Land responded in an interview that it was a half-billion-dollar investment. Other estimates have put it higher. In any case, the SX-70 was a design masterpiece. It was estimated that the reflex-viewing system cost millions of dollars and required more than two-and-a-half years of engineering effort. Engineering for the eyepiece alone cost $2 million.

Land's expectations of the camera's success were as lavish as his investment in the camera. At $180 per camera, company projections were that first-year sales would reach several million. By some accounts, sales of 5,000,000 units were predicted. Yet despite such optimism, the camera met with only limited public support. By the end of its first year in 1973, only 470,000 SX-70 cameras had been sold. It would take several years, many design changes, and significant price cuts before the camera would gain widespread market acceptance—all at the cost of sacrificing many of the camera's original features. Land's personal vision of the instant camera had missed what the market wanted.

Most important, in his quest for the perfect instant camera he had failed to take into account lessons that his company had already learned about consumers' needs. Before the SX-70, Polaroid's experience with both its black-and-white and its color cameras was that demand was intimately tied to price. Consumers wanted an inexpensive, easy-to-use, instant camera. Their foremost desire was not a perfect picture but a relatively good instant picture at a low price.

In the 1960s, the marketplace had powerfully demonstrated its needs to Polaroid after the company first introduced its color system in 1963. When the Colorpack cameras priced at $100 met with only limited market interest, Polaroid introduced a version at $75 and, by 1969, a $30 Colorpack. At the $30 price level, volume dramatically expanded, and 4,000,000 units were sold by 1973. Consumers wanted instant photography but only at an inexpensive price. So how could 5,000,000 SX-70s at $180 a piece be sold when only 4,000,000 Colorpack cameras had been sold at $30 each? Clearly they could not. Dr. Land's vision was a personal ideal, one that was not shared by consumers at a price of $180 per camera.

What happened to Land that he failed to learn from the past? There are several possible explanations. For one, his initial vision of instant photography had been correct; people really did want instant photographs. This initial success, however, may have convinced him of the invincibility of his ideas. Second, Land was an engineer at heart; he loved the technology more than the marketing of the product. His very background made him product- and technology-driven, not so much marketplace-driven. Finally and most important, I believe that Land, like other leaders, came to identify with his vision to an unhealthy extreme: The vision personified him.

A similar example is seen in Henry Ford, who was willing to build a Model T of any color as long as it was black. The vision in essence becomes so much a part of the leader's personality that he or she is unwilling or unable to consider information to the contrary from staff members or from the marketplace. Convinced by past successes of their invincibility, such leaders plow ahead without considering other viewpoints—a sure course toward failure.

Becoming a "Pyrrhic Victor"

In the quest to achieve a vision, a leader may be so driven as to ignore the costly implications of his strategic aims. Ambition and the miscalculation of necessary resources can lead to a "Pyrrhic victory" for the leader. The term "Pyrrhic victory" comes from an incident in Ancient Greece: Pyrrhus, the King of Epirus, sustained such heavy losses in defeating the Romans that despite his numerous victories over them, his entire empire was ultimately undermined. Thus the costs of a "Pyrrhic" victory deplete the resources that are needed for future success.

In this scenario, the leader is usually driven by a desire to expand or accelerate the realization of his vision. The initial vision appears correct, and early successes essentially delude or weaken the leader's ability to realistically assess his resources and marketplace realities. The costs that must be paid for acquisitions or market share ultimately become unsustainable and threaten the long term viability of the leader's organization.

Robert Campeau is the quintessential Pyrrhic victor. After amassing a fortune as a real estate developer, he proceeded to expand his empire into retailing with a series of purchases in the mid-1980s totalling $13.4 billion. He did this despite the fact that he knew little about the business of retailing itself. His celebrated purchase of the Allied and Federated Department Stores alone cost him some $400 million in bankers' and lawyers' fees and added $11.7 billion of debt to the Campeau Corporation. They also transformed him overnight into the most powerful retailer in the world. The price of course was an enormous amount of debt—much of it in the form of high-interest junk bonds that would soon demand most of the company's operating cash to service.

When asked how he planned to successfully integrate and enhance the profitability of these new and unrelated acquisitions, Campeau explained that it was only a matter of consolidating various operations, selling off assets to pay off company debt, and motivating management by giving them stock options. With an air of great confidence, he commented: "I own the best department stores in the world, and they will be damned profitable." He also envisioned enormous potential for synergy between his retailing and real estate operations. His plans included the building of some 50 U.S. shopping malls anchored by his newly acquired retail stores. These projects, which included 17 new Bloomingdale's stores, were estimated at a cost of $1.5 billion. In comments to the press, he stated: "Most retail managements don't know much about real estate and finance . . . [but] real estate is the gravy on top of these great retailing deals." For Campeau, his newly acquired stores sat on prime land—ripe for future deals. It was an intriguing and untried dream.

Ironically, these bold strategic moves were all made during a sales slowdown in the department store industry and in a country glutted with shopping malls. As well, the two chains he had acquired were prestigious but also notoriously inefficient. None of these factors seemed to impede Campeau, who was intent on building an empire.

Despite his rosy projections for the future, Campeau's kingdom quickly unraveled within a few years. After struggling to meet a crushing debt load, Campeau's retail operations ran out of operating cash in August 1989. By January 1990 his company stood on the edge of bankruptcy, and so did Campeau himself. The projections of great profitability for the retail operations had never materialized. New and last-minute junk-bond financing to keep the company alive came at a dear price, with interest rates as high as 17.75%. But this would not save the company as soaring debt-servicing costs forced Campeau to sell off company stock to others and to default on company loans. Even the company's crown jewel—Bloomingdale's—was soon put up for sale. Campeau's own personal fortune of $500 million was said to have all but evaporated by February 1990.

Campeau's tragic error in this case was tied as much to blind ambition as it was to poor strategic and financing decision. His history of successes in the real estate field, in combination with an ambitious personality, led this visionary leader to dream of ever-greater expansion, but in new and unfamiliar territories. The idea of an "empire" became more important than the satisfaction of enjoying his present successes. Failing to see that he lacked the long-term resources or skills needed to sustain his grand plan, he continued to acquire companies and debt at an alarming rate.

Then, too, in wishing to maintain an image of self-confidence, he may have denied or minimized the existence of any problems. Already an autocratic leader, Campeau became even more autocratic. For example, he himself assumed the position of chairman of the board at both Federated and Allied, a job he had originally and sensibly promised to an executive of a highly successful retail chain. He wanted to run his new and glamorous acquisitions personally. Sadly, this scenario is all too typical of the Pyrrhic victor whose ambitions stymie his ability to assess goals and resources realistically. Investment bankers and subordinates may further encourage visions of grandeur. As serious problems emerge, their importance is minimized. Once a crisis stage is reached, the leader exerts greater personal control and becomes less able to hear the counsel of advisors or staff members who might be helpful. In the worst case, such as Campeau's, the organization's resources are exhausted and the company fails.

Chasing a Vision Before Its Time

Sometimes a leader's perceptions of the market are so exaggerated or so significantly ahead of their time that the marketplace fails to sustain the leader's venture. The organization's resources are mobilized and spent on a mission that ultimately fails to produce the expected results. In this case, the leader is perhaps too visionary or too idealistic. He or she is unable to see that the time is not ripe, so the vision goes on to failure or, at best, a long dormancy.

Robert Lipp, former president of Chemical Bank, is an example of a visionary charismatic who in one project was essentially too far ahead of his time. He had championed a vision of home banking in the early 1980s. Sensing that the personal computer was revolutionizing many aspects of everyday life, Lipp and others at Chemical Bank expected personal banking to be the next beneficiary of the personal computer revolution. Through a modem, phone line, software supplied by the bank, and a personal computer at home, individuals could instruct their banks to carry out certain transactions. A service fee of $8 to $15 a month was charged for personal users and $20 to $50 a month for small businesses. From the user's viewpoint, home banking provided convenience in bill paying and ease of access to accounts. While on travel, the user could instruct the system to pay bills on exact due dates.

For banks, electronic home banking was very appealing. The printing, processing, and return of some 41 billion checks annually in the United States amounted to $41 billion. This figure represented 20% of the annual revenues of banks belonging to the Federal Reserve System. Home banking offered the possibility of a tremendous reduction in operating costs.

In 1983, Chemical Bank under Lipp's guidance introduced a home banking system called the Pronto Two with a goal of four million customers within several years. By 1988, however, the total nationwide users of home banking systems had reached only 100,000 people. An article in *Business Week* (February 29, 1988) remarked: "When Chemical Bank unveiled the idea of home banking in 1983, it projected that 10% of its customers would eventually pay bills and make banking transactions from their home computer. Talk about misplaced optimism. Today, if you're among those who deal with any bank by personal computer, you're in a minority of a mere 100,000 people—and that includes a number of small business operators." Only 30 banks were offering the service by 1988, out of a total of 14,000 banks nationwide.

What Chemical and others later discovered was that several inherent problems with home banking led to consumer resistance. First, customers were reluctant to give up the "float" between when they wrote a check and when it was cashed. With home banking, once the computer authorizes a payment, it is immediately debited from the customer's account.

Second, some investment—for a computer and a modem—was required on the customer's part. It is estimated that only 10% of personal computer owners had modems—and the number of personal computers in homes was limited. Finally, it was a matter of opinion whether writing a paper check was not just as simple and convenient as paying bills by personal computer. Given the costs of such computer systems, it was believed that only by providing a wider range of services, such as home shopping services, would home banking's appeal increase—and that a period of 10 to 15 years was required for market acceptance.

In Lipp's case, his vision was essentially premature for its market. Part of the problem could be attributed to the difficulty of trying to predict a future event for which there is no history. It is extremely difficult to accurately estimate the demand for a particular product or service; the leader is essentially relying on his or her forecast of resources and market trends. The margin for error in these situations is high, and the costs and time horizons for introducing a new product or service are often underestimated. Such miscalculations can forestall a vision.

Two other factors may play important roles. In their own excitement over an idea, leaders may fail to adequately test-market a new product or service or fail to hear naysayers or overlook contrary signs from the environment. Again, because of successes in other projects (Lipp had had several outstanding ones), they may delude themselves into believing they know their markets more accurately than they actually do. Or their spellbinding ability to lead may not be backed up by an adequate understanding of marketplace trends.

HOW LEADERS COME TO DENY FLAWS IN THEIR VISIONS

All three of these cases share certain characteristics that cause leaders to deny the flaws in their visions. Often, for example, leaders will perceive that their course of action is producing negative results, yet they persist. Why this happens can be explained by a process called "cognitive dissonance," which prevents the leader from changing his course. Simply put, individuals act to keep the commitments they have made because failing to do so would damage their favorable perceptions of themselves. For example, studies have found that executives will sometimes persist in an ineffective course of action simply because they feel they have committed themselves to the decision. This same process, I suspect, occurs with leaders.

Others in the organization, who tend to become dependent on a visionary leader, may perpetuate the problem through their own actions. They may idealize their leader excessively and thus ignore negative aspects and exaggerate the good qualities. As a result, they may carry out their leader's orders unquestioningly—and leaders may in certain cases encourage such behavior because of their needs to dominate and be admired. The resulting sense of omnipotence encourages denial of market and organizational realities. The danger is that leaders will surround themselves with "yes people" and thus fail to receive information that might be important but challenging to the mission. Their excessive confidence and the desire for heroic recognition encourages them to undertake large, risky ventures—but because of their overreliance on themselves and their cadre of "yes people," strategic errors go unnoticed. Bold but poorly thought-out strategies will be designed and implemented. The leader's vision, in essence, becomes a vehicle for his or her own needs for attention and visibility.

Finally, problems with "group-think" can occur where the leader's advisors delude themselves into agreement with the leader or dominant others. In such a case, decision-making becomes distorted, and a more thorough and objective review of possible alternatives to a problem are all but precluded. This is especially true of groups that are very cohesive, highly committed to their success, under pressure, and possessing favorable opinions of themselves—common characteristics in the organizations of powerful and charismatic leaders. When group-think occurs, the opinions of the leader and advisors with closely allied views come to dominate decision making. Doubts that others might have are kept hidden for fear of disapproval. It is more important "to go along to get along" rather than to consider contrary viewpoints.

John DeLorean is an example of a leader who may have purposely created group-think situations. One executive of the DeLorean Motor Company, after being dismissed by DeLorean from the company board, commented: "He told me he knew how some of the things the board was doing bothered my conscience. He said he wanted me to keep a clear conscience and not to worry as much as I did, so he had dropped me from the board. . . . When I told him he couldn't bear having anyone disagree with him so he had to stack the board his way, John . . . just nodded and said, "That's right. It's my company and I'm going to do what I want to do—when you get your own company, you can do the same' " (Hill Levin, *Grand Delusions,* Viking, 1983, pg. 248).

MANIPULATION THROUGH IMPRESSION MANAGEMENT AND COMMUNICATION SKILLS

Because some leaders are gifted at communicating, it may be quite easy for them to misuse this ability. For instance, they may present information that makes their visions appear more realistic or more appealing than the visions actually are. They may also use their language skills to screen out problems in the larger environment or to foster an illusion of control when, in reality, things are out of control. Exhibit 2 highlights a number of these possible problem areas.

While at General Motors John DeLorean was particularly adept at employing skills of articulation and impression management to promote himself. For example, he would often claim responsibility for projects without acknowledging the contributions of others. His aim was simply to manipulate information so that he appeared as the originating genius. In the case of the highly successful Pontiac GTO, DeLorean claimed to be the engineer at Pontiac who conceived the idea of combining a lighter

EXHIBIT 2
Potential liabilities in the leader's communications and impression management skills.

Exaggerated self-descriptions.
Exaggerated claims for the vision.
A technique of fulfilling stereotypes and images of uniqueness to manipulate audiences.
A habit of gaining commitment by restricting negative information and maximizing positive information.
Use of anecdotes to distract attention away from negative statistical information.
Creation of an illusion of control through affirming information and attributing negative outcomes to external causes.

version of the Tempest body with a powerful engine to create the GTO. In reality, the idea was suggested by a GM colleague.

In *Current Biography,* DeLorean is described as owning "more than 200 patents, including those for the recessed windshield wipers and the overhead-cam engine." However, Hill Levin in his biography of DeLorean reported that the U.S. Patent Office listed a total of 52 patents, none for the wipers or for the overhead cam. Exaggeration of personal deeds was perhaps DeLorean's way of building the legend. What we see with some leaders is that their need for personal recognition and visibility is so high that they feel compelled to distort reality to enhance their own image.

When leaders rely greatly on their impression management skills in communicating, they do themselves a disservice. For instance, research in impression management indicates not only that one's self-descriptions are effective in deceiving an audience, but also that they may deceive the presenter as well. This is especially true when an audience reinforces and approves of the individual's image. Such positive responses encourage leaders to internalize their own self-enhancing descriptions. Especially when exaggeration is only moderate, leaders tend to internalize and believe such claims. So DeLorean may ultimately have come to believe in his own responsibility for the Pontiac GTO.

Considerable research has also been performed on people who are ingratiators—people who play to their audiences by telling them what they want to hear. Two particular tactics that I suspect charismatic leaders use to ingratiate themselves with their audiences are to (1) fulfill stereotypes and (2) create an image of uniqueness.

Research shows that if individuals behave in ways that fulfill the positive stereotypes of an audience they are more likely to interact successfully with them. This can be achieved by espousing the beliefs, values, and behaviors associated with the stereotype and appearing as the stereotype is expected to look. For example, DeLorean supposedly went to great efforts to present the image of a young, highly successful executive with an entrepreneurial spirit. He underwent cosmetic surgery, dieted from 200 pounds to 160, lifted weights, dyed his grey hair black. He flew only first class. When he ate out, he always obtained the best table. To many, his image fulfilled the stereotype of the successful businessman.

DeLorean used the second tactic—to demonstrate uniqueness—through his unconventional actions while working at General Motors and his tales of innovations at the automobile giant. These stories created the image of a highly successful, unique individual excelling in the corporate world.

In terms of how or what a leader communicates, according to Charles Schwenk, there are several tactics that individuals can use to gain commitment from others even when the circumstances are unethical. Because our ability to process information is limited, we rely on simple biases to reduce the amount of information needed to make a decision. By playing on these biases, a leader can create or heighten commitment to a course of action. They may manipulate information so as to encourage biases in others that will increase confidence in and commitment to the leader's strategic choices. For example, leaders can withhold information that is not favorable to a cause and present instead more positive information. Or they may relate anecdotes designed to draw attention away from statistical information that reflects negatively on their plans.

DeLorean's management of investors in his automobile venture offers one example of this process. If investors had looked at history, they would have found that the odds of his succeeding were slim. Not since the founding of the four major auto companies had a new automobile company succeeded, and there had been many attempts in the interim. Moreover, there was negative statistical information in the company prospectus that might have dissuaded investors. But instead of focusing on such important statistical information, the investors allowed themselves to be swayed by DeLorean's personal character and his impressive press coverage while at General Motors. Could it be that DeLorean aimed to create a flashy image in the minds of investors in order to draw their attention away from other sources of information?

Anecdotal information may be used by the leader not only to influence decision makers' choices, but also to increase their confidence in a choice. The sheer amount of information the leader provides may act to build overconfidence. Various studies of decision making indicate that more information apparently permits people to generate more reasons for justifying their decisions and, in turn, increases the confidence of others in the decisions. Leaders might also create an illusion of control by selectively providing information that affirms they are in control and attributes failures or problems to external causes. All of these tactics may be used by leaders to mislead their direct reports and their investors.

MANAGEMENT PRACTICES THAT BECOME LIABILITIES

The managerial practices of leaders also have certain inherent liabilities. Some leaders are known for their excessively impulsive, autocratic management style. Others become so disruptive through their unconventional behavior that their organizations mobilize against them. Moreover, leaders can at times be poor at managing their superiors and peers. In general, some of the very management practices that make leaders unique may also lead to their downfall.

Leaders' liabilities fall into several categories: (1) the way they manage relations with important others, (2) their management style with direct reports, and (3) their thoroughness and attention to certain administrative detail. Typical problems associated with each of these categories are shown in Exhibit 3. We will start with the first category: managing relations with important others.

Managing Upwards and Sideways

Some leaders—particularly charismatic leaders in large organizations—seem to be very poor at managing upwards and sideways. Because they are usually unconventional advocates of radical reform, they may often alienate others in the organization, including their own bosses. The charismatic leader's unconventional actions may trigger the ire of forces within the organization which then act to immobilize him or her. Leaders' aggressive style may also alienate many potential supporters and ultimately leave them without sufficient political support for their ambitious plans. This problem is common when charismatic leaders are brought in from the outside; their radically different values and approaches may alienate the rest of the organization.

This kind of situation occurred at General Motors when Ross Perot was made a board member. Once on the board, Perot became one of the company's most outspo-

EXHIBIT 3
Potential liabilities of a leader's management practices.

Poor management of people networks, especially superiors and peers.
Unconventional behavior that alienates.
Creation of disruptive "in-group/out-group" rivalries.
An autocratic, controlling management style.
An informal/impulsive style that is disruptive and dysfunctional.
Alteration between idealizing and devaluing others, particularly direct reports.
Creation of excessive dependence in others.
Failure to manage details and effectively act as an administrator.
Attention to the superficial.
Absence from operations.
Failure to develop successors of equal ability.

ken critics. As an entrepreneur, he was quite naturally accustomed to running his own show, and after his company, Electronic Data Systems (EDS), merged with GM he insisted that any changes made in EDS procedures be cleared through him. His style and outspokenness were so much at odds with the General Motors culture that the company offered Perot $700 million in stock to step down from the board—an offer he finally accepted.

A second problem related to managing relations within large organizations is the tendency of certain leaders to cultivate a feeling of being "special" among members of their operating units. This practice is often accompanied by a corresponding depreciation of other parts of the corporation. In short, the leader creates an "us versus them" attitude. Although this heightens the motivation of the leader's group, it further alienates other groups that may be important for resources or political support. Steven Jobs did this with the MacIntosh division at Apple Computer. Even though the company's Apple II Computer provided the profits, Jobs consistently downplayed that division's importance. He essentially divided the company into two rivals. He was fond of telling people in the MacIntosh division, "This is the cream of Apple. This is the future of Apple." He even went so far as telling marketing managers for Apple II that they worked for an outdated, clumsy organization. Jobs's later departure from Apple stemmed in part from morale problems he created within the company by using this tactic.

In another case, the charismatic president of a division in a large corporation used as his group's emblem a mascot symbol of the TV cartoon character Roadrunner. (In the cartoon, Roadrunner was particularly adept at outwitting a wily coyote.) To him, his division managers were the "roadrunners" who were smarter and faster than the corporate "coyotes" who laid roadblocks in their path. He also had a habit of ignoring corporate staff requests for reports or information, and he returned their reports with "STUPID IDEA" stamped on the front cover. Although such behaviors and tactics fostered a sense of camaraderie and aggressiveness within the charismatic leader's division, they were ultimately detrimental both to the leader and to the organization. In this case, the executive eventually stepped down from the organization.

Relationships with Subordinates

Highly directive and visionary leaders are often described as autocratic. Jobs, for example, has been described as dictatorial. I suspect that in many cases the vision is such a personification of the leader that he or she becomes obsessed about its perfection or implementation. Leaders' natural impatience with the pace of the vision's achievement exacerbates the problem and encourages them to be more hands-on, more controlling.

There also appears to be, at times, an impulsive dynamic at work in the way leaders manage—and at such times they will override subordinates' suggestions or insights. Again, this occurs especially in relation to accomplishing the vision. DeLorean is described as increasing his production of the DeLorean car by 50% in the belief that his product would become an overnight sensation. Production went to an annual rate of 30,000 cars. This was done in spite of market research that showed total annual sales of between 4,000 and 10,000 cars. A company executive lamented, "Our figures showed that this was a viable company with half the production. If the extravagence had been cut out of New York, we could have broken even making just 6,000 cars a year. But that wasn't fast enough for John. First he had to build his paper empire in the stock market. A creditable success was not enough for him" (ibid., pg. 282).

Steven Jobs is known to have darted in and out of operations causing havoc: "He would leap-frog back and forth among various projects, dictating designs, with little or no knowledge of whether or not the technology even existed to make his ideas work" (L. Butcher, *Accidental Millionaire,* Paragon House, 1988, pp. 140–141).

Another potential problem can arise from a style of informality when managing the hierarchy of an organization—this is especially true of charismatic leaders. Advantages of this style are that leaders are highly visible, approachable, and able to react quickly to issues and problems. The drawback is that they often violate the chain of command by going around direct reports and thus undercut their direct reports' authority. If a particular project or idea interests them, they do not hesitate to become involved, sometimes to the detriment of the project managers' responsibilities. DeLorean would drop in on his engineers to suggest what seemed trivial ideas. One company engineer said: "He came in one day to say we should hook into the cooling system and make a little icebox for a six-pack of beer behind the driver's seat. Or, another time, he told us to work on a sixty-watt radio speaker that could be detached and hung outside the car for picnics" (H. Levin, ibid., pg. 267).

Administrative Skills

Some visionary leaders are so absorbed by the "big picture" that they fail to understand essential details—except for "pet" projects in which they become excessively involved. Iacocca, for instance, turned over most of the day-to-day operations to others as he became increasingly famous. As a result, he lost touch with new model planning. He himself admitted: "If I made one mistake, it was delegating all the product development and not going to a single meeting" (ibid., pg. 267). A DeLorean executive complained "He [John DeLorean] just didn't have time for the details of the project. But attention to detail is everything" (ibid., p. 267). Then, too, leaders may get so caught up in corporate stardom that they become absentee leaders. Again, Iacocca is an example. His success at Chrysler led to his becoming a best-selling author, a U.S. presidential prospect, and the head of the $277 million fund-raising campaign for the Statue of Liberty—all of which distracted him from the important task of leading Chrysler.

Because these individuals are often excited by ideas, they may at times be poor implementors. Once an idea begins to appear as a tangible reality, I suspect they feel the need to move on to the next challenge, thereby leaving subordinates scrambling to pick up the pieces. Furthermore, because some leaders have high needs for visibility, they gravitate toward activities that afford them high people contact and recognition. Such activities are generally not performed at a desk while paying careful attention to the details.

Succession Problems

A true leader is usually a strong figure and, as noted, often one upon whom subordinates develop dependencies. Thus it is difficult for others with leadership potential to develop fully in the shadow of such leaders. For while they may actively coach their subordinates, I suspect that it is extremely difficult for them to develop others to be leaders *of equal power.* Leaders simply enjoy the limelight too much to share it, so when they ultimately depart, a leadership vacuum is created. Moreover, under charismatic leadership authority may be highly centralized around the leader—and this is an arrangement that, unfortunately, weakens the authority structures that are normally dispersed throughout an organization.

It's clear that many of the qualities of a strong leader have both a positive and a negative face. That's why the presence of leaders entails risks for their direct reports, their organizations, and at times their societies. They must be managed with care. The negatives, however, must always be weighed in light of the positives. For companies and society, the need for organizational change and strategic vision may be so great that the risks of confrontation, unconventionality, and so on may seem a small price to pay. It is also possible that organizations and educational institutions can train, socialize, and manage future leaders in ways that will minimize their negative qualities.

SELECTED BIBLIOGRAPHY

For an in-depth look at the psychological dynamics of the dark side of leaders, we recommend *The Neurotic Organization* (Jossey-Bass, 1984) by Manfred Kets de Vries and Danny Miller and "Personality, Culture, and Organization" (*The Academy of Management Review,* April 1986), also by Manfred Kets de Vries and Danny Miller.

Works that provide an informative treatment on the topic of impression management include *The Presentation of Self in Everyday Life* (Doubleday-Anchor, 1959) by Erving Goffman and *Impression Management* (Brooks/Cole, 1980) by B.R. Schlenker. Books and articles that deal more systematically with the issue of commitment to a course of action as well as communicating information are *A Theory of Cognitive Dissonance* (Row, Peterson, 1957) by L. Festinger; Charles R. Schwenk's "Information, Cognitive Bias, and Commitment to a Course of Action" (*The Academy of Management Review,* April 1986); Barry Staw's "Knee Deep in the Big Muddy: A Study of

Escalating Commitment to a Chosen Course of Action" (*Organizational Behavior and Human Performance,* June 1976); and "The Escalation of Commitment to a Course of Action" (*The Academy of Management Review,* October 1981). The definitive work on group-think is *Victims of Group Think* (Houghton-Mifflin, 1972) by I. L. Janis.

Readers wishing more depth on the individual case studies of leaders should consult the following sources. For Edwin Land and the SX-70 camera, see G.W. Merry's Polaroid-Kodak Case Study (Harvard Business School, 1976) and P.C. Wensberg's *Land's Polaroid* (Houghton Mifflin, 1987). Several articles on Robert Campeau include "Buy-Out Bomb" (*Wall Street Journal,* Jan. 11, 1990), Kate Ballen's "Campeau Is on a Shopper's High" (*Fortune,* Aug. 15, 1988), and Eric Berg's "Is Campeau Himself Bankrupt?" (*New York Times,* Feb. 2, 1990). Two interesting sources on John DeLorean are Michael Daly's "The Real DeLorean Story" (*New York,* Nov. 8, 1982) and Hill Levin's *Grand Delusions* (Viking Press, 1983). *Accidental Millionaire* (Paragon House, 1988) by Lee Butcher presents a darker-side view of Steven Jobs. Two articles on the home banking industry and its slow takeoff are Efrem Sigel's "Is Home Banking for Real?" (*Datamation,* Sept. 15, 1986) and Laura Zinn's "Home Banking Is Here—If You Want It" (*Business Week,* Feb. 29, 1988).

Substitutes for Leadership: Effective Alternatives to Ineffective Leadership

Jon P. Howell
David E. Bowen
Peter W. Dorfman
Steven Kerr
Philip M. Podsakoff

Leadership has been recognized through the ages as a primary means of influencing the behavior of others. Research into the keys to effective and ineffective leadership has also been going on for quite some time. The earliest assumption was that effective leaders possessed particular traits that distinguished them from ineffective leaders. Effective leaders were thought to be dynamic, intelligent, dependable, high-achieving individuals—so, since traits are hard to change, problems caused by poor leadership were considered best solved by *replacing the leader* with someone who possessed more of the key traits. Regrettably, researchers were unable to identify leader traits that systematically improved organizational effectiveness. Yet leader replacement continues to be a very popular tool in the executive toolkit.

Partly in response to the limitation of trait theory, research in the late 1940s began to focus on relationships between leader behaviors and employee performance, in search of behaviors exhibited by effective leaders that were not displayed by those less effective. With this approach, effective leaders need not possess magical traits but, instead, provide strong direction and support while encouraging subordinates to participate in important decisions. This emphasis on leader behaviors still permitted replacement of a weak leader but allowed an additional remedy as well: namely, *changing the leader's behavior* through some form of training. Probably the most disappointing aspect of research on leader behaviors is that no strong, consistent relationships between particular leader behaviors and organizational effectiveness have ever been found. This has not prevented many off-the-shelf training programs from becoming popular, however, nor the marketers of such programs from becoming prosperous.

SITUATIONAL THEORIES

By the late 1950s it became evident that an approach was needed that didn't depend on ideal traits and universal behaviors. One answer was "situational theory," which starts with the assumption that there are no traits, and no behaviors, that automatically constitute effective leadership. The key is the fit between a leader's style and the situation the leader faces; thus the leader who is highly effective in one situation may be totally ineffective in another. For instance, although General George Patton led the 3rd Army to outstanding performance in World War II, one could hardly imagine the effective use of his leadership style in Mahatma Gandhi's situation against the British in India.

According to situational theories, effective leaders must correctly identify the behaviors each situation requires and then be flexible enough to exhibit these behaviors. Leaders who are behaviorally inflexible, or who lack the necessary diagnostic skills, must be either trained or replaced—the same remedies identified by researchers of leader traits and behaviors. An alternative is to let the leader alone but *change the situations so that the fit is improved.*

Various situational leadership theories have spawned a large number of intervention strategies, many of them competent and some of them useful. However, an assumption underlies all these theories that is wholly unsupported by the research literature. This assumption is that, though different situations require different leadership styles, in *every* situation there is *some* leadership style that will be effective. It has been shown in numerous studies, however, that circumstances often counteract the potential power of leadership, making it virtually impossible in some situations for leaders to have much impact regardless of their style or how good the fit is between leader and situation.

SUBSTITUTES FOR LEADERSHIP

Fortunately, additional remedies for problems stemming from weak leadership— remedies not articulated in any of the earlier trait, behavioral, or situational approaches—have been identified. Such remedies derive from acceptance of the conclusion, based on the research studies referenced earlier, that many organizations contain "substitutes for leadership"—attributes of subordinates, tasks, and organizations that provide task guidance and incentives to perform to such a degree that they virtually negate the leader's ability to either improve or impair subordinate performance. To the extent that powerful leadership substitutes exist, formal leadership, however displayed, tends to be unproductive and can even be counterproductive. In comparison with situational leadership approaches, research on leadership substitutes focuses on whether subordinates are receiving needed task guidance and incentives to perform without taking it for granted that the formal leader is the primary supplier.

Closely Knit Teams of Highly Trained Individuals

Consider the positive impact of substitutes in the following example. Todd LaPorte, Gene Rochlin, and Karlene Roberts are three researchers studying such highly stressful organizational situations as those involving pilots who land jet fighters on a nuclear carrier and air-traffic controllers who direct traffic into San Francisco. They have found that directive leadership is relatively unimportant compared with the work experience and training of individuals in closely knit work groups. This is particularly evident ". . . in the white heat of danger, when the whole system threatens to collapse. . . . The stress creates a need for competence among colleagues who by necessity develop close working relationships with each other." All such individuals are trained extensively and daily, regardless of their position in the hierarchy, to redirect operations or bring them to an abrupt halt. This can involve ignoring orders from managers who are removed from the front line of action. Here the experience and continuous training of individuals, along with the close relationships among members of a work group, substitute for the manager's directive leadership.

By creating alternate sources of task guidance and incentives to perform, substitutes for leadership may have a temporary negative effect on morale among leaders who perceive a loss of power. However, leadership substitutes can also serve as important remedies where there are organizational problems, particularly in situations where the leader is not the source of the problems or where, if the leader is the source, replacement, training, and improving the leader-situation fit are overly expensive, politically infeasible, or too time-consuming to be considered.

A principal advantage of the substitutes construct is that it identifies a remedy for problems stemming from weak leadership in addition to replacement, training, or situational engineering. The remedy is to intentionally, systematically *create substitutes for hierarchical leadership.* In fact, whereas weak, powerhungry leaders invariably regard substitutes as frustrating and necessarily dysfunctional (when they are aware of them at all), strong leaders understand and are comfortable with the idea that effective results can be achieved when task guidance and incentives to perform emanate from sources other than themselves. When other sources are deficient, the hierarchical superior is in a position to play a dominant role; when strong incentives and guidance derive from other sources, the hierarchical superior has less opportunity, but also less need, to exert his or her influence.

Intrinsic Satisfaction

The degree of intrinsic satisfaction that employees derive from their work task is a strong leadership substitute in a large manufacturer of camping equipment in the western United States. The company produces sleeping bags that range from top-of-the-line lightweight backpackers to low-cost models filled with floor sweepings from a mattress factory. Manufacturing personnel are required to rotate among all the lines, so no one group gains a territorial claim to a particular product. Management reports that for workers on the top-quality down-filled bags, supervisory direction has become relatively unnecessary, yet output and quality typically exceed management expectations. Workers report pride in working on this line and usually solve production problems themselves or with co-workers.

The production of bottom-line bags is very different. Quality problems are commonplace, workers cooperate less to overcome the problems, and workers seem to care little about meeting output or quality standards. The constant supervision required to address these problems raises indirect costs. Consultants observing the various production lines during a typical day report that supervisors slowly gravitate away from high-quality lines toward the lowest-quality lines. Thus the workers' intrinsic satisfaction from producing a high-quality product alleviates the need for most supervisory leadership.

Computer Technology

Edward E. Lawler III has noticed that companies with computer-integrated manufacturing and networked computer systems rely on computers to take over many of the supervisor's leadership functions. Feedback is provided by computerized productivity and quality data; directions for certain tasks are entered into the information system;

even error detection and goal setting are incorporated in some interactive systems. When individual workers have access to operating data and to a network that allows them to ask employees at other locations to help solve problems, they become more independent of their managers and arrive at solutions among themselves. Spans of control greater than 100 are not unheard of in these organizations. Computerized information technology is therefore providing a substitute for certain types of managerial leadership.

Effective leadership, then, depends upon a leader's ability to supply subordinates with task guidance and incentives to perform to the extent that these are not provided by other sources. The inverse of this assertion is equally valid. Leadership substitutes can contribute to organizational effectiveness by supplying subordinates with task guidance and incentives to perform that are not being provided by the hierarchical superior. From this perspective it makes sense for a leader or someone above the leader to create substitutes when, for example, the leader must be frequently absent, has a large span of control, or is saddled with time-consuming nonmanagerial duties. Substitutes are also useful when a leader departs before a successor has been identified or there is a need to manage employees who are geographically dispersed or who, as in the following example, are culturally resistant to hierarchical supervision.

Extensive Professional Education

Professional employees may come to their firms with so much formal education that they can perform most work assignments without relying upon technical guidance from their hierarchical superior. Their education also often includes a strong socialization component, instilling in them a desire for autonomous, self-controlling behavior. The result may be that they neither need or will readily accept a leader's direction. In such instances, professional education and socialization can serve as substitutes for formal leadership: A 1981 study by Jeffrey Ford found that extensive subordinate education acted as a substitute for directive and supportive leadership in a book publishing firm, a branch bank, and a midwestern university.

USING LEADERSHIP SUBSTITUTES TO SOLVE ORGANIZATIONAL PROBLEMS

The notion that professional education and socialization can substitute for traditional formal leadership identifies an important potential problem, but it can be turned to advantage if a leader is sensitive to the situation and builds collegial systems of task-related guidance and interpersonal support. This approach can be found in most well-run hospitals and universities, where deliberately designed substitutes for leadership abound.

Thus charges of medical malfeasance are often investigated by peer review teams, and university promotion and tenure decisions depend greatly on assessments by faculty colleagues who lack formal authority. Indeed, many a dean has learned that the same criticism that would be bitterly denied if it came from him or her is grudgingly accepted if the source is a peer-review committee. The trick is to develop norms and structures that consistently produce feedback when feedback is needed, rather than merely an occasional spontaneous outburst when circumstances become intolerable.

Team Approaches

Tracy Kidder's *The Soul of a New Machine* provides an excellent account of how a key manager at Data General utilized subordinates' professional norms and standards as a substitute for leadership to produce a faster computer than the competition's. The company at that time was competitive, highly political, and resource-poor, but the computer-design engineers were young, creative, well trained, and highly motivated. Recognizing the futility of relying on directive leadership and meager financial re- wards, the leader obtained work space that encouraged considerable interaction among team members and discouraged interaction outside the team. He articulated key para- meters and project deadlines, stayed out of members' personal disputes, obtained re- sources for the team, and buffered them from organization politics. Reflecting the atti- tude of team members, Kidder observes, "They were building the machine all by themselves, without any significant help from their leader."

Task guidance and incentives to perform may derive from a number of sources other than the leader, including organized staff groups, internal and external consul- tants, and competent peers at all organizational levels. In the Columbus, Ohio Police Department, the creation of two-person patrol units and field-training officer positions effectively substituted for the guidance and support traditionally provided by hierar- chical leaders, thus making time available for them to attend to other tasks. Where one-person patrols without field-training officers were utilized, leader guidance and support continued to be essential. (An ancillary benefit of substituting peer for hierar- chical sources of task guidance is that it is often easier for subordinates to admit inad- equacies to and request assistance from their co-workers than from their boss.)

High-Ability Independent Workers

Even when subordinates haven't much formal education, ability combined with expe- rience can serve as a substitute for hierarchical leadership. Cummins Engine Com- pany, General Motors Corporation, and Procter and Gamble all have reduced supervi- sory personnel and managerial overhead by selecting and developing high-ability, independent workers who require little or no supervision. Paul Reeves, a key produc- tion foreman for Harmon Auto Parts, taught workers to take over his job by helping them increase their ability and experience so that their responsibilities could also be increased. Each worker voluntarily spent half-days with him—asking questions, dis- cussing his responses and, eventually, helping him perform his duties. When Reeves was promoted, the group continued to operate effectively without a foreman.

In Place of Hierarchical Feedback

Among the most important elements of task guidance is performance feedback. In the absence of feedback, ability to perform cannot be improved and motivation to perform cannot be sustained. Most organizations assign responsibility for feedback to the hierarchical superior, even in cases where the superior works at a physical distance from employees or doesn't know enough about their technical specialties to give them credible feedback.

However, many organizations have come to the realization that feedback from clients and peers, and feedback provided by the task itself, can serve as powerful substitutes for hierarchical feedback. Charles Manz and Hank Sims, two organizational researchers, described the operation of one such feedback system in a nonunion small-parts manufacturing plant. A subsidiary of a large U.S. corporation, the plant was organized around the concept of self-managed work teams from its inception in the early 1970s.

Each team of eight to twelve members is assigned a set of closely related production tasks, and the teams are buffered from each other by physical space and stores of in-process inventory. Each team prepares its own budgets, makes within-team job assignments, keeps track of quality control statistics and hours worked, and handles member absenteeism and discipline problems. Team members are trained in conducting meetings and in group problem solving. A hierarchical leader is responsible for each team, but this person is not supposed to supply either task guidance or interpersonal support, aside from encouraging self-observation, self-evaluation, and self-reinforcement. Manz and Sims found, in fact, that the most effective teams were those whose leaders did refrain from providing guidance and support. Leaders of effective teams spent much of their time representing the team to higher management, obtaining resources for the team, training new members, and coaching team members with respect to peer feedback and peer evaluation.

Substitutes by Procedure

The detailed work rules, guidelines, policies, and procedures existing in many organizations also serve to some extent as substitutes for hierarchical leadership by providing important non-leader sources of task guidance. Researchers Jon Howell and Peter Dorfman found this to be the case in a medium-size hospital, as did Robert Miles and M. M. Petty in county-level social service agencies. This type of leadership substitute can be particularly useful in situations where consistent behavior is imperative. For example, units of a firm increase the firm's legal exposure by acting inconsistently with respect to hiring, firing, leaves of absence, promotions, or other human resources actions. In other instances, such as pricing or purchasing activities, variation may be legal but cost-ineffective. It is quite common in these cases for organizations to install procedures, rules and guidelines to replace or forestall managerial discretion.

LEADERSHIP NEUTRALIZERS

Thus far we have discussed only leadership substitutes, whose effect is to make it both less possible and less necessary for leaders to influence subordinate satisfaction and performance, replacing the leader's impact with impact of their own. Leadership "neutralizers" are attributes of subordinates, tasks, and organizations that also interfere with a leader's attempts to influence subordinates. Unlike leadership substitutes, however, neutralizers do not replace the leader's impact over subordinates, but rather create an "influence vacuum" that can have serious negative consequences.

Physical Distances

For example, when subordinates work at a physical distance from their leader, many recommended leadership practices have limited usefulness or are nearly impossible to perform. A case in point is found at Kinko's, which provides professional copying services at widely dispersed locations nationwide. Regional managers at Kinko's are continually frustrated by not being able to provide enough direction, guidance, and personal support for the new store managers because physical distances are too great for much personal interaction. In other organizations, subordinates and leaders may not share a common time zone; indeed, they may scarcely share the same work day.

Spatial distance will be increasingly important as a potential leadership neutralizer in the future because, as the number of firms with international operations continues to rise, managers will increasingly be required to supervise subordinates across great distances. Furthermore, the growing importance of the U.S. service sector means that more and more employees will be working at home or at their client's work site.

Reward Systems

Organizational reward systems can also be important neutralizers of the hierarchical leadership's effects. Rewards may be awarded strictly according to seniority, for example, or attractive rewards may be unavailable to subordinates. Leaders tend to have little influence on corporate "rebels" because, in part, the rebels are not attracted to the typical rewards available in corporate bureaucracies. Union contracts also may mandate that all employees within a given job classification be paid the same wage rate, and civil service policies may require that promotions be based on objective examinations. In other cases, rewards may be controlled by higher management in ways that prevent the immediate supervisor from exerting influence. This occurs, for example, in firms requiring numerous one-over-one approvals before a salary recommendation takes effect. Other firms permit leaders to influence the amount of rewards, but their timing is wholly constrained by fiscal periods or employee anniversary dates.

Bypassing Management Structure

A very different type of neutralization occurs when someone at a higher level repeatedly bypasses a level of management to deal directly with that manager's subordinates. Another neutralizer is the continual countermanding by higher management of a leader's orders and instructions. These neutralizers often occur in instances where an organization's founder has finally, reluctantly, hired a subordinate manager to oversee operations and where a union's potential for mischief is so feared that supervisory efforts aimed at maintaining discipline are routinely reversed at higher levels.

Although normally dysfunctional, leadership neutralizers can occasionally be used to advantage. One such occasion occurred in a petrochemical processing firm where, because of his technical expertise and involvement in several critical projects, an interpersonally incompetent director of design engineering could not be replaced. As an interim solution until he could be phased out, his day-to-day contact with employees was sharply curtailed, he was given numerous technical (nonleader) assignments, and his influence over salary and personnel decisions was considerably reduced. In this instance the "influence vacuum" caused by creating leadership neutralizers was deemed preferable to the state of leadership that previously existed.

LEADERSHIP ENHANCERS

Leader "enhancers" are attributes of employees, tasks, and organizations that amplify a leader's impact on the employees. For example, cohesive work groups with strong norms in support of cooperation with management can crystallize ambiguous goals and role definitions, augment overly subtle leader-provided feedback, and otherwise increase the power of weak, inconsistent leaders—for better or for worse. A study of four large hospitals found that development of a culture with strong performance norms greatly enhanced the impact of the head nurse's directive leadership style.

The creation of leadership enhancers makes particular sense when a leader has both the skill to manage effectively and personal goals consonant with organizational objectives but is prevented by one or more neutralizers from being effective. One way to amplify such a leader's power is to alter the organization's reward system. For example, make additional resources available, grant more discretion concerning the distribution of existing resources, or increase subordinates' dependency on the leader for desired physical and financial resources. Another type of enhancement is to give the leader access to key information and prestigious people at high levels—for example, as a member of a visible, prestigious task force. Enhancement in this case derives from connecting the leader to sources of power and important information, as well as from signaling to others that the leader probably has considerable influence with those at the top.

STRATEGIES FOR IMPROVING LEADERSHIP EFFECTIVENESS

Exhibit 1 outlines some typical leadership problems and effective coping strategies using leadership substitutes, neutralizers, and enhancers. Exhibit 2 provides specific information about how to implement these alternative leadership strategies.

Is the Leader to Blame?

When evaluating alternative strategies for addressing a problematic situation (for example, one characterized by high employee absenteeism, grievances, and turnover or by low morale and performance), a good first step is to assess whether the leader is primarily to blame for deficiencies or whether responsibility resides more with the particular situation. Admittedly difficult under the best of circumstances, such an assessment is complicated by our tendency to attribute, correctly or not, poor performance to individuals rather than to situations. As a result, higher management all too often tries to remedy poor unit performance by replacing the leader—sometimes fol-

EXHIBIT 1
Eleven managerial leadership problems and effective coping strategies.*

Leadership problems	Enhancer/neutralizer	Substitutes
Leader doesn't keep on top of details in the department; co-ordination among subordi-nates is difficult.	Not useful.	Develop self-managed work teams; encourage team mem-bers to interact within and across departments.
Competent leadership is re-sisted through noncompliance or passive resistance.	*Enhancers:* Increase employ-ees' dependence on leader through greater leader control of rewards/resources; in-crease their perception of leader's influence outside of work group.	Develop collegial systems of guidance for decision making.
Leader doesn't provide sup-port or recognition for jobs well done.	Not useful.	Develop a reward system that operates independently of the leader. Enrich jobs to make them inherently satisfying.
Leader doesn't set targets or goals, or clarify roles for em-ployees.	Not useful.	Emphasize experience and ability in selecting subordi-nates. Establish group goal-setting. Develop an organiza-tional culture that stresses high performance expecta-tions.
A leader behaves inconsis-tently over time.	*Enhancers:* These are dysfunctional. *Neutralizer:* Remove rewards from leader's control.	Develop group goal-setting and group rewards.
An upper-level manager regu-larly bypasses a leader in dealing with employees, or countermands the leader's directions.	*Enhancers:* Increase leader's control over rewards and re-sources; build leader's image via in-house champion or visi-ble "important" responsibilities. *Neutralizer:* Physically dis-tance subordinates from up-per-level manager.	Increase the professionaliza-tion of employees.
A unit is in disarray or out of control.	Not useful.	Develop highly formalized plans, goals, routines, and ar-eas of responsibility.
Leadership is brutal, autocratic.	*Enhancers:* These are dysfunctional. *Neutralizers:* Physically dis-tance subordinates; remove rewards from leader's control.	Establish group goal-setting and peer performance appraisal.
There is inconsistency across different organizational units.	Not useful.	Increase formalization. Set up a behaviorally focused reward system.
Leadership is unstable over time; leaders are rotated and/or leave office frequently.	Not useful.	Establish competent advisory staff units. Increase profes-sionalism of employees.
Incumbent management is poor; there's no heir apparent.	*Enhancers:* These are dysfunctional. *Neutralizer:* Assign nonleader duties to problem managers.	Emphasize experience and ability in selecting employees. Give employees more training.

* The suggested solutions are examples of many possibilities for each problem.

EXHIBIT 2
Creative strategies for improving leadership effectiveness.

Creating substitutes for leader directiveness and supportiveness	Creating enhancers for leader directiveness and supportiveness
Develop collegial systems of guidance: • Peer appraisals to increase acceptability of feedback by subordinates. • Quality circles to increase workers' control over production quality. • Peer support networks; mentor systems.	Increase subordinates' perceptions of leader's influence/expertise: • Provide a visible champion or leader. • Give leader important organizational responsibilities. • Build leader's image through in-house publications and other means.
Improve performance-oriented organizational formalization: • Automatic organization reward system (such as commissions or gainsharing). • Group management-by-objectives (MBO) program. • Company mission statements and codes of conduct (as at Johnson & Johnson).	Build organizational climate: • Reward small wins to increase subordinates' confidence. • Emphasize ceremony and myth to encourage team spirit. • Develop superordinate goals to encourage cohesiveness and high performance norms.
Increase administrative staff availability: • Specialized training personnel. • Troubleshooters for human relations problems. • Technical advisors to assist production operators.	Increase subordinates' dependence on leader: • Create crises requiring immediate action. • Increase leader centrality in providing information. • Eliminate one-over-one approvals.
Increase professionalism of subordinates: • Staffing based on employee professionalism. • Development plans to increase employees' abilities and experience. • Encourage active participation in professional associations.	Increase leader's position power: • Change title to increase status. • Increase reward power. • Increase resource base.
Redesign jobs to increase: • Performance feedback from the task. • Ideological importance of jobs.	Create cohesive work groups with high performance norms: • Provide physical setting conducive to teamwork. • Encourage subordinates' participation in group problem solving. • Increase group's status. • Create intergroup competition.
Start team-building activities to develop group self-management skills such as: • Solving work-related problems on their own. • Resolving interpersonal conflicts among members. • Providing interpersonal support to members.	

lowing many sessions of well-intentioned but ineffectual training—with another leader who is bound to fail for the same situational reasons that doomed his or her predecessor. (For a current example of this misguided approach to improving organizational effectiveness, see your local newspaper's sports section this week, or last week, or next week.)

Harold H. Kelley's influential work on causal attributional processes offers a useful guide to assessing whether a problem can fairly be attributed to a particular leader rather than to the leader's situation. According to Kelley, three key questions are:

- *Consistency.* Does a leader consistently fail to provide necessary guidance and support to subordinates, and is he or she therefore repeatedly ineffective over time?
- *Distinctiveness.* Is a leader more effective in some situations than others, or does his or her ineffectiveness extend across a wide variety of situations?
- *Consensus.* Are other leaders in similar situations—for example, managers of sister units—effective or ineffective in the performance of their duties?

Another useful way to consider the question of whether a leader or the situation is primarily responsible for an existing problem is to try to view the leader "out of context," as if videotaped in extreme close-up so that the leader's effects on subordinates and the environment cannot be viewed. If the leader is apparently doing all the right things, training or replacement is unlikely to be successful.

Is Replacement a Solution?

When analysis reveals that, in fact, the leader is the probable source of a problem, training or replacement may well be appropriate. However, even when analysis leads to the conclusion that the leader should be replaced, replacement may not really be a viable solution. That is, the pool of suitable replacements may be thin, the leader's boss may lack authority to transfer or terminate, or the paper trail may be weak and the legal exposure excessive. Similarly, although analysis may indicate that leadership training could be productive, the manager in question might not be educable, or the problem may require a speedier solution.

Can the situation be altered to improve the fit? Since all situational leadership theories share the conviction that some type of hierarchical leadership will always be needed, they focus solely upon the leader-situational fit. If the leader is the primary source of task guidance and motivational stimuli needed by employees to perform their tasks, then he or she is clearly a major catalyst of performance in that situation, and improving the leader-situation fit could be an effective remedy for various organizational problems. However, in circumstances where task guidance and incentives to perform stem primarily from nonleader sources, such remedies as replacing leaders, training leaders, and improving the leader-situation fit are unlikely to be effective.

A DECISION-TREE APPROACH

At this point, there may seem to be too many considerations in identifying an optimal solution to the problem of ineffective leadership. One way to resolve this problem is for the executive to consider the key diagnostic questions sequentially.

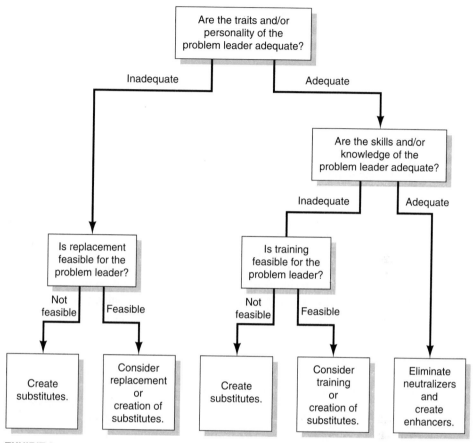

EXHIBIT 3
A decision tree for overcoming ineffective managerial leadership.

Exhibit 3 articulates the key questions that must be answered to identify the most effective approach to resolving a leadership problem. These questions must be carefully evaluated if the most appropriate solution is to be identified. As the decision tree shown in Exhibit 3 demonstrates, different answers to the questions point to different solutions to a particular leadership problem.

In two of the situations described in Exhibit 3, creation of leadership substitutes is identified as the best solution. In these situations the leader possesses either a trait or a skill inadequacy, and replacement and training are not feasible. Such inadequacies could describe an insensitive, autocratic manager who stifles subordinates or a leader whose inconsistent behavior sends confusing signals to subordinates. Some type of substitute must be created to neutralize the potentially damaging effects of an incapable leader and to provide the guidance and/or positive feelings needed by employees.

One situation in Exhibit 3 calls for a solution based on eliminating leadership neutralizers and creating leadership enhancers. Here the leader apparently is not deficient in traits or skills, so some environmental factor probably is preventing the leader from having the positive influence that is within his or her capability. These neutralizers must be identified and removed.

In two situations identified in Exhibit 3, more than one solution strategy is suggested. In these situations the leader's traits or skills are inadequate, and either replacement or training is a feasible option to consider. Since substitutes also have the capacity to positively affect subordinate behaviors and feelings, three strategies could lead to effective resolution: replacement, training, or the creation of substitutes for leadership. It would be necessary to assess the relative merits of each. Problems in these categories include disarray in the leader's unit, lack of cooperation among subordinates, their noncompliance with important leader requests, and a leader ready to leave with no apparent successor.

EVALUATING ALTERNATIVE SOLUTIONS

In assessing the relative merits of replacement, training, and substitutes for leadership, managers must be concerned with two questions: Will the solution remedy the problem, and what will it cost? In many instances, more than one solution may remedy the problem, but they often differ when it comes to overall benefits and costs.

Several factors must be considered in evaluating the advantages and disadvantages of each possible solution:

• *Durability.* This refers to the length of time a remedy remains in effect. For replacement, of course, this factor depends on the length of tenure of the new incumbent. Training often is not durable; substitutes can be very durable. For example, a clearly articulated set of procedures (organizational formalization) or a challenging job (intrinsic satisfaction) can be enduring sources of guidance and motivation.

• *Reversibility.* The ability to undo a remedy once it has been implemented is also important. Replacement and training are difficult to reverse, but substitutes tend to be easily reversible.

• *Symptom specificity.* Can the solution be directed toward only the undesirable attributes of the leader and not spill over to the leader's desirable attributes? For example, if a leader is deficient in giving subordinates guidance, can this be remedied without sacrificing other things the leader does well—offering support, exercising upward influence, etc? Clearly, replacement is not symptom-specific; the leader goes, taking with him or her not only the bad but the good as well. Training and substitutes are symptom-specific because they can be directed at only the undesirable attributes.

• *Single-source dependency.* Does a given solution make the organization dependent on a single source of guidance and support? Replacement and training create continuing dependence on the hierarchical leader. Substitutes, however, can provide a diversified portfolio of solutions to problems of leadership effectiveness.

• *Time to implement a particular solution.* This factor often favors replacement, particularly if someone is already identified. Certain training programs are very time-consuming. The amount of time necessary to build substitutes into the environment depends on the nature of the substitute.

• *Development of the leader.* This is the major focus of leadership training. Replacement typically fails to address this benefit. The effect of substitutes is uncertain because some may negate or eliminate the need for certain types of leadership, and others may enhance the leader's effectiveness.

• *Affordability.* The cost of a solution will vary with the situation. Replacement of a leader from outside can be expensive; promotion from within may be inexpensive. In-house training may not be costly, whereas training consultants can be expensive. Implementation of substitutes varies from rules and regulation changes (at little cost) to major job-design efforts (at substantial cost).

This discussion suggests that substitutes for leadership are often a superior alternative to the conventional remedies of replacement and training. Creating leadership substitutes in no way implies abolishing the leadership function; rather, it is in itself an act of leadership. Just as the conductor of a symphony orchestra should not and cannot be eliminated, he or she need not worry about directing individual symphony members on instrumental techniques or musical structure. The musical score and the high level of training and commitment of professional musicians obviate the need for the conductor to spend time on these matters; instead, the conductor creates a unique expression of the music from an ensemble of competent individuals. Can any organization ask more of its leaders?

SELECTED BIBLIOGRAPHY

Citations describing the historical aspects of leadership theory include Bernard M. Bass's *Bass and Stogdill's Handbook of Leadership* (Free Press, 1990) and the second edition of Gary Yukl's *Leadership in Organizations* (Prentice Hall, 1989). Articles that deal with the optimal leadership strategy under specific conditions include Robert Tannenbaum and Warren H. Schmidt's "How to Choose a Leadership Pattern" and Fred Fiedler's "Engineer the Job to Fit the Manager" in *Harvard Business Review* (May-June 1973 and October 1965, respectively).

The seminal article introducing the "substitutes for leadership" construct written by Steve Kerr and John Jermier is "Substitutes for Leadership: Their Meaning and Measurement" in *Organizational Behavior and Human Performance* (December 1978). Further development and refinement of the concept can be found in the article "Moderator Variables in Leadership Research" by Jon P. Howell, Peter W. Dorfman, and Steven Kerr in *Academy of Management Review* (March 1986).

The leadership substitute citation by Tracy Kidder at Data General is found in his engaging account of the highly competitive and stressful computer business, *The Soul of a New Machine* (Little, Brown, 1981). Self-managed work teams continue to be a hot topic in organizational development literature. An article by Charles C. Manz and Hank P. Sims Jr., "Leading Workers to Lead Themselves: The External Leadership of Self-Managing Work Teams" in *Administrative Science Quarterly* (March 1987) gives a good account of this substitute. Additional thorough empirical investigations of substitutes include both articles by Jon P. Howell and Peter W. Dorfman "Leadership and Substitutes for Leadership Among Professional and Nonprofessional Workers" in *Journal of Applied Science Behavior* (Vol. 22, No. 1, 1986) and "Substitutes for Leadership: Test of a Construct" in *Academy of Management Journal* (December 1981), and in Robert H. Miles and M. M. Petty's "Leadership Effectiveness in Small Bureaucracies" in *Academy of Management Journal* (June 1977). The substitutes example that describes life on an aircraft carrier is titled "The Secret of Life at the Limits: Cogs Become Big Wheels" in *Smithsonian Magazine* (July 1989). The article by Edward E. Lawler III that provides insight into high-tech examples of substitutes is "Substitutes for Hierarchy" in *Organizational Dynamics* (Summer 1981).

Harold H. Kelley's work in explaining the fundamental process of attribution theory, "Attribution Theory in Social Psychology," appears in *Nebraska Symposium on Motivation* (Nebraska Press, 1967), edited by David Levine. It has provided a new paradigm for leadership theory and research. Bobby J. Calder is credited as being among the first to apply attribution theory to leadership processes in his chapter "An Attribution Theory of Leadership" in *New Directions in Organizational Behavior* (St. Clair, 1977), edited by Barry M. Staw and Gerald R. Salancik. Robert Lord has further developed the information processing approach to leadership. Lord's "information processing paradigm" helps to better understand the importance of determining whether it is the leader, the leader's situation, or both at the root of any leadership problem. [See, for example, Robert G. Lord, Roseanne J. Foti, and Christy L. DeVader's article "A Test of Leadership Categorization Theory" in *Organizational Behavior and Human Performance* (December 1984).]

CHAPTER 9: Questions for Discussion

1 Do you agree with Kotter's distinction between "management" and "leadership"? Could you make a counterargument that the distinction is somewhat artificial?
2 Could one make the argument that the distinction between "transformational" leaders and "transactional" leaders is simply a distinction between "effective" and "ineffective" leaders?
3 In the article by Bass, most of the examples of transformational leaders from the corporate world are CEOs. How likely is it that a number of "transformational" leaders could be found at all levels in the *same* organization, not just at the CEO level?
4 Similar to Question 3, how much total "transformational leadership" can a particular organization tolerate?
5 Could a truly transformational leader within an organization be an effective immediate subordinate of a higher-level transformational leader? Why? Why not?
6 In your opinion, are the views of Krantz and Conger too negative regarding charismatic leaders? Should most organizations with which you are familiar attempt to develop more charismatic leaders? What, if any, would be the possible consequences?
7 Thinking about organizations you have worked in or observed, what are some of the best examples you can cite of "substitutes for leadership"? Were they effective? Did they make a major difference in the need for leadership?

IMPLEMENTING
ORGANIZATIONAL CHANGE

In a sense, this chapter can be seen as a continuation of the preceding one on "Leadership Challenges." The reason, of course, is that implementing organizational change is one of the major, if not *the* major, challenges that leaders and would-be leaders face in confronting today's fast-paced rate of change in the external environment. Certainly, if there were ever a time when the idea that "what worked last year probably won't work next year" is applicable, it is the period we are in at the turn of the decade, century, and millennium. This is true not only for the world of business, where the notion of constant change is so frequently invoked, but also in other institutional areas including, but not limited to, government and higher education. Thus, the challenge of implementing change is nearly universal for almost all types of organizations and in almost all areas of society.

OVERVIEW OF THE READINGS

The basic premises of the opening article by Nadler and Tushman are that "organizational transformations need to be initiated and implemented rapidly" and that "different kinds of organizational changes will require very different kinds of leadership." They acknowledge the importance of a charismatic leadership style for some conditions, but argue that such behavior is "a necessary but not a sufficient component" of effective major change efforts. What is needed in addition, they contend, is "instrumental leadership" that gives attention to more prosaic matters such as structures and managerial processes. From the perspective of these authors and the propositions they advance, "it appears that effective organizational reorientation requires both charismatic and instrumental leadership. . . . Either one alone is insufficient for the achievement of change." They also particularly stress the importance, overlooked in many discussions of leadership, of "institutionalizing" the leadership of change, that is, of extending throughout the organization the responsibility for advancing major change and not leaving the leadership role solely to a few executives at the top.

In the next article, Howell and Higgins provide empirical data on the role of "champions" (those who actively identify with a particular change and persist in promoting and defending it to make sure it becomes a reality and a success) in bringing about technological innovation. Here, again, the phenomenon of "charismatic" leader behaviors is invoked, with the authors finding that champions of project innovations exhibit more of such behaviors than do nonchampions. Their results also indicate that the use of multiple influence tactics (refer back to the article by Yukl et al. in Chapter 4) tends to differentiate champions from their peers.

In the final article in this chapter, and a fitting final article for this book, Senge focuses on leaders' roles in building "learning organizations." He advances the axiom that "over the long run, superior performance depends on superior learning," not just for individuals, of course, but especially for organizations. The article makes a major distinction between "adaptive learning," which occurs as the reaction to situations, compared to "generative learning," which *anticipates* situations. Senge believes that both types of learning are critical for organizations, but he also indicates that generative learning does not come easily to the typical organization and must be specifically fostered by leaders. Leaders who want to encourage generative learning, according to Senge, must stimulate "creative tension," the perceived gap between a desired reality and the current reality, and they must become "designers, teachers, and stewards." This in turn will require new skills and new tools and a deliberately systemic way of thinking about issues if a true learning organization is to be developed.

Interestingly once again, while the focus of the three readings in this chapter is heavily on the role of leadership in stimulating and guiding organizational change through a minefield of potential obstacles, each article also utilizes the concept of motivation at critical points. Thus, Nadler and Tushman talk about one of the specific roles of the leader in organizational change situations being "the direct generation of energy—motivation to act—among members," and they also stress the fact that expectancy theories of motivation form the basis for instrumental leadership that "involves managing environments to create conditions that motivate desired behavior." Howell and Higgins refer to transformational leaders as "providing a strong motivational force for change." Senge emphasizes that with a problem-solving approach to change, "the motivation for change is extrinsic"; with the creative tension approach that he advocates, "the motivation is intrinsic." A fair conclusion across the three articles in this chapter would be that consideration of both leadership and motivation is critical for understanding the process and potential success of organization change, whether that change is incremental or revolutionary.

Beyond the Charismatic Leader: Leadership and Organizational Change

David A. Nadler
Michael L. Tushman

Like never before, discontinuous organization change is an important determinant of organization adaptation. Responding to regulatory, economic, competitive and/or technological shifts through more efficiently pushing the same organization systems and processes just does not work.[1] Rather, organizations may need to manage through periods of both incremental as well as revolutionary change.[2] Further, given the intensity of global competition in more and more industries, these organizational transformations need to be initiated and implemented rapidly. Speed seems to count.[3] These trends put a premium on executive leadership and the management of system-wide organization change.

There is a growing knowledge base about large-scale organization change.[4] This literature is quite consistent on at least one aspect of effective system-wide change—namely, executive leadership matters. The executive is a critical actor in the drama of organization change.[5] Consider the following examples:

At Fuji-Xerox, Yotaro Kobayashi's response to declining market share, lack of new products, and increasing customer complaints was to initiate widespread organization change. Most fundamentally, Kobayashi's vision was to change the way Fuji-Xerox conducted its business. Kobayashi and his team initiated the "New Xerox Movement" through Total Quality Control. The core values of quality, problem solving, teamwork, and customer emphasis were espoused and acted upon by Kobayashi and his team. Further, the executive team at Fuji instituted a dense infrastructure of objectives, measures, rewards, tools, education and slogans all in service of TQC and the "New Xerox." New heroes were created. Individuals and teams were publicly celebrated to reinforce to the system those behaviors that reflected the best of the new Fuji-Xerox. Kobayashi continually reinforced, celebrated, and communicated his TQC vision. Between 1976–1980, Fuji-Xerox gained back its market share, developed an impressive set of new products, and won the Deming prize.[6]

Much of this Fuji-Xerox learning was transferred to corporate Xerox and further enhanced by Dave Kearns and his executive team. Beginning in 1983, Kearns clearly expressed his "Leadership Through Quality" vision for the corporation. Kearns established a Quality Task Force and Quality Office with respected Xerox executives. This broad executive base developed the architecture of Leadership Through Quality. This effort included quality principles, tools, education, required leadership actions, rewards, and feedback mechanisms. This attempt to transform the entire corporation was initiated at the top and diffused throughout the firm through overlapping teams. These teams were pushed by Kearns and his team to achieve extraordinary gains. While not completed, this transformation has helped Xerox regain lost market share and improve product development efforts.[7]

At General Electric, Jack Welch's vision of a lean, aggressive organization with all the benefits of size but the agility of small firms is being driven by a set of interrelated actions. For example, the "work-out" effort is a corporate-wide endeavor, spearheaded by Welch, to get the bureaucracy out of a large-old organization and, in turn, to liberate GE employees to be their best. This effort is more than Welch. Welch's vision is being implemented by a senior task force which has initiated work-out efforts in Welch's own top team as well as in each GE business area. These efforts consist of training, problem solving, measures, rewards, feedback procedures, and outside expertise. Similarly, sweeping changes at SAS under Carlzon, at ICI under Harvey-Jones, by Anderson at NCR, and at Honda each emphasize the importance of visionary leadership along with executive teams, systems, structures and processes to transfer an individual's vision of the future into organizational reality.[8]

On the other hand, there are many examples of visionary executives who are unable to translate their vision into organization action. For example, Don Burr's vision at People Express not only to "make a better world" but also to grow rapidly and expand to capture the business traveller was not coupled with requisite changes in organization infrastructure, procedures, and/or roles. Further, Burr was unable to build a cohesive senior team to help execute his compelling vision. This switch in vision, without a committed senior team and associated structure and systems, led to the rapid demise of People Express.

Vision and/or charisma is not enough to sustain large-system change. While a necessary condition in the management of discontinuous change, we must build a model of leadership that goes beyond the inspired individual; a model that takes into account the complexities of system-wide change in large, diverse, geographically complex organizations. We attempt to develop a framework for the extension of charismatic leadership by building on the growing leadership literature,[9] the literature on organization evolution,[10] and our intensive consulting work with executives attempting major organization change.[11]

ORGANIZATIONAL CHANGE AND RE-ORGANIZATION

Organizations go through change all the time. However, the nature, scope, and intensity of organizational changes vary considerably. Different kinds of organizational changes will require very different kinds of leadership behavior in initiating, energizing, and implementing the change. Organization changes vary along the following dimensions:

- *Strategic and Incremental Changes*—Some changes in organizations, while significant, only affect selected components of the organization. The fundamental aim of such change is to enhance the effectiveness of the organization, but within the general framework of the strategy, mode of organizing, and values that already are in place. Such changes are called *incremental changes*. Incremental changes happen all the time in organizations, and they need not be small. Such things as changes in organization structure, the introduction of new technology, and significant modifications of personnel practices are all large and significant changes, but ones which usually occur within the existing definition and frame of reference of the organization. Other changes have an impact on the whole system of the organization and fundamentally redefine what the organization is or change its basic framework, including strategy, structure, people, processes, and (in some cases) core values. These changes are called *strategic organizational changes*. The Fuji-Xerox, People Express, ICI, and SAS cases are examples of system-wide organization change.

• *Reactive and Anticipatory Changes*—Many organizational changes are made in direct response to some external event. These changes, which are forced upon the organization, are called *reactive*. The Xerox, SAS and ICI transformations were all initiated in response to organization performance crisis. At other times, strategic organizational change is initiated not because of the need to respond to a contemporaneous event, but rather because senior management believes that change in anticipation of events still to come will provide competitive advantage. These changes are called *anticipatory*. The GE and People Express cases as well as more recent system-wide changes at ALCOA and Cray Research are examples of system-wide change initiated in anticipation of environmental change.

If these two dimensions are combined, a basic typology of different changes can be described (see Figure 1).

Change which is incremental and anticipatory is called *tuning*. These changes are not system-wide redefinitions, but rather modifications of specific components, and they are initiated in anticipation of future events. Incremental change which is initiated reactively is called *adaptation*. Strategic change initiated in anticipation of future events is called *re-orientation,* and change which is prompted by immediate demands is called *re-creation.*[12]

Research on patterns of organizational life and death across several industries has provided insight into the patterns of strategic organizational change.[13] Some of the key findings are as follows:

• *Strategic organization changes are necessary.* These changes appear to be environmentally driven. Various factors—be they competitive, technological, or regulatory—drive the organization (either reactively or in anticipation) to make system-wide changes. While strategic organization change does not guarantee success, those organizations that fail to change, generally fail to survive. Discontinuous environmental change seems to require discontinuous organization change.

• *Re-creations are riskier.* Re-creations are riskier endeavors than reorientations if only because they are initiated under crisis conditions and under sharp time constraints. Further, re-creations almost always involve a change in core values. As core values are most resistant to change, re-creations always trigger substantial individual resistance to change and heightened political behavior. Re-creations that do succeed

FIGURE 1

Types of organizational changes.

	Incremental	Strategic
Anticipatory	**Tuning**	**Re-orientation**
Reactive	**Adaptation**	**Re-creation**

usually involve changes in the senior leadership of the firm, frequently involving replacement from the outside. For example, the reactive system-wide changes at U.S. Steel, Chrysler, and Singer were all initiated by new senior teams.

• *Re-orientations are associated more with success.* Re-orientations have the luxury of time to shape the change, build coalitions, and empower individuals to be effective in the new organization. Further, re-orientations give senior managers time to prune and shape core values in service of the revised strategy, structure, and processes. For example, the proactive strategic changes at Cray Research, ALCOA, and GE each involved system-wide change as well as the shaping of core values ahead of the competition and from a position of strength.

Re-orientations are, however, risky. When sweeping changes are initiated in advance of precipitating external events, success is contingent on making appropriate strategic bets. As re-orientations are initiated ahead of the competition and in advance of environmental shifts, they require visionary executives. Unfortunately, in real time, it is unclear who will be known as visionary executives (e.g., Welch, Iacocca, Rollwagen at Cray Research) and who will be known as failures (e.g., Don Burr at People Express, or Larry Goshorn at General Automation). In turbulent environments, not to make strategic bets is associated with failure. Not all bets will pay off, however. The advantages of re-orientations derive from the extra implementation time and from the opportunity to learn from and adapt to mistakes.[14]

As with re-creations, executive leadership is crucial in initiating and implementing strategic re-orientations. The majority of successful re-orientations involve change in the CEO and substantial executive team change. Those most successful firms, however, have executive teams that are relatively stable yet are still capable of initiating several re-orientations (e.g., Ken Olsen at DEC and An Wang at Wang).

There are, then, quite fundamentally different kinds of organizational changes. The role of executive leadership varies considerably for these different types of organizational changes. Incremental change typically can be managed by the existing management structures and processes of the organization, sometimes in conjunction with special transition structures.[15] In these situations, a variety of leadership styles may be appropriate, depending upon how the organization is normally managed and led. In strategic changes, however, the management process and structure itself is the subject of change; therefore, it cannot be relied upon to manage the change. In addition, the organization's definition of effective leadership may also be changing as a consequence of the re-orientation or re-creation. In these situations, leadership becomes a very critical element of change management.

This article focuses on the role of executive leadership in strategic organization change, and in particular, the role of leadership in re-orientations. Given organization and individual inertia, re-orientations can not be initiated or implemented without sustained action by the organization's leadership. Indeed, re-orientations are frequently driven by new leadership, often brought in from outside the organization.[16] A key challenge for executives facing turbulent environments, then, is to learn how to effectively initiate, lead, and manage re-orientations. Leadership of strategic re-orientations requires not only charisma, but also substantial instrumental skills in building executive teams, roles, and systems in support of the change, as well as institutional skills in diffusing leadership throughout the organization.

THE CHARISMATIC LEADER

While the subject of leadership has received much attention over the years, the more specific issue of leadership during periods of change has only recently attracted serious attention.[17] What emerges from various discussions of leadership and organizational change is a picture of the special kind of leadership that appears to be critical during times of strategic organizational change. While various words have been used to portray this type of leadership, we prefer the label "charismatic" leader. It refers to a special quality that enables the leader to mobilize and sustain activity within an organization through specific personal actions combined with perceived personal characteristics.

The concept of the charismatic leader is not the popular version of the great speech maker or television personality. Rather, a model has emerged from recent work aimed at identifying the nature and determinants of a particular type of leadership that successfully brings about changes in an individual's values, goals, needs, or aspirations. Research on charismatic leadership has identified this type of leadership as observable, definable, and having clear behavioral characteristics.[18] We have attempted to develop a first cut description of the leader in terms of patterns of behavior that he/she seems to exhibit. The resulting approach is outlined in Figure 2, which lists three major types of behavior that characterize these leaders and some illustrative kinds of actions.

The first component of charismatic leadership is *envisioning*. This involves the creation of a picture of the future, or of a desired future state with which people can identify and which can generate excitement. By creating vision, the leader provides a vehicle for people to develop commitment, a common goal around which people can rally, and a way for people to feel successful. Envisioning is accomplished through a range of different actions. Clearly, the simplest form is through articulation of a compelling vision in clear and dramatic terms. The vision needs to be challenging, meaningful, and worthy of pursuit, but it also needs to be credible. People must believe that it is possible to succeed in the pursuit of the vision. Vision is also communicated in other ways, such as through expectations that the leader expresses and through the leader personally demonstrating behaviors and activities that symbolize and further that vision.

The second component is *energizing*. Here the role of the leader is the direct generation of energy—motivation to act—among members of the organization. How is this done? Different leaders engage in energizing in different ways, but some of the most common include demonstration of their own personal excitement and energy, com-

FIGURE 2
The charismatic leader.

Envisioning
- articulating a compelling vision
- setting high expectations
- modeling consistent behaviors

Energizing
- demonstrating personal excitement
- expressing personal confidence
- seeking, finding, & using success

Enabling
- expressing personal support
- empathizing
- expressing confidence in people

bined with leveraging that excitement through direct personal contact with large numbers of people in the organization. They express confidence in their own ability to succeed. They find, and use, successes to celebrate progress towards the vision.

The third component is *enabling*. The leader psychologically helps people act or perform in the face of challenging goals. Assuming that individuals are directed through a vision and motivated by the creation of energy, they then may need emotional assistance in accomplishing their tasks. This enabling is achieved in several ways. Charismatic leaders demonstrate empathy—the ability to listen, understand, and share the feelings of those in the organization. They express support for individuals. Perhaps most importantly, the charismatic leader tends to express his/her confidence in people's ability to perform effectively and to meet challenges.

Yotaro Kobayashi at Fuji-Xerox and Paul O'Neil at ALCOA each exhibit the characteristics of charismatic leaders. In Kobayashi's transformation at Fuji, he was constantly espousing his New Xerox Movement vision for Fuji. Kobayashi set high standards for his firm (e.g., the 3500 model and the Deming Prize), for himself, and for his team. Beyond espousing this vision for Fuji, Kobayashi provided resources, training, and personal coaching to support his colleagues' efforts in the transformation at Fuji. Similarly, Paul O'Neil has espoused a clear vision for ALCOA anchored on quality, safety, and innovation. O'Neil has made his vision compelling and central to the firm, has set high expectations for his top team and for individuals throughout ALCOA and provides continuous support and energy for his vision through meetings, task forces, video tapes, and extensive personal contact.

Assuming that leaders act in these ways, what functions are they performing that help bring about change? First, they provide a psychological focal point for the energies, hopes, and aspirations of people in the organization. Second, they serve as powerful role models whose behaviors, actions and personal energy demonstrate the desired behaviors expected throughout the firm. The behaviors of charismatic leaders provide a standard to which others can aspire. Through their personal effectiveness and attractiveness they build a very personal and intimate bond between themselves and the organization. Thus, they can become a source of sustained energy; a figure whose high standards others can identify with and emulate.

Limitations of the Charismatic Leader   Even if one were able to do all of the things involved in being a charismatic leader, it might still not be enough. In fact, our observations suggest that there are a number of inherent limitations to the effectiveness of charismatic leaders, many stemming from risks associated with leadership which revolves around a single individual. Some of the key potential problems are:

• *Unrealistic Expectations*—In creating a vision and getting people energized, the leader may create expectations that are unrealistic or unattainable. These can backfire if the leader cannot live up to the expectations that are created.

• *Dependency and Counterdependency*—A strong, visible, and energetic leader may spur different psychological responses. Some individuals may become overly dependent upon the leader, and in some cases whole organizations become dependent. Everyone else stops initiating actions and waits for the leader to provide direction; individuals may become passive or reactive. On the other extreme, others may be uncomfortable with strong personal presence and spend time and energy demonstrating how the leader is wrong—how the emperor has no clothes.

• *Reluctance to Disagree with the Leader*—The charismatic leader's approval or disapproval becomes an important commodity. In the presence of a strong leader, people may become hesitant to disagree or come into conflict with the leader. This may, in turn, lead to stifling conformity.

• *Need for Continuing Magic*—The charismatic leader may become trapped by the expectation that the magic often associated with charisma will continue unabated. This may cause the leader to act in ways that are not functional, or (if the magic is not produced) it may cause a crisis of leadership credibility.

• *Potential Feelings of Betrayal*—When and if things do not work out as the leader has envisioned, the potential exists for individuals to feel betrayed by their leader. They may become frustrated and angry, with some of that anger directed at the individual who created the expectations that have been betrayed.

• *Disenfranchisement of Next Levels of Management*—A consequence of the strong charismatic leader is that the next levels of management can easily become disenfranchised. They lose their ability to lead because no direction, vision, exhortation, reward, or punishment is meaningful unless it comes directly from the leader. The charismatic leader thus may end up underleveraging his or her management and/or creating passive/dependent direct reports.

• *Limitations of Range of the Individual Leader*—When the leadership process is built around an individual, management's ability to deal with various issues is limited by the time, energy, expertise, and interest of that individual. This is particularly problematic during periods of change when different types of issues demand different types of competencies (e.g., markets, technologies, products, finance) which a single individual may not possess. Different types of strategic changes make different managerial demands and call for different personal characteristics. There may be limits to the number of strategic changes that one individual can lead over the life of an organization.

In light of these risks, it appears that the charismatic leader is a necessary component—but not a sufficient component—of the organizational leadership required for effective organizational re-organization. There is a need to move beyond the charismatic leader.

INSTRUMENTAL LEADERSHIP

Effective leaders of change need to be more than just charismatic. Effective re-orientations seem to be characterized by the presence of another type of leadership behavior which focuses not on the excitement of individuals and changing their goals, needs or aspirations, but on making sure that individuals in the senior team and throughout the organization behave in ways needed for change to occur. An important leadership role is to build competent teams, clarify required behaviors, build in measurement, and administer rewards and punishments so that individuals perceive that behavior consistent with the change is central for them in achieving their own goals.[19] We will call this type of leadership *instrumental leadership,* since it focuses on the management of teams, structures, and managerial processes to create individual instrumentalities. The basis of this approach is in expectancy theories of motivation, which propose that individuals will perform those behaviors that they perceive as instrumental for acquiring valued outcomes.[20] Leadership, in this context, involves managing environments to create conditions that motivate desired behavior.[21]

In practice, instrumental leadership of change involves three elements of behavior (see Figure 3). The first is *structuring.* The leader invests time in building teams that have the required competence to execute and implement the re-orientation[22] and in creating structures that make it clear what types of behavior are required throughout the organization. This may involve setting goals, establishing standards, and defining roles and responsibilities. Re-orientations seem to require detailed planning about what people will need to do and how they will be required to act during different phases of the change. The second element of instrumental leadership is *controlling.* This involves the creation of systems and processes to measure, monitor, and assess both behavior and results and to administer corrective action.[23] The third element is *rewarding*, which includes the administration of both rewards and punishments contingent upon the degree to which behavior is consistent with the requirements of the change.

Instrumental leadership focuses on the challenge of shaping consistent behaviors in support of the re-orientation. The charismatic leader excites individuals, shapes their aspirations, and directs their energy. In practice, however, this is not enough to sustain patterns of desired behavior. Subordinates and colleagues may be committed to the vision, but over time other forces may influence their behavior, particularly when they are not in direct personal contact with the leader. This is particularly relevant during periods of change when the formal organization and the informal social system may lag behind the leader and communicate outdated messages or reward traditional behavior. Instrumental leadership is needed to ensure compliance over time consistent with the commitment generated by charismatic leadership.

At Xerox, for example, David Kearns used instrumental leadership to further enliven his Leadership Through Quality efforts.[24] Beyond his own sustained behaviors in

FIGURE 3

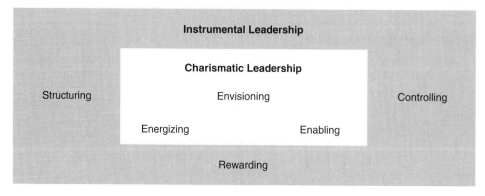

support of the Leadership Through Quality effort, Kearns and his Quality Office developed a comprehensive set of roles, processes, teams, and feedback and audit mechanisms for getting customer input and continuous improvement into everyday problem solving throughout Xerox. Individuals and teams across the corporation were evaluated on their ability to continuously meet customer requirements. These data were used in making pay, promotion, and career decisions.

The Role of Mundane Behaviors   Typical descriptions of both charismatic and instrumental leaders tend to focus on significant events, critical incidents, and grand gestures. Our vision of the change manager is frequently exemplified by the key speech or public event that is a potential watershed event. While these are important arenas for leadership, leading large-system change also requires sustained attention to the myriad of details that make up organizational life. The accumulation of less dramatic, day-to-day activities and mundane behaviors serves as a powerful determinant of behavior.[25] Through relatively unobtrusive acts, through sustained attention to detail, managers can directly shape perceptions and culture in support of the change effort. Examples of mundane behavior that when taken together can have a great impact include:

- allocation of time; calendar management
- asking questions, following up
- shaping of physical settings
- public statements
- setting agendas of events or meetings
- use of events such as lunches, meetings, to push the change effort
- summarization—post hoc interpretation of what occurred
- creating heroes
- use of humor, stories, and myths
- small symbolic actions, including rewards and punishments

In each of these ways, leaders can use daily activities to emphasize important issues, identify desirable behavior, and help create patterns and meaning out of the various transaction that make up organizational life.

The Complementarity of Leadership Approaches   It appears that effective organizational re-orientation requires both charismatic and instrumental leadership. Charismatic leadership is needed to generate energy, create commitment, and direct individuals towards new objectives, values or aspirations. Instrumental leadership is required to ensure that people really do act in a manner consistent with their new goals. Either one alone is insufficient for the achievement of change.

The complementarity of leadership approaches and the necessity for both creates a dilemma.[26] Success in implementing these dual approaches is associated with the personal style, characteristics, needs, and skills of the executive. An individual who is adept at one approach may have difficulty executing the other. For example, charismatic leaders may have problems with tasks involved in achieving control. Many charismatic leaders are motivated by a strong desire to receive positive feedback from those around them.[27] They may therefore have problems delivering unpleasant messages, dealing with performance problems, or creating situations that could attract negative feelings.[28]

Only exceptional individuals can handle the behavioral requirements of both charismatic and instrumental leadership styles. While such individuals exist, an alternative may be to involve others in leadership roles, thus complementing the strengths and weaknesses of one individual leader.[29] For example, in the early days at Honda, it took the steadying, systems-oriented hand of Takeo Fujisawa to balance the fanatic, impatient, visionary energy of Soichiro Honda. Similarly, at Data General, it took Alsing and Rasala's social, team, and organization skills to balance and make more humane Tom West's vision and standards for the Eclipse team.[30] Without these complementary organization and systems skills, Don Burr was unable to execute his proactive system-wide changes at People Express.

The limitations of the individual leader pose a significant challenge. Charismatic leadership has a broad reach. It can influence many people, but is limited by the frequency and intensity of contact with the individual leader. Instrumental leadership is also limited by the degree to which the individual leader can structure, observe, measure and reward behavior. These limitations present significant problems for achieving re-orientations. One implication is that structural extensions of leadership should be created in the process of managing re-orientations.[31] A second implication is that human extensions of leadership need to be created to broaden the scope and impact of leader actions. This leads to a third aspect of leadership and change—the extension of leadership beyond the individual leader, or the creation of institutionalized leadership throughout the organization.

INSTITUTIONALIZING THE LEADERSHIP OF CHANGE

Given the limitations of the individual charismatic leader, the challenge is to broaden the range of individuals who can perform the critical leadership functions during periods of significant organizational change. There are three potential leverage points for the extension of leadership—the senior team, broader senior management, and the development of leadership throughout the organization (see Figure 4).

Leveraging the Senior Team   The group of individuals who report directly to the individual leader—the executive or senior team—is the first logical place to look for opportunities to extend and institutionalize leadership. Development of an effective, visible, and dynamic senior team can be a major step in getting around the problems and limitations of the individual leader.[32] Examples of such executive teams include the Management Committee established at Corning by Jamie Houghton or Bob Allen's Executive Committee at AT&T. Several actions appear to be important in enhancing the effectiveness of the senior team.

• *Visible Empowerment of the Team*—A first step is the visible empowerment of the team, or "anointing" the team as extensions of the individual leader. There are two different aspects to this empowerment: objective and symbolic. Objective empowerment involves providing team members with the autonomy and resources to serve effectively. Symbolic empowerment involves communicating messages (through infor-

FIGURE 4

mation, symbols, and mundane behaviors) to show the organization that these individuals are indeed extensions of the leader, and ultimately key components of the leadership. Symbolic empowerment can be done through the use of titles, the designation of organizational structures, and the visible presence of individuals in ceremonial roles.

• *Individual Development of Team Members*—Empowerment will fail if the individuals on the team are not capable of executing their revised leadership roles. A major problem in re-orientations is that the members of the senior team frequently are the product of the very systems, structures, and values that the re-orientation seeks to change. Participating in the change, and more importantly, leading it, may require a significant switching of cognitive gears.[33] Re-orientations demand that senior team members think very differently about the business and about managing. This need for personal change at the most senior level has implications for the selection of senior team members (see below). It also may mean that part of the individual leader's role is to help coach, guide, and support individuals in developing their own leadership capabilities. Each individual need not (and should not) be a "clone" of the individual leader; but each should be able to initiate credible leadership actions in a manner consistent with their own personal styles. Ultimately, it also puts a demand on the leader to deal with those who will not or can not make the personal changes required for helping lead the re-orientation.

• *Composition of the Senior Team*—The need for the senior team to implement change may mean that the composition of that team may have to be altered. Different skills, capabilities, styles, and value orientations may be needed to both lead the changes as well as to manage in the reconfigured organization.[34] In fact, most successful re-orientations seem to involve some significant changes in the make-up of the senior team. This may require outplacement of people as well as importing new people, either from outside the organization, or from outside the coalition that has traditionally led the organization.[35]

• *The Inducement of Strategic Anticipation*—A critical issue in executing re-orientations is strategic anticipation. By definition, a re-orientation is a strategic organizational change that is initiated in anticipation of significant external events. Re-orientation occurs because the organization's leadership perceives competitive advantage from initiating change earlier rather than later. The question is, who is responsible for thinking about and anticipating external events, and ultimately deciding that re-orientation is necessary? In some cases, the individual leader does this, but the task is enormous. This is where the senior team can be helpful, because as a group it can scan a larger number of events and potentially be more creative in analyzing the environment and the process of anticipation.

Companies that are successful anticipators create conditions in which anticipation is more likely to occur. They invest in activities that foster anticipation, such as environmental scanning, experiments or probes inside the organization (frequently on the periphery), and frequent contacts with the outside. The senior team has a major role in initiating, sponsoring, and leveraging these activities.[36]

• *The Senior Team as a Learning System*—For a senior team to benefit from its involvement in leading change, it must become an effective system for learning about the business, the nature of change, and the task of managing change. The challenge is to both bond the team together, while avoiding insularity. One of the costs of such team structures is that they become isolated from the rest of the organization, they develop patterns of dysfunctional conformity, avoid conflict, and over time develop patterns of learned incompetence. These group processes diminish the team's capacity for effective strategic anticipation, and decrease the team's ability to provide effective leadership of the re-orientation.[37]

There are several ways to enhance a senior team's ability to learn over time. One approach is to work to keep the team an open system, receptive to outside ideas and information. This can be accomplished by creating a constant stream of events that expose people to new ideas and/or situations. For example, creating simulations, using critical incident techniques, creating near histories, are all ways of exposing senior teams to novel situations and sharpening problem-solving skills.[38] Similarly, senior teams can open themselves to new ideas via speakers or visitors brought in to meet with the team, visits by the team to other organizations, frequent contact with customers, and planned informal data collection through personal contact (breakfasts, focus groups, etc.) throughout the organization. A second approach involves the shaping and management of the internal group process of the team itself. This involves working on effective group leadership, building effective team member skills, creating meeting management discipline, acquiring group problem-solving and information-processing skills, and ultimately creating norms that promote effective learning, innovation, and problem solving.[39]

David Kearns at Xerox and Paul O'Neil at ALCOA made substantial use of senior teams in implementing their quality-oriented organization transformations. Both executives appointed senior quality task forces composed of highly respected senior executives. These task forces were charged with developing the corporate-wide architecture of the change effort. To sharpen their change and quality skills these executives made trips to Japan and to other experienced organizations, and were involved in extensive education and problem-solving efforts in their task forces and within their own divisions. These task forces put substance and enhanced energy into the CEO's broad vision. These executives were, in turn, role models and champions of the change efforts in their own sectors.

As a final note, it is important to remember that frequently there are significant obstacles in developing effective senior teams to lead re-orientations. The issues of skills and selection have been mentioned. Equally important is the question of power and succession. A team is most successful when there is a perception of common fate. *Individuals have to believe that the success of the team will, in the long run, be more salient to them than their individual short-run success.* In many situations, this can be accomplished through appropriate structures, objectives, and incentives. But these actions may fail when there are pending (or anticipated) decisions to be made concerning senior management succession. In these situations, the quality of collaboration tends to deteriorate significantly, and effective team leadership of change becomes problematic. The individual leader must manage the timing and process of succession in relation to the requirements for team leadership, so that conflicting (and mutually exclusive) incentives are not created by the situation.[40]

Broadening Senior Management A second step in moving beyond individual leadership of change is the further extension of the leadership beyond the executive or senior team to include a broader set of individuals who make up the senior management of the organization. This would include individuals one or two levels down from the executive team. At Corning, the establishment of two groups—the Corporate Policy Group (approximately the top 35) and the Corporate Management Group (about the top 120)—are examples of mechanisms used by Houghton to broaden the definition of senior management. This set of individuals is in fact the senior operating management of most sizeable organizations and is looked upon as senior management by the majority of employees. In many cases (and particularly during times of change) they do not feel like senior management, and thus they are not positioned to lead the change. They feel like participants (at best) and victims (at worst). This group can be particularly problematic since they may be more embedded in the current system of organizing and managing than some of the senior team. They may be less prepared to change, they frequently have molded themselves to fit the current organizational style, and they may feel disenfranchised by the very act of developing a strong executive team, particularly if that team has been assembled by bringing in people from outside of the organization.

The task is to make this group feel like senior management, to get them signed up for the change, and to motivate and enable them to work as an extension of the senior team. Many of the implications are similar to those mentioned above in relation to the top team; however, there are special problems of size and lack of proximity to the individual charismatic leader. Part of the answer is to get the senior team to take responsibility for developing their own teams as leaders of change. Other specific actions may include:

• *Rites of Passage*—Creating symbolic events that help these individuals to feel more a part of senior management.

• *Senior Groups*—Creating structures (councils, boards, committees, conferences) to maintain contact with this group and reinforce their sense of participation as members of senior management.

• *Participation in Planning Change*—Involving these people in the early diagnosing of the need to change and the planning of change strategies associated with the re-orientation. This is particularly useful in getting them to feel more like owners, rather than victims of the change.

• *Intensive Communication*—Maintaining a constant stream of open communication to and from this group. It is the lack of information and perspective that psychologically disenfranchises these individuals.

Developing Leadership in the Organization A third arena for enhancing the leadership of re-organizations is through organizational structures, systems, and process for leadership development consistent with the re-orientation. Frequently leadership development efforts lag behind the re-orientation. The management development system of many organizations often works effectively to create managers who will fit well with the organizational environment that the leadership seeks to abandon. There needs to be a strategic and anticipatory thinking about the leadership development process, including the following:

• *Definition of Managerial Competence*—A first step is determining the skills, capabilities, and capacities needed to manage and lead effectively in the re-orientation and post re-orientation period. Factors that have contributed to managerial success in the past may be the seeds of failure in the future.

• *Sourcing Managerial Talent*—Re-orientations may require that the organization identify significantly different sources for acquiring leaders or potential leaders. Senior managers should be involved in recruiting the hiring. Because of the lead time involved, managerial sourcing has to be approached as a long-term (five to ten years) task.

• *Socialization*—As individuals move into the organization and into positions of leadership, deliberate actions must be taken to teach them how the organization's social system works. During periods of re-orientation, the socialization process ought to lead rather than lag behind the change.

• *Management Education*—Re-orientation may require managers and leaders to use or develop new skills, competencies, or knowledge. This creates a demand for effective management education. Research indicates that the impact of passive internal management education on the development of effective leaders may be minimal when compared with more action-oriented educational experiences. The use of educational events to expose people to external settings or ideas (through out-of-company education) and to socialize individuals through action-oriented executive education may be more useful than attempts to teach people to be effective leaders and managers.[41]

• *Career Management*—Research and experience indicate that the most potent factor in the development of effective leaders is the nature of their job experiences.[42] The challenge is to ensure that middle and lower level managers get a wide range of experiences over time. Preparing people to lead re-orientations may require a greater emphasis on the development of generalists through cross-functional, divisional, and/or multinational career experiences.[43] Diverse career experiences help individuals develop a broad communication network and a range of experiences and competences all of which are vital in managing large-system change. This approach to careers implies the sharing of the burden of career management between both the organization and the employee as well as the deliberate strategy of balancing current contribution with investment for the future when placing people in job assignments.[44]

• *Seeding Talent*—Developing leadership for change may also require deliberate leveraging of available talent. This implies thoughtful placement of individual leaders in different situations and parts of the organization, the use of transfers, and the strategic placement of high-potential leaders.[45]

Perhaps the most ambitious and most well-documented effort at developing leadership throughout the organization is Welch's actions at GE. Welch has used GE's Management Development Institute at Crotonville as an important lever in the transformation of GE. Based on Welch's vision of a lean, competitive, agile organization with businesses leading in their respective markets, Crotonville has been used as a staging area for the revolution at GE. With Welch's active involvement, Crotonville's curriculum has moved from a short-term cognitive orientation towards longer-term problem solving and organization change. The curriculum has been developed to shape experiences and sharpen skills over the course of an individual's career in service of developing leaders to fit into the new GE.[46]

SUMMARY

In a world characterized by global competition, deregulation, sharp technological change, and political turmoil, discontinuous organization change seems to be a determinant of organization adaptation. Those firms that can initiate and implement discontinuous organization change more rapidly and/or prior to the competition have a competitive advantage. While not all change will be successful, inertia or incremental change in the face of altered competitive arenas is a recipe for failure.

Executive leadership is the critical factor in the initiation and implementation of large-system organization change. This article has developed an approach to the leadership of discontinuous organization change with particular reference to re-orientations—discontinuous change initiated in advance of competitive threat and/or performance crisis. Where incremental change can be delegated, strategic change must be driven by senior management. Charismatic leadership is a vital aspect of managing large-system change. Charismatic leaders provide vision, direction, and energy. Thus the successes of O'Neil at ALCOA, Welch at GE, Kearns at Xerox, and Rollwagen and Cray are partly a function of committed, enthusiastic, and passionate individual executives.

Charisma is not, however, enough to effect large-system change. Charismatic leadership must be bolstered by instrumental leadership through attention to detail on roles, responsibilities, structures, and rewards. Further, as many organizations are too large and complex for any one executive and/or senior team to directly manage, responsibility for large-system change must be institutionalized throughout the management system. The leadership of strategic organization change must be pushed throughout the organization to maximize the probability that managers at all levels own and are involved in executing the change efforts and see the concrete benefits of making the change effort work. O'Neil, Welch, Kearns, and Rollwagen are important catalysts in their organizations. Their successes to date are, however, not based simply on strong personalities. Each of these executives has been able to build teams, systems, and managerial processes to leverage and add substance to his vision and energy. It is this interaction of charisma, attention to systems and processes, and widespread involvement at multiple levels that seems to drive large-system change.

Even with inspired leadership, though, no re-orientation can emerge fully developed and planned. Re-orientations take time to implement. During this transition period, mistakes are made, environments change and key people leave. Given the turbulence of competitive conditions, the complexity of large-system change and individual cognitive limitations, the executive team must develop its ability to adapt to new conditions and, as importantly, learn from both its successes and failures. As organizations can not remain stable in the face of environmental change, so too must the management of large-system change be flexible. This ability of executive teams to build in learning and to build in flexibility into the process of managing large-system organizational change is a touchstone for proactively managing re-orientations.

REFERENCES

1 R. Solow, M. Dertouzos, and R. Lester, *Made in America* (Cambridge, MA: MIT Press, 1989).
2 See M.L. Tushman, W. Newman, and E. Romanelli, "Convergence and Upheaval: Managing the Unsteady Pace of Organizational Evolution," *California Management Review,* 29/1 (Fall 1986): 29–44.
3 E.g., K. Imai, I. Nonaka, and H. Takeuchi, "Managing the New Product Development Process: How Japanese Companies Learn and Unlearn," in K. Clark and R. Hayes, *The Uneasy Alliance* (Cambridge, MA: Harvard University Press, 1985).
4 E.g., A. Pettigrew, *The Awakening Giant: Continuity and Change at ICI* (London: Blackwell, 1985); J.R. Kimberly and R.E. Quinn, *New Futures: The Challenge of Managing Corporate Transitions* (Homewood, IL: Dow Jones-Irwin, 1984); Y. Allaire and M. Firsirotu, "How to Implement Radical Strategies in Large Organizations," *Sloan Management Review* (Winter 1985).
5 E.g., J. Gabbaro, *The Dynamics of Taking Charge* (Cambridge, MA: Harvard Business School Press, 1987); L. Greiner and A. Bhambri, "New CEO Intervention and Dynamics of Deliberate Strategic Change," *Strategic Management Journal,* 10 (1989): 67–86; N.M. Tichy and M.A. Devanna, *The Transformational Leader* (New York, NY: John Wiley & Sons, 1986); D. Hambrick, "The Top Management Team: Key to Strategic Success," *California Management Review*, 30/1 (Fall 1987):88–108.
6 Y. Kobayashi, "Quality Control in Japan: The Case of Fuji Xerox," *Japanese Economic Studies* (Spring 1983).
7 G. Jacobson and J. Hillkirk, *Xerox: American Samurai* (New York, NY: Macmillan, 1986).
8 For SAS, see J. Carlzon, *Moments of Truth* (Cambridge, MA: Ballinger, 1987); for ICI, see Pettigrew, op. cit.; for NCR, see R. Rosenbloom, *From Gears to Chips: The Transformation of NCR in the Digital Era* (Cambridge, MA: Harvard University Press, 1988); for

Honda, see I. Nonaka, "Creating Organizational Order Out of Chaos: Self-Renewal in Japanese Firms," *California Management Review,* 30/3 (Spring 1988):57–73.

9 Gabbaro, op. cit.; H. Levinson and S. Rosenthal, *CEO: Corporate Leadership in Action* (New York, NY: Basic Books, 1984); Greiner and Bhambri, op. cit.

10 Tushman et al., op. cit.; R. Greenwood and C. Hinings, "Organization Design Types, Tracks, and the Dynamics of Strategic Change," *Organization Studies,* 9/3 (1988):293–316; D. Miller and P. Friesen, *Organizations: A Quantum View* (Englewood Cliffs, NJ: Prentice-Hall, 1984).

11 D.A. Nadler and M.L. Tushman, "Organizational Framebending: Principles for Managing Re-orientation," *Academy of Management Executive,* 3 (1989):194–202.

12 For a more detailed discussion of this framework, see Nadler and Tushman, ibid.

13 Tushman et al., op. cit.; Greiner and Bhambri, op. cit.; Greenwood and Hinings, op. cit.; B. Virany and M.L. Tushman, "Changing Characteristics of Executive Teams in an Emerging Industry," *Journal of Business Venturing,* 1 (1986):261–274; M.L. Tushman and E. Romanelli, "Organizational Evolution: A Metamorphosis Model of Convergence and Re-orientation," in B.M. Staw and L.L. Cummings, eds., *Research in Organizational Behavior,* 5 (Greenwich, CT: JAI Press, 1985), pp. 171–222.

14 J. March, L. Sproull, and M. Tamuz, "Learning from Samples of One or Fewer," *Organization Science,* 2 (1991):14–39.

15 R. Beckhard and R. Harris, *Organizational Transitions* (Reading, MA: Addison-Wesley, 1977).

16 See R. Vancil, *Passing the Baton* (Cambridge, MA: Harvard Business School Press, 1987).

17 J.M. Burns, *Leadership* (New York, NY: Harper & Row, 1978); W. Bennis and B. Nanus, *Leaders: The Strategies for Taking Charge* (New York, NY: Harper & Row, 1985); N.M. Tichy and D. Ulrich, "The Leadership Challenge: A Call for the Transformational Leader," *Sloan Management Review* (Fall 1984); Tichy and Devanna, op. cit.

18 D.E. Berlew, "Leadership and Organizational Excitement," in D.A. Kolb, I.M. Rubin, and J.M. McIntyre, eds., *Organizational Psychology* (Englewood Cliffs, NJ: Prentice-Hall, 1974); R. J. House, "A 1976 Theory of Charismatic Leadership," in J.G. Hunt and L.L. Larson, eds., *Leadership: The Cutting Edge* (Carbondale, IL: Southern Illinois University Press, 1977); Levinson and Rosenthall, op. cit.; B.M. Bass, *Performance Beyond Expectations* (New York, NY: Free Press, 1985); R. House et al., "Personality and Charisma in the U.S. Presidency," Wharton Working Paper, 1989.

19 Hambrick, op. cit.; D. Ancona and D. Nadler, "Teamwork at the Top: Creating High Performing Executive Teams," *Sloan Management Review* (in press).

20 V.H. Vroom, *Work and Motivation* (New York, NY: John Wiley & Sons, 1964); J.P. Campbell, M.D. Dunnette, E.E. Lawler, and K. Weick, *Managerial Behavior, Performances, and Effectiveness* (New York, NY: McGraw-Hill, 1970).

21 R.J. House, "Path-Goal Theory of Leadership Effectiveness," *Administrative Science Quarterly,* 16 (1971):321–338; G.R. Oldham, "The Motivational Strategies Used by Supervisors: Relationships to Effectiveness Indicators," *Organizational Behavior and Human Performance,* 15 (1976):66–86.

22 See Hambrick, op. cit.

23 E.E. Lawler and J.G. Rhode, *Information and Control in Organizations* (Pacific Palisades, CA: Goodyear, 1976).

24 Jacobson and Hillkirk, op. cit.

25 Gabbaro, op. cit.; T.J. Peters, "Symbols, Patterns, and Settings: An Optimistic Case for Getting Things Done," *Organizational Dynamics* (Autumn 1978).

26 R.J. House, "Exchange and Charismatic Theories of Leadership," in G. Reber, ed., *Ency-*

clopedia of Leadership (Stuttgart: C.E. Poeschel-Verlag, 1987).

27 M. Kets de Vries and D. Miller, "Neurotic Style and Organization Pathology," *Strategic Management Journal* (1984).

28 Levinson and Rosenthal, op. cit.

29 Hambrick, op. cit.

30 T. Kidder, *Soul of the New Machine* (Boston, MA: Little, Brown, 1981).

31 These are discussed in Nadler and Tushman, op. cit.

32 Hambrick, op. cit.

33 M. Louis and R. Sutton, *Switching Cognitive Gears* (Stanford, CA: Stanford University Press, 1987).

34 C. O'Reilly, D. Caldwell, and W. Barnett, "Work Group Demography, Social Integration, and Turnover," *Administrative Science Quarterly,* 34, (1989):21–37.

35 Hambrick, op. cit.; Virany and Tushman, op. cit.

36 See D. Ancona, "Top Management Teams: Preparing for the Revolution," in J. Carroll, ed., *Social Psychology in Business Organizations* (New York, NY: Erlbaum Associates, in press).

37 Louis and Sutton, op. cit.

38 March et al., op. cit.

39 See also C. Gersick, "Time and Transition in Work Teams," *Academy of Management Journal,* 31, (1988):9–41; Ancona and Nadler, op. cit.

40 See Vancil, op. cit.

41 N. Tichy, "GE's Crotonville: A Staging Ground for Corporate Revolution," *Academy of Management Executive,* 3 (1989):99–106.

42 E.g., Gabbaro, op. cit.; V. Pucik, "International Management of Human Resources," in C. Fombrun et al., *Strategic Human Resource Management* (New York, NY: John Wiley & Sons, 1984).

43 Pucik, op. cit.

44 M. Devanna, C. Fombrun, and N. Tichy, "A Framework for Strategic Human Resource Management," in C. Fombrun et al., *Strategic Human Resource Management* (New York, NY: John Wiley & Sons, 1984).

45 Hambrick, op. cit.

46 Tichy, op. cit.

Leadership Behaviors, Influence Tactics, and Career Experiences of Champions of Technological Innovation

Jane M. Howell
Christopher A. Higgins

This research examines the leadership behaviors, influence tactics, and career experiences of champions of technological innovations. Content analysis of the interview transcripts of a matched sample of 25 champions and nonchampions indicated that champions exhibited more charismatic leader behaviors and used a wider variety of influence tactics than nonchampions. Champions also held more job positions, worked in more divisions and geographic locations, and had greater previous innovation experience during their careers than nonchampions. Implications of the findings for organization theory and practice and directions for future research are discussed.

Leadership research has focused on a variety of outcomes such as satisfaction, effectiveness, and performance (Bass, 1990). Despite the considerable attention devoted to these outcome variables, relatively few studies have examined the link between leadership and innovation. Recent theoretical developments may change this trend. Of particular importance is the development of transformational and charismatic theories of leadership which focus on proactive leader behaviors that may be essential to innovation and creativity (Avolio & Bass, 1988; Bass, 1985; Conger & Kanungo, 1987; House, 1977; Tichy & Devanna, 1986). These transformational leaders are described as providing a strong motivational force for change by questioning and altering traditional techniques, rules, and regulations which support the status quo (Bass, 1985; Conger & Kanungo, 1987; House, 1977).

One area that merges the phenomena of transformational and charismatic leadership and innovation is the role of the champion. Champions are individuals who emerge in organizations and make "a decisive contribution to the innovation by actively and enthusiastically promoting its progress through the critical [organizational] stages" (Achilladelis, Jervis, & Robertson, 1971, p. 14). Donald Schön's (1963) discussion of champions serves as the starting point for most writers concerned with championship. He argued that to overcome the obstacles against technological change, champions are needed who personally identify with the idea, actively and vigorously promote the idea through informal channels, and willingly risk their position and credibility to ensure the innovation's success. In support of Schön's argument, many field and case studies have demonstrated that innovation success is strongly related to the presence of a champion (e.g., Achilladelis, Jervis, & Robertson, 1971; Burgelman, 1983; Ettlie, Bridges, & O'Keefe, 1984; Roberts, 1968; Rothwell et al., 1974).

While champions are recognized as playing a key role in the innovation process, our knowledge about how these individuals operate in organizations is limited. Previous studies of champions suffer from several methodological problems and thus cast

From *Leadership Quarterly,* 1990, 1 (4), 249–264. © 1990, JAI Press Inc. Reprinted by permission.

doubt on the validity and interpretability of their findings. First, prior research has paid little attention to the valid measurement of individual attributes of champions such as leadership and influence. Most studies rely on the researchers' impressions of the individuals rather than systematic qualitative or quantitative measurement. Second, comparison groups for champions are not identified in any study. Therefore, it is unclear to what extent champions actually differ from managers in general. Third, the method employed to identify champions in prior research is often not delineated (e.g., Burgelman, 1983; Dean, 1987; Maidique, 1980; Souder, 1981). Often, individual responses, uncorroborated by others, are used to identify champions (Ettlie, 1983; Ettlie, Bridges, & O'Keefe, 1984; Frohman, 1978; Roberts, 1968). This method is problematic since bias may be introduced due to the tendency to report oneself as a champion, a socially desirable label.

The methodological problems of previous research call into question the adequacy of our current knowledge about champions. Accordingly, in a prior study, we tested a model of champion emergence that combined personality characteristics, leader behaviors, and influence tactics (Howell & Higgins, 1990). Analyses of questionnaire responses and interview transcripts of 25 matched pairs of champions and nonchampions revealed that in comparison to nonchampions, champions reported significantly more transformational leader behaviors, displayed higher risk-taking propensity and innovativeness, initiated more influence attempts, and used a greater variety of influence strategies. While the general individual attributes of champions and nonchampions were delineated using broad constructs and categories, an in-depth exploration of the tactics, behaviors, and career histories of champions was not reported.

The present study extends our previous research by conducting a fine-grained analysis of the specific charismatic behaviors, influence tactics, and career experiences of champions and nonchampions. While the capacity of champions to influence others has been widely discussed, there has been no attempt to integrate findings with the theoretical and empirical literature regarding leadership and social influence processes in organizations. Moreover, researchers have not systematically measured the leadership behaviors and influence attempts of champions, or explored whether champions differ from other managers in the amount and quality of their influence. Additionally, the extent to which career experiences contribute to the development and emergence of champions has not been investigated. Through the present study, a richer understanding of how champions emerge as informal leaders in organizations to promote innovations may be possible.

Leadership Behavior

The literature on champions and innovation underscores the capacity of champions to inspire and enthuse others with their vision of the potential of an innovation, to persist in promoting their vision despite strong opposition, to show extraordinary confidence in themselves and their mission, and to gain the commitment of others to support the innovation (Burgelman, 1983; Dean, 1987; Maidique, 1980; Schön, 1963). These behaviors are similar to the qualities of transformational leaders who develop, intellectually stimulate, and inspire followers to transcend their own self-interests for a higher collective purpose (Bass, 1985; Burns, 1978).

While these general descriptors are useful for understanding champions' leadership behavior, greater insights into how champions get others committed to the innovation can be gleaned by examining the specific behaviors exhibited by champions. House, Woycke, and Fodor (1988) clearly specified the behaviors of charismatic leaders. These behaviors include articulating a mission or vision in ideological terms, demonstrating a high degree of self-confidence, communicating high performance expectations to followers and confidence in followers' ability to meet such expectations, and showing individualized consideration toward followers (House et al., 1988, p. 105). In addition, Conger and Kanungo (1987) theorized that charismatic leaders assess environmental constraints and resources needed to bring about change within their organization, and engage in unconventional, countercultural, and innovative behavior while leading their followers toward the realization of their vision. Collectively, these charismatic behaviors may distinguish champions from nonchampions. From this we hypothesize as follows:

Hypothesis 1. Champions will exhibit charismatic leader behaviors, that is, articulate ideological goals, display unconventional behavior, express confidence in others, show environmental sensitivity, demonstrate self-confidence, communicate high expectations, and display individualized consideration to a greater extent than nonchampions.

Influence Tactics

Case studies of innovation have clearly documented that champions actively engage in influence attempts to promote their ideas. According to Schön's (1963) study of radical military innovations, champions were capable of using any and every means of informal sales and pressure to succeed. Burgelman's (1983) investigation of the internal corporate venturing process revealed that champions strongly influenced the dispositions of top managers toward a new corporate venture by keeping them informed and enthusiastic about a particular area of development and by articulating a convincing strategy for the new field. In his study of decision processes involved in the adoption of advanced manufacturing technology, Dean (1987) found that due to the pervasive effect of the technology on the organization, champions needed to secure support from a disparate set of organizational actors. To convince these actors of the necessity of the innovation, champions relied on a variety of influence strategies including rational justification, pressure from above, repeated informal expression of enthusiasm and confidence about the innovation, imminency of request to purchase, and information sharing with potential coalition members. Drawing on the results of extensive fieldwork and comparative research on innovation, Kanter (1988) argued that the effectiveness of the political activity in which the champion engaged was largely accountable for whether an idea ever moved into the later phase of innovation production. In particular, coalition building, the process of acquiring power by selling the project to potential allies, was an essential task for champions.

In addition to case studies of innovation, the literature on social influence processes in organizations sheds further light on the factors that determine an individual's choice of influence tactics, including the perceived relative power of the influence target and the reason for exercising influence (Ansari & Kapoor, 1987; Frost, 1987; Kipnis, Schmidt, & Wilkinson, 1980; Porter, Allen, & Angle, 1981; Yukl & Falbe, 1990). The intended direction of influence plays a role in determining the choice of strategies. Different strategies are needed when the target is a subordinate, peer, or supervisor. Studies of upward influence reveal that rational informational persuasion is preferred over less rational and sanction-based strategies (Ansari & Kapoor, 1987; Mowday, 1979; Porter et al., 1981; Schilit & Locke, 1982; Yukl & Falbe, 1990). When influencing peers, rationality, coalition, and exchange are the selected methods of influence while assertiveness, rationality, coalition, exchange, consultation, and inspirational appeals are the tactics of choice when influencing subordinates (Kipnis et al., 1980; Yukl & Falbe, 1990).

Situational factors also determine the choice of influence tactic. Kipnis et al. (1980), in their investigation of intraorganizational influence tactics, reported that individuals rely on different influence strategies when they are seeking personal assistance, assigning work, attempting to improve others' performance, obtaining benefits, or initiating change. In particular, they found that when individuals try to convince others to accept new ideas, they use a variety of influence tactics, including rationality, assertiveness, ingratiation, coalition, and exchange.

In our earlier study of champions and technological innovation, we reported that champions engaged in more frequent influence attempts and utilized a greater variety of influence tactics than nonchampions to convince multiple stakeholders of the necessity of the innovation (Howell & Higgins, 1990). However, the specific influence tactics utilized by champions and nonchampions to convince people of the importance of technology were not delineated. Since champions attempt to influence superiors, peers, and subordinates to appreciate and pay attention to new ideas, needs, and opportunities, they may use a wide range of influence tactics.

Hypothesis 2. Champions will utilize a wider variety of influence strategies, including friendliness, bargaining, sanctions, reason, assertiveness, higher authority, and coalition than nonchampions.

Career Experience

The literature on championship suggests that certain career experiences or events influence the likelihood of champion emergence. Schön (1963) alluded to the importance of organizational experience by acknowledging that champions must know and understand how to use the company's informal system of relationships to create and sell ideas. In addition, champions' interests must cut across different functional areas that are essential to product or process development. In a study of 29 paired comparisons of successful and unsuccessful attempts to innovate in the chemical and scientific instruments industries, Achilladelis and his associates (1971) reported that champions of successful innovations had more varied experience than champions of unsuccessful innovations.

In her discussion of the structural and social patterns that facilitate the innovation process, Kanter (1988) contended that potential innovators benefit from diversity and breadth of experience, links to users and outsiders, and integration across fields. Moreover, since champions often have to draw on resources from other departments or areas, their work is facilitated by network formation and collaboration across areas through frequent mobility, including lateral career moves. These contentions are consistent with prior research, which suggested that cosmopolitan rather than local orientations were an important factor in high rates of innovation (Robertson & Wind, 1983; Rogers & Shoemaker, 1971).

An examination of the antecedents to charismatic and transformational leadership is informative regarding the type of career experiences conducive to innovation. For example, Gibbons (cited in Avolio & Gibbons, 1988) analyzed leadership development based on retrospective life histories generated from in-depth clinical interviews with 16 senior corporate executives. These executives were described by their followers as transformational and transactional, pure transformational, pure transactional, or laissez-faire leaders. Analysis of the qualitatively generated data suggested seven key elements that captured some of the significant antecedents to the development of pure transformational leaders. One important element was that the leader had many previous leadership opportunities and experiences in a variety of settings. However, because of the limited sample size ($N = 16$) and because retrospective analysis is subject to errors of omission and intrusion, Gibbons's findings require further replication if external validity is to be established.

Drawing on anecdotal material about charismatic leaders' careers, Conger (1989) suggested that a comprehensive understanding of product, service, or industry during early career, and exposure to and experimentation with innovative ideas and tactics, were vital experiential factors contributing to the development of charismatic leaders. He speculated that through these diverse career experiences, individuals were able to develop a comprehensive understanding of an industry or product and, in turn, were better equipped to detect shortcomings and emerging opportunities in their respective markets. Since these speculations are based on the author's interpretations or popular writings about business leaders (labeled as charismatic by the business press), rigorous empirical investigation of the career experiences of charismatic leaders is warranted.

The requisite career experiences of charismatic and transformational leaders are also common to creative individuals. Based on a content analysis of interview transcripts of 120 R&D scientists, Amabile (1988) distilled the qualities of individuals that influence creativity. She reported that diverse experience (i.e., broad general knowledge and experience in a wide range of domains) was among the salient qualities of problem solvers that served to enhance creativity. In particular, diverse experience promoted a cognitive style favorable to adopting new perspectives on problems. Based on the literature cited earlier, we hypothesize as follows:

> **Hypothesis 3.** Champions will have greater exposure to different positions, functions, divisions, geographic locations, and industries and greater involvement in innovations during their careers than nonchampions.

The hypotheses were tested in a study of information technology innovations in 25 large Canadian companies. A matched sample of champions and nonchampions were interviewed about their involvement in the introduction and implementation of the innovations. Content analysis of the interview transcripts was conducted for the presence of themes related to leader behavior, influence tactics, and career experiences.

METHODS

Description of Innovations

In the current study, an innovation was defined as the adoption of a new product or process that reflected the application of information technology (Pennings, 1987). Specifically, information technology innovations that required hands-on interaction with a computer-based system through a computer keyboard were examined. Three criteria for selecting these innovations were established. The first criterion was that the technological innovations were designed for use by managers and/or professionals. At management levels, adoption of information technology is usually voluntary rather than mandatory. Consequently, champions may be needed to promote the introduction and implementation of these technologies. The second criterion was that the innovation was implemented (i.e., adopted in practice) within the 18 months prior to the study to ensure more accurate recall of the innovation process by participants. The third criterion was that the innovation represented a significant financial investment to the company, which ensured that the innovation was visible in the organization and had a potentially important impact on managerial work.

Derivation of Sample

Through a survey of 350 chief executive officers (CEOs) of Canadian firms listed on the *Financial Post 500*, an annual enumeration of the largest Canadian companies (in terms of sales), 88 organizations which had recently implemented a technological innovation were identified.

Based on the survey responses, 56 innovations appeared to meet the three selection criteria for inclusion in the study. Preliminary interviews were conducted with executives from these companies. During these interviews, the investigators explained to the executives the background and general purpose of the study and obtained from them an in-depth description of the innovation. Based on these interviews, 28 information technology innovations that met the established criteria were identified. All 28 organizations agreed to participate in the study.

Procedure

Individuals who played a major role in the innovation were identified by a two-stage process. First, a company executive identified the central individuals involved in the introduction and implementation of the innovation. After interviewing these key individuals, others were often identified as playing an important role in the innovation. These individuals were also interviewed. For each innovation, an average of five key individuals were interviewed. In total, 153 interviews were conducted and tape recorded. On average, the interviews lasted 1.5 hours.

The interviews with key individuals were conducted using a structured protocol. The first part of the interview focused on reliably identifying champions and non-champions and is discussed in detail in the next section. The remainder of the interview focused on (a) the key individual's personal involvement in the innovation; (b) the receptiveness and commitment of users to the innovation; (c) the methods of influence used by the individual to initiate the innovation and to overcome resistance; (d) the motivation of the individual to participate in the innovation and the recognition received; (e) the personal and organizational risk associated with involvement in the innovation; (f) the identification of factors contributing to the success or failure of the innovation; and (g) the career history of the individual and his or her involvement in previous innovations.

Transcripts of the interviews were content analyzed for leadership behaviors, influence tactics, and career experiences of champions and nonchampions. The content analysis procedure is described in a subsequent section.

Identification of Champions and Nonchampions

The first part of the interview focused on identifying champions and nonchampions through peer nomination. The reliable identification of champions was a key component of the current research, and peer nomination was used, as it has been shown to be a highly reliable and valid technique (Kane & Lawler, 1978; Love, 1981).

The peer nomination procedure worked as follows. Initially, via an open-ended question, the respondent was asked to identify the key people associated with the innovation and to describe the roles each of them played. The respondent was subsequently given a list of five role definitions derived from the innovation literature. Four of these roles—project champion, technical innovator, business innovator, chief executive—were drawn from Achilladelis et al. (1971). An additional role, user champion, was derived from the information systems literature (Curley & Gremillion, 1983). Each key individual then identified the person or persons who clearly fit each of these roles.

The criterion for accurately identifying project champions was complete (100%) agreement among the key individuals regarding the person who played a particular role in championing the project. Using this criterion, 25 project champions were identified. For three projects, unanimous agreement regarding the designation of the project champion was not obtained.

To test the hypotheses of the present study, a comparison group, labeled "nonchampions," was established based on four criteria. First, nonchampions and champions were involved in the same innovation within the same organization. Therefore, pairing a champion and a nonchampion for each innovation controlled for the cost, type, importance, success or complexity of the innovations, company size, and industry. Second, both nonchampions and champions played active, informal roles in the promotion of the innovation. However, in comparison to champions, nonchampions could not be consensually identified as playing a specific role in the innovation (i.e., project champion, technical innovator, business innovator, chief executive, user champion) according to the peer nomination procedure. This implied that the champions and nonchampions were highly comparable in technical knowledge (since champions and nonchampions were not identified as the technical innovator) and position power (since champions and nonchampions were not identified as the business innovator, chief executive, or user champion). Third, champions and nonchampions were peers at the same organizational level. That is, there was no formal reporting relationship between them. Finally, champions and nonchampions were self-appointed to the project.

It was not within their job mandate to seek out and promote new technological inno-vations. Thus, differences between champions and nonchampions could not be attrib-uted to role requirements or assigned positions such as project leader.

To confirm that champions and nonchampions were similar on specific demo-graphic variables paired t tests were conducted. The results indicated that champions and nonchampions were not signficantly different with regard to age ($t(24) = 0.61$; $p > .05$) and salary ($t(24) = 0.62$; $p > .05$). In addition, chi-squared tests revealed that champions and nonchampions were not significantly different in job level ($\chi^2(3) = 2.39$; $p = .49$), functional area ($\chi^2(3) = 3.84$; $p = .28$), and educational level ($\chi^2(1) = 1.09$; $p = .29$). Thus, any differences found between the two groups could not be at-tributed to differences in these demographic characteristics.

The final sample consisted of 25 pairs of champions and nonchampions. The 50 participants, all of whom were male, had an average age of 45 years and were at exec-utive (52%) or middle management (48%) levels across a variety of functional areas including accounting, engineering, finance, general management, information sys-tems, and marketing.

Content Analysis

The transcripts of the champion and nonchampion interviews were content analyzed for the presence of themes relating to leadership behavior, influence tactics, and career experience, using the same procedure as House et al. (1988). Descriptions of leader-ship behaviors were developed using charismatic and transformational leadership the-ories as a guide (Bass, 1985; Conger & Kanungo, 1987; House et al., 1988). Descrip-tions of influence tactics were adopted from Kipnis and Schmidt (1982). Drawing on the innovation and charismatic leadership literature, career experience categories were developed (Amabile, 1988; Avolio & Gibbons, 1988; Conger, 1989; Kanter, 1988).

Transcripts separate from those to be used in the study were selected to clarify the operationalization of the leadership behaviors and influence tactics. Three individuals independently coded these practice passages, discussed their ratings, and then clarified the descriptions when necessary. Five iterations of rating and discussion were com-pleted before it was felt that there was an unambiguous operationalization of each leadership behavior and influence tactic. The final coding of these practice passages became the key on which the coders were trained and eventually tested (House et al., 1988).

University students were recruited to code the interview transcripts. They were given a test to ensure that their reading comprehension was adequate for the material they would have to code. Of 12 students who took the reading test, seven passed. Six of these students were hired to code the transcripts.

Students were randomly assigned to code leader behaviors and influence tactics. Using precoded practice material and a description of leader and influence behaviors, the students were trained so they understood and were able to code the interviews ac-curately. The six students trained to code leader behaviors or influence tactics met the established criterion of 75% agreement with the key. In total, the training required 12 hours. During the coding of the actual interview transcripts, interrater agreement was assessed after every five transcripts to ensure that the students maintained or exceeded the 75% agreement criterion. The identification of champions and nonchampions was disguised so coders could not determine the identity of the people to which the transcripts applied. In addition, coders were unaware of the hypotheses of the study. In total, over 1,000 pages of transcripts were analyzed. There were no significant differences in the lengths of champion and nonchampion interview transcripts.

Measures

Leadership Behavior   To determine if champions, in comparison to nonchampions, engaged more frequently in behaviors that theoretically distinguish charismatic and noncharismatic leaders, a content analysis of the interview transcripts was conducted. Each interview passage was coded separately for the presence or absence of the individual's display of self-confidence; strong conviction about ideological goals; communication of individualized consideration for others; expression of high expectations for others; communication of confidence in others' ability to accomplish tasks; demonstration of unconventional, innovative, or countercultural behavior; and assessment of environmental resources and constraints for bringing about change (Bass, 1985; Conger & Kanungo, 1987; House et al., 1988).

Influence Tactics   The variety of influence tactics utilized by champions and nonchampions was assessed using the same content analysis technique described earlier. Passages describing strategies were coded based on Kipnis and Schmidt's (1982) description of seven different influence tactics including building coalitions, appealing to higher authority, bargaining, presenting rational arguments, using friendliness and ingratiation, applying sanctions, and being assertive.

Career Experience   Passages describing career experiences were coded to determine the extent to which champions and nonchampions had experience in different (a) job positions, (b) functional areas, (c) divisions, (d) companies in the same industry, (e) companies in different industries, and (f) geographic locations (Amabile, 1988; Avolio & Gibbons, 1988; Conger, 1989; Kanter, 1988). In addition, the number of previous innovations in which champions and nonchampions had been involved was counted.

Data Analysis

Three discriminant analyses were conducted to determine if champions and nonchampions could be distinguished on the basis of (a) charismatic leadership behaviors, (b) influence tactics, and (c) career experiences. Discriminant analysis requires that the discriminating variables be drawn from a population with a multivariate normal distribution and that the covariance matrices of the two groups not be significantly different (Klecka, 1980). For each discriminant analysis, Kolmogorov–Smirnov tests indicated that the normality criterion was satisfied. Box's M test confirmed that the covariance matrices were equal.

RESULTS

Hypothesis 1 stated that champions would display more charismatic behaviors than nonchampions. In support of this hypothesis, the discriminant function for the leadership variables was significant (Wilks Lambda = .64; $\chi^2[5]$ = 19.17; $p < .01$) and the overall classification rate was 82% (see Table 1). The structure coefficients, which are the simple bivariate correlations between each variable and the discriminant function, can be used to determine the relative importance of the individual variables (Klecka, 1980). Variables with correlations greater than .3 were as follows, in order of importance: ideological goals, unconventional behavior, confidence in others, self-confidence, and environmental sensitivity.

Hypothesis 2 posited that champions would utilize a greater variety of influence tactics than nonchampions. In accordance with this hypothesis, the discriminant function was significant (Wilks Lambda = .49; $\chi^2[7]$ = 30.09; $p < .01$) and the overall classification result was 90% (see Table 2). Inspection of the structure coefficients revealed that coalition, reason, higher authority, and assertiveness were the influence tactics that best differentiated between champions and nonchampions. Three influence tactics—sanctions, bargaining, and friendliness—did not discriminate between champions and nonchampions.

Hypothesis 3, which postulated that champions would have greater exposure to different positions, functional areas, divisions, geographic locations, and industries, and greater involvement in innovations during their careers than nonchampions, was supported. The discriminant function was significant (Wilks Lambda = .67; $\chi^2[7]$ = 17.06; $p < .05$) and the overall classification result was 82% (see Table 3). Inspection of the

TABLE 1

DISCRIMINANT ANALYSIS FOR THE CHARISMATIC LEADER BEHAVIORS OF CHAMPIONS AND NONCHAMPIONS[†]

Classification matrix	Predicted group membership	
Group	Champion	Nonchampion
Champion	76%	24%
Nonchampion	12%	88%
Percent correctly classified = 82%		

Structure matrix	Loading
Ideological goals	0.64
Unconventional behavior	0.57
Confidence in others	0.57
Self-confidence	0.33
Environmental sensitivity	0.32

[†]Inspection of the data revealed that two charismatic leader behaviors, communicating high performance expectations and showing individualized consideration for others, were not present in either the champion or nonchampion interviews. These variables were omitted from the analysis.

Note: N = 25 champions and 25 nonchampions.

TABLE 2

DISCRIMINANT ANALYSIS FOR THE INFLUENCE TACTICS USED BY CHAMPIONS
AND NONCHAMPIONS

Classification matrix	Predicted group membership	
Group	Champion	Nonchampion
Champion	88%	12%
Nonchampion	8%	92%
Percent correctly classified = 90%		

Structure matrix	Loading
Coalition	.45
Reason	.45
Higher authority	.31
Assertiveness	.31
Sanctions	.27
Bargaining	.18
Friendliness	.02

Note: N = 25 champions and 25 nonchampions.

structure coefficients revealed that all variables had values exceeding .3, with the exception of experience in different companies in different industries.

DISCUSSION

The results of the current study demonstrate that charismatic leadership can be empirically linked to innovation through the role played by champions. This link has not been made to date. More specifically, the findings suggest that fundamental components of a champion's capacity to introduce innovations are the articulation of a compelling vision of the innovation's potential for the organization, the expression of confidence in others to participate effectively in the initiative, the display of unconventional, innovative actions to achieve goals, the belief in one's capacities to initiate change, and the assessment of environmental resources and constraints for bringing about change. Collectively, these charismatic behaviors suggest that champions use their imagination to envision new possibilities and proactively guide the innovation to fruition.

To date, charismatic and transformational leadership theory has focused on formal leaders (Avolio & Bass, 1988; Bass, 1985; Conger & Kanungo, 1987; House, 1977). This study extends charismatic and transformational leadership theory to include informal, emergent leaders such as the champions studied in this research. This theoretical extension is important since it implies that both formal and informal leaders must be examined to appreciate fully the process of innovation in organizations.

Our analyses further indicate that champions rely on coalition, reason, higher authority, and assertiveness to convince others to accept the innovative idea. These findings are consistent with case studies of innovation which suggest that champions use

TABLE 3

DISCRIMINANT ANALYSIS FOR THE CAREER EXPERIENCES OF CHAMPIONS
AND NONCHAMPIONS

Classification matrix	Predicted group membership	
Group	Champion	Nonchampion
Champion	80%	20%
Nonchampion	16%	84%
Percent correctly classified = 82%		

Structure matrix	Loading
Previous innovations	.71
Divisions	.67
Geographic areas	.66
Positions	.64
Functional areas	.30
Companies/same industry	.30
Companies/different industry	.15

Note: N = 25 champions and 25 nonchampions.

many means of influence to promote their ideas (Dean, 1987; Maidique, 1980; Schön, 1963). They are also consistent with Kipnis et al.'s (1980) investigation of the tactics used by employees to influence their bosses, coworkers, or subordinates when initiating change. Indeed, the champion's ability to gather information that allows him or her to formulate successful influence strategies, to marshall a wide range of supportive political tactics, and to be astute at using them to influence others may be critical to the innovation's ultimate success. An important issue for future research is how champions access, recognize, and harness power to their advantage in different situations. For example, depending on the level of support for innovation within the organization, or the leadership styles of their influence targets, champions may use radically different types, sequences, and combinations of influence processes to introduce and sell their idea to various stakeholders.

Since a new technology often introduces crucial uncertainties in organizations, it represents an opportunity for individuals to gain influence (Burkhardt & Brass, 1990). Those who are able to decrease uncertainty for themselves and others can increase their power and centrality (Hickson, Hinings, Lee, Schneck, & Pennings, 1971; Pfeffer, 1981; Tushman & Romanelli, 1983). Studies of the communicative patterns of innovation pioneers and early adopters indicate that they hold positions of centrality in influence networks (Becker, 1970; Burkhardt & Brass, 1990). Many researchers have demonstrated that individuals occupying central positions in communication networks are likely to be perceived as powerful and influential (Brass, 1984; Hickson et al., 1971; Pettigrew, 1972). The findings of the current study suggest that champions rely on highly communicative types of influence strategies, such as coalition formation and reasoning, to create support for their innovations. Based on these results, an hypothesis for future research is that, in comparison to nonchampions, champions are more centrally situated in communication networks and are more adept at using this source of power to their advantage.

The results of the present study further reveal that in contrast to nonchampions, champions' career experiences within the organization involved many different job positions spanning multiple functional areas, divisions, and geographic locations. Moreover, champions had greater experience working in different companies within the same industry than nonchampions. These findings are striking since champions and nonchampions were matched on age, salary, job level, functional area, and educational level variables. The results imply that through broad exposure during their careers within their industry, and particularly within their organization, champions may have had more opportunities than nonchampions for building information networks for the discovery of new ideas, for developing a unique vantage point from which to view emerging trends and therefore opportunities that others might not detect, and for creating interpersonal contacts necessary for future coalition building. This interpretation is consistent with Granovetter's (1983) analyses of the strength of structural relationships, which suggest that weak social ties, that is, brief contacts with numerous acquaintances, provide occasions for learning about new ideas and practices.

The involvement of champions in previous innovations may have enabled them to establish credibility in effectively managing risky projects which, in turn, may have positively influenced their perceived competence and latitude for innovation. This explanation is consistent with Hollander's (1978) idiosyncratic credit theory. He theorized that individuals who conform to group norms early in their membership in the group and show characteristics of competence will amass idiosyncratic credits. If individuals continue to gain credits, then they attain a threshold permitting deviations from group norms, that is, innovative behavior. Longitudinal studies of the career histories of champions might reveal if they amass credits prior to embarking on innovative projects.

In addition, since champions had many experiences with innovation projects during their careers, they may have gained both knowledge and self-confidence in launching and implementing successful innovations thereby increasing their willingness to undertake new projects. According to Bandura (1986), expectations about self-efficacy are directly related to people's perception of their success in dealing with past situations and to their expectations about future success. Thus, the knowledge champions may have acquired through previous experience and the strategies they have developed in the past to deal with ambiguity or uncertainty may also influence how they select information and respond to new situations. In his study of the relationship between organizational socialization tactics and role and personal outcomes, Jones (1986) found that self-efficacy moderated this learning process. When newcomers possessed high levels of self-efficacy, socialization tactics produced a stronger innovative role orientation than when newcomers possessed low levels of self-efficacy. Drawing on the aforementioned theoretical and empirical arguments, an interesting question for future research is whether champions have higher self-efficacy and outcome expectancies than nonchampions, which contributes to their innovative role orientation.

The results of the present study suggest that individuals who have champion potential can be identified through the use of validated tests measuring charismatic leadership and influence tactics (Bass & Avolio, 1990; Kipnis et al., 1982). If potential champions are identified via psychological assessment, then managers could provide them with an appropriate environment and career experiences conducive to innovation. For example, by assigning potential champions to projects requiring creative problem solving and imaginative solutions, innovation skills and self-confidence in tackling challenging projects may be fostered. In addition, managers could help potential champions build extensive communication networks through job rotations spanning multiple divisions and geographic locations.

One limitation of the present study is that the findings are based on same-source data. It could, therefore, be argued that the sources of information reflect a common source bias. This argument is considerably weakened by two observations. The first observation concerns the use of peer nomination, whereby key individuals blind to the explicit purpose and hypotheses of the study independently nominated the champion. Unanimous agreement regarding the identity of the champion was required for classification. Second, coders blind to the hypotheses of the study conducted the content analysis of the interview transcripts.

The use of retrospective data represents a second limitation of this research. Nisbett and Wilson (1977) concluded that in salient situations individuals' recall of events was likely to reflect the actual events. Since the technological innovations studied in this research represented major changes within the organization, these situations appeared highly salient to organizational members. Hence, it is a reasonable assumption that the events reported by the key individuals are representative of the actual situation.

A final limitation of the study is the relatively small size of 25 champion and nonchampion pairs. Clearly, we would have more statistical conclusion validity with a larger sample. However, the careful matching of champions and nonchampions on a variety of demographic characteristics as well as the rigorous procedure for selecting champions give us confidence in the results.

This study provides an empirical link between charismatic leadership, influence tactics, career experiences, and innovation via championship. Charismatic leadership theory has been extended to include informal leaders engaged in innovation. Moreover, the distinctive career histories of champions implies that they may have greater opportunities for building information networks and interpersonal contacts necessary for discovering and building support for new ideas. These findings provide a basis for future theoretical and empirical work on champions as emergent charismatic leaders.

REFERENCES

Achilladelis, B., P. Jervis, & A. Robertson. (1971). *A study of success and failure in industrial innovation.* Sussex, England: University of Sussex Press.
Amabile, T. M. (1988). A model of creativity and innovation in organizations. In B. M. Staw & L. L. Cummings (Eds.). *Research in organizational behavior* (Vol. 10, pp. 123–167). Greenwich, CT: JAI Press.
Ansari, M. A., & A. Kapoor. (1987). Organizational context and upward influence tactics. *Organizational Behavior and Human Decision Processes, 40,* 39–49.
Avolio, B. J., & B. M. Bass. (1988). Charisma and beyond. In J. G. Hunt, B. R. Baliga, H. P.

Dachler, & C. A. Schriesheim (Eds.), *Emerging leadership vistas* (pp. 29–49). Lexington, MA: D. C. Heath.

Avolio, B. J., & T. C. Gibbons. (1988). Developing transformational leaders: A life span approach. In J. A. Conger & R. N. Kanungo (Eds.), *Charismatic leadership* (pp. 276–308). San Francisco: Jossey-Bass.

Bandura, A. (1986). *Social foundations of thought and action: A social cognitive theory.* Englewood Cliffs, NJ: Prentice-Hall.

Bass, B. M. (1990). *Bass & Stogdill's handbook of leadership.* New York: Free Press.

———. (1985). *Leadership and performance beyond expectations.* New York: Free Press.

Bass, B. M., & B. J. Avolio. (1990). *Transformational leadership development: Manual for the Multifactor Leadership Questionnaire.* Palo Alto, CA: Consulting Psychologists Press.

Becker, M. G. (1970). Sociometric location and innovativeness: Reformation and extension of the diffusion model. *American Sociological Review, 35,* 267–282.

Brass, D. J. (1984). Being in the right place: A structural analysis of individual influence in an organization. *Administrative Science Quarterly, 29,* 518–539.

Burgelman, R. A. (1983). A process model of internal corporate venturing in the diversified major firm. *Administrative Science Quarterly, 8,* 223–244.

Burkhardt, M. E., & D. J. Brass. (1990). Changing patterns or patterns of change: The effects of a change in technology on social network power and structure. *Administrative Science Quarterly, 35,* 104–127.

Burns, J. M. (1978). *Leadership.* New York: Harper & Row.

Conger, J. A. (1989). *The charismatic leader.* San Francisco: Jossey-Bass.

Conger, J. A., & R. N. Kanungo. (1987). Toward a behavioral theory of charismatic leadership in organizational settings. *Academy of Management Review, 12,* 637–647.

Curley, K. F., & L. L. Gremillion. (1983). The role of the champion in DSS implementation. *Information and Management, 6,* 203–209.

Dean, J. W. (1987). Building the future: The justification process for new technology. In J. M. Pennings & A. Buitendam (Eds.), *New technology as organizational innovation* (pp. 35–58). Cambridge, MA: Ballinger.

Ettlie, J. E. (1983). A note on the relationship between managerial change values, innovative intentions and innovative technology outcomes in food sector firms. *R & D. Management, 13,* 231–244.

Ettlie, J. E., W. P. Bridges, & R. D. O'Keefe. (1984). Organization strategy and structural differences for radical versus incremental innovation. *Management Science, 30,* 682–695.

Frohman, A. L. (1978). The performance of innovation: Managerial roles. *California Management Review, 20,* 12.

Frost, P. J. (1987). Power, politics and influence. In F. M. Jablin, L. L. Putnam, K. H. Roberts, and L. W. Porter (Eds.), *Handbook of organizational communication* (pp. 503–548). Beverly Hills, CA: Sage.

Granovetter, M. (1983). The strength of weak ties—A network theory revisited. In R. Collins (Ed.), *Sociological theory 1983* (pp. 201–233). San Francisco: Jossey-Bass.

Hickson, D. J., C. R. Hinings, C. A. Lee, R. E. Schneck, & J. M. Pennings. (1971). A strategic contingencies theory of intraorganizational power. *Administrative Science Quarterly, 16,* 216–229.

Hollander, E. P. (1978). *Leadership dynamics.* New York: Free Press.

House, R. J. (1977). A 1976 theory of charismatic leadership. In J. G. Hunt & L. L. Larson (Eds.), *Leadership: The cutting edge* (pp. 189–207). Carbondale, IL: Southern Illinois University Press.

House, R. J., J. Woycke, & E. M. Fodor. (1988). Charismatic and noncharismatic leaders: Differences in behavior and effectiveness. In J. A. Conger & R. N. Kanungo (Eds.), *Charis-*

matic leadership (pp. 98–121). San Francisco: Jossey-Bass.

Howell, J. M., & P. J. Frost. (1989). A laboratory study of charismatic leadership. *Organizational Behavior and Human Decision Processes, 43,* 243–269.

Howell, J. M., & C. A. Higgins. (1990). Champions of technological innovation. *Administrative Science Quarterly, 35,* 317–341.

Jones, G. R. (1986). Socialization tactics, self-efficacy, and newcomers' adjustments to organizations. *Academy of Management Journal, 29,* 262–279.

Kane, J. S., & E. E. Lawler. (1978). Methods of peer assessment. *Psychological Bulletin, 35,* 555–586.

Kanter, R. M. (1988). When a thousand flowers bloom: Structural, collective, and social conditions for innovation in organization. In B. M. Staw & L. L. Cummings (Eds.), *Research in organizational behavior* (Vol. 10, pp. 169–211). Greenwich, CT: JAI Press.

Kipnis, D., & S. M. Schmidt. (1982). *Profiles of organizational influence strategies.* Toronto: University Associates.

Kipnis, D., S. M. Schmidt, & I. Wilkinson. (1980). Intraorganizational influence tactics: Exploration in getting one's ways. *Journal of Applied Psychology, 65,* 440–452.

Klecka, W. R. (1980). *Discriminant analysis.* Beverly Hills, CA: Sage.

Love, K. G. (1981). Comparison of peer assessment methods: Reliability, validity, friendship bias, and user reaction. *Journal of Applied Psychology, 66,* 451–457.

Maidique, M. A. (1980). Entrepreneurs, champions, and technological innovation. *Sloan Management Review, 21,* 59–76.

Mowday, R. T. (1979). Leader characteristics, self-confidence, and methods of upward influence in organizational decision situations. *Academy of Management Journal, 22,* 709–725.

Nisbett, R. E., & T. D. Wilson. (1977). Telling more than we can know: Verbal reports on mental processes. *Psychological Review, 814,* 231–259.

Pennings, J. M. (1987). On the nature of new technology as organizational innovation. In J. M. Pennings & A. Buitendam (Eds.), *New technology as organizational innovation* (pp. 3–12). Cambridge, MA: Ballinger.

Pettigrew, A. (1972). Information control as a source of power. *Sociology, 6,* 187–204.

Pfeffer, J. (1981). *Power in organizations.* Marshfield, MA: Pitman.

Porter, L. W., R. W. Allen, & H. L. Angle. (1981). The politics of upward influence in organizations. In B. M. Staw & L. L. Cummings (Eds.), *Research in organizational behavior* (Vol. 3, pp. 109–149). Greenwich, CT: JAI Press.

Roberts, E. B. (1968). A basic study of innovators: How to keep and capitalize on their talents. *Research Management, 11,* 249–266.

Robertson, T., & Y. Wind. (1983). Organizational cosmopolitanism and innovation. *Academy of Management Journal, 26,* 332–338.

Rogers, E. M., & F. F. Shoemaker. (1971). *Communication of innovations: A cross-cultural approach* (2nd ed.). New York: Free Press.

Rothwell, R., C. Freeman, A. Horsley, V. T. P. Jervis, A. B. Robertson, & J. Townsend. (1974). SAPPHO updated—Project SAPPHO phase II. *Research Policy, 3,* 258–291.

Schilit, W. K., & E. A. Locke. (1982). A study of upward influence in organizations. *Administrative Science Quarterly, 27,* 304–316.

Schön, D. A. (1963). Champions for radical new inventions. *Harvard Business Review, 41,* 77–86.

Souder, W. E. (1981). Encouraging entrepreneurship in the large corporations. *Research Management, 24,* 18–22.

Tichy, N. M., & M. A. Devanna. (1986). *The transformational leader.* New York: Wiley.

Tushman, M., & D. Nadler. (1986). Organizing for innovation. *California Management Review.*

28, 74–92.

Tushman, M. L., & E. Romanelli. (1983). Uncertainty, social location and influence in decision making: A sociometric analysis. *Management Science, 29,* 12–23.

Yukl, G., & C. M. Falbe. (1990). Influence tactics and objectives in upward, downward, and lateral influence attempts. *Journal of Applied Psychology, 75,* 132–140.

The Leader's New Work: Building Learning Organizations

Peter M. Senge

Human beings are designed for learning. No one has to teach an infant to walk, or talk, or master the spatial relationships needed to stack eight building blocks that don't topple. Children come fully equipped with an insatiable drive to explore and experiment. Unfortunately, the primary institutions of our society are oriented predominantly toward controlling rather than learning, rewarding individuals for performing for others rather than for cultivating their natural curiosity and impulse to learn. The young child entering school discovers quickly that the name of the game is getting the right answer and avoiding mistakes—a mandate no less compelling to the aspiring manager.

"Our prevailing system of management has destroyed our people," writes W. Edwards Deming, leader in the quality movement.[1] "People are born with intrinsic motivation, self-esteem, dignity, curiosity to learn, joy in learning. The forces of destruction begin with toddlers—a prize for the best Halloween costume, grades in school, gold stars, and on up through the university. On the job, people, teams, divisions are ranked—reward for the one at the top, punishment at the bottom. MBO, quotas, incentive pay, business plans, put together separately, division by division, cause further loss, unknown and unknowable."

Ironically, by focusing on performing for someone else's approval, corporations create the very conditions that predestine them to mediocre performance. Over the long run, superior performance depends on superior learning. A Shell study showed that, according to former planning director Arie de Geus, "a full one-third of the Fortune '500' industrials listed in 1970 had vanished by 1983."[2] Today, the average lifetime of the largest industrial enterprises is probably less than *half* the average lifetime of a person in an industrial society. On the other hand, de Geus and his colleagues at Shell also found a small number of companies that survived for seventy-five years or longer. Interestingly, the key to their survival was the ability to run "experiments in the margin," to continually explore new business and organizational opportunities that create potential new sources of growth.

If anything, the need for understanding how organizations learn and accelerating that learning is greater today than ever before. The old days when a Henry Ford, Alfred Sloan, or Tom Watson *learned for the organization* are gone. In an increasingly dynamic, interdependent, and unpredictable world, it is simply no longer possible for anyone to "figure it all out at the top." The old model, "the top thinks and the local acts," must now give way to integrating thinking and acting at all levels. While the challenge is great, so is the potential payoff. "The person who figures out how to harness the collective genius of the people in his or her organization," according to former Citibank CEO Walter Wriston, "is going to blow the competition away."

From *Sloan Management Review,* Fall 1990, 7–23. Reprinted by permission. Copyright 1990 by Sloan Management Review Association. All rights reserved.

Adaptive Learning and Generative Learning

The prevailing view of learning organizations emphasizes increased adaptability. Given the accelerating pace of change, or so the standard view goes, "the most successful corporation of the 1990s," according to *Fortune* magazine, "will be something called a learning organization, a consummately adaptive enterprise."[3] As the Shell study shows, examples of traditional authoritarian bureaucracies that responded too slowly to survive in changing business environments are legion.

But increasing adaptiveness is only the first stage in moving toward learning organizations. The impulse to learn in children goes deeper than desires to respond and adapt more effectively to environmental change. The impulse to learn, at its heart, is an impulse to be generative, to expand our capability. This is why leading corporations are focusing on *generative* learning, which is about creating, as well as *adaptive* learning, which is about coping.[4]

The total quality movement in Japan illustrates the evolution from adaptive to generative learning. With its emphasis on continuous experimentation and feedback, the total quality movement has been the first wave in building learning organizations. But Japanese firms' view of serving the customer has evolved. In the early years of total quality, the focus was on "fitness to standard," making a product reliably so that it would do what its designers intended it to do and what the firm told its customers it would do. Then came a focus on "fitness to need," understanding better what the customer wanted and then providing products that reliably met those needs. Today, leading edge firms seek to understand and meet the "latent need" of the customer—what customers might truly value but have never experienced or would never think to ask for. As one Detroit executive commented recently, "You could never produce the Mazda Miata solely from market research. It required a leap of imagination to see what the customer *might want*."[5]

Generative learning, unlike adaptive learning, requires new ways of looking at the world, whether in understanding customers or in understanding how to better manage a business. For years, U.S. manufacturers sought competitive advantage in aggressive controls on inventories, incentives against overproduction, and rigid adherence to production forecasts. Despite these incentives, their performance was eventually eclipsed by Japanese firms who saw the challenges of manufacturing differently. They realized that eliminating delays in the production process was the key to reducing instability and improving cost, productivity, and service. They worked to build networks of relationships with trusted suppliers and to redesign physical production processes so as to reduce delays in materials procurement, production set up, and in-process inventory—a much higher-leverage approach to improving both cost and customer loyalty.

As Boston Consulting Group's George Stalk has observed, the Japanese saw the significance of delays because they saw the process of order entry, production scheduling, materials procurement, production, and distribution *as an integrated system*. "What distorts the system so badly is time," observed Stalk—the multiple delays between events and responses. "These distortions reverberate throughout the system, producing disruptions, waste, and inefficiency."[6] Generative learning requires seeing the systems that control events. When we fail to grasp the systemic source of problems, we are left to "push on" symptoms rather than eliminate underlying causes. The best we can ever do is adaptive learning.

The Leader's New Work

"I talk with people all over the country about learning organizations, and the response is always very positive," says William O'Brien, CEO of the Hanover Insurance companies. "If this type of organization is so widely preferred, why don't people create such organizations? I think the answer is leadership. People have no real comprehension of the type of commitment it requires to build such an organization."[7]

Our traditional view of leaders—as special people who set the direction, make the key decisions, and energize the troops—is deeply rooted in an individualistic and non-systemic worldview. Especially in the West, leaders are *heroes*—great men (and occasionally women) who rise to the fore in times of crisis. So long as such myths prevail, they reinforce a focus on short-term events and charismatic heroes rather than on systemic forces and collective learning.

Leadership in learning organizations centers on subtler and ultimately more important work. In a learning organization, leaders' roles differ dramatically from that of the charismatic decision maker. Leaders are designers, teachers, and stewards. These roles require new skills: the ability to build shared vision, to bring to the surface and challenge prevailing mental models, and to foster more systemic patterns of thinking. In short, leaders in learning organizations are responsible for *building organizations* where people are continually expanding their capabilities to shape their future—that is, leaders are responsible for learning.

CREATIVE TENSION: THE INTEGRATING PRINCIPLE

Leadership in a learning organization starts with the principle of creative tension.[8] Creative tension comes from seeing clearly where we want to be, our "vision," and telling the truth about where we are, our "current reality." The gap between the two generates a natural tension (see Figure 1).

Creative tension can be resolved in two basic ways: by raising current reality toward the vision, or by lowering the vision toward current reality. Individuals, groups, and organizations who learn how to work with creative tension learn how to use the energy it generates to move reality more reliably toward their visions.

The principle of creative tension has long been recognized by leaders. Martin Luther King, Jr., once said, "Just as Socrates felt that it was necessary to create a tension in the mind, so that individuals could rise from the bondage of myths and half truths . . . so must we . . . create the kind of tension in society that will help men rise from the dark depths of prejudice and racism."[9]

Without vison there is no creative tension. Creative tension cannot be generated from current reality alone. All the analysis in the world will never generate a vision. Many who are otherwise qualified to lead fail to do so because they try to substitute analysis for vision. They believe that, if only people understood current reality, they would surely feel the motivation to change. They are then disappointed to discover that people "resist" the personal and organizational changes that must be made to alter reality. What they never grasp is that the natural energy for changing reality comes from holding a picture of what might be that is more important to people than what is.

But creative tension cannot be generated from vision alone; it demands an accurate

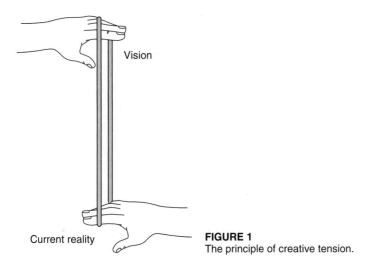

FIGURE 1
The principle of creative tension.

picture of current reality as well. Just as King had a dream, so too did he continually strive to "dramatize the shameful conditions" of racism and prejudice so that they could no longer be ignored. Vision without understanding of current reality will more likely foster cynicism than creativity. The principle of creative tension teaches that *an accurate picture of current reality is just as important as a compelling picture of a desired future.*

Leading through creative tension is different than solving problems. In problem solving, the energy for change comes from attempting to get away from an aspect of current reality that is undesirable. With creative tension, the energy for change comes from the vision, from what we want to create, juxtaposed with current reality. While the distinction may seem small, the consequences are not. Many people and organizations find themselves motivated to change only when their problems are bad enough to cause them to change. This works for a while, but the change process runs out of steam as soon as the problems driving the change become less pressing. With problem solving, the motivation for change is extrinsic. With creative tension, the motivation is intrinsic. This distinction mirrors the distinction between adaptive and generative learning.

NEW ROLES

The traditional authoritarian image of the leader as "the boss calling the shots" has been recognized as oversimplified and inadequate for some time. According to Edgar Schein, "Leadership is intertwined with culture formation." Building an organization's culture and shaping its evolution is the "unique and essential function" of leadership.[10] In a learning organization, the critical roles of leadership—designer, teacher, and steward—have antecedents in the ways leaders have contributed to building organizations in the past. But each role takes on new meaning in the learning organization and, as will be seen in the following sections, demands new skills and tools.

Leader as Designer

Imagine that your organization is an ocean liner and that you are "the leader." What is your role?

I have asked this question of groups of managers many times. The most common answer, not surprisingly, is "the captain." Others say, "The navigator, setting the direction." Still others say, "The helmsman, actually controlling the direction," or, "The engineer down there stoking the fire, providing energy," or, "The social director, making sure everybody's enrolled, involved, and communicating." While these are legitimate leadership roles, there is another which, in many ways, eclipses them all in importance. Yet rarely does anyone mention it.

The neglected leadership role is the *designer* of the ship. No one has a more sweeping influence than the designer. What good does it do for the captain to say, "Turn starboard 30 degrees," when the designer has built a rudder that will only turn to port, or which takes six hours to turn to starboard? It's fruitless to be the leader in an organization that is poorly designed.

The functions of design, or what some have called "social architecture," are rarely visible; they take place behind the scenes. The consequences that appear today are the result of work done long in the past, and work today will show its benefits far in the future. Those who aspire to lead out of a desire to control, or gain fame, or simply to be at the center of the action, will find little to attract them to the quiet design work of leadership.

But what, specifically, is involved in organizational design? "Organization design is widely misconstrued as moving around boxes and lines," says Hanover's O'Brien. "The first task of organization design concerns designing the governing ideas of purpose, vision, and core values by which people will live." Few acts of leadership have a more enduring impact on an organization than building a foundation of purpose and core values.

In 1982, Johnson & Johnson found itself facing a corporate nightmare when bottles of its bestselling Tylenol were tampered with, resulting in several deaths. The corporation's immediate response was to pull all Tylenol off the shelves of retail outlets. Thirty-one million capsules were destroyed, even though they were tested and found safe. Although the immediate cost was significant, no other action was possible given the firm's credo. Authored almost forty years earlier by president Robert Wood Johnson, Johnson & Johnson's credo states that permanent success is possible only when modern industry realizes that:

- service to its customers comes first;
- service to its employees and management comes second;
- service to the community comes third, and
- service to its stockholders, last.

Such statements might seem like motherhood and apple pie to those who have not seen the way a clear sense of purpose and values can affect key business decisions.

Johnson & Johnson's crisis management in this case was based on that credo. It was simple, it was right, and it worked.

If governing ideas consititue the first design task of leadership, the second design task involves the policies, strategies, and structures that translate guiding ideas into business decisions. Leadership theorist Philip Selznick calls policy and structure the "institutional embodiment of purpose."[11] "Policy making (the rules that guide decisions) ought to be separated from decision making," says Jay Forrester.[12] "Otherwise, short-term pressures will usurp time from policy creation."

Traditionally, writers like Selznick and Forrester have tended to see policy making and implementation as the work of a small number of senior managers. But that view is changing. Both the dynamic business environment and the mandate of the learning organization to engage people at all levels now make it clear that this second design task is more subtle. Henry Mintzberg has argued that strategy is less a rational plan arrived at in the abstract and implemented throughout the organization than an "emergent phenomenon." Successful organizations "craft strategy" according to Mintzberg, as they continually learn about shifting business conditions and balance what is desired and what is possible.[13] The key is not getting the right strategy but fostering strategic thinking. "The choice of individual action is only part of . . . the policy-maker's need," according to Mason and Mitroff.[14] "More important is the need to achieve insight into the nature of the complexity and to formulate concepts and world views for coping with it."

Behind appropriate policies, strategies, and structures are effective learning processes; their creation is the third key design responsibility in learning organizations. This does not absolve senior managers of their strategic responsibilities. Actually, it deepens and extends those responsibilities. Now, they are not only responsible for ensuring that an organization have well-developed strategies and policies, but also for ensuring that processes exist whereby these are continually improved.

In the early 1970s, Shell was the weakest of the big seven oil companies. Today, Shell and Exxon are arguably the strongest, both in size and financial health. Shell's ascendance began with frustration. Around 1971 members of Shell's "Group Planning" in London began to foresee dramatic change and unpredictability in world oil markets. However, it proved impossible to persuade managers that the stable world of steady growth in oil demand and supply they had known for twenty years was about to change. Despite brilliant analysis and artful presentation, Shell's planners realized, in the words of Pierre Wack, that they "had failed to change behavior in much of the Shell organization."[15] Progress would probably have ended there, had the frustration not given way to a radically new view of corporate planning.

As they pondered this failure, the planners' view of their basic task shifted: "We no longer saw our task as producing a documented view of the future business environment five or ten years ahead. Our real target was the microcosm (the 'mental model') of our decision makers." Only when the planners reconceptualized their basic task as fostering learning rather than devising plans did their insights begin to have an impact. The initial tool used was "scenario analysis," through which planners encouraged operating managers to think through how they would manage in the future under different possible scenarios. It mattered not that the managers believed the planners' scenarios absolutely, only that they became engaged in ferreting out the implications. In this way, Shell's planners conditioned managers to be mentally prepared for a shift from low prices to high prices and from stability to instability. The results were significant. When OPEC became a reality, Shell quickly responded by increasing local operating company control (to enhance maneuverability in the new political environment), building buffer stocks, and accelerating development on non-OPEC sources—actions that its competitors took much more slowly or not at all.

Somewhat inadvertently, Shell planners had discovered the leverage of designing institutional learning processes, whereby, in the words of former planning director de Geus, "Management teams change their shared mental models of their company, their markets, and their competitors."[16] Since then, "planning as learning" has become a by-word at Shell, and Group Planning has continually sought out new learning tools that can be integrated into the planning process. Some of these are described below.

Leader as Teacher

"The first responsibility of a leader," writes retired Herman Miller CEO Max de Pree, " is to define reality."[17] Much of the leverage leaders can actually exert lies in helping people achieve more accurate, more insightful, and more *empowering* views of reality.

Leader as teacher does *not* mean leader as authoritarian expert whose job it is to teach people the "correct" view of reality. Rather, it is about helping everyone in the organization, oneself included, to gain more insightful views of current reality. This is in line with a popular emerging view of leaders as coaches, guides, or facilitators.[18] In learning organizations, this teaching role is developed further by virtue of explicit attention to people's mental models and by the influence of the systems perspective.

The role of leader as teacher starts with bringing to the surface people's mental models of important issues. No one carries an organization, a market, or a state of technology in his or her head. What we carry in our heads are assumptions. These mental pictures of how the world works have a significant influence on how we perceive problems and opportunities, identify courses of action, and make choices.

One reason that mental models are so deeply entrenched is that they are largely tacit. Ian Mitroff, in his study of General Motors, argues that an assumption that prevailed for years was that, in the United States, "Cars are status symbols. Styling is therefore more important than quality."[19] The Detroit automakers didn't say, "We have a *mental model* that all people care about is styling." Few actual managers would even say publicly that all people care about is styling. So long as the view remained unexpressed, there was little possibility of challenging its validity or forming more accurate assumptions.

But working with mental models goes beyond revealing hidden assumptions. "Reality," as perceived by most people in most organizations, means pressures that must be borne, crises that must be reacted to, and limitations that must be accepted. Leaders as teachers help people *restructure their views of reality* to see beyond the superficial conditions and events into the underlying causes of problems—and therefore to see new possibilities for shaping the future.

Specifically, leaders can influence people to view reality at three distinct levels: events, patterns of behavior, and systemic structure.

Systemic Structure
(Generative)
↓
Patterns of Behavior
(Responsive)
↓
Events
(Reactive)

The key question becomes *where do leaders predominantly focus their own and their organization's attention?*

Contemporary society focuses predominantly on events. The media reinforces this perspective, with almost exclusive attention to short-term, dramatic events. This focus leads naturally to explaining what happens in terms of those events: "The Dow Jones average went up sixteen points because high fourth-quarter profits were announced yesterday."

Pattern-of-behavior explanations are rarer, in contemporary culture, than event explanations, but they do occur. "Trend analysis" is an example of seeing patterns of behavior. A good editorial that interprets a set of current events in the context of long-term historical changes is another example. Systemic, structural explanations go even further by addressing the question, "What cause the patterns of behavior?"

In some sense, all three levels of explanation are equally true. But their usefulness is quite different. Event explanations—who did what to whom—doom their holders to a reactive stance toward change. Pattern-of-behavior explanations focus on identifying long-term trends and assessing their implications. They at least suggest how, over time, we can respond to shifting conditions. Structural explanations are the most powerful. Only they address the underlying causes of behavior at a level such that patterns of behavior can be changed.

By and large, leaders of our current institutions focus their attention on events and patterns of behavior, and, under their influence, their organizations do likewise. That is why contemporary organizations are predominantly reactive, or at best responsive—rarely generative. On the other hand, leaders in learning organizations pay attention to all three levels, but focus especially on systemic structure; largely by example, they teach people throughout the organization to do likewise.

Leader as Steward

This is the subtlest role of leadership. Unlike the roles of designer and teacher, it is almost solely a matter of attitude. It is an attitude critical to learning organizations.

While stewardship has long been recognized as an aspect of leadership, its source is still not widely understood. I believe Robert Greenleaf came closest to explaining real stewardship, in his seminal book *Servant Leadership.*[20] There, Greenleaf argues that "The servant leader *is* servant first. . . . It begins with the natural feeling that one wants to serve, to serve *first.* This conscious choice brings one to aspire to lead. That person is sharply different from one who is leader first, perhaps because of the need to assuage an unusual power drive or to acquire material possessions."

Leaders' sense of stewardship operates on two levels: stewardship for the people they lead and stewardship for the larger purpose or mission that underlies the enterprise. The first type arises from a keen appreciation of the impact one's leadership can have on others. People can suffer economically, emotionally, and spiritually under inept leadership. If anything, people in a learning organization are more vulnerable because of their commitment and sense of shared ownership. Appreciating this naturally instills a sense of responsibility in leaders. The second type of stewardship arises from a leader's sense of personal purpose and commitment to the organization's larger mission. People's natural impulse to learn is unleashed when they are engaged in an endeavor they consider worthy of their fullest commitment. Or, as Lawrence Miller puts it, "Achieving return on equity does not, as a goal, mobilize the most noble forces of our soul."[21]

Leaders engaged in building learning organizations naturally feel part of a larger purpose that goes beyond their organization. They are part of changing the way businesses operate, not from a vague philanthropic urge, but from a conviction that their efforts will produce more productive organizations, capable of achieving higher levels of organizational success and personal satisfaction than more traditional organizations. Their sense of stewardship was succinctly captured by George Bernard Shaw when he said,

> This is the true joy in life, the being used for a purpose you consider a mighty one, the being a force of nature rather than a feverish, selfish clod of ailments and grievances complaining that the world will not devote itself to making you happy.

NEW SKILLS

New leadership roles require new leadership skills. These skills can only be developed, in my judgment, through a lifelong commitment. It is not enough for one or two individuals to develop these skills. They must be distributed widely throughout the organization. This is one reason that understanding the *disciplines* of a learning organization is so important. These disciplines embody the principles and practices that can widely foster leadership development.

Three critical areas of skills (disciplines) are building shared vision, surfacing and challenging mental models, and engaging in systems thinking.[22]

Building Shared Vision

How do individual visions come together to create shared visions? A useful metaphor is the hologram, the three-dimensional image created by interacting light sources.

If you cut a photograph in half, each half shows only part of the whole image. But if you divide a hologram, each part, no matter how small, shows the whole image intact. Likewise, when a group of people come to share a vision for an organization, each person sees an individual picture of the organization at its best. Each shares responsibility for the whole, not just for one piece. But the component pieces of the hologram are not identical. Each represents the whole image from a different point of view. It's something like poking holes in a window shade; each hole offers a unique angle for viewing the whole image. So, too, is each individual's vision unique.

When you add up the pieces of a hologram, something interesting happens. The image becomes more intense, more lifelike. When more people come to share a vision, the vision becomes more real in the sense of a mental reality that people can truly imagine achieving. They now have partners, co-creators; the vision no longer rests on their shoulders alone. Early on, when they are nurturing an individual vision, people may say it is "my vision." But, as the shared vision develops, it becomes both "my vision" and "our vision."

The skills involved in building shared vision include the following:

• **Encouraging Personal Vision.** Shared visions emerge from personal visions. It is not that people only care about their own self-interest—in fact, people's values usually include dimensions that concern family, organization, community, and even the world. Rather, it is that people's capacity for caring is *personal.*

• **Communicating and Asking for Support.** Leaders must be willing to continually share their own vision, rather than being the official representative of the corporate vision. They also must be prepared to ask, "Is this vision worthy of your commitment?" This can be difficult for a person used to setting goals and presuming compliance.

• **Visioning as an Ongoing Process.** Building shared vision is a never-ending process. At any one point there will be a particular image of the future that is predominant, but that image will evolve. Today, too many managers want to dispense with the "vision business" by going off and writing the Official Vision Statement. Such statements almost always lack the vitality, freshness, and excitement of a genuine vision that comes from people asking, "What do we really want to achieve?"

• **Blending Extrinsic and Intrinsic Visions.** Many energizing visions are extrinsic—that is, they focus on achieving something relative to an outsider, such as a competitor. But a goal that is limited to defeating an opponent can, once the vision is achieved, easily become a defensive posture. In contrast, intrinsic goals like creating a new type of product, taking an established product to a new level, or setting a new standard for customer satisfaction can call forth a new level of creativity and innovation. Intrinsic and extrinsic visions need to coexist; a vision solely predicated on defeating an adversary will eventually weaken an organization.

• **Distinguishing Positive from Negative Visions.** Many organizations only truly pull together when their survival is threatened. Similarly, most social movements aim at eliminating what people don't want: for example, anti-drugs, anti-smoking, or anti-nuclear arms movements. Negative visions carry a subtle message of powerlessness: people will only pull together when there is sufficient threat. Negative visions also tend to be short term. Two fundamental sources of energy can motivate organizations: fear and aspiration. Fear, the energy source behind negative visions, can produce extraordinary changes in short periods, but aspiration endures as a continuing source of learning and growth.

Surfacing and Testing Mental Models

Many of the best ideas in organizations never get put into practice. One reason is that new insights and initiatives often conflict with established mental models. The leadership task of challenging assumptions without invoking defensiveness requires reflection and inquiry skills possessed by few leaders in traditional controlling organizations.[23]

- **Seeing Leaps of Abstraction.** Our minds literally move at lightning speed. Ironically, this often slows our learning, because we leap to generalizations so quickly that we never think to test them. We then confuse our generalizations with the observable data upon which they are based, treating the generalizations *as if they were data.* The frustrated sales rep reports to the home office that "customers don't really care about quality, price is what matters," when what actually happened was that three consecutive large customers refused to place an order unless a larger discount was offered. The sales rep treats her generalization, "customers care only about price," as if it were absolute fact rather than an assumption (very likely an assumption reflecting her own views of customers and the market). This thwarts future learning because she starts to focus on how to offer attractive discounts rather than probing behind the customers' statements. For example, the customers may have been so disgruntled with the firm's delivery or customer service that they are unwilling to purchase again without larger discounts.

- **Balancing Inquiry and Advocacy.** Most managers are skilled at articulating their views and presenting them persuasively. While important, advocacy skills can become counterproductive as managers rise in responsibility and confront increasingly complex issues that require collaborative learning among different, equally knowledgeable people. Leaders in learning organizations need to have both inquiry *and* advocacy skills.[24]

Specifically, when advocating a view, they need to be able to:
- explain the reasoning and data that led to their view;
- encourage others to test their view (e.g., Do you see gaps in my reasoning? Do you disagree with the data upon which my view is based?); and
- encourage others to provide different views (e.g., Do you have either different data, different conclusions, or both?).

When inquiring into another's views, they need to:
- actively seek to understand the other's view, rather than simply restating their own view and how it differs from the other's view; and
- make their attributions about the other and the other's view explicit (e.g., Based on your statement that . . . ; I am assuming that you believe . . . ; Am I representing your views fairly?).

If they reach an impasse (others no longer appear open to inquiry), they need to:
- ask what data or logic might unfreeze the impasse, or if an experiment (or some other inquiry) might be designed to provide new information.

- **Distinguishing Espoused Theory from Theory in Use.** We all like to think that we hold certain views, but often our actions reveal deeper views. For example, I may proclaim that people are trustworthy, but never lend friends money and jealously guard my possessions. Obviously, my deeper mental model (my theory in use), differs from my espoused theory. Recognizing gaps between espoused views and theories in use (which often requires the help of others) can be pivotal to deeper learning.

- **Recognizing and Defusing Defensive Routines.** As one CEO in our research program puts it, "Nobody ever talks about an issue at the 8:00 business meeting exactly the same way they talk about it at home that evening or over drinks at the end of the day." The reason is what Chris Argyris calls "defensive routines," entrenched habits used to protect ourselves from the embarrassment and threat that come with exposing our thinking. For most of us, such defenses began to build early in life in response to pressures to have the right answers in school or at home. Organizations add new levels of performance anxiety and thereby amplify and exacerbate this defensiveness. Ironically, this makes it even more difficult to expose hidden mental models, and thereby lessens learning.

The first challenge is to recognize defensive routines, then to inquire into their operation. Those who are best at revealing and defusing defensive routines operate with a high degree of self-disclosure regarding their own defensiveness (e.g., I notice that I am feeling uneasy about how this conversation is going. Perhaps I don't understand it or it is threatening to me in ways I don't yet see. Can you help me see this better?).

Systems Thinking

We all know that leaders should help people see the big picture. But the actual skills whereby leaders are supposed to achieve this are not well understood. In my experience, successful leaders often *are* "systems thinkers" to a considerable extent. They focus less on day-to-day events and more on underlying trends and forces of change. But they do this almost completely intuitively. The consequence is that they are often unable to explain their intuitions to others and feel frustrated that others cannot see the world the way they do.

One of the most significant developments in management science today is the gradual coalescence of managerial systems thinking as a field of study and practice. This field suggests some key skills for future leaders:

• **Seeing Interrelationships, Not Things, and Processes, Not Snapshots.** Most of us have been conditioned throughout our lives to focus on things and to see the world in static images. This leads us to linear explanations of systemic phenomenon. For instance, in an arms race each party is convinced that the other is *the cause* of problems. They react to each new move as an isolated event, not as part of a process. So long as they fail to see the interrelationships of these actions, they are trapped.

• **Moving beyond Blame.** We tend to blame each other or outside circumstances for our problems. But it is poorly designed systems, not incompetent or unmotivated individuals, that cause most organizational problems. Systems thinking shows us that there is no outside—that you and the cause of your problems are part of a single system.

• **Distinguishing Detail Complexity from Dynamic Complexity.** Some types of complexity are more important strategically than others. Detail complexity arises when there are many variables. Dynamic complexity arises when cause and effect are distant in time and space, and when the consequences over time of interventions are subtle and not obvious to many participants in the system. The leverage in most management situations lies in understanding dynamic complexity, not detail complexity.

• **Focusing on Areas of High Leverage.** Some have called systems thinking the "new dismal science" because it teaches that most obvious solutions don't work—at best, they improve matters in the short run, only to make things worse in the long run. But there is another side to the story. Systems thinking also shows that small, well-focused actions can produce significant, enduring improvements, if they are in the right place. Systems thinkers refer to this idea as the principle of "leverage." Tackling a difficult problem is often a matter of seeing where the high leverage lies, where a change—with a minimum of effort—would lead to lasting, significant improvement.

• **Avoiding Symptomatic Solutions.** The pressures to intervene in management systems that are going awry can be overwhelming. Unfortunately, given the linear thinking that predominates in most organizations, interventions usually focus on symptomatic fixes, not underlying causes. This results in only temporary relief, and it tends to create still more pressures later on for further, low-leverage intervention. If leaders acquiesce to these pressures, they can be sucked into an endless spiral of increasing intervention. Sometimes the most difficult leadership acts are to refrain from intervening through popular quick fixes and to keep the pressure on everyone to identify more enduring solutions.

While leaders who can articulate systemic explanations are rare, those who *can* will leave their stamp on an organization. One person who had this gift was Bill Gore, the founder and long-time CEO of W.L. Gore and Associates (makers of Gore-Tex and other synthetic fiber products). Bill Gore was adept at telling stories that showed how the organization's core values of freedom and individual responsibility required particular operating policies. He was proud of his egalitarian organization, in which there were (and still are) no "employees," only "associates," all of whom own shares in the company and participate in its management. At one talk, he explained the company's policy of controlled growth: "Our limitation is not financial resources. Our limitation is the rate at which we can bring in new associates. Our experience has been that if we try to bring in more than a 25 percent per year increase, we begin to bog down. Twenty-five percent per year growth is a real limitation; you can do much better than that with an authoritarian organization." As Gore tells the story, one of the associates, Esther Baum, went home after this talk and reported the limitation to her husband. As it happened, he was an astronomer and mathematician at Lowell Observatory. He said, "That's a very interesting figure." He took out a pencil and paper and calculated and said, "Do you realize that in only fifty-seven and a half years, everyone in the world will be working for Gore?"

Through this story, Gore explains the systemic rationale behind a key policy, limited growth rate—a policy that undoubtedly caused a lot of stress in the organization. He suggests that, at larger rates of growth, the adverse effects of attempting to integrate too many new people too rapidly would begin to dominate. (This is the "limits to growth" systems archetype explained below.) The story also reaffirms the organization's commitment to creating a unique environment for its associates and illustrates the types of sacrifices that the firm is prepared to make in order to remain true to its vision. The last part of the story shows that, despite the self-imposed limit, the company is still very much a growth company.

The consequences of leaders who lack systems thinking skills can be devastating. Many charismatic leaders manage almost exclusively at the level of events. They deal in visions and in crises, and little in between. Under their leadership, an organization hurtles from crisis to crisis. Eventually, the worldview of people in the organization becomes dominated by events and reactiveness. Many, especially those who are deeply committed, become burned out. Eventually, cynicism comes to pervade the organization. People have no control over their time, let alone their destiny.

Similar problems arise with the "visionary strategist," the leader with vision who sees both patterns of change and events. This leader is better prepared to manage change. He or she can explain strategies in terms of emerging trends, and thereby foster a climate that is less reactive. But such leaders still impart a responsive orientation rather than a generative one.

Many talented leaders have rich, highly systemic intuitions but cannot explain those intuitions to others. Ironically, they often end up being authoritarian leaders, even if they don't want to, because only they see the decisions that need to be made. They are unable to conceptualize their strategic insights so that these can become public knowledge, open to challenge and further improvement.

NEW TOOLS

Developing the skills described above requires new tools—tools that will enhance leaders' conceptual abilities and foster communication and collaborative inquiry. What follows is a sampling of tools starting to find use in learning organizations.

Systems Archetypes

One of the insights of the budding, managerial systems-thinking field is that certain types of systemic structures recur again and again. Countless systems grow for a period, then encounter problems and cease to grow (or even collapse) well before they have reached intrinsic limits to growth. Many other systems get locked in runaway vicious spirals where every actor has to run faster and faster to stay in the same place. Still others lure individual actors into doing what seems right locally, yet which eventually causes suffering for all.[25]

Some of the system archetypes that have the broadest relevance include:

• **Balancing Process with Delay.** In this archetype, decision makers fail to appreciate the time delays involved as they move toward a goal. As a result, they overshoot the goal and may even produce recurring cycles. Classic example: Real estate developers who keep starting new projects until the market has gone soft, by which time an eventual glut is guaranteed by the properties still under construction.

• **Limits to Growth.** A reinforcing cycle of growth grinds to a halt, and may even reverse itself, as limits are approached. The limits can be resource constraints, or external or internal responses to growth. Classic examples: Product life cycles that peak prematurely due to poor quality or service, the growth and decline of communication in a management team, and the spread of a new movement.

• **Shifting the Burden.** A short-term "solution" is used to correct a problem, with seemingly happy immediate results. As this correction is used more and more, fundamental long-term corrective measures are used less. Over time, the mechanisms of the fundamental solution may atrophy or become disabled, leading to even greater reliance on the symptomatic solution. Classic example: Using corporate human resource staff to solve local personnel problems, thereby keeping managers from developing their own interpersonal skills.

• **Eroding Goals.** When all else fails, lower your standards. This is like "shifting the burden," except that the short-term solution involves letting a fundamental goal, such as quality standards or employee morale standards, atrophy. Classic example: A company that responds to delivery problems by continually upping its quoted delivery times.

• **Escalation.** Two people or two organizations, who each see their welfare as depending on a relative advantage over the other, continually react to the other's advances. Whenever one side gets ahead, the other is threatened, leading it to act more aggressively to reestablish its advantage, which threatens the first, and so on. Classic examples: Arms race, gang warfare, price wars.

• **Tragedy of the Commons.**[26] Individuals keep intensifying their use of a commonly available but limited resource until all individuals start to experience severely diminishing returns. Classic examples: Sheepherders who keep increasing their flocks until they overgraze the common pasture; divisions in a firm that share a common salesforce and compete for the use of sales reps by upping their sales targets, until the salesforce burns out from overextension.

• **Growth and Underinvestment.** Rapid growth approaches a limit that could be eliminated or pushed into the future, but only by aggressive investment in physical and human capacity. Eroding goals or standards cause investment that is too weak, or too slow, and customers get increasingly unhappy, slowing demand growth and thereby making the needed investment (apparently) unnecessary or impossible. Classic example: Countless once-successful growth firms that allowed product or service quality to erode, and were unable to generate enough revenues to invest in remedies.

The Archetype template is a specific tool that is helping managers identify archetypes operating in their own strategic areas (see Figure 2).[27] The template shows the basic structural form of the archetype but lets managers fill in the variables of their own situation. For example, the shifting the burden template involves two balancing processes ("B") that compete for control of a problem symptom. The upper, symptomatic solution provides a short-term fix that will make the problem symptom go away for a while. The lower, fundamental solution provides a more enduring solution. The side effect feedback ("R") around the outside of the diagram identifies unintended exacerbating effects of the symptomatic solution, which, over time, make it more and more difficult to invoke the fundamental solution.

Several years ago, a team of managers from a leading consumer goods producer used the shifting the burden archetype in a revealing way. The problem they focused on was financial stress, which could be dealt with in two different ways: by running marketing promotions (the symptomatic solution) or by product innovation (the fundamental solution). Marketing promotions were fast. The company was expert in their design and implementation. The results were highly predictable. Product innovation was slow and much less predictable, and the company had a history over the past ten years of product-innovation mismanagement. Yet only through innovation could they retain a leadership position in their industry, which had slid over the past ten to twenty years. What the managers saw clearly was that the more skillful they became at pro-

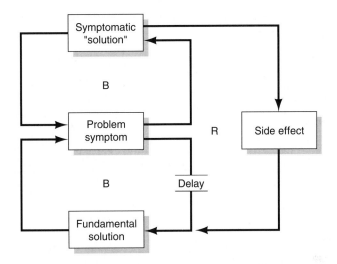

In the "shifting the burden" template, two balancing processes (B) compete for control of a problem symptom. Both solutions affect the symptom, but only the fundamental solution treats the cause. The symptomatic "solution" creates the additional side effect (R) of deferring the fundamental solution, making it harder and harder to achieve.

FIGURE 2
"Shifting the burden" archetype template.

motions, the more they shifted the burden away from product innovation. But what really struck home was when one member identified the unintended side effect: the last three CEOs had all come from advertising function, which had become the politically dominant function in the corporation, thereby institutionalizing the symptomatic solution. Unless the political values shifted back toward product and process innovation, the managers realized, the firm's decline would accelerate—which is just the shift that has happened over the past several years.

Charting Strategic Dilemmas

Management teams typically come unglued when confronted with core dilemmas. A classic example was the way U.S. manufacturers faced the low cost–high quality choice. For years, most assumed that it was necessary to choose between the two. Not surprisingly, given the short-term pressures perceived by most managements, the prevailing choice was low cost. Firms that chose high quality usually perceived themselves as aiming exclusively for a high quality, high price market niche. The consequences of this perceived either-or choice have been disastrous, even fatal, as U.S. manufacturers have encountered increasing international competition from firms that have chosen to consistently improve quality *and* cost.

In a recent book, Charles Hampden-Turner presented a variety of tools for helping management teams confront strategic dilemmas creatively.[28] He summarizes the process in seven steps:

- **Eliciting the Dilemmas.** Identifying the opposed values that form the "horns" of the dilemma, for example, cost as opposed to quality, or local initiative as opposed to central coordination and control. Hampden-Turner suggests that humor can be a distinct asset in this process since "the admission that dilemmas even exist tends to be difficult for some companies."
- **Mapping.** Locating the opposing values as two axes and helping managers identify where they see themselves, or their organization, along the axes.
- **Processing.** Getting rid of nouns to describe the axes of the dilemma. Present participles formed by adding "ing" convert rigid nouns into processes that imply movement. For example, central control versus local control becomes "strengthening national office" and "growing local initiatives." This loosens the bond of implied opposition between the two values. For example, it becomes possible to think of "strengthening national services from which local branches can benefit."
- **Framing/Contextualizing.** Further softening the adversarial structure among different values by letting "each side in turn be the frame or context for the other." This shifting of the "figure-ground" relationship undermines any implicit attempts to hold one value as intrinsically superior to the other, and thereby to become mentally closed to creative strategies for continuous improvement of both.
- **Sequencing.** Breaking the hold of static thinking. Very often, values like low cost and high quality appear to be in opposition because we think in terms of a point in time, not in terms of an ongoing process. For example, a strategy of investing in new process technology and developing a new production-floor culture of worker responsibility may take time and money in the near term, yet reap significant long-term financial rewards.
- **Waving/Cycling.** Sometimes the strategic path toward improving both values involves cycles where both values will get "worse" for a time. Yet, at a deeper level, learning is occurring that will cause the next cycle to be at a higher plateau for both values.
- **Synergizing.** Achieving synergy where significant improvement is occurring along all axes of all relevant dilemmas. (This is the ultimate goal, of course.) Synergy, as Hampden-Turner points out, is a uniquely systemic notion, coming from the Greek *syn-ergo* of "work together."

"The Left-Hand Column": Surfacing Mental Models

The idea that mental models can dominate business decisions and that these models are often tacit and even contradictory to what people espouse can be very threatening to managers who pride themselves on rationality and judicious decision making. It is important to have tools to help managers discover for themselves how their mental models operate to undermine their own intentions.

One tool that has worked consistently to help managers see their own mental models in action is the "left-hand column" exercise developed by Chris Argyris and his colleagues. This tool is especially helpful in showing how we leap from data to generalization without testing the validity of our generalizations.

When working with managers, I start this exercise by selecting a specific situation in which I am interacting with other people in a way that is not working, that is not producing the learning that is needed. I write out a sample of the exchange, with the script on the right-hand side of the page. On the left-hand side, I write what I am thinking but not saying at each stage in the exchange (see sidebar).

The left-hand column exercise not only brings hidden assumptions to the surface, it shows how they influence behavior. In the example, I make two key assumptions about Bill: he lacks confidence and he lacks initiative. Neither may be literally true, but both are evident in my internal dialogue, and both influence the way I handle the situation. Believing that he lacks confidence, I skirt the fact that I've heard the presentation was a bomb. I'm afraid that if I say it directly, he will lose what little confidence he has, or he will see me as unsupportive. So I bring up the subject of the presentation obliquely. When I ask Bill what we should do next, he gives no specific course of action. Believing he lacks initiative, I take this as evidence of his laziness; he is content to do nothing when action is definitely required. I conclude that I will have to manufacture some form of pressure to motivate him, or else I will simply have to take matters into my own hands.

The exercise reveals the elaborate webs of assumptions we weave, within which we become our own victims. Rather than dealing directly with my assumptions about Bill

---

THE LEFT-HAND COLUMN: AN EXERCISE

Imagine my exchange with a colleague, Bill, after he made a big presentation to our boss on a project we are doing together. I had to miss the presentation, but I've heard that it was poorly received.

Me: How did the presentation go?
Bill: Well, I don't know. It's really too early to say. Besides, we're breaking new ground here.
Me: Well, what do you think we should do? I believe that the issues you were raising are important.
Bill: I'm not so sure. Let's just wait and see what happens.
Me: You may be right, but I think we may need to do more than just wait.

Now, here is what the exchange looks like with my "left-hand column":

What I'm thinking	What is said
Everyone says the presentation was a bomb.	*Me:* How did the presentation go?
Does he really not know how bad it was? Or is he not willing to face up to it?	*Bill:* Well, I don't know. It's too early to say. Besides, we're breaking new ground here. *Me:* Well, what do you think we should do? I believe that the issues you were raising are important.
He really is afraid to see the truth. If he only had more confidence, he could probably learn from a situation like this.	*Bill:* I'm not so sure. Let's just wait and see what happens.
I can't believe he doesn't realize how disastrous that presentation was to our moving ahead.	*Me:* You may be right, but I think we may need to do more than just wait.
I've got to find some way to light a fire under the guy.	

LEARNING AT HANOVER INSURANCE

Hanover Insurance has gone from the bottom of the property and liability industry to a position among the top 25 percent of U.S. insurance companies over the past twenty years, largely through the efforts of CEO William O'Brien and his predecessor, Jack Adam. The following comments are excerpted from a series of interviews Senge conducted with O'Brien as background for his book.

Senge: Why do you think there is so much change occurring in management and organizations today? Is it primarily because of increased competitive pressures?

O'Brien: That's a factor, but not the most significant factor. The ferment in management will continue until we find models that are more congruent with human nature.

One of the great insights of modern psychology is the hierarchy of human needs. As Maslow expressed this idea, the most basic needs are food and shelter. Then comes belonging. Once these three basic needs are satisfied, people begin to aspire toward self-respect and esteem, and toward self-actualization—the fourth- and fifth-order needs.

Our traditional hierarchical organizations are designed to provide for the first three levels, but not the fourth and fifth. These first three levels are now widely available to members of industrial society, but our organizations do not offer people sufficient opportunities for growth.

Senge: How would you assess Hanover's progress to date?

O'Brien: We have been on a long journey away from a traditional hierarchical culture. The journey began with everyone understanding some guiding ideas about purpose, vision, and values as a basis for participative management. This is a better way to begin building a participative culture than by simply "letting people in on decision making." Before there can be meaningful participation, people must share certain values and pictures about where we are trying to go. We discovered that people have a real need to feel that they're part of an enobling mission. But developing shared visions and values is not the end, only the beginning.

Next we had to get beyond mechanical, linear thinking. The essence of our job as managers is to deal with "divergent" problems—problems that have no simple answer. "Convergent" problems—problems that have a "right" answer—should be solved locally. Yet we are deeply conditioned to see the world in terms of convergent problems. Most managers try to force-fit simplistic solutions and undermine the potential for learning when divergent problems arise. Since everyone handles the linear issues fairly well, companies that learn how to handle divergent issues will have a great advantage.

The next basic stage in our progression was coming to understand inquiry and advocacy. We learned that real openness is rooted in people's ability to continually inquire into their own thinking. This requires exposing yourself to being wrong—not something that most managers are rewarded for. But learning is very difficult if you cannot look for errors or incompleteness in your own ideas.

What all this builds to is the capability throughout an organization to manage mental models. In a locally controlled organization, you have the fundamental challenge of learning how to help people make good decisions without coercing them into making *particular* decisions. By managing mental models, we create "self-concluding" decisions—decisions that people come to themselves—which will result in deeper conviction, better implementation, and the ability to make better adjustments when the situation changes.

Senge: What concrete steps can top managers take to begin moving toward learning organizations?

O'Brien: Look at the signals you send through the organization. For example, one critical signal is how you spend your time. It's hard to build a learning organization if people are unable to take the time to think through important matters. I rarely set up an appointment for less than one hour. If the subject is not worth an hour, it shouldn't be on my calendar.

Senge: Why is this so hard for so many managers?

O'Brien: It comes back to what you believe about the nature of your work. The authoritarian manger has a "chain gang" mental model: "The speed of the boss is the speed of the gang. I've got to keep things moving fast, because I've got to keep people working." In a learning organization, the manager shoulders an almost sacred responsibility: to create conditions that enable people to have happy and productive lives. If you understand the effects the ideas we are discussing can have on the lives of people in your organization, you will take the time.

and the situation, we talk around the subject. The reasons for my avoidance are self-evident: I assume that if I raised my doubts, I would provoke a defensive reaction that would only make matters worse. But the price of avoiding the issue is high. Instead of determining how to move forward to resolve our problems, we end our exchange with no clear course of action. My assumptions about Bill's limitations have been reinforced. I resort to a manipulative strategy to move things forward.

The exercise not only reveals the need for skills in surfacing assumptions, but that we are the ones most in need of help. There is no one right way to handle difficult situations like my exchange with Bill, but any productive strategy revolves around a high level of self-disclosure and willingness to have my views challenged. I need to recognize my own leaps of abstraction regarding Bill, share the events and reasoning that are leading to my concern over the project, and be open to Bill's views on both. The skills to carry on such conversations without invoking defensiveness take time to develop. But if both parties in a learning impasse start by doing their own left-hand column exercise and sharing them with each other, it is remarkable how quickly everyone recognizes their contribution to the impasse and progress starts to be made.

Learning Laboratories: Practice Fields for Management Teams

One of the most promising new tools is the learning laboratory or "microworld": constructed microcosms of real-life settings in which management teams can learn how to learn together.

The rationale behind learning laboratories can best be explained by analogy. Although most management teams have great difficulty learning (enhancing their collective intelligence and capacity to create), in other domains team learning is the norm rather than the exception—team sports and the performing arts, for example. Great basketball teams do not start off great. They learn. But the process by which these teams learn is, by and large, absent from modern organizations. The process is a continual movement between practice and performance.

The vision guiding current research in management learning laboratories is to design and construct effective practice fields for management teams. Much remains to be done, but the broad outlines are emerging.

First, since team learning in organizations is an individual-to-individual and individual-to-system phenomenon, learning laboratories must combine meaningful business issues with meaningful interpersonal dynamics. Either alone is incomplete.

Second, the factors that thwart learning about complex business issues must be eliminated in the learning lab. Chief among these is the inability to experience the long-term, systemic consequences of key strategic decisions. We all learn best from experience, but we are unable to experience the consequences of many important organizational decisions. Learning laboratories remove this constraint through system dynamics simulation games that compress time and space.

Third, new learning skills must be developed. One constraint on learning is the inability of managers to reflect insightfully on their assumptions, and to inquire effectively into each other's assumptions. Both skills can be enhanced in a learning laboratory, where people can practice surfacing assumptions in a low-risk setting. A note of caution: It is far easier to design an entertaining learning laboratory than it is to have an impact on real management practices and firm traditions outside the learning lab. Research on management simulations has shown that they often have greater entertainment value than educational value. One of the reasons appears to be that many simulations do not offer deep insights into systemic structures causing business problems. Another reason is that they do not foster new learning skills. Also, there is no connection between experiments in the learning lab and real life experiments. These are significant problems that research on learning laboratory design is now addressing.

DEVELOPING LEADERS AND LEARNING ORGANIZATIONS

In a recently published retrospective on organization development in the 1980s, Marshall Sashkin and N. Warner Burke observe the return of an emphasis on developing leaders who can develop organizations.[29] They also note Schein's critique that most top executives are not qualified for the task of developing culture.[30] Learning organizations represent a potentially significant evolution of organizational culture. So it should come as no surprise that such organizations will remain a distant vision until the leadership capabilities they demand are developed. "The 1990s may be the period," suggest Sashkin and Burke, "during which organization development and (a new sort of) management development are reconnected."

I believe that this new sort of management development will focus on the roles, skills, and tools for leadership in learning organizations. Undoubtedly, the ideas offered above are only a rough approximation of this new territory. The sooner we begin seriously exploring the territory, the sooner the initial map can be improved—and the sooner we will realize an age-old vision of leadership:

> The wicked leader is he who the people despise.
> The good leader is he who the people revere.
> The great leader is he who the people say, "We did it ourselves."
>
> Lao Tsu

REFERENCES

1 P. Senge, *The Fifth Discipline: The Art and Practice of the Learning Organization* (New York: Doubleday/Currency, 1990).

2 A.P. de Geus, "Planning as Learning," *Harvard Business Review,* March-April 1988, pp. 70–74.

3 B. Domaine, *Fortune,* 3 July 1989, pp. 48–62.

4 The distinction between adaptive and generative learning has its roots in the distinction between what Argyris and Schon have called their "single-loop" learning, in which individuals or groups adjust their behavior relative to fixed goals, norms, and assumptions, and "double-loop" learning, in which goals, norms, and assumptions, as well as behavior, are open to change (e.g., see C. Argyris and D. Schon, *Organizational Learning: A Theory-in-Action Perspective* (Reading, Massachusetts: Addison-Wesley, 1978)).

5 All unattributed quotes are from personal communications with the author.

6 G. Stalk, Jr., "Time: The Next Source of Competitive Advantage," *Harvard Business Review,* July-August 1988, pp. 41–51.

7 Senge (1990).

8 The principle of creative tension comes from Robert Fritz' work on creativity. See R. Fritz, *The Path of Least Resistance* (New York: Ballantine, 1989) and *Creating* (New York: Ballantine, 1990).

9 M.L. King, Jr., "Letter from Birmingham Jail," *American Visions,* January-February 1986, pp. 52–59.

10 E. Schein, *Organizational Culture and Leadership* (San Francisco: Jossey-Bass, 1985). Similar views have been expressed by many leadership theorists. For example, see: P. Selznick, *Leadership in Administration* (New York: Harper & Row, 1957); W. Bennis and B. Nanus, *Leaders* (New York: Harper & Row, 1985); and N.M. Tichy and M.A. Devanna, *The Transformational Leader* (New York: John Wiley & Sons, 1986).

11 Selznick (1957).

12 J.W. Forrester, "A New Corporate Design," *Sloan Management Review* (formerly *Industrial Management Review*), Fall 1965, pp. 5–17.

13 See, for example, H. Mintzberg, "Crafting Strategy," *Harvard Business Review,* July-August 1987, pp. 66–75.

14 R. Mason and I. Mitroff, *Challenging Strategic Planning Assumptions* (New York: John Wiley & Sons, 1981), p. 16.

15 P. Wack, "Scenarios: Uncharted Waters Ahead," *Harvard Business Review,* September-October 1985, pp. 73–89.

16 de Geus (1988).

17 M. de Pree, *Leadership Is an Art* (New York: Doubleday, 1989) p. 9.

18 For example, see T. Peters and N. Austin, *A Passion for Excellence* (New York: Random House, 1985) and J.M. Kouzes and B.Z. Posner, *The Leadership Challenge* (San Francisco: Jossey-Bass, 1987).

19 I. Mitroff, *Break-Away Thinking* (New York: John Wiley & Sons, 1988), pp. 66–67.

20 R.K. Greenleaf, *Servant Leadership: A Journey into the Nature of Legitimate Power and Greatness* (New York: Paulist Press, 1977).

21 L. Miller, *American Spirit: Visions of a New Corporate Culture* (New York: William Morrow, 1984), p. 15.

22 These points are condensed from the practices of the five disciplines examined in Senge (1990).

23 The ideas below are based to a considerable extent on the work of Chris Argyris, Donald Schon, and their Action Science colleagues: C. Argyris and D. Schon, *Organizational Learning: A Theory-in-Action Perspective* (Reading, Massachusetts: Addison-Wesley, 1978); C. Argyris, R. Putnam, and D. Smith, *Action Science* (San Francisco: Jossey-Bass, 1985); C. Argyris, *Strategy, Change, and Defensive Routines* (Boston: Pitman, 1985); and C. Argyris, *Overcoming Organizational Defenses* (Englewood Cliffs, New Jersey: Prentice-Hall, 1990).

24 I am indebted to Diana Smith for the summary points below.

25 The system archetypes are one of several systems diagraming and communication tools. See D.H. Kim, "Toward Learning Organizations: Integrating Total Quality Control and Systems Thinking" (Cambridge, Massachusetts: MIT Sloan School of Management, Working Paper No. 3037-89-BPS, June 1989).

26 This archetype is closely associated with the work of ecologist Garrett Hardin, who coined its label: G. Hardin, "The Tragedy of the Commons," *Science*, 13 December 1968.

27 These templates were originally developed by Jennifer Kemeny, Charles Kiefer, and Michael Goodman of Innovation Associates, Inc., Framingham, Massachusetts.

28 C. Hampden-Turner, *Charting the Corporate Mind* (New York: The Free Press, 1990).

29 M. Sashkin and W.W. Burke, "Organization Development in the 1980s" and "An End-of-the-Eighties Retrospective," in *Advances in Organization Development,* ed. F. Masarik (Norwood, New Jersey: Ablex, 1990).

30 E. Schein (1985).

CHAPTER 10: Questions for Discussion

1 How easy or difficult would it be for a typical manager to be able to demonstrate *both* charismatic *and* instrumental leadership? Would most managers be able to shift from one to the other mode as needed?

2 What are the problems of "institutionalizing" leadership throughout an organization, as Nadler and Tushman advocate, when the organization is headed by a very charismatic CEO?

3 Would you expect that someone who functions as a "champion" of one particular technological innovation could do it again on other different projects? Put another way, is the pattern of behaviors that Howell and Higgins term "championing" a generalizable ability?

4 Are "learning organizations" likely to be developed much more frequently in the future, or will only a small percentage of organizations be able to demonstrate the qualities of true learning organizations?

5 How easy, or difficult, is it for a leader to be able to maintain an acceptable level of "creative tension" without increasing it or decreasing it too much? Is consistent and continuing creative tension of an appropriate level only an "ideal," or is it a realistic objective for most leaders?

CONCLUDING COMMENTS

As discussed in Chapter 1, in order to survive, organizations must be able to recruit members and encourage them to engage in both role and extra-role behaviors. Further, it was argued that fulfilling these behavioral requirements has become much more difficult as organizations operate within increasingly turbulent and competitive environments, marked by such factors as the globalization of the world's markets, changing government regulations, the growing sophistication of capital markets, and advances in information technologies. As organizations make fundamental modifications to their goals to accommodate environmental shifts, managers are faced with the challenges of attracting and retaining employees and then energizing and leading them in achieving these *changing* objectives. Under such conditions, researchers and managers must draw on both the topics of motivation and leadership in order to understand behavior in organizations.

This book has presented a combination of text and scholarly readings on current theories, research, and applications in motivation and leadership. Further, the volume has been structured to take the reader from the general to the specific. Thus, after introducing the study of motivation and leadership in Chapter 1 and the primary theoretical models of Chapters 2 and 3, we looked at a number of key topics as they relate to motivation and leadership, such as social influence and power, job attitudes, cross-cultural influences, reward systems, high-involvement management systems, and organizational change. Throughout the book, we have also examined the interplay between motivation and leadership as they *jointly* determine work behavior.

Taken together, the text and associated reading provide a comprehensive picture of the role of motivation and leadership in organizational settings. In this concluding chapter we want to call the reader's attention to three remaining points. First, it is essential to recognize the importance of the work context in any efforts to motivate and lead employees in organizations. Second, it is useful to understand where we are in the theoretical development of the field; that is, what are the current conceptual issues facing the topics of motivation and leadership and what remains to be learned? Finally, it is important to consider why contemporary organizations do not necessarily make use of what is currently known about motivating and leading employees.

WORK AS A CONTEXT FOR UNDERSTANDING MOTIVATION AND LEADERSHIP

If one objective of increased knowledge about behavioral processes is to improve both work attitudes and performance, then there is clearly a need to consider the nature and meaning of work as a contextual variable. That is, what functions are currently served by work in a modern society? How does the nature of work influence employees' self-identity or their perception of events around them? Without an understanding of the meaning of work to individuals and groups, it is difficult to appreciate fully how managerial attempts to influence employee behavior through motivation and leadership are seen, interpreted—or responded to—by subordinates. It is also difficult actually to manage! Without an understanding of context, managerial efforts will be severely limited.

We can identify at least four aspects of work that are relevant for understanding the context in which influence attempts take place.

Reciprocity or Exchange   To begin with, implicit within the very concept of work is the notion of reciprocity, or exchange. Whether an individual is a corporate executive, a factory worker, or a Peace Corps volunteer, everyone receives some form of reward for his or her services. These rewards may be primarily *extrinsic,* such as money, or they may be primarily *intrinsic,* such as the personal satisfaction from a job well done. In either case, the individual comes to the job with certain expectations about the type and amount of rewards he or she should receive for services rendered. To the extent that such expectations are largely met in the workplace, we would expect the individual to be relatively satisfied and to continue his or her effort. In fact, this concept of reciprocity is at the heart of several theories of work motivation, such as equity theory (see Chapter 2), as well as of certain leadership models, such as leader-member exchange and path-goal theory (see Chapter 3). Reciprocity, or exchange, is also fundamental to understanding—or managing—reward systems in organizations, as discussed in Chapter 7.

Social Interaction   In addition, work often—although not always—serves several social functions. The workplace often provides opportunities for meeting new people and developing friendships. Indeed, many employees spend more time interacting with their coworkers than they do with their own families. As we saw in Chapter 4, social factors in the workplace often represent potent influences on work behavior that are frequently overlooked by managers. It remains to be seen, however, whether this social role of work will continue to be as strong as it presently is in view of the increasing tendency to conduct work "off site." The emergence of telecommuting and similar new forms of work may significantly reduce the social opportunities traditionally provided by the workplace.

Status or Rank   A person's job is often a source of status or rank in society. For example, a corporation president is generally accorded higher status—and, as such, frequently receives greater privileges—than technicians or secretaries, who, in turn, are typically accorded higher status than manual laborers. Despite our idealized views of social equality, the fact remains that what we do at work often transcends the boundaries of the work organization. Thus, a CEO may hold high status in the community because of his or her position in the firm, regardless of his or her contributions to the community itself. Such status can serve as both a source of rewards and an incentive for the CEO, motivating the individual to invest time or money in community enterprises (see Chapter 7). Thus, work can be simultaneously a source of social differentiation and a source of social integration.

Personal Identity   Finally, work frequently carries special meanings for employees. From a psychological standpoint, work can be an important source of identity, self-esteem, and self-actualization. It can provide fulfillment by giving employees a sense of purpose and by clarifying their value to society. Conversely, work can also be a source of frustration, boredom, and feelings of meaninglessness, depending on the characteristics of the individual and the nature of the task. People tend to evaluate themselves according to what they accomplish. If they see their job as interfering with the achievement of their full potential, they may find it increasingly difficult to retain their sense of self-confidence or purpose at work. Such feeling can lead to reduced job involvement, decreased job satisfaction, reduced motivational levels, and increased absenteeism and turnover. On the other hand, if employees see their jobs as a source of personal fulfillment and challenge, motivation and satisfaction should increase. In fact, this premise is at the heart of the recent efforts to develop high-involvement management techniques, as discussed in Chapter 8. Hence, the nature of the job—and the meaning it has for employees—can have a profound effect on employee attitudes and behavior.

THEORIES OF MOTIVATION AND LEADERSHIP: SOME CONCLUDING OBSERVATIONS

Chapter 2 presented an in-depth overview of what researchers have learned about employee motivation and work behavior. Both cognitive and noncognitive theories were discussed. The seven articles presented in that chapter highlighted several key issues currently facing theory development in the field. Taking the articles together, one is led to the conclusion that many of the theories are moving toward at least limited convergence. For example, the principle of reciprocity, whether in the form of performance-contingent rewards or procedural justice, has become a key feature of most contemporary motivation theories. Moreover, there is now a clear recognition of the role in motivated behavior of learning and self-confidence in one's own abilities. The notion of goal-directedness—most clearly articulated in goal-setting approaches—seems to be pervasive in most current theories. Finally, in most extant frameworks the importance of feedback loops as a source of reinforcement for or against a given course of action is highlighted. While the specific theories may differ at the margins, it could be argued that complex theories of motivation increasingly overlap with respect to variables and processes. This convergence is largely the result of the accumulation of learning over the years, and it has implications for managers in search of lessons for the future.

In Chapter 3, we looked in some detail at contemporary theories of leadership. Again we see a convergence of sorts across these theories, but not nearly to the extent as with theories of motivation. For example, whether we are using the classic "trait" approach or the more contemporary "charismatic" theory, we pay heed to relatively stable personal characteristics of the leader that inspire others to follow. Indeed, the nature and quality of this vertical bond between leaders and followers frequently forms the heart of the theory itself. Moreover, as with motivation theories, the notion of reciprocity is prevalent; leaders and followers are continually negotiating both short- and long-term psychological contracts that influence behaviors. Finally, most contemporary theories of leadership incorporate—explicitly or implicitly—the prevailing corporate culture as a factor in leader success. Charismatic theories do this directly, while LMX and the normative decision model do so in a more indirect fashion. Nevertheless, the nature and quality of a group or organization's culture—including its perceived levels of trust, perceptions about the fairness of reward systems, and emphasis on performance—play a central role in setting the context for leadership efforts. Moreover, we can envision numerous situations where "substitutes for leadership" may actually be more effective in achieving desired effects than overt leadership attempts, as discussed in Chapter 9. At the heart of all of these points is the issue of influence, since leadership (and its "substitutes") is ultimately a question of one's ability to influence followers to invest their collective energies toward a specific goal. It matters little whether this collective effort is based upon the charisma of the leader or the participative decision processes that led the group to accept the goals; in either case, leadership rests upon the ability of the leader or manager to cause his or her followers to want to join in a collaborative enterprise. Without this influence, leadership does not exist.

Throughout this book, we have seen that motivation and leadership are really two sides of the same coin. For example, we saw in Chapter 3 that the path-goal theory of leadership is, in fact, based on the expectancy/valence theory of motivation. Interestingly, although the principal researchers who study leadership and motivation tend to be different, their research objectives are quite similar. While leadership researchers focus on how managers attempt to gain follower compliance, motivation researchers focus on what causes followers to comply. While leadership researchers look principally—although not exclusively—at the characteristics of the leader, motivation researchers look principally—although, again, not exclusively—at the characteristics of followers. Both focus their analyses on the interplay between individuals and groups and their surrounding environments and on the subsequent attitudes and behaviors that flow from these interactions. Both base their analyses on efforts to develop a deeper understanding of the causes of human behavior in organizations. When taken together *and studied simultaneously,* they significantly enhance our understanding of organizational dynamics as they relate to both goal-directed employee behavior and organizational effectiveness.

Beyond the general discussions of motivation and leadership processes, we also focused attention on a variety of more specific topics that are in some ways influenced by these processes. The readings associated with these topics (Chapters 4–10) reveal the scope of motivational and leadership processes in organizational settings. For example, we saw in Chapter 4 that the effective use of power in organizations relies heavily on an understanding of what motivates people. Leaders must be motivated by something—perhaps a feeling of responsibility to the group or its mission—in order to attempt to exert power over others. Similarly, followers must be motivated by some factor—whether it be a personal characteristic or an expectation—to follow. Without motivated behavior, power has little effect in organizations.

Gender has also been shown to play a role in motivation and leadership, but not in the way one might expect. In Chapter 4, for example, we saw that the influence of gender on managerial behavior is more complex than first believed. Based upon a meta-analytic review of available research, it was shown that men and women exhibited few stylistic differences in their approach to leadership when these behaviors occurred within an organizational context. However, when similar behaviors occurred in nonorganizational contexts, significant differences frequently occurred. Thus, we are again reminded of the importance of recognizing organizational—that is, work—contexts in leadership attempts. We are also reminded of the necessity to be alert to simplistic (or stereotypical) beliefs about gender differences in management. Women managers are not necessarily more "people-oriented" while men are more "task-oriented," and, indeed, the within-group variance here is probably larger than the between-group variance.

Job attitudes also play a crucial role in both motivated behavior and in leadership attempts. For instance, we saw in Chapter 5 that job dissatisfaction can lead to a variety of organizational ills, including reduced organizational citizenship behavior, reduced job effort and performance, and increased absenteeism and turnover. Low levels of employee commitment to the organization can lead to similar problems (see in Chapter 4). This conclusion is especially troubling because a manager or a firm may often be unable to do much to change the reward system or the corporate culture in a way to enhance job attitudes; that is, we often overestimate the ability of a manager actually to improve the situation. Moreover, as noted in Chapter 5, some employees may come to work with predisposed attitudes that may be difficult to change under any circumstances. Despite an organization's best efforts, some employees are just not "happy campers." Thus, despite the hundreds, or even thousands, of studies conducted over the decades on job attitudes, we seem actually to understand very little about how to foster significant attitude changes over time.

We also learned that cross-cultural or cross-national differences can influence both motivation and leadership. Western conceptions of both motivation and leadership are largely predicated upon beliefs that most employees and leaders have an internal desire to achieve and be recognized. These beliefs run contrary to many Eastern beliefs. For instance, the Japanese have a saying that "the nail that sticks out gets hammered down," meaning that bringing attention to oneself is to be avoided; indeed, it may be punished. Only *group* accomplishment is to be praised. Similarly, many Western models of management—including most of those discussed in this text—assume a future-oriented perspective. That is, we assume that employees will respond to certain incentive systems in the hopes of being rewarded in the future. However, in some Middle Eastern societies, it is considered presumptuous to make predictions about future events; what is important is what happens now. In such cases, future promises by managers for present efforts may fall on deaf ears. In some societies hierarchy is valued; in others it is not. In some societies people are hired and promoted based upon family connections; in others they are hired and promoted based upon merit. And so on. Chapter 6 discussed this subject in detail. We revisit it simply to remind the reader of the profound effects cultural differences can sometimes have on employee behavior and performance. As we approach the so-called "global village," recognition of these differences and their effects on employee—and managerial—behavior takes on increasing significance.

Even within one nation, employee reactions to managerial actions can vary significantly. We saw this in Chapter 7 in the readings on reward systems. Textbooks typically extol the virtues of "pay-for-performance" incentive systems. While popular—and effective—in many organizational settings, it is important to remember that most people are motivated by a constellation of factors, and monetary rewards represent only one such factor. Some people will work hard for other potential rewards (for example, increased time off), while others may simply not work hard under any circumstances. Thus, some organizations have experimented with "cafeteria" compensation systems to try to accommodate differences in employee preferences, but such systems are difficult and costly to implement and administer. Managers need to remain alert to individual needs and preferences and to try to make the system work as well as possible within the confines of organizational policies and union contracts.

Finally, in view of the accelerating pace of technological change and innovation, it is increasingly important for organizations in many industrial sectors of the economy to hire and develop employees who can both accept primary responsibility for task completion and learn continually on the job. As Eric Hoffer once observed, "in a time of drastic change, it is the *learners* who will inherit the future; the *learned* will find themselves equipped to live in a world that no longer exists." As many organizational analysts and managers have suggested, managing organizational change—and the accompanying issue of employee development—is increasingly a "live-or-die" issue for many companies. In this regard, the president of BMW (the innovative auto manufacturer) recently noted that, in the future, the big companies will not overtake the small ones; rather, the fast companies will overtake the slow ones! Such assertions point to an important need for organizations and their managers to prepare both their organizations and their employees for perpetual change and continual learning. Whether we look at virtual corporations, strategic alliances, or network organizational forms, employees must remain flexible and must learn and change with the firm. One organizational response to this challenge is to implement what has been called high-involvement management systems, in which employees at all levels of the organization are given greater responsibility for managing their own part of the business and are rewarded accordingly (see Chapter 8). Approaches such as this give meaning to the phrase *developing* human resources.

MOTIVATION AND LEADERSHIP IN PRACTICE

As we have seen throughout this book, we have learned a fair amount about work motivation and leadership effectiveness in the past several decades. However, when we survey current management practices relating to these topics, we frequently discover a sizable discrepancy between theory and practice; many contemporary organizations simply do not make use of what we currently know about motivating and leading employees. Why is this? Several possible explanations exist:

• Some managers continue to hold conservative beliefs about how much employees really want to contribute on the job. They frequently assume that most employees are lazy or indifferent to organizational needs, and they rely largely on "carrot-and-stick" incentives. This is the case despite the large body of data showing that most employees sincerely want to be actively involved in helping organizations to succeed.

• Some managers feel that motivation and leadership are no longer critical issues in the workplace due to the increase in technologically driven manufacturing processes. Since production control is frequently no longer in the hands of employees, why worry about such things as employee attitudes? Such a position ignores the impact that turnover, absenteeism, strikes, output restrictions, sabotage, and the like can have on productivity, even with automated technology. Of course, the potential effects of motivation and leadership on performance are greatly enhanced for jobs—and there are many of them, especially in the service sector—that are not highly automated.

• Some labor leaders continue to believe that increased productivity will lead to reduced employment. They resist efforts to improve job performance by any means. Ironically, the economic trends of the past two decades have demonstrated almost the opposite. Inefficient industries have closed, while companies characterized by high productivity—combined with state-of-the-art technologies—have frequently expanded their employee base as their businesses have grown.

The creation of a stimulating, productive, and satisfying work environment can be beneficial for both management and employees if genuine and realistic concern is shown by all parties. If all parties are to derive some benefit from such an environment, however, the concerns of the employee must be clearly recognized and taken into account. The pivotal role in this process belongs to managers because of their influence in determining the characteristics of the performance environment.

NAME INDEX

SUBJECT INDEX